Introduction to
Psychology

Director of Content:
Katherine Binder

Project Manager & Lead Editor:
Cory Eno

New Course Development Manager:
Laura Brown

Editors:
Caitlin Coleman,
Caitlin Edahl,
Cory Eno

Assistant Editors:
Wright Bailey,
Steven Steinbacher

VP Research & Development: Marcel Prevuznak

Creative Services Manager:
Joshua A. Walker

Content Operations Manager:
Robert Alexander

Contributing Designers:
Brandon Aiton,
Trudy Gove,
Kenneth Hanson,
Patrick Thompson,
Tee Jay Zajac

Cover Design:
Patrick Thompson

Composition Assistance:
Integra Software Services Pvt. Ltd.,
QSI (Pvt.) Ltd.

A division of Quant Systems, Inc.

546 Long Point Road
Mount Pleasant, SC 29464

Printed in the United States of America 🇺🇸

10 9 8 7 6 5 4 3 2 1

ISBN: 978-1-64277-295-1

Table of Contents

Chapter 3

States of Consciousness

Chapter 4

Sensation and Perception

Chapter 5

Learning

Chapter 15
Therapy and Treatment

★ Introduction to Psychology

Content Highlights (Key Features)

★ Real-World Applications

Relevant examples, scenarios, and exercises are embedded in the text to encourage students to see the connections between psychology and the world around them. This application lies at the heart of the textbook.

Figure 3: Voting for government officials in the United States is private to reduce the pressure of conformity.

★ Verified Quizlet Sets

Vocabulary is central to psychology, and students can practice with Verified Quizlet sets for every lesson and chapter that have been created specifically for *Introduction to Psychology*.

Flash Forward

Ready to dig into the vocabulary? Get some practice with this Hawkes Verified Quizlet set (hawkes.biz/psych5q4)!

Flash Back

Now that you've worked through the chapter, sharpen your vocabulary with this Hawkes Verified Quizlet set (hawkes.biz/psychch5)!

★ Further Resources

Students are presented with opportunities to connect content to outside sources. These sources include current events, research, short essays, TedTalks and other instructional videos, case studies, and more. Students are provided with links to easily visit these resources.

Further Resources

For more information, watch this video (hawkes.biz/observationallearning) of Dr. Brian Collin summarizing Albert Bandura's study on observational learning.

★ Group Activities

Collaborative exercises pepper the text and direct students to work with one another to converse, brainstorm, and apply key lesson content via discussion and hands-on activities. All activities require little to no outside materials!

Group Activity

Watson's experiment is considered unethical by today's standards. As a group, identify the modern standards that would be violated by this experiment today.

★ Helpful Hints

Review further explanations and instructional tips and tricks that break down complex concepts and help students retain information more easily.

Helpful Hint

Our tendency to give ourselves the benefit of the doubt, but not to do the same for others, may stem from an evolutionary source. Giving ourselves an external explanation for negative behavior can increase our confidence, which may allow us to take more beneficial risks. Read this article (hawkes.biz/fae) to explore the fundamental attribution error.

★ Reflection Questions

These questions prompt students to stop and think. They often ask students to reflect on how their own lives, connect with the content, and/or ask them to consider further implications associated with complex ideas or controversial studies.

Reflection Questions

Figure 6: Do you think the link between marijuana use and schizophrenia should be considered by legislators who are considering legalizing marijuana? Why or why not?

★ Dig Deeper

These sections allow students to understand complex topics through a further examination of related ideas and case studies.

Dig Deeper

The Myth of Mental Illness

In the 1950s and 1960s, the concept of mental illness was widely criticized. One of the major criticisms focused on the notion that mental illness was a "myth that justifies psychiatric intervention in socially disapproved behavior" (Wakefield, 1992). Thomas Szasz (1960), a noted psychiatrist, was perhaps the biggest proponent of this view. Szasz argued that the notion of mental illness was invented by society (and the mental health establishment) to stigmatize and subjugate people whose behavior violates accepted social and legal norms. Indeed, Szasz suggested that what appear to be symptoms of mental illness are more appropriately characterized as "problems in living" (Szasz, 1960).

★ Everyday Connections

This feature helps students understand how psychological topics play a role in the real world by providing examples rooted in relevance.

♀ Everyday Connection

Solving Puzzles

Take a look at the "Puzzling Scales" logic puzzle below (Figure 4). Sam Loyd, a well-known puzzle master, created and refined countless puzzles throughout his lifetime (Cyclopedia of Puzzles, n.d.).

Figure 3: Did you figure it out? (The answer is at the end of this lesson.) Once you understand how to crack this puzzle, you won't forget.

Figure 2: How long did it take you to solve this sudoku puzzle? (You can see the answer at the end of this lesson.)

★ What Do You Think?

Students have a chance to critically evaluate scenarios that are often controversial or met with varying opinions.

What Do You Think?

Deaf Culture

In the United States and other places around the world, deaf people have their own language, schools, and customs. This is called deaf culture. In the United States, deaf individuals often communicate using American Sign Language (ASL); ASL has no verbal component and is based entirely on visual signs and gestures. The primary mode of communication is signing. One of the values of deaf culture is to continue traditions like using sign language rather than teaching deaf children to try to speak, read lips, or have cochlear implant surgery.

★ Connect the Concepts

This feature uses real-world examples to connect related psychological concepts from various areas of the field.

♀ Connect the Concepts

Tweens, Teens, and Social Norms

My 11-year-old daughter, Jessica, recently told me she needed shorts and shirts for the summer and that she wanted me to take her to a store at the mall that is popular with preteens and teens to buy them. I have noticed that many girls have clothes from that store, so I tried teasing her. I said, "All the shirts say 'Aero' on the front. If you are wearing a shirt like that and you have a substitute teacher, and the other girls are all wearing that type of shirt, won't the substitute teacher think you are all named 'Aero?'"

★ On Your Own Activities

Interactive activities prompt students to apply what they're learning in real time. Students are encouraged to practice their understanding of concepts through open-ended prompts, matching exercises, multiple-choice questions, and more.

☑ On Your Own

Select the answer that best completes the following statements.

1. People with low congruence would have a:

   ☐ higher likelihood of being maladjusted

   ☐ greater sense of self-worth

2. People with high congruence would have a:

   ☐ higher likelihood of being maladjusted

   ☐ greater sense of self-worth

★ Chapter Review

At the end of each chapter, students are encouraged to review the key components of the content. This review includes a recap of key terms and definitions as well as lesson summaries.

 Chapter 6 Review

Lesson Summaries

6.1 What Is Cognition?

Cognitive psychology is the study of cognition, or the brain's ability to think, perceive, plan, analyze, and remember. Concepts and their corresponding prototypes help us quickly organize our thinking by creating categories into which we can sort new information. Schemata are clusters of related concepts. Some schemata involve routines of thought and behavior, and these help us function properly in various situations without having to "think twice" about them. Schemata also show up in social situations and routines of daily behavior.

★ Chapter Projects

These projects promote collaboration, relevance, and creativity while exploring the practical side of psychology. Through activities using real-world applications based on the chapter's content, students work together to create meaningful connections.

🔖 Chapter Project

Purpose

In this project, you will work with a peer to develop case studies for two individuals, both college students. Your task is to use the content in this chapter to create these two case studies. And, because creativity is a concept covered in this chapter, you are invited to be creative as you "build your characters." **The purpose of this project is to provide you an opportunity for empathy-building and perspective-taking, as you consider the genetic and environmental influences on the development of thinking, language, and intelligence.**

★ Answer Key

Located in the back of the book, the Answer Key provides answers to all odd numbered exercises in each section. This allows students to check their work to ensure that they are accurately applying the methods and skills they have learned.

☑ Comprehensive Material

Introduction to Psychology takes an expansive approach to course content in order to meet the varying needs and goals of instructors and students. Additionally, both introductory and advanced topics provide students with a text that fully prepares them for current and future psychology courses.

💡 Answer Key

Chapter 3

1. c. hypothalamus   **13.** c. cataplexy

3. b. circadian   **15.** c. SIDS

5. c. pituitary gland   **17.** c. tolerance

7. b. melatonin   **19.** a. psychological dependence

9. c. stage 3 and stage 4 **21.** a. hypnosis

11. c. depression

Tips for Success

★ How to Read a Psychology Textbook

☑ Don't Skim

When reading psychology textbooks, look at everything: titles, definitions, case studies, text in the margins, and any text that is highlighted, outlined, or in bold. Also pay close attention to any tables, figures, charts, and graphs.

☑ Start at the Beginning

Don't start in the middle of an assigned section. You may miss an important concept or point of research that is crucial to understanding the rest of the material in the section.

☑ Highlight and Annotate

Put your book to good use and don't be afraid to add comments and highlighting. If you don't understand something in the text, reread it a couple of times. If it is still not clear, note the text with a question mark or some other notation, so you can ask your instructor about it.

☑ Use Available Resources

Many textbooks reference websites and resources to help you understand the content. These resources may contain videos that help explain more complex steps or concepts. Try searching the internet for additional explanations of topics you don't understand.

☑ Try Reading the Materials Aloud

Reading aloud makes you focus on every word in the sentence. Leaving out a word in a sentence or math problem could give it a totally different meaning, so be sure to read the text carefully and reread if necessary.

★ Tips for Success in a Psychology Course

☑ Take Notes

Take notes in class using a method that works for you. There are many different note-taking strategies, such as the Cornell Method and Concept Mapping. You can try researching these and other methods to see if they might work better than your current note-taking system.

☑ Stay Organized

As you review your notes each day, be sure to label them using categories such as definition, concept, example, and procedure. Try highlighting each category with a different colored highlighter.

☑ Use Study Aids

Use note cards to help you remember definitions and concepts. Use the front of the card for the vocabulary term and write the definition on the back of the card, along with a description in your own words.

☑ Understand, Don't Memorize

Don't try to memorize concepts without understanding them. Try describing or explaining them in your own words or look for patterns, so you don't have to memorize them.

☑ Manage your Time

Don't spend more than 10 to 15 minutes working on a single question. If you can't figure out the answer, put it aside and work on another one. You may learn something from the next question that will help you with the one you couldn't do. Mark the questions that you skip so that you can ask your instructor about it during the next class. It may also help to work a similar, but perhaps easier, problem.

★ Do I Need a Psychology Tutor?

☑ Alternatives to Tutoring

Before getting a tutor, you might consider setting up a meeting with your instructor during their office hours to get help. Unfortunately, you may find that your instructor's office hours don't coincide with your schedule or don't provide enough time for one-on-one help. Another alternative is to put together a study group of classmates from your psychology class. Working in groups and explaining your work to others can be very beneficial to your understanding of psychology. Study groups work best if there are three to six members. Having too many people in a study group may make it difficult to schedule a time for all group members to meet. A large study group may also increase distractions.

☑ Where to Find a Tutor

Many schools have both group and individual tutoring available. In most cases, the cost of this tutoring is included in tuition costs. If your college offers tutoring through a learning lab or tutoring center, then you should take advantage of it. You may need to complete an application to be considered for tutoring, so be sure to get the necessary paperwork at the start of each semester to increase your chances of getting a tutoring time that works well with your schedule. You might be able to find a tutor by asking your instructor for references or by asking friends who have taken higher-level psychology classes than you have. You can also try researching the internet for local reputable tutoring organizations in your area.

☑ What to Look for in a Tutor

Whether you obtain a tutor through your college or hire a personal tutor, look for someone who has experience, educational qualifications, and who is friendly and easy to work with. If you find that the tutor's personality or learning style isn't similar to yours, then you should look for a different tutor that matches your style. It may take some effort to find a tutor who works well with you.

☑ How to Prepare for a Tutoring Session

To get the most out of your tutoring session, come prepared by bringing your text, class notes, and any homework or questions you need help with. If you know ahead of time what you will be working on, communicate this to the tutor, so they can also come prepared. You should attempt the homework prior to the session and write notes or questions for the tutor. Do not use the tutor to do your homework for you. The tutor will explain to you how to do the work and let you work some problems on your own while he or she observes. Ask the tutor to explain the steps aloud while working through a problem. Be sure to do the same so that the tutor can correct any mistakes in your reasoning. Take notes during your tutoring session and ask the tutor if he or she has any additional resources such as websites, videos, or handouts that may help you.

Psychology and You: Conflict Resolution

Purpose

We encounter conflict in our lives every day. From minor disagreements to disruptive altercations, our lives are filled with opportunities to resolve conflict and find harmony with those around us. **The purpose of this assignment it to better understand and apply principles of conflict resolution in your own life.**

Instructional Content

For this assignment, your instructor will place you in a small group of approximately four people. There are two parts to this assignment, which are to be completed as a group. By the time you are assigned to your group, you should have already read this article on conflict resolution (hawkes.biz/conflict).

Directions

Part 1 – Why You Should Resolve Conflict

As a group, discuss each of the following scenarios. Then, in 250+ words each (i.e., 3 x 250+ words), illustrate at least one of the reasons given in the article as to why they should resolve the conflict. Feel free to take liberties with the scenarios, adding specific information that might be important to note in considering why this conflict should be resolved.

Note: Your groups may "divide and conquer" the actual writing of these three responses, but you may only do that after 5–10 minutes of group discussion on each scenario regarding what direction the writer(s) should go. The writer(s) should take notes and ask clarifying questions during the discussion.

Scenarios:

1. Dominic and Jackson are freshman who were randomly paired together as roommates. They have very different expectations when it comes to dorm room cleanliness.

2. Harriot and Olga are college students who are working as camp counselors for the summer, and they do not agree about how to correct bad behaviors in their ten-year-old campers. While Harriot tends to be more patient and hands-off, making suggestions about how the children can change bad behavior, Olga is quick to raise her voice and stop the behavior immediately before it gets out of hand.

3. Boris, Sandra, Jose, and Starr are taking a business course on entrepreneurship. They have been placed together for a final project that is worth 50% of their individual final grades. Their task is to put together a business plan for a brand-new business. They have the option to create a new product (e.g., a soft drink, a smartphone, etc.) OR a new service (e.g., a nail salon, a painting company, etc.). While Boris and Starr both come from families who have started service-based businesses and would prefer to go that direction, Jose and Sandra had already privately discussed a number of new product ideas. The pairs are now at a standoff, and the stakes are high (Remember, this is worth 50% of final grade!).

Part 2 – Successfully Resolving a Conflict

As a group, choose any one of these scenarios to extend into a seven-step plan for conflict resolution (based on the article). Each section of the plan should be 150+ words.

Note: Your group should spend 10–15 minutes discussing which direction to go and what steps to take before starting this writing assignment.

Part 3 – Reflection

As your group discussed Parts 1 and 2 of this assignment, you were collectively forced to make a number of decisions. It is likely that there was not agreement at every juncture. Your task now is to reflect, individually, on any conflict or disagreement (experienced, perceived, or privately felt) that came up in your group discussions. In 500+ words, apply what you learned in the article to what you experienced in your group negotiation. Provide specific examples, and display mastery of your understanding of the article by integrating at least five ideas from it. Be sure to cite your source each time!

Finally, in 250+ words, discuss how this article, assignment, AND reflection (all three) might benefit your academics, relationships, OR work. Choose one: be specific.

✔ Checklist

Part 1 – Why You Should Resolve Conflict

☐ Read the given article.

☐ Read and discuss with your group all three scenarios.

☐ Write 250+ words per conflict about why the conflict should be resolved.

Part 2 – Successfully Resolving a Conflict

☐ Discuss with your group which conflict scenario to resolve.

☐ Write a seven-step plan for conflict resolution (150+ words per step).

Part 3 – Reflection

☐ Discuss Parts 1 and 2.

☐ Write 500+ words reflecting on the experience and what you learned.

☐ Integrate at least five ideas from the article.

☐ Cite all your sources.

☐ Write a 250+ word reflection/application.

☐ Discuss the article, assignment, and previous reflection.

☐ Discuss how what you learned might benefit one of the following: academics, relationships, or work.

Psychology and You: Group Dynamics

Purpose

We all find ourselves playing different roles in different groups throughout our lives. The dynamics of these groups, and how we perceive and react to them, can have a significant impact on the success of these groups and the individuals in them. **The purpose of this project is to help you better understand group dynamics, particularly as they pertain to groups that a college student may be involved in.**

Instructional Content

For this assignment, your instructor will place you in a small group of approximately five people. There are two parts to this assignment, which are to be completed as a group. By the time you are assigned to your group, you should have already read this article on group dynamics (hawkes.biz/groupdynamics).

Directions

Part 1 – Role Play

1. Determine what the relationship of the group is. For example, are they in a class together, in a club, on a team, coworkers at a coffee shop, etc.? Be specific.

2. Determine what sort of decision the group is trying to make. For example, problem solve the cafeteria food, get more funding for the Ping-Pong Club, sort out summer holidays on the work schedule, etc. Be creative, but realistic.

3. Browse the assigned reading on group dynamics to specifically choose roles that are inspired by what we know about how groups work.

4. Based on the reading, create the five characters' roles for the role play.

5. On five note cards, write the card number, the character's role, and the corresponding group dynamic concept, theory, or principle associated with that role.

   For example:

   • Card 1

   • Concept: Social Loafing

   • Role: You are there to let everyone else do the work.

6. Once all five cards are completed, find five classmates (or another group) to role play this scenario. Don't forget to tell the entire class the nature of the relationship of the group and what sort of decision they are trying to make in their five-minute conversation. Do not tell the class what the roles are.

Part 2 – Identify Group Dynamics

After completing the role-playing scenarios, return to the online reading about group dynamics. As a group, identify and reflect upon 10 different concepts or principles from the reading that may have been at work in your own group's dynamics. Then write a reflection for each of the 10 different concepts. Each reflection should be a minimum of 100 words and should contain specific references to your group's behaviors, interactions, or activities. You may "divide and conquer" the work in groups, but no work should be done individually. All ten reflections should be discussed as a group before the final product is submitted and should be formatted in the following way:

Concept 1: **Your first group dynamic concept** – Your paragraph of reflection

Concept 2: **Your second group dynamic concept** – Your paragraph of reflection

Concept 3: …and so on…

✅ Checklist

Part 1 – Role Play

- ☐ Read the article on group dynamics.
- ☐ Determine the relationship of the group and the decision it is trying to make.
- ☐ Assign five characters' roles based on the group dynamics described in the article.
- ☐ Create the note cards for each character.
- ☐ Role play scenario with another group.

Part 2 – Identify Group Dynamics

- ☐ Reflect on 10 different concepts that may be at play in your group's scenario.
- ☐ Write a 100+ word reflection for each concept referencing your group's behaviors, interaction, or activities.
- ☐ Discuss your group's reflection.
- ☐ Format reflection correctly.

Introduction to
Psychology

Chapter 1
Psychological Science

Chapter Introduction

📷 **Figure 1:** Psychology is the scientific study of mind and behavior.

Clive Wearing is an accomplished musician who lost his ability to form new memories when he became sick at the age of 46. While he can remember how to play the piano perfectly, he cannot remember what he ate for breakfast just an hour ago (Sacks, 2007).

James Wannerton experiences a taste sensation that is associated with the sound of words. His former girlfriend's name tastes like rhubarb (Mundasad, 2013).

John Nash is a brilliant mathematician and Nobel Prize winner. However, while he was a professor at MIT, he would tell people that *The New York Times* contained coded messages from extraterrestrial beings that were intended for him. He also began to hear voices and became suspicious of the people around him. Soon thereafter, Nash was diagnosed with schizophrenia and admitted to a state-run mental institution (O'Connor & Robertson, 2002). Nash was the subject of the 2001 movie *A Beautiful Mind*.

Why did these people have these experiences? How does the human brain work? And what is the connection between the brain's internal processes and people's external behaviors? This course will introduce you to various ways that the field of psychology has explored these questions.

Flash Forward

Ready to dig into the vocabulary? Get some practice with this Hawkes Verified Quizlet set (hawkes.biz/psych1q1)!

1.1 What Is Psychology?

In Greek mythology, Psyche was a mortal woman whose beauty was so great that it rivaled that of the goddess Aphrodite. The goddess sent her brother, Eros, to make Psyche fall in love with the ugliest man in the world, but the plan backfired. Eros pricked himself with the tip of his own arrow and fell in love with Psyche himself. Eros hid his face from Psyche and abandoned her when she didn't respect this wish. Through her persistence, Psyche was reunited with Eros and transformed into a goddess herself.

Psyche came to represent the human soul's triumph over the misfortunes of life in the pursuit of true happiness (Bulfinch, 1855); in fact, the word *psyche* means soul, and it is often represented as a butterfly. The word *psychology* was coined at a time when the concepts of soul and mind were not as clearly distinguished (Green, 2001). The root *ology* denotes scientific study of, and *psychology* refers to the scientific study of the mind. Since science studies only observable phenomena and the mind is not directly observable, we expand this definition to the scientific study of mind and behavior.

Reflection Questions

Based on what you already know about psychology, what do you think it means to study the mind and behavior?

The scientific study of any aspect of the world uses the scientific method to acquire knowledge. A typical use of the scientific method, might go something like this:

Scientific Method

1. A researcher with a question about how or why something happens will propose a tentative explanation called a hypothesis.

2. That hypothesis fits into the context of a scientific theory, which is a broad explanation for some aspect of the natural world.

3. The researcher then makes observations or carries out an experiment. This is to test the validity of the hypothesis.

4. That test and its results are published so that others can check the results or build on them.

✎ On Your Own

Is the following statement a testable hypothesis?

A bird sings because it is happy.

☐ Yes   ☐ No

Science deals only with things that are perceivable and measurable, such as matter or energy. It may be simple to measure differences in size, shape, and structure of different substances, but the study of psychology deals with measuring things that are not so concrete. Researchers cannot take out a ruler and measure emotional states or consciousness.

An important component of psychological research is finding ways to measure psychological constructs, such as anxiety, using operational definitions. A psychologist who wants to measure anxiety may ask study subjects about how often they have negative feelings about events that may occur in the future.

The scientific method is also a form of empiricism. An **empirical method** for acquiring knowledge is one based on observation, including experimentation, rather than a method based only on forms of logical argument.

☑ On Your Own

Pretend you are a researcher and use the table below to identify what you will measure, how you will measure the phenomena, and what your hypothesis is based on the theory described.

Theory	Lack of sleep negatively impacts performance.	Alcohol slows reaction time.	Dogs communicate using facial expressions.
What to measure?	Performance, sleep		
How to measure it?	Record hours of sleep each night and test scores		
Hypothesis	Individuals who get less than 6 hours of sleep each night for 3 straight weeks will have lower test scores than those who get more than 6 hours of sleep each night.		

Psychology was initially considered to be a component of philosophy and biology until the late 1800s when it became its own academic discipline. Due to the influence of others on our behavior, thought, and emotion, psychology is considered a social science. Today, psychology is one of the more popular courses in undergraduate programs of study in the United States.

Merits of an Education in Psychology

Currently, psychology is one of the most popular majors on college campuses across the United States (Johnson & Lubin, 2011). About six percent of all bachelor degrees granted in the United States are in the discipline of psychology (U.S. Department of Education, 2013). A number of well-known individuals were psychology majors. Just a few famous names on this list are Facebook's creator Mark Zuckerberg, television personality and political satirist Jon Stewart, actress Natalie Portman, and filmmaker Wes Craven (Halonen, 2011).

Why should you pursue an education in psychology? Psychology teaches students critical thinking skills and the scientific method. Critical thinking is the active application of a set of skills to information for the understanding and evaluation of that information. The evaluation of information—assessing its reliability and usefulness—is an important skill in a world full of competing "facts," many of which are designed to be misleading. Psychology students also can develop better communication skills, which can be useful in both personal and professional settings (American Psychological Association, 2011).

Group Activity

Discuss in a small group why you each decided to take a psychology course. What do you hope to get out of it?

In addition to these broad-based skills, psychology students come to understand the complex factors that shape one's behavior. They appreciate the interaction of our biology, our environment, and our experiences in determining who we are and how we will behave. Psychology students also learn about basic principles that guide how we think and behave, and they come to recognize the tremendous diversity that exists across individuals and across cultural boundaries (American Psychological Association, 2011).

Further Resources

Watch a brief video (hawkes.biz/psychologymajor) that describes some of the questions a student should consider before deciding to major in psychology.

History of Psychology

Compared to earlier disciplines like human physiology, psychology is a relatively young science with its experimental roots in the 19th century. As mentioned, anyone interested in exploring issues related to the mind generally did so in a philosophical context prior to the 1800s. Two men, working in the 19th century, are generally credited as being the founders of psychology as a science and academic discipline that was distinct from philosophy. Their names were Wilhelm Wundt and William James. Next, we will look at the shifts in paradigms that have influenced psychology from Wundt and James through today.

Wundt and Structuralism

Wilhelm Wundt (1832–1920) was a German scientist who established one of the first psychology laboratories at the University of Leipzig in 1879 (Figure 2). The goal of Wundt's research was to identify the basic components of conscious experience.

Wundt would observe study participants' behavior and their internal experiences during a series of tasks. He used **introspection** (he called it "internal perception"), a process by which someone examines their own conscious experience as objectively as possible, making the human mind like any other aspect of nature that a scientist observed. Wundt's process included trained observers and several trials with multiple participants. His attempt to understand the structure or characteristics of the mind was known as **structuralism**. Wundt summarized his research and structuralism in his famous book entitled *Principles of Physiological Psychology*, which was published in 1873.

(a)

(b)

Figure 2: (a) Wilhelm Wundt is credited as one of the founders of psychology. He created the first laboratory for psychological research. (b) This photo shows him seated and surrounded by fellow researchers and equipment in his laboratory in Germany.

In the laboratory, Wundt and his students conducted experiments on things like reaction times. A subject, sometimes in a room isolated from the scientist, would receive a stimulus such as a light, image, or sound. The subject's reaction to the stimulus would be to push a button, and an apparatus would record the time to reaction. Wundt could measure reaction time to one-thousandth of a second (Nicolas & Ferrand, 1999). Despite his efforts to train individuals in the process of introspection, the process remained highly subjective, and there was very little agreement between individuals. As a result, structuralism fell out of favor with the passing of Wundt's student Edward Titchener in 1927 (Gordon, 1995).

🖉 On Your Own

Pick up an object in the room. Use the table below to describe your experience.

Experience	Response
Behavior: how did you respond after picking it up?	
Thoughts: what were you thinking?	
Sensations: what did you feel, smell, touch, taste, or see?	

James and Functionalism

William James (1842–1910) was the first American psychologist who espoused a different perspective on how psychology should operate (Figure 3). James was introduced to Darwin's theory of evolution by natural selection and accepted it as an explanation of an organism's characteristics. Key to that theory is the idea that natural selection leads to organisms that are adapted to their environment, including their behavior. Adaptation means that a trait of an organism has a function for the survival and reproduction of the individual because it has been naturally selected.

As James saw it, psychology's purpose was to study the function of behavior in the world, and as such, his perspective was known as functionalism. **Functionalism** focused on how mental activities helped an organism fit into its environment. It also has a second, more subtle meaning in that functionalists were more interested in the operation of the whole mind rather than of its individual parts, which were the focus of structuralism. Like Wundt, James believed that introspection could serve as one means by which someone might study mental activities, but James also relied on more objective measures, including the use of various recording devices and examinations of concrete products of mental activities and anatomy and physiology (Gordon, 1995).

Figure 3: William James was the first American psychologist.

✎   **On Your Own**

Complete the table by identifying two behaviors you engage in and how they help you adapt to your environment.

Behavior	Adaptation
Wearing team colors to a football game	If I fit in with other fans, they'll know I'm part of the group, and it will increase the chances of interacting positively with them.

Pioneering Women

Figure 4: While women are ubiquitous in psychology today, it was the perseverance of women like Mary Whiton Calkins and Margaret Floy Washburn that broke sexist barriers and paved the way.

Early psychology was not without barriers for marginalized groups, but several individuals challenged those limitations and built successful careers. Women faced the same discriminatory attitudes and policies as the discipline grew that they did elsewhere in their lives. Mary Whiton Calkins (1863–1930) studied under William James and completed the requirements for a PhD in psychology from Harvard. Her male cohorts dropped out of the program, and Harvard refused to grant her the degree she earned, but Calkins was ultimately undeterred. She became the first female president of the APA (American Psychological Association) in 1905 and made significant contributions to the field in pursuing the concept of the self. Calkins also used her experience to enrich the movement for women's suffrage, arguing against "the ignorant satisfaction with things as they are" (Stanton & Anthony, 2013, p. 575). Following Calkins as the second female president of the APA was Margaret Floy Washburn. When Washburn earned her PhD in psychology from Cornell in 1894, she also earned the distinction of being the first woman to be awarded the degree. Beyond these milestones, Washburn was a significant early contributor to comparative psychology, known best for her study of animal consciousness and behavior that culminated in her book *The Animal Mind* (Washburn, 2010).

Dig Deeper

Feminist Psychology

The science of psychology has had an impact on human wellbeing, both positive and negative. The dominant influence of Western, White, and male academics in the early history of psychology meant that psychology developed with the biases inherent in those individuals, which often had negative consequences for members of society that were not White or male. Women, members of ethnic minorities in both the United States and other countries, and individuals with sexual orientations other than heterosexual had difficulties entering the field of psychology and, therefore, influencing its development. They also suffered from the attitudes of White, male psychologists, who were not immune to the nonscientific attitudes prevalent in the society in which they developed and worked. Until the 1960s, the science of psychology was largely a "womanless" psychology (Crawford & Marecek, 1989), meaning that few women were able to practice psychology, so they had little influence on what was studied. In addition, the experimental subjects of psychology were mostly men, which resulted from underlying assumptions that gender had no influence on psychology and that women were not of sufficient interest to study.

An article by Naomi Weisstein, first published in 1968 (Weisstein, 1993), stimulated a feminist revolution in psychology by presenting a critique of psychology as a science. She also specifically criticized male psychologists for constructing the psychology of women entirely out of their own cultural biases and without careful experimental tests to verify any of their characterizations of women. Weisstein used, as examples, statements by prominent psychologists in the 1960s, such as this quote by Bruno Bettleheim: "...we must start with the realization that, as much as women want to be good scientists or engineers, they want first and foremost to be womanly companions of men and to be mothers." Weisstein's critique formed the foundation for the subsequent development of a feminist psychology that attempted to be free of the influence of male cultural biases on our knowledge of the psychology of women and, indeed, of both genders.

Crawford & Marecek (1989) identified several feminist approaches to psychology that can be described as feminist psychology. These include re-evaluating and discovering the contributions of women to the history of psychology, studying psychological gender differences, and questioning the male bias present across the practice of the scientific approach to knowledge.

Figure 5: Elizabeth Loftus is an American cognitive psychologist and famous for her research on the misinformation effect, eyewitness memory, and false memories. She leads in a field that was once dominated by men.

Freud and Psychoanalytic Theory

Perhaps one of the most influential and well-known figures in psychology's history was Sigmund Freud (Figure 6). Freud (1856–1939) was an Austrian neurologist who theorized that many of his patients' problems arose from the unconscious mind. In Freud's view, the unconscious mind was a repository of feelings and urges of which we have no awareness. Gaining access to the unconscious, then, was crucial to the successful resolution of the patient's problems. According to Freud, the unconscious mind could be accessed through dream analysis, by examinations of the first words that came to people's minds, and through seemingly innocent slips of the tongue. **Psychoanalytic theory** focuses on the role of a person's unconscious, as well as early childhood experiences, and this particular perspective dominated clinical psychology for several decades (Thorne & Henley, 2005).

Freud's ideas were influential, and you will learn more about them when you study lifespan development, personality, and therapy. For instance, many therapists believe strongly in the unconscious and the impact of early childhood experiences on the rest of a person's life. The method of psychoanalysis, which involves patients talking about their experiences and selves, while not invented by Freud, was certainly popularized by him and is still used today.

Figure 6: Sigmund Freud was a highly influential figure in the history of psychology.

> **Reflection Questions**
>
> Do you agree with Freud that dreams have meaning in your day-to-day life? Why or why not?

Many of Freud's other ideas, however, are controversial. For example, Freud's early theories proposed the Oedipus complex, which is a young boy's unconscious sexual desire for the mother paired with hatred for the family. Conversely, Freud suggested that young girls experience penis envy, or anxiety, when they realize they do not have a penis. Although these theories among others drew criticism, Drew Westen (1998) argues that many of the criticisms of Freud's ideas are misplaced in that they attack his older ideas without considering his later writings.

Westen also argues that critics fail to consider the success of the broad ideas that Freud introduced or developed, such as the importance of childhood experiences in adult motivations, the role of unconscious versus conscious motivations in driving our behavior, the fact that motivations can cause conflicts that affect behavior, the effects of mental representations of ourselves and others in guiding our interactions, and the development of personality over time. More modern iterations of Freud's clinical approach have been empirically demonstrated to be effective (Knekt et al., 2008; Shedler, 2010). Some current practices in psychotherapy involve examining unconscious aspects of the self and relationships, often through the relationship between the therapist and the client.

Wertheimer, Koffka, Köhler, and Gestalt Psychology

Investigate Figures A and B below. You might say that Figure A is a square made up of 36 circles, and Figure B is 3 columns of 12 circles. Your perception of both figures was not just the parts of the figure but how the parts connected to form the whole. If you were asked to look at each of the individual parts of two figures below, or the 36 circles in Figure A and the 36 circles in Figure B, without allowing you to look at the whole picture, you would have likely perceived Figure A and B to be the same. Gestalt psychology operates on the principle that the whole is greater than the sum of its parts.

a.   b.

Figure 7: (a) Figure A is 36 circles in the shape of a square. (b) Figure B is 36 circles in the shape of a square but spaced differently than Figure A.

The word *Gestalt* roughly translates to "whole"; a major emphasis of Gestalt psychology deals with the fact that although a sensory experience can be broken down into individual parts, how those parts relate to each other as a whole is often what the individual responds to in perception. Max Wertheimer (1880–1943), Kurt Koffka (1886–1941), and Wolfgang Köhler (1887–1967) were three German psychologists who were credited with introducing psychologists in the United States to Gestalt principles after escaping Nazi Germany.

Unfortunately, in moving to the United States, these men were forced to abandon much of their work and were unable to continue to conduct research on a large scale. These factors along with the rise of behaviorism (described next) in the United States prevented principles of Gestalt psychology from being as influential in the United States as they had been in their native Germany (Thorne & Henley, 2005). Despite these issues, several Gestalt principles are still very influential today. Considering the human individual as a whole rather than as a sum of individually measured parts became an important foundation in humanistic theory late in the century.

Structuralism, Freud, and the Gestalt psychologists were all concerned in one way or another with describing and understanding inner experience. But other researchers had concerns that inner experience could be a legitimate subject of scientific inquiry and chose instead to exclusively study behavior, the objectively observable outcome of mental processes.

Pavlov, Watson, Skinner, and Behaviorism

Early work in the field of behavior was conducted by the Russian physiologist Ivan Pavlov (1849–1936) who was the founder of classical conditioning. Pavlov played the sound of a metronome and presented meat powder to groups of dogs. Eventually, the dogs would learn to salivate to the sound of the metronome without the presence of the meat powder. Pavlov's work was able to demonstrate that an otherwise neutral stimulus, like a metronome, can be paired with a stimulus that causes a reflex, to produce a similar response.

Figure 8: Ivan Pavlov is known as the founder of classical conditioning.

John B. Watson (1878–1958) was an influential American psychologist whose most famous work occurred during the early 20th century at Johns Hopkins University (Figure 9). In contrast to Wundt and James, Watson thought that analysis of the mind was impossible and directed the focus of psychology toward **behaviorism**, or the study of observing and controlling behavior. A major object of study in this approach was learned behavior and its interaction with the inborn qualities of an organism. Behaviorists commonly used animals in experiments under the assumption that what was learned using animal models could, to some degree, be applied to human behavior.

Reflection Questions

What factors do you think led Watson to believe that analysis of the mind was impossible?

B.F. Skinner (1904–1990) was an American psychologist. Like Watson, Skinner was a behaviorist, and he concentrated on how behavior was affected by its consequences, which is called operant conditioning. Therefore, Skinner spoke of reinforcement and punishment as major factors in driving behavior. Reinforcement is adding a stimulus that increases the likelihood of a behavior, while punishment is a stimulus that reduces the likelihood of a behavior. As a part of his research, Skinner developed a chamber that allowed the careful study of the principles of modifying behavior through reinforcement and punishment. This device, known as an operant conditioning chamber (or more familiarly, a Skinner box), has remained a crucial resource for researchers studying behavior (Thorne & Henley, 2005).

Figure 9: John B. Watson is known as the father of behaviorism within psychology.

— Speaker

— Lights

— Lever

— Dispenser

Figure 10: B.F. Skinner is famous for his research on operant conditioning. Modified versions of the operant conditioning chamber, or Skinner box, are still widely used in research settings today.

The Skinner box is a chamber that isolates the subject from the external environment and has a behavior indicator such as a lever or a button. When the animal pushes the lever or button, the box delivers a positive reinforcement of the behavior (such as food), a punishment (such as a noise), or a token conditioner (such as a light) that is correlated with either the positive reinforcement or punishment. Skinner's focus on positive and negative reinforcement of learned behaviors had a lasting influence in psychology that has waned somewhat since the growth of research in cognitive psychology. Despite this, conditioned learning is still used in human behavioral modification.

📷 **Figure 11:** These students are conducting an experiment on a pigeon using a Skinner box.

Reflection Questions

Think about a time when you used operant conditioning to try and control a person or an animal's behavior. Was it successful?

Overall, behaviorism is largely responsible for establishing psychology as a scientific discipline through its objective methods and, especially, experimentation. In addition, it is used in behavioral and cognitive-behavioral therapy. Behavior modification is commonly used in certain classroom settings. The research conducted from behaviorism has shed light on the environmental influences on human behavior.

Maslow, Rogers, and Humanism

During the early 20th century, American psychology was dominated by behaviorism and psychoanalysis. However, some psychologists were uncomfortable with what they viewed as limited perspectives being so influential to the field. They objected to the pessimism and determinism (all actions driven by the unconscious) of Freud. They also disliked the simplicity of behaviorism as the mind is much more complex. Some psychologists began to form their own ideas that emphasized personal control, intentionality, and a true predisposition for "good" as important for our self-concept and our behavior. Thus, humanism emerged.

Humanism is a perspective within psychology that emphasizes the potential for good that is innate to all humans. Two of the most well-known proponents of humanistic psychology are Abraham Maslow and Carl Rogers (O'Hara, n.d.). Humanism attempts to distinguish psychology from the physical and biological sciences by emphasizing self-concept, well-being, and progress through psychotherapy. Abraham Maslow (1908–1970) was an American psychologist who is best known for proposing a hierarchy of human needs in motivating behavior (Figure 12). Maslow asserted that so long as basic needs necessary for survival were met (e.g., food, water, shelter), higher-level needs (e.g., social needs) would begin to motivate behavior. According to Maslow, the highest-level needs relate to self-actualization, a process by which we work to achieve our full potential.

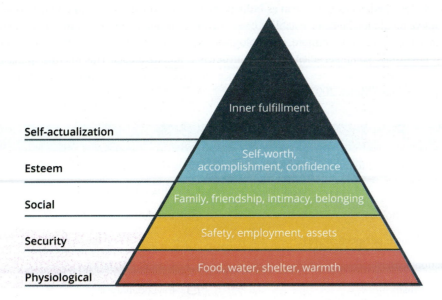

🖻 **Figure 12:** Maslow's hierarchy of needs is shown.

Carl Rogers (1902–1987) was also an American psychologist who, like Maslow, emphasized the potential for good that exists within all people (Figure 13). Rogers used a therapeutic technique known as client-centered therapy in helping his clients deal with problematic issues that resulted in their seeking psychotherapy.

Unlike a psychoanalytic approach in which the therapist plays an important role in interpreting what conscious behavior reveals about the unconscious mind, client-centered therapy involves the patient taking a lead role in the therapy session. Rogers believed that a therapist needed to display three features to maximize the effectiveness of this particular approach: unconditional positive regard, genuineness, and empathy. Unconditional positive regard refers to the fact that the therapist accepts clients for who they are, no matter what they might say. Provided these factors, Rogers believed that people were more than capable of dealing with and working through their own issues (Thorne & Henley, 2005).

Humanism has been influential to psychology as a whole. Both Maslow and Rogers are well-known names among students of psychology (you will read more about both men later in this text), and their ideas have influenced many scholars. Furthermore, Rogers' client-centered approach to therapy is still commonly used in psychotherapeutic settings today (O'Hara, n.d.).

🖻 **Figure 13:** Carl Rogers, shown in this portrait, developed a client-centered therapy method that has been influential in clinical settings.

Reflection Questions

Do you favor humanism over psychoanalysis and behaviorism? Why or why not?

Further Resources

View a brief video (hawkes. biz/rogersapproach) of Carl Rogers describing his therapeutic approach.

The Cognitive Revolution

The early work of the humanistic psychologists redirected attention to the individual human as a whole and as a conscious and self-aware being. By the 1950s, new disciplinary perspectives in linguistics, neuroscience, and computer science were emerging, and these areas revived interest in the mind as a focus of scientific inquiry. This perspective has come to be known as the cognitive revolution (Miller, 2003). By 1967, Ulric Neisser published the first textbook entitled *Cognitive Psychology*, which served as a core text in cognitive psychology courses around the country (Thorne & Henley, 2005).

Although no one person is entirely responsible for starting the cognitive revolution, Noam Chomsky was very influential in the early days of this movement (Figure 14). Chomsky (1928–), an American linguist, was dissatisfied with the influence that behaviorism had had on psychology. He believed that psychology's focus on behavior was short-sighted and that the field had to re-incorporate mental functioning into its purview if it were to offer any meaningful contributions to understanding behavior (Miller, 2003).

European psychology had never really been as influenced by behaviorism as had American psychology; and thus, the cognitive revolution helped reestablish lines of communication between European psychologists and their American counterparts. Furthermore, psychologists began to cooperate with scientists in other fields, like anthropology, linguistics, computer science, and neuroscience, among others. This interdisciplinary approach is referred to as the cognitive sciences, and the influence and prominence of this perspective resonates in modern-day psychology (Miller, 2003).

Figure 14: Noam Chomsky was very influential in beginning the cognitive revolution.

✎ On Your Own

Which perspective is most focused on the unconscious mind?

☐ Behaviorism   ☐ Structuralism

☐ Gestalt psychology   ☐ Psychoanalysis

The first psychological perspective was:

☐ Functionalism   ☐ Gestalt psychology

☐ Structuralism   ☐ Psychoanalysis

Which psychological perspective focuses on studying observable actions?

☐ Functionalism   ☐ Behaviorism

☐ Structuralism   ☐ Gestalt psychology

Which perspective focuses on the whole making up more than the sum of its parts?

☐ Gestalt psychology   ☐ Functionalism

☐ Structuralism   ☐ Behaviorism

Multicultural Psychology

Culture has important impacts on individuals and social psychology, yet the effects of culture on psychology are under-studied. There is a risk that psychological theories and data derived from White, American settings could be assumed to apply to individuals and social groups from other cultures, and this is unlikely to be true (Betancourt & López, 1993). One weakness in the field of cross-cultural psychology is that in looking for differences in psychological attributes across cultures, there remains a need to go beyond simple descriptive statistics (Betancourt & López, 1993). In this sense, it has remained a descriptive science, rather than one seeking to determine cause and effect. For example, a study of characteristics of individuals seeking treatment for a binge eating disorder in Hispanic-American, African-American, and Caucasian-American individuals found significant differences between groups (Franko et al., 2012). The study concluded that results from studying any one of the groups could not be extended to the other groups, and yet potential causes of the differences were not measured.

This history of multicultural psychology in the United States is a long one. The role of African-American psychologists in researching the cultural differences between the African-American individual and social psychology is but one example. At Clark University in 1920, Francis Cecil Sumner (1895–1954) became the first African American to earn a PhD. Sumner studied racial bias and influenced a generation of black psychologists from his position as department chair at Howard University. Among those affected by Sumner's work was Kenneth Clark (Jackson, 2001). Along with his wife, Mamie, Clark greatly contributed to the understanding of the adverse effects of segregation on younger African Americans. Their work was used as evidence in the landmark Supreme Court case *Brown v. Board of Education* (Clark, 2002). Much of the work of early African-American psychologists (and a general focus of much work in the first half of the 20th century in psychology in the United States) was dedicated to testing, more specifically intelligence testing (Black et al., 2004). That emphasis has continued, particularly because of the importance of testing in determining opportunities for children, but other areas of exploration in African-American psychology research include learning style, sense of community and belonging, and spiritualism (Black et al., 2004).

The field was further enriched by the work of George Sanchez (1906–1972). Sanchez was a prominent Latino psychologist who studied the impact of cultural bias in intelligence testing, further demonstrating the real-world applications of social psychology (Ramirez, 2004).

Despite the daunting barriers in front of them, these pioneering psychologists contributed their voices to a growing chorus that embodied an evolving, modernizing field. The American Psychological Association has several ethnically based organizations for professional psychologists that facilitate interactions among members. Since psychologists belonging to specific ethnic groups or cultures have the most interest in studying the psychology of their communities, these organizations provide an opportunity for the growth of research on the impact of culture on individual and social psychology.

Figure 15: Kenneth Clark and his wife, Mamie, conducted work on the effects of segregation that was used as evidence in *Brown v. Board of Education*.

✍ On Your Own

Rank *structuralism, functionalism, psychoanalysis, Gestalt psychology, behaviorism, cognitive psychology,* and the *multicultural perspective of psychology* from 1 (your most favorite) to 7 (your least favorite) and explain why.

Rank	Perspective	Reason why
1		
2		
3		
4		
5		
6		
7		

Further Resources

Listen to a news story (hawkes.biz/psychincourt) about the influence of an African American's psychology research on the historic *Brown v. Board of Education* civil rights case.

Summary

Psychology derives from the roots *psyche* (meaning "soul") and *-ology* (meaning "scientific study of"). Thus, psychology is defined as the scientific study of mind and behavior. Students of psychology develop critical thinking skills, become familiar with the scientific method, and recognize the complexity of behavior.

Before the time of Wundt and James, questions about the mind were considered by philosophers. However, both Wundt and James helped create psychology as a distinct scientific discipline. Wundt was a structuralist, which meant he believed that our cognitive experience was best understood by breaking that experience into its component parts. He thought this was best accomplished by introspection.

William James was the first American psychologist, and he was a proponent of functionalism. This particular perspective focused on how mental activities served as adaptive responses to an organism's environment. Like

Wundt, James also relied on introspection; however, his research approach also incorporated more objective measures as well.

Psychology has not been exempt from the barriers that prevented people from entering the field based on race or gender. Despite this, the field has been heavily influenced and enriched by contributions of pioneering psychologists like Mary Whiton Calkins and Francis Cecil Sumner who overcame those barriers and made it both more representative and more inclusive.

Sigmund Freud believed that understanding the unconscious mind was absolutely critical to understanding conscious behavior. This was especially true for individuals that he saw who suffered from various hysterias and neuroses. Freud relied on dream analysis, slips of the tongue, and free association as means to access the unconscious. Psychoanalytic theory remained a dominant force in clinical psychology for several decades.

Gestalt psychology was very influential in Europe. Gestalt psychology takes a holistic view of an individual and his experiences. As the Nazis came to power in Germany, Wertheimer, Koffka, and Köhler immigrated to the United States. Although they left their laboratories and their research behind, they did introduce America to Gestalt ideas. Some of the principles of Gestalt psychology are still very influential in the study of sensation and perception.

One of the most influential schools of thought within psychology's history was behaviorism. Behaviorism focused on making psychology an objective science by studying overt behavior and deemphasizing the importance of unobservable mental processes. John Watson is often considered the father of behaviorism, and B.F. Skinner's contributions to our understanding of the principles of operant conditioning cannot be underestimated.

As behaviorism and psychoanalytic theory took hold of so many aspects of psychology, some began to become dissatisfied with psychology's picture of human nature. Thus, a humanistic movement within psychology began to take hold. Humanism focuses on the potential of all people for good. Both Maslow and Rogers were influential in shaping humanistic psychology.

During the 1950s, the landscape of psychology began to change. A science of behavior began to shift back to its roots of focus on mental processes. The emergence of neuroscience and computer science aided this transition. Ultimately, the cognitive revolution took hold, and people came to realize that cognition was crucial to a true appreciation and understanding of behavior.

1.2 Contemporary Psychology

Flash Forward

Ready to dig into the vocabulary? Get some practice with this Hawkes Verified Quizlet set (hawkes.biz/psych1q2)!

Contemporary psychology is a diverse field that is influenced by all of the historical perspectives described in the preceding section. Reflective of the discipline's diversity is the diversity seen within the **American Psychological Association (APA)** and the Association for Psychological Science (APS).

APA

- Professional organization representing diverse psychologists in the United States

- Largest organization of psychologists in the world

- Advances and disseminates psychological knowledge to improve understanding of the mind and behavior

- 56 divisions, including religion, sports, behavioral neuroscience, and comparative psychology

- Members (including affiliate and associate members) span from students to doctoral-level psychologists and can be found in educational settings, criminal justice, hospitals, the armed forces, and industry

Source: American Psychological Association, 2014

APS

- Founded in 1988

- Advanced the scientific orientation of psychology

- Result of disagreements between members of the scientific and clinical branches of psychology within the APA

- Publishes five research journals and engages in education and advocacy with funding agencies

- Significant proportion of its members are international although the majority is located in the United States

Other organizations provide networking and collaboration opportunities for professionals of several ethnic or racial groups working in psychology, such as the National Latina/o Psychological Association (NLPA), the Asian American Psychological Association (AAPA), the Association of Black Psychologists (ABPsi), and the Society of Indian Psychologists (SIP). Most of these groups are also dedicated to studying psychological and social issues within their specific communities.

This section will provide an overview of the major subdivisions within psychology today in the order in which they are introduced throughout the remainder of this textbook. This is not meant to be an exhaustive listing, but it will provide insight into the major areas of research and practice of modern-day psychologists.

Biopsychology and Evolutionary Psychology

As the name suggests, **biopsychology** explores how biology influences our behavior. While biological psychology is a broad field, many biological psychologists want to understand how the structure and function of the nervous system are related to behavior (Figure 1).

As such, they often combine the research strategies of both psychologists and physiologists to accomplish this goal (as discussed in Carlson, 2013).

Further Resources

Please visit this website (hawkes.biz/apadivisions) to learn more about the divisions within the APA.

Student resources (hawkes.biz/aparesources) are also provided by the APA.

Central Nervous System

Brain

Spinal cord

(a)

Peripheral Nervous System

Nerve

(b)

Figure 1: Biological psychologists study how the structure and function of the nervous system generate behavior.

Biopsychology

Broad Scope of Topics:

- Sensory and motor systems
- Sleep
- Drug use and abuse
- Ingestive behavior
- Reproductive behavior
- Neurodevelopment
- Biological connections to psychological disorders

Given the broad areas of interest falling under the purview of biological psychology, it will probably come as no surprise that individuals from all sorts of backgrounds are involved in this research, including biologists, medical professionals, physiologists, and chemists. This interdisciplinary approach is often referred to as neuroscience, of which biological psychology is a component (Carlson, 2013).

Are you particularly moody, or maybe more even-keel? Are there certain traits you find more attractive in others? Do you think these things come naturally to you?

While biopsychology typically focuses on the immediate causes of behavior based in the physiology of humans or other animals, evolutionary psychology seeks to study the ultimate biological causes of behavior. In fact, the discipline is among the newest schools of thought to wade into the nature versus nurture debate with a focus on causes that reach back deeply into human history.

Because behavior is impacted by genetics, a behavior will demonstrate adaptation to its surroundings. These surroundings include the physical environment and, since interactions between organisms can be important to survival and reproduction, the social environment.

The study of behavior in the context of evolution has its origins with Charles Darwin, the co-discoverer of the theory of evolution by natural selection. Darwin was well aware that behaviors should be adaptive, believing that traits and behaviors did not survive without being advantageous to survival.

Evolutionary psychology, and specifically, the evolutionary psychology of humans, has enjoyed a resurgence in recent decades. Evolutionary psychologists look at genetics and behaviors associated with species-specific survival to apply to current conditions. For example, humans are predisposed to be more attentive to dangerous stimuli and remember it later. In prehistoric days, being hypervigilant helped reduced deaths caused by large animals. In current days, most of us are not in the position of prey; however, we still remember threatening stimuli. Some evolutionary psychologists attribute rates in depression and anxiety to this type of evolution-based behavior. In general, we expect all human cultures to express a behavior if it is caused genetically since the genetic differences among human groups are small. The approach taken by most evolutionary psychologists is to predict the outcome of a behavior in a particular situation based on evolutionary theory and then to make observations, or conduct experiments, to determine whether the results match the theory.

There are many areas of human behavior for which evolution can make predictions. Examples include memory, mate choice, relationships between kin, friendship and cooperation, parenting, social organization, and status (Confer et al., 2010).

Evolutionary psychologists have had success in finding experimental correspondence between observations and expectations. In one example, in a study of mate preference differences between men and women that spanned 37 cultures, Buss (1989) found that women valued earning potential factors greater than men, and men valued potential reproductive factors (youth and attractiveness) greater than women in their prospective mates. In general, the predictions were in line with the predictions of evolution although there were deviations in some cultures.

Further Resources

Capgras syndrome is a neuro-psychological condition also known as "imposter syndrome" or "Capgras delusion." People who experience this syndrome will have an irrational belief that someone they know or recognize has been replaced by an imposter.

Want to hear more about Capgras and other mysteries of the brain? Check out this Ted Talk (hawkes.biz/psychdelusion) from V.S. Ramachandran.

Figure 2: Chimpanzees and their behavior are studied to gain insight into human behavior.

Sensation and Perception

Imagine walking between buildings as you move from one class to another. You are inundated with sights, sounds, touch sensations, and smells. You also experience the temperature of the air around you and maintain your balance as you make your way. Do you ever wonder why you see certain colors as they are, or how music can make you feel the way it does? People working in the domain of sensation and perception set out to answer questions just like these.

Sensation remains constant, but your perception can vary (Figure 3). That is because perception is unique to the individual. As we'll see in a later chapter, our experience of the world is not as simple as the sum total of all of the sensory information (or sensation) together. Rather, our experience (or perception) is complex and is influenced by where we focus our attention, our previous experiences, and even our cultural backgrounds.

Figure 3: When you look at this image, you may see a duck or a rabbit. The sensory information remains the same, but your perception can vary dramatically.

Cognitive Psychology

How do you remember a phone number, or a grocery list, or a childhood injury? Do your experiences and the way you think about them affect decisions you make or the way you react to a situation?

The cognitive revolution in the second half of the 20th century created an impetus for psychologists to focus their attention on better understanding the mind and mental processes that underlie behavior. Thus, **cognitive psychology** is the area of psychology that focuses on studying cognitions, or thoughts, and their relationship to our experiences and our actions.

Like biological psychology, cognitive psychology is broad in its scope and often involves collaborations among people from a diverse range of disciplinary backgrounds. This has led some to coin the term *cognitive science* to describe the interdisciplinary nature of this area of research (Miller, 2003).

Group Activity

Think that naming a color is an easy task of perception? Gather a group of friends and head on over to take the Stroop test (hawkes.biz/strooptest). Be sure to have something to record your time on each task.

Cognitive Processes

- Concepts
- Attention
- Problem solving

- Decision making
- Judgement
- Language

- Memory

Cognitive psychologists have research interests that span a spectrum of topics, ranging from attention and problem solving to language and memory. The approaches used in studying these topics are equally diverse.

Further Resources

View a brief video (hawkes. biz/cognitivepsych) recapping some of the major concepts explored by cognitive psychologists.

Further Resources

Piaget proposed several stages of development that can be observed at different ages. Check out this video (hawkes.biz/piagetstages) to see each stage.

Aoccdrnig to a rscheearch at Cmabrigde Uinervtisy, it deosn't mttaer in waht oredr the ltteers in a wrod are, the olny iprometnt tihng is taht the frist and lsat ltteer be in the rghit pclae. The rset can be a toatl mses, and you can sitll raed it wouthit porbelm. Tihs is bcuseae the huamn mnid deos not raed ervey lteter by istlef but the wrod as a wlohe.

Figure 4: According to a researcher at Cambridge University, reading sensation and perception occur so quickly, we often overlook typos. This image can be read and comprehended even though all would agree, it is only closely related to English words.

Given such diversity, cognitive psychology is not captured in one chapter of this text per se; rather, various concepts related to cognitive psychology will be covered in relevant portions of the chapters on sensation and perception, thinking and intelligence, memory, lifespan development, social psychology, and therapy.

Developmental Psychology

How have you changed over time? Did you pass through a set of clearly marked stages on your way to adulthood, or do you think it's more complicated than that?

Developmental psychology is the scientific study of development across a lifespan. Developmental psychologists are interested in processes related to physical maturation. However, their focus is not limited to the physical changes associated with aging, as they also focus on changes in cognitive skills, moral reasoning, social behavior, and other psychological attributes.

Early developmental psychologists focused primarily on changes that occurred through reaching adulthood, providing enormous insight into the differences in physical, cognitive, and social capacities that exist between very young children and adults.

Figure 5: Jean Piaget is famous for his theories regarding changes in cognitive ability that occur as we move from infancy to adulthood.

For instance, research by Jean Piaget (Figure 5) demonstrated that very young children do not demonstrate object permanence. Object permanence refers to the understanding that physical things continue to exist, even if they are hidden from us. If you were to show an adult a toy, and then hide it behind a curtain, the adult knows that the toy still exists. However, very young infants act as if a hidden object no longer exists. The age at which object permanence is achieved is somewhat controversial (Munakata, McClelland, Johnson, and Siegler, 1997).

While Piaget and others such as Erik Erikson were focused on cognitive changes during infancy and childhood as we move to adulthood, there is an increasing interest in extending research into the changes that occur much later in life. This may be reflective of changing population demographics of developed nations as a whole and a greater concern for understanding what happens to us as we age.

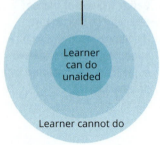

Figure 6: The Zone of Proximal Development describes the process of learning things through examples or leading questions, which helps us move from things we can't do to things we can do.

Reflection Questions

Developmental psychologists have proposed several methods of learning. Vyotsky proposed the concept of scaffolding and the Zone of Proximal Development (Figure 6). The theory explains how individuals move from areas of knowledge they already have to areas of new skills through the use of assistance.

Can you think of activities you engaged in as a child, or skills you have tried to teach another, that utilizes the scaffolding method?

Personality Psychology

If you asked a few people who know you well, what would they say about your personality? How would the traits they see in you compare to those you see in yourself?

Personality psychology focuses on patterns of thoughts and behaviors that make each individual unique. Several theorists (e.g., Freud and Maslow) that we have already discussed in our historical overview of psychology, and the American psychologist Gordon Allport, contributed to early theories of ideas about personality. They all made attempts to explain how an individual's personality develops from his or her given perspective.

For example, Freud proposed that personality arose as a result of conflicts between the conscious and unconscious parts of the mind. Specifically, Freud theorized that an individual went through various psychosexual stages of development. According to Freud, adult personality would result from the resolution of various conflicts that centered on the migration of erogenous (or sexual pleasure-producing) zones from the oral (mouth) to the anus to the phallus to the genitals. Like many of Freud's theories, this particular idea was controversial and did not lend itself to experimental tests (Person, 1980).

Freud's model of personality structure

Figure 7: Freud's model of personality includes major division between the conscious and unconscious and the id, ego, and superego.

More recently, the study of personality has taken on a more quantitative approach. Rather than explaining how personality arises, research is focused on identifying personality traits, measuring these traits, and determining how these traits interact in a particular context to determine how a person will behave in any given situation.

Personality traits are relatively consistent patterns of thought and behavior, and many have proposed that five trait dimensions are sufficient to capture the variations in personality seen across individuals. These five dimensions are known as the "Big Five," or the Five Factor model, and include dimensions of conscientiousness, agreeableness, neuroticism, openness, and extraversion (Figure 8).

Each of these traits has been demonstrated to be relatively stable over the lifespan (e.g., Rantanen, Metsäpelto, Feldt, Pulkinnen, and Kokko, 2007; Soldz & Vaillant, 1999; McCrae & Costa, 2008) and is influenced by genetics (e.g., Jang, Livesly, and Vernon, 1996).

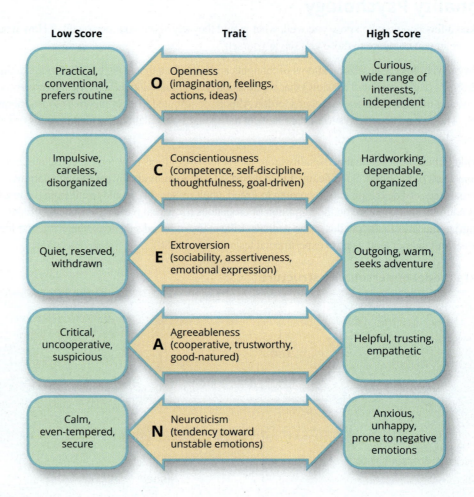

Figure 8: Each of the dimensions of the Five Factor model is shown in this figure. The provided description would describe someone who scored highly on that given dimension. Someone with a lower score on a given dimension could be described in opposite terms.

Further Resources

Wonder how you rate on the Big Five Factors? Take this online test (hawkes.biz/big5factors) to find out!

Social Psychology

Do you act differently when certain people are around? Have you ever done something because you felt social pressure?

Social psychology focuses on how we interact with and relate to others.

Social Psychology

Broad Scope of Topics:

- Explaining our own behavior vs. the behavior of others
- Authority
- Power
- Prejudice
- Attraction
- Conflict
- Impact of social situations on our behavior and thought patterns

Group Activity

Identify a common social norm and then construct an experiment in which you violate this norm. You should observe how others react to you and also how it makes you feel. You may want to have some helpers who can help observe others' responses, but the experiment should ultimately be your own.

Before you begin the assignment, pay attention to the people around you or in the situation where you plan to violate a social norm. How are they acting? Observe how this changes when you break the norm.

To get you started, here are some norms you might violate:

- social distance norms
- conversational norms
- gender norms
- volume norms

Still having difficulty deciding on a norm? Check out this BuzzFeed video (hawkes.biz/psychnorms).

PLEASE NOTE: A man who decides to grow a beard has not violated a norm, even if he has never worn a beard before. A man who decides to grow a beard and dye it pink has violated a norm because it is normative for the males of this era to avoid dying their beards.

BE VERY CAREFUL NOT TO DO ANYTHING ILLEGAL OR THAT PUTS YOU OR OTHERS IN DANGER!

After doing your experiment, answer at least three of the following questions:

1. What social sanctions resulted from your norm violation? Who created and/or enforced them? How?

2. How do race, class, and/or gender affect your deviance (others perception of it, your ability to do it, different sanctions that might be brought against different groups or person engaging in the same act)?

3. What theories best explain the deviance that you have engaged in?

4. What if you could not change your norm violation? How would others see you? How would you cope? How would it affect your life and those around you?

5. During your time as a "deviant," how uncomfortable were you? What normally keeps you in line? How hard is it to break an unspoken rule? How are the unspoken rules enforced?

Figure 9: Are you more likely to perceive someone as an authority by the way they're dressed?

While there are many interesting examples of social psychological research, and you will read about many of these in a later chapter of this text, one of the more controversial and memorable experiments in this field was orchestrated by Stanley Milgram.

Milgram was an American social psychologist who is most famous for research that he conducted on obedience. After the Holocaust, in 1961, a Nazi war criminal, Adolf Eichmann, who was accused of committing mass atrocities, was put on trial. Many people wondered how German soldiers were capable of torturing prisoners in concentration camps, and they were unsatisfied with the excuses given by soldiers that they were simply following orders. At the time, most psychologists agreed that few people would be willing to inflict such extraordinary pain and suffering solely in the interest of obeying orders. Milgram decided to conduct research to determine whether or not this was true.

Milgram found that nearly two-thirds of his participants were willing to deliver what they believed to be lethal shocks to another person just because they were instructed to do so by an authority figure (in this case, a man dressed in a lab coat). This was in spite of the fact that participants received payment for merely showing up for the research study and could have chosen not to inflict pain or more serious consequences on another person by withdrawing from the study.

No one was actually hurt or harmed in any way, but Milgram's experiment was a clever ruse that took advantage of research confederates, those who pretend to be participants in a research study but who are actually working for the researcher and have clear, specific directions on how to behave during the research study (Hock, 2009). Milgram's and others' studies that involved deception and potential emotional harm to

Further Resources

What other discoveries about the human condition have social psychologists found? Check out this article (hawkes.biz/socialpsychexperiments) on "Why We Do Dumb or Irrational Things: 10 Brilliant Social Psychology Experiments."

study participants catalyzed the development of ethical guidelines for conducting psychological research that discourage the use of deception of research subjects, unless it can be argued not to cause harm, and, in general, require informed consent of participants.

Industrial-Organizational Psychology

Industrial-organizational psychology (I-O psychology) is a subfield of psychology that applies psychological theories, principles, and research findings in industrial and organizational settings. I-O psychologists are often involved in issues related to personnel management, organizational structure, and workplace environment. Businesses often seek the aid of I-O psychologists to make the best hiring decisions as well as to create an environment that results in high levels of employee productivity and efficiency. In addition to its applied nature, I-O psychology also involves conducting scientific research on behavior within I-O settings (Riggio, 2013).

Health Psychology

Health psychology focuses on how health is affected by the interaction of biological, psychological, and sociocultural factors. This particular approach is known as the **biopsychosocial model** (Figure 10). Health psychologists are interested in helping individuals achieve better health through public policy, education, intervention, and research. Health psychologists might conduct research that explores the relationship between one's genetic makeup, patterns of behavior, relationships, psychological stress, and health. They may research effective ways to motivate people to address patterns of behavior that contribute to poorer health (MacDonald, 2013).

📷 **Figure 10:** The biopsychosocial model suggests that health/illness is determined by an interaction of biological, social, and psychological factors.

Sport and Exercise Psychology

Researchers in **sport and exercise psychology** study the psychological aspects of sport performance, including motivation and performance anxiety, and the effects of sports on mental and emotional well-being. Research is also conducted on similar topics as they relate to physical exercise in general. The discipline also includes topics that are broader than sport and exercise but that are related to interactions between mental and physical performance under demanding conditions, such as firefighting, military operations, artistic performance, and surgery.

✎ On Your Own

Within the field of sport psychology, two types of psychology are practiced. The first deals with mental-skills training, like teaching athletes to use psychological skills to control anxiety. The other deals with more traditional psychological therapy. Sport psychologists use therapeutic techniques, such as cognitive-behavioral therapy, and apply them to sports performance to deal with the underlying issues that affect an athlete.

Sport psychologists have worked with Olympic athletes for the last several decades. Can you think of different issues that Olympic athletes may face? Complete the table below.

What are some issues Olympic athletes face that can be addressed by mental-skills training and therapy?	
Mental Skills Training	**Therapy**

Clinical Psychology

Clinical psychology is the area of psychology that focuses on the diagnosis and treatment of psychological disorders and other problematic patterns of behavior. As such, it is generally considered to be a more applied area within psychology; however, some clinicians are also actively engaged in scientific research. **Counseling psychology** is a similar discipline that focuses on emotional, social, vocational, and health-related outcomes in individuals who are considered psychologically healthy.

(a)   (b)   (c)

Figure 11: Clinical psychologists use a variety of therapy styles, including (a) individual counseling, (b) group therapy, and (c) the use of play and token economies for children.

As mentioned earlier, both Freud and Rogers provided perspectives that have been influential in shaping how clinicians interact with people seeking psychotherapy. While aspects of the psychoanalytic theory are still found among some of today's therapists who are trained from a psychodynamic perspective, Roger's ideas about client-centered therapy have been especially influential in shaping how many clinicians operate. Furthermore, both behaviorism and the cognitive revolution have shaped clinical practice in the forms of behavioral therapy, cognitive therapy, and cognitive-behavioral therapy (Figure 12). Issues related to the diagnosis and treatment of psychological disorders and problematic patterns of behavior will be discussed in detail in later chapters of this text.

Figure 12: Cognitive-behavioral therapists take cognitive processes and behaviors into account when providing psychotherapy. This is one of several strategies that may be used by practicing clinical psychologists.

By far, this is the area of psychology that receives the most attention in popular media, and many people mistakenly assume that all psychology is clinical psychology.

Forensic Psychology

Forensic psychology is a branch of psychology that deals with questions of psychology as they arise in the context of the justice system. For example, forensic psychologists (and forensic psychiatrists) will assess a person's competency to stand trial, assess the state of mind of a defendant, act as consultants on child custody cases, consult on sentencing and treatment recommendations, and advise on issues such as eyewitness testimony and children's testimony (American Board of Forensic Psychology, 2014). In these capacities, they will typically act as expert witnesses called by either side in a court case to provide their research- or experience-based opinions. As expert witnesses, forensic psychologists must have a good understanding of the law and provide information in the context of the legal system rather than just within the realm of psychology. Forensic psychologists are also used in the jury selection process and witness preparation. They may also be involved in providing psychological treatment within the criminal justice system. Criminal profilers are a relatively small proportion of psychologists that act as consultants to law enforcement.

Figure 13: Forensic psychologists use their training to impact the criminal justice system.

Reflection Questions

Think about the following questions:

- Is the phenomenon of false or "implanted" memories real?

- What are memories, and are they as accurate as we believe them to be?

- Consider the role of the eyewitness in identifying the person who committed the crime. Are you more likely to believe the victim if there is a witness to the sexual assault? Why might we discredit a victim, if they are unable to remember certain aspects of the crime or assailant?

For more, check out the research of Elizabeth Loftus and her "Lost in the Mall" studies.

Careers in Psychology

When most people think of a career in psychology, they imagine a therapist sitting on a couch, listening to their patient's problems, while doodling on a notepad. As one can see from the many branches of psychology described previously, clinical psychology is just one career option. Individuals seeking to be clinical psychologists, as well as those wishing to work in academic settings, will likely need an advanced, or graduate degree. The most common graduate degree is the **PhD**, or Doctor of Philosophy. The process of earning one's PhD takes many years and a great deal of training and is marked by a ceremonial "hooding" at graduation (Figure 14).

Figure 14: Doctoral degrees are generally conferred in formal ceremonies involving special attire and rites.

The requirements to earn a PhD vary from country to country and even from school to school, but usually, individuals earning this degree must complete a dissertation. A **dissertation** is essentially a long research paper or bundled published articles describing research that was conducted as a part of the candidate's doctoral training. In the United States, a dissertation generally has to be defended before a committee of expert reviewers before the degree is conferred.

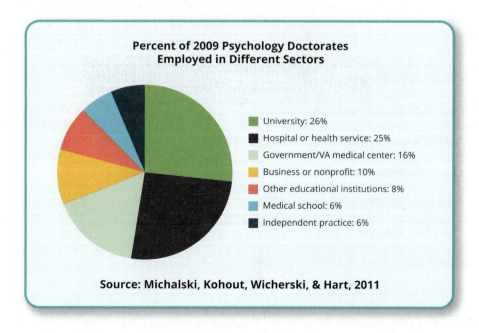

Figure 15: Individuals earning a PhD in psychology have a range of employment options.

Further Resources

The APA provides career information (hawkes.biz/apacareers) about various areas of psychology.

Further Resources

For more information on graduate schools in psychology, check out this video series (hawkes.biz/apagradschool) by the APA.

While earning a doctoral degree in psychology is a lengthy process, usually taking between 5–6 years of graduate study (DeAngelis, 2010), there are a number of careers that can be attained with a master's degree in psychology. People who wish to provide psychotherapy can become licensed to serve as various types of professional counselors (Hoffman, 2012). Relevant master's degrees are also sufficient for individuals seeking careers as school psychologists (National Association of School Psychologists, n.d.), in some capacities related to sport psychology (American Psychological Association, 2014), or as consultants in various industrial settings (Landers, 2011). Undergraduate coursework in psychology may be applicable to other careers, such as psychiatric social work or psychiatric nursing, where assessments and therapy may be a part of the job.

In some areas in psychology, it is common for individuals who have recently earned their PhD to seek out positions in **postdoctoral training programs** that are available before going on to serve as faculty. In most cases, young scientists will complete one or two postdoctoral programs before applying for a full-time faculty position. Postdoctoral training programs allow young scientists to further develop their research programs and broaden their research skills under the supervision of other professionals in the field.

Individuals who wish to become practicing clinical psychologists have another option for earning a doctoral degree, which is known as a PsyD. A **PsyD** is a Doctor of Psychology degree that is increasingly popular among individuals interested in pursuing careers in clinical psychology. PsyD programs generally place less emphasis on research-oriented skills and focus more on application of psychological principles in the clinical context (Norcorss & Castle, 2002).

As mentioned in the opening section of this chapter, an undergraduate education in psychology is associated with a knowledge base and skill set that many employers find quite attractive. It should come as no surprise, then, that individuals earning bachelor's degrees in psychology find themselves in a number of different careers, as shown in Table 1. Examples of a few such careers can involve serving as case managers, working in sales, working in human resource departments, and teaching in high schools. The rapidly growing realm of health care professions is another field in which an education in psychology is helpful and sometimes required. For example, the Medical College Admission Test (MCAT) exam that people must take to be admitted to medical school now includes a section on the psychological foundations of behavior.

Further Resources

Want to know more about the possible career opportunities with a degree in psychology? Check out this website (hawkes.biz/psychcareers) detailing different careers in psychology.

Ranking	Occupation
1	Mid- and top-level management (executive, administrator)
2	Sales
3	Social work
4	Other management positions
5	Human resources (personnel, training)
6	Other administrative positions
7	Insurance, real estate, business
8	Marketing and sales
9	Health care (nurse, pharmacist, therapist)
10	Finance (accountant, auditor)

Table 1: Top Occupations Employing Graduates with a BA in Psychology (Fogg, Harrington, Harrington, & Shatkin, 2012)

Summary

Psychology is a diverse discipline that is made up of several major subdivisions with unique perspectives. Biological psychology involves the study of the biological bases of behavior. Sensation and perception refer to the area of psychology that is focused on how information from our sensory modalities is received, and how this information is transformed into our perceptual experiences of the world around us. Cognitive psychology is concerned with the relationship that exists between thought and behavior, and developmental psychologists study the physical and cognitive changes that occur throughout one's lifespan. Personality psychology focuses on individuals' unique patterns of behavior, thought, and emotion. Industrial and organizational psychology, health psychology, sport and exercise psychology, forensic psychology, and clinical psychology are all considered applied areas of psychology. Industrial and organizational psychologists apply psychological concepts to I-O settings. Health psychologists look for ways to help people live healthier lives. Sport and exercise psychologists study the interactions between thoughts, emotions, and physical performance in sports, exercise, and other activities. Forensic psychologists carry out activities related to psychology in association with the justice system, and clinical psychology involves the diagnosis and treatment of psychological disorders and other problematic behavioral patterns.

Generally, academic careers in psychology require doctoral degrees. However, there are a number of nonacademic career options for people who have master's degrees in psychology. While people with bachelor's degrees in psychology have more limited psychology-related career options, the skills acquired as a function of an undergraduate education in psychology are useful in a variety of work contexts.

1.3 Why Is Research Important?

Flash Forward

Ready to dig into the vocabulary? Get some practice with this Hawkes Verified Quizlet set (hawkes.biz/psych1q3)!

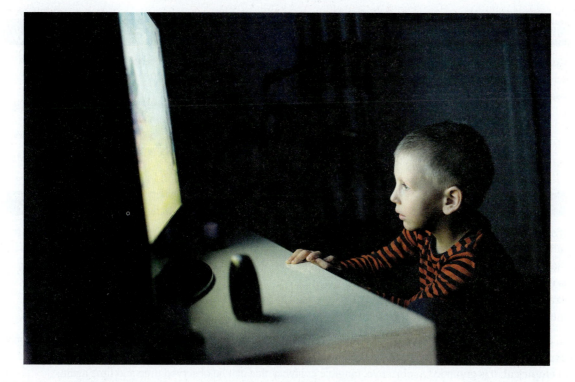

Figure 1: How does television content impact children's behavior?

Have you ever wondered whether the violence you see on television affects your behavior? Are you more likely to behave aggressively in real life after watching people behave violently in dramatic situations on the screen? Or, could seeing fictional violence actually release aggression from your system, causing you to be more peaceful? How are children influenced by the media they are exposed to? A psychologist interested in the relationship between behavior and exposure to violent images might ask these very questions.

The topic of violence in the media today is contentious. Since ancient times, humans have been concerned about the effects of new technologies on our behaviors and thinking processes. The Greek philosopher Socrates, for example, worried that writing—a new technology at that time—would diminish people's ability to remember because they could rely on written records rather than committing information to memory. Currently, many people have stopped memorizing phone numbers. If a cell phone is lost, the owner may only be able to remember one or two numbers. Technology is impacting our ability to remember.

In our world of quickly changing technologies, questions about the effects of media continue to emerge. Many of us find ourselves with a strong opinion on these issues, only to find the person next to us bristling with the opposite view.

How can we go about finding answers that are supported not by mere opinion but by evidence that we can all agree on? The findings of psychological research can help us navigate issues like this.

Figure 2: Some of our ancestors, across the world and over the centuries, believed that trephination—the practice of making a hole in the skull, as shown here—allowed evil spirits to leave the body, thus curing mental illness and other disorders.

Scientific Research

Scientific research is a critical tool for successfully navigating our complex world. Without it, we would be forced to rely solely on intuition, other people's authority, and blind luck. While many of us feel confident in our abilities to decipher and interact with the world around us, history is filled with examples of how very wrong we can be when we fail to recognize the need for evidence in supporting claims. At various times in history, we would have been certain that the sun revolved around a flat earth, that the earth's continents did not move, and that mental illness was caused by possession (Figure 2). It is through systematic scientific research that we divest ourselves of our preconceived notions and superstitions and gain an objective understanding of ourselves and our world.

✎ On Your Own

Read through the following paragraphs and select the sentence that contains the characteristics of scientific knowledge.

> The goal of all scientists is to better understand the world around them. Psychologists focus their attention on understanding behavior, as well as the cognitive (mental) and physiological (body) processes that underlie behavior. The hallmark of scientific research is that there is evidence to support a claim. Scientific knowledge is empirical: it is grounded in objective, tangible evidence that is consistent over time, regardless of who is observing.

If someone is crying, we can see their behavior; it is observable. However, the reason for the behavior is more difficult to determine. Is the person crying due to sadness, pain, or even happiness? Sometimes we can learn the reason for someone's behavior by simply asking them. But there are situations in which an individual is either too uncomfortable or unwilling to answer the question honestly or does not know the reason. For example, infants would not be able to explain why they are crying. In such circumstances, the psychologist must be creative in finding ways to better understand behavior.

In contrast to other methods that people use to understand the behavior of others, such as intuition and personal experience, the hallmark of scientific research is that there is evidence to support a claim. Scientific knowledge is **empirical**: it is grounded in objective, tangible evidence that can be observed time and time again, regardless of who is observing.

Use of Research Information

We should strive to think critically about all the information we encounter by exercising a degree of healthy skepticism. When someone makes a claim, we should examine the claim from different perspectives.

- What is the expertise of the person(s) making the claim?

- What might he/she/they gain if the claim is valid?

- Does the claim seem justified given the evidence?

- What do other researchers think of the claim?

This is especially important when we consider how much of the information in advertising campaigns and on the internet claims to be based on "scientific evidence" when instead it is a belief or perspective to sell a product or draw attention to a perspective.

We should be informed consumers of the information made available to us because decisions based on this information have significant consequences. One such consequence can be seen in politics and public policy.

Imagine that you have been elected as the governor of your state. One of your responsibilities is to manage the state budget and determine how to best spend your constituents' tax dollars. As the new governor, you need to decide whether to continue funding the D.A.R.E. (Drug Abuse Resistance Education) program in public schools (Figure 3). This program typically involves police officers coming into the classroom to educate students about the dangers of becoming involved with alcohol and other drugs. According to the D.A.R.E. website (hawkes.biz/dare1), this program has been very popular since its inception in 1983, and it is currently operating in 75% of school districts in the United States and in more than 40 countries worldwide. Sounds like an easy decision, right? However, on closer review, you discover that the vast majority of research into this program consistently suggests that participation has little, if any, effect on whether or not someone uses alcohol or other drugs (Clayton, Cattarello, & Johnstone, 1996; Ennett, Tobler, Ringwalt, & Flewelling, 1994; Lynam et al., 1999; Ringwalt, Ennett, & Holt, 1991). If you are committed to being a good steward of taxpayer money, will you fund this particular program, or will you try to find other programs that research has consistently demonstrated to be effective?

🖼 **Figure 3:** The D.A.R.E. program continues to be popular in schools around the world despite research suggesting that it is ineffective.

Ultimately, it is not just politicians who can benefit from using research in guiding their decisions. We all might look to research from time to time when making decisions in our lives. Imagine you just found out that a close friend has breast cancer or that one of your young relatives has recently been diagnosed with autism. In either case, you want to know which treatment options are most successful with the fewest side effects. How would you find that out? You would probably talk with your doctor and personally review the research that has been done on various treatment options—always with a critical eye to ensure that you are as informed as possible.

In the end, research is what makes the difference between facts and opinions. **Facts** are observable realities, and **opinions** are personal judgments, conclusions, or attitudes that may or may not be accurate. In the scientific community, facts can be established only using evidence collected through empirical research.

Figure 4: In the 4th century BCE, Aristotle documented the process of deductive reasoning.

The Process of Scientific Research

Scientific knowledge is advanced through a process known as the scientific method. Ideas (in the form of theories and hypotheses) are tested against the real world (in the form of empirical observations), and those empirical observations lead to more ideas that are tested against the real world, and so on. In this sense, the scientific process is circular. The types of reasoning within the circle are called deductive and inductive. In **deductive reasoning**, ideas are tested against the empirical world; in **inductive reasoning**, empirical observations lead to new ideas (Figure 5). These processes are inseparable, like inhaling and exhaling, but different research approaches place different emphasis on the deductive and inductive aspects.

Figure 5: Psychological research relies on both inductive and deductive reasoning.

In the scientific context, deductive reasoning begins with a generalization—one hypothesis—that is then used to reach conclusions about the real world. If the hypothesis is correct, then the logical conclusions reached through deductive reasoning should also be correct. A deductive reasoning argument might go something like this: all living things require energy to survive (this would be your hypothesis or premise). Ducks are living things. Therefore, ducks require energy to survive (logical conclusion). In this example, the hypothesis is correct; therefore, the conclusion is correct as well. Sometimes, however, an incorrect hypothesis may lead to a logical but incorrect conclusion. Consider this argument: all ducks are born with the ability to see. Quackers is a duck. Therefore, Quackers was born with the ability to see. This conclusion may or may not be correct. Quackers could have been born blind.

Scientists use deductive reasoning to empirically test their hypotheses. Returning to the example of the ducks, researchers might design a study to test the hypothesis that if all living things require energy to survive, then ducks will be found to require energy to survive.

Deductive reasoning starts with a generalization that is tested against real-world observations; however, inductive reasoning moves in the opposite direction. Inductive reasoning uses empirical observations to construct broad generalizations. Unlike deductive reasoning, conclusions drawn from inductive reasoning may or may not be correct, regardless of the observations on which they are based. For instance, you may notice that your favorite fruits—apples, bananas, and oranges—all grow on trees; therefore, you assume that all fruit must grow on trees. This would be an example of inductive reasoning, and clearly, the existence of strawberries, blueberries, and kiwi demonstrate that this generalization is not correct despite it being based on a number of direct observations. Scientists use inductive reasoning to formulate theories, which in turn generate hypotheses that are tested with deductive reasoning. In the end, science involves both deductive and inductive processes.

Descriptive research approaches, such as case studies, naturalistic observation, and archival research (which you will read about in the next section) are heavily weighted on the side of empirical observations. Thus, they are closely associated with inductive processes as researchers gather massive amounts of observations and seek interesting patterns (new ideas) in the data. Experimental research, on the other hand, puts great emphasis on deductive reasoning.

We've stated that theories and hypotheses are ideas, but what sort of ideas are they, exactly? A **theory** is a well-developed set of ideas that propose an explanation for observed phenomena. Theories are repeatedly checked against the world, but they tend to be too complex to be tested all at once; instead, researchers create hypotheses to test specific aspects of a theory.

✑ On Your Own

What are the characteristics of a theory and a hypothesis?

Theory	Hypothesis

A **hypothesis** is a testable prediction about how the world will behave if our idea is correct, and it is often worded as an if-then statement (e.g., if I study all night, then I will get a passing grade on the test). The hypothesis is extremely important because it bridges the gap between the realm of ideas and the real world. As specific hypotheses are tested, theories are modified and refined to reflect and incorporate the result of these tests (Figure 6).

Helpful Hint

Deductive reasoning consists of three parts: an initial statement (called a premise), a second related statement, and a conclusion that relates the premise and the second statement.

Further Resources

Play this "Deal Me In" interactive card game (hawkes.biz/inductive) to practice using inductive reasoning.

Helpful Hint

Think of a theory as an umbrella. Everything under the umbrella stays dry, like a person's head, arms, legs. A body is made up of individual units and all are kept dry under the umbrella if it is positioned correctly.

A hypothesis is used to test an individual body part under the umbrella (e.g., right leg) rather than everything under the umbrella.

📷 **Figure 6:** The scientific method of research includes proposing hypotheses, conducting research, and creating or modifying theories based on results.

To see how this process works, let's consider a specific theory and a hypothesis that might be generated from that theory. As you'll learn in a later chapter, the James-Lange theory of emotion asserts that emotional experience relies on the physiological arousal associated with the emotional state. If you walked out of your home and discovered a very aggressive snake waiting on your doorstep, your heart would begin to race and your stomach churn. According to the James-Lange theory, these physiological changes would result in your feeling of fear. A hypothesis that could be derived from this theory might be that a person who is unaware of the physiological arousal that the sight of the snake elicits will not feel fear.

A scientific hypothesis is also **falsifiable**, or capable of being shown to be incorrect. Recall from the introductory chapter that Sigmund Freud had lots of interesting ideas to explain various human behaviors (Figure 7). However, a major criticism of Freud's theories is that many of his ideas are not falsifiable; for example, it is impossible to imagine empirical observations that would disprove the existence of the id, the ego, and the superego—the three elements of personality described in Freud's theories. Despite this, Freud's theories are widely taught in introductory psychology texts because of their historical significance for personality psychology and psychotherapy, and these remain the root of all modern forms of therapy.

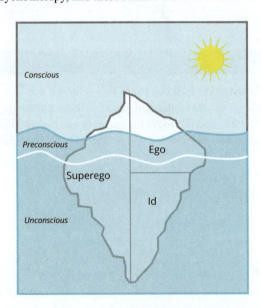

📷 **Figure 7:** Many of the specifics of Freud's theories, such as his division of the mind into id, ego, and superego, have fallen out of favor in recent decades because they are not falsifiable. In broader strokes, his views set the stage for much of psychological thinking today, such as the unconscious nature of the majority of psychological processes.

In contrast, the James-Lange theory does generate falsifiable hypotheses, such as the one described above. Some individuals who suffer significant injuries to their spinal columns are unable to feel the bodily changes that often accompany emotional experiences. Therefore, we could test the hypothesis by determining how emotional experiences differ between individuals who have the ability to detect these changes in their physiological arousal and those who do not. In fact, this research has been conducted and while the emotional experiences of people deprived of an awareness of their physiological arousal may be less intense, they still experience emotion (Chwalisz, Diener, & Gallagher, 1988).

Scientific research's dependence on falsifiability allows for great confidence in the information that it produces. Typically, by the time information is accepted by the scientific community, it has been tested repeatedly.

Summary

Scientists are engaged in explaining and understanding how the world around them works, and they are able to do so by coming up with theories that generate hypotheses that are testable and falsifiable. Theories that stand up to their tests are retained and refined, while those that do not are discarded or modified. In this way, research enables scientists to separate fact from simple opinion. Having good information generated from research aids in making wise decisions both in public policy and in our personal lives.

1.4 Approaches to Research

There are many research methods available to psychologists in their efforts to understand, describe, and explain behavior and the cognitive and biological processes that underlie it. Some methods rely on observational techniques. Other approaches involve interactions between the researcher and the individuals who are being studied—ranging from a series of simple questions to extensive, in-depth interviews—to well-controlled experiments. Sometimes researchers will use two or more approaches in a research study. Each research method has unique strengths and weaknesses, and each method is only appropriate for certain types of research questions.

Further Resources

Watch this video (hawkes.biz/incorrectresearch) about research to learn about some of the problems researchers encounter and how research results are often incorrectly reported in the media.

Flash Forward

Ready to dig into the vocabulary? Get some practice with this Hawkes Verified Quizlet set (hawkes.biz/psych1q4)!

✎ On Your Own

What are the pros and cons of different research methods? Fill in the table below.

Method	PROS	CONS
Archival data		
Case studies		
Naturalistic observation		
Surveys		

Group Activity

Data can belong to multiple categories. Go to the Census Bureau datasets (hawkes.biz/psychdata) and download a data set. This data set is archival in nature but also comes from a survey.

With group members:

1. Determine what some of the variables are (variables are the columns of data). You may need to download a codebook that explains what each column means.

2. Look at the variables in the data set.

3. With group members, discuss which variables may be related.

4. Take a vote and choose two variables.

5. Make a prediction about what the relationship is between the two variables (none, positive correlation, negative correlation).

6. Using Microsoft Excel, you can check your prediction using the Formula tab, More functions, Statistical, or CORREL.

The methods described thus far are correlational in nature. This means that researchers can examine relationships that might exist between two or more variables of interest. However, correlational data cannot be used to make claims about cause-and-effect relationships. Researchers can find a relationship between two variables (or more), but the only way a researcher can claim that the relationship between the variables is cause-and-effect is to perform an experiment. In experimental research, which will be discussed later in this chapter, there is a tremendous amount of control over variables of interest. While this is a powerful approach, experiments are often conducted in very artificial settings. This calls into question whether the results of an experiment would generalize to real-world settings. In addition, many of the questions that psychologists would like to answer cannot be pursued through experimental research because of ethical concerns.

Reflection Questions

A researcher is interested in the long-term effects of child abuse. She believes that child abuse can lead to depression symptoms in adults.

1. What are the pros and cons of using archival research? Survey research? Case studies?

2. A research assistant suggests naturalistic observation. Is this a good idea?

3. How would you design this experiment? What are the ethical challenges to using this design?

Clinical or Case Studies

In 2011, *The New York Times* published a feature story on Krista and Tatiana Hogan, Canadian twin girls. These twins are unique because Krista and Tatiana are conjoined twins, connected at the head. There is evidence that the two girls are connected in a part of the brain called the thalamus, which is a major sensory relay center. Most incoming sensory information is sent through the thalamus before reaching higher regions of the cerebral cortex for processing.

Further Resources

To learn more about Krista and Tatiana, watch this *New York Times* video (hawkes.biz/casestudy) about their lives.

The implications of this potential connection meant that it might be possible for one twin to experience the sensations of the other twin. For instance, if Krista is watching a particularly funny television program, Tatiana might smile or laugh even if she is not watching the program. This possibility has generated the interest of many neuroscientists who seek to understand how the brain uses sensory information.

These twins represent an enormous resource in the study of the brain, and since their condition is very rare, it is likely that with permission, scientists will follow these girls very closely throughout their lives to gain as much information as possible (Dominus, 2011).

✍ On Your Own

What are the pros and cons of case studies?

PROS	CONS

Further Resources

The Shakers are a religious group who live in communes in New England. They are known for making furniture and for practicing celibacy. Because of their celibacy, there are only a few remaining members. Researchers and journalists have spent time in Shaker communities to document (hawkes.biz/observestudy) how they live.

In observational research, scientists are conducting a **clinical** or **case study** when they focus on one person or just a few individuals. Indeed, some scientists spend their entire careers studying just 10–20 individuals. Why would they do this? Obviously, when they focus their attention on a very small number of people, they can gain a tremendous amount of insight into those cases. The richness of information that is collected in clinical or case studies is unmatched by any other single research method. This allows the researcher to have a very deep understanding of the individuals and the particular phenomenon being studied.

If clinical or case studies provide so much information, why are they not used more frequently by researchers? As it turns out, the major benefit of case studies is also a weakness. As mentioned earlier, this approach is often used when studying individuals who are interesting to researchers because they have a rare characteristic. Therefore, the individuals who serve as the focus of case studies are not like most other people. If scientists ultimately want to explain all behavior, focusing attention on such a special group of people can make it difficult to generalize any observations to the larger population. **Generalizing** refers to the ability to apply the findings of a research project to larger segments of society. Again, case studies provide enormous amounts of information, but since the cases are so specific, the potential to apply what is learned to the average person may be very limited.

Further Resources

In *The Man Who Mistook His Wife for a Hat: And Other Clinical Tales*, Dr. Oliver Sacks describes case studies of patients with a rare neurological disorder. You can read more about this book in this archived *New York Times* review (hawkes.biz/rarecasestudy).

Naturalistic Observation

If you want to understand how behavior occurs, one of the best ways to gain information is to simply observe the behavior in its natural context. This type of observational study is called **naturalistic observation**: observing behavior in its natural setting.

However, people might change their behavior in unexpected ways if they know they are being observed. How do researchers obtain accurate information when people tend to hide their natural behavior? This is very similar to the phenomenon mentioned earlier in this chapter: many individuals do not feel comfortable answering a question honestly.

To better understand peer exclusion, Suzanne Fanger collaborated with colleagues at the University of Texas to observe the behavior of preschool children on a playground. How did the observers remain inconspicuous over the duration of the study? They equipped a few of the children with wireless microphones (which the children quickly forgot about) and observed while taking notes from a distance. Also, the children in that preschool (a "laboratory preschool") were accustomed to having observers on the playground (Fanger, Frankel, & Hazen, 2012).

It is critical that the observer be as unobtrusive and as inconspicuous as possible; when people know they are being watched, they are less likely to behave naturally. If you have any doubt about this, ask yourself how your driving behavior might differ in two situations: in the first situation, you are driving down a deserted highway during the middle of the day; in the second situation, you are being followed by a police car down the same deserted highway (Figure 2).

🖼 **Figure 1:** A playground is an ideal place for naturalistic observation of childhood social behavior.

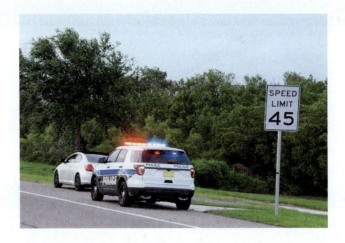

Figure 2: Seeing a police car behind you would probably affect your driving behavior.

It should be pointed out that naturalistic observation is not limited to research involving humans. Indeed, some of the best-known examples of naturalistic observation involve researchers going into the field to observe various kinds of animals in their own environments. As with human studies, the researchers maintain their distance and avoid interfering with the animal subjects so as not to influence their natural behaviors. Scientists have used this technique to study social hierarchies and interactions among animals ranging from ground squirrels to gorillas. The information provided by these studies is invaluable in understanding how those animals organize socially and communicate with one another.

The anthropologist Jane Goodall, for example, spent nearly five decades observing the behavior of chimpanzees in Africa (Figure 3). As an illustration of the types of concerns that a researcher might encounter in naturalistic observation, some scientists criticized Goodall for giving the chimps names instead of referring to them by numbers—using names was thought to undermine the emotional detachment required for the objectivity of the study (McKie, 2010).

(a)   (b)

Figure 3: (a) Jane Goodall made a career of conducting naturalistic observations of (b) chimpanzee behavior.

The greatest benefit of naturalistic observation is the validity, or accuracy, of information collected unobtrusively in a natural setting. Having individuals behave as they normally would in a given situation means that there is a higher degree of ecological validity, or realism, than we might achieve with other research approaches. Because of this, our ability to generalize the findings of the research to real-world situations is enhanced. If completed correctly, we don't need to worry about people or animals modifying their behavior simply because they are being observed. Sometimes, we might assume that reality TV shows give us a glimpse into authentic human behavior. However, the principle of inconspicuous observation is violated as reality stars are followed by camera crews and are interviewed on camera for personal confessionals. Given that environment, we must doubt how natural and realistic their behaviors are.

The major downside of naturalistic observation is that experiments are often difficult to set up and control. In a restroom study, what if you stood in the restroom all day prepared to record people's hand washing behavior and no one came in? Or, what if you have been closely observing a troop of gorillas for weeks only to find that they migrated to a new place while you were sleeping in your tent? The benefit of realistic data comes at a cost. As a researcher you have no control of when (or if) you have behavior to observe. In addition, this type of observational research often requires significant investments of time, money, and a good dose of luck.

✎ On Your Own

What are the pros and cons of naturalistic observation?

PROS	CONS

Sometimes studies involve structured observation. In these cases, people are observed while engaging in set, specific tasks. An excellent example of structured observation comes from the Strange Situation by Mary Ainsworth (you will read more about this in the chapter on lifespan development). The Strange Situation is a procedure used to evaluate attachment styles that exist between an infant and caregiver. In this scenario, caregivers bring their infants into a room filled with toys. The Strange Situation involves several phases, including a stranger coming into the room, the caregiver leaving the room, and the caregiver's return to the room. The infant's behavior is closely monitored at each phase, but it is the behavior of the infant upon being reunited with the caregiver that is most telling in terms of characterizing the infant's attachment style with the caregiver.

Another potential problem in observational research is **observer bias**. Generally, people who act as observers are closely involved in the research project and may unconsciously skew their observations to fit their research goals or expectations. To protect against this type of bias, researchers should have clear criteria established for the types of behaviors recorded and how those behaviors should be classified. In addition, researchers often compare observations of the same event by multiple observers, in order to test **inter-rater reliability**: a measure of reliability that assesses the consistency of observations by different observers.

Surveys

Often, psychologists develop surveys as a means of gathering data. **Surveys** are lists of questions to be answered by research participants and can be delivered as paper-and-pencil questionnaires, administered electronically, or conducted verbally (Figure 4). Generally, the survey itself can be completed in a short time, and the ease of administering a survey makes it easy to collect data from a large group.

Further Resources

Watch this video (hawkes. biz/strangesituation) of the Strange Situation experiment.

Dear Visitor,

Your opinion is important to us.

We would like to invite you to participate in a short survey to gather your opinions and feedback on your news consumption habits.

The survey will take approximately 10-15 minutes.
Simply click the "Yes" button below to launch the survey.

Would you like to participate?

YES   NO

Figure 4: Surveys can be administered in a number of ways, including electronically administered research, like the survey shown here.

Surveys allow researchers to gather data from larger samples than may be afforded by other research methods. A **sample** is a subset of individuals selected from a **population**, which is the overall group of individuals that the researchers are interested in. Researchers study the sample and seek to generalize their findings to the population (Figure 5).

Figure 5: A sample of children can represent the entire school population.

✎ On Your Own

Read through the following paragraphs and select a sentence that identifies the weaknesses of surveys.

There are both strengths and weaknesses of surveys in comparison to case studies. By using surveys, we can collect information from a larger sample of people. A larger sample is better able to reflect the actual diversity of the population, thus allowing better generalizability. Therefore, if our sample is sufficiently large and diverse, we can assume that the data we collect from the survey can be generalized to the larger population with more certainty than the information collected through a case study. However, given the greater number of people involved, we are not able to collect the same depth of information on each person that would be collected in a case study. Another potential weakness of surveys is that people don't always give accurate responses when they self-report. They may lie, misremember, or answer questions in a way that they think makes them look good. For example, people may report drinking less alcohol than is accurate. This is especially a threat for sensitive questions involving things like health, drug and alcohol use, sexual behavior, childhood abuse history, and domestic abuse history.

Any number of research questions can be answered through the use of surveys. One real-world example is the research conducted by Jenkins, Ruppel, Kizer, Yehl, and Griffin (2012) about the backlash against the U.S. Arab-American community following the terrorist attacks of September 11, 2001. Jenkins and colleagues wanted to determine to what extent these negative attitudes toward Arab-Americans still existed nearly a decade after the attacks occurred. In one study, 140 research participants filled out a survey with 10 questions, including questions asking directly about the participant's overt prejudicial attitudes toward people of various ethnicities. The survey also asked indirect questions about how likely the participant would be to interact with a person of a given ethnicity in a variety of settings (such as, "How likely do you think it is that you would introduce yourself to a person of Arab-American descent?"). The results of the research suggested that participants were unwilling to report prejudicial attitudes toward any ethnic group. However, there were significant differences between their pattern of responses to questions about social interaction with Arab-Americans compared to other ethnic groups: they indicated less willingness to participate in social interaction with Arab-Americans compared to the other ethnic groups. This suggested that the participants harbored subtle forms of prejudice against Arab-Americans despite their assertions that this was not the case (Jenkins et al., 2012).

Archival Research

Some researchers gain access to large amounts of data without interacting with a single research participant. Instead, they use existing records to answer various research questions. This type of research approach is known as archival research. **Archival research** relies on looking at past records or data sets to look for interesting patterns or relationships.

For example, a researcher might access the academic records of all individuals who enrolled in college within the past ten years and calculate how long it took them to complete their degrees, as well as course loads, grades, and extracurricular involvement. Archival research could provide important information about who is most likely to complete their education, and it could help identify important risk factors for struggling students (Figure 6).

(a)   (b)

🖼 **Figure 6:** A researcher doing archival research examines records, whether archived as a (a) hardcopy or (b) electronically.

In comparing archival research to other research methods, there are several important distinctions. For one, the researcher employing archival research never directly interacts with research participants. Therefore, the investment of time and money to collect data is considerably less with archival research. Additionally, researchers have no control over what information was originally collected. Therefore, research questions have to be tailored, so they can be answered within the structure of the existing data sets. There is also no guarantee of consistency between the records from one source to another, which might make comparing and contrasting different data sets problematic.

> ### ☑ On Your Own
>
> What are the pros and cons of archival research?
>
> | PROS | CONS |
> | --- | --- |
> | | |
> | | |
> | | |
> | | |

Further Resources

For further information about ongoing prejudice and violence towards Arab-Americans and Muslims read the MDPI article (hawkes.biz/prejudice) on the radicalization of Islam in the United States. You should also check out the Pew Research Center's report (hawkes.biz/violence2) on violence against Muslims. There is also a PRI article (hawkes.biz/hatecrime) analyzing hate crime against Muslims.

Longitudinal and Cross-Sectional Research

Sometimes we want to see how people change over time, as in studies of human development and lifespan. When we test the same group of individuals repeatedly over an extended period of time, we are conducting longitudinal research. **Longitudinal research** is a research design in which data-gathering is administered repeatedly over an extended period of time. For example, we may survey a group of individuals about their dietary habits at age 20, retest them a decade later at age 30, and then again at age 40.

CHARACTERISTICS OF LONGITUDINAL STUDIES

- **What:** Data are gathered from same group of participants over a long period of time

- **When it is used:** Long-term health studies, following individuals with childhood abuse histories, follow a cohort over time (better understand risk factors)

- **Why:** Powerful statistical design because each participant serves as his/her/their own control

- **Challenges:** Substantial time and financial investment, participants or researchers may leave the project

Often longitudinal studies are employed when researching various diseases in an effort to understand specific risk factors. Such studies often involve tens of thousands of individuals who are followed for several decades. Given the enormous number of people involved in these studies, researchers can feel confident that their findings can be generalized to the larger population. The Cancer Prevention Study-3 (CPS-3) is one of a series of longitudinal studies sponsored by the American Cancer Society and aimed at determining predictive risk factors associated with cancer. When participants enter the study, they complete a survey about their lives and family histories, providing information on factors that might cause or prevent the development of cancer. Then every few years the participants receive additional surveys to complete. In the end, hundreds of thousands of participants will be tracked over 20 years to determine which of them develop cancer and which do not.

Clearly, this type of research is important and potentially very informative. For instance, earlier longitudinal studies sponsored by the American Cancer Society provided some of the first scientific demonstrations of the now well-established links between increased rates of cancer and smoking (American Cancer Society, n.d.) (Figure 7).

Figure 7: Longitudinal research like the CPS-3 help us to better understand how smoking is associated with cancer and other diseases.

Research participants must also be willing to continue their participation for an extended period of time, and this can be problematic. People move, get married and take new names, get ill, and eventually die. Even without significant life changes, some people may simply choose to discontinue their participation in the project. As a result, the **attrition** rates, or reduction in the number of research participants due to dropouts, in longitudinal studies are quite high and increases over the course of a project. For this reason, researchers using this approach typically recruit many participants fully expecting that a substantial number will drop out before the end. As the study progresses, they continually check whether the sample still represents the larger population and make adjustments as necessary.

Another approach is cross-sectional research. In **cross-sectional research**, a researcher compares multiple segments of the population at the same time. Using the dietary habits example above, the researcher might directly compare different groups of people by age. Instead of studying a group of people for 20 years to see how their dietary habits changed from decade to decade, the researcher would study a group of 20-year-old individuals and compare them to a group of 30-year-old individuals and a group of 40-year-old individuals. While cross-sectional research requires a shorter-term investment, it is also limited by differences that exist between the different generations (or cohorts) that have nothing to do with age per se but rather reflect the social and cultural experiences of different generations of individuals that make them different from one another.

CHARACTERISTICS OF CROSS-SECTIONAL STUDIES

- **What:** Data are gathered from participants at one point in time and subgroups are compared (e.g., age groups, gender, education level, etc.)

- **When it is used:** Used most frequently for attitudinal and polling research

- **Why:** Provides a snapshot in time and is cheaper than longitudinal research

- **Challenges:** Cannot examine changes in groups over time, or generational differences due to different experiences

To illustrate this concept, consider the following survey findings. In recent years there has been significant growth in the popular support of same-sex marriage. Many studies on this topic break down survey participants into different age groups. In general, younger people are more supportive of same-sex marriage than are those who are older (Jones, 2013). Does this mean that as we age, we become less open to the idea of same-sex marriage, or does this mean that older individuals have different perspectives because of the social climates in which they grew up? Longitudinal research is a powerful approach because the same individuals are involved in the research project over time, which means that the researchers need to be less concerned with differences among cohorts affecting the results of their study.

Summary

The clinical or case study involves studying just a few individuals for an extended period of time. While this approach provides an incredible depth of information, the ability to generalize these observations to the larger population is problematic. Naturalistic observation involves observing behavior in a natural setting and allows for the collection of valid, true-to-life information from realistic situations. However, naturalistic observation does not allow for much control and often requires quite a bit of time and money to perform. Researchers strive to ensure that their tools for collecting data are both reliable (consistent and replicable) and valid (accurate).

Surveys can be administered in a number of ways and make it possible to collect large amounts of data quickly. However, the depth of information that can be collected through surveys is somewhat limited compared to a clinical or case study.

Archival research involves studying existing data sets to answer research questions.

Longitudinal research has been incredibly helpful to researchers who need to collect data on how people change over time. Cross-sectional research compares multiple segments of a population at a single time.

📷 **Figure 8:** Longitudinal research looks at the same individuals in a study over time.

1.5 Analyzing Findings

Correlational Research

A **correlation** means that there is a relationship between two or more variables. When two variables are correlated, it simply means that as one variable changes, so does the other. For example, when ice cream sales increase, so do drowning deaths. Why are these variables correlated? During the hot months of the summer, people are more likely to eat ice cream and swim. The more people swim, the more likely there are to be drowning deaths. However, this does not mean that eating an ice cream cone is going to cause you to drown to death. Just because two variables like ice cream sales and drowning deaths are correlated, we can't assume that one causes the other.

A **positive correlation** means that the variables move in the same direction. Put another way, when one variable increases, the other variable increases; when the same variable decreases, the other variable decreases. The example of ice cream sales and drowning deaths is a positive correlation. When ice cream sales go up, likely during the summer months, so do drowning deaths. Conversely, when ice cream sales go down, during the winter months, so do drowning deaths. Another example is as height increases so does weight.

Flash Forward

Ready to dig into the vocabulary? Get some practice with this Hawkes Verified Quizlet set (hawkes.biz/psych1q5)!

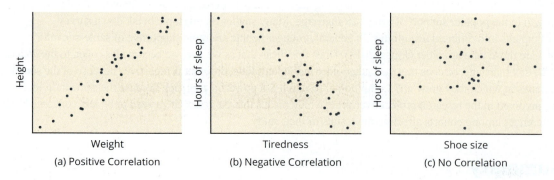

Figure 1: Scatterplots are a graphical view of the strength and direction of correlations. The stronger the correlation, the closer the data points are to a straight line. In these examples, we see that there is (a) a positive correlation between weight and height, (b) a negative correlation between tiredness and hours of sleep, and (c) no correlation between shoe size and hours of sleep.

A **negative correlation** means that the variables move in opposite directions. If two variables are negatively correlated, a decrease in one variable is associated with an increase in the other and vice versa. An example of a negative correlation is exercise and body weight. If diet doesn't change, we might expect that when exercise increases, body weight decreases. In contrast, when exercise decreases, body weight might increase. One might expect a negative correlation to exist between someone's tiredness during the day and the number of hours they slept the previous night: the amount of sleep decreases as the feelings of tiredness increase. In a real-world example of negative correlation, student researchers at the University of Minnesota found a weak negative correlation ($r = -0.29$) between the average number of days per week that students got fewer than 5 hours of sleep and their GPA (Lowry, Dean, & Manders, 2010). Keep in mind that a negative correlation is not the same as no correlation. For example, we would probably find no correlation between hours of sleep and shoe size.

Further Resources

Manipulate this interactive scatterplot (hawkes.biz/correlation) to practice your understanding of positive and negative correlation.

✎ On Your Own

Identify your own positive and negative correlations using the table below.

Correlation Type	Variable 1	Variable 2
Positive		
Negative		

A **correlation coefficient** is usually represented by the letter r. r values range from -1 to $+1$. The closer the number is to 1 (be it negative or positive), the more strongly related the variables are and the more predictable changes in one variable will be as the other variable changes. Let's assume that you bring your umbrella to school with you every day it rains, and you don't bring it when it doesn't rain. In this case, the correlation between you bringing your umbrella and the likelihood of it raining, would be $+1$. Let's say you forget to bring your umbrella when it rains one day, or the weather man calls for rain and it doesn't, so you bring your umbrella on some days when it doesn't rain. In this case, the correlation coefficient of you bringing your umbrella on days when it rains may be 0.6, 0.7, or 0.8.

The closer the number is to zero, the weaker the relationship, and the less predictable the relationships between the variables becomes. For instance, a correlation coefficient of 0.9 indicates a far stronger relationship than a correlation coefficient of 0.3. If the variables are not related to one another at all, the correlation coefficient is 0 (like in shoe size and hours of sleep).

Correlation Does Not Indicate Causation

Correlational research is useful because it allows us to discover the strength and direction of relationships that exist between two variables. However, correlation is limited because establishing the existence of a relationship tells us little about **cause and effect**. While variables are sometimes correlated because one does cause the other, it could also be that some other factor, a **confounding variable**, is causing the systematic movement in our variables of interest. In the ice cream/drowing deaths example mentioned earlier, temperature is a confounding variable that could account for the relationship between the two variables.

☑ On Your Own

Researchers found that being the higher birth order (being a younger sibling) is associated with a higher risk for Down syndrome. Which of the following could be classified as a confounding variable in this study?

- ☐ Age of sibling
- ☐ Age of mother
- ☐ There are no confounding variables.

Unfortunately, people mistakenly make claims of causation as a function of correlations all the time. Such claims are especially common in advertisements and news stories. For example, recent research found that people who eat cereal on a regular basis achieve healthier weights than those who rarely eat cereal (Frantzen, Treviño, Echon, Garcia-Dominic, & DiMarco, 2013; Barton et al., 2005). Does eating cereal really cause an individual to maintain a healthy weight? It is possible that individuals who are obese may avoid meals in attempt to maintain a healthy weight, thus being less likely to eat cereal. If this was the case, the positive correlation between cereal and a healthy weight is not because eating cereal causes weight loss but because people who weigh more are less likely to eat cereal. While correlational research is invaluable in identifying relationships among variables, a major limitation is the inability to establish causality. The next section describes how scientific experiments can help psychologists understand causal relationships between two or more variables.

🖼 **Figure 2:** Does eating cereal really cause someone to be a healthy weight?

Illusory Correlations

The temptation to make erroneous cause-and-effect statements based on correlational research is not the only way we tend to misinterpret data. We also tend to make the mistake of illusory correlations, especially with unsystematic observations. **Illusory correlations**, or false correlations, occur when people believe that relationships exist between two things when no such relationship exists. One well-known illusory correlation is the supposed effect that the moon's phases have on human behavior. Many people passionately assert that human behavior is affected by the phase of the moon, and specifically, that people act strangely when the moon is full (Figure 3).

There is no denying that the moon exerts a powerful influence on our planet. The ebb and flow of the ocean's tides are tightly tied to the gravitational forces of the moon. Many people believe, therefore, that it is logical that we are affected by the moon as well. After all, our bodies are largely made up of water. A meta-analysis of nearly 40 studies consistently demonstrated, however, that the relationship between the moon and our behavior does not exist (Rotton & Kelly, 1985). While we may pay more attention to odd behavior during the full phase of the moon, the rates of odd behavior remain constant throughout the lunar cycle.

🖼 **Figure 3:** Many people believe that a full moon makes people behave oddly.

Why are we so apt to believe in illusory correlations like this? Often we read or hear about them and simply accept the information as valid. Or, we have a hunch about how something works and then look for evidence to support that hunch, ignoring evidence that would tell us our hunch is false; this is known as **confirmation bias**. Other times, we find illusory correlations based on the information that comes most easily to mind, even if that information is severely limited. And while we may feel confident that we can use these relationships to better understand and predict the world around us, illusory correlations can have significant drawbacks. For example, research suggests that illusory correlations—in which certain behaviors are inaccurately attributed to certain groups—are involved in the formation of prejudicial attitudes that can ultimately lead to discriminatory behavior (Fiedler, 2004).

Causality: Conducting Experiments and Using the Data

As you've learned, the only way to establish that there is a cause-and-effect relationship between two variables is to conduct a scientific experiment. An experiment uses controlled settings and conditions to be able to conclude with a degree of certainty that one variable causes a change in another variable. Many experiments are conducted in a laboratory setting so that researchers can control conditions.

The Experimental Hypothesis

A hypothesis is an educated prediction of what will happen in a given study. The hypothesis is often made by observations in the real world or by review of previous research. If you believe watching violent television causes children to behave more violently, you may set up an experiment to test this hypothesis. The study can either confirm that watching violent TV shows results in an increase in violent behavior, or you may also find that this is not the case (Figure 4).

Designing an Experiment

Figure 4: Seeing behavior like this right after a child watches violent television programming might lead you to hypothesize that viewing violent television programming leads to an increase in the display of violent behaviors.

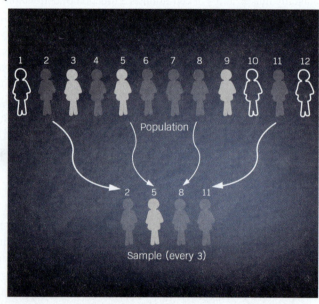

Figure 5: Samples strive to represent the population accurately.

The most basic experimental design involves two groups: the experimental group and the control group. The two groups are designed to be the same except for one difference—experimental manipulation. The **experimental group** gets the experimental manipulation—that is, the treatment or variable being tested (in this case, violent TV images)—and the **control group** does not. Since experimental manipulation is the only difference between the experimental and control groups, we can be sure that any differences between the two are due to experimental manipulation rather than chance.

In an influential study on observational learning, Albert Bandura hypothesized that watching adults engage in violent behavior on television can cause children to be aggressive in real life. His experimental group included children who watched a video of adults punching, kicking, and hitting a doll. Next, the children were placed in a room with the doll, and their behavior was observed.

As expected, the children in the experimental group were likely to punch, hit, and kick the doll as observed in the video. Bandura might be able to conclude with these results that children can learn aggressive behavior from observing adults. If he only included an control group, critics may not have argued that most children, especially boys, would punch, hit, or kick a doll regardless of watching a video. To address this criticism,

Bandura put a control group of children, who did not watch the video, in the room with the doll and observed their behavior. By comparing the results of the experimental group to a control, Bandura could make causal conclusions about the relationship between watching adults model aggressive behavior and children's behavior.

Consistent with his hypothesis, Bandura found that children in the experimental group acted more aggressively toward the dolls than those in the control group. How did Bandura determine if the children were aggressive? You can't exactly get out a ruler and measure aggression. In psychology research, a lot of abstract concepts are measured like aggression, anxiety, depression, and so forth. An **operational definition** is an explanation of how the specific variable was measured. In Bandura's study, each aggressive action, such as a hit, kick, or punch, was added up to determine the child's score.

What if Bandura organized the children into experimental and control groups himself? He might be motivated to pick children who looked like they would be more aggressive for the experimental group. Bandura might count aggressive acts that were questionable for the experimental group but not for the control group to confirm his hypothesis.

Figure 6: Does violent content cause children to become more aggressive?

✎ On Your Own

Joe is trying to determine the effects of exercise on weight loss. One group of men runs 30 minutes a day on the treadmill, whereas the other group does not run 30 minutes on a treadmill. Their weight is measured before and after the study. Which of the following would be considered the experimental group?

☐ The men who ran on the treadmill

☐ The men who did not run on the treadmill

☐ The weight the men gained or lost

In our example of how violent television programming might affect violent behavior in children, we have the experimental group view violent television programming for a specified time and then measure their violent behavior. We measure the violent behavior in our control group after they watch nonviolent television programming for the same amount of time. It is important for the control group to be treated similarly to the experimental group, with the exception that the control group does not receive the experimental manipulation. Therefore, we have the control group watch non-violent television programming for the same amount of time as the experimental group.

We also need to precisely define, or operationalize, what is considered violent and nonviolent. An operational definition is a description of how we will measure our variables, and it is important in allowing others to understand exactly how and what a researcher measures in a particular experiment. In operationalizing violent behavior, we might choose to count only physical acts like kicking or punching as instances of this behavior, or we also may choose to include angry verbal exchanges. Whatever we determine, it is important that we operationalize violent behavior in such a way that anyone who hears about our study for the first time knows exactly what we mean by violence. This aids peoples' ability to interpret our data as well as their capacity to repeat our experiment should they choose to do so.

Once we have operationalized what is considered violent television programming and what is considered violent behavior from our experiment participants, we need to establish how we will run our experiment. In this case, we might have participants watch a 30-minute television program (either violent or nonviolent, depending on their group membership) before sending them out to a playground for an hour where their behavior is observed and the number and type of violent acts is recorded.

Experimenter bias refers to the possibility that a researcher's expectations might skew the results of the study. Remember, conducting an experiment requires a lot of planning, and the people involved in the research project have a vested interest in supporting their hypotheses. If the observers knew which child was in which group, it might influence how much attention they paid to each child's behavior as well as how they interpreted that behavior. **Random assignment** is a process that ensures each participant has an equal chance of being assigned to the experimental or control group. Since Bandura used a random

> **Group Activity**
>
> In groups, come up with your own operational definition for a variable that might be measured in a psychology study. Remember to explain exactly how you are going to measure it.

assignment to divide the participants into experimental and control groups, his study is less likely to be affected by experimenter bias.

By being blind to which participant is in which group, we protect against those biases. The situation described previously is a **single-blind study**, meaning that the participants are unaware as to which group they are in (experiment or control group), while the researcher who developed the experiment knows which participants are in each group. In a **double-blind study**, both the researchers and the participants are blind to group assignments.

Why would a researcher want to run a study where no one knows who is in which group? The **placebo effect** occurs when expectations or beliefs influence or determine our experience in a given situation. In other words, simply expecting something to happen can change your perception of the event. For example, you may take a sugar pill that you believe is an anti-depressant and feel better simply because you were under the impression that the anti-depressant is working. To control for the placebo effect, experimenters randomly assign study participants into an experimental and placebo group. The placebo group may take a pill filled with sugar or some other non-effective substance instead of the actual treatment drug. If participants knew they were taking a placebo pill, then people's expectations for the treatment would be lowered, and it would not be an accurate measure of the placebo effect. This is why participants cannot know if they are receiving the actual treatment or a placebo pill (Figure 7).

Figure 7: Providing the control group with a placebo treatment protects against bias caused by expectancy.

Independent and Dependent Variables

An **independent variable** is manipulated or controlled by the experimenter. In a well-designed experimental study, the independent variable is the only important difference between the experimental and control groups. In Bandura's study, a child's viewing of the aggressive adult behavior before playing with the doll would be the independent variable. A **dependent variable** is what the researcher measures to see how much effect the independent variable had. In Bandura's example, the dependent variable is the number of aggressive acts the children had toward the dolls. We expect that the dependent variable will change as a function of the independent variable. In other words, the dependent variable *depends* on the independent variable. In Bandura's study, the aggressive actions *depended* on if they watched the video of the adults modeling aggressive behavior. A researcher looking at violent television content and its impact on children would be considering whether a child's display of violent acts *depends* on the television content she is watching (Figure 8).

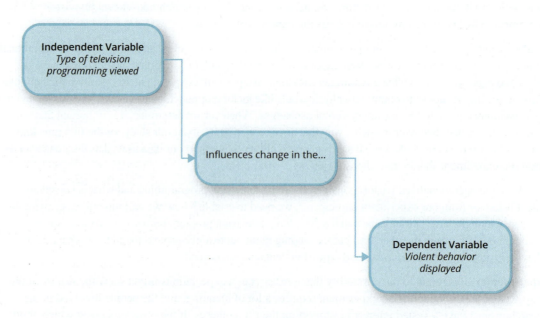

Figure 8: In an experiment, manipulations of the independent variable are expected to result in changes in the dependent variable.

Selecting and Assigning Experimental Participants

Participants are the individuals who are involved in the psychological research or actively participate in the process. The group of participants in a study are referred to as the sample. The population is characteristic of people that the results of the study would apply to, so a sample is a subset of that population. In published research studies, discussions of the sample will often include statistics on age, ethnicity, gender, and other relevant variables. For example, a study assessing a weight loss program for individuals with obesity may include only Caucasian males. The results of this study may suggest that this weight loss program could be used for any individuals who are obese. The population in this case, would be individuals who are obese. Given that the study only includes Caucasian male participants, the results do not apply for individuals with different gender or ethnic backgrounds.

A researcher's goal is to obtain a sample that is representative of the population, which was not the case in the previous example. A **random sample** is when every member of the population regardless of age, gender, or ethnicity has an equal chance of being selected as a part of the study. Random sampling is ideal because researchers can conclude that the participants in the study are representative of a larger population.

Issues to Consider

While experiments allow scientists to make cause-and-effect claims, they are not without problems. True experiments require the experimenter to manipulate an independent variable, and that can complicate many questions that psychologists might want to address. For instance, imagine that you want to know what effect sex (the independent variable) has on spatial memory (the dependent variable). Although you can certainly look for differences between males and females on a task that taps into spatial memory, you cannot directly control a person's sex. We categorize this type of research approach as quasi-experimental and recognize that we cannot make cause-and-effect claims in these circumstances.

Experimenters are also limited by ethical constraints. For instance, you would not be able to conduct an experiment designed to determine if experiencing abuse as a child leads to lower levels of self-esteem among adults. To conduct such an experiment, you would need to randomly assign some experimental participants to a group that receives abuse, and that experiment would be unethical.

Interpreting Experimental Findings

Once data is collected from both the experimental and the control groups, a **statistical analysis** is conducted to find out if there are meaningful differences between the two groups. For example, Bandura had to conduct statistical tests to determine if there was a significant or meaningful difference in aggressive acts between the children that watched the video and those that did not. In many cases significance means 95% confidence, so Bandura's tests revealed with 95% confidence that children who watched a video of adults modeling aggressive behavior are significantly more likely to punch, kick, or hit the doll than children who did not.

Reporting Research

Research psychologists write up the findings of their study for publication in a **peer-reviewed journal**. The peer review process provides some degree of quality control for psychological research. Publications in a peer review psychology journal generally follow formatting guidelines from the American Psychological Association (APA). After an article is sent for publication, several research scientists read it and look for flaws in the study design, methods, analysis, and conclusion. An important consideration that is made by reviewers is how much the study advances the discipline's knowledge. Ultimately, the journal editor will compile the peer reviewers' feedback and determine whether the article will be published in its current state, published with revisions, or not accepted for publication. Peer review also ensures that the research is described clearly enough to allow other scientists to **replicate** it, meaning they can repeat the experiment using different samples to determine reliability.

Further Resources

The Online Writing Lab (OWL) (hawkes.biz/owlpurdue) at Purdue University can walk you through the APA writing guidelines.

Dig Deeper

The Vaccine-Autism Myth and Retraction of Published Studies

Some scientists have claimed that routine childhood vaccines cause some children to develop autism, and in fact, several peer-reviewed publications published research making these claims. Since the initial reports, large-scale epidemiological research has suggested that vaccinations are not responsible for causing autism and that it is much safer to have your child vaccinated than not. Furthermore, several of the original studies making this claim have since been retracted.

A published piece of work can be rescinded when data is called into question because of falsification, fabrication, or serious research design problems. Once rescinded, the scientific community is informed that there are serious problems with the original publication. Retractions can be initiated by the researcher who led the study, by research collaborators, by the institution that employed the researcher, or by the editorial board of the journal in which the article was originally published. In the vaccine-autism case, the retraction was made because of a significant conflict of interest in which the leading researcher had a financial interest in establishing a link between childhood vaccines and autism (Offit, 2008). Unfortunately, the initial studies received so much media attention that many parents around the world became hesitant to have their children vaccinated (Figure 9). For more information about how the vaccine/autism story unfolded, as well as the repercussions of this story, take a look at Paul Offit's book *Autism's False Prophets: Bad Science, Risky Medicine, and the Search for a Cure.*

Figure 9: Some people still think vaccinations cause autism.

Reliability and Validity

Reliability refers to the ability to consistently produce a given result. In the context of psychological research, this would mean that any instruments or tools used to collect data do so in consistent, reproducible ways. **Validity** is the extent to which a given instrument or tool accurately measures what it's supposed to measure. Let's say you take an intelligence test and on one day you receive a score of 120, and you take it another day and score an 80. Given that the scores produce inconsistent results over time, this test would be considered unreliable. Let's assume on this first attempt (where you made the score of 120), you tried your absolute best, but on the second attempt you purposefully answered questions wrong (and made a score of 80). The inconsistent results would not be due to the unreliability of the test, it would be due to your lack of effort. Given that intelligence tests depend on the examinee giving their best effort, the second attempt would be considered invalid because the test did not accurately measure your intellectual ability. In another example, assume that you used a ruler to measure the length of someone's foot and reported it as their weight. You would get scores that are reliable, given that foot size can be measured in a consistent reproducible way. The results would be invalid because foot size is not an accurate measurement of weight.

☑ On Your Own

Answer the following questions on reliability and validity.

1. If a psychological measure is measuring what it's supposed to measure, but yielding inconsistent results over time, the study would be:

☐ Both reliable and valid   ☐ Reliable, not valid

☐ Neither reliable nor valid   ☐ Valid, not reliable

2. Beth conducts an assessment on anxiety, and individuals with depression score higher on it than those with anxiety disorders. However, individuals tend to make consistent scores over time.

☐ Both reliable and valid   ☐ Reliable, not valid

☐ Neither reliable nor valid   ☐ Valid, not reliable

3. Jacob is a math teacher. On his math test, the high performing students scored better than the low performing students. Students were given the test again and received similar scores.

☐ Both reliable and valid   ☐ Reliable, not valid

☐ Neither reliable nor valid   ☐ Valid, not reliable

Summary

A correlation is described with a correlation coefficient, r, which ranges from -1 to $+1$. The correlation coefficient tells us about the nature (positive or negative) and the strength of the relationship between two or more variables. Correlations do not tell us anything about causation—regardless of how strong the relationship is between variables. Researchers can test cause-and-effect hypotheses by conducting experiments. Ideally, experimental participants are randomly selected from the population of interest. Then, the participants are randomly assigned to the experimental and control groups. Sometimes, the researcher and the participants are blind to group membership to prevent their expectations from influencing the results.

The independent variable often includes comparisons between the experimental and control groups. The dependent variable is how the effect of the independent variable is measured. Once data is collected from both groups, it is analyzed statistically to determine if there are meaningful differences between the groups. Psychologists then report their research findings in peer-reviewed journal articles. Research published in this format is checked by several other psychologists who serve as a filter separating ideas that are supported by evidence from ideas that are not. Replication has an important role in ensuring the legitimacy of published research. In the long run, only those findings that are capable of being replicated consistently will achieve consensus in the scientific community.

☑ **On Your Own**

Design your own study by answering the questions in the table below.

Questions	Response
What is your hypothesis?	
Who will participate in your study?	
What are the conditions for the experimental group?	
What are the stipulations for the control group?	
What is the independent variable?	
What is the dependent variable?	
What are the possible conclusions?	

1.6 Ethics

Today, scientists agree that good research is ethical in nature and is guided by a basic respect for human dignity and safety. However, as you will read, this has not always been the case. Modern researchers must demonstrate that the research they perform is ethically sound. This section presents how ethical considerations affect the design and implementation of research conducted today.

Research Involving Human Participants

Any experiment involving the participation of human subjects is governed by extensive, strict guidelines designed to ensure that the experiment does not result in harm. Any research institution that receives federal support for research involving human participants must have access to an **institutional review board (IRB)**. An IRB is a committee of individuals often made up of members of the institution's administration, scientists, and community members (Figure 1). The purpose of an IRB is to review proposals for research that involves human participants. An IRB reviews these proposals with the principles mentioned above in mind, and generally, approval from an IRB is required for the experiment to proceed.

An institution's IRB requires several components in any experiment it approves. For one, each participant must sign an informed consent form before they can participate in the experiment. An **informed consent** form provides a written description of what participants can expect during the experiment, which includes:

- The potential risks and implications of the research.

- Participation in the study is voluntary.

- Participant can discontinue the study at any time without penalty.

- Informed consent guarantees that any data collected in the experiment will remain completely confidential.

- Parents or legal guardians must sign the consent form for children under the age of 18.

Flash Forward

Ready to dig into the vocabulary? Get some practice with this Hawkes Verified Quizlet set (hawkes.biz/ psych1q6)!

📷 **Figure 1:** An institution's IRB meets regularly to review experimental proposals that involve human participants.

Further Resources

Visit this website (hawkes. biz/consentform) to see an example of a consent form.

✍ On Your Own

Using the table below, explain why you think each of the following was included in the informed consent process.

Consent Form Process	Why it should be included?
The potential risks and implications of the research.	
Participation in the study is voluntary.	
Participant can discontinue the study at any time without penalty.	
Informed consent guarantees that any data collected in the experiment will remain completely confidential.	
Parents or legal guardians must sign the consent form for children under the age of 18.	

While the informed consent form should be as honest as possible in describing exactly what participants will be doing, sometimes deception is necessary to prevent participants' knowledge of the exact research question from affecting the results of the study. **Deception** involves purposely misleading experiment participants to maintain the integrity of the experiment but not to the point where the deception could be considered harmful. For example, if we are interested in how our opinion of someone is affected by their attire, we wouldn't want to tell participants that that is the purpose of our study. If we did, then it would likely affect the results.

Reflection Questions

Design a study of your own that might require deception.

We might use deception in describing the experiment to prevent that knowledge from affecting participants' responses. In cases where deception is involved, participants must receive a full **debriefing** upon conclusion of the study—complete, honest information about the purpose of the experiment, how the data collected will be used, the reasons why deception was necessary, and information about how to obtain additional information about the study.

Reflection Questions
Using your example study, how would you debrief the subjects?

Dig Deeper

Ethics and the Tuskegee Syphilis Study

Figure 2: A participant in the Tuskegee Syphilis Study receives an injection.

Unfortunately, the ethical guidelines that exist for research today were not always applied in the past. In 1932, poor, rural, Black, male sharecroppers from Tuskegee, Alabama, were recruited to participate in an experiment conducted by the U.S. Public Health Service, with the aim of studying syphilis in Black men (Figure 2). In exchange for free medical care, meals, and burial insurance, 600 men agreed to participate in the study. A little more than half of the men tested positive for syphilis, and they served as the experimental group (given that the researchers could not randomly assign participants to groups, this represents a quasi-experiment). The remaining syphilis-free individuals served as the control group. However, those individuals that tested positive for syphilis were never informed that they had the disease.

While there was no treatment for syphilis when the study began, by 1947 penicillin was recognized as an effective treatment for the disease. Despite this, no penicillin was administered to the participants in this study, and the participants were not allowed to seek treatment at any other facilities if they continued in the study. Over the course of 40 years, many of the participants unknowingly spread syphilis to their wives (and subsequently their children born from their wives) and eventually died because they never received treatment for the disease. This study was discontinued in 1972 when the experiment was discovered by the national press (Tuskegee University, n.d.). The resulting outrage over the experiment led directly to the National Research Act of 1974 and the strict ethical guidelines for research on humans described in this lesson.

Why is this study unethical? How were the men who participated and their families harmed as a function of this research?

Further Resources
Visit this website (hawkes.biz/tuskegee) to learn more about the Tuskegee Syphilis Study.

✎ On Your Own

Where do researchers need to apply to in order to ensure that their study is ethical for human subjects?

☐ Debriefing   ☐ Informed consent   ☐ Institutional Review Board

Research Involving Animal Subjects

Figure 3: Rats, like the one shown here, often serve as the subjects of animal research.

Many psychologists conduct research involving animal subjects. Often, these researchers use rodents (Figure 3) or birds as the subjects of their experiments—the APA estimates that 90% of all animal research in psychology uses these species (American Psychological Association, n.d.). Because many basic processes in animals are sufficiently similar to those in humans, these animals are acceptable substitutes for research that would be considered unethical in human participants.

This does not mean that animal researchers are immune to ethical concerns. Indeed, the humane and ethical treatment of animal research subjects is a critical aspect of this type of research. Researchers must design their experiments to minimize any pain or distress experienced by animals serving as research subjects.

Whereas IRBs review research proposals that involve human participants, animal experimental proposals are reviewed by an **Institutional Animal Care and Use Committee (IACUC)**. An IACUC consists of institutional administrators, scientists, veterinarians, and community members. This committee is charged with ensuring that all experimental proposals require the humane treatment of animal research subjects. It also conducts semi-annual inspections of all animal facilities to ensure that the research protocols are being followed. No animal research project can proceed without the committee's approval.

☑ On Your Own

The process of informing a participant about the procedures of the study and their rights as a human subject is called?

☐ Debriefing   ☐ Informed consent   ☐ Institutional Review Board

---

Summary

Ethics in research is an evolving field, and some practices that were accepted or tolerated in the past would be considered unethical today. Researchers are expected to adhere to basic ethical guidelines when conducting experiments that involve human participants. Any experiment involving human participants must be approved by an IRB. Participation in experiments is voluntary and requires informed consent of the participants. If any deception is involved in the experiment, each participant must be fully debriefed upon the conclusion of the study.

Animal research is also held to a high ethical standard. Researchers who use animals as experimental subjects must design their projects so that pain and distress are minimized. Animal research requires the approval of an IACUC, and all animal facilities are subject to regular inspections to ensure that animals are being treated humanely.

🔖 **Chapter 1 Project**

Purpose

You've learned about different research methods, and you've been introduced to experiments and correlations. Students often have a very difficult time understanding experiments and correlations and often confuse aspects of them. **The purpose of this project is to help you to understand experiments and correlations, and to learn the difference between them.** Doing this project in pairs would be great! It will probably make you less likely to fall into this experiment-correlation confusion.

You will need to have an understanding of experiments and correlations, as well as descriptive research methods, variables, and the other basics of psychological research methods. Lessons 1.3–1.5 will help you there. Feel free to go to outside, web-based resources if you want some more clarification on any of these things.

Directions

You will design two studies: one experimental and one correlational. You will not actually DO the studies. You will just develop them, which is going to take some creativity (which good researchers are full of). There are a couple of things to note as we begin:

- Each study will use the same variables (whichever you choose)

- Each study will intend to ask a question that could be somehow helpful to the average student's life (e.g., in areas of school, work, relationships, health, etc.)

For <u>each</u> of the studies:

1. Identify your hypothesis.

2. Identify your participants and explain what you are doing with your participants.

3. Identify your operationally defined variables (two for each study).

4. Write a paragraph or two to describe all aspects of each study, right up to the point where you would actually do the study.

5. Imagine you did the studies and that your hypotheses were supported. Include a simple statement of what conclusion can be drawn from each study.

6. Include a final statement about how such psychological findings could be helpful to students.

Finally, write a single paragraph to explain the differences between the findings of your two studies (i.e., how correlation and experiments are different).

Materials

None required. Trifold poster board as optional follow-up. See below.

Going a step further? Create a visually stimulating trifold poster with your experimental design depicted on the left, your correlational design depicted on the right, and the center of the folder with connecting information (e.g., differences and similarities of the methods, how these research questions help students, etc.). Be ready to present your poster to your peers.

✅ **Checklist**

Experimental Study

- ☐ Hypothesis
- ☐ Participants (and what you'll do with them)
- ☐ Independent & dependent variables
- ☐ Experimental & control conditions
- ☐ Study narrative (1-2 paragraphs)
- ☐ Simple conclusion statement
- ☐ Helpful to students?

Correlational Study

- ☐ Hypothesis
- ☐ Participants (and what you'll do with them)
- ☐ Independent & dependent variables
- ☐ Study narrative (1-2 paragraphs)
- ☐ Simple conclusion statement
- ☐ Helpful to students?

Comparison

- ☐ Explain differences in findings from your studies (1 paragraph)

⚑ Chapter 1 Review

Lesson Summaries

1.1 What Is Psychology?

Psychology derives from the roots *psyche* (meaning "soul") and *-ology* (meaning "scientific study of"). Thus, psychology is defined as the scientific study of mind and behavior. Students of psychology develop critical thinking skills, become familiar with the scientific method, and recognize the complexity of behavior.

Before the time of Wundt and James, questions about the mind were considered by philosophers. However, both Wundt and James helped create psychology as a distinct scientific discipline. Wundt was a structuralist, which meant he believed that our cognitive experience was best understood by breaking that experience into its component parts. He thought this was best accomplished by introspection.

William James was the first American psychologist, and he was a proponent of functionalism. This particular perspective focused on how mental activities served as adaptive responses to an organism's environment. Like Wundt, James also relied on introspection; however, his research approach also incorporated more objective measures as well.

Psychology has not been exempt from the barriers that prevented people from entering the field based on race or gender. Despite this, the field has been heavily influenced and enriched by contributions of pioneering psychologists like Mary Whiton Calkins and Francis Cecil Sumner who overcame those barriers and made it both more representative and more inclusive.

Sigmund Freud believed that understanding the unconscious mind was absolutely critical to understanding conscious behavior. This was especially true for individuals that he saw who suffered from various hysterias and neuroses. Freud relied on dream analysis, slips of the tongue, and free association

as means to access the unconscious. Psychoanalytic theory remained a dominant force in clinical psychology for several decades.

Gestalt psychology was very influential in Europe. Gestalt psychology takes a holistic view of an individual and his experiences. As the Nazis came to power in Germany, Wertheimer, Koffka, and Köhler immigrated to the United States. Although they left their laboratories and their research behind, they did introduce America to Gestalt ideas. Some of the principles of Gestalt psychology are still very influential in the study of sensation and perception.

One of the most influential schools of thought within psychology's history was behaviorism. Behaviorism focused on making psychology an objective science by studying overt behavior and deemphasizing the importance of unobservable mental processes. John Watson is often considered the father of behaviorism, and B.F. Skinner's contributions to our understanding of the principles of operant conditioning cannot be underestimated.

As behaviorism and psychoanalytic theory took hold of so many aspects of psychology, some began to become dissatisfied with psychology's picture of human nature. Thus, a humanistic movement within psychology began to take hold. Humanism focuses on the potential of all people for good. Both Maslow and Rogers were influential in shaping humanistic psychology.

During the 1950s, the landscape of psychology began to change. A science of behavior began to shift back to its roots of focus on mental processes. The emergence of neuroscience and computer science aided this transition. Ultimately, the cognitive revolution took hold, and people came to realize that cognition was crucial to a true appreciation and understanding of behavior.

1.2 Contemporary Psychology

Psychology is a diverse discipline that is made up of several major subdivisions with unique perspectives. Biological psychology involves the study of the biological bases of behavior. Sensation and perception refer to the area of psychology that is focused on how information from our sensory modalities is received, and how this information is transformed into our perceptual experiences of the world around us. Cognitive psychology is concerned with the relationship that exists between thought and behavior, and developmental psychologists study the physical and cognitive changes that occur throughout one's lifespan. Personality psychology focuses on individuals' unique patterns of behavior, thought, and emotion. Industrial and organizational psychology, health psychology, sport and exercise psychology, forensic psychology, and clinical psychology are all considered applied areas of psychology. Industrial and organizational psychologists apply psychological concepts to I-O settings. Health psychologists look for ways to help people live healthier lives. Sport and exercise psychologists study the interactions between thoughts, emotions, and physical performance in sports, exercise, and other activities. Forensic psychologists carry out activities related to psychology in association with the justice system, and clinical psychology involves the diagnosis and treatment of psychological disorders and other problematic behavioral patterns.

Generally, academic careers in psychology require doctoral degrees. However, there are a number of nonacademic career options for people who have master's degrees in psychology. While people with bachelor's degrees in psychology have more limited psychology-related career options, the skills acquired as a function of an undergraduate education in psychology are useful in a variety of work contexts.

1.3 Why Is Research Important?

Scientists are engaged in explaining and understanding how the world around them works, and they are able to do so by coming up with theories that generate hypotheses that are testable and falsifiable. Theories that stand up to their tests are retained and refined, while those that do not are discarded or modified. In this way, research enables scientists to separate fact from simple opinion. Having good information generated from research aids in making wise decisions both in public policy and in our personal lives.

1.4 Approaches to Research

The clinical or case study involves studying just a few individuals for an extended period of time. While this approach provides an incredible depth of information, the ability to generalize these observations to the larger population is problematic. Naturalistic observation involves observing behavior in a natural setting and allows for the collection of valid, true-to-life information from realistic situations. However, naturalistic observation does not allow for much control and often requires quite a bit of time and money to perform. Researchers strive to ensure that their tools for collecting data are both reliable (consistent and replicable) and valid (accurate).

Surveys can be administered in a number of ways and make it possible to collect large amounts of data quickly. However, the depth of information that can be collected through surveys is somewhat limited compared to a clinical or case study.

Archival research involves studying existing data sets to answer research questions.

Longitudinal research has been incredibly helpful to researchers who need to collect data on how people change over time. Cross-sectional research compares multiple segments of a population at a single time.

1.5 Analyzing Findings

A correlation is described with a correlation coefficient, r, which ranges from −1 to +1. The correlation coefficient tells us about the nature (positive or negative) and the strength of the relationship between two or more variables. Correlations do not tell us anything about causation—regardless of how strong the relationship is between variables. Researchers can test cause-and-effect hypotheses by conducting experiments. Ideally, experimental participants are randomly selected from the population of interest. Then, the participants are randomly assigned to the experimental and control groups. Sometimes, the researcher and the participants are blind to group membership to prevent their expectations from influencing the results.

The independent variable often includes comparisons between the experimental and control groups. The dependent variable is how the effect of the independent variable is measured. Once data is collected from both groups, it is analyzed statistically to determine if there are meaningful differences between the groups. Psychologists then report their research findings in peer-reviewed journal articles. Research published in this format is checked by several other psychologists who serve as a filter separating ideas that are supported by evidence from ideas that are not. Replication has an important role in ensuring the legitimacy of published research. In the long run, only those findings that are capable of being replicated consistently will achieve consensus in the scientific community.

1.6 Ethics

Ethics in research is an evolving field, and some practices that were accepted or tolerated in the past would be considered unethical today. Researchers are expected to adhere to basic ethical guidelines when conducting experiments that involve human participants. Any experiment involving human participants must be approved by an IRB. Participation in

experiments is voluntary and requires informed consent of the participants. If any deception is involved in the experiment, each participant must be fully debriefed upon the conclusion of the study.

Animal research is also held to a high ethical standard. Researchers who use animals as experimental subjects must design their projects so that pain and distress are minimized. Animal research requires the approval of an IACUC, and all animal facilities are subject to regular inspections to ensure that animals are being treated humanely.

Key Terms

> ### Flash Back
> Now that you've worked through the chapter, sharpen your vocabulary with this Hawkes Verified Quizlet set (hawkes.biz/psychch1)!

American Psychological Association
Professional organization representing psychologists in the United States

Archival Research
Method of research using past records or data sets to answer various research questions or to search for interesting patterns or relationships

Attrition
Reduction in number of research participants as some drop out of the study over time

Behaviorism
Focus on observing and controlling behavior

Biopsychosocial model
Perspective that asserts that biology, psychology, and social factors interact to determine an individual's health

Biopsychology
Study of how biology influences behavior

Cause-and-Effect Relationship
Changes in one variable cause the changes in the other variable; can be determined only through an experimental research design

Clinical or Case Study
Observational research study focusing on one or a few people

Clinical Psychology

Area of psychology that focuses on the diagnosis and treatment of psychological disorders and other problematic patterns of behavior

Cognitive Psychology

Study of cognitions, or thoughts, and their relationship to experiences and actions

Confirmation Bias

Tendency to ignore evidence that disproves ideas or beliefs

Confounding Variable

Unanticipated outside factor that affects both variables of interest, often giving the false impression that changes in one variable causes changes in the other variable when, in actuality, the outside factor causes changes in both variables

Control Group

Serves as a basis for comparison and controls for chance factors that might influence the results of the study—by holding such factors constant across groups so that the experimental manipulation is the only difference between groups

Correlation

Relationship between two or more variables; when two variables are correlated, one variable changes as the other does

Correlation Coefficient

Number from −1 to +1 indicating the strength and direction of the relationship between variables and usually represented by r

Counseling Psychology

Area of psychology that focuses on improving emotional, social, vocational, and other aspects of the lives of psychologically healthy individuals

Cross-Sectional Research

Compares multiple segments of a population at a single time

Debriefing

When an experiment involves deception, participants are told complete and truthful information about the experiment at its conclusion

Deception

Purposely misleading experiment participants in order to maintain the integrity of the experiment

Deductive Reasoning

Results are predicted based on a general premise

Dependent Variable

Variable that the researcher measures to see how much effect the independent variable had

Developmental Psychology

Scientific study of development across a lifespan

Dissertation

Long paper on research that was conducted as a part of the candidate's doctoral training

Double-Blind Study

Experiment in which both the researchers and the participants are blind to group assignments

Empirical

Grounded in objective, tangible evidence that can be observed time and time again, regardless of who is observing

Empirical Method

Method for acquiring knowledge based on observation, including experimentation, rather than a method based only on forms of logical argument or previous authorities

Experimental Group

Group designed to answer the research question; experimental manipulation is the only difference between the experimental and control groups, so any differences between the two are due to experimental manipulation rather than chance

Experimenter Bias

Researcher expectations skew the results of the study

Fact

Objective and verifiable observation, established using evidence collected through empirical research

Falsifiable

Able to be disproven by experimental results

Forensic Psychology

Area of psychology that applies the science and practice of psychology to issues within and related to the justice system

Functionalism

Focuses on how mental activities help an organism adapt to its environment

Generalize

Inferring that the results for a sample apply to the larger population

Humanism

Perspective within psychology that emphasizes the potential for good that is innate to all humans

Hypothesis

(Plural: *hypotheses*) tentative and testable statement about the relationship between two or more variables

Illusory Correlation

Seeing relationships between two things when in reality no such relationship exists

Independent Variable

Variable that is influenced or controlled by the experimenter; in a sound experimental study, the independent variable is the only important difference between the experimental and control group

Inductive Reasoning

Conclusions are drawn from observations

Informed Consent

Process of informing a research participant about what to expect during an experiment, any risks involved, and the implications of the research and then obtaining the person's consent to participate

Institutional Animal Care and Use Committee (IACUC)

Committee of administrators, scientists, veterinarians, and community members that reviews proposals for research involving non-human animals

Institutional Review Board (IRB)

Committee of administrators, scientists, and community members that reviews proposals for research involving human participants

Inter-rater Reliability

Measure of agreement among observers on how they record and classify a particular event

Introspection

Process by which someone examines their own conscious experience in an attempt to break it into its component parts

Longitudinal Research

Studies in which the same group of individuals is surveyed or measured repeatedly over an extended period of time

Naturalistic Observation

Observation of behavior in its natural setting

Negative Correlation

Two variables change in different directions, with one becoming larger as the other becomes smaller; a negative correlation is not the same thing as no correlation

Observer Bias

When observations may be skewed to align with observer expectations

-ology

Suffix that denotes "scientific study of"

Operational Definition

Description of what actions and operations will be used to measure the dependent variables and manipulate the independent variables

Opinion

Personal judgments, conclusions, or attitudes that may or may not be accurate

Participants

Subjects of psychological research

Peer-Reviewed Journal Article

Article read by several other scientists (usually anonymously) with expertise in the subject matter, who provide feedback regarding the quality of the manuscript before it is accepted for publication

Personality Psychology

Study of patterns of thoughts and behaviors that make each individual unique

Personality Trait

Consistent pattern of thought and behavior

PhD

(Doctor of philosophy) doctoral degree conferred in many disciplinary perspectives housed in a traditional college of liberal arts and sciences

Placebo Effect

People's expectations or beliefs influencing or determining their experience in a given situation

Population

Overall group of individuals that the researchers are interested in

Positive Correlation

Two variables change in the same direction, both becoming either larger or smaller

Postdoctoral Training Program

Allows young scientists to further develop their research programs and broaden their research skills under the supervision of other professionals in the field

Psyche

Greek word for *soul*

Psychoanalytic Theory

Focus on the role of the unconscious in affecting conscious behavior

Psychology

Scientific study of the mind and behavior

PsyD

(Doctor of psychology) doctoral degree that places less emphasis on research-oriented skills and focuses more on application of psychological principles in the clinical context

Random Assignment

Method of experimental group assignment in which all participants have an equal chance of being assigned to either group

Random Sample

Subset of a larger population in which every member of the population has an equal chance of being selected

Reliability

Consistency and reproducibility of a given result

Replicate

Repeating an experiment using different samples to determine the research's reliability

Sample

Subset of individuals selected from the larger population

Single-Blind Study

Experiment in which the researcher knows which participants are in the experimental group and which are in the control group

Sport and Exercise Psychology

Area of psychology that focuses on the interactions between mental and emotional factors and physical performance in sports, exercise, and other activities

Statistical Analysis

Determines how likely any difference between experimental groups is due to chance

Structuralism

Understanding the conscious experience through introspection

Survey

List of questions to be answered by research participants—given as paper-and-pencil questionnaires, administered electronically, or conducted verbally—allowing researchers to collect data from a large number of people

Theory

Well-developed set of ideas that propose an explanation for observed phenomena

Validity

Accuracy of a given result in measuring what it is designed to measure

💡 Exercises

Review Questions

1. Which of the following was mentioned as a skill to which psychology students would be exposed?

   a. Critical thinking

   b. Use of the scientific method

   c. Critical evaluation of sources of information

   d. All of the above

2. *Psyche* is a Greek word meaning _____.

   a. essence

   b. soul

   c. behavior

   d. love

3. Before psychology became a recognized academic discipline, matters of the mind were undertaken by those in _____.

   a. biology

   b. chemistry

   c. philosophy

   d. physics

4. In the scientific method, a hypothesis is a(n) _____.

   a. observation

   b. measurement

   c. test

   d. proposed explanation

5. Based on your reading, which theorist would have been most likely to agree with this statement? Perceptual phenomena are best understood as a combination of their components.

   a. William James

   b. Max Wertheimer

   c. Carl Rogers

   d. Noam Chomsky

6. _____ is most well-known for proposing his hierarchy of needs.

   a. Noam Chomsky

   b. Carl Rogers

   c. Abraham Maslow

   d. Sigmund Freud

7. Rogers believed that providing genuineness, empathy, and _____ in the therapeutic environment for his clients was critical to their being able to deal with their problems.

   a. structuralism

   b. functionalism

   c. Gestalt

   d. unconditional positive regard

8. The operant conditioning chamber (aka _____ box) is a device used to study the principles of operant conditioning.

   a. Skinner

   b. Watson

   c. James

   d. Koffka

9. A researcher interested in how changes in the cells of the hippocampus (a structure in the brain related to learning and memory) are related to memory formation would be most likely to identify as a _____ psychologist.

   a. biological

   b. health

   c. clinical

   d. social

10. An individual's consistent pattern of thought and behavior is known as a(n) _____.

    a. psychosexual stage

    b. object permanence

    c. personality

    d. perception

11. In Milgram's controversial study on obedience, nearly _____ of the participants were willing to administer what appeared to be lethal electrical shocks to another person because they were told to do so by an authority figure.

   a. 1/3

   b. 2/3

   c. 3/4

   d. 4/5

12. A researcher interested in what factors make an employee best suited for a given job would most likely identify as a(n) _____ psychologist.

   a. personality

   b. clinical

   c. social

   d. I-O

13. If someone wanted to become a psychology professor at a 4-year college, then s/he would probably need a _____ degree in psychology.

   a. bachelor of science

   b. bachelor of art

   c. master's

   d. PhD

14. The _____ places less emphasis on research and more emphasis on application of therapeutic skills.

   a. PhD

   b. PsyD

   c. postdoctoral training program

   d. dissertation

15. Which of the following degrees would be the minimum required to teach psychology courses in high school?

   a. PhD

   b. PsyD

   c. Master's degree

   d. Bachelor's degree

16. One would need at least a(n) _____ degree to serve as a school psychologist.

   a. associate's

   b. bachelor's

   c. master's

   d. doctoral

17. Scientific hypotheses are _____ and falsifiable.

   a. observable

   b. original

   c. provable

   d. testable

18. _____ are defined as observable realities.

   a. Behaviors

   b. Facts

   c. Opinions

   d. Theories

19. Scientific knowledge is _____.

   a. intuitive

   b. empirical

   c. permanent

   d. subjective

20. A major criticism of Freud's early theories involves the fact that his theories _____.

   a. were too limited in scope

   b. were too outrageous

   c. were too broad

   d. were not testable

21. Sigmund Freud developed his theory of human personality by conducting in-depth interviews over an extended period of time with a few clients. This type of research approach is known as a(n) _____.

   a. archival research

   b. case study

   c. naturalistic observation

   d. survey

22. _____ involves observing behavior in individuals in their natural environments.

    a.   Archival research

    b.   Case study

    c.   Naturalistic observation

    d.   Survey

23. The major limitation of case studies is _____.

    a.   the superficial nature of the information collected in this approach

    b.   the lack of control that the researcher has in this approach

    c.   the inability to generalize the findings from this approach to the larger population

    d.   the absence of inter-rater reliability

24. The benefit of naturalistic observation studies is _____.

    a.   the honesty of the data that is collected in a realistic setting

    b.   how quick and easy these studies are to perform

    c.   the researcher's capacity to make sure that data is collected as efficiently as possible

    d.   the ability to determine cause and effect in this particular approach

25. Using existing records to try to answer a research question is known as _____.

    a.   naturalistic observation

    b.   survey research

    c.   longitudinal research

    d.   archival research

26. _____ involves following a group of research participants for an extended period of time.

    a.   Archival research

    b.   Longitudinal research

    c.   Naturalistic observation

    d.   Cross-sectional research

27. A(n) _____ is a list of questions developed by a researcher that can be administered in paper form.

    a.   archive

    b.   case study

    c.   naturalistic observation

    d.   survey

28. Longitudinal research is complicated by high rates of _____.

    a.   deception

    b.   observation

    c.   attrition

    d.   generalization

29. Height and weight are positively correlated. This means that as height _____ weight _____.

    a.   There is not relationship between height and weight.

    b.   increases; decreases

    c.   decreases; increases

    d.   increases; increases

30. Which of the following correlation coefficients indicates the strongest relationship between two variables?

    a.   −.90

    b.   −.50

    c.   +.80

    d.   +.25

31. Which statement best illustrates a negative correlation between the number of hours spent watching TV the week before an exam and the grade on that exam?

    a.   Watching too much television leads to poor exam performance.

    b.   Smart students watch less television.

    c.   Viewing television interferes with a student's ability to prepare for the upcoming exam.

    d.   Students who watch more television perform more poorly on their exams.

32. The correlation coefficient indicates the weakest relationship when _____.

    a. it is closest to 0

    b. it is closest to −1

    c. it is positive

    d. it is negative

33. _____ means that everyone in the population has the same likelihood of being asked to participate in the study.

    a. Operationalizing

    b. Placebo effect

    c. Random assignment

    d. Random sampling

34. The _____ is controlled by the experimenter, while the _____ represents the information collected and statistically analyzed by the experimenter.

    a. dependent variable; independent variable

    b. independent variable; dependent variable

    c. placebo effect; experimenter bias

    d. experiment bias; placebo effect

35. Researchers must _____ important concepts in their studies so others will have a clear understanding of exactly how those concepts were defined.

    a. randomly assign

    b. randomly select

    c. operationalize

    d. generalize

36. Sometimes, researchers will administer a(n) _____ to participants in the control group to control for the effects that participant expectation might have on the experiment.

    a. dependent variable

    b. independent variable

    c. statistical analysis

    d. placebo

37. _____ is to animal research as _____ is to human research.

    a. Informed consent; deception

    b. IACUC; IRB

    c. IRB; IACUC

    d. Deception; debriefing

38. Researchers might use _____ when providing participants with the full details of the experiment to prevent skewing their responses.

    a. informed consent

    b. deception

    c. ethics

    d. debriefing

39. A person's participation in a research project must be _____.

    a. confidential

    b. rewarded

    c. voluntary

    d. public

40. Before participating in an experiment, individuals should read and sign the _____ form.

    a. informed consent

    b. debriefing

    c. IRB

    d. ethics

Critical Thinking Questions

41. Why do you think psychology courses like this one are often requirements of so many different programs of study?

42. Why do you think many people might be skeptical about psychology being a science?

43. How did the object of study in psychology change over the history of the field since the 19th century?

44. In part, what aspect of psychology was the behaviorist approach to psychology a reaction to?

45. Given the incredible diversity among the various areas of psychology that were described in this chapter, how do they all fit together?

46. What are the potential ethical concerns associated with Milgram's research on obedience?

47. Why is an undergraduate education in psychology so helpful in a number of different lines of work?

48. Other than a potentially greater salary, what would be the reasons an individual would continue on to get a graduate degree in psychology?

49. In this chapter, the D.A.R.E. program was described as an incredibly popular program in schools across the United States despite the fact that research consistently suggests that this program is largely ineffective. How might one explain this discrepancy?

50. The scientific method is often described as self-correcting and cyclical. Briefly describe your understanding of the scientific method with regard to these concepts.

51. In this chapter, conjoined twins, Krista and Tatiana, were described as being potential participants in a case study. In what other circumstances would you think that this particular research approach would be especially helpful and why?

52. Presumably, reality television programs aim to provide a realistic portrayal of the behavior displayed by the characters featured in such programs. This chapter pointed out why this is not really the case. What changes could be made in the way that these programs are produced that would result in more honest portrayals of realistic behavior?

53. Which of the research methods discussed in this chapter would be best suited to research the effectiveness of the D.A.R.E. program in preventing the use of alcohol and other drugs? Why?

54. Aside from biomedical research, what other areas of research could greatly benefit by both longitudinal and archival research?

55. Earlier in this chapter, we read about research suggesting that there is a correlation between eating cereal and weight. Cereal companies that present this information in their advertisements could lead someone to believe that eating more cereal causes healthy weight. Why would they make such a claim, and what arguments could you make to counter this cause-and-effect claim?

56. Recently a study was published in the journal, *Nutrition and Cancer*, which established a negative correlation between coffee consumption and breast cancer. Specifically, it was found that women consuming more than 5 cups of coffee a day were less likely to develop breast cancer than women who never consumed coffee (Lowcock, Cotterchio, Anderson, Boucher, & El-Sohemy, 2013). Imagine you see a newspaper story about this research that says, "Coffee Protects Against Cancer." Why is this headline misleading, and why would a more accurate headline draw less interest?

57. Sometimes, true random sampling can be very difficult to obtain. Many researchers make use of convenience samples as an alternative. For example, one popular convenience sample would involve students enrolled in Introduction to Psychology courses. What are the implications of using this sampling technique?

58. Peer review is an important part of publishing research findings in many scientific disciplines. This process is normally conducted anonymously; in other words, the author of the article being reviewed does not know who is reviewing the article, and the reviewers are unaware of the author's identity. Why would this be an important part of this process?

59. Some argue that animal research is inherently flawed in terms of being ethical because unlike human participants, animals do not consent to be involved in research. Do you agree with this perspective? Given that animals do not consent to be involved in research projects, what sorts of extra precautions should be taken to ensure that they receive the most humane treatment possible?

60. At the end of the last lesson, you were asked to design a basic experiment to answer some question of interest. What ethical considerations should be made with the study you proposed to ensure that your experiment would conform to the scientific community's expectations of ethical research?

Biopsychology

Chapter Introduction

📷 **Figure 1:** Identical twins at a gestational age of 15 weeks, shown in coronal and sagittal plane, respectively.

Jim Lewis and Jim Springer were identical twins who were separated at 1 month old and separately raised. When the 39-year-old twins reunited in 1979, they discovered they both suffered from tension headaches, were prone to nail biting, smoked Salem cigarettes, drove the same type of car, and even vacationed at the same location in Florida. Indeed, behaviors that were believed to be due to social influence, such as religious belief and social attitudes, have been shown to have a strong genetic influence in large, longitudinal studies such as the Minnesota Study of Twins Reared Apart. There is still a debate on the role of nurture (social influence and environment) versus nature (genes), but if we're going to understand human behavior, it is best to start at the beginning.

This chapter strives to explain the biological mechanisms that underlie behavior. These physiological and anatomical foundations are the basis for many areas of psychology. In this chapter, you will learn how genetics influence both physiological and psychological traits. You will become familiar with the structure and function of the nervous system. And, finally, you will learn how the nervous system interacts with the endocrine system.

Flash Forward

Ready to dig into the vocabulary? Get some practice with this Hawkes Verified Quizlet set (hawkes.biz/psych2q1)!

2.1 Human Genetics

Psychological researchers study genetics in order to better understand the biological basis that contributes to certain behaviors. While all humans share certain biological mechanisms, we are each unique. And while our bodies have many of the same parts—brains and hormones and cells with genetic codes—these are expressed in a wide variety of behaviors, thoughts, and reactions.

- Why do two people infected by the same disease have different outcomes: one surviving and one succumbing to the ailment?

- How are genetic diseases passed through family lines?

- Are there genetic components to psychological disorders, such as depression or schizophrenia?

- To what extent might there be a psychological basis to health conditions such as childhood obesity?

Further Resources

Visit this website (hawkes.biz/sicklecell) to learn more about how a mutation in DNA leads to sickle-cell anemia.

To explore these questions, let's start by focusing on a specific disease, sickle-cell anemia, and how it might affect two infected sisters. Sickle-cell anemia is a genetic condition in which red blood cells, which are normally round, take on a crescent-like shape (Figure 2). The changed shape of these cells affects how they function: sickle-shaped cells can clog blood vessels and block blood flow, leading to high fever, severe pain, swelling, and tissue damage.

Normal blood cells

Sickle-shaped blood cells

Figure 2: Normal blood cells travel freely through the blood vessels, while sickle-shaped cells form blockages preventing blood flow.

Many people with sickle-cell anemia—and the particular genetic mutation that causes it—die at an early age. While the notion of "survival of the fittest" may suggest that people suffering from this disease have a low survival rate and, therefore, the disease will become less common, this is not the case. Despite the negative evolutionary effects associated with this genetic mutation, the sickle-cell gene remains relatively common among people of African descent. Why is this? The explanation is illustrated with the following scenario.

Imagine two young women—Luwi and Sena—who are sisters in rural Zambia, Africa. Luwi carries the gene for sickle-cell anemia; Sena does not carry the gene. Sickle-cell carriers have one copy of the sickle-cell gene but do not have full-blown sickle-cell anemia. They experience symptoms only if they are severely dehydrated or are deprived of oxygen (as in mountain climbing). Carriers are thought to be immune from malaria (an often deadly disease that is widespread in tropical climates) because changes in their blood chemistry and immune functioning prevent the malaria parasite from having its effects (Gong, Parikh, Rosenthal, & Greenhouse, 2013). However, full-blown sickle-cell anemia, with two copies of the sickle-cell gene, does not provide immunity to malaria.

While walking home from school, both sisters are bitten by mosquitos carrying the malaria parasite. Luwi does not get malaria because she carries the sickle-cell mutation. Sena, on the other hand, develops malaria and dies just two weeks later. Luwi survives and eventually has children, to whom she may pass on the sickle-cell mutation.

Malaria is rare in the United States, so the sickle-cell gene benefits nobody: the gene manifests primarily in health problems—minor in carriers, severe in the full-blown disease—with no health benefits for carriers. However, the situation is quite different in other parts of the world. In parts of Africa where malaria is prevalent, having the sickle-cell mutation does provide health benefits for carriers (protection from malaria).

Charles Darwin describes this in the **theory of evolution by natural selection** (Figure 3). In simple terms, the theory states that organisms that are better suited for their environment will survive and reproduce, while those that are poorly suited for their environment will die off. In our example, we can see that as a carrier, Luwi's mutation is highly adaptive in her African homeland; however, if she resided in the United States (where malaria is much less common), her mutation could prove costly—with a high probability of the disease in her descendants and minor health problems of her own.

(a)   (b)

📷 **Figure 3:** (a) In 1859, Charles Darwin proposed his theory of evolution by natural selection in his book *On the Origin of Species*. (b) The book contains just one illustration: this diagram that shows how species evolve over time through natural selection.

Dig Deeper

Two Perspectives on Genetics and Behavior

It's easy to get confused about two fields that study the interaction of genes and the environment, such as the fields of evolutionary psychology and behavioral genetics. How can we tell them apart?

In both fields, it is understood that genes not only code for particular traits but also contribute to certain patterns of cognition and behavior. Evolutionary psychology focuses on how universal patterns of behavior and cognitive processes have evolved over time. Therefore, variations in cognition and behavior would make individuals more or less successful in reproducing and passing those genes to their offspring. Evolutionary psychologists study a variety of psychological phenomena that may have evolved as adaptations, including fear response, food preferences, mate selection, and cooperative behaviors (Confer et al., 2010).

Figure 4: Psychologists study the relationship between an individual's genetics and behavior.

Whereas evolutionary psychologists focus on universal patterns that evolved over millions of years, behavioral geneticists study how individual differences arise, in the present, through the interaction of genes and the environment. When studying human behavior, behavioral geneticists often employ twin and adoption studies to research questions of interest. Twin studies compare the rates that a given behavioral trait is shared among identical and fraternal twins; adoption studies compare those rates among biologically related relatives and adopted relatives. Both approaches provide some insight into the relative importance of genes and environment for the expression of a given trait.

Genetic Variation

Genetic variation, the genetic difference between individuals, is what contributes to a species' adaptation to its environment. In humans, genetic variation begins with an egg, about 100 million sperm, and fertilization. Fertile women ovulate roughly once per month, releasing an egg from follicles in the ovary. During the egg's journey from the ovary through the fallopian tubes, to the uterus, a sperm may fertilize an egg.

The egg and the sperm each contain 23 chromosomes. **Chromosomes** are long strings of genetic material known as **deoxyribonucleic acid (DNA)**. DNA is a helix-shaped molecule made up of nucleotide base pairs. In each chromosome, sequences of DNA make up **genes** that control or partially control a number of visible characteristics, known as traits, such as eye color, hair color, and so on. A single gene may have multiple possible variations, or alleles. An **allele** is a specific version of a gene. So, a given gene may code for the trait of hair color, and the different alleles of that gene affect which hair color an individual has.

When a sperm and egg fuse, their 23 chromosomes pair up and create a zygote with 23 pairs of chromosomes. Therefore, each parent contributes half the genetic information carried by the offspring; the resulting physical characteristics of the offspring (called the phenotype) are determined by the interaction of genetic material supplied by the parents (called the genotype). A person's **genotype** is the genetic makeup of that individual. **Phenotype**, on the other hand, refers to the individual's inherited physical characteristics, which are a combination of genetic and environmental influences (Figure 5).

(a)   (b)

📷 **Figure 5:** (a) Genotype refers to the genetic makeup of an individual based on the genetic material (DNA) inherited from one's parents. (b) Phenotype describes an individual's observable characteristics, such as hair color, skin color, height, and build.

✏️ On Your Own

Identify the trait as a genotype or phenotype. Then, check the box next to the correct answer.

1. Susceptibility to cancer:

☐ Genotype   ☐ Phenotype

2. Freckles:

☐ Genotype   ☐ Phenotype

3. Lactose intolerance:

☐ Genotype   ☐ Phenotype

4. The ability to roll one's tongue:

☐ Genotype   ☐ Phenotype

Most traits are controlled by multiple genes, but some traits are controlled by one gene. A characteristic like cleft chin, for example, is influenced by a single gene from each parent. In this example, we will call the gene for cleft chin "B," and the gene for smooth chin "b." Cleft chin is a dominant trait, which means that having the **dominant allele** either from one parent (Bb) or both parents (BB) will always result in the phenotype associated with the dominant allele. When someone has two copies of the same allele, they are said to be **homozygous** for that allele. When someone has a combination of alleles for a given gene, they are said to be **heterozygous**. For example, smooth chin is a recessive trait, which means that an individual will only display the smooth chin phenotype if they are homozygous for that **recessive allele** (bb).

Imagine that a woman with a cleft chin mates with a man with a smooth chin. What type of chin will their child have? The answer to that depends on which alleles each parent carries. If the woman is homozygous for cleft chin (BB), her offspring will always have cleft chin. It gets a little more complicated, however, if the mother is heterozygous for this gene (Bb). Since the father has a smooth chin—therefore homozygous for the recessive allele (bb)—we can expect the offspring to have a 50% chance of having a cleft chin and a 50% chance of having a smooth chin (Figure 6).

Mother (Bb)

	B	b
Father (bb) b	Bb	bb
b	Bb	bb

(a)

(b)

Figure 6: (a) A Punnett square is a tool used to predict how genes will interact in the production of offspring. The capital B represents the dominant allele, and the lowercase b represents the recessive allele. In the example of the cleft chin, where B is cleft chin (dominant allele), wherever a pair contains the dominant allele, B, you can expect a cleft chin phenotype. You can expect a smooth chin phenotype only when there are two copies of the recessive allele, bb. (b) A cleft chin, shown here, is an inherited trait.

✍ On Your Own

Look at the following list and determine if it is a dominant trait (which will appear if only one allele is present) or a recessive trait (which must have two alleles present to appear).

1. Widow's peak:

   ☐ Dominant

   ☐ Recessive

2. Attached earlobes:

   ☐ Dominant

   ☐ Recessive

3. Lateral roll of the tongue:

   ☐ Dominant

   ☐ Recessive

4. Left-handedness:

   ☐ Dominant

   ☐ Recessive

5. Curly hair:

   ☐ Dominant

   ☐ Recessive

Dig Deeper

The Curious Case of the Peppered Moth and Infective Inheritance

In the early 19th century, the peppered moth was a predominantly white-winged moth, with black speckles. Then in 1848, during the peak of the industrial revolution, a black variant of the moth was discovered in Manchester, England. By 1895, 95% of the Mancunian peppered moths were black. This dark variant spread across industrial Britain until the entomologist JW Tutt suggested that the moths evolved to the darker color to remain camouflaged. Sure enough, following the 1956 Clean Air Act, the black form of the moth began to decline with the return of the white form, which was bettered camouflaged on lichen-covered tree bark.

Figure 7: The peppered moth, in both black and white variants

So far, we have discussed traits that involve just one gene, but few human characteristics are controlled by a single gene. Most traits are **polygenic**: controlled by more than one gene. Height is one example of a polygenic trait, as are skin color and weight.

Where do harmful genes that contribute to diseases come from? Gene mutations provide one source of harmful genes. A **mutation** is a sudden, permanent change in a gene. While many mutations can be harmful or lethal, once in a while, a mutation benefits an individual by giving that person an advantage over those who do not have the mutation. Recall that the theory of evolution asserts that individuals best adapted to their particular environments are more likely to reproduce and pass on their genes to future generations. In order for this process to occur, there must be competition—more technically, there must be variability in genes (and resultant traits) that allow for variation in adaptability to the environment. If a population consisted of identical individuals, then any dramatic changes in the environment would affect everyone in the same way, and there would be no variation in selection. In contrast, diversity in genes and associated traits allows some individuals to perform slightly better than others when faced with environmental change. This creates a distinct advantage for individuals best suited for their environments in terms of successful reproduction and genetic transmission.

Gene-Environment Interactions

Genes do not exist in a vacuum. Although we are all biological organisms, we also exist in an environment that is incredibly important in determining not only when and how our genes express themselves but also in what combination. Each of us represents a unique interaction between our genetic makeup and our environment; range of reaction is one way to describe this interaction. **Range of reaction** asserts that our genes set the boundaries within which we can operate, and our environment interacts with the genes to determine where in that range we will fall. For example, if an individual's genetic makeup predisposes her to high levels of intellectual potential and she is reared in a rich, stimulating environment, then she will be more likely to achieve her full potential than if she were raised under conditions of significant deprivation.

According to the concept of range of reaction, genes set definite limits on potential, and environment determines how much of that potential is achieved. Some disagree with this theory and argue that genes do not set a limit on a person's potential.

Another perspective on the interaction between genes and the environment is the concept of **genetic environmental correlation**. Stated simply, our genes influence our environment, and our environment influences the expression of our genes (Figure 8). Not only do our genes and environment interact, as in range of reaction, but they also influence one another bidirectionally. For example, the child of a professional basketball player would probably be exposed to basketball from an early age. Such exposure might allow the child to realize his or her full genetic, athletic potential. Thus, the parents' genes, which the child shares, influence the child's environment, and that environment, in turn, is well suited to support the child's genetic potential.

Further Resources

Want to know more about atypical evolution, including the rise of super-bugs? Check out this podcast from Radiolab (hawkes.biz/evolution).

Figure 8: Learning about the construction industry early in life could help genes of aptitude for math and science express themselves.

> ### Reflection Questions
>
> What is the role of genetics in how we express gender?

In another approach to gene-environment interactions, the field of **epigenetics** looks beyond the genotype itself and studies how the same genotype can be expressed in different ways. In other words, researchers study how the same genotype can lead to very different phenotypes. As mentioned earlier, gene expression is often influenced by environmental context in ways that are not entirely obvious. For instance, identical twins share the same genetic information (**identical twins** develop from a single fertilized egg that split, so the genetic material is exactly the same in each; in contrast, **fraternal twins** develop from two different eggs fertilized by different sperm, so the genetic material varies as with non-twin siblings). But even with identical genes, there remains an incredible amount of variability in how gene expression can unfold over the course of each twin's life. Sometimes, one twin will develop a disease, and the other will not. In one example, Tiffany, an identical twin, died from cancer at age 7, but her twin, now 19 years old, has never had cancer. Although these individuals share an identical genotype, their phenotypes differ as a result of how that genetic information is expressed over time. The epigenetic perspective is very different from range of reaction because here the genotype is not fixed and limited.

Genes affect more than our physical characteristics. Indeed, scientists have found genetic linkages to a number of behavioral characteristics, ranging from basic personality traits to sexual orientation to spirituality (for examples, see Mustanski et al., 2005; Comings, Gonzales, Saucier, Johnson, & MacMurray, 2000). Genes are also associated with temperament and a number of psychological disorders, such as depression and

Further Resources

Want inspiration? Check out McKenna Pope (hawkes.biz/geneenvironment), who convinced one of the largest toy companies in the world to change the way that they marketed one of their best-selling products when she was just 13 years old.

Further Resources

Visit this site (hawkes.biz/twinstudies) for an engaging video primer on the epigenetics of twin studies.

schizophrenia. So while it is true that genes provide the biological blueprints for our cells, tissues, organs, and body, they also have significant impact on our experiences and our behaviors.

Let's look at the following findings regarding schizophrenia in light of our three views of gene-environment interactions. Which view do you think best explains this evidence?

In a study of people who were given up for adoption, adoptees whose biological mothers had schizophrenia *and* who had been raised in a disturbed family environment were much more likely to develop schizophrenia or another psychotic disorder than were any of the other groups in the study:

Figure 9: Scientific studies suggest there are genetic linkages to psychological disorders, such as schizophrenia.

- Of adoptees whose biological mothers had schizophrenia (high genetic risk) and who were raised in disturbed family environments, 36.8% were likely to develop schizophrenia.

- Of adoptees whose biological mothers had schizophrenia (high genetic risk) and who were raised in healthy family environments, 5.8% were likely to develop schizophrenia.

- Of adoptees with a low genetic risk (whose mothers did not have schizophrenia) and who were raised in disturbed family environments, 5.3% were likely to develop schizophrenia.

- Of adoptees with a low genetic risk (whose mothers did not have schizophrenia) and who were raised in healthy family environments, 4.8% were likely to develop schizophrenia (Tienari et al., 2004).

The study shows that adoptees with high genetic risk were especially likely to develop schizophrenia only if they were raised in disturbed home environments. This research lends credibility to the notion that both genetic vulnerability and environmental stress are necessary for schizophrenia to develop and that genes alone do not tell the full tale.

Summary

Genes are sequences of DNA that code for a particular trait. Different versions of a gene are called alleles—sometimes alleles can be classified as dominant or recessive. A dominant allele always results in the dominant phenotype. In order to exhibit a recessive phenotype, an individual must be homozygous for the recessive allele. Genes affect both physical and psychological characteristics. Ultimately, how and when a gene is expressed and what the outcome will be—in terms of both physical and psychological characteristics—is a function of the interaction between our genes and our environments.

Flash Forward

Ready to dig into the vocabulary? Get some practice with this Hawkes Verified Quizlet set (hawkes.biz/psych2q2)!

2.2 Cells of the Nervous System

Imagine you are at your favorite coffee shop and a person approaches you and begins to start a conversation. From the tone and familiarity, you assume it may be someone you are friends with, but you don't know because you have a condition called prosopagnosia, or the inability to recognize faces. Prosopagnosia, or face-blindness, is the disorder in which the ability to recognize familiar faces, including one's own face (self-recognition), is impaired, while other aspects of visual processing remain intact. Although nearly 2% of the population has prosopagnosia, many are not aware of it until later in life. This disorder is connected to a specific region in the brain called the fusiform gyrus, a bundle of neurons responsible for decoding visual information into perceptions of faces.

The nervous system is composed of two basic cell types: glial cells (also known as glia) and neurons. The average human brain has about 100 billion neurons (or nerve cells) and many more glial cells, which serve to support and protect the neurons. **Glial cells**, which outnumber neurons ten to one, are traditionally thought to play a supportive role to neurons, both physically and metabolically. Glial cells provide scaffolding on which the nervous system is built, help neurons line up closely with each other to allow neuronal communication, provide insulation to neurons, transport nutrients and waste products, and mediate immune responses.

Neurons, on the other hand, serve as interconnected information processors that are essential for all of the tasks of the nervous system. This section briefly describes the structure and function of neurons.

> ✎ **On Your Own**
>
> Consider the different functions of the cells in the nervous system. List a few of the tasks that neurons and glial cells are responsible for in the table below.
>
> | Neuron | Glial Cell |
> |--------|-----------|
> | | |
> | | |
> | | |

Figure 1: Although we can detect a face in this salad, those with prosopagnosia would not be able to perceive the whole as a face.

Neuron Structure

Neurons are the central building blocks of the nervous system, 100 billion strong at birth. Like all cells, neurons consist of several different parts, each serving a specialized function (Figure 2). A neuron's outer surface is made up of a **semipermeable membrane**. This membrane allows smaller molecules and molecules without an electrical charge to pass through it while stopping larger or highly charged molecules.

Figure 2: This illustration shows a prototypical neuron, which is being myelinated.

The nucleus of the neuron is located in the **soma**, or cell body. The soma has branching extensions known as dendrites. The neuron is a small information processor, and **dendrites** serve as input sites where signals are received from other neurons. These signals are transmitted electrically across the soma and down a major extension from the soma known as the **axon**, which ends at multiple terminal buttons. The **terminal buttons** contain **synaptic vesicles** that house **neurotransmitters**, the chemical messengers of the nervous system.

Part of the Neuron	Location and Appearance	Function
Dendrite	End of neuron; jagged finger-like structures near the ends of other neurons	Receives information (neurotransmitters) from other neurons that excite or inhibit the stimulation of the rest of the neuron
Soma	Middle of the neuron; blob-like appearance	Contains the nucleus and produces neurotransmitters
Axon	Leaving the soma; long, cable-like structure	Carries the vesicle full of neurotransmitters from the soma to the terminal buttons
Terminal Button	End of neuron, attached to axon; tube-like structures with larger pads at the end	Releases the neurotransmitters into the synaptic gap; has receptors to regulate neurotransmitters in the gap; recycles unused neurotransmitters
Synaptic Vesicle	Inside the soma; travels down the axon, on microtubules, spherical membrane	Contains the neurotransmitters in transport from the soma, through the axon, and empties contents into synaptic gap

Group Activity

Recruit 4–6 people to stand in front of the room in a line, holding hands. The first person is the dendrite, the last person is the terminal button, and those in between are the axon. Have another person, not part of the neuron, spray the hand of the dendrite with water from a small spray bottle (the dendrite should not be looking but only feeling for the spray). Once the dendrite feels the "incoming message" they should squeeze the hand of next person in line, and that person then squeezes the hand next on the line until the terminal button receives the message and raises their hand. Try this multiple times, using more or less powerful spray, and answer the following questions.

- How fast was each transmission?

- How does the amount of water sprayed (neurotransmitters) impact the relay?

- How is the all-or-none principle displayed in this activity?

Axons range in length from a fraction of an inch to several feet. In some axons, glial cells form a fatty substance known as the **myelin sheath**, which coats the axon and acts as an insulator, increasing the speed at which the signal travels. The myelin sheath is crucial for the normal operation of the neurons within the nervous system: the loss of the insulation it provides can be detrimental to normal function.

To understand how this works, let's consider an example. Multiple sclerosis (MS), an autoimmune disorder, involves a large-scale loss of the myelin sheath on axons throughout the nervous system. The resulting interference in the electrical signal prevents the quick transmittal of information by neurons and can lead to a number of symptoms, such as dizziness, fatigue, loss of motor control, and sexual dysfunction. While some treatments may help to modify the course of the disease and manage certain symptoms, there is currently no known cure for multiple sclerosis.

Figure 3: In people who suffer from multiple sclerosis, the myelin sheaths on some of their neurons are destroyed by the body's own immune cells.

In healthy individuals, the neuronal signal moves rapidly down the axon to the terminal buttons, where synaptic vesicles release neurotransmitters into the synapse (Figure 4). The **synapse** is a very small space between two neurons and is an important site where communication between neurons occurs. Once neurotransmitters are released into the synapse, they travel across the small space and bind with corresponding receptors on the dendrite of an adjacent neuron. **Receptors**, or proteins on the cell surface where neurotransmitters attach, vary in shape, with different shapes "matching" different neurotransmitters.

How does a neurotransmitter "know" which receptor to bind to? The neurotransmitter and the receptor have what is referred to as a lock-and-key relationship—specific neurotransmitters fit specific receptors similar to how a key fits a lock. The neurotransmitter binds to any receptor that it fits.

Neuronal Communication

Now that we have learned about the basic structures of the neuron and the role that these structures play in neuronal communication, let's take a closer look at the signal itself—how it moves through the neuron and then jumps to the next neuron and where the process is repeated.

We begin at the neuronal membrane. The neuron exists in a fluid environment—it is surrounded by extracellular fluid and contains intracellular fluid (i.e., cytoplasm). The neuronal membrane keeps these two fluids separate. This difference in charge across the membrane is called the **membrane potential**.

The type of molecules (ions) that are present inside the fluids of the cell are mostly negatively charged, while the ions outside of the cell (extracellular fluid) are positively charged. It is the movement of these ions from areas of high concentration to areas of less concentration that creates an electrical charge.

Between signals, the neuron membrane's potential is held in a state of readiness, called the **resting potential**. Like a rubber band stretched out and waiting to spring into action, ions line up on either side of the cell membrane, ready to rush across the membrane when the neuron goes active and the membrane opens its gates (i.e., a sodium-potassium pump that allows movement of ions across the membrane). Ions in high-concentration areas are ready to move to low-concentration areas, and positive ions are ready to move to areas with a negative charge.

In the resting state, sodium (Na^+) is at higher concentrations outside the cell, so it will tend to move into the cell. Potassium (K^+), on the other hand, is more concentrated inside the cell and will tend to move out of the cell (Figure 5). In addition, the inside of the cell is slightly negatively charged compared to the outside. This provides an additional force on sodium, causing it to move into the cell.

Figure 4: The synapse is the space between the terminal button of one neuron and the dendrite of another neuron. Neurotransmitters are released into the synapse where they bind to receptors on the neighboring dendrite.

Helpful Hint

Much of what we know about how neurons work comes from experiments performed on the giant axon of the squid. The giant axon extends from the head to the tail of the squid and is used to move the squid's tail. It can be up to 1 millimeter in diameter, which is easily seen with the naked eye.

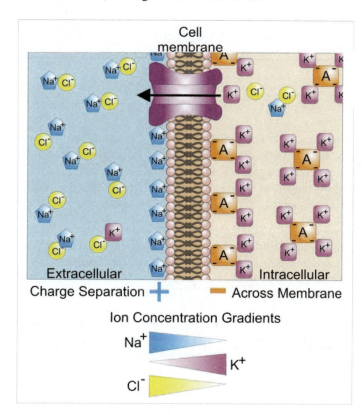

Figure 5: A neuron waits in a state of readiness called resting potential.

From this resting potential state, the neuron receives a signal and its state changes abruptly (Figure 6). When a neuron receives signals at the dendrites—due to neurotransmitters from an adjacent neuron binding to its receptors—small pores, or gates, open on the neuronal membrane, allowing Na^+ ions, propelled by both charge and concentration differences, to move into the cell. With this influx of positive ions, the internal charge of the cell becomes more positive. If that charge reaches a certain level, called the **threshold of excitation**, the neuron becomes active, and the action potential begins.

Many additional pores open, causing a massive influx of Na^+ ions and a huge positive spike in the membrane potential, the peak action potential. At the peak of the spike, the sodium gates close and the potassium gates open. As positively charged potassium ions leave, the cell quickly begins repolarization. At first, it hyperpolarizes, becoming slightly more negative than the resting potential, and then it levels off, returning to the resting potential.

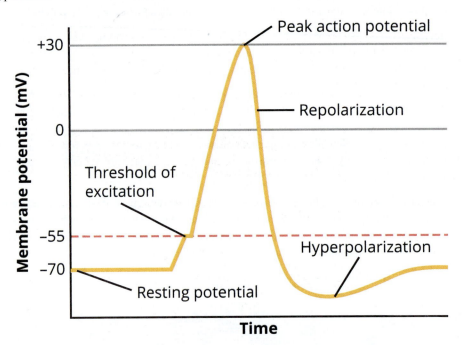

Figure 6: During the action potential, the electrical charge across the membrane changes dramatically.

Further Resources

Watch this video (hawkes. biz/neuroncomm) that walks through the process of neuronal communication, along with real-time animation.

This positive spike constitutes the **action potential:** the electrical signal that typically moves from the cell body down the axon to the axon terminals. The electrical signal moves down the axon like a wave; at each point, some of the sodium ions that enter the cell diffuse to the next section of the axon, raising the charge past the threshold of excitation and triggering a new influx of sodium ions. The action potential moves all the way down the axon to the terminal buttons.

The action potential is an **all-or-none** phenomenon. In simple terms, this means that an incoming signal from another neuron is either sufficient or insufficient to reach the threshold of excitation. There is no in-between, and there is no turning off an action potential once it starts. Think of it like sending an email or a text message. You can think about sending it all you want, but the message is not sent until you hit the send button. Furthermore, once you send the message, there is no stopping it.

Because it is all or none, the action potential is recreated, or propagated, at its full strength at every point along the axon. Much like the lit fuse of a firecracker, it does not fade away as it travels down the axon. It is this all-or-none property that explains the fact that your brain perceives an injury to a distant body part like your toe as equally painful as one to your nose.

✎ On Your Own

Label the diagram and describe what is happening at each step in the process.

🖼 **Figure 7:** The membrane permeability of a neuron during an action potential

A	
B	
C	
D	
E	

1	
2	
3	
4	

As noted earlier, when the action potential arrives at the terminal button, the synaptic vesicles release their neurotransmitters into the synapse. The neurotransmitters travel across the synapse and bind to receptors on the dendrites of the adjacent neuron, and the process repeats itself in the new neuron (assuming the signal is sufficiently strong to trigger an action potential). Once the signal is delivered, excess neurotransmitters in the synapse drift away, are broken down into inactive fragments, or are reabsorbed in a process known as reuptake. **Reuptake** involves the neurotransmitter being pumped back into the neuron that released it, in order to clear the synapse (Figure 8). Clearing the synapse serves both to provide a clear "on" and "off" state between signals and to regulate the production of neurotransmitter (full synaptic vesicles provide signals that no additional neurotransmitters need to be produced).

Reuptake

Neurotransmitter

🖼 **Figure 8:** Reuptake involves moving a neurotransmitter from the synapse back into the axon terminal from which it was released.

Further Resources

Click through this interactive simulation (hawkes.biz/ neuroncomm2) for a closer look at neuronal communication.

Neuronal communication is often referred to as an electrochemical event. The movement of the action potential down the length of the axon is an electrical event, and movement of the neurotransmitter across the synaptic space represents the chemical portion of the process.

Neurotransmitters and Drugs

There are several different types of neurotransmitters released by different neurons, and we can speak in broad terms about the kinds of functions associated with different neurotransmitters (Table 1). Much of what psychologists know about the functions of neurotransmitters comes from research on the effects of drugs in psychological disorders. Psychologists who take a **biological perspective** and focus on the physiological causes of behavior assert that psychological disorders like depression and schizophrenia are associated with imbalances in one or more neurotransmitter systems. In this perspective, psychotropic medications can help improve the symptoms associated with these disorders. **Psychotropic medications** are drugs that treat psychiatric symptoms by restoring neurotransmitter balance.

Neurotransmitter	Involved in	Potential Effect on Behavior
Acetylcholine	Muscle action, memory	Increased arousal, enhanced cognition
Beta-endorphin	Pain, pleasure	Decreased anxiety, decreased tension
Dopamine	Mood, sleep, learning	Increased pleasure, suppressed appetite
Gamma-aminobutyric acid (GABA)	Brain function, sleep	Decreased anxiety, decreased tension
Glutamate	Memory, learning	Increased learning, enhanced memory
Norepinephrine	Heart, intestines, alertness	Increased arousal, suppressed appetite
Serotonin	Mood, sleep	Modulated mood, suppressed appetite

Table 1: Major Neurotransmitters and How They Affect Behavior

Psychoactive drugs can act as agonists or antagonists for a given neurotransmitter system. **Agonists** are chemicals that mimic a neurotransmitter at the receptor site and, thus, strengthen its effects. An **antagonist**, on the other hand, blocks or impedes the normal activity of a neurotransmitter at the receptor. Agonist and antagonist drugs are prescribed to correct the specific neurotransmitter imbalances underlying a person's condition. For example, Parkinson's disease, a progressive nervous system disorder, is associated with low levels of dopamine. Therefore, dopamine agonists, which mimic the effects of dopamine by binding to dopamine receptors, are one treatment strategy.

> **Further Resources**
>
> Play Mouse Party (hawkes.biz/drugbrain) to see how different drugs affect the brain at a synaptic level.

✎ On Your Own

Determine if the following are acting as an agonist or an antagonist.

1. MDMA increases the release of serotonin precursor and inhibits the reuptake of serotonin.

☐ Agonist   ☐ Antagonist

2. Alcohol opens specific potassium channels, hyperpolarizing the neuron.

☐ Agonist   ☐ Antagonist

3. Marijuana operates on the cannabinoid receptors to allow it to open more easily.

☐ Agonist   ☐ Antagonist

Certain symptoms of schizophrenia are associated with overactive dopamine neurotransmission. The antipsychotics used to treat these symptoms are antagonists for dopamine—they block dopamine's effects by binding its receptors without activating them. Thus, they prevent dopamine released by one neuron from signaling information to adjacent neurons.

In contrast to agonists and antagonists, which both operate by binding to receptor sites, reuptake inhibitors prevent unused neurotransmitters from being transported back to the neuron. This leaves more neurotransmitters in the synapse for a longer time, increasing its effects. Depression, which has been consistently linked with reduced serotonin levels, is commonly treated with selective serotonin reuptake inhibitors (SSRIs). By preventing reuptake, SSRIs strengthen the effect of serotonin, giving it more time to interact with serotonin receptors on dendrites. Common SSRIs on the market today include Prozac, Paxil, and Zoloft. The drug LSD is structurally very similar to serotonin, and it affects the same neurons and receptors as serotonin.

Psychotropic drugs are not instant solutions for people suffering from psychological disorders. Often, an individual must take a drug for several weeks before seeing improvement, and many psychoactive drugs have significant negative side effects. Furthermore, individuals vary dramatically in how they respond to the drugs. To improve chances for success, it is not uncommon for people receiving pharmacotherapy to undergo psychological and/or behavioral therapies as well. Some research suggests that combining drug therapy with other forms of therapy tends to be more effective than any one treatment alone (for one such example, see March et al., 2007).

Summary

Glia and neurons are the two cell types that make up the nervous system. While glia generally play supporting roles, the communication between neurons is fundamental to all of the functions associated with the nervous system. Neuronal communication is made possible by the neuron's specialized structures. The soma contains the cell nucleus, and the dendrites extend from the soma in tree-like branches. The axon is another major extension of the cell body; axons are often covered by a myelin sheath, which increases the speed of transmission of neural impulses. At the end of the axon are terminal buttons that contain synaptic vesicles filled with neurotransmitters.

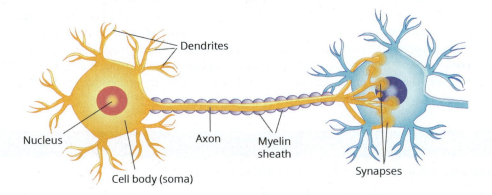

Figure 9: Neuron communication is essential to functions related to the nervous system.

Neuronal communication is an electrochemical event. The dendrites contain receptors for neurotransmitters released by nearby neurons. If the signals received from other neurons are sufficiently strong, an action potential will travel down the length of the axon to the terminal buttons, resulting in the release of neurotransmitters into the synapse. Action potentials operate on the all-or-none principle and involve the movement of Na^+ and K^+ across the neuronal membrane.

Different neurotransmitters are associated with different functions. Often, psychological disorders involve imbalances in a given neurotransmitter system. Therefore, psychotropic drugs are prescribed in an attempt to bring the neurotransmitters back into balance. Drugs can act either as agonists or as antagonists for a given neurotransmitter system.

2.3 Parts of the Nervous System

The nervous system can be divided into two major subdivisions: the **central nervous system (CNS)** and the **peripheral nervous system (PNS)**, shown in Figure 1. The CNS is comprised of the brain and spinal cord; the PNS connects the CNS to the rest of the body. In this section, we focus on the peripheral nervous system; later, we'll look at the brain and spinal cord.

Flash Forward

Ready to dig into the vocabulary? Get some practice with this Hawkes Verified Quizlet set (hawkes.biz/psych2q3)!

Central Nervous System

Peripheral Nervous System

Brain

Spinal cord

Nerve

(a)

(b)

Figure 1: The nervous system is divided into two major parts: (a) the Central Nervous System and (b) the Peripheral Nervous System.

Peripheral Nervous System

The peripheral nervous system is made up of thick bundles of axons, called nerves, carrying messages back and forth between the brain, the spinal cord, and the muscles, organs, and senses in the periphery of the body (i.e., everything outside the CNS). The PNS has two major subdivisions: the somatic nervous system and the autonomic nervous system.

The **somatic nervous system** is associated with the relay of sensory and motor information to and from the brain; therefore, it consists of motor neurons and sensory neurons. Each nerve is basically a two-way superhighway, containing thousands of axons, both efferent and afferent. Motor neurons, carrying instructions from the brain to the muscles, are efferent fibers (*efferent* means "moving away from"). Sensory neurons, carrying sensory information to the CNS, are afferent fibers (*afferent* means "moving toward").

✎ On Your Own

Which of the following tells muscles what to do?

☐ Somatic Neurons   ☐ Motor Neurons   ☐ Sensory Neurons

The **autonomic nervous system** controls our internal organs and glands and is generally considered to be outside the realm of voluntary control. It can be further subdivided into the sympathetic and parasympathetic divisions (Figure 2). The **sympathetic nervous system** is involved in preparing the body for stress-related activities; the **parasympathetic nervous system** is associated with returning the body to routine, day-to-day operations. The two systems have complementary functions, operating in tandem to maintain the body's homeostasis. **Homeostasis** is a state of equilibrium, in which biological conditions (such as body temperature) are maintained at optimal levels.

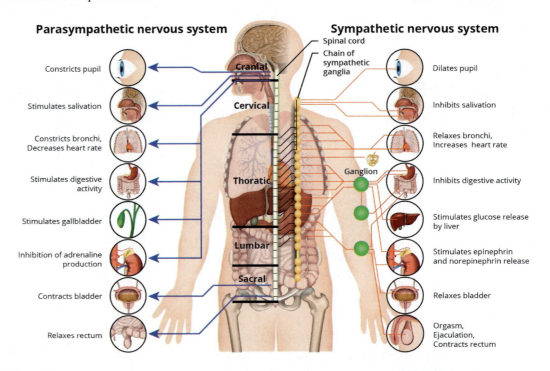

🖼 **Figure 2:** The sympathetic and parasympathetic divisions of the autonomic nervous system have the opposite effects on various systems.

The sympathetic nervous system is activated when we are faced with stressful or high-arousal situations. The activity of this system was adaptive for our ancestors, increasing their chances of survival. Imagine, for example, that one of our early ancestors, out hunting small game, suddenly disturbs a large bear with her cubs. At that moment, his body undergoes a series of changes—a direct function of sympathetic activation—preparing him to face the threat. His pupils dilate, his heart rate and blood pressure increase, his bladder relaxes, his liver releases glucose, and adrenaline surges into his bloodstream. This constellation of physiological changes, known as the **fight-or-flight response**, allows the body access to energy reserves and heightened sensory capacity so that it might fight off a threat or run away to safety.

✎ On Your Own

Answer the following questions about functions of the central and peripheral nervous systems.

1. Fight or flight:

☐ Sensory Neurons   ☐ Sympathetic Nervous System

☐ Parasympathetic Nervous System   ☐ Peripheral Neurons

2. Rest and digest:

☐ Sympathetic Nervous System   ☐ Parasympathetic Nervous System

☐ Motor Neurons   ☐ Sensory Neurons

3. Carrying tactile information from your hands to the brain:

☐ Sympathetic Nervous System   ☐ Sensory Neurons

☐ Parasympathetic Nervous System   ☐ Motor Neurons

4. Dilated pupils:

☐ Sympathetic Nervous System   ☐ Parasympathetic Nervous System

☐ Motor Neurons   ☐ Sensory Neurons

5. Activated after you eat a big meal:

☐ Sympathetic Nervous System   ☐ Sensory Neurons

☐ Parasympathetic Nervous System   ☐ Motor Neurons

Our ancestors lived in a world of real physical threats, such as getting attacked by a bear. During a situation when you are getting attacked by a bear, your sympathetic nervous system is activated, and you are prepared to fight or flight (run away). Now, you might not be in a bear fight any time soon, but your brain and body are still prepared for such madness. Modern day humans experience increased sympathetic activity from psychological threats or stressful situations, such as giving a presentation or taking an important test. Recent research suggests that an increase in susceptibility to heart disease (Chandola, Brunner, & Marmot, 2006) and impaired function of the immune system (Glaser & Kiecolt-Glaser, 2005) are among the many negative consequences of persistent and repeated exposure to stressful situations.

Further Resources

Reinforce what you've learned about the nervous system by playing this BBC-produced interactive game (hawkes.biz/nervoussystem) about the nervous system.

Reflection Questions

What are some ways you can increase parasympathetic nervous system activity?

Once the threat has been resolved, whether it is a bear, a big test, or having to walk down a long hallway with a casual acquaintance after you've already said goodbye, the parasympathetic nervous system takes over and returns bodily functions to a relaxed state. Our heart rate and blood pressure return to normal, our pupils constrict, we regain control of our bladders, and our livers begin to store glucose in the form of glycogen for future use.

Summary

The brain and spinal cord make up the central nervous system. The peripheral nervous system is comprised of the somatic and autonomic nervous systems. The somatic nervous system transmits sensory and motor signals to and from the central nervous system. The autonomic nervous system controls the function of our organs and glands and can be divided into the sympathetic and parasympathetic divisions. Sympathetic activation [handwritten note: Spinal cord connects brain to outside world

Relay station (very smart)

Routes message to and from, own system of automatic processes (reflexes)]

...c activation is associated with normal functioning under

The Brain and Spinal Cord

...d of billions of interconnected neurons and glia. It is a ...ed into distinct lobes. Each lobe is associated with certain ...ain interact with one another to provide the foundation for ...uss the overall organization of the brain and the functions ...n the spinal cord.

...he brain to the outside world. Because of it, the brain can ...y smart one. It not only routes messages to and from the brain, but it also has its own system of automatic processes, called reflexes.

The top of the spinal cord merges with the brain stem, where the basic processes of life are controlled, such as breathing and digestion. In the opposite direction, the spinal cord ends just below the ribs, it does not extend all the way to the base of the spine.

The spinal cord is functionally organized in 30 segments, corresponding with the vertebrae. Each segment is connected to a specific part of the body through the peripheral nervous system. Nerves branch out from the spine at each vertebra. Sensory nerves bring messages in; motor nerves send messages out to the muscles and organs. Messages travel to and from the brain through every segment.

The brain stem controls breathing and digestion.

The spinal cord directs responses to withdraw from heat, knee reflexes, and other automatic responses. This saves processing time.

Sensory nerves bring messages to spinal cord; motor nerves send messages to muscles and organs.

Figure 1: The spinal cord connects the brain to the outside world.

When a sensory message meets certain parameters, the spinal cord initiates an automatic reflex. The signal passes from the sensory nerve to a simple processing center, which initiates a motor command. Seconds are saved because messages don't have to go the brain, be processed, and get sent back. In matters of survival, the spinal reflexes allow the body to react extraordinarily fast.

The spinal cord is protected by bony vertebrae and cushioned in cerebrospinal fluid, but injuries still occur. When the spinal cord is damaged in a particular segment, all lower segments are cut off from the brain, causing paralysis. Therefore, the lower on the spine damage is, the fewer functions an injured individual loses.

☑ On Your Own

Select an automatic reflex from the boxes below.

- ☐ ducking when someone swings at you
- ☐ hand recoils from a heat source
- ☐ feeling that someone's watching you

The Two Hemispheres

The surface of the brain, known as the **cerebral cortex**, is very uneven, characterized by a distinctive pattern of folds or bumps, known as **gyri** (singular: *gyrus*), and grooves, known as **sulci** (singular: *sulcus*), shown in Figure 2. These gyri and sulci form important landmarks that allow us to separate the brain into functional centers. The most prominent sulcus, known as the **longitudinal fissure**, is the deep groove that separates the brain into two halves or **hemispheres**: the left hemisphere and the right hemisphere.

Figure 2: The surface of the brain is covered with gyri and sulci. A deep sulcus is called a fissure, such as the longitudinal fissure that divides the brain into left and right hemispheres.

There is evidence of some specialization of function, referred to as **lateralization**, in each hemisphere, mainly regarding differences in language ability. What we do know is that the left hemisphere controls the right half of the body although the brain has the flexibility to rewire certain pathways in the event of a brain injury.

The two hemispheres are connected by a thick band of neural fibers known as the corpus callosum, consisting of about 200 million axons. The **corpus callosum** allows the two hemispheres to communicate with each other and allows for information being processed on one side of the brain to be shared with the other side.

Normally, we are not aware of the different roles that our two hemispheres play in day-to-day functions, but there are people who come to know the capabilities and functions of their two hemispheres quite well. In some cases of severe epilepsy, doctors elect to sever the corpus callosum as a means of controlling the spread of seizures (Figure 3). While this is an effective treatment option, it results in individuals who have split brains.

After surgery, these split-brain patients show a variety of interesting behaviors. For instance, a split-brain patient is unable to name a picture that is shown in the patient's left visual field because the information is only available in the largely nonverbal right hemisphere. However, they can recreate the picture with their left hand, which is also controlled by the right hemisphere. When the more verbal left hemisphere sees the

Helpful Hint

There has been much research and discussion about brain differences between males and females. A meta-analysis (review of multiple studies on the same topic) of 126 studies conducted between 1990 and 2013 and reported by Ruigrock et al. (2014) in *Neuroscience and Biobehavioral Reviews* indicated that the male brain, on average, has a larger volume than females, and there appear to be regional size differences (specific areas) in the amygdala, hippocampus, and insula (impacting limbic structures and language).

Figure 3: The corpus callosum connects the left and right hemispheres of the brain. This image shows a scientist spreading apart a dissected sheep brain apart to show the corpus callosum.

picture that the hand drew, the patient can identify the picture (assuming the left hemisphere can interpret what was drawn by the left hand).

Much of what we know about the functions of different areas of the brain comes from studying changes in the behavior and ability of individuals who have suffered damage to the brain. For example, researchers study the behavioral changes caused by strokes to learn about the functions of specific brain areas. A stroke, caused by an interruption of blood flow to a region in the brain, causes a loss of brain function in the affected region. The damage can be in a small area, and if it is, this gives researchers the opportunity to link any resulting behavioral changes to a specific area. The types of deficits displayed after a stroke will be largely dependent on where in the brain the damage occurred.

Consider Theona, an intelligent, self-sufficient woman, who is 62 years old. Recently, she suffered a stroke in the front portion of her right hemisphere. As a result, she has great difficulty moving her left leg. (As you learned earlier, the right hemisphere controls the left side of the body; also, the brain's main motor centers are located at the front of the head, in the frontal lobe.) Theona has also experienced behavioral changes. For example, while in the produce section of the grocery store, she sometimes eats grapes, strawberries, and apples directly from their bins before paying for them. This behavior—which would have been very embarrassing to her before the stroke—is consistent with damage in another region in the frontal lobe—the prefrontal cortex, which is associated with judgment, reasoning, and impulse control.

Further Resources

Watch this video (hawkes.biz/splitbrain) from Scientific American Frontiers about a severed corpus callosum.

✐ On Your Own

Select the effect of a brain injury below that would be likely in the following scenario:

Theona had a stroke in her right frontal lobe.

☐ Loss of movement in right leg   ☐ Altered impulse control

☐ Loss of speech

Forebrain Structures

The cerebral cortex is associated with higher level processes such as consciousness, thought, emotion, reasoning, language, and memory.

Subcortical structures (below cerebral cortex):

- thalamus
- hypothalamus
- pituitary gland
- limbic system (collection of structures)

Each cerebral hemisphere can be subdivided into four lobes, each associated with different functions.

Lobes of the Brain

The four lobes of the brain are the frontal, parietal, temporal, and occipital lobes (Figure 5). The **frontal lobe** is located in the forward part of the brain, extending back to a fissure known as the central sulcus. It contains the **motor cortex**, which is involved in planning and coordinating movement; the **prefrontal cortex**, which is responsible for higher-level cognitive functioning; and **Broca's area**, which is essential for language production.

Figure 4: The brain and its parts can be divided into three main categories: the forebrain, midbrain, and hindbrain.

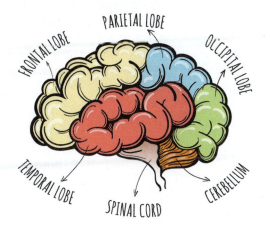

📖 **Figure 5:** The lobes of the brain serve a variety of functions.

People who suffer damage to Broca's area have great difficulty producing language of any form (Figure 5). For example, Padma was an electrical engineer who was socially active and a caring, involved mother. About twenty years ago, she was in a car accident and suffered damage to her Broca's area. She completely lost the ability to speak and form any kind of meaningful language. There is nothing wrong with her mouth or her vocal cords, but she is unable to produce words. She can follow directions but can't respond verbally, and she can read but no longer write. She can do routine tasks like running to the market to buy milk, but she could not communicate verbally if a situation called for it.

The brain's **parietal lobe** contains the **somatosensory cortex**, which is essential for processing sensory information from across the body, such as touch, temperature, and pain. The somatosensory cortex is organized topographically, which means that spatial relationships that exist in the body are maintained on the surface of the somatosensory cortex (Figure 6). For example, the portion of the cortex that processes sensory information from the hand is adjacent to the portion that processes information from the wrist.

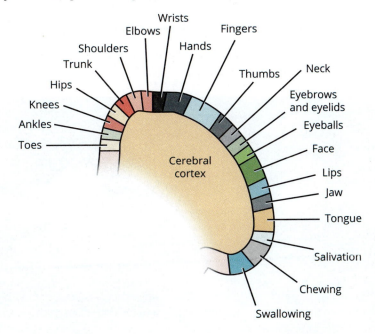

📖 **Figure 6:** Spatial relationships in the body are mirrored in the organization of the somatosensory cortex.

The **temporal lobe** is located on the side of the head (temporal means "near the temples") and is associated with hearing, memory, emotion, and some aspects of language. The **auditory cortex**, the main area responsible for processing auditory information, is located within the temporal lobe. **Wernicke's area**, important for speech comprehension, is also located here. Whereas individuals with damage to Broca's area have difficulty producing language, those with damage to Wernicke's area can produce sensible language, but they are unable to understand it (Figure 7).

Damage will cause problems with speech comprehension.

Wernicke's area

Broca's area

Damage will cause issues with speech production.

📷 **Figure 7:** Damage to either Broca's area or Wernicke's area can result in language deficits. The types of deficits are very different, however, depending on which area is affected.

The **occipital lobe** is located at the very back of the brain and contains the primary visual cortex, which is responsible for interpreting incoming visual information. The occipital cortex is organized retinotopically, which means there is a close relationship between the position of an object in a person's visual field and the position of that object's representation on the cortex. We'll learn much more about how visual information is processed in the occipital lobe when we look at sensation and perception.

Other Areas of the Forebrain

Other areas of the **forebrain**, located beneath the cerebral cortex, include the thalamus and the limbic system. The **thalamus** is a sensory relay for the brain. (Figure 8).

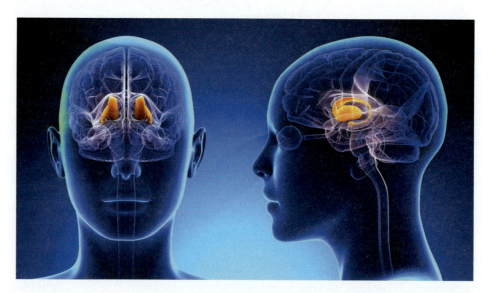

📷 **Figure 8:** The thalamus serves as the relay center of the brain where most senses are routed for processing, except for smell.

The **limbic system** is involved in processing both emotion and memory. Interestingly, the sense of smell projects directly to the limbic system; therefore, not surprisingly, smell can evoke emotional responses in ways that other sensory modalities cannot. The three most important structures of the limbic system are the **hippocampus**, the **amygdala**, and the **hypothalamus** (Figure 9).

BASAL GANGLIA
control of movements, learning, habit, cognition, and emotion

THALAMUS
regulation of sleep, consciousness, and alertness

HYPOTHALAMUS
controls body temperature, hunger, fatigue, sleep

AMYGDALA
memory, decision-making, and emotional responses

HIPPOCAMPUS
memory, navigation

Figure 9: The limbic system is involved in mediating emotional response and memory.

The Case of Henry Molaison (H.M.)

In 1953, Henry Gustav Molaison (H.M.) was a 27-year-old man who experienced severe seizures. In an attempt to control his seizures, H.M. underwent brain surgery to remove his hippocampus and amygdala. Following the surgery, H.M.'s seizures became much less severe, but he also suffered some unexpected—and devastating—consequences of the surgery: he lost his ability to form many types of new memories. He was able to learn new skills, but afterward, he had no recollection of learning them. He could not remember new faces, and he was unable to remember events, even immediately after they occurred. Researchers were fascinated by his experience, and he is considered one of the most studied cases in medical and psychological history (Hardt, Einarsson, & Nader, 2010; Squire, 2009).

Midbrain and Hindbrain Structures

The **midbrain** is comprised of structures located deep within the brain, between the forebrain and the hindbrain.

Reticular formation (extends up into the forebrain and down into the hindbrain):

- regulates sleep/wake cycle
- regulates arousal

- regulates alertness
- regulates motor activity

Substantia nigra (Latin for "black substance") and **ventral tegmental area (VTA)**:

- produce dopamine
- are involved in Parkinson's disease

- are involved in mood, reward, and addiction

(Berridge & Robinson, 1998; Gardner, 2011; George, Le Moal, & Koob, 2012)

Further Resources

Clive Wearing, an accomplished musician, lost the ability to form new memories when his hippocampus was damaged through illness. Check out the first few minutes of this documentary video (hawkes.biz/braindamage) for an introduction to this man and his condition.

⊠ Figure 10: The substantia nigra and ventral tegmental area (VTA) are located in the midbrain.

Hindbrain Structures

The **hindbrain** is located at the back of the head and looks like an extension of the spinal cord. It contains the medulla, pons, and cerebellum (Figure 11). The medulla, pons, and midbrain together are known as the brainstem.

> The **medulla** controls the automatic processes of the autonomic nervous system, such as:
>
> - breathing
> - blood pressure
> - heart rate

> The **pons** (means "bridge"):
>
> - connects brain and spinal cord
> - regulates brain activity during sleep

> The **cerebellum** (Latin for "little brain"):
>
> - receives messages from muscles, tendons, joints, and structures in our ear to control balance, coordination, movement, and motor skills
> - believed to be involved in processing some memories, such as procedural memory or memory involved in learning and remembering how to perform tasks

Pons

Cerebellum

Medulla

🖼 **Figure 11:** The pons, medulla, and cerebellum make up the hindbrain.

✎ On Your Own

Identify the area of the brain with the structures it contains.

1. Contains the limbic system

   ☐ Forebrain   ☐ Midbrain   ☐ Hindbrain

2. Contains a structure believed to be involved in procedural memory

   ☐ Forebrain   ☐ Midbrain   ☐ Hindbrain

3. Contains a structure involved in Parkinson's disease

   ☐ Forebrain   ☐ Midbrain   ☐ Hindbrain

Figure 12: Families are often faced with difficult decisions about the medical response to patients declared brain dead.

What Do You Think?

Brain Dead and on Life Support

What would you do if your spouse or loved one was declared brain dead but his or her body was being kept alive by medical equipment? Whose decision should it be to remove a feeding tube? Should medical care costs be a factor?

On February 25, 1990, a Florida woman named Terri Schiavo went into cardiac arrest, apparently triggered by a bulimic episode. She was eventually revived, but her brain had been deprived of oxygen for a long time. Brain scans indicated that there was no activity in her cerebral cortex, and she suffered from severe and permanent cerebral atrophy. Basically, Schiavo was in a vegetative state. Medical professionals determined that she would never again be able to move, talk, or respond in any way. To remain alive, she required a feeding tube, and there was no chance that her situation would ever improve.

On occasion, Schiavo's eyes would move, and sometimes she would groan. Despite the doctors' insistence to the contrary, her parents believed that these were signs that she was trying to communicate with them.

After 12 years, Schiavo's husband argued that his wife would not have wanted to be kept alive with no feelings, sensations, or brain activity. Her parents, however, were very much against removing her feeding tube. Eventually, the case made its way to the courts, both in the state of Florida and at the federal level. By 2005, the courts found in favor of Schiavo's husband, and the feeding tube was removed on March 18, 2005. Schiavo died 13 days later.

Why did Schiavo's eyes sometimes move, and why did she groan? Although the parts of her brain that control thought, voluntary movement, and feeling were completely damaged, her brainstem was still intact. Her medulla and pons maintained her breathing and caused involuntary movements of her eyes and the occasional groans. Over the 15-year period that she was on a feeding tube, Schiavo's medical costs may have topped $7 million (Arnst, 2003).

These questions were brought to popular conscience 25 years ago in the case of Terri Schiavo, and they persist today. In 2013, a 13-year-old girl who suffered complications after tonsil surgery was declared brain dead. There was a battle between her family, who wanted her to remain on life support, and the hospital's policies regarding persons declared brain dead. In another complicated 2013–14 case in Texas, a pregnant EMT professional declared brain dead was kept alive for weeks, despite her spouse's directives, which were based on her wishes should this situation arise. In this case, state laws designed to protect an unborn fetus came into consideration until doctors determined the fetus unviable.

Decisions surrounding the medical response to patients declared brain dead are complex. What do you think about these issues?

Brain Imaging

You have learned how brain injury can provide information about the functions of different parts of the brain. Increasingly, however, we are able to obtain that information using brain imaging techniques on individuals who have not suffered brain injury. In this section, we take a more in-depth look at some of the techniques that are available for imaging the brain, including techniques that rely on radiation, magnetic fields, or electrical activity within the brain.

Techniques Involving Radiation

A **computerized tomography (CT) scan** involves taking multiple x-rays of a particular section of a person's body or brain (Figure 13). The x-rays pass through tissues of different densities at different rates, allowing a computer to construct an overall image of the area of the body being scanned. A CT scan is often used to determine whether someone has a tumor or significant brain atrophy.

📷 **Figure 13:** A CT scan can be used to show brain tumors and hemorrhages (Left to Right: Normal brain, Brain tumor, Cerebral infarction, Intracerebral hemorrhage).

Positron emission tomography (PET) scans create pictures of the living, active brain (Figure 14). An individual receiving a PET scan drinks or is injected with a mildly radioactive substance called a tracer. Once in the bloodstream, the amount of tracer in any given region of the brain can be monitored. As brain areas become more active, more blood flows to that area. A computer monitors the movement of the tracer and creates a rough map of active and inactive areas of the brain during a given behavior.

PET scans show little detail, are unable to pinpoint events precisely in time, and require that the brain be exposed to radiation; therefore, this technique has been replaced by the fMRI as an alternative diagnostic tool.

However, combined with CT, PET technology is still being used in certain contexts. For example, CT/PET scans allow better imaging of the activity of neurotransmitter receptors and open new avenues in schizophrenia research. In this hybrid CT/PET technology, CT contributes clear images of brain structures, while PET shows the brain's activity.

📷 **Figure 14:** A PET scan is helpful for showing activity in different parts of the brain.

Techniques Involving Magnetic Fields

In **magnetic resonance imaging (MRI)**, a person is placed inside a machine that generates a strong magnetic field. The magnetic field causes the hydrogen atoms in the body's cells to move. When the magnetic field is turned off, the hydrogen atoms emit electromagnetic signals as they return to their original positions. Tissues of different densities give off different signals, which a computer interprets and displays on a monitor. **Functional magnetic resonance imaging (fMRI)** operates on the same principles, but it shows changes in brain activity over time by tracking blood flow and oxygen levels. The fMRI provides more detailed images of the brain's structure, as well as better accuracy in time, than is possible in PET scans (Figure 15). With their high level of detail, MRI and fMRI are often used to compare the brains of healthy individuals to the brains of

> **Further Resources**
>
> Visit this virtual lab (hawkes. biz/mri) to learn more about MRI and fMRI.

individuals diagnosed with psychological disorders. This comparison helps determine what structural and functional differences exist between these populations.

📷 **Figure 15:** An fMRI shows activity in the brain over time. This image shows a researcher checking fMRI images.

Techniques Involving Electrical Activity

In some situations, it is helpful to gain an understanding of the overall activity of a person's brain, without needing information on the actual location of the activity. **Electroencephalography (EEG)** serves this purpose by providing a measure of a brain's electrical activity. An array of electrodes is placed around a person's head (Figure 16). The signals received by the electrodes result in a printout of the electrical activity of his or her brain, or brainwaves, showing both the frequency (number of waves per second) and amplitude (height) of the recorded brainwaves, with an accuracy within milliseconds. Such information is especially helpful to researchers studying sleep patterns among individuals with sleep disorders.

📷 **Figure 16:** Using caps with electrodes, modern EEG research can study the precise timing of overall brain activities.

🖉 On Your Own

Summarize brain tests and their functions.

Type of Brain Imaging:	Used for:
CT Scan	
PET Scan	
MRI	
fMRI	
EEG	

Reflection Questions

What would you do if you were told that a family member is braindead, and there is no hope for recovery of brain function? Would you continue or discontinue life support? What if your family member had a living will that specified that life support be discontinued in these circumstances? Would you honor their wishes?

Summary

The brain consists of two hemispheres, each controlling the opposite side of the body. Each hemisphere can be subdivided into different lobes: frontal, parietal, temporal, and occipital. In addition to the lobes of the cerebral cortex, the forebrain includes the thalamus (sensory relay) and limbic system (emotion and memory circuit).

The midbrain contains the reticular formation, which is important for sleep and arousal, as well as the substantia nigra and ventral tegmental area. These structures are important for movement, reward, and addictive processes. The hindbrain contains the structures of the brainstem (medulla, pons, and midbrain), which control automatic functions like breathing and blood pressure. The hindbrain also contains the cerebellum, which helps coordinate movement and certain types of memories.

Individuals with brain damage have been studied extensively to provide information about the role of different areas of the brain, and recent advances in technology allow us to glean similar information by imaging brain structure and function. These techniques include CT, PET, MRI, fMRI, and EEG.

2.5 The Endocrine System

The **endocrine system** consists of a series of glands that produce chemical substances known as **hormones** (Figure 1). Like neurotransmitters, hormones are chemical messengers that must bind to a receptor in order to send their signal. However, unlike neurotransmitters, which are released in close proximity to cells with their receptors, hormones are secreted into the bloodstream and travel throughout the body, affecting any cells that contain receptors for them. Thus, whereas neurotransmitters' effects are localized, the effects of hormones are widespread. Also, hormones are slower to take effect and tend to be longer lasting.

Flash Forward

Ready to dig into the vocabulary? Get some practice with this Hawkes Verified Quizlet set (hawkes.biz/psych2q5)!

Hypothalamus

Pituitary glands

Pineal gland

Thyroid and parathyroid glands

Thymus

Pancreas

Ovary (in female)

Adrenal glands

Placenta (during pregnancy)

Testicle (in male)

Figure 1: The major glands of the endocrine system are shown.

Hormones are involved in regulating all sorts of bodily functions, and they are ultimately controlled through interactions between the hypothalamus (in the central nervous system) and the pituitary gland (in the endocrine system). Imbalances in hormones are related to disorders. This section explores some of the major glands that make up the endocrine system and the hormones secreted by these glands.

> ### Reflection Questions
> How is it evolutionarily advantageous for our neurotransmitters to be fast-acting and our hormones to be released and act more slowly?

Further Resources

Watch this video (hawkes.biz/endocrine) to learn more about how the endocrine system works.

Major Glands

Pituitary gland (descends from the hypothalamus at the base of the brain)

- "Master gland"—messenger hormones control all endocrine glands
- Carries out instructions from hypothalamus
- Secretes growth hormone
- Secretes endorphins for pain relief
- Secretes hormones that regulate fluid levels

Thyroid gland (located in the neck)

- Releases hormones that regulate growth, metabolism, and appetite
- Graves' disease (hyperthyroidism):
  - *Secretes too much thyroxine*
  - *Causes agitation, bulging eyes, weight loss*
- Hypothyroidism:
  - *Secretes too little thyroxine*
  - *Causes tiredness and feeling cold*

Fortunately, thyroid disorders are often treatable with medications that help reestablish a balance in the hormones secreted by the thyroid.

Adrenal glands (sit on top of kidneys)

- Secrete hormones involved in stress response:
  - *Epinephrine (adrenaline)*
  - *Norepinephrine (noradrenaline)*

Pancreas (organ that secretes hormones that regulate blood sugar)

- Insulin (lower blood sugar)
- Glucagon (increase blood sugar)

People who suffer from **diabetes** do not produce enough insulin; therefore, they must take medications that stimulate or replace insulin production, and they must closely control the amount of sugars and carbohydrates they consume.

Gonads

- Secrete sexual hormones, which are important in reproduction:

  - *Female ovaries secrete estrogens and progesterone*

  - *Male testes secrete androgens (e.g., testosterone)*

- Mediate sexual motivation and behavior

✐ On Your Own

Which gland matches the descriptions below?

1. Known as the master gland

   ☐ Adrenal gland   ☐ Thyroid gland   ☐ Pituitary gland

   ☐ Gonads   ☐ Pancreas

2. Sits on top of the kidneys

   ☐ Adrenal gland   ☐ Thyroid gland   ☐ Pituitary gland

   ☐ Gonads   ☐ Pancreas

3. Located in the neck

   ☐ Adrenal gland   ☐ Thyroid gland   ☐ Pituitary gland

   ☐ Gonads   ☐ Pancreas

4. Dysfunction can cause diabetes

   ☐ Adrenal gland   ☐ Thyroid gland   ☐ Pituitary gland

   ☐ Gonads   ☐ Pancreas

5. Secretes testosterone in males

   ☐ Adrenal gland   ☐ Thyroid gland   ☐ Pituitary gland

   ☐ Gonads   ☐ Pancreas

Group Activity

The percentage of Americans who are overweight continues to increase. As a result, Type II diabetes diagnoses are increasing in children and teenagers. Research the average weight for adult men and women in the 1970s, 1990s, and in 2015. Has it increased or decreased? If so, by how much? Come up with some possible explanations for your findings.

Figure 2: Performance-enhancing drugs, such as steroids, can cause changes in mood and behavior.

Dig Deeper

Athletes and Anabolic Steroids

Although it is against federal laws and many professional athletic associations (e.g., The National Football League) have banned their use, anabolic steroid drugs continue to be used by amateur and professional athletes. The drugs are believed to enhance athletic performance. Anabolic steroid drugs mimic the effects of the body's own steroid hormones, like testosterone and its derivatives. These drugs have the potential to provide a competitive edge by increasing muscle mass, strength, and endurance although not all users may experience these results. Moreover, use of performance-enhancing drugs (PEDs) does not come without risks. Anabolic steroid use has been linked with a wide variety of potentially negative outcomes, ranging in severity from largely cosmetic (acne) to life threatening (heart attack). Furthermore, use of these substances can result in profound changes in mood and can increase aggressive behavior (National Institute on Drug Abuse, 2001).

Baseball player Alex Rodriguez (A-Rod) was at the center of a media storm regarding his use of illegal PEDs. Rodriguez's performance on the field was unparalleled while using the drugs; his success played a large role in negotiating a contract that made him the highest paid player in professional baseball. Although Rodriguez maintains that he had not used PEDs for the several years, he received a substantial suspension in 2013 that cost him more than 20 million dollars in earnings (Gaines, 2013).

- What are your thoughts on athletes and doping?
- Should the use of PEDs be banned? What makes you say that?
- What advice would you give an athlete who was considering using PEDs?

Summary

The glands of the endocrine system secrete hormones to regulate normal body functions. The hypothalamus serves as the interface between the nervous system and the endocrine system, and it controls the secretions of the pituitary. The pituitary serves as the master gland, controlling the secretions of all other glands. The thyroid secretes thyroxine, which is important for basic metabolic processes and growth; the adrenal glands secrete hormones involved in the stress response; the pancreas secretes hormones that regulate blood sugar levels; and the ovaries and testes produce sex hormones that regulate sexual motivation and behavior.

Chapter 2 Project

Purpose

Test anxiety is real. Millions of students all over the country experience this vague sense of unease when it comes to testing.

Psychology gives us insight into what is going on with our bodies in response to something like test anxiety. In fact, when a person understands their body's response to anxiety, it can be helpful in dealing with it. **The purpose of this project is to better understand how the body's structures (i.e., parts), functions (i.e., what those parts do), and systems operate when a student experiences test anxiety.**

Directions

On a piece of very large paper or poster board, label and explain the role and/or process of biological structures, functions, and systems that are activated when a student is experiencing test anxiety. You should thoroughly address the role of each the following:

1. Brain Structures

2. Brain Functions

3. Neurotransmitters

4. Neural Transmission

5. The Nervous System

6. The Endocrine System

Begin with an outline of the body and brain. You should also display visually, an understanding of neural transmission. You should specifically address test anxiety on your poster.

Materials

Large piece of paper or poster board (20+ inches width) required. Pencil crayons or colored markers encouraged.

☑ Checklist

Biopsychological Components of Test Anxiety

☐ Brain Structures

☐ Brain Functions

☐ Neurotransmitters

☐ Neural Transmission

☐ The Nervous System

☐ The Endocrine System

For each component:

☐ Label

☐ Explain role in test anxiety

Chapter 2 Review

Lesson Summaries

2.1 Human Genetics

Genes are sequences of DNA that code for a particular trait. Different versions of a gene are called alleles—sometimes alleles can be classified as dominant or recessive. A dominant allele always results in the dominant phenotype. In order to exhibit a recessive phenotype, an individual must be homozygous for the recessive allele. Genes affect both physical and psychological characteristics. Ultimately, how and when a gene is expressed and what the outcome will be—in terms of both physical and psychological characteristics—is a function of the interaction between our genes and our environments.

2.2 Cells of the Nervous System

Glia and neurons are the two cell types that make up the nervous system. While glia generally play supporting roles, the communication between neurons is fundamental to all of the functions associated with the nervous system. Neuronal communication is made possible by the neuron's specialized structures. The soma contains the cell nucleus, and the dendrites extend from the soma in tree-like branches. The axon is another major extension of the cell body; axons are often covered by a myelin sheath, which increases the speed of transmission of neural impulses. At the end of the axon are terminal buttons that contain synaptic vesicles filled with neurotransmitters.

Neuronal communication is an electrochemical event. The dendrites contain receptors for neurotransmitters released by nearby neurons. If the signals received from other neurons are sufficiently strong, an action potential will travel down the length of the axon to the terminal buttons, resulting in the release of neurotransmitters into the synapse. Action potentials operate on the all-or-none principle and involve the movement of Na^+ and K^+ across the neuronal membrane.

Different neurotransmitters are associated with different functions. Often, psychological disorders involve imbalances in a given neurotransmitter system. Therefore, psychotropic drugs are prescribed in an attempt to bring the neurotransmitters back into balance. Drugs can act either as agonists or as antagonists for a given neurotransmitter system.

2.3 Parts of the Nervous System

The brain and spinal cord make up the central nervous system. The peripheral nervous system is comprised of the somatic and autonomic nervous systems. The somatic nervous system transmits sensory and motor signals to and from the central nervous system. The autonomic nervous system controls the function of our organs and glands and can be divided into the sympathetic and parasympathetic divisions. Sympathetic activation prepares us for fight or flight, while parasympathetic activation is associated with normal functioning under relaxed conditions.

2.4 The Brain and Spinal Cord

The brain consists of two hemispheres, each controlling the opposite side of the body. Each hemisphere can be subdivided into different lobes: frontal, parietal, temporal, and occipital. In addition to the lobes of the cerebral cortex, the forebrain includes the thalamus (sensory relay) and limbic system (emotion and memory circuit).

The midbrain contains the reticular formation, which is important for sleep and arousal, as well as the substantia nigra and ventral tegmental area. These structures are important for movement, reward, and addictive processes. The hindbrain contains the structures of the brainstem (medulla, pons, and midbrain), which control automatic functions like breathing and blood pressure. The hindbrain also contains the cerebellum, which helps coordinate movement and certain types of memories.

Individuals with brain damage have been studied extensively to provide information about the role of different areas of the brain, and recent advances in technology allow us to glean similar information by imaging brain structure and function. These techniques include CT, PET, MRI, fMRI, and EEG.

2.5 The Endocrine System

The glands of the endocrine system secrete hormones to regulate normal body functions. The hypothalamus serves as the interface between the nervous system and the endocrine system, and it controls the secretions of the pituitary. The pituitary serves as the master gland, controlling the secretions of all other glands. The thyroid secretes thyroxine, which is important for basic metabolic processes and growth; the adrenal glands secrete hormones involved in the stress response; the pancreas secretes hormones that regulate blood sugar levels; and the ovaries and testes produce sex hormones that regulate sexual motivation and behavior.

Key Terms

Flash Back

Now that you've worked through the chapter, sharpen your vocabulary with this Hawkes Verified Quizlet set (hawkes.biz/psychch2)!

Action Potential

Electrical signal that moves down the neuron's axon

Adrenal Gland

Sits atop our kidneys and secretes hormones involved in the stress response

Agonist

Drug that mimics or strengthens the effects of a neurotransmitter

Allele

Specific version of a gene

All-or-None

Phenomenon that the incoming signal from another neuron is either sufficient or insufficient to reach the threshold of excitation

Amygdala

Structure in the limbic system involved in our experience of emotion and tying emotional meaning to our memories

Antagonist

Drug that blocks or impedes the normal activity of a given neurotransmitter

Auditory Cortex

Strip of cortex in the temporal lobe that is responsible for processing auditory information

Autonomic Nervous System

Controls our internal organs and glands

Axon

Major extension of the soma

Biological Perspective

View that psychological disorders like depression and schizophrenia are associated with imbalances in one or more neurotransmitter systems

Broca's Area

Region in the left hemisphere that is essential for language production

Central Nervous System (CNS)

Brain and spinal cord

Cerebellum

Hindbrain structure that controls our balance, coordination, movement, and motor skills, and it is thought to be important in processing some types of memory

Cerebral Cortex

Surface of the brain that is associated with our highest mental capabilities

Chromosome

Long strand of genetic information

Computerized Tomography (CT) Scan

Imaging technique in which a computer coordinates and integrates multiple x-rays of a given area

Corpus Callosum

Thick band of neural fibers connecting the brain's two hemispheres

Dendrite

Branch-like extension of the soma that receives incoming signals from other neurons

Deoxyribonucleic Acid (DNA)

Helix-shaped molecule made of nucleotide base pairs

Diabetes

Disease related to insufficient insulin production

Dominant Allele

Allele whose phenotype will be expressed in an individual that possesses that allele

Electroencephalography (EEG)

Recording the electrical activity of the brain via electrodes on the scalp

Endocrine System

Series of glands that produce chemical substances known as hormones

Epigenetics

Study of gene-environment interactions, such as how the same genotype leads to different phenotypes

Fight-or-Flight Response

Activation of the sympathetic division of the autonomic nervous system, allowing access to energy reserves and heightened sensory capacity so that we might fight off a given threat or run away to safety

Forebrain

Largest part of the brain, containing the cerebral cortex, the thalamus, and the limbic system, among other structures

Fraternal Twins

Twins who develop from two different eggs fertilized by different sperm, so their genetic material varies the same as in non-twin siblings

Frontal Lobe

Part of the cerebral cortex involved in reasoning, motor control, emotion, and language; contains motor cortex

Functional Magnetic Resonance Imaging (fMRI)

MRI that shows changes in metabolic activity over time

Gene

Sequence of DNA that controls or partially controls physical characteristics

Genetic Environmental Correlation

View of gene-environment interaction that asserts our genes affect our environment, and our environment influences the expression of our genes

Genotype

Genetic makeup of an individual

Glial Cell

Nervous system cell that provides physical and metabolic support to neurons, including neuronal insulation and communication and nutrient and waste transport

Gonad

Secretes sexual hormones, which are important for successful reproduction, and mediates both sexual motivation and behavior

Gyrus

(Plural: *gyri*) bump or ridge on the cerebral cortex

Hemisphere

Left or right half of the brain

Heterozygous

Consisting of two different alleles

Hindbrain

Division of the brain containing the medulla, pons, and cerebellum

Hippocampus

Structure in the temporal lobe associated with learning and memory

Homeostasis

State of equilibrium—biological conditions, such as body temperature, are maintained at optimal levels

Homozygous

Consisting of two identical alleles

Hormone

Chemical messenger released by endocrine glands

Hypothalamus

Forebrain structure that regulates sexual motivation and behavior and a number of homeostatic processes; serves as an interface between the nervous system and the endocrine system

Identical Twins

Twins that develop from the same sperm and egg

Lateralization

Concept that each hemisphere of the brain is associated with specialized functions

Limbic System

Collection of structures involved in processing emotion and memory

Longitudinal Fissure

Deep groove in the brain's cortex

Magnetic Resonance Imaging (MRI)

Magnetic fields used to produce a picture of the tissue being imaged

Medulla

Hindbrain structure that controls automated processes like breathing, blood pressure, and heart rate

Membrane Potential

Difference in charge across the neuronal membrane

Midbrain

Division of the brain located between the forebrain and the hindbrain; contains the reticular formation

Motor Cortex

Strip of cortex involved in planning and coordinating movement

Mutation

Sudden, permanent change in a gene

Myelin Sheath

Fatty substance that insulates axons

Neuron

Cells in the nervous system that act as interconnected information processors, which are essential for all of the tasks of the nervous system

Neurotransmitter

Chemical messenger of the nervous system

Occipital Lobe

Part of the cerebral cortex associated with visual processing; contains the primary visual cortex

Pancreas

Secretes hormones that regulate blood sugar

Parasympathetic Nervous System

Associated with routine, day-to-day operations of the body

Parietal Lobe

Part of the cerebral cortex involved in processing various sensory and perceptual information; contains the primary somatosensory cortex

Peripheral Nervous System (PNS)

Connects the brain and spinal cord to the muscles, organs, and senses in the periphery of the body

Phenotype

Individual's inheritable physical characteristics

Pituitary Gland

Secretes a number of key hormones, which regulate fluid levels in the body, and a number of messenger hormones, which direct the activity of other glands in the endocrine system

Polygenic

Multiple genes affecting a given trait

Pons

Hindbrain structure that connects the brain and spinal cord; involved in regulating brain activity during sleep

Positron Emission Tomography (PET) Scan

Involves injecting individuals with a mildly radioactive substance and monitoring changes in blood flow to different regions of the brain

Prefrontal Cortex

Area in the frontal lobe responsible for higher-level cognitive functioning

Psychotropic Medication

Drugs that treat psychiatric symptoms by restoring neurotransmitter balance

Range of Reaction

Asserts our genes set the boundaries within which we can operate, and our environment interacts with the genes to determine where in that range we will fall

Receptor

Protein on the cell surface where neurotransmitters attach

Recessive Allele

Allele whose phenotype will be expressed only if an individual is homozygous for that allele

Resting Potential

The state of readiness of a neuron membrane's potential between signals

Reticular Formation

Midbrain structure important in regulating the sleep/wake cycle, arousal, alertness, and motor activity

Reuptake

Neurotransmitter is pumped back into the neuron that released it

Semipermeable Membrane

Cell membrane that allows smaller molecules or molecules without an electrical charge to pass through it while stopping larger or highly charged molecules

Soma

Cell body

Somatic Nervous System

Relays sensory and motor information to and from the CNS

Somatosensory Cortex

Essential for processing sensory information from across the body, such as touch, temperature, and pain

Substantia Nigra

Midbrain structure where dopamine is produced; involved in control of movement

Sulcus

(Plural: *sulci*) depressions or grooves in the cerebral cortex

Sympathetic Nervous System

Involved in stress-related activities and functions

Synapse

Small gap between two neurons where communication occurs

Synaptic Vesicle

Storage site for neurotransmitters

Temporal Lobe

Part of cerebral cortex associated with hearing, memory, emotion, and some aspects of language; contains primary auditory cortex

Terminal Button

Axon terminal containing synaptic vesicles

Thalamus

Sensory relay for the brain

Theory of Evolution by Natural Selection

States that organisms that are better suited for their environments will survive and reproduce compared to those that are poorly suited for their environments

Threshold of Excitation

Level of charge in the membrane that causes the neuron to become active

Thyroid

Secretes hormones that regulate growth, metabolism, and appetite

Ventral Tegmental Area (VTA)

Midbrain structure where dopamine is produced; associated with mood, reward, and addiction

Wernicke's Area

Important for speech comprehension

🔆   Exercises

Review Questions

1. A(n) _____ is a sudden, permanent change in a sequence of DNA.

    a.   allele

    b.   chromosome

    c.   epigenetic

    d.   mutation

2. _____ refers to a person's genetic makeup, while _____ refers to a person's physical characteristics.

    a.   Phenotype; genotype

    b.   Genotype; phenotype

    c.   DNA; gene

    d.   Gene; DNA

3. _____ is the field of study that focuses on genes and their expression.

    a.   Social psychology

    b.   Evolutionary psychology

    c.   Epigenetics

    d.   Behavioral neuroscience

4. Humans have _____ pairs of chromosomes.

    a.   15

    b.   23

    c.   46

    d.   78

5. The _____ receive(s) incoming signals from other neurons.

    a.   soma

    b.   terminal buttons

    c.   myelin sheath

    d.   dendrites

6. A(n) _____ facilitates or mimics the activity of a given neurotransmitter system.

    a.   axon

    b.   SSRI

    c.   agonist

    d.   antagonist

7. Multiple sclerosis involves a breakdown of the _____.

    a.   soma

    b.   myelin sheath

    c.   synaptic vesicles

    d.   dendrites

8. An action potential involves Na^+ moving _____ the cell and K^+ moving _____ the cell.

    a.   inside; outside

    b.   outside; inside

    c.   inside; inside

    d.   outside; outside

9. Our ability to make our legs move as we walk across the room is controlled by the _____ nervous system.

    a.   autonomic

    b.   somatic

    c.   sympathetic

    d.   parasympathetic

10. If your _____ is activated, you will feel relatively at ease.

    a.   somatic nervous system

    b.   sympathetic nervous system

    c.   parasympathetic nervous system

    d.   spinal cord

11. The central nervous system is comprised of _____.

    a.   sympathetic and parasympathetic nervous systems

    b.   organs and glands

    c.   somatic and autonomic nervous systems

    d.   the brain and spinal cord

12. Sympathetic activation is associated with _____.

    a. pupil dilation

    b. storage of glucose in the liver

    c. increased heart rate

    d. both A and C (pupil dilation and increased heart rate)

13. The _____ is a sensory relay station where all sensory information, except for smell, goes before being sent to other areas of the brain for further processing.

    a. amygdala

    b. hippocampus

    c. hypothalamus

    d. thalamus

14. Damage to the _____ disrupts one's ability to comprehend language, but it leaves one's ability to produce words intact.

    a. amygdala

    b. Broca's Area

    c. Wernicke's Area

    d. occipital lobe

15. A(n) _____ uses magnetic fields to create pictures of a given tissue.

    a. EEG

    b. MRI

    c. PET scan

    d. CT scan

16. Which of the following is not a structure of the forebrain?

    a. Thalamus

    b. Hippocampus

    c. Amygdala

    d. Substantia nigra

17. The two major hormones secreted from the pancreas are:

    a. estrogen and progesterone

    b. norepinephrine and epinephrine

    c. thyroxine and oxytocin

    d. glucagon and insulin

18. The _____ secretes messenger hormones that direct the function of the rest of the endocrine glands.

    a. ovary

    b. thyroid

    c. pituitary

    d. pancreas

19. The _____ gland secretes epinephrine.

    a. adrenal

    b. thyroid

    c. pituitary

    d. master

20. The _____ secretes hormones that regulate the body's fluid levels.

    a. adrenal

    b. pituitary

    c. testes

    d. thyroid

Critical Thinking Questions

21. The theory of evolution by natural selection requires variability of a given trait. Why is variability necessary, and where does it come from?

22. Cocaine has two effects on synaptic transmission: it impairs reuptake of dopamine, and it causes more dopamine to be released into the synapse. Would cocaine be classified as an agonist or antagonist? Why?

23. Drugs such as lidocaine and novocaine act as Na^+ channel blockers. In other words, they prevent sodium from moving across the neuronal membrane. Why would this particular effect make these drugs such effective local anesthetics?

24. What are the implications of compromised immune function as a result of exposure to chronic stress?

25. Examine Figure 2 in Lesson 2.3, illustrating the effects of sympathetic nervous system activation. How would all of these things play into the fight-or-flight response?

26. Before the advent of modern imaging techniques, scientists and clinicians relied on autopsies of people who suffered brain injury with resultant change in behavior to determine how different areas of the brain were affected. What are some of the limitations associated with this kind of approach?

27. Which of the techniques discussed would be viable options for you to determine how activity in the reticular formation is related to sleep and wakefulness? Why?

28. Hormone secretion is often regulated through a negative feedback mechanism, which means that once a hormone is secreted, it will cause the hypothalamus and pituitary to shut down the production of signals necessary to secrete the hormone in the first place. Most oral contraceptives are made of small doses of estrogen and/or progesterone. Why would this be an effective means of contraception?

29. Chemical messengers are used in both the nervous system and the endocrine system. What properties do these two systems share? What properties are different? Which one would be faster? Which one would result in long-lasting changes?

Chapter 3

States of Consciousness

Chapter Introduction

📷 **Figure 1:** Sleep, which we all experience, is a quiet and mysterious pause in our daily lives.

Our lives involve regular, dramatic changes in the degree to which we are aware of our surroundings and our internal states. While awake, we feel alert and aware of the many important things going on around us. Our experiences change dramatically while we are in deep sleep and once again when we are dreaming.

This chapter will discuss states of consciousness with a particular emphasis on sleep. The different stages of sleep will be identified, and sleep disorders will be described. The chapter will close with discussions of altered states of consciousness produced by psychoactive drugs, hypnosis, and meditation.

Flash Forward

Ready to dig into the vocabulary? Get some practice with this Hawkes Verified Quizlet set (hawkes.biz/psych3q1)!

3.1 What Is Consciousness?

Consciousness describes our awareness of internal and external stimuli. Awareness of internal stimuli includes feeling pain, hunger, thirst, sleepiness, and being aware of our thoughts and emotions. Awareness of external stimuli includes seeing the light from the sun, feeling the warmth of a room, and hearing the voice of a friend.

We experience different states of consciousness and different levels of awareness on a regular basis. We might even describe consciousness as a continuum that ranges from full awareness to a deep sleep. **Sleep** is a state marked by relatively low levels of physical activity and reduced sensory awareness that is distinct from periods of rest that occur during wakefulness. **Wakefulness** is characterized by high levels of sensory awareness, thought, and behavior. In between these extremes are states of consciousness related to daydreaming, intoxication as a result of alcohol or other drug use, meditative states, hypnotic states, and altered states of consciousness following sleep deprivation. We might also experience unconscious states of being via drug-induced anesthesia for medical purposes. Often, we are not completely aware of our surroundings, even when we are fully awake. For instance, have you ever daydreamed while driving home from work or school without really thinking about the drive itself? You were capable of engaging in all of the complex tasks involved with operating a motor vehicle even though you were not aware of doing so. Many of these processes, like much of psychological behavior, are rooted in our biology.

Biological Rhythms

Biological rhythms are internal rhythms of biological activity. A woman's menstrual cycle is an example of a biological rhythm—a recurring, cyclical pattern of bodily changes. One complete menstrual cycle takes about 28 days—a lunar month—but many biological cycles are much shorter. For example, body temperature fluctuates cyclically over a 24-hour period (Figure 2). Alertness is associated with higher body temperatures, and sleepiness with lower body temperatures.

Figure 2: This chart illustrates the circadian change in body temperature over 28 hours in a group of eight young men. Body temperature rises throughout the waking day, peaks in the afternoon, and falls during sleep with the lowest point occurring during the very early morning hours.

This pattern of temperature fluctuation, which repeats every day, is one example of a circadian rhythm. A **circadian rhythm** is a biological rhythm that takes place over a period of about 24 hours. Our sleep-wake cycle, which is linked to our environment's natural light-dark cycle, is perhaps the most obvious example of a circadian rhythm, but we also have daily fluctuations in heart rate, blood pressure, blood sugar, and body temperature. Some circadian rhythms play a role in changes in our state of consciousness.

If we have biological rhythms, then is there some sort of biological clock? In the brain, the hypothalamus, which lies above the pituitary gland, is a main center of homeostasis. **Homeostasis** is the tendency to maintain a balance, or optimal level, within a biological system.

The brain's clock mechanism is located in an area of the hypothalamus known as the **suprachiasmatic nucleus (SCN)**. The axons of light-sensitive neurons in the retina provide information to the SCN based on the amount of light present, allowing this internal clock to be synchronized with the outside world (Klein, Moore, & Reppert, 1991; Welsh, Takahashi, & Kay, 2010) (Figure 3).

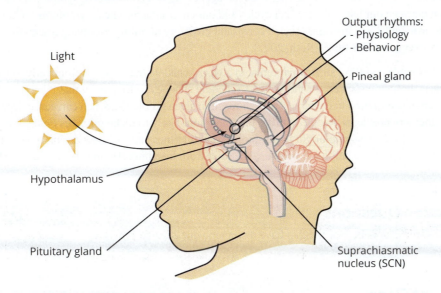

Figure 3: The suprachiasmatic nucleus (SCN) serves as the brain's clock mechanism. The clock sets itself with light information received through projections from the retina.

Problems with Circadian Rhythms

Generally, and for most people, our circadian cycles are aligned with the outside world. For example, most people sleep during the night and are awake during the day. One important regulator of sleep-wake cycles is the hormone **melatonin**. The **pineal gland**, an endocrine structure located inside the brain that releases melatonin, is thought to be involved in the regulation of various biological rhythms and of the immune system during sleep (Hardeland, Pandi-Perumal, & Cardinali, 2006). Melatonin release is stimulated by darkness and inhibited by light.

There are individual differences with regards to our sleep-wake cycle. For instance, some people would say they are morning larks, while others would consider themselves to be night owls. These individual differences in circadian patterns of activity are known as a person's chronotype, and research demonstrates that morning larks and night owls differ with regard to sleep regulation (Taillard, Philip, Coste, Sagaspe, & Bioulac, 2003). **Sleep regulation** refers to the brain's control of switching between sleep and wakefulness as well as coordinating this cycle with the outside world.

> ### Further Resources
> Watch this brief video (hawkes.biz/circadianrhythms) describing circadian rhythms and how they affect sleep.

✍ On Your Own

Which of the following brain structures are *not* directly involved in circadian rhythm?

☐ The Pineal Gland ☐ Suprachiasmatic Nucleus ☐ Substantia Gelatinosa

Which of the following is released from the pineal gland during darkness?

☐ Melatonin ☐ Adrenaline ☐ Dopamine

Disruptions of Normal Sleep

Whether lark, owl, or somewhere in between, there are situations in which a person's circadian clock gets out of synchrony with the external environment. One way that this happens involves traveling across multiple time zones. When we do this, we often experience jet lag. **Jet lag** is a collection of symptoms that results from the mismatch between our internal circadian cycles and our environment. These symptoms include fatigue, sluggishness, irritability, and **insomnia** (i.e., a consistent difficulty in falling or staying asleep for at least three nights a week over a month's time) (Roth, 2007).

In a different example, **rotating shift work** refers to a work schedule that changes from early to late on a daily or weekly basis. In such instances, the individual's schedule changes so frequently that it becomes difficult for a normal circadian rhythm to develop. This can result in sleep problems, which can cause depression, anxiety, and memory problems. People who are tired are more likely to make mistakes on the job (Gold et al., 1992; Presser, 1995). Exposure to bright lights during wakeful times and darkness during times where you are supposed to be asleep can be helpful to people who suffer from insomnia (Huang, Tsai, Chen, & Hsu, 2013).

> ### Reflection Questions
> What are some factors in your life that have disrupted your circadian rhythm?

Figure 4: For better sleep, one can follow these helpful tips.

Insufficient Sleep

A person with a **sleep debt** does not get enough sleep on a chronic basis. The consequences of sleep debt include decreased levels of alertness and mental efficiency. While there is tremendous variation in any given individual's sleep needs, the National Sleep Foundation (n.d.) cites research to estimate that newborns require the most sleep (between 12 and 18 hours a night) and that this amount declines to just 7–9 hours by the time we are adults. Research suggests that by the time we are 65 years old, we average fewer than 7 hours of sleep per day (Ohayon, Carskadon, Guilleminault, & Vitiello, 2004). Table 1 shows recommended amounts of sleep at different ages.

Age	Recommended	May be appropriate	Not recommended
0–3 months	12–18 hours	11–13 hours 18–19 hours	Less than 11 hours More than 19 hours
4 months–11 months	12–15 hours	10–11 hours 16–18 hours	Less than 10 hours More than 18 hours
1–2 years	11–14 hours	9–10 hours 15–16 hours	Less than 9 hours More than 16 hours
3–5 years	10–13 hours	8–9 hours 14 hours	Less than 8 hours More than 14 hours
6–13 years	9–11 hours	7–8 hours 12 hours	Less than 7 hours More than 12 hours
14–17 years	8–10 hours	7 hours 11 hours	Less than 7 hours More than 11 hours
18–25 years	7–9 hours	6 hours 10 hours	Less than 6 hours More than 10 hours
≥65 years	7–8 hours	5–6 hours 9 hours	Less than 5 hours More than 9 hours

Table 1: Sleep Needs at Different Ages

Sleep debt and sleep deprivation have significant negative psychological and physiological consequences (Figure 5). As mentioned earlier, lack of sleep can lead one to experience depression-like symptoms. Research also suggests that sleep deprivation affects cognitive and motor function as much as, if not more than, alcohol intoxication (Williamson & Feyer, 2000). It is also important to note that individuals with other health related problems are more likely to experience sleep debt. For example, people who are obese have higher levels of stress hormones, reduced immune system functioning, and are more likely to experience sleep debt (Banks & Dinges, 2007).

Reflection Questions

Have you noticed changes in your circadian rhythm before? Describe what the experience was like.

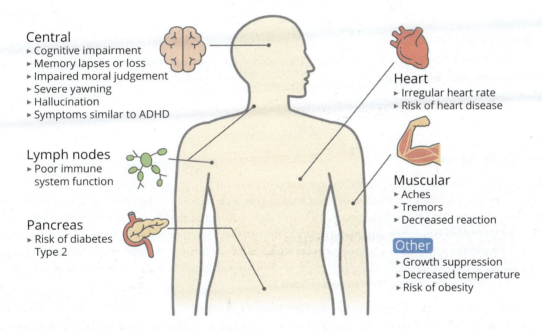

Central
▸ Cognitive impairment
▸ Memory lapses or loss
▸ Impaired moral judgement
▸ Severe yawning
▸ Hallucination
▸ Symptoms similar to ADHD

Lymph nodes
▸ Poor immune
  system function

Pancreas
▸ Risk of diabetes
  Type 2

Heart
▸ Irregular heart rate
▸ Risk of heart disease

Muscular
▸ Aches
▸ Tremors
▸ Decreased reaction

Other
▸ Growth suppression
▸ Decreased temperature
▸ Risk of obesity

Figure 5: This figure illustrates some of the negative consequences of sleep deprivation. While cognitive deficits may be the most obvious, many body systems are negatively impacted by lack of sleep.

Summary

States of consciousness vary over the course of the day and throughout our lives. Important factors in these changes are the biological rhythms and, more specifically, the circadian rhythms generated by the suprachiasmatic nucleus (SCN). Typically, our biological clocks are aligned with our external environment, and light tends to be an important cue in setting this clock. When people travel across multiple time zones or work rotating shifts, they can experience disruptions of their circadian cycles that can lead to insomnia, sleepiness, and decreased alertness. Bright light therapy has shown promising in dealing with circadian disruptions. If people go extended periods of time without sleep, they will accrue a sleep debt and potentially experience adverse psychological and physiological consequences.

Further Resources

To assess your own sleeping habits, read this article (hawkes.biz/sleepneeds) about sleep needs.

Flash Forward

Ready to dig into the vocabulary? Get some practice with this Hawkes Verified Quizlet set (hawkes.biz/psych3q2)!

3.2 Sleep and Why We Sleep

We spend approximately one-third of our lives sleeping. Given the average life expectancy for U.S. citizens falls between 73 and 79 years old (Singh & Siahpush, 2006), we can expect to spend approximately 25 years asleep. Compared to some species, that may be a small or large amount.

Consider the examples below:

Species	Sleep Patterns
Bullfrogs	Need little sleep; responsive to stimuli while resting
Dolphins	Extended gaps in sleep without apparent negative consequences
Rats	Die after two weeks of sleep deprivation

Why do humans devote so much time to sleeping? Is it absolutely essential that we sleep? This section will consider these questions and explore various explanations for why we sleep.

Reflection Questions

Are you impacted by getting too little sleep? Too much sleep? What are some ways in which sleep affects your body and your mind?

What Is Sleep?

You have read that sleep is distinguished by low levels of physical activity and reduced sensory awareness. As discussed by Siegel (2008), a definition of sleep must also include mention of the interplay of the circadian and homeostatic mechanisms that regulate sleep. Homeostatic regulation of sleep is evidenced by sleep rebound following sleep deprivation. **Sleep rebound** refers to the fact that a sleep-deprived individual will tend to take a shorter time to fall asleep during subsequent opportunities for sleep. Sleep is characterized by certain patterns of activity of the brain that can be visualized using electroencephalography (EEG), and different phases of sleep can be differentiated using EEG as well (Figure 2).

Figure 1: An individual's biological clock tells the brain when to sleep and when to wake.

Sleep-wake cycles seem to be controlled by multiple brain areas acting in conjunction with one another. Some of these areas include the thalamus, the hypothalamus, and the pons. As already mentioned, the hypothalamus contains the SCN—the biological clock of the body—in addition to other nuclei that, in conjunction with the thalamus, regulate slow-wave sleep. The pons is important for regulating rapid eye movement (REM) sleep (National Institutes of Health, n.d.).

Sleep is also associated with the secretion and regulation of a number of hormones from several endocrine glands including melatonin, follicle stimulating hormone (FSH), luteinizing hormone (LH), and growth hormone (National Institutes of Health, n.d.). The pineal gland releases melatonin during sleep (Figure 3). Melatonin is thought to be involved in the regulation of various biological rhythms and the immune system (Hardeland et al., 2006). During sleep, the pituitary gland secretes both FSH and LH, which are important in regulating the reproductive system (Christensen et al., 2012; Sofikitis et al., 2008). The pituitary gland also secretes growth hormone during sleep, which plays a role in physical growth and maturation as well as other metabolic processes (Bartke, Sun, & Longo, 2013).

Figure 2: This is a segment of a polysomnogram (PSG), a recording of several physical variables during sleep. Polysomnogram show an individual's EEG output, and the waveforms are characteristics of a specific stage of sleep. Other curves show other sleep-related data, such as body temperature, muscle activity, and heartbeat.

Figure 3: The pineal and pituitary glands secrete a number of hormones during sleep.

On Your Own

Which gland is being described in the following examples?

1. This gland releases melatonin during sleep.

    ☐ Pineal Gland   ☐ Pituitary Gland

2. This gland plays a role in developing physical growth and maturation.

    ☐ Pineal Gland   ☐ Pituitary Gland

Why Do We Sleep?

Given the central role that sleep plays in our lives and the number of adverse consequences that have been associated with sleep deprivation, one would think that we would have a clear understanding of why it is that we sleep. Unfortunately, this is not the case; however, several hypotheses have been proposed to explain the function of sleep.

Group Activity

As a group, brainstorm all of the ways in which you expend energy throughout the day. Based on this list, do you feel that this perspective on why we sleep makes sense?

Adaptive Function of Sleep

One popular hypothesis of sleep involves evolutionary psychology. **Evolutionary psychology** is a discipline that studies how universal patterns of behavior and cognitive processes have evolved over time as a result of natural selection. Variations and adaptations in cognition and behavior make individuals more or less successful in reproducing and passing their genes to their offspring. One hypothesis might argue that sleep is essential to restore resources that are expended during the day. Just as bears hibernate in the winter when resources are scarce, perhaps people sleep at night to reduce their energy expenditures.

While this is an intuitive explanation of sleep, there is little research that supports this explanation. In fact, it has been suggested that there is no reason to think that energetic demands could not be addressed with periods of rest and inactivity (Frank, 2006; Rial et al., 2007), and some research has actually found a negative correlation between energetic demands and the amount of time spent sleeping (Capellini, Barton, McNamara, Preston, & Nunn, 2008).

Another evolutionary hypothesis of sleep holds that our sleep patterns evolved as an adaptive response to predatory risks, which increase in darkness. Thus, we sleep in safe areas to reduce the chance of harm. Again, this is an intuitive and appealing explanation for why we sleep. Perhaps our ancestors spent extended periods of time asleep to reduce attention to themselves from potential predators. Comparative research indicates, however, that the relationship that exists between predatory risk and sleep is very complex and equivocal.

Below are two common arguments from this research:

Argument #1	Species that face higher predatory risks sleep fewer hours than other species. (Capellini et al., 2008)
Argument #2	There is no relationship between the amount of time a given species spends in deep sleep and its predation risk. (Lesku, Roth, Amlaner, & Lima, 2006)

Figure 4: Studies suggest that species that do not face predatory risk sleep more that others. A male lion spends 18 to 20 hours a day sleeping.

✎ On Your Own

In the space below, reflect on which argument you agree with more. Does it make sense to you that creatures facing high risks of survival sleep more or less than others? Or do you feel that there is likely no comparison?

It is quite possible that sleep serves no single universally adaptive function, and different species have evolved different patterns of sleep in response to their unique evolutionary pressures. While we have discussed the negative outcomes associated with sleep deprivation, it should be pointed out that there are many benefits that are associated with adequate amounts of sleep. The National Sleep Foundation (n.d.) sites the below benefits:

- Maintaining a healthy weight
- Lowering stress levels
- Improving your mood

- Increasing motor coordination
- Benefiting cognition and memory formation

Figure 5: Visit the National Sleep Foundation's website to learn helpful sleep tools and tips: (hawkes.biz/sleeptips1).

Cognitive Function of Sleep

Another theory regarding why we sleep involves sleep's importance for cognitive function and memory formation (Rattenborg, Lesku, Martinez-Gonzalez, & Lima, 2007). Indeed, we know sleep deprivation results in disruptions in cognition and memory deficits (Brown, 2012), leading to impairments in our abilities to maintain attention, make decisions, and recall long-term memories. Moreover, these impairments become more severe as the amount of sleep deprivation increases (Alhola & Polo-Kantola, 2007). Furthermore, slow-wave sleep after learning a new task can improve resultant performance on that task (Huber, Ghilardi, Massimini, & Tononi, 2004) and seems essential for effective memory formation (Stickgold, 2005). Understanding the impact of sleep on cognitive function should help you understand that cramming all night for a test may be not effective and can even prove counterproductive.

Sleep has also been associated with other cognitive benefits. Research indicates that included among these possible benefits are increased capacities for creative thinking (Cai, Mednick, Harrison, Kanady, & Mednick, 2009; Wagner, Gais, Haider, Verleger, & Born, 2004), language learning (Fenn, Nusbaum, & Margoliash, 2003; Gómez, Bootzin, & Nadel, 2006), and inferential judgments (Ellenbogen, Hu, Payne, Titone, & Walker, 2007). It is possible that even the processing of emotional information is influenced by certain aspects of sleep (Walker, 2009).

✒ On Your Own

Which term is best defined in the following examples?

This phenomenon refers to the fact that a sleep-deprived individual will tend to take a shorter time to fall asleep during opportunities for sleep.

- ☐ Natural selection
- ☐ Evolutionary psychology
- ☐ Sleep debt
- ☐ Sleep rebound

A discipline that studies how universal patterns of behavior and cognitive processes have evolved over time as a result of natural selection.

- ☐ Evolutionary psychology
- ☐ Natural selection
- ☐ Sleep rebound

Summary

Since we devote a very large portion of time to sleep, our brains have complex systems that control various aspects of it. Several hormones important for physical growth and maturation are secreted during sleep. While the reasons for sleep remain something of a mystery, there is some evidence to suggest that it is very important to learning and memory.

3.3 Stages of Sleep

Sleep is not a uniform state of being. Instead, sleep is composed of several different stages that can be differentiated from one another by the patterns of brain wave activity that occur during each stage. These changes in brain wave activity can be visualized using EEG and are distinguished from one another by both the frequency and amplitude of brain waves (Figure 1). Sleep can be divided into two different general phases: REM sleep and non-REM (NREM) sleep. **Rapid eye movement (REM) sleep** is characterized by darting movements of the eyes under closed eyelids. Brain waves during REM sleep appear very similar to brain waves during wakefulness. In contrast, **non-REM (NREM) sleep** sleep is subdivided into four stages distinguished from each other and from wakefulness by characteristic patterns of brain waves. The first four stages of sleep are NREM sleep, while the fifth and final stage of sleep is REM sleep. In this section, we will discuss each of these stages of sleep and their associated patterns of brain wave activity.

Further Resources

Watch this brief video (hawkes.biz/sleepdeprived) describing sleep deprivation in college students.

Here's another brief video (hawkes.biz/sleeptips) describing sleep tips for college students.

Watch this brief video (hawkes.biz/sleepmemory) describing the relationship between sleep and memory.

Flash Forward

Ready to dig into the vocabulary? Get some practice with this Hawkes Verified Quizlet set (hawkes.biz/psych3q3)!

Figure 1: While we sleep, brainwaves can be monitored to examine brain activity.

NREM Stages of Sleep

The first stage of NREM sleep is known as stage 1 sleep. **Stage 1 sleep** is a transitional phase that occurs between wakefulness and sleep, the period during which we drift off to sleep.

> **Stage 1 Sleep**
>
> - Transitional phase
> - Reduction in rates of respiration and heart rate
> - Marked decrease in overall muscle tension
> - Decrease in core body temperature

In terms of brain wave activity, stage 1 sleep is associated with both alpha and theta waves. The early portion of stage 1 sleep produces **alpha waves**, which are relatively low frequency (8–13 Hz), high amplitude patterns of electrical activity (waves) that become synchronized (Figure 2). This pattern of brain wave activity resembles that of someone who is relaxed, yet awake. As an individual continues through stage 1 sleep, there is an increase in theta wave activity. **Theta waves** are even lower frequency (4–7 Hz), higher amplitude brain waves than alpha waves. It is relatively easy to wake someone from stage 1 sleep; in fact, people often report that they have not been asleep if they are awoken during stage 1 sleep.

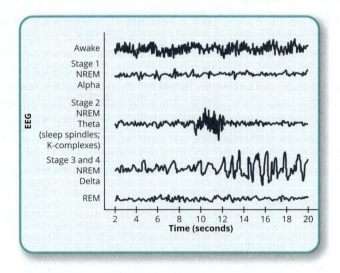

📷 **Figure 2:** Brainwave activity changes dramatically across the different stages of sleep.

As we move into **stage 2 sleep**, the body goes into a state of deep relaxation. Theta waves still dominate the activity of the brain, but they are interrupted by brief bursts of activity known as sleep spindles (Figure 3). A **sleep spindle** is a rapid burst of higher frequency brain waves that may be important for learning and memory (Fogel & Smith, 2011; Poe, Walsh, & Bjorness, 2010). In addition, the appearance of K-complexes is often associated with stage 2 sleep. A **K-complex** is a high amplitude pattern of brain activity that may in some cases occur in response to environmental stimuli. Thus, K-complexes might serve as a bridge to higher levels of arousal in response to what is going on in our environments (Halász, 1993; Steriade & Amzica, 1998).

Figure 3: Stage 2 sleep is characterized by the appearance of both sleep spindles and K-complexes.

Stage 3 and **stage 4** of sleep are often referred to as deep sleep or slow-wave sleep because these stages are characterized by low frequency (up to 4 Hz), high amplitude **delta waves** (Figure 4). During this time, an individual's heart rate and respiration slow dramatically. It is much more difficult to awaken someone from sleep during stage 3 and stage 4 than during earlier stages. Interestingly, individuals who have increased levels of alpha brain wave activity (more often associated with wakefulness and transition into stage 1 sleep) during stage 3 and stage 4 often report that they do not feel refreshed upon waking, regardless of how long they slept (Stone, Taylor, McCrae, Kalsekar, & Lichstein, 2008).

(a)

(b)

Figure 4: (a) Delta waves, which are low frequency and high amplitude, characterize (b) slow-wave stage 3 and stage 4 sleep.

REM Sleep

As mentioned earlier, REM sleep is marked by rapid movements of the eyes. During REM sleep:

- the brain waves are similar to those observed when a person is awake (Figure 5)

- dreaming occurs

- muscle systems are paralyzed with the exception of circulation and respiration

- there is high brain activity and lack of muscle tone (i.e., paradoxical sleep)

Like NREM sleep, REM has been implicated in various aspects of learning and memory (Wagner, Gais, & Born, 2001) although there is disagreement within the scientific community about how important both NREM and REM sleep are for normal learning and memory (Siegel, 2001).

(a)   (b)

▨ **Figure 5:** (a) A period of rapid eye movement is marked by the short red line segment. The brain waves associated with REM sleep, outlined in the red box in (a), look very similar to those seen (b) during wakefulness.

If people are deprived of REM sleep and then allowed to sleep without disturbance, they will spend more time in REM sleep in what would appear to be an effort to recoup the lost time in REM. This is known as the REM rebound, and it suggests that REM sleep is also homeostatically regulated. Aside from the role that REM sleep may play in processes related to learning and memory, REM sleep may also be involved in emotional processing and regulation. In such instances, REM rebound may actually represent an adaptive response to stress in nondepressed individuals by suppressing the emotional salience of aversive events that occurred in wakefulness (Suchecki, Tiba, & Machado, 2012).

☑ On Your Own

For the stages of sleep below, indicate which waveforms are happening in each. For some stages, more than one waveform is associated.

Stage 1	Stage 2	Stage 3	Stage 4

While sleep deprivation in general is associated with a number of negative consequences (Brown, 2012), the consequences of REM deprivation appear to be less profound (as discussed in Siegel, 2001). In fact, some have suggested that REM deprivation can actually be beneficial in some circumstances. For instance, REM sleep deprivation has been demonstrated to improve symptoms of people suffering from major depression, and many effective antidepressant medications suppress REM sleep (Riemann, Berger, & Volderholzer, 2001; Vogel, 1975).

It should be pointed out that some reviews of the literature challenge this finding, suggesting that sleep deprivation that is not limited to REM sleep is just as effective or more effective at alleviating depressive symptoms among some patients suffering from depression. In either case, why sleep deprivation improves the mood of some patients is not entirely understood (Giedke & Schwärzler, 2002). Recently, however, some have suggested that sleep deprivation might change emotional processing so that various stimuli are more likely to be perceived as positive in nature (Gujar, Yoo, Hu, & Walker, 2011). The hypnogram below (Figure 6) shows a person's passage through the stages of sleep.

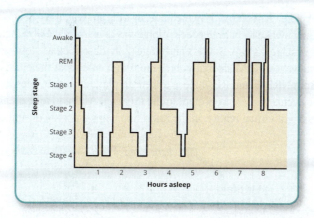

▣ **Figure 6:** A hypnogram is a diagram of the stages of sleep as they occur during a period of sleep. This hypnogram illustrates how an individual moves through the various stages of sleep.

Dreams

The meaning of dreams varies across different cultures and periods of time. By the late 19th century, German psychiatrist Sigmund Freud had become convinced that dreams represented an opportunity to gain access to the unconscious. By analyzing dreams, Freud thought people could increase self-awareness and gain valuable insight to help them deal with the problems they faced in their lives. Freud made distinctions between the manifest content and the latent content of dreams. **Manifest content** is the actual content, or storyline, of a dream. **Latent content**, on the other hand, refers to the hidden meaning of a dream. For instance, if a woman dreams about being chased by a snake, Freud might have argued that this represents the woman's fear of sexual intimacy, with the snake serving as a symbol of a man's penis.

Freud was not the only theorist to focus on the content of dreams. The 20th century Swiss psychiatrist Carl Jung believed that dreams allowed us to tap into the collective unconscious. The **collective unconscious**, as described by Jung, is a theoretical repository of information he believed to be shared by everyone. According to Jung, certain symbols in dreams reflected universal archetypes with meanings that are similar for all people regardless of culture or location.

The sleep and dreaming researcher Rosalind Cartwright, however, believes that dreams simply reflect life events that are important to the dreamer. Unlike Freud and Jung, Cartwright's ideas about dreaming have found empirical support. For example, she and her colleagues published a study in which women going through divorce were asked several times over a five-month period to report the degree to which their former spouses were on their minds. These same women were awakened during REM sleep in order to provide a detailed account of their dream content. There was a significant positive correlation between the degree to which women thought about their former spouses during waking hours and the number of times their former spouses appeared as characters in their dreams (Cartwright, Agargun, Kirkby, & Friedman, 2006). Recent research (Horikawa, Tamaki, Miyawaki, & Kamitani, 2013) has uncovered new techniques by which researchers may effectively detect and classify the visual images that occur during dreaming by using fMRI for neural measurement of brain activity patterns, opening the way for additional research in this area.

Further Resources

Read this article (hawkes.biz/dreams) to learn more about the use of dream analysis in therapy.

▣ **Figure 7:** Carl Jung first proposed the idea of a collective unconscious.

Recently, neuroscientists have also become interested in understanding why we dream. For example, Hobson (2009) suggests that dreaming may represent a state of protoconsciousness. In other words, dreaming involves constructing a virtual reality in our heads that we might use to help us during wakefulness. Among a variety of neurobiological evidence, John Hobson cites research on lucid dreams as an opportunity to better understand dreaming in general. **Lucid dreams** are dreams in which certain aspects of wakefulness are maintained during a dream state. In a lucid dream, a person becomes aware of the fact that they are dreaming, and as such, they can control the dream's content (LaBerge, 1990).

Group Activity

Discuss why you think we dream. What is the purpose?

Summary

The different stages of sleep are characterized by the patterns of brain waves associated with each stage. As a person transitions from being awake to falling asleep, alpha waves are replaced by theta waves. Sleep spindles and K-complexes emerge in stage 2 sleep. Stage 3 and stage 4 are described as slow-wave sleep that is marked by a predominance of delta waves. REM sleep involves rapid movements of the eyes, paralysis of voluntary muscles, and dreaming. Both NREM and REM sleep appear to play important roles in learning and memory. Dreams may represent life events that are important to the dreamer. Alternatively, dreaming may represent a state of protoconsciousness, or a virtual reality, in the mind that helps a person during consciousness.

Figure 8: This figure shows and summarizes the different stages of the sleep cycle.

3.4 Sleep Problems and Disorders

For many of us, sleep isn't easy. And while there are a lot of reasons why we might not get a good night's sleep, such as staring at our phones for hours before we hit the pillow, some people suffer from more pervasive issues. There are several kinds of sleep disturbances, and they can affect not only the person experiencing them but others, too.

Flash Forward

Ready to dig into the vocabulary? Get some practice with this Hawkes Verified Quizlet set (hawkes.biz/psych3q4)!

Insomnia

Insomnia, a consistent difficulty in falling or staying asleep, is the most common of the sleep disorders. Individuals with insomnia often spend a significant time in their bed without falling asleep. They may wake up in the middle of the night and have difficulty going back to sleep (Roth, 2007).

There may be many factors that contribute to insomnia, including age, drug use, exercise, mental status, and bedtime routines. For example, taking a stimulant medication too close to bedtime can interfere with sleep. People who do not burn off enough calories during the day may have more difficulty sleeping. As a result, mental health professionals often recommend increasing physical activity for patients who experience insomnia. In some cases, people turn to over-the-counter (OTC) or prescribed sleep medications to help them sleep. However, sleep medications can cause dependence and alter the nature of one's sleep cycle, which may increase insomnia over time.

Reflection Questions

Have you ever experienced insomnia? Describe what it was like and why you think you were unable to sleep.

Mental health professionals often use **cognitive-behavioral therapy (CBT)**, which is a type of psychotherapy that has shown to be effective in treating insomnia (Savard, Simard, Ivers, & Morin, 2005; Williams, Roth, Vatthauer, & McCrae, 2013). The therapist will often work with the client to change sleep-related behaviors. For example, the therapist may ask the client to only go to their bed when they are tired and ready to sleep. This strategy will help the client associated the bed with sleep and not any other activities. To measure progress, the therapist may ask her client to keep a daily record of when they go to bed and how many hours they slept each night to track progress. The client and therapist may adjust their goals related to which strategies are most successful at increasing sleep hygiene.

Figure 1: Insomnia is the most common sleeping disorder. There are many factors that can lead to insomnia.

Parasomnias

A **parasomnia** is one of a group of sleep disorders in which unwanted, disruptive motor activity and/or experiences during sleep play a role. Parasomnias can occur in either REM or NREM phases of sleep. Sleepwalking, restless leg syndrome, and night terrors are all examples of parasomnias (Mahowald & Schenck, 2000).

Sleepwalking

Sleepwalking (also called somnambulism) is a parasomnia where the sleeper engages in relatively complex behaviors ranging from wandering about to driving an automobile. During periods of sleepwalking, sleepers often have their eyes open, but they are not responsive to attempts to communicate with them (Mahowald & Schenck, 2000). Historically, somnambulism has been treated with a variety of pharmacotherapies ranging from benzodiazepines to antidepressants, but the efficacy of these treatments is questionable (Guilleminault et al., 2005).

Further Resources

For more information about insomnia and treatment problems, visit the National Sleep Foundation website: hawkes.biz/insomnia

Figure 2: According to the National Sleep Foundation, an individual is more likely to sleepwalk if they have not received enough sleep.

Dig Deeper

A Sleepwalking Defense?

On January 16, 1997, Scott Falater sat down to dinner with his wife and children and told them about difficulties he was experiencing on a project at work. After dinner, he prepared some materials to use in leading a church youth group the following morning, and then he attempted to repair the family's swimming pool pump before retiring to bed. The following morning, he awoke to barking dogs and unfamiliar voices from downstairs. As he went to investigate what was going on, he was met by a group of police officers who arrested him for the murder of his wife (Cartwright, 2004; CNN, 1999).

Yarmila Falater's body was found in the family's pool with 44 stab wounds. A neighbor called the police after witnessing Falater standing over his wife's body before dragging her into the pool. Upon a search of the premises, police found blood-stained clothes and a bloody knife in the trunk of Falater's car, and he had blood stains on his neck.

Remarkably, Falater insisted that he had no recollection of hurting his wife in any way. His children and his wife's parents all agreed that Falater had an excellent relationship with his wife, and they couldn't think of a reason that would provide any sort of motive to murder her (Cartwright, 2004).

Scott Falater had a history of regular episodes of sleepwalking as a child, and he had even behaved violently toward his sister once when she tried to prevent him from leaving their home in his pajamas during a sleepwalking episode. He suffered from no apparent anatomical brain anomalies or psychological disorders. It appeared that Scott Falater had killed his wife in his sleep, or at least, that is the defense he used when he was tried for his wife's murder (Cartwright, 2004; CNN, 1999). In Falater's case, a jury found him guilty of first degree murder in June of 1999 (CNN, 1999); however, there are other murder cases where the sleepwalking defense has been used successfully. As scary as it sounds, many sleep researchers believe that homicidal sleepwalking is possible in individuals suffering from the types of sleep disorders described in this lesson (Broughton et al., 1994; Cartwright, 2004; Mahowald, Schenck, & Cramer Bornemann, 2005; Pressman, 2007).

Reflection Questions

Do you think Falater should have been convicted of murder if he has a sleepwalking disorder? Why or why not?

REM Sleep Behavior Disorder (RBD)

Figure 3: Individuals who experience RBD can perform certain behaviors, such as yelling or punching, during disturbing dreams.

REM sleep behavior disorder (RBD) occurs when the muscle paralysis associated with the REM sleep phase does not occur. Individuals who suffer from RBD have high levels of physical activity during REM sleep, especially during disturbing dreams. People with Parkinson's disease and other neurodegenerative disorders have a much higher likelihood to be diagnosed with RBD than the general population (Ferini-Strambi, 2011). These behaviors vary widely, but they can include kicking, punching, scratching, yelling, and behaving like they have been frightened or attacked. People who suffer from this disorder can injure themselves or their sleeping partners when engaging in these behaviors. Furthermore, these types of behaviors ultimately disrupt sleep although affected individuals have no memories that these behaviors have occurred (Arnulf, 2012).

RBD is often treated with medication such as Clonazepam, an anti-anxiety medication with sedative properties, and melatonin (a hormone secreted by the pineal gland). In addition, the sleeping environment is often modified to make it a safer place for those suffering from RBD and the people living with them (Zangini, Calandra-Buonaura, Grimaldi, & Cortelli, 2011).

Other Parasomnias

A person with **restless leg syndrome** has uncomfortable sensations in the legs during periods of inactivity or when trying to fall asleep. This discomfort is relieved by deliberately moving the legs, which contributes to difficulty in falling or staying asleep. Restless leg syndrome is quite common and can be associated with other medical diagnoses, such as chronic kidney disease and diabetes (Mahowald & Schenck, 2000). Benzodiazepines, opiates, and anticonvulsants have been used to treat restless leg syndrome (Restless Legs Syndrome Foundation, n.d.).

Night terrors result in a sense of panic in the sufferer and are often accompanied by screams, which happen during NREM phase of sleep (Provini, Tinuper, Bisulli, & Lagaresi, 2011; Mahowald & Schenck, 2000). Although individuals suffering from night terrors appear to be awake, they generally have no memories of the events and attempts to console them are ineffective. Typically, individuals suffering from night terrors will fall back asleep again within a short time. Generally, treatment for night terrors is unnecessary unless there is some underlying medical or psychological condition that is contributing to the night terrors (Mayo Clinic, n.d.).

Figure 4: Individuals who experience restless leg syndrome can not resist the tendency to move their legs, which can cause trouble falling asleep.

🗎 On Your Own

John is a diabetic who reports sleep disturbances without a neurodegenerative disorder such as Parkinson's disease. His sleep partner stated that he moves during sleep but has never gotten up and walked around, had violent movements, or screamed. Based on what you know about John, which of the following sleep disorders is John most likely to have?

☐ REM Sleep Disorder   ☐ Restless Leg Syndrome   ☐ Night Terrors

Sleep Apnea

Sleep apnea is when a sleeper is unable to breath during sleep. People with sleep apnea may not be aware of the disruptions in sleep. While people are often unaware of their sleep apnea, they are keenly aware of some of the adverse consequences of insufficient sleep. For example, it is not uncommon for people suffering from undiagnosed or untreated sleep apnea to fear that their careers will be affected by the lack of sleep (Henry & Rosenthal, 2013, p. 52).

Obstructive sleep apnea occurs when an individual's airway becomes blocked during sleep, and air is prevented from entering the lungs. In contrast, **central sleep apnea** is a result of disrupted brain signals that cause periods of interrupted breathing (White, 2005).

One of the most common treatments for sleep apnea involves the use of a special device during sleep. A **continuous positive airway pressure (CPAP)** device includes a mask that fits over the sleeper's nose and mouth, which is connected to a pump that pumps air into the person's airways, forcing them to remain open, as shown in Figure 5. This treatment option has proven to be effective for people suffering from mild to severe cases of sleep apnea (McDaid et al., 2009). However, alternative treatment options are available because some people do not regularly wear their CPAP devices. A new EPAP (expiratory positive air pressure) device has shown promise in double-blind trials as one such alternative (Berry, Kryger, & Massie, 2011).

Chuck's wife reported that he is an extremely loud snorer and goes through periods where he does not breath during sleep. However, they found that his airway is not blocked during sleep. Which of the following best describes Chuck's condition?

☐ Parasomnia   ☐ Obstructive Sleep Apnea   ☐ Central Sleep Apnea

📷 **Figure 5:** A typical CPAP device used in the treatment of sleep apnea is affixed to the head with straps and a mask that covers the nose and mouth.

For each sleep disorder, provide a definition and the recommended treatment.

Sleep Disorder	Definition	Treatment
Insomnia		
Parasomnia		
Sleep Apnea		
Narcolepsy		

SIDS

Sudden infant death syndrome (SIDS) is when an infant stops breathing during sleep and dies. Infants younger than 12 months appear to be at the highest risk for SIDS, and boys are at greater risk than girls. Risk factors for SIDS include premature birth, smoking within the home, and hyperthermia. There may also be differences in both brain structure and function in infants that die from SIDS (Berkowitz, 2012; Mage & Donner, 2006; Thach, 2005).

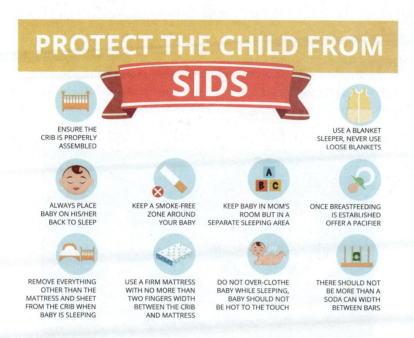

PROTECT THE CHILD FROM SIDS

ENSURE THE CRIB IS PROPERLY ASSEMBLED

USE A BLANKET SLEEPER, NEVER USE LOOSE BLANKETS

ALWAYS PLACE BABY ON HIS/HER BACK TO SLEEP

KEEP A SMOKE-FREE ZONE AROUND YOUR BABY

KEEP BABY IN MOM'S ROOM BUT IN A SEPARATE SLEEPING AREA

ONCE BREASTFEEDING IS ESTABLISHED OFFER A PACIFIER

REMOVE EVERYTHING OTHER THAN THE MATTRESS AND SHEET FROM THE CRIB WHEN BABY IS SLEEPING

USE A FIRM MATTRESS WITH NO MORE THAN TWO FINGERS WIDTH BETWEEN THE CRIB AND MATTRESS

DO NOT OVER-CLOTHE BABY WHILE SLEEPING, BABY SHOULD NOT BE HOT TO THE TOUCH

THERE SHOULD NOT BE MORE THAN A SODA CAN WIDTH BETWEEN BARS

Figure 6: There are a number of ways to protect infants from SIDS.

Research suggests that infants should be placed on their backs when put down to sleep, and their cribs should not contain any items which pose suffocation threats, such as blankets, pillows, or padded crib bumpers (cushions that cover the bars of a crib). Infants should not have caps placed on their heads when put down to sleep to prevent overheating, and people in the child's household should abstain from smoking in the home. Recommendations like these have helped to decrease the number of infant deaths from SIDS in recent years (Mitchell, 2009; Task Force on Sudden Infant Death Syndrome, 2011).

Narcolepsy

Unlike the other sleep disorders described in this section, a person with **narcolepsy** cannot resist falling asleep at inopportune times. These sleep episodes are often associated with **cataplexy**, which is a lack of muscle tone or muscle weakness, and in some cases involves complete paralysis of the voluntary muscles.

Narcoleptic episodes are often triggered by states of heightened arousal or stress. The typical episode can last from a minute or two to half an hour. Once awakened from a narcoleptic attack, people report that they feel refreshed (Chokroverty, 2010). Regular narcoleptic episodes can interfere with the ability to perform one's job or complete schoolwork, and in some situations, narcolepsy can result in significant harm and injury (e.g., driving a car or operating machinery or other potentially dangerous equipment).

> ### Reflection Questions
> Have you ever fallen asleep during a task where you were supposed to be awake? What was that experience like?

Narcolepsy is associated with reduced levels of the signaling molecule hypocretin in some areas of the brain (De la Herrán-Arita & Drucker-Colín, 2012; Han, 2012), and the traditional stimulant drugs do not have direct effects on this system. Therefore, it is quite likely that new medications that are developed to treat narcolepsy will be designed to target the hypocretin system. Currently, narcolepsy is treated using psychomotor stimulant drugs, such as amphetamines, which promote an increased level of neural activity (Mignot, 2012).

Summary

Insomnia is a common experience in which people have difficulty falling or staying asleep. Parasomnias involve unwanted motor behavior or experiences throughout the sleep cycle and include RBD, sleepwalking, restless leg syndrome, and night terrors. Sleep apnea occurs when individuals stop breathing during their sleep, and in the case of sudden infant death syndrome, infants will stop breathing during sleep and die. Narcolepsy involves an irresistible urge to fall asleep during waking hours and is often associated with cataplexy and hallucination.

📷 **Figure 7:** For many people, getting a good night's sleep is difficult. Some people experience problems or disorders that affect their amount of sleep.

Flash Forward

Ready to dig into the vocabulary? Get some practice with this Hawkes Verified Quizlet set (hawkes.biz/psych3q5)!

3.5 Substance Use and Abuse

While we all experience altered states of consciousness in the form of sleep on a regular basis, some people use drugs and other substances that result in altered states of consciousness as well. This section will present information relating to the use of various psychoactive drugs and problems associated with such use. This will be followed by brief descriptions of the effects of some of the more well-known drugs commonly used today.

Substance Use Disorders

The Diagnostic and Statistical Manual of Mental Disorders, *Fifth Edition* (DSM-5) is used by clinicians to diagnose individuals suffering from various psychological disorders. Drug use disorders are addictive disorders, and the criteria for specific substance (drug) use disorders are described in DSM-5.

📷 **Figure 1:** Clinicians use the DSM-5 as a guide to classify and diagnose mental disorders.

Criteria for Substance Abuse Disorder

- Uses more of substance than originally intended
- Continues use despite experiencing adverse consequences
- Shows compulsive pattern of use
- Physical and psychological dependence

Physical dependence involves changes in normal bodily functions—the user will experience withdrawal from the drug upon cessation of use. In contrast, a person who has **psychological dependence** has an emotional rather than physical need for the drug and may use the drug to relieve psychological distress. **Tolerance** is linked to physiological dependence, and it occurs when a person requires more and more of a drug to achieve effects previously experienced at lower doses. Tolerance can cause the user to increase the amount of drug used to a dangerous level—even to the point of overdose and death.

☑ On Your Own

Read the situations below and determine if the scenario describes a physical or psychological dependence.

Situation	Type of Dependence
James, a usual coffee drinker, feels sluggish and out of touch when he misses his normal two cups of coffee in the morning.	
When Anni, an ex-smoker, sits at the bar, she looks longingly at the person next to her who is smoking. She feels that old familiar urge to smoke.	
When Julianne stops using heroin, she feels ill as if she will throw up at any moment. She also starts to experience chills and a general feeling of unease.	

Drug **withdrawal** includes a variety of negative symptoms experienced when drug use is discontinued. These symptoms tend to be the opposite of the effects of the drug. For example, withdrawal from sedative drugs often produces unpleasant arousal and agitation. In addition to withdrawal, many individuals who are diagnosed with substance use disorders will also develop tolerance to these substances. Psychological dependence, or drug craving, is a recent addition to the diagnostic criteria for substance use disorder in DSM-5. This is an important factor because we can develop tolerance and experience withdrawal from any number of drugs that we do not abuse. In other words, physical dependence in and of itself is of limited utility in determining whether or not someone has a substance use disorder.

Drug Categories

The effects of all psychoactive drugs occur through their interactions with our endogenous neurotransmitter systems. Many of these drugs, and their relationships, are shown in Figure 2. As you have learned, drugs can act as agonists or antagonists of a given neurotransmitter system. An agonist facilitates the activity of a neurotransmitter system, and antagonists impede neurotransmitter activity.

Group Activity

In a group of two or three classmates, generate a list of drugs that individuals develop tolerance to or experience withdrawal from but that are not generally drugs of abuse.

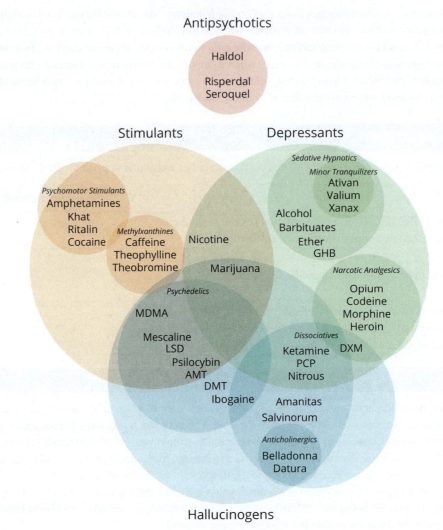

Figure 2: This figure illustrates various drug categories and the overlap among them.

✎ On Your Own

For the following questions, identify if the drug is considered an agonist or an antagonist.

1. Drug X causes the serotonin reuptake pump to run backwards.

☐ Agonist   ☐ Antagonist

2. Drug A blocks receptors on the postsynaptic cell.

☐ Agonist   ☐ Antagonist

3. Drug M causes excess release of norepinephrine.

☐ Agonist   ☐ Antagonist

Alcohol and Other Depressants

Ethanol, which we commonly refer to as alcohol, is in a class of psychoactive drugs known as depressants (Figure 3). A **depressant** is a drug that tends to suppress central nervous system activity. Other depressants include barbiturates and benzodiazepines. These drugs share in common their ability to serve as agonists of the gamma-Aminobutyric acid (GABA) neurotransmitter system. Because GABA has a quieting effect on the brain, GABA agonists also have a quieting effect; these types of drugs are often prescribed to treat both anxiety and insomnia.

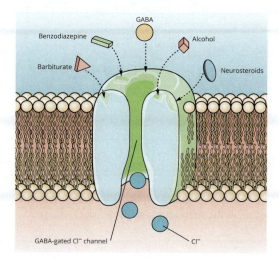

Figure 3: The GABA-gated chloride (Cl⁻) channel is embedded in the cell membrane of certain neurons. The channel has multiple receptor sites where alcohol, barbiturates, and benzodiazepines bind to exert their effects. The binding of these molecules opens the chloride channel, allowing negatively-charged chloride ions (Cl⁻) into the neuron's cell body. Changing its charge in a negative direction pushes the neuron *away* from firing; thus, activating a GABA neuron has a quieting effect on the brain.

Acute alcohol administration results in a variety of changes to consciousness. In addition, if a pregnant woman consumes alcohol, her infant may be born with a cluster of birth defects and symptoms collectively called fetal alcohol spectrum disorder (FASD) or fetal alcohol syndrome (FAS).

Common Effects of Alcohol on the Individual

Low Doses

- Feelings of sedation
- Decreases in reaction time and visual activity
- Lowered levels of alertness
- Reductions in behavioral control

Figure 4: People can become physically dependent on depressants, such as alcohol, which increases the likelihood of abuse.

Excessive Doses

- Complete loss of consciousness
- Difficulty remembering events that occurred

With repeated use of many central nervous system depressants, such as alcohol, a person becomes physically dependent upon the substance and will exhibit signs of both tolerance and withdrawal. Psychological dependence on these drugs is also possible. Therefore, the abuse potential of central nervous system depressants is relatively high.

Drug withdrawal is usually an aversive experience, and it can be a life-threatening process in individuals who have a long history of very high doses of alcohol and/or barbiturates. This is of such concern that people who are trying to overcome addiction to these substances should only do so under medical supervision.

Stimulants

Stimulants are drugs that tend to increase overall levels of neural activity. Many of these drugs act as agonists of the dopamine neurotransmitter system. Dopamine activity is often associated with reward and craving; therefore, drugs that affect dopamine neurotransmission often have abuse liability.

Stimulant Drugs

- Cocaine
- Amphetamines
- Cathinones
- MDMA
- Nicotine
- Caffeine

Cocaine can be taken in multiple ways. While many users snort cocaine, use intravenous injection, and ingestion are also common. The freebase version of cocaine, known as crack, is a potent, smokable version of the drug. Like many other stimulants, cocaine agonizes the dopamine neurotransmitter system by blocking the reuptake of dopamine in the neuronal synapse.

Figure 5: Crack rocks like these are smoked to achieve a high. Compared with other routes of administration, smoking a drug allows it to enter the brain more rapidly, which can often enhance the user's experience.

Dig Deeper

Crack Cocaine

Crack (Figure 5) is often considered to be more addictive than cocaine itself because it is smokable and reaches the brain very quickly. Crack is often less expensive than other forms of cocaine; therefore, it tends to be a more accessible drug for individuals from impoverished segments of society. During the 1980s, many drug laws were rewritten to punish crack users more severely than cocaine users. This led to discriminatory sentencing with low-income, inner-city minority populations receiving the harshest punishments. The wisdom of these laws has recently been called into question, especially given research that suggests crack may not be more addictive than other forms of cocaine, as previously thought (Haasen & Krausz, 2001; Reinerman, 2007).

Amphetamines have a mechanism of action quite similar to cocaine in that they block the reuptake of dopamine in addition to stimulating its release (Figure 6). While amphetamines are often abused, they are also commonly prescribed to children diagnosed with attention deficit hyperactivity disorder (ADHD). It may seem counterintuitive that stimulant medications are prescribed to treat a disorder that involves hyperactivity, but the therapeutic effect comes from increases in neurotransmitter activity within certain areas of the brain associated with impulse control.

Further Resources

Read this interesting newspaper article (hawkes. biz/crack) describing myths about crack cocaine.

Dopamine

Reuptake

Bound cocaine

Cocaine

Postsynaptic cell

Figure 6: As one of their mechanisms of action, cocaine and amphetamines block the reuptake of dopamine from the synapse into the presynaptic cell.

In recent years, methamphetamine (meth) use has become increasingly widespread. **Methamphetamine** is a type of amphetamine that can be made from ingredients that are readily available (e.g., medications containing pseudoephedrine, a compound found in many over-the-counter cold and flu remedies). Despite recent changes in laws designed to make obtaining pseudoephedrine more difficult, methamphetamine continues to be an easily accessible and relatively inexpensive drug option (Shukla, Crump, & Chrisco, 2012).

The cocaine, amphetamine, cathinones, and MDMA users seek a **euphoric high**, feelings of intense elation and pleasure, especially in those users who take the drug via intravenous injection or smoking. Repeated use of these stimulants can have significant adverse consequences.

Symptoms of Stimulant Use

- Nausea
- Elevated blood pressure
- Increased heart rate

- Feelings of anxiety
- Hallucinations
- Paranoia

Normal brain functioning is altered after repeated use of these drugs. For example, repeated use can lead to overall depletion among the monoamine neurotransmitters (dopamine, norepinephrine, and serotonin). People may engage in compulsive use of these stimulant substances in part to try to reestablish normal levels of these neurotransmitters (Jayanthi & Ramamoorthy, 2005; Rothman, Blough, & Baumann, 2007).

Caffeine is another stimulant drug. While it is probably the most commonly used drug in the world, the potency of this particular drug pales in comparison to the other stimulant drugs described in this section. Generally, people use caffeine to maintain increased levels of alertness and arousal. Caffeine is found in many common medicines (such as weight loss drugs), beverages, foods, and even cosmetics (Herman & Herman, 2013). While caffeine may have some indirect effects on dopamine neurotransmission, its primary mechanism of action involves antagonizing adenosine activity (Porkka-Heiskanen, 2011).

Figure 7: Caffeine, like other stimulants, can be very addictive.

☑ On Your Own

Which neurotransmitter system does each drug impact?

Drug	Neurotransmitter System
Depressants	
Cocaine	
Amphetamines	
Caffeine	

Although caffeine is generally considered a relatively safe drug, high blood levels of caffeine can result in insomnia, agitation, muscle twitching, nausea, irregular heartbeat, and even death (Reissig, Strain, & Griffiths, 2009; Wolt, Ganetsky, & Babu, 2012).

Reflection Questions

Think about your own experience with caffeine. Do you feel it has an impact on you? If so, what has that impact been?

Nicotine is highly addictive, and the use of tobacco products is associated with increased risks of heart disease, stroke, and a variety of cancers. Nicotine exerts its effects through its interaction with acetylcholine receptors. Acetylcholine functions as a neurotransmitter in motor neurons. In the central nervous system, it plays a role in arousal and reward mechanisms. Nicotine is most commonly used in the form of tobacco products like cigarettes or chewing tobacco; therefore, there is a tremendous interest in developing effective smoking cessation techniques. To date, people have used a variety of nicotine replacement therapies in addition to various psychotherapeutic options in an attempt to discontinue their use of tobacco products. In general, smoking cessation programs may be effective in the short term, but it is unclear whether these effects persist (Cropley, Theadom, Pravettoni, & Webb, 2008; Levitt, Shaw, Wong, & Kaczorowski, 2007; Smedslund, Fisher, Boles, & Lichtenstein, 2004).

Opioids

Opioids have analgesic properties; that is, they decrease pain. Humans have an endogenous opioid neurotransmitter system—the body makes small quantities of opioid compounds that bind to opioid receptors reducing pain and producing euphoria. Thus, opioid drugs, which mimic this endogenous painkilling mechanism, have an extremely high potential for abuse. Natural opioids, called **opiates**, are derivatives of opium, which is a naturally occurring compound found in the poppy plant. There are now several synthetic versions of opiate drugs (correctly called opioids) that have very potent painkilling effects, and they are often abused. For example, the National Institutes of Drug Abuse has sponsored research that suggests the misuse and abuse of the prescription pain killers hydrocodone and oxycodone are significant public health concerns (Maxwell, 2006). In 2013, the U.S. Food and Drug Administration recommended tighter controls on their medical use.

Further Resources

Watch this video (hawkes.biz/opiods) to get a glimpse into the life of one woman who turned to painkillers for relief from trauma.

Opiods

- Heroin
- Morphine
- Methadone
- Codeine

Figure 8: Heroin is commonly cooked on a spoon and then injected using a syringe.

Historically, heroin has been a major opioid drug of abuse (Figure 8). Heroin can be snorted, smoked, or injected intravenously. Like the stimulants described earlier, the use of heroin is associated with an initial feeling of euphoria followed by periods of agitation. Because heroin is often administered via intravenous injection, users often bear needle track marks on their arms and, like all abusers of intravenous drugs, have an increased risk for contraction of both tuberculosis and HIV. Additionally, because of the black market, heroin users are increasingly exposed to other, more potent, opioids like fentanyl. This powerful synthetic opioid (originally developed pharmaceutically as a patch) is sometimes mixed with heroin or disguised as more powerful heroin and has contributed to the rising number of opioid overdoses in recent years.

Reflection Questions

Did you know that heroin was made by Bayer pharmaceuticals and was marketed as a cough suppressant during the days of rampant tuberculosis? What are your thoughts on the origins of this drug of abuse?

Aside from their utility as analgesic drugs, opioid-like compounds are often found in cough suppressants, anti-nausea, and anti-diarrhea medications. Given that withdrawal from a drug often involves an experience opposite to the effect of the drug, it should be no surprise that opioid withdrawal resembles a severe case of the flu. While opioid withdrawal can be extremely unpleasant, it is not life-threatening (Julien, 2005). Still, people experiencing opioid withdrawal may be given methadone to make withdrawal from the drug less difficult. **Methadone** is a synthetic opioid that is less euphorigenic than heroin and similar drugs. **Methadone clinics** help people who previously struggled with opioid addiction manage withdrawal symptoms through the use of methadone. Other drugs, including the opioid buprenorphine, have also been used to alleviate symptoms of opiate withdrawal.

Codeine is an opioid with relatively low potency. It is often prescribed for minor pain, and it is available over-the-counter in some countries. Like all opioids, codeine does have abuse potential. In fact, abuse of prescription opioid medications is becoming a major concern worldwide (Aquina, Marques-Baptista, Bridgeman, & Merlin, 2009; Casati, Sedefov, & Pfeiffer-Gerschel, 2012).

Hallucinogens

A **hallucinogen** is one of a class of drugs that results in profound alterations in sensory and perceptual experiences (Figure 9). In some cases, users experience vivid visual hallucinations. It is also common for these types of drugs to cause hallucinations of body sensations (e.g., feeling as if you are a giant) and a skewed perception of the passage of time.

As a group, hallucinogens are incredibly varied in terms of the neurotransmitter systems they affect. In general, these drugs are not thought to possess the same sort of abuse potential as other classes of drugs discussed in this section.

Figure 9: Psychedelic images like this are often associated with hallucinogenic compounds.

Hallucinogen	Affected Neurotransmitter System
Mescaline	Serotonin (agonist)
LSD	Serotonin (agonist)
PCP	Glutamate (receptor antagonist)
Ketamine	Glutamate (receptor antagonist)

Dig Deeper

Medical Marijuana

Figure 10: Many states are passing laws that are legalizing the medical and/or recreational use of marijuana.

While the possession and use of marijuana is illegal in many states, as of early 2019 it is now legal in 11 states and the District of Columbia to possess limited quantities of marijuana for recreational use (Table 1). In 13 more states, recreational use and possession have been decriminalized, meaning that penalties have been reduced for those infractions. In contrast, medical marijuana use is now legal in well over half of the United States (33 states) and in the territories of Guam and Puerto Rico. Medical marijuana is marijuana that is prescribed by a doctor for the treatment of a health condition. For example, people who undergo chemotherapy will often be prescribed marijuana to stimulate their appetites and prevent excessive weight loss resulting from the side effects of chemotherapy treatment. Marijuana may also have some promise in the treatment of a variety of medical conditions (Mather, Rauwendaal, Moxham-Hall, & Wodak, 2013; Robson, 2014; Schicho & Storr, 2014).

State-level Marijuana Policy (2019)

Legal for Adult Recreational & Medical Use	Legal for Medical Use Only	
Alaska	Arizona	New Hampshire
California	Arkansas	New Jersey
Colorado	Connecticut	New Mexico
Illinois	Delaware	New York
Maine	Florida	North Dakota
Massachusetts	Hawaii	Ohio
Michigan	Louisiana	Oklahoma
Nevada	Maryland	Pennsylvania
Oregon	Minnesota	Rhode Island
Vermont	Missouri	Utah
Washington	Montana	West Virginia

Table 1: Medical and recreational marijuana are becoming more and more common in the United States.

Although medical marijuana laws have been passed on a state-by-state basis, federal laws still classify this as an illicit substance, making conducting research on the potentially beneficial medicinal uses of marijuana problematic. There is quite a bit of controversy within the scientific community as to the extent to which marijuana might have medicinal benefits due to a lack of large-scale, controlled research (Bostwick, 2012). As a result, many scientists have urged the federal government to allow for relaxation of current marijuana laws and classifications in order to facilitate a more widespread study of the drug's effects (Aggarwal et al., 2009; Bostwick, 2012; Kogan & Mechoulam, 2007).

Until recently, the United States Department of Justice routinely arrested people involved and seized marijuana used in medicinal settings. In the latter part of 2013, however, the United States Department of Justice issued a memo (the Cole Memo) indicating that they would not continue to challenge state medical marijuana laws. This shift in policy may be in response to the scientific community's recommendations and/or reflect changing public opinion regarding marijuana. Former Attorney General Jeff Sessions officially rescinded the Cole Memo in 2018, and the confirmation hearings for his successor included questions about the future of a federal stance on marijuana. This highlights the fact that politics can often be well behind both science and the attitudes of the general public, as well as a source of confusion for people trying to make personal, medical, and business decisions. It also underscores the wider societal impact that drug policy can have, as marijuana use and possession are key components of pressing issues like opioid addiction and criminal justice reform.

Summary

Substance use disorder is defined in DSM-5 as a compulsive pattern of drug use despite negative consequences. Both physical and psychological dependence are important parts of this disorder. Alcohol, barbiturates, and benzodiazepines are central nervous system depressants that affect GABA neurotransmission. Cocaine, amphetamine, cathinones, and MDMA are all central nervous stimulants that agonize dopamine neurotransmission, while nicotine and caffeine affect acetylcholine and adenosine, respectively. Opiate drugs serve as powerful analgesics through their effects on the endogenous opioid neurotransmitter system, and hallucinogenic drugs cause pronounced changes in sensory and perceptual experiences. The hallucinogens are variable with regards to the specific neurotransmitter systems they affect.

3.6 Other States of Consciousness

Our states of consciousness change as we move from wakefulness to sleep. We also alter our consciousness through the use of various psychoactive drugs. This final section will consider hypnotic and meditative states as additional examples of altered states of consciousness experienced by some individuals.

Flash Forward

Ready to dig into the vocabulary? Get some practice with this Hawkes Verified Quizlet set (hawkes.biz/psych3q6)!

Hypnosis

Hypnosis is a state of extreme self-focus and attention in which minimal attention is given to external stimuli. There are a number of a reasons why hypnosis is used. Below are a few common examples:

- It has been known to alter peoples' thoughts and perceptions.

- It can draw out information believed to be buried deeply in someone's memory.

- It can be an effective tool for those particularly open to the power of suggestion.

- It can be a form of therapeutic treatment.

Brain imaging studies have demonstrated that hypnotic states are associated with global changes in brain functioning meaning that changes can occur across the entire brain. (Del Casale et al., 2012; Guldenmund, Vanhaudenhuyse, Boly, Laureys, & Soddu, 2012).

Historically, hypnosis has been viewed with some suspicion because of its portrayal in popular media and entertainment (Figure 1). Therefore, it is important to make a distinction between hypnosis as an empirically based therapeutic approach versus as a form of entertainment. Contrary to popular belief, individuals undergoing hypnosis usually have clear memories of the hypnotic experience and are in control of their own behaviors. While hypnosis may be useful in enhancing memory or a skill, such enhancements are very modest in nature (Raz, 2011).

Figure 1: Popular portrayals of hypnosis have led to some widely-held misconceptions.

Myths and Truths about Hypnosis

Myth	People can be made to do embarrassing things.
Truth	People are aware of what they do under hypnosis.
Myth	The hypnotist can control my mind.
Truth	People remain in control while under hypnosis.

Further Resources

Do you think there is merit to hypnosis? Read this article (hawkes.biz/hypnosis) from *Time* magazine and see what science has to say about it.

How exactly does a hypnotist bring a participant to a state of hypnosis? While there are variations, there are four parts that appear consistent in bringing people into the state of suggestibility associated with hypnosis (National Research Council, 1994). These components include:

- The participant is asked to focus on one thing, such as the hypnotist's words or a ticking watch.

- The participant is made comfortable and is directed to be relaxed and sleepy.

- The participant is told to be open to the process of hypnosis, trust the hypnotist, and let go.

- The participant is encouraged to use his or her imagination.

These steps encourage a heightened suggestibility of hypnosis.

People vary in terms of their ability to be hypnotized, but a review of available research suggests that most people are at least moderately hypnotizable (Kihlstrom, 2013). Hypnosis in conjunction with other techniques is used for a variety of therapeutic purposes and has shown to be at least somewhat effective for pain management, treatment of depression and anxiety, smoking cessation, and weight loss (Alladin, 2012; Elkins, Johnson, & Fisher, 2012; Golden, 2012; Montgomery, Schnur, & Kravits, 2012).

Group Activity

With your group, discuss any experiences you've had or seen relating to hypnosis. Do you feel the previously described steps would be effective on you? Do you feel you would be open to the idea?

✎ On Your Own

Use the space below to brainstorm additional scenarios in which you feel people could benefit from hypnosis.

_____

_____

_____

_____

_____

Some scientists are working to determine whether the power of suggestion can affect cognitive processes such as learning, with a view of using hypnosis in educational settings (Wark, 2011). Furthermore, there is some evidence that hypnosis can alter processes that were once thought to be automatic and outside the purview of voluntary control, such as reading (Lifshitz, Aubert Bonn, Fischer, Kashem, & Raz, 2013; Raz, Shapiro,

Fan, & Posner, 2002). However, it should be noted that others have suggested that the automaticity of these processes remains intact (Augustinova & Ferrand, 2012).

> ### Reflection Questions
>
> There are some who believe that practices like hypnosis are immoral. Why do you think people would make this argument? Do you see any merit in this perspective? Why or why not?

How does hypnosis work? Two theories attempt to answer this question. One theory views hypnosis as dissociation, and the other theory views it as the performance of a social role. Let's compare elements of each theory.

Theory	Belief	Evolution of Theory
Dissociation Theory	Hypnosis is a dissociated state of consciousness, much like when you may drive to work, but you are only minimally aware of the process of driving because your attention is focused elsewhere.	This theory was born from Ernest Hilgard's research into hypnosis and pain. Hilgard induced participants into hypnosis and placed their arms into ice water. Participants were told they would not feel pain, but they could press a button if they did; while they reported not feeling pain, they did press the button, suggesting a dissociation of consciousness while in a hypnotic state.
Social-Cognitive Theory	People in hypnotic states are simply performing the social role of a hypnotized person.	This theory was born of the belief that people's behavior is shaped by their expectations of how they should act in a given situation. Some view a hypnotized person's behavior not as an altered or dissociated state of consciousness but as their fulfillment of the social expectations for that role.

Meditation

Meditation is the act of focusing on a single target, such as breath or a repeated sound, to increase awareness of the moment. While hypnosis is generally achieved through the interaction of a therapist and the person being treated, an individual can perform meditation alone. Often, people wishing to learn meditation receive some training in techniques to achieve a meditative state. A meditative state, as shown by EEG recordings of newly-practicing meditators, is not an altered state of consciousness per se; however, patterns of brain waves exhibited by expert meditators may represent a unique state of consciousness (Fell, Axmacher, & Haupt, 2010).

Although there are a number of different techniques in use, the central feature of all meditation is clearing the mind in order to achieve a state of relaxed awareness and focus (Chen et al., 2013; Lang et al., 2012). Mindfulness meditation has recently become popular. In this variation of meditation, the meditator's attention is focused on some internal process or an external object (Zeidan, Grant, Brown, McHaffie, & Coghill, 2012).

While there are a number of ways to practice meditation, the health benefits are fairly consistent. They include the following benefits.

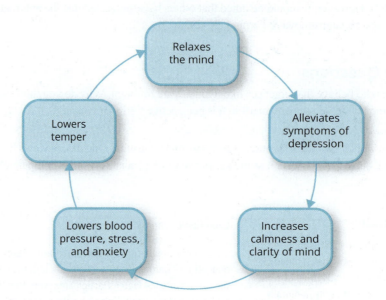

▣ **Figure 2:** Meditation has been shown to improve physical and mental health.

Meditative techniques have their roots in religious practices (Figure 3), but their use has grown in popularity among practitioners of alternative medicine. Research indicates that meditation may help reduce blood pressure, and the American Heart Association suggests that meditation might be used in conjunction with more traditional treatments as a way to manage hypertension although there is not sufficient data for a recommendation to be made (Brook et al., 2013). Like hypnosis, meditation also shows promise in stress management, sleep quality (Caldwell, Harrison, Adams, Quin, & Greeson, 2010), treatment of mood and anxiety disorders (Chen et al., 2013; Freeman et al., 2010; Vøllestad, Nielsen, & Nielsen, 2012), and pain management (Reiner, Tibi, & Lipsitz, 2013).

(a)   (b)

▣ **Figure 3:** (a) This is a statue of a meditating Buddha, representing one of the many religious traditions of which meditation plays a part. (b) People practicing meditation may experience an alternate state of consciousness.

Further Resources

Feeling stressed? Think meditation might help? These instructional videos (hawkes. biz/meditation) teach you how to use Buddhist meditation techniques to alleviate stress.

Summary

Hypnosis is a focus on the self that involves suggested changes of behavior and experience. Meditation involves relaxed, yet focused, awareness. Both hypnotic and meditative states may involve altered states of consciousness that have potential application for the treatment of a variety of physical and psychological disorders.

Chapter 3 Project

Purpose

As within many areas of psychology, the average person holds both accurate and inaccurate beliefs about consciousness. Of course, as psychological scientists, we determine what we know about any topic through empiricism. **The purpose of this project is to have you explain how a variety of areas of consciousness could have a positive effect in a student's life.**

Directions

This project has three parts:

Part 1: Identify three interesting things you did not previously understand about consciousness but learned in this chapter. For each concept/theory discuss: i) how this previous knowledge may have hindered you as a college student, and ii) how accurate knowledge could be beneficial. Be specific and be sure to give in-depth examples.

Part 2: Identify three other interesting things from this chapter. For each concept/theory discuss how it could be beneficial to you as a college student. Be specific and be sure to give in-depth examples.

Part 3: Using the six concepts/theories you discussed above, write a hand-written letter to an incoming college freshman (e.g., Dear Diego…), providing advice about college success. Your letter will consist of a brief introduction and then six paragraphs, one related to each topic you explored above. Since this incoming freshman has never taken a psychology course, you will need to find a way to explain this content in an <u>accessible</u> and <u>helpful</u> way, all while conveying the importance of science "as a way of knowing" to display mastery.

Materials

None required.

✔ Checklist

Part 1

☐ Three interesting things about consciousness

☐ How not knowing those things could hinder you as a college student

☐ How understanding those things could benefit you

Part 2

☐ Three additional interesting things about consciousness

☐ How understanding these things could be beneficial to you as a college student

Part 3

☐ Letter to incoming freshman

☐ Introduction

☐ One paragraph for each of the topics in parts 1 & 2

☐ Accessible and helpful advice based on this content

🏁 Chapter 3 Review

Lesson Summaries

3.1 What Is Consciousness?

States of consciousness vary over the course of the day and throughout our lives. Important factors in these changes are the biological rhythms, and, more specifically, the circadian rhythms generated by the suprachiasmatic nucleus (SCN). Typically, our biological clocks are aligned with our external environment, and light tends to be an important cue in setting this clock. When people travel across multiple time zones or work rotating shifts, they can experience disruptions of their circadian cycles that can lead to insomnia, sleepiness, and decreased alertness. Bright light therapy has shown to be promising in dealing with circadian disruptions. If people go extended periods of time without sleep, they will accrue a sleep debt and potentially experience adverse psychological and physiological consequences.

3.2 Sleep and Why We Sleep

Since we devote a very large portion of time to sleep, our brains have complex systems that control various aspects of it. Several hormones important for physical growth and maturation are secreted during sleep. While the reasons for sleep remain something of a mystery, there is some evidence to suggest that it is very important to learning and memory.

3.3 Stages of Sleep

The different stages of sleep are characterized by the patterns of brain waves associated with each stage. As a person transitions from being awake to falling asleep, alpha waves are replaced by theta waves. Sleep spindles and K-complexes emerge in stage 2 sleep. Stage 3 and stage 4 are described as slow-wave sleep that is marked by a predominance of delta waves. REM sleep involves rapid movements of the eyes, paralysis of voluntary muscles, and dreaming. Both NREM and REM sleep appear to play important roles in learning and memory. Dreams may represent life events that are important to the dreamer. Alternatively, dreaming may represent a state of protoconsciousness, or a virtual reality, in the mind that helps a person during consciousness.

3.4 Sleep Problems and Disorders

Insomnia is a common experience in which people have difficulty falling or staying asleep. Parasomnias involve unwanted motor behavior or experiences throughout the sleep cycle and include RBD, sleepwalking, restless leg syndrome, and night terrors. Sleep apnea occurs when individuals stop breathing during their sleep, and in the case of sudden infant death syndrome, infants will stop breathing during sleep and die. Narcolepsy involves an irresistible urge to fall asleep during waking hours and is often associated with cataplexy and hallucination.

3.5 Substance Use and Abuse

Substance use disorder is defined in DSM-5 as a compulsive pattern of drug use despite negative consequences. Both physical and psychological dependence are important parts of this disorder. Alcohol, barbiturates, and benzodiazepines are central nervous system depressants that affect GABA neurotransmission. Cocaine, amphetamine, cathinones, and MDMA are all central nervous system stimulants that agonize dopamine neurotransmission, while nicotine and caffeine affect acetylcholine and adenosine, respectively. Opiate drugs serve as powerful analgesics through their effects on the endogenous opioid neurotransmitter system, and hallucinogenic drugs cause pronounced changes in sensory and perceptual experiences. The hallucinogens are variable with regards to the specific neurotransmitter systems they affect.

3.6 Other States of Consciousness

Hypnosis is a focus on the self that involves suggested changes of behavior and experience. Meditation involves relaxed, yet focused, awareness. Both hypnotic and meditative states may involve altered states of consciousness that have potential application for the treatment of a variety of physical and psychological disorders.

Key Terms

Flash Back

Now that you've worked through the chapter, sharpen your vocabulary with this Hawkes Verified Quizlet set (hawkes.biz/psychch3)!

Alpha Wave

Type of relatively low frequency, relatively high amplitude brain wave that becomes synchronized; characteristic of the beginning of stage 1 sleep

Biological Rhythm

Internal cycle of biological activity

Cataplexy

Lack of muscle tone or muscle weakness, and in some cases complete paralysis of the voluntary muscles

Central Sleep Apnea

Sleep disorder with periods of interrupted breathing due to a disruption in signals sent from the brain that regulate breathing

Circadian Rhythm

Biological rhythm that occurs over approximately 24 hours

Codeine

Opiate with relatively low potency often prescribed for minor pain

Cognitive-Behavioral Therapy

Psychotherapy that focuses on cognitive processes and problem behaviors that is sometimes used to treat sleep disorders such as insomnia

Collective Unconscious

Theoretical repository of information shared by all people across cultures, as described by Carl Jung

Consciousness

Awareness of internal and external stimuli

Continuous Positive Airway Pressure (CPAP)

Device used to treat sleep apnea; includes a mask that fits over the sleeper's nose and mouth, which is connected to a pump that pumps air into the person's airways, forcing them to remain open

Delta Wave

Type of low frequency, high amplitude brain wave characteristic of stage 3 and stage 4 sleep

Depressant

Drug that tends to suppress central nervous system activity

Euphoric High

Feelings of intense elation and pleasure from drug use

Evolutionary Psychology

Discipline that studies how universal patterns of behavior and cognitive processes have evolved over time as a result of natural selection

Hallucinogen

One of a class of drugs that results in profound alterations in sensory and perceptual experiences, often with vivid hallucinations

Homeostasis

Tendency to maintain a balance, or optimal level, within a biological system

Hypnosis

State of extreme self-focus and attention in which minimal attention is given to external stimuli

Insomnia

Consistent difficulty in falling or staying asleep for at least three nights a week over a month's time

Jet Lag

Collection of symptoms brought on by travel from one time zone to another that results from the mismatch between our internal circadian cycles and our environment

K-Complex

Very high amplitude pattern of brain activity associated with stage 2 sleep that may occur in response to environmental stimuli

Latent Content

Hidden meaning of a dream, per Sigmund Freud's view of the function of dreams

Lucid Dream

People become aware that they are dreaming and can control the dream's content

Manifest Content

Storyline of events that occur during a dream, per Sigmund Freud's view of the function of dreams

Meditation

Clearing the mind in order to achieve a state of relaxed awareness and focus

Melatonin

Hormone secreted by the endocrine gland that serves as an important regulator of the sleep-wake cycle

Methadone

Synthetic opioid that is less euphorogenic than heroin and similar drugs; used to manage withdrawal symptoms in opiate users

Methadone Clinic

Uses methadone to treat withdrawal symptoms in opiate users

Methamphetamine

Type of amphetamine that can be made from pseudoephedrine, an over-the-counter drug; widely manufactured and abused

Narcolepsy

Sleep disorder in which the sufferer cannot resist falling to sleep at inopportune times

Night Terror

Sleep disorder in which the sleeper experiences a sense of panic and may scream or attempt to escape from the immediate environment

Non-REM (NREM) Sleep

Period of sleep outside periods of rapid eye movement (REM) sleep

Obstructive Sleep Apnea

Sleep disorder defined by episodes when breathing stops during sleep as a result of blockage of the airway

Opiate/Opioid

One of a category of drugs that has strong analgesic properties; opiates are produced from the resin of the opium poppy; includes heroin, morphine, methadone, and codeine

Parasomnia

One of a group of sleep disorders characterized by unwanted, disruptive motor activity and/or experiences during sleep

Physical Dependence

Changes in normal bodily functions that cause a drug user to experience withdrawal symptoms upon cessation of use

Pineal Gland

Endocrine structure located inside the brain that releases melatonin

Psychological Dependence

Emotional, rather than a physical, need for a drug which may be used to relieve psychological distress

Rapid Eye Movement (REM) Sleep

Period of sleep characterized by brain waves very similar to those during wakefulness and by darting movements of the eyes under closed eyelids

REM Sleep Behavior Disorder (RBD)

Sleep disorder in which the muscle paralysis associated with the REM sleep phase does not occur; sleepers have high levels of physical activity during REM sleep, especially during disturbing dreams

Restless Leg Syndrome

Sleep disorder in which the sufferer has uncomfortable sensations in the legs when trying to fall asleep that are relieved by moving the legs

Rotating Shift Work

Work schedule that changes from early to late on a daily or weekly basis

Sleep

State marked by relatively low levels of physical activity and reduced sensory awareness that is distinct from periods of rest that occur during wakefulness

Sleep Apnea

Sleep disorder defined by episodes during which breathing stops during sleep

Sleep Debt

Result of insufficient sleep on a chronic basis

Sleep Rebound

Sleep-deprived individuals will experience shorter sleep latencies during subsequent opportunities for sleep

Sleep Regulation

Brain's control of switching between sleep and wakefulness as well as coordinating this cycle with the outside world

Sleep Spindle

Rapid burst of high frequency brain waves during stage 2 sleep that may be important for learning and memory

Sleepwalking

(Also, *somnambulism*) sleep disorder in which the sleeper engages in relatively complex behaviors

Stage 1 Sleep

First stage of sleep; transitional phase that occurs between wakefulness and sleep; the period during which a person drifts off to sleep

Stage 2 Sleep

Second stage of sleep; the body goes into deep relaxation; characterized by the appearance of sleep spindles

Stage 3 Sleep

Third stage of sleep; deep sleep characterized by low frequency, high amplitude delta waves

Stage 4 Sleep

Fourth stage of sleep; deep sleep characterized by low frequency, high amplitude delta waves

Stimulant

Drug that tends to increase overall levels of neural activity; includes caffeine, nicotine, amphetamines, and cocaine

Sudden Infant Death Syndrome (SIDS)

Infant (one year old or younger) with no apparent medical condition suddenly dies during sleep

Suprachiasmatic Nucleus (SCN)

Area of the hypothalamus in which the body's biological clock is located

Theta Wave

Type of low frequency, high amplitude brain wave characteristic of stage 1 and stage 2 sleep

Tolerance

State of requiring increasing quantities of the drug to gain the desired effect

Wakefulness

Characterized by high levels of sensory awareness, thought, and behavior

Withdrawal

Variety of negative symptoms experienced when drug use is discontinued

Exercises

Review Questions

1. The body's biological clock is located in the _____.

    a. hippocampus

    b. thalamus

    c. hypothalamus

    d. pituitary gland

2. _____ occurs when there is a chronic deficiency in sleep.

    a. Jet lag

    b. Rotating shift work

    c. Circadian rhythm

    d. Sleep debt

3. _____ cycles occur roughly once every 24 hours.

    a. Biological

    b. Circadian

    c. Rotating

    d. Conscious

4. _____ is one way in which people can help reset their biological clocks.

    a. Light-dark exposure

    b. Coffee consumption

    c. Alcohol consumption

    d. Napping

5. Growth hormone is secreted by the _____ while we sleep.

    a. pineal gland

    b. thyroid

    c. pituitary gland

    d. pancreas

6. The _____ plays a role in controlling slow-wave sleep.

    a. hypothalamus

    b. thalamus

    c. pons

    d. both a and b

7. _____ is a hormone secreted by the pineal gland that plays a role in regulating biological rhythms and immune function.

    a. Growth hormone

    b. Melatonin

    c. LH

    d. FSH

8. _____ appears to be especially important for enhanced performance on recently learned tasks.

    a. Melatonin

    b. Slow-wave sleep

    c. Sleep deprivation

    d. Growth hormone

9. _____ is (are) described as slow-wave sleep.

    a. Stage 1

    b. Stage 2

    c. Stage 3 and stage 4

    d. REM sleep

10. Sleep spindles and K-complexes are most often associated with _____ sleep.

    a. stage 1

    b. stage 2

    c. stage 3 and stage 4

    d. REM

11. Symptoms of _____ may be improved by REM deprivation.

    a. schizophrenia

    b. Parkinson's disease

    c. depression

    d. generalized anxiety disorder

12. The _____ content of a dream refers to the true meaning of the dream.

    a. latent

    b. manifest

    c. collective unconscious

    d. important

13. _____ is loss of muscle tone or control that is often associated with narcolepsy.

   a. RBD

   b. CPAP

   c. Cataplexy

   d. Insomnia

14. An individual may suffer from _____ if there is a disruption in the brain signals that are sent to the muscles that regulate breathing.

   a. central sleep apnea

   b. obstructive sleep apnea

   c. narcolepsy

   d. SIDS

15. The most common treatment for _____ involves the use of amphetamine-like medications.

   a. sleep apnea

   b. RBD

   c. SIDS

   d. narcolepsy

16. _____ is another word for sleepwalking.

   a. Insomnia

   b. Somnambulism

   c. Cataplexy

   d. Narcolepsy

17. _____ occurs when a drug user requires more and more of a given drug in order to experience the same effects of the drug.

   a. Withdrawal

   b. Psychological dependence

   c. Tolerance

   d. Reuptake

18. Cocaine blocks the reuptake of _____.

   a. GABA

   b. glutamate

   c. acetylcholine

   d. dopamine

19. _____ refers to drug craving.

   a. Psychological dependence

   b. Antagonism

   c. Agonism

   d. Physical dependence

20. LSD affects _____ neurotransmission.

   a. dopamine

   b. serotonin

   c. acetylcholine

   d. norepinephrine

21. _____ is most effective in individuals that are very open to the power of suggestion.

   a. Hypnosis

   b. Meditation

   c. Mindful awareness

   d. Cognitive therapy

22. _____ has its roots in religious practice.

   a. Hypnosis

   b. Meditation

   c. Cognitive therapy

   d. Behavioral therapy

23. Meditation may be helpful in _____.

   a. pain management

   b. stress control

   c. treating the flu

   d. both a and b

24. Research suggests that cognitive processes, such as learning, may be affected by _____.

   a. hypnosis

   b. meditation

   c. mindful awareness

   d. progressive relaxation

Critical Thinking Questions

25. Health care professionals often work rotating shifts. Why is this problematic? What can be done to deal with potential problems?

26. Generally, humans are considered diurnal, which means we are awake during the day and asleep during the night. Many rodents, on the other hand, are nocturnal. Why do you think different animals have such different sleep-wake cycles?

27. If theories that assert sleep is necessary for restoration and recovery from daily energetic demands are correct, what do you predict about the relationship that would exist between individuals' total sleep duration and their level of activity?

28. How could researchers determine if given areas of the brain are involved in the regulation of sleep?

29. Differentiate the evolutionary theories of sleep and make a case for the one with the most compelling evidence.

30. Freud believed that dreams provide important insight into the unconscious mind. He maintained that a dream's manifest content could provide clues into an individual's unconscious. What potential criticisms exist for this particular perspective?

31. Some people claim that sleepwalking and talking in your sleep involve individuals acting out their dreams. Why is this particular explanation unlikely?

32. One of the recommendations that therapists will make to people who suffer from insomnia is to spend less waking time in bed. Why do you think spending waking time in bed might interfere with the ability to fall asleep later?

33. How is narcolepsy with cataplexy similar to and different from REM sleep?

34. The negative health consequences of both alcohol and tobacco products are well-documented. A drug like marijuana, on the other hand, is generally considered to be as safe, if not safer than these legal drugs. Why do you think marijuana use continues to be illegal in many parts of the United States?

35. Why are programs designed to educate people about the dangers of using tobacco products just as important as developing tobacco cessation programs?

36. What advantages exist for researching the potential health benefits of hypnosis?

37. What types of studies would be most convincing regarding the effectiveness of meditation in the treatment for some type of physical or mental disorder?

Chapter 4

Sensation and Perception

Chapter Introduction

🖼 **Figure 1:** If you were standing in the midst of this street scene, you would be absorbing and processing numerous pieces of sensory input.

Imagine standing on a city street corner. You might be struck by movement everywhere as cars and people go about their business, by the sound of a street musician's melody or a horn honking in the distance, by the smell of exhaust fumes or of food being sold by a nearby vendor, and by the sensation of hard pavement under your feet.

We rely on our sensory systems to provide important information about our surroundings. We use this information to successfully navigate and interact with our environment so that we can find nourishment, seek shelter, maintain social relationships, and avoid potentially dangerous situations.

This chapter will provide an overview of how sensory information is received and processed by the nervous system and how that affects our conscious experience of the world. We begin by learning the distinction between sensation and perception. Then we consider the physical properties of light and sound stimuli, along with an overview of the basic structures and functions of the major sensory systems. The chapter will close with a discussion of a historically important theory of perception called Gestalt.

Flash Forward

Ready to dig into the vocabulary? Get some practice with this Hawkes Verified Quizlet set (hawkes.biz/psych4q1)!

4.1 Sensation versus Perception

Sensation

What does it mean to sense something? Sensory receptors are specialized neurons that respond to specific types of stimuli. When sensory information is detected by a sensory receptor, **sensation** has occurred. For example, light that enters the eye causes chemical changes in cells that line the back of the eye. These cells relay messages, in the form of action potentials (as you learned when studying biopsychology), to the central nervous system. The conversion from sensory stimulus energy to action potential is known as **transduction**.

🖼 **Figure 2:** Our senses bring information to the brain for processing. While we are familiar with the five senses, our bodies have systems for balance, position, movement, pain, and temperature as well.

You have probably known since elementary school that we have five senses: vision, hearing (audition), smell (olfaction), taste (gustation), and touch (somatosensation). It turns out that this notion of five senses is oversimplified. We also have sensory systems that provide information about balance (the vestibular sense), body position and movement (proprioception and kinesthesia), pain (nociception), and temperature (thermoception).

The sensitivity of a given sensory system to the relevant stimuli can be expressed as an absolute threshold. **Absolute threshold** refers to the minimum amount of stimulus energy that must be present for the stimulus to be detected 50% of the time. Another way to think about this is by asking how dim can a light be or how soft can a sound be and still be detected half of the time. The sensitivity of our sensory receptors can be quite amazing. It has been estimated that on a clear night, the most sensitive sensory cells in the back of the eye can detect a candle flame 30 miles away (Okawa & Sampath, 2007). Under quiet conditions, the hair cells (the receptor cells of the inner ear) can detect the tick of a clock 20 feet away (Galanter, 1962).

It is also possible for us to get messages that are presented below the threshold for conscious awareness—these are called **subliminal messages**. A stimulus reaches a physiological threshold when it is strong enough to excite sensory receptors and send nerve impulses to the brain: this is an absolute threshold. A message below that threshold is said to be subliminal: we receive it, but we are not consciously aware of it. Over the years there has been a great deal of speculation about the use of subliminal messages in advertising, rock music, and self-help audio programs. Research evidence shows that in laboratory settings, people can process and respond to information outside of awareness. But this does not mean that we obey these messages like zombies; in fact, hidden messages have little effect on behavior outside the laboratory (Kunst-Wilson & Zajonc, 1980; Rensink, 2004; Nelson, 2008; Radel, Sarrazin, Legrain, & Gobancé, 2009; Loersch, Durso, & Petty, 2013).

Absolute thresholds are generally measured under incredibly controlled conditions in situations that are optimal for sensitivity. Sometimes, we are more interested in how much difference in stimuli is required to detect a difference between them. This is known as the **just noticeable difference (jnd)** or difference threshold. Unlike the absolute threshold, the difference threshold changes depending on the stimulus intensity. As an example, imagine yourself in a very dark movie theater. If an audience member were to receive a text message on her cell phone, which caused her screen to light up, chances are that many people would notice the change in illumination in the theater. However, if the same thing happened in a brightly lit arena during a basketball game, very few people would notice. The cell phone brightness does not change, but its ability to be detected as a change in illumination varies dramatically between the two contexts. Ernst Weber proposed this theory of change in difference threshold in the 1830s, and it has become known as Weber's law: the difference threshold is a constant fraction of the original stimulus, as the example illustrates.

What are the differences between absolute threshold and difference threshold?

Absolute

Minimum amount of stimulus energy required for stimulus to be detected 50% of the time

Difference

Changes depending on stimulus intensity

Perception

While our sensory receptors are constantly collecting information from the environment, it is ultimately how we interpret that information that affects how we interact with the world. **Perception** refers to the way sensory information is organized, interpreted, and consciously experienced. Perception involves both bottom-up and top-down processing. **Bottom-up processing** refers to the fact that perceptions are built from sensory input. On the other hand, how we interpret those sensations is influenced by our available knowledge, our experiences, and our thoughts. This is called **top-down processing**.

One way to think of this concept is that sensation is a physical process, whereas perception is psychological. For example, upon walking into a kitchen and smelling the scent of baking cinnamon rolls, the *sensation* is the scent receptors detecting the odor of cinnamon, but the *perception* may be, "Mmm, this smells like the bread Grandma used to bake when the family gathered for holidays."

Although our perceptions are built from sensations, not all sensations result in perception. In fact, we often don't perceive stimuli that remain relatively constant over prolonged periods of time. This is known as **sensory adaptation**. Imagine entering a classroom with an old analog clock. Upon first entering the room, you can hear the ticking of the clock; as you begin to engage in conversation with classmates or listen to your professor greet the class, you are no longer aware of the ticking. The clock is still ticking, and that information is still affecting sensory receptors of the auditory system. The fact that you no longer perceive the sound demonstrates sensory adaptation and shows that while closely associated, sensation and perception are different.

Group Activity

Subliminal messages occur in all types of media every day. Form groups of 4 or 5 and assign each member of the group a type of media (magazines, TV, social, radio, etc.). Each member should locate 5 to 10 examples of subliminal messages in their assigned type of media (to be determined by the professor). Bring in examples of your findings to class and share with everyone in the group. Did all members get the same messages or different ones? Does everyone agree on the message?

Further Resources

Watch this video (hawkes.biz/processing) for more on bottom-up and top-down processing.

Figure 3: A ticking clock in the classroom might be noticed at first, but as other stimuli get your attention, you'll adapt and not perceive the ticking.

Reflection Questions

If someone lost one of their senses do you think their perceptions would alter? An example might be losing a sense of smell and no longer being able to equate cinnamon with Grandma's baked goods. Would another sense take over, and how would it work?

There is another factor that affects sensation and perception: attention. Attention plays a significant role in determining what is sensed versus what is perceived. Imagine you are at a party full of music, chatter, and laughter. You get involved in an interesting conversation with a friend, and you tune out all the background noise. If someone interrupted you to ask what song had just finished playing, you would probably be unable to answer that question.

Further Resources

See for yourself how inattentional blindness works by checking out this selective attention test (hawkes.biz/ attention) from Simons and Chabris (1999).

One of the most interesting demonstrations of how important attention is in determining our perception of the environment occurred in a famous study conducted by Daniel Simons and Christopher Chabris (1999). In this study, participants watched a video of people dressed in black and white passing basketballs. Participants were asked to count the number of times the team in white passed the ball. During the video, a person dressed in a black gorilla costume walks among the two teams. You would think that someone would notice the gorilla, right? Nearly half of the people who watched the video didn't notice the gorilla at all despite the fact that he was clearly visible for nine seconds. Because participants were so focused on the number of times the white team was passing the ball, they completely tuned out other visual information. Failure to notice something that is completely visible because of a lack of attention is called **inattentional blindness**.

In a similar experiment, researchers tested inattentional blindness by asking participants to observe images moving across a computer screen. They were instructed to focus on either white or black objects, disregarding the other color. When a red cross passed across the screen, about one third of subjects did not notice it (Figure 4) (Most, Simons, Scholl, & Chabris, 2000).

Further Resources

Have you ever felt your phone vibrate in your pocket and go to check it only to see you have no new notifications? This is a newly emerging phenomenon that is occurring as technology becomes more ingrained in our every day lives. Studies are currently being conducted into these "phantom vibrations." To read more, visit these websites:

hawkes.biz/phantom

hawkes.biz/phantom2

Figure 4: Nearly one third of participants in a study did not notice that a red cross passed on the screen because their attention was focused on the black or white figures.

Motivation can also affect perception. Have you ever been expecting a really important phone call, and while taking a shower, you think you hear the phone ringing, only to discover that it is not? If so, then you have experienced how motivation to detect a meaningful stimulus can shift our ability to discriminate between a true sensory stimulus and background noise. The ability to identify a stimulus when it is embedded in a distracting background is called **signal detection theory**. This might also explain why a mother is awakened by a quiet murmur from her baby but not by other sounds that occur while she is asleep. Signal detection theory has practical applications, such as increasing air traffic controller accuracy. Controllers need to be able to detect planes among many signals (blips) that appear on the radar screen and follow those planes as they move through the sky. In fact, the original work of the researcher who developed signal detection theory was focused on improving the sensitivity of air traffic controllers to plane blips (Swets, 1964).

Our perceptions can also be affected by our beliefs, values, prejudices, expectations, and life experiences. As you will see later in this chapter, individuals who are deprived of the experience of binocular vision during critical periods of development have trouble perceiving depth (Fawcett, Wang, & Birch, 2005). The shared experiences of people within a given cultural context can have pronounced effects on perception. For example, Marshall Segall, Donald Campbell, and Melville Herskovits (1963) published the results of a multinational study in which they demonstrated that individuals from Western cultures were more prone to experience certain types of visual illusions than individuals from non-Western cultures, and vice versa. One such illusion that Westerners were more likely to experience was the Müller-Lyer illusion (Figure 5): the lines appear to be different lengths, but they are actually the same length.

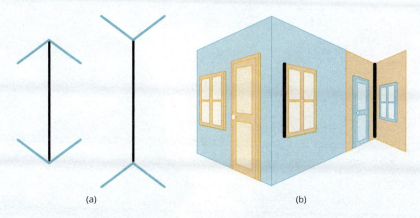

(a)   (b)

🖼 **Figure 5:** In the Müller-Lyer illusion, lines appear to be different lengths although they are identical. (a) Arrows at the ends of lines may make the line on the right appear longer although the lines are the same length. (b) When applied to a three-dimensional image, the line on the right again may appear longer although both black lines are the same length.

These perceptual differences were consistent with differences in the types of environmental features experienced on a regular basis by people in a given cultural context. People in Western cultures, for example, have a perceptual context of buildings with straight lines, what Segall's study called a carpentered world (Segall et al., 1966). In contrast, people from certain non-Western cultures with an uncarpentered view, such as the Zulu of South Africa, whose villages are made up of round huts arranged in circles, are less susceptible to this illusion (Segall et al., 1999). It is not just vision that is affected by cultural factors. Indeed, research has demonstrated that the ability to identify an odor and rate its pleasantness and its intensity varies cross-culturally (Ayabe-Kanamura, Saito, Distel, Martínez-Gómez, & Hudson, 1998).

Children described as thrill seekers are more likely to show taste preferences for intense sour flavors (Liem, Westerbeek, Wolterink, Kok, & de Graaf, 2004), which suggests that basic aspects of personality might affect perception. Furthermore, individuals who hold positive attitudes toward reduced-fat foods are more likely to rate foods labeled as reduced fat as tasting better than people who have less positive attitudes about these products (Aaron, Mela, & Evans, 1994).

Reflection Questions

Do you enjoy intense sour flavors? If yes, do you consider yourself a thrill seeker? Do agree with the findings of Liem, Westerbeek, Wolterink, Kok, & de Graaf?

✎   **On Your Own**

Optical Illusion

Look at the image below and record what you see in the space provided. Most people see two images depending on what they focus on. Why do you think we have trouble seeing two things at once?

Summary

Sensation occurs when sensory receptors detect sensory stimuli. Perception involves the organization, interpretation, and conscious experience of those sensations. All sensory systems have both absolute and difference thresholds, which refer to the minimum amount of stimulus energy or the minimum amount of difference in stimulus energy required to be detected about 50% of the time, respectively. Sensory adaptation, selective attention, and signal detection theory can help explain what is perceived and what is not. In addition, our perceptions are affected by a number of factors, including beliefs, values, prejudices, culture, and life experiences.

4.2 Waves and Wavelengths

Visual and auditory stimuli both occur in the form of waves. Although the two stimuli are different in terms of composition, the wave forms share similar characteristics that are especially important to our visual and auditory perceptions. In this section, we describe the physical properties of the waves as well as the perceptual experiences associated with them.

Flash Forward

Ready to dig into the vocabulary? Get some practice with this Hawkes Verified Quizlet set (hawkes.biz/psych4q2)!

Amplitude and Wavelength

Two physical characteristics of a wave are amplitude and wavelength (Figure 1). The **amplitude** of a wave is the height of a wave as measured from the highest point on the wave (**peak** or **crest**) to the lowest point on the wave (**trough**). **Wavelength** refers to the length of a wave from one peak to the next.

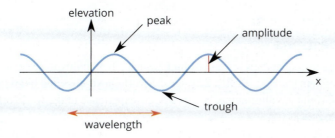

Figure 1: The amplitude, or height, of a wave is measured from the peak to the trough. The wavelength is measured from peak to peak.

Wavelength is directly related to the frequency of a given wave form. **Frequency** refers to the number of waves that pass a given point in a particular time period and is often expressed in terms of **hertz (Hz)**, or cycles per second. Longer wavelengths will have lower frequencies, and shorter wavelengths will have higher frequencies (Figure 2).

Figure 2: This figure illustrates waves of differing wavelengths/frequencies. At the top of the figure, the red wave has a long wavelength/short frequency. Moving from top to bottom, the wavelengths decrease and frequencies increase.

Light Waves

The **visible spectrum** is the portion of the larger **electromagnetic spectrum** that we can see. As Figure 3 shows, the electromagnetic spectrum encompasses all of the electromagnetic radiation that occurs in our environment and includes gamma rays, x-rays, ultraviolet light, visible light, infrared light, microwaves, and radio waves. The visible spectrum in humans is associated with wavelengths that range from 380 to 740 nm—a very small distance since a nanometer (nm) is one billionth of a meter. Other species can detect other portions of the electromagnetic spectrum. For instance, honeybees can see light in the ultraviolet range (Wakakuwa, Stavenga, & Arikawa, 2007), and some snakes can detect infrared radiation in addition to more traditional visual light cues (Chen, Deng, Brauth, Ding, & Tang, 2012; Hartline, Kass, & Loop, 1978).

Figure 3: Light that is visible to humans makes up only a small portion of the electromagnetic spectrum.

Reflection Questions

People have often assumed that dogs are color-blind. Instead, their ability to see color is slightly different from that of humans. Specifically, they see the world in yellows and blues (without the ability to perceive green). Given that information, how is a dog's experience of the world different from your own?

In humans, light wavelength is associated with perception of color (Figure 4). Within the visible spectrum, our experience of red is associated with longer wavelengths, greens are intermediate, and blues and violets are shorter in wavelength. (An easy way to remember this is the mnemonic ROYGBIV: **r**ed, **o**range, **y**ellow, **g**reen, **b**lue, **i**ndigo, **v**iolet.) The amplitude of light waves is associated with our experience of brightness or intensity of color, with larger amplitudes appearing brighter.

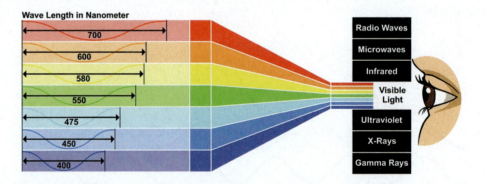

Figure 4: Different wavelengths of light are associated with our perception of different colors.

☑ On Your Own

Fill out the tables with the following information.

1. Jeremy is wearing a brightly colored red shirt. In this case, describe the light waves that are coming from his shirt in terms of amplitude and frequency.

Amplitude	
Frequency	

2. Natalie's jeans are a faded blue. Describe the light waves that are coming from her jeans in terms of amplitude and frequency.

Amplitude	
Frequency	

Reflection Questions

How would your life differ if you could see beyond the visible spectrum that humans are able to perceive?

Sound Waves

Like light waves, the physical properties of sound waves are associated with various aspects of our perception of sound. The frequency of a sound wave is associated with our perception of that sound's **pitch**. High-frequency sound waves are perceived as high-pitched sounds, while low-frequency sound waves are perceived as low-pitched sounds. The audible range of sound frequencies is between 20 and 20,000 Hz, with greatest sensitivity to those frequencies that fall in the middle of this range.

As was the case with the visible spectrum, other species show differences in their audible ranges. For instance, chickens have a very limited audible range, from 125 to 2,000 Hz. Mice have an audible range from 1,000 to 91,000 Hz, and the beluga whale's audible range is from 1,000 to 123,000 Hz. Our pet dogs and cats have audible ranges of about 70–45,000 Hz and 45–64,000 Hz, respectively (Strain, 2003).

The loudness of a given sound is closely associated with the amplitude of the sound wave. Higher amplitudes are associated with louder sounds.

Further Resources

Can people really break glasses with only their voices? It is real science! Check out this video (hawkes.biz/soundwaves) to find out how.

☑ On Your Own

Fill out the tables with the following information.

1. Describe a loud, high pitch sound in terms of frequency and amplitude.

Amplitude	
Frequency	

2. Describe a soft, low pitch sound in terms of frequency and amplitude.

Amplitude	
Frequency	

Loudness is measured in terms of **decibels (dB)**, a logarithmic unit of sound intensity. A typical conversation would correlate with 60 dB; a rock concert might check in at 120 dB (Figure 5). A whisper 5 feet away or rustling leaves are at the low end of our hearing range; sounds like a window air conditioner, a normal conversation, and even heavy traffic or a vacuum cleaner are within a tolerable range. However, there is the potential for hearing damage from about 80 dB to 130 dB: these are sounds of a food processor, power lawnmower, heavy truck (25 feet away), subway train (20 feet away), live rock music, and a jackhammer. The threshold for pain is about 130 dB, a jet plane taking off or a revolver firing at close range (Dunkle, 1982).

Further Resources

Watch this brief video (hawkes.biz/perceivedloudness) demonstrating how frequency and amplitude interact in our perception of loudness.

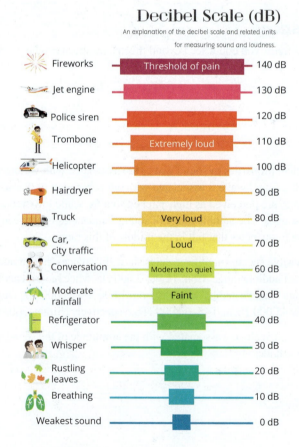

Decibel Scale (dB)

An explanation of the decibel scale and related units for measuring sound and loudness.

Fireworks	Threshold of pain — 140 dB
Jet engine	— 130 dB
Police siren	— 120 dB
Trombone	Extremely loud — 110 dB
Helicopter	— 100 dB
Hairdryer	— 90 dB
Truck	Very loud — 80 dB
Car, city traffic	Loud — 70 dB
Conversation	Moderate to quiet — 60 dB
Moderate rainfall	Faint — 50 dB
Refrigerator	— 40 dB
Whisper	— 30 dB
Rustling leaves	— 20 dB
Breathing	— 10 dB
Weakest sound	— 0 dB

🖼 **Figure 5:** This figure illustrates the loudness of common sounds.

✎ On Your Own

Think about the sounds you encounter in your everyday life. Using the information provided in the lesson, create a list of the sounds you encounter listed from the most to least harmful.

Most Harmful Sounds (higher dB)
Least Harmful Sounds (lower dB)

Reflection Questions

How likely do you think it is that you have already suffered some level of hearing loss? What have you experienced in your life that may have caused damage?

Although wave amplitude is generally associated with loudness, there is some interaction between frequency and amplitude in our perception of loudness within the audible range. For example, a 10 Hz sound wave is inaudible no matter the amplitude of the wave. A 1,000 Hz sound wave, on the other hand, would vary dramatically in terms of perceived loudness as the amplitude of the wave increased.

Of course, different musical instruments can play the same musical note at the same level of loudness, yet they still sound quite different. This is known as the timbre of a sound. **Timbre** refers to a sound's purity, and it is affected by the complex interplay of frequency, amplitude, and timing of sound waves.

Further Resources

Follow this link (hawkes.biz/hearingtest) to test your hearing using mosquito ringtones!

Summary

Both light and sound can be described in terms of wave forms with physical characteristics like amplitude, wavelength, and timbre. Wavelength and frequency are inversely related so that longer waves have lower frequencies, and shorter waves have higher frequencies. In the visual system, a light wave's wavelength is generally associated with color, and its amplitude is associated with brightness. In the auditory system, a sound's frequency is associated with pitch, and its amplitude is associated with loudness.

4.3 Vision

We use our vision to create mental representations of the world around us (Figure 1). This helps us find our way and interact with the people and objects in our everyday lives. This section will provide an overview of the basic anatomy and function of the visual system. In addition, we will explore our ability to perceive color and depth.

Flash Forward

Ready to dig into the vocabulary? Get some practice with this Hawkes Verified Quizlet set (hawkes.biz/psych4q3)!

Figure 1: Our eyes take in sensory information that helps us understand the world around us.

Anatomy of the Visual System

The eye is the major sensory organ involved in vision (Figure 2). Light waves are transmitted across the cornea and enter the eye through the pupil. The **cornea** is the transparent covering over the eye. It serves as a barrier between the inner eye and the outside world, and it is involved in focusing light waves that enter the eye. The **pupil** is the small opening in the eye through which light passes, and the size of the pupil can change as a function of light levels as well as emotional arousal. When light levels are low, the pupil will become dilated, or expanded, to allow more light to enter the eye. When light levels are high, the pupil will constrict, or become smaller, to reduce the amount of light that enters the eye. The pupil's size is controlled by muscles that are connected to the **iris**, which is the colored portion of the eye.

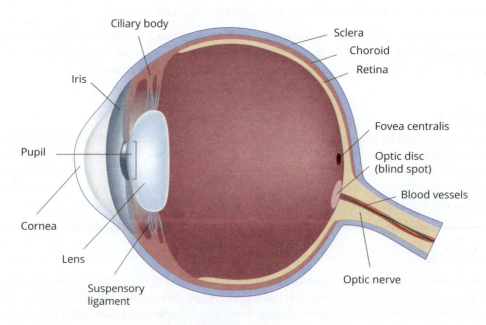

Figure 2: The anatomy of the eye is illustrated in this diagram.

After passing through the pupil, light crosses the **lens**, a curved, transparent structure that serves to provide additional focus. The lens is attached to muscles that can change its shape to aid in focusing light that is reflected from near or far objects. In a normal-sighted individual, the lens will focus images perfectly on a small indentation in the back of the eye known as the **fovea**, which is part of the **retina**, the light-sensitive lining of the eye. The fovea contains densely packed specialized photoreceptor cells (Figure 3). These **photoreceptor** cells, known as cones, are light-detecting cells. The **cones** are specialized types of photoreceptors that work best in bright light conditions. Cones are very sensitive to acute detail and provide tremendous spatial resolution. They are also directly involved in our ability to perceive color.

While cones are concentrated in the fovea, where images tend to be focused, rods, another type of photoreceptor, are located throughout the remainder of the retina. **Rods** are specialized photoreceptors that work well in low light conditions, and while they lack the spatial resolution and color function of the cones, they are involved in our vision in dimly lit environments as well as in our perception of movement on the periphery of our visual field.

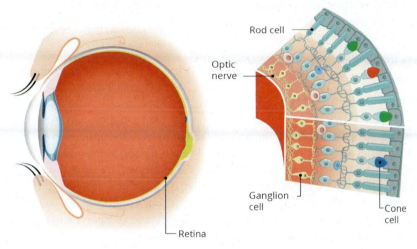

SECTION OF RETINA

📷 **Figure 3:** The two types of photoreceptors are shown in this image.

✍ On Your Own

Match the correct component of the eye with each of the following functions.

1. Photoreceptors that serve our vision in dimly lit environments

   ☐ Retina   ☐ Cornea   ☐ Rods

2. Changes size due to light levels or emotional arousal

   ☐ Iris   ☐ Pupil   ☐ Cones

3. Small indentation where the lens focuses an image

   ☐ Cornea   ☐ Iris   ☐ Fovea

We have all experienced the different sensitivities of rods and cones when making the transition from a brightly lit environment to a dimly lit environment. Imagine going to see a blockbuster movie on a clear summer day. As you walk from the brightly lit lobby into the dark theater, you notice that you immediately have difficulty seeing much of anything. After a few minutes, you begin to adjust to the darkness and can see the interior of the theater. In the bright environment, your vision was dominated primarily by cone activity. As you move to the dark environment, rod activity dominates, but there is a delay in transitioning between the phases. If your rods do not transform light into nerve impulses as easily and efficiently as they should, you will have difficulty seeing in dim light, a condition known as night blindness.

Group Activity

Complete the following steps then answer the questions.

1. Form groups of two.

2. Take five different pieces of colored paper (all the same size, all different colors).

3. Lower the lights to the point of just being able to see.

4. Wait ten minutes, and then have one partner hold up a piece of paper while the other partner states what they think the color is.

5. The partner holding the paper up should record this perceived color on the back of the sheet.

6. Repeat this for each sheet and then switch roles.

7. Compare results with your partner and then with the rest of the class.

- Were there any similarities in your perceived colors?

- Notable differences?

- Why do you think the results ended up this way?

- What do you know about our vision in low light conditions that helps explain this?

Rods and cones are connected (via several interneurons) to retinal ganglion cells. Axons from the retinal ganglion cells converge and exit through the back of the eye to form the **optic nerve**. The optic nerve carries visual information from the retina to the brain. There is a point in the visual field called the **blind spot**: even when light from a small object is focused on the blind spot, we do not see it. We are not consciously aware of our blind spots for two reasons: first, each eye gets a slightly different view of the visual field; therefore, the blind spots do not overlap. Second, our visual system fills in the blind spot so that although we cannot respond to visual information that occurs in that portion of the visual field, we are also not aware that information is missing.

The optic nerve from each eye merges just below the brain at a point called the **optic chiasm**. As Figure 4 shows, the optic chiasm is an X-shaped structure that sits just below the cerebral cortex at the front of the brain. At the point of the optic chiasm, information from the right visual field (which comes from both eyes) is sent to the left side of the brain, and information from the left visual field is sent to the right side of the brain.

Once inside the brain, visual information is sent via a number of structures to the occipital lobe at the back of the brain for processing. Visual information might be processed in parallel pathways, which can generally be described as the "what pathway" and the "where/how pathway." The "what pathway" is involved in object recognition and identification, while the "where/how pathway" is involved with location in space and how one might interact with a particular visual stimulus (Milner & Goodale, 2008; Ungerleider & Haxby, 1994). For example, when you see a ball rolling down the street, the "what pathway" identifies what the object is, and the "where/how pathway" identifies its location or movement in space.

The Visual Projection Pathway

📷 **Figure 4:** This illustration shows the optic chiasm at the front of the brain and the pathways to the occipital lobe at the back of the brain, where visual sensations are processed into meaningful perceptions.

Color and Depth Perception

We do not see the world in black and white; neither do we see it as two-dimensional (2-D) or flat (just height and width, no depth). Let's look at how color vision works and how we perceive three dimensions (height, width, and depth).

Reflection Questions

What do you think the world would look like if we could only view it in two dimensions?

Color Vision

Normal-sighted individuals have three different types of cones that mediate color vision. Each of these cone types is maximally sensitive to a slightly different wavelength of light. According to the **trichromatic theory of color vision**, shown in Figure 5, all colors in the spectrum can be produced by combining red, green, and blue. The three types of cones are each receptive to one of the colors.

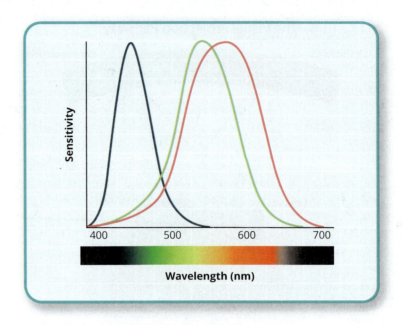

📷 **Figure 5:** This figure illustrates the different sensitivities for the three cone types found in a normal-sighted individual.

📷 **Figure 6:** Stare at the white dot for 30–60 seconds and then move your eyes to a blank piece of white paper. What do you see? This is known as a negative afterimage, and it provides empirical support for the opponent-process theory of color vision.

Further Resources

Watch this video (hawkes. biz/colorvision) to see the first part of a documentary explaining color vision in more detail.

One of the most famous experiments on depth perception, the Visual Cliff, was conducted by Elanor Gibson in 1960. Watch this video (hawkes.biz/ depthperception) to learn more about how infants responded to various depth cues.

The trichromatic theory of color vision is not the only theory. Another major theory of color vision is known as the **opponent-process theory**. According to this theory, color is coded in opponent pairs: black-white, yellow-blue, and green-red. The basic idea is that some cells of the visual system are excited by one of the opponent colors and inhibited by the other. So, a cell that was excited by wavelengths associated with green would be inhibited by wavelengths associated with red, and vice versa. One of the implications of opponent processing is that we do not experience greenish-reds or yellowish-blues as colors. Another implication is that this leads to the experience of negative afterimages. An **afterimage** describes the continuation of a visual sensation after removal of the stimulus. For example, when you stare briefly at the sun and then look away from it, you may still perceive a spot of light although the stimulus (the sun) has been removed. When color is involved in the stimulus, the color pairings identified in the opponent-process theory lead to a negative afterimage. You can test this concept using the flag in Figure 6.

But these two theories—the trichromatic theory of color vision and the opponent-process theory—are not mutually exclusive. Research has shown that they just apply to different levels of the nervous system. For visual processing on the retina, trichromatic theory applies: the cones are responsive to three different wavelengths that represent red, blue, and green. But once the signal moves past the retina on its way to the brain, the cells respond in a way consistent with opponent-process theory (Land, 1959; Kaiser, 1997).

Depth Perception

Our ability to perceive spatial relationships in three-dimensional (3-D) space is known as **depth perception**. With depth perception, we can describe things as being in front, behind, above, below, or to the side of other things.

Our world is three-dimensional, so it makes sense that our mental representation of the world has three-dimensional properties. We use a variety of cues in a visual scene to establish our sense of depth. Some of these are **binocular cues**, which means that they rely on the use of both eyes. One example of a binocular depth cue is **binocular disparity**, the slightly different view of the world that each of our eyes receives. To experience this slightly different view, do this simple exercise: extend your arm fully and extend one of your fingers and focus on that finger. Now, close your left eye without moving your head, then open your left eye and close your right eye without moving your head. You will notice that your finger seems to shift as you alternate between the two eyes because of the slightly different view each eye has of your finger.

A 3-D movie works on the same principle: the special glasses you wear allow the two slightly different images projected onto the screen to be seen separately by your left and your right eye. As your brain processes these images, you have the illusion that the leaping animal or running person is coming right toward you.

Although we rely on binocular cues to experience depth in our 3-D world, we can also perceive depth in 2-D arrays. Think about all the paintings and photographs you have seen. Generally, you pick up on depth in these images even though the visual stimulus is 2-D. When we do this, we are relying on a number of **monocular cues**, or cues that require only one eye. If you think you can't see depth with one eye, note that you don't bump into things when using only one eye while walking—and in fact, we have more monocular cues than binocular cues.

An example of a monocular cue would be what is known as linear perspective. **Linear perspective** refers to the fact that we perceive depth when we see two parallel lines that seem to converge in an image (Figure 8). Some other monocular depth cues are interposition, the partial overlap of objects, and the relative size and closeness of images to the horizon.

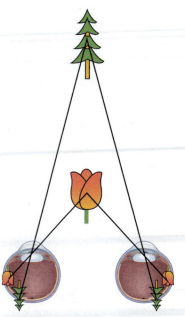

Figure 7: In this image, notice how the tree appears to be on different sides of the flower within each eye. This is caused by binocular disparity.

Figure 8: We perceive depth in a two-dimensional figure like this one through the use of monocular cues such as linear perspective, like the parallel lines converging as the road narrows in the distance.

Dig Deeper

Stereoblindness

Bruce Bridgeman was born with an extreme case of lazy eye that resulted in him being stereoblind, or unable to respond to binocular cues of depth. He relied heavily on monocular depth cues, but he never had a true appreciation of the 3-D nature of the world around him. This all changed one night in 2012 while Bruce was seeing a movie with his wife.

The movie the couple was going to see was shot in 3-D, and even though he thought it was a waste of money, Bruce paid for the 3-D glasses when he purchased his ticket. As soon as the film began, Bruce put on the glasses and experienced something completely new. For the first time in his life he appreciated the true depth of the world around him. Remarkably, his ability to perceive depth persisted outside of the movie theater.

There are cells in the nervous system that respond to binocular depth cues. Normally, these cells require activation during early development in order to persist, so experts familiar with Bruce's case (and others like his) assume that at some point in his development, Bruce must have experienced at least a fleeting moment of binocular vision. It was enough to ensure the survival of the cells in the visual system tuned to binocular cues. The mystery now is why it took Bruce nearly 70 years to have these cells activated (Peck, 2012).

Summary

Light waves cross the cornea and enter the eye at the pupil. The eye's lens focuses this light so that the image is focused on a region of the retina known as the fovea. The fovea contains cones that possess high levels of visual acuity and operate best in bright light conditions. Rods are located throughout the retina and operate best under dim light conditions. Visual information leaves the eye via the optic nerve. Information from each visual field is sent to the opposite side of the brain at the optic chiasm. Visual information then moves through a number of brain sites before reaching the occipital lobe, where it is processed.

Two theories explain color perception. The trichromatic theory asserts that three distinct cone groups are tuned to slightly different wavelengths of light, and it is the combination of activity across these cone types that results in our perception of all the colors we see. The opponent-process theory of color vision asserts that color is processed in opponent pairs and accounts for the interesting phenomenon of a negative afterimage. We perceive depth through a combination of monocular and binocular depth cues.

Figure 9: What is going on in this image? Is the ball rolling along the surface or is the surface being moved beneath the ball?

Flash Forward

Ready to dig into the vocabulary? Get some practice with this Hawkes Verified Quizlet set (hawkes.biz/psych4q4)!

4.4 Hearing

Our auditory system converts pressure waves into meaningful sounds. This translates into our ability to hear the sounds of nature, to appreciate the beauty of music, and to communicate with one another through spoken language. This lesson will provide an overview of the basic anatomy and function of the auditory system. It will include a discussion of how the sensory stimulus is translated into neural impulses, where in the brain that information is processed, how we perceive pitch, and how we know where sound is coming from.

Anatomy of the Auditory System

The ear can be separated into multiple sections.

Outer Ear	Middle Ear	Inner Ear
Pinna	Malleus (ossicle)	Semi-circular canals
Auditory canal	Incus (ossicle)	Cochlea
Tympanic membrane	Stapes (ossicle)	

The outer ear includes the **pinna**, which is the visible part of the ear that protrudes from our heads, the auditory canal, and the **tympanic membrane** (or eardrum). The middle ear contains three tiny bones known as the ossicles, which are named the **malleus** (or hammer), **incus** (or anvil), and the **stapes** (or stirrup). The inner ear contains the semi-circular canals, which are involved in balance and movement (the vestibular sense), and the cochlea. The **cochlea** is a fluid-filled, snail-shaped structure that contains the sensory receptor cells (hair cells) of the auditory system (Figure 1).

Figure 1: The ear is divided into outer, middle, and inner divisions.

Sound waves travel along the auditory canal and strike the tympanic membrane, causing it to vibrate. This vibration results in movement of the three ossicles. As the ossicles move, the stapes presses into a thin membrane of the cochlea known as the oval window. As the stapes presses into the oval window, the fluid inside the cochlea begins to move, which in turn stimulates **hair cells**, which are auditory receptor cells of the inner ear embedded in the basilar membrane. The **basilar membrane** is a thin strip of tissue within the cochlea.

The activation of hair cells is a mechanical process: the stimulation of the hair cell ultimately leads to activation of the cell. As hair cells become activated, they generate neural impulses that travel along the auditory nerve to the brain. Auditory information is shuttled to the inferior colliculus, the medial geniculate nucleus of the thalamus, and finally to the auditory cortex in the temporal lobe of the brain for processing. Like the visual system, there is also evidence suggesting that information about auditory recognition and localization is processed in parallel streams (Rauschecker & Tian, 2000; Renier et al., 2009).

☑ **On Your Own**

Using the information learned in this lesson, recreate the auditory pathway below, starting from the auditory canal and ending in the auditory cortex.

Auditory Canal

_____

_____

_____

_____

_____

_____

_____

Auditory Cortex

_____

Pitch Perception

Different frequencies of sound waves are associated with differences in our perception of the pitch of those sounds. Low-frequency sounds are lower pitched, and high-frequency sounds are higher pitched.

☑ **On Your Own**

Select the correct sound wave for a high-pitched sound.

☐ High frequency   ☐ High amplitude

How does the auditory system differentiate among various pitches?

Several theories have been proposed to account for pitch perception. We'll discuss two of them here: temporal theory and place theory. The **temporal theory** of pitch perception asserts that frequency is coded by the activity level of a sensory neuron. This would mean that a given hair cell would fire action potentials related to the frequency of the sound wave. While this is a very intuitive explanation, we detect such a broad range of frequencies (20–20,000 Hz) that the frequency of action potentials fired by hair cells cannot account for the entire range. Because of properties related to sodium channels on the neuronal membrane that are involved in action potentials, there is a point at which a cell cannot fire any faster (Shamma, 2001).

☑ On Your Own

Answer the short answer questions below.

1. Explain the temporal theory of pitch perception in your own words.

_____

_____

2. If a sound were roughly 20 Hz compared to 20,000 Hz, how would this information be coded according to the temporal theory?

_____

_____

The **place theory** of pitch perception suggests that different portions of the basilar membrane are sensitive to sounds of different frequencies. More specifically, the base of the basilar membrane responds best to high frequencies and the tip of the basilar membrane responds best to low frequencies. Therefore, hair cells that are in the base portion would be labeled as high-pitch receptors, while those in the tip of basilar membrane would be labeled as low-pitch receptors (Shamma, 2001).

In reality, both theories explain different aspects of pitch perception. At frequencies up to about 4,000 Hz, it is clear that both the rate of action potentials and place contribute to our perception of pitch. However, much higher frequency sounds can only be encoded using place cues (Shamma, 2001).

Reflection Questions

For individuals who experience hearing loss, they often lose the ability to hear the highest pitches.

How would both the temporal theory and place theory of pitch perception explain these losses?

Sound Localization

The ability to locate sound in our environments is an important part of hearing. Localizing sound could be considered similar to the way that we perceive depth in our visual fields. Like the monocular and binocular cues that provided information about depth, the auditory system uses both **monaural** (one-eared) and **binaural** (two-eared) cues to localize sound.

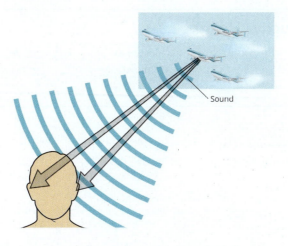

Sound

📷 **Figure 2:** Localizing sound involves the use of both monaural and binaural cues.

Each pinna interacts with incoming sound waves differently, depending on the sound's source relative to our bodies. This interaction provides a monaural cue that is helpful in locating sounds that occur above or below and in front or behind us. The sound waves received by your two ears from sounds that come from directly above, below, in front, or behind you would be identical; therefore, monaural cues are essential (Grothe, Pecka, & McAlpine, 2010).

Binaural cues, on the other hand, provide information on the location of a sound along a horizontal axis by relying on differences in patterns of vibration of the eardrum between our two ears. If a sound comes from an off-center location, it creates two types of binaural cues: interaural level differences and interaural timing differences. **Interaural level difference** refers to the fact that a sound coming from the right side of your body is more intense at your right ear than at your left ear because of the attenuation of the sound wave as it passes through your head. **Interaural timing difference** refers to the small difference in the time at which a given sound wave arrives at each ear (Figure 2). Certain brain areas monitor these differences to construct where along a horizontal axis a sound originates (Grothe et al., 2010).

☑ On Your Own

Answer the short answer questions below.

1. If you are sitting with your eyes closed, and your left ear and your right ear both receive a sound that is 15 dB at the same time, where is the sound coming from?

_____

_____

2. If you are sitting with your eyes closed, and your left ear receives a sound that is 20 dB 500-milliseconds earlier than a 15 dB sound that is received by your right ear, where is the sound coming from? How do you know?

_____

_____

Hearing Loss

Deafness is the partial or complete inability to hear. Some people are born deaf, which is known as **congenital deafness**. In other cases, individuals can suffer from **conductive hearing loss**.

Causes of Conductive Hearing Loss

- Age
- Genetics
- Exposure to extreme noise
- Illnesses
- Damage due to toxins

(a)   (b)

Figure 3: Environmental factors that can lead to conductive hearing loss include regular exposure to loud music or construction equipment. (a) Rock musicians and (b) construction workers are at risk for this type of hearing loss.

Given the mechanical nature by which the sound wave stimulus is transmitted from the eardrum through the ossicles to the oval window of the cochlea, some degree of hearing loss is inevitable. With conductive hearing loss, hearing problems are associated with a failure in the vibration of the eardrum and/or movement of the ossicles. These problems are often dealt with through devices like hearing aids that amplify incoming sound waves to make vibration of the eardrum and movement of the ossicles more likely to occur.

Reflection Questions

Which do you think would be a more difficult situation for you: congenital deafness or total conductive hearing loss in your 20s? Why?

When the hearing problem is associated with a failure to transmit neural signals from the cochlea to the brain, it is called **sensorineural hearing loss**. One disease that results in sensorineural hearing loss is Ménière's disease. Although not well understood, **Ménière's disease** results in a degeneration of inner ear structures that can lead to hearing loss, tinnitus (constant ringing or buzzing), **vertigo** (a sense of spinning), and an increase in pressure within the inner ear (Semaan & Megerian, 2011). This kind of loss cannot be treated with hearing aids, but some individuals might be candidates for a cochlear implant as a treatment option. **Cochlear implants** are electronic devices that consist of a microphone, a speech processor, and an electrode array. The device receives incoming sound information and directly stimulates the auditory nerve to transmit information to the brain.

Further Resources

Watch this video (hawkes. biz/cochlearimplants) that describes cochlear implant surgeries and how they work.

What Do You Think?

Deaf Culture

In the United States and other places around the world, deaf people have their own language, schools, and customs. This is called deaf culture. In the United States, deaf individuals often communicate using American Sign Language (ASL); ASL has no verbal component and is based entirely on visual signs and gestures. The primary mode of communication is signing. One of the values of deaf culture is to continue traditions like using sign language rather than teaching deaf children to try to speak, read lips, or have cochlear implant surgery.

When a child is diagnosed as deaf, parents have difficult decisions to make. Should the child be enrolled in mainstream schools and taught to verbalize and read lips? Or should the child be sent to a school for deaf children to learn ASL and have significant exposure to deaf culture? Do you think there might be differences in the way that parents approach these decisions depending on whether or not they are also deaf?

Figure 4: A cochlear implant can be used to treat sensorineural hearing loss.

Summary

Sound waves are funneled into the auditory canal and cause vibrations of the eardrum; these vibrations move the ossicles. As the ossicles move, the stapes presses against the oval window of the cochlea, which causes fluid inside the cochlea to move. As a result, hair cells embedded in the basilar membrane become enlarged, which sends neural impulses to the brain via the auditory nerve.

Pitch perception and sound localization are important aspects of hearing. Our ability to perceive pitch relies on both the firing rate of the hair cells in the basilar membrane as well as their location within the membrane. In terms of sound localization, both monaural and binaural cues are used to locate where sounds originate in our environment.

Individuals can be born deaf, or they can develop deafness as a result of age, genetic predisposition, and/or environmental causes. Hearing loss that results from a failure of the vibration of the eardrum or the resultant movement of the ossicles is called conductive hearing loss. Hearing loss that involves a failure of the transmission of auditory nerve impulses to the brain is called sensorineural hearing loss.

4.5 The Other Senses

> **Flash Forward**
>
> Ready to dig into the vocabulary? Get some practice with this Hawkes Verified Quizlet set (hawkes.biz/psych4q5)!

Vision and hearing have received an incredible amount of attention from researchers over the years. While there is still much to be learned about how these sensory systems work, we have a much better understanding of them than of our other sensory modalities. In this lesson, we will explore our chemical senses (taste and smell) and our body senses (touch, temperature, pain, balance, and body position).

The Chemical Senses

Taste (gustation) and smell (olfaction) are called chemical senses because both have sensory receptors that respond to molecules in the food we eat or in the air we breathe. There is a pronounced interaction between our chemical senses. For example, when we describe the flavor of a given food, we are really referring to both gustatory and olfactory properties of the food working in combination.

Taste (Gustation)

You have learned since elementary school that there are four basic groupings of taste: sweet, salty, sour, and bitter. Research demonstrates, however, that we have at least six taste groupings. Umami is our fifth taste. **Umami** is actually a Japanese word that roughly translates to *yummy*, and it is associated with a taste for monosodium glutamate (Kinnamon & Vandenbeuch, 2009). There is also a growing body of experimental evidence suggesting that we possess a taste for the fatty content of a given food (Mizushige, Inoue, & Fushiki, 2007).

✐ On Your Own

Look at the following photo and consider what taste bud groupings might be activated by the different ingredients.

📷 **Figure 1:** What does Hawaiian pizza taste like?

Taste Bud Grouping	Ingredient

Molecules from the food and beverages we consume dissolve in our saliva and interact with taste receptors on our tongue and in our mouth and throat. **Taste buds** are formed by groupings of taste receptor cells with hair-like extensions that protrude into the central pore of the taste bud (Figure 2).

📷 **Figure 2:** (a) Taste buds are composed of a number of individual taste receptors cells that transmit information to nerves. (b) This micrograph shows a close-up view of the tongue's surface.

Taste buds have a life cycle of ten days to two weeks, so even destroying some by burning your tongue won't have any long-term effect; they just grow right back. Taste molecules bind to receptors on this extension and cause chemical changes within the sensory cell that result in neural impulses being transmitted to the brain via different nerves, depending on where the receptor is located. Taste information is transmitted to the medulla, thalamus, and limbic system, and ultimately to the gustatory cortex, which is tucked underneath the overlap between the frontal and temporal lobes (Maffei, Haley, & Fontanini, 2012; Roper, 2013).

☑ On Your Own

Recreate the gustatory pathway below, starting from the taste receptors and ending in the gustatory cortex.

Taste Receptors

Gustatory Cortex

Smell (Olfaction)

Olfactory receptor cells are located in a mucous membrane at the top of the nose. Small hair-like extensions from these receptors serve as the sites for odor molecules dissolved in the mucus to interact with chemical receptors located on these extensions (Figure 3). Once an odor molecule has bound a given receptor, chemical changes within the cell result in signals being sent to the **olfactory bulb**: a bulb-like structure at the tip of the frontal lobe where the olfactory nerves begin. From the olfactory bulb, information is sent to regions of the limbic system and to the primary olfactory cortex, which is located very near the gustatory cortex (Lodovichi & Belluscio, 2012; Spors et al., 2013).

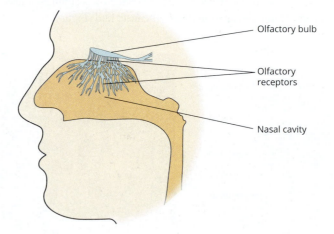

Olfactory bulb

Olfactory receptors

Nasal cavity

Figure 3: Olfactory receptors are the hair-like parts that extend from the olfactory bulb into the mucous membrane of the nasal cavity.

There is tremendous variation in the sensitivity of the olfactory systems of different species. We often think of dogs as having far superior olfactory systems than our own, and indeed, dogs can do some remarkable things with their noses. There is some evidence to suggest that dogs can "smell" dangerous drops in blood glucose levels as well as cancerous tumors (Wells, 2010). Dogs' extraordinary olfactory abilities may be due to the increased number of functional genes for olfactory receptors (between 800 and 1,200), compared to the fewer than 400 observed in humans and other primates (Niimura & Nei, 2007).

Reflection Questions

How might your life differ if you had the olfactory system of a dog? What would be the benefits? Challenges?

Many species respond to chemical messages, known as **pheromones**, sent by another individual (Wysocki & Preti, 2004). Pheromonal communication often involves providing information about the reproductive status of a potential mate. So, for example, when a female rat is ready to mate, she secretes pheromonal signals that draw attention from nearby male rats. Pheromonal activation is actually an important component in eliciting sexual behavior in the male rat (Furlow, 1996, 2012; Purvis & Haynes, 1972; Sachs, 1997). There has also been a good deal of research (and controversy) about pheromones in humans (Comfort, 1971; Russell, 1976; Wolfgang-Kimball, 1992; Weller, 1998).

Further Resources

Should you buy perfumes and colognes that contain "pheromones?" Check out this video (hawkes.biz/pheromones) to see the results of a social experiment to determine if they are effective.

Touch, Thermoception, and Nociception

A number of receptors are distributed throughout the skin to respond to various touch-related stimuli (Figure 4). These receptors include Meissner's corpuscles, Pacinian corpuscles, Merkel's disks, and Ruffini corpuscles. **Meissner's corpuscles** respond to pressure and lower frequency vibrations, and **Pacinian corpuscles** detect transient pressure and higher frequency vibrations. **Merkel's disks** respond to light pressure, while **Ruffini corpuscles** detect stretch (Abraira & Ginty, 2013).

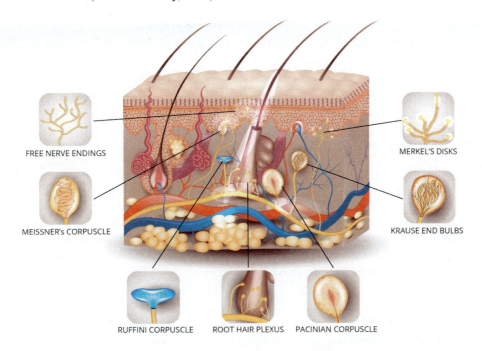

FREE NERVE ENDINGS

MERKEL'S DISKS

MEISSNER's CORPUSCLE

KRAUSE END BULBS

RUFFINI CORPUSCLE   ROOT HAIR PLEXUS   PACINIAN CORPUSCLE

Figure 4: There are many types of sensory receptors located in the skin, each attuned to specific touch-related stimuli.

✎ On Your Own

Stephanie holds her yoga tree pose, enjoying the muscle elongation she feels in her right quadricep. In this situation, which of Stephanie's receptors are activated?

☐ Meissner's corpuscles   ☐ Pacinian corpuscles   ☐ Ruffini corpuscles

In addition to the receptors located in the skin, there are also a number of free nerve endings that serve sensory functions. These nerve endings respond to a variety of different types of touch-related stimuli and serve as sensory receptors for both **thermoception** (temperature perception) and **nociception** (a signal indicating potential harm and maybe pain) (Garland, 2012; Petho & Reeh, 2012; Spray, 1986). Sensory information collected from the receptors and free nerve endings travels up the spinal cord and is transmitted to regions of the medulla, thalamus, and ultimately to the somatosensory cortex, which is located in the postcentral gyrus of the parietal lobe.

✎ On Your Own

Using the information learned in this lesson, recreate the sensory pathway below, starting from the sensory receptors and ending in the somatosensory cortex.

Sensory Receptors

Somatosensory Cortex

Pain Perception

Pain is an unpleasant experience that involves both physical and psychological components. Feeling pain is quite adaptive because it makes us aware of an injury, and it motivates us to remove ourselves from the cause of that injury. In addition, pain also makes us less likely to suffer additional injury because we will be gentler with our injured body parts.

Generally speaking, pain can be considered to be neuropathic or inflammatory in nature. Pain that signals some type of tissue damage is known as **inflammatory pain**. In some situations, pain results from damage to neurons of either the peripheral or central nervous system. As a result, pain signals that are sent to the brain get exaggerated. This type of pain is known as **neuropathic pain**. Multiple treatment options for pain relief range from relaxation therapy to the use of analgesic medications to deep brain stimulation. The most effective treatment option for a given individual will depend on a number of considerations, including the severity and persistence of the pain and any medical/psychological conditions.

Reflection Questions

How might your life be improved if you were unable to feel pain? Would there be drawbacks?

Further Resources

Watch this video (hawkes. biz/pain) to learn more about congenital insensitivity to pain.

Some individuals are born without the ability to feel pain. This very rare genetic disorder is known as **congenital insensitivity to pain** (or **congenital analgesia**). While those with congenital analgesia can detect differences in temperature and pressure, they cannot experience pain. As a result, they often suffer significant injuries. Young children have serious mouth and tongue injuries because they have bitten themselves repeatedly. Not surprisingly, individuals suffering from this disorder have much shorter life expectancies due to their injuries and secondary infections of injured sites (U.S. National Library of Medicine, 2013).

The Vestibular Sense, Proprioception, and Kinesthesia

The **vestibular sense** contributes to our ability to maintain balance and body posture. As Figure 5 shows, the major sensory organs (utricle, saccule, and the three semicircular canals) of this system are located next to the cochlea in the inner ear. The vestibular organs are fluid-filled and have hair cells, similar to the ones found in the auditory system, which respond to movement of the head and gravitational forces. When these hair cells are stimulated, they send signals to the brain via the vestibular nerve. Although we may not be consciously aware of our vestibular system's sensory information under normal circumstances, its importance is apparent when we experience motion sickness and/or dizziness related to infections of the inner ear (Khan & Chang, 2013).

Figure 5: The major sensory organs of the vestibular system are located next to the cochlea in the inner ear. These include the utricle, saccule, and the three semicircular canals (posterior, superior, and horizontal).

In addition to maintaining balance, the vestibular system collects information critical for controlling movement and the reflexes that move various parts of our bodies to compensate for changes in body position. Therefore, both **proprioception** (perception of body position) and **kinesthesia** (perception of the body's movement through space) interact with information provided by the vestibular system.

These sensory systems also gather information from receptors that respond to stretch and tension in muscles, joints, skin, and tendons (Lackner & DiZio, 2005; Proske, 2006; Proske & Gandevia, 2012). Proprioceptive and kinesthetic information travel to the brain via the spinal column. Several cortical regions in addition to the cerebellum receive information from and send information to the sensory organs of the proprioceptive and kinesthetic systems.

Summary

Taste (gustation) and smell (olfaction) are chemical senses that employ receptors on the tongue and in the nose that bind directly with taste and odor molecules in order to transmit information to the brain for processing. Our ability to perceive touch, temperature, and pain is mediated by a number of receptors and free nerve endings that are distributed throughout the skin and various tissues of the body. The vestibular sense helps us maintain a sense of balance through the response of hair cells in the utricle, saccule, and semicircular canals that respond to changes in head position and gravity. Our proprioceptive and kinesthetic systems provide information about body position and body movement through receptors that detect stretch and tension in the muscles, joints, tendons, and skin of the body.

Flash Forward

Ready to dig into the vocabulary? Get some practice with this Hawkes Verified Quizlet set (hawkes.biz/psych4q6)!

4.6 Gestalt Principles of Perception

In the early part of the 20th century, Max Wertheimer published a paper demonstrating that individuals perceived motion in rapidly flickering static images—an insight that came to him as he used a child's toy tachistoscope. Wertheimer, and his assistants Wolfgang Köhler and Kurt Koffka, who later became his partners, believed that perception involved more than simply combining sensory stimuli. This belief led to a new movement within the field of psychology known as **Gestalt psychology**. The word *Gestalt* literally means "form or pattern," but its use reflects the idea that the whole is different from the sum of its parts.

In other words, the brain creates a perception that is more than simply the sum of available sensory inputs, and it does so in predictable ways. Gestalt psychologists translated these predictable ways into principles by which we organize sensory information. As a result, Gestalt psychology has been extremely influential in the area of sensation and perception (Rock & Palmer, 1990).

One Gestalt principle is the **figure-ground relationship**. According to this principle, we tend to segment our visual world into figure and ground.

Figure-Ground Relationships

1	Figure: object or person that is the focus
2	Ground: background to the primary focus

Figure 1: The concept of figure-ground relationship explains that we segment our visual world.

As Figure 2 shows, our perception can vary tremendously, depending on what is perceived as figure and what is perceived as ground. Presumably, our ability to interpret sensory information depends on what we label as figure and what we label as ground in any particular case although this assumption has been called into question (Peterson & Gibson, 1994; Vecera & O'Reilly, 1998).

Another Gestalt principle for organizing sensory stimuli into meaningful perception is **proximity**. This principle asserts that things that are close to one another tend to be grouped together, as Figure 3 illustrates.

Figure 2: The concept of figure-ground relationship explains why this image can be perceived either as a vase or as a pair of faces.

(a)   (b)

Figure 3: The Gestalt principle of proximity suggests that you see (a) one block of dots on the left side and (b) three columns on the right side.

How we read something provides another illustration of the proximity concept. For example, we read this sentence like this, notl iket hiso rt hat. We group the letters of a given word together because there are no spaces between the letters, and we perceive words because there are spaces between each word. Here are some more examples:

- Cany oum akes enseo ft hiss entence?

- What doth es e wor dsmea n?

Group Activity

In a small group, discuss examples of times when you have grouped items based on their proximity to each other.

We might also use the principle of **similarity** to group things in our visual fields. According to this principle, things that are alike tend to be grouped together (Figure 4). For example, when watching a football game, we tend to group individuals based on the colors of their uniforms. When watching an offensive drive, we can get a sense of the two teams simply by grouping along this dimension.

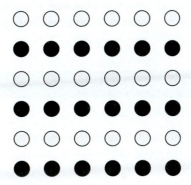

Figure 4: When looking at this array of dots, we likely perceive alternating rows of black and white. We are grouping these dots according to the principle of similarity.

Two additional Gestalt principles are the law of continuity (or good continuation) and closure. The law of **continuity** suggests that we are more likely to perceive continuous, smooth flowing lines rather than jagged, broken lines (Figure 5). The principle of **closure** states that we organize our perceptions into complete objects rather than as a series of parts (Figure 6).

Figure 5: Good continuation would suggest that we are more likely to perceive this as two overlapping lines, rather than four lines meeting in the center.

Figure 6: Closure suggests that we will perceive a complete circle and rectangle rather than a series of segments.

According to Gestalt theorists, **pattern perception**, or our ability to discriminate among different figures and shapes, occurs by following the principles described previously. You probably feel fairly certain that your perception accurately matches the real world, but this is not always the case. Our perceptions are based on **perceptual hypotheses**: educated guesses that we make while interpreting sensory information. These hypotheses are informed by a number of factors, including our personalities, experiences, and expectations. We use these hypotheses to generate our perceptual set. For instance, research has demonstrated that those who are given verbal priming produce a biased interpretation of complex ambiguous figures (Goolkasian & Woodbury, 2010).

✎ On Your Own

Select the best answer for each of the following questions.

1. When entering into the dark movie theater, Talitha assumes that people who are sitting next to each other are groups of friends, and she tries to find the group of five people who may be the people she is supposed to meet for the movie. Which Gestalt principle is at work?

☐ Closure   ☐ Similarity

☐ Proximity   ☐ Good continuation

2. When trying to find the router wire in the mess of computer and printer wires, David assumes that the wire continues in a relatively linear path. Which Gestalt principle is at work?

☐ Closure   ☐ Similarity

☐ Proximity   ☐ Good continuation

Dig Deeper

The Depths of Perception: Bias, Prejudice, and Cultural Factors

In this chapter, you have learned that perception is a complex process. Built from sensations but influenced by our own experiences, biases, prejudices, and cultures, perceptions can be very different from person to person. Research suggests that implicit racial prejudice and stereotypes affect perception. For instance, several studies have demonstrated that non-Black participants identify weapons faster and are more likely to identify non-weapons as weapons when the image of the weapon is paired with the image of a Black person (Payne, 2001; Payne, Shimizu, & Jacoby, 2005). Furthermore, White individuals' decisions to shoot an armed target in a video game is made more quickly when the target is Black (Correll, Park, Judd, & Wittenbrink, 2002; Correll, Urland, & Ito, 2006). This research is important, considering the number of very high-profile cases in the last few decades in which young Blacks were killed by people who claimed to believe that the unarmed individuals were armed and/or represented some threat to their personal safety.

Summary

Gestalt theorists have been incredibly influential in the areas of sensation and perception. Gestalt principles such as figure-ground relationship, grouping by proximity or similarity, the law of good continuation, and closure are all used to help explain how we organize sensory information. Our perceptions are not infallible, and they can be influenced by bias, prejudice, and other factors.

Chapter 4 Project

Purpose

In this chapter, you have learned about sensation and perception, our connection with the outside world. **The purpose of this project is to investigate 1) how sensation and perception contribute to success in multiple areas of your daily life, 2) how the lack of functioning senses would be detrimental to people's lives, and 3) how the nervous system is involved in sensation and perception.**

Directions

Answer the following questions, which build upon one another. Your answers should be robust, including examples or illustrations, and should be thoroughly explained in your own words.

Part 1 - Choose any one of the five senses. Describe three ways that this sense helps you in particular tasks that are related to being successful in three different areas of your life (e.g., relationship, work, school, etc. – one per area). The three tasks should be specific (e.g., type on a computer, communicate with my boyfriend, know when something is burning as a cook at a restaurant, etc.) and you should explain how it is related to success. List them as bullet points 1, 2, and 3.

Part 2 - Now, choose any one of the three tasks and write a paragraph that describes both the electrical and chemical process of sensory communication associated with the task (you may need to revisit Chapter 2 or outside sources). Also, explain the role transduction plays in moving this information from the outside world, through to sensation and perception.

Part 3 - If this sense did not work correctly, characterize three negative outcomes that could happen in your (present) life as a result. Be specific and thorough.

Part 4 - Use a search engine to find a case where someone did not have this functioning sense (Use critical thinking to determine if it is a reputable source. Include a reference for it, with a link). Describe this person's situation, as if you were writing to a friend to explain it. Provide specific examples of its impact in this person's life. Use Chapter 2 and online sources to assess and describe which parts of the brain are involved in processing this sense. If you can further determine which neurotransmitters are involved, please list them and their general function in the brain. If you cannot determine this for certain, make a statement about which neurotransmitters you think might be involved, and why.

Materials

None required.

✅ Checklist

Part 1 - Senses in everyday life

- ☐ Choose a sense
- ☐ Life Area #1
  - ☐ Task 1
  - ☐ How is this sense related to success?
- ☐ Life Area #2
  - ☐ Task 2
  - ☐ How is this sense related to success?
- ☐ Life Area #3
  - ☐ Task 3
  - ☐ How is this sense related to success?

Part 2 - Sensory communication (1 paragraph)

- ☐ Electrical & chemical communication for 1 task
- ☐ Transduction

Part 3 - Problems with chosen sense

- ☐ Potential negative outcomes in your present life
  - ☐ Negative outcome #1
  - ☐ Negative outcome #2
  - ☐ Negative outcome #3

Part 4 - Explain a real-life example

- ☐ Find a reputable case study of someone without chosen functioning sense
- ☐ Informal explanation with specific examples
- ☐ Describe parts of the brain involved in chosen sense
- ☐ Explain how they are involved
- ☐ Which neurotransmitters? Why?

⚐ Chapter 4 Review

Lesson Summaries

4.1 Sensation versus Perception

Sensation occurs when sensory receptors detect sensory stimuli. Perception involves the organization, interpretation, and conscious experience of those sensations. All sensory systems have both absolute and difference thresholds, which refer to the minimum amount of stimulus energy or the minimum amount of difference in stimulus energy required to be detected about 50% of the time, respectively. Sensory adaptation, selective attention, and signal detection theory can help explain what is perceived and what is not. In addition, our perceptions are affected by a number of factors, including beliefs, values, prejudices, culture, and life experiences.

4.2 Waves and Wavelengths

Both light and sound can be described in terms of wave forms with physical characteristics like amplitude, wavelength, and timbre. Wavelength and frequency are inversely related so that longer waves have lower frequencies, and shorter waves have higher frequencies. In the visual system, a light wave's wavelength is generally associated with color, and its amplitude is associated with brightness. In the auditory system, a sound's frequency is associated with pitch, and its amplitude is associated with loudness.

4.3 Vision

Light waves cross the cornea and enter the eye at the pupil. The eye's lens focuses this light so that the image is focused on a region of the retina known as the fovea. The fovea contains cones that possess high levels of visual acuity and operate best in bright light conditions. Rods are located throughout the retina and operate best under dim light conditions. Visual information leaves the eye via the optic nerve. Information from each visual field is sent to the opposite side of the brain at the optic chiasm. Visual information then moves through a number of brain sites before reaching the occipital lobe, where it is processed.

Two theories explain color perception. The trichromatic theory asserts that three distinct cone groups are tuned to slightly different wavelengths of light, and it is the combination of activity across these cone types that results in our perception of all the colors we see. The opponent-process theory of color vision asserts that color is processed in opponent pairs and accounts for the interesting phenomenon of a negative afterimage. We perceive depth through a combination of monocular and binocular depth cues.

4.4 Hearing

Sound waves are funneled into the auditory canal and cause vibrations of the eardrum; these vibrations move the ossicles. As the ossicles move, the stapes presses against the oval window of the cochlea, which causes fluid inside the cochlea to move. As a result, hair cells embedded in the basilar membrane become enlarged, which sends neural impulses to the brain via the auditory nerve.

Pitch perception and sound localization are important aspects of hearing. Our ability to perceive pitch relies on both the firing rate of the hair cells in the basilar membrane as well as their location within the membrane. In terms of sound localization, both monaural and binaural cues are used to locate where sounds originate in our environment.

Individuals can be born deaf, or they can develop deafness as a result of age, genetic predisposition, and/or environmental causes. Hearing loss that results from a failure of the vibration of the eardrum or the resultant movement of the ossicles is called conductive hearing loss. Hearing loss that involves a failure of the transmission of auditory nerve impulses to the brain is called sensorineural hearing loss.

4.5 The Other Senses

Taste (gustation) and smell (olfaction) are chemical senses that employ receptors on the tongue and in the nose that bind directly with taste and odor molecules in order to transmit information to the brain for processing. Our ability to perceive touch, temperature, and pain is mediated by a number of receptors and free nerve endings that are distributed throughout the skin and various tissues of the body. The vestibular sense helps us maintain a sense of balance through the response of hair cells in the utricle, saccule, and semicircular canals that respond to changes in head position and gravity. Our proprioceptive and kinesthetic systems provide information about body position and body movement through receptors that detect stretch and tension in the muscles, joints, tendons, and skin of the body.

4.6 Gestalt Principles of Perception

Gestalt theorists have been incredibly influential in the areas of sensation and perception. Gestalt principles such as figure-ground relationship, grouping by proximity or similarity, the law of good continuation, and closure are all used to help explain how we organize sensory information. Our perceptions are not infallible, and they can be influenced by bias, prejudice, and other factors.

Key Terms

Flash Back

Now that you've worked through the chapter, sharpen your vocabulary with this Hawkes Verified Quizlet set (hawkes.biz/psychch4)!

Absolute Threshold

Minimum amount of stimulus energy that must be present for the stimulus to be detected 50% of the time

Afterimage

Continuation of a visual sensation after removal of the stimulus

Amplitude

Height of a wave

Basilar Membrane

Thin strip of tissue within the cochlea that contains the hair cells which serve as the sensory receptors for the auditory system

Binaural Cue

Two-eared cue to localize sound

Binocular Cue

Cue that relies on the use of both eyes

Binocular Disparity

Slightly different view of the world that each eye receives

Blind Spot

Point where we cannot respond to visual information in that portion of the visual field

Bottom-Up Processing

System in which perceptions are built from sensory input

Closure

Organizing our perceptions into complete objects rather than as a series of parts

Cochlea

Fluid-filled, snail-shaped structure that contains the sensory receptor cells of the auditory system

Cochlear Implant

Electronic device that consists of a microphone, a speech processor, and an electrode array to directly stimulate the auditory nerve to transmit information to the brain

Conductive Hearing Loss

Failure in the vibration of the eardrum and/or movement of the ossicles

Cone

Specialized photoreceptor that works best in bright light conditions and detects color

Congenital Deafness

Deafness from birth

Congenital Insensitivity to Pain (Congenital Analgesia)

Genetic disorder that results in the inability to experience pain

Cornea

Transparent covering over the eye

Deafness

Partial or complete inability to hear

Decibel (dB)

Logarithmic unit of sound intensity

Depth Perception

Ability to perceive depth

Electromagnetic Spectrum

All the electromagnetic radiation that occurs in our environment

Figure-Ground Relationship

Segmenting our visual world into figure and ground

Fovea

Small indentation in the retina that contains cones

Frequency

Number of waves that pass a given point in a given time period

Gestalt Psychology

Field of psychology based on the idea that the whole is different from the sum of its parts

Good Continuation

(Also, *continuity*) we are more likely to perceive continuous, smooth flowing lines rather than jagged, broken lines

Hair Cell

Auditory receptor cell of the inner ear

Hertz (Hz)

Cycles per second; measure of frequency

Inattentional Blindness

Failure to notice something that is completely visible because of a lack of attention

Incus

Middle ear ossicle; also known as the *anvil*

Inflammatory Pain

Signal that some type of tissue damage has occurred

Interaural Level Difference

Sound coming from one side of the body is more intense at the closest ear because of the attenuation of the sound wave as it passes through the head

Interaural Timing Difference

Small difference in the time at which a given sound wave arrives at each ear

Iris

Colored portion of the eye

Just Noticeable Difference

Difference in stimuli required to detect a difference between the stimuli

Kinesthesia

Perception of the body's movement through space

Lens

Curved, transparent structure that provides additional focus for light entering the eye

Linear Perspective

Perceive depth in an image when two parallel lines seem to converge

Malleus

Middle ear ossicle; also known as the *hammer*

Meissner's Corpuscle

Touch receptor that responds to pressure and lower frequency vibrations

Ménière's Disease

Results in a degeneration of inner ear structures that can lead to hearing loss, tinnitus, vertigo, and an increase in pressure within the inner ear

Merkel's Disk

Touch receptor that responds to light touch

Monaural Cue

One-eared cue to localize sound

Monocular Cue

Cue that requires only one eye

Neuropathic Pain

Pain from damage to neurons of either the peripheral or central nervous system

Nociception

Sensory signal indicating potential harm and maybe pain

Olfactory Bulb

Bulb-like structure at the tip of the frontal lobe, where the olfactory nerves begin

Olfactory Receptor

Sensory cell for the olfactory system

Opponent-Process Theory of Color Perception

Color is coded in opponent pairs: black-white, yellow-blue, and red-green

Optic Chiasm

X-shaped structure that sits just below the brain's ventral surface; represents the merging of the optic nerves from the two eyes and the separation of information from the two sides of the visual field to the opposite side of the brain

Optic Nerve

Carries visual information from the retina to the brain

Pacinian Corpuscle

Touch receptor that detects transient pressure and higher frequency vibrations

Pattern Perception

Ability to discriminate among different figures and shapes

Peak

(Also, *crest*) highest point of a wave

Perception

Way that sensory information is interpreted and consciously experienced

Perceptual Hypothesis

Educated guess used to interpret sensory information

Pheromone

Chemical message sent by another individual

Photoreceptor

Light-detecting cell

Pinna

Visible part of the ear that protrudes from the head

Pitch

Perception of a sound's frequency

Place Theory of Pitch Perception

Different portions of the basilar membrane are sensitive to sounds of different frequencies

Proprioception

Perception of body position

Proximity

Things that are close to one another tend to be grouped together

Pupil

Small opening in the eye through which light passes

Retina

Light-sensitive lining of the eye

Rod

Specialized photoreceptor that works well in low light conditions

Ruffini Corpuscle

Touch receptor that detects stretch

Sensation

What happens when sensory information is detected by a sensory receptor

Sensorineural Hearing Loss

Failure to transmit neural signals from the cochlea to the brain

Sensory Adaptation

Not perceiving stimuli that remain relatively constant over prolonged periods of time

Signal Detection Theory

Change in stimulus detection as a function of current mental state

Similarity

Things that are alike tend to be grouped together

Stapes

Middle ear ossicle; also known as the *stirrup*

Subliminal Message

Message presented below the threshold of conscious awareness

Taste Bud

Grouping of taste receptor cells with hair-like extensions that protrude into the central pore of the taste bud

Temporal Theory of Pitch Perception

Sound's frequency is coded by the activity level of a sensory neuron

Thermoception

Temperature perception

Timbre

Sound's purity

Top-Down Processing

Interpretation of sensations is influenced by available knowledge, experiences, and thoughts

Transduction

Conversion from sensory stimulus energy to action potential

Trichromatic Theory of Color Perception

Color vision is mediated by the activity across the three groups of cones

Trough

Lowest point of a wave

Tympanic Membrane

Eardrum

Umami

Taste for monosodium glutamate

Vertigo

Spinning sensation

Vestibular Sense

Contributes to our ability to maintain balance and body posture

Visible Spectrum

Portion of the electromagnetic spectrum that we can see

Wavelength

Length of a wave from one peak to the next peak

Exercises

Review Questions

1. _____ refers to the minimum amount of stimulus energy required to be detected 50% of the time.

    a. Absolute threshold

    b. Difference threshold

    c. Just noticeable difference

    d. Transduction

2. Decreased sensitivity to an unchanging stimulus is known as _____.

    a. transduction

    b. difference threshold

    c. sensory adaptation

    d. inattentional blindness

3. _____ involves the conversion of sensory stimulus energy into neural impulses.

    a. Sensory adaptation

    b. Inattentional blindness

    c. Difference threshold

    d. Transduction

4. _____ occurs when sensory information is organized, interpreted, and consciously experienced.

    a. Sensation

    b. Perception

    c. Transduction

    d. Sensory adaptation

5. Which of the following correctly matches the pattern in our perception of color as we move from short wavelengths to long wavelengths?

    a. Red to orange to yellow

    b. Yellow to orange to red

    c. Yellow to red to orange

    d. Orange to yellow to red

6. The visible spectrum includes light that ranges from about _____.

    a. 400–700 nm

    b. 200–900 nm

    c. 20–20,000 Hz

    d. 10–20 dB

7. The electromagnetic spectrum includes _____.

    a. radio waves

    b. x-rays

    c. infrared light

    d. all of the above

8. The audible range for humans is _____.

    a. 380–740 Hz

    b. 10–20 dB

    c. less than 300 dB

    d. 20–20,000 Hz

9. The quality of a sound that is affected by frequency, amplitude, and timing of the sound wave is known as _____.

    a. pitch

    b. tone

    c. electromagnetic

    d. timbre

10. The _____ is a small indentation of the retina that contains cones.

    a. optic chiasm

    b. optic nerve

    c. fovea

    d. iris

11. _____ operate best under bright light conditions.

    a. Cones

    b. Rods

    c. Retinal ganglion cells

    d. Striate cortex

12. _____ depth cues require the use of both eyes.

    a. Monocular

    b. Binocular

    c. Linear perspective

    d. Accommodating

13. If you were to stare at a green dot for a relatively long period of time and then shift your gaze to a blank white screen, you would see a _____ negative afterimage.

    a. blue

    b. yellow

    c. black

    d. red

14. Hair cells located near the base of the basilar membrane respond best to _____ sounds.

    a. low-frequency

    b. high-frequency

    c. low-amplitude

    d. high-amplitude

15. The three ossicles of the middle ear are known as _____.

    a. malleus, incus, and stapes

    b. hammer, anvil, and stirrup

    c. pinna, cochlea, and utricle

    d. both a and b (malleus, incus, and stapes and hammer, anvil, and stirrup)

16. Hearing aids might be effective for treating _____.

    a. Ménière's disease

    b. sensorineural hearing loss

    c. conductive hearing loss

    d. interaural time differences

17. Cues that require two ears are referred to as _____ cues.

    a. monocular

    b. monaural

    c. binocular

    d. binaural

18. Chemical messages often sent between two members of a species to communicate something about reproductive status are called _____.

    a. hormones

    b. pheromones

    c. Merkel's disks

    d. Meissner's corpuscles

19. Which taste is associated with monosodium glutamate?

    a. Sweet

    b. Bitter

    c. Umami

    d. Sour

20. _____ serve as sensory receptors for temperature and pain stimuli.

    a. Free nerve endings

    b. Pacinian corpuscles

    c. Ruffini corpuscles

    d. Meissner's corpuscles

21. Which of the following is involved in maintaining balance and body posture?

    a. Auditory nerve

    b. Nociceptors

    c. Olfactory bulb

    d. Vestibular system

22. According to the principle of _____, objects that occur close to one another tend to be grouped together.

    a. similarity

    b. good continuation

    c. proximity

    d. closure

23. Our tendency to perceive things as complete objects rather than as a series of parts is known as the principle of _____.

    a. closure

    b. good continuation

    c. proximity

    d. similarity

24. According to the law of _____, we are more likely to perceive smoothly flowing lines rather than choppy or jagged lines.

    a. closure

    b. good continuation

    c. proximity

    d. similarity

25. The main point of focus in a visual display is known as the _____.

    a. closure

    b. perceptual set

    c. ground

    d. figure

Critical Thinking Questions

26. Not everything that is sensed is perceived. Do you think there could ever be a case where something could be perceived without being sensed?

27. Please generate a novel example of how just noticeable difference can change as a function of stimulus intensity.

28. Why do you think other species have such different ranges of sensitivity for both visual and auditory stimuli compared to humans?

29. Why do you think humans are especially sensitive to sounds with frequencies that fall in the middle portion of the audible range?

30. Compare the two theories of color perception. Are they completely different?

31. Color is not a physical property of our environment. What function (if any) do you think color vision serves?

32. Given what you've read about sound localization, from an evolutionary perspective, how does sound localization facilitate survival?

33. How can temporal and place theories both be used to explain our ability to perceive the pitch of sound waves with frequencies up to 4,000 Hz?

34. Many people experience nausea while traveling in a car, plane, or boat. How might you explain this as a function of sensory interaction?

35. If you heard someone say that they would do anything not to feel the pain associated with significant injury, how would you respond given what you've just read?

36. Do you think women experience pain differently than men? Why do you think this is?

37. The central tenet of Gestalt psychology is that the whole is different from the sum of its parts. What does this mean in the context of perception?

Learning

Chapter Introduction

The summer sun shines brightly on a deserted stretch of beach. Suddenly, a tiny grey head emerges from the sand, then another and another. Soon the beach is teeming with loggerhead sea turtle hatchlings (Figure 1). Although only minutes old, the hatchlings know exactly what to do. They continue toward the water, instinctively. Some are quickly snapped up by gulls circling overhead, and others become lunch for hungry ghost crabs that dart out of their holes. Despite these dangers, the hatchlings are driven to leave the safety of their nest and find the ocean.

Figure 1: Loggerhead sea turtle hatchlings are born knowing how to find the ocean and how to swim. Unlike the sea turtle, humans must learn how to swim (and surf).

Not far down this same beach, Ben and his son, Julian, paddle out into the ocean on surfboards. A wave approaches. Julian crouches on his board, then jumps up and rides the wave for a few seconds before losing his balance. He emerges from the water in time to watch his father ride the face of the wave.

Unlike baby sea turtles, which know how to find the ocean and swim with no help from their parents, we are not born knowing how to swim or surf. Yet we pride ourselves on our ability to learn. Have you ever asked yourself how it is that we learn? What processes are at work? This chapter focuses on the primary ways in which learning occurs.

Flash Forward

Ready to dig into the vocabulary? Get some practice with this Hawkes Verified Quizlet set (hawkes.biz/psych5q1)!

5.1 What Is Learning?

Birds build nests and migrate as winter approaches. Infants suckle at their mother's breast. Dogs shake water off wet fur. Salmon swim upstream to spawn, and spiders spin intricate webs. What do these seemingly unrelated behaviors have in common? They all are *unlearned* behaviors. Humans and animals have a number of unlearned behaviors that often start at birth.

✎ **On Your Own**

Look at the table below. Fill it in with your own examples of species and their unlearned behaviors.

Species	Unlearned Behavior
Birds	Build nests and migrate
Infants	Suckle at mother's breast
Dogs	Shake water off of fur
Salmon	Swim upstream
Spiders	Spin intricate webs

Both instincts and reflexes are innate behaviors that organisms are born with. **Reflexes** are a motor or neural reaction to a specific stimulus in the environment. They tend to be simpler than instincts, involve the activity of specific body parts and systems, and involve more primitive centers of the central nervous system (e.g., the spinal cord and the medulla). Examples include:

- The knee-jerk reflex

- The contraction of the pupil in bright light

In contrast, **instincts** are innate behaviors that are triggered by a broader range of events. They are more complex patterns of behavior, involve movement of the organism as a whole (e.g., sexual activity and migration), and involve higher brain centers. Examples include:

- The aging process

- The desire to survive

Both reflexes and instincts help an organism adapt to its environment and do not have to be learned. For example, every healthy human baby has a sucking reflex, present at birth. Babies are born knowing how to suck on a nipple, whether artificial (from a bottle) or human. Nobody teaches the baby to suck, just as no one teaches a sea turtle hatchling to move toward the ocean. Learning, like reflexes and instincts, allows an organism to adapt to its environment.

Group Activity

As a group, discuss why you feel humans and other species are born with instincts and reflexes? Other than the ability to adapt to one's environment, what other benefits come with unlearned behaviors?

But unlike instincts and reflexes, learned behaviors involve change and experience; **learning** is a relatively permanent change in behavior or knowledge that results from experience. In contrast to the innate behaviors discussed previously, learning involves acquiring knowledge and skills through experience. In our surfing scenario, Julian will have to spend much more time training with his surfboard before he learns how to ride like his father.

Any complex learning process involves a complex interaction of conscious and unconscious processes. Learning has traditionally been studied in terms of its simplest components—the associations our minds automatically make between events. Our minds have a natural tendency to connect events that occur closely together or in sequence. **Associative learning** occurs when an organism makes connections between stimuli or events that occur together in the environment. You will see that associative learning is central to all three basic learning processes discussed in this chapter.

Figure 2: Different types of learning can involve conscious or unconscious processes.

It is helpful to have a brief overview of each learning process above as you begin to explore how learning is understood from a psychological perspective.

In classical conditioning, also known as Pavlovian conditioning, organisms learn to associate events—or stimuli—that repeatedly happen together. We experience this process throughout our daily lives. For example, you might see a flash of lightning in the sky during a storm and then hear a loud boom of thunder. The sound of the thunder naturally makes you jump (loud noises have that effect by reflex). Because lightning reliably predicts the impending boom of thunder, you may associate the two and jump when you see lightning. Psychological researchers study this associative process by focusing on behaviors as they can be seen and measured. Researchers often ask if one stimulus triggers a reflex, can we train a different stimulus to trigger that same reflex?

✍ On Your Own

Select an option below that exemplifies classical conditioning.

☐ You flinch at the sight of a needle.

☐ You imitate your friend's fashion style.

☐ You shudder at a scary movie title.

In operant conditioning, organisms learn to associate events—a behavior and its consequence (**reinforcement** or punishment). A pleasant consequence encourages more of that behavior in the future, whereas a punishment deters the behavior. More specifically, **positive reinforcement** refers to giving the organism something in order to encourage behavior, while **positive punishment** refers to giving something to an organism in order to deter behavior. Let's consider the examples below:

Positive Reinforcement   You tell your dog, Leroy, to sit, and give him a treat when he does. After repeated experiences, Leroy begins to associate the act of sitting with receiving a treat. He learns that the consequence of sitting is that he gets a doggie biscuit (Figure 3).

Positive Punishment   You want Leroy to be in your yard when you aren't with him, so he receives a small shock when crossing the boundary of an invisible electric fence. If Leroy is punished when trying to exceed the fence, he becomes conditioned to avoid that behavior.

Figure 3: In operant conditioning, a response is associated with a consequence. This dog has learned that certain behaviors result in receiving a treat.

Observational learning extends the effective range of both classical and operant conditioning. In contrast to classical and operant conditioning, in which learning occurs only through direct experience, observational learning is the process of watching others and then imitating what they do. A lot of learning among humans and other animals comes from observational learning. To get an idea of the extra effective range that observational learning brings, consider Ben and his son Julian from the introduction. How might observation help Julian learn to surf, as opposed to learning by trial and error alone? By watching his father, he can imitate the moves that bring success and avoid the moves that lead to failure.

Reflection Questions

Can you think of something you have learned to do simply by watching someone else?

All of the approaches covered in this chapter are part of a particular tradition in psychology, called behaviorism, which we discuss in the next section. However, these approaches do not represent the entire study of learning. Separate traditions of learning have taken shape within different fields of psychology, such as memory and cognition, so you will find that other chapters will round out your understanding of the topic.

Over time these traditions tend to converge. For example, in this chapter you will see how cognition has come to play a larger role in behaviorism, whose more extreme adherents once insisted that behaviors are triggered by the environment with no intervening thought.

✎ On Your Own

Read the questions below and select the types of learning being described.

Sam learns that he loses video games for the day if he screams at his brother. This is an example of:

☐ Classical conditioning   ☐ Operant conditioning   ☐ Observational learning

Jonathan learns that dinner is always on the table at 6 p.m. and begins to feel hungry right around 5:50 p.m. This is an example of:

☐ Classical conditioning   ☐ Operant conditioning   ☐ Observational learning

When Michael plays with the toy gun, his younger brother Thomas immediately tries to imitate the behaviors. This is an example of:

☐ Classical conditioning   ☐ Operant conditioning   ☐ Observational learning

---

Summary

Instincts and reflexes are innate behaviors—they occur naturally and do not involve learning. In contrast, learning is a change in behavior or knowledge that results from experience. There are three main types of learning: classical conditioning, operant conditioning, and observational learning. Both classical and operant conditioning are forms of associative learning where associations are made between events that occur together. Observational learning is just as it sounds: learning by observing others.

5.2 Classical Conditioning

Does the name Ivan Pavlov ring a bell? Even if you are new to the study of psychology, chances are that you have heard of Pavlov and his famous dogs.

Pavlov (1849–1936), a Russian scientist, performed extensive research on dogs and is best known for his experiments in classical conditioning (Figure 1). As we discussed briefly in the previous section, **classical conditioning** is a process by which we learn to associate stimuli and, consequently, to anticipate events.

Pavlov's Work

In his studies with dogs, Pavlov surgically implanted tubes inside dogs' cheeks to collect saliva. He then measured the amount of saliva produced in response to various foods. Over time, Pavlov (1927) observed that the dogs began to salivate not only at the taste of food, but also at the sight of food, an empty food bowl, and even at the sound of the laboratory assistants' footsteps. He was able to train the dogs to salivate in response to stimuli that clearly had nothing to do with food, such as the sound of a metronome, a light, and a touch on the leg. Through his experiments, Pavlov realized that an organism has two types of responses to its environment:

1. unconditioned (unlearned) responses, or reflexes, and

2. conditioned (learned) responses.

In Pavlov's experiments, the dogs salivated each time meat powder was presented to them. The meat powder in this situation was an **unconditioned stimulus (UCS)**: a stimulus that elicits a reflexive response in an

> **Flash Forward**
>
> Ready to dig into the vocabulary? Get some practice with this Hawkes Verified Quizlet set (hawkes.biz/psych5q2)!

Ivan Pavlov

Figure 1: Ivan Pavlov's research on the digestive system of dogs unexpectedly led to his discovery of the learning process now known as classical conditioning.

organism. The dogs' salivation was an **unconditioned response (UCR)**: a natural (unlearned) reaction to a given stimulus. Before conditioning, think of the dogs' stimulus and response like this:

Meat powder (UCS)→Salivation (UCR)

In classical conditioning, a neutral stimulus is presented immediately before an unconditioned stimulus. Pavlov would sound a tone (like a metronome or buzzer) and then give the dogs the meat powder (Figure 2). The tone was the **neutral stimulus (NS)**, which is a stimulus that does not naturally elicit a response. Prior to conditioning, the dogs did not salivate when they just heard the tone.

Quite simply this pairing means:

Tone (NS) + Meat Powder (UCS)→Salivation (UCR)

When Pavlov paired the tone with the meat powder over and over again, the previously neutral stimulus (the tone) also began to elicit salivation from the dogs. Thus, the neutral stimulus became the **conditioned stimulus (CS)**, which is a stimulus that elicits a response after repeatedly being paired with an unconditioned stimulus. Eventually, the dogs began to salivate to the tone alone, just as they previously had salivated at the sound of the assistants' footsteps. The behavior caused by the conditioned stimulus is called the **conditioned response (CR)**. In the case of Pavlov's dogs, they had learned to associate the tone (CS) with being fed, and they began to salivate (CR) in anticipation of food.

Tone (CS)→Salivation (CR)

Before Conditioning

During Conditioning   **After Conditioning**

Figure 2: Before conditioning, an unconditioned stimulus (food) produces an unconditioned response (salivation), and a neutral stimulus (bell) does not produce a response. During conditioning, the unconditioned stimulus (food) is presented repeatedly just after the presentation of the neutral stimulus (bell). After conditioning, the neutral stimulus alone produces a conditioned response (salivation), thus becoming a conditioned stimulus.

Further Resources

Now that you have learned about the process of classical conditioning, do you think you can condition Pavlov's dog? Visit this website (hawkes.biz/pavlov) to play the game.

Further Resources

Check out this video of Dr. Brian Collin explaining classical conditioning. (hawkes.biz/classicalconditioning)

Real World Application of Classical Conditioning

How does classical conditioning work in the real world? Let's say you have a cat named Buck. Every time Buck hears the crack of a can, he comes down the steps to get his food.

✐ On Your Own

Read the options below and select the correct answer.

In the video example from the Further Resources, the sound of the can opening is which component of classical conditioning?

☐ Unconditioned Stimulus   ☐ Unconditioned Response

☐ Conditioned Stimulus   ☐ Conditioned Response

Which of the following would be the unconditioned response?

☐ Responding to the sound of the can   ☐ Responding to the smell of food

☐ The sound of the can   ☐ The smell of the cat food

Further Resources

Watch this video of Buck getting his food. (hawkes.biz/ conditioningapplication)

Let's say you use an electric can opener. Buck begins to associate the electric can opener with the food. If the electric can opener is stored in a cabinet, then Buck will begin to associate the squeak of the cabinet with the electric can opener, which is associated with food. Pairing a new neutral stimulus (cabinet noise) with the conditioned stimulus (sound of the can opener) is called **higher-order conditioning**, or **second-order conditioning**. This means you are using the conditioned stimulus of the can opener to condition another stimulus: the squeaky cabinet (Figure 3). It is hard to achieve anything above second-order conditioning. For example, if you ring a bell, open the cabinet, use the can opener, and then feed Buck, Buck will likely never get excited when hearing the bell alone.

Higher-Order / Second-Order Conditioning

Electric can opener	Food	Salivation
Conditioned stimulus (CS)	Unconditioned stimulus (UCS)	Unconditioned response (UCR)

Squeaky cabinet door	Electric can opener	Salivation
Second-order stimulus	Conditioned stimulus (CS)	Conditioned response (CR)

Squeaky cabinet door	Salivation
Second-order stimulus	Conditioned response (CR)

📷 **Figure 3:** In higher-order conditioning, an established conditioned stimulus is paired with a new neutral stimulus (the second-order stimulus) so that eventually the new stimulus also elicits the conditioned response, without the initial conditioned stimulus being presented.

Classical Conditioning at Stingray City

Kate and her husband Scott recently vacationed in the Cayman Islands and booked a boat tour to Stingray City, where they could feed and swim with the southern stingrays. The boat captain explained how the normally solitary stingrays have become accustomed to interacting with humans. About 40 years ago, fishermen began to clean fish and conch (unconditioned stimulus) at a particular sandbar near a barrier reef, and large numbers of stingrays would swim in to eat (unconditioned response) what the fishermen threw into the water; this continued for years. By the late 1980s, word of the large group of stingrays spread among scuba divers, who then started feeding them by hand. Over time, the southern stingrays in the area were classically conditioned much like Pavlov's dogs. When they hear the sound of a boat engine (neutral stimulus that becomes a conditioned stimulus), they know that they will get to eat (conditioned response).

As soon as Kate and Scott reached Stingray City, over two dozen stingrays surrounded their tour boat. The couple slipped into the water with bags of squid, the stingrays' favorite treat. The swarm of stingrays bumped and rubbed up against their legs like hungry cats (Figure 4). Kate and Scott were able to feed, pet, and even kiss (for luck) these amazing creatures. Then all the squid was gone and so were the stingrays.

🖼 **Figure 4:** Stingrays can be classically conditioned to associate the sound of a boat motor with food provided by tourists.

✏️ **On Your Own**

Classical conditioning also applies to humans, even babies. For example, Sara buys formula in blue canisters for her six-month-old daughter, Angelina. Whenever Sara takes out a formula container, Angelina gets excited, tries to reach toward the food, and most likely salivates. Why does Angelina get excited when she sees the formula canister? What are the UCS, CS, UCR, and CR here?

Term	Example
Unconditioned Stimulus	
Unconditioned Response	
Conditioned Stimulus	
Conditioned Response	

General Processes in Classical Conditioning

In classical conditioning, the initial period of learning is known as **acquisition**, an organism learns to connect a neutral stimulus and an unconditioned stimulus. During acquisition, the neutral stimulus becomes the conditioned stimulus. What happens when learning is not used for a while—when what was learned lies dormant? As we just discussed, Pavlov found that when he repeatedly presented the bell (conditioned stimulus) without the meat powder (unconditioned stimulus) extinction occurred; the dogs stopped salivating to the bell.

📷 **Figure 5:** This is the curve of acquisition, extinction, and spontaneous recovery. The rising curve shows the conditioned response quickly getting stronger through the repeated pairing of the conditioned stimulus and the unconditioned stimulus (acquisition). Then the curve decreases, which shows how the conditioned response weakens when only the conditioned stimulus is presented (extinction). After a break or pause from conditioning, the conditioned response reappears (spontaneous recovery).

Extinction is the decrease in the conditioned response when the unconditioned stimulus is no longer presented with the conditioned stimulus. However, after a couple of hours of resting from this extinction training, the dogs again began to salivate when Pavlov rang the bell. What do you think would happen with Buck's behavior if your electric can opener broke, and you did not use it for several months? When you finally got it fixed and started using it to open Buck's food again, Buck would remember the association between the can opener and his food—he would get excited and run to the kitchen when he heard the sound. The behavior of Pavlov's dogs and Buck illustrates a concept Pavlov called **spontaneous recovery**: the return of a previously extinguished conditioned response following a rest period (Figure 5).

🖉 On Your Own

Taste aversion is a type of conditioning in which an interval of several hours may pass between the conditioned stimulus (something ingested) and the unconditioned stimulus (nausea or illness). Here's how it works. Between classes, you and a friend grab a quick lunch from a food cart on campus. You share a dish of chicken curry and head off to your next class. A few hours later, you feel nauseous and become ill. Now you will not eat chicken curry, and even the smell of it will make you sick. Identify which of the following is the UCS, UCR, CS, and CR using this example.

Example	Term
Bacteria	
Getting sick	
Chicken curry	
Not eating chicken curry	

Acquisition and extinction involve the strengthening and weakening, respectively, of a learned association. Two other learning processes—stimulus discrimination and stimulus generalization—are involved in distinguishing which stimuli will trigger the learned association. When an organism learns to respond differently to various stimuli that are similar, it is called **stimulus discrimination**.

On the other hand, when an organism demonstrates the conditioned response to stimuli that are similar to the condition stimulus, it is called **stimulus generalization**. The more similar a stimulus is to the condition stimulus, the more likely the organism is to give the conditioned response.

Sometimes, classical conditioning can lead to habituation. **Habituation** occurs when we learn not to respond to a stimulus that is presented repeatedly without change. As the stimulus occurs over and over, we learn not to focus our attention on it.

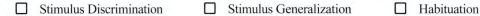

✐ On Your Own

Read the options below and select the correct answer.

Since the electric mixer sounds very similar to the can opening, Buck may come running after hearing its sound. This is an example of:

☐ Stimulus Discrimination   ☐ Stimulus Generalization   ☐ Habituation

Imagine that your neighbor or roommate constantly has the television blaring. This background noise is distracting and makes it difficult for you to focus when you're studying. However, over time, you become accustomed to the stimulus of the television noise, and eventually you hardly notice it any longer.

☐ Stimulus Discrimination   ☐ Stimulus Generalization   ☐ Habituation

🖼 **Figure 6:** John B. Watson used the principles of classical conditioning in the study of human emotion.

Behaviorism

John B. Watson, shown in Figure 6, is considered the founder of behaviorism. Behaviorism is a school of thought that arose during the first part of the 20th century, which incorporates elements of Pavlov's classical conditioning (Hunt, 2007). Watson championed the idea that all behavior can be studied as a simple stimulus-response reaction in terms of observable behavior, without regard for internal processes. According to Watson, human behavior, just like animal behavior, is primarily the result of conditioned responses.

Watson believed the same principles could be extended to the conditioning of human emotions (Watson, 1919). Thus began Watson's work with his graduate student Rosalie Rayner and a baby called Little Albert. Through their experiments with Little Albert, Watson and Rayner (1920) demonstrated how fears can be conditioned.

Through these experiments, Little Albert was exposed to and conditioned to fear certain things. Initially, he was presented with various neutral stimuli, including a rabbit, a dog, a monkey, masks, cotton wool, and a white rat. He was not afraid of any of these things. Then Watson, with the help of Rayner, conditioned Little Albert to associate these stimuli with an emotion—fear. For example, Watson handed Little Albert the white rat, and Little Albert enjoyed playing with it. Then Watson made a loud sound, by striking a hammer against a metal bar hanging behind Little Albert's head, each time Little Albert touched the rat. Little Albert was frightened by the sound—demonstrating a reflexive fear of sudden loud noises—and began to cry. Watson repeatedly paired the loud sound with the white rat. Soon, Little Albert became frightened by the white rat alone.

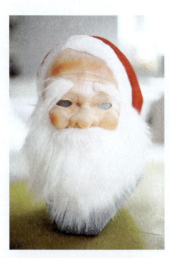

🖼 **Figure 7:** Through stimulus generalization, Little Albert came to fear furry things, including Watson in a Santa Claus mask.

Days later, Little Albert demonstrated stimulus generalization—he became afraid of other furry things: a rabbit, a furry coat, and even a Santa Claus mask (Figure 7). Watson had succeeded in conditioning a fear response in Little Albert, thus demonstrating that emotions could become conditioned responses. It had been Watson's intention to produce a phobia—a persistent, excessive fear of a specific object or situation—through conditioning alone.

☑ On Your Own

Identify which of the following are the UCS, UCR, CS, and CR in the table.

Term	Example
	Loud noise
	Fear
	Animals; Santa Claus mask
	Fear toward conditioned animals and Santa Claus

💡 Everyday Connection

Advertising and Associative Learning

Advertising executives are pros at applying the principles of associative learning. Think about the car commercials you have seen on television. Many of them feature an attractive model. By associating the model with the car being advertised, you come to see the car as being desirable (Cialdini, 2008). You may be asking yourself, does this advertising technique actually work? According to Cialdini (2008), men who viewed a car commercial that included an attractive model later rated the car as being faster, more appealing, and better designed than did men who viewed an advertisement for the same car minus the model.

Have you ever noticed how quickly advertisers cancel contracts with a famous athlete following a scandal? As far as the advertiser is concerned, that athlete is no longer associated with positive feelings; therefore, the athlete cannot be used as an unconditioned stimulus to condition the public to associate positive feelings (the unconditioned response) with their product (the conditioned stimulus).

Now that you are aware of how associative learning works, see if you can find examples of these types of advertisements on television, in magazines, or on the Internet.

Summary

Pavlov's pioneering work with dogs contributed greatly to what we know about learning. His experiments explored the type of associative learning we now call classical conditioning. In classical conditioning, organisms learn to associate events that repeatedly happen together. Pavlov's experiments show how stimulus-response bonds are formed. Watson, the founder of behaviorism, was greatly influenced by Pavlov's work. He tested humans by conditioning fear in an infant known as Little Albert. His findings suggest that classical conditioning can explain how some fears develop.

5.3 Operant Conditioning

Our last lesson focused on the type of associative learning known as classical conditioning. Remember that in classical conditioning, something in the environment triggers a reflex automatically, and researchers train the organism to react to a different stimulus.

Now we turn to the second type of associative learning, **operant conditioning**. In operant conditioning, organisms learn to associate a behavior and its consequence (Table 1). A pleasant consequence makes that behavior more likely to be repeated in the future. For example, Spirit, a dolphin at the National Aquarium in Baltimore, does a flip in the air when her trainer blows a whistle. The consequence is that she gets a fish.

	Classical Conditioning	Operant Conditioning
Conditioning approach	An unconditioned stimulus (such as food) is paired with a neutral stimulus (such as a bell). The neutral stimulus eventually becomes the conditioned stimulus, which brings about the conditioned response (salivation).	The target behavior is followed by reinforcement or punishment to either strengthens or weakens it so that the learner is more or less likely to exhibit the behavior in the future.
Stimulus timing	The stimulus occurs immediately before the response.	The stimulus (either reinforcement or punishment) occurs soon after the response.

Table 1: Classical and Operant Conditioning Compared

Psychologist B.F. Skinner saw that classical conditioning is limited to existing behaviors that are reflexively elicited, and it doesn't account for new behaviors, such as riding a bike. He proposed a theory about how such behaviors come about. Skinner believed that behavior is motivated by the consequences we receive for the behavior: the reinforcements and punishments. His idea that learning is the result of consequences is based on the **law of effect**, which was first proposed by psychologist Edward Thorndike.

Figure 1: Psychologist Edward Thorndike introduced the law of effect.

Law of Effect

Behaviors that are followed by consequences that are satisfying to the organism are more likely to be repeated.

- *If an organism does something that brings about a desired result, the organism is more likely to do it again.*

- *If an organism does something that does not bring about a desired result, the organism is less likely to do it again.*

An example of the law of effect is in employment. One of the reasons (and often the main reason) we show up for work is because we get paid to do so. If we stop getting paid, we will likely stop showing up—even if we love our job.

Reflection Questions

Edward Thorndike tested the law of effect by placing cats in puzzle boxes that had to be manipulated in order for the cat to escape. How do you think the cats' behaviors differed from the first time in the box, to the fifth, to the final trial?

Further Resources

Watch this brief video clip (hawkes.biz/ operantconditioning) to learn more about operant conditioning; Skinner is interviewed, and operant conditioning of pigeons is demonstrated.

Working with Thorndike's law of effect as his foundation, Skinner began conducting scientific experiments on animals (mainly rats and pigeons) to determine how organisms learn through operant conditioning (Skinner, 1938). He placed these animals inside an operant conditioning chamber, which has come to be known as a "Skinner box" (Figure 2). A Skinner box contains a lever (for rats) or disk (for pigeons) that the animal can press or peck for a food reward via the dispenser. Speakers and lights can be associated with certain behaviors. A recorder counts the number of responses made by the animal.

Figure 2: B.F. Skinner developed operant conditioning for the systematic study of how behaviors are strengthened or weakened according to their consequences. In a Skinner box, a rat presses a lever in an operant conditioning chamber to receive a food reward.

In discussing operant conditioning, we use several everyday words—*positive*, *negative*, *reinforcement*, and *punishment*—in a specialized manner. **In operant conditioning, positive and negative do not mean good and bad.**

Figure 3: It's important to grasp the specific vocabulary used in reference to operant conditioning.

Reinforcement can be positive or negative, and punishment can also be positive or negative. All reinforcers (positive or negative) *increase* the likelihood of a behavioral response. All punishers (positive or negative) *decrease* the likelihood of a behavioral response. Now let's combine these four terms: *positive reinforcement*, *negative reinforcement*, *positive punishment*, and *negative punishment* (Table 2).

	Reinforcement	Punishment
Positive	Something is *added* to *increase* the likelihood of a behavior.	Something is *added* to *decrease* the likelihood of a behavior.
Negative	Something is *removed* to *increase* the likelihood of a behavior.	Something is *removed* to *decrease* the likelihood of a behavior.

Table 2: Positive and Negative Reinforcement and Punishment

Reinforcement

The most effective way to teach a person or animal a new behavior is with positive reinforcement. In positive reinforcement, a desirable stimulus is added to increase a behavior.

Consider the examples below:

- Five-year-old Jerome gets a toy if he cleans his room.

- Janine gets paid $5 for each *A* she earns on her report card.

- Shakita gets praise and high fives when she completes her homework each night.

Let's pause for a moment. Some people might say, "Why should I reward my child for doing what is expected?" But in fact we are constantly and consistently rewarded in our lives.

Consider the examples of consistent rewards currently present in daily life:

- Paychecks

- High grades

- Acceptance into preferred schools

- Praise for a job well done

- Praise for passing a driver's test

Figure 4: Another common example of operant conditioning is teaching a dog to shake. When he gives you his paw in response to the command "shake," he is positively reinforced when the consequence of that behavior is a treat.

Positive reinforcement as a learning tool is extremely effective. It has been found that one of the most effective ways to increase achievement in school districts with below-average reading scores was to pay the children to read. Specifically, second-grade students in Dallas were paid $2 each time they read a book and passed a short quiz about the book. The result was a significant increase in reading comprehension (Fryer, 2010). If Skinner were alive today, he would probably think this was a great idea. He was a strong proponent of using operant conditioning principles to influence students' behavior at school. In fact, in addition to the Skinner box, he also invented what he called a teaching machine that was designed to reward small steps in learning (Skinner, 1961)—an early forerunner of computer-assisted learning. His teaching machine tested students' knowledge as they worked through various school subjects. If students answered questions correctly, they received immediate positive reinforcement and could continue; if they answered incorrectly, they did not receive any reinforcement. The idea was that students would spend additional time studying the material to increase their chance of being reinforced the next time (Skinner, 1961).

Reflection Questions

In 1998, a book about the Nurtured Heart approach hit shelves. Within the book, the authors described a method by which parents should notice each time their children acted in non-disruptive ways and to reward that behavior by commenting or actively seeing the child in those times of good (or neutral) behavior. What would Skinner think about this program?

In **negative reinforcement**, an undesirable stimulus is removed to increase a behavior. For example, car manufacturers use the principles of negative reinforcement in their seatbelt systems, which go "beep, beep, beep" until you fasten your seatbelt. The annoying sound stops when you exhibit the desired behavior, increasing the likelihood that you will buckle up in the future. Negative reinforcement is also used frequently in horse training. Riders apply pressure—by pulling the reins or squeezing their legs—and then remove the pressure when the horse performs the desired behavior, such as turning or speeding up. The pressure is the negative stimulus that the horse wants to remove.

☑ On Your Own

Provide examples of positive and negative reinforcement that you've experienced or used in your own life.

Positive Reinforcement	Negative Reinforcement

Punishment

Many people confuse negative reinforcement with punishment in operant conditioning, but they are two very different mechanisms. Remember that reinforcement, even when it is negative, always increases a behavior. In contrast, **punishment** always decreases a behavior. In positive punishment, you add an undesirable stimulus to decrease a behavior. An example of positive punishment is scolding a student to get the student to stop texting in class. In this case, a stimulus (the reprimand) is added in order to decrease the behavior (texting in class). In **negative punishment**, you remove an aversive stimulus to decrease behavior. For example, when a child misbehaves, a parent can take away a favorite toy. In this case, a stimulus (the toy) is removed in order to decrease the behavior.

Punishment, especially when it is immediate, is one way to decrease undesirable behavior. For example, imagine your four-year-old son, Brandon, hit his younger brother. You have Brandon write 100 times "I will not hit my brother" (positive punishment). Chances are he won't repeat this behavior. While strategies like this are common today, in the past children were often subject to physical punishment, such as spanking. It's important to be aware of some of the drawbacks in using physical punishment on children.

First, punishment may teach fear. Brandon may become fearful of hitting his brother, but he also may become fearful of the person who delivered the punishment—you, his parent. Similarly, children who are punished by teachers may come to fear the teacher and try to avoid school (Gershoff et al., 2010). Consequently, most schools in the United States have banned corporal punishment. Second, punishment may cause children to become more aggressive and prone to antisocial behavior and delinquency (Gershoff, 2002). They see their parents resort to spanking when they become angry and frustrated, so, in turn, they may act out this same behavior when they become angry and frustrated. For example, because you spank Brenda when you are angry with her for her misbehavior, she might start hitting her friends when they won't share their toys.

Figure 5: As a child, were you ever told to go stand facing a wall for timeout? This is a form of negative punishment many of us are all too familiar with.

Results of Spanking

Fear of stimulus that resulted in spanking

Fear of disciplinarian (i.e., parent/teacher)

Increased aggression

Increased antisocial behaviors

Figure 6: Make sure you are aware of some of the potential drawbacks related to spanking.

Further Resources

Watch this video clip (hawkes.biz/ punishmentvsreinforcement) to see how an episode of *The Big Bang Theory* explains the common confusion between negative reinforcement and positive punishment. Did they get anything wrong?

While positive punishment can be effective in some cases, Skinner suggested that the use of punishment should be weighed against the possible negative effects. Today's psychologists and parenting experts favor reinforcement over punishment—they recommend that you catch your child doing something good and reward her for it.

Shaping

In his operant conditioning experiments, Skinner often used an approach called shaping. Instead of rewarding only the target behavior, in **shaping**, we reward successive approximations of a target behavior. Why is shaping needed? Remember that in order for reinforcement to work, the organism must first display the behavior. Shaping is needed because it is extremely unlikely that an organism will display anything but the simplest of behaviors spontaneously. In shaping, behaviors are broken down into many small, achievable steps. The specific steps used in the process are the following:

1.   Reinforce any response that resembles the desired behavior.

2.   Then reinforce the response that more closely resembles the desired behavior. You will no longer reinforce the previously reinforced response.

3.   Next, begin to reinforce the response that even more closely resembles the desired behavior.

4.   Continue to reinforce closer and closer approximations of the desired behavior.

5.   Finally, only reinforce the desired behavior.

🖼 **Figure 7:** Two students can be seen conducting an experiment on pigeons using a Skinner box.

Shaping is often used in teaching a complex behavior or chain of behaviors. Skinner used shaping to teach pigeons not only relatively simple behaviors, such as pecking a disk in a Skinner box, but also many unusual and entertaining behaviors, such as turning in circles, walking in figure eights, and even playing ping pong; the technique is commonly used by animal trainers today. An important part of shaping is stimulus discrimination. Recall Pavlov's dogs—he trained them to respond to the tone of a bell and not to similar tones or sounds. This discrimination is also important in operant conditioning and in shaping behavior.

Group Activity

Brainstorm how you would use shaping to train a dog to fetch a newspaper from the curb and bring it back into the house.

Further Resources

Here is a brief video of (hawkes.biz/skinner) Skinner's pigeons playing ping pong.

Reflection Questions

How could shaping be applied to humans? For example, let's say you wanted to shape a child to clean his or her room? How would you do this?

Primary and Secondary Reinforcers

Rewards such as stickers, praise, money, toys, and more can be used to reinforce learning. Let's go back to Skinner's rats again. How did the rats learn to press the lever in the Skinner box? They were rewarded with food each time they pressed the lever. For animals, food would be an obvious reinforcer.

What would be a good reinforcer for humans? If you gave Joaquin, the soccer player, a piece of candy every time he made a goal, you would be using a **primary reinforcer**. Primary reinforcers are reinforcers that have innate reinforcing qualities. These kinds of reinforcers are not learned. Examples of primary reinforcers include the following:

> **Figure 8:** Primary reinforcers are innately reinforcing.

Organisms do not lose their drive for these primary reinforcers. For most people, jumping in a cool lake on a very hot day would be reinforcing, and the cool lake would be innately reinforcing—the water would cool the person off (a physical need), as well as provide pleasure.

A **secondary reinforcer** has no inherent value and only has reinforcing qualities when linked with a primary reinforcer. Praise, linked to affection, is one example of a secondary reinforcer, like when you call out "Great shot!" every time Joaquin makes a goal. Another example, money, is only worth something when you can use it to buy other things—either things that satisfy basic needs (food, water, shelter—all primary reinforcers) or other secondary reinforcers. If you were on a remote island in the middle of the Pacific Ocean and you had stacks of money, the money would not be useful if you could not spend it.

✏ On Your Own

In the past few weeks, what primary reinforcers have you purchased with money?

_____

_____

_____

_____

What about the stickers on the behavior chart? They also are secondary reinforcers. Sometimes, instead of stickers on a sticker chart, a token is used. Tokens, which are also secondary reinforcers, can then be traded in for rewards and prizes. Entire behavior management systems, known as token economies, are built around the use of these kinds of token reinforcers. Token economies have been found to be very effective at modifying behavior in a variety of settings such as schools, prisons, and mental hospitals. For example, a study by Cangi and Daly (2013) found that use of a token economy increased appropriate social behaviors and reduced inappropriate behaviors in a group of school children with autism. Some children with autism can exhibit disruptive behaviors, such as pinching and hitting. When the children in the study exhibited appropriate behavior (not hitting or pinching), they received a "quiet hands" token. When they hit or pinched, they lost a token. The children could then exchange specified amounts of tokens for minutes of playtime.

Group Activity

Brainstorm with a small group how you might employ a token economy to increase your level of studying for this class.

Behavior Modification in Children

Parents and teachers often use behavior modification to change a child's behavior. Behavior modification uses the principles of operant conditioning to accomplish behavior change so that undesirable behaviors are switched for more socially acceptable ones. Some teachers and parents create a sticker chart, in which several behaviors are listed (Figure 9). Sticker charts are a form of token economies, as described in the text. Each time children perform the behavior, they get a sticker, and after a certain number of stickers, they get a prize, or reinforcer. The goal is to increase acceptable behaviors and decrease misbehavior. Remember, it is best to reinforce desired behaviors, rather than to use punishment. In the classroom, the teacher can reinforce a wide range of behaviors, from students raising their hands, to walking quietly in the hall, to turning in their homework. At home, parents might create a behavior chart that rewards children for things such as putting away toys, brushing their teeth, and helping with dinner. In order for behavior modification to be effective, the reinforcement needs to be connected with the behavior; the reinforcement must matter to the child and be done consistently.

Time-out is another popular technique used in behavior modification with children. It operates on the principle of negative punishment. When a child demonstrates an undesirable behavior, she is removed from the desirable activity at hand (Figure 10). For example, say that Sophia and her brother Mario are playing with building blocks. Sophia throws some blocks at her brother, so you give her a warning that she will go to time-out if she does it again. A few minutes later, she throws more blocks at Mario. You remove Sophia from the room for a few minutes. When she comes back, she doesn't throw blocks.

There are several important points that you should know if you plan to implement time-out as a behavior modification technique. First, make sure the child is being removed from a desirable activity and placed in a less desirable location. If the activity is something undesirable for the child, this technique will backfire because it is more enjoyable for the child to be removed from the activity. Second, the length of the time-out is important. The general rule of thumb is one minute for each year of the child's age. Sophia is five; therefore, she sits in a time-out for five minutes. Setting a timer helps children know how long they have to sit in time-out. Finally, as a caregiver, keep several guidelines in mind over the course of a time-out: remain calm when directing your child to time-out; ignore your child during time-out (because caregiver attention may reinforce misbehavior); and give the child a hug or a kind word when time-out is over.

Figure 9: Sticker charts are a form of positive reinforcement and a tool for behavior modification. Once this little girl earns a certain number of stickers for demonstrating a desired behavior, she will be rewarded with a trip to the ice cream parlor.

(a) (b)

Figure 10: Time-out is a popular form of negative punishment used by caregivers. When a child misbehaves, he or she is removed from a desirable activity in an effort to decrease the unwanted behavior. For example, (a) a child might be playing on the playground with friends and push another child; (b) the child who misbehaved would then be removed from the activity for a short period of time.

Reinforcement Schedules

Remember, the best way to teach a person or animal a behavior is to use positive reinforcement. For example, Skinner used positive reinforcement to teach rats to press a lever in a Skinner box. At first, the rat might randomly hit the lever while exploring the box, and out would come a pellet of food. After eating the pellet, what do you think the hungry rat did next? It hit the lever again and received another pellet of food. Each time the rat hit the lever, a pellet of food came out. When an organism receives a reinforcer each time it displays a behavior, it is called **continuous reinforcement**. This reinforcement schedule is the quickest way to teach someone a behavior, and it is especially effective in training a new behavior. Let's look back at the dog that was learning to sit earlier in the chapter. Now, each time he sits, you give him a treat. Timing is important here: you will be most successful if you present the reinforcer immediately after he sits, so that he can make an association between the target behavior (sitting) and the consequence (getting a treat).

Once a behavior is trained, researchers and trainers often turn to another type of reinforcement schedule—partial reinforcement. In **partial reinforcement**, also referred to as intermittent reinforcement, the person or animal does not get reinforced every time they perform the desired behavior. There are several different types of partial reinforcement schedules (Table 3). These schedules are described as either fixed or variable and as either interval or ratio. *Fixed* refers to the number of responses between reinforcements, or the amount of time between reinforcements, which is set and unchanging. *Variable* refers to the number of responses or amount of time between reinforcements, which varies or changes. *Interval* means the schedule is based on the time between reinforcements, and *ratio* means the schedule is based on the number of responses between reinforcements.

Figure 11: Using continuous reinforcement is the best way to begin training your puppy to sit, but after the behavior is learned, you can switch to partial reinforcement.

Reinforcement Schedule	Description	Result	Example
Fixed interval	Reinforcement is delivered at predictable time intervals (e.g., every 15 minutes).	Moderate response rate with significant pauses after reinforcement	Hospital patient uses patient-controlled, doctor-timed pain relief
Variable interval	Reinforcement is delivered at unpredictable time intervals (e.g., after 5, then 7, then 10, then 3 minutes).	Moderate yet steady response rate	Checking Facebook
Fixed ratio	Reinforcement is delivered after a predictable number of responses (e.g., every 6 responses).	High response rate with pauses after reinforcement	Piecework factory worker getting paid for every *x* number of items manufactured
Variable ratio	Reinforcement is delivered after an unpredictable number of responses (e.g., after 1, 4, 5, and 9 responses).	High and steady response rate	Gambling

Table 3: Reinforcement Schedules

Now let's combine these four terms. A **fixed interval reinforcement schedule** is when behavior is rewarded after a set amount of time. For example, June undergoes major surgery in a hospital. During recovery, she is expected to experience pain and will require prescription medications for pain relief. June is given an IV drip with a patient-controlled painkiller. Her doctor sets a limit: one dose per hour. June pushes a button when pain becomes difficult, and she receives a dose of medication. Since the reward (pain relief) only occurs on a fixed interval, there is no point in exhibiting the behavior when it will not be rewarded.

✎ On Your Own

Which example best represents a fixed interval reinforcement schedule?

☐ Continuously putting coins in a slot machine

☐ Receiving a weekly paycheck

☐ Receiving a cookie for every five homework problems completed

☐ Pop quizzes in class

With a **variable interval reinforcement schedule**, the person or animal gets the reinforcement based on varying amounts of time, which are unpredictable. Say that Manuel is the manager at a fast-food restaurant. Every once in a while, someone from the quality control division comes to Manuel's restaurant. If the restaurant is clean and the service is fast, everyone on that shift earns a $20 bonus. Manuel never knows when the quality control person will show up, so he always tries to keep the restaurant clean and ensures that his employees provide prompt and courteous service. His productivity regarding prompt service and keeping a clean restaurant are steady because he wants his crew to earn the bonus.

✎ On Your Own

Which example best represents a variable interval reinforcement schedule?

☐ When running a marathon, there is a drink station every mile.

☐ You get paid for each square foot of tile you lay in the kitchen.

☐ You keep checking your email for an important message.

☐ You receive bonuses for sales, but the required number of sales changes weekly.

With a **fixed ratio reinforcement schedule**, there are a set number of responses that must occur before the behavior is rewarded. Carla sells glasses at an eyeglass store, and she earns a commission every time she sells a pair of glasses. She always tries to sell people more pairs of glasses, including prescription sunglasses or a backup pair, so she can increase her commission. She does not care if the person really needs the prescription sunglasses; Carla just wants her bonus. The quality of what Carla sells does not matter because her commission is not based on quality; it's only based on the number of pairs sold. This distinction in the quality of performance can help determine which reinforcement method is most appropriate for a particular situation. Fixed ratios are better suited to optimize the quantity of output, whereas a fixed interval, in which the reward is not quantity based, can lead to a higher quality of output.

✎ On Your Own

Which example best represents a fixed ratio reinforcement schedule?

☐ A regular six-month dental check-up

☐ A door-to-door salesman

☐ Mom sends a "check-in" text every day but at random times throughout the day

☐ Receiving a dollar each time you pass out 20 flyers

In a **variable ratio reinforcement schedule**, the number of responses needed for a reward varies. This is the most powerful partial reinforcement schedule. An example of the variable ratio reinforcement schedule is gambling. Imagine that Sarah—generally a smart, thrifty woman—visits Las Vegas for the first time. She is not a gambler, but out of curiosity, she puts a quarter into the slot machine and then another and another. Nothing happens. Two dollars in quarters later, her curiosity is fading, and she is just about to quit. But then, the machine lights up, bells go off, and Sarah gets 50 quarters back. That's more like it! Sarah gets back to inserting quarters with renewed interest, and a few minutes later she has used up all her gains and is $10 in the hole. Now might be a sensible time to quit. And yet, she keeps putting money into the slot machine because she never knows when the next reinforcement is coming. She keeps thinking that with the next quarter she could win $50, $100, or even more. Because the reinforcement schedule in most types of gambling has a variable ratio schedule, people keep trying and hoping that the next time they will win big. This is one of the reasons that gambling is so addictive—and so resistant to extinction.

Figure 12: The excitement of winning and the unpredictability of reinforcement during gambling is often enough to keep players going during a losing streak.

✎ On Your Own

Which example best represents a variable ratio reinforcement schedule?

- ☐ Your weekly Thursday night phone conversation with your mom
- ☐ Asking random people at the mall to complete a survey
- ☐ Getting a free ice cream after six previous purchases
- ☐ Setting the kitchen timer for 10 minutes to bake the cookies

---

In operant conditioning, extinction of a reinforced behavior occurs at some point after reinforcement stops, and the speed at which this happens depends on the reinforcement schedule. In a variable ratio schedule, the point of extinction comes very slowly, as described above. But in the other reinforcement schedules, extinction may come quickly. For example, if June presses the button for the pain relief medication before the allotted time her doctor has approved, no medication is administered. She is on a fixed interval reinforcement schedule (dosed hourly), so extinction occurs quickly when reinforcement doesn't come at the expected time. Among the reinforcement schedules, variable ratio is the most productive and the most resistant to extinction. Fixed interval is the least productive and the easiest to extinguish (Figure 13).

Figure 13: The four reinforcement schedules yield different response patterns. The variable ratio schedule is unpredictable and yields high and steady response rates, with little if any pause after reinforcement (e.g., gambler). A fixed ratio schedule is predictable and produces a high response rate, with a short pause after reinforcement (e.g., eyeglass saleswoman). The variable interval schedule is unpredictable and produces a moderate, steady response rate (e.g., restaurant manager). The fixed interval schedule yields a scallop-shaped response pattern, reflecting a significant pause after reinforcement (e.g., surgery patient).

⊘ Connect the Concepts

Gambling and the Brain

Skinner (1953) stated, "If the gambling establishment cannot persuade a patron to turn over money with no return, it may achieve the same effect by returning part of the patron's money on a variable-ratio schedule" (p. 397).

Skinner uses gambling as an example of the power and effectiveness of conditioning behavior based on a variable ratio reinforcement schedule. In fact, Skinner was so confident in his knowledge of gambling addiction that he even claimed he could turn a pigeon into a pathological gambler ("Skinner's Utopia," 1971). Beyond the power of variable ratio reinforcement, gambling seems to work on the brain in the same way as some addictive drugs. The Illinois Institute for Addiction Recovery (n.d.) reports evidence suggesting that pathological gambling is an addiction similar to a chemical addiction (Figure 14). Specifically, gambling may activate the reward centers of the brain, much like cocaine does. Research has shown that some pathological gamblers have lower levels of the neurotransmitter (brain chemical) known as norepinephrine than do normal gamblers (Roy, et al., 1988). According to a study conducted by Alec Roy and colleagues, norepinephrine is secreted when a person feels stress, arousal, or thrill; pathological gamblers use gambling to increase their levels of this neurotransmitter. Another researcher, neuroscientist Hans Breiter, has done extensive research on gambling and its effects on the brain. Breiter (as cited in Franzen, 2001) reports that "monetary reward in a gambling-like experiment produces brain activation very similar to that observed in a cocaine addict receiving an infusion of cocaine" (para. 1). Deficiencies in serotonin (another neurotransmitter) might also contribute to compulsive behavior, including a gambling addiction.

It may be that pathological gamblers' brains are different than those of other people, and perhaps this difference may somehow have led to their gambling addiction, as these studies seem to suggest. However, it is very difficult to ascertain the cause because it is impossible to conduct a true experiment (it would be unethical to try to turn randomly assigned participants into problem gamblers). Therefore, it may be that causation actually moves in the opposite direction—perhaps the act of gambling somehow changes neurotransmitter levels in some gamblers' brains. It also is possible that some overlooked factor, or confounding variable, played a role in both the gambling addiction and the differences in brain chemistry.

🖼 **Figure 14:** Some research suggests that pathological gamblers use gambling to compensate for abnormally low levels of the hormone norepinephrine, which is associated with stress and is secreted in moments of arousal and thrill.

Cognition and Latent Learning

Although strict behaviorists such as Skinner and Watson refused to believe that cognition (such as thoughts and expectations) plays a role in learning, another behaviorist, Edward C. Tolman, had a different opinion. Tolman's experiments with rats demonstrated that organisms can learn even if they do not receive immediate reinforcement (Tolman & Honzik, 1930; Tolman, Ritchie, & Kalish, 1946). This finding was in conflict with the prevailing idea at the time that reinforcement must be immediate in order for learning to occur, thus suggesting a cognitive aspect to learning.

In the experiments, Tolman placed hungry rats in a maze with no reward for finding their way through it. He also studied a comparison group that was rewarded with food at the end of the maze. As the unreinforced rats explored the maze, they developed a **cognitive map**: a mental picture of the layout of the maze (Figure 15). After 10 sessions in the maze without reinforcement, food was placed in a goal box at the end of the maze. As soon as the rats became aware of the food, they were able to find their way through the maze quickly, just as quickly as the comparison group, which had been rewarded with food all along. This phenomenon is known as **latent learning**: learning that occurs but is not observable in behavior until there is a reason to demonstrate it.

Figure 15: Psychologist Edward Tolman found that rats use cognitive maps to navigate through a maze. Have you ever worked your way through various levels on a video game? You learned when to turn left or right, move up or down. In that case, you were relying on a cognitive map, just like the rats in a maze.

Latent learning also occurs in humans. Children may learn by watching the actions of their parents but only demonstrate it at a later date, when the learned material is needed. For example, suppose that Ravi's dad drives him to school every day. In this way, Ravi learns the route from his house to his school, but he's never driven there himself, so he has not had a chance to demonstrate that he's learned the way. One morning, Ravi's dad has to leave early for a meeting, so he can't drive Ravi to school. Instead, Ravi follows the same route on his bike that his dad would have taken in the car. This demonstrates latent learning. Ravi had learned the route to school but had no need to demonstrate this knowledge earlier.

💡 Everyday Connection

This Place Is Like a Maze

Have you ever gotten lost in a building and couldn't find your way back out? While that can be frustrating, you're not alone. At one time or another, we've all gotten lost in places like museums, hospitals, or university libraries. Whenever we go someplace new, we build a mental representation—or cognitive map—of the location, as Tolman's rats built a cognitive map of their maze. However, some buildings are confusing because they include many areas that look alike or have short lines of sight. Because of this, it's often difficult to predict what's around a corner or decide whether to turn left or right to get out of a building. Psychologist Laura Carlson (2010) suggests that what we place in our cognitive map can impact our success in navigating through the environment. She suggests that paying attention to specific features upon entering a building, such as a picture on the wall, a fountain, a statue, or an escalator, adds information to our cognitive map that can be used later to help find our way out of the building.

Further Resources

Watch this video (hawkes. biz/carlson) to learn more about Carlson's studies on cognitive maps and navigation in buildings.

Summary

Operant conditioning is based on the work of B.F. Skinner. Operant conditioning is a form of learning in which the motivation for a behavior happens *after* the behavior is demonstrated. An animal or a human receives a consequence after performing a specific behavior. The consequence is either a reinforcer or a punisher. All reinforcement (positive or negative) *increases* the likelihood of a behavioral response. All punishment (positive or negative) *decreases* the likelihood of a behavioral response. Several types of reinforcement schedules are used to reward behavior depending on either a set or variable period of time.

Flash Forward

Ready to dig into the vocabulary? Get some practice with this Hawkes Verified Quizlet set (hawkes.biz/psych5q4)!

5.4 Observational Learning (Modeling)

Previous sections of this chapter focused on classical and operant conditioning, which are forms of associative learning. In **observational learning**, we learn by watching others and then imitating, or modeling, what they do or say. The individuals performing the imitated behavior are called **models**. Research suggests that this imitative learning involves a specific type of neuron, called a mirror neuron (Hickock, 2010; Rizzolatti, Fadiga, Fogassi, & Gallese, 2002; Rizzolatti, Fogassi, & Gallese, 2006).

Humans and other animals are capable of observational learning. As you will see, the phrase "monkey see, monkey do" really is accurate (Figure 1). The same could be said about other animals. For example, in a study of social learning in chimpanzees, researchers gave juice boxes with straws to two groups of captive chimpanzees. The first group dipped the straw into the juice box, and then sucked on the small amount of juice at the end of the straw. The second group sucked through the straw directly, getting much more juice. When the first group, the "dippers," observed the second group, "the suckers," what do you think happened? All of the "dippers" in the first group switched to sucking through the straws directly. By simply observing the other chimps and modeling their behavior, they learned that this was a more efficient method of getting juice (Yamamoto, Humle, and Tanaka, 2013).

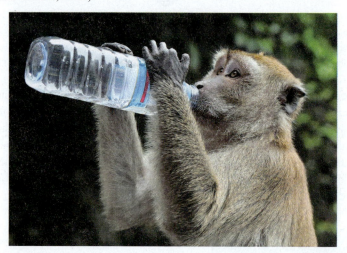

📷 **Figure 1:** This monkey learned to drink water from a plastic bottle by seeing the behavior modeled by a human.

Imitation is much more obvious in humans, but is imitation really the sincerest form of flattery? Consider Claire's experience with observational learning. Claire's nine-year-old son, Jay, was getting into trouble at school and was defiant at home. Claire feared that Jay would end up like her brothers, two of whom were in prison. One day, after yet another bad day at school and another negative note from the teacher, Claire, at her wit's end, spanked her son to get him to behave. Later that night, as she put her children to bed, Claire witnessed her four-year-old daughter, Anna, spanking her teddy bear. Claire was shocked, realizing that Anna was imitating her mother. It was then that Claire knew she wanted to discipline her children in a different manner.

Further Resources

For more information, watch this video (hawkes.biz/observationallearning) of Dr. Brian Collin summarizing Albert Bandura's study on observational learning.

Like Tolman, whose experiments with rats suggested a cognitive component to learning, psychologist Albert Bandura's ideas about learning were different from those of strict behaviorists. Bandura and other researchers proposed a brand of behaviorism called social learning theory, which took cognitive processes into account. According to Bandura, pure behaviorism could not explain why learning can take place in the absence of external reinforcement. He felt that internal mental states must also have a role in learning and that observational learning involves much more than imitation. In imitation, a person simply copies what the model does. Observational learning is much more complex. According to Lefrançois (2012) there are a couple ways that observational learning can occur:

- You learn a new response.

    - After watching your coworker get chewed out by your boss for coming in late, you start leaving home 10 minutes earlier so that you won't be late.

- You choose whether or not to imitate the model depending on what you saw happen to the model.

  - When learning to surf, Julian might watch how his father pops up successfully on his surfboard and then attempt to do the same thing.

  - Julian might learn not to touch a hot stove after watching his father get burned on a stove.

✎ On Your Own

Record three examples of observational learning in the space below.

	Example
1	
2	
3	

Bandura identified three kinds of models: live, verbal, and symbolic. A live model demonstrates a behavior in person, as when Ben stood up on his surfboard so that Julian could see how he did it. A verbal instructional model does not perform the behavior but instead explains or describes the behavior, as when a soccer coach tells his young players to kick the ball with the side of the foot, not with the toe. A symbolic model can be fictional characters or real people who demonstrate behaviors in books, movies, television shows, video games, or Internet sources (Figure 2).

(a)   (b)

🖼 **Figure 2:** (a) Yoga students learn by observation as their yoga instructor demonstrates the correct stance and movement for her students (live model). (b) Models don't have to be present for learning to occur: through symbolic modeling, this child can learn a behavior by watching someone demonstrate it on television.

Steps in the Modeling Process

Bandura argued that in order to learn the behavior you need to pay attention to the model, remember what the model did, and be motivated to copy the model.

Simply put, he felt the following steps were necessary:

1. Attention

2. Retention

3. Reproduction

4. Motivation

Figure 3: Young children will often imitate their mothers and play with makeup.

If you saw that the model was reinforced for her behavior, you will be more motivated to copy her. This is known as **vicarious reinforcement**. On the other hand, if you observed the model being punished, you would be less motivated to copy her. This is called **vicarious punishment**.

✒ On Your Own

Four-year-old Allison watched her older sister Kaitlyn playing in their mother's makeup and then saw Kaitlyn get a time-out when their mother came in. Now, Allison is less likely to play with her mother's makeup in the future. This is an example of what:

☐ Vicarious Punishment   ☐ Vicarious Reinforcement   ☐ Classical Conditioning

---

Further Resources

Watch this video clip (hawkes. biz/bandura) to see a portion of the famous Bobo doll experiment, including an interview with Albert Bandura.

Bandura researched modeling behavior, particularly children's modeling of adults' aggressive and violent behaviors (Bandura, Ross, & Ross, 1961). He conducted an experiment with a five-foot inflatable doll that he called a Bobo doll. In the experiment, children's aggressive behavior was influenced by whether the teacher was punished for her behavior. In one scenario, a teacher acted aggressively with the doll, hitting, throwing, and even punching the doll while a child watched. There were two types of responses by the children to the teacher's behavior. When the teacher was punished for her bad behavior, the children decreased their tendency to act as she had. When the teacher was praised or ignored (and not punished for her behavior), the children imitated what she did, and even what she said. They punched, kicked, and yelled at the doll.

Bandura concluded that we watch and learn, and that this learning can have both prosocial and antisocial effects. Prosocial (positive) models can be used to encourage socially acceptable behavior. Children observe and learn from their parents, even their parents' behaviors. If you want your children to read, then read to them. Let them see you reading. Keep books in your home. Talk about your favorite books. If you want your children to be healthy, then let them see you eat right and exercise, and spend time engaging in physical fitness activities together. The same holds true for qualities like kindness, courtesy, and honesty.

Reflection Questions

Who has been a prosocial model in your life? What kinds of behaviors did they model for you?

The antisocial effects of observational learning are also worth mentioning. As you saw from the example of Claire at the beginning of this section, her daughter viewed Claire's aggressive behavior and copied it. Research suggests that this may help to explain why abused children often grow up to be abusers themselves (Murrell, Christoff, & Henning, 2007). In fact, about 30% of abused children become abusive parents (U.S. Department of Health & Human Services, 2013). We tend to do what we know. Abused children, who grow up witnessing their parents deal with anger and frustration through violent and aggressive acts, often learn to behave in that manner themselves. Sadly, it's a vicious cycle that's difficult to break.

Some studies suggest that violent television shows, movies, and video games may also have antisocial effects although further research needs to be done to understand the correlational and causational aspects of media violence and behavior. This is a highly complicated area of research, and there are many variables that come into play. Some studies have found a link between viewing violence and aggression seen in children (Anderson & Gentile, 2008; Kirsch, 2010; Miller, Grabell, Thomas, Bermann, & Graham-Bermann, 2012). These findings may not be surprising, given that a child graduating from high school has been exposed to around 200,000 violent acts including murder, robbery, torture, bombings, beatings, and rape through various forms of media (Huston et al., 1992). Not only might viewing media violence affect aggressive behavior by teaching people to act that way in real life situations, but it has also been suggested that repeated exposure to violent acts also desensitizes people to it. Psychologists are working to understand this dynamic.

Figure 4: Researchers are working to better understand the dynamic between viewing violence and participating in it.

Further Resources

Check out this 2019 study (hawkes.biz/violenceexposure) that found that violent video games were not associated with aggressive adolescent behavior.

Summary

According to Bandura, learning can occur by watching others and then modeling what they do or say. This is known as observational learning. There are specific steps in the process of modeling that must be followed if learning is to be successful. These steps include attention, retention, reproduction, and motivation. Through modeling, Bandura has shown that children learn many things both good and bad simply by watching their parents, siblings, and others.

🔖 Chapter 5 Project

Purpose

Learning theories help to explain many things in the life of a student, from dating behaviors, to studying behaviors, to test anxiety, to confidence in sports and activities, to learning better study habits just by watching other peers.

The purpose of this project is to master learning theories by applying them to the student experience.

This will be done in two ways:

1. **Application** – Many students can understand textbook or online examples of different types of learning, but have difficulty applying that knowledge to multiple contexts. An ability to apply displays better learning.

2. **Integration** – The three learning theories are often not mutually exclusive in real-world experiences. An ability to integrate them displays better learning.

Directions

On your own or with a partner, you will design four integrated, applied learning scenarios that are college-student-specific, and which explain a variety of behaviors and thought processes. Here are the step by step directions. For each of the four scenarios:

1. Provide a brief narrative of the integrated learning scenario (as it relates to the life of a typical college student). For example, "Jenny went to class…" or "Drake is having a problem with his friend…" This single narrative should include Classical Conditioning, one specific type of Operant Conditioning, and Observational Learning.

2. Explain how this narrative scenario includes **Classical Conditioning** by identifying the following:

   • Unconditioned Stimulus

   • Unconditioned Response

   • Conditioned Stimulus

   • Conditioned Response

3. Explain how this narrative scenario includes **Operant Conditioning** by identifying the following:

   • The Target Behavior

   • The Consequence

   • Whether it is Positive Reinforcement, Negative Reinforcement, Positive Punishment, or Negative Punishment

Please note: Each of your four examples should use a different type of Operant Conditioning, so that you can display a clear understanding of each one.

4. Explain how this narrative scenario includes **Observational Learning** by identifying the following:

   • The Model

   • What Was Learned

   • The Motivation (see Bandura's "Steps in the Modeling Process" in Lesson 5.4)

Finally, based on what was has been learned through this assignment, each group member should submit a 300-word reflection that addresses the following:

5. The role that these three theories of learning have played in your current experiences as a college student. These should be related specifically to success or failure in college.

6. Two learning-based changes which, if implemented, could increase your success as a college student.

Please note: Individual reflections should illustrate knowledge of Classical Conditioning, Operant Conditioning, and Observational Learning.

Materials

None required.

✓ Checklist

Scenario 1

- ☐ Narrative; includes all three types of learning
- ☐ Explain how it shows Classical Conditioning
- ☐ Identify US, UR, CS, & CR
- ☐ Explain how it shows Operant Conditioning
- ☐ Identify Target Behavior, Consequence, Type of Operant Conditioning
- ☐ Explain how it shows Observational Learning
- ☐ Identify Model, Learned Behavior, Motivation

Scenario 2

- ☐ Narrative; includes all three types of learning
- ☐ Explain how it shows Classical Conditioning
- ☐ Identify US, UR, CS, & CR
- ☐ Explain how it shows Operant Conditioning
- ☐ Identify Target Behavior, Consequence, Type of Operant Conditioning
- ☐ Explain how it shows Observational Learning
- ☐ Identify Model, Learned Behavior, Motivation

Scenario 3

- ☐ Narrative; includes all three types of learning
- ☐ Explain how it shows Classical Conditioning
- ☐ Identify US, UR, CS, & CR
- ☐ Explain how it shows Operant Conditioning
- ☐ Identify Target Behavior, Consequence, Type of Operant Conditioning
- ☐ Explain how it shows Observational Learning
- ☐ Identify Model, Learned Behavior, Motivation

Scenario 4

- ☐ Narrative; includes all three types of learning
- ☐ Explain how it shows Classical Conditioning
- ☐ Identify US, UR, CS, & CR
- ☐ Explain how it shows Operant Conditioning
- ☐ Identify Target Behavior, Consequence, Type of Operant Conditioning
- ☐ Explain how it shows Observational Learning
- ☐ Identify Model, Learned Behavior, Motivation

Individual Reflection (min. 300 words)

- ☐ Role each of the three types of learning have played in your success or failure in college life
- ☐ Two learning-based changes that could contribute to your success in college

Chapter 5 Review

Lesson Summaries

5.1 What Is Learning?

Instincts and reflexes are innate behaviors—they occur naturally and do not involve learning. In contrast, learning is a change in behavior or knowledge that results from experience. There are three main types of learning: classical conditioning, operant conditioning, and observational learning. Both classical and operant conditioning are forms of associative learning where associations are made between events that occur together. Observational learning is just as it sounds: learning by observing others.

5.2 Classical Conditioning

Pavlov's pioneering work with dogs contributed greatly to what we know about learning. His experiments explored the type of associative learning we now call classical conditioning. In classical conditioning, organisms learn to associate events that repeatedly happen together. Pavlov's experiments show how stimulus-response bonds are formed. Watson, the founder of behaviorism, was greatly influenced by Pavlov's work. He tested humans by conditioning fear in an infant known as Little Albert. His findings suggest that classical conditioning can explain how some fears develop.

5.3 Operant Conditioning

Operant conditioning is based on the work of B.F. Skinner. Operant conditioning is a form of learning in which the motivation for a behavior happens *after* the behavior is demonstrated. An animal or a human receives a consequence after performing a specific behavior. The consequence is either a reinforcer or a punisher. All reinforcement (positive or negative) *increases* the likelihood of a behavioral response. All punishment (positive or negative) *decreases* the likelihood of a behavioral response. Several types of reinforcement schedules are used to reward behavior depending on either a set or variable period of time.

5.4 Observational Learning (Modeling)

According to Bandura, learning can occur by watching others and then modeling what they do or say. This is known as observational learning. There are specific steps in the process of modeling that must be followed if learning is to be successful. These steps include attention, retention, reproduction, and motivation. Through modeling, Bandura has shown that children learn many things both good and bad simply by watching their parents, siblings, and others.

Key Terms

Flash Back

Now that you've worked through the chapter, sharpen your vocabulary with this Hawkes Verified Quizlet set (hawkes.biz/psychch5)!

Acquisition

Period of initial learning in classical conditioning in which a human or an animal begins to connect a neutral stimulus and an unconditioned stimulus so that the neutral stimulus will begin to elicit the conditioned response

Associative Learning

Form of learning that involves connecting certain stimuli or events that occur together in the environment (classical and operant conditioning)

Classical Conditioning

Learning in which the stimulus or experience occurs before the behavior and then gets paired or associated with the behavior

Cognitive Map

Mental picture of the layout of the environment

Conditioned Response (CR)

Response caused by the conditioned stimulus

Conditioned Stimulus (CS)

Stimulus that elicits a response due to its being paired with an unconditioned stimulus

Continuous Reinforcement

Rewarding a behavior every time it occurs

Extinction

Decrease in the conditioned response when the unconditioned stimulus is no longer paired with the conditioned stimulus

Fixed Interval Reinforcement Schedule

Behavior is rewarded after a set amount of time

Fixed Ratio Reinforcement Schedule

Set number of responses must occur before a behavior is rewarded

Habituation

When we learn not to respond to a stimulus that is presented repeatedly without change

Higher-Order Conditioning

(Also, *second-order conditioning*) using a conditioned stimulus to condition a neutral stimulus

Instinct

Unlearned knowledge, involving complex patterns of behavior; instincts are thought to be more prevalent in lower animals than in humans

Latent Learning

Learning that occurs, but it may not be evident until there is a reason to demonstrate it

Law of Effect

Behavior that is followed by consequences satisfying to the organism will be repeated and behaviors that are followed by unpleasant consequences will be discouraged

Learning

Change in behavior or knowledge that is the result of experience

Model

Person who performs a behavior that serves as an example (in observational learning)

Negative Punishment

Taking away a pleasant stimulus to decrease or stop a behavior

Negative Reinforcement

Taking away an undesirable stimulus to increase a behavior

Neutral Stimulus (NS)

Stimulus that does not initially elicit a response

Observational Learning

Type of learning that occurs by watching others

Operant Conditioning

Form of learning in which the stimulus/experience happens after the behavior is demonstrated

Partial Reinforcement

Rewarding behavior only some of the time

Positive Punishment

Adding an undesirable stimulus to stop or decrease a behavior

Positive Reinforcement

Adding a desirable stimulus to increase a behavior

Primary Reinforcer

Has innate reinforcing qualities (e.g., food, water, shelter, sex)

Punishment

Implementation of a consequence in order to decrease a behavior

Reflex

Unlearned, automatic response by an organism to a stimulus in the environment

Reinforcement

Implementation of a consequence in order to increase a behavior

Secondary Reinforcer

Has no inherent value unto itself and only has reinforcing qualities when linked with something else (e.g., money, gold stars, poker chips)

Shaping

Rewarding successive approximations toward a target behavior

Spontaneous Recovery

Return of a previously extinguished conditioned response

Stimulus Discrimination

Ability to respond differently to similar stimuli

Stimulus Generalization

Demonstrating the conditioned response to stimuli that are similar to the conditioned stimulus

Unconditioned Response (UCR)

Natural (unlearned) behavior to a given stimulus

Unconditioned Stimulus (UCS)

Stimulus that elicits a reflexive response

Variable Interval Reinforcement Schedule

Behavior is rewarded after unpredictable amounts of time have passed

Variable Ratio Reinforcement Schedule

Number of responses differ before a behavior is rewarded

Vicarious Punishment

Process where the observer sees the model punished, making the observer less likely to imitate the model's behavior

Vicarious Reinforcement

Process where the observer sees the model rewarded, making the observer more likely to imitate the model's behavior

☀ Exercises

Review Questions

1. Which of the following is an example of a reflex that occurs at some point in the development of a human being?

    a. Child riding a bike

    b. Teen socializing

    c. Infant sucking on a nipple

    d. Toddler walking

2. Learning is best defined as a relatively permanent change in behavior that _____.

    a. is innate

    b. occurs as a result of experience

    c. is found only in humans

    d. occurs by observing others

3. Two forms of associative learning are _____ and _____.

    a. classical conditioning; operant conditioning

    b. classical conditioning; Pavlovian conditioning

    c. operant conditioning; observational learning

    d. operant conditioning; learning conditioning

4. In _____ the stimulus or experience occurs before the behavior and then gets paired with the behavior.

    a. associative learning

    b. observational learning

    c. operant conditioning

    d. classical conditioning

5. A stimulus that does not initially elicit a response in an organism is a(n) _____.

    a. unconditioned stimulus

    b. neutral stimulus

    c. conditioned stimulus

    d. unconditioned response

6. In Watson and Rayner's experiments, Little Albert was conditioned to fear a white rat, and then he began to be afraid of other furry white objects. This demonstrates _____.

    a. higher order conditioning

    b. acquisition

    c. stimulus discrimination

    d. stimulus generalization

7. Extinction occurs when _____.

    a. the conditioned stimulus is presented repeatedly without being paired with an unconditioned stimulus

    b. the unconditioned stimulus is presented repeatedly without being paired with a conditioned stimulus

    c. the neutral stimulus is presented repeatedly without being paired with an unconditioned stimulus

    d. the neutral stimulus is presented repeatedly without being paired with a conditioned stimulus

8. In Pavlov's work with dogs, the secretions were _____.

   a. unconditioned responses

   b. conditioned responses

   c. unconditioned stimuli

   d. conditioned stimuli

9. _____ is when you take away a pleasant stimulus to stop a behavior.

   a. Positive reinforcement

   b. Negative reinforcement

   c. Positive punishment

   d. Negative punishment

10. Which of the following is not an example of a primary reinforcer?

   a. Food

   b. Money

   c. Water

   d. Sex

11. Rewarding successive approximations toward a target behavior is _____.

   a. shaping

   b. extinction

   c. positive reinforcement

   d. negative reinforcement

12. Slot machines reward gamblers with money according to which reinforcement schedule?

   a. Fixed ratio

   b. Variable ratio

   c. Fixed interval

   d. Variable interval

13. The person who performs a behavior that serves as an example is called a _____.

   a. teacher

   b. model

   c. instructor

   d. coach

14. In Bandura's Bobo doll study, when the children who watched the aggressive model were placed in a room with the doll and other toys, they _____.

   a. ignored the doll

   b. played nicely with the doll

   c. played with tinker toys

   d. kicked and threw the doll

15. Which is the correct order of steps in the modeling process?

   a. Attention, retention, reproduction, motivation

   b. Motivation, attention, reproduction, retention

   c. Attention, motivation, retention, reproduction

   d. Motivation, attention, retention, reproduction

16. Who proposed observational learning?

   a. Ivan Pavlov

   b. John B. Watson

   c. Albert Bandura

   d. B.F. Skinner

Critical Thinking Questions

17. Compare and contrast classical and operant conditioning. How are they alike? How do they differ?

18. What is the difference between a reflex and a learned behavior?

19. If the sound of your toaster popping up toast causes your mouth to water, what are the UCS, CS, and CR?

20. Explain how the processes of stimulus generalization and stimulus discrimination are considered opposites.

21. How does a neutral stimulus become a conditioned stimulus?

22. What is a Skinner box, and what is its purpose?

23. What is the difference between negative reinforcement and punishment?

24. What is shaping, and how would you use shaping to teach a dog to roll over?

25. What is the effect of prosocial modeling and antisocial modeling?

26. Cara is 17 years old. Cara's mother and father both drink alcohol every night. They tell Cara that drinking is bad, and she shouldn't do it. Cara goes to a party where beer is being served. What do you think Cara will do? Why?

Chapter 6
Thinking and Intelligence

Chapter Introduction

Figure 1: Thinking is an important part of our human experience, and one that has captivated people for centuries. Today, it is one area of psychological study. The 19th-century *Girl with a Book* by José Ferraz de Almeida Júnior, the 20th-century sculpture *The Thinker* by August Rodin, and Shi Ke's 10th-century painting *Huike Thinking* all reflect the fascination with the process of human thought.

Why is it so difficult to break habits like reaching for your ringing phone even when you shouldn't, such as when you're driving? How does a person who has never seen or touched snow in real life develop an understanding of the concept of snow? How do young children acquire the ability to learn language with no formal instruction? Psychologists who study thinking explore questions like these.

Cognitive psychologists also study intelligence. What is intelligence, and how does it vary from person to person? Are "street smarts" a kind of intelligence, and if so, how do they relate to other types of intelligence? What does an IQ test really measure? These questions and more will be explored in this chapter as you study thinking and intelligence.

In other chapters, we discuss the cognitive processes of perception, learning, and memory. In this chapter, we will focus on high-level cognitive processes. As a part of this discussion, we will consider thinking and briefly explore the development and use of language. We will also discuss problem solving and creativity before ending with a discussion of how intelligence is measured and how our biology and environments interact to affect intelligence. After finishing this chapter, you will have a greater appreciation of the higher-level cognitive processes that contribute to our distinctiveness as a species.

Flash Forward

Ready to dig into the vocabulary? Get some practice with this Hawkes Verified Quizlet set (hawkes.biz/psych6q1)!

6.1 What Is Cognition?

Imagine all of your thoughts as if they were physical entities, swirling rapidly inside your mind. How is it possible that the brain is able to move from one thought to the next in an organized, orderly fashion? The brain is endlessly perceiving, processing, planning, organizing, and remembering—it is always active. Yet, you don't notice most of your brain's activity as you move throughout your daily routine. This is only one facet of the complex processes involved in cognition. Simply put, **cognition** is thinking, and it encompasses the processes associated with perception, knowledge, problem solving, judgment, language, and memory. Scientists who study cognition are searching for ways to understand how we integrate, organize, and utilize our conscious cognitive experiences without being aware of all of the unconscious work that our brains are doing (for example, Kahneman, 2011).

Cognition

Upon waking each morning, you begin thinking—contemplating the tasks that you must complete that day. In what order should you run your errands? Should you go to the gym, the grocery store, or the library first? Can you get these things done before you head to class, or will they need to wait until school is done? These thoughts are one example of cognition at work. Exceptionally complex, cognition is an essential feature of human consciousness, yet not all aspects of cognition are consciously experienced.

Cognitive psychology is the field of psychology dedicated to examining how people think. It attempts to explain how and why we think the way we do by studying the interactions among human thinking, emotion, creativity, language, and problem solving, in addition to other cognitive processes. Cognitive psychologists strive to determine and measure different types of intelligence, why some people are better at problem solving than others, and how emotional intelligence affects success in the workplace, among countless other topics. They also sometimes focus on how we organize thoughts and information gathered from our environments into meaningful categories of thought, which will be discussed later.

Concepts and Prototypes

The human senses serve as the interface between the mind and the external environment, receiving stimuli and translating it into nervous impulses that are processed in the brain. The brain uses the relevant pieces to create sensory memory, which can lead to thoughts. Thoughts can be expressed through language or stored in memory for future use. When thoughts are formed, the brain also pulls information from emotions and memories to bring into consciousness (Figure 2).

Figure 2: Sensations and information are received by our brains, filtered through emotions and memories, and processed to become thoughts.

Concepts are categories or groupings of linguistic information, images, ideas, or memories, such as life experiences. For example, mammals are a group of animals that have fur, produce milk, and the females carry the species. Concepts are, in many ways, big ideas that are generated by observing details and categorizing and combining these details into cognitive structures. You use concepts to see the relationships among the different elements of your experiences and to keep the information in your mind organized and accessible.

Concepts are informed by our semantic memory (you will learn more about semantic memory in a later chapter) and are present in every aspect of our lives; however, one of the easiest places to notice concepts is inside a classroom, where they are discussed explicitly. When you study United States history, for example, you learn about more than just individual events that have happened in America's past. You absorb a large quantity of information by listening to and participating in discussions, examining maps, and reading first-hand accounts of people's lives. Your brain analyzes these details and develops an overall understanding of American history. In the process, your brain gathers details that inform and refine your understanding of related concepts like democracy, power, and freedom.

Concepts can be complex and abstract, like justice, or more concrete, like types of birds. In psychology, for example, Piaget's stages of development are abstract concepts. Some concepts, like tolerance, are agreed upon by many people because they have been used in various ways over many years. Other concepts, like the characteristics of your ideal friend or your family's birthday traditions, are personal and individualized. In this way, concepts touch every aspect of our lives, from our many daily routines to the guiding principles behind the way governments function.

Another technique used by your brain to organize information is the identification of prototypes for the concepts you have developed. A **prototype** is the best example or representation of a concept. For example, for the category of civil disobedience, your prototype could be Rosa Parks. Her peaceful resistance to segregation on a city bus in Montgomery, Alabama, is a recognizable example of civil disobedience. Or your prototype could be Mohandas Gandhi, sometimes called Mahatma Gandhi (*Mahatma* is an honorific title.) (Figure 3).

Mohandas Gandhi served as a nonviolent force for independence for India while simultaneously demanding that Buddhist, Hindu, Muslim, and Christian leaders—both Indian and British—collaborate peacefully. Although he was not always successful in preventing violence around him, his life provides a steadfast example of the civil disobedience prototype (Constitutional Rights Foundation, 2013). Just as concepts can be abstract or concrete, we can make a distinction between concepts that are functions of our direct experience with the world and those that are more artificial in nature.

Natural and Artificial Concepts

In psychology, concepts can be divided into two categories, natural and artificial. **Natural concepts** are created "naturally" through your experiences and can be developed from either direct or indirect experiences. For example, if you live in Essex Junction, Vermont, you have probably had a lot of direct experience with snow. You've watched it fall from the sky, you've seen lightly falling snow that barely covers the windshield of your car, and you've shoveled out 18 inches of fluffy white snow as you've thought, "This is perfect for skiing." You've thrown snowballs at your best friend and gone sledding down the steepest hill in town. In short, you know snow. You know what it looks like, smells like, tastes like, and feels like. If, however, you've lived your whole life on the island of Saint Vincent in the Caribbean, you may never have actually seen snow, much less tasted, smelled, or touched it. You know snow from the indirect experience of seeing pictures of falling snow—or from watching films that feature snow as part of the setting. Either way, snow is a natural concept because you can construct an understanding of it through direct observations or experiences of snow (Figure 4).

Further Resources

Watch this video of the original Salt March led by Mohandas Gandhi in 1930. (hawkes.biz/gandhi)

Figure 3: In 1930, Mohandas Gandhi led a group in peaceful protest against a British tax on salt in India.

(a)

(b)

Figure 4: (a) Our concept of snow is an example of a natural concept—one that we understand through direct observation and experience. (b) In contrast, artificial concepts are ones that we know by a specific set of characteristics that they always exhibit, such as what defines different basic shapes.

An **artificial concept**, on the other hand, is a concept that is defined by a specific set of characteristics. Various properties of geometric shapes, like squares and triangles, serve as useful examples of artificial concepts. A triangle always has three angles and three sides. A square always has four equal sides and four right angles. Mathematical formulas, like the equation for area (length × width) are artificial concepts defined by specific sets of characteristics that are always the same. Artificial concepts can enhance the understanding of a topic by building on one another. For example, before learning the concept of "area of a square" (and the formula to find it), you must understand what a square is. Once the concept of "area of a square" is understood, an understanding of area for other geometric shapes can be built upon the original understanding of area. The use of artificial concepts to define an idea is crucial to communicating with others and engaging in complex thought. According to Goldstone and Kersten (2003), concepts act as building blocks and can be connected in countless combinations to create complex thoughts.

Schemata

A **schema** is a mental construct consisting of a cluster or collection of related concepts (Bartlett, 1932).

When a schema is activated, you are more likely to recall or think about concepts, memories, and emotions that are related to that schema. A **role schema** makes assumptions about how individuals in certain roles will behave (Callero, 1994). For example, imagine you meet someone who introduces himself as a firefighter. When this happens, your brain automatically activates the "firefighter schema" and begins making assumptions that this person is brave, selfless, and community-oriented. However, this individual may not be brave, he might just be working as a firefighter to pay the bills while studying to become an accountant.

Figure 5: What event schema do you perform when riding in an elevator?

An **event schema**, also known as a **cognitive script**, is a set of behaviors that often go in a specific order and can often feel like a routine. Think about what you do when you walk into an elevator (Figure 5). First, the doors open, and you wait to let exiting passengers leave the elevator car. Then, you step into the elevator and turn around to face the doors, looking for the correct button to push. Since you expect the behaviors for getting in an elevator to go in this order, it is your cognitive script for getting on an elevator.

✎   **On Your Own**

Which of the following *best* represents a cognitive script?

☐ Teresa knows that a lizard is a reptile.

☐ Homer thinks that a man he meets is not going to be talkative because he is an accountant.

☐ Jerry knows that he leaves for work after he finishes pouring his coffee.

Because event schemata are automatic, they can be difficult to change. Imagine that you are driving home from work or school. This event schema involves getting in the car, shutting the door, and buckling your seatbelt before putting the key in the ignition. You might perform this script two or three times each day. As you drive home, you hear your phone's ring tone. Typically, the event schema that occurs when you hear your phone ringing involves locating the phone and answering it or responding to your latest text message. So without thinking, you reach for your phone, which could be in your pocket, in your bag, or on the passenger seat of the car. This powerful event schema is informed by your pattern of behavior and the pleasurable stimulation that a phone call or text message gives your brain. Because it is a schema, it is extremely challenging for us to stop reaching for the phone even though we know that we endanger our own lives and the lives of others while we do it (Neyfakh, 2013) (Figure 6).

🖼 **Figure 6:** Texting while driving is dangerous, but it is a difficult event schema for some people to resist.

Remember the elevator? It feels almost impossible to walk in and *not* face the door. Our powerful event schema dictates our behavior in the elevator, and it is no different with our phones. Current research suggests that it is the habit, or event schema, of checking our phones in many different situations that makes refraining from checking them while driving especially difficult (Bayer & Campbell, 2012). Because texting and driving has become a dangerous epidemic in recent years, psychologists are looking at ways to help people interrupt the "phone schema" while driving. Event schemata like these are the reason why many habits are difficult to break once they have been acquired. As we continue to examine thinking, keep in mind how powerful the forces of concepts and schemata are to our understanding of the world.

Summary

Cognitive psychology is the study of cognition, or the brain's ability to think, perceive, plan, analyze, and remember. Concepts and their corresponding prototypes help us quickly organize our thinking by creating categories into which we can sort new information. Schemata are clusters of related concepts. Some schemata involve routines of thought and behavior, and these help us function properly in various situations without having to "think twice" about them. Schemata also show up in social situations and routines of daily behavior.

Flash Forward

Ready to dig into the vocabulary? Get some practice with this Hawkes Verified Quizlet set (hawkes.biz/psych6q2)!

6.2 Language

Language is a communication system that involves using words and systematic rules to organize those words to transmit information from one individual to another.

Lexicon refers to the words of a given language or its vocabulary. **Grammar** refers to the set of rules that are used to convey meaning by use of the lexicon (Fernández & Cairns, 2011). For instance, English grammar dictates that most verbs receive an *-ed* at the end to indicate past tense. Semantics and syntax are part of a language's grammar.

A **phoneme** (e.g., the sounds "ah" vs. "eh") is a basic sound unit of a given language, and different languages have different sets of phonemes. Phonemes are combined to form **morphemes**, which are the smallest units of language that convey some type of meaning (e.g., "I" is both a phoneme and a morpheme). We use semantics and syntax to construct language. **Semantics** refers to the process by which we derive meaning from morphemes and words. **Syntax** refers to the way words are organized into sentences (Chomsky, 1965; Fernández & Cairns, 2011).

Figure 1: This cuneiform symbol, "ama-gi," literally means "return to mother" and refers to "the restoration of persons and property to their original status." It may be the earliest written reference to the concept of freedom.

☑ On Your Own

Write the following terms next to the example that best describes them: *grammar*, *lexicon*, *phoneme*, *morpheme*, *semantics*, and *syntax*.

Term	Example
	"eh" "b"
	The five words baby Beth knows are her what?
	It's "the dog has a ball," not "dog ball a has the."
	"ology," "psych"
	Psychology is derived from *psych* ("the mind") and *ology* ("the study of") to make "the study of the mind."
	A system that involves words and rules to organize words used to communicate with others

Language Development

B.F. Skinner (1957) proposed that language is learned through reinforcement. Noam Chomsky (1965) criticized this behaviorist approach, asserting instead that the mechanisms underlying language acquisition are biologically determined (Chomsky, 1965; Fernández & Cairns, 2011). One of Chomsky's arguments (1965) are that regardless of culture or the type of language spoken, it is more easily learned in early childhood than at any other point in the lifespan (Johnson & Newport, 1989; Lenneberg, 1967; Singleton,

1995). Research has shown that babies are born being able to discriminate sounds of all human languages. However, by the time they are one year old, they can only discriminate among the phonemes that are used in the languages that they are exposed to (Jensen, 2011; Werker & Lalonde, 1988; Werker & Tees, 1984).

The use of language develops in the absence of formal instruction and appears to follow a very similar pattern in children from vastly different cultures and backgrounds. It would seem, therefore, that we are born with a biological predisposition to acquire a language (Chomsky, 1965; Fernández & Cairns, 2011). Moreover, it appears that there is a critical period for language acquisition.

> ## Dig Deeper
>
> ### The Case of Genie
>
> In the fall of 1970, a social worker in the Los Angeles area found a 13-year-old girl who was being raised in extremely neglectful and abusive conditions. The girl, who came to be known as Genie, had lived most of her life tied to a potty chair or confined to a crib in a small room that was kept closed with the curtains drawn. For a little over a decade, Genie had virtually no social interaction and no access to the outside world. As a result of these conditions, Genie was unable to stand up, chew solid food, or speak (Fromkin, Krashen, Curtiss, Rigler, & Rigler, 1974; Rymer, 1993). The police took Genie into protective custody.
>
> Genie's abilities improved dramatically following her removal from her abusive environment, and early on, it appeared she was acquiring language—much later than would be predicted by critical period hypotheses that had been posited at the time (Fromkin et al., 1974). Genie managed to amass an impressive vocabulary in a relatively short amount of time. However, she never developed a mastery of the grammatical aspects of language (Curtiss, 1981). Perhaps being deprived of the opportunity to learn language during a critical period impeded Genie's ability to fully acquire and use language.

The stages of language and communication development are displayed in Table 1. Children begin to learn about language from a very early age. In fact, it appears that this is occurring even before we are born. Newborns show preference for their mother's voice and appear to be able to discriminate between the language spoken by their mother and other languages. Babies are also attuned to the languages being used around them and show preferences for videos of faces that are moving in synchrony with the audio of spoken language versus videos that do not synchronize with the audio (Blossom & Morgan, 2006; Pickens, 1994; Spelke & Cortelyou, 1981). After the first few months of life, babies enter what is known as the babbling stage, during which time they tend to produce single syllables that are repeated over and over. As time passes, more variations appear in the syllables that they produce, which is likely the baby practicing how to talk (Fernández & Cairns, 2011). In many cases, a child's first word is uttered some time between the ages of 1 year to 18 months. During the next few months, the child will be able to say words but not phrases. A child in this stage may say *cookie*, which means that she wants a cookie. By age 18 to 36 months, the child should be able to use simple sentences of two or three words. After age three, the child should be able to speak in complex sentences and have regular every day conversations. During this time, children commit an error called **overgeneralization**, which is an extension of a language rule to an exception to the rule. For example, we add an *s* to the end of most animals to indicate there is more than one of them. A child may refer to more than one mouse as *mouses* instead of *mice*.

Figure 2: Language development occurs in stages.

You may recall that each language has its own set of phonemes that are used to generate morphemes, words, and so on. Babies can discriminate among the sounds that make up a language (for example, they can tell the difference between the *s* in *vision* and the *ss* in *fission*); early on, they can differentiate between the sounds of all human languages, even those that do not occur in the languages that are used in their environments. However, by the time that they are about 1 year old, they can only discriminate among those phonemes that are used in the language or languages in their environments (Jensen, 2011; Werker & Lalonde, 1988; Werker & Tees, 1984).

Stage	Age	Developmental Language and Communication
1	0–3 months	Reflexive communication
2	3–8 months	Reflexive communication; interest in others
3	8–13 months	Intentional communication; sociability
4	12–18 months	First words
5	18–24 months	Simple sentences of two words
6	2–3 years	Sentences of three or more words
7	3–5 years	Complex sentences; has conversations

Table 1: Stages of Language and Communication Development

✎ On Your Own

Answer the following questions about language development.

Assuming a child develops at a normal pace, what age would they most likely start committing overgeneralization errors?

☐ One year old   ☐ Three years old   ☐ Seven years old

Assuming a child is developing on a normal trajectory, when would you expect them to say their first word?

☐ One year old   ☐ Two years old   ☐ Four years old

Further Resources

Watch this video (hawkes.biz/babies) to learn more about how babies lose the ability to discriminate among all possible human phonemes as they age.

Language and Thought

When we speak one language, we agree that words are representations of ideas, people, places, and events. The given language that children learn is connected to their culture and surroundings. But can words themselves shape the way we think about things? Psychologists have long investigated the question of whether language shapes thoughts and actions, or whether our thoughts and beliefs shape our language. Two researchers, Edward Sapir and Benjamin Lee Whorf, began this investigation in the 1940s. They wanted to understand how the language habits of a community encourage members of that community to interpret language in a particular manner (Sapir, 1941/1964). Sapir and Whorf proposed that language determines thought, suggesting, for example, that a person whose community language did not have past-tense verbs would have difficulty thinking about the past (Whorf, 1956).

Reflection Questions

What are your thoughts on the Linguistic Relativity Hypothesis? Do you think language can limit thought? Why or why not?

Researchers have since identified this view as too absolute, pointing out a lack of empiricism behind what Sapir and Whorf proposed (Abler, 2013; Boroditsky, 2011; van Troyer, 1994). Today, psychologists continue to study and debate the relationship between language and thought.

What Do You Think?

The Meaning of Language

Think about what you know of other languages; perhaps you even speak multiple languages. Imagine for a moment that your closest friend fluently speaks more than one language. Do you think that friend thinks differently, depending on which language is being spoken? You may know a few words that are not translatable from their original language into English. For example, the Portuguese word *saudade* originated during the 15th century when Portuguese sailors left home to explore the seas and travel to Africa or Asia. Those left behind described the emptiness and fondness they felt as *saudade* (Figure 3). The word came to express many meanings, including loss, nostalgia, yearning, warm memories, and hope. There is no single word in English that includes all of those emotions in a single description. Do words such as *saudade* indicate that different languages produce different patterns of thought in people? What do you think?

Figure 3: These two works of art depict saudade. (a) Saudade de Nápoles, which is translated into "missing Naples," was painted by Bertha Worms in 1895. (b) Almeida Júnior painted Saudade in 1899.

Language may indeed influence the way that we think, an idea known as linguistic determinism. One recent demonstration of this phenomenon involved differences in the way that English and Mandarin Chinese speakers talk and think about time. English speakers tend to talk about time using terms that describe changes along a horizontal dimension, for example, saying something like "I'm running behind schedule" or "Don't get ahead of yourself." While Mandarin Chinese speakers also describe time in horizontal terms, it is not uncommon to also use terms associated with a vertical arrangement. For example, the past might be described as being "up" and the future as being "down." It turns out that these differences in language translate into differences in performance on cognitive tests designed to measure how quickly an individual can recognize temporal relationships. Specifically, when given a series of tasks with vertical priming, Mandarin Chinese speakers were faster at recognizing temporal relationships between months. Indeed, Boroditsky (2001) sees these results as suggesting that "habits in language encourage habits in thought" (p. 12).

One group of researchers who wanted to investigate how language influences thought compared how English speakers and the Dani people of Papua New Guinea think and speak about color. The Dani have two words for color: one word for *light* and one word for *dark*. In contrast, the English language has 11 color words. Researchers hypothesized that the number of color terms could limit the ways that the Dani people conceptualized color. However, the Dani were able to distinguish colors with the same ability as English speakers despite having fewer words at their disposal (Berlin & Kay, 1969). A recent review of research aimed at determining how language might affect something like color perception suggests that language can influence perceptual phenomena, especially in the left hemisphere of the brain. You may recall from earlier chapters that the left hemisphere is associated with language for most people. However, the right (less linguistic hemisphere) of the brain is less affected by linguistic influences on perception (Regier & Kay, 2009).

Summary

Language is a communication system that has both a lexicon and a system of grammar. Language acquisition occurs naturally and effortlessly during the early stages of life, and this acquisition occurs in a predictable sequence for individuals around the world. Language has a strong influence on thought, and the concept of how language may influence cognition remains an area of study and debate in psychology.

Flash Forward

Ready to dig into the vocabulary? Get some practice with this Hawkes Verified Quizlet set (hawkes.biz/psych6q3)!

6.3 Problem Solving

We've all got problems. Sometimes these problems are straightforward: if you forgot to get ice for your party, but your first guest has already arrived, you could text someone who hasn't arrived yet and have them pick it up for you. Problem solved.

Sometimes, however, the problems we encounter are more complex. Let's say your car breaks down, and you don't have the money to fix it right away. You have to get to school and to work, and you have family members who rely on you for rides. What should you do? First, you need to identify the problem, and potentially its many parts, and then apply a strategy for solving the problem.

Problem-Solving Strategies

A **problem-solving strategy** is a plan of action used to find a solution. Different strategies have different action plans associated with them (Table 1). For example, a well-known strategy is **trial and error**, which means to continue trying different solutions until the problem is solved.

An **algorithm** is a problem-solving formula that provides you with step-by-step instructions used to achieve a desired outcome (Kahneman, 2011). An example of this is a recipe with highly detailed instructions that produce the same result every time they are performed.

A **heuristic** is a mental shortcut that is used to help us solve problems. Although heuristics may help us save time, they are not always the best for making rational decisions. **Working backwards** is a useful heuristic in which you begin solving the problem by focusing on the result. For example, let's say you are doing your math homework. You look up the answer in the book, and try to use that to help you figure out how the problem was solved.

Different types of heuristics are used in different types of situations, but the impulse to use a heuristic occurs when one of five conditions is met (Pratkanis, 1989):

Figure 1: Heuristics serve as mental shortcuts.

- When one is faced with too much information

- When the time is limited

- When the decision to be made isn't important

- When there is access to very little information to use in making the decision

- When an appropriate heuristic happens to come to mind in the same moment

Method	Description	Example
Heuristic	General problem-solving framework	Working backwards; breaking a task into steps
Trial and error	Continue trying different solutions until problem is solved	Restarting phone, turning off Wi-Fi, turning off Bluetooth in order to determine why your phone is malfunctioning
Algorithm	Step-by-step problem-solving formula	Instruction manual for installing new software on your computer

Table 1: Problem-Solving Strategies

✎ On Your Own

Keisha has a leak in her kitchen sink. She goes on YouTube and finds a video that goes through the instructions for how to fix the leak. This best exemplifies which of the following?

☐ Algorithm   ☐ Trial and Error   ☐ Heuristic

Solving Puzzles

Problem-solving abilities can improve with practice. Many people challenge themselves every day with puzzles and other mental exercises to sharpen their problem-solving skills. Sudoku puzzles appear daily in most newspapers. Typically, a sudoku puzzle is a 9×9 grid. The simple sudoku below (Figure 2) is a 4×4 grid. To solve the puzzle, fill in the empty boxes with a single digit: 1, 2, 3, or 4. Here are the rules: the numbers must total 10 in each bolded box, each row, and each column; however, each digit can only appear once in a bolded box, row, and column. Time yourself as you solve this puzzle, and compare your time with a classmate.

Here is another popular type of puzzle (Figure 3) that challenges your spatial reasoning skills. Connect all nine dots with four connecting straight lines without lifting your pencil from the paper.

Take a look at the "Puzzling Scales" logic puzzle below (Figure 4). Sam Loyd, a well-known puzzle master, created and refined countless puzzles throughout his lifetime (Cyclopedia of Puzzles, n.d.).

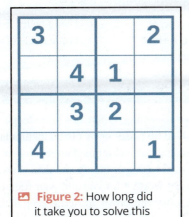

🖼 **Figure 2:** How long did it take you to solve this sudoku puzzle? (You can see the answer at the end of this lesson.)

🖼 **Figure 3:** Did you figure it out? (The answer is at the end of this lesson.) Once you understand how to crack this puzzle, you won't forget.

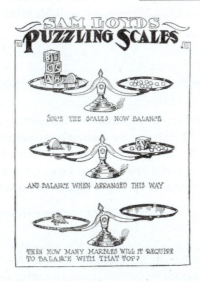

🖼 **Figure 4:** What steps did you take to solve this puzzle? (You can read the solution at the end of this lesson.)

Pitfalls to Problem Solving

A **mental set** is where you persist in approaching a problem in a way that has worked in the past but is clearly not working now.

Functional fixedness is a type of mental set where you cannot perceive an object being used for something other than what it was designed for. During the *Apollo 13* mission to the moon, NASA engineers at Mission Control had to overcome functional fixedness to save the lives of the astronauts aboard the spacecraft. An explosion in a module of the spacecraft damaged multiple systems. The astronauts were in danger of being poisoned by rising levels of carbon dioxide because of problems with the carbon dioxide filters. The engineers found a way for the astronauts to use spare plastic bags, tape, and air hoses to create a makeshift air filter, which saved the lives of the astronauts.

> ### Further Resources
>
> Check out this *Apollo 13* scene (hawkes.biz/functionalfixedness) where a group of NASA engineers are given the task of overcoming functional fixedness.

✎ On Your Own

Which of the following is *not* an example of a mental set that causes functional fixedness?

☐ Only using a water bottle to store water that you drink

☐ Only using a hammer to drive a nail into a surface

☐ Using water from a water bottle to clean a stain on a shirt

In order to make good decisions, we use our knowledge and our reasoning. Often, this knowledge and reasoning is sound and solid. Sometimes, however, we are swayed by biases or by others manipulating a situation. Let's say you and three friends wanted to rent a house and had a combined target budget of $1,600 per month. The realtor shows you only very run-down houses for $1,600 per month and then shows you a very nice house for $2,000 per month. Even though it would have been worth it for you and your friends to spend $100 extra each a month for a nice house, you may have stuck to the run-down houses to keep within the $1,600 per month price point.

Why would the realtor show you the run-down houses and the nice house? The realtor may be challenging your anchoring bias. An **anchoring bias** occurs when you focus on one piece of information when making a decision or solving a problem. In this case, you're so focused on the amount of money you are willing to spend that you may not recognize what kinds of houses are available at that price point.

> ### Reflection Questions
>
> In your opinion, how can sales people use the anchoring bias to their advantage?

Confirmation bias is the tendency to focus on information that confirms your existing beliefs. For example, if you are trying to prove that Michael Jordan was the greatest basketball player of all time, as opposed to Lebron James, you may only reference statistical categories where Michael Jordan outperformed Lebron James. However, you might ignore categories where Lebron James outperformed Michael Jordan. In this instance, you would be ignoring other information that is valuable to constructing a more informed opinion.

> ### Reflection Questions
>
> Think of a time when you or someone you know committed confirmation bias. What was the situation, and why do you think you or the person in question ignored the other facts of the argument?

Hindsight bias leads you to believe that the event you just experienced was predictable even though it really wasn't. In other words, you knew all along that things would turn out the way they did. During Super Bowl XLIX, the Seattle Seahawks were on the one-yard line trailing 28 to 24 with 26 seconds left and one of the best running backs in the game, Marshawn Lynch, in the backfield. The popular call would have been to hand the ball to Lynch who may have scored easily, which would have resulted in the Seahawks taking a 30-28 lead and likely a Super Bowl XLIX victory. However, Seahawks coach Pete Carroll elected to throw the ball, which resulted in an interception by Patriots defensive back Malcolm Butler. Butler's interception clinched Super Bowl XLIX for the Patriots. Carroll's call to throw the ball is one of the most criticized decisions in the history of the sport. Many football analysts and commentators "knew all along that you shouldn't throw the football on the goal line." However, if the Seahawks scored on that same play rather than getting the ball intercepted, Carroll would have most likely been revered and praised for making the same exact decision.

Reflection Questions

Think of a time when you or someone you know committed hindsight bias? What do you think about the situation led you to do it?

Figure 5: Do all Canadians love hockey?

Representative bias is when you unintentionally stereotype someone or something like assuming someone is a hockey fan because they live in Canada (and hockey is popular in Canada). The **availability heuristic** is a heuristic in which you make a decision based on information that is readily available (Aronson, 1995; Kahneman, 2011). If you watch a lot of TV shows about home break-ins, you may think your odds of your house getting broken into are a lot higher than they really are. The reason is that you can easily think of examples when people's homes have gotten broken into.

✐ On Your Own

Without using any resources or checking the internet, which city do you think has more people, New York City, NY, USA or Seoul, South Korea?

☐ New York City, NY, USA   ☐ Seoul, South Korea   ☐ Both have the
                                                                                same population.

✐ On Your Own

Complete the table by writing a description of each of the following biases in your own words.

Bias	Description
Confirmation	
Hindsight	
Representative	
Availability	
Anchoring	

Further Resources

Watch this clever music video (hawkes.biz/cognitivebias) that a high school teacher made to explain these and other cognitive biases to his AP psychology students.

Were you able to determine how many marbles are needed to balance the scales in Figure 4? You need nine. Were you able to solve the problems in Figure 2 and Figure 3? Here are the answers (Figure 6).

 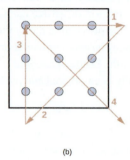

(a)   (b)

📈 **Figure 6:** Here are the solutions to the puzzles in Figure 2 and Figure 3.

Summary

Many different strategies exist for solving problems. Typical strategies include trial and error, applying algorithms, and using heuristics. To solve a large, complicated problem, it often helps to break the problem into smaller steps that can be accomplished individually, leading to an overall solution. Roadblocks to problem solving include mental sets, functional fixedness, and various biases that can cloud decision-making skills.

Flash Forward

Ready to dig into the vocabulary? Get some practice with this Hawkes Verified Quizlet set (hawkes.biz/ psych6q4)!

6.4 What Are Intelligence and Creativity?

A four-and-a-half-year-old boy sits at the kitchen table with his father, who is reading a new story aloud to him. He turns the page to continue reading, but before he can begin, the boy says, "Wait, Daddy!" He points to the words on the new page and reads aloud, "Go, Pig! Go!" The father stops and looks at his son. "Can you read that?" he asks. "Yes, Daddy!" And he points to the words and reads again, "Go, Pig! Go!"

This father was not actively teaching his son to read even though the child constantly asked questions about letters, words, and symbols that they saw everywhere: in the car, in the store, on the television. The father wondered about what else his son might understand and decided to try an experiment.

Grabbing a sheet of blank paper, he wrote several simple words in a list: *mom, dad, dog, bird, bed, truck, car,* and *tree*. He put the list down in front of the boy and asked him to read the words. "Mom, dad, dog, bird, bed, truck, car, tree," he read, slowing down to carefully pronounce *bird* and *truck*. Then he asks, "Did I do it, Daddy?" And the father replied, "You sure did! That is very good." The father gave his little boy a warm hug and continued reading the story about the pig, all the while wondering if his son's abilities were an indication of exceptional intelligence or simply a normal pattern of linguistic development. Like the father in this example, psychologists have wondered what constitutes intelligence and how it can be measured.

Classifying Intelligence

What exactly is intelligence? The way that researchers have defined the concept of intelligence has been modified many times since the birth of psychology. British psychologist Charles Spearman believed intelligence consisted of one general factor, called *g*, which could be measured and compared among individuals. Spearman focused on the commonalities among various intellectual abilities and deemphasized what made each unique. Long before modern psychology developed, however, ancient philosophers, such as Aristotle, held a similar view (Cianciolo & Sternberg, 2004).

(a)   (b)

🖼 **Figure 1:** (a) This is a representation of Spearman's *g* factor of intelligence. Each purple oval represents a factor related to intelligence, such as verbal fluency. (b) Gardener's Multiple Intelligence Theory argues that each individual has strengths and weaknesses in at least eight types of intelligence.

Other psychologists believe that instead of a single factor, intelligence is a collection of distinct abilities. In the 1940s, Raymond Cattell proposed a theory of intelligence that divided general intelligence into two components: **crystallized intelligence** and **fluid intelligence** (Cattell, 1963).

Crystallized Intelligence

- Acquired knowledge and the ability to retrieve it

- Used when learning, remembering, and recalling information

- Helps us overcome concrete, straightforward problems

- **Example**: *Demonstrating that you have mastered the information covered in this course*

Fluid Intelligence

- Ability to see complex relationships and solve problems

- Used when tackling complex, abstract challenges in your daily life

- **Example**: *Navigating your way home after being detoured to an unfamiliar route because of road construction*

Other theorists and psychologists believe that intelligence should be defined in more practical terms. For example, what types of behaviors help you get ahead in life? Which skills promote success? Think about this for a moment. Being able to recite all 45 presidents of the United States in order is an excellent party trick, but will knowing this make you a better person?

Further Resources

Try this test (hawkes.biz/fluidintelligence) to check out your fluid intelligence.

Robert Sternberg developed another theory of intelligence, which he titled the **triarchic theory of intelligence** because it sees intelligence as comprised of three parts (Sternberg, 1988): **practical**, **creative**, and **analytical intelligence** (Figure 2).

Figure 2: Sternberg's theory identifies three types of intelligence: practical, creative, and analytical.

Practical Intelligence

- Sometimes compared to "street smarts"

- Finding solutions that work in your everyday life by applying knowledge based on your experiences

- Appears to be separate from traditional understanding of IQ; individuals who score high in practical intelligence may or may not have comparable scores in creative and analytical intelligence (Sternberg, 1988)

- **Example**: *When your friends want to find something to eat in a new city, you use an app to find locations and reviews for restaurants closest to you.*

Analytical Intelligence

- Closely aligned with academic problem solving and computations

- Demonstrated by an ability to analyze, evaluate, judge, compare, and contrast

- **Example**: *When solving a challenging math problem, you analyze different aspects of the problem and then solve it section by section.*

Creative Intelligence

- Marked by inventing or imagining a solution to a problem or situation

- Can include finding a novel solution to an unexpected problem or producing a beautiful work of art or a well-developed short story

- **Example**: *When camping, you figure out a way to brew coffee, despite the fact that the coffee pot was forgotten by your friend Mark. Classic Mark.*

☑ On Your Own

Marcel, Marie, and Meriel are traveling abroad to Paris, France. Once they arrive, they find that they are lost and unable to navigate the public transportation from the airport to their hostel near the Eiffel Tower.

Read the following descriptions and determine whether they represent creative, analytical, or practical intelligence.

1. Marcel decides to ask a person manning a ticket booth for help. Marcel is demonstrating which kind of intelligence?

☐ Creative ☐ Practical ☐ Analytical

2. Marie walks up to the Metro Map and locates the airport and the Eiffel Tower and figures out which train they should get on. Marie is demonstrating which kind of intelligence?

☐ Creative ☐ Practical ☐ Analytical

3. Meriel suggests that should just follow the majority of people, as they are likely heading into the center of Paris, too. Meriel is demonstrating which kind of intelligence?

☐ Creative ☐ Practical ☐ Analytical

Multiple Intelligences Theory was developed by Howard Gardner, a Harvard psychologist and former student of Erik Erikson. Gardner's theory, which has been refined for more than thirty years, is a more recent development among theories of intelligence. In Gardner's theory, each person possesses at least eight intelligences. Among these eight intelligences, a person typically excels in some and falters in others (Gardner, 1983). Table 1 describes each type of intelligence.

Intelligence Type	Characteristics	Representative Career
Linguistic intelligence	Perceives different functions of language, different sounds and meanings of words; may easily learn multiple languages	Journalist, novelist, poet, teacher
Logical-mathematical intelligence	Capable of seeing numerical patterns; strong ability to use reason and logic	Scientist, mathematician
Musical intelligence	Understands and appreciates rhythm, pitch, and tone; may play multiple instruments or perform as a vocalist	Composer, performer
Bodily kinesthetic intelligence	High ability to control the movements of the body and use the body to perform various physical tasks	Dancer, athlete, athletic coach, yoga instructor
Spatial intelligence	Ability to perceive the relationship between objects and how they move in space	Choreographer, sculptor, architect, aviator, sailor
Interpersonal intelligence	Ability to understand and be sensitive to the various emotional states of others	Counselor, social worker, salesperson
Intrapersonal intelligence	Ability to access personal feelings and motivations and use them to direct behavior and reach personal goals	Key component of personal success over time
Naturalist intelligence	High capacity to appreciate the natural world and interact with the species within it	Biologist, ecologist, environmentalist

Table 1: Multiple Intelligences

Gardner's theory is relatively new and needs additional research to better establish empirical support. At the same time, his ideas challenge the traditional idea of intelligence to include a wider variety of abilities although it has been suggested that Gardner simply relabeled what other theorists called *cognitive styles* as *intelligences*

(Morgan, 1996). Furthermore, developing traditional measures of Gardner's intelligences is extremely difficult (Furnham, 2009; Gardner & Moran, 2006; Klein, 1997).

Gardner's inter- and intrapersonal intelligences are often combined into a single type: emotional intelligence. **Emotional intelligence** encompasses the ability to understand the emotions of yourself and others, show empathy, understand social relationships and cues, regulate your own emotions, and respond in culturally appropriate ways (Parker, Saklofske, & Stough, 2009). People with high emotional intelligence typically have well-developed social skills. Some researchers, including Daniel Goleman, the author of *Emotional Intelligence: Why It Can Matter More than IQ*, argue that emotional intelligence is a better predictor of success than traditional intelligence (Goleman, 1995). However, emotional intelligence has been widely debated, with researchers pointing out inconsistencies in how it is defined and described, as well as questioning results of studies on a subject that is difficult to measure and study empirically (Locke, 2005; Mayer, Salovey, & Caruso, 2004).

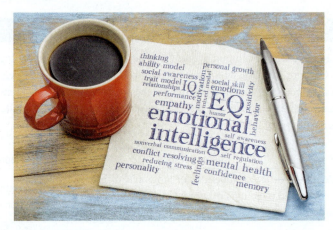

Figure 3: Emotional intelligence is the ability to understand your own emotions and how they relate to and affect others.

Intelligence can also have different meanings and values in different cultures. If you live on a small island where most people get their food by fishing from boats, it would be important to know how to fish and how to repair a boat. If you were an exceptional angler, your peers would probably consider you intelligent. If you were also skilled at repairing boats, your intelligence might be known across the whole island.

Think about your own family's culture. In Irish families, hospitality and telling an entertaining story are marks of the culture. If you are a skilled storyteller, other members of Irish culture are likely to consider you intelligent. What values are important for Latino families? Italian families?

Some cultures place a high value on working together as a collective. In these cultures, the importance of the group supersedes the importance of individual achievement. When you visit such a culture, how well you relate to the values of that culture exemplifies your **cultural intelligence**, sometimes referred to as *cultural competence*.

Creativity

Creativity is the ability to generate, create, or discover new ideas, solutions, and possibilities. Very creative people often have intense knowledge about something, work on it for years, look at novel solutions, seek out the advice and help of other experts, and take risks. Although creativity is often associated with the arts, it is actually a vital form of intelligence that drives people in many disciplines to discover something new. Creativity can be found in every area of life, from the way you decorate your residence to a new way of understanding how a cell works.

Creativity is often assessed as a function of one's ability to engage in **divergent thinking**. Divergent thinking can be described as thinking "outside the box"; it allows an individual to arrive at unique, multiple solutions to a given problem. In contrast, **convergent thinking** describes the ability to provide a correct or well-established answer or solution to a problem (Cropley, 2006; Gilford, 1967).

♀ Everyday Connection

Creativity

Dr. Tom Steitz, the Sterling Professor of biochemistry and biophysics at Yale University, has spent his career looking at the structure and specific aspects of RNA molecules and how their interactions could help produce antibiotics and ward off diseases. As a result of his lifetime of work, he won the Nobel Prize in chemistry in 2009. He wrote, "Looking back over the development and progress of my career in science, I am reminded how vitally important good mentorship is in the early stages of one's career development and constant face-to-face conversations, debate, and discussions with colleagues at all stages of research. Outstanding discoveries, insights, and developments do not happen in a vacuum" (Steitz, 2010, para. 39). Based on Steitz's comment, it becomes clear that someone's creativity, although an individual strength, benefits from interactions with others. Think of a time when your creativity was sparked by a conversation with a friend or classmate. How did that person influence you and what problem did you solve using creativity?

Figure 4: Dr. Steitz's work on RNA and his career experiences remind us that our creativity can be greatly influenced by interactions with others.

Further Resources

Do you think our current educational model fosters creativity? Watch this TED Talk (hawkes.biz/creativity) from Ken Robinson on his argument that schools kill creativity.

Want more on creativity? Check out this playlist (hawkes.biz/creativity2) from TED.

Summary

Intelligence is a complex characteristic of cognition. Many theories have been developed to explain what intelligence is and how it works. Sternberg generated his triarchic theory of intelligence, whereas

Gardner posited that intelligence is comprised of many factors. Still others focus on the importance of emotional intelligence. Finally, creativity seems to be a facet of intelligence, but it is extremely difficult to measure objectively.

Flash Forward

Ready to dig into the vocabulary? Get some practice with this Hawkes Verified Quizlet set (hawkes.biz/psych6q5)!

6.5 Measures of Intelligence

While you're likely familiar with the term *IQ* and associate it with the idea of intelligence, what does it really mean? *IQ* stands for **intelligence quotient** and describes a score earned on a test designed to measure intelligence. There are many ways psychologists describe intelligence (or more aptly, intelligences). Similarly, IQ tests—the tools designed to measure intelligence—have been the subject of debate throughout their development and use.

> **Reflection Questions**
>
> When might an IQ test be used? What do we learn from the results, and how might people use this information?

IQ tests are expensive to administer and must be given by a licensed psychologist. Intelligence testing has been considered useful for education and social policy. In this lesson, we will explore what intelligence tests measure, how they are scored, and how they were developed.

Measuring Intelligence

It seems that the human understanding of intelligence is somewhat limited when we focus on traditional or academic-type intelligence. How then can intelligence be measured? How do we ensure that IQ tests function as valid measures of intelligence?

The IQ test has been synonymous with intelligence for over a century. In the late 1800s, Sir Francis Galton developed the first broad test of intelligence (Flanagan & Kaufman, 2004). Although he was not a psychologist, his contributions are still influential today (Gordon, 1995). Reliable intelligence testing began in earnest during the early 1900s with a researcher named Alfred Binet (Figure 1). Binet was asked by the French government to develop an intelligence test to use on children to determine which ones might have difficulty in school; it included many verbally based tasks. American researchers soon realized the value of such testing.

(a)   (b)

🖼 **Figure 1:** (a) French psychologist Alfred Binet helped to develop intelligence testing. (b) This page is from a 1908 version of the Binet-Simon Intelligence Scale. Children being tested were asked which face, of each pair, was prettier.

Louis Terman, a Stanford professor, modified Binet's work by standardizing the administration of the test and tested thousands of different-aged children to establish an average score for each age. As a result, the test was normed and standardized, which means that it was administered consistently to a large enough representative sample of the population that the range of scores resulted in a bell curve (bell curves will be discussed later). Let's review these concepts:

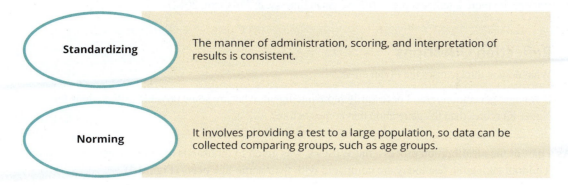

Standardizing   The manner of administration, scoring, and interpretation of results is consistent.

Norming   It involves providing a test to a large population, so data can be collected comparing groups, such as age groups.

🖼 **Figure 2:** Standardization and norming are two concepts that IQ testing seeks to fulfill.

The resulting data provide norms, or referential scores, by which to interpret future scores. Norms are not expectations of what a given group *should* know but a demonstration of what that group *does* know. **Norming** and **standardizing** the test ensures that new scores are reliable. This new version of the test was called the Stanford-Binet Intelligence Scale (Terman, 1916). Remarkably, an updated version of this test is still widely used today.

In 1939, David Wechsler, a psychologist who spent part of his career working with World War I veterans, developed a new IQ test in the United States. Wechsler combined several subtests from other intelligence tests used between 1880 and World War I. These subtests tapped into a variety of verbal and nonverbal skills because Wechsler believed that intelligence encompassed "the global capacity of a person to act purposefully, to think rationally, and to deal effectively with his environment" (Wechsler, 1958, p. 7). He named the test the Wechsler-Bellevue Intelligence Scale (Wechsler, 1981).

> **Further Resources**
>
> Interested in taking the Stanford-Binet Intelligence Assessment? Visit this site (hawkes.biz/stanford) for a few different versions of the test.

✎ On Your Own

Answer the following questions in the space below.
Do you agree with Wechsler's definition of what encompasses intelligence? Why or why not? What do you think reflects signs of intelligence?

This combination of subtests became one of the most extensively used intelligence tests in the history of psychology. Although its name was later changed to the Wechsler Adult Intelligence Scale (WAIS) and has been revised several times, the aims of the test remain virtually unchanged since its inception (Boake, 2002). Today, there are three intelligence tests credited to Wechsler:

1. The Wechsler Adult Intelligence Scale—fourth edition (WAIS-IV)

2. The Wechsler Intelligence Scale for Children (WISC-V)

3. The Wechsler Preschool and Primary Scale of Intelligence—IV (WPPSI-IV) (Wechsler, 2012)

These tests are used widely in schools and communities throughout the United States, and they are periodically normed and standardized as a means of recalibration. Interestingly, the periodic recalibrations have led to an interesting observation known as the Flynn effect. Named after James Flynn, who was among the first to describe this trend, the **Flynn effect** refers to the observation that each generation has a significantly higher IQ than the last. Flynn himself argues, however, that increased IQ scores do not necessarily mean that younger generations are more intelligent per se (Flynn, Shaughnessy, & Fulgham, 2012).

> **Reflection Questions**
>
> What do you think causes the Flynn effect?
>
> If younger generations aren't necessarily more intelligent, what are some possible explanations for higher IQ scores than the generation that comes before?

As a part of the recalibration process, the WISC-V was given to thousands of children across the country, and children taking the test today are compared with their same-age peers (Figure 3).

The WISC-V is composed of 14 subtests, which comprise five categories, which then render an IQ score. The five categories are as follows:

Verbal Comprehension

Visual Spatial

Fluid Reasoning

Working Memory

Processing Speed

▣ **Figure 3:** These categories comprise the 14 subtests of the WISC-V.

When the test is complete, individuals receive a score for each of the five indices and a Full Scale IQ score. The method of scoring reflects the understanding that intelligence is comprised of multiple abilities in several cognitive realms and focuses on the mental processes that the child used to arrive at his or her answers to each test item.

Ultimately, we are still left with the question of how valid intelligence tests are. Certainly, the most modern versions of these tests tap into more than verbal competencies, yet the specific skills that should be assessed in IQ testing, the degree to which any test can truly measure an individual's intelligence, and the use of the results of IQ tests are still issues of debate (Gresham & Witt, 1997; Flynn, Shaughnessy, & Fulgham, 2012; Richardson, 2002; Schlinger, 2003).

What Do You Think?

Intellectually Disabled Criminals and Capital Punishment

The case of *Atkins v. Virginia* was a landmark case in the United States Supreme Court. On August 16, 1996, two men, Daryl Atkins and William Jones, robbed, kidnapped, and then shot and killed Eric Nesbitt, a local airman from the U.S. Air Force. A clinical psychologist evaluated Atkins and testified at the trial that Atkins had an IQ of 59. The mean IQ score is 100. The psychologist concluded that Atkins was "mildly mentally retarded."

The jury found Atkins guilty, and he was sentenced to death. Atkins and his attorneys appealed to the Supreme Court. In June 2002, the Supreme Court reversed a previous decision and ruled that executions of "mentally retarded" criminals are "cruel and unusual punishments" prohibited by the Eighth Amendment. The court wrote in their decision:

> Clinical definitions of mental retardation require not only subaverage intellectual functioning, but also significant limitations in adaptive skills. Mentally retarded persons frequently know the difference between right and wrong and are competent to stand trial. Because of their impairments, however, by definition they have diminished capacities to understand and process information, to communicate, to abstract from mistakes and learn from experience, to engage in logical reasoning, to control impulses, and to understand others' reactions. Their deficiencies do not warrant an exemption from criminal sanctions but diminish their personal culpability. (*Atkins v. Virginia*, 2002, par. 5)

The court also decided that there was a state legislature consensus against the execution of individuals with intellectual disabilities and that this consensus should stand for all of the states. The Supreme Court ruling left it up to the states to determine their own definitions of intellectual disability. The definitions vary among states as to who can be executed. In the Atkins case, a jury decided that because he had many contacts with his lawyers and thus was provided with intellectual stimulation, his IQ had reportedly increased, and he was now smart enough to be executed. He was given an execution date and then received a stay of execution after it was revealed that lawyers for co-defendant, William Jones, coached Jones to "produce a testimony against Mr. Atkins that did match the evidence" (Liptak, 2008). After the revelation of this misconduct, Atkins was re-sentenced to life imprisonment.

Atkins v. Virginia (2002) highlights several issues regarding society's beliefs around intelligence. In the Atkins case, the Supreme Court decided that intellectual disability *does* affect decision making and therefore should affect the nature of the punishment such criminals receive. Where, however, should the lines of intellectual disability be drawn? In May 2014, the Supreme Court ruled in a related case (*Hall v. Florida*) that IQ scores cannot be used as a final determination of a prisoner's eligibility for the death penalty (Roberts, 2014).

Group Activity

As a group, discuss and react to the story about *Atkins v. Virginia*. Do you agree with the court's ruling? Why or why not?

✎ On Your Own

Fill in the box with each psychologist's contributions to IQ testing.

Psychologist	Contributions to IQ Testing
Sir Francis Galton	
Alfred Binet	
Louis Terman	
David Wechsler	

Figure 4: This is a portrait of Sir Francis Galton from the 1890s.

The Bell Curve

The results of intelligence tests follow the bell curve, a graph in the general shape of a bell. When the bell curve is used in psychological testing, the graph demonstrates a normal distribution of a trait, in this case, intelligence, in the human population. Many human traits naturally follow the bell curve. For example, if you lined up all your female schoolmates according to height, it is likely that a large cluster of them would be the average height for an American woman: 5'4"–5'6". This cluster would fall in the center of the bell curve, representing the average height for American women (Figure 5). There would be fewer women who stand closer to 4'11" or 5'11".

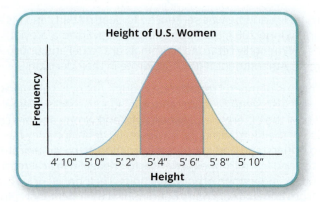

Figure 5: Are you of below-average, average, or above-average height?

The trick to finding a bell curve in nature is to use a large sample size. Without a large sample size, it is less likely that the bell curve will represent the wider population. A **representative sample** is a subset of the population that accurately represents the general population. If, for example, you measured the height of the women in your classroom only, you might not actually have a representative sample. Perhaps the women's basketball team wanted to take this course together, and they are all in your class. Because basketball players tend to be taller than average, the women in your class may not be a good representative sample of the population of American women. But if your sample included all the women at your school, it is more likely that their heights would form a natural bell curve.

The same principles apply to intelligence tests scores. Individuals earn a score called an intelligence quotient (IQ). Over the years, different types of IQ tests have evolved, but the way scores are interpreted remains the same. The average IQ score on an IQ test is 100. **Standard deviations** describe how data are dispersed in a population and give context to large data sets. The bell curve uses the standard deviation to show how all scores are dispersed from the average score (Figure 6). In modern IQ testing, one standard deviation is 15 points. So a score of 85 would be described as "one standard deviation below the mean." How would you describe a score of 115 and a score of 70? Any IQ score that falls within one standard deviation above and below the mean (between 85 and 115) is considered average, and 68% of the population has IQ scores in this range. An IQ score of 130 or above is considered a superior level.

Figure 6: The majority of people have an IQ score between 85 and 115.

Only 2.2% of the population has an IQ score below 70 (American Psychological Association [APA], 2013). A score of 70 or below indicates significant cognitive delays, major deficits in adaptive functioning, and difficulty meeting "community standards of personal independence and social responsibility" when compared to same-aged peers (APA, 2013, p. 37). An individual in this IQ range would be considered to have an intellectual disability and exhibit deficits in intellectual functioning and adaptive behavior (American Association on Intellectual and Developmental Disabilities, 2013). Formerly known as *mental retardation*, the accepted term now is *intellectual disability*, and it has four subtypes: mild, moderate, severe, and profound (Table 1). *The Diagnostic and Statistical Manual of Psychological Disorders* lists criteria for each subgroup (APA, 2013).

Intellectual Disability Subtype	Percentage of Intellectually Disabled Population	Description
Mild	85%	3rd- to 6th-grade skill level in reading, writing, and math; may be employed and live independently
Moderate	10%	Basic reading and writing skills; functional self-care skills; requires some oversight
Severe	5%	Functional self-care skills; requires oversight of daily environment and activities
Profound	<1%	May be able to communicate verbally or nonverbally; requires intensive oversight

Table 1: Characteristics of Cognitive Disorders

On the other end of the intelligence spectrum are those individuals whose IQs fall into the highest ranges. Consistent with the bell curve, about 2% of the population falls into this category. People are considered gifted if they have an IQ score of 130 or higher, or superior intelligence in a particular area. Long ago, popular belief suggested that people of high intelligence were maladjusted. This idea was disproven through a groundbreaking study of gifted children. In 1921, Lewis Terman began a longitudinal study of over 1,500 children with IQs over 135 (Terman, 1925). His findings showed that these children became well-educated, successful adults who were, in fact, well-adjusted (Terman & Oden, 1947). Additionally, Terman's study showed that the subjects were above average in physical build and attractiveness, dispelling an earlier popular notion that highly intelligent people were "weaklings." Some people with very high IQs elect to join Mensa, an organization dedicated to identifying, researching, and fostering intelligence. Members must have an IQ score in the top 2% of the population, and they may be required to pass other exams in their application to join the group.

Dig Deeper

What's in a Name? Mental Retardation

In the past, individuals with IQ scores below 70 and significant adaptive and social functioning delays were diagnosed with mental retardation. When this diagnosis was first named, the title held no social stigma. In time, the degrading word *retard* sprang from this diagnostic term. *Retard* was frequently used as a taunt until the words *mentally retarded* and *retard* became an insult. As such, the DSM-5 now labels this diagnosis as *intellectual disability*. Many states once had a Department of Mental Retardation to serve those diagnosed with such cognitive delays, but most have changed their name to Department of Developmental Disabilities or something similar in language. The Social Security Administration still uses the term *mental retardation* but is considering eliminating it from its programming (Goad, 2013).

Reflection Questions

Do you think changing the title of the previous department has any impact on how people regard those with developmental disabilities? Does a different name give people more dignity, and if so, how? Does it change the expectations for those with developmental or cognitive disabilities?

Why Measure Intelligence?

The value of IQ testing is most evident in educational or clinical settings. Children who seem to be experiencing learning difficulties or severe behavioral problems can be tested to ascertain whether their difficulties can be partly attributed to an IQ score that is significantly different from the mean for their age group. Without IQ testing—or another measure of intelligence—children and adults needing extra support might not be identified effectively. IQ testing is also used in courts to determine whether a defendant has special or extenuating circumstances that preclude him from participating in a trial. People also use IQ testing results to seek disability benefits from the Social Security Administration. The usefulness and benefits of IQ testing are vast. Consider the following case study:

> Candace, a 14-year-old girl experiencing problems at school, was referred for a court-ordered psychological evaluation. She was in regular education classes in ninth grade and was failing every subject. Candace had never been a stellar student but had always been passed to the next grade. She would frequently curse at her teachers who called on her in class. She also got into fights with other students and occasionally shoplifted. When she arrived for the evaluation, Candace immediately said that she hated everything about school, including the teachers, the rest of the staff, the building, and the homework. Her parents stated that they felt their daughter was picked on because she was of a different race than the teachers and most of the other students. When asked why she cursed at her teachers, Candace replied, "They only call on me when I don't know the answer. I don't want to say, 'I don't know' all of the time and look like an idiot in front of my friends. The teachers embarrass me." She was given a battery of tests, including an IQ test. Her score on the IQ test was 68.

Reflection Questions

What does Candace's score say about her ability to excel or even succeed in a regular education class without assistance?

✏ On Your Own

Answer the following questions about measuring intelligence.

1. You took an intelligence test and scored a 130. When asked how you did, you reply:

☐ "I scored one standard deviation below the mean."

☐ "I scored two standard deviations below the mean."

☐ "I scored one standard deviation above the mean."

☐ "I scored two standard deviations above the mean."

2. The first person to develop an intelligence test was:

☐ Alfred Binet

☐ Louis Terman

☐ David Wechsler

☐ Sir Francis Galton

3. You took an intelligence test and scored a 90. You would be considered:

☐ above average   ☐ average

☐ below average   ☐ intellectually disabled

Summary

In this lesson, we learned about the history of intelligence testing and some of the challenges regarding intelligence testing. Intelligence tests began in earnest with Binet; Wechsler later developed intelligence tests that are still in use today: the WAIS-IV and WISC-V. The bell curve shows the range of scores that encompass average intelligence as well as standard deviations.

6.6 The Source of Intelligence

A young girl, born of teenage parents, lives with her grandmother in rural Mississippi. They are in serious poverty, but they do their best to get by with what they have. She learns to read when she is just 3 years old. As she grows older, she longs to live with her mother, who now resides in Wisconsin. She moves there at age 6. At 9 years of age, she is raped. During the next several years, several different male relatives repeatedly molest her, and her life unravels. She turns to drugs and sex to fill the deep, lonely void inside her. Her mother then sends her to Nashville to live with her father, who imposes strict behavioral expectations upon her, and over time, her wild life settles once again. She begins to experience success in school and, at 19 years old, becomes the youngest and first African-American female news anchor ("Dates and Events," n.d.). The woman—Oprah Winfrey—has gone on to become a media giant known for both her intelligence and her empathy.

Flash Forward

Ready to dig into the vocabulary? Get some practice with this Hawkes Verified Quizlet set (hawkes.biz/psych6q6)!

High Intelligence: Nature or Nuture?

Is intelligence determined by genetics? Researchers from the Minnesota Study of Twins Reared Apart found that identical twins raised together and identical twins raised apart exhibit a higher correlation between their IQ scores than siblings or fraternal twins raised together (Bouchard, Lykken, McGue, Segal, & Tellegen, 1990). The findings from this study suggest that intelligence is partially determined by genetics (Figure 1). A separate study suggests that although genetics seem to be in control of the level of intelligence, environmental influences help determine if a child reaches his or her full potential (Bartels, Rietveld, Van Baal, & Boomsma, 2002).

Reflection Questions

What about a child's environment do you think is most important for them to achieve their full intellectual potential?

📊 **Figure 1:** The correlations of IQs of unrelated versus related persons reared apart or together suggest a genetic component to intelligence.

Range of Reaction is the theory that each person responds to the environment in a unique way based on his or her genetic makeup. According to this idea, your genetic potential is a fixed quantity, but whether you reach your full intellectual potential is dependent upon the environmental stimulation you experience, especially in childhood.

Children and adults who come from certain minority ethnic groups or come from more impoverished socioeconomic backgrounds, tend to have lower IQ scores. For example, Arthur Jensen made a controversial conclusion that African Americans had lower conceptual and analytical abilities than Caucasian and Asian Americans (Modgil & Routledge, 1987; Williams, 1970; Jensen, 1969). He also posited that intelligence was made up of two types of abilities: Level I and Level II. In his theory, Level I is responsible for rote memorization, whereas Level II is responsible for conceptual and analytical abilities. According to his findings, Level I remains consistent among the human race. Level II, however, exhibits differences among ethnic groups (Modgil & Routledge, 1987). Jensen's most controversial conclusion was that Level II intelligence is most prevalent among Asians and least prevalent among African Americans with Caucasians falling in the middle. Robert Williams was among those who called out racial bias in Jensen's results (Williams, 1970).

More recent research has indicated that children growing up in poverty, which includes a higher proportion of African Americans than Caucasian and Asian Americans, do not have their basic needs of safety, food, and shelter met on a consistent basis. Even when these children do have their needs met, they may frequently worry that they will lose them in the future. As a result, this excessive worry can lead to reduced prefrontal brain functioning, which can impact performance on IQ tests (Kishyama, Boyce, Jimenez, Perry, & Knight, 2009). These factors may explain these results.

Parents of African-American students filed a case against the State of California in 1979 because they believed that the testing method used to identify students with learning disabilities was culturally unfair. They argued that the tests were normed and standardized using white children (*Larry P. v. Riles*). The testing method used by the state disproportionately identified African-American children as intellectually disabled. These results identify the cultural biases that exist with intelligence testing and the importance of cultural sensitivity in the practice of psychological assessment. According to a summary of the case, *Larry P. v. Riles* :

> In violation of Title VI of the Civil Rights Act of 1964, the Rehabilitation Act of 1973, and the Education for All Handicapped Children Act of 1975, defendants have utilized standardized intelligence tests that are racially and culturally biased, have a discriminatory impact against

Black children, and have not been validated for the purpose of essentially permanent placements of Black children into educationally dead-end, isolated, and stigmatizing classes for the so-called educable mentally retarded. Further, these federal laws have been violated by defendants' general use of placement mechanisms that, taken together, have not been validated and result in a large over-representation of Black children in the special E.M.R. classes. (*Larry P. v. Riles*, par. 6)

Examples like this reveal the limitations of intelligence testing.

Reflection Questions

What do you think IQ test makers can do to ensure that intelligence tests are culturally sensitive?

What Are Learning Disabilities?

Learning disabilities are cognitive disorders that affect different areas of cognition, particularly language or reading. It should be pointed out that learning disabilities are not the same thing as intellectual disabilities. Learning disabilities are considered specific neurological impairments rather than global intellectual or developmental disabilities. A person with a language disability has difficulty understanding or using spoken language, whereas someone with a reading disability, such as dyslexia, has difficulty processing what he or she is reading.

Furthermore, learning disabilities tend to exhibit comorbidity with other disorders, like attention-deficit hyperactivity disorder (ADHD). Anywhere between 30–70% of individuals with diagnosed cases of ADHD also have some sort of learning disability such as dyslexia or dysgraphia (Riccio, Gonzales, & Hynd, 1994).

☑ On Your Own

Which of the following is not a learning disability?

- ☐ Attention Deficit Hyperactivity Disorder (ADHD)
- ☐ Dyslexia
- ☐ Bipolar Disorder

Dysgraphia

Children with **dysgraphia** have a learning disability that results in a struggle to write legibly (Smits-Engelsman & Van Galen, 1997). Dysgraphia can exist independently of intelligence. For example, a child with an extremely high IQ can still suffer from dysgraphia. Students with dysgraphia need academic accommodations to help them succeed in school, such as alternative assignment opportunities (Barton, 2003). These alternative assignment opportunities may include an oral exam. Children with dysgraphia can be treated by an occupational therapist, but it is unclear how well these treatments work (Zwicker, 2005).

Dyslexia

Dyslexia is the most common learning disability in children. An individual with **dyslexia** exhibits an inability to correctly process letters. The neurological mechanism for sound processing does not work properly in someone with dyslexia. As a result, dyslexic children may not understand which letter is associated with what sound. Children with dyslexia are at an extreme disadvantage from their peers because they must learn words by memorizing them because they can't sound them out. A child with dyslexia may mix up letters within words and sentences or skip whole words while reading. Letter reversals, such as those shown in Figure 2, are a hallmark of this learning disability (Berninger, 2008).

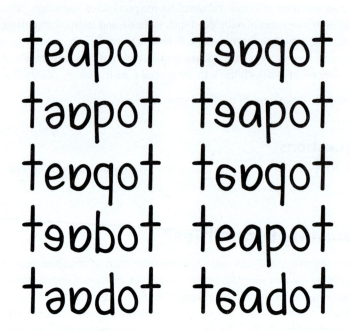

🖼 **Figure 2:** These written words show variations of the word *teapot* as written by individuals with dyslexia.

✐ **On Your Own**

Complete the following sentence.

A child with a high IQ:

☐ Could have dysgraphia, but not dyslexia

☐ Could have dyslexia, but not dysgraphia

☐ Could have either dyslexia, dysgraphia, or both

Summary

Genetics and environment affect intelligence and the challenges of certain learning disabilities.

The intelligence levels of all individuals seem to benefit from rich stimulation in their early environments.

Highly intelligent individuals, however, may have a built-in resiliency that allows them to overcome difficult obstacles in their upbringing. Learning disabilities can cause major challenges for children who are learning to read and write. Unlike developmental disabilities, learning disabilities are strictly neurological in nature and are not related to intelligence levels. Students with dyslexia, for example, may have extreme difficulty learning to read, but their intelligence levels are typically average or above average.

Chapter 6 Project

Purpose

In this project, you will work with a peer to develop case studies for two individuals, both college students. Your task is to use the content in this chapter to create these two case studies. And, because creativity is a concept covered in this chapter, you are invited to be creative as you "build your characters." **The purpose of this project is to provide you an opportunity for empathy-building and perspective-taking, as you consider the genetic and environmental influences on the development of thinking, language, and intelligence.**

Directions

For <u>each</u> written case study, use <u>at least two</u> concepts or ideas from each of the lessons in this chapter (i.e., 6.1-6.6), for a total of 12 concepts per case study. Place these chosen concepts in a table like the one below. Your case studies may have no more than six of the twelve concepts in common, so that you can consider diversity in college students.

Chapter 6	College Student Case Study 1	College Student Case Study 2
6.1 – Concept 1 (Example)	**Schemata**	**Prototype**
6.1 – Concept 1		
6.1 – Concept 2		
6.2 – Concept 1		
6.2 – Concept 2		
6.3 – Concept 1		
6.3 – Concept 2		
6.4 – Concept 1		
6.4 – Concept 2		
6.5 – Concept 1		
6.5 – Concept 2		
6.6 – Concept 1		
6.6 – Concept 2		

Each written case study should begin by providing some background on the individual (e.g., name, gender, ethnicity, family background, etc.). Following this background, you should display a clear understanding of each concept in your table, by showing how it is at work or how it has been experienced in this person's life. Since you will use narrative (i.e., story) to illustrate your understanding of these concepts, you should expect each case study to be at least 750 words. All concepts should be applied within the case study and should be typed in **boldface** when used, either directly within the narrative if it is suitable, or in parentheses after an illustration is given.

Finally, you are encouraged to think in divergent ways (see Lesson 6.4). For the greatest impact of this assignment, try to make at least one of your characters very different from you in terms of gender, ethnicity, socioeconomic status, educational background and opportunity, etc. Your case study should also "flow." That is, it should read like a real college student's life (or case), integrating stories and using chronological history.

Materials

None required.

✏ Checklist

Case Study 1

☐ 2 concepts from lessons 6.1-6.6 (total of twelve)

☐ Background information

☐ Clear demonstration of each concept at work in case study

☐ Narrative approach; 750 words

☐ Concepts in **bold**

☐ Demonstrates diversity

Case Study 2

☐ 2 concepts from lessons 6.1-6.6 (total of twelve)

☐ Background information

☐ Clear demonstration of each concept at work in case study

☐ Narrative approach; 750 words

☐ Concepts in **bold**

☐ Demonstrates diversity

🏁 Chapter 6 Review

Lesson Summaries

6.1 What Is Cognition?

Cognitive psychology is the study of cognition, or the brain's ability to think, perceive, plan, analyze, and remember. Concepts and their corresponding prototypes help us quickly organize our thinking by creating categories into which we can sort new information. Schemata are clusters of related concepts. Some schemata involve routines of thought and behavior, and these help us function properly in various situations without having to "think twice" about them. Schemata also show up in social situations and routines of daily behavior.

6.2 Language

Language is a communication system that has both a lexicon and a system of grammar. Language acquisition occurs naturally and effortlessly during the early stages of life, and this acquisition occurs in a predictable sequence for individuals around the world. Language has a strong influence on thought, and the concept of how language may influence cognition remains an area of study and debate in psychology.

6.3 Problem Solving

Many different strategies exist for solving problems. Typical strategies include trial and error, applying algorithms, and using heuristics. To solve a large, complicated problem, it often helps to break the problem into smaller steps that can be accomplished individually, leading to an overall solution. Roadblocks to problem solving include a mental set, functional fixedness, and various biases that can cloud decision-making skills.

6.4 What Are Intelligence and Creativity?

Intelligence is a complex characteristic of cognition. Many theories have been developed to explain what intelligence is and how it works. Sternberg generated his triarchic theory of intelligence, whereas Gardner posited that intelligence is comprised of many factors. Still others focus on the importance of emotional intelligence. Finally, creativity seems to be a facet of intelligence, but it is extremely difficult to measure objectively.

6.5 Measures of Intelligence

In this lesson, we learned about the history of intelligence testing and some of the challenges regarding intelligence testing. Intelligence tests began in earnest with Binet; Wechsler later developed intelligence tests that are still in use today: the WAIS-IV and WISC-V. The bell curve shows the range of scores that encompass average intelligence as well as standard deviations.

6.6 The Source of Intelligence

Genetics and environment affect intelligence and the challenges of certain learning disabilities.

The intelligence levels of all individuals seem to benefit from rich stimulation in their early environments.

Highly intelligent individuals, however, may have a built-in resiliency that allows them to overcome difficult obstacles in their upbringing. Learning disabilities can cause major challenges for children who are learning to read and write. Unlike developmental disabilities, learning disabilities are strictly neurological in nature and are not related to intelligence levels.

Students with dyslexia, for example, may have extreme difficulty learning to read, but their intelligence levels are typically average or above average.

Key Terms

Flash Back

Now that you've worked through the chapter, sharpen your vocabulary with this Hawkes Verified Quizlet set (hawkes.biz/psychch6)!

Algorithm
Problem-solving strategy characterized by a specific set of instructions

Analytical Intelligence
Aligned with academic problem solving and computations

Anchoring Bias
Faulty heuristic in which you fixate on a single aspect of a problem to find a solution

Artificial Concept
Concept that is defined by a very specific set of characteristics

Availability Heuristic
Faulty heuristic in which you make a decision based on information readily available to you

Cognition
Thinking, including perception, learning, problem solving, judgment, and memory

Cognitive Psychology
Field of psychology dedicated to studying every aspect of how people think

Cognitive Script
Set of behaviors that are performed the same way each time; also referred to as an *event schema*

Concept
Category or grouping of linguistic information, objects, ideas, or life experiences

Confirmation Bias

Faulty heuristic in which you focus on information that confirms your beliefs

Convergent Thinking

Providing correct or established answers to problems

Creative Intelligence

Ability to produce new products, ideas, or inventing a new, novel solution to a problem

Creativity

Ability to generate, create, or discover new ideas, solutions, and possibilities

Crystallized Intelligence

Characterized by acquired knowledge and the ability to retrieve it

Cultural Intelligence

Ability with which people can understand and relate to those in another culture

Divergent Thinking

Ability to think "outside the box" to arrive at novel solutions to a problem

Dysgraphia

Learning disability that causes extreme difficulty in writing legibly

Dyslexia

Common learning disability in which letters are not processed properly by the brain

Emotional Intelligence

Ability to understand emotions and motivations in yourself and others

Event Schema

Set of behaviors that are performed the same way each time; also referred to as a *cognitive script*

Fluid Intelligence

Ability to see complex relationships and solve problems

Flynn Effect

Observation that each generation has a significantly higher IQ than the previous generation

Functional Fixedness

Inability to see an object as useful for any other use other than the one for which it was intended

Grammar

Set of rules that are used to convey meaning through the use of a lexicon

Heuristic

Mental shortcut that saves time when solving a problem

Hindsight Bias

Belief that the event just experienced was predictable even though it really wasn't

Intelligence Quotient

(Also, *IQ*) score on a test designed to measure intelligence

Language

Communication system that involves using words to transmit information from one individual to another

Lexicon

The words of a given language

Mental Set

Continually using an old solution to a problem without results

Morpheme

Smallest unit of language that conveys some type of meaning

Multiple Intelligences Theory

Gardner's theory that each person possesses at least eight types of intelligence

Natural Concept

Mental groupings that are created "naturally" through your experiences

Norming

Administering a test to a large population, so data can be collected to reference the normal scores for a population and its groups

Overgeneralization

Extension of a rule that exists in a given language to an exception to the rule

Phoneme

Basic sound unit of a given language

Practical Intelligence

Also known as "street smarts"

Problem-Solving Strategy

Method for solving problems

Prototype

Best representation of a concept

Range of Reaction

Each person's response to the environment is unique based on his or her genetic make-up

Representative Bias

Faulty heuristic in which you stereotype someone or something without a valid basis for your judgment

Representative Sample

Subset of the population that accurately represents the general population

Role Schema

Set of expectations that define the behaviors of a person occupying a particular role

Schema

(Plural: *schemata*) mental construct consisting of a cluster or collection of related concepts

Semantics

Process by which we derive meaning from morphemes and words

Standard Deviation

Measure of variability that describes the difference between a set of scores and their mean

Standardization

Method of testing in which administration, scoring, and interpretation of results are consistent

Syntax

Manner by which words are organized into sentences

Trial and Error

Problem-solving strategy in which multiple solutions are attempted until the correct one is found

Triarchic Theory of Intelligence

Sternberg's theory of intelligence; three facets of intelligence: practical, creative, and analytical

Working Backwards

Heuristic in which you begin to solve a problem by focusing on the end result

Exercises

Review Questions

1. Cognitive psychology is the branch of psychology that focuses on the study of _____.

    a. human development

    b. human thinking

    c. human behavior

    d. human society

2. Which of the following is an example of a prototype for the concept of leadership on an athletic team?

    a. The equipment manager

    b. The scorekeeper

    c. The team captain

    d. The quietest member of the team

3. Which of the following is an example of an artificial concept?

    a. Mammals

    b. A triangle's area

    c. Gemstones

    d. Teachers

4. An event schema is also known as a cognitive _____.

    a. stereotype

    b. concept

    c. script

    d. prototype

5. _____ provides general principles for organizing words into meaningful sentences.

    a. Linguistic determinism

    b. Lexicon

    c. Semantics

    d. Syntax

6. _____ are the smallest unit of language that carry meaning.

    a. Lexicon

    b. Phonemes

    c. Morphemes

    d. Syntax

7. The meaning of words and phrases is determined by applying the rules of _____.

    a. lexicon

    b. phonemes

    c. overgeneralization

    d. semantics

8. _____ is (are) the basic sound units of a spoken language.

    a. Syntax

    b. Phonemes

    c. Morphemes

    d. Grammar

9. A specific formula for solving a problem is called _____.

    a. an algorithm

    b. a heuristic

    c. a mental set

    d. trial and error

10. A mental shortcut in the form of a general problem-solving framework is called _____.

    a. an algorithm

    b. a heuristic

    c. a mental set

    d. trial and error

11. Which type of bias involves becoming fixated on a single trait of a problem?

    a. Anchoring bias

    b. Confirmation bias

    c. Representative bias

    d. Availability bias

12. Which type of bias involves relying on a false stereotype to make a decision?

    a. Anchoring bias

    b. Confirmation bias

    c. Representative bias

    d. Availability bias

13. Fluid intelligence is characterized by _____.

    a. being able to recall information

    b. being able to create new products

    c. being able to understand and communicate with different cultures

    d. being able to see complex relationships and solve problems

14. Which of the following is not one of Gardner's Multiple Intelligences?

    a. Creative

    b. Spatial

    c. Linguistic

    d. Musical

15. Which theorist put forth the triarchic theory of intelligence?

    a. Goleman

    b. Gardner

    c. Sternberg

    d. Steitz

16. When you are examining data to look for trends, which type of intelligence are you using most?

    a. Practical

    b. Analytical

    c. Emotional

    d. Creative

17. In order for a test to be normed and standardized it must be tested on _____.

    a. a group of same-age peers

    b. a representative sample

    c. children with mental disabilities

    d. children of average intelligence

18. The mean score for a person with an average IQ is _____.

    a. 70

    b. 130

    c. 85

    d. 100

19. Who developed the IQ test most widely used today?

    a. Sir Francis Galton

    b. Alfred Binet

    c. Louis Terman

    d. David Wechsler

20. The DSM-5 now uses _____ as a diagnostic label for what was once referred to as mental retardation.

    a. autism and developmental disabilities

    b. lowered intelligence

    c. intellectual disability

    d. cognitive disruption

21. Where does high intelligence come from?

    a. Genetics

    b. Environment

    c. Both A and B

    d. Neither A nor B

22. Arthur Jensen believed that _____.

    a. genetics was solely responsible for intelligence

    b. environment was solely responsible for intelligence

    c. intelligence level was determined by race

    d. IQ tests do not take socioeconomic status into account

23. What is a learning disability?

    a. A developmental disorder

    b. A neurological disorder

    c. An emotional disorder

    d. An intellectual disorder

24. Which of the following statements is true?

    a. Poverty always affects whether individuals are able to reach their full intellectual potential.

    b. An individual's intelligence is determined solely by the intelligence levels of his siblings.

    c. The environment in which an individual is raised is the strongest predictor of her future intelligence.

    d. There are many factors working together to influence an individual's intelligence level.

Critical Thinking Questions

25. Describe a social schema that you would notice at a sporting event.

26. Explain why event schemata have so much power over human behavior.

27. How do words not only represent our thoughts but also represent our values?

28. How could grammatical errors actually be indicative of language acquisition in children?

29. What is functional fixedness, and how can overcoming it help you solve problems?

30. How does an algorithm save you time and energy when solving a problem?

31. Describe a situation in which you would need to use practical intelligence.

32. Describe a situation in which cultural intelligence would help you communicate better.

33. Why do you think different theorists have defined intelligence in different ways?

34. Compare and contrast the benefits of the Stanford-Binet IQ test and Wechsler's IQ tests.

35. What evidence exists for a genetic component to an individual's IQ?

36. Describe the relationship between learning disabilities and intellectual disabilities to intelligence.

Chapter 7

Memory

Chapter Introduction

Take a few minutes to imagine what your day might be like if you could not remember anything you had learned. You would have to figure out how to get dressed, what clothing you should wear, and how to work buttons and zippers. You would need someone to teach you how to brush your teeth and tie your shoes. Who would you ask for help with these tasks since you wouldn't recognize the faces of these people in your house? Wait…is this even your house? You feel hungry. You'd like something to eat, but you don't know where the food is kept or even how to prepare it. This is getting confusing. Maybe it would be best to just go back to bed. A bed…what's a bed?

🖼 **Figure 1:** Imagine feeling a sense of confusion as a result of complete memory loss.

We have an amazing capacity for memory, but how, exactly, do we process and store information? Are there different kinds of memory, and if so, what characterizes the different types? How do we retrieve our memories? And why do we forget? This chapter will explore these questions as we learn about memory.

7.1 How Memory Functions

Memory is an information processing system; therefore, we often compare it to a computer. **Memory** is the set of processes used to encode, store, and retrieve information over different periods of time (Figure 2).

📷 **Figure 2:** Encoding involves the input of information into the memory system. Storage is the retention of the encoded information. Retrieval, or getting the information out of memory and back into awareness, is the third function.

Encoding

We get information into our brains through a process called **encoding**, which is the input of information into the memory system. Once we receive sensory information from the environment, our brains label or code it. We organize the information with other similar information and connect new concepts to existing concepts. Encoding information occurs through automatic processing and effortful processing.

If someone asks you what you ate for lunch today, more than likely you could recall this information quite easily. This is known as **automatic processing**, or the encoding of details like time, space, frequency, and the meaning of words. Automatic processing is usually done without any conscious awareness. Recalling the last time you studied for a test is another example of automatic processing. But what about the actual test material you studied? It probably required a lot of work and attention on your part in order to encode that information. This is known as **effortful processing** (Figure 3).

What are the most effective ways to ensure that important memories are well encoded? Even a simple sentence is easier to recall when it is meaningful (Anderson, 1984). Read the following sentences (Bransford & McCarrell, 1974), then look away and count backwards from 30 by threes to zero, and then try to write down the sentences without looking at them again.

1. The notes were sour because the seams split.

2. The voyage wasn't delayed because the bottle shattered.

3. The haystack was important because the cloth ripped.

How well did you do? By themselves, the statements that you wrote down were most likely confusing and difficult for you to recall. Now, try writing them again, using the following prompts: bagpipe, ship christening, and parachutist. Next, count backwards from 40 by fours, then check yourself to see how well you recalled the sentences this time. You can see that the sentences are now much more memorable because each of the sentences was placed in context. Material is far better encoded when you make it meaningful.

The encoding of words and their meaning is known as **semantic encoding**. William Bousfield (1935) found that people use a strategy called semantic clustering when they are asked to remember words. Semantic clustering is recalling a list of words in categories based on their meaning.

📷 **Figure 3:** When you first learn new skills such as driving a car, you have to put forth effort and attention to encode information about how to start a car, how to brake, how to handle a turn, and so on. Once you know how to drive, you can encode additional information about this skill automatically.

📷 **Figure 4:** Chunking ideas and concepts can help people remember and make meaning out of them.

Visual encoding is the encoding of images, and **acoustic encoding** is the encoding of sounds. If you were asked to recall words from the following list: *car*, *level*, *dog*, *truth*, *book*, and *value*; you would be more likely to recall *car*, *dog*, and *book* because you can recall images of these words. In contrast, you may have difficulty recalling more abstract words like *level*, *truth*, and *value*. Higher imagery words, such as *car*, *dog*, and *book* are easier to remember than low imagery words (Paivio, 1986).

Craik and Tulving concluded that we process verbal information best through semantic encoding, especially if we apply what is called the self-reference effect. Words that had been encoded semantically were better remembered than those encoded visually or acoustically. This is because semantic encoding involves a deeper level of processing than the shallower visual or acoustic encoding. The **self-reference effect** is the tendency for an individual to have better memory for information that relates to oneself in comparison to material that has less personal relevance (Rogers, Kuiper & Kirker, 1977).

✎ On Your Own

Based on the information presented so far in this lesson, which of the following is the most effective study strategy?

☐ Explaining the terms and concepts in the chapter to a friend or family member and applying examples of the content to your own life.

☐ Studying the important charts, graphs, and visuals that are presented in the textbook.

☐ Listening to a recording of the chapter as much as you can throughout the day.

Reflection Questions

What are some ways that you can incorporate semantic encoding and the self-reference effect into the classes you are taking now?

Storage

Storage is the creation of a permanent record of information.

According to Richard Atkinson and Richard Shiffrin (1968), a memory goes through three stages to be stored. These are sensory memory, short-term memory, and then long-term memory.

Figure 5: According to the Atkinson-Shiffrin model of memory, information passes through three distinct stages in order for it to be stored in long-term memory.

The **Atkinson-Shiffrin model** is just one approach to memory. Others, such as Baddeley and Hitch (1974), have proposed a model where short-term memory itself has different forms. In this model, storing memories in short-term memory is like opening different files on a computer and adding information. The type of short-term memory (or computer file) depends on the type of information received. There are memories in visual-spatial form, as well as memories of spoken or written material, and they are stored in three short-term systems: a visuospatial sketchpad, an episodic buffer, and a phonological loop. According to Baddeley and Hitch, a central executive part of memory supervises or controls the flow of information to and from the three short-term systems.

Sensory Memory

In the Atkinson-Shiffrin model, stimuli from the environment are processed first in **sensory memory**: storage of brief sensory events, such as sights, sounds, and tastes. It is very brief storage—up to a couple of seconds. We are constantly bombarded with sensory information, and we cannot absorb all of it, or even most of it. And most of it has no impact on our lives. J.R. Stroop found that people will name a color more easily if it appears printed in that color. This phenomenon is called the Stroop effect. Try an experiment: name the colors of the words you are given in Figure 6. Do not read the words, but say the color the word is printed in. For example, upon seeing the word *yellow* in green print, you should say "green," not "yellow."

Red	Blue	Yellow
Orange	Purple	Orange
Green	Yellow	Black
Yellow	Green	Red
Purple	Blue	Purple

Figure 6: The Stroop effect describes why it is difficult for us to name a color when the word and the color of the word are different.

Short-Term Memory

Short-term memory (STM) is a temporary storage system that processes incoming sensory memory; sometimes it is called working memory. Short-term memory can also represent everything that you are consciously aware of at a given second. The average person can hold something in short-term memory for approximately 20 seconds. George Miller (1956), in his research on the capacity of memory, found that most people can retain between five and nine items in STM. **Rehearsal** is the conscious repetition of information with the goal of storing it into long-term memory. The process of storing a short-term memory into long-term memory is called **memory consolidation**.

To test the capacity of your own short-term memory, have a partner read the strings of random numbers in Figure 7 out loud to you, beginning each string by saying, "Ready?" and ending each by saying, "Recall," at which point you should try to write down the string of numbers from memory. Note the longest string at which you got the series correct.

9754	68259	913825	5316842	86951372	719384273
6419	67148	648327	5963827	51739826	163875942

Figure 7: Work through this series of numbers using the recall exercise explained previously to determine the longest string of digits that you can store.

Reflection Questions

How did you do on the previous exercise? Did it confirm that you had a good, bad, or average short-term memory? Why or why not?

Long-Term Memory

Long-term memory (LTM) is the continuous storage of memories for everything that has happened to you in your life. Unlike short-term memory, the storage capacity of LTM has no limits. Long-term memory is divided into two types: explicit and implicit (Figure 8). **Explicit memories** are those we consciously try to remember and recall. For example, if you are studying for your chemistry exam, the material you are learning will be part of your explicit memory. **Implicit memories**, or non-declarative memories, are memories that are not part of our consciousness; they are formed from behaviors such as driving a car or riding a bike.

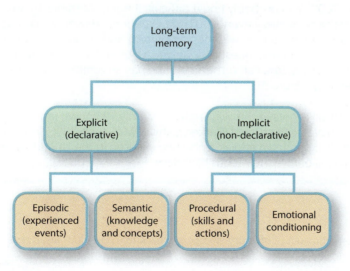

Figure 8: There are two components of long-term memory: explicit and implicit. Explicit memory includes episodic and semantic memory. Implicit memory includes procedural memory and things learned through conditioning.

Procedural memory is a type of implicit memory: it stores information about how to do things. It is the memory for skilled actions, such as how to brush your teeth, how to drive a car, or how to swim the crawl (freestyle) stroke.

Declarative memory has to do with the storage of facts and events we personally experienced. Explicit (declarative) memory has two parts: semantic memory and episodic memory.

Semantic memory has to do with language and knowledge about language. For example, knowing that George Washington was the first president of the United States would be a semantic memory.

Episodic memory is information about events we have personally experienced. An example of episodic memory may be your memory for what happened on your most recent birthday.

✍ On Your Own

Using the table below, give an example of the following types of memory.

Memory Type	Example
Explicit	
Implicit	
Episodic	
Semantic	
Procedural	

📷 **Figure 9:** Marilu Henner's super autobiographical memory is known as hyperthymesia.

Further Resources

Watch these Part 1 (hawkes. biz/automemory) and Part 2 (hawkes.biz/automemory2) video clips on superior autobiographical memory from the television news show *60 Minutes*.

💡 Everday Connection

Can You Remember Everything You Ever Did or Said?

Episodic memories are also called autobiographical memories. Let's quickly test your autobiographical memory. What were you wearing exactly five years ago today? What did you eat for lunch on April 10, 2009? You probably find it difficult, if not impossible, to answer these questions. Can you remember every event you have experienced over the course of your life—meals, conversations, clothing choices, weather conditions, and so on? Most likely none of us could even come close to answering these questions; however, American actress Marilu Henner, best known for the television show *Taxi*, can remember. She has an amazing and highly superior autobiographical memory (Figure 9).

Very few people can recall events in this way; right now, only 12 known individuals have this ability, and only a few have been studied (Parker, Cahill & McGaugh 2006). And although hyperthymesia normally appears in adolescence, two children in the United States appear to have memories from well before their tenth birthdays.

Retrieval

The act of getting information out of memory storage and back into conscious awareness, or short-term memory, is known as **retrieval**.

Recall is what we most often think about when we talk about memory retrieval; it means you can access information without cues.

Recognition happens when you identify information that you have previously learned after encountering it again.

The third form of retrieval is **relearning**, or learning information that you previously learned.

✐ On Your Own

Answer the following questions about retrieval.

1. Fill-in-the-blank and short answer tests rely on what aspect of retrieval?

☐ Recall   ☐ Recognition   ☐ Relearning

2. A multiple-choice quiz would rely on which aspect of retrieval?

☐ Recall   ☐ Recognition   ☐ Relearning

Reflection Questions

What type of test would you rather have, an essay or a multiple-choice test? What do you think this says about your preferred method of retrieval?

Summary

Memory is a system or process that stores what we learn for future use. Our memory has three basic functions: encoding, storing, and retrieving information. Encoding is the act of getting information into our memory system through automatic or effortful processing. Storage is retention of the information, and retrieval is the act of getting information out of storage and into conscious awareness through recall, recognition, and relearning.

The idea that information is processed through three memory systems is called the Atkinson-Shiffrin (A-S) model of memory. First, environmental stimuli enter our sensory memory for a period of less than a second to a few seconds. Those stimuli that we notice and pay attention to then move into short-term memory (also called working memory). According to the A-S model, if we rehearse this information, then it moves into long-term memory for permanent storage. Other models like that of Baddeley and Hitch suggest there is more of a feedback loop between short-term memory and long-term memory.

Long-term memory has a practically limitless storage capacity and is divided into implicit and explicit memory. Finally, retrieval is the act of getting memories out of storage and back into conscious awareness. This is done through recall, recognition, and relearning.

7.2 Parts of the Brain Involved with Memory

Are memories stored in just one part of the brain, or are they stored in many different parts of the brain? Karl Lashley began exploring this problem about 100 years ago by making lesions in the brains of animals, such as rats and monkeys. He was searching for evidence of the **engram**: the group of neurons that serve as the "physical representation of memory" (Josselyn, 2010). First, Lashley (1950) trained rats to find their way through a maze. Then, he used the tools available at the time—in this case, a soldering iron—to create lesions in the rats' brains, specifically in the cerebral cortex. He did this because he was trying to erase the engram, or the original memory trace, that the rats had of the maze.

Flash Forward

Ready to dig into the vocabulary? Get some practice with this Hawkes Verified Quizlet set (hawkes.biz/psych7q2)!

📷 **Figure 1:** For decades, rats have been used to help advance findings in modern science.

Lashley did not find evidence of the engram, and the rats were still able to find their way through the maze, regardless of the size or location of the lesion. Based on his creation of lesions and the animals' reaction, he formulated the **equipotentiality hypothesis**: if part of one area of the brain involved in memory is damaged, another part of the same area can take over that memory function (Lashley, 1950). Although Lashley's early work did not confirm the existence of the engram, modern psychologists are making progress locating it. Eric Kandel, for example, spent decades working on the synapse, the basic structure of the brain, and its role in controlling the flow of information through neural circuits needed to store memories (Mayford, Siegelbaum, & Kandel, 2012).

Many scientists believe that the entire brain is involved with memory. However, since Lashley's research, other scientists have been able to look more closely at the brain and memory. They have argued that memory is processed in specific parts of the brain, and specific neurons can be recognized for their involvement in forming memories. The main parts of the brain involved with memory are the amygdala, the hippocampus, the cerebellum, and the prefrontal cortex (Figure 2).

Further Resources

Watch this video (hawkes.biz/engrams) to hear Dr. Ryan, an assistant professor in neuroscience at Trinity College in Dublin, Ireland, explain engrams.

📷 **Figure 2:** The amygdala is involved in fear and fear memories. The hippocampus is associated with declarative and episodic memory as well as recognition memory. The cerebellum plays a role in processing procedural memories, such as how to play the piano. The prefrontal cortex appears to be involved in remembering semantic tasks.

The Amygdala

First, let's look at the role of the **amygdala** in memory formation. The main job of the amygdala is to regulate emotions, such as fear and aggression (Figure 2). The amygdala plays a part in how memories are stored because storage is influenced by stress hormones. For example, one researcher experimented with rats and the fear response (Josselyn, 2010). Using Pavlovian conditioning, a neutral tone was paired with a foot shock to the rats. This produced a fear memory in the rats. After being conditioned, each time they heard the tone, they would freeze (a defense response in rats), indicating a memory for the impending shock. Then the researchers induced cell death in neurons in the lateral amygdala, which is the specific area of the brain responsible for fear memories. They found that the fear memory faded (became extinct). Because of its role in processing emotional information, the amygdala is also involved in memory consolidation: the process of transferring new learning into long-term memory. The amygdala seems to facilitate encoding memories at a deeper level when the event is emotionally arousing.

Group Activity

In a small group, make a list of ways in which the rats' defensive response of freezing might be adaptive from an evolutionary perspective. Next, discuss and list examples of how the "fight-or-flight" response in humans is adaptive. As a class, share your lists and discuss what they have in common.

Reflection Questions

Do you think it is okay to hurt animals if it is for research purposes? Why or why not?

The Hippocampus

Another group of researchers also experimented with rats to learn how the hippocampus functions in memory processing (Figure 2). They created lesions in the hippocampi of the rats and found that the rats demonstrated memory impairment on various tasks, such as object recognition and maze running. They concluded that the hippocampus is involved in memory, specifically normal recognition memory as well as spatial memory (when the memory tasks are like recall tests) (Clark, Zola, & Squire, 2000). Another job of the hippocampus is to project information to cortical regions that give memories meaning and connect them with other connected memories. It also plays a part in memory consolidation: the process of transferring new learning into long-term memory.

Injury to this area leaves us unable to process new declarative memories. One famous patient, known for years only as H.M., had both his left and right temporal lobes (hippocampi) removed in an attempt to help control the seizures he had been suffering from for years (Corkin, Amaral, González, Johnson, & Hyman, 1997). As a result, his declarative memory was significantly affected, and he could not form new semantic knowledge. He lost the ability to form new memories, yet he could still remember information and events that had occurred prior to the surgery.

Figure 3: The brain's health determines one's ability to store memories.

The Cerebellum and Prefrontal Cortex

Although the hippocampus seems to be more of a processing area for explicit memories, you could still lose it and be able to create implicit memories (procedural memory, motor learning, and classical conditioning), thanks to your cerebellum (Figure 2). For example, one classical conditioning experiment is to accustom subjects to blink when they are given a puff of air. When researchers damaged the cerebellums of rabbits, they discovered that the rabbits were not able to learn the conditioned eye-blink response (Steinmetz, 1999; Green & Woodruff-Pak, 2000).

Other researchers have used brain scans, including positron emission tomography (PET) scans, to learn how people process and retain information. From these studies, it seems the prefrontal cortex is involved. In one study, participants had to complete two different tasks: either looking for the letter *a* in words (considered a perceptual task) or categorizing a noun as either living or non-living (considered a semantic task) (Kapur et al., 1994). Participants were then asked which words they had previously seen. Recall was much better for the semantic task than for the perceptual task. According to PET scans, there was much more activation in the left inferior prefrontal cortex in the semantic task. In another study, encoding was associated with left frontal activity, while retrieval of information was associated with the right frontal region (Craik et al., 1999).

Further Resources

For a closer look at how memory works, view this video (hawkes.biz/memory) on the quirks of memory.

Further Resources

Watch this video (hawkes. biz/cerebellum) to hear Richard Thompson explain the classical conditioning experiment in rabbits that paired a puff of air and blinking.

On Your Own

Identify the four parts of the brain involved in forming and encoding memories and the role each part plays.

Part of the Brain	Role in Memory
	1. processes emotional information 2. transfers new information into long-term memory
	1. recognition memory 2. spatial memory 3. sends information to cortex and connects with related memories 4. transfers new information into long-term memory
	Create implicit memories: 1. procedural memory (order in which to do things) 2. motor learning 3. classical conditioning
	1. process information 2. memory retention

Neurotransmitters

There also appear to be specific neurotransmitters involved with the process of memory, such as epinephrine, dopamine, serotonin, glutamate, and acetylcholine (Myhrer, 2003). There continues to be discussion and debate among researchers as to which neurotransmitter plays which specific role (Blockland, 1996). Although we don't yet know which role each neurotransmitter plays in memory, we do know that communication among neurons via neurotransmitters is critical for developing new memories. Repeated activity by neurons leads to increased neurotransmitters in the synapses and more efficient and more synaptic connections. This is how memory consolidation occurs.

It is also believed that strong emotions trigger the formation of strong memories, and weaker emotional experiences form weaker memories; this is called **arousal theory** (Christianson, 1992). For example, strong emotional experiences can trigger the release of neurotransmitters, as well as hormones, which strengthen memory; therefore, our memory for an emotional event is usually better than our memory for a non-emotional event. When humans and animals are stressed, the brain secretes more of the neurotransmitter glutamate, which helps them remember the stressful event (McGaugh, 2003). This is clearly evidenced by what is known as the flashbulb memory phenomenon.

📷 **Figure 4:** Moments of high emotional stress are more likely to stay in our memory.

✍ On Your Own

Identify the connection between emotion and memory formation.

1. Strong emotions:

☐ form weak memories   ☐ can trigger neurotransmitter and
                                         hormone release

2. Arousal theory predicts which emotional experiences form strong and weak memories.

☐ False   ☐ True

A **flashbulb memory** is an exceptionally clear recollection of an important event (Figure 5). Where were your older siblings or parents when the 9/11 terrorist attacks occurred? Have they ever talked about it? Most likely they can remember where they were and what they were doing. In fact, a Pew Research Center (2011) survey found that of those Americans who were age 8 or older at the time of the event, 97% can recall the moment they learned of this event, even more than a decade after it happened.

📷 **Figure 5:** Most people can remember where they were when they first heard about the 9/11 terrorist attacks. This is an example of a flashbulb memory: a record of an atypical and unusual event that has very strong emotional associations.

Dig Deeper

Inaccurate and False Memories

Flashbulb memories can have decreased accuracy with the passage of time, even with very important events. For example, on at least three occasions, when asked how he heard about the terrorist attacks of 9/11, President George W. Bush responded inaccurately. In January 2002, less than 4 months after the attacks, the then sitting President Bush was asked how he heard about the attacks. He responded:

> I was sitting there, and my Chief of Staff—well, first of all, when we walked into the classroom, I had seen this plane fly into the first building. There was a TV set on. And you know, I thought it was pilot error, and I was amazed that anybody could make such a terrible mistake. (Greenberg, 2004, p. 2)

Contrary to what President Bush recalled, no one saw the first plane hit, except people on the ground near the Twin Towers. The first plane was not videotaped because it was a normal Tuesday morning in New York City, until the first plane hit.

Some people attributed Bush's wrong recall of the event to conspiracy theories. However, there is a much more benign explanation: human memory, even flashbulb memories, can be frail. In fact, memory can be so frail that we can convince a person an event happened to them, even when it did not. In studies, research participants will recall hearing a word even though they never heard the word. For example, participants were given a list of 15 sleep-related words, but the word *sleep* was not on the list. Participants recalled hearing the word *sleep* even though they did not actually hear it (Roediger & McDermott, 2000). The researchers who discovered this named the theory after themselves and a fellow researcher, calling it the Deese-Roediger-McDermott paradigm.

Summary

Beginning with Karl Lashley, researchers and psychologists have been searching for the engram, which is the physical trace of memory. Lashley did not find the engram, but he did suggest that memories are distributed throughout the entire brain rather than stored in one specific area. Now we know that three brain areas do play significant roles in the processing and storage of different types of memories: the cerebellum, hippocampus, and amygdala. The cerebellum processes procedural memories; the hippocampus encodes new memories; and the amygdala helps determine what memories to store and plays a part in determining where the memories are stored based on whether we have a strong or weak emotional response to the event. Strong emotional experiences can trigger the release of neurotransmitters and hormones, which strengthen memory, so that memory for an emotional event is usually stronger than memory for a non-emotional event. This is shown by what is known as the flashbulb memory phenomenon: our ability to remember significant life events. However, our memory for life events (autobiographical memory) is not always accurate.

Flash Forward

Ready to dig into the vocabulary? Get some practice with this Hawkes Verified Quizlet set (hawkes.biz/psych7q3)!

7.3 Problems with Memory

You may pride yourself on your amazing ability to remember the birthdates and ages of all your friends and family members, or you may be able to recall vivid details of your 5th birthday party at Chuck E. Cheese's. However, all of us have at times felt frustrated, and even embarrassed, when our memories have failed us. There are several reasons why this happens.

Amnesia

Amnesia is the loss of long-term memory that occurs as the result of disease, physical trauma, or psychological trauma. Psychologist Endel Tulving (2002) and his colleagues at the University of Toronto studied K.C. for years. K.C. suffered a traumatic head injury in a motorcycle accident and then had severe amnesia. Tulving writes, "the outstanding fact about K.C.'s mental make-up is his utter inability to remember any events, circumstances, or situations from his own life. His episodic amnesia covers his whole life, from birth to the present. The only exception is the experiences that, at any time, he has had in the last minute or two" (Tulving, 2002, p. 14).

Anterograde Amnesia

There are two common types of amnesia: **anterograde amnesia** and retrograde amnesia (Figure 2).

Anterograde Amnesia

- commonly caused by brain trauma, such as a blow to the head

- cannot remember new information

- can remember information and events that happened prior to injury

- hippocampus is usually affected (McLeod, 2011)

- inability to transfer information from short-term to long-term memory; that is, the inability to consolidate memories

- usually unable to form new episodic or semantic memories

- usually able to form new procedural memories (Bayley & Squire, 2002)

Retrograde Amnesia

Retrograde amnesia is loss of memory for events that occurred before the trauma.

Retrograde Amnesia

- cannot remember some or all of past events

- difficulty remembering episodic memories

Figure 1: Forgetfulness can be frustrating, but there's usually a reason why it happens.

Figure 2: Memories can disappear gradually or all at once.

Further Resources

Watch this video (hawkes.biz/amnesia) to explore the case of Clive Wearing, who after suffering a brain injury can only recognize his wife. Each time he sees her, it is like he hasn't seen her for a very long time. His memory lasts only seconds.

Further Resources

View this video (hawkes.biz/amnesia2) profiling Scott Bolzan's amnesia and his attempts to get his life back.

Hollywood has been fascinated with the amnesia plot for nearly a century, going all the way back to the film *Garden of Lies* from 1915 to more recent movies such as the Jason Bourne spy thrillers. However, for real-life sufferers of retrograde amnesia, like former NFL football player Scott Bolzan, the story is not a Hollywood movie. Bolzan fell, hit his head, and deleted 46 years of his life in an instant. He is now living with one of the most extreme cases of retrograde amnesia on record.

What are the differences in memory retrieval and memory formation in the two amnesia types?

Amnesia Type	Impact on Memory Retrieval	Impact on Memory Formation
anterograde	can remember events prior to event that caused amnesia	cannot form new episodic or semantic memories but can form new procedural memories
retrograde	cannot remember events prior to event that caused amnesia	can form new memories

Reflection Questions

In the movie *Eternal Sunshine of the Spotless Mind* (2004), Clementine and Joel go through a procedure that removes all memory of their relationship. If you could take a pill or undergo a procedure to erase memories from your past, would you choose to do so? Why or why not?

Memory Construction and Reconstruction

The formulation of new memories is sometimes called **construction**, and the process of bringing up old memories is called **reconstruction**. Yet as we retrieve our memories, we also tend to alter and modify them. A memory pulled from long-term storage into short-term memory is flexible. New events can be added, and we can change what we think we remember about past events, resulting in inaccuracies and distortions. People may not intend to distort facts, but it can happen in the process of retrieving old memories and combining them with new memories (Roediger and DeSoto, in press).

✏ On Your Own

Identify whether each of the following statements is true or false.

1. Reconstruction of memory occurs through a rewind and play process that is like watching a video.

   ☐ False   ☐ True

2. Our prior experiences are added to the encoding of new memories, called the construction of memory.

   ☐ False   ☐ True

Suggestibility

Suggestibility describes the effects of misinformation from external sources that leads to the creation of false memories. When someone witnesses a crime, that person's memory of the details of the crime is very important in catching the suspect. However, because memory is so fragile, witnesses can be easily (and often accidentally) misled due to the problem of suggestibility. In the fall of 2002, two snipers in the D.C. area shot people at a gas station, in a Home Depot parking lot, and walking down the street. These attacks went on for over three weeks and resulted in the deaths of 10 people. During this time, as you can imagine, people were terrified to leave their homes, go shopping, or even walk through their neighborhoods. Police officers and the FBI worked frantically to solve the crimes, and a tip hotline was set up. Law enforcement received over 140,000 tips, which resulted in approximately 35,000 possible suspects (Newseum, n.d.).

> **Further Resources**
>
> Read this *New York Times* postmortem (hawkes.biz/suggestibility) of the D.C. sniper investigation. The D.C. snipers were peacefully taken into custody; they were sleeping when they were found by Montgomery County (MD) police. The older sniper, John Muhammed, was executed in 2009 while the younger sniper, Lee Malvo was imprisoned for life due to his age when the shootings were committed.

📷 **Figure 3:** Do you think you would remember a vehicle present at the scene of a crime?

Most of the tips were dead ends until a white van was spotted at the site of one of the shootings. The police chief went on national television with a picture of the white van. After the news conference, several other eyewitnesses called to say that they too had seen a white van fleeing from the scene of the shooting. At the time, there were more than 70,000 white vans in the area. Police officers, as well as the public, focused almost exclusively on white vans because they believed the eyewitnesses. Other tips were ignored. When the suspects were finally caught, they were driving a blue sedan.

As illustrated by this example, we are vulnerable to the power of suggestion, simply based on something we see on the news, or we can claim to remember something that in fact is only a suggestion someone made. It is the suggestion that is the cause of the false memory.

Eyewitness Misidentification

Even though memory and the process of reconstruction can be fragile, police officers, prosecutors, and the courts often rely on eyewitness identification and testimony in the prosecution of criminals. However, faulty eyewitness identification and testimony can lead to wrongful convictions (Figure 4).

Further Resources

Psychologist Dr. Elizabeth Loftus has spent most of her career studying the reliability of memory. Watch this TEDTalk (hawkes.biz/falsememory), where Dr. Loftus describes the fallibility of memory.

Figure 4: In studying cases where DNA evidence has exonerated people from crimes, the Innocence Project discovered that eyewitness misidentification is the leading cause of wrongful convictions (Benjamin N. Cardozo School of Law, Yeshiva University, 2009).

In North Carolina in 1984, Ronald Cotton was misidentified by Jennifer Thompson, a 22-year-old college student brutally raped at knifepoint. She was hesitant to identify Cotton as her rapist but was encouraged by unintended cues and suggestions by police officers. In contrast to her hesitation in picking Cotton out of a police lineup, at the trial, Thompson reported absolutely no doubt that she was raped by Ronald Cotton.

After Cotton was convicted of the rape, he was sent to prison for life plus 50 years. After four years in prison, he was able to get a new trial. Jennifer Thompson once again testified against him. This time, Ronald Cotton was given two life sentences. After serving 11 years in prison, DNA evidence finally demonstrated that Ronald Cotton did not commit the rape, was innocent, and had served over a decade in prison for a crime he did not commit.

📷 **Figure 5:** Purposeful and accidental pressures have often led victims to choose innocent individuals out of a police lineup.

Ronald Cotton's story, unfortunately, is not unique. There are also people convicted and placed on death row, who were later exonerated. The Innocence Project is a non-profit group that works to exonerate falsely convicted people, including those convicted by eyewitness testimony. To learn more, you can visit their website (hawkes.biz/innocence1).

Ever since Loftus published her first studies on the suggestibility of eyewitness testimony in the 1970s, social scientists, police officers, therapists, and legal practitioners have been aware of the flaws in interview practices. **Consequently, steps have been taken to decrease the suggestibility of witnesses:**

- Modify how witnesses are questioned.

  - When interviewers use neutral and less leading language, children more accurately recall what happened and who was involved (Goodman, 2006; Pipe, 1996; Pipe, Lamb, Orbach, & Esplin, 2004).

- Change how police lineups are conducted.

  - Use a blind photo lineup, so the person administering the lineup doesn't know which photo belongs to the suspect, minimizing the possibility of giving leading cues.

- Judges in some states now inform jurors about the possibility of misidentification.

- Judges can also suppress eyewitness testimony if they deem it unreliable.

Dig Deeper

Preserving Eyewitness Memory: the Elizabeth Smart Case

Contrast the Cotton case with what happened in the Elizabeth Smart case. When Elizabeth was 14 years old and fast asleep in her bed at home, she was abducted at knifepoint. Her nine-year-old sister, Mary Katherine, was sleeping in the same bed and watched, terrified, as her beloved older sister was abducted. Mary Katherine was the sole eyewitness to this crime and was very fearful. In the coming weeks, the Salt Lake City police and the FBI proceeded with caution with Mary Katherine. They did not want to implant any false memories or mislead her in any way. They did not show her police line-ups or push her to do a composite sketch of the abductor. They knew if they corrupted her memory, Elizabeth might never be found. For several months, there was little or no progress on the case. Then, about 4 months after the kidnapping, Mary Katherine first recalled that she had heard the abductor's voice prior to that night (he had worked one time as a handyman at the family's home), and then she was able to name the person whose voice it was. The family contacted the press and others recognized him—after a total of 9 months, the suspect was caught, and Elizabeth Smart was returned to her family.

📷 **Figure 6:** Elizabeth Smart, pictured above, speaks of her abduction 10 years after she had been rescued.

The Misinformation Effect

Cognitive psychologist Elizabeth Loftus has conducted extensive research on memory. She has studied false memories as well as recovered memories of childhood sexual abuse. Loftus also developed the **misinformation effect paradigm**, which holds that after exposure to incorrect information, a person may misremember the original event.

According to Loftus, an eyewitness's memory of an event is very flexible due to the misinformation effect.

To test this theory, Loftus and John Palmer (1974) asked 45 U.S. college students to estimate the speed of cars using different forms of questions. The participants were shown films of car accidents and were asked to play the role of the eyewitness and describe what happened. They were asked, "About how fast were the cars going when they (smashed, collided, bumped, hit, contacted) each other?" The participants estimated the speed of the cars based on the verb used (Figure 7).

(a)

(b)

Figure 7: When people are asked leading questions about an event, their memory of the event may be altered.

In a follow-up one week later, participants were asked if they saw any broken glass (none was shown in the accident pictures). Participants who had been in the *smashed* group were more than twice as likely to indicate that they did remember seeing glass. Loftus and Palmer demonstrated that a leading question encouraged them to not only remember the cars were going faster but to also falsely remember that they saw broken glass.

Controversies over Repressed and Recovered Memories

The idea that memories of traumatic events could be repressed has been a theme in the field of psychology, beginning with Sigmund Freud, and the controversy surrounding the idea continues today.

Recall of false autobiographical memories is called **false memory syndrome**. This syndrome has received a lot of publicity, particularly as it relates to memories of events that do not have independent witnesses—often the only witnesses to the abuse are the perpetrator and the victim (e.g., sexual abuse).

The False Memory Debate

- **Belief in Recovered Memories**

    - **Premise:** trauma in children causes repressed memories

    - **Treatment:** trauma recalled through hypnosis and guided imagery

    - **Evidence:** 59% of 450 men and women with a history of child sexual abuse did not recall experiences (Briere & Conte, 1993).

    - **Outcome:** The Recovered Memory Project was created so that victims of childhood sexual abuse can recall these memories and allow the healing process to begin (Cheit, 2007; Devilly, 2007).

- **Opponents of Recovered Memories**

    - **Premise:** believes trauma occurs but not repression

Figure 8: Those involved in crime are sometimes impacted by false memory.

- **Treatment:** believes questioning by others results in false memories of abuse (Loftus)

- **Evidence:** 55% of three-year-old children falsely reported being touched in the genital area during an exam (Ceci & Brooks, 1993, 1995).

Forgetting

Forgetting refers to loss of information from long-term memory. We all forget things, like a loved one's birthday, someone's name, or where we put our car keys. As you've come to see, memory is fragile, and forgetting can be frustrating and even embarrassing. But why do we forget? To answer this question, we will look at several perspectives on forgetting.

Encoding Failure

Sometimes memory loss happens before the actual memory process begins, which is called encoding failure. Encoding failure occurs when memory is not stored because we did not pay attention to details and did not actively work to process the information.

For instance, think of how many times in your life you've seen a penny. Can you accurately recall what the front of a U.S. penny looks like? When researchers Raymond Nickerson and Marilyn Adams (1979) asked this question, they found that most Americans can't recall the specifics of what a penny looks like. The reason is most likely encoding failure. Most of us never encode the details of the penny. We only encode enough information to be able to distinguish it from other coins. If we don't encode the information, then it's not in our long-term memory, so we will not be able to remember it.

📷 **Figure 9:** It is difficult to notice fake money on sight since this information is often not encoded.

Memory Errors

Psychologist Daniel Schacter (2001), a well-known memory researcher, offers seven ways our memories fail us. He calls them the seven sins of memory and categorizes them into three groups: forgetting, distortion, and intrusion (Table 1).

Sin	Type	Description	Example
Transience	Forgetting	Accessibility of memory decreases over time	Forget events that occurred long ago
Absentmindedness	Forgetting	Forgetting caused by lapses in attention	Forget where your phone is
Blocking	Forgetting	Accessibility of information is temporarily blocked	Tip of the tongue
Misattribution	Distortion	Source of memory is confused	Recalling a dream memory as a waking memory
Suggestibility	Distortion	False memories	Results from leading questions
Bias	Distortion	Memories distorted by current belief system	Align memories to current beliefs

Further Resources

In this Crash Course Psychology video called "Episode 14: Remembering and Forgetting (hawkes.biz/forgetting)," you can learn about how memories are encoded and stored and why it is sometimes hard to retrieve memories.

Sin	Type	Description	Example
Persistence	Intrusion	Inability to forget undesirable memories	Traumatic events

Table 1: Schacter's Seven Sins of Memory

In 1885, German psychologist Hermann Ebbinghaus analyzed the process of memorization.

1.   First, he memorized lists of nonsense syllables.

2.   Then he measured how much he learned (retained) when he attempted to relearn each list.

3.   He tested himself over different periods of time from 20 minutes later to 30 days later.

The result is his famous forgetting curve (Figure 10). **Due to storage decay, an average person will lose 50% of the memorized information after 20 minutes and 70% of the information after 24 hours (Ebbinghaus, 1885/1964).** Your memory for new information decays quickly and then eventually levels out.

Figure 10: The Ebbinghaus forgetting curve shows how quickly memory for new information decays.

Examples of Memory Errors

- **transience:** cannot recall details of a book read many years ago. Storage decay means that unused information tends to fade with the passage of time.

- **absentmindedness:** cannot remember why you walked into a room. These lapses in memory are caused by breaks in attention or our focus being somewhere else.

- **blocking:** information is on the tip of your tongue but cannot be recalled. In this case, you are unable to access stored information (Figure 11).

- **misattribution:** confuse the source of your information. This happens when you create a false memory about the source of the information on your own.

- **suggestibility:** create a false memory based on information from others.

- **bias:** current feelings and world view distort your memory of past events. There are several types of bias.

    - <u>Stereotypical bias</u> involves racial and gender biases. For example, when Asian-American and European-American research participants were presented with a list of names, they more frequently incorrectly remembered typical African-American names to be associated with the

Figure 11: Blocking is also known as tip-of-the-tongue (TOT) phenomenon. The memory is right there, but you can't seem to recall it, just like not being able to remember the name of that very famous actor, Leonardo Di Caprio.

occupation of basketball player, and they more frequently incorrectly remembered typical White names to be associated with the occupation of politician (Payne, Jacoby, & Lambert, 2004).

- Egocentric bias involves enhancing our memories of the past (Payne et al., 2004). Did you really score the winning goal in that big soccer match, or did you just assist?

- Hindsight bias happens when we think an outcome was inevitable after the fact. This is the "I-knew-it-all-along" phenomenon. The reconstructive nature of memory contributes to hindsight bias (Carli, 1999). We remember untrue events that seem to confirm that we knew the outcome all along.

- **persistence:** you keep remembering something, to the point where you can't "get it out of your head," and it interferes with your ability to concentrate on other things. It's a failure of our memory system because we involuntarily recall unwanted memories, particularly unpleasant ones (Figure 12). For instance, you witness a horrific car accident on the way to work one morning, and you can't concentrate on work because you keep remembering the scene.

Figure 12: Many veterans of military conflicts involuntarily recall unwanted, unpleasant memories.

✎ On Your Own

Identify the memory error in the following scenarios.

1. Your phone rings as you enter your house. You put down your stuff to answer your phone, and now you can't find your keys.

☐ Bias   ☐ Persistence   ☐ Absentmindedness

2. While Maya was teaching, she couldn't remember the name of a singer she wanted to use as an example.

☐ Misattribution   ☐ Blocking   ☐ Suggestibility

Interference

Sometimes information is stored in our memory, but for some reason, it is inaccessible. This is known as interference, and there are two types: proactive interference and retroactive interference (Figure 13).

Proactive interference occurs when old information interferes with recall of newly learned information. For instance, you can recall your home phone number from childhood but not your new cell phone number.

Retroactive interference happens when information learned more recently hinders the recall of older information. For example, this week you are studying about Freud's psychoanalytic theory. Next week, you study the humanistic perspective of Maslow and Rogers. Thereafter, you have trouble remembering Freud's psychosexual stages of development because you can only remember Maslow's hierarchy of needs.

Reflection Questions

Can you remember your home phone number from when you were 5 years old? What about your first cell phone number? Can you remember your best friend's phone number? If you can't, what type(s) of interference is this, or is it a memory error?

Figure 13: Sometimes forgetting is caused by a failure to retrieve information. This can be due to interference, either retroactive or proactive.

Summary

All of us at times have felt dismayed, frustrated, and even embarrassed when our memories have failed us. Our memory is flexible and prone to many errors, which is why eyewitness testimony has been found to be largely unreliable. There are several reasons why forgetting occurs. In cases of brain trauma or disease, forgetting may be due to amnesia. Another reason we forget is due to encoding failure. We can't remember something if we never stored it in our memory in the first place. Schacter presented seven memory errors that also contribute to forgetting. Sometimes, information is actually stored in our memory, but we cannot access it due to interference. Proactive interference happens when old information hinders the recall of newly learned information. Retroactive interference happens when information learned more recently hinders the recall of older information.

7.4 Ways to Enhance Memory

Most of us suffer from memory failures of one kind or another, and most of us would like to improve our memories so that we don't forget where we put the car keys or, more importantly, the material we need to know for an exam. In this lesson, we'll look at some ways to help improve your memory and some strategies for more effective studying.

Memory-Enhancing Strategies

What are some everyday ways we can improve our memory, including recall? To help make sure information goes from short-term memory to long-term memory, you can use **memory-enhancing strategies**.

> ### Flash Forward
>
> Ready to dig into the vocabulary? Get some practice with this Hawkes Verified Quizlet set (hawkes.biz/psych7q4)!

Figure 1: Do you ever wish you could save a hard drive of information to store in your memory?

Memory-Enhancing Strategies

Rehearsal / Elaborative rehearsal

Chunking

Mnemonic devices

Expressive writing

Saying words aloud

Figure 2: There are several different strategies you can use to improve your memory.

One strategy is rehearsal, or the conscious repetition of information to be remembered (Craik & Watkins, 1973). Think about how you learned your multiplication tables as a child. You may recall that $6 \times 6 = 36$, $6 \times 7 = 42$, and $6 \times 8 = 48$. Memorizing these facts is rehearsal.

Another strategy is **chunking**: you organize information into manageable bits or chunks (Bodie, Powers, & Fitch-Hauser, 2006). Chunking is useful when trying to remember information like dates and phone numbers. Instead of trying to remember 5205550467, you remember the number as 520-555-0467. So, if you met an interesting person at a party, and you wanted to remember his phone number, you would naturally chunk it, and you could repeat the number over and over, which is the rehearsal strategy.

Reflection Questions

Think of a time when you used chunking to remember information. Why do you suppose chunking works as a memory aid?

Further Resources

Try this fun activity (hawkes. biz/memoryenhance) that employs a memory-enhancing strategy.

You could also enhance memory by using **elaborative rehearsal**: a technique in which you think about the meaning of the new information and its relation to knowledge already stored in your memory (Tigner, 1999). For example, in this case, you could remember that 520 is an area code for Arizona, and the person you met is from Arizona. This would help you better remember the 520 prefix. If the information is retained, it goes into long-term memory.

Mnemonic devices are memory aids that help us organize information for encoding (Figure 3).

Use Mnemonic for the Following Items

Figure 3: You can use mnemonic devices to help you remember parts of a system, steps, stages, and phrases.

Brian needs to learn the order of the planets in the solar system, but he's having a hard time remembering the correct order. His friend Kelly suggests a mnemonic device that can help him remember. Kelly tells Brian to simply remember the name Mr. VEM J. SUN, and he can easily recall the correct order of the planets: **M**ercury, **V**enus, **E**arth, **M**ars, **J**upiter, **S**aturn, **U**ranus, and **N**eptune. You might use a mnemonic device to help you remember:

- someone's name

- a mathematical formula

- the seven levels of Bloom's taxonomy

Figure 4: Mnemonic devices like this one can help us remember how to recognize and respond to emergencies. FAST is used to help a person having a stroke. It stands for "face drooping, "arm weakness," "speech difficulties," and "time to call emergency services."

If you have ever watched the television show *Modern Family*, you might have seen Phil Dunphy explain how he remembers names:

> The other day I met this guy named Carl. Now, I might forget that name, but he was wearing a Grateful Dead t-shirt. What's a band like the Grateful Dead? Phish. Where do fish live? The ocean. What else lives in the ocean? Coral. Hello, Co-arl. (Wrubel & Spiller, 2010)

It seems the more vivid or unusual the mnemonic, the easier it is to remember. The key to using any mnemonic successfully is to find a strategy that works for you.

Some other strategies that are used to improve memory include expressive writing and saying words aloud. Expressive writing helps boost your short-term memory, particularly if you write about a traumatic experience in your life. Masao Yogo and Shuji Fujihara (2008) had participants write for 20-minute intervals several times per month. The participants were instructed to write about a traumatic experience, their best possible future selves, or a trivial topic. The researchers found that this simple writing task increased short-term memory capacity after five weeks but only for the participants who wrote about traumatic experiences. Psychologists can't explain why this writing task works, but it does.

What if you want to remember items you need to pick up at the store? Simply say them out loud to yourself. A series of studies (MacLeod, Gopie, Hourihan, Neary, & Ozubko, 2010) found that saying a word out loud improves your memory for the word because it increases the word's distinctiveness. Do you feel silly saying random grocery items aloud? This technique works equally well if you just mouth the words. Using these techniques increased participants' memory for the words by more than 10%. These techniques can also be used to help you study.

Reflection Questions

How can you apply the concepts of elaborative rehearsal, chunking, and mnemonic devices to learning psychology?

Figure 5: Memory techniques can be useful when studying for class.

How to Study Effectively

Based on the information presented in this chapter, here are some strategies and suggestions to help you hone your study techniques (Figure 5). The key with any of these strategies is to figure out what works best for you.

Use elaborative rehearsal: In a famous article, Craik and Lockhart (1972) discussed their belief that information we process more deeply goes into long-term memory. Their theory is called **levels of processing**. If we want to remember a piece of information, we should think about it more deeply and link it to other information and memories to make it more meaningful. For example, if we are trying to remember that the hippocampus is involved with memory processing, we might envision a hippopotamus with excellent memory, which might help us better remember the name and function of the hippocampus.

- **Apply the self-reference effect**: As you go through the process of elaborative rehearsal, it would be even more beneficial to make the material you are trying to memorize personally meaningful to you. When you do this, you are building a web of retrieval cues that will help you access the material when you want to remember it. To make use of the self-reference effect, you could:

  - Write notes in your own words.

  - Write definitions from the text, and then rewrite them in your own words.

  - Relate the material to something you have already learned for another class.

  - Think how you can apply the concepts to your own life.

- **Don't forget the forgetting curve**: As you know, the information you learn drops off rapidly with time. Even if you think you know the material, study it again right before test time to increase the likelihood the information will remain in your memory. Overlearning can help prevent storage decay.

- **Rehearse, rehearse, rehearse**: Review the material over time, in spaced and organized study sessions. Link the new information to other information you already know well.

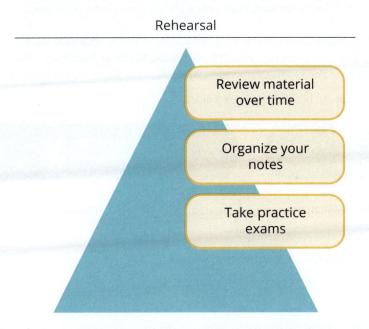

Rehearsal

Review material over time

Organize your notes

Take practice exams

📷 **Figure 6:** Using different rehearsal techniques when studying can increase how much you remember.

- **Be aware of interference**: To reduce the likelihood of interference, study during a quiet time without interruptions or distractions (like television or music).

- **Keep moving**: Of course, you already know that exercise is good for your body, but did you also know it's also good for your mind? Research suggests that regular aerobic exercise (anything that gets your heart rate elevated) is beneficial for memory (van Praag, 2008). Aerobic exercise promotes neurogenesis: the growth of new brain cells in the hippocampus, an area of the brain known to play a role in memory and learning.

- **Get enough sleep**: While you are sleeping, your brain is still at work. During sleep the brain organizes and consolidates information to be stored in long-term memory (Abel & Bäuml, 2013).

- **Make use of mnemonic devices**: As you learned earlier in this lesson, mnemonic devices often help us to remember and recall information. There are different types of mnemonic devices, such as the acronym.

Acronym | Word formed by first letter of each word you want to remember

📷 **Figure 7:** Acronyms are formed by using the first letter in each word you are trying to remember.

For example, even if you live near one, you might have difficulty recalling the names of all five Great Lakes. What if I told you to think of the word *Homes*? HOMES is an acronym that represents Huron, Ontario, Michigan, Erie, and Superior: the five Great Lakes.

Another type of mnemonic device is an acrostic.

Figure 8: An acrostic is like an acronym, but it uses a phrase instead of a single word.

For example, if you are taking a math test and you are having difficulty remembering the order of operations, recalling the following sentence will help you: "Please Excuse My Dear Aunt Sally." The order of mathematical operations is **P**arentheses, **E**xponents, **M**ultiplication, **D**ivision, **A**ddition, **S**ubtraction.

There also are jingles that can be used as memory aides.

Figure 9: Jingles are a common advertising technique that get you to remember the product long after you are first exposed to it.

An example of a jingle could be *i before e, except after c.*

Summary

There are many ways to combat the inevitable failures of our memory system. Some common strategies that can be used in everyday situations include mnemonic devices, rehearsal, self-referencing, and adequate sleep. These same strategies can also help you study more effectively.

Chapter 7 Project

Purpose

The way we go about remembering something is very complex. Only through further exploration can we truly appreciate the impact that memory has on our daily lives. The purpose of this project is to further reflect on memory and apply it to your everyday life. You are going examine your own memories over a week and apply the information that you learned to those memories.

Directions

For a period of a week, you will spend at least 5 days of your choice reflecting on a particular memory you encoded, stored, or retrieved. Decide on the days and times that you want to assess your memory. Do your best to vary the time of day (i.e., day 1: morning shortly after you wake up; day 2: during lunch; day 3: evening; day 4: when you are out with friends, etc.). The goal is to have you tap into as many memories as possible.

Then, get a small notebook (small enough you can keep on you) or use your phone to jot down the memory that you experience and the time of day. Once you have at least 5 days' worth of memories, you are going to classify each one based on the terminology in this chapter in the order below:

1. Describe your memory in at least 50 words.

2. Decide if you're encoding, storing, or retrieving information.

   A. If encoding…

      i. Did you use automatic processing or effortful processing?

      ii. Was it semantic?

      iii. Was it visual or acoustic?

   B. If storing…

      i. Was it sensory, short-term, or long-term memory?

      ii. If in long-term memory…

         1. Was it explicit or implicit?

            a. If explicit…was it episodic or semantic?

            b. If implicit…was it procedural or emotional conditioning?

   C. If retrieving…

      i. Was it recall, recognition, or relearning?

3. Decide what part of the brain you think was used in that memory and provide an explanation as to why you think that part was used.

Materials

A small notebook or phone to take notes on

☑ **Checklist**

☐ 5 days' worth of memories

☐ Memories are recorded at different times of the day.

☐ Each memory has the following:

    ☐ Described in at least 50 words

    ☐ Categorized as encoding, storing, or retrieving information

        ☐ Additional categorization as needed

    ☐ The part of the brain the memory is using

        ☐ Why you think this part of the brain is used

🏁 Chapter 7 Review

Lesson Summaries

7.1 How Memory Functions

Memory is a system or process that stores what we learn for future use. Our memory has three basic functions: encoding, storing, and retrieving information. Encoding is the act of getting information into our memory system through automatic or effortful processing. Storage is retention of the information, and retrieval is the act of getting information out of storage and into conscious awareness through recall, recognition, and relearning.

The idea that information is processed through three memory systems is called the Atkinson-Shiffrin (A-S) model of memory. First, environmental stimuli enter our sensory memory for a period of less than a second to a few seconds. Those stimuli that we notice and pay attention to then move into short-term memory (also called working memory). According to the A-S model, if we rehearse this information, then it moves into long-term memory for permanent storage. Other models like that of Baddeley and Hitch suggest there is more of a feedback loop between short-term memory and long-term memory.

Long-term memory has a practically limitless storage capacity and is divided into implicit and explicit memory. Finally, retrieval is the act of getting memories out of storage and back into conscious awareness. This is done through recall, recognition, and relearning.

7.2 Parts of the Brain Involved with Memory

Beginning with Karl Lashley, researchers and psychologists have been searching for the engram, which is the physical trace of memory. Lashley did not find the engram, but he did suggest that memories are distributed throughout the entire brain rather than stored in one specific area. Now we know that three brain areas do play significant roles in the processing and storage of different types of memories: the cerebellum, hippocampus, and amygdala. The cerebellum processes procedural memories; the hippocampus encodes new memories; and the amygdala helps determine what memories to store and plays a part in determining where the memories are stored based on whether we have a strong or weak emotional response to the event. Strong emotional experiences can trigger the release of neurotransmitters and hormones, which strengthen memory, so that memory for an emotional event is usually stronger than memory for a non-emotional event. This is shown by what is known as the flashbulb memory phenomenon: our ability to remember significant life events. However, our memory for life events (autobiographical memory) is not always accurate.

7.3 Problems with Memory

All of us at times have felt dismayed, frustrated, and even embarrassed when our memories have failed us. Our memory is flexible and prone to many errors, which is why eyewitness testimony has been found to be largely unreliable. There are several reasons why forgetting occurs. In cases of brain trauma or disease, forgetting may be due to amnesia. Another reason we forget is due to encoding failure. We can't remember something if we never stored it in our memory in the first place. Schacter presented seven memory errors that also contribute to forgetting. Sometimes, information is actually stored in our memory, but we cannot access it due to interference. Proactive interference happens when old information hinders the recall of newly learned information. Retroactive interference happens when information learned more recently hinders the recall of older information.

7.4 Ways to Enhance Memory

There are many ways to combat the inevitable failures of our memory system. Some common strategies that can be used in everyday situations include mnemonic devices, rehearsal, self-referencing, and adequate sleep. These same strategies can also help you study more effectively.

Key Terms

Flash Back

Now that you've worked through the chapter, sharpen your vocabulary with this Hawkes Verified Quizlet set (hawkes.biz/psychch7)!

Absentmindedness
Lapses in memory that are caused by breaks in attention or our focus being somewhere else

Acoustic Encoding
Input of sounds, words, and music

Amnesia
Loss of long-term memory that occurs as the result of disease, physical trauma, or psychological trauma

Anterograde Amnesia
Loss of memory for events that occur after the brain trauma

Arousal Theory
Strong emotions trigger the formation of strong memories and weaker emotional experiences form weaker memories

Atkinson-Shiffrin Model (A-S)
Memory model that states we process information through three systems: sensory memory, short-term memory, and long-term memory

Automatic Processing

Encoding of informational details like time, space, frequency, and the meaning of words

Bias

How feelings and view of the world distort memory of past events

Blocking

Memory error in which you cannot access stored information

Chunking

Organizing information into manageable bits or chunks

Construction

Formulation of new memories

Declarative Memory

Type of long-term memory of facts and events we personally experience

Effortful Processing

Encoding of information that takes effort and attention

Elaborative Rehearsal

Thinking about the meaning of the new information and its relation to knowledge already stored in your memory

Encoding

Input of information into the memory system

Engram

Physical trace of memory

Episodic Memory

Type of declarative memory that contains information about events we have personally experienced, also known as *autobiographical memory*

Equipotentiality Hypothesis

Some parts of the brain can take over for damaged parts in forming and storing memories

Explicit Memory

Memories we consciously try to remember and recall

False Memory Syndrome

Recall of false autobiographical memories

Flashbulb Memory

Exceptionally clear recollection of an important event

Forgetting

Loss of information from long-term memory

Implicit Memory

Memories that are not part of our consciousness

Levels of Processing

Information that is thought of more deeply becomes more meaningful and thus better committed to memory

Long-Term Memory (LTM)

Continuous storage of information

Memory

System or process that stores what we learn for future use

Memory Consolidation

Active rehearsal to move information from short-term memory into long-term memory

Memory-Enhancing Strategy

Technique to help make sure information goes from short-term memory to long-term memory

Misattribution

Memory error in which you confuse the source of your information

Misinformation Effect Paradigm

After exposure to incorrect information, a person may misremember the original event

Mnemonic Device

Memory aids that help organize information for encoding

Persistence

Failure of the memory system that involves the involuntary recall of unwanted memories, particularly unpleasant ones

Proactive Interference

Old information hinders the recall of newly learned information

Procedural Memory

Type of long-term memory for making skilled actions, such as how to brush your teeth, how to drive a car, and how to swim

Recall

Accessing information without cues

Recognition

Identifying previously learned information after encountering it again, usually in response to a cue

Reconstruction

Process of bringing up old memories that might be distorted by new information

Rehearsal

Conscious repetition of information to be remembered

Relearning

Learning information that was previously learned

Retrieval

Act of getting information out of long-term memory storage and back into conscious awareness

Retroactive Interference

Information learned more recently hinders the recall of older information

Retrograde Amnesia

Loss of memory for events that occurred prior to brain trauma

Self-Reference Effect

Tendency for an individual to have better memory for information that relates to oneself in comparison to material that has less personal relevance

Semantic Encoding

Input of words and their meaning

Semantic Memory

Type of declarative memory about words, concepts, and language-based knowledge and facts

Sensory Memory

Storage of brief sensory events, such as sights, sounds, and tastes

Short-Term Memory (STM)

(Also, *working memory*) holds about seven bits of information before it is forgotten or stored, as well as information that has been retrieved and is being used

Storage

Creation of a permanent record of information

Suggestibility

Effects of misinformation from external sources that leads to the creation of false memories

Transience

Memory error in which unused memories fade with the passage of time

Visual Encoding

Input of images

💡 **Exercises**

Review Questions

1. _____ is another name for short-term memory.

    a. Sensory memory

    b. Episodic memory

    c. Working memory

    d. Implicit memory

2. The storage capacity of long-term memory is _____.

    a. one or two bits of information

    b. seven bits, plus or minus two

    c. limited

    d. essentially limitless

3. The three functions of memory are _____.

    a. automatic processing, effortful processing, and storage

    b. encoding, processing, and storage

    c. automatic processing, effortful processing, and retrieval

    d. encoding, storage, and retrieval

4. This physical trace of memory is known as the _____.

    a. engram

    b. Lashley effect

    c. Deese-Roediger-McDermott Paradigm

    d. flashbulb memory effect

5. An exceptionally clear recollection of an important event is a(n) _____.

    a. engram

    b. arousal theory

    c. flashbulb memory

    d. equipotentiality hypothesis

6. _____ is when our recollections of the past are done in a self-enhancing manner.

    a. Stereotypical bias

    b. Egocentric bias

    c. Hindsight bias

    d. Enhancement bias

7. Tip-of-the-tongue phenomenon is also known as _____.

    a. persistence

    b. misattribution

    c. transience

    d. blocking

8. The formulation of new memories is sometimes called _____, and the process of bringing up old memories is called _____.

    a. construction; reconstruction

    b. reconstruction; construction

    c. production; reproduction

    d. reproduction; production

9. When you are learning how to play the piano, the statement "every good boy does fine" can help you remember the notes E, G, B, D, and F for the lines of the treble clef. This is an example of a(n) _____.

    a. jingle

    b. acronym

    c. acrostic

    d. acoustic

10. According to a study by Yogo and Fujihara (2008), if you want to improve your short-term memory, you should spend time writing about _____.

    a. your best possible future self

    b. a traumatic life experience

    c. a trivial topic

    d. your grocery list

11. The self-referencing effect refers to _____.

    a. making the material you are trying to memorize personally meaningful to you

    b. making a phrase of all the first letters of the words you are trying to memorize

    c. making a word formed by the first letter of each of the words you are trying to memorize

    d. saying words you want to remember out loud to yourself

12. Memory aids that help organize information for encoding are _____.

    a. mnemonic devices

    b. memory-enhancing strategies

    c. elaborative rehearsal

    d. effortful processing

Critical Thinking Questions

13. Compare and contrast implicit and explicit memory.

14. According to the Atkinson-Shiffrin model, name and describe the three stages of memory.

15. Compare and contrast the two ways in which we encode information.

16. What might happen to your memory system if you sustained damage to your hippocampus?

17. Compare and contrast the two types of interference.

18. Compare and contrast the two types of amnesia.

19. What is the self-reference effect, and how can it help you study more effectively?

20. You and your roommate spent all of last night studying for your psychology test. You think you know the material; however, you suggest that you study again the next morning an hour prior to the test. Your roommate asks you to explain why you think this is a good idea. What do you tell her?

Chapter 8

Lifespan Development

Chapter Introduction

📷 **Figure 1:** How have you changed since childhood? How are you the same? What will your life be like 25 years from now? Fifty years from now? Lifespan development studies how you change as well as how you remain the same over the course of your life.

Welcome to the story of your life. In this chapter, we explore the fascinating tale of how you have grown and developed into the person you are today. We also look at some ideas about who you will grow into as time marches on. Yours is a story of lifespan development (Figure 1), from the start of life to wherever it takes you.

The process of human growth and development is more obvious in infancy and childhood, yet your development is happening this moment and will continue, minute by minute, for the rest of your life. Who you are today and who you will be in the future depends on a blend of genetics, environment, culture, relationships, and more, as you continue through each phase of life. You have experienced firsthand much of what is discussed in this chapter. Now consider what psychological science has to say about your physical, cognitive, and psychosocial development, from the womb to the tomb.

Flash Forward

Ready to dig into the vocabulary? Get some practice with this Hawkes Verified Quizlet set (hawkes.biz/psych8q1)!

8.1 What Is Lifespan Development?

My heart leaps up when I behold
A rainbow in the sky:
So was it when my life began;
So is it now I am a man;
So be it when I shall grow old,
Or let me die!
The Child is father of the Man;
I could wish my days to be
Bound each to each by natural piety. (Wordsworth, 1802)

In this poem, William Wordsworth writes, "the Child is father of the Man." What does this seemingly incongruous statement mean, and what does it have to do with lifespan development? Wordsworth might be suggesting that the person he is as an adult depends largely on the experiences he had in childhood.

> **Reflection Questions**
>
> To what extent do you believe that the adult you are today was influenced by the child you were? To what extent is a child fundamentally different from the adult he/she becomes?

Developmental psychologists study how humans change and grow from conception through childhood, adolescence, adulthood, and death. They view development as a lifelong process that can be studied scientifically across three developmental domains—physical, cognitive, and psychosocial development. We refer to these domains throughout the chapter.

Physical Development — Growth and changes in body, brain, senses, motor skills, health, and wellness

Cognitive Development — Learning, attention, memory, language, thinking, reasoning, and creativity

Psychosocial Development — Emotions, personality, and social relationships

Figure 2: As we grow, it's not just our physical self that is changing, but our cognitive and psychosocial processes change as well.

♀ Connect the Concepts

Research Methods in Developmental Psychology

You've learned about a variety of research methods used by psychologists. Developmental psychologists use many of these approaches in order to better understand how individuals change mentally and physically over time. These methods include naturalistic observations, case studies, surveys, and experiments, among others.

Naturalistic observations involve observing behavior in its natural context. A developmental psychologist might observe how children behave on a playground, at a daycare center, or in the child's own home. While this research approach provides a glimpse into how children behave in their natural settings, researchers have very little control over the types and/or frequencies of displayed behavior.

In a case study, developmental psychologists collect a great deal of information from one individual in order to better understand physical and psychological changes over the lifespan. This particular approach is an excellent way to better understand individuals, who are exceptional in some way, but it is especially prone to researcher bias in interpretation, and it is difficult to generalize conclusions to the larger population.

In one classic example of this research method being applied to a study of lifespan development, Sigmund Freud analyzed the development of a child known as "Little Hans" (Freud, 1909/1949). Freud's findings helped inform his theories of psychosexual development in children, which you will learn about later in this chapter. Little Genie, the subject of a case study discussed in the chapter on thinking and intelligence, provides another example of how psychologists examine developmental milestones through detailed research on a single individual. In Genie's case, her neglectful and abusive upbringing led to her being unable to speak until, at age 13, she was removed from that harmful environment. As she learned to use language, psychologists were able to compare how her language acquisition abilities differed when occurring in her late-stage development compared to the typical acquisition of those skills during the ages of infancy through early childhood (Fromkin, Krashen, Curtiss, Rigler, & Rigler, 1974; Curtiss, 1981).

The survey method asks individuals to self-report important information about their thoughts, experiences, and beliefs. This particular method can provide large amounts of information in relatively short amounts of time; however, validity of data collected in this way relies on honest self-reporting, and the data is relatively shallow when compared to the depth of information collected in a case study.

Experiments involve significant control over extraneous variables and manipulation of the independent variable. As such, experimental research allows developmental psychologists to make causal statements about certain variables that are important for the developmental process. Because experimental research must occur in a controlled environment, researchers must be cautious about whether behaviors observed in the laboratory translate to an individual's natural environment.

Later in this chapter, you will learn about several experiments in which toddlers and young children observe scenes or actions so that researchers can determine at what age specific cognitive abilities develop. For example, children may observe a quantity of liquid poured from a short, fat glass into a tall, skinny glass. As the experimenters question the children about what occurred, the subjects' answers help psychologists understand at what age a child begins to comprehend that the volume of liquid remained the same even though the shapes of the containers differs.

✎ On Your Own

Identify the type of research that would best fit the following scenario.

If a researcher wanted to discover how kids select play partners on the playground by solely watching the children engage with others, he/she would be using:

- ☐ An experiment
- ☐ A survey
- ☐ A case study
- ☐ An observational study

Across these three domains—physical, cognitive, and psychosocial—the **normative approach** to development is also discussed. This approach asks, "What is normal development?" In the early decades of the 20th century, normative psychologists studied large numbers of children at various ages to determine norms (i.e., average ages) of when most children reach specific developmental milestones in each of the three domains (Gesell, 1933, 1939, 1940; Gesell & Ilg, 1946; Hall, 1904). Although children develop at slightly different rates, we can use these age-related averages as general guidelines to compare children with same-age peers to determine the approximate ages they should reach specific normative events called **developmental milestones**.

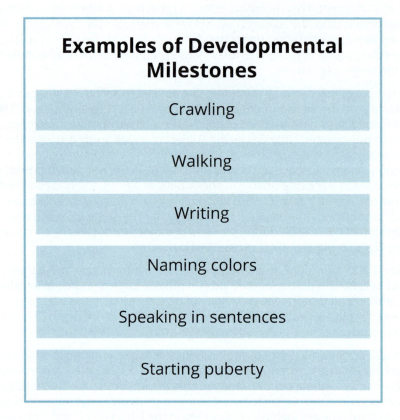

Examples of Developmental Milestones

Crawling

Walking

Writing

Naming colors

Speaking in sentences

Starting puberty

📷 **Figure 3:** Generally, children reach certain developmental milestones around the same age.

Not all normative events are universal, meaning they are not experienced by all individuals across all cultures. Biological milestones, such as puberty, tend to be universal, but social milestones, such as the age when children begin formal schooling, are not necessarily universal; instead, they affect most individuals in a particular culture (Gesell & Ilg, 1946). For example, in developed countries children begin school around 5 or 6 years old, but in developing countries, like Nigeria, children often enter school at an advanced age, if at all (Huebler, 2005; United Nations Educational, Scientific, and Cultural Organization [UNESCO], 2013).

To better understand the normative approach, imagine two new mothers, Louisa and Kimberly, who are close friends and have children around the same age. Louisa's daughter is 14 months old, and Kimberly's son is 12 months old. According to the normative approach, the average age a child starts to walk is 12 months. However, at 14 months Louisa's daughter still isn't walking. She tells Kimberly she is worried that something might be wrong with her baby. Kimberly is surprised because her son started walking when he was only 10 months old.

Reflection Questions

In the case of Louisa, should she be worried about her daughter? Should she be worried if her daughter is not yet walking by 15 months? 18 months?

Issues in Developmental Psychology

There are many different theoretical approaches regarding human development. As we evaluate them in this chapter, recall that developmental psychology focuses on how people change, and keep in mind that all the approaches that we present in this chapter address questions of change:

- Is the change smooth or uneven (continuous versus discontinuous)?

- Is this pattern of change the same for everyone, or are there many different patterns of change (one course of development versus many courses)?

- How do genetics and environment interact to influence development (nature versus nurture)?

Is Development Continuous or Discontinuous?

Continuous development views development as a cumulative process, gradually improving on existing skills (Figure 4). With this type of development, there is gradual change. Consider, for example, a child's physical growth: adding inches to her height year by year. In contrast, theorists who view development as **discontinuous** believe that development takes place in unique stages: it occurs at specific times or ages. With this type of development, the change is more sudden, such as an infant's ability to conceive object permanence.

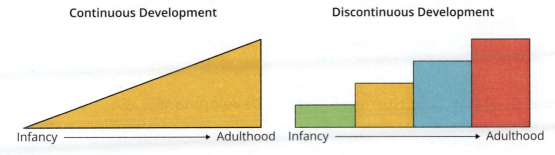

Continuous Development   **Discontinuous Development**

Infancy ⟶ Adulthood   Infancy ⟶ Adulthood

📷 **Figure 4:** The concept of continuous development can be visualized as a smooth slope of progression, whereas discontinuous development sees growth in more discrete stages.

Is There One Course of Development or Many?

- Is development essentially the same, or universal, for all children (i.e., there is one course of development)?

- Does development follow a different course for each child, depending on the child's specific genetics and environment (i.e., there are many courses of development)?

- Do people across the world share more similarities or more differences in their development?

- How much do culture and genetics influence a child's behavior?

Stage theories hold that the sequence of development is universal. For example, in cross-cultural studies of language development, children from around the world reach language milestones in a similar sequence (Gleitman & Newport, 1995). Infants in all cultures coo before they babble. They begin babbling at about the same age and utter their first word around 12 months old. Yet we live in diverse contexts that have a unique effect on each of us. For example, researchers once believed that motor development follows one course for all children regardless of culture. However, child care practices vary by culture, and different practices have been found to accelerate or inhibit achievement of developmental milestones such as sitting, crawling, and walking (Karasik, Adolph, Tamis-LeMonda, & Bornstein, 2010).

For instance, let's look at the Aché society in Paraguay. They spend a significant amount of time foraging in forests. While foraging, Aché mothers carry their young children, rarely putting them down in order to protect them from getting hurt in the forest. Consequently, their children walk much later, around 23–25 months old, in comparison to infants in Western cultures who begin to walk around 12 months old. However, as Aché children become older, they are allowed more freedom to move about, and by about age 9, their motor skills surpass those of U.S. children of the same age; Aché children are able to climb trees up to 25 feet tall and use machetes to chop their way through the forest (Kaplan & Dove, 1987). As you can see, our development is influenced by multiple contexts, so the timing of basic motor functions may vary across cultures. However, the functions themselves are present in all societies (Figure 5).

Group Activity

Brainstorm three examples of development that are continuous and three examples of development that are discontinuous.

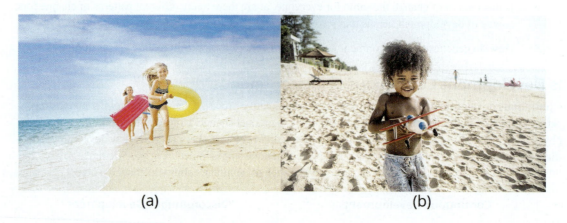

(a)   (b)

⬜ **Figure 5:** All children across the world love to play. Whether in (a) Florida or (b) South Africa, children enjoy exploring sand, sunshine, and the sea.

How Do Nature and Nurture Influence Development?

Are we who we are because of **nature** (biology and genetics), or are we who we are because of **nurture** (our environment and culture)?

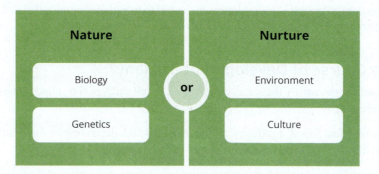

⬜ **Figure 6:** Nature involves biology and genetics, while nurture involves environment and culture.

This longstanding question is known in psychology as the nature versus nurture debate. It seeks to understand how our personalities and traits are the product of our genetic makeup and biological factors, and how they are shaped by our environment, including our parents, peers, and culture.

Reflection Questions

Why do biological children sometimes act like their parents? Is it because of genetics or early childhood environment? How can siblings from the same family be so different?

We are all born with specific genetic traits inherited from our parents, such as eye color, height, and certain personality traits. Beyond our basic genotype, however, there is a deep interaction between our genes and our environment. Our unique experiences in our environment influence whether and how particular traits are expressed, and at the same time, our genes influence how we interact with our environment (Diamond, 2009; Lobo, 2008). This chapter will show that there is a reciprocal interaction between nature and nurture as they both shape who we become, but the debate continues as to the relative contributions of each.

Dig Deeper

The Achievement Gap: How Does Socioeconomic Status Affect Development?

The achievement gap refers to the persistent difference in grades, test scores, and graduation rates that exist among students of different ethnicities, races, and—in certain subjects—sexes (Winerman, 2011). Research suggests that these achievement gaps are strongly influenced by differences in socioeconomic factors that exist among the families of these children. While researchers acknowledge that programs aimed at reducing such socioeconomic discrepancies would likely aid in equalizing the aptitude and performance of children from different backgrounds, they recognize that such large-scale interventions would be difficult to achieve. Therefore, it is recommended that programs aimed at fostering aptitude and achievement among disadvantaged children may be the best option for dealing with issues related to academic achievement gaps (Duncan & Magnuson, 2005).

Low-income children perform significantly more poorly than their middle- and high-income peers on a number of educational variables:

- Significantly lower standardized test scores
- Lower graduation rates
- Lower college entrance rates
- Higher school dropout rates

There have been attempts to correct the achievement gap through state and federal legislation, but what if the problems start before the children even enter school?

Psychologists Betty Hart and Todd Risley (2006) spent their careers looking at early language ability and progression of children in various income levels. In one longitudinal study, they found that although all the parents in the study engaged and interacted with their children, middle- and high-income parents interacted with their children differently than low-income parents. After analyzing 1,300 hours of parent-child interactions, the researchers found that middle- and high-income parents talk to their children significantly more, starting when the children are infants. By 3 years old, high-income children knew almost double the number of words known by their low-income counterparts, and they had heard an estimated total of 30 million more words than the low-income counterparts (Hart & Risley, 2003). And the gaps only become more pronounced. Before entering kindergarten, high-income children score 60% higher on achievement tests than their low-income peers (Lee & Burkam, 2002).

There are solutions to this problem. At the University of Chicago, experts are working with low-income families, visiting them at their homes, and encouraging them to speak more to their children on a daily and hourly basis. Other experts are designing preschools in which students from diverse economic backgrounds are placed in the same classroom. In this research, low-income children made significant gains in their language development, likely as a result of attending the specialized preschool (Schechter & Byeb, 2007). What other methods or interventions could be used to decrease the achievement gap? What types of activities could be implemented to help the children of your community or a neighboring community?

Summary

Lifespan development explores how we change and grow from conception to death. This field of psychology is studied by developmental psychologists. They view development as a lifelong process that can be studied scientifically across three developmental domains: physical, cognitive, and psychosocial. There are several theories of development that focus on the following issues: whether development is continuous or discontinuous, whether development follows one course or many, and the relative influence of nature versus nurture on development.

Flash Forward

Ready to dig into the vocabulary? Get some practice with this Hawkes Verified Quizlet set (hawkes.biz/psych8q2)!

8.2 Lifespan Theories

There are many theories regarding how babies and children grow and develop into happy, healthy adults. We explore several of these theories in this lesson.

Psychosexual Theory of Development

Sigmund Freud (1856–1939) believed that personality develops during early childhood and shapes our personalities as adults. He viewed development as discontinuous; he believed that each of us must pass through a series of stages during childhood called the stages of **psychosexual development**. These stages are based on pleasure-seeking urges that are centered on different erogenous zones. They included oral, anal, phallic, latency, and genital stages. Psychologists today dispute Freud's psychosexual stages as a legitimate explanation for how one's personality develops. However, what we can take away from Freud's theory is that personality is shaped, in some part, by experiences we have in childhood.

Psychosocial Theory of Development

Erik Erikson (1902–1994), another stage theorist, took Freud's theory and modified it as psychosocial theory. Erikson's **psychosocial development** theory emphasizes the social nature of our development rather than its sexual nature. While Freud believed that personality is shaped only in childhood, Erikson proposed that personality development takes place all through the lifespan (Figure 1). Erikson suggested that how we interact with others is what affects our sense of self, or what he called the ego identity.

Figure 1: Erik Erikson proposed the psychosocial theory of development, arguing that personality development takes place throughout the lifespan.

Erikson proposed that we are motivated by a need to achieve competence in certain areas of our lives. According to psychosocial theory, we experience eight stages of development over our lifespan, from infancy through late adulthood. At each stage, there is a conflict, or task, that we need to resolve. Successful completion of each developmental task results in a sense of competence and a healthy personality. Failure to master these tasks leads to feelings of inadequacy.

According to Erikson (1963), trust is the basis of our development during infancy (birth to 12 months). Therefore, the primary task of this stage is trust versus mistrust. Infants are dependent upon their caregivers, so caregivers who are responsive and sensitive to their infant's needs help their baby to develop a sense of trust; their baby will see the world as a safe, predictable place. Unresponsive caregivers who do not meet their baby's needs can engender feelings of anxiety, fear, and mistrust; their baby may see the world as unpredictable.

As toddlers (ages 1–3 years) begin to explore their world, they learn that they can control their actions and act on the environment to get results. They begin to show clear preferences for certain elements of the environment, such as food, toys, and clothing. A toddler's main task is to resolve the issue of autonomy versus shame and doubt by working to establish independence. This is the "me do it" stage. For example, we might observe a budding sense of autonomy in a 2-year-old child who wants to choose her clothes and dress herself. Although her outfits might not be appropriate for the situation, her input in such basic decisions has an effect on her sense of independence. If denied the opportunity to act on her environment, she may begin to doubt her abilities, which could lead to low self-esteem and feelings of shame.

Once children reach the preschool stage (ages 3–6 years), they are capable of initiating activities and asserting control over their world through social interactions and play. According to Erikson, preschool children must resolve the task of initiative versus guilt. By learning to plan and achieve goals while interacting with others, preschool children can master this task. Those who do will develop self-confidence and feel a sense of purpose. Those who are unsuccessful at this stage—with their initiative misfiring or stifled—may develop feelings of guilt.

Reflection Questions

How might over-controlling parents stifle a child's initiative?

During the elementary school stage (ages 6–12), children face the task of industry versus inferiority. Children begin to compare themselves to their peers to see how they measure up. They either develop a sense of pride and accomplishment in their schoolwork, sports, social activities, and family life, or they feel inferior and inadequate when they don't measure up.

Reflection Questions

What are some things parents and teachers can do to help children develop a sense of competence and a belief in themselves and their abilities?

In adolescence (ages 12–18), children face the task of identity versus role confusion. According to Erikson, an adolescent's main task is developing a sense of self. Adolescents struggle with questions such as "Who am I?" and "What do I want to do with my life?" Along the way, most adolescents try on many different selves to see which ones fit. Adolescents who are successful at this stage have a strong sense of identity and are able to remain true to their beliefs and values in the face of problems and other people's perspectives. What happens to apathetic adolescents, who do not make a conscious search for identity, or those who are pressured to conform to their parents' ideas for the future? These teens will have a weak sense of self and experience role confusion. They are unsure of their identity and confused about the future.

People in early adulthood (i.e., 20s through early 40s) are concerned with intimacy versus isolation. After we have developed a sense of self in adolescence, we are ready to share our life with others. Erikson said that we must have a strong sense of self before developing intimate relationships with others. Adults who do not develop a positive self-concept in adolescence may experience feelings of loneliness and emotional isolation.

When people reach their 40s, they enter the time known as middle adulthood, which extends to the mid-60s. The social task of middle adulthood is generativity versus stagnation. Generativity involves finding your life's work and contributing to the development of others through activities such as volunteering, mentoring, and raising children. Those who do not master this task may experience stagnation, having little connection with others and little interest in productivity and self-improvement.

Reflection Questions

What stage of Erikson's theory are you in right now? How do you feel like you are progressing through it?

From the mid-60s to the end of life, we are in the period of development known as late adulthood. Erikson's task at this stage is called integrity versus despair. He said that people in late adulthood reflect on their lives and feel either a sense of satisfaction or a sense of failure. People who feel proud of their accomplishments feel a sense of integrity, and they can look back on their lives with few regrets. However, people who are not successful at this stage may feel as if their lives have been wasted. They focus on what "would have," "should have," and "could have" been. They face the end of their lives with feelings of bitterness, depression, and despair. Table 1 summarizes the stages of Erikson's theory.

Stage	Age (years)	Developmental Task	Description
1	0–1	Trust vs. mistrust	Trust (or mistrust) that basic needs, such as nourishment and affection, will be met
2	1–3	Autonomy vs. shame/doubt	Develop a sense of independence in many tasks
3	3–6	Initiative vs. guilt	Take initiative on some activities—may develop guilt when unsuccessful or boundaries overstepped
4	7–11	Industry vs. inferiority	Develop self-confidence in abilities when competent or sense of inferiority when not
5	12–18	Identity vs. confusion	Experiment with and develop identity and roles
6	19–39	Intimacy vs. isolation	Establish intimacy and relationships with others
7	40–64	Generativity vs. stagnation	Contribute to society and be part of a family
8	65+	Integrity vs. despair	Assess and make sense of life and meaning of contributions

Table 1: Erikson's Psychosocial Stages of Development

Cognitive Theory of Development

Jean Piaget (1896–1980) is another stage theorist who focused on children's cognitive growth. Piaget's discontinuous theory states that children learn **schemata**, which are mental models used to help us categorize and interpret information. We have schemata for everything such as driving a car, naming animals, or getting around your campus. **Assimilation** is taking information from a pre-existing schema and applying it to a new situation. In contrast, **accommodation** describes when they change their schemata based on new information. For example, 2-year-old Blake learned the schema for dogs because his family has a Labrador retriever.

Figure 2: Toddlers will sometimes assimilate by applying schema for one animal, like dogs, to others, like cats.

Blake thought all furry four-legged creatures were dogs, so he called Buck, his neighbor's cat, a dog. After his mom tells Blake that Buck is a cat, he has to accommodate his schema for dogs based on his new experience. Now, he has a schema for dogs and a new one for cats. Piaget thought development unfolds in a series of stages approximately associated with age ranges. He proposed a theory of **cognitive development** that unfolds in four stages: sensorimotor, preoperational, concrete operational, and formal operational (Table 2).

Age (years)	Stage	Description	Developmental issues
0–2	Sensorimotor	World experienced through senses and actions	Object permanence Stranger anxiety
2–6	Preoperational	Use words and images to represent things but lack logical reasoning	Pretend play Egocentrism Language development
7–11	Concrete operational	Understand concrete events and analogies logically; perform arithmetical operations	Conservation Mathematical transformations
12+	Formal operational	Formal operations Utilize abstract reasoning	Abstract logic Moral reasoning

Table 2: Piaget's Stages of Cognitive Development

✍ On Your Own

Use the table to give an example of assimilation and accomodation.

Term	Example
What are you learning how to do?	
Assimilation	
Accommodation	

Figure 3: The game peek-a-boo is based on a child's understanding of object permanence.

The first stage is the **sensorimotor stage**, which lasts from birth to about two years old. During this stage, children learn about the world through their senses and motor behavior. Young children put objects in their mouths to see if the items are edible, and once they can grasp objects, they may shake or bang them to see if they make sounds. According to Piaget, young infants do not remember an object after it has been removed from sight. Piaget studied infants' reactions when a toy was first shown to an infant and then hidden under a blanket. Infants who had already developed object permanence would reach for the hidden toy, indicating that they knew it still existed, whereas infants who had not developed object permanence would appear confused. Children usually develop **object permanence**, which is knowing something still exists even when it is not seen, around five to eight months.

Piaget's second stage is the **preoperational stage**, which is from approximately 2 to 7 years old. In this stage, children can use symbols to represent words, images, and ideas, which is why children in this stage engage in pretend play. Children also begin to use language in the preoperational stage, but they cannot understand adult logic or mentally manipulate information. Their logic is based on their own personal knowledge of the world so far, rather than on conventional knowledge. For example, Keiko and Kenny's dad gave a slice of pizza to 10-year-old Keiko and another slice to her 3-year-old brother, Kenny. Kenny's pizza slice was cut into five pieces, so Kenny told his sister that he got more pizza than she did. Children in this stage cannot perform mental operations because they have not developed an understanding of **conservation**, which is the idea that even if you change the appearance of something, it is still equal in size as long as nothing has been removed or added.

During this stage, we also expect children to display **egocentrism**, which means that the child is not able to take the perspective of others. A child at this stage thinks that everyone sees, thinks, and feels just as they do. Let's look at Kenny and Keiko again. Keiko's birthday is coming up, so their mom takes Kenny to the toy store to choose a present for his sister. He selects an Iron Man action figure for her, thinking that if he likes the toy, his sister will too.

Piaget's third stage is the **concrete operational stage**, which occurs from about 7 to 11 years old. In this stage, children can think logically about real (concrete) events; they can add, subtract, multiply, and divide. In this stage, children also master the concept of conservation: even if something changes shape, its mass, volume, and number stay the same.

Children in this stage understand **reversibility**, which means that objects can be changed and then returned back to their original form or condition.

The fourth, and last, stage in Piaget's theory is the **formal operational stage**, which is from about age 11 to adulthood. The difference between the concrete and formal operational stages is that children in the formal operational stage can also deal with abstract ideas and hypothetical situations. Children in this stage can use abstract thinking to problem solve, look at alternative solutions, and test these solutions. In adolescence, a renewed egocentrism occurs. For example, a 15-year-old with a very small pimple on her face might think it is huge and incredibly visible under the mistaken impression that others must share her perceptions.

✎ On Your Own

Which of the following is first mastered in the concrete operational stage?

☐ Object permanence   ☐ Conservation   ☐ Abstract thinking

Beyond Formal Operational Thought

As with other major contributors of theories of development, several of Piaget's ideas have come under criticism based on the results of further research. For example, researchers suggest that children reach cognitive milestones earlier than Piaget describes (Baillargeon, 2004; de Hevia & Spelke, 2010). According to Piaget, the highest level of cognitive development is formal operational thought, which develops between 11 and 20 years old. Adolescents are typically not as good as adults at making decisions that involve emotion and risk taking. As such, many developmental psychologists disagree with Piaget, suggesting a fifth stage of cognitive development, known as the postformal stage (Basseches, 1984; Commons & Bresette, 2006; Sinnott, 1998).

Reflection Questions

Do you think that cognitive development stops at age 20, or do you think there is a postformal stage? Why?

Theory of Moral Development

Psychologist Lawrence Kohlberg (1927–1987) believed that moral development, like cognitive development, follows a series of stages. He proposed hypothetical moral dilemmas to people of all ages like the one below, which is referred to as the Heinz dilemma:

> In Europe, a woman was near death from a special kind of cancer. There was one drug that the doctors thought might save her. It was a form of radium that a druggist in the same town had recently discovered. The drug was expensive to make, but the druggist was charging ten times what the drug cost him to make. He paid $200 for the radium and charged $2,000 for a small dose of the drug. The sick woman's husband, Heinz, went to everyone he knew to borrow the money, but he could only get together about $1,000, which is half of what it cost. He told the druggist that his wife was dying and asked him to sell it cheaper or let him pay later. But the druggist said, "No, I discovered the drug, and I'm going to make money from it." So Heinz got desperate and broke into the man's store to steal the drug for his wife. Should the husband have done that? (Kohlberg, 1969, p. 379)

Reflection Questions

If you only had two options, to steal the drug and not steal the drug, which one would you choose and why?

Kohlberg identified a pattern in how people's reasoning through these types of dilemmas change as they get older, which laid the framework for his **stages of moral reasoning** (Figure 4). The pre-conventional level is a reason that reflects the consequences of the action. For example, I shouldn't steal the drug to avoid punishment, or I should steal the drug because I get to have my wife. A conventional response reflects the laws and rules of society or maintaining societal norms. Someone in the conventional stage may choose to steal the drug because "most people would steal a drug to save their wife" or not steal the drug because "it is against the law to steal." Post-conventional reasoning is a justification that goes beyond the rules and norms to support social cooperation.

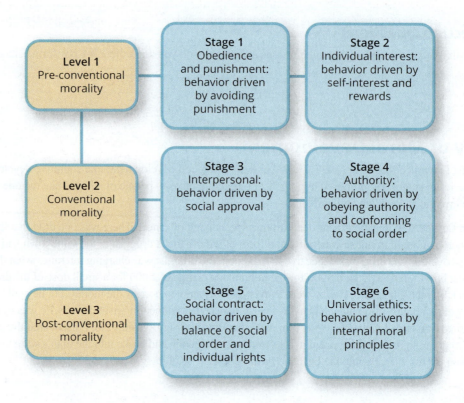

🖼 **Figure 4:** Kohlberg identified three levels of moral reasoning: pre-conventional, conventional, and post-conventional. Each level is associated with increasingly complex stages of moral development.

Kohlberg (1969) felt that more males than females move past stage four in their moral development. These ideas were not well received by Carol Gilligan, a research assistant of Kohlberg, who consequently developed her own ideas of moral development. In her groundbreaking book, *In a Different Voice: Psychological Theory and Women's Development*, Gilligan (1982) criticizes her former mentor's theory because it was based only on upper-class White men and boys. For example, she argues that women would prefer stage three, the one emphasizing interpersonal relationships, while men would prefer stage four, the one emphasizing societal rules and norms. Gilligan argues (1982) that these differences represent a difference in orientation between males and females disputing that fact that males are more advanced in moral reasoning than females.

> **Reflection Questions**
>
> Do you agree with Kohlberg, that stage four should be higher than stage three? Do you side with Gilligan that stage three and four are a difference in gender orientation? Explain your response.

Many psychologists agree with Kohlberg's theory of moral development but point out that moral reasoning is very different from moral behavior. Sometimes what we say we would do in a situation is not what we actually do in that situation. For example, people who reason at the post-conventional level also make decisions that are related to the consequence of the behavior.

Summary

There are many theories regarding how babies and children grow and develop into happy, healthy adults. Sigmund Freud suggested that we pass through a series of psychosexual stages in which our energy is focused on certain erogenous zones on the body. Eric Erikson said that our social interactions and successful completion of social tasks shape our sense of self. Jean Piaget proposed a theory of cognitive development that explains how children think and reason as they move through various stages. Lawrence Kohlberg turned his attention to moral development. He said that we pass through three levels of moral thinking that build on our cognitive development.

8.3 Stages of Development

From the moment we are born until the moment we die, we continue to develop.

As discussed at the beginning of this chapter, developmental psychologists often divide our development into three areas:

- physical development

- cognitive development

- psychosocial development

Mirroring Erikson's stages, lifespan development is divided into different stages that are based on age. We will discuss prenatal, infant, child, adolescent, and adult development.

Prenatal Development

How did you come to be who you are? From beginning as a one-cell structure to your birth, your prenatal development occurred in an orderly and delicate sequence.

There are three stages of prenatal development: germinal, embryonic, and fetal. Let's take a look at what happens to the developing baby in each of these stages.

Germinal Stage (Weeks 1–2)

In our discussion of biopsychology, you learned about genetics and DNA. A mother and father's DNA is passed on to the child at the moment of conception. **Conception** occurs when sperm fertilizes an egg and forms a zygote (Figure 2). A **zygote** begins as a one-cell structure that is created when a sperm and egg merge. The genetic makeup and sex of the baby are set at this point. During the first week after conception, the zygote divides and multiplies, going from a one-cell structure to two cells, then four cells, then eight cells, and so on. This process of cell division is called **mitosis** (Figure 1). Mitosis is a fragile process, and fewer than one-half of all zygotes survive beyond the first two weeks (Hall, 2004).

5 days after conception

• 100 cells

9 months after conception

• Billions of cells

 Figure 1: The process of mitosis turns a single cell into billions of cells.

As the cells divide, they become more specialized, forming different organs and body parts. In the germinal stage, the mass of cells has yet to attach itself to the lining of the mother's uterus. Once it does, the next stage begins.

Figure 2: Sperm and ovum fuse at the point of conception.

Embryonic Stage (Weeks 3–8)

📷 **Figure 3:** This is an embryo 7 weeks after conception.

After the zygote divides for about 7–10 days and has 150 cells, it travels down the fallopian tubes and implants itself in the lining of the uterus. Upon implantation, this multi-cellular organism is called an **embryo**. Now blood vessels grow, forming the placenta. The **placenta** is a structure connected to the uterus that provides nourishment and oxygen from the mother to the developing embryo via the umbilical cord. Basic structures of the embryo start to develop into areas that will become the head, chest, and abdomen. During the embryonic stage:

- the heart begins to beat

- the organs form and begin to function

- the neural tube forms along the back of the embryo, developing into the spinal cord and brain

Fetal Stage (Weeks 9–40)

When the organism is about nine weeks old, the embryo is called a fetus. At this stage, the fetus is about the size of a kidney bean and begins to take on the recognizable form of a human being as the "tail" begins to disappear.

📷 **Figure 4:** Ultrasounds like this can observe the development of a fetus.

From 9–12 weeks, the sex organs begin to differentiate. At about 16 weeks, the fetus is approximately 4.5 inches long. Fingers and toes are fully developed, and fingerprints are visible. By the time the fetus reaches the sixth month of development (24 weeks), it weighs up to 1.4 pounds. Hearing has developed, so the fetus can respond to sounds. The internal organs, such as the lungs, heart, stomach, and intestines, have formed enough that a fetus born prematurely at this point has a chance to survive outside of the mother's womb. Throughout the fetal stage the brain continues to grow and develop, nearly doubling in size from weeks 16 to 28. Around 36 weeks, the fetus is almost ready for birth. It weighs about 6 pounds and is about 18.5 inches long, and by week 37, all of the fetus's organ systems are developed enough that it could survive outside the mother's uterus without many of the risks associated with premature birth. The fetus continues to gain weight and grow in length until approximately 40 weeks. By then, the fetus has little room to move around and birth becomes imminent. The progression through the stages is shown in Figure 5.

9 weeks
Fetal stage begins

12 weeks
Sex organs differentiate

16 weeks
Fingers and toes develop

20 weeks
Hearing begins

24 weeks
Lungs begin to develop

28 weeks
Brain grows rapidly

32 weeks
Bones fully develop

36 weeks
Muscles fully develop

40 weeks
Full-term development

Figure 5: During the fetal stage, the baby's brain develops, and the body adds size and weight until the fetus reaches full-term development.

✎ On Your Own

At which age have fingers and toes fully developed?

☐ 16 weeks ☐ 24 weeks ☐ 36 weeks

Prenatal Influences

During each prenatal stage, genetic and environmental factors can affect development. The developing fetus is completely dependent on the mother for life. It is important that the mother takes good care of herself and receives **prenatal care**, which is medical care received during pregnancy that monitors the health of both the mother and the fetus (Figure 6). According to the National Institutes of Health ([NIH], 2013), routine prenatal care is important because it can reduce the risk of complications for the mother and fetus during pregnancy. In fact, women who are trying to become pregnant or who may become pregnant should discuss pregnancy

Further Resources

Watch this video (hawkes.biz/prenatal) for an amazing, in-depth look at prenatal development and the process of birth.

planning with their doctor. They may be advised, for example, to take a vitamin containing folic acid, which helps prevent certain birth defects, or to monitor aspects of their diet or exercise routines.

Recall that when the zygote attaches to the wall of the mother's uterus, the placenta is formed. The placenta provides nourishment and oxygen to the fetus. Most everything the mother ingests, including food, liquid, and even medication, travels through the placenta to the fetus, hence the common phrase "eating for two." Anything the mother is exposed to in the environment affects the fetus; if the mother is exposed to something harmful, the child can show life-long effects.

📷 **Figure 6:** A pregnant woman receives an examination as part of her prenatal care.

> ## Reflection Questions
>
> Some people encourage pregnant women to literally "eat for two," as in they should double their caloric intake when pregnant. What might be some drawbacks to this mentality?

A **teratogen** is any environmental agent—biological, chemical, or physical—that causes damage to the developing embryo or fetus. There are different types of teratogens. Alcohol and most drugs cross the placenta and affect the fetus. Alcohol is not safe to drink in any amount during pregnancy. Alcohol use during pregnancy has been found to be the leading preventable cause of intellectual disabilities in children in the United States (Maier & West, 2001). Excessive maternal drinking while pregnant can cause fetal alcohol spectrum disorders with life-long consequences for the child ranging in severity (Table 1).

Facial Feature	Potential Effect of Fetal Alcohol Syndrome
Head size	Below-average head circumference
Eyes	Smaller than average eye opening, skin folds at corners of eyes
Nose	Low nasal bridge, short nose
Midface	Smaller than average midface size
Lip and philtrum	Thin upper lip, indistinct philtrum

Table 1: Fetal Alcohol Syndrome Facial Features

Fetal alcohol spectrum disorders (FASD) are a collection of birth defects associated with heavy consumption of alcohol during pregnancy. Children with FASD may have:

- a small head size
- abnormal facial features
- poor judgment
- poor impulse control
- higher rates of ADHD
- more learning issues
- lower IQ scores

These developmental problems and delays persist into adulthood (Streissguth et al., 2004). Based on studies conducted on animals, it also has been suggested that a mother's alcohol consumption during pregnancy may predispose her child to perceive alcohol as tasting and smelling better (Youngentob et al., 2007).

Smoking is also considered a teratogen because nicotine travels through the placenta to the fetus. When the mother smokes, the developing baby experiences a reduction in blood oxygen levels.

Increased Risks Associated with Smoking when Pregnant
Premature birth
Infants with low birth weight
Stillbirth
Sudden infant death syndrome

Heroin, cocaine, methamphetamine, almost all prescription medicines, and most over-the counter medications are also considered teratogens. Babies born with a heroin addiction need heroin just like an adult addict. The child will need to be gradually weaned from the heroin under medical supervision; otherwise, the child could have seizures and die. Other teratogens include radiation, viruses such as HIV and herpes, and rubella (German measles). Women in the United States are much less likely to be afflicted with rubella because most women received childhood immunizations or vaccinations that protect the body from disease.

Each organ of the fetus develops during a specific period in the pregnancy, called the **critical or sensitive period** (Figure 7). For example, research with primate models of FASD has demonstrated that the time during which a developing fetus is exposed to alcohol can dramatically affect the appearance of facial characteristics associated with fetal alcohol syndrome. Specifically, this research suggests that alcohol exposure that is limited to day 19 or 20 of gestation can lead to significant facial abnormalities in the offspring (Ashley, Magnuson, Omnell, & Clarren, 1999). Certain regions of the brain also show sensitive periods during which they are most susceptible to the teratogenic effects of alcohol (Tran & Kelly, 2003).

9 weeks
Fetal stage begins

12 weeks
Sex organs differentiate

16 weeks
Fingers and toes develop

20 weeks
Hearing begins

24 weeks
Lungs begin to develop

28 weeks
Brain grows rapidly

32 weeks
Bones fully develop

36 weeks
Muscles fully develop

40 weeks
Full-term development

Figure 7: During the fetal stage, the baby's brain develops, and the body adds size and weight until the fetus reaches full-term development.

What Do You Think?

Should Women Who Use Drugs During Pregnancy Be Arrested and Jailed?

As you now know, women who use drugs or alcohol during pregnancy can cause serious lifelong harm to their child. Some people have advocated mandatory screenings for women who are pregnant and have a history of drug abuse, and if the women continue using, to arrest, prosecute, and incarcerate them (Figdor & Kaeser, 1998). This policy was tried in Charleston, South Carolina, as recently as 20 years ago. The policy was called the Interagency Policy on Management of Substance Abuse During Pregnancy and had disastrous results.

> The Interagency Policy applied to patients attending the obstetrics clinic at MUSC, which primarily serves patients who are indigent or on Medicaid. It did not apply to private obstetrical patients. The policy required patient education about the harmful effects of substance abuse during pregnancy....[A] statement also warned patients that protection of unborn and newborn children from the harms of illegal drug abuse could involve the Charleston police, the Solicitor of the Ninth Judicial Court, and the Protective Services Division of the Department of Social Services (DSS). (Jos, Marshall, & Perlmutter, 1995, pp. 120–121)

This policy seemed to deter women from seeking prenatal care, deterred them from seeking other social services, and was applied solely to low-income women, resulting in lawsuits. The program was canceled after 5 years, during which 42 women were arrested. A federal agency later determined that the program involved human experimentation without the approval and oversight of an institutional review board (IRB).

Reflection Questions

In the excerpt above, what were the flaws in the program and how would you correct them? What are the ethical implications of charging pregnant women with child abuse?

Infancy Through Childhood

The average newborn weighs approximately 7.5 pounds. Although small, a newborn is not completely helpless because his reflexes and sensory capacities help him interact with the environment from the moment of birth. All healthy babies are born with **newborn reflexes**: inborn automatic responses to particular forms of stimulation. Reflexes help the newborn survive until it is capable of more complex behaviors—these reflexes are crucial to survival. They are present in babies whose brains are developing normally and usually disappear around 4–5 months old.

How do you think these reflexes promote survival in the first months of life?

Reflexes

Rooting	Turn head to a stroke on the cheek
Sucking	Automatic sucking motions
Grasping	Grasp anything placed into palm
Moro	Spread arms, pull them back in, cry in response to feeling like child is falling

Figure 8: Typically, newborns demonstrate these reflexes for several months after birth.

Further Resources

Take a few minutes to view this brief video clip (hawkes.biz/ newbornreflexes) illustrating several newborn reflexes.

What can young infants see, hear, and smell? Newborn infants' sensory abilities are significant, but their senses are not yet fully developed. Many of a newborn's innate preferences facilitate interaction with caregivers and other humans. Although vision is their least developed sense, newborns already show a preference for faces. Babies who are just a few days old also prefer human voices, they will listen to voices longer than sounds that do not involve speech (Vouloumanos & Werker, 2004), and they seem to prefer their mother's voice over a stranger's voice (Mills & Melhuish, 1974). In an interesting experiment, 3-week-old babies were given pacifiers that played a recording of the infant's mother's voice and of a stranger's voice. When the infants heard their mother's voice, they sucked more strongly at the pacifier (Mills & Melhuish, 1974). Newborns also have a strong sense of smell. For instance, newborn babies can distinguish the smell of their own mother from that of others. In a study by MacFarlane (1978), 1-week-old babies who were being breastfed were placed between two gauze pads. One gauze pad was from the bra of a nursing mother who was a stranger, and the other gauze pad was from the bra of the infant's own mother. More than two-thirds of the week-old babies turned toward the gauze pad with their mother's scent.

Group Activity

In a small group, discuss whether or not a baby turning towards a gauze pad of his or her mother's scent indicates that the infant knows it is the mother's scent. Are there any other reasons a child would demonstrate this behavior?

Physical Development

In infancy, toddlerhood, and early childhood, the body's **physical development** is rapid (Figure 9). On average, newborns weigh between 5 and 10 pounds, and a newborn's weight typically doubles in six months and triples in one year. By 2 years old the weight will have quadrupled, so we can expect that a 2-year-old should weigh between 20 and 40 pounds. The average length of a newborn is 19.5 inches, increasing to 29.5 inches by 12 months and 34.4 inches by 2 years old (WHO Multicentre Growth Reference Study Group, 2006).

During infancy and childhood, growth does not occur at a steady rate (Carel, Lahlou, Roger, & Chaussain, 2004). Growth slows between 4 and 6 years old; during this time children gain 5–7 pounds and grow about 2–3 inches per year. Once girls reach 8–9 years old, their growth rate outpaces that of boys due to a pubertal growth spurt. This growth spurt continues until around 12 years old, coinciding with the start of the menstrual cycle. By 10 years old, the average girl weighs 88 pounds, and the average boy weighs 85 pounds.

We are born with all of the brain cells that we will ever have—about 100–200 billion neurons (nerve cells) whose function is to store and transmit information (Huttenlocher & Dabholkar, 1997). However, the nervous system continues to grow and develop. Each neural pathway forms thousands of new connections during infancy and toddlerhood. This period of rapid neural growth is called blooming. Neural pathways continue to develop through puberty. The blooming period of neural growth is then followed by a period of pruning, where neural connections are reduced. It is thought that pruning causes the brain to function more efficiently, allowing for mastery of more complex skills (Hutchinson, 2011). Blooming occurs during the first few years of life, and pruning continues through childhood and into adolescence in various areas of the brain.

Figure 9: Children experience rapid physical changes through infancy and early childhood.

The size of our brains increases rapidly. For example, the brain of a 2-year-old is 55% of its adult size, and by 6 years old the brain is about 90% of its adult size (Tanner, 1978). During early childhood (ages 3–6), the frontal lobes grow rapidly. Recalling our discussion of the 4 lobes of the brain earlier in this course, the frontal lobes are associated with:

- planning
- reasoning
- memory
- impulse control

Therefore, by the time children reach school age, they are developmentally capable of controlling their attention and behavior. Through the elementary school years, the frontal, temporal, occipital, and parietal lobes all grow in size. The brain growth spurts experienced in childhood tend to follow Piaget's sequence of cognitive development so that significant changes in neural functioning account for cognitive advances (Kolb & Whishaw, 2009; Overman, Bachevalier, Turner, & Peuster, 1992).

Motor development occurs in an orderly sequence as infants move from reflexive reactions (e.g., sucking and rooting) to more advanced motor functioning.

Motor Development

1. Hold head up
2. Sit with assistance and then unassisted
3. Crawl
4. Walk

Figure 10: Motor development continues throughout infancy and childhood.

Motor skills refer to our ability to move our bodies and manipulate objects. **Fine motor skills** focus on the muscles in our fingers, toes, and eyes, and enable coordination of small actions (e.g., grasping a toy, writing with a pencil, and using a spoon). **Gross motor skills** focus on large muscle groups that control our arms and legs and involve larger movements (e.g., balancing, running, and jumping).

As motor skills develop, there are certain developmental milestones that young children should achieve (Table 2). For each milestone there is an average age, as well as a range of ages in which the milestone should be reached. An example of a developmental milestone is sitting. On average, most babies sit alone at 7 months old. Sitting involves both coordination and muscle strength, and 90% of babies achieve this milestone between 5 and 9 months old. In another example, babies on average are able to hold up their head at 6 weeks old, and 90% of babies achieve this between 3 weeks and 4 months old. If a baby is not holding up his head by 4 months old, he is showing a delay. If the child is displaying delays on several milestones, that is reason for concern, and the parent or caregiver should discuss this with the child's pediatrician. Some developmental delays can be identified and addressed through early intervention.

Age (years)	Physical	Personal/Social	Language	Cognitive
2	Kicks a ball; walks up and down stairs	Plays alongside other children; copies adults	Points to objects when named; puts 2–4 words together in a sentence	Sorts shapes and colors; follows 2-step instructions
3	Climbs and runs; pedals tricycle	Takes turns; express-es many emotions; dresses self	Names familiar things; uses pronouns	Plays make believe; works toys with parts (levers, handles)
4	Catches balls; uses scissors	Prefers social play to solo play; knows likes and interests	Knows songs and rhymes by memory	Names colors and numbers; begins writing letters
5	Hops and swings; uses fork and spoon	Distinguishes real from pretend; likes to please friends	Speaks clearly; uses full sentences	Counts to 10 or higher; prints some letters and copies basic shapes

Table 2: Developmental Milestones, Ages 2–5 Years

Cognitive Development

In addition to rapid physical growth, young children also exhibit significant development of their cognitive abilities. Piaget thought that children's ability to understand objects—such as learning that a rattle makes a noise when shaken—was a cognitive skill that develops slowly as a child matures and interacts with the environment. Today, developmental psychologists think Piaget was incorrect. Researchers have found that even very young children understand objects and how they work long before they have experience with those objects (Baillargeon, 1987; Baillargeon, Li, Gertner, & Wu, 2011). For example, children as young as 3 months old demonstrated knowledge of the properties of objects that they had only viewed and did not have prior experience with them. In one study, 3-month-old infants were shown a truck rolling down a track and behind a screen. The box, which appeared solid but was actually hollow, was placed next to the track. The truck rolled past the box as would be expected. Then the box was placed on the track to block the path of the truck. When the truck was rolled down the track this time, it continued unimpeded. The infants spent significantly more time looking at this impossible event (Figure 11). Baillargeon (1987) concluded that they knew solid objects cannot pass through each other. Baillargeon's findings suggest that very young children have an understanding of objects and how they work, which Piaget (1954) would have said is beyond their cognitive abilities due to their limited experiences in the world.

Further Resources

Watch this video (hawkes.biz/baillargeon) for more on the Baillargeon ramp experiment.

(a)   (b)   (c)

Figure 11: In Baillargeon's study, infants observed a truck (a) roll down an unobstructed track, (b) roll down an unobstructed track with an obstruction (box) beside it, and (c) roll down and pass through what appeared to be an obstruction.

Just as there are physical milestones that we expect children to reach, there are also cognitive milestones. It is helpful to be aware of these milestones as children gain new abilities to think, problem solve, and communicate. For example, infants shake their head "no" around 6–9 months, and they respond to verbal requests to do things like "wave bye-bye" or "blow a kiss" around 9–12 months. Remember Piaget's ideas about object permanence? We can expect children to grasp the concept that objects continue to exist even when they are not in sight by around 8 months old. Because toddlers (i.e., 12–24 months old) have mastered object permanence, they enjoy games like hide and seek, and they realize that when someone leaves the room they will come back (Loop, 2013). Toddlers also point to pictures in books and look in appropriate places when you ask them to find objects.

Preschool-age children (i.e., 3–5 years old) also make steady progress in cognitive development. Children in this age group are able to:

- count
- name colors
- tell you their name and age
- make some decisions on their own, such as choosing an outfit to wear
- understand basic time concepts and sequencing (e.g., before and after)

- predict what will happen next in a story
- enjoy the use of humor in stories
- think symbolically
- enjoy pretend play and inventing elaborate characters and scenarios
- experience curiosity

An important cognitive change occurs in children this age. Recall that Piaget described 2–3 year olds as egocentric, meaning that they do not have an awareness of others' points of view. Between 3 and 5 years old, children come to understand that people have thoughts, feelings, and beliefs that are different from their own. This is known as theory-of-mind (TOM). Children can use this skill to tease others, persuade their parents to purchase a candy bar, or understand why a sibling might be angry. When children develop TOM, they can recognize that others have false beliefs (Dennett, 1987; Callaghan et al., 2005).

Cognitive skills continue to expand in middle and late childhood (6–11 years old). Thought processes become more logical and organized when dealing with concrete information (Figure 12). Children at this age understand concepts such as the past, present, and future, giving them the ability to plan and work toward goals. Additionally, they can process complex ideas such as addition and subtraction and cause-and-effect relationships. However, children's attention spans tend to be limited until they are around 11 years old. After that point, it begins to improve through adulthood.

Figure 12: Because they understand luck and fairness, children in middle and late childhood (6–11 years old) are able to follow rules for games.

One well-researched aspect of cognitive development is language acquisition. As mentioned earlier, the order in which children learn language structures is consistent across children and cultures (Hatch, 1983). You've also learned that some psychological researchers have proposed that children possess a biological predisposition for language.

Starting before birth, babies begin to develop language and communication skills. At birth, babies:

- recognize their mother's voice

- can discriminate between the language(s) spoken by their mothers and foreign languages

- show preferences for faces that are moving in synchrony with audible language (Blossom & Morgan, 2006; Pickens, 1994; Spelke & Cortelyou, 1981)

Children communicate information through gesturing long before they speak, and there is some evidence that gesture usage predicts subsequent language development (Iverson & Goldin-Meadow, 2005). In terms of producing spoken language, babies begin to coo almost immediately. Cooing is a one-syllable combination of a consonant and a vowel sound (e.g., *coo* or *ba*). Interestingly, babies replicate sounds from their own languages. A baby whose parents speak French will coo in a different tone than a baby whose parents speak Spanish or Urdu. After cooing, the baby starts to babble. Babbling begins with repeating a syllable, such as *ma-ma*, *da-da*, or *ba-ba*. When a baby is about 12 months old, we expect her to say her first word for meaning and to start combining words for meaning at about 18 months.

At about 2 years old, a toddler uses between 50 and 200 words; by 3 years old, they have a vocabulary of up to 1000 words and can speak in sentences. During the early childhood years, children's vocabulary increases at a rapid pace. This is sometimes referred to as the "vocabulary spurt" and has been claimed to involve an expansion in vocabulary at a rate of 10–20 new words per week. Recent research may indicate that while some children experience these spurts, it is far from universal (as discussed in Ganger & Brent, 2004). It has been estimated that 5 year olds understand about 6000 words, speak 2000 words, and can define words and question their meanings. They can rhyme and name the days of the week. Seven year olds speak fluently and use slang and clichés (Stork & Widdowson, 1974).

Figure 13: Children go through specific stages of language acquisition before being able to speak fluently.

> ## Reflection Questions
>
> Does your receptive vocabulary outpace your productive vocabulary? Why do you think this might be the case?

What accounts for such dramatic language learning by children? Behaviorist B.F. Skinner thought that we learn language in response to reinforcement or feedback, such as through parental approval or through being understood. For example, when a two-year-old child asks for juice, he might say, "me juice," to which his mother might respond by giving him a cup of apple juice. Noam Chomsky (1957) criticized Skinner's theory and proposed that we are all born with an innate capacity to learn language. Chomsky called this mechanism a language acquisition device (LAD). Who is correct? Both Chomsky and Skinner are right. Remember that we are a product of both nature and nurture. Researchers now believe that language acquisition is partially inborn and partially learned through our interactions with our linguistic environment (Gleitman & Newport, 1995; Stork & Widdowson, 1974).

> ## Group Activity
> Generate examples that would support Skinner's ideas of language development. What about Chomsky's ideas?

Attachment

Psychosocial development occurs as children form relationships, interact with others, and understand and manage their feelings. In social and emotional development, forming healthy attachments is very important and is the major social milestone of infancy. **Attachment** is a long-standing connection or bond with others. Developmental psychologists are interested in how infants reach this milestone. They ask such questions as:

- How do parent and infant attachment bonds form?

- How does neglect affect these bonds?

- What accounts for children's attachment differences?

Researchers Harry Harlow, John Bowlby, and Mary Ainsworth conducted studies designed to answer these questions. In the 1950s, Harlow conducted a series of experiments on monkeys. He separated newborn monkeys from their mothers. Each monkey was presented with two surrogate mothers. One surrogate monkey was made out of wire mesh, and she could dispense milk. The other monkey was softer and made from cloth but could not dispense milk. Research shows that the monkeys preferred the soft, cuddly cloth monkey even though she did not provide any nourishment. The baby monkeys spent their time clinging to the cloth monkey and only went to the wire monkey when they needed to be fed (Figure 14).

Prior to this study, the medical and scientific communities generally thought that babies become attached to the people who provide their nourishment. However, Harlow (1958) concluded that there was more to the mother-child bond than nourishment. Feelings of comfort and security are the critical components to maternal-infant bonding, which leads to healthy psychosocial development.

> ### Reflection Questions
> What would you say to a father who was jealous of the closeness his wife shared with their newborn because she was able to feed the baby?

Figure 14: Research has shown that baby monkeys tend to cling to the cloth monkey even though they receive no nourishment from it.

Building on the work of Harlow and others, John Bowlby developed the concept of attachment theory. He defined attachment as the affectional bond or tie that an infant forms with the mother (Bowlby, 1969). An infant must form this bond with a primary caregiver in order to have normal social and emotional development. In addition, Bowlby proposed that this attachment bond is powerful and continues throughout life. He used the concept of secure base to define a healthy attachment between parent and child (1988). A **secure base** is a parental presence that gives the child a sense of safety as he explores his surroundings.

Figure 15: Healthy attachment relies on multiple factors.

While Bowlby thought attachment was an all-or-nothing process, Mary Ainsworth's (1970) research showed otherwise. Ainsworth wanted to know if children differ in the ways they bond, and if so, why. To find the answers, she used the Strange Situation procedure to study attachment between mothers and their infants (1970). In the Strange Situation, the mother (or primary caregiver) and the infant (age 12–18 months) are placed in a room together. There are toys in the room, and the caregiver and child spend some time alone in the room. After the child has had time to explore her surroundings, a stranger enters the room. The mother then leaves her baby with the stranger. After a few minutes, she returns to comfort her child.

Figure 16: Mutually enjoyable interactions promote the mother-infant bond.

Based on how the infants/toddlers responded to the separation and reunion, Ainsworth identified three types of parent-child attachments: secure, avoidant, and resistant (Ainsworth & Bell, 1970). A fourth style, known as disorganized attachment, was later described (Main & Solomon, 1990). The most common type of attachment—also considered the healthiest—is called **secure attachment** (Figure 17). In this type of attachment, the toddler prefers his parent over a stranger. The attachment figure is used as a secure base to explore the environment and is sought out in times of stress. Securely attached children were distressed when their caregivers left the room in the Strange Situation experiment, but when their caregivers returned, the securely attached children were happy to see them. Securely attached children have caregivers who are sensitive and responsive to their needs.

Figure 17: In secure attachment, the parent provides a secure base for the toddler, allowing him to securely explore his environment.

Secure Attachment

Prefer caregiver over stranger

Caregiver is secure base

Caregiver sought when stressed

Distressed when caregiver leaves

Happy to see caregiver upon return

With **avoidant attachment**, the child is unresponsive to the parent, does not use the parent as a secure base, and does not care if the parent leaves. The toddler reacts to the parent the same way she reacts to a stranger. When the parent does return, the child is slow to show a positive reaction. Ainsworth theorized that these children were most likely to have a caregiver who was insensitive and inattentive to their needs (Ainsworth, Blehar, Waters, & Wall, 1978).

Avoidant Attachment

Child unresponsive to caregiver

Caregiver is not a secure base

Does not care if caregiver leaves

Reacts similarly to caregiver and stranger

Slow to show positive reaction to return

In cases of **resistant attachment**, children tend to show clingy behavior, but then they reject the attachment figure's attempts to interact with them (Ainsworth & Bell, 1970). These children do not explore the toys in the room, as they are too fearful. During separation in the Strange Situation, they became extremely disturbed and angry with the parent. When the parent returns, the children are difficult to comfort. Resistant attachment is the result of the caregivers' inconsistent level of response to their child.

Further Resources

Watch this video (hawkes.biz/strangesituation) to view a clip of the Strange Situation. Try to identify which type of attachment baby Lisa exhibits.

Resistant Attachment

Clingy behavior to caregiver

Reject the caregiver's interactions

Too fearful to explore

Disturbed and angry at separation

Difficult to comfort on return

Finally, children with **disorganized attachment** behaved oddly in the Strange Situation. They freeze, run around the room in an erratic manner, or try to run away when the caregiver returns (Main & Solomon, 1990). This type of attachment is seen most often in kids who have been abused. Research has shown that abuse disrupts a child's ability to regulate their emotions.

While Ainsworth's research has found support in subsequent studies, it has also met criticism. Some researchers have pointed out that a child's temperament may have a strong influence on attachment (Gervai, 2009; Harris, 2009), and others have noted that attachment varies from culture to culture, a factor not accounted for in Ainsworth's research (Rothbaum, Weisz, Pott, Miyake, & Morelli, 2000; van Ijzendoorn & Sagi-Schwartz, 2008).

Self-Concept

Just as attachment is the main psychosocial milestone of infancy, the primary psychosocial milestone of childhood is the development of a positive sense of self. How does self-awareness develop? Infants don't have a self-concept, which is an understanding of who they are. If you place a baby in front of a mirror, she will reach out to touch her image, thinking it is another baby. However, by about 18 months, a toddler will recognize that the person in the mirror is herself. How do we know this? In a well-known experiment, a researcher placed a red dot of paint on children's noses before putting them in front of a mirror (Amsterdam, 1972). Commonly known as the mirror test, this behavior is demonstrated by humans and a few other species and is considered evidence of self-recognition (Archer, 1992). At 18 months old, they would touch their own noses when they saw the paint, surprised to see a spot on their faces. By 24–36 months old, children can name and/or point to themselves in pictures, clearly indicating self-recognition.

Further Resources

The mirror test has become popular as a test of animal self-awareness. Which animals are capable of recognizing themselves? Check out this video (hawkes.biz/selfconcept) to find out!

Children from 2–4 years old display a great increase in social behavior once they have established a self-concept. They enjoy playing with other children, but they have difficulty sharing their possessions. Also, through play children explore and come to understand their gender roles and can label themselves as a girl or boy (Chick, Heilman-Houser, & Hunter, 2002). By 4 years old, children can:

- cooperate with other children
- share when asked
- separate from parents with little anxiety
- exhibit autonomy
- initiate tasks
- carry out plans

Success in these areas contributes to a positive sense of self. Once children reach 6 years old, they can identify themselves in terms of group memberships: "I'm a first grader!" School-age children compare themselves to their peers and discover that they are competent in some areas and less so in others (recall Erikson's task of industry versus inferiority). At this age, children recognize their own personality traits as well as some other traits they would like to have. For example, 10-year-old Layla says, "I'm kind of shy. I wish I could be more talkative like my friend Alexa."

Development of a positive self-concept is important to healthy development.

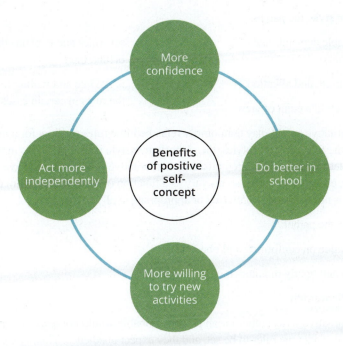

Figure 18: Positive self concept allows for healthy development.

Formation of a positive self-concept begins in Erikson's toddlerhood stage, when children establish autonomy and become confident in their abilities. Development of self-concept continues in elementary school, when children compare themselves to others. When the comparison is favorable, children feel a sense of competence and are motivated to work harder and accomplish more. Self-concept is re-evaluated in Erikson's adolescence stage, as teens form an identity. They internalize the messages they have received regarding their strengths and weaknesses, keeping some messages and rejecting others. Adolescents who have achieved identity formation are capable of contributing positively to society (Erikson, 1968).

What can parents do to nurture a healthy self-concept? Diana Baumrind (1971, 1991) thinks parenting style may be a factor. The way we parent is an important factor in a child's socioemotional growth. Baumrind developed and refined a theory describing four parenting styles: authoritative, authoritarian, permissive, and uninvolved.

Figure 19: Baumrind identified four types of parenting styles: authoritarian, authoritative, permissive, and uninvolved.

With the **authoritative style**, the parent:

- gives reasonable demands and consistent limits
- expresses warmth and affection
- listens to the child's point of view

- sets rules and explains the reasons behind them
- is flexible and willing to make exceptions to the rules in certain cases

For example, an authoritative parent may temporarily relax bedtime rules to allow for a nighttime swim during a family vacation. Of the four parenting styles, the authoritative style is the one that is most encouraged in modern American society. American children raised by authoritative parents tend to have high self-esteem and social skills. However, effective parenting styles vary as a function of culture, and as Small (1999) pointed out, the authoritative style is not necessarily preferred or appropriate in all cultures.

In **authoritarian style**, the parent:

- places high value on conformity and obedience
- is often strict and tightly monitors their children
- expresses little warmth

In contrast to the authoritative style, authoritarian parents probably would not relax bedtime rules during a vacation because they consider the rules to be set, and they expect obedience. This style can create anxious, withdrawn, and unhappy kids. However, it is important to point out that authoritarian parenting is as beneficial as the authoritative style in some ethnic groups (Russell, Crockett, & Chao, 2010). For instance, first-generation Chinese-American children raised by authoritarian parents did just as well in school as their peers who were raised by authoritative parents (Russell et al., 2010).

Reflection Questions

Would you say that success in school is the best measure of the effectiveness of the authoritarian parenting style? Why or why not?

In the **permissive style**, the parent:

- is highly nurturing
- rarely uses punishment

- allows the child to run the show
- may play the role of friend rather than parent

In terms of our example of vacation bedtimes, permissive parents might not have bedtime rules at all—instead they allow the child to choose his bedtime whether on vacation or not. Not surprisingly, children raised by permissive parents tend to lack self-discipline, and the permissive parenting style is negatively associated with grades (Dornbusch, Ritter, Leiderman, Roberts, & Fraleigh, 1987). The permissive style may also contribute to other risky behaviors such as alcohol abuse (Bahr & Hoffman, 2010), risky sexual behavior especially among female children (Donenberg, Wilson, Emerson, & Bryant, 2002), and increased display of disruptive behaviors by male children (Parent et al., 2011). However, there are some positive outcomes associated with children raised by permissive parents. They tend to have higher self-esteem, better social skills, and report lower levels of depression (Darling, 1999).

With the **uninvolved style** of parenting, the parents:

- are indifferent, uninvolved, and sometimes referred to as neglectful
- don't respond to the child's needs
- make relatively few demands

This could be because of severe depression or substance abuse, or other factors, such as the parents' extreme focus on work. These parents may provide for the child's basic needs but little else. The children raised in this parenting style are usually emotionally withdrawn, fearful, anxious, perform poorly in school, and are at an increased risk of substance abuse (Darling, 1999).

Figure 20: Extreme focus on work can lead to neglecting your child's needs.

✎ On Your Own

Choose the parenting style that most accurately reflects the following descriptions.

1. Which parenting style results in children who lack self-discipline?

☐ Permissive   ☐ Uninvolved   ☐ Authoritarian

2. Which parenting style has been shown to increase anxiety and withdrawal in children?

☐ Authoritative   ☐ Permissive   ☐ Authoritarian

3. Which parenting style has been associated with high self-esteem?

☐ Uninvolved   ☐ Authoritarian   ☐ Permissive

As you can see, parenting styles influence childhood adjustment, but could a child's temperament likewise influence parenting? **Temperament** refers to innate traits that influence how one thinks, behaves, and reacts with the environment. Children with easy temperaments demonstrate positive emotions, adapt well to change, and are capable of regulating their emotions. Conversely, children with difficult temperaments demonstrate negative emotions and have difficulty adapting to change and regulating their emotions. Difficult children are much more likely to challenge parents, teachers, and other caregivers (Thomas, 1984). Therefore, it's possible that easy children (i.e., social, adaptable, and easy to soothe) tend to elicit warm and responsive parenting, whereas demanding, irritable, withdrawn children evoke irritation in their parents or cause their parents to withdraw (Sanson & Rothbart, 1995).

 Figure 21: Allowing kids to play and explore outside is beneficial for their development. Encouraging kids to get involved with the garden may increase their interest in eating more vegetables.

The Importance of Play and Recess

According to the American Academy of Pediatrics (2007), unstructured play is an integral part of a child's development. It builds creativity, problem-solving skills, and social relationships. Play also allows children to develop a theory-of-mind as they imaginatively take on the perspective of others.

Outdoor play allows children the opportunity to directly experience and sense the world around them. While doing so, they may collect objects that they come across and develop lifelong interests and hobbies. They also benefit from increased exercise, and engaging in outdoor play can actually increase how much they enjoy physical activity. This helps support the development of a healthy heart and brain. Unfortunately, research suggests that today's children are engaging in less and less outdoor play (Clements, 2004). Perhaps, it is no surprise to learn that lowered levels of physical activity in conjunction with easy access to calorie-dense foods with little nutritional value are contributing to alarming levels of childhood obesity (Karnik & Kanekar, 2012).

Despite the adverse consequences associated with reduced play, some children are over-scheduled and have little free time to engage in unstructured play. In addition, some schools have taken away recess time for children in a push for students to do better on standardized tests, and many schools commonly use loss of recess as a form of punishment.

- Do you agree with these practices?

- Why or why not?

Adolescence

Adolescence is a socially constructed concept. In pre-industrial society, children were considered adults when they reached physical maturity, but today we have an extended time between childhood and adulthood called adolescence. **Adolescence** is the period of development that begins at puberty and ends at emerging adulthood, which is discussed later. In the United States, adolescence is seen as a time to develop independence from parents while remaining connected to them (Figure 22). The typical age range of adolescence is from 12 to 18 years, and this stage of development also has some predictable physical, cognitive, and psychosocial milestones.

🖼 **Figure 22:** Peers are a primary influence on our development in adolescence.

Physical Development

As noted above, adolescence begins with puberty. While the sequence of physical changes in puberty is predictable, the onset and pace of puberty vary widely. Several physical changes occur during puberty, such as **adrenarche** and **gonadarche**, the maturing of the adrenal glands and sex glands, respectively. Also during this time, primary and secondary sexual characteristics develop and mature. **Primary sexual characteristics** are organs specifically needed for reproduction, like the uterus and ovaries in females and testes in males. **Secondary sexual characteristics** are physical signs of sexual maturation that do not directly involve sex organs, such as development of breasts and hips in girls and development of facial hair and a deepened voice in boys. Girls experience **menarche**, the beginning of menstrual periods, usually around 12–13 years old, and boys experience **spermarche**, the first ejaculation, around 13–14 years old.

During puberty, both sexes experience a rapid increase in height (i.e., growth spurt). For girls, this begins between 8 and 13 years old, with adult height reached between 10 and 16 years old. Boys begin their growth spurt slightly later, usually between 10 and 16 years old and reach their adult height between 13 and 17 years old. Both nature (i.e., genes) and nurture (e.g., nutrition, medications, and medical conditions) can influence height.

Because rates of physical development vary so widely among teenagers, puberty can be a source of pride or embarrassment. Early maturing boys tend to be stronger, taller, and more athletic than their later maturing peers.

Early Maturing Girls

Teased or admired

Higher risk for depression and eating disorders

Higher risk for substance abuse

Early Maturing Boys

More popular, confident, independent

At greater risk for substance abuse

At greater risk for early sexual activity

Figure 23: Early maturing boys and girls are at higher risk for certain activities.

Late blooming boys and girls (i.e., they develop more slowly than their peers) may feel self-conscious about their lack of physical development. Negative feelings are particularly a problem for late maturing boys, who are at a higher risk for depression and conflict with parents (Graber et al., 1997) and more likely to be bullied (Pollack & Shuster, 2000).

The adolescent brain also remains under development. Up until puberty, brain cells continue to bloom in the frontal region. Adolescents engage in increased risk-taking behaviors and emotional outbursts possibly because the frontal lobes of their brains are still developing (Figure 24). Recall that this area is responsible for judgment, impulse control, and planning, and it is still maturing into early adulthood (Casey, Tottenham, Liston, & Durston, 2005).

Further Resources

According to neuroscientist Jay Giedd in the Frontline video "Inside the Teenage Brain" (2013), "It's sort of unfair to expect [teens] to have adult levels of organizational skills or decision-making before their brains are finished being built." Watch this segment on "The Wiring of the Adolescent Brain" (hawkes. biz/adolescentbrain) to find out more about the developing brain during adolescence.

Human Brain Anatomy

Figure 24: Brain growth continues into the early 20s. The development of the frontal lobe, in particular, is important during this stage.

Cognitive Development

More complex thinking abilities emerge during adolescence. Some researchers suggest this is due to increases in processing speed and efficiency rather than as the result of an increase in mental capacity—in other words, due to improvements in existing skills rather than development of new ones (Bjorkland, 1987; Case, 1985). During adolescence, teenagers move beyond concrete thinking and become capable of abstract thought. Recall that Piaget refers to this stage as formal operational thought. Teen thinking is also characterized by the ability to:

- consider multiple points of view
- imagine hypothetical situations
- debate ideas and opinions (e.g., politics, religion, and justice)
- form new ideas (Figure 25)

In addition, it's not uncommon for adolescents to question authority or challenge established societal norms.

Cognitive empathy, also known as theory-of-mind (which we discussed earlier with regard to egocentrism), relates to the ability to take the perspective of others and feel concern for others (Shamay-Tsoory, Tomer, & Aharon-Peretz, 2005). Cognitive empathy begins to increase in adolescence and is an important component of social problem solving and conflict avoidance. According to one longitudinal study, levels of cognitive empathy begin rising in girls around 13 years old and around 15 years old in boys (Van der Graaff et al., 2013). Teens who reported having supportive fathers with whom they could discuss their worries were found to be better able to take the perspective of others (Miklikowska, Duriez, & Soenens, 2011).

Psychosocial Development

Adolescents continue to refine their sense of self as they relate to others. Erikson referred to the task of the adolescent as one of identity versus role confusion. Thus, in Erikson's view, an adolescent's main questions are "Who am I?" and "Who do I want to be?" Some adolescents adopt the values and roles that their parents expect for them. Other teens develop identities that are in opposition to their parents but align with a peer group. This is common as peer relationships become a central focus in adolescents' lives.

Figure 25: Teenage thinking is characterized by the ability to reason logically and solve hypothetical problems such as how to design, plan, and build a structure.

As adolescents work to form their identities, they pull away from their parents, and the peer group becomes important (Shanahan, McHale, Osgood, & Crouter, 2007). Despite spending less time with their parents, most teens report positive feelings toward them (Moore, Guzman, Hair, Lippman, & Garrett, 2004). Warm and healthy parent-child relationships have been associated with positive child outcomes, such as better grades and fewer school behavior problems, in the United States as well as in other countries (Hair et al., 2005).

It appears that most teens don't experience adolescent storm and stress to the degree once famously suggested by G. Stanley Hall, a pioneer in the study of adolescent development. Only small numbers of teens have major conflicts with their parents (Steinberg & Morris, 2001), and most disagreements are minor (Figure 26). For example, in a study of over 1,800 parents of adolescents from various cultural and ethnic groups, Barber (1994) found that conflicts occurred over day-to-day issues, such as homework, money, curfews, clothing, chores, and friends. These types of arguments tend to decrease as teens develop (Galambos & Almeida, 1992).

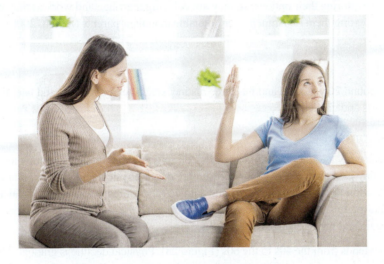

📷 **Figure 26:** Although it is commonly accepted as a given, most teens don't have major conflicts with their parents.

Reflection Questions
Many parents fear the adolescent years with their children due to the popular belief that it is a period of storm and stress, yet the research does not support this notion. Why do you think the idea persists?

Group Activity
In a small group, discuss everyone's thoughts regarding when a person officially becomes an adult. How does culture influence your answers?

Emerging Adulthood

The next stage of development is **emerging adulthood**. This is a relatively newly defined period of lifespan development spanning from 18 years old to the mid-20s, characterized as an in-between time where identity exploration is focused on work and love.

There are many ways to answer the question of when a person becomes an adult. In the United States, you are legally considered an adult at 18 years old. But other definitions of adulthood vary widely; in sociology, for example, a person may be considered an adult when she:

- becomes self-supporting
- chooses a career
- gets married
- starts a family

The ages at which we achieve these milestones vary from person to person as well as from culture to culture. For example, in the African country of Malawi, 15-year-old Njemile was married at 14 years old and had her first child at 15 years old. In her culture she is considered an adult. Children in Malawi take on adult responsibilities such as marriage and work (e.g., carrying water, tending babies, and working fields) as

📷 **Figure 27:** In Malawi, it isn't unusual for girls to be married by 14 years old and have their first child at 15 years old.

early as 10 years old. In stark contrast, independence in Western cultures is taking longer and longer, effectively delaying the onset of adult life.

Why is it taking twentysomethings so long to grow up? It seems that emerging adulthood is a product of both Western culture and our current times (Arnett, 2000). People in developed countries are living longer, allowing the freedom to take an extra decade to start a career and family. Changes in the workforce also play a role. For example, 50 years ago, a young adult with a high school diploma could immediately enter the work force and climb the corporate ladder. That is no longer the case. Bachelor's and even graduate degrees are required more and more often—even for entry-level jobs (Arnett, 2000). In addition, many students are taking longer (five or six years) to complete a college degree as a result of working and going to school at the same time. After graduation, many young adults return to the family home because they have difficulty finding a job. Changing cultural expectations may be the most important reason for the delay in entering adult roles. Young people are spending more time exploring their options, so they are delaying marriage and work as they change majors and jobs multiple times, putting them on a much later timetable than their parents (Arnett, 2000).

Adulthood

Adulthood begins around 20 years old and has three distinct stages: early, middle, and late. Each stage brings its own set of rewards and challenges.

Physical Development

By the time we reach early adulthood (20 to early 40s), our physical maturation is complete although our height and weight may increase slightly. In young adulthood, our physical abilities are at their peak, including muscle strength, reaction time, sensory abilities, and cardiac functioning. Most professional athletes are at the top of their game during this stage. Many women have children in the young adulthood years, so they may see additional weight gain and breast changes.

Middle adulthood extends from the 40s to the 60s (Figure 28). Physical decline is gradual. The skin loses some elasticity, and wrinkles are among the first signs of aging. Visual acuity decreases during this time. Women experience a gradual decline in fertility as they approach the onset of menopause, the end of the menstrual cycle, around 50 years old. Both men and women tend to gain weight: in the abdominal area for men and in the hips and thighs for women. Hair begins to thin and turn gray.

Figure 28: Physical declines of middle and late adulthood can be minimized with proper exercise, nutrition, and an active lifestyle.

Late adulthood is considered to extend from the 60s on. This is the last stage of physical change. The skin continues to lose elasticity, reaction time slows further, and muscle strength diminishes. Smell, taste, hearing, and vision, so sharp in our twenties, decline significantly. The brain may also no longer function at optimal levels, leading to problems like memory loss, dementia, and Alzheimer's disease in later years.

Further Resources

Aging doesn't mean a person can't explore new pursuits, learn new skills, and continue to grow. Watch this inspiring story (hawkes.biz/physicalaging) about Neil Unger who is a newbie to the world of skateboarding at 60 years old.

Cognitive Development

Because we spend so many years in adulthood (more than any other stage), cognitive changes are numerous. In fact, research suggests that adult cognitive development is a complex, ever changing process that may be even more active than cognitive development in infancy and early childhood (Fischer, Yan, & Stewart, 2003).

Unlike our physical abilities, which peak in our mid-20s and then begin a slow decline, our cognitive abilities remain steady throughout early and middle adulthood. Our crystallized intelligence tends to hold steady as we age—it may even improve. For example, adults show relatively stable to increasing scores on intelligence tests until their mid-30s to mid-50s (Bayley & Oden, 1955).

Further Resources

There is good news for the middle age brain. View this brief video (hawkes.biz/adultcognitive) to find out what it is.

Figure 29: Crystallized intelligence can either stay the same or improve as we age.

However, in late adulthood we begin to experience a decline in another area of our cognitive abilities—fluid intelligence. These processes become slower.

Figure 30: Fluid intelligence tends to decline as we age.

How can we delay the onset of cognitive decline? Mental and physical activity seems to play a part (Figure 31). Research has found adults who engage in mentally and physically stimulating activities experience less cognitive decline and have a reduced incidence of mild cognitive impairment and dementia (Hertzog, Kramer, Wilson, & Lindenberger, 2009; Larson et al., 2006; Podewils et al., 2005).

Psychosocial Development

There are many theories about the social and emotional aspects of aging. Some aspects of healthy aging include activities, social connectedness, and the role of a person's culture. According to many theorists, including George Vaillant (2002), who studied and analyzed over 50 years of data, we need to have and continue to find meaning throughout our lives. For those in early and middle adulthood, meaning is found through work (Sterns & Huyck, 2001) and family life (Markus, Ryff, Curan, & Palmersheim, 2004). These areas relate to the tasks that Erikson referred to as generativity and intimacy. As mentioned previously, adults tend to define themselves by what they do—their careers. Earnings peak during this time, yet job satisfaction is more closely tied to work that:

Figure 31: Cognitive activities such as playing mahjong, chess, or other games, can keep you mentally fit. The same is true for solo pastimes like reading and completing crossword puzzles.

- involves contact with other people
- is interesting
- provides opportunities for advancement
- allows some independence (Mohr & Zoghi, 2006)

Reflection Questions

Does your future career meet the criteria above? How might being unemployed or being in a dead-end job challenge adult well-being?

Further Resources

To learn more, view this video (hawkes.biz/aging) on aging in America.

Positive relationships with significant others in our adult years have been found to contribute to a state of well-being (Ryff & Singer, 2009). Most adults in the United States identify themselves through their relationships with family—particularly with spouses, children, and parents (Markus et al., 2004). While raising children can be stressful, especially when they are young, research suggests that parents reap the rewards down the road, as adult children tend to have a positive effect on parental well-being (Umberson, Pudrovska, & Reczek, 2010). Having a stable marriage has also been found to contribute to well-being throughout adulthood (Vaillant, 2002).

Another aspect of positive aging is believed to be social connectedness and social support. As we get older, **socioemotional selectivity theory** suggests that our social support and friendships dwindle in number but remain as close, if not more close, than in our earlier years (Carstensen, 1992) (Figure 32).

Figure 32: Social support is important as we age.

Summary

At conception the egg and sperm cell are united to form a zygote, which will begin to divide rapidly. This marks the beginning of the first stage of prenatal development (germinal stage), which lasts about two weeks. Then the zygote implants itself into the lining of the woman's uterus, marking the beginning of the second stage of prenatal development (embryonic stage), which lasts about six weeks. The embryo begins to develop body and organ structures, and the neural tube forms, which will later become the brain and spinal cord. The third phase of prenatal development (fetal stage) begins at 9 weeks and lasts until birth. The body, brain, and organs grow rapidly during this stage. During all stages of pregnancy it is important that the mother receive prenatal care to reduce health risks to herself and to her developing baby.

Newborn infants weigh about 7.5 pounds. Doctors assess a newborn's reflexes, such as the sucking, rooting, and moro reflexes. Our physical, cognitive, and psychosocial skills grow and change as we move through developmental stages from infancy through late adulthood. Attachment in infancy is a critical component of healthy development. Parenting styles have been found to have an effect on childhood outcomes of well-being. The transition from adolescence to adulthood can be challenging due to the timing of puberty and due to the extended amount of time spent in emerging adulthood. Although physical decline begins in middle adulthood, cognitive decline does not begin until later. Activities that keep the body and mind active can help maintain good physical and cognitive health as we age. Social supports through family and friends remain important as we age.

8.4 Death and Dying

You may have heard the old adage, "Don't take life too seriously. Nobody gets out alive anyway" (Figure 1). No matter what your life story, it inevitably ends with a transition to death. Often, our culture and individual backgrounds influence how we view death. In some cultures, death is embraced as a natural part of life. In contrast, until about 50 years ago in the United States, a doctor might not inform someone that they were dying, and so the majority of deaths occurred in hospitals.

In 1967, that reality began to change with Cicely Saunders, who created the first modern hospice in England. The aim of **hospice** is to help provide a death with dignity and pain management in a humane and comfortable environment, which is usually outside of a hospital setting. In 1974, Florence Wald founded the first hospice in the United States. Today, hospice provides care for 1.65 million Americans and their families. Because of hospice care, many terminally ill people are able to spend their last days at home.

Research has indicated that hospice care is beneficial for the patient (Brumley, Enquidanos, & Cherin, 2003; Brumley et al., 2007; Godkin, Krant, & Doster, 1984) for the following reasons:

- Higher levels of satisfaction

- Ability to stay in their homes

- Not completely dependent on strangers for care (Brumley et al., 2007)

- Longer life expectancy (Connor, Pyenson, Fitch, Spence, & Iwasaki, 2007; Temel et al., 2010)

Additionally, hospice is beneficial for the patient's family (Rhodes, Mitchell, Miller, Connor, & Teno, 2008; Godkin et al., 1984). Family members receive emotional support and are regularly informed of their loved one's treatment and condition. The family member's burden of care is also reduced (McMillan et al., 2006). Both the patient and the patient's family members report increased family support, increased social support, and improved coping while receiving hospice services (Godkin et al., 1984).

Facing the imminent reality of one's own death can be extremely difficult. How do you think you might react if you were diagnosed with a terminal illness? Elizabeth Kübler-Ross (1969), who worked with the founders of hospice care, described the process of an individual accepting his own death. She proposed five stages of grief: denial, anger, bargaining, depression, and acceptance.

Figure 1: In some cultures, people's bodies may be buried in a cemetery after death.

🖼 **Figure 2:** The five stages of grief can occur in any order.

Most individuals experience these stages, but the stages may occur in different orders, depending on the individual. In addition, not all people experience all of the stages. It is also important to note that some psychologists believe that the more a dying person fights death, the more likely he is to remain stuck in the denial phase. This could make it difficult for the dying person to face death with dignity. However, other psychologists believe that not facing death until the very end is an adaptive coping mechanism for some people.

Whether due to illness or old age, not everyone facing death or the loss of a loved one experiences the negative emotions outlined in the Kübler-Ross model (Nolen-Hoeksema & Larson, 1999).

> Research suggests that people with religious or spiritual beliefs are better able to cope with death because of their hope in an afterlife and because of social support from religious or spiritual associations (Hood, Spilka, Hunsberger, & Corsuch, 1996; McIntosh, Silver, & Wortman, 1993; Paloutzian, 1996; Samarel, 1991; Wortman & Park, 2008).

Further Resources

Watch the full version of Randy Pausch's lecture (hawkes.biz/randypausch).

Take Randy Pausch, who was a well-loved and respected professor at Carnegie Mellon University. Diagnosed with terminal pancreatic cancer in his mid-40s and given only 3–6 months to live, Pausch focused on living in a fulfilling way in the time he had left. Instead of becoming angry and depressed, he presented his now famous last lecture called "Really Achieving Your Childhood Dreams." In his moving, yet humorous talk, he shares his insights on seeing the good in others, overcoming obstacles, and experiencing zero gravity, among many other things. Despite his terminal diagnosis, Pausch lived the final year of his life with joy and hope, showing us that our plans for the future still matter, even if we know that we are dying.

☑ **On Your Own**

1. In what year was hospice care first started in the United States?

☐ 1967   ☐ 1974   ☐ 1986

2. Today, how many individuals are cared for by hospice care?

☐ 1 million   ☐ 2 million
☐ 1.65 million   ☐ 2.65 million

Summary

Death marks the endpoint of our lifespan. There are many ways that we might react when facing death.
Kübler-Ross developed a five-stage model of grief as a way to explain this process. Many people
facing death choose hospice care, which allows their last days to be spent at home in a comfortable,
supportive environment.

Chapter 8 Project

Purpose

A good way to understand how an individual changes over the lifespan is to observe them. However, that takes a long time. An alternative research method that is often used in developmental psychology is a cross-sectional design, where different individuals, at various stages of the lifespan, are studied all at once. **The purpose of this assignment is to help you identify and understand the theories and concepts of lifespan psychology using the cross-sectional research method with three individuals at various stages of the lifespan.** You will interview each individual and collect raw data (i.e., interview notes) and provide that raw data as well as a summary report that focuses on how this individual exemplifies an aspect of developmental psychology.

Directions

You will be assigned a partner for this project. The two of you will then choose three people to interview from different developmental stages. For each of those people, you will be focused on one domain of lifespan psychology (i.e., physical, cognitive, or social). Since you will be conducting interviews, you can choose any individual who can carry on a conversation (yes, young children can carry on a conversation). For each individual, after you ask a set of common preliminary interview questions (see the list below), you will also ask five domain-specific questions that you develop.

Common Preliminary Interview Questions (should be asked to everyone):

1. What is your name?

2. How old are you?

3. How do you spend most of your time?

4. Please tell me about something that is important to you.

5. Please tell me about an accomplishment you are proud of.

6. Please tell me about something you are looking forward to.

7. Please share with me a very important event in your life. Why was it important?

Your final submitted paper will have three sections:

Part 1 - Introduction

Part 2 - Developmental reports (3)

Part 3 - Interview notes from each report (3)

Part 1 - Introduction

Please begin your final report with the following information:

Student 1:

Student 2:

	Interviewee Name and Relationship	Developmental Stage	Developmental Domain	Specific Theory or Content
Individual 1				
Individual 2				
Individual 3				

Part 2 - Developmental Reports

Begin by listing the five-or-more questions that you came up with to better understand some specific lifespan psychology content (i.e., theory or principle). Then write a 500–1,000 word report that illustrates your insights and knowledge about the developmental domain. For example:

Developmental Report 1

    Individual: Jane Doe, grandmother

    Developmental Stage: Late adulthood

    Developmental Domain: Social

    Specific Theory or Content: Erikson's Integrity vs. Despair

Questions:

1. *Example* - Looking back, how do you feel about the course of your life to now?

2.

3.

4.

5.

Erikson's Integrity vs. Despair in Jane Doe (500–1,000 words)

Part 3 - Interview Notes

These should be typed notes from your interview sessions. They need not be of essay-quality. Bullet points are acceptable.

> **Hint: it is highly recommended that you have one student take notes while the other student fully engages in the interview. You must both be present for all three interviews.*

Materials

None required.

☑ Checklist

- ☐ Introduction
- ☐ Person 1 Developmental Report
  - ☐ Name and relationship
  - ☐ Developmental stage
  - ☐ Developmental domain
  - ☐ Specific theory or content
  - ☐ 500–1,000 word report
- ☐ Person 2 Developmental Report
  - ☐ Name and relationship
  - ☐ Developmental stage
  - ☐ Developmental domain
  - ☐ Specific theory or content
  - ☐ 500–1,000 word report

- ☐ Person 3 Developmental Report
  - ☐ Name and relationship
  - ☐ Developmental stage
  - ☐ Developmental domain
  - ☐ Specific theory or content
  - ☐ 500–1,000 word report
- ☐ Interview notes
  - ☐ Person 1
  - ☐ Person 2
  - ☐ Person 3

🏁 Chapter 8 Review

Lesson Summaries

8.1 What Is Lifespan Development?

Lifespan development explores how we change and grow from conception to death. This field of psychology is studied by developmental psychologists. They view development as a lifelong process that can be studied scientifically across three developmental domains: physical, cognitive, and psychosocial. There are several theories of development that focus on the following issues: whether development is continuous or discontinuous, whether development follows one course or many, and the relative influence of nature versus nurture on development.

8.2 Lifespan Theories

There are many theories regarding how babies and children grow and develop into happy, healthy adults. Sigmund Freud suggested that we pass through a series of psychosexual stages in which our energy is focused on certain erogenous zones on the body. Eric Erikson said that our social interactions and successful completion of social tasks shape our sense of self. Jean Piaget proposed a theory of cognitive development that explains how children think and reason as they move through various stages. Lawrence Kohlberg turned his attention to moral development. He said that we pass through three levels of moral thinking that build on our cognitive development.

8.3 Stages of Development

At conception the egg and sperm cell are united to form a zygote, which will begin to divide rapidly. This marks the beginning of the first stage of prenatal development (germinal stage), which lasts about two weeks. Then the zygote implants itself into the lining of the woman's uterus, marking the beginning of the second stage of prenatal development (embryonic stage), which lasts about six weeks. The embryo begins to develop body and organ structures, and the neural tube forms, which will later become the brain and spinal cord. The third phase of prenatal development (fetal stage) begins at 9 weeks and lasts until birth. The body, brain, and organs grow rapidly during this stage. During all stages of pregnancy it is important that the mother receive prenatal care to reduce health risks to herself and to her developing baby.

Newborn infants weigh about 7.5 pounds. Doctors assess a newborn's reflexes, such as the sucking, rooting, and moro reflexes. Our physical, cognitive, and psychosocial skills grow and change as we move through developmental stages from infancy through late adulthood. Attachment in infancy is a critical component of healthy development. Parenting styles have been found to have an effect on childhood outcomes of well-being. The transition from adolescence to adulthood can be challenging due to the timing of puberty and due to the extended amount of time spent in emerging adulthood. Although physical decline begins in middle adulthood, cognitive decline does not begin until later. Activities that keep the body and mind active can help maintain good physical and cognitive health as we age. Social supports through family and friends remain important as we age.

8.4 Death and Dying

Death marks the endpoint of our lifespan. There are many ways that we might react when facing death. Kübler-Ross developed a five-stage model of grief as a way to explain this process. Many people facing death choose hospice care, which allows their last days to be spent at home in a comfortable, supportive environment.

Key Terms

Flash Back

Now that you've worked through the chapter, sharpen your vocabulary with this Hawkes Verified Quizlet set (hawkes.biz/psychch8)!

Accommodation
Adjustment of a schema by changing a scheme to accommodate new information different from what was already known

Adolescence
Period of development that begins at puberty and ends at early adulthood

Adrenarche
Maturing of the adrenal glands

Assimilation
Adjustment of a schema by adding information similar to what is already known

Attachment
Long-standing connection or bond with others

Authoritarian Parenting Style
Parents place a high value on conformity and obedience, are often rigid, and express little warmth to the child

Authoritative Parenting Style
Parents give children reasonable demands and consistent limits, express warmth and affection, and listen to the child's point of view

Avoidant Attachment
Characterized by child's unresponsiveness to parent, does not use the parent as a secure base, and does not care if parent leaves

Cognitive Development
Domain of lifespan development that examines learning, attention, memory, language, thinking, reasoning, and creativity

Cognitive Empathy

Ability to take the perspective of others and to feel concern for others

Conception

When a sperm fertilizes an egg and forms a zygote

Concrete Operational Stage

Third stage in Piaget's theory of cognitive development; from about 7 to 11 years old, children can think logically about real (concrete) events

Conservation

Idea that even if you change the appearance of something, it is still equal in size, volume, or number as long as nothing is added or removed

Continuous Development

View that development is a cumulative process: gradually improving on existing skills

Critical (Sensitive) Period

Time during fetal growth when specific parts or organs develop

Developmental Milestone

Approximate ages at which children reach specific normative events

Discontinuous Development

View that development takes place in unique stages, which happen at specific times or ages

Disorganized Attachment

Characterized by the child's odd behavior when faced with the parent; type of attachment seen most often with kids that are abused

Egocentrism

Preoperational child's difficulty in taking the perspective of others

Embryo

Multi-cellular organism in its early stages of development

Emerging Adulthood

Newly defined period of lifespan development from 18 years old to the mid-20s; young people are taking longer to complete college, get a job, get married, and start a family

Fine Motor Skills

Use of muscles in fingers, toes, and eyes to coordinate small actions

Formal Operational Stage

Final stage in Piaget's theory of cognitive development; from age 11 and up, children are able to deal with abstract ideas and hypothetical situations

Gonadarche

Maturing of the sex glands

Gross Motor Skills

Use of large muscle groups to control arms and legs for large body movements

Hospice

Service that provides a death with dignity; pain management in a humane and comfortable environment; usually outside of a hospital setting

Menarche

Beginning of menstrual period; around 12–13 years old

Mitosis

Process of cell division

Motor Skills

Ability to move our body and manipulate objects

Nature

Genes and biology

Newborn Reflexes

Inborn automatic response to a particular form of stimulation that all healthy babies are born with

Normative Approach

Study of development using norms, or average ages, when most children reach specific developmental milestones

Nurture

Environment and culture

Object Permanence

Idea that even if something is out of sight, it still exists

Permissive Parenting Style

Parents make few demands and rarely use punishment

Physical Development

Domain of lifespan development that examines growth and changes in the body and brain, the senses, motor skills, and health and wellness

Placenta

Structure connected to the uterus that provides nourishment and oxygen to the developing baby

Prenatal Care

Medical care during pregnancy that monitors the health of both the mother and the fetus

Preoperational Stage

Second stage in Piaget's theory of cognitive development; from ages 2 to 7, children learn to use symbols and language but do not understand mental operations and often think illogically

Primary Sexual Characteristics

Organs specifically needed for reproduction

Psychosexual Development

Process proposed by Freud in which pleasure-seeking urges focus on different erogenous zones of the body as humans move through five stages of life

Psychosocial Development

Process proposed by Erikson in which social tasks are mastered as humans move through eight stages of life from infancy to adulthood

Resistant Attachment

Characterized by the child's tendency to show clingy behavior and rejection of the parent when she attempts to interact with the child

Reversibility

Principle that objects can be changed but then returned back to their original form or condition

Schema

(Plural: *schemata*) concept (mental model) that is used to help us categorize and interpret information

Secondary Sexual Characteristics

Physical signs of sexual maturation that do not directly involve sex organs

Secure Attachment

Characterized by the child using the parent as a secure base from which to explore

Secure Base

Parental presence that gives the infant/toddler a sense of safety as he explores his surroundings

Sensorimotor Stage

First stage in Piaget's theory of cognitive development; from birth through age 2, a child learns about the world through senses and motor behavior

Socioemotional Selectivity Theory

Social support/friendships dwindle in number but remain as close, if not more close, than in earlier years

Spermarche

First male ejaculation

Stage of Moral Reasoning

Process proposed by Kohlberg; humans move through three stages of moral development

Temperament

Innate traits that influence how one thinks, behaves, and reacts with the environment

Teratogen

Biological, chemical, or physical environmental agent that causes damage to the developing embryo or fetus

Uninvolved Parenting Style

Parents are indifferent, uninvolved, and sometimes referred to as neglectful; they don't respond to the child's needs and make relatively few demands

Zygote

Structure created when a sperm and egg merge at conception; begins as a single cell and rapidly divides to form the embryo and placenta

⚡ Exercises

Review Questions

1. The view that development is a cumulative process, gradually adding to the same type of skills is known as _____.

    a. nature

    b. nurture

    c. continuous development

    d. discontinuous development

2. Developmental psychologists study human growth and development across three domains. Which of the following is not one of these domains?

    a. Cognitive

    b. Psychological

    c. Physical

    d. Psychosocial

3. How is lifespan development defined?

    a. The study of how we grow and change from conception to death

    b. The study of how we grow and change in infancy and childhood

    c. The study of physical, cognitive, and psychosocial growth in children

    d. The study of emotions, personality, and social relationships

4. The idea that even if something is out of sight, it still exists is called _____.

    a. egocentrism

    b. object permanence

    c. conservation

    d. reversibility

5. Which theorist proposed that moral thinking proceeds through a series of stages?

    a. Sigmund Freud

    b. Erik Erikson

    c. John Watson

    d. Lawrence Kohlberg

6. According to Erikson's theory of psychosocial development, what is the main task of the adolescent?

    a. Developing autonomy

    b. Feeling competent

    c. Forming an identity

    d. Forming intimate relationships

7. Which of the following is the correct order of prenatal development?

    a. Zygote, fetus, embryo

    b. Fetus, embryo zygote

    c. Fetus, zygote, embryo

    d. Zygote, embryo, fetus

8. The time during fetal growth when specific parts or organs develop is known as _____.

    a. critical period

    b. mitosis

    c. conception

    d. pregnancy

9. What begins as a single-cell structure that is created when a sperm and egg merge at conception?

    a. Embryo

    b. Fetus

    c. Zygote

    d. Infant

10. Using scissors to cut out paper shapes is an example of _____.

    a. gross motor skills

    b. fine motor skills

    c. large motor skills

    d. small motor skills

11. The child uses the parent as a base from which to explore her world in which attachment style?

    a. Secure

    b. Insecure avoidant

    c. Insecure ambivalent-resistant

    d. Disorganized

12. The frontal lobes become fully developed _____.

    a. at birth

    b. at the beginning of adolescence

    c. at the end of adolescence

    d. by 25 years old

13. Who created the very first modern hospice?

    a. Elizabeth Kübler-Ross

    b. Cicely Saunders

    c. Florence Wald

    d. Florence Nightingale

14. Although they can occur in any order, which of the following is the order of stages Elizabeth Kübler-Ross outlined in her five-stage model of grief?

    a. Denial, bargaining, anger, depression, acceptance

    b. Anger, depression, bargaining, acceptance, denial

    c. Denial, anger, bargaining, depression, acceptance

    d. Anger, acceptance, denial, depression, bargaining

Critical Thinking Questions

15. Describe the nature versus nurture controversy, and give an example of a trait and how it might be influenced by each?

16. Compare and contrast continuous and discontinuous development.

17. Why should developmental milestones only be used as a general guideline for normal child development?

18. What is the difference between assimilation and accommodation? Provide examples of each.

19. Why was Carol Gilligan critical of Kohlberg's theory of moral development?

20. What is egocentrism? Provide an original example.

21. What are some known teratogens, and what kind of damage can they do to the developing fetus?

22. What is prenatal care and why is it important?

23. Describe what happens in the embryonic stage of development. Describe what happens in the fetal stage of development.

24. What makes a personal quality part of someone's personality?

25. Describe some of the newborn reflexes. How might they promote survival?

26. Compare and contrast the four attachment styles and describe the kinds of childhood outcomes we can expect with each.

27. What is emerging adulthood and what are some factors that have contributed to this new stage of development?

28. Describe the five stages of grief and provide examples of how a person might react in each stage.

29. What is the purpose of hospice care?

Chapter 9
Emotion and Motivation

Chapter Introduction

Figure 1: Emotions can change in an instant, especially in response to an unexpected event. Surprise, fear, anger, and sadness are some immediate emotions that people experienced in the aftermath of the April 15, 2013 Boston Marathon bombing. What are emotions? What causes them? What motivated some bystanders to immediately help others while other people ran for safety?

What makes us behave as we do? What drives us to eat? What drives us toward sex? Is there a biological basis to explain the feelings we experience? How universal are emotions?

In this chapter, we will explore issues relating to both motivation and emotion. We will begin with a discussion of several theories that have been proposed to explain motivation and why we engage in a given behavior. You will learn about the physiological needs that drive some human behaviors, as well as the importance of our social experiences in influencing our actions.

Next, we will consider both eating and having sex as examples of motivated behaviors. What are the physiological mechanisms of hunger and satiety? What understanding do scientists have of why obesity occurs, and what treatments exist for obesity and eating disorders? How has research into human sex and sexuality evolved over the past century? How do psychologists understand and study the human experience of sexual orientation and gender identity? These questions—and more—will be explored.

This chapter will close with a discussion of emotion. You will learn about several theories that have been proposed to explain how emotion occurs, the biological underpinnings of emotion, and the universality of emotions.

Flash Forward

Ready to dig into the vocabulary? Get some practice with this Hawkes Verified Quizlet set (hawkes.biz/psych9q1)!

9.1 Motivation

Why do we do the things we do? What motivations underlie our behaviors? **Motivation** describes the wants or needs that direct behavior toward a goal. In addition to biological motives, motivations can be **intrinsic** (arising from internal factors) or **extrinsic** (arising from external factors) (Figure 2). Intrinsically motivated behaviors are performed because of the sense of personal satisfaction that they bring, whereas extrinsically motivated behaviors are performed in order to receive something from others.

Intrinsic Motivation
(from within)
Autonomy
Mastery
Purpose

Extrinsic Motivation
(from outside)
Compensation
Punishment
Reward

Figure 2: Intrinsic motivation comes from within the individual, while extrinsic motivation comes from outside the individual.

✐ On Your Own

What are your intrinsic and extrinsic motivations for being in college?

Intrinsic Motivations	Extrinsic Motivations

In reality, our motivations are often a mix of both intrinsic and extrinsic factors, but the nature of the mix of these factors might change over time (often in ways that seem counter-intuitive). There is an old adage that says, "Choose a job that you love, and you will never have to work a day in your life," meaning that if you enjoy your occupation, work doesn't seem like…well, work. Some research suggests that this isn't necessarily the case (Daniel & Esser, 1980; Deci, 1972; Deci, Koestner, & Ryan, 1999). According to this research, receiving some sort of extrinsic reinforcement (i.e., getting paid) for engaging in behaviors that we enjoy leads to those behaviors no longer providing that same enjoyment. As a result, we might spend less time engaging in these reclassified behaviors in the absence of any extrinsic reinforcement.

Consider these examples:

- Odessa loves baking, so she bakes for fun in her free time. However, once she starts working in the bakery department, she no longer has the desire to bake when she is not working (Figure 3).

- Nicole enjoys designing video games, but once she is employed with a local video game company, she no longer looks forward to the task as she once did.

- Michael loves children, so he thinks that the best job would be to work with them frequently. Instead, he finds that the constant exposure to children makes him rethink his own future as a parent.

What Odessa and the others have experienced is called the overjustification effect—intrinsic motivation is diminished when extrinsic motivation is given. This can lead to extinguishing the intrinsic motivation and creating a dependence on extrinsic rewards for continued performance (Deci et al., 1999).

Figure 3: Research suggests that when something we love to do, like icing cakes, becomes our job, our intrinsic and extrinsic motivations to do it may change.

Other studies suggest that intrinsic motivation may not be so vulnerable to the effects of extrinsic reinforcements, and in fact, reinforcements such as verbal praise might actually increase intrinsic motivation (Arnold, 1976; Cameron & Pierce, 1994). In that case, Odessa's motivation to bake in her free time might remain high if, for example, customers regularly compliment her baking or cake decorating skills.

These apparent discrepancies in the researchers' findings may be understood by considering several factors. For one, physical reinforcement (such as money) and verbal reinforcement (such as praise) may affect an individual in very different ways. In fact, tangible rewards (i.e., money) tend to have more negative effects on intrinsic motivation than do intangible rewards (i.e., praise).

Figure 4: Instrinsic motivation can be affected both negatively and positively depending on the type of reward.

Furthermore, the expectation of the extrinsic motivator by an individual is crucial: if the person expects to receive an extrinsic reward, then intrinsic motivation for the task tends to be reduced. If, however, there is no such expectation, and the extrinsic motivation is presented as a surprise, then intrinsic motivation for the task tends to persist (Deci et al., 1999).

In educational settings, students are more likely to experience intrinsic motivation to learn when they feel a sense of belonging and respect in the classroom. This internalization can be enhanced if the evaluative aspects of the classroom are de-emphasized and if students feel that they exercise some control over the learning environment. Furthermore, providing students with activities that are challenging, yet doable, along with a rationale for engaging in various learning activities can enhance intrinsic motivation for those tasks (Niemiec & Ryan, 2009).

Ways to Foster Intrinsic Motivation in Class

Figure 5: There are different strategies that are effective for increasing instrinsic motivation in class.

Consider Hakim, a first-year law student with two courses this semester: Family Law and Criminal Law. The Family Law professor has a rather intimidating classroom; he likes to put students on the spot with tough questions, which often leaves students feeling belittled or embarrassed. Grades are based exclusively on quizzes and exams, and the instructor posts results of each test on the classroom door. In contrast, the Criminal Law professor facilitates classroom discussions and respectful debates in small groups. The majority of the course grade is not exam-based but centers on a student-designed research project on a crime issue of the student's choice. Research suggests that Hakim will be less intrinsically motivated in his Family Law course, where students are intimidated in the classroom setting, and there is an emphasis on teacher-driven evaluations. Alternatively, Hakim is likely to experience a higher level of intrinsic motivation in his Criminal Law course, where the class setting encourages inclusive collaboration and a respect for ideas and where students have more influence over their learning activities.

Reflection Questions

Have you ever consider what kind of things keep you motivated? Money? Success? Love? Do different things motivate you in different situations?

Theories about Motivation

William James (1842–1910) was an important contributor to early research into motivation, and he is often referred to as the father of psychology in the United States. James theorized that behavior was driven by a number of instincts, which aid survival (Figure 6). From a biological perspective, an **instinct** is a species-specific pattern of behavior that is not learned. There was, however, considerable controversy among James and his contemporaries over the exact definition of instinct. James proposed several dozen special human instincts, but many of his contemporaries had their own lists that differed. A mother's protection of her baby, the urge to lick sugar, and hunting prey were among the human behaviors proposed as true instincts during James's era. This view—that human behavior is driven by instincts—received a fair amount of criticism because of the undeniable role of learning in shaping all sorts of human behavior. In fact, as early as the 1900s, some instinctive behaviors were experimentally demonstrated to result from associative learning (recall when you learned about Watson's conditioning of fear response with "Little Albert") (Faris, 1921).

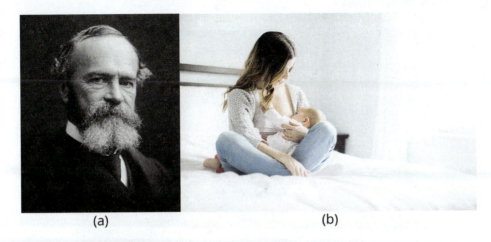

(a)   (b)

Figure 6: (a) William James proposed the instinct theory of motivation, asserting that behavior is driven by instincts. (b) In humans, instincts may include behaviors such as an infant's rooting for a nipple and sucking.

Reflection Questions

Do humans have instincts that do not differ across individuals? Identify at least 5 instincts.

Another early theory of motivation proposed that the maintenance of homeostasis is particularly important in directing behavior. You may recall from your earlier reading that homeostasis is the tendency to maintain a balance, or optimal level, within a biological system. In a body system, a control center (which is often part of the brain) receives input from receptors (which are often complexes of neurons). The control center directs effectors (which may be other neurons) to correct any imbalance detected by the control center.

According to the **drive theory** of motivation, deviations from homeostasis create physiological needs. These needs result in psychological drive states that direct behavior to meet the need and, ultimately, bring the system back to homeostasis. When it comes to ingestive behavior, you experience the following when you go without food for a period of time:

1   Drop in blood sugar levels

2   Physiological need state

3   Drive state (i.e., hunger)

4   Consume food

Figure 7: Going without food causes a specific physiological response that encourages you to eat.

Eating will eliminate the hunger, and your blood sugar levels will return to normal (Figure 8). Interestingly, drive theory also emphasizes the role that habits play in the type of behavioral response in which we engage. A **habit** is a pattern of behavior in which we regularly engage. Once we have engaged in a behavior that successfully reduces a drive, we are more likely to engage in that behavior whenever faced with that drive in the future (Graham & Weiner, 1996).

Figure 8: Hunger and subsequent eating are the result of complex physiological processes that maintain homeostasis.

Extensions of drive theory take into account levels of arousal as potential motivators. As you recall from your study of learning, these theories assert that there is an optimal level of arousal that we all try to maintain (Figure 9). If we are underaroused, we become bored and will seek out some sort of stimulation. On the other hand, if we are overaroused, we will engage in behaviors to reduce our arousal (Berlyne, 1960). Most students have experienced this need to maintain optimal levels of arousal over the course of their academic career. Think about how much stress students experience toward the end of spring semester. They feel overwhelmed with seemingly endless exams, papers, and major assignments that must be completed on time. They probably yearn for the rest and relaxation that awaits them over the extended summer break. However, once they finish the semester, it doesn't take too long before they begin to feel bored. Generally, by the time the next semester is beginning in the fall, many students are quite happy to return to school. This is an example of how arousal theory works.

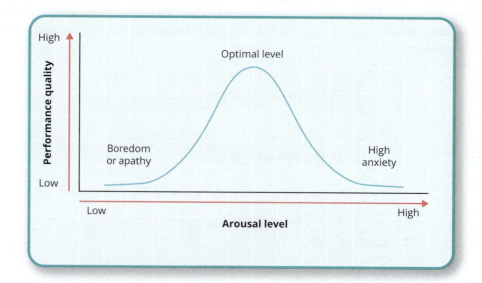

Figure 9: The concept of optimal arousal in relation to performance on a task is depicted here. Performance is maximized at the optimal level of arousal, and it tapers off during under- and overarousal.

So what is the optimal level of arousal? What level leads to the best performance? Research shows that moderate arousal is generally best; when arousal is very high or very low, performance tends to suffer (Yerkes & Dodson, 1908).

Optimal arousal level is more complex than a simple answer that the middle level is always best. Researchers Robert Yerkes (pronounced "Yerk-EES") and John Dodson discovered that the optimal arousal level depends on the complexity and difficulty of the task to be performed (Figure 10). This relationship is known as **Yerkes-Dodson law**, which holds that a simple task is performed best when arousal levels are relatively high and complex tasks are best performed when arousal levels are lower.

Group Activity

In a small group, discuss your arousal level with regard to taking an exam for this class. How does your arousal correlate with your performance?

Figure 10: Task performance is best when arousal levels are in a middle range, with difficult tasks best performed under lower levels of arousal and simple tasks best performed under higher levels of arousal.

Self-Efficacy and Social Motives

Self-efficacy is an individual's belief in her own capability to complete a task, which may include a previous successful completion of the exact task or a similar task. Albert Bandura (1994) theorized that an individual's sense of self-efficacy plays a pivotal role in motivating behavior. Bandura argues that motivation derives from expectations that we have about the consequences of our behaviors, and it is the appreciation of our capacity to engage in a given behavior that will determine what we do and the future goals that we set for ourselves. For example, if you have a sincere belief in your ability to achieve at the highest level, you are more likely to take on challenging tasks and to not let setbacks dissuade you from seeing the task through to the end.

Reflection Questions

Think back to a recent challenge you faced. Did you approach the problem with high or low self-efficacy?

A number of theorists have focused their research on understanding social motives (McAdams & Constantian, 1983; McClelland & Liberman, 1949; Murray et al., 1938). Among the motives they describe are needs for achievement, affiliation, and intimacy.

Social Motives

Need for achievement	Drives accomplishment and performance.
Need for affiliation	Encourages positive interactions with others.
Need for intimacy	Causes people to seek deep, meaningful relationships.

Figure 11: We are driven socially by a need for achievement, affiliation, and intimacy.

Henry Murray et al. (1938) categorized these needs into domains. For example, the need for achievement and recognition falls under the domain of ambition. Dominance and aggression were recognized as needs under the domain of human power, and play was a recognized need in the domain of interpersonal affection.

Maslow's Hierarchy of Needs

While the theories of motivation described earlier relate to basic biological drives, individual characteristics, or social contexts, Abraham Maslow (1943) proposed a **hierarchy of needs** that spans the spectrum of motives ranging from the biological to the individual to the social. These needs are often depicted as a pyramid (Figure 12).

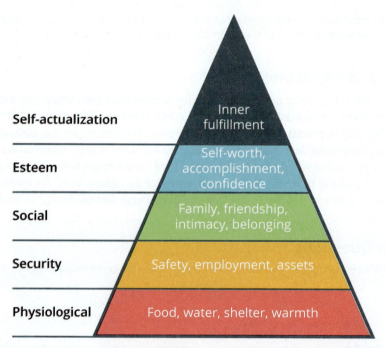

Figure 12: Maslow's hierarchy of needs is illustrated here. In some versions of the pyramid, cognitive and aesthetic needs are also included between esteem and self-actualization. Others include another tier at the top of the pyramid for self-transcendence.

At the base of the pyramid are all of the physiological needs that are necessary for survival. These are followed by basic needs for security and safety, the need to be loved and to have a sense of belonging, and the need to have self-worth and confidence. The top tier of the pyramid is self-actualization, which is a need that essentially equates to achieving one's full potential, and it can only be realized when needs lower on the pyramid have been met. To Maslow and humanistic theorists, self-actualization reflects the humanistic emphasis on positive aspects of human nature. Maslow suggested that this is an ongoing, life-long process and that only a small percentage of people actually achieve a self-actualized state (Francis & Kritsonis, 2006; Maslow, 1943).

According to Maslow (1943), one must satisfy lower-level needs before addressing those needs that occur higher in the pyramid.

Consider the following examples:

- Shaterra is struggling to find enough food to meet her nutritional requirements, so would she be worried about her level of popularity in school?

- Jarred lives in a bad neighborhood where he is constantly fearful of his home being broken into. In this case, do you think he would be overly concerned with how he performs in school?

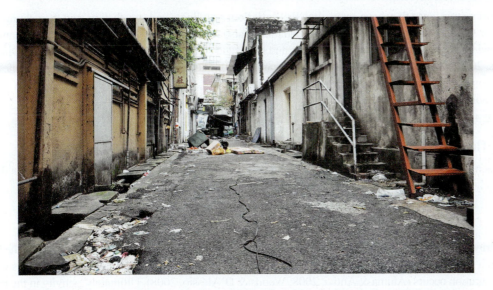

📷 **Figure 13:** Unsafe environments and circumstances may lead to difficulty in meeting basic needs.

> **Further Resources**
> Check out this interactive exercise (hawkes.biz/maslow) that illustrates some of the important concepts in Maslow's hierarchy of needs.

It should be pointed out that Maslow's theory has been criticized for its subjective nature and its inability to account for phenomena that occur in the real world (Leonard, 1982). Other research has more recently addressed that late in life, Maslow proposed a self-transcendence level above self-actualization—to represent striving for meaning and purpose beyond the concerns of oneself (Koltko-Rivera, 2006). For example, people sometimes make self-sacrifices in order to make a political statement or in an attempt to improve the conditions of others. Mohandas K. Gandhi, a world-renowned advocate for independence through nonviolent protest, on several occasions went on hunger strikes to protest a particular situation. People may starve themselves or otherwise put themselves in danger displaying higher-level motives beyond their own needs.

Summary

Motivation to engage in a given behavior can come from internal and/or external factors. Multiple theories have been put forward regarding motivation. More biologically oriented theories deal with the ways that instincts and the need to maintain bodily homeostasis motivate behavior. Bandura postulated that our sense of self-efficacy motivates behaviors, and there are a number of theories that focus on a variety of social motives. Abraham Maslow's hierarchy of needs is a model that shows the relationship among multiple motives that range from lower-level physiological needs to the very high level of self-actualization.

Flash Forward

Ready to dig into the vocabulary? Get some practice with this Hawkes Verified Quizlet set (hawkes.biz/psych9q2)!

9.2 Hunger and Eating

Eating is essential for survival, and it is no surprise that a drive-like hunger exists to ensure that we seek out sustenance. While this lesson will focus primarily on the physiological mechanisms that regulate hunger and eating, powerful social, cultural, and economic influences also play important roles. This lesson will explain the regulation of hunger, eating, and body weight and will discuss the adverse consequences of disordered eating.

Physiological Mechanisms

There are a number of physiological mechanisms that serve as the basis for hunger. When our stomachs are empty, they contract, causing both hunger pangs and the secretion of chemical messages that travel to the brain to serve as a signal to initiate feeding behavior. When our blood glucose levels drop, the pancreas and liver generate a number of chemical signals that induce hunger (Konturek et al., 2003; Novin, Robinson, Culbreth, & Tordoff, 1985) and thus initiate feeding behavior.

For most people, once they have eaten, they feel **satiation**, or fullness and satisfaction, and their eating behavior stops. Like the initiation of eating, satiation is also regulated by several physiological mechanisms. As blood glucose levels increase, the pancreas and liver send signals to shut off hunger and eating (Drazen & Woods, 2003; Druce, Small, & Bloom, 2004; Greary, 1990). The food's passage through the gastrointestinal tract also provides important satiety signals to the brain (Woods, 2004), and fat cells release **leptin**, a satiety hormone.

📷 **Figure 1:** Some people place great happiness in eating food. This scenario often has neurological roots.

Reflection Questions

When your body tells you that you've eaten enough food, do you generally listen to it? How often do you ignore this message and choose to overeat?

The various hunger and satiety signals that are involved in the regulation of eating are integrated in the brain. Research suggests that several areas of the hypothalamus and hindbrain are especially important sites where this integration occurs (Ahima & Antwi, 2008; Woods & D'Alessio, 2008). Ultimately, activity in the brain determines whether or not we engage in feeding behavior (Figure 2).

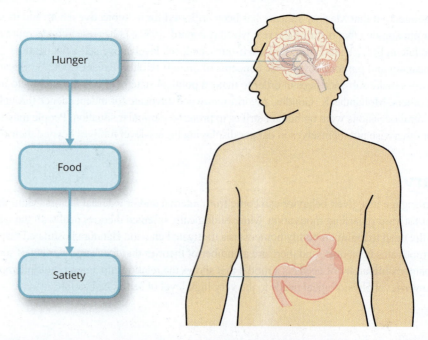

📷 **Figure 2:** Hunger and eating are regulated by a complex interplay of hunger and satiety signals that are integrated in the brain.

✏️ On Your Own

Which of the following is part of the satiety process?

☐ Pancreas   ☐ Gastrointestinal Tract   ☐ All answers are correct.

☐ Liver   ☐ Leptin

Metabolism and Body Weight

Our body weight is affected by a number of factors, including gene-environment interactions, and the number of calories we consume versus the number of calories we burn in daily activity. If our caloric intake exceeds our caloric use, our bodies store excess energy in the form of fat. Our energy expenditure is obviously affected by our levels of activity, but our body's metabolic rate also comes into play. A person's **metabolic rate** is the amount of energy that is expended in a given period of time, and there is tremendous individual variability in our metabolic rates. People with high rates of metabolism are able to burn off calories more easily than those with lower rates of metabolism.

✏️ On Your Own

Which part of the brain is most closely linked to regulating hunger and satiety?

☐ Occipital Lobe   ☐ Amygdala

☐ Hippocampus   ☐ Hypothalamus

Although some people are able to make extreme changes to their weight through diet and exercise, most people's weight fluctuates within a narrow margin. The **set-point theory** argues that when an individual diets and exercises, their metabolic rate will naturally slow down to keep that individual at their same ideal body weight. In contrast, the theory suggests the opposite will happen if an individual consumes more food and exercises less. The set-point theory has not received empirical support. For example, a research study indicated that metabolic rates did not change in individuals who had lost weight (Weinsier et al., 2000). However, people still use the set-point theory to help explain how body weight is maintained.

> ### Reflection Questions
> Do you agree with the set-point theory, or do you think body weight over time is influenced mostly by diet or exercise?

Obesity

Nearly two in three adults and one in six children are classified as overweight or obese (CDC, 2012). Being extremely overweight or obese increases one's risk for type 2 diabetes, sleep apnea, colon cancer, breast cancer, infertility, and arthritis. A body mass index is calculated by taking an individual's weight divided by their height. An adult with a body mass index (BMI) between 25 and 29.9 is considered **overweight**, 30 or higher is considered **obese**, and a BMI over 40 is considered **morbidly obese** (Figure 4). BMI is not always an accurate measure of an individual's health and physical fitness. An athlete, for example, may have a high BMI because the tool doesn't distinguish between the body's percentage of fat and muscle in a person's weight. As such, BMI is a good measure to study populations rather than individuals. Research suggests genetics, socioeconomic status, and physical environment are contributing factors to obesity (CDC, 2012).

Figure 3: Obesity is a growing problem in the United States.

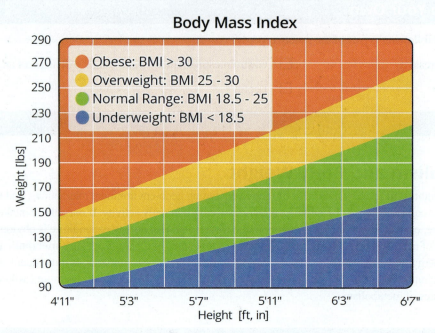

Body Mass Index

Obese: BMI > 30
Overweight: BMI 25 - 30
Normal Range: BMI 18.5 - 25
Underweight: BMI < 18.5

Weight [lbs] — *Height [ft, in]*

🖼 **Figure 4:** This chart shows how adult BMI is calculated. Individuals find their height on the *x*-axis and their weight on the *y*-axis to determine their BMI.

✍ On Your Own

According to the CDC, a BMI of 31 is considered:

☐ Normal   ☐ Obese

☐ Overweight   ☐ Morbidly Obese

Reflection Questions

Why do you think socioeconomic status might be related to obesity?

Patients who suffer from obesity and are unable to lose weight through diet and exercise may be recommended for bariatric surgery. **Bariatric surgery** is a type of surgery specifically aimed at weight reduction, and it involves modifying the gastrointestinal system to reduce the amount of food that can be eaten and/or limiting how much of the digested food can be absorbed (Figure 5) (Mayo Clinic, 2013). A recent meta-analysis suggests that bariatric surgery is more effective than non-surgical treatment for obesity in the two years immediately following the procedure, but to date, no long-term studies yet exist (Gloy et al., 2013).

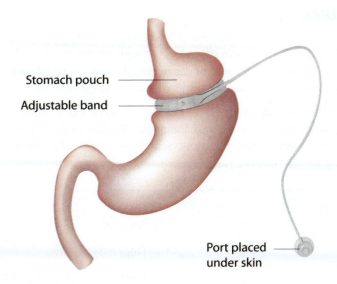

Stomach pouch

Adjustable band

Port placed
under skin

Figure 5: Gastric banding surgery creates a small pouch of stomach, reducing the size of the stomach that can be used for digestion.

Further Resources

Watch this video (hawkes. biz/bariatric) that describes two different types of bariatric surgeries.

Dig Deeper

Prader-Willi Syndrome

Prader-Willi Syndrome (PWS) is a genetic disorder that results in persistent feelings of intense hunger and reduced rates of metabolism. Typically, affected children have to be supervised around the clock to ensure that they do not engage in excessive eating. Currently, PWS is the leading genetic cause of morbid obesity in children, and it is associated with a number of cognitive deficits and emotional problems (Figure 6).

While genetic testing can be used to make a diagnosis, there are a number of behavioral diagnostic criteria associated with PWS. From birth to 2 years of age, lack of muscle tone and poor sucking behavior may serve as early signs of PWS. Developmental delays are seen between the ages of 6 and 12, and excessive eating and cognitive deficits associated with PWS usually onset a little later.

While the exact mechanisms of PWS are not fully understood, there is evidence that affected individuals have hypothalamic abnormalities. This is not surprising given the hypothalamus's role in regulating hunger and eating. However, as you will learn in the next lesson of this chapter, the hypothalamus is also involved in the regulation of sexual behavior. Consequently, many individuals suffering from PWS fail to reach sexual maturity during adolescence.

There is no current treatment or cure for PWS. However, if weight can be controlled in these individuals, then their life expectancies are significantly increased. (Historically, sufferers of PWS often died in adolescence or early adulthood.) Advances in the use of various psychoactive medications and growth hormones continue to enhance the quality of life for individuals with PWS (Cassidy & Driscoll, 2009; Prader-Willi Syndrome Association, 2012).

Figure 6: Eugenia Martínez Vallejo, depicted in this 1680 painting, may have had Prader-Willi Syndrome. At just eight years old, she weighed approximately 120 pounds, and she was nicknamed "La Monstrua" (the monster).

Eating Disorders

📖 **Figure 7:** Some people with eating disorders have a morphed sense of their physical image.

While nearly two out of three U.S. adults struggle with issues related to being overweight, a smaller, but significant, portion of the population has eating disorders that typically result in being normal weight or underweight. Often, these individuals are fearful of gaining weight. Individuals who suffer from bulimia nervosa and anorexia nervosa face many adverse health consequences (Mayo Clinic, 2012a, 2012b).

People suffering from **bulimia nervosa** engage in binge eating behavior that is followed by an attempt to compensate for the large amount of food consumed. Purging the food by inducing vomiting or through the use of laxatives are two common compensatory behaviors. Some affected individuals engage in excessive amounts of exercise to compensate for their binges.

Impacts of Bulimia

- Kidney failure
- Heat failure
- Tooth decay
- Anxiety
- Depression
- Increased risk of substance abuse

The lifetime prevalence rate for bulimia nervosa is estimated at around 1% for women and less than 0.5% for men (Smink, van Hoeken, & Hoek, 2012).

As of the 2013 release of *The Diagnostic and Statistical Manual, fifth edition,* **binge eating disorder** is a disorder recognized by the American Psychiatric Association (APA). Unlike with bulimia, eating binges are not followed by inappropriate behavior, such as purging, but they are followed by distress, including feelings of guilt and embarrassment. The resulting psychological distress distinguishes binge eating disorder from overeating (American Psychiatric Association [APA], 2013).

Anorexia nervosa is an eating disorder characterized by the maintenance of a body weight well below average through starvation and/or excessive exercise. Individuals suffering from anorexia nervosa often have a **distorted body image**, referenced in literature as a type of body dysmorphia, meaning that they view themselves as overweight even though they are not.

Further Resources

Watch this news story (hawkes.biz/anorexia) about an Italian advertising campaign that raised public awareness of anorexia nervosa.

Impacts of Anorexia

- Bone loss
- Heart failure
- Kidney failure
- Amenorrhea (cessation of menstrual period)
- Reduced function of the gonads
- Anxiety disorders
- Mood disorders
- Substance abuse
- Death

Estimates of the prevalence of anorexia nervosa vary from study to study but generally range from just under one percent to just over four percent in women. Generally, prevalence rates are considerably lower for men (Smink et al., 2012).

While both anorexia and bulimia nervosa occur in men and women of many different cultures, Caucasian females from Western societies tend to be the most at-risk population. Recent research indicates that females between the ages of 15 and 19 are most at risk, and it has long been suspected that these eating disorders are culturally-bound phenomena that are related to messages of a thin ideal often portrayed in popular media and the fashion world (Figure 8) (Smink et al., 2012). While social factors play an important role in the development of eating disorders, there is also evidence that genetic factors may predispose people to these disorders (Collier & Treasure, 2004).

Reflection Questions

Why do you think eating disorders are more common in the United States than other areas of the world?

Figure 8: Young women in our society are inundated with images of extremely thin models (sometimes accurately depicted and sometimes digitally altered to make them look even thinner). These images may contribute to eating disorders.

Summary

Hunger and satiety are highly regulated processes that result in a person maintaining a fairly stable weight that is resistant to change. When more calories are consumed than expended, a person will store excess energy as fat. Being significantly overweight substantially adds to a person's health risks and problems, including cardiovascular disease, type 2 diabetes, certain cancers, and other medical issues.

Sociocultural factors that emphasize thinness as a beauty ideal and a genetic predisposition contribute to the development of eating disorders in many young females, though eating disorders span ages and genders.

9.3 Sexual Behavior

Like food, sex is an important part of our lives. From an evolutionary perspective, the reason is obvious—perpetuation of the species. Sexual behavior in humans, however, involves much more than reproduction. This lesson provides an overview of research that has been conducted on human sexual behavior and motivation. We will close with a discussion of issues related to gender and sexual orientation.

Flash Forward

Ready to dig into the vocabulary? Get some practice with this Hawkes Verified Quizlet set (hawkes.biz/psych9q3)!

Figure 1: Gender and sexuality are a critical part of the human experience.

Physiological Mechanisms of Sexual Behavior and Motivation

Much of what we know about the physiological mechanisms that underlie sexual behavior and motivation comes from animal research. As you've learned, the hypothalamus plays an important role in motivated behaviors, and sex is no exception. In fact, lesions to an area of the hypothalamus called the medial preoptic area completely disrupt a male rat's ability to engage in sexual behavior. Surprisingly, medial preoptic lesions do not change how hard a male rat is willing to work to gain access to a sexually receptive female (Figure 2). This suggests that the ability to engage in sexual behavior and the motivation to do so may be mediated by neural systems distinct from one another.

🖼 **Figure 2:** A male rat that cannot engage in sexual behavior still seeks receptive females, suggesting that the ability to engage in sexual behavior and the motivation to do so are mediated by different systems in the brain.

Animal research suggests that limbic system structures such as the amygdala and nucleus accumbens are especially important for sexual motivation. Damage to these areas results in a decreased motivation to engage in sexual behavior while leaving the ability to do so intact (Figure 3) (Everett, 1990). Similar dissociations of sexual motivation and sexual ability have also been observed in the female rat (Becker, Rudick, & Jenkins, 2001; Jenkins & Becker, 2001).

🖼 **Figure 3:** The medial preoptic area, an area of the hypothalamus, is involved in the ability to engage in sexual behavior, but it does not affect sexual motivation. In contrast, the amygdala and nucleus accumbens are involved in motivation for sexual behavior, but they do not affect the ability to engage in it.

📷 **Figure 4:** Different areas of the brain are involved in different aspects of sexual behavior.

Although human sexual behavior is much more complex than that seen in rats, some parallels between animals and humans can be drawn from this research. The worldwide popularity of drugs used to treat erectile dysfunction (Conrad, 2005) speaks to the fact that sexual motivation and the ability to engage in sexual behavior can also be dissociated in humans. Moreover, disorders that involve abnormal hypothalamic function are often associated with hypogonadism (reduced function of the gonads) and reduced sexual function (e.g., Prader-Willi syndrome).

Given the hypothalamus's role in endocrine function, it is not surprising that hormones secreted by the endocrine system also play important roles in sexual motivation and behavior. For example, many animals show no sign of sexual motivation in the absence of the appropriate combination of sex hormones from their gonads. While this is not the case for humans, there is considerable evidence that sexual motivation for both men and women varies as a function of circulating testosterone levels (Bhasin, Enzlin, Coviello, & Basson, 2007; Carter, 1992; Sherwin, 1988).

☑ On Your Own

Answer the following short answer questions.

1. In an experiment, a male rat actively seeks out access to a new room that houses a receptive female but does not initiate mating upon arrival into the room. What deficit might the adult male rat have?

    _____

    _____

2. In an experiment, a male rat is fully capable of mating but does not appear interested in the sexually receptive female place in his cage. What deficit might the adult male rat have?

    _____

    _____

Kinsey's Research

Before the late 1940s, access to reliable, empirically-based information on sex was limited. Physicians were considered authorities on all issues related to sex, despite the fact that they had little to no training in these issues, and it is likely that most of what people knew about sex had been learned either through their own experiences or by talking with their peers. Convinced that people would benefit from a more open dialogue on

📷 **Figure 5:** Alfred Kinsey, shown here in 1955, established the Kinsey Institute for Research, Sex, Gender, and Reproduction at Indiana University. This institute continues to be a site of important psychological studies.

Group Activity

In a small group, briefly research and discuss the limitations of the Kinsey study. How would you have changed it to improve its validity?

issues related to human sexuality, Dr. Alfred Kinsey of Indiana University initiated large-scale survey research on the topic (Figure 5).

The results of some of these efforts were published in two books—*Sexual Behavior in the Human Male* and *Sexual Behavior in the Human Female*—which were published in 1948 and 1953, respectively (Bullough, 1998).

At the time, the Kinsey reports were quite sensational. Never before had the American public seen its private sexual behavior become the focus of scientific scrutiny on such a large scale. The books, which were filled with statistics and scientific lingo, sold remarkably well to the general public, and people began to engage in open conversations about human sexuality. As you might imagine, not everyone was happy that this information was being published. In fact, these books were banned in some countries. Ultimately, the controversy resulted in Kinsey losing funding that he had secured from the Rockefeller Foundation to continue his research efforts (Bancroft, 2004).

Although Kinsey's research has been widely criticized as being riddled with sampling and statistical errors (Jenkins, 2010), there is little doubt that this research was very influential in shaping future research on human sexual behavior and motivation. Kinsey described a remarkably diverse range of sexual behaviors and experiences reported by the volunteers participating in his research. Behaviors that had once been considered exceedingly rare or problematic were demonstrated to be much more common and innocuous than previously imagined (Bancroft, 2004; Bullough, 1998).

📷 **Figure 6:** The more research findings Kinsey reported, the more people realized that many of their sexual behaviors and patterns were common.

Among the results of Kinsey's research were the findings that women are as interested and experienced in sex as their male counterparts, that both males and females masturbate without adverse health consequences, and that homosexual acts are fairly common (Bancroft, 2004). Kinsey also developed a continuum known as the Kinsey scale that is still commonly used today to categorize an individual's sexual orientation (Jenkins, 2010). **Sexual orientation** is an individual's emotional and erotic attractions to same-sexed individuals (**homosexual**), opposite-sexed individuals (**heterosexual**), or both (**bisexual**).

Reflection Questions

The Kinsey Scale for sexual orientation indicates that sexual orientation is on a continuum which can range from exclusively heterosexual to exclusively homosexual with a variety of shades in between. Do you feel that a continuum best represents sexual orientation? Why or why not?

Masters and Johnson's Research

In 1966, William Masters and Virginia Johnson published a book detailing the results of their observations of nearly 700 people who agreed to participate in their study of physiological responses during sexual behavior.

Unlike Kinsey, who used personal interviews and surveys to collect data, Masters and Johnson observed people having intercourse in a variety of positions, and they observed people masturbating, manually or with the aid of a device. While this was occurring, researchers recorded measurements of physiological variables, such as blood pressure and respiration rate, as well as measurements of sexual arousal, such as vaginal lubrication and penile tumescence (swelling associated with an erection). In total, Masters and Johnson observed nearly 10,000 sexual acts as a part of their research (Hock, 2008).

Based on these observations, Masters and Johnson divided the **sexual response cycle** into four phases that are fairly similar in men and women: **excitement**, **plateau**, **orgasm**, and **resolution** (Figure 7).

Figure 7: This graph illustrates the different phases of the sexual response cycle as described by Masters and Johnson.

While many women can quickly repeat the sexual response cycle, men must pass through a longer refractory period as part of resolution. The **refractory period** is a period of time that follows an orgasm during which an individual is incapable of experiencing another orgasm. In men, the duration of the refractory period can vary dramatically from individual to individual with some refractory periods as short as several minutes and others as long as a day. As men age, their refractory periods tend to span longer periods of time.

Figure 8: The female sexual response cycle goes through the same stages as the male sexual response cycle.

Male Sexual Response Cycle

Excitement
Erection of the penis

Plateau
Full erection, presence of pre-ejaculatory fluid

Orgasm
Pelvic contractions with release of seminal fluid

Resolution
Return to unaroused state

Figure 9: Males have longer refractory periods than females.

Further Resources

Multiple studies have investigated the issue of average and preferred penis size. Read this article (hawkes.biz/sexresearch) for a summary of some of the major findings.

In addition to the insights that their research provided with regards to the sexual response cycle and the multi-orgasmic potential of women, Masters and Johnson also collected important information about reproductive anatomy. Their research demonstrated the oft-cited statistic of the average size of a flaccid and an erect penis (3 and 6 inches, respectively) as well as dispelling long-held beliefs about relationships between the size of a man's erect penis and his ability to provide sexual pleasure to his female partner. Furthermore, they determined that the vagina is a very elastic structure that can conform to penises of various sizes (Hock, 2008).

On Your Own

When Suzanne experiences a clitoral erection and increased lubrication during a sexual encounter, she is in which stage of the sexual response cycle?

☐ Excitement   ☐ Orgasm

☐ Plateau   ☐ Resolution

Sexual Orientation

As mentioned earlier, a person's sexual orientation is their emotional and erotic attraction toward another individual (Figure 10). While the majority of people identify as heterosexual, there is a sizable population of people within the United States who identify as either homosexual or bisexual. Research suggests that somewhere between 3% and 10% of the population identifies as homosexual (Kinsey, Pomeroy, & Martin, 1948; LeVay, 1996; Pillard & Bailey, 1995).

📷 **Figure 10:** Between 3% and 10% of the adult population identifies as homosexual.

Issues of sexual orientation have long fascinated scientists interested in determining what causes one individual to be heterosexual while another is homosexual. For many years, people believed that these differences arose because of different socialization and familial experiences. However, research has consistently demonstrated that the family backgrounds and experiences are very similar among heterosexuals and homosexuals (Bell, Weinberg, & Hammersmith, 1981; Ross & Arrindell, 1988).

Genetic and biological mechanisms have also been proposed, and the balance of research evidence suggests that sexual orientation has an underlying biological component. For instance, over the past 25 years, research has demonstrated gene-level contributions to sexual orientation (Bailey & Pillard, 1991; Hamer, Hu, Magnuson, Hu, & Pattatucci, 1993; Rodriguez-Larralde & Paradisi, 2009), with some researchers estimating that genes account for at least half of the variability seen in human sexual orientation (Pillard & Bailey, 1998). Other studies report differences in brain structure and function between heterosexuals and homosexuals (Allen & Gorski, 1992; Byne et al., 2001; Hu et al., 2008; LeVay, 1991; Ponseti et al., 2006; Rahman & Wilson, 2003a; Swaab & Hofman, 1990), and even differences in basic body structure and function have been observed (Hall & Kimura, 1994; Lippa, 2003; Loehlin & McFadden, 2003; McFadden & Champlin, 2000; McFadden & Pasanen, 1998; Rahman & Wilson, 2003b). In aggregate, the data suggests that to a significant extent, sexual orientations are something with which we are born.

Underlying Biological Components

Figure 11: Research suggests that sexual orientation has a biological component.

Misunderstandings about Sexual Orientation

Regardless of how sexual orientation is determined, research has made clear that sexual orientation is not a choice, but rather it is a relatively stable characteristic of a person that cannot be changed. Claims of successful gay conversion therapy have received wide criticism from the research community due to significant concerns with research design, recruitment of experimental participants, and interpretation of data. As such, there is no credible scientific evidence to suggest that individuals can change their sexual orientation (Jenkins, 2010).

> ### Reflection Questions
>
> Do you believe that reparative therapy for homosexuality is ethical? If a family member or close friend was going to enter into this type of therapy, what would you say to him or her?

Dr. Robert Spitzer, the author of one of the most widely-cited examples of successful conversion therapy, apologized to both the scientific community and the gay community for his mistakes, and he publicly recanted his own paper in a public letter addressed to the editor of *Archives of Sexual Behavior* in the spring of 2012 (Carey, 2012). In this letter, Spitzer wrote,

> I was considering writing something that would acknowledge that I now judge the major critiques of the study as largely correct.…I believe I owe the gay community an apology for my study making unproven claims of the efficacy of reparative therapy. I also apologize to any gay person who wasted time or energy undergoing some form of reparative therapy because they believed that I had proven that reparative therapy works with some "highly motivated" individuals. (Becker, 2012, pars. 2, 5)

Further Resources

Read this draft (hawkes.biz/spitzer) of Dr. Spitzer's letter.

Citing research that suggests not only that gay conversion therapy is ineffective, but also potentially harmful, legislative efforts to make such therapy illegal have either been enacted (e.g., it is now illegal in California) or are underway across the United States, and many professional organizations have issued statements against this practice (Human Rights Campaign, n.d.).

Gender Identity

Many people conflate sexual orientation with gender identity because of stereotypical attitudes that exist about homosexuality. In reality, these are two related, but different, issues. **Gender identity** refers to one's sense of being male or female. Generally, our gender identities correspond to our chromosomal and phenotypic sex, but

this is not always the case. When individuals do not feel comfortable identifying with the gender associated with their biological sex, then they experience gender dysphoria. **Gender dysphoria** is a diagnostic category in the fifth edition of *The Diagnostic and Statistical Manual of Mental Disorders* (DSM-5) that describes individuals who do not identify as the gender that most people would assume they are. This dysphoria must persist for at least six months and result in significant distress or dysfunction to meet DSM-5 diagnostic criteria. In order for children to be assigned this diagnostic category, they must verbalize their desire to become the other gender.

Many people who are classified as gender dysphoric seek to live their lives in ways that are consistent with their own gender identity. This involves dressing in opposite-sex clothing and assuming an opposite-sex identity. These individuals may also undertake **transgender hormone therapy** in an attempt to make their bodies look more like the opposite sex, and in some cases, they elect to have surgeries to alter the appearance of their external genitalia to resemble that of their gender identity (Figure 13). While these may sound like drastic changes, gender dysphoric individuals take these steps because their bodies seem to them to be a mistake of nature, and they seek to correct this mistake.

Further Resources

The idea that children can suffer from gender dysphoria has been a controversial issue. Watch this video (hawkes.biz/genderdysphoria) to witness a few stories from youth who are transgender.

Figure 12: Some establishments are changing their gender-specific bathrooms to one available to anyone, despite their gender identity.

Figure 13: Chaz Bono, a transgender male, is a well-known person who transitioned from female to male. In the 1970s, the world knew Chaz as Chastity Bono, the daughter of the famous entertaining duo Sonny and Cher. Later in life, Chaz transitioned to align his physical body with his gender identity.

Cultural Factors in Sexual Orientation and Gender Identity

Issues related to sexual orientation and gender identity are very much influenced by sociocultural factors. Even the ways in which we define sexual orientation and gender vary from one culture to the next. While in the United States exclusive heterosexuality is viewed as the norm, there are societies that have different attitudes regarding homosexual behavior. In fact, in some instances, periods of exclusively homosexual behavior are socially prescribed as a part of normal development and maturation. For example, in parts of New Guinea, young boys are expected to engage in sexual behavior with other boys for a given period of time because it is believed that doing so is necessary for these boys to become men (Baldwin & Baldwin, 1989).

There has been a binary, or two-gendered, culture in the United States, which tended to classify an individual as either male or female. However, this has changed significantly in recent years. It may seem like a big shift in America, but in some cultures, there are additional gender variants resulting in more than two gender categories. For example, in Thailand, you can be male, female, or kathoey. A kathoey is an individual who would be described as intersexed or transgendered in the United States (Tangmunkongvorakul, Banwell, Carmichael, Utomo, & Sleigh, 2010).

Further Resources

Hear firsthand about the transgender experience and the disconnect that occurs when one's self-identity does not align with one's body. In this brief video (hawkes.biz/transgender), Chaz Bono discusses the difficulties of growing up identifying as male while living in a female body.

Reflection Questions

American culture is changing regarding gender identity. The decisions by platforms such as Facebook to include dozens of gender options (hawkes.biz/genderoptions) has led to both praise and derision. Likewise, the Trump administration's restrictions on transgender individuals in the military (hawkes.biz/transgender2), as well as attempts to define gender (hawkes.biz/definegender) as anatomically-based and binary, have drawn vocal critics and supporters.

- Why do you think gender is such an emotionally charged front in America's culture wars?

- How can psychology and scientific thinking help bring resolution to these disagreements?

Further Resources

To learn more about the life of David Reimer, visit the page found here. (hawkes.biz/davidreimer)

Dig Deeper

The Case of David Reimer

In August of 1965, Janet and Ronald Reimer of Winnipeg, Canada, welcomed the birth of their twin sons, Bruce and Brian. Within a few months, the twins were experiencing urinary problems; doctors recommended the problems could be alleviated by having the boys circumcised. A malfunction of the medical equipment used to perform the circumcision resulted in Bruce's penis being irreparably damaged. Distraught, Janet and Ronald looked to expert advice on what to do with their baby boy. By happenstance, the couple became aware of Dr. John Money at Johns Hopkins University and his theory of psychosexual neutrality (Colapinto, 2000).

Dr. Money had spent a considerable amount of time researching transgendered individuals and individuals born with ambiguous genitalia. As a result of this work, he developed a theory of psychosexual neutrality. His theory asserted that we are essentially neutral at birth with regard to our gender identity and that we don't assume a concrete gender identity until we begin to master language. Furthermore, Dr. Money believed that the way in which we are socialized in early life is ultimately much more important than our biology in determining our gender identity (Money, 1962).

Dr. Money encouraged Janet and Ronald to bring the twins to Johns Hopkins University, and he convinced them that they should raise Bruce as a girl. Left with few other options at the time, Janet and Ronald agreed to have Bruce's testicles removed and to raise him as a girl. When they returned home to Canada, they brought with them Brian and his "sister," Brenda, along with specific instructions to never reveal to Brenda that she had been born a boy (Colapinto, 2000).

Early on, Dr. Money shared with the scientific community the great success of this natural experiment that seemed to fully support his theory of psychosexual neutrality (Money, 1975). Indeed, in early interviews with the children it appeared that Brenda was a typical little girl who liked to play with "girly" toys and do "girly" things.

However, Dr. Money was less than forthcoming with information that seemed to argue against the success of the case. In reality, Brenda's parents were constantly concerned that their little girl wasn't really behaving as most girls did, and by the time Brenda was nearing adolescence, it was painfully obvious to the family that she was really having a hard time identifying as a female. In addition, Brenda was becoming increasingly reluctant to continue her visits with Dr. Money to the point that she threatened suicide if her parents made her go back to see him again.

At that point, Janet and Ronald disclosed the true nature of Brenda's early childhood to their daughter. While initially shocked, Brenda reported that things made sense to her now, and ultimately, by the time she was an adolescent, Brenda had decided to identify as a male. Thus, she became David Reimer.

David was quite comfortable in his masculine role. He made new friends and began to think about his future. Although his castration had left him infertile, he still wanted to be a father. In 1990, David married a single mother and loved his new role as a husband and father. In 1997, David was made aware that Dr. Money was continuing to publicize his case as a success supporting his theory of psychosexual neutrality. This prompted David and his brother to go public with their experiences in attempt to discredit the doctor's publications. While this revelation created a firestorm in the scientific community for Dr. Money, it also triggered a series of unfortunate events that ultimately led to David committing suicide in 2004 (O'Connell, 2004).

This sad story speaks to the complexities involved in gender identity. While the Reimer case had earlier been paraded as a hallmark of how socialization trumped biology in terms of gender identity, the truth of the story made the scientific and medical communities more cautious in dealing with cases that involve intersex children and how to deal with their unique circumstances. In fact, stories like this one have prompted measures to prevent unnecessary harm and suffering to children who might have issues with gender identity. For example, in 2013, a law took effect in Germany allowing parents of intersex children to classify their children as indeterminate so that children can self-assign the appropriate gender once they have fully developed their own gender identities (Paramaguru, 2013).

Further Resources

Watch this news story (hawkes.biz/davidreimer2) about the experiences of David Reimer and his family.

Summary

The hypothalamus and structures of the limbic system are important in sexual behavior and motivation. There is evidence to suggest that our motivation to engage in sexual behavior and our ability to do so are related, but separate, processes. Alfred Kinsey conducted large-scale survey research that demonstrated the incredible diversity of human sexuality. William Masters and Virginia Johnson observed individuals engaging in sexual behavior in developing their concept of the sexual response cycle. While often confused, sexual orientation and gender identity are related, but distinct, concepts.

9.4 Emotion

As we move through our daily lives, we experience a variety of emotions. An **emotion** is a subjective state of being that we often describe as our feelings (Figure 2). The words *emotion* and *mood* are sometimes used interchangeably, but psychologists use these words to refer to two different things.

Flash Forward

Ready to dig into the vocabulary? Get some practice with this Hawkes Verified Quizlet set (hawkes.biz/psych9q4)!

Figure 1: Emotion and mood are two related but different concepts.

Here we will focus on emotion, and you will learn more about mood in the chapter that covers psychological disorders.

🖼️ **Figure 2:** Toddlers can cycle through emotions quickly, being extremely happy one moment and extremely angry the next.

We can be at the heights of joy or in the depths of despair. We might feel angry when we are betrayed, fear when we are threatened, and surprised when something unexpected happens. This lesson will outline some of the most well-known theories explaining our emotional experience and provide insight into the biological basis of emotion. We will close with a discussion of the ubiquitous nature of facial expressions of emotion and our abilities to recognize those expressions in others.

Theories of Emotion

Our emotional states are combinations of physiological arousal, psychological appraisal, and subjective experiences. Together, these are known as the **components of emotion**.

Components of Emotion

🖼️ **Figure 3:** The three components of emotion all combine into our emotional state.

Emotional appraisals are informed by our experiences, backgrounds, and cultures. Therefore, different people may have different emotional experiences even when faced with similar circumstances. Over time, several different theories of emotion, discussed next, have been proposed to explain how the various components of emotion interact with one another.

The **James-Lange theory** of emotion asserts that emotions arise from physiological arousal.

Recall what you have learned about the sympathetic nervous system and our fight-or-flight response when threatened. If you were to encounter some threat in your environment, like a venomous snake in your backyard, your sympathetic nervous system would initiate significant physiological arousal, which would make your heart race and increase your respiration rate. According to the James-Lange theory of emotion, you would only experience a feeling of fear after this physiological arousal had taken place. Furthermore, different arousal patterns would be associated with different feelings.

Figure 4: How would you react coming face to face with something like this?

✎ On Your Own

Select the scenario that best fits the James-Lange theory of emotion.

☐ Johnson walks through the haunted house. When the zombie jumps out to scare him, his heart begins to pound and then he feels fear.

☐ Johnson walks through the haunted house. When the zombie jumps out to scare him, his heart begins to pound, and he cognitively labels the experience as fear.

☐ Johnson walks through the haunted house. When the zombie jumps out to scare him, his heart begins to pound, and he simultaneously feels fear.

Reflection Questions

Think about a time when your body reacted in fear before you had a chance to even consciously experience that you were afraid.

Other theorists, however, doubted that the physiological arousal that occurs with different types of emotions is distinct enough to result in the wide variety of emotions that we experience. Thus, the **Cannon-Bard theory** of emotion was developed. According to this view, physiological arousal and emotional experience occur simultaneously, yet independently (Lang, 1994). So, when you see the venomous snake, you feel fear at exactly the same time that your body mounts its fight-or-flight response. This emotional reaction would be separate and independent of the physiological arousal even though they occur at the same time.

✎ On Your Own

Select the scenario that best fits the Cannon-Bard theory of emotion.

☐ When Tristan sees Emma on their wedding day, his heart leaps in his chest at the same time that he feels a surge of love for his soon-to-be bride.

☐ When Tristan sees Emma on their wedding day, his heart leaps in his chest, and he then feels a surge of love for his soon-to-be bride.

☐ When Tristan sees Emma on their wedding day, his heart leaps in his chest. He realizes this experience represents love.

The James-Lange and Cannon-Bard theories have each garnered some empirical support in various research paradigms. For instance, Chwalisz, Diener, and Gallagher (1988) conducted a study of the emotional experiences of people who had spinal cord injuries. They reported that individuals who were incapable of receiving autonomic feedback because of their injuries still experienced emotion; however, there was a tendency for people with less awareness of autonomic arousal to experience less intense emotions. More recently, research investigating the facial feedback hypothesis suggested that suppression of facial expression of emotion lowered the intensity of some emotions experienced by participants (Davis, Senghas, & Ochsner, 2009). In both of these examples, neither theory is fully supported because physiological arousal does not seem to be necessary for the emotional experience, but this arousal does appear to be involved in enhancing the intensity of the emotional experience.

Reflection Questions

Imagine a situation in which you feel fear, but you do not experience the physiological component of fear—no heart racing, no sweaty palms. Would you feel as afraid in this situation?

The **Schachter-Singer two-factor theory** of emotion is another variation on theories of emotions that takes into account both physiological arousal and the emotional experience. According to this theory, emotions are composed of two factors: physiological and cognitive. In other words, physiological arousal is interpreted in context to produce the emotional experience. In revisiting our example involving the venomous snake in your backyard, the two-factor theory maintains that the snake elicits sympathetic nervous system activation that is labeled as fear given the context, and our experience is that of fear.

Further Resources

The Schachter and Singer (1962) study provides some basis for the idea of emotional contagion—participants took on the emotions of those around them when they did not expect to feel physiological reactions in the study. Are we being affected by others' emotions in other aspects of our lives? Check out this video (hawkes.biz/emotionalcontagion) about emotional contagion on Facebook.

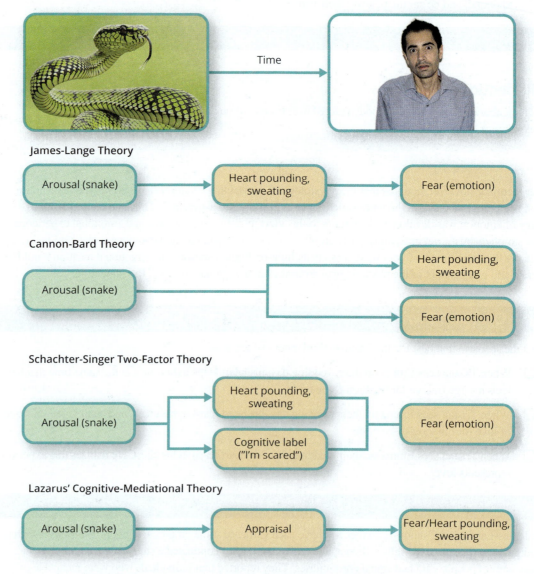

Figure 5: This figure illustrates the major assertions of the James-Lange, Cannon-Bard, Lazarus' cognitive-mediational, and Schachter-Singer two-factor theories of emotion.

It is important to point out that Schachter and Singer believed that physiological arousal is very similar across the different types of emotions that we experience, and therefore, the cognitive appraisal of the situation is critical to the actual emotion experienced. In fact, it might be possible to misattribute arousal to an emotional experience if the circumstances were right (Schachter & Singer, 1962).

To test their idea, Schachter and Singer performed a clever experiment. Male participants were randomly assigned to one of several groups. Some of the participants received injections of epinephrine that caused bodily changes that mimicked the fight-or-flight response of the sympathetic nervous system; however, only some of these men were told to expect these reactions as side effects of the injection. The other men that received injections of epinephrine were told either that the injection would have no side effects or that it would result in a side effect unrelated to a sympathetic response, such as itching feet or headache. After receiving these injections, participants waited in a room with someone else they thought was another subject in the research project. In reality, the other person was a confederate of the researcher. The confederate engaged in scripted displays of euphoric or angry behavior (Schachter & Singer, 1962).

When those subjects who were told that they should expect to feel symptoms of physiological arousal were asked about any emotional changes that they had experienced related to either euphoria or anger (depending on how their confederate behaved), they reported none. However, the men who weren't expecting physiological arousal as a function of the injection were more likely to report that they experienced euphoria or anger as a function of their assigned confederate's behavior. While everyone that received an injection of epinephrine experienced the same physiological arousal, only those who were not expecting the arousal used context to interpret the arousal as a change in emotional state (Schachter & Singer, 1962).

Strong emotional responses are associated with strong physiological arousal.

Figure 6: Imagine how you would feel if someone unexpectedly starting showcasing anger after this experiment.

Signs of Physiological Arousal

- Increased heart rate

- Increased respiration rate

- Sweating

These signs might serve as a tool to determine whether someone is telling the truth or not. The assumption is that most of us would show signs of physiological arousal if we were being dishonest with someone. A **polygraph**, or lie detector test, measures the physiological arousal of an individual responding to a series of questions.

Someone trained in reading these tests would look for answers to questions that are associated with increased levels of arousal as potential signs that the respondent may have been dishonest on those answers. While polygraphs are still commonly used, their validity and accuracy are highly questionable because there is no evidence that lying is associated with any particular pattern of physiological arousal (Saxe & Ben-Shakhar, 1999).

The relationship between our experiencing of emotions and our cognitive processing of them, and the order in which these occur, remains a topic of research and debate. Lazarus (1991) developed the **cognitive-mediational theory** that asserts our emotions are determined by our appraisal of the stimulus. This appraisal mediates between the stimulus and the emotional response, and it is immediate and often unconscious. In contrast to the Schachter-Singer model, the appraisal precedes a cognitive label. You will learn more about Lazarus's appraisal concept when you study stress, health, and lifestyle.

Further Resources

While the use of lie detectors remains very common, including a prominent example during the 2018 Supreme Court confirmation hearing of Justice Kavanaugh, there is very little evidence that they actually work. Read this article (hawkes.biz/polygraph) about the unreliable nature of polygraph tests.

Additionally, watch this clip (hawkes.biz/polygraph2) from *Adam Ruins Everything* about why lie detectors don't detect lies.

Group Activity

Partner up with a few other students and generate a list of pros and cons for using a polygraph test to determine if an individual is telling the truth. What problems might there be with polygraphs? Should polygraphs be admissible (allowed) in court?

Reflection Questions

Think about an experience where your appraisal might differ from others, resulting in a different experience of emotion for you than most people. For example, a person who has owned a pet tarantula is less likely to react with fear when confronted with a spider due to the difference in cognitive appraisal of the stimulus.

Two other prominent views arise from the work of Robert Zajonc and Joseph LeDoux. Zajonc asserted that some emotions occur separately from or prior to our cognitive interpretation of them, such as feeling fear in response to an unexpected loud sound (Zajonc, 1998). He also believed in what we might casually refer to as a gut feeling—that we can experience an instantaneous and unexplainable like or dislike for someone or something (Zajonc, 1980). LeDoux also views some emotions as requiring no cognition: some emotions completely bypass contextual interpretation. His research into the neuroscience of emotion has demonstrated the amygdala's primary role in fear (Cunha, Monfils, & LeDoux, 2010; LeDoux 1996, 2002). A fear stimulus is processed by the brain through one of two paths: from the thalamus (where it is perceived) directly to the amygdala or from the thalamus through the cortex and then to the amygdala. The first path is quick, while the second enables more processing of details of the stimulus. In the following section, we will look more closely at the neuroscience of emotional response.

✍ On Your Own

Select the theory of emotion that best fits the following scenario:

James calls Linda to ask her out on a date. As soon as she answers, his heart leaps in his chest, and he thinks about how terrified he is to ask her out. His fear causes him to make idle small talk about tomorrow's assignment, and then he ends the conversation without completing his goal.

☐ James-Lange theory   ☐ Schachter-Singer two-factor theory

☐ Cannon-Bard theory   ☐ Lazarus' cognitive-mediational theory

The Biology of Emotions

Earlier, you learned about the limbic system, which is the area of the brain involved in emotion and memory (Figure 7).

Hypothalamus

Amygdala   Hippocampus

🖼 **Figure 7:** The limbic system, which includes the hypothalamus, thalamus, amygdala, and the hippocampus, is involved in mediating emotional response and memory.

Components of the Limbic System

Hypothalamus
Activates sympathetic nervous system

Thalamus
Sensory relay center

Amygdala
Processes emotional information

Hippocampus
Integrates emotional experience with cognition

Figure 8: Each part of the limbic system has a specialized job in mediating emotions.

Amygdala

The amygdala has received a great deal of attention from researchers interested in understanding the biological basis for emotions, especially fear and anxiety (Blackford & Pine, 2012; Goosens & Maren, 2002; Maren, Phan, & Liberzon, 2013). The amygdala is composed of various subnuclei, including the basolateral complex and the central nucleus (Figure 9). The **basolateral complex** has dense connections with a variety of sensory areas of the brain. It is critical for classical conditioning and for attaching emotional value to learning processes and memory. The **central nucleus** plays a role in attention, and it has connections with the hypothalamus and various brainstem areas to regulate the autonomic nervous and endocrine systems' activity (Pessoa, 2010).

Further Resources

Watch this video (hawkes.biz/brainparts) for a refresher on the parts of the brain involved in the limbic system.

Figure 9: The anatomy of the basolateral complex and central nucleus of the amygdala are illustrated in this diagram.

Animal research has demonstrated that there is increased activation of the amygdala in rat pups that have odor cues paired with electrical shock when their mother is absent. This leads to an aversion to the odor cue that suggests the rats learned to fear the odor cue. Interestingly, when the mother was present, the rats actually showed a preference for the odor cue despite its association with an electrical shock. This preference was associated with no increases in amygdala activation. This suggests a differential effect on the amygdala by the *context* (the presence or absence of the mother) determined whether the pups learned to fear the odor or to be attracted to it (Moriceau & Sullivan, 2006).

Raineki, Cortés, Belnoue, and Sullivan (2012) demonstrated that, in rats, negative early life experiences could alter the function of the amygdala and result in adolescent patterns of behavior that mimic human mood disorders. In this study, rat pups received either abusive or normal treatment during postnatal days 8–12. There were two forms of abusive treatment and one control group.

> **Forms of Treatment**
>
> - The first form of abusive treatment had an insufficient bedding condition. The mother rat had insufficient bedding material in her cage to build a proper nest that resulted in her spending more time away from her pups trying to construct a nest and less time nursing her pups.
>
> - The second form of abusive treatment had an associative learning task that involved pairing odors and an electrical stimulus in the absence of the mother, as described above.
>
> - The control group was in a cage with sufficient bedding and was left undisturbed with their mothers during the same time period.

The rat pups that experienced abuse were much more likely to exhibit depressive-like symptoms during adolescence when compared to controls. These depressive-like behaviors were associated with increased activation of the amygdala.

Human research also suggests a relationship between the amygdala and psychological disorders of mood or anxiety. Changes in amygdala structure and function have been demonstrated in adolescents who are either at-risk or have been diagnosed with various mood and/or anxiety disorders (Miguel-Hidalgo, 2013; Qin et al., 2013). It has also been suggested that functional differences in the amygdala could serve as a biomarker to differentiate individuals suffering from bipolar disorder from those suffering from major depressive disorder (Fournier, Keener, Almeida, Kronhaus, & Phillips, 2013).

Hippocampus

As mentioned earlier, the hippocampus is also involved in emotional processing. Like the amygdala, research has demonstrated that hippocampal structure and function are linked to a variety of mood and anxiety disorders. Individuals suffering from posttraumatic stress disorder (PTSD) show marked reductions in the volume of several parts of the hippocampus, which may result from decreased levels of neurogenesis and dendritic branching (the generation of new neurons and the generation of new dendrites in existing neurons, respectively) (Wang et al., 2010). While it is impossible to make a causal claim with correlational research like this, studies have demonstrated behavioral improvements and hippocampal volume increases following either pharmacological or cognitive-behavioral therapy in individuals suffering from PTSD (Bremner & Vermetten, 2004; Levy-Gigi, Szabó, Kelemen, & Kéri, 2013).

Facial Expression and Recognition of Emotions

Culture can impact the way in which people display emotion. A **cultural display rule** is one of a collection of culturally specific standards that govern the types and frequencies of displays of emotions that are acceptable (Malatesta & Haviland, 1982). Therefore, people from varying cultural backgrounds can have very different cultural display rules of emotion. For example, research has shown that individuals from the United States

Figure 10: Soldiers are at high-risk for PTSD upon returning home from war.

express negative emotions like fear, anger, and disgust both alone and in the presence of others, while Japanese individuals only do so while alone (Matsumoto, 1990). Furthermore, individuals from cultures that tend to emphasize social cohesion are more likely to engage in suppression of emotional reaction, so they can evaluate which response is most appropriate in a given context (Matsumoto, Yoo, & Nakagawa, 2008).

Other distinct cultural characteristics might be involved in emotionality. For instance, there may be gender differences involved in emotional processing. While research into gender differences in emotional display is equivocal, there is some evidence that men and women may differ in regulation of emotions (McRae, Ochsner, Mauss, Gabrieli, & Gross, 2008).

Reflection Questions

What constraints do you have on how you can express your emotions? Are they culturally-based? Gender-based? Something else?

Despite different emotional display rules, our ability to recognize and produce facial expressions of emotion appears to be universal. In fact, even congenitally blind individuals produce the same facial expression of emotions, despite their never having the opportunity to observe these facial displays of emotion in other people. This would seem to suggest that the pattern of activity in facial muscles involved in generating emotional expressions is universal, and indeed, this idea was suggested in the late 19th century in Charles Darwin's book *The Expression of Emotions in Man and Animals* (1872). In fact, there is substantial evidence for seven universal emotions that are each associated with distinct facial expressions. These include happiness, surprise, sadness, fright, disgust, contempt, and anger (Figure 11) (Ekman & Keltner, 1997).

Happiness   Surprise   Sadness   Fright

Disgust   Contempt   Anger

Figure 11: The seven universal facial expressions of emotion are shown.

Reflection Questions

Does smiling make you happy? Or does being happy make you smile?

The **facial feedback hypothesis** asserts that facial expressions are capable of influencing our emotions, meaning that smiling can make you feel happier (Buck, 1980; Soussignan, 2001; Strack, Martin, & Stepper, 1988). Recent research explored how Botox, which paralyzes facial muscles and limits facial expression, might affect emotion. Havas, Glenberg, Gutowski, Lucarelli, and Davidson (2010) discovered that depressed individuals reported less depression after paralysis of their frowning muscles with Botox injections.

Of course, emotion is not only displayed through facial expression. We also use the tone of our voices, various behaviors, and body language to communicate information about our emotional states. **Body language** is the expression of emotion in terms of body position or movement. Research suggests that we are quite sensitive to the emotional information communicated through body language, even if we're not consciously aware of it (de Gelder, 2006; Tamietto et al., 2009).

◌ Connect the Concepts

Autism Spectrum Disorder and Expression of Emotions

Autism spectrum disorder (ASD) is a set of neurodevelopmental disorders characterized by repetitive behaviors and communication and social problems. Children who have autism spectrum disorders have difficulty recognizing the emotional states of others, and research has shown that this may stem from an inability to distinguish various nonverbal expressions of emotion (i.e., facial expressions) from one another (Hobson, 1986). In addition, there is evidence to suggest that autistic individuals also have difficulty expressing emotion through tone of voice and by producing facial expressions (Macdonald et al., 1989). Difficulties with emotional recognition and expression may contribute to the impaired social interaction and communication that characterize autism; therefore, various therapeutic approaches have been explored to address these difficulties. Various educational curricula, cognitive-behavioral therapies, and pharmacological therapies have shown some promise in helping autistic individuals process emotionally relevant information (Bauminger, 2002; Golan & Baron-Cohen, 2006; Guastella et al., 2010).

Figure 12: Folks with autism often struggle with expressing emotions accurately.

Summary

Emotions are subjective experiences that consist of physiological arousal and cognitive appraisal. Various theories have been put forward to explain our emotional experiences. The James-Lange theory asserts that emotions arise as a function of physiological arousal. The Cannon-Bard theory maintains that emotional experience occurs simultaneous to and independent of physiological arousal. The Schachter-Singer two-factor theory suggests that physiological arousal receives cognitive labels as a function of the relevant context and that these two factors together result in an emotional experience.

The limbic system is the brain's emotional circuit, which includes the amygdala and the hippocampus. Both of these structures are implicated in playing a role in normal emotional processing as well as in psychological mood and anxiety disorders. Increased amygdala activity is associated with learning to fear, and it is seen in individuals who are at risk for or suffering from mood disorders. The volume of the hippocampus has been shown to be reduced in individuals suffering from posttraumatic stress disorder.

The ability to produce and recognize facial expressions of emotions seems to be universal regardless of cultural background. However, there are cultural display rules, which influence how often and under what circumstances various emotions can be expressed. Tone of voice and body language also serve as a means by which we communicate information about our emotional states.

Chapter 9 Project

Purpose

College is challenging and requires quite a lot of adjustment. For example, a student may be faced with the challenge of balancing social life with academic responsibility or with dealing with the feelings of new roles and more complex relationships. In fact, college students may never be as aware of their own motivations and emotions until they are faced with some of these new situations. **The purpose of this project is to help you reflect on your own experiences as a college student, in light of psychological theories of motivation and emotion.**

Directions

There are three parts to this project:

Part 1 - The Reflection

Part 2 - The Application

Part 3 - The Plan

Part 1 – The Reflection

Reflect on the changes that you have experienced in coming to college, in the following four areas:

- Relationships

- Responsibilities

- Independence

- Identity

There is not a "right" way to reflect upon these categories; simply write 150+ words for each one as you consider how these things changed for you when you became a college student. **Note: Don't do this before you read about the requirements in Part 2.**

Part 2 – The Application

For each of these reflections, choose one concept or theory from Chapter 9 that might help you better understand your student experience. You may choose any concepts or theories you like, though each one should apply to <u>one</u> of your four areas of reflection. When choosing your specific concepts or theories, you should be sure to cover each of the following categories:

9.1 Intrinsic Motivation AND Extrinsic Motivation (required)

9.1 Motivation (any, other than intrinsic and extrinsic motivation)

9.2 Hunger and Eating (any)
OR 9.3 Sexual Behavior (any)

9.4 Emotion (any)

In 150+ words, apply one of each of the chosen concepts to one of your reflections. Your application should display deep understanding of that concept or theory. In total you will have four sets of 300+ word reflections and applications.

Part 3 – The Plan

To complete this project, you will first need to read and understand Chapter 9. Then, to begin, and to help you organize your writing, fill in this table to match your chosen concepts/theories to your reflections:

	Theme of Your Reflection (150+ words)	Category (9.1 E/I Motivation, 9.1, 9.2 or 9.3, and 9.4)	Chosen Concept or Theory to Apply to Reflection (150+ words)
Relationships			
Responsibilities			
Independence			
Identity			

Please submit this table along with your four reflections and applications.

Materials

None required.

✅ Checklist

- ☐ Reflection
  - ☐ Relationships (150+ words)
  - ☐ Responsibilities (150+ words)
  - ☐ Independence (150+ words)
  - ☐ Identity (150+ words)
- ☐ Application
  - ☐ Covers all of the given categories (9.1 E/I Motivation, 9.1, 9.2 or 9.3, and 9.4)
  - ☐ Relationships (150+ words)
    - ☐ Connected to concept or theory
    - ☐ Connected to relevant category

- ☐ Responsibilities (150+ words)
  - ☐ Connected to concept or theory
  - ☐ Connected to relevant category
- ☐ Independence (150+ words)
  - ☐ Connected to concept or theory
  - ☐ Connected to relevant category
- ☐ Identity (150+ words)
  - ☐ Connected to concept or theory
  - ☐ Connected to relevant category

Chapter 9 Review

Lesson Summaries

9.1 Motivation

Motivation to engage in a given behavior can come from internal and/or external factors. Multiple theories have been put forward regarding motivation. More biologically oriented theories deal with the ways that instincts and the need to maintain bodily homeostasis motivate behavior. Bandura postulated that our sense of self-efficacy motivates behaviors, and there are a number of theories that focus on a variety of social motives. Abraham Maslow's hierarchy of needs is a model that shows the relationship among multiple motives that range from lower-level physiological needs to the very high level of self-actualization.

9.2 Hunger and Eating

Hunger and satiety are highly regulated processes that result in a person maintaining a fairly stable weight that is resistant to change. When more calories are consumed than expended, a person will store excess energy as fat. Being significantly overweight substantially adds to a person's health risks and problems, including cardiovascular disease, type 2 diabetes, certain cancers, and other medical issues.

Sociocultural factors that emphasize thinness as a beauty ideal and a genetic predisposition contribute to the development of eating disorders in many young females, though eating disorders span ages and genders.

9.3 Sexual Behavior

The hypothalamus and structures of the limbic system are important in sexual behavior and motivation. There is evidence to suggest that our motivation to engage in sexual behavior and our ability to do so are related, but separate, processes. Alfred Kinsey conducted large-scale survey research that demonstrated the incredible diversity of human sexuality. William Masters and Virginia Johnson observed individuals engaging in sexual behavior in developing their concept of the sexual response cycle. While often confused, sexual orientation and gender identity are related, but distinct, concepts.

9.4 Emotion

Emotions are subjective experiences that consist of physiological arousal and cognitive appraisal. Various theories have been put forward to explain our emotional experiences. The James-Lange theory asserts that emotions arise as a function of physiological arousal. The Cannon-Bard theory maintains that emotional experience occurs simultaneous to and independent of physiological arousal. The Schachter-Singer two-factor theory suggests that physiological arousal receives cognitive labels as a function of the relevant context and that these two factors together result in an emotional experience.

The limbic system is the brain's emotional circuit, which includes the amygdala and the hippocampus. Both of these structures are implicated in playing a role in normal emotional processing as well as in psychological mood and anxiety disorders. Increased amygdala activity is associated with learning to fear, and it is seen in individuals who are at risk for or suffering from mood disorders. The volume of the hippocampus has been shown to be reduced in individuals suffering from posttraumatic stress disorder.

The ability to produce and recognize facial expressions of emotions seems to be universal regardless of cultural background. However, there are cultural display rules, which influence how often and under what circumstances various emotions can be expressed. Tone of voice and body language also serve as a means by which we communicate information about our emotional states.

Key Terms

Flash Back

Now that you've worked through the chapter, sharpen your vocabulary with this Hawkes Verified Quizlet set (hawkes.biz/psychch9)!

Anorexia Nervosa

Eating disorder characterized by an individual maintaining body weight that is well below average through starvation and/or excessive exercise

Bariatric Surgery

Type of surgery that modifies the gastrointestinal system to reduce the amount of food that can be eaten and/or limiting how much of the digested food can be absorbed

Basolateral Complex

Part of the brain with dense connections with a variety of sensory areas of the brain; it is critical for classical conditioning and attaching emotional value to memory

Binge Eating Disorder

Type of eating disorder characterized by binge eating and associated distress

Bisexual

Emotional and erotic attractions to both same-sexed individuals and opposite-sexed individuals

Body Language

Emotional expression through body position or movement

Bulimia Nervosa

Type of eating disorder characterized by binge eating followed by purging

Cannon-Bard Theory of Emotion

Physiological arousal and emotional experience occur at the same time

Central Nucleus

Part of the brain involved in attention and has connections with the hypothalamus and various brainstem areas to regulate the autonomic nervous and endocrine systems' activity

Cognitive-Mediational Theory

Our emotions are determined by our appraisal of the stimulus

Components of Emotion

Physiological arousal, psychological appraisal, and subjective experience

Cultural Display Rule

One of the culturally specific standards that governs the types and frequencies of emotions that are acceptable

Distorted Body Image

Individuals view themselves as overweight even though they are not

Drive Theory

Deviations from homeostasis create physiological needs that result in psychological drive states that direct behavior to meet the need and ultimately bring the system back to homeostasis

Emotion

Subjective state of being often described as feelings

Excitement

Phase of the sexual response cycle that involves sexual arousal

Extrinsic Motivation

Motivation that arises from external factors or rewards

Facial Feedback Hypothesis

Facial expressions are capable of influencing our emotions

Gender Dysphoria

Diagnostic category in DSM-5 for individuals who do not identify as the gender associated with their biological sex

Gender Identity

Individual's sense of being male or female

Habit

Pattern of behavior in which we regularly engage

Heterosexual

Emotional and erotic attractions to opposite-sexed individuals

Hierarchy of Needs

Spectrum of needs ranging from basic biological needs to social needs to self-actualization

Homosexual

Emotional and erotic attractions to same-sexed individuals

Instinct

Species-specific pattern of behavior that is unlearned

Intrinsic Motivation

Motivation based on internal feelings rather than external rewards

James-Lange Theory of Emotion

Emotions arise from physiological arousal

Leptin

Satiety hormone

Metabolic Rate

Amount of energy that is expended in a given period of time

Morbid Obesity

Adult with a BMI over 40

Motivation

Wants or needs that direct behavior toward some goal

Obese

Adult with a BMI of 30 or higher

Orgasm

Peak phase of the sexual response cycle associated with rhythmic muscle contractions (and ejaculation)

Overweight

Adult with a BMI between 25 and 29.9

Plateau

Phase of the sexual response cycle that falls between excitement and orgasm

Polygraph

Lie detector test that measures physiological arousal of individuals as they answer a series of questions

Refractory Period

Time immediately following an orgasm during which an individual is incapable of experiencing another orgasm

Resolution

Phase of the sexual response cycle following orgasm during which the body returns to its unaroused state

Satiation

Fullness; satisfaction

Schachter-Singer Two-Factor Theory of Emotion

Emotions consist of two factors: physiological and cognitive

Self-Efficacy

Individual's belief in his own capabilities or capacities to complete a task

Set-Point Theory

Assertion that each individual has an ideal body weight, or set point, that is resistant to change

Sexual Orientation

Emotional and erotic attraction to same-sexed individuals, opposite-sexed individuals, or both

Sexual Response Cycle

Divided into four phases including excitement, plateau, orgasm, and resolution

Transgender Hormone Therapy

Use of hormones to make one's body look more like the opposite-sex

Yerkes-Dodson Law

Simple tasks are performed best when arousal levels are relatively high, while complex tasks are best performed when arousal is lower

💡 Exercises

Review Questions

1. Need for _____ refers to maintaining positive relationships with others.

   a. achievement

   b. affiliation

   c. intimacy

   d. power

2. _____ proposed the hierarchy of needs.

   a. William James

   b. David McClelland

   c. Abraham Maslow

   d. Albert Bandura

3. _____ is an individual's belief in her capability to complete some task.

   a. Physiological needs

   b. Self-esteem

   c. Self-actualization

   d. Self-efficacy

4. Carl mows the yard of his elderly neighbor each week for $20. What type of motivation is this?

   a. Extrinsic

   b. Intrinsic

   c. Drive

   d. Biological

5. According to your reading, nearly _____ of the adult population in the United States can be classified as obese.

   a. one half

   b. one third

   c. one fourth

   d. one fifth

6. _____ is a chemical messenger secreted by fat cells that acts as an appetite suppressant.

   a. Orexin

   b. Angiotensin

   c. Leptin

   d. Ghrelin

7. _____ is characterized by episodes of binge eating followed by attempts to compensate for the excessive amount of food that was consumed.

   a. Prader-Willi syndrome

   b. Morbid obesity

   c. Anorexia nervosa

   d. Bulimia nervosa

8. In order to be classified as morbidly obese, an adult must have a BMI of _____.

   a. less than 25

   b. 25–29.9

   c. 30–39.9

   d. 40 or more

9. Animal research suggests that in male rats the _____ is critical for the ability to engage in sexual behavior but not for the motivation to do so.

   a. nucleus accumbens

   b. amygdala

   c. medial preoptic area of the hypothalamus

   d. hippocampus

10. During the _____ phase of the sexual response cycle, individuals experience rhythmic contractions of the pelvis that are accompanied by uterine contractions in women and ejaculation in men.

    a. excitement

    b. plateau

    c. orgasm

    d. resolution

11. Which of the following findings was not a result of the Kinsey study?

    a. Sexual desire and sexual ability can be separate functions.

    b. Females enjoy sex as much as males.

    c. Homosexual behavior is fairly common.

    d. Masturbation has no adverse consequences.

12. If someone is uncomfortable identifying with the gender normally associated with their biological sex, then he could be classified as experiencing _____.

    a. homosexuality

    b. bisexuality

    c. heterosexuality

    d. gender dysphoria

13. Individuals suffering from posttraumatic stress disorder have been shown to have reduced volumes of the _____.

    a. amygdala

    b. hippocampus

    c. hypothalamus

    d. thalamus

14. According to the _____ theory of emotion, emotional experiences arise from physiological arousal.

    a. James-Lange

    b. Cannon-Bard

    c. Schachter-Singer two-factor

    d. Darwinian

15. Which of the following is not one of the seven universal emotions described in this chapter?

    a. Contempt

    b. Disgust

    c. Melancholy

    d. Anger

16. Which of the following theories of emotion would suggest that polygraphs should be quite accurate at differentiating one emotion from another?

    a. Cannon-Bard theory

    b. James-Lange theory

    c. Schachter-Singer two-factor theory

    d. Darwinian theory

Critical Thinking Questions

17. How might someone espousing an arousal theory of motivation explain visiting an amusement park?

18. Schools often use concrete rewards to increase adaptive behaviors. How might this be a disadvantage for students intrinsically motivated to learn? What are educational implications of the potential for concrete rewards to diminish intrinsic motivation for a given task?

19. The index that is often used to classify people as being underweight, normal weight, overweight, obese, or morbidly obese is called BMI. Given that BMI is calculated solely on weight and height, how could it be misleading?

20. As indicated in this chapter, Caucasian women from industrialized, Western cultures tend to be at the highest risk for eating disorders like anorexia and bulimia nervosa. Why might this be?

21. While much research has been conducted on how an individual develops a given sexual orientation, many people question the validity of this research citing that the participants used may not be representative. Why do you think this might be a legitimate concern?

22. There is no reliable scientific evidence that gay conversion therapy actually works. What kinds of evidence would you need to see in order to be convinced by someone arguing that she had successfully converted her sexual orientation?

23. Imagine you find a venomous snake crawling up your leg just after taking a drug that prevented sympathetic nervous system activation. What would the James-Lange theory predict about your experience?

24. Why can we not make causal claims regarding the relationship between the volume of the hippocampus and PTSD?

Personality

Chapter Introduction

Figure 1: What makes individuals have different personalities?

Three months before William Jefferson Blythe III was born, his father died in a car accident. He was raised in Hope, Arkansas, by his mother, Virginia Dell, and his grandparents. When he turned 4, his mother married Roger Clinton, Jr., an alcoholic who physically abused William's mother. Six years later, Virginia gave birth to her son, Roger. William, who later took the last name Clinton from his stepfather, became the 42nd president of the United States. While Bill Clinton was making his political ascendance, his half-brother, Roger Clinton, was arrested numerous times for drug charges, including possession, conspiracy to distribute cocaine, and driving under the influence. Two brothers, raised by the same people, took radically different paths in their lives. Why did they make the choices they did? What internal forces shaped their decisions? Personality psychology can help us answer these questions.

Flash Forward

Ready to dig into the vocabulary? Get some practice with this Hawkes Verified Quizlet set (hawkes.biz/psych10q1)!

10.1 What Is Personality?

Personality refers to the long-standing traits and patterns that propel individuals to consistently think, feel, and behave in specific ways. Our personality is what makes us unique individuals. Each person has an idiosyncratic pattern of enduring, long-term characteristics and a manner in which he or she interacts with other individuals and the world. Our personalities are thought to be long term, stable, and not easily changed. The word *personality* comes from the Latin word *persona*. In the ancient world, a persona was a mask worn by an actor. While we tend to think of a mask as being worn to conceal one's identity, the theatrical mask was originally used to represent a specific personality trait.

Figure 2: Happy, sad, impatient, shy, fearful, curious, helpful. What characteristics describe your personality?

Reflection Questions

Think about how your personality compares to your family, friends, classmates, or coworkers. What personality strengths do you see in yourself? In others?

Historical Perspectives

The concept of personality has been studied for at least 2,000 years, beginning with Hippocrates in 370 BCE (Fazeli, 2012). Hippocrates theorized that personality traits and human behaviors are based on four separate temperaments associated with four fluids ("humors") of the body (Clark & Watson, 2008; Eysenck & Eysenck, 1985; Lecci & Magnavita, 2013; Noga, 2007):

1. Choleric temperament (yellow bile from the liver)

2. Melancholic temperament (black bile from the kidneys)

3. Sanguine temperament (red blood from the heart)

4. Phlegmatic temperament (white phlegm from the lungs)

Centuries later, the influential Greek physician and philosopher Galen built on Hippocrates's theory, suggesting that both diseases and personality differences could be explained by imbalances in the humors and that each person exhibits one of the four temperaments (Clark & Watson, 2008; Stelmack & Stalikas, 1991). For example:

Temperament	Traits
Choleric	Passionate, ambitious, bold
Melancholic	Reserved, anxious, unhappy
Sanguine	Joyful, eager, optimistic
Phlegmatic	Calm, reliable, thoughtful

Galen's theory was prevalent for over 1,000 years and continued to be popular through the Middle Ages.

In 1780, Franz Gall, a German physician, proposed that the distances between bumps on the skull reveal a person's personality traits, character, and mental abilities (Figure 3). According to Gall, measuring these distances revealed the sizes of the brain areas underneath, providing information that could be used to determine whether a person was friendly, prideful, murderous, kind, good with languages, and so on. Initially, phrenology was very popular; however, it was soon discredited for lack of empirical support and has long been relegated to the status of pseudoscience (Fancher, 1979).

(a)   (b)

Figure 3: The pseudoscience of measuring the areas of a person's skull is known as phrenology. (a) Gall developed a chart that depicted which areas of the skull corresponded to particular personality traits or characteristics (Hothersall, 1995). (b) An 1825 lithograph depicts Gall examining the skull of a young woman.

In the centuries after Galen, other researchers contributed to the development of his four primary temperament types, most prominently Immanuel Kant (in the 18th century) and psychologist Wilhelm Wundt (in the 19th century) (Eysenck, 2009; Stelmack & Stalikas, 1991; Wundt, 1874/1886). Kant agreed with Galen that everyone could be sorted into one of the four temperaments and that there was no overlap between the four categories (Eysenck, 2009). He developed a list of traits that could be used to describe the personality of a person from each of the four temperaments (Figure 4). However, Wundt suggested that a better description of personality could be achieved using two major axes:

1. Emotional/non-emotional

2. Changeable/unchangeable

The first axis separated strong from weak emotions, and the second axis divided the changeable temperaments (Eysenck, 2009).

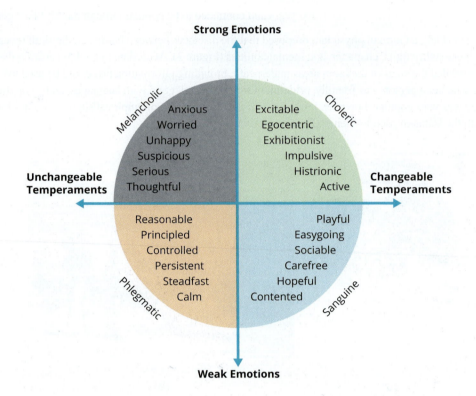

📷 **Figure 4:** Developed from Galen's theory of the four temperaments, Kant proposed trait words to describe each temperament. Wundt later suggested the arrangement of the traits on two major axes.

✍ On Your Own

Consult the previous chart and indicate which manner of emotions fits each temperament (i.e., strong emotions + unchangeable).

Temperaments and their Qualities
Melancholic
Choleric
Phlegmatic
Sanguine

Sigmund Freud's psychodynamic perspective of personality was the first comprehensive theory of personality, explaining a wide variety of both normal and abnormal behaviors. According to Freud, unconscious drives influenced by sex and aggression, along with childhood sexuality, are the forces that influence our personality. Freud attracted many followers who modified his ideas to create new theories about personality. These theorists, referred to as neo-Freudians, generally agreed with Freud that childhood experiences matter, but they reduced the emphasis on sex and focused more on the social environment and effects of culture on personality. The perspective of personality proposed by Freud and his followers was the dominant theory of personality for the first half of the 20th century.

Other major theories then emerged, including the learning, humanistic, biological, evolutionary, trait, and cultural perspectives. In this chapter, we will explore these various perspectives on personality in depth.

Further Resources

View this video (hawkes.biz/psychpersonality) for a brief overview of some of the psychological perspectives on personality.

Summary

Personality has been studied for over 2,000 years, beginning with Hippocrates. More recent theories of personality have been proposed, including Freud's psychodynamic perspective, which holds that personality is formed through early childhood experiences. Other perspectives then emerged in reaction to the psychodynamic perspective, including the learning, humanistic, biological, trait, and cultural perspectives.

10.2 Freud and the Psychodynamic Perspective

Sigmund Freud (1856–1939) is probably the most controversial and misunderstood psychological theorist. When reading Freud's theories, it is important to remember that he was a medical doctor, not a psychologist. There was no such thing as a degree in psychology at the time that he received his education, which can help us understand some of the controversy over his theories today. However, Freud was the first to systematically study and theorize the workings of the unconscious mind in the manner that we associate with modern psychology. Freud referred to the unconscious mind as mental activity that we are unaware of and unable to access.

> **Flash Forward**
>
> Ready to dig into the vocabulary? Get some practice with this Hawkes Verified Quizlet set (hawkes.biz/psych10q2)!

Levels of Consciousness

To explain the concept of conscious versus unconscious experience, Freud compared the mind to an iceberg (Figure 1). He said that only about one-tenth of our mind is **conscious**, and the rest of our mind is unconscious. Our **unconscious** refers to that mental activity of which we are unaware and are unable to access (Freud, 1923). According to Freud, unacceptable urges and desires are kept in our unconscious through a process called repression. For example, we sometimes say things that we don't intend to say by unintentionally substituting another word for the one we meant. You've probably heard of a Freudian slip, the term used to describe this. Freud suggested that slips of the tongue are actually sexual or aggressive urges, accidentally slipping out of our unconscious. Speech errors such as this are quite common. Seeing them as a reflection of unconscious desires, linguists today have found that slips of the tongue tend to occur when we are tired, nervous, or not at our optimal level of cognitive functioning (Motley, 2002).

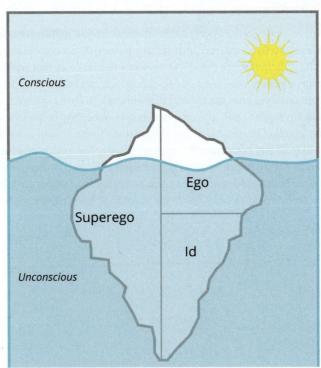

Conscious

Ego

Superego

Id

Unconscious

🖼 **Figure 1:** Freud believed that we are only aware of a small amount of our mind's activities and that most of it remains hidden from us in our unconscious. The information in our unconscious affects our behavior although we are unaware of it.

According to Freud, our personality develops from a conflict between two forces: our biological aggressive and pleasure-seeking drives versus our internal (socialized) control over these drives. Our personality is the result of our efforts to balance these two competing forces. Freud suggested that we can understand this by imagining three interacting systems within our minds. He called them the id, ego, and superego (Figure 2).

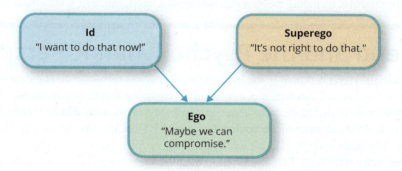

📷 **Figure 2:** The job of the ego, or self, is to balance the aggressive/pleasure-seeking drives of the id with the moral control of the superego.

The unconscious **id** contains our most primitive drives or urges and is present from birth. It directs impulses for hunger, thirst, and sex. Freud believed that the id operates on what he called the "pleasure principle," in which the id seeks immediate gratification. Through social interactions with parents and others in a child's environment, the ego and superego develop to help control the id. The **superego** develops as a child interacts with others, learning the social rules for right and wrong. The superego acts as our conscience; it is our moral compass that tells us how we should behave. It strives for perfection and judges our behavior, leading to feelings of pride or—when we fall short of the ideal—feelings of guilt. In contrast to the instinctual id and the rule-based superego, the **ego** is the rational part of our personality. It's what Freud considered to be the self, and it is the part of our personality that is seen by others. Its job is to balance the demands of the id and superego in the context of reality; thus, it operates on what Freud called the "reality principle." The ego helps the id satisfy its desires in a realistic way.

The id and superego are in constant conflict because the id wants instant gratification regardless of the consequences, but the superego tells us that we must behave in socially acceptable ways. Thus, the ego's job is to find the middle ground. It helps satisfy the id's desires in a rational way that will not lead us to feelings of guilt. According to Freud, a person who has a strong ego, which can balance the demands of the id and the superego, has a healthy personality. Freud maintained that imbalances in the system can lead to **neurosis** (a tendency to experience negative emotions), anxiety disorders, or unhealthy behaviors. For example, a person who is dominated by their id might be narcissistic and impulsive. A person with a dominant superego might be controlled by feelings of guilt and deny themselves even socially acceptable pleasures; conversely, if the superego is weak or absent, a person might become a psychopath. An overly dominant superego might be seen in an over-controlled individual whose rational grasp on reality is so strong that they are unaware of their emotional needs or in a neurotic who is overly defensive (overusing ego defense mechanisms).

☑ On Your Own

Identify a conflict between the id and the superego like the one described previously. Explain the perspective of the id and the superego and how the individual's ego might resolve the problem.

Term	Response
Conflict	
Id Perspective	
Superego Perspective	
Ego Resolution	

Defense Mechanisms

Freud believed that feelings of anxiety result from the ego's inability to mediate the conflict between the id and superego. When this happens, Freud believed that the ego seeks to restore balance through various protective measures known as defense mechanisms (Figure 3). When certain events, feelings, or yearnings cause an individual anxiety, the individual wishes to reduce that anxiety. To do that, the individual's unconscious mind uses ego **defense mechanisms**, unconscious protective behaviors that aim to reduce anxiety. The ego, usually conscious, resorts to unconscious strivings to protect the ego from being overwhelmed by anxiety. When we use defense mechanisms, we are unaware that we are using them. Further, they operate in various ways that distort reality. According to Freud, we all use ego defense mechanisms.

While everyone uses defense mechanisms, Freud believed that overuse of them may be problematic. For example, let's say Joe Smith is a high school football player. Deep down, Joe feels sexually attracted to males. His conscious belief is that being gay is immoral and that if he were gay, his family would disown him and he would be ostracized by his peers. Therefore, there is a conflict between his conscious beliefs (being gay is wrong and will result in being ostracized) and his unconscious urges (attraction to males). The idea that he might be gay causes Joe to have feelings of anxiety. How can he decrease his anxiety? Joe may find himself acting very "macho," making gay jokes, and picking on a school peer who is gay. This way, Joe's unconscious impulses are further submerged.

There are several different types of defense mechanisms. For instance, in repression, anxiety-causing memories from consciousness are blocked. As an analogy, let's say your car is making a strange noise, but because you do not have the money to get it fixed, you just turn up the radio so that you no longer hear the strange noise. Eventually you forget about it. Similarly, in the human psyche, if a memory is too overwhelming to deal with, it might be **repressed** and thus removed from conscious awareness (Freud, 1920). This repressed memory might cause symptoms in other areas.

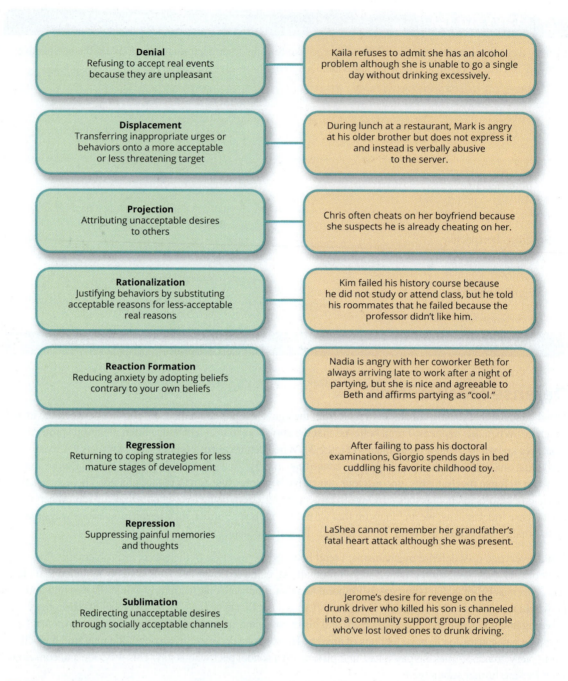

Denial
Refusing to accept real events because they are unpleasant

Kaila refuses to admit she has an alcohol problem although she is unable to go a single day without drinking excessively.

Displacement
Transferring inappropriate urges or behaviors onto a more acceptable or less threatening target

During lunch at a restaurant, Mark is angry at his older brother but does not express it and instead is verbally abusive to the server.

Projection
Attributing unacceptable desires to others

Chris often cheats on her boyfriend because she suspects he is already cheating on her.

Rationalization
Justifying behaviors by substituting acceptable reasons for less-acceptable real reasons

Kim failed his history course because he did not study or attend class, but he told his roommates that he failed because the professor didn't like him.

Reaction Formation
Reducing anxiety by adopting beliefs contrary to your own beliefs

Nadia is angry with her coworker Beth for always arriving late to work after a night of partying, but she is nice and agreeable to Beth and affirms partying as "cool."

Regression
Returning to coping strategies for less mature stages of development

After failing to pass his doctoral examinations, Giorgio spends days in bed cuddling his favorite childhood toy.

Repression
Suppressing painful memories and thoughts

LaShea cannot remember her grandfather's fatal heart attack although she was present.

Sublimation
Redirecting unacceptable desires through socially acceptable channels

Jerome's desire for revenge on the drunk driver who killed his son is channeled into a community support group for people who've lost loved ones to drunk driving.

Figure 3: Defense mechanisms are unconscious protective behaviors that work to reduce anxiety.

Another defense mechanism is **reaction formation**, in which someone expresses feelings, thoughts, and behaviors opposite to their inclinations. In the above example, Joe made fun of a homosexual peer while himself being attracted to males. In **regression**, an individual acts much younger than their age. For example, a four-year-old child who resents the arrival of a newborn sibling may act like a baby and revert to drinking out of a bottle. In **projection**, a person refuses to acknowledge her own unconscious feelings and instead sees those feelings in someone else. Other defense mechanisms include **rationalization**, **displacement**, and **sublimation**.

☑   **On Your Own**

Provide an example of the following defense mechanisms.

Defense Mechanism	Example
Regression	
Sublimation	
Projection	
Rationalization	
Denial	

Stages of Psychosexual Development

Freud believed that personality develops during early childhood, and childhood experiences shape our personalities as well as our behavior as adults. He asserted that we develop via a series of stages during childhood. Each of us must pass through these childhood stages, and if we do not have the proper nurturing and parenting during a stage, we will be stuck, or fixated, in that stage, even as adults.

In each **psychosexual stage of development**, the child's pleasure-seeking urges, coming from the id, are focused on a different area of the body, called an erogenous zone. The stages are oral, anal, phallic, latency, and genital (Table 1).

Freud's psychosexual development theory is quite controversial. To understand the origins of the theory, it is helpful to be familiar with the political, social, and cultural influences of Freud's day in Vienna at the turn of the 20th century. During this era, a climate of sexual repression, combined with limited understanding and education surrounding human sexuality, heavily influenced Freud's perspective. Given that sex was a taboo topic, Freud assumed that negative emotional states (neuroses) stemmed from suppression of unconscious sexual and aggressive urges. For Freud, his own recollections and interpretations of patients' experiences and dreams were sufficient proof that psychosexual stages were universal events in early childhood.

Stage	Age (years)	Erogenous Zone	Major Conflict	Adult Fixation Example
Oral	0–1	Mouth	Weaning off breast or bottle	Smoking, overeating
Anal	1–3	Anus	Toilet training	Neatness, messiness
Phallic	3–6	Genitals	Oedipus/Electra complex	Vanity, overambition
Latency	6–12	None	None	None
Genital	12+	Genitals	None	None

Table 1: Freud's Stages of Psychosexual Development

Oral Stage

In the **oral stage** (birth to 1 year), pleasure is focused on the mouth. Eating and the pleasure derived from sucking (nipples, pacifiers, and thumbs) play a large part in a baby's first year of life. At around 1 year of age, babies are weaned from the bottle or breast, and this process can create conflict if not handled properly by caregivers. According to Freud, an adult who smokes, drinks, overeats, or bites her nails is fixated in the oral stage of her psychosexual development; she may have been weaned too early or too late, resulting in these fixation tendencies, all of which seek to ease anxiety.

Figure 4: According to Freud, fixation in the oral stage results in an adult who smokes, drinks, overeats, or bites his or her nails.

Anal Stage

After passing through the oral stage, children enter what Freud termed the **anal stage** (1–3 years). During this stage, children are going through toilet training. Freud asserted that parents who offer praise and rewards encourage positive results and can help children feel competent. However, parents who are harsh in toilet training can cause a child to become fixated at the anal stage, leading to the development of an anal-retentive personality. The anal-retentive personality is stingy and stubborn, has a compulsive need for order and neatness, and might be considered a perfectionist. If parents are too lenient in toilet training, the child might also become fixated and display an anal-expulsive personality. The anal-expulsive personality is messy, careless, disorganized, and prone to emotional outbursts.

Phallic Stage

Freud's third stage of psychosexual development is the **phallic stage** (3–6 years), corresponding to the age when children become aware of their bodies and recognize the differences between boys and girls. Conflict arises when the child feels a desire for the opposite-sex parent and jealousy and hatred toward the same-sex parent. The Oedipus complex is a phenomenon where a boy sees his father as a rival for his mother's attention. In contrast, the Electra complex is when a girl sees her mother as a rival for her father's attention. A more controversial and criticized aspect of Freud's theory was penis envy, where a girl is angry at her mother for not providing her with a penis (Freud, 1931/1968; Scott, 2005).

Latency Period

Following the phallic stage of psychosexual development is a period known as the **latency period** (6 years to puberty). This period is not considered a stage because sexual feelings are dormant as children focus on other pursuits, such as school, friendships, hobbies, and sports. Children generally engage in activities with peers of the same sex, which serves to consolidate a child's gender-role identity.

Genital Stage

The final stage is the **genital stage**, which starts in puberty when the young person directs urges to more socially acceptable partners. According to Freud, individuals who successfully completed the previous stages and reach the genital stage with no fixations are said to be well-balanced, healthy adults.

☑ On Your Own

Identify the stage described in the following scenarios.

1. Heidi is more interested in school and her friends than getting into romantic relationships with boys. She no longer sees her mother as competition for her father's attention. Heidi is most likely in which of the following stages of development?

☐ Oral Stage   ☐ Phallic Stage   ☐ Genital Stage

☐ Anal Stage   ☐ Latency Period

2. Deontay gets jealous when his father kisses his mother. According to Freud, which of the following stages would Deontay be in?

☐ Oral Stage   ☐ Phallic Stage   ☐ Genital Stage

☐ Anal Stage   ☐ Latency Period

3. Yolanda has just hit puberty. Which of the following stages would she be in according to Freud?

☐ Oral Stage   ☐ Phallic Stage   ☐ Genital Stage

☐ Anal Stage   ☐ Latency Period

Reflection Questions

Freud's theories are very controversial because of their strong emphasis on sex and gender bias. What aspects of Freud's theories do you think make sense? What aspects do you disagree with? What is the reason for your opinion?

Summary

Sigmund Freud presented the first comprehensive theory of personality. He was also the first to recognize that much of our mental life takes place beyond our conscious awareness. Freud also proposed three components to our personality: the id, ego, and superego. The job of the ego is to balance the sexual and aggressive drives of the id with the moral ideal of the superego. Freud also said that personality develops through a series of psychosexual stages. In each stage, pleasure focuses on a specific erogenous zone. Failure to resolve a stage can lead one to become fixated in that stage, leading to unhealthy personality traits. Successful resolution of the stages leads to a healthy adult.

Flash Forward

Ready to dig into the vocabulary? Get some practice with this Hawkes Verified Quizlet set (hawkes.biz/psych10q3)!

10.3 Neo-Freudians: Adler, Erikson, Jung, and Horney

Freud attracted many followers who modified his ideas to create new theories about personality. These theorists, referred to as neo-Freudians, generally agreed with Freud that childhood experiences matter but deemphasized sex, focusing more on the social environment and effects of culture on personality. Four notable neo-Freudians include Alfred Adler, Erik Erikson, Carl Jung (pronounced "Yoong"), and Karen Horney (pronounced "HORN-eye").

Alfred Adler

Alfred Adler founded a school of psychology called **individual psychology**, which focuses on our drive to compensate for feelings of inferiority. Adler (1937, 1956) proposed the concept of the inferiority complex. An **inferiority complex** refers to a person's feelings that they lack worth and don't measure up to the standards of others or of society. Adler proposed that we may feel inferior when we are not measuring up in the following fundamental social tasks:

- Occupational tasks (careers)

- Societal tasks (friendship)

- Love tasks (finding an intimate partner for a long-term relationship)

One of Adler's major contributions to personality psychology was the idea that our birth order shapes our personality. He proposed that older siblings, who start out as the focus of their parents' attention but later must share that attention once a new child joins the family, compensate by becoming overachievers. The youngest children, according to Adler, may be spoiled, leaving the middle child with the opportunity to minimize the negative dynamics of the youngest and oldest children.

Figure 1: Alfred Adler proposed the concept of the inferiority complex.

> **Reflection Questions**
>
> How are the dynamics with your siblings? Do you agree with Adler? Is the oldest sibling an overachiever? Is the youngest child spoiled? What about the middle child? Do they minimize negative dynamics between the youngest and oldest sibling?

Further Resources

One of Adler's major contributions to personality psychology was the idea that our birth order shapes our personality. Follow this link (hawkes.biz/adler) to view a summary of birth order theory.

Erik Erikson

Erik Erikson's theory of psychosocial development emphasized the social relationships that are important at each stage of personality development. Erikson identified eight stages, each of which represents a conflict or developmental task (Table 1). The development of a healthy personality and a sense of competence depend on the successful completion of each task.

Stage	Age (years)	Developmental Task	Description
1	0–1	Trust vs. mistrust	Trust (or mistrust) that basic needs, such as nourishment and affection, will be met
2	1–3	Autonomy vs. shame/doubt	Sense of independence in many tasks develops
3	3–6	Initiative vs. guilt	Take initiative on some activities; may develop guilt when success not met or boundaries overstepped
4	7–11	Industry vs. inferiority	Develop self-confidence in abilities when competent or sense of inferiority when not
5	12–18	Identity vs. confusion	Experiment with and develop identity and roles
6	19–39	Intimacy vs. isolation	Establish intimacy and relationships with others
7	40–64	Generativity vs. stagnation	Contribute to society and be part of a family
8	65+	Integrity vs. despair	Assess and make sense of life and meaning of contributions

Table 1: Erikson's Psychosocial Stages of Development

Reflection Questions

What stage of Erikson's theory would you say you are in now? What about the previous stages? How have you resolved them?

Carl Jung

Carl Jung (Figure 2) focused on **analytical psychology**, which emphasizes balancing opposing forces of conscious and unconscious thought and experience within one's personality. According to Jung, this work is a continuous learning process—mainly occurring in the second half of life—of becoming aware of unconscious elements and integrating them into consciousness. The **collective unconscious** is a universal version of the personal unconscious, holding mental patterns, or memory traces, which are common to all of us (Jung, 1928). Jung believed in **archetypes**, which are universal themes in cultures expressed through literature, art, and drama. Jung said that these themes reflect the common experiences of people the world over, such as facing death, becoming independent, and striving for mastery. In Jung's view, the task of integrating these unconscious archetypal aspects of the self is part of the self-realization process in the second half of life.

Jung also proposed two attitudes or approaches toward life: extroversion and introversion (Jung, 1923) (Table 2). If you are an extrovert, then you are a person who is energized by being around others. If you are an introvert, your energy is derived from your inner psychic activity. Jung believed a balance between extroversion and introversion best served the goal of self-realization.

Figure 2: Carl Jung was interested in exploring the collective unconscious.

Introvert	Extrovert
Energized by being alone	Energized by being with others
Avoids attention	Seeks attention
Speaks slowly and softly	Speaks quickly and loudly
Thinks before speaking	Thinks out loud
Stays on one topic	Jumps from topic to topic
Prefers written communication	Prefers verbal communication
Pays attention easily	Distractible
Cautious	Acts first, thinks later

Table 2: Introverts and Extroverts

Reflection Questions

Based on the descriptions listed in Table 2, would you consider yourself more of an introvert, an extrovert, or in the middle? Why?

Further Resources

Jung's view of extroverted and introverted types serves as a basis of the Myers-Briggs Type Indicator (MBTI). This questionnaire describes a person's degree of introversion versus extroversion, thinking versus feeling, intuition versus sensation, and judging versus perceiving. This site (hawkes. biz/mbti) provides a modified questionnaire based on the MBTI.

For a look at some criticism of the MBTI, check out this article (hawkes.biz/mbti2) from *The New Yorker*.

💡 Connect the Concepts

Are Archetypes Genetically Based?

Jung proposed that human responses to archetypes are similar to instinctual responses in animals. One criticism of Jung is that there is no evidence that archetypes are biologically based or similar to animal instincts (Roesler, 2012). Jung formulated his ideas about 100 years ago, and great advances have been made in the field of genetics since that time. We've found that human babies are born with certain capacities, including the ability to acquire language. However, we've also found that symbolic information (such as archetypes) is not encoded on the genome and that babies cannot decode symbolism, refuting the idea of a biological basis to archetypes. Rather than being seen as purely biological, more recent research suggests that archetypes emerge directly from our experiences and are reflections of linguistic or cultural characteristics (Young-Eisendrath, 1995). Today, most Jungian scholars believe that the collective unconscious and archetypes are based on both innate and environmental influences, with the differences being in the role and degree of each (Sotirova-Kohli et al., 2013).

Karen Horney

Karen Horney was one of the first women trained as a Freudian psychoanalyst. During the Great Depression, Horney moved from Germany to the United States, and subsequently moved away from Freud's teachings. Like Jung, Horney believed that each individual has the potential for self-realization and that the goal of psychoanalysis should be moving toward a healthy self rather than exploring early childhood patterns of dysfunction. Horney also disagreed with the Freudian idea that girls have penis envy and are jealous of male biological features. According to Horney, any jealousy is most likely culturally based, due to the greater privileges that males often have, meaning that the differences between men's and women's personalities are culturally based, not biologically based. She further suggested that men have womb envy because they cannot give birth.

📷 **Figure 3:** Karen Horney argued that the way we cope with anxiety and insecurity as children can impact our relationships and coping strategies in adulthood.

Horney's theories focused on the role of unconscious anxiety. She suggested that normal growth can be blocked by basic anxiety stemming from needs not being met, such as childhood experiences of loneliness and/or isolation. How do children learn to handle this anxiety? Horney suggested three styles of coping (Table 3).

Coping Style	Description	Example
Moving toward people	Affiliation and dependence	Child seeking positive attention and affection from parent; adult needing love
Moving against people	Aggression and manipulation	Child fighting or bullying other children; adult who is abrasive and verbally hurtful or who exploits others
Moving away from people	Detachment and isolation	Child withdrawn from the world and isolated; adult loner

Table 3: Horney's Coping Styles

The first coping style, *moving toward people*, relies on affiliation and dependence. These children become dependent on their parents and other caregivers in an effort to receive attention and affection, which provides relief from anxiety (Burger, 2008). When these children grow up, they tend to use this same coping strategy to deal with relationships, expressing an intense need for love and acceptance (Burger, 2008). The second coping style, *moving against people*, relies on aggression and assertiveness. Children with this coping style find that fighting is the best way to deal with an unhappy home situation, and they deal with their feelings of insecurity by bullying other children (Burger, 2008). As adults, people with this coping style tend to lash out with hurtful comments and exploit others (Burger, 2008). The third coping style, *moving away from people*, centers on detachment and isolation. These children handle their anxiety by withdrawing from the world. They need privacy and tend to be self-sufficient. When these children are adults, they continue to avoid such things as love and friendship, and they also tend to gravitate toward careers that require little interaction with others (Burger, 2008).

Horney believed these three styles are ways in which people typically cope with day-to-day problems; however, the three coping styles can become neurotic strategies if they are used rigidly and compulsively, leading a person to become alienated from others.

> **Reflection Questions**
>
> What are your tendencies in dealing with anxiety? Do you move away from people, move toward people, or move against people? What do you think explains these tendencies?

✐ On Your Own

Answer each of the following questions about the neo-Freudian theories of personality.

1. Which neo-Freudian psychologist came up with the concepts of introversion and extroversion?

   ☐ Adler   ☐ Jung

   ☐ Erikson   ☐ Horney

2. Which psychologists' theory best explains why Pam is bullying other children?

   ☐ Adler   ☐ Jung

   ☐ Erikson   ☐ Horney

3. Who came up with a theory that outlines a series of conflicts that explain development throughout the lifespan?

   ☐ Adler   ☐ Jung

   ☐ Erikson   ☐ Horney

Summary

The neo-Freudians were psychologists whose work followed from Freud's. They generally agreed with Freud that childhood experiences matter, but they decreased the emphasis on sex and focused more on the social environment and effects of culture on personality. Some of the notable neo-Freudians are Alfred Adler, Carl Jung, Erik Erikson, and Karen Horney. The neo-Freudian approaches have been criticized because they tend to be philosophical rather than based on sound scientific research. For example, Jung's conclusions about the existence of the collective unconscious are based on myths, legends, dreams, and art. In addition, as with Freud's psychoanalytic theory, the neo-Freudians based much of their theories of personality on information from their patients.

Flash Forward

Ready to dig into the vocabulary? Get some practice with this Hawkes Verified Quizlet set (hawkes.biz/psych10q4)!

10.4 Learning Approaches

In contrast to the psychodynamic approaches of Freud and the neo-Freudians, which relate personality to inner (and hidden) processes, the learning approaches focus only on observable behavior. This illustrates one significant advantage of the learning approaches over psychodynamics: because learning approaches involve observable, measurable phenomena, they can be scientifically tested.

The Behavioral Perspective

Behaviorists do not believe in biological determinism: they do not see personality traits as inborn. Instead, they view personality as significantly shaped by the reinforcements and consequences outside of the organism. In other words, people behave in a consistent manner based on prior learning. B.F. Skinner, a strict behaviorist, believed that environment was solely responsible for all behavior, including the enduring, consistent behavior patterns studied by personality theorists.

As you may recall from your study on the psychology of learning, Skinner (1953) proposed that we increase the behaviors that lead to positive consequences, and we decrease the behaviors that lead to negative consequences. Skinner disagreed with Freud's idea that personality is fixed in childhood. He argued that personality develops over our entire life, not only in the first few years. Our responses can change as we come across new situations; therefore, we can expect more variability over time in personality than Freud would anticipate. For example, consider a young woman, Greta, a risk taker. She drives fast and participates in dangerous sports such as hang gliding and kiteboarding. But after she gets married and has children, the system of reinforcements and punishments in her environment changes. Speeding and extreme sports are no longer reinforced, so she no longer engages in those behaviors. In fact, Greta now describes herself as a cautious person.

Figure 1: Hang gliding is a risky sport, and we're more likely to take risks when those choices are reinforced.

The Social-Cognitive Perspective

Albert Bandura agreed with Skinner that personality develops through learning. He disagreed, however, with Skinner's strict behaviorist approach to personality development because he felt that thinking and reasoning are important components of learning. He presented a **social-cognitive theory** of personality that emphasizes both learning and cognition as sources of individual differences in personality. In social-cognitive theory, the concepts of reciprocal determinism, observational learning, and self-efficacy all play a part in personality development.

Reciprocal Determinism

In contrast to Skinner's idea that the environment alone determines behavior, Bandura (1990) proposed the concept of **reciprocal determinism**, in which cognitive processes, behavior, and context all interact, each factor influencing and being influenced by the others simultaneously (Figure 2).

Figure 2: Bandura proposed the idea of reciprocal determinism: our behavior, cognitive processes, and situational context all influence each other.

- *Cognitive processes* refer to all characteristics previously learned, including beliefs, expectations, and personality characteristics.

- *Behavior* refers to anything that we do that may be rewarded or punished.

- *Context* in which the behavior occurs refers to the environment or situation, which includes rewarding/punishing stimuli.

Consider, for example, that you're at a festival and one of the attractions is bungee jumping from a bridge. Do you do it? In this example, the behavior is bungee jumping. Cognitive factors that might influence this behavior include your beliefs, values, and past experiences with similar behaviors. Finally, context refers to the reward structure for the behavior. According to reciprocal determinism, all of these factors are in play.

✎ On Your Own

Answer the following questions based on the bungee jumping example in the following table.

Factor	Question	Response
Behavior	Would you go bungee jumping?	
Situational Factors	What situation would make you more likely to go bungee jumping? What situation would make you less likely to go bungee jumping?	
Cognitive Factors	What beliefs, values, and past experiences contribute to your decision to go or not go bungee jumping?	

Observational Learning

Bandura's key contribution to learning theory was the idea that much learning is vicarious. We learn by observing someone else's behavior and its consequences, which Bandura called observational learning. He felt that this type of learning also plays a part in the development of our personality. Just as we learn individual behaviors, we learn new behavior patterns when we see them performed by other people or models. Drawing on the behaviorists' ideas about reinforcement, Bandura suggested that whether we choose to imitate a model's behavior depends on whether we see the model reinforced or punished. Through observational learning, we come to learn what behaviors are acceptable and rewarded in our culture, and we also learn to inhibit deviant or socially unacceptable behaviors by seeing what behaviors are punished.

Reflection Questions

Can you think of an example where you learned from someone else's mistake? How do you think this changed how you think about the behavior in question?

We can see the principles of reciprocal determinism at work in observational learning. For example, personal factors determine which behaviors in the environment a person chooses to imitate, and those environmental events in turn are processed cognitively according to other personal factors.

Self-Efficacy

Bandura (1977, 1995) has studied a number of cognitive and personal factors that affect learning and personality development and most recently has focused on the concept of self-efficacy. **Self-efficacy** is our level of confidence in our own abilities, developed through our social experiences. Self-efficacy affects how we approach challenges and reach goals. In observational learning, self-efficacy is a cognitive factor that affects which behaviors we choose to imitate as well as our success in performing those behaviors.

People who have high self-efficacy believe that their goals are within reach, have a positive view of challenges and see them as tasks to be mastered, develop a deep interest in and strong commitment to the activities in which they are involved, and quickly recover from setbacks. Conversely, people with low self-efficacy avoid challenging tasks because they doubt their ability to be successful, tend to focus on failure and negative outcomes, and lose confidence in their abilities if they experience setbacks. Feelings of self-efficacy can be specific to certain situations. For instance, a student might feel confident in her ability in English class but much less so in math class.

Julian Rotter and Locus of Control

Julian Rotter (1966) proposed the concept of **locus of control**, which refers to our beliefs about the power we have over our lives. In Rotter's view, people possess either an internal or an external locus of control (Figure 3). Those of us with an internal locus of control ("internals") tend to believe that most of our outcomes are the direct result of our efforts. Those of us with an external locus of control ("externals") tend to believe that our outcomes are outside of our control. Externals see their lives as being controlled by other people, luck, or chance.

Figure 3: Locus of control occurs on a continuum from internal to external.

Researchers have found that people with an internal locus of control (Benassi, Sweeney, & Durfour, 1988; Lefcourt, 1982; Maltby, Day, & Macaskill, 2007; Whyte, 1977, 1978, 1980):

- Perform better academically
- Achieve more in their careers
- Are more independent

- Are healthier
- Are more able to cope with setbacks
- Are less likely to be depressed

Let's say you didn't spend much time studying for your psychology test and went out to dinner with friends instead. When you receive your test score, you see that you earned a *D*. If you possess an internal locus of control, you would most likely admit that you did poorly because you didn't spend enough time studying and decide to study more for the next test. On the other hand, if you possess an external locus of control, you might conclude that the test was too hard and not bother studying for the next test because you figure you wouldn't do well anyway.

Identify the most likely responses for the following scenarios.

1. Gerald didn't make the basketball team. Which of the following responses would best represent an external locus of control?

☐ "I don't care about making the basketball team anyway."

☐ "The coach was never going to pick me anyway."

☐ "I didn't get picked because I did not practice enough."

2. Let's assume you failed your math test. Which of the following explanations would be an internal locus of control?

☐ "I am stupid."

☐ "I didn't study hard enough."

☐ "The class is just too hard."

Walter Mischel and the Person-Situation Debate

Walter Mischel was a student of Julian Rotter and taught for years at Stanford, where he was a colleague of Albert Bandura. Mischel surveyed several decades of empirical psychological literature regarding trait prediction of behavior, and his conclusion shook the foundations of personality psychology. Mischel found that the data did not support the central principle of the field—that a person's personality traits are consistent across situations. His report triggered a decades-long period of self-examination, known as the person-situation debate, among personality psychologists.

Mischel suggested that perhaps we were looking for consistency in the wrong places. He found that although behavior was inconsistent across different situations, it was much more consistent within situations—so that a person's behavior in one situation would likely be repeated in a similar one. And as you will see next regarding his famous "marshmallow test," Mischel also found that behavior is consistent in equivalent situations across time.

One of Mischel's most notable contributions to personality psychology was his ideas on self-regulation.

According to Lecci & Magnavita (2013), "Self-regulation is the process of identifying a goal or set of goals and, in pursuing these goals, using both internal (e.g., thoughts and affect) and external (e.g., responses of anything or anyone in the environment) feedback to maximize goal attainment" (p. 6.3).

Self-regulation is also known as will power. When we talk about will power, we tend to think of it as the ability to delay gratification. For example, Bettina's teenage daughter made strawberry cupcakes, and they looked delicious. However, Bettina forfeited the pleasure of eating one because she is training for a 5K race and wants to be fit and do well in the race. Would you be able to resist getting a small reward now in order to get a larger reward later? This is the question Mischel investigated in his now-classic marshmallow test.

Mischel designed a study to assess self-regulation in young children. In the marshmallow study, Mischel and his colleagues placed a preschool child in a room with one marshmallow on the table. The child was told that he could either eat the marshmallow now, or wait until the researcher returned to the room, and then he could have two marshmallows (Mischel, Ebbesen & Raskoff, 1972). This was repeated with hundreds of preschoolers. What Mischel and his team found was that young children differ in their degree of self-control. Mischel and his colleagues continued to follow this group of preschoolers through high school, and what do you think they discovered? The children who had more self-control in preschool (the ones who waited for the bigger reward) were more successful in high school. They had higher SAT scores, had positive peer relationships, and were less likely to have substance abuse issues; as adults, they also had more stable marriages (Mischel, Shoda, & Rodriguez, 1989; Mischel et al., 2010). On the other hand, those children who had poor self-control in preschool (the ones who grabbed the one marshmallow) were not as successful in high school, and they were found to have academic and behavioral problems.

☑ On Your Own

If you were a child in Mischel's study, would you have eaten the marshmallow? Use Bandura's concepts of reciprocal determinism to explain why or why not.

Factor	Question	Response
Behavior	Would you have eaten the marshmallow before the experimenter returned?	
Situational Factors	What situation would make you more likely to eat the marshmallow? What situation would have made you less likely to eat the marshmallow?	
Cognitive Factors	What beliefs, values, and past experiences would contribute to your decision to eat or not eat the marshmallow?	

Today, the debate is mostly resolved, and most psychologists consider both the situation and personal factors in understanding behavior. For Mischel (1993), people are situation processors. The children in the marshmallow test each processed, or interpreted, the rewards structure of that situation in their own way. Mischel's approach to personality stresses the importance of both the situation and the way the person perceives the situation. Instead of behavior being determined by the situation, people use cognitive processes to interpret the situation and then behave in accordance with that interpretation.

Figure 4: What do you think you would have chosen to do in the marshmallow test?

Summary

Behavioral theorists view personality as significantly shaped and impacted by the reinforcements and consequences outside of the organism. People behave in a consistent manner based on prior learning. B.F. Skinner, a prominent behaviorist, said that we demonstrate consistent behavior patterns because we have developed certain response tendencies. Mischel focused on how personal goals play a role in the self-regulation process. Albert Bandura said that one's environment can determine behavior, but at the same time, people can influence the environment with both their thoughts and behaviors, which is known as reciprocal determinism. Bandura also emphasized how we learn from watching others. He felt that this type of learning also plays a part in the development of our personality. Bandura discussed the concept of self-efficacy, which is our level of confidence in our own abilities. Rotter proposed the concept of locus of control, which refers to our beliefs about the power we have over our lives. He said that people fall along a continuum between a purely internal and a purely external locus of control. Finally, Mischel focused on how self-regulation patterns in early childhood can predict academic success and social behavior in adolescence.

Flash Forward

Ready to dig into the vocabulary? Get some practice with this Hawkes Verified Quizlet set (hawkes.biz/psych10q5)!

10.5 Humanistic Approaches

Humanism is touted as a reaction to two psychological movements and their believed effects on society:

Pessimistic determinism of *psychoanalysis* → Too much emphasis on psychological disturbance

Behaviorists' view of humans passively reacting to the enviroment → Making people seem like lifeless robots

📷 **Figure 1:** What makes individuals have different personalities?

It does not suggest that psychoanalytic, behaviorist, and other points of view are incorrect but argues that these perspectives do not recognize the depth and meaning of human experience and fail to recognize the innate capacity for self-directed change and transforming personal experiences.

✍ On Your Own

Re-read the paragraph above, and in your own words, recap the reasons that proponents of humanism feel the other perspectives are inadequate.

_____

_____

This perspective focuses on how healthy people develop. One pioneering humanist, Abraham Maslow, studied people who he considered to be healthy, creative, and productive, including Albert Einstein, Eleanor Roosevelt, Thomas Jefferson, Abraham Lincoln, and others. Maslow (1950, 1970) found that such people share similar characteristics including:

- Openness
- Creativity
- A loving spirit

- Spontaneity
- Compassion
- Concern for others

- Acceptance of themselves

You may have learned about one of the best-known humanistic theories, Maslow's hierarchy of needs, in which Maslow proposes that human beings have certain needs in common and that these needs must be met in a certain order. The highest need is the need for self-actualization, which is the achievement of our fullest potential.

Another humanistic theorist was Carl Rogers. One of Rogers's main ideas about personality regards **self-concept**, our thoughts and feelings about ourselves. How would you respond to the following question?

Who am I?

If your response to the above question is primarily positive, then you tend to feel good about who you are, and you see the world as a safe and positive place. If your response is mainly negative, then you may feel unhappy with who you are. Rogers further divided the self into two categories:

1. The ideal self

2. The real self

The **ideal self** is the person that you would like to be; the **real self** is the person you actually are.

Reflection Questions

Take some time to think about the above terms. How do these versions of self compare in your own life?

Rogers focused on the idea that we need to achieve consistency between these two selves. We experience **congruence** when our thoughts about our real self and ideal self are very similar—in other words, when our self-concept is accurate. High congruence leads to a greater sense of self-worth and a healthy, productive life. Parents can help their children achieve this by giving them unconditional positive regard, or unconditional love. According to Rogers (1980), "As persons are accepted and prized, they tend to develop a more caring attitude towards themselves" (p. 116). Conversely, when there is a great discrepancy between our ideal and actual selves, we experience a state Rogers called **incongruence**, which can lead to maladjustment. Both Rogers's and Maslow's theories focus on individual choices and do not believe that biology is deterministic of these factors.

☑ On Your Own

Select the answer that best completes the following statments.

1. People with low congruence would have a:

☐ higher likelihood of being maladjusted   ☐ greater sense of self-worth

2. People with high congruence would have a:

☐ higher likelihood of being maladjusted   ☐ greater sense of self-worth

---

Summary

Humanistic psychologists Abraham Maslow and Carl Rogers focused on the growth potential of healthy individuals. They believed that people strive to become self-actualized. Both Rogers's and Maslow's theories greatly contributed to our understanding of the self. They emphasized free will and self-determination, with each individual desiring to become the best person they can become.

Flash Forward

Ready to dig into the vocabulary? Get some practice with this Hawkes Verified Quizlet set (hawkes.biz/psych10q6)!

10.6 Biological Approaches

Reflection Questions

How much of our personality is in-born and biological? How much is influenced by the environment and culture we are raised in?

Psychologists who favor the biological approach believe that inherited predispositions as well as physiological processes can be used to explain differences in our personalities (Burger, 2008).

In the field of behavioral genetics, the Minnesota Study of Twins Reared Apart—a well-known study of the genetic basis for personality—conducted research with twins from 1979 to 1999. In studying 350 pairs of twins, including pairs of identical and fraternal twins reared together and apart, researchers found that identical twins, whether raised together or apart, have very similar personalities (Bouchard, 1994; Bouchard, Lykken, McGue, Segal, & Tellegen, 1990; Segal, 2012). These findings suggest the heritability of some personality traits. **Heritability** refers to the proportion of difference among people that is attributed to genetics.

Some of the traits that the study reported as having more than a 0.50 heritability ratio include:

Group Activity

As a group, brainstorm areas in which you believe identical twins would be similar with regard to personality.

- leadership
- a sense of well-being
- resistance to stress

- obedience to authority
- feelings of alienation
- fearfulness

The implication is that some aspects of our personalities are largely controlled by genetics; however, it's important to point out that traits are not determined by a single gene but by a combination of many genes, as well as by epigenetic factors that control whether the genes are expressed.

Further Resources

To what extent is our personality dictated by our genetic makeup? View this video (hawkes.biz/personalitygenes) to learn more.

Temperament

Most contemporary psychologists believe temperament has a biological basis due to its appearance very early in our lives (Rothbart, 2011). Thomas and Chess (1977) found that babies could be categorized into one of three temperaments: easy, difficult, or slow to warm up. However, environmental factors (family interactions, for example) and maturation can affect the ways in which children's personalities are expressed (Carter et al., 2008).

Research suggests that there are two dimensions of our temperament that are important parts of our adult personality—reactivity and self-regulation (Rothbart, Ahadi, & Evans, 2000).

Figure 1: The two dimensions of our adult personality are reactivity and self-regulation.

For example, one person may immediately respond to new stimuli with a high level of anxiety while another barely notices it.

♀ **Connect the Concepts**

Body Type and Temperament

Is there an association between your body type and your temperament? The constitutional perspective, which examines the relationship between the structure of the human body and behavior, seeks to answer this question (Genovese, 2008). The first comprehensive system of constitutional psychology was proposed by American psychologist William H. Sheldon (1940, 1942). He believed that your body type can be linked to your personality. Sheldon's life's work was spent observing human bodies and temperaments. Based on his observations and interviews of hundreds of people, he proposed three body/personality types, which he called somatotypes.

The three somatotypes are:

- ectomorphs

- endomorphs

- mesomorphs

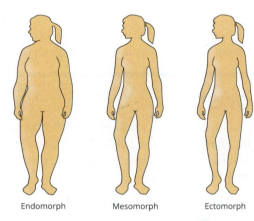

Endomorph   Mesomorph   Ectomorph

🖼 **Figure 2:** Sheldon proposed three somatotypes: endomorphs, mesomorphs, and ectomorphs. Do you think Sheldon's ideas about somatotypes are generally accurate about most people?

Ectomorphs are thin with a small bone structure and very little fat on their bodies. According to Sheldon, the ectomorph personality is anxious, self-conscious, artistic, thoughtful, quiet, and private. They enjoy intellectual stimulation and feel uncomfortable in social situations. Actors Adrien Brody and Nicole Kidman would be characterized as ectomorphs.

Endomorphs are the opposite of ectomorphs. Endomorphs have narrow shoulders and wide hips, and carry extra fat on their round bodies. Sheldon described endomorphs as being relaxed, comfortable, good-humored, even-tempered, sociable, and tolerant. Endomorphs enjoy affection and detest disapproval. Queen Latifah and Jack Black would be considered endomorphs.

The third somatotype is the mesomorph. This body type falls between the ectomorph and the endomorph. Mesomorphs have a large bone structure, well-defined muscles, broad shoulders, narrow waists, and attractive, strong bodies. According to Sheldon, mesomorphs are adventurous, assertive, competitive, and fearless. They are curious and enjoy trying new things but can also be obnoxious and aggressive. Channing Tatum and Scarlett Johannson would likely be mesomorphs.

Sheldon (1949) also conducted further research into somatotypes and criminality. He measured the physical proportions of hundreds of juvenile delinquent boys in comparison to male college students and found that problem youth were primarily mesomorphs. Why might this be? Perhaps it's because they are quick to anger and don't have the restraint demonstrated by ectomorphs. Maybe it's because a person with a mesomorphic body type reflects high levels of testosterone, which may lead to more aggressive behavior. Can you think of other explanations for Sheldon's findings?

Sheldon's method of somatotyping is not without criticism, as it has been considered largely subjective (Carter & Heath, 1990; Cortés & Gatti, 1972; Parnell, 1958). More systematic and controlled research methods did not support his findings (Eysenck, 1970). Consequently, it's not uncommon to see his theory labeled as pseudoscience, much like Gall's theory of phrenology (Rafter, 2007; Rosenbaum, 1995). However, studies involving correlations between somatotype, temperament, and children's school performance (Sanford et al., 1943; Parnell); somatotype and performance of pilots during wartime (Damon, 1955); and somatotype and temperament (Peterson, Liivamagi, & Koskel, 2006) did support his theory.

Reflection Questions

Which somatotype are you? Do you agree with the personality description that fits your body type?

Summary

Some aspects of our personalities are largely controlled by genetics; however, environmental factors (such as family interactions) and maturation can affect the ways in which children's personalities are expressed.

10.7 Trait Theorists

Flash Forward

Ready to dig into the vocabulary? Get some practice with this Hawkes Verified Quizlet set (hawkes.biz/psych10q7)!

Trait theorists believe personality can be understood via the approach that all people have certain **traits**, or characteristic ways of behaving. One trait theorist, Gordon Allport (Allport & Odbert, 1936), found 4,500 words in the English language that could describe people. He organized these personality traits into three categories: cardinal traits, central traits, and secondary traits.

- A cardinal trait is one that dominates your entire personality.

- Central traits are those that make up our personalities (such as loyal, kind, agreeable, friendly, sneaky, wild, and grouchy).

- Secondary traits are present under specific circumstances and include preferences and attitudes. For example, one person can only sleep on the left side of the bed, and yet another always orders her salad dressing on the side.

☑ On Your Own

Using the following table, describe a cardinal trait, central trait, and a secondary trait that you possess.

Trait Type	Response
Cardinal	
Central	
Secondary	

Raymond Cattell (1946, 1957) narrowed down the list to about 171 traits. Cattell (1957) identified 16 factors or dimensions of personality: warmth, reasoning, emotional stability, dominance, liveliness, rule-consciousness, social boldness, sensitivity, vigilance, abstractedness, private-ness, apprehension, openness to change, self-reliance, perfectionism, and tension (Table 1).

Cattell developed a personality assessment based on these 16 factors, called the 16PF. Instead of a trait being present or absent, each dimension is scored over a continuum, from high to low. For example, your level of warmth describes how warm, caring, and nice to others you are. If you score low on this index, you tend to be distant and cold. A high score on this index signifies you are supportive and comforting.

Factor	Low Score	High Score
Warmth	Reserved, detached	Outgoing, supportive
Intellect	Concrete thinker	Analytical
Emotional stability	Moody, irritable	Stable, calm
Aggressiveness	Docile, submissive	Controlling, dominant
Liveliness	Somber, prudent	Adventurous, spontaneous
Dutifulness	Unreliable	Conscientious
Social assertiveness	Shy, restrained	Uninhibited, bold
Sensitivity	Tough-minded	Sensitive, caring
Paranoia	Trusting	Suspicious
Abstractness	Conventional	Imaginative
Introversion	Open, straightforward	Private, shrewd
Anxiety	Confident	Apprehensive
Open-mindedness	Closeminded, traditional	Curious, experimental
Independence	Outgoing, social	Self-sufficient
Perfectionism	Disorganized, casual	Organized, precise
Tension	Relaxed	Stressed

Table 1: Personality Factors Measured by the 16PF Questionnaire

Further Resources

Follow this link (hawkes.biz/16pf) to an assessment based on Cattell's 16PF questionnaire to see which personality traits dominate your personality.

Psychologists Hans and Sybil Eysenck were personality theorists (Figure 1) who focused on **temperament**, the inborn, genetically based personality differences. The Eysencks (Eysenck, 1990, 1992; Eysenck & Eysenck, 1963) viewed people as having two specific personality dimensions: extroversion/introversion and neuroticism/stability.

According to their theory, people high on the trait of extroversion are sociable, outgoing, and readily connect with others, whereas people high on the trait of introversion have a higher need to be alone, engage in solitary behaviors, and limit their interactions with others. In the neuroticism/stability dimension, people high on neuroticism tend to be anxious and even with low stress, their bodies and emotional state tend to go into a flight-or-fight reaction. In contrast, people high on stability tend to need more stimulation to activate their flight-or-fight reaction and are considered more emotionally stable. Based on these two dimensions, the Eysencks' theory divides people into four quadrants. These quadrants are sometimes compared with the four temperaments described by the Greeks: melancholic, choleric, phlegmatic, and sanguine (Figure 2).

Later, the Eysencks added a third dimension: psychoticism versus superego control (Eysenck, Eysenck & Barrett, 1985). In this dimension, people who are high on psychoticism tend to be independent thinkers, cold, nonconformists, impulsive, antisocial, and hostile, whereas people who are high on superego control tend to have high impulse control—they are more altruistic, empathetic, cooperative, and conventional (Eysenck, Eysenck & Barrett, 1985).

Figure 1: Hans and Sybil Eysenck believed that our personality traits are influenced by our genetic inheritance.

Figure 2: The Eysencks described two factors to account for variations in our personalities: extroversion/introversion and emotional stability/instability.

Another personality theory, called the **Five Factor Model**, effectively hits a middle ground, with its five factors referred to as the Big Five personality traits (Figure 3). The five traits include the following:

- *Openness to experience* is characterized by imagination, feelings, actions, and ideas. People who score high on this trait tend to be curious and have a wide range of interests.

- *Conscientiousness* is characterized by competence, self-discipline, thoughtfulness, and achievement-striving (goal-directed behavior). People who score high on this trait are hardworking and dependable. Numerous studies have found a positive correlation between conscientiousness and academic success (Akomolafe, 2013; Chamorro-Premuzic & Furnham, 2008; Conrad & Patry, 2012; Noftle & Robins, 2007; Wagerman & Funder, 2007).

- *Extroversion* is characterized by sociability, assertiveness, excitement-seeking, and emotional expression. People who score high on this trait are usually described as outgoing and warm. Not surprisingly, people who score high on both extroversion and openness are more likely to participate in adventure and risky sports due to their curious and excitement-seeking nature (Tok, 2011).

- *Agreeableness* is the tendency to be pleasant, cooperative, trustworthy, and good-natured. People who score low on agreeableness tend to be described as rude and uncooperative, yet one recent study reported that men who scored low on this trait earned more money than men who were considered more agreeable (Judge, Livingston, & Hurst, 2012).

- *Neuroticism* is the tendency to experience negative emotions. People high on neuroticism tend to experience emotional instability and are characterized as angry, impulsive, and hostile. Watson and Clark (1984) found that people reporting high levels of neuroticism also tend to report feeling anxious and unhappy. In contrast, people who score low in neuroticism tend to be calm and even-tempered.

Reflection Questions

Do you think you would score high or low on certain Five Factor Model personality traits? If so, which ones and why?

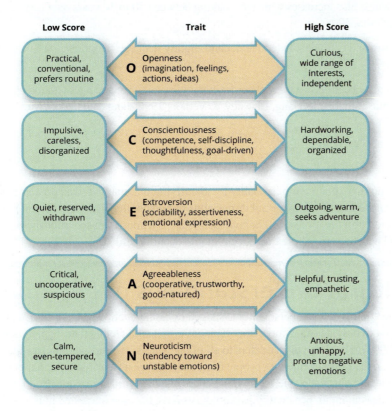

🖼 **Figure 3:** In the Five Factor Model, each person has five traits that are scored on a continuum from high to low. In the center column, notice that the first letter of each trait spells the mnemonic OCEAN.

✎ On Your Own

Answer the following questions based on the Five Factor Model.

1. Tom has never missed a day of school and makes straight *A*'s at school. This information suggests that Tom would score high in:

☐ Neuroticism   ☐ Extroversion   ☐ Openness

☐ Agreeableness   ☐ Conscientiousness

2. Mary loves to travel to foreign countries because she is very curious about how their lives differ from those in the United States. She loves trying new foreign cuisines and enjoys trying new activities. She has even been skydiving before. Mary also has a very diverse group of friends. Based on the information presented, Mary would likely score high in which of the following Five Factor Model traits?

☐ Neuroticism   ☐ Extroversion   ☐ Openness

☐ Agreeableness   ☐ Conscientiousness

The Big Five personality factors each represent a range between two extremes. In reality, most of us tend to lie somewhere midway along the continuum of each factor, rather than at polar ends. It's important to note that the Big Five traits are relatively stable over our lifespan, with some tendency for the traits to increase or decrease slightly. Researchers have found that:

- Conscientiousness increases through young adulthood into middle age, as we become better able to manage our personal relationships and careers (Donnellan & Lucas, 2008).

- Agreeableness also increases with age, peaking between 50 to 70 years old (Terracciano, McCrae, Brant, & Costa, 2005).

- Neuroticism and extroversion tend to decline slightly with age (Donnellan & Lucas; Terracciano et al.).

The Big Five traits have been shown to exist across ethnicities, cultures, and ages and may have substantial biological and genetic components (Jang, Livesley, & Vernon, 1996; Jang et al., 2006; McCrae & Costa, 1997; Schmitt et al., 2007).

Summary

Trait theorists attempt to explain our personality by identifying our stable characteristics and ways of behaving. They have identified important dimensions of personality. The Five Factor Model is the most widely accepted trait theory today. The five factors are openness, conscientiousness, extroversion, agreeableness, and neuroticism. These traits occur along a continuum.

10.8 Cultural Understandings of Personality

As you have learned in this chapter, personality is shaped by both genetic and environmental factors. The culture in which you live is one of the most important environmental factors that shapes your personality (Triandis & Suh, 2002). The term **culture** refers to all of the beliefs, customs, art, and traditions of a particular society. Culture is transmitted to people through language as well as through the modeling of culturally acceptable and nonacceptable behaviors that are either rewarded or punished (Triandis & Suh, 2002). With these ideas in mind, personality psychologists have become interested in the role of culture in understanding personality. They ask whether personality traits are the same across cultures or if there are variations. It appears that there are both universal and culture-specific aspects that account for variation in people's personalities.

Figure 1: Our cultures can greatly impact the way we think and interact.

Further Resources

To find out about your personality and where you fall on the Big Five traits, follow this link (hawkes.biz/big5test) to take the Big Five personality test.

Flash Forward

Ready to dig into the vocabulary? Get some practice with this Hawkes Verified Quizlet set (hawkes.biz/psych10q8)!

Group Activity

Socialization is the process where a child slowly acquires a set of habits, attitudes, traits, and ways of behaving that allows him to operate in the group he is a member of.

In small groups, list different types of learned behaviors or beliefs that depend on where we are born or where we grow up. How might that impact how others perceive a child's personality?

Why might it be important to consider cultural influences on personality? Western ideas about personality may not be applicable to other cultures (Benet-Martinez & Oishi, 2008). In fact, there is evidence that the strength of personality traits varies across cultures. Let's take a look at some of the Big Five factors (conscientiousness, neuroticism, openness, and extroversion) across cultures. As you will learn when you study social psychology, Asian cultures are more collectivist, and people in these cultures tend to be less extroverted. People in Central and South American cultures tend to score higher on openness to experience, whereas Europeans score higher on neuroticism (Benet-Martinez & Karakitapoglu-Aygun, 2003).

According to this study, there also seem to be regional personality differences within the United States (Figure 3). Researchers analyzed responses from over 1.5 million individuals in the United States and found that there are three distinct regional personality clusters: Cluster 1, which is in the Upper Midwest and Deep South, is dominated by people who fall into the "friendly and conventional" personality; Cluster 2, which includes the West, is dominated by people who are more relaxed, emotionally stable, calm, and creative; and Cluster 3, which includes the Northeast, has more people who are stressed, irritable, and depressed. People who live in Clusters 2 and 3 are also generally more open (Rentfrow et al., 2013).

Figure 2: Aboriginal men play music on a didgeridoo and wooden instruments.

One explanation for the regional differences is **selective migration** (Rentfrow et al., 2013). Selective migration is the concept that people choose to move to places that are compatible with their personalities and needs. For example, a person high on the agreeable scale would likely want to live near family and friends and would choose to settle or remain in such an area. In contrast, someone high on openness would prefer to settle in a place that is recognized as diverse and innovative (such as California).

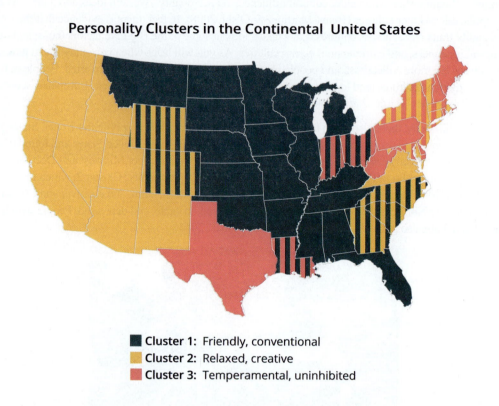

Personality Clusters in the Continental United States

■ Cluster 1: Friendly, conventional
■ Cluster 2: Relaxed, creative
■ Cluster 3: Temperamental, uninhibited

Figure 3: Researchers found three distinct regional personality clusters in the United States. People tend to be friendly and conventional in the Upper Midwest and Deep South; relaxed, emotionally stable, and creative in the West; and stressed, irritable, and depressed in the Northeast (Rentfrow et al., 2013).

Personality in Individualist and Collectivist Cultures

Individualist cultures and collectivist cultures place emphasis on different basic values. People who live in individualist cultures tend to believe that independence, competition, and personal achievement are important. Individuals in Western nations such as the United States, England, and Australia score high on individualism (Oyserman, Coon, & Kemmelmier, 2002). People who live in collectivist cultures value social harmony, respectfulness, and group needs over individual needs. Individuals who live in countries in Asia, Africa, and South America score high on collectivism (Hofstede, 2001; Triandis, 1995). These values influence personality. For example, Yang (2006) found that people in individualist cultures displayed more personally oriented personality traits, whereas people in collectivist cultures displayed more socially oriented personality traits.

Reflection Questions

Consider your personal experience with collectivistic and individualistic cultures, in real life, through media, etc., and answer the following questions:

1. In which culture would you expect a greater degree of happiness? Why?

2. In which culture would you expect a higher crime rate? Why?

3. How might students in such cultures react differently to personal success and failure?

4. How and why might individuals in these two cultures have different orientations to dealing with time? What would be an easy way to examine cross-cultural comparisons to time orientation?

One answer: "In which culture would you expect a greater degree of happiness? In a survey of nations that included 75% of the world's population, the level of happiness was positively associated with the degree to which a country was rated as individualistic (Diener, Diener, & Diener, 1995). Feelings of independence and autonomy tend to contribute to a greater sense of life satisfaction for those individuals living in individualistic cultures (Lucas & Diener, 2008). Such individuals tend to be happier because their life choices reflect their personal needs and values to a greater degree than individuals whose choices reflect more the needs and values of others. For example, a young female who is allowed to marry someone she selects for herself after deciding to attend college is likely to feel more happy than a young female who marries the man selected by her parents and enters the family business instead of pursuing her desire to attend college" (Carducci, 2012).

Read this study summary (hawkes.biz/culturepersonality) to find out what research has to say about the differences between cultures and personality.

Approaches to Studying Personality in a Cultural Context

There are three approaches that can be used to study personality in a cultural context: the *cultural-comparative approach*, the *indigenous approach*, and the *combined approach*, which incorporates elements of both views. Since ideas about personality have a Western basis, the cultural-comparative approach seeks to test Western ideas about personality in other cultures to determine whether they can be generalized and if they have cultural validity (Cheung van de Vijver, & Leong, 2011). For example, recall from the lesson on the trait perspective that researchers used the cultural-comparative approach to test the universality of McCrae and Costa's Five Factor Model. They found applicability in numerous cultures around the world, with the Big Five traits being stable in many cultures (McCrae & Costa, 1997; McCrae et al., 2005). The indigenous approach came about in reaction to the dominance of Western approaches to the study of personality in non-Western settings (Cheung et al., 2011). Because Western-based personality assessments cannot fully capture the personality constructs of other cultures, the indigenous model has led to the development of personality assessment instruments that are based on constructs relevant to the culture being studied (Cheung et al., 2011). The third approach to cross-cultural studies of personality is the combined approach, which serves as a bridge between Western and indigenous psychology as a way of understanding both universal and cultural variations in personality (Cheung et al., 2011).

Summary

The culture in which you live is one of the most important environmental factors that shapes your personality. Western ideas about personality may not be applicable to other cultures. In fact, there is evidence that the strength of personality traits varies across cultures. Individualist cultures and collectivist cultures place emphasis on different basic values. People who live in individualist cultures tend to believe that independence, competition, and personal achievement are important. People who live in collectivist cultures value social harmony, respectfulness, and group needs over individual needs. There are three approaches that can be used to study personality in a cultural context: the cultural-comparative approach, the indigenous approach, and the combined approach, which incorporates both elements of both views.

Flash Forward

Ready to dig into the vocabulary? Get some practice with this Hawkes Verified Quizlet set (hawkes.biz/psych10q9)!

10.9 Personality Assessment

Roberto, Mikhail, and Nat are college friends who all want to be police officers. Roberto is quiet and shy, lacks self-confidence, and usually follows others. He is a kind person but lacks motivation. Mikhail is loud and boisterous, a leader. He works hard but is impulsive and drinks too much on the weekends. Nat is thoughtful and well liked. He is trustworthy but sometimes he has difficulty making quick decisions. Of these three men, who would make the best police officer? What qualities and personality factors make someone a good police officer? What makes someone a bad or dangerous police officer?

A police officer's job is very stressful, and law enforcement agencies want to make sure they hire the right people. Personality testing is often used for this purpose—to screen applicants for employment and job training. Personality tests are also used in criminal cases and custody battles and to assess psychological disorders. This lesson explores the best known among the many different types of personality tests.

Self-Report Inventories

Self-report inventories are a kind of objective test used to assess personality. They typically use multiple-choice items or numbered scales, which represent a range from 1 (strongly disagree) to 5 (strongly agree). They often are called Likert scales after their developer, Rensis Likert (1932) (Figure 1).

Figure 1: If you've ever taken a survey, you are probably familiar with Likert-type scale questions. Most personality inventories employ these types of response scales.

One of the most widely used personality inventories is the **Minnesota Multiphasic Personality Inventory (MMPI)**, first published in 1943, with 504 true/false questions, and updated to the MMPI-2 in 1989, with 567 questions. The MMPI-2 takes 1–2 hours to complete and responses include 10 scales: hypochondriasis, depression, hysteria, psychopathic deviance (social deviance), masculinity versus femininity, paranoia, psychasthenia (obsessive/compulsive qualities), schizophrenia, hypomania, and social introversion. In 2008, the test was again revised, using more advanced methods, to the MMPI-2-RF. This version takes about one-half the time to complete and has only 338 questions (Figure 2). Despite the new test's advantages, the MMPI-2 is more established and is still more widely used. Although the MMPI was originally developed to assist in the clinical diagnosis of psychological disorders, it is now also used for occupational screening, such as in law enforcement and in college, career, and marital counseling (Ben-Porath & Tellegen, 2008).

1. I like gardening magazines.

True   False

2. I am unhappy with my sex life.

True   False

3. I feel like no one understands me.

True   False

4. I think I would enjoy the work of a teacher.

True   False

5. I am not easy awakened by noise.

True   False

Figure 2: These true/false questions resemble the kinds of questions you would find on the MMPI.

In addition to clinical scales, the tests also have validity and reliability scales. These scales help distinguish between responses that represent one's true self or if they are trying to put on a positive or negative impression. For example, someone who applies to a job may present themselves more positively, whereas an individual who is feigning a mental disorder may over report their symptoms. Impression management is an important aspect of psychological testing, which should be considered in any self-report psychological assessment.

Projective Tests

Another method for assessment of personality is **projective testing**. This kind of test relies on one of the defense mechanisms proposed by Freud—projection—as a way to assess unconscious processes. During this type of testing, a series of ambiguous cards is shown to the person being tested, who then is encouraged to project his feelings, impulses, and desires onto the cards—by telling a story, interpreting an image, or completing a sentence. A challenge with projective tests is that scores and interpretations can vary from clinician to clinician, which makes it less valid and reliable (Aronow, Weiss, & Rezinkoff, 2001; Lilienfeld, Wood, & Garb, 2000).

Many projective tests have undergone standardization procedures (for example, Exner, 2002) and can be used to assess whether someone has unusual thoughts, has a high level of anxiety, or is likely to become volatile. Some examples of projective tests are the Rorschach Inkblot Test, the Thematic Apperception Test (TAT), the Contemporized-Themes Concerning Blacks test, the TEMAS (Tell-Me-A-Story), and the Rotter Incomplete Sentence Blank (RISB).

The **Rorschach Inkblot Test** was developed in 1921 by a Swiss psychologist named Hermann Rorschach (pronounced "ROAR-shock"). It is a series of symmetrical inkblot cards that are presented to a client by a psychologist. Upon presentation of each card, the psychologist asks the client, "What might this be?" What the test-taker sees reveals unconscious feelings and struggles (Piotrowski, 1987; Weiner, 2003). The Rorschach has been standardized using the Exner system and is effective in measuring depression, psychosis, and anxiety.

Figure 3: The Rorschach inkblot is one of the most commonly known forms of projective tests.

A second projective test is the **Thematic Apperception Test (TAT)**, created in the 1930s by Henry Murray, an American psychologist, and a psychoanalyst named Christiana Morgan. A person taking the TAT is shown 8–12 ambiguous pictures and is asked to tell a story about each picture. The stories give insight into their social world, revealing hopes, fears, interests, and goals. The storytelling format helps to lower a person's resistance divulging unconscious personal details (Cramer, 2004). The TAT has been used in clinical settings to evaluate psychological disorders, and more recently, it has been used in counseling settings to help clients gain a better understanding of themselves and achieve personal growth. Standardization of test administration is virtually nonexistent among clinicians, and the test tends to be modest to low on validity and reliability (Aronow, Weiss, & Rezinkoff, 2001; Lilienfeld, Wood, & Garb, 2000). Despite these shortcomings, the TAT has been one of the most widely used projective tests.

A third projective test is the **Rotter Incomplete Sentence Blank (RISB)** developed by Julian Rotter in 1950 (recall his theory of locus of control, covered earlier in this chapter). There are three forms of this test for use with different age groups: the school form, the college form, and the adult form. The tests include 40 incomplete sentences that people are asked to complete as quickly as possible (Figure 5). The average time for completing the test is approximately 20 minutes, as responses are only 1–2 words in length. This test is similar to a word association test, and like other types of projective tests, it is presumed that responses will reveal desires, fears, and struggles. The RISB is used in screening college students for adjustment problems and in career counseling (Holaday, Smith, & Sherry, 2010; Rotter & Rafferty 1950).

Figure 4: Inkblots can come in a variety of styles, but standardization can increase reliability and validity.

1. I feel...

2. I regret...

3. At home...

4. My mother...

5. My greatest worry...

Figure 5: These incomplete sentences resemble the types of questions on the RISB. How would you complete these sentences?

For many decades, these traditional projective tests have been used in cross-cultural personality assessments. However, it was found that test bias limited their usefulness (Hoy-Watkins & Jenkins-Moore, 2008). It is difficult to assess the personalities and lifestyles of members of widely divergent ethnic/cultural groups using personality instruments based on data from a single culture or race (Hoy-Watkins & Jenkins-Moore, 2008). For example, when the TAT was used with African-American test takers, the result was often shorter story length and low levels of cultural identification (Duzant, 2005). Therefore, it was vital to develop other personality assessments that explored factors such as race, language, and level of acculturation (Hoy-Watkins & Jenkins-Moore, 2008). To address this need, Robert Williams developed the first culturally specific projective test designed to reflect the everyday life experiences of African Americans (Hoy-Watkins & Jenkins-Moore, 2008).

The updated version of the instrument is the **Contemporized-Themes Concerning Blacks Test (C-TCB)** (Williams, 1972). The C-TCB contains 20 color images that show scenes of African-American lifestyles. When the C-TCB was compared with the TAT for African Americans, it was found that use of the C-TCB led to increased story length, higher degrees of positive feelings, and stronger identification with the C-TCB (Hoy, 1997; Hoy-Watkins & Jenkins-Moore, 2008).

The **TEMAS Multicultural Thematic Apperception Test** is another tool designed to be culturally relevant to minority groups, especially Hispanic youths. TEMAS—standing for "Tell Me a Story" but also a play on the Spanish word *temas* (*themes*)—uses images and storytelling cues that relate to minority culture (Constantino, 1982).

☑ On Your Own

Based on what you know about psychological assessments, which test do you think has the highest reliability?

☐ Rorschach Inkblot Test   ☐ Thematic Apperception Test   ☐ MMPI-2

Summary

Personality tests are techniques designed to measure one's personality. They are used to diagnose psychological problems as well as to screen candidates for college and employment.

There are two types of personality tests: self-report inventories and projective tests. The MMPI is one of the most common self-report inventories. It asks a series of true/false questions that are designed to provide a clinical profile of an individual.

Projective tests use ambiguous images or other ambiguous stimuli to assess an individual's unconscious fears, desires, and challenges. The Rorschach Inkblot Test, the TAT, the RISB, and the C-TCB are all forms of projective tests.

🔖 Chapter 10 Project

Purpose

Personality refers to the long-standing traits and patterns that propel individuals to consistently think, feel, and behave in specific ways; it is what makes each individual unique. Psychologists study the factors that contribute to personality development. These factors are varied and include biological and social influences. **The purpose of this project is to better understand what personality is and how it is influenced.**

Directions

For this project, you will be studying one person. You may choose to study yourself or someone you know well, such as a parent or close friend. If you choose to study someone else, share the scope of this project with them and obtain permission to use them as your subject before beginning.

After identifying your subject, consider and/or discuss who your subject is as a person and the factors that have helped to shape their traits, characteristics, and coping mechanisms. It may help to create a list of interview questions based on information from the chapter in order to fully investigate this question. Take notes as you explore the question "Who Am I?" with your subject.

After completing your exploration of personality with your subject, answer the following questions. Your answers should reflect an understanding of your subject's personality as well as an understanding of the key concepts from psychology pertaining to personality and personality development. Use specific information from the chapter to build and support the points you make about who your subject is and the factors that helped to shape them.

1. Briefly describe your subject and their personality. In your discussion, specifically describe how your subject sees their real and ideal self. Is there congruence?

2. Identity your subject's key cardinal, central, and secondary personality traits. Record them in the following table.

Cardinal Traits	Central Traits	Secondary Traits

3. Describe your subject's social context. How has it influenced their personality and the behaviors they engage in?

4. Identify which archetypes have influenced your subject's personality. Discuss the impact these archetypes have had.

5. Which, if any, traits does your subject identify as inherited? In other words, how has heritability influenced your subject's temperament?

Materials

None required.

✅ Checklist

- ☐ Description of subject
- ☐ Subject's key cardinal, central, and secondary traits identified
- ☐ Description of subject's social context
- ☐ Subject's archetypes identified and discussed
- ☐ Description of inherited traits

Chapter 10 Review

Lesson Summaries

10.1 What Is Personality?

Personality has been studied for over 2,000 years, beginning with Hippocrates. More recent theories of personality have been proposed, including Freud's psychodynamic perspective, which holds that personality is formed through early childhood experiences. Other perspectives then emerged in reaction to the psychodynamic perspective, including the learning, humanistic, biological, trait, and cultural perspectives.

10.2 Freud and the Psychodynamic Perspective

Sigmund Freud presented the first comprehensive theory of personality. He was also the first to recognize that much of our mental life takes place beyond our conscious awareness. Freud also proposed three components to our personality: the id, ego, and superego. The job of the ego is to balance the sexual and aggressive drives of the id with the moral ideal of the superego. Freud also said that personality develops through a series of psychosexual stages. In each stage, pleasure focuses on a specific erogenous zone. Failure to resolve a stage can lead one to become fixated in that stage, leading to unhealthy personality traits. Successful resolution of the stages leads to a healthy adult.

10.3 Neo-Freudians: Adler, Erikson, Jung, and Horney

The neo-Freudians were psychologists whose work followed from Freud's. They generally agreed with Freud that childhood experiences matter, but they decreased the emphasis on sex and focused more on the social environment and effects of culture on personality. Some of the notable neo-Freudians are Alfred Adler, Carl Jung, Erik Erikson, and Karen Horney. The neo-Freudian

approaches have been criticized because they tend to be philosophical rather than based on sound scientific research. For example, Jung's conclusions about the existence of the collective unconscious are based on myths, legends, dreams, and art. In addition, as with Freud's psychoanalytic theory, the neo-Freudians based much of their theories of personality on information from their patients.

10.4 Learning Approaches

Behavioral theorists view personality as significantly shaped and impacted by the reinforcements and consequences outside of the organism. People behave in a consistent manner based on prior learning. B.F. Skinner, a prominent behaviorist, said that we demonstrate consistent behavior patterns because we have developed certain response tendencies. Mischel focused on how personal goals play a role in the self-regulation process. Albert Bandura said that one's environment can determine behavior, but at the same time, people can influence the environment with both their thoughts and behaviors, which is known as reciprocal determinism. Bandura also emphasized how we learn from watching others. He felt that this type of learning also plays a part in the development of our personality. Bandura discussed the concept of self-efficacy, which is our level of confidence in our own abilities. Rotter proposed the concept of locus of control, which refers to our beliefs about the power we have over our lives. He said that people fall along a continuum between a purely internal and a purely external locus of control. Finally, Mischel focused on how self-regulation patterns in early childhood can predict academic success and social behavior in adolescence.

10.5 Humanistic Approaches

Humanistic psychologists Abraham Maslow and Carl Rogers focused on the growth potential of healthy individuals. They believed that people strive to become self-actualized. Both Rogers's and Maslow's theories greatly contributed to our understanding of the self. They emphasized free will and self-determination, with each individual desiring to become the best person they can become.

10.6 Biological Approaches

Some aspects of our personalities are largely controlled by genetics; however, environmental factors (such as family interactions) and maturation can affect the ways in which children's personalities are expressed.

10.7 Trait Theorists

Trait theorists attempt to explain our personality by identifying our stable characteristics and ways of behaving. They have identified important dimensions of personality. The Five Factor Model is the most widely accepted trait theory today. The five factors are openness, conscientiousness, extroversion, agreeableness, and neuroticism. These traits occur along a continuum.

10.8 Cultural Understandings of Personality

The culture in which you live is one of the most important environmental factors that shapes your personality. Western ideas about personality may not be applicable to other cultures. In fact, there is evidence that the strength of personality traits varies across cultures. Individualist cultures and collectivist cultures place emphasis on different basic values. People who live in individualist cultures tend to believe that independence, competition, and personal achievement are important. People who live in collectivist cultures value social harmony, respectfulness, and group needs over individual needs. There are three approaches that can be used to study personality in a cultural context: the cultural-comparative approach, the indigenous approach, and the combined approach, which incorporates both elements of both views.

10.9 Personality Assessment

Personality tests are techniques designed to measure one's personality. They are used to diagnose psychological problems as well as to screen candidates for college and employment.

There are two types of personality tests: self-report inventories and projective tests. The MMPI is one of the most common self-report inventories. It asks a series of true/false questions that are designed to provide a clinical profile of an individual.

Projective tests use ambiguous images or other ambiguous stimuli to assess an individual's unconscious fears, desires, and challenges. The Rorschach Inkblot Test, the TAT, the RISB, and the C-TCB are all forms of projective tests.

Key Terms

Flash Back

Now that you've worked through the chapter, sharpen your vocabulary with this Hawkes Verified Quizlet set (hawkes.biz/psychch10)!

Anal Stage

Psychosexual stage in which children experience pleasure in their bowel and bladder movements

Analytical Psychology

Jung's theory focusing on the balance of opposing forces within one's personality and the significance of the collective unconscious

Archetype

Pattern that exists in our collective unconscious across cultures and societies

Collective Unconsious

Common psychological tendencies that have been passed down from one generation to the next

Congruence

State of being in which our thoughts about our real and ideal selves are very similar

Conscious

Mental activity (thoughts, feelings, and memories) that we can access at any time

Contemporized-Themes Concerning Blacks Test (C-TCB)

Projective test designed to be culturally relevant to African Americans, using images that relate to African-American culture

Culture

All of the beliefs, customs, art, and traditions of a particular society

Defense Mechanism

Unconscious protective behaviors designed to reduce ego anxiety

Displacement

Ego defense mechanism in which a person transfers inappropriate urges or behaviors toward a more acceptable or less threatening target

Ego

Aspect of personality that represents the self, or the part of one's personality that is visible to others

Five Factor Model

Theory that personality is composed of five factors or traits, including openness, conscientiousness, extroversion, agreeableness, and neuroticism

Genital Stage

Psychosexual stage in which the focus is on mature sexual interests

Heritability

Proportion of difference among people that is attributed to genetics

Id

Aspect of personality that consists of our most primitive drives or urges, including impulses for hunger, thirst, and sex

Ideal Self

Person we would like to be

Incongruence

State of being in which there is a great discrepancy between our real and ideal selves

Individual Psychology

School of psychology proposed by Adler that focuses on our drive to compensate for feelings of inferiority

Inferiority Complex

Refers to a person's feelings that they lack worth and don't measure up to others' or to society's standards

Latency Period

Psychosexual stage in which sexual feelings are dormant

Locus of Control

Beliefs about the power we have over our lives; an external locus of control is the belief that our outcomes are outside of our control; an internal locus of control is the belief that we control our own outcomes

Minnesota Multiphasic Personality Inventory (MMPI)

Personality test composed of a series of true/false questions in order to establish a clinical profile of an individual

Neurosis

Tendency to experience negative emotions

Oral Stage

Psychosexual stage in which an infant's pleasure is focused on the mouth

Personality

Long-standing traits and patterns that propel individuals to consistently think, feel, and behave in specific ways

Phallic Stage

Psychosexual stage in which the focus is on the genitals

Projection

Ego defense mechanism in which a person confronted with anxiety disguises their unacceptable urges or behaviors by attributing them to other people

Projective Test

Personality assessment in which a person responds to ambiguous stimuli, revealing hidden feelings, impulses, and desires

Psychosexual Stages of Development

Stages of child development in which a child's pleasure-seeking urges are focused on specific areas of the body called erogenous zones

Rationalization

Ego defense mechanism in which a person confronted with anxiety makes excuses to justify behavior

Reaction Formation

Ego defense mechanism in which a person confronted with anxiety swaps unacceptable urges or behaviors for their opposites

Real Self

Person we actually are

Reciprocal Determinism

Belief that one's environment can determine behavior, but at the same time, people can influence the environment with both their thoughts and behaviors

Regression

Ego defense mechanism in which a person confronted with anxiety returns to a more immature behavioral state

Repression

Ego defense mechanism in which anxiety-related thoughts and memories are kept in the unconscious

Rorschach Inkblot Test

Projective test that employs a series of symmetrical inkblot cards that are presented to a client by a psychologist in an effort to reveal the person's unconscious desires, fears, and struggles

Rotter Incomplete Sentence Blank (RISB)

Projective test that is similar to a word association test in which a person completes sentences in order to reveal their unconscious desires, fears, and struggles

Selective Migration

Concept that people choose to move to places that are compatible with their personalities and needs

Self-Concept

Our thoughts and feelings about ourselves

Self-Efficacy

Someone's level of confidence in their own abilities

Social-Cognitive Theory

Bandura's theory of personality that emphasizes both cognition and learning as sources of individual differences in personality

Sublimation

Ego defense mechanism in which unacceptable urges are channeled into more appropriate activities

Superego

Aspect of the personality that serves as one's moral compass, or conscience

TEMAS Multicultural Thematic Apperception Test

Projective test designed to be culturally relevant to minority groups, especially Hispanic youths, using images and storytelling that relate to minority culture

Temperament

How a person reacts to the world, including their activity level, starting when they are very young

Thematic Apperception Test (TAT)

Projective test in which people are presented with ambiguous images, and they then make up stories to go with the images in an effort to uncover their unconscious desires, fears, and struggles

Traits

Characteristic ways of behaving

Unconscious

Mental activity of which we are unaware and unable to access

⚡ Exercises

Review Questions

1. Personality is thought to be _____.

    a. short term and easily changed

    b. a pattern of short-term characteristics

    c. unstable and short term

    d. long term, stable, and not easily changed

2. The long-standing traits and patterns that propel individuals to consistently think, feel, and behave in specific ways are known as _____.

    a. psychodynamic

    b. temperament

    c. humors

    d. personality

3. _____ is credited with the first comprehensive theory of personality.

    a. Hippocrates

    b. Gall

    c. Wundt

    d. Freud

4. An early science that tried to correlate personality with measurements of parts of a person's skull is known as _____.

    a. phrenology

    b. psychology

    c. physiology

    d. personality psychology

5. The id operates on the _____ principle.

    a. reality

    b. pleasure

    c. instant gratification

    d. guilt

6. The ego defense mechanism in which a person who is confronted with anxiety returns to a more immature behavioral stage is called _____.

    a. repression

    b. regression

    c. reaction formation

    d. rationalization

7. The Oedipus complex occurs in the _____ stage of psychosexual development.

    a. oral

    b. anal

    c. phallic

    d. latency

8. The universal bank of ideas, images, and concepts that have been passed down through the generations from our ancestors refers to _____.

    a. archetypes

    b. intuition

    c. collective unconscious

    d. personality types

9. Self-regulation is also known as _____.

    a. self-efficacy

    b. will power

    c. internal locus of control

    d. external locus of control

10. Your level of confidence in your own abilities is known as _____.

    a. self-efficacy

    b. self-concept

    c. self-control

    d. self-esteem

11. Jane believes that she got a bad grade on her psychology paper because her professor doesn't like her. Jane most likely has an _____ locus of control.

   a. internal

   b. external

   c. intrinsic

   d. extrinsic

12. Self-concept refers to _____ .

   a. our level of confidence in our own abilities

   b. all of our thoughts and feelings about ourselves

   c. the belief that we control our own outcomes

   d. the belief that our outcomes are outside of our control

13. The idea that people's ideas about themselves should match their actions is called _____ .

   a. confluence

   b. conscious

   c. conscientiousness

   d. congruence

14. The way a person reacts to the world, starting when they are very young, including the person's activity level is known as _____ .

   a. traits

   b. temperament

   c. heritability

   d. personality

15. Brianna is 18 months old. She cries frequently, is hard to soothe, and wakes frequently during the night. According to Thomas and Chess, she would be considered _____ .

   a. an easy baby

   b. a difficult baby

   c. a slow to warm up baby

   d. a colicky baby

16. According to the findings of the Minnesota Study of Twins Reared Apart, identical twins, whether raised together or apart have _____ personalities.

   a. slightly different

   b. very different

   c. slightly similar

   d. very similar

17. Temperament refers to _____ .

   a. inborn, genetically based personality differences

   b. characteristic ways of behaving

   c. conscientiousness, agreeableness, neuroticism, openness, and extroversion

   d. degree of introversion-extroversion

18. According to the Eysencks' theory, people who score high on neuroticism tend to be _____ .

   a. calm

   b. stable

   c. outgoing

   d. anxious

19. The United States is considered a(n) _____ culture.

   a. collectivistic

   b. individualist

   c. traditional

   d. nontraditional

20. The concept that people choose to move to places that are compatible with their personalities and needs is known as _____ .

   a. selective migration

   b. personally oriented personality

   c. socially oriented personality

   d. individualism

21. Which of the following is *not* a projective test?

   a. Minnesota Multiphasic Personality Inventory (MMPI)

   b. Rorschach Inkblot Test

   c. Thematic Apperception Test (TAT)

   d. Rotter Incomplete Sentence Blank (RISB)

22. A personality assessment in which a person responds to ambiguous stimuli, revealing unconscious feelings, impulses, and desires is a _____.

    a. self-report inventory

    b. projective test

    c. Minnesota Multiphasic Personality Inventory (MMPI)

    d. Myers-Briggs Type Indicator (MBTI)

23. Which personality assessment employs a series of true/false questions?

    a. Minnesota Multiphasic Personality Inventory (MMPI)

    b. Thematic Apperception Test (TAT)

    c. Rotter Incomplete Sentence Blank (RISB)

    d. Myers-Briggs Type Indicator (MBTI)

Critical Thinking Questions

24. What makes a personal quality part of someone's personality?

25. How might the common expression "daddy's girl" be rooted in the idea of the Electra complex?

26. Describe the personality of someone who is fixated at the anal stage.

27. Describe the difference between extroverts and introverts in terms of what is energizing to each.

28. Discuss Horney's perspective on Freud's concept of penis envy.

29. Compare the personalities of someone who has high self-efficacy to someone who has low self-efficacy.

30. Compare and contrast Skinner's perspective on personality development to Freud's.

31. How might a temperament mix between parent and child affect family life?

32. How stable are the Big Five traits over one's lifespan?

33. Compare the personality of someone who scores high on agreeableness to someone who scores low on agreeableness.

34. Why might it be important to consider cultural influences on personality?

35. Why might a prospective employer screen applicants using personality assessments?

36. Why would a clinician give someone a projective test?

Chapter Introduction

📷 **Figure 1:** Trayvon Martin, 17, was shot to death at the hands of George Zimmerman, a volunteer neighborhood watchman, in 2012. While Zimmerman claimed it was in self-defense, hundreds of people rallied to question the role of racial bias in the murder.

Humans are diverse, and sometimes our differences are fault lines of tension and conflict between us. A poignant example is that of Trayvon Martin, a 17-year-old African American who was shot by a neighborhood watch volunteer, George Zimmerman, in a predominantly White neighborhood in 2012. Zimmerman grew suspicious of the boy dressed in a hoodie and pursued Martin. A physical altercation ended with Zimmerman fatally shooting Martin. Zimmerman claimed that he acted in self-defense; Martin was unarmed. A Florida jury found Zimmerman not guilty of second degree murder nor of manslaughter.

Several groups protested what they deemed racial profiling and brutality against an unarmed Black male. Zimmerman, who has a Peruvian mother and a German father, was accused of being racist. Some media coverage was criticized for inflaming racial politics in their coverage.

In spite of conflicts such as these, people also work together to create positive change. Martin's death, and the controversy surrounding the deaths of many more young, unarmed Black men, united a broad coalition of Americans who have brought increased attention to racial discrimination and criminal justice in the years that followed. After the 9/11 terrorist attacks, Muslims in America faced increased discrimination, yet people also rallied together and charitable donations skyrocketed (Brown & Minty, 2006). This chapter explores how the presence of other people influences the behavior of individuals, dyads, and groups. Social factors can determine whether human behavior tends toward conflict or harmony.

Flash Forward

Ready to dig into the vocabulary? Get some practice with this Hawkes Verified Quizlet set (hawkes.biz/psych11q1)!

11.1   What Is Social Psychology?

Social psychology examines how people affect one another, and it looks at the power of the situation. Social psychologists assert that an individual's thoughts, feelings, and behaviors are very much influenced by social situations. Essentially, people will change their behavior to align with the social situation at hand. If we are in a new situation or are unsure how to behave, we will take our cues from other individuals.

The field of social psychology studies topics at both the intra- and interpersonal levels. Intrapersonal topics (those that pertain to the individual) include emotions and attitudes, the self, and social cognition (the ways in which we think about ourselves and others). Interpersonal topics (those that pertain to dyads and groups) include helping behavior (Figure 2), aggression, prejudice and discrimination, attraction and close relationships, and group processes and intergroup relationships.

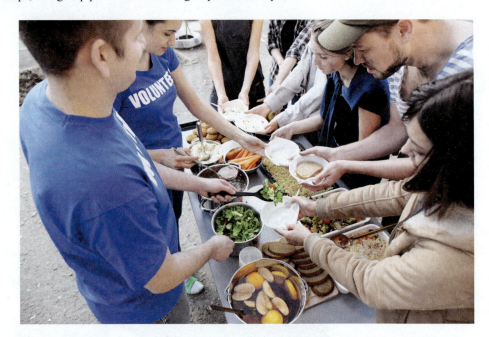

Figure 2: Social psychology deals with all kinds of interactions between people, spanning a wide range of how we connect: from moments of confrontation to moments of working together and helping others, as shown here.

Social psychologists focus on how people construe or interpret situations and how these interpretations influence their thoughts, feelings, and behaviors (Ross & Nisbett, 1991). Thus, social psychology studies individuals in a social context and how situational variables interact to influence behavior. We will discuss the intrapersonal processes of self-presentation and cognitive dissonance and attitude change; we will also look at the interpersonal processes of conformity and obedience, aggression and altruism, and, finally, love and attraction.

Situational and Dispositional Influences on Behavior

Behavior is a product of both the situation (e.g., cultural influences, social roles, and the presence of bystanders) and the person (e.g., personality characteristics). Subfields of psychology tend to focus on one influence or behavior over others. **Situationism** is the view that our behavior and actions are determined by our immediate environment and surroundings. In contrast, **dispositionism** holds that our behavior is determined by internal factors (Heider, 1958). An **internal factor** is an attribute of a person and includes personality traits and temperament. Social psychologists have tended to take the situationist perspective, whereas personality psychologists have promoted the dispositionist perspective. Modern approaches to social psychology, however, take both the situation and the individual into account when studying human behavior (Fiske, Gilbert, & Lindzey, 2010). In fact, the field of social-personality psychology has emerged to study the complex interaction of internal and situational factors that affect human behavior (Mischel, 1977; Richard, Bond, & Stokes-Zoota, 2003).

📝 **On Your Own**

Read the following scenarios and determine if the person is making a situational or dispositional attribution.

1. Today, Julie arrived late for work. Her boss thinks that she is disorganized and lazy and that is why she was late to work.

☐ Julie's boss is making a situational attribution.

☐ Julie's boss is making a dispositional attribution.

2. While driving home from school, Mike cuts off another driver when merging on to the freeway. The driver behind him thinks, "Boy, that guy must be in a rush!"

☐ The other driver is making a situational attribution.

☐ The other driver is making a dispositional attribution.

3. Makayla got a poor grade on her last psychology exam. Makayla now thinks that she isn't smart enough to be successful in college.

☐ Makayla is making a situational attribution.

☐ Makayla is making a dispositional attribution.

Fundamental Attribution Error

In the United States, the predominant culture tends to favor a dispositional approach in explaining human behavior. We tend to think that people are in control of their own behaviors, and, therefore, any behavior change must be due to something internal, such as their personality, habits, or temperament.

> ### Reflection Questions
>
> Why do you think that Americans tend to take a dispositional approach? What values or historical developments might contribute to this cultural norm?

According to some social psychologists, people tend to overemphasize internal factors as explanations—or attributions—for the behavior of other people. They tend to assume that the behavior of another person is a *trait* of that person and underestimate the power of the situation on the behavior of others. They tend to fail to recognize when the behavior of another is due to situational variables and, thus, to the person's *state*. This erroneous assumption is called the **fundamental attribution error** (Ross, 1977; Riggio & Garcia, 2009).

To better understand, imagine this scenario:

> Greg returns home from work, and upon opening the front door, his wife happily greets him and inquires about his day. Instead of greeting his wife, Greg yells at her, "Leave me alone!"

Why did Greg yell at his wife? How would someone committing the fundamental attribution error explain Greg's behavior? The most common response is that Greg is a mean, angry, or unfriendly person (his traits). This is an internal or dispositional explanation. However, imagine that Greg was just laid off from his job due to company downsizing. Would your explanation for Greg's behavior change? Your revised explanation might be that Greg was frustrated and disappointed for losing his job; therefore, he was in a bad mood (his state). This is an external or situational explanation for Greg's behavior.

The fundamental attribution error is so powerful that people often overlook obvious situational influences on behavior. A classic example was demonstrated in a series of experiments known as the quizmaster study (Ross, Amabile, & Steinmetz, 1977). Student participants were randomly assigned to play the role of a questioner (the quizmaster) or a contestant in a quiz game. Questioners developed difficult questions to which they knew the answers, and they presented these questions to the contestants. The contestants answered

🖼 **Figure 3:** Greg's negative behavior is likely the result of external factors.

> **Helpful Hint**
>
> Our tendency to give ourselves the benefit of the doubt, but not to do the same for others, may stem from an evolutionary source. Giving ourselves an external explanation for negative behavior can increase our confidence, which may allow us to take more beneficial risks. Read this article (hawkes.biz/fae) to explore the fundamental attribution error.

the questions correctly only 4 out of 10 times (Figure 4). After the task, the questioners and contestants were asked to rate their own general knowledge compared to the average student. Questioners did not rate their general knowledge higher than the contestants, but the contestants rated the questioners' intelligence higher than their own. In a second study, observers of the interaction also rated the questioner as having more general knowledge than the contestant. The obvious influence on performance is the situation. The questioners wrote the questions, so of course they had an advantage. Both the contestants and observers made an internal attribution for the performance. They concluded that the questioners must be more intelligent than the contestants.

Figure 4: In the quizmaster study, people tended to disregard the influence of the situation and wrongly concluded that a questioner's knowledge was greater than their own.

As demonstrated in the previous example, the fundamental attribution error is considered a powerful influence in how we explain the behaviors of others. However, it should be noted that some researchers have suggested that the fundamental attribution error may not be as powerful as it is often portrayed. In fact, a recent review of more than 173 published studies suggests that several factors (e.g., high levels of idiosyncrasy of the character and how well hypothetical events are explained) play a role in determining just how influential the fundamental attribution error is (Malle, 2006).

Is the Fundamental Attribution Error a Universal Phenomenon?

You may be able to think of examples of the fundamental attribution error in your life. Do people in all cultures commit the fundamental attribution error? Research suggests that they do not. People from an **individualistic culture**, that is, a culture that focuses on individual achievement and autonomy, have the greatest tendency to commit the fundamental attribution error. Individualistic cultures, found in western countries, such as the United States, Canada, and the United Kingdom, promote a focus on the individual. Therefore, a person's disposition is thought to be the primary explanation for her behavior. In contrast, people from a **collectivistic culture**, that is, a culture that focuses on communal relationships with others, such as family, friends, and community (Figure 5), are less likely to commit the fundamental attribution error (Markus & Kitayama, 1991; Triandis, 2001).

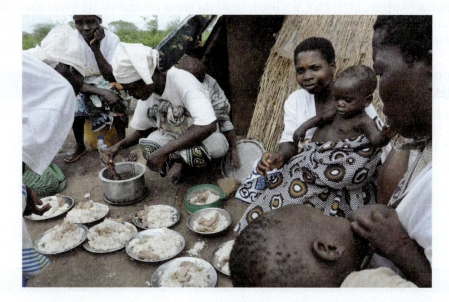

Figure 5: People from collectivistic cultures are more likely to emphasize relationships with others than to focus primarily on the individual. Activities such as preparing a meal, hanging out, and playing a game engage people in a group.

Why do you think this is the case? Collectivistic cultures, which tend to be found in east Asian countries and in Latin American and African countries, focus on the group more than on the individual (Nisbett, Peng, Choi, & Norenzayan, 2001). This focus on others provides a broader perspective that takes into account both situational and cultural influences on behavior; thus, a more nuanced explanation of the causes of others' behavior becomes more likely. Table 1 compares individualistic and collectivistic cultures.

Individualistic Culture	Collectivistic Culture
Achievement oriented	Relationship oriented
Focus on autonomy	Focus on group autonomy
Dispositional perspective	Situational perspective
Independent	Interdependent
Analytic thinking style	Holistic thinking style

Table 1: Characteristics of Individualistic and Collectivistic Cultures

Actor-Observer Bias

Returning to our earlier example, Greg knew that he lost his job, but an observer would not know. So a naïve observer would tend to attribute Greg's hostile behavior to Greg's disposition rather than to the situational cause. Why do you think we underestimate the influence of the situation on the behaviors of others? One reason is that we often don't have all the information we need to make a situational explanation for another person's behavior. The only information we might have is what is observable. Due to this lack of information, we have a tendency to assume the behavior is due to a dispositional, or internal, factor. When it comes to explaining our own behaviors, however, we have much more information available to us. If you came home from school or work angry and yelled at your dog or a loved one, what would your explanation be? You might say you were very tired or feeling unwell and needed quiet time—a situational explanation. The **actor-observer bias** is the phenomenon of attributing other people's behavior to internal factors (fundamental attribution error) while attributing our own behavior to situational forces (Jones & Nisbett, 1971; Nisbett,

Caputo, Legant, & Marecek, 1973; Choi & Nisbett, 1998). As actors of behavior, we have more information available to explain our own behavior. However as observers, we have less information available; therefore, we tend to default to a dispositionist perspective.

Figure 6: Icebergs are often used to illustrate the human psyche; the visible portions are clearly exposed, but the iceberg's true shape depends on the larger portions that are concealed beneath the surface.

✎ On Your Own

What are the similarities and differences between actor-observer bias and the fundamental attribution error?

Similarities	Differences

One study on the actor-observer bias investigated reasons male participants gave for why they liked their girlfriend (Nisbett et al., 1973). When asked why participants liked their own girlfriend, participants focused on internal, dispositional qualities of their girlfriends (for example, her pleasant personality). The participants' explanations rarely included causes internal to themselves, such as dispositional traits (for example, "I need companionship."). In contrast, when speculating why a male friend liked his girlfriend, participants were equally likely to give dispositional and external explanations. This supports the idea that actors tend to provide few internal explanations but many situational explanations for their own behavior. In contrast, observers tend to provide more dispositional explanations for a friend's behavior (Figure 7).

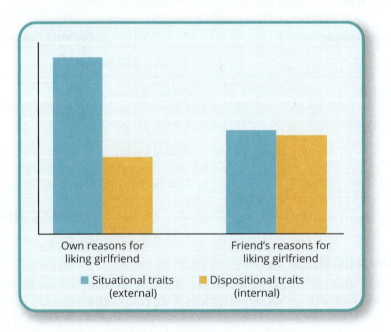

Figure 7: Actor-observer bias is evident when subjects explain their own reasons for liking a girlfriend versus their impressions of others' reasons for liking a girlfriend.

Self-Serving Bias

Following an outcome, self-serving bias are those attributions that enable us to see ourselves in favorable light (for example, making internal attributions for success and external attributions for failures). When you do well at a task, for example acing an exam, it is in your best interest to make a dispositional attribution for your behavior ("I'm smart.") instead of a situational one ("The exam was easy."). The tendency of an individual to take credit by making dispositional or internal attributions for positive outcomes but situational or external attributions for negative outcomes is known as the **self-serving bias** (Miller & Ross, 1975). This bias serves to protect self-esteem. You can imagine that if people always made situational attributions for their behavior, they would never be able to take credit and feel good about their accomplishments.

We can understand self-serving bias by digging more deeply into **attribution**, a belief about the cause of a result. One model of attribution proposes three main dimensions: locus of control (internal versus external), stability (stable versus unstable), and controllability (controllable versus uncontrollable). In this context, stability refers the extent to which the circumstances that result in a given outcome are changeable. The circumstances are considered stable if they are unlikely to change. Controllability refers to the extent to which the circumstances that are associated with a given outcome can be controlled. Obviously, those things that we have the power to control would be labeled controllable (Weiner, 1979).

Consider the example of how we explain our favorite sports team's wins. Research shows that we make internal, stable, and controllable attributions for our team's victory (Figure 8) (Grove, Hanrahan, & McInman, 1991). For example, we might tell ourselves that our team is talented (internal), consistently works hard (stable), and uses effective strategies (controllable). In contrast, we are more likely to make external, unstable, and uncontrollable attributions when our favorite team loses. For example, we might tell ourselves that the other team has more experienced players or that the referees were unfair (external), the other team played at home (unstable), and the cold weather affected our team's performance (uncontrollable).

▶ **Figure 8:** We tend to believe that our team wins because it's better but loses for reasons it cannot control (Roesch & Amirkham, 1997).

✎ On Your Own

Which of the following is *not* an example of the self-serving bias?

- ☐ Maggie won first place in her 400 meter race. She tells herself that all of the practice and hard work paid off.

- ☐ Patrick was a candidate for his student council presidency. He lost the election. Patrick believes that he lost because his opponent bribed voters with cookies.

- ☐ Elena received a failing grade on her statistics exam. She believes she is not smart enough to pass the class.

Group Activity

1. Jot down a list of your personal strengths and your perceived weaknesses.

2. Now, tally up the number of strengths and weaknesses in your respective lists.

3. Then, as a group or class, list examples of strengths and weaknesses and write them down in a central location.

4. Examine the list of "weaknesses." How many are truly negative or are less serious or "self problems" ("Well, I sometimes work too hard and expect too much of myself.")? How might this reflect a self-serving bias?

Just-World Hypothesis

One consequence of westerners' tendency to provide dispositional explanations for behavior is victim blame (Jost & Major, 2001). When people experience bad fortune, others tend to assume that they somehow are responsible for their own fate. A common ideology, or worldview, in the United States is the just-world hypothesis. The **just-world hypothesis** is the belief that people get the outcomes they deserve (Lerner & Miller, 1978). In order to maintain the belief that the world is a fair place, people tend to think that good people experience positive outcomes, and bad people experience negative outcomes (Jost, Banaji, & Nosek, 2004; Jost & Major, 2001). The ability to think of the world as a fair place, where people get what they deserve, allows us to feel that the world is predictable and that we have some control over our life outcomes (Jost et al., 2004; Jost & Major, 2001). For example, if you want to experience positive outcomes, you just need to work hard to get ahead in life.

Can you think of a negative consequence of the just-world hypothesis? One negative consequence is people's tendency to blame poor individuals for their plight. What common explanations are given for why people live in poverty? Have you heard statements such as, "The poor are lazy and just don't want to work" or "Poor people just want to live off the government?" What types of explanations are these, dispositional or situational? These dispositional explanations are clear examples of the fundamental attribution error. Blaming poor people for their poverty ignores situational factors that impact them, such as high unemployment rates, recession, poor educational opportunities, and the familial cycle of poverty (Figure 9). Other research shows that people who hold just-world beliefs have negative attitudes toward people who are unemployed and people living with HIV/AIDS (Sutton & Douglas, 2005). In the United States and other countries, victims of sexual assault may find themselves blamed for their abuse. Victim advocacy groups, such as Domestic Violence Ended (DOVE), attend court in support of victims to ensure that blame is directed at the perpetrators of sexual violence, not the victims.

> **Further Resources**
>
> Want to assess your belief in a just world? Check out this quiz (hawkes.biz/justworldquiz) to see how you measure up.

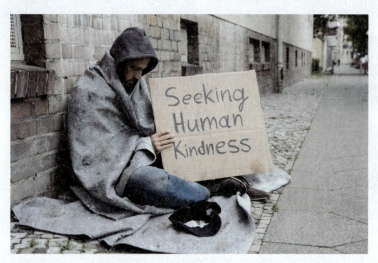

🖼 **Figure 9:** People who hold just-world beliefs tend to blame the people in poverty for their circumstances, ignoring situational and cultural causes of poverty.

> **Reflection Questions**
>
> Research shows that we are hardwired to blame the victim. Check out this blog (hawkes.biz/justworld) from the *Atlantic* on the role of just-world belief and the #metoo movement.
>
> Can you think of other examples in current news that demonstrate the effect of the just-world belief?

Summary

Social psychology is the subfield of psychology that studies the power of the situation to influence individuals' thoughts, feelings, and behaviors. Psychologists categorize the causes of human behavior as those due to internal factors, such as personality, or those due to external factors, such as cultural and other social influences. Behavior is better explained, however, by using both approaches. Lay people tend to over-rely on dispositional explanations for behavior and ignore the power of situational influences, a perspective called the fundamental attribution error. People from individualistic cultures are more likely to display this bias versus people from collectivistic cultures. Our explanations for our own and others' behaviors can be biased due to not having enough information about others' motivations for behaviors and by providing explanations that bolster our self-esteem.

11.2 Self-Presentation

As you've learned, social psychology is the study of how people affect one another's thoughts, feelings, and behaviors. We have discussed situational perspectives and social psychology's emphasis on the ways in which a person's environment, including culture and other social influences, affect behavior. In this lesson, we examine situational forces that have a strong influence on human behavior including social roles, social norms, and scripts. We discuss how humans use the social environment as a source of information, or as cues, on how to behave. Situational influences on our behavior have important consequences, such as whether we will help a stranger in an emergency or how we would behave in an unfamiliar environment.

> **Flash Forward**
>
> Ready to dig into the vocabulary? Get some practice with this Hawkes Verified Quizlet set (hawkes.biz/ psych11q2)!

✐ On Your Own

Describe how you might react in each of the following situations.

Situation	Reaction
You arrive to a new class and don't know anyone. All of your peers are quiet, and most are playing on their phones or flipping through books.	
The woman next to you at a coffee shop is sitting alone, and she suddenly begins choking.	
You want to walk across the street even though there is a red light. There is a large crowd next to you waiting for the light to change.	

🖼 **Figure 1:** These photographs are from the 1862 book *Mécanisme de la Physionomie Humaine* by Guillaume Duchenne. Through electric stimulation, he determined which muscles were responsible for different facial expressions. Facial expressions are just one type of social cue that help us communicate.

Social Roles

One major social determinant of human behavior is our social roles. A **social role** is a pattern of behavior that is expected of a person in a given setting or group (Hare, 2003). Each one of us has several social roles. You may be, at the same time, a student, a parent, an aspiring teacher, a son or daughter, a spouse, and a lifeguard. How do these social roles influence your behavior?

Social roles are defined by culturally shared knowledge. That is, nearly everyone in a given culture knows what behavior is expected of a person in a given role. For example, what is the social role for a student? If you look around a college classroom, you will likely see students engaging in studious behavior, taking notes, listening to the professor, reading the textbook, and sitting quietly at their desks (Figure 2). Of course, you may see students deviating from the expected studious behavior such as texting on their phones or scrolling through Reddit on their laptops, but in all cases, the students that you observe are attending class—a part of the social role of students.

Figure 2: Being a student is just one of the many social roles you have.

On Your Own

Look at the following photo and consider what social roles are present here. Underneath the photo, record any common social behaviors you observe based on these roles.

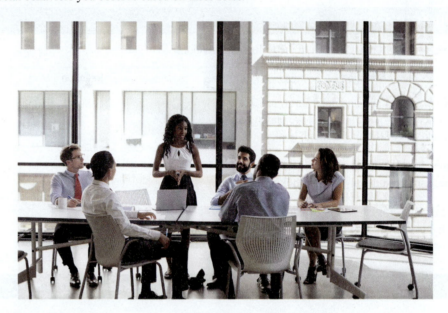

Figure 3: What kinds of social behaviors are demonstrated in this photo?

Behavioral Observations

Social roles, and our related behaviors, can vary across different settings. How do you behave when you are engaging in the role of son or daughter and attending a family function? Now imagine how you behave when you are engaged in the role of employee at your workplace. It is very likely that your behavior will be different. Perhaps you are more relaxed and outgoing with your family, making jokes and doing silly things. But at your workplace you might speak more professionally, and although you may be friendly, you are also serious and focused on getting the work completed. These are examples of how our social roles influence and often dictate our behavior to the extent that identity and personality can vary with context (that is, in different social groups) (Malloy, Albright, Kenny, Agatstein & Winquist, 1997).

Social Norms

As discussed previously, social roles are defined by a culture's shared knowledge of what is expected behavior of an individual in a specific role. This shared knowledge comes from social norms. A **social norm** is a group's expectation of what is appropriate and acceptable behavior for its members—how they are supposed to behave and think (Deutsch & Gerard, 1955; Berkowitz, 2004).

- How are we expected to act?

- What are we expected to talk about?

- What are we expected to wear?

In our discussion of social roles, we noted that colleges have social norms for students just like workplaces have social norms for employees' behaviors. Social norms are everywhere including in families, gangs, and on social media outlets.

Figure 4: Shaking hands after a sports match or game is considered a social norm.

> ### Reflection Questions
>
> What are some social norms when using Snapchat? How do people react when these norms not followed?

Consider the following examples:

- In Oscar's family, it is considered rude to bring your phone to the dinner table.

- In order to be accepted into the fraternity, all aspiring members must treat current fraternity brothers with the utmost respect.

- At Yolanda's place of employment, it is believed that discussing politics is delicate and should, therefore, be avoided.

💡 Connect the Concepts

Tweens, Teens, and Social Norms

My 11-year-old daughter, Jessica, recently told me she needed shorts and shirts for the summer and that she wanted me to take her to a store at the mall that is popular with preteens and teens to buy them. I have noticed that many girls have clothes from that store, so I tried teasing her. I said, "All the shirts say 'Aero' on the front. If you are wearing a shirt like that and you have a substitute teacher, and the other girls are all wearing that type of shirt, won't the substitute teacher think you are all named 'Aero'?"

My daughter replied, in typical 11-year-old fashion, "Mom, you are not funny. Can we please go shopping?"

I tried a different tactic. I asked Jessica if having clothing from that particular store will make her popular. She replied, "No, it will not make me popular. It is what the popular kids wear. It will make me feel happier." How can a label or name brand make someone feel happier? Think back to

> **Further Resources**
>
> Good literature often reflects truths about society. Take some time to read Shirley Jackson's "The Lottery," (hawkes.biz/socialnorms) and consider what it suggests about the power of social norms.

what you've learned about lifespan development. What is it about pre-teens and young teens that make them want to fit in (Figure 5)? Does this change over time? Think back to your high school experience, or look around your college campus. What is the main name brand clothing you see? What messages do we get from the media about how to fit in?

Figure 5: Young people struggle to become independent at the same time they are desperately trying to fit in with their peers.

Scripts

Because of social roles, people tend to know what behavior is expected of them in specific, familiar settings. A **script** is a person's knowledge about the sequence of events expected in a specific setting (Schank & Abelson, 1977). How do you act on the first day of school, when you walk into an elevator, or are at a restaurant? For example, at a restaurant in the United States, if we want the server's attention, we try to make eye contact. In Brazil, you would make the sound "psst" to get the server's attention. You can see the cultural differences in scripts. To an American, saying "psst" to a server might seem rude, yet to a Brazilian, trying to make eye contact might not seem an effective strategy. Scripts are important sources of information to guide behavior in given situations. Can you imagine being in an unfamiliar situation and not having a script for how to behave? This could be uncomfortable and confusing. How could you find out about social norms in an unfamiliar culture?

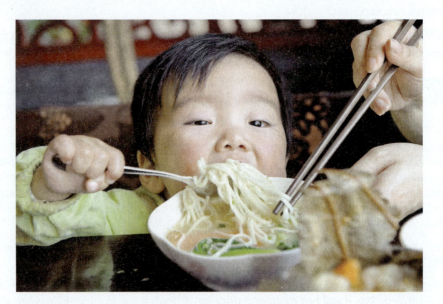

Figure 6: Slurping is often perceived as rude in the U.S., but in Japanese and other Asian cultures, slurping noodles is a sign of appreciation and recognition of a delicious meal.

✎ On Your Own

Read through the following scenario and select any examples of scripts in action.

> Marcy woke up to a lazy Sunday with no plans and no obligations. "How rare," she thought, as she stumbled to the kitchen to pour a cup of coffee. She concocted her plan: head downtown, visit the local library, and look for an outfit for next week's interview. After checking out a few new reads, Marcy walked to the corner and put her hand in the air to catch a taxi. She hopped out near Crave—a new boutique she'd been wanting to check out. Marcy perused the store and found a sweater she liked that was just out of reach. She waved to a store employee to get his attention.

✎ On Your Own

Answer the following questions about social norms, roles, and scripts.

1. A group standard for how it's members should act, think, and feel in certain situations is an example of a:

☐ Social Role   ☐ Social Norm   ☐ Script

2. Kate knows that as a student, she should pay attention and listen to her teacher during class. This example best fits which of the following terms:

☐ Social Role   ☐ Social Norm   ☐ Script

3. Kristy knows that when the teacher of her class starts talking, she must stop talking and begin taking notes. This example best fits which of the following terms:

☐ Social Role   ☐ Social Norm   ☐ Script

Zimbardo's Stanford Prison Experiment

The famous **Stanford prison experiment**, conducted by social psychologist Philip Zimbardo and his colleagues at Stanford University, demonstrated the power of social roles, social norms, and scripts. In the summer of 1971, an advertisement was placed in a California newspaper asking for male volunteers to participate in a study about the psychological effects of prison life. More than 70 men volunteered, and these volunteers then underwent psychological testing to eliminate candidates who had underlying psychiatric issues, medical issues, or a history of crime or drug abuse. The pool of volunteers was whittled down to 24 healthy male college students. Each student was paid $15 per day and was randomly assigned to play the role of either a prisoner or a guard in the study.

A mock prison was constructed in the basement of the psychology building at Stanford. Participants assigned to play the role of prisoners were "arrested" at their homes by Palo Alto police officers, booked at a police station, and subsequently taken to the mock prison. The experiment was scheduled to run for several weeks. To the surprise of the researchers, both the "prisoners" and "guards" assumed their roles with zeal. In fact, on day 2, some of the prisoners revolted, and the guards quelled the rebellion by threatening the prisoners with night sticks. In a relatively short time, the guards came to harass the prisoners in an increasingly sadistic manner through a complete lack of privacy, lack of basic comforts such as mattresses to sleep on, and degrading chores and late-night counts.

> **Group Activity**
>
> As a group, discuss what you've learned about research methods. Based on this, why do you think it is important that these participants were randomly assigned?

📷 **Figure 7:** It didn't take long for prisoners to be berated and dehumanized in the famous Stanford prison experiment.

📷 **Figure 8:** Iraqi prisoners of war were abused by their American captors in Abu Ghraib prison during the second Iraq war.

The prisoners, in turn, began to show signs of severe anxiety and hopelessness—they began tolerating the guards' abuse. Even the Stanford professor who designed the study and was the head researcher, Philip Zimbardo, found himself acting as if the prison was real and his role, as prison supervisor, was real as well. After only six days, the experiment had to be ended due to the participants' deteriorating behavior. Zimbardo explained,

> At this point it became clear that we had to end the study. We had created an overwhelmingly powerful situation—a situation in which prisoners were withdrawing and behaving in pathological ways, and in which some of the guards were behaving sadistically. Even the "good" guards felt helpless to intervene, and none of the guards quit while the study was in progress. Indeed, it should be noted that no guard ever came late for his shift, called in sick, left early, or demanded extra pay for overtime work. (Zimbardo, 2013)

Reflection Questions

What is your reaction to this experiment? Why do you think both the prisoners and the guards were so quick to adapt to their roles? What does this suggest about the ways in which human beings rise to, and fall from, power?

Further Resources

Visit this website (hawkes. biz/zimbardo) to hear an NPR interview with Philip Zimbardo where he discusses the parallels between the Stanford prison experiment and the Abu Ghraib prison in Iraq.

The Stanford prison experiment demonstrated the power of social roles, norms, and scripts in affecting human behavior. The guards and prisoners enacted their social roles by engaging in behaviors appropriate to the role. Review the following table to see the specific behaviors each group displayed.

Prisoners	Guards
Followed orders	Gave orders
Acted submissive	Acted powerful
Rebelled: threw pillows, trashed cells	Instituted punishments: forced push-ups, removed privacy
Exhibited symptoms of mental breakdown	Exhibited symptoms of power-hungry authority

However, according to Zimbardo, none of the participants suffered long-term harm (Alexander, 2001).

The Stanford prison experiment has some parallels with the abuse of prisoners of war by U.S. Army troops and CIA personnel at the Abu Ghraib prison in 2003 and 2004. The offenses at Abu Ghraib were documented by photographs of the abuse, some taken by the abusers themselves (Figure 8).

Summary

Human behavior is largely influenced by our social roles, norms, and scripts. In order to know how to act in a given situation, we have shared cultural knowledge of how to behave depending on our role in society. Social norms dictate the behavior that is appropriate or inappropriate for each role. Each social role has scripts that help humans learn the sequence of appropriate behaviors in a given setting. The famous Stanford prison experiment is an example of how the power of the situation can dictate the social roles, norms, and scripts we follow in a given situation, even if this behavior is contrary to our typical behavior.

11.3 Attitudes and Persuasion

Social psychologists have documented how the power of the situation can influence our behaviors. Now we turn to how the power of the situation can influence our attitudes and beliefs. **Attitude** is our evaluation of a person, an idea, or an object. We have attitudes for many things ranging from products that we might pick up in the supermarket to important social issues. Typically, attitudes are favorable or unfavorable: positive or negative (Eagly & Chaiken, 1993). And they have three components: an affective component (feelings), a behavioral component (the effect of the attitude on behavior), and a cognitive component (belief and knowledge) (Rosenberg & Hovland, 1960).

Let's say you hold a positive attitude toward recycling. How would that attitude be manifested in its three components?

📷 **Figure 1:** Attitudes can be broken down into three components.

Affective Component	Behavioral Component	Cognitive Component
"It makes me feel good to recycle."	You recycle as often as you can.	Favorable thoughts like, "Recycling is the responsible thing to do."

Positive Attitude Toward Recycling

Our attitudes and beliefs are not only influenced by external forces but also by internal influences that we control. Like our behavior, our attitudes and thoughts are not always changed by situational pressures, but they can be consciously changed by our own free will. In this lesson, we discuss the conditions under which we would want to change our own attitudes and beliefs.

Flash Forward

Ready to dig into the vocabulary? Get some practice with this Hawkes Verified Quizlet set (hawkes.biz/psych11q3)!

Group Activity

How can an attitude you might not even be aware of impact your behavior, even before you have the chance to act?

Consider your attitude towards mathematics. Take this assessment (hawkes.biz/attitudes) and discuss with your peers how your score may reflect your feelings about math.

What Is Cognitive Dissonance?

Social psychologists have documented that feeling good about ourselves and maintaining positive self-esteem is a powerful motivator of human behavior (Tavris & Aronson, 2008). In the United States, members of the predominant culture typically think very highly of themselves and view themselves as good people who are above average on many desirable traits (Ehrlinger, Gilovich, & Ross, 2005). Often, our behavior, attitudes, and beliefs are affected when we experience a threat to our self-esteem or positive self-image. Psychologist Leon Festinger (1957) defined **cognitive dissonance** as psychological discomfort arising from holding two or more inconsistent attitudes, behaviors, or cognitions (thoughts, beliefs, or opinions). Festinger's theory of cognitive dissonance states that when we experience a conflict in our behaviors, attitudes, or beliefs that runs counter to our positive self-perceptions, we experience psychological discomfort (dissonance). For example, if you believe smoking is bad for your health but you continue to smoke, you experience conflict between your belief and behavior (Figure 3).

Figure 2: A lawyer might experience cognitive dissonance defending a guilty client; making false statements and convincing others of false innocence may contradict his or her identity as both a lawyer and an honest person.

Figure 3: Cognitive dissonance is aroused by inconsistent beliefs and behaviors. Believing cigarettes are bad for your health but smoking cigarettes anyway can cause cognitive dissonance. To reduce cognitive dissonance, individuals can change their behavior, as in quitting smoking, or change their belief, such as discounting the evidence that smoking is harmful.

Group Activity

Part 1

Please indicate whether or not you agree with the following statements by recording your responses on a separate piece of paper.

1. Texting while driving is dangerous.

   • Yes   • No
2. It is important to stay informed about proposed legislation that affects my community.

   • Yes   • No
3. Soft drinks/sodas are unhealthy beverages.

   • Yes   • No
4. Poverty is a serious problem that needs to be addressed.

   • Yes   • No
5. Smoking is an unhealthy behavior.

   • Yes   • No

Part 2

Please indicate whether or not you have performed each of the following behaviors by recording your responses on a separate piece of paper.

1. I text when I am driving.

   • Yes   • No
2. I am able to name at least one bill affecting my community that was passed in the last year by the legislators in my county or my state.

3. I drink soft drinks/sodas.

   • Yes   • No
4. Within the last year, I have donated money or engaged in volunteer work to address the problem of poverty.

   • Yes   • No
5. Within the last year, I have smoked a cigarette.

   • Yes   • No

Part 3

Compare your answers in Part 1 (Attitude Survey) to your answers in Part 2 (Behavior Survey).

Part 4

Reflect on the following questions, and share your answers in small groups.

1. Did you experience cognitive dissonance? Why or why not?

2. What thoughts were going through your head as you completed the Behavior Survey and had answers that were incongruent with your Attitude Survey?

3. What was your emotional reaction to experiencing dissonance?

4. What strategies did you use to try and lessen your experience of dissonance?

(From Breaking the Prejudice Habit [hawkes.biz/breaking])

Later research documented that only conflicting cognitions that threaten individuals' positive self-image cause dissonance (Greenwald & Ronis, 1978). Additional research found that dissonance is not only psychologically uncomfortable but also can cause physiological arousal (Croyle & Cooper, 1983) and activate regions of the brain important in emotions and cognitive functioning (van Veen, Krug, Schooler, & Carter, 2009). When we experience cognitive dissonance, we are motivated to decrease it because it is psychologically, physically, and mentally uncomfortable. We can reduce cognitive dissonance by bringing our cognitions, attitudes, and behaviors in line—that is, making them harmonious. This can be done in different ways, such as:

- changing our discrepant behavior (e.g., stop smoking)

- changing our cognitions through rationalization or denial (e.g., telling ourselves that health risks can be reduced by smoking filtered cigarettes)

- adding a new cognition (e.g., "Smoking suppresses my appetite, so I don't become overweight, which is good for my health.")

A classic example of cognitive dissonance is John, a 20-year-old who enlists in the military. During boot camp he is awakened at 5:00 a.m., is chronically sleep deprived, yelled at, covered in sand flea bites, physically bruised and battered, and mentally exhausted (Figure 4). It gets worse. Recruits that make it to week 11 of boot camp have to do 54 hours of continuous training.

Figure 4: A person who has chosen a difficult path must deal with cognitive dissonance in addition to many other discomforts.

Not surprisingly, John is miserable. No one likes to be miserable. In this type of situation, people can change their beliefs, their attitudes, or their behaviors. The last option, a change of behaviors, is not available to John. He has signed on to the military for four years, and he cannot legally leave.

If John keeps thinking about how miserable he is, it is going to be a very long four years. He will be in a constant state of cognitive dissonance. As an alternative to this misery, John can change his beliefs or attitudes. He can tell himself, "I am becoming stronger, healthier, and sharper. I am learning discipline and how to defend myself and my country. What I am doing is really important." If this is his belief, he will realize that he is becoming stronger through his challenges. He then will feel better and not experience cognitive dissonance, which is an uncomfortable state.

The Effect of Initiation

The military example demonstrates the observation that a difficult initiation into a group influences us to like the group *more*, due to the justification of effort. We do not want to have wasted time and effort to join a group that we eventually leave.

A classic experiment by Aronson and Mills (1959) demonstrated this justification of effort effect. College students volunteered to join a campus group that would meet regularly to discuss the psychology of sex. Participants were randomly assigned to one of three conditions: no initiation, an easy initiation, and a difficult initiation into the group. After participating in the first discussion, which was deliberately made very boring, participants rated how much they liked the group. Participants who underwent a difficult initiation process to join the group rated the group more favorably than did participants with an easy initiation or no initiation (Figure 5).

🏞 **Figure 5:** Justification of effort has a distinct effect on a person liking a group. Students in the difficult initiation condition liked the group more than students in other conditions due to the justification of effort effect.

Similar effects can be seen in a more recent study of how student effort affects course evaluations. Heckert, Latier, Ringwald-Burton, and Drazen (2006) surveyed 463 undergraduates enrolled in courses at a midwestern university about the amount of effort that their courses required of them. In addition, the students were also asked to evaluate various aspects of the course. Given what you've just read, it will come as no surprise that those courses that were associated with the highest level of effort were evaluated as being more valuable than those that did not. Furthermore, students indicated that they learned more in courses that required more effort, regardless of the grades that they received in those courses (Heckert et al., 2006).

Reflection Questions

There has been at least one hazing-related death in the U.S. every year since the early 1960s.

Conduct a Google search on "Hazing Death" or visit the Wikipedia site listing hazing deaths in the United States. Read any one story and consider the following:

- Why would an individual allow themselves to be hazed, even to the point of death?

- How is hazing a form of cognitive dissonance?

- What social groups utilize hazing (or other forms of cognitive dissonance) to increase group cohesion?

Besides the classic military example and group initiation, can you think of other examples of cognitive dissonance?

Here's one more example:

> Marco and Maria live in Fairfield County, Connecticut, which is one of the wealthiest areas in the United States and has a very high cost of living. Marco telecommutes from home and Maria does not work outside of the home. They rent a very small house for more than $3000 a month. Maria shops at consignment stores for clothes and economizes where she can. They complain that they never

have any money and that they cannot buy anything new. When asked why they do not move to a less expensive location, since Marco telecommutes, they respond that Fairfield County is beautiful, they love the beaches, and they feel comfortable there.

How does the theory of cognitive dissonance apply to Marco and Maria's choices?

Persuasion

In the previous section, we discussed that the motivation to reduce cognitive dissonance leads us to change our attitudes, behaviors, and/or cognitions to make them consonant. **Persuasion** is the process of changing our attitude toward something based on some kind of communication. Much of the persuasion we experience comes from outside forces. How do people convince others to change their attitudes, beliefs, and behaviors (Figure 6)? What communications do you receive that attempt to persuade you to change your attitudes, beliefs, and behaviors?

A subfield of social psychology studies persuasion and social influence, providing us with a plethora of information on how humans can be persuaded by others.

Figure 6: We encounter attempts at persuasion everywhere. Persuasion is not limited to formal advertising; we are confronted with it throughout our everyday world.

Communication Type	Factors that Impact Persuasion
Source of the communication	Attractiveness of speaker Perceived credibility of speaker
Nature of the communication	Quality of message Sincerity of communication
Receiver/audience of the communication	Intelligence of message receiver Age of message receiver

Yale Attitude Change Approach—Case Study

The topic of persuasion has been one of the most extensively researched areas in social psychology (Fiske et al., 2010). During the Second World War, Carl Hovland extensively researched persuasion for the U.S. Army. After the war, Hovland continued his exploration of persuasion at Yale University. Out of this work came a model called the Yale attitude change approach, which describes the conditions under which people tend to change their attitudes. Hovland demonstrated that certain features of the source of a persuasive message, the content of the message, and the characteristics of the audience will influence the persuasiveness of a message (Hovland, Janis, & Kelley, 1953).

Features of the source of the persuasive message include the credibility of the speaker (Hovland & Weiss, 1951) and the physical attractiveness of the speaker (Eagly & Chaiken, 1975; Petty, Wegener, & Fabrigar, 1997). Thus, speakers who are credible, or have expertise on the topic, and who are deemed as trustworthy are more persuasive than less credible speakers. Similarly, more attractive speakers are more persuasive than less attractive speakers. The use of famous actors and athletes to advertise products on television and in print relies on this principle. The immediate and long-term impact of the persuasion also depends, however, on the credibility of the messenger (Kumkale & Albarracín, 2004).

Figure 7: Michael Phelps, a well-decorated Olympic athlete, was endorsed by Kellogg's, but the company revoked their sponsorship after photos of his marijuana use surfaced on the Internet in 2009.

Features of the message itself that affect persuasion include subtlety (the quality of being important, but not obvious) (Petty & Cacioppo, 1986; Walster & Festinger, 1962); sidedness (that is, having more than one side) (Crowley & Hoyer, 1994; Igou & Bless, 2003; Lumsdaine & Janis, 1953); timing (Haugtvedt & Wegener, 1994; Miller & Campbell, 1959), and whether both sides are presented. Messages that are more subtle are more persuasive than direct messages. Arguments that occur first, such as in a debate, are more influential if messages are given back-to-back. However, if there is a delay after the first message, and before the audience needs to make a decision, the last message presented will tend to be more persuasive (Miller & Campbell, 1959).

Features of the audience that affect persuasion are attention (Albarracín & Wyer, 2001; Festinger & Maccoby, 1964), intelligence, self-esteem (Rhodes & Wood, 1992), and age (Krosnick & Alwin, 1989). In order to be persuaded, audience members must be paying attention. People with lower intelligence are more easily persuaded than people with higher intelligence; whereas people with moderate self-esteem are more easily persuaded than people with higher or lower self-esteem (Rhodes & Wood, 1992). Finally, younger adults aged 18–25 are more persuadable than older adults.

Elaboration Likelihood Model

An especially popular model that describes the dynamics of persuasion is the elaboration likelihood model of persuasion (Petty & Cacioppo, 1986). The elaboration likelihood model considers the variables of the attitude change approach—that is, features of the source of the persuasive message, contents of the message, and characteristics of the audience are used to determine when attitude change will occur. According to the elaboration likelihood model of persuasion, there are two main routes that play a role in delivering a persuasive message: central and peripheral (Figure 8).

📖 **Figure 8:** Persuasion can take one of two paths, and the durability of the end result depends on the path.

The **central route** is logic driven and uses data and facts to convince people of an argument's worthiness. For example, a car company seeking to persuade you to purchase their model will emphasize the car's safety features and fuel economy. This is a direct route to persuasion that focuses on the quality of the information. In order for the central route of persuasion to be effective in changing attitudes, thoughts, and behaviors, the argument must be strong and, if successful, will result in lasting attitude change.

The central route to persuasion works best when the target of persuasion, or the audience, is analytical and willing to engage in processing the information. From an advertiser's perspective, what products would be best sold using the central route to persuasion? What audience would most likely be influenced to buy the product?

One example is buying a computer. It is likely, for example, that small business owners might be especially influenced by the focus on the computer's quality and features such as processing speed and memory capacity.

The **peripheral route** is an indirect route that uses peripheral cues to associate positivity with the message (Petty & Cacioppo, 1986). Instead of focusing on the facts and a product's quality, the peripheral route relies on association with positive characteristics, such as positive emotions and celebrity endorsement. For example, having a popular athlete advertise athletic shoes is a common method used to encourage young adults to purchase the shoes. This route to attitude change does not require much effort or information processing. This method of persuasion may promote positivity toward the message or product, but it typically results in a less permanent attitude or behavior change. The audience does not need to be analytical or motivated to process the message. In fact, a peripheral route to persuasion may not even be noticed by the audience, like with product placement. Product placement refers to putting a product with a clear brand name or brand identity in a TV show or movie to promote the product (Gupta & Lord, 1998). For example, one season of the reality series *American Idol* prominently showed the panel of judges drinking out of cups that displayed the Coca-Cola logo. What other products would be best sold using the peripheral route to persuasion?

One example is clothing: a retailer may focus on celebrities that are wearing the same style of clothing.

📖 **Figure 9:** Revlon endorses celebrities like Halle Berry, Jessica Alba, and Emma Stone. Why do you think Revlon selected these individuals as brand ambassadors?

Foot-in-the-Door Technique

Further Resources

Curious about the industry of persuasion? Watch this *Frontline* episode (hawkes.biz/persuasion) called "The Persuaders."

Researchers have tested many persuasion strategies that are effective in selling products and changing people's attitudes, ideas, and behaviors. One effective strategy is the foot-in-the-door technique (Cialdini, 2001; Pliner, Hart, Kohl, & Saari, 1974). Using the **foot-in-the-door technique**, the persuader gets a person to agree to a small favor or to buy a small item, only to later request a larger favor or purchase of a bigger item. The foot-in-the-door technique was demonstrated in a study by Freedman and Fraser (1966) in which participants who agreed to post a small sign in their yard or sign a petition were more likely to agree to put a large sign in their yard than people who declined the first request (Figure 10). Research on this technique also illustrates the principle of consistency (Cialdini, 2001): our past behavior often directs our future behavior, and we have a desire to maintain consistency once we have a committed to a behavior.

Figure 10: With the foot-in-the-door technique, a small request, such as wearing a campaign button, can turn into a large request, such as putting campaigns signs in your yard.

✎ On Your Own

Which of the following is an example of the foot-in-the-door technique?

- ☐ Alisa, a student applying to graduate school, asks her professor if she will write one letter of recommendation for her. After receiving the letter, the student then asks the professor if she will submit letters of recommendation to four more schools, to which the professor agrees.

- ☐ Tyrell, whose job involves a lot of travel, asks his boss if he can have a company car. His boss denies the request but gives him a $1/hr raise.

- ☐ Mike is planning on buying a new car. He makes a deal with the car sales guy for what Mike thinks is a great price. However, after he has agreed to the lower price, he finds out that to get power windows and power locks, he will have to pay extra. Mike buys the car anyway.

A common application of foot-in-the-door is when teens ask their parents for a small permission (for example, extending curfew by a half hour) and then ask them for something larger. Having granted the smaller request increases the likelihood that parents will acquiesce with the later, larger request.

How would a store owner use the foot-in-the-door technique to sell you an expensive product? For example, say that you are buying the latest model smartphone, and the salesperson suggests you purchase the best data plan. You agree to this. The salesperson then suggests a bigger purchase—the three-year extended warranty. After agreeing to the smaller request, you are more likely to also agree to the larger request. You may have encountered this if you have bought a car. When salespeople realize that a buyer intends to purchase a certain model, they might try to get the customer to pay for more available options for the car.

📷 **Figure 11:** The children's book *If You Give a Mouse a Cookie* by Laura Numeroff illustrates the foot-in-the-door concept perfectly. "If you give a mouse a cookie, he'll ask for a glass of milk. When you give him the milk, he'll probably ask you for a straw. When he's finished, he'll ask you for a napkin..." and so on.

Summary

Attitudes are our evaluations or feelings toward a person, idea, or object and typically are positive or negative. Our attitudes and beliefs are influenced not only by external forces but also by internal influences that we control. An internal form of attitude change is cognitive dissonance or the tension we experience when our thoughts, feelings, and behaviors are in conflict. In order to reduce dissonance, individuals can change their behavior, attitudes, or cognitions or add a new cognition. External forces of persuasion include advertising; the features of advertising that influence our behaviors include the source, message, and audience. There are two primary routes to persuasion. The central route to persuasion uses facts and information to persuade potential consumers. The peripheral route uses positive association with cues such as beauty, fame, and positive emotions.

11.4 Conformity, Compliance, and Obedience

Now, we'll discuss additional ways in which people influence others. The topics of conformity, social influence, obedience, and group processes demonstrate the power of the social situation to change our thoughts, feelings, and behaviors. We begin this lesson with a discussion of a famous social psychology experiment that demonstrated how susceptible humans are to outside social pressures.

Conformity

Solomon Asch conducted several experiments in the 1950s to determine how people are affected by the thoughts and behaviors of other people. In one study, Asche had participants enter a classroom with a group of **confederates**, which are people that are aware of the experiment and work for the researcher. The participants, however, assumed that the confederates were other participants in the study. In the classroom, the participants were asked to judge which of three line segments was closest in length to line segment *x* (Figure 1).

> **Flash Forward**
>
> Ready to dig into the vocabulary? Get some practice with this Hawkes Verified Quizlet set (hawkes.biz/psych11q4)!

📷 **Figure 1:** These line segments illustrate the judgment task in Asch's conformity study. Which line on the right—*a*, *b*, or *c*—is the same length as line *x* on the left?

Each group of participants had only one true, naïve subject. The remaining members of the group were confederates of the researcher. Confederates are used to manipulate social situations as part of the research design, and the true, naïve participants believe that confederates are, like them, uninformed participants in the experiment. In Asch's study, the confederates identified a line segment that was obviously shorter than the target line—a wrong answer. The naïve participant then had to identify aloud the line segment that best matched the target line segment.

How often do you think the true participant aligned with the confederates' response? That is, how often do you think the group influenced the participant, and the participant gave the wrong answer? Asch (1955) found that 76% of participants conformed to group pressure at least once by indicating the incorrect line. **Conformity** is the change in a person's behavior to go along with the group, even if he does not agree with the group. Why would people give the wrong answer? What factors would increase or decrease someone giving in or conforming to group pressure?

> ### Reflection Question
>
> What factors do you think make a person more likely to yield to group pressure?

The **Asch effect** is the influence of the group majority on an individual's judgment.

What factors make a person more likely to yield to group pressure? Research shows that the size of the majority, the presence of another dissenter, and the public or relatively private nature of responses are key influences on conformity.

📷 **Figure 2:** The Asch effect is the influence of group majority on an individual.

- *The size of the majority:* The greater the number of people in the majority, the more likely an individual will conform. There is, however, an upper limit (a point where adding more members does not increase conformity). In Asch's study, conformity increased with the number of people in the majority—up to seven individuals. At numbers beyond seven, conformity leveled off and decreased slightly (Asch, 1955).

- *The presence of another dissenter:* If there is at least one dissenter, conformity rates drop to near zero (Asch, 1955).

- *The public or private nature of the responses:* When responses are made publicly (in front of others), conformity is more likely; however, when responses are made privately (e.g., writing down the response), conformity is less likely (Deutsch & Gerard, 1955).

The finding that conformity is more likely to occur when responses are public than when they are private is the reason government elections require voting in secret, so we are not coerced by others (Figure 3). The Asch effect can be easily seen in children when they have to publicly vote for something. For example, if the teacher asks whether the children would rather have extra recess, no homework, or candy, once a few children vote, the rest will comply and go with the majority. In a different classroom, the majority might vote differently, and most of the children would comply with that majority. When someone's vote changes if it is made in public versus private, this is known as compliance. Compliance can be a form of conformity. Compliance is going along with a request or demand, even if you do not agree with the request. In Asch's studies, the participants complied by giving the wrong answers but privately did not accept that the obvious wrong answers were correct.

Reflection Question

How do you think you would have responded if you were in Asch's study?

Figure 3: Voting for government officials in the United States is private to reduce the pressure of conformity.

Now that you have learned about the Asch line experiments, why do you think the participants conformed? The correct answer to the line segment question was obvious, and it was an easy task. Researchers have categorized the motivation to conform into two types: normative social influence and informational social influence (Deutsch & Gerard, 1955).

In **normative social influence**, people conform to the group norm to fit in, to feel good, and to be accepted by the group. However, with **informational social influence**, people conform because they believe the group is competent and has the correct information, particularly when the task or situation is ambiguous. What type of social influence was operating in the Asch conformity studies? Since the line judgment task was unambiguous, participants did not need to rely on the group for information. Instead, participants complied to fit in and avoid ridicule, an instance of normative social influence.

✎ On Your Own

Which of the following types of influence was Asch's study?

☐ Normative social influence   ☐ Informational social influence   ☐ Active social influence

Figure 4: The term *influencer* now refers to individuals with a large social media platform and/or follower base. How does this newly coined term relate to conformity and compliance?

An example of informational social influence may be what to do in an emergency situation. Imagine that you are in a movie theater watching a film and what seems to be smoke comes in the theater from under the emergency exit door. You are not certain that it is smoke—it might be a special effect for the movie, such as a fog machine. When you are uncertain, you will tend to look at the behavior of others in the theater. If other people show concern and get up to leave, you are likely to do the same. However, if others seem unconcerned, you are likely to stay put and continue watching the movie (Figure 5).

Figure 5: People in crowds tend to take cues from others and act accordingly. The audience at this rock concert is standing, dancing, and participating in crowd surfing. How would the crowd behavior differ at an educational lecture?

How would you have behaved if you were a participant in Asch's study? Many students say they would not conform, that the study is outdated, and that people nowadays are more independent. To some extent this may be true. Research suggests that overall rates of conformity may have reduced since the time of Asch's research. Furthermore, efforts to replicate Asch's study have made it clear that many factors determine how likely it is that someone will demonstrate conformity to the group. These factors include the participant's age, gender, and socio-cultural background (Bond & Smith, 1996; Larsen, 1990; Walker & Andrade, 1996).

Stanley Milgram's Experiment

Conformity is one effect of the influence of others on our thoughts, feelings, and behaviors. Another form of social influence is obedience to authority. **Obedience** is the change of an individual's behavior to comply with a demand by an authority figure. People often comply with the request because they are concerned about a consequence if they do not comply. To demonstrate this phenomenon, we review another classic social psychology experiment.

Stanley Milgram was a social psychology professor at Yale who was influenced by the trial of Adolf Eichmann, a Nazi war criminal. Eichmann's defense for the atrocities he committed was that he was "just following orders." Milgram (1963) wanted to test the validity of this defense, so he designed an experiment and initially recruited 40 men for his experiment. The volunteer participants were led to believe that they were participating in a study to improve learning and memory. The participants were told that they were to teach other students (learners) correct answers to a series of test items. The participants were shown how to use a device that they were told delivered electric shocks of different intensities to the learners. The participants were told to shock the learners if they gave a wrong answer to a test item—that the shock would help them to learn. The participants gave (or believed they gave) the learners shocks, which increased in 15-volt increments, all the way up to 450 volts. The participants did not know that the learners were confederates and that the confederates did not actually receive shocks.

In response to a string of incorrect answers from the learners, the participants obediently and repeatedly shocked them. The confederate learners cried out for help, begged the participant teachers to stop, and even complained of heart trouble. Yet, when the researcher told the participant-teachers to continue the shock, 65% of the participants continued the shock to the maximum voltage and to the point that the learner became unresponsive (Figure 6).

Figure 6: The Milgram experiment showed the surprising degree to which people obey authority. Two out of three (65%) participants continued to administer shocks to an unresponsive learner.

Reflection Questions

What do you think makes someone obey authority to the point of causing serious harm to another person?

Several variations of the original Milgram experiment were conducted to test the boundaries of obedience, which include the following:

- When the setting of the experiment was moved to an office building, the percentage of participants who delivered the highest shock dropped to 48%.

- When the learner was in the same room as the teacher, the highest shock rate dropped to 40%.

- When the teachers' and learners' hands were touching, the highest shock rate dropped to 30%.

- When the researcher gave the orders by phone, the rate dropped to 23%.

These variations show that when the humanity of the person being shocked increased, obedience decreased. Similarly, when the authority of the experimenter decreased, so did obedience.

This case is still very applicable today. What does a person do if an authority figure orders something done? What if the person believes it is incorrect, or worse, unethical? In a study by Martin and Bull (2008), midwives privately filled out a questionnaire regarding best practices and expectations in delivering a baby. Then, a more senior midwife and supervisor asked the junior midwives to do something they had previously stated they were opposed to. Most of the junior midwives were obedient to authority, going against their own beliefs.

Groupthink

When in group settings, we are often influenced by the thoughts, feelings, and behaviors around us. Whether it is due to normative or informational social influence, groups have power to influence individuals. Another phenomenon of group conformity is groupthink. **Groupthink** is the modification of the opinions of members of a group to align with what they believe is the group consensus (Janis, 1972). In group situations, the group often takes action that individuals would not perform outside the group setting because groups make more extreme decisions than individuals do. Moreover, groupthink can hinder opposing trains of thought. This elimination of diverse opinions contributes to faulty decision making.

Figure 7: What do you think about the tag line of this World War II poster? What if the command goes against the soldier's morals or beliefs? Should he or she still obey?

Maintaining harmony	Avoiding dissent from leader	Isolation from alternative information
People value maintaining group harmony over making sound decisions.	People in the group may not want to disagree with the leader.	People in groups may be isolated from hearing new or alternative viewpoints that may conflict with those in the group.

Causes of Groupthink

Dig Deeper

Groupthink in the U.S. Government

There have been several instances of groupthink in the U.S. government. One example occurred when the United States led a small coalition of nations to invade Iraq in March 2003. This invasion occurred because a small group of advisors and former President George W. Bush were convinced that Iraq represented a significant terrorism threat with a large stockpile of weapons of mass destruction at its disposal. Although some of these individuals may have had some doubts about the credibility of the information available to them at the time, in the end, the group arrived at a consensus that Iraq had weapons of mass destruction and represented a significant threat to national security. It later came to light that Iraq did not have weapons of mass destruction but not until the invasion was well underway. As a result, 6,000 American soldiers were killed and many more civilians died. How did the Bush administration arrive at their conclusions?

Do you see evidence of groupthink?

There are several symptoms of groupthink including the following:

- Perceiving the group as invulnerable or invincible or that it can do no wrong

- Believing the group is morally correct

- Group members withholding information to avoid disrupting the group consensus

- The squashing of dissenting group members' opinions

- The shielding of the group leader from dissenting views

- Perceiving an illusion of unanimity among group members

- Holding stereotypes or negative attitudes toward the out-group or others' with differing viewpoints (Janis, 1972)

Given the causes and symptoms of groupthink, how can it be avoided? There are several strategies that can improve group decision making including seeking outside opinions, voting in private, having the leader withhold position statements until all group members have voiced their views, conducting research on all viewpoints, weighing the costs and benefits of all options, and developing a contingency plan (Janis, 1972; Mitchell & Eckstein, 2009).

Figure 8: Groupthink can suppress the expression of opposing views and opinions.

✎ On Your Own

Why do you think the following strategies would be effective in improving group decision making (Janis, 1972; Mitchell & Eckstein, 2009)? Include your answers in the following table.

Strategy	Why does this improve group decision making?
Seeking outside opinions?	
Voting in private?	
Having a leader withhold positions until all group members voted?	
Conduct research on all viewpoints?	
Weighing the costs and benefits of decisions?	

Group Polarization

Another phenomenon that occurs within group settings is group polarization. **Group polarization** (Teger & Pruitt, 1967) is the strengthening of an original group attitude after the discussion of views within a group. That is, if a group initially favors a viewpoint, after discussion the group consensus is likely a stronger endorsement of the viewpoint. Conversely, if the group was initially opposed to a viewpoint, group discussion would likely lead to stronger opposition. Group polarization explains many actions taken by groups that would not be undertaken by individuals. Group polarization can be observed at political conventions, when platforms of the party are supported by individuals who, when not in a group, would decline to support them. A more everyday example is a group's discussion of how attractive someone is. Does your opinion change if you find someone attractive, but your friends do not agree? If your friends vociferously agree, might you then find this person even more attractive?

> **Reflection Questions**
>
> Describe a time when your opinion of something changed because of a group discussion. What was the opinion, and why do you think you changed it?

Social Facilitation

Social facilitation occurs when an individual performs better when an audience is watching than when the individual performs the behavior alone. This occurs when people are performing a task for which they are skilled. For example, skilled basketball players will be more likely to make a free throw basket when surrounded by a cheering audience than when playing alone in the gym (Figure 9). However, there are instances when even skilled athletes can have difficulty under pressure. For example, if an athlete is less skilled or nervous about making a free throw, having an audience may hinder rather than help. In sum, social facilitation is likely to occur for easy tasks, or tasks at which we are skilled, but worse performance may occur when performing in front of others, depending on the task.

Figure 9: The attention of the crowd can motivate a skilled athlete.

Social Loafing

Social loafing is the exertion of less effort by a person working together with a group. Social loafing occurs when our individual performance cannot be evaluated separately from the group. Thus, group performance declines on easy tasks (Karau & Williams, 1993).

> **Reflection Questions**
>
> When you've worked on a group project, have you had to contribute more than your fair share because your group members weren't putting in the work? Have you exerted less effort on a project because you knew that you were graded as a group? Describe what your experience was like.

Essentially, individual group members loaf and let other group members pick up the slack. Because each individual's efforts cannot be evaluated, individuals become less motivated to perform well. For example, consider a group of people cooperating to clean litter from the roadside. Some people will exert a great amount of effort, while others will exert little effort. Yet the entire job gets done, and it may not be obvious who worked hard and who didn't.

As a college student you may have experienced social loafing while working on a group project. You may have had to do more than your share of the work. This may happen when a professor assigns a group grade instead of individual grades. If the professor doesn't know how much effort each student contributed to a project, some students may be inclined to let more conscientious students do more of the work. The chance of social loafing in student work groups increases as the size of the group increases (Shepperd & Taylor, 1999).

Figure 10: Many students have experienced social loafing during group projects, whether they are the ones loafing or pulling the extra weight.

Interestingly, the opposite of social loafing occurs when the task is complex and difficult (Bond & Titus, 1983; Geen, 1989). Remember the previous discussion of choking under pressure? This happens when you perform a difficult task and your individual performance can be evaluated. In a group setting, such as the student work group, if your individual performance cannot be evaluated, there is less pressure for you to do well, and thus less anxiety or physiological arousal (Latané, Williams, & Harkens, 1979). This puts you in a relaxed state in which you can perform your best, if you choose (Zajonc, 1965). If the task is a difficult one, many people feel motivated and believe that their group needs their input to do well on a challenging project (Jackson & Williams, 1985). Given what you learned about social loafing, what advice would you give a new professor about how to design group projects? If you suggested that individuals' efforts should not be evaluated, to prevent the anxiety of choking under pressure, but that the task must be challenging, you have a good understanding of the concepts discussed in this section. Alternatively, you can suggest that individuals' efforts should be evaluated, but the task should be easy so as to facilitate performance.

✎ On Your Own

Please indicate the type of social influence that goes along with the description.

Description	Type of Social Influence
Changing your behavior to go along with the group even if you do not agree with the group	
Going along with a request or demand	
Conformity to a group norm to fit in, feel good, and be accepted by the group	
Conformity to a group norm prompted by the belief that the group is competent and has the correct information	
Changing your behavior to please an authority figure or to avoid aversive consequences	
Group members modify their opinions to match what they believe is the group consensus	
Strengthening of the original group attitude after discussing views within a group	
Improved performance when an audience is watching versus when the individual performs the behavior alone	
Exertion of less effort by a person working in a group because individual performance cannot be evaluated separately from the group, thus causing performance decline on easy tasks	

Summary

The power of the situation can lead people to conform, or go along with the group, even in the face of inaccurate information. Conformity to group norms is driven by two motivations, the desire to fit in and be liked and the desire to be accurate and gain information from the group.

Authority figures also have influence over our behaviors, and many people become obedient and follow orders even if the orders are contrary to their personal values.

Conformity to group pressures can also result in groupthink, or the faulty decision-making process that results from cohesive group members trying to maintain group harmony.

Group situations can improve human behavior through facilitating performance on easy tasks but inhibiting performance on difficult tasks. The presence of others can also lead to social loafing when individual efforts cannot be evaluated.

11.5 Prejudice and Discrimination

Flash Forward

Ready to dig into the vocabulary? Get some practice with this Hawkes Verified Quizlet set (hawkes.biz/psych11q5)!

Human conflict can result in crime, war, and mass murder, such as genocide. Prejudice and discrimination can often be causes of human conflict, which explains how strangers come to hate one another to the extreme of causing others harm. It's also important to realize that prejudice and discrimination affect everyone. In this lesson, we will examine the definitions of prejudice and discrimination, examples of these concepts, and causes of these biases.

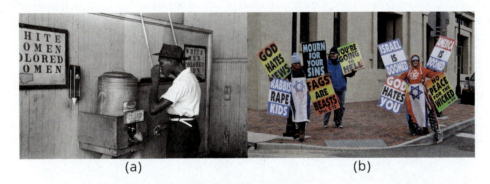

(a)   (b)

📷 **Figure 1:** Prejudice and discrimination occur across the globe. (a) An African-American male drinks from a designated "colored" water fountain in Oklahoma in 1939 during the era of racial segregation as a practice of discrimination. (b) Members of the Westboro Baptist Church, widely identified as a hate group, engage in discrimination based on religion and sexual orientation.

Understanding Prejudice and Discrimination

🖉 **On Your Own**

Define *prejudice*, *stereotype*, and *discrimination* in your own words.

Term	Example
Prejudice	
Stereotype	
Discrimination	

As we discussed in the chapter opening story of Trayvon Martin, humans are very diverse, and although we share many similarities, we also have many differences. The social groups we belong to help form our identities (Tajfel, 1974). These differences may be difficult for some people to reconcile, which may lead to prejudice toward people who are different. **Prejudice** is a negative attitude and feeling toward an individual based solely on one's membership in a particular social group (Allport, 1954; Brown, 2010). Prejudice is common against people who are members of an unfamiliar cultural group. Thus, certain types of education, contact, interactions, and building relationships with members of different cultural groups can reduce the tendency toward prejudice. In fact, simply imagining interacting with members of different cultural groups might affect prejudice. Indeed, when experimental participants were asked to imagine themselves positively interacting with someone from a different group, this led to an increased positive attitude toward the other group and an increase in positive traits associated with the other group. Furthermore, imagined social interaction can reduce anxiety associated with inter-group interactions (Crisp & Turner, 2009). What are some examples of social groups that you belong to that contribute to your identity? Social groups can include gender, race, ethnicity, nationality, social class, religion, sexual orientation, profession, and many more. And, as is true for social roles, you can simultaneously be a member of more than one social group. An example of prejudice is having a negative attitude toward people who are not born in the United States. Although people holding this prejudiced attitude do not know all people who were not born in the United States, they dislike them due to their status as foreigners.

Prejudice often begins in the form of a **stereotype**—that is, a specific belief or assumption about individuals based solely on their membership in a group, regardless of their individual characteristics. Stereotypes become overgeneralized and applied to all members of a group. For example, someone holding prejudiced attitudes toward older adults, may believe that older adults are slow and incompetent (Cuddy, Norton, & Fiske, 2005; Nelson, 2004). We cannot possibly know each individual person of advanced age to know that all older adults are slow and incompetent. Therefore, this negative belief is overgeneralized to all members of the group even though many of the individual group members may in fact be spry and intelligent.

— Herr Baron, der Bub stiehlt Ihnen Ihr Sacktuch!
— Lassen sen geihn, mer hab'n aach klein angefangen.

📷 **Figure 2:** This is a caricature based on a stereotype of Jewish stock-exchange speculators that appeared in the German satirical magazine *Fliegende Blätter* in 1851. The caption reads: "Herr Baron, that lad's stealing your handkerchief!" "Let him go, we once started small too." Widespread use and acceptance of stereotypes like these can directly contribute to dangerous social conditions and even be used to wrongly justify violence.

Reflection Questions

What are some stereotypes and prejudices that you hold about people who are from a race, gender, and age group different from your own? How did this attitude develop?

✎   **On Your Own**

Choose the term that is defined or represented by the following examples.

Thoughts and generalizations about people

☐   Prejudice   ☐   Stereotype   ☐   Discrimination

Feelings about groups of people that can be positive or negative

☐   Prejudice   ☐   Stereotype   ☐   Discrimination

"Yankees fans are arrogant and obnoxious."

☐   Prejudice   ☐   Stereotype   ☐   Discrimination

"I would never hire nor become friends with a person if I knew he or she was a Yankees fan."

☐   Prejudice   ☐   Stereotype   ☐   Discrimination

Another example of a well-known stereotype involves beliefs about racial differences among athletes. As Hodge, Burden, Robinson, and Bennett (2008) point out, Black male athletes are often believed to be more athletic, yet less intelligent, than their White male counterparts. These beliefs persist despite a number of high profile examples to the contrary. Sadly, such beliefs often influence how these athletes are treated by others and how they view themselves and their own capabilities. Whether or not you agree with a stereotype, stereotypes are generally well-known within a given culture (Devine, 1989).

Sometimes people will act on their prejudiced attitudes toward a group of people, and this behavior is known as discrimination. **Discrimination** is negative action toward an individual as a result of one's membership in a particular group (Allport, 1954; Dovidio & Gaertner, 2004). As a result of holding negative beliefs (stereotypes) and negative attitudes (prejudice) about a particular group, people often treat the target of prejudice poorly, such as excluding older adults from their circle of friends. Have you ever been the target of discrimination? If so, how did this negative treatment make you feel?

So far, we've discussed stereotypes, prejudice, and discrimination as negative thoughts, feelings, and behaviors because these are typically the most problematic. However, it is important to also point out that people can hold positive thoughts, feelings, and behaviors toward individuals based on group membership; for example, they would show preferential treatment for people who are like themselves—that is, who share the same gender, race, or favorite sports team.

Types of Prejudice and Discrimination

When we meet strangers we automatically process three pieces of information about them: their race, gender, and age (Ito & Urland, 2003). Why are these aspects of an unfamiliar person so important? Why don't we instead notice whether their eyes are friendly, whether they are smiling, their height, the type of clothes they are wearing? Although these secondary characteristics are important in forming a first impression of a stranger, the social categories of race, gender, and age provide a wealth of information about an individual. This information, however, often is based on stereotypes. We may have different expectations of strangers depending on their race, gender, and age.

Racism

Racism is prejudice and discrimination against an individual based solely on one's membership in a specific racial group (such as toward African Americans, Asian Americans, Latinos, Native Americans, or European Americans). What are some stereotypes of various racial or ethnic groups? Research suggests cultural stereotypes for Asian Americans include cold, sly, and intelligent; for Latinos, cold and unintelligent; for European Americans, cold and intelligent; and for African Americans, aggressive,

Further Resources

This video (hawkes.biz/discrimination) demonstrates the concepts of prejudice, stereotypes, and discrimination. In the video, a social experiment is conducted in a park where three people try to steal a bike out in the open. The race and gender of the thief is varied: a White male teenager, a Black male teenager, and a White female. Does anyone try to stop them? The treatment of the teenagers in the video demonstrates the concept of racism.

🖼 **Figure 3:** In the same way discrimination includes negative treatment of a certain group, it also includes preferential treatments of certain groups.

📷 **Figure 4:** South Carolina Senator Tim Scott spoke about how he experienced racial profiling while driving. "I do not know many African-American men who do not have a very similar story to tell—no matter their profession, no matter their income, no matter their disposition in life."

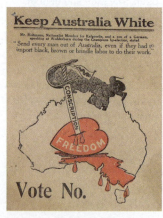

📷 **Figure 5:** This is an anti-conscription leaflet imploring voters to "Keep Australia White." A horde of Asians bearing a dragon flag is shown to the north.

athletic, and more likely to be law breakers (Devine & Elliot, 1995; Fiske, Cuddy, Glick, & Xu, 2002; Sommers & Ellsworth, 2000; Dixon & Linz, 2000).

Racism exists for many racial and ethnic groups. For example, Blacks are significantly more likely to have their vehicles searched during traffic stops than Whites, particularly when Blacks are driving in predominately White neighborhoods, (a phenomenon often termed "DWB," or "driving while Black") (Rojek, Rosenfeld, & Decker, 2012).

Mexican Americans and other Latino groups also are targets of racism from the police and other members of the community. For example, when purchasing items with a personal check, Latino shoppers are more likely than White shoppers to be asked to show formal identification (Dovidio et al., 2010).

In one case of alleged harassment by the police, several East Haven, Connecticut, police officers were arrested on federal charges due to reportedly continued harassment and brutalization of Latinos. When the accusations came out, the Mayor of East Haven was asked, "What are you doing for the Latino community today?" The Mayor responded, "I might have tacos when I go home; I'm not quite sure yet" ("East Haven Mayor," 2012). This statement undermines the important issue of racial profiling and police harassment of Latinos while belittling Latino culture by emphasizing an interest in a food product stereotypically associated with Latinos.

Racism is prevalent toward many other groups in the United States including Native Americans, Arab Americans, Jewish Americans, and Asian Americans. Have you witnessed racism toward any of these racial or ethnic groups? Are you aware of racism in your community?

One reason modern forms of racism, and prejudice in general, are hard to detect is related to the dual attitudes model (Wilson, Lindsey, & Schooler, 2000). Humans have two forms of attitudes: explicit attitudes, which are conscious and controllable, and implicit attitudes, which are unconscious and uncontrollable (Devine, 1989; Olson & Fazio, 2003). Because holding egalitarian views is socially desirable (Plant & Devine, 1998), most people do not show extreme racial bias or other prejudices on measures of their explicit attitudes. However, measures of implicit attitudes often show evidence of mild to strong racial bias or other prejudices (Greenwald, McGee, & Schwartz, 1998; Olson & Fazio, 2003).

Sexism

Sexism is prejudice and discrimination toward individuals based on their sex. Typically, sexism takes the form of men holding biases against women, but either sex can show sexism toward their own or their opposite sex. Like racism, sexism may be subtle and difficult to detect. Common forms of sexism in modern society include gender role expectations, such as expecting women to be the caretakers of the household. Sexism also includes people's expectations for how members of a gender group should behave. For example, women are expected to be friendly, passive, and nurturing, and when women behave in an unfriendly, assertive, or neglectful manner, they often are disliked for violating their gender role (Rudman, 1998). Research by Laurie Rudman (1998) finds that when female job applicants self-promote, they are likely to be viewed as competent, but they may be disliked and are less likely to be hired because they violated gender expectations for modesty. Sexism can exist on a societal level such as in hiring, employment opportunities, and education. Women are less likely to be hired or promoted in male-dominated professions such as engineering, aviation, and construction (Figure 6) (Blau, Ferber, & Winkler, 2010; Ceci & Williams, 2011).

📷 **Figure 6:** In 2016, five women of the U.S. women's national soccer team filed a law suit against the U.S. Soccer Federation on the basis of wage discrimination. The women's team, despite more wins and higher viewer ratings, receives lower compensation than the men's team for friendly and non-friendly matches, base salary, World Cup wins, and Olympic wins.

> ### Reflection Questions
> Have you ever experienced or witnessed sexism? Why do you think there are perceptions about certain jobs as being more male- or female-oriented?

Ageism

People often form judgments and hold expectations about people based on their age. These judgments and expectations can lead to **ageism**, or prejudice and discrimination toward individuals based solely on their age. Typically, ageism occurs against older adults, but ageism also can occur toward younger adults. Think of expectations you hold for older adults. How could someone's expectations influence the feelings they hold toward individuals from older age groups? Ageism is widespread in U.S. culture (Nosek, 2005), and a common ageist attitude toward older adults is that they are incompetent, physically weak, and slow (Greenberg, Schimel, & Martens, 2002), and some people consider older adults less attractive. Some cultures, however, including some Asian, Latino, and African-American cultures, both outside and within the United States afford older adults respect and honor.

> ### Reflection Questions
> Ageism can also occur toward younger adults.
>
> Have you ever experienced ageism? How did it impact you?

Homophobia

Another form of prejudice is **homophobia**: prejudice and discrimination of individuals based solely on their sexual orientation. Like ageism, homophobia is a widespread prejudice in U.S. society that is tolerated by many people (Herek & McLemore, 2013; Nosek, 2005). Negative feelings often result in discrimination, such as the exclusion of lesbian, gay, bisexual, and transgender (LGBT) people from social groups and the avoidance of LGBT neighbors and co-workers. Individuals from the LGBT community often get turned down for jobs they are qualified for because of their sexual orientation.

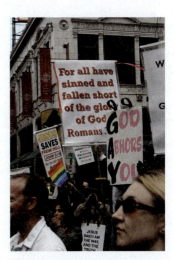

📷 **Figure 7:** Here are some protesters at a pride parade in Seattle.

Reflection Questions

Have you experienced or witnessed homophobia in real life? If not, have you witnessed it portrayed in media? What stereotypes, prejudiced attitudes, and discrimination were evident?

Dig Deeper

Research into Homophobia

Some people are quite passionate in their hatred for non-heterosexuals in our society. In some cases, people have been tortured and/or murdered simply because they were not heterosexual. This passionate response has led some researchers to question what motives might exist for homophobic people. Adams, Wright, & Lohr (1996) conducted a study investigating this issue and their results were quite an eye-opener.

In this experiment, male college students were given a scale that assessed how homophobic they were; those with extreme scores were recruited to participate in the experiment. In the end, 64 men agreed to participate and were split into two groups: homophobic men and non-homophobic men. Both groups of men were fitted with a penile plethysmograph, an instrument that measures changes in blood flow to the penis and serves as an objective measurement of sexual arousal.

All men were shown segments of sexually explicit videos. One of these videos involved a sexual interaction between a man and a woman (heterosexual clip). One video displayed two females engaged in a sexual interaction (homosexual female clip), and the final video displayed two men engaged in a sexual interaction (homosexual male clip). Changes in penile tumescence were recorded during all three clips, and a subjective measurement of sexual arousal was also obtained. While both groups of men became sexually aroused to the heterosexual and female homosexual video clips, only those men who were identified as homophobic showed sexual arousal to the homosexual male video clip. While all men reported that their erections indicated arousal for the heterosexual and female homosexual clips, the homophobic men indicated that they were not sexually aroused (despite their erections) to the male homosexual clips. Adams et al. (1996) suggest that these findings may indicate that homophobia is related to homosexual arousal that the homophobic individuals either deny or are unaware of.

Why Do Prejudice and Discrimination Exist?

Prejudice and discrimination persist in society due to social learning and conformity to social norms. Children learn prejudiced attitudes and beliefs from society: their parents, teachers, friends, the media, and other sources of socialization, such as Facebook (O'Keeffe & Clarke-Pearson, 2011). If certain types of prejudice and discrimination are acceptable in a society, there may be normative pressures to conform and share those prejudiced beliefs, attitudes, and behaviors. For example, public and private schools are still somewhat segregated by social class. Historically, only children from wealthy families could afford to attend private schools, whereas children from middle- and low-income families typically attended public schools.

Reflection Questions

If a child from a low-income family received a merit scholarship to attend a private school, what concerns might her parents have about her treatment by classmates?

Stereotypes and Self-Fulfilling Prophecy

When we hold a stereotype about a person, we have expectations that he or she will fulfill that stereotype. A **self-fulfilling prophecy** is an expectation held by a person that alters his or her behavior in a way that tends to make it true. When we hold stereotypes about a person, we tend to treat the person according to our expectations. This treatment can influence the person to act according to our stereotypic expectations, thus confirming our stereotypic beliefs. Research by Rosenthal and Jacobson (1968) found that disadvantaged students whose teachers expected them to perform well had higher grades than disadvantaged students whose teachers expected them to do poorly.

> ### Reflection Questions
>
> Have you ever fallen prey to the self-fulfilling prophecy or confirmation bias? Were you the source or target?

Consider this example of cause and effect in a self-fulfilling prophecy: if an employer expects an openly gay male job applicant to be incompetent, the potential employer might treat the applicant negatively during the interview by engaging in less conversation, making little eye contact, and generally behaving coldly toward the applicant (Hebl, Foster, Mannix, & Dovidio, 2002). In turn, the job applicant will perceive that the potential employer dislikes him, and he will respond by giving shorter responses to interview questions, making less eye contact, and generally disengaging from the interview. After the interview, the employer will reflect on the applicant's behavior, which seemed cold and distant, and the employer will conclude, based on the applicant's poor performance during the interview, that the applicant was, in fact, incompetent. Thus, the employer's stereotype—gay men are incompetent and do not make good employees—is reinforced. Do you think this job applicant is likely to be hired? Treating individuals according to stereotypic beliefs can lead to prejudice and discrimination.

Another dynamic that can reinforce stereotypes is confirmation bias. When interacting with the target of our prejudice, we tend to pay attention to information that is consistent with our stereotypic expectations and ignore information that is inconsistent with our expectations. In this process, known as **confirmation bias**, we seek out information that supports our stereotypes and ignore information that is inconsistent with our stereotypes (Wason & Johnson-Laird, 1972). In the job interview example, the employer may not have noticed that the job applicant was friendly, engaging, and provided competent responses to the interview questions in the beginning of the interview. Instead, the employer focused on the job applicant's performance in the later part of the interview, after the applicant changed his demeanor and behavior to match the interviewer's negative treatment.

Social class stereotypes of individuals tend to arise when information about the individual is ambiguous. If information is unambiguous, stereotypes do not tend to arise (Baron et al., 1995).

Figure 8: Confirmation bias has been described as an internal "yes man" that echoes back existing beliefs.

In-Groups and Out-Groups

As discussed previously in this lesson, we all belong to a gender, race, age, and social economic group. These groups provide a powerful source of our identity and self-esteem (Tajfel & Turner, 1979). These groups serve as our in-groups. An **in-group** is a group that we identify with or see ourselves as belonging to. A group that we don't belong to, or an **out-group**, is a group that we view as fundamentally different from us. For example, if you are female, your gender in-group includes all females, and your gender out-group includes all males (Figure 9). People often view gender groups as being fundamentally different from each other in personality traits, characteristics, social roles, and interests. Because we often feel a strong sense of belonging and emotional connection to our in-groups, we develop in-group bias: a preference for our own group over other groups. This **in-group bias** can result in prejudice and discrimination because the out-group is perceived as different and is less preferred than our in-group.

Figure 9: Children become aware of their gender in-group and out-group at a very young age.

Despite the group dynamics that seem only to push groups toward conflict, there are forces that promote reconciliation between groups: the expression of empathy, acknowledgment of past suffering on both sides, and the halt of destructive behaviors.

One function of prejudice is to help us feel good about ourselves and maintain a positive self-concept. This need to feel good about ourselves extends to our in-groups: we want to feel good and protect our in-groups. We seek to resolve threats individually and at the in-group level. This often happens by blaming an out-group for the problem. **Scapegoating** is the act of blaming an out-group when the in-group experiences frustration or is blocked from obtaining a goal (Allport, 1954).

✎ On Your Own

Using the following table, identify one in-group and one out-group for your gender, race/ethnicity, religion, and sexual orientation. For both your in-group and the out-group you listed, identify a stereotype, an prejudiced statement against the group, and an example of discrimination that may be common for that group.

Question	Gender	Race/Ethnicity	Religion	Sexual Orientation
Your in-group				
Your out-group				
Stereotype of your in-group				
Stereotype of the out-group you listed				
Prejudiced statement against your in-group				
Prejudiced statement against the out-group you listed				
Example of discrimination against your in-group				
Example of discrimination against the out-group you listed				

Summary

As diverse individuals, humans can experience conflict when interacting with people who are different from each other. Prejudice, or negative feelings and evaluations, is common when people are from a different social group (i.e., out-group). Negative attitudes toward out-groups can lead to discrimination.

Prejudice and discrimination against others can be based on gender, race, ethnicity, social class, sexual orientation, or a variety of other social identities.

In-groups who feel threatened may blame the out-groups for their plight, thus using the out-group as a scapegoat for their frustration.

11.6 Aggression

Throughout this chapter, we have discussed how people interact and influence one another's thoughts, feelings, and behaviors in both positive and negative ways. People can work together to achieve great things, such as helping each other in emergencies: recall the heroism displayed during the 9/11 terrorist attacks. People also can do great harm to one another, such as conforming to group norms that are immoral and obeying authority to the point of murder: consider the mass conformity of Nazis during WWII. In this lesson, we will discuss a negative side of human behavior—aggression.

> **Flash Forward**
>
> Ready to dig into the vocabulary? Get some practice with this Hawkes Verified Quizlet set (hawkes.biz/psych11q6)!

Aggression

Humans engage in **aggression** when they seek to cause harm or pain to another person. Aggression takes two forms depending on one's motives: hostile or instrumental. **Hostile aggression** is motivated by feelings of anger with intent to cause pain; a fight in a bar with a stranger is an example of hostile aggression. In contrast, **instrumental aggression** is motivated by achieving a goal and does not necessarily involve intent to cause pain (Berkowitz, 1993); a contract killer who murders for hire displays instrumental aggression.

Figure 1: Humans and animals show aggression for many different reasons.

✎ On Your Own

Fill in the following chart with examples of both hostile and instrumental aggression.

Hostile Aggression	Instrumental Aggression

There are many different theories as to why aggression exists. Some researchers argue that aggression serves an evolutionary function (Buss, 2004). Men are more likely than women to show aggression (Wilson & Daly, 1985). From the perspective of evolutionary psychology, human male aggression, like that in nonhuman primates, likely serves to display dominance over other males, both to protect a mate and to perpetuate the male's genes (Figure 2). Sexual jealousy is part of male aggression; males endeavor to make sure their mates are not copulating with other males, thus ensuring their own paternity of the female's offspring. Although aggression provides an obvious evolutionary advantage for men, women also engage in aggression. Women typically display instrumental forms of aggression, with their aggression serving as a means to an end (Dodge & Schwartz, 1997). For example, women may express their aggression covertly, for example, by communication that impairs the social standing of another person. Another theory that explains one of the functions of human aggression is frustration aggression theory (Dollard, Doob, Miller, Mowrer, & Sears, 1939). This theory states that when humans are prevented from achieving an important goal, they become frustrated and aggressive.

Figure 2: Human males and nonhuman male primates endeavor to gain and display dominance over other males, as demonstrated in the behavior of these gorillas.

Bullying

A modern form of aggression is bullying. As you learn in your study of child development, socializing and playing with other children is beneficial for children's psychological development. However, as you may have experienced as a child, not all play behavior has positive outcomes. Some children are aggressive and want to play roughly. Other children are selfish and do not want to share toys. One form of negative social interactions among children that has become a national concern is bullying. **Bullying** is repeated negative treatment of another person, often an adolescent, over time (Olweus, 1993). A one-time incident in which one child hits another child on the playground would not be considered bullying: bullying is repeated behavior. The negative treatment typical in bullying is the attempt to inflict harm, injury, or humiliation, and bullying can include physical or verbal attacks. However, bullying doesn't have to be physical or verbal, it can be psychological. Research finds gender differences in how girls and boys bully others (American Psychological Association, 2010; Olweus, 1993). Boys tend to engage in direct, physical aggression, such as physically harming others. Girls tend to engage in indirect, social forms of aggression, such as spreading rumors, ignoring, or socially isolating others. Based on what you have learned about child development and social roles, why do you think boys and girls display different types of bullying behavior?

Bullying involves three parties: the bully, the victim, and witnesses or bystanders. The act of bullying involves an imbalance of power with the bully holding more power—physically, emotionally, and/or socially—over the victim. The experience of bullying can be positive for the bully, who may enjoy a boost to self-esteem. However, there are several negative consequences of bullying for the victim and also for the bystanders. How do you think bullying negatively impacts adolescents? Being the victim of bullying is associated with decreased mental health, including experiencing anxiety and depression (APA, 2010). Victims of bullying may underperform in schoolwork (Bowen, 2011). Bullying also can result in the victim committing suicide (APA, 2010). How might bullying negatively affect witnesses?

📷 **Figure 3:** Bullying can be physical or verbal.

Although there is not one single personality profile for who becomes a bully and who becomes a victim of bullying (APA, 2010), researchers have identified some patterns in children who are at a greater risk of being bullied (Olweus, 1993):

- Children who are emotionally reactive are at a greater risk for being bullied. Bullies may be attracted to children who get upset easily because the bully can quickly get an emotional reaction from them.

- Children who are different from others are likely to be targeted for bullying. Children who are overweight, cognitively impaired, or racially or ethnically different from their peer group may be at higher risk.

- Gay, lesbian, bisexual, and transgender teens are at very high risk of being bullied and hurt.

Cyberbullying

With the rapid growth of technology, and widely available mobile technology and social networking media, a new form of bullying has emerged: cyberbullying (Hoff & Mitchell, 2009). **Cyberbullying**, like bullying, is repeated behavior that is intended to cause psychological or emotional harm to another person. What is unique about cyberbullying is that it is typically covert, concealed, done in private, and the bully can remain anonymous. This anonymity gives the bully power, and the victim may feel helpless, unable to escape the harassment, and unable to retaliate (Spears, Slee, Owens, & Johnson, 2009).

Reflection Questions

More than half of bullying situations (57%) stop when a peer intervenes on behalf of the student being bullied (Hawkins, Pepler, & Craig, 2001).

What do you think are the barriers for a peer to stand up to a bully on behalf of another?

Why do you think that bullying ends more easily when another defends the target of the bullying?

Cyberbullying can take many forms, including harassing a victim by spreading rumors, creating a website defaming the victim, and ignoring, insulting, laughing at, or teasing the victim (Spears et al., 2009). In cyberbullying, it is more common for girls to be the bullies and victims because cyberbullying is nonphysical and is a less direct form of bullying (Figure 4) (Hoff & Mitchell, 2009). Interestingly, girls who become cyberbullies often have been the victims of cyberbullying at one time (Vandebosch & Van Cleemput, 2009). The effects of cyberbullying are just as harmful as traditional bullying and include the victim feeling frustration, anger, sadness, helplessness, powerlessness, and fear. Victims will also experience lower self-esteem (Hoff & Mitchell, 2009; Spears et al., 2009). Furthermore, recent research suggests that both cyberbullying victims and perpetrators are more likely to experience suicidal ideation, and they are more likely to attempt suicide than individuals who have no experience with cyberbullying (Hinduja & Patchin, 2010).

What features of technology make cyberbullying easier and perhaps more accessible to young adults? What can parents, teachers, and social networking websites, like Facebook, do to prevent cyberbullying?

📷 **Figure 4:** Because cyberbullying is not physical in nature, cyberbullies and their victims are most often female; however, there is much evidence that male homosexuals are frequently victims of cyberbullying as well (Hinduja & Patchin, 2011).

📷 **Figure 5:** Diffusion of responsibility likely contributes to the bystander effect.

The Bystander Effect

The discussion of bullying highlights the problem of witnesses not intervening to help a victim. This is a common occurrence, as the following well-publicized event demonstrates.

In 1964, in Queens, New York, a 19-year-old woman named Kitty Genovese was attacked by a person with a knife near the back entrance to her apartment building and again in the hallway inside her apartment building. When the attack occurred, she screamed for help numerous times and eventually died from her stab wounds. This story became famous because reportedly numerous residents in the apartment building heard her cries for help and did nothing—neither helping her nor summoning the police—though these facts have been disputed.

Based on this case, researchers Latané and Darley (1968) described a phenomenon called the bystander effect. The **bystander effect** is a phenomenon in which a witness or bystander does not volunteer to help a victim or person in distress. Instead, they just watch what is happening. Social psychologists hold that we make these decisions based on the social situation, not our own personality variables. Why do you think the bystanders didn't help Genovese? What are the benefits to helping her? What are the risks? It is very likely you listed more costs than benefits to helping. In this situation, bystanders likely feared for their own lives—if they went to her aid, the attacker might harm them. However, how difficult would it have been to make a phone call to the police from the safety of their apartments? Why do you think no one helped in any way? Social psychologists claim that diffusion of responsibility is the likely explanation. **Diffusion of responsibility** is the tendency for no one in a group to help because the responsibility to help is spread throughout the group (Bandura, 1999). Because there were many witnesses to the attack on Genovese, as evidenced by the number of lit apartment windows in the building, individuals assumed someone else must have already called the police. The responsibility to call the police was diffused across the number of witnesses to the crime. Have you ever passed an accident on the freeway and assumed that a victim or certainly another motorist has already reported the accident? In general, the greater the number of bystanders, the less likely any one person will help.

Summary

Aggression is seeking to cause another person harm or pain. Hostile aggression is motivated by feelings of anger with intent to cause pain, and instrumental aggression is motivated by achieving a goal and does not necessarily involve intent to cause pain. Bullying is an international public health concern that largely affects the adolescent population. Bullying is repeated behaviors that are intended to inflict harm on the victim and can take the form of physical, psychological, emotional, or social abuse. Bullying has negative mental health

Group Activity

As you read, the bystander effect can be very powerful, holding people back from helping, especially when someone is desperately in need.

Test out the theory in real life. In pairs or small groups, go out into the community and create a situation in which one of the group member needs assistance, such as carrying a heavy load while trying to open the door. Have the person struggle alone while the other members watch to see if anyone comes to aid. Then, in a different location or time, re-create the situation. Except this time, have the other group members offer to help. See how many strangers offer to help as well.

consequences for youth including suicide. Cyberbullying is a newer form of bullying that takes place in an online environment where bullies can remain anonymous and victims are helpless to address the harassment. Despite the social norm of helping others in need, when there are many bystanders witnessing an emergency, diffusion of responsibility will lead to a lower likelihood of any one person helping.

11.7   Prosocial Behavior

You've learned about many of the negative behaviors of social psychology, but the field also studies many positive social interactions and behaviors. What makes people like each other? With whom are we friends? Whom do we date? Researchers have documented several features of the situation that influence whether we form relationships with others. There are also universal traits that humans find attractive in others. In this lesson, we discuss conditions that make forming relationships more likely, what we look for in friendships and romantic relationships, the different types of love, and a theory explaining how our relationships are formed, maintained, and terminated.

Flash Forward

Ready to dig insto the vocabulary? Get some practice with this Hawkes Verified Quizlet set (hawkes.biz/psych11q7)!

Prosocial Behavior and Altruism

Do you voluntarily help others? Voluntary behavior with the intent to help other people is called **prosocial behavior**. Why do people help other people? Is personal benefit, such as feeling good about oneself, the only reason people help one another? Research suggests there are many other reasons. **Altruism** is people's desire to help others even if the costs outweigh the benefits of helping. In fact, people acting in altruistic ways may disregard the personal costs associated with helping (Figure 1). For example, news accounts of the 9/11 terrorist attacks on the World Trade Center in New York reported an employee in the first tower helped his co-workers make it to the exit stairwell. After helping a co-worker to safety, he went back in the burning building to help additional co-workers. In this case, the costs of helping were great, and the hero lost his life in the destruction (Stewart, 2002).

🖼 **Figure 1:** In the event of a crisis, people often spring into action and offer immediate help without weighing the costs.

Some researchers suggest that altruism operates on empathy. **Empathy** is the capacity to understand another person's perspective, to feel what he or she feels. An empathetic person makes an emotional connection with others and feels compelled to help (Batson, 1991). Other researchers argue that altruism is a form of selfless helping that is not motivated by benefits or feeling good about oneself. Certainly, after helping, people feel good about themselves, but some researchers argue that this is a consequence of altruism, not a cause. Other researchers argue that helping is always self-serving because our egos are involved, and we receive benefits from helping (Cialdini, Brown, Lewis, Luce, & Neuberg 1997). It is challenging to determine experimentally the true motivation for helping, whether is it largely self-serving (egoism) or selfless (altruism). Thus, a debate on whether pure altruism exists continues.

Group Activity

In small groups, discuss the difference between apathy, empathy, and sympathy.

Now, have the members of the group think of a situation from your own lives in which empathy may be needed.

- What would an apathetic, sympathetic, or empathetic response be?

- What would the potential impact of each response be?

Forming Relationships

What do you think is the single most influential factor in determining with whom you become friends and whom you form romantic relationships? You might be surprised to learn that the answer is simple: the people with whom you have the most contact. This most important factor is proximity. You are more likely to be friends with people you have regular contact with. For example, there are decades of research that shows that you are more likely to become friends with people who live in your dorm, your apartment building, or your immediate neighborhood than with people who live farther away (Festinger, Schachler, & Back, 1950). It is simply easier to form relationships with people you see often because you have the opportunity to get to know them.

> ## Reflection Questions
>
> The mere-exposure effect is a psychological phenomenon by which people tend to develop a preference for things merely because they are familiar with them. This is an extension of proximity effects in regards to attraction. In other words, the more we see it, the more familiar we are with it, the more we like it.
>
> Can you think of a person, a song, TV show, or product that you started to like after being exposed to it several times?

Similarity is another factor that influences who we form relationships with. We are more likely to become friends or lovers with someone who is similar to us in background, attitudes, and lifestyle. In fact, there is no evidence that opposites attract. Rather, we are attracted to people who are most like us (Figure 2) (McPherson, Smith-Lovin, & Cook, 2001).

Figure 2: People tend to be attracted to similar people. Many couples share a cultural background. This can be quite obvious in a ceremony such as a wedding and more subtle (but no less significant) in the day-to-day workings of a relationship.

Why do you think we are attracted to people who are similar to us? Sharing things in common will certainly make it easy to get along with others and form connections. When you and another person share similar music taste, hobbies, food preferences, and so on, deciding what to do with your time together might be easy. **Homophily** is the tendency for people to form social networks, including friendships, marriages, business relationships, and many other types of relationships, with others who are similar (McPherson et al., 2001).

Once we form relationships with people, we desire reciprocity. **Reciprocity** is the give and take in relationships. We contribute to relationships, but we expect to receive benefits as well. That is, we want our relationships to be a two-way street. We are more likely to like and engage with people who like us back. Self-disclosure is part of the two-way street. **Self-disclosure** is the sharing of personal information (Laurenceau, Barrett, & Pietromonaco, 1998). We form more intimate connections with people with whom we disclose important information about ourselves. Indeed, self-disclosure is a characteristic of healthy intimate relationships, as long as the information disclosed is consistent with our own views (Cozby, 1973).

Figure 3: Reciprocity within relationships is a two-way street.

Attraction

We have discussed how proximity and similarity lead to the formation of relationships and that reciprocity and self-disclosure are important for relationship maintenance. But, what features of a person do we find attractive? We don't form relationships with everyone that lives or works near us, so how is it that we decide which specific individuals we will select as friends and lovers?

Researchers have documented several characteristics in men and women that humans find attractive. First, we look for friends and lovers who are physically attractive. People differ in what they consider attractive, and attractiveness is culturally influenced. Research, however, suggests that some universally attractive features in women include large eyes, high cheekbones, a narrow jaw line, a slender build (Buss, 1989), and a lower waist-to-hip ratio (Singh, 1993). For men, attractive traits include being tall, having broad shoulders, and a narrow waist (Buss, 1989). Both men and women with high levels of facial and body symmetry are generally considered more attractive than asymmetric individuals (Fink, Neave, Manning, & Grammer, 2006; Penton-Voak et al., 2001; Rikowski & Grammer, 1999). Social traits that people find attractive in potential female mates include warmth, affection, and social skills; in males, the attractive traits include achievement, leadership qualities, and job skills (Regan & Berscheid, 1997).

(a)   (b)

Figure 4: Here are some examples of the matching hypothesis: famous couples (a) Blake Lively and Ryan Reynolds and (b) Beyoncé and Jay-Z.

Although humans want mates who are physically attractive, this does not mean that we look for the most attractive person possible. In fact, this observation has led some to propose what is known as the matching hypothesis, which asserts that people tend to pick someone they view as their equal in physical attractiveness, and social desirability (Taylor, Fiore, Mendelsohn, & Cheshire, 2011). For example, you and most people you know likely would say that a very attractive movie star is out of your league. So, even if you had proximity to that person, you likely would not ask them out on a date because you believe you likely would be rejected. People weigh a potential partner's attractiveness against the likelihood of success with that person. If you think you are particularly unattractive (even if you are not), you likely will seek partners that are fairly unattractive (that is, unattractive in physical appearance or in behavior).

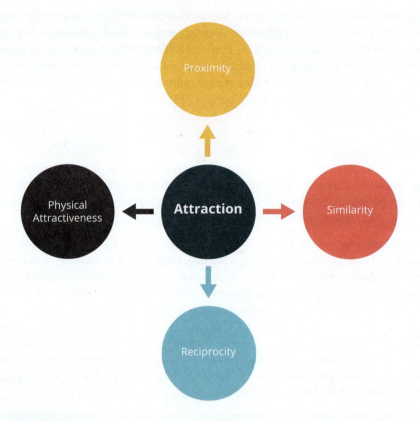

Figure 5: There are several factors that influence attraction.

Sternberg's Triangular Theory of Love

We typically love the people with whom we form relationships, but the type of love we have for our family, friends, and lovers differs. Robert Sternberg (1986) proposed that there are three components of love: intimacy, passion, and commitment. These three components form a triangle that defines multiple types of love: this is known as Sternberg's **triangular theory of love** (Figure 6). Intimacy is the sharing of details and intimate thoughts and emotions. Passion is the physical attraction—the flame in the fire. Commitment is standing by the person—the "in sickness and health" part of the relationship.

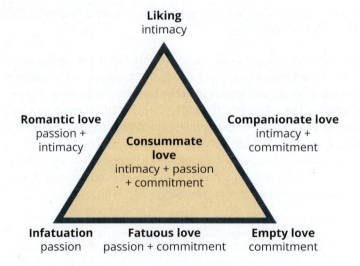

Figure 6: According to Sternberg's triangular theory of love, seven types of love can be described from combinations of three components: intimacy, passion, and commitment.

Sternberg (1986) states that a healthy relationship will have all three components of love—intimacy, passion, and commitment—which is described as **consummate love** (Figure 7). However, different aspects of love might be more prevalent at different life stages. Other forms of love include liking, which is defined as having intimacy but no passion or commitment. Infatuation is the presence of passion without intimacy or commitment. Empty love is having commitment without intimacy or passion. **Companionate love**, which is characteristic of close friendships and family relationships, consists of intimacy and commitment but no passion. **Romantic love** is defined by having passion and intimacy but no commitment. Finally, fatuous love is defined by having passion and commitment but no intimacy, such as a long-term sexual love affair. Can you describe other examples of relationships that fit these different types of love?

Figure 7: According to Sternberg, consummate love describes a healthy relationship containing intimacy, passion, and commitment.

✏ On Your Own

Read the following examples and determine what type of love is being described.

1. In 2004, Britney Spears and her childhood friend, Jason Alexander, got married in Las Vegas. The marriage lasted for 55 hours.

☐ Empty Love   ☐ Fatuous Love   ☐ Companionate Love

2. Marcus and Danessa met at a party a month ago and fell in love "at first sight." They have been together every free moment since.

☐ Romantic Love   ☐ Fatuous Love   ☐ Consummate Love

Social Exchange Theory

We have discussed why we form relationships, what attracts us to others, and different types of love. But what determines whether we are satisfied with and stay in a relationship? One theory that provides an explanation is social exchange theory. According to **social exchange theory**, we act as naïve economists in keeping a tally of the ratio of costs and benefits of forming and maintaining a relationship with others (Figure 8) (Rusbult & Van Lange, 2003).

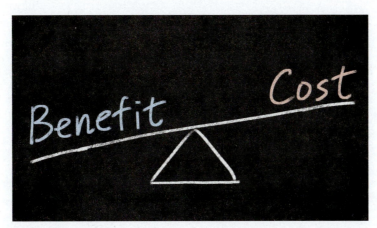

Figure 8: Acting like naïve economists, people may keep track of the costs and benefits of maintaining a relationship. Typically, only those relationships in which the benefits outweigh the costs will be maintained.

People are motivated to maximize the benefits of social exchanges, or relationships, and minimize the costs. People prefer to have more benefits than costs, or to have nearly equal costs and benefits, but most people are dissatisfied if their social exchanges create more costs than benefits. Let's discuss an example. If you have ever decided to commit to a romantic relationship, you probably considered the advantages and disadvantages of your decision. What are the benefits of being in a committed romantic relationship? You may have considered having companionship, intimacy, and passion but also being comfortable with a person you know well. What are the costs of being in a committed romantic relationship? You may think that over time boredom from being with only one person may set in; moreover, it may be expensive to share activities such as attending movies and going to dinner. However, the benefits of dating your romantic partner presumably outweigh the costs, or you wouldn't continue the relationship.

Summary

Altruism is a pure form of helping others out of empathy, which can be contrasted with egoistic motivations for helping. Forming relationships with others is a necessity for social beings. We typically form relationships with people who are close to us in proximity and people with whom we share similarities. We expect reciprocity and self-disclosure in our relationships. We also want to form relationships with people who are physically attractive, though standards for attractiveness vary by culture and gender. There are many types of love that are determined by various combinations of intimacy, passion, and commitment; consummate love, which is the ideal form of love, contains all three components. When determining satisfaction and whether to maintain a relationship, individuals often use a social exchange approach and weigh the costs and benefits of forming and maintaining a relationship.

Chapter 11 Project

Purpose

The failure to recognize the power of a situation or social context on other's individual behavior and instead attributing the behavior to the person's state or personality is referred to as the fundamental attribution error. The fundamental attribution error is most commonly committed in individualistic cultures that promote a focus on individual achievements verses communal relationships.

Social psychologists argue that people's behaviors, thoughts, and attitudes are strongly influenced by their social settings, situations, and interactions with others. Thus, understanding the role of the social world on behavior is critical and is the central tenant of social psychology. **The purpose of this project is to broaden your understanding of the social forces that influence individual behavior and examine the impacts of social settings, groups, and scripts on everyday life.**

Directions

This project includes two parts:

Part 1 – The Response

Part 2 – The Reflection

Part 1 – The Response:

Provide two examples for each of the following questions. Create a table like the one below.

Question	Example 1	Example 2
Identify two social settings you regularly participate in, such as school or church. Briefly describe each.		
Describe your social role in each setting.		
Describe the social norms for each setting.		
Describe the social scripts you follow in each setting.		
Describe the role, if any, of conformity, compliance, and/or obedience in each setting.		
Describe the social groups you interact with and/or participate in in each setting.		
What, if any, initiation did you complete to become part of these groups?		
What stereotypes or prejudices, if any, do you experience through participation in these social groups?		
What benefits or exchanges do you receive from participating in these social interactions?		

Part 2 – The Reflection:

Go back through your responses and write a 150+ word paragraph on what you learned, what surprised you, and what questions you now have.

Then, write a second paragraph considering if what you discovered connects with the concept of social impact.

Materials

None required.

✅ **Checklist**

☐ All questions are answered for both examples

☐ Reflection

    ☐ 150+ words

    ☐ Connection to the concept of social impact

🏁 Chapter 11 Review

Lesson Summaries

11.1 What Is Social Psychology?

Social psychology is the subfield of psychology that studies the power of the situation to influence individuals' thoughts, feelings, and behaviors. Psychologists categorize the causes of human behavior as those due to internal factors, such as personality, or those due to external factors, such as cultural and other social influences. Behavior is better explained, however, by using both approaches. Lay people tend to over-rely on dispositional explanations for behavior and ignore the power of situational influences, a perspective called the fundamental attribution error. People from individualistic cultures are more likely to display this bias versus people from collectivistic cultures. Our explanations for our own and others' behaviors can be biased due to not having enough information about others' motivations for behaviors and by providing explanations that bolster our self-esteem.

11.2 Self-Presentation

Human behavior is largely influenced by our social roles, norms, and scripts. In order to know how to act in a given situation, we have shared cultural knowledge of how to behave depending on our role in society. Social norms dictate the behavior that is appropriate or inappropriate for each role. Each social role has scripts that help humans learn the sequence of appropriate behaviors in a given setting. The famous Stanford prison experiment is an example of how the power of the situation can dictate the social roles, norms, and scripts we follow in a given situation, even if this behavior is contrary to our typical behavior.

11.3 Attitudes and Persuasion

Attitudes are our evaluations or feelings toward a person, idea, or object and typically are positive or negative. Our attitudes and beliefs are influenced not only by external forces but also by internal influences that we control. An internal form of attitude change is cognitive dissonance or the tension we experience when our thoughts, feelings, and behaviors are in conflict. In order to reduce dissonance, individuals can change their behavior, attitudes, or cognitions or add a new cognition. External forces of persuasion include advertising; the features of advertising that influence our behaviors include the source, message, and audience. There are two primary routes to persuasion. The central route to persuasion uses facts and information to persuade potential consumers. The peripheral route uses positive association with cues such as beauty, fame, and positive emotions.

11.4 Conformity, Compliance, and Obedience

The power of the situation can lead people to conform, or go along with the group, even in the face of inaccurate information. Conformity to group norms is driven by two motivations, the desire to fit in and be liked and the desire to be accurate and gain information from the group.

Authority figures also have influence over our behaviors, and many people become obedient and follow orders even if the orders are contrary to their personal values.

Conformity to group pressures can also result in groupthink, or the faulty decision-making process that results from cohesive group members trying to maintain group harmony.

Group situations can improve human behavior through facilitating performance on easy tasks but inhibiting performance on difficult tasks. The presence of others can also lead to social loafing when individual efforts cannot be evaluated.

11.5 Prejudice and Discrimination

As diverse individuals, humans can experience conflict when interacting with people who are different from each other. Prejudice, or negative feelings and evaluations, is common when people are from a different social group (i.e., out-group). Negative attitudes toward out-groups can lead to discrimination.

Prejudice and discrimination against others can be based on gender, race, ethnicity, social class, sexual orientation, or a variety of other social identities.

In-groups who feel threatened may blame the out-groups for their plight, thus using the out-group as a scapegoat for their frustration.

11.6 Aggression

Aggression is seeking to cause another person harm or pain. Hostile aggression is motivated by feelings of anger with intent to cause pain, and instrumental aggression is motivated by achieving a goal and does not necessarily involve intent to cause pain. Bullying is an international public health concern that largely affects the adolescent population. Bullying is repeated behaviors that are intended to inflict harm on the victim and can take the form of physical, psychological, emotional, or social abuse. Bullying has negative mental health consequences for youth including suicide. Cyberbullying is a newer form of bullying that takes place in an online environment where bullies can remain anonymous and victims are helpless to address the harassment. Despite the social norm of helping others in need, when there are many bystanders witnessing an emergency, diffusion of responsibility will lead to a lower likelihood of any one person helping.

11.7 Prosocial Behavior

Altruism is a pure form of helping others out of empathy, which can be contrasted with egoistic motivations for helping. Forming relationships with others is a necessity for social beings. We typically form relationships with people who are close to us in proximity and people with whom we share similarities. We expect reciprocity and self-disclosure in our relationships. We also want to form relationships with people who are physically attractive, though standards for attractiveness vary by culture and gender. There are many types of love that are determined by various combinations of intimacy, passion, and commitment; consummate love, which is the ideal form of love, contains all three components. When determining satisfaction and whether to maintain a relationship, individuals often use a social exchange approach and weigh the costs and benefits of forming and maintaining a relationship.

Key Terms

Flash Back

Now that you've worked through the chapter, sharpen your vocabulary with this Hawkes Verified Quizlet set (hawkes.biz/psychch11)!

Actor-Observer Bias

Phenomenon of explaining other people's behaviors are due to internal factors and our own behaviors are due to situational forces

Ageism

Prejudice and discrimination toward individuals based solely on their age

Aggression

Seeking to cause harm or pain to another person

Altruism

Humans' desire to help others even if the costs outweigh the benefits of helping

Asch Effect

Group majority influences an individual's judgment, even when that judgment is inaccurate

Attitude

Evaluations of or feelings toward a person, idea, or object that are typically positive or negative

Attribution

Explanation for the behavior of other people

Bullying

A person, often an adolescent, being treated negatively repeatedly and over time

Bystander Effect

Situation in which a witness or bystander does not volunteer to help a victim or person in distress

Central Route Persuasion

Logic-driven arguments using data and facts to convince people of an argument's worthiness

Cognitive Dissonance

Psychological discomfort that arises from a conflict in a person's behaviors, attitudes, or beliefs that runs counter to one's positive self-perception

Collectivistic Culture

Culture that focuses on communal relationships with others such as family, friends, and community

Companionate Love

Type of love consisting of intimacy and commitment, but not passion; associated with close friendships and family relationships

Confederate

Person who works for a researcher and is aware of the experiment, but who acts as a participant; used to manipulate social situations as part of the research design

Confirmation Bias

Seeking out information that supports our stereotypes while ignoring information that is inconsistent with our stereotypes

Conformity

When individuals change their behavior to go along with the group even if they do not agree with the group

Consummate Love

Type of love occurring when intimacy, passion, and commitment are all present

Cyberbullying

Repeated behavior that is intended to cause psychological or emotional harm to another person and that takes place online

Diffusion of Resonsibility

Tendency for no one in a group to help because the responsibility to help is spread throughout the group

Discrimination

Negative actions toward individuals as a result of their membership in a particular group

Dispositionism

Describes a perspective common to personality psychologists, which asserts that our behavior is determined by internal factors, such as personality traits and temperament

Empathy

Capacity to understand another person's perspective—to feel what he or she feels

Foot-in-the-Door Technique

Persuasion of one person by another person, encouraging a person to agree to a small favor, or to buy a small item, only to later request a larger favor or purchase of a larger item

Fundamental Attribution Error

Tendency to overemphasize internal factors as attributions for behavior and underestimate the power of the situation

Group Polarization

Strengthening of the original group attitude after discussing views within the group

Groupthink

Group members modify their opinions to match what they believe is the group consensus

Homophily

Tendency for people to form social networks, including friendships, marriages, business relationships, and many other types of relationships, with others who are similar

Homophobia

Prejudice and discrimination against individuals based solely on their sexual orientation

Hostile Aggression

Aggression motivated by feelings of anger with intent to cause pain

Individualistic Culture

Culture that focuses on individual achievement and autonomy

Informational Social Influence

Conformity to a group norm prompted by the belief that the group is competent and has the correct information

In-Group

Group that we identify with or see ourselves as belonging to

In-Group Bias

Preference for our own group over other groups

Instrumental Aggression

Aggression motivated by achieving a goal and does not necessarily involve intent to cause pain

Internal Factor

Internal attribute of a person, such as personality traits or temperament

Just-World Hypothesis

Ideology common in the United States that people get the outcomes they deserve

Normative Social Influence

Conformity to a group norm to fit in, feel good, and be accepted by the group

Obedience

Change of behavior to please an authority figure or to avoid aversive consequences

Out-Group

Group that we don't belong to—one that we view as fundamentally different from us

Peripheral Route Persuasion

One person persuades another person; an indirect route that relies on association of peripheral cues (such as positive emotions and celebrity endorsement) to associate positivity with a message

Persuasion

Process of changing our attitude toward something based on some form of communication

Prejudice

Negative attitudes and feelings toward individuals based solely on their membership in a particular group

Prosocial Behavior

Voluntary behavior with the intent to help other people

Racism

Prejudice and discrimination toward individuals based solely on their race

Reciprocity

Give and take in relationships

Romantic Love

Type of love consisting of intimacy and passion but no commitment

Scapegoating

Act of blaming an out-group when the in-group experiences frustration or is blocked from obtaining a goal

Script

Person's knowledge about the sequence of events in a specific setting

Self-Disclosure

Sharing personal information in relationships

Self-Fulfilling Prophecy

Treating stereotyped group members according to our biased expectations only to have this treatment influence the individual to act according to our stereotypic expectations, thus confirming our stereotypic beliefs

Self-Serving Bias

Tendency for individuals to take credit by making dispositional or internal attributions for positive outcomes and situational or external attributions for negative outcomes

Sexism

Prejudice and discrimination toward individuals based on their sex

Situationism

Describes a perspective that behavior and actions are determined by the immediate environment and surroundings; a view promoted by social psychologists

Social Exchange Theory

Humans act as naïve economists in keeping a tally of the ratio of costs and benefits of forming and maintain a relationship, with the goal to maximize benefits and minimize costs

Social Facilitation

Improved performance when an audience is watching versus when the individual performs the behavior alone

Social Loafing

Exertion of less effort by a person working in a group because individual performance cannot be evaluated separately from the group, thus causing performance decline on easy tasks

Social Norm

Group's expectations regarding what is appropriate and acceptable for the thoughts and behavior of its members

Social Psychology

Field of psychology that examines how people impact or affect each other, with particular focus on the power of the situation

Social Role

Socially defined pattern of behavior that is expected of a person in a given setting or group

Stanford Prison Experiment

Stanford University conducted an experiment in a mock prison that demonstrated the power of social roles, social norms, and scripts

Stereotype

Specific beliefs or assumptions about individuals based solely on their membership in a group, regardless of their individual characteristics

Triangular Theory of Love

Model of love based on three components: intimacy, passion, and commitment; several types of love exist, depending on the presence or absence of each of these components

Exercises

Review Questions

1. As a field, social psychology focuses on _____ in predicting human behavior.

   a. personality traits

   b. genetic predispositions

   c. biological forces

   d. situational factors

2. Making internal attributions for your successes and making external attributions for your failures is an example of _____.

   a. actor-observer bias

   b. fundamental attribution error

   c. self-serving bias

   d. just-world hypothesis

3. Collectivistic cultures are to _____ as individualistic cultures are to _____.

   a. dispositional; situational

   b. situational; dispositional

   c. autonomy; group harmony

   d. just-world hypothesis; self-serving bias

4. According to the actor-observer bias, we have more information about _____.

   a. situational influences on behavior

   b. influences on our own behavior

   c. influences on others' behavior

   d. dispositional influences on behavior

5. A(n) _____ is a set of group expectations for appropriate thoughts and behaviors of its members.

   a. social role

   b. social norm

   c. script

   d. attribution

6. On his first day of soccer practice, Jose suits up in a t-shirt, shorts, and cleats and runs out to the field to join his teammates. Jose's behavior is reflective of _____.

   a. a script

   b. social influence

   c. good athletic behavior

   d. normative behavior

7. When it comes to buying clothes, teenagers often follow social norms; this is likely motivated by _____.

   a. following parents' rules

   b. saving money

   c. fitting in

   d. looking good

8. In the Stanford prison experiment, even the lead researcher succumbed to his role as a prison supervisor. This is an example of the power of _____ influencing behavior.

   a. scripts

   b. social norms

   c. conformity

   d. social roles

9. Attitudes describe our _____ of people, objects, and ideas.

   a. treatment

   b. evaluations

   c. cognitions

   d. knowledge

10. Cognitive dissonance causes discomfort because it disrupts our sense of _____.

    a. dependency

    b. unpredictability

    c. consistency

    d. power

11. In order for the central route to persuasion to be effective, the audience must be _____ and _____.

    a. analytical; motivated

    b. attentive; happy

    c. intelligent; unemotional

    d. gullible; distracted

12. Examples of cues used in peripheral route persuasion include all of the following except _____.

    a. celebrity endorsement

    b. positive emotions

    c. attractive models

    d. factual information

13. In the Asch experiment, participants conformed due to _____ social influence.

    a. informational

    b. normative

    c. inspirational

    d. persuasive

14. Under what conditions will informational social influence be more likely?

    a. When individuals want to fit in

    b. When the answer is unclear

    c. When the group has expertise

    d. Both b and c

15. Social loafing occurs when _____.

    a. individual performance cannot be evaluated

    b. the task is easy

    c. both a and b

    d. none of the above

16. If group members modify their opinions to align with a perceived group consensus, then _____ has occurred.

    a. group cohesion

    b. social facilitation

    c. groupthink

    d. social loafing

17. Prejudice is to _____ as discrimination is to _____.

    a. feelings; behavior

    b. thoughts; feelings

    c. feelings; thoughts

    d. behavior; feelings

18. Which of the following is not a type of prejudice?

    a. Homophobia

    b. Racism

    c. Sexism

    d. Individualism

19. _____ occurs when the out-group is blamed for the in-group's frustration.

    a. Stereotyping

    b. In-group bias

    c. Scapegoating

    d. Ageism

20. When we seek out information that supports our stereotypes we are engaged in _____.

    a. scapegoating

    b. confirmation bias

    c. self-fulfilling prophecy

    d. in-group bias

21. Typically, bullying from boys is to _____ as bullying from girls is to _____.

    a. emotional harm; physical harm

    b. physical harm; emotional harm

    c. psychological harm; physical harm

    d. social exclusion; verbal taunting

22. Which of the following adolescents is least likely to be targeted for bullying?

    a. A child with a physical disability

    b. A transgender adolescent

    c. An emotionally sensitive boy

    d. The captain of the football team

23. The bystander effect likely occurs due to _____.

    a. desensitization to violence

    b. people not noticing the emergency

    c. diffusion of responsibility

    d. emotional insensitivity

24. Altruism is a form of prosocial behavior that is motivated by _____.

    a. feeling good about oneself

    b. selfless helping of others

    c. earning a reward

    d. showing bravery to bystanders

25. After moving to a new apartment building, research suggests that Sam will be most likely to become friends with _____.

    a. his next door neighbor

    b. someone who lives three floors up in the apartment building

    c. someone from across the street

    d. his new postal delivery person

26. What trait do both men and women tend to look for in a romantic partner?

    a. Sense of humor

    b. Social skills

    c. Leadership potential

    d. Physical attractiveness

27. According to the triangular theory of love, what type of love is defined by passion and intimacy but no commitment?

    a. Consummate love

    b. Empty love

    c. Romantic love

    d. Liking

28. According to social exchange theory, humans want to maximize the _____ and minimize the _____ in relationships.

    a. intimacy; commitment

    b. benefits; costs

    c. costs; benefits

    d. passion; intimacy

Critical Thinking Questions

29. Compare and contrast situational influences and dispositional influences and give an example of each. Explain how situational influences and dispositional influences might explain inappropriate behavior.

30. Provide an example of how people from individualistic and collectivistic cultures would differ in explaining why they won an important sporting event.

31. Why didn't the "good" guards in the Stanford prison experiment object to other guards' abusive behavior? Were the student prisoners simply weak people? Why didn't they object to being abused?

32. Describe how social roles, social norms, and scripts were evident in the Stanford prison experiment. How can this experiment be applied to everyday life? Are there any more recent examples where people started fulfilling a role and became abusive?

33. Give an example (one not used in class or your text) of cognitive dissonance and how an individual might resolve this.

34. Imagine that you work for an advertising agency, and you've been tasked with developing an advertising campaign to increase sales of Bliss Soda. How would you develop an advertisement for this product that uses a central route of persuasion? How would you develop an ad using a peripheral route of persuasion?

35. Describe how seeking outside opinions can prevent groupthink.

36. Compare and contrast social loafing and social facilitation.

37. Some people seem more willing to openly display prejudice regarding sexual orientation than prejudice regarding race and gender. Speculate on why this might be.

38. When people blame a scapegoat, how do you think they choose evidence to support the blame?

39. Compare and contrast hostile and instrumental aggression.

40. What evidence discussed in Lesson 11.6 suggests that cyberbullying is difficult to detect and prevent?

41. Describe what influences whether relationships will be formed.

42. The evolutionary theory argues that humans are motivated to perpetuate their genes and reproduce. Using an evolutionary perspective, describe traits in men and women that humans find attractive.

Chapter 12
Industrial-Organizational Psychology

Chapter Introduction

(a)   (b)   (c)

🖼 **Figure 1:** What does an office look like? For people who telecommute, their workspace may be adapted to fit their lifestyle.

In July 2012, Yahoo!, one of the largest and oldest web companies, announced the appointment of Marissa Mayer as CEO. Yahoo! had struggled to define itself and excel in the industry for several years, and the appointment of Mayer, a top Google executive, made big news. Among her many decisions, in February 2013, Mayer announced that employees would no longer be allowed to telecommute. Telecommuting is representative of many management innovations that have been made in recent years, largely by tech companies. Telecommuting reflects a belief on the part of companies that employees are responsible, self-motivating, and perhaps work best when they are left alone. It also has an impact on work–family balance, though which way is yet unclear. And telecommuting reflects the more general trend of increasing overlap between workers' time spent *on the job* and time spent *off the job*.

The reversal of this policy at Yahoo! brought controversy and a lot of questions about what it meant. Mayer has stayed largely quiet on her reasoning behind the decision, except to say that it was meant to better the company. She finally addressed her decision briefly at the 2013 Great Place to Work conference (Tkaczyk, 2013) by saying, among other things, that while "people are more productive when they're alone, they're more collaborative and innovative when they're together." Interestingly, shortly after the Yahoo! change, Bank of America, IBM, and Best Buy also eliminated telecommuting as an option for their employees.

Did the change make these companies more innovative or more productive? How has the change affected employees, particularly working parents and those taking care of elderly relatives? Was the change introduced in the most effective way? These questions are commonly studied by a branch of psychology called industrial and organizational psychology.

Flash Forward

Ready to dig into the vocabulary? Get some practice with this Hawkes Verified Quizlet set (hawkes.biz/psych12q1)!

12.1 What Is Industrial and Organizational Psychology?

In 2012, people who worked in the United States spent an average of 56.4 hours per week working (Bureau of Labor Statistics—U.S. Department of Labor, 2013). Sleeping was the only other activity they spent more time on with an average of 61.2 hours per week. The workday is a significant portion of workers' time and energy. It impacts their lives and their family's lives in positive and negative physical and psychological ways. **Industrial and organizational (I-O) psychology** is a branch of psychology that studies how human behavior and psychology affect work and how they are affected by work.

Industrial and organizational psychologists work in four main contexts: academia, government, consulting firms, and business. Most I-O psychologists have a master's or doctorate degree. The field of I-O psychology can be divided into three broad areas (Figure 2): industrial, organizational, and human factors. **Industrial psychology** is concerned with describing job requirements and assessing individuals for their ability to meet those requirements. In addition, once employees are hired, industrial psychology studies and develops ways to train, evaluate, and respond to those evaluations. As a consequence of its concern for candidate characteristics, industrial psychology must also consider issues of legality regarding discrimination in hiring.

Further Resources

The story goes like this: Theophilus Van Kannel hated chivalry. There was nothing he despised more than trying to walk in or out of a building and locking horns with other men in a game of "oh, you first. I insist." But most of all, Theophilus Van Kannel hated opening doors for women.

He set about inventing his way out of social phobia. And that's how, in 1888, Theophilus Van Kannel was awarded U.S. Patent #387571 A for a "Storm-door structure," which would soon become known as the revolving door.

Want to know more about one of the first human factors designs? Check out this podcast (hawkes.biz/humanfactorsdesigns) by 99% Invisible.

(a)   (b)

Figure 2: (a) Industrial psychology focuses on hiring and maintaining employees. (b) Organizational psychology is interested in employee relationships and organizational culture.

Organizational psychology is a discipline interested in how the relationships among employees affect those employees and the performance of a business. This includes studying worker satisfaction, motivation, and commitment. This field also studies management, leadership, and organizational culture, as well as how an organization's structures, management and leadership styles, social norms, and role expectations affect individual behavior. As a result of its interest in worker well-being and relationships, organizational psychology also considers the subjects of harassment, including sexual harassment, and workplace violence.

Human factors psychology is the study of how workers interact with the tools of work and how to design those tools to optimize workers' productivity, safety, and health. These studies can involve interactions as straightforward as the fit of a desk, chair, and computer to a human having to sit on the chair at the desk using the computer for several hours each day (Figure 3). They can also include the examination of how humans interact with complex displays and their ability to interpret them accurately and quickly. In Europe, this field is referred to as ergonomics.

MONITOR
Adjust distance and height: top of the monitor at eye-level and slightly tilted.

ARMS
Relax shoulders, forearms parallel to the floor. Minimal bend at the wrist.

CHAIR
Should have a backrest and armrests, adjust height.

LEGS
Thighs parallel to the floor.

FEET
Parallel to the floor, use a footrest if necessary.

18/24 in (45-70 cm)

Figure 3: Human factors psychology is the study of interactions between humans, tools, and work systems.

The Historical Development of Industrial and Organizational Psychology

Industrial and organizational psychology had its origins in the early 20th century. Several influential early psychologists studied issues that today would be categorized as industrial psychology: James Cattell (1860–1944) at Columbia, Hugo Münsterberg (1863–1916) at Harvard, Walter Dill Scott (1869–1955) at Northwestern, Robert Yerkes (1876–1956) and Walter Bingham (1880–1952) at Dartmouth, and Lillian Gilbreth (1878–1972) at Purdue. Cattell, Münsterberg, and Scott had been students of Wilhelm Wundt, the father of experimental psychology. Some of these researchers had been involved in work in the area of industrial psychology before World War I. Cattell's contribution to industrial psychology is largely reflected in his founding of a psychological consulting company, which is still operating today, called the Psychological Corporation and in the accomplishments of students at Columbia in the area of industrial psychology. In 1913, Münsterberg published *Psychology and Industrial Efficiency*, which covered topics such as employee selection, employee training, and effective advertising.

Scott was one of the first psychologists to apply psychology to advertising, management, and personnel selection. In 1903, Scott published two books: *The Theory of Advertising* and *Psychology of Advertising*. They are the first books to describe the use of psychology in the business world. By 1911, he published two more books, *Influencing Men in Business* and *Increasing Human Efficiency in Business*. In 1916, a newly formed division in the Carnegie Institute of Technology hired Scott to conduct applied research on employee selection (Katzell & Austin, 1992).

The focus of all this research was in what we now know as industrial psychology; it was only later in the century that the field of organizational psychology developed as an experimental science (Katzell & Austin, 1992). In addition to their academic positions, these researchers also worked directly for businesses as consultants.

The involvement of the United States in World War I in April 1917 catalyzed the participation in the military effort of psychologists working in this area. Yerkes organized a group under the Surgeon General's Office (SGO) that developed methods for screening and selecting enlisted men. They developed the Army Alpha test to measure mental abilities. The Army Beta test was a non-verbal form of the test that was administered to

Group Activity

Take a moment to consider the following questions:

- What do you hope to get out of this psychology class?

- How do you know if the class has met your expectations?

In three separate groups, define a set of expectations for your class, your instructor, and you as a student. Each groups should then create a measure or evaluation to assess your assigned target (class, instructor, student).

How easy is it to evaluate a class or the performance of a person? We know when something or someone does not meet our expectations, but how often do we consider our expectations at the beginning of a class?

Further Resources

Find out what I-O psychologists do on the Society for Industrial and Organizational Psychology (hawkes.biz/iopsych) (SIOP) website—a professional organization for people working in the discipline.

illiterate and non-English-speaking draftees. Scott and Bingham organized a group under the Adjutant General's Office (AGO) with the goal to develop selection methods for officers. They created a catalogue of occupational needs for the Army, essentially a job-description system and a system of performance ratings and occupational skill tests for officers (Katzell & Austin, 1992).

After the war, work on personnel selection continued. For example, Millicent Pond, who received a PhD from Yale University, worked at several businesses and was director of employment test research at Scoville Manufacturing Company. She researched the selection of factory workers, comparing the results of pre-employment tests with various indicators of job performance. These studies were published in a series of research articles in the *Journal of Personnel Research* in the late 1920s (Vinchur & Koppes, 2014).

From 1929 to 1932, Elton Mayo (1880–1949) and his colleagues began a series of studies at a plant near Chicago, Western Electric's Hawthorne Works (Figure 6). This long-term project took industrial psychology beyond just employee selection and placement to a study of more complex problems of interpersonal relations, motivation, and organizational dynamics. These studies mark the origin of organizational psychology. They began as research into the effects of the physical work environment (e.g., level of lighting in a factory), but the researchers found that the psychological and social factors in the factory were of more interest than the physical factors. These studies also examined how human interaction factors, such as supervisorial style, enhanced or decreased productivity.

Figure 4: This is a recruitment advertisement for the U.S. Navy.

Figure 5: This is a recruitment advertisement for the U.S. Army.

Figure 6: Hawthorne Works provided the setting for several early I-O studies.

Analysis of the findings by later researchers led to the term the **Hawthorne effect**, which describes the increase in performance of individuals who are noticed, watched, and paid attention to by researchers or supervisors (Figure 7). What the original researchers found was that any change in a variable, such as lighting levels, led to an improvement in productivity; this was true even when the change was negative, such as a return to poor lighting. The effect faded when the attention faded (Roethlisberg & Dickson, 1939). The Hawthorne-effect concept endures today as an important experimental consideration in many fields and a factor that has to be accounted for in an experiment. In other words, an experimental treatment of some kind may produce an effect simply because it involves greater attention of the researchers on the participants (McCarney et al., 2007).

📷 **Figure 7:** Researchers discovered that employees performed better when researchers or supervisors observed and interacted with them, a dynamic termed the Hawthorne effect.

In the 1930s, researchers began to study employees' feelings about their jobs. Kurt Lewin also conducted research on the effects of various leadership styles, team structure, and team dynamics (Katzell & Austin, 1992). Lewin is considered the founder of social psychology and much of his work and that of his students produced results that had important influences in organizational psychology. Lewin and his students' research included an important early study that used children to study the effect of leadership style on aggression, group dynamics, and satisfaction (Lewin, Lippitt, & White, 1939). Lewin was also responsible for coining the term *group dynamics*, and he was involved in studies of group interactions, cooperation, competition, and communication that bear on organizational psychology.

Parallel to these studies in industrial and organizational psychology, the field of human factors psychology was also developing. Frederick Taylor was an engineer who saw that if one could redesign the workplace, there would be an increase in both output for the company and wages for the workers. In 1911, he put forward his theory in a book titled *The Principles of Scientific Management* (Figure 8). His book examines management styles, personnel selection and training, as well as the work itself, using time and motion studies.

Further Resources

Watch this video (hawkes.biz/hawthorne) to hear first-hand accounts of the original Hawthorne studies from those who participated in the research.

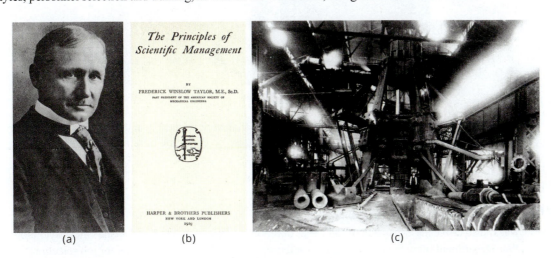

(a)   (b)   (c)

📷 **Figure 8:** (a) Frederick Taylor (1911) strived to engineer workplaces to increase productivity, based on the ideas he set forth in (b) his book *The Principles of Scientific Management*. (c) Taylor designed this steam hammer at the Midvale Steel Company.

One of the examples of Taylor's theory in action involved workers handling heavy iron ingots. Taylor showed that the workers could be more productive by taking work rests. This method of rest increased worker productivity from 12.5 to 47.0 tons moved per day with less reported fatigue as well as increased wages for the workers who were paid by the ton. At the same time, the company's cost was reduced from 9.2 cents to 3.9 cents per ton. Despite these increases in productivity, Taylor's theory received a great deal of criticism at the time because it was believed that it would exploit workers and reduce the number of workers needed. Also controversial was the underlying concept that only a manager could determine the most efficient method of working, and that while at work, a worker was incapable of this. Taylor's theory was underpinned by the notion that a worker was fundamentally lazy and the goal of Taylor's scientific management approach was to maximize productivity without much concern for worker well-being. His approach was criticized by unions and those sympathetic to workers (Van De Water, 1997).

Lillian Gilbreth was another influential I-O psychologist who strove to find ways to increase productivity (Figure 9). Using time and motion studies, Gilbreth and her husband, Frank, worked to make workers more efficient by reducing the number of motions required to perform a task. She not only applied these methods to industry but also to the home, office, shops, and other areas. She investigated employee fatigue and time management stress and found many employees were motivated by money and job satisfaction. In 1914, Gilbreth wrote the book titled, *The Psychology of Management: The Function of the Mind in Determining, Teaching, and Installing Methods of Least Waste*, and she is known as the mother of modern management. Some of Gilbreth's contributions are still in use today: you can thank her for the idea to put shelves inside on refrigerator doors, and she also came up with the concept of using a foot pedal to operate the lid of trash can (Gilbreth, 1914, 1998; Koppes, 1997; Lancaster, 2004). Gilbreth was the first woman to join the American Society of Mechanical Engineers in 1926, and in 1966, she was awarded the Hoover Medal of the American Society of Civil Engineers.

Taylor and Gilbreth's work improved productivity, but these innovations also improved the fit between technology and the human using it. The study of machine-human fit is known as ergonomics or human factors psychology.

(a)   (b)

📷 **Figure 9:** Lillian Gilbreth studied efficiency improvements that were applicable in the workplace, home, and other areas. She is credited with the idea of (a) putting shelves on the inside of refrigerator doors and (b) foot-pedal-operated garbage cans.

From WWII to Today

World War II also drove the expansion of industrial psychology. Bingham was hired as the chief psychologist for the War Department (now the Department of Defense) and developed new systems for job selection, classification, training, ad performance review, plus methods for team development, morale change, and attitude change (Katzell & Austin, 1992). Other countries, such as Canada and the United Kingdom, likewise saw growth in I-O psychology during World War II (McMillan, Stevens, & Kelloway, 2009). In the years after the war, both industrial psychology and organizational psychology became areas of significant research effort. Concerns about the fairness of employment tests arose, and the ethnic and gender biases in various tests were evaluated with mixed results. In addition, a great deal of research went into studying job satisfaction and employee motivation (Katzell & Austin, 1992). Today, I-O psychology is a diverse and deep field of research and practice, as you will learn about in the rest of this chapter. The Society for Industrial and Organizational Psychology (SIOP), a division of the APA, lists 8,000 members (SIOP, 2014) and the Bureau of Labor Statistics—U.S. Department of Labor (2013) has projected this profession will have the greatest growth of all job classifications in the 20 years following 2012. On average, a person with a master's degree in industrial-organizational psychology will earn over $80,000 a year, while someone with a doctorate will earn over $110,000 a year (Khanna, Medsker, & Ginter, 2012).

✍ On Your Own

Think about the contribution of each founding member of I-O psychology, and fill out the following summary.

What were the major contributions of the founding members of I-O psychology	
Founding Member	**Contribution**
Hugo Münsterberg	
James Cattell	
Walter Dill Scott	
Robert Yerkes	
Elton Mayo	
Frederick Taylor	
Lillian Gilbreth	

Summary

The field of I-O psychology had its birth in industrial psychology and the use of psychological concepts to aid in personnel selection. However, with research such as the Hawthorne study, it was found that productivity was affected more by human interaction and not physical factors; the field of industrial psychology expanded to include organizational psychology. Both WWI and WWII had a strong influence on the development of an expansion of industrial psychology in the United States and elsewhere. The tasks the psychologists were assigned led to development of tests and research in how the psychological concepts could assist industry and other areas. This movement aided in expanding industrial psychology to include organizational psychology.

Flash Forward

Ready to dig into the vocabulary? Get some practice with this Hawkes Verified Quizlet set (hawkes.biz/psych12q2)!

12.2 Industrial Psychology: Selecting and Evaluating Employees

The branch of I-O psychology known as industrial psychology focuses on identifying and matching persons to tasks within an organization. This involves **job analysis**, which means accurately describing the task or job.

Selecting Employees

A job analysis is approached in two ways. The first approach, the task-oriented approach, requires listing tasks based on how frequently they need to be performed, level of difficulty, and importance to the job. The second approach, or the worker-oriented approach called job specification, describes the knowledge, skills, and abilities (KSAs) required of the worker to successfully perform the job (Dierdorff & Wilson, 2003). Research suggests that the reliability and accuracy of a job analysis can depend on the nature of the descriptions and the source for the job analysis. For example, Dierdorff & Wilson (2003) found that job analyses developed from descriptions provided by people holding the job themselves were less reliable than other sources.

The United States Department of Labor maintains a database, O*Net (hawkes.biz/onet), which includes previously compiled job analyses for a wide variety of jobs in different occupations. Each occupation in the list includes key performance areas, work context, activities, education requirements, interests, personality, and work styles necessary for success at the position. In addition, you can see the average earnings and projected job growth in that industry.

✐ On Your Own

Identify a job that you think would fit well with the following personality traits, and explain why you think that might be the case.

Personality Characteristic	Definition	Job	Reason
Agreeableness	Place high value on the approval of others		
Conscientiousness	Organized and careful to perform the task well		
Extroversion	Enjoy the company of others		

Candidate Analysis and Testing

The process to narrow down potential candidates can involve testing, an interview, work samples, or other exercises. The goal of these exercises are to match personality characteristics that would ensure good performance on the job. For example, a high rating of agreeableness might be desirable in a customer support position. However, someone who is too high in agreeableness may prefer agreeing with the customer even if they have a misperception about a product or service, which would not lead to resolution of the complaint. As a result, multiple forms of assessment should be conducted to determine a candidate's best fit for the position (Arthur, Woehr, & Graziano, 2001). Other types of tests that may be given to candidates include IQ tests, integrity tests, and physical tests, such as drug tests or physical fitness tests.

What Do You Think?

Using Cutoff Scores to Determine Job Selection

Many positions require applicants to take tests as part of the selection process. The organization may set cutoff scores (i.e., a score below which a candidate will not move forward) for each test to determine whether the applicant moves on to the next stage. For example, there was the case of Robert Jordan, a 49-year-old college graduate who applied for a position with the police force in New London, Connecticut. As part of the selection process, Jordan took the Wonderlic Personnel Test (WPT), a test designed to measure cognitive ability.

Jordan did not make it to the interview stage because his WPT score of 33, equivalent to an IQ score of 125 (100 is the average IQ score), was too high. The New London Police department policy is to not interview anyone who has a WPT score over 27 (equivalent to an IQ score over 104) because they believe anyone who scores higher would be bored with police work. The average score for police officers nationwide is the equivalent of an IQ score of 104 (*Jordan v. New London*, 2000; ABC News, 2000).

Jordan sued the police department alleging that his rejection was discrimination, and his civil rights were violated because he was denied equal protection under the law. The 2nd U.S. Circuit Court of Appeals upheld a lower court's decision that the city of New London did not discriminate against him because the same standards were applied to everyone who took the exam (*The New York Times*, 1999).

What do you think? When might universal cutoff points make sense in a hiring decision, and when might they eliminate otherwise potentially strong employees?

Figure 1: Potential candidates for police officers must take several tests including an IQ test.

Interviews

Information derived from job analysis usually forms the basis for the types of questions asked in the interview process, which is common for most jobs in the United States. In an unstructured interview, the interviewer does not determine the questions beforehand, and the responses are not scored with a standardized system. In a structured interview, the questions are prepared in advanced and scored the same for each candidate. An advantage of the structured interview over the unstructured interview is that the structured interview is easier to compare across multiple candidates. In fact, research suggests that structured interviews are more effective than unstructured interviews at predicting job performance of a candidate (McDaniel, Whetzel, Schmidt & Maurer, 1994).

Reflection Questions

What tips have you learned to improve your performance at job interviews?

💡 Everyday Connection

Preparing for a Job Interview

You might be wondering if psychology research can tell you how to succeed in a job interview. As you can imagine, most research is concerned with the employer's interest in choosing the most appropriate candidate for the job, a goal that makes sense for the candidate, too. But suppose you are not the only qualified candidate for the job; is there a way to increase your chances of being hired? A limited amount of research has addressed this question.

As you might expect, non-verbal cues are important in an interview. Liden, Martin, & Parsons (1993) found that lack of eye contact and smiling on the part of the applicant led to lower applicant ratings. Studies of impression management on the part of an applicant have shown that self-promotion

Figure 2: What gives you a favorable first impression?

behaviors generally have a positive impact on interviewers (Gilmore & Ferris, 1989). Different personality types use different forms of impression management; for example, extroverts use verbal self-promotion, and applicants high in agreeableness use non-verbal methods such as smiling and eye contact. However, it is possible to overdo self-promotion with experienced interviewers (Howard & Ferris, 1996). Barrick, Swider, & Stewart (2010) examined the effect of first impressions during the rapport building that typically occurs before an interview begins. They found that initial judgments by interviewers during this period were related to job offers and that the judgments were about the candidate's competence and not just likability. Levine & Feldman (2002) looked at the influence of several non-verbal behaviors in mock interviews on candidates' likability and projections of competence. Likability was affected positively by greater smiling behavior. Interestingly, other behaviors affected likability differently depending on the gender of the applicant. Men who displayed higher eye contact were less likable; women were more likable when they made greater eye contact. However, for this study male applicants were interviewed by men, and female applicants were interviewed by women. In a study carried out in a real setting, DeGroot & Gooty (2009) found that non-verbal cues affected interviewers' assessments about candidates. They looked at visual cues, which can often be modified by the candidate and vocal (non-verbal) cues, which are more difficult to modify. They found that interviewer judgment was positively affected by visual and vocal cues of conscientiousness, visual and vocal cues of openness to experience, and vocal cues of extroversion.

You might recognize these traits from the Big Five personality assessment.

What is the take home message from the limited research that has been done? Learn to be aware of your behavior during an interview. You can do this by practicing and soliciting feedback from mock interviews. Pay attention to any non-verbal cues you are projecting, and work at presenting non-verbal cues that project confidence and positive personality traits. And finally, pay attention to the first impression you are making as it may also have an impact in the interview.

Training

Overall, training is effective when the employee is held accountable to know that information through testing, evaluation of learning outcomes on the job, and overall productivity at work (Arthur, Bennett, Edens, and Bell, 2003). Training usually begins for new employees with an orientation period during which they are provided information about the company and administrative policies, such as time tracking and benefits. In addition, employees will learn how to use new hardware or software tools needed to perform the job. An important goal of orientation training is to educate the new employee about the organizational culture, values, visions, hierarchies, and norms (Figure 3).

Figure 3: Training usually begins with an orientation period during which a new employee learns about company policies, practices, and culture.

In an examination of a large number of studies on the effectiveness of organizational training to meet its goals, Arthur, Bennett, Edens, & Bell (2003) found that training was effective when measured by the immediate response of the employee to the training effort, evaluation of learning outcomes (e.g., a test at the end of the training), behavioral measurements of job activities by a supervisor, and results-based criteria (e.g., productivity or profits). The examined studies represented diverse forms of training including self-instruction, lecture and discussion, and computer-assisted training.

Mentoring is a form of informal training in which an experienced employee guides the work of a new employee. In some situations, mentors will be formally assigned to a new employee, while in others a mentoring relationship may develop informally.

Mentoring effects on the mentor and the employee being mentored, the protégé, have been studied in recent years. In a review of mentoring studies, Eby, Allen, Evans, Ng, & DuBois (2008) found significant but small effects of mentoring on performance (i.e., behavioral outcomes), motivation and satisfaction, and actual career outcomes. In a more detailed review, Allen, Eby, Poteet, Lentz, & Lima (2004) found that mentoring positively affected a protégé's compensation and number of promotions compared with non-mentored employees. In addition, protégés were more satisfied with their careers and had greater job satisfaction. All of the effects were small but significant. Eby, Durley, Evans, & Ragins (2006) examined mentoring effects on the mentor and found that mentoring was associated with greater job satisfaction and organizational commitment. Gentry, Weber, & Sadri (2008) found that mentoring was positively related with performance ratings by supervisors. Allen, Lentz, & Day (2006) found in a comparison of mentors and non-mentors that mentoring led to greater reported salaries and promotions.

Reflection Questions

Do you think it important to having a mentor when starting a career? Why or why not?

Mentoring is recognized as particularly important to the career success of women (McKeen & Bujaki, 2007) by creating connections to informal networks, adopting a style of interaction that male managers are comfortable with, and overcoming discrimination in job promotions.

Gender combinations in mentoring relationships are also an area of active study. Ragins & Cotton (1999) studied the effects of gender on the outcomes of mentoring relationships and found that protégés with a history of male mentors had significantly higher compensation especially for male protégés. The study found that female mentor-male protégé relationships were considerably rarer than the other gender combinations.

Evaluating Employees

Industrial and organizational psychologists are typically involved in designing performance-appraisal systems for organizations. These systems are designed to evaluate whether each employee is performing her job satisfactorily. Industrial and organizational psychologists study, research, and implement ways to make work evaluations as fair and positive as possible; they also work to decrease the subjectivity involved with performance ratings. Fairly evaluated work helps employees do their jobs better, improves the likelihood of people being in the right jobs for their talents, maintains fairness, and identifies company and individual training needs.

Performance appraisals are typically documented several times a year, often with a formal process and an annual face-to-face brief meeting between an employee and his supervisor. It is important that the original job analysis plays a role in performance appraisal as well as any goals that have been set by the employee or by the employee and supervisor. The meeting is often used for the supervisor to communicate specific concerns about the employee's performance and to positively reinforce elements of good performance. It may also be used to discuss specific performance rewards, such as a pay increase, or consequences of poor performance, such as a probationary period. Part of the function of performance appraisals for the organization is to document poor performance to bolster decisions to terminate an employee.

Performance appraisals are becoming more complex processes within organizations and are often used to motivate employees to improve performance and expand their areas of competence, in addition to assessing their job performance. In this capacity, performance appraisals can be used to identify opportunities for training or indicate whether a particular training program has been successful. One approach to performance appraisal is called the 360-degree feedback appraisal (Figure 4). In this system, the employee's appraisal derives from a combination of ratings by supervisors, peers, employees supervised by the employee, and from the employee herself. Occasionally, outside observers may be used as well, such as customers. The purpose of the 360-degree system is to give the employee (who may be a manager) and supervisor different perspectives of the employee's job performance; the system should help employees make improvements through their own efforts or through training. The system is also used in a traditional performance-appraisal context, providing the supervisor with more information with which to make decisions about the employee's position and compensation (Tornow, 1993a).

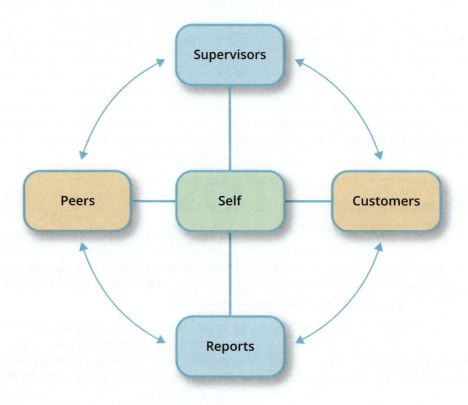

Figure 4: In a 360-degree feedback appraisal, supervisors, customers, direct reports, peers, and the employee himself rate an employee's performance.

✎ On Your Own

What are the advantages of 360-degree feedback performance appraisals?

☐ They are reliable.

☐ They include information from multiple sources.

☐ They provide only specific information to one job or task.

Reflection Questions

If you were CEO of a large company, would you include 360-degree feedback appraisals to evaluate employees' performances? Why or why not?

The purpose of job appraisals are to provide employees with a platform to gain feedback on their performance. However, most employees solicit feedback on their performance if it is not offered at their organization (DeNisi & Kluger, 2000). Furthermore, there are questions on whether or not performance evaluations even serve a positive purpose at the organization. For example, Schreader, Becton, & Portis (2007) argue that performance appraisal systems are used incorrectly because it often does not consider the organizations values and how they operate (Fletcher, 2001).

Bias and Protections in Hiring

Interview rankings can be influenced by factors other than knowledge, skills, and abilities necessary for the position. For example, research has found that:

- Similar body language to the interviewer can increase the likelihood that the candidate will be hired (Bye, Horverak, Sandal, Sam, & Vijver, 2014).

- The regional accent of the employee can influence hiring decisions (Rakić, Steffens, & Mummendey 2011).

- Hiring managers have demonstrated bias against candidates that are overweight or obese (Agerström & Rooth, 2011).

- Physically attractive candidates are more likely to get hired, get positive performance reviews, and get a promotion than less attractive candidates (Hosoda, Stone-Romero, & Coats, 2003).

Hiring managers may discriminate by choosing not to hire an employee because he or she belongs to a specific group rather than because of his or her knowledge, skills, and abilities (Figure 5). As a result, there are numerous local, state, and federal laws in the United States that prevent discriminatory hiring practices. For example, it is illegal for a potential employer to ask your age, marital status, disability status, race, or religion in an interview. Unless membership in that group directly affects potential job performance, a decision based on group membership is discriminatory.

(a)   (b)   (c)

🖼 **Figure 5:** (a) Pregnancy, (b) religion, and (c) age are some of the criteria on which hiring decisions cannot legally be made.

Reflection Questions

What do you think organizations can do to prevent discriminatory hiring practices on the job?

The U.S. Equal Employment Opportunity Commission (EEOC)

The **U.S. Equal Employment Opportunity Commission (EEOC)** is responsible for enforcing federal laws that make it illegal to discriminate against a job applicant or an employee because of the person's race, color, religion, sex (including pregnancy), national origin, age (40 or older), disability, or genetic information. Figure 6 provides some of the legal language from laws that have been passed to prevent discrimination.

The United States has several specific laws regarding fairness and avoidance of discrimination. The Equal Pay Act requires equal pay for men and women in the same workplace who are performing equal work. Despite the law, persistent inequities in earnings between men and women exist. Corbett & Hill (2012) studied one facet of the gender gap by looking at earnings in the first year after college in the United States. Just comparing the earnings of women to men, women earn about 82 cents for every dollar a man earns in their first year out of college. However, some of this difference can be explained by education, career, and life choices, such as choosing majors with lower earning potential or specific jobs within a field that have less responsibility. When these factors were corrected, the study found an unexplained seven-cents-on-the-dollar gap in the first year after college that can be attributed to gender discrimination in pay. This approach to analysis of the gender pay gap, called the human capital model, has been criticized. Lips (2013) argues that the education, career, and life choices can, in fact, be constrained by necessities imposed by gender discrimination. This suggests that removing these factors entirely from the gender gap equation leads to an estimate of the size of the pay gap that is too small.

Selected Text from Legislation Prohibiting Employment Discrimination

Title VII of the Civil Rights Act of 1964

It shall be an unlawful employment practice for an employer (1) to fail or refuse to hire or to discharge any individual, or otherwise to discriminate against any individual with respect to his compensation, terms, conditions, or privileges of employment, because of such individual's race, color, religion, sex, or national origin; or (2) to limit, segregate, or classify his employees or applicants for employment in any way which would deprive or tend to deprive any individual of employment opportunities or otherwise adversely affects his status as an employee, because of such individual's race, color, religion, sex, or national origin.

The Age Discrimination in Employment Act of 1967

It shall be an unlawful employer (1) to fail or refuse to hire or to discharge any individual, or otherwise discriminate against any individual with respect to his compensation, terms, conditions, or privileges of employment, because of such individual's age.

Titles I and V of the Americans with Disabilities Act of 1990 (ADA)

No covered entity shall discriminate against a qualified individual on the basis of disability in regard to job application procedures, the hiring, advancement, of discharge of employees, employee compensation, job training, and other terms, conditions, and privileges of employment.... the term "discriminate against a qualified individual on the basis of disability" includes... not making reasonable accommodations to the known physical or mental limitations of an otherwise qualified individual with a disability who is an applicant or employee, unless such covered entity can demonstrate that the accommodation would impose an undue hardship on the operation of the business of such covered entity.

Figure 6: The laws shown here protect employees in the U.S. from discriminatory practices.

Reflection Questions

What do you think can be done to reduce the gender pay gap?

Title VII of the Civil Rights Act of 1964 makes it illegal to treat individuals unfavorably because of their race or color of their skin: an employer cannot discriminate based on skin color, hair texture, or other **immutable characteristics**, which are traits of an individual that are fundamental to her identity, in hiring, benefits, promotions, or termination of employees. The Pregnancy Discrimination Act of 1978 amends the Civil Rights Act; it prohibits job (e.g., employment, pay, and termination) discrimination of a woman because she is pregnant as long as she can perform the work required.

The Supreme Court ruling in *Griggs v. Duke Power Co.* made it illegal under Title VII of the Civil Rights Act to include educational requirements in a job description (e.g., high school diploma) that negatively impacts one race over another if the requirement cannot be shown to be directly related to job performance.

The EEOC (2014) received more than 94,000 charges of various kinds of employment discrimination in 2013. Many of the filings are for multiple forms of discrimination and include charges of retaliation for making a claim, which itself is illegal. Only a small fraction of these claims become suits filed in a federal court although the suits may represent the claims of more than one person. In 2013, there were 148 suits filed in federal courts.

Federal legislation does not protect employees in the private sector from discrimination related to sexual orientation and gender identity. These groups include lesbian, gay, bisexual, and transgender individuals. There is evidence of discrimination derived from surveys of workers, studies of complaint filings, wage comparison studies, and controlled job-interview studies (Badgett, Sears, Lau, & Ho, 2009). Federal legislation protects federal employees from such discrimination, and the District of Columbia and 20 states have laws protecting public and private employees from discrimination for sexual orientation (American Civil Liberties Union, n.d). Most of the states with these laws also protect against discrimination based on gender identity. Gender identity, as discussed in the lesson on sexual behavior, refers to one's sense of being male or female.

Many cities and counties have adopted local legislation preventing discrimination based on sexual orientation or gender identity (Human Rights Campaign, 2013a), and some companies have recognized a benefit to explicitly stating that their hiring must not discriminate on these bases (Human Rights Campaign, 2013b).

Americans with Disabilities Act (ADA)

The **Americans with Disabilities Act (ADA)** of 1990 states people may not be discriminated against due to the nature of their disability. A disability is defined as a physical or mental impairment that limits one or more major life activities such as hearing, walking, and breathing. If a disability is disclosed, an employer must make reasonable accommodations for the performance of a disabled employee's job. This might include making the work facility handicapped accessible with ramps, providing readers for blind personnel, or allowing for more frequent breaks. The ADA has now been expanded to include individuals with alcoholism, former drug use, obesity, or psychiatric disabilities. The premise of the law is that disabled individuals can contribute to an organization, and they cannot be discriminated against because of their disabilities (O'Keefe & Bruyere, 1994).

The Civil Rights Act and the Age Discrimination in Employment Act make provisions for **bona fide occupational qualifications (BFOQs)**, which are requirements of certain occupations for which denying an individual employment would otherwise violate the law. For example, there may be cases in which religion, national origin, age, and sex are bona fide occupational qualifications. There are no BFOQ exceptions that apply to race although the first amendment protects artistic expressions, such as films, in making race a requirement of a role. Clearcut examples of BFOQs would be hiring someone of a specific religion for a leadership position in a worship facility or for an executive position in religiously affiliated institutions, such as the president of a university with religious ties. Age has been determined to be a BFOQ for airline pilots; hence, there are mandatory retirement ages for safety reasons. Sex has been determined as a BFOQ for guards in male prisons.

Gender is the most common reason for invoking a BFOQ as a defense against accusing an employer of discrimination (Manley, 2009). Courts have established a three-part test for sex-related BFOQs that are often used in other types of legal cases for determining whether a BFOQ exists. The first of these is whether all or substantially all women would be unable to perform a job. This is the reason most physical limitations, such as "able to lift 30 pounds," fail as reasons to discriminate because most women are able to lift this weight. The second test is the "essence of the business" test, in which having to choose the other gender would undermine the essence of the business operation. This test was the reason the now defunct Pan American World Airways (i.e., Pan Am) was told it could not hire only female flight attendants. Hiring men would not have undermined the essense of this business. On a deeper level, this means that hiring cannot be made purely on customers' or others' preferences. The third and final test is whether the employer cannot make reasonable alternative accomodations, such as reassigning staff so that a woman does not have to work in a male-only part of a jail or other gender-specific facility. Privacy concerns are a major reason why discrimination based on gender is upheld by the courts, for example in situations such as hires for nursing or custodial staff (Manley, 2009). Most cases of BFOQs are decided on a case-by-case basis, and these court decisions inform policy and future case decisions.

Figure 7: Hooters restaurants only hire female wait staff.

What Do You Think?

Hooters and BFOQ Laws

The restaurant chain Hooters, which hires only female wait staff and has them dress in a sexually provocative manner, is commonly cited as a discriminatory employer. The chain would argue that the female employees are an essential part of their business in that they market through sex appeal, and the wait staff attracts customers. Men have filed discrimination charges against Hooters in the past for not hiring them as wait staff simply because they are men. The chain has avoided a court decision on their hiring practices by settling out of court with the plaintiffs in each case. Do you think their practices violate the Civil Rights Act? See if you can apply the three court tests to this case, and make a decision about whether a case that went to trial would find in favor of the plaintiff or the chain.

Summary

Industrial psychology studies the attributes of jobs, applicants of those jobs, and methods for assessing fit to a job. These procedures include job analysis, applicant testing, and interviews. It also studies and puts into place procedures for the orientation of new employees and ongoing training of employees. The process of hiring employees can be vulnerable to bias, which is illegal, and industrial psychologists must develop methods for adhering to the law in hiring. Performance appraisal systems are an active area of research and practice in industrial psychology.

Flash Forward

Ready to dig into the vocabulary? Get some practice with this Hawkes Verified Quizlet set (hawkes.biz/psych12q3)!

12.3 Organizational Psychology: The Social Dimension of Work

Organizational psychology is the second major branch of study and practice within the discipline of industrial and organizational psychology. In organizational psychology, the focus is on social interactions and their effect on the individual and on the functioning of the organization. In this lesson, you will learn about the work organizational psychologists have done to understand job satisfaction, different styles of management, different styles of leadership, organizational culture, and teamwork.

Job Satisfaction

Some people love their jobs, some people tolerate their jobs, and some people cannot stand their jobs. **Job satisfaction** describes the degree to which individuals enjoy their job.

Reflection Questions

Have you ever felt highly satisfied or dissatisfied with your job? How did it affect your thoughts, feelings, and motivation to perform?

It was described by Edwin Locke (1976) as the state of feeling resulting from appraising one's job experiences. While job satisfaction results from both how we think about our work (our cognition) and how we feel about our work (our affect) (Saari & Judge, 2004), it is described in terms of affect. Job satisfaction is impacted by the work itself, our personality, and the culture we come from and live in (Saari & Judge, 2004).

Job satisfaction is typically measured after a change in an organization, such as a shift in the management model, to assess how the change affects employees. It may also be routinely measured by an organization to assess one of many factors expected to affect the organization's performance. In addition, polling companies like Gallup regularly measure job satisfaction on a national scale to gather broad information on the state of the economy and the workforce (Saad, 2012).

Job satisfaction is measured using questionnaires that employees complete. Sometimes a single question might be asked in a very straightforward way to which employees respond using a rating scale, such as a Likert. A Likert scale (typically) provides five possible answers to a statement or question that allows respondents to indicate their positive-to-negative strength of agreement or strength of feeling regarding the question or statement. Thus, the possible responses to a question such as "How satisfied are you with your job today?" might be "Very satisfied," "Somewhat satisfied," "Neither satisfied, nor dissatisfied," "Somewhat dissatisfied," and "Very dissatisfied." More commonly, the survey will ask a number of questions about the employee's satisfaction to determine more precisely why he is satisfied or dissatisfied. Sometimes these surveys are created for specific jobs; at other times, they are designed to apply to any job. Job satisfaction can be measured at a global level, meaning how satisfied in general the employee is with work, or at the level of specific factors intended to measure which aspects of the job lead to satisfaction (Table 1).

Factor	Description
Autonomy	Individual responsibility, control over decisions
Work content	Variety, challenge, role clarity
Communication	Feedback
Financial rewards	Salary and benefits
Growth and development	Personal growth, training, education
Promotion	Career advancement opportunity
Coworkers	Professional relations or adequacy
Supervision and feedback	Support, recognition, fairness
Workload	Time pressure, tedium
Work demands	Extra work requirements, insecurity of position

Table 1: Factors Involved in Job Satisfaction—Dissatisfaction

Research has suggested that the work-content factor, which includes variety, difficulty level, and role clarity of the job, is the strongest predictive factor of overall job satisfaction (Saari & Judge, 2004). In contrast, there is a weak correlation between pay level and job satisfaction (Judge, Piccolo, Podsakoff, Shaw, & Rich, 2010). Judge et al. (2010) suggested that individuals adjust or adapt to higher pay levels: higher pay no longer provides the satisfaction the individual initially felt when her salary increased.

Why should we care about job satisfaction? Or more specifically, why should an employer care about job satisfaction? Measures of job satisfaction are somewhat correlated with job performance; in particular, they appear to relate to organizational citizenship or discretionary behaviors on the part of an employee that further the goals of the organization (Judge & Kammeyer-Mueller, 2012). Job satisfaction is related to general life satisfaction although there has been limited research on how the two influence each other or whether personality and cultural factors affect both job and general life satisfaction. One carefully controlled study suggested that the relationship is reciprocal: job satisfaction affects life satisfaction positively, and vice versa (Judge & Watanabe, 1993). Of course, organizations cannot control life satisfaction's influence on job satisfaction. Job satisfaction, specifically low job satisfaction, is also related to withdrawal behaviors, such as leaving a job or absenteeism (Judge & Kammeyer-Mueller, 2012). The relationship with turnover itself, however, is weak (Judge & Kammeyer-Mueller, 2012). Finally, it appears that job satisfaction is related to organizational performance, which suggests that implementing organizational changes to improve employee job satisfaction will improve organizational performance (Judge & Kammeyer-Mueller, 2012).

There is opportunity for more research in the area of job satisfaction. Weiss (2002) suggests that the concept of job satisfaction measurements have combined both emotional and cognitive concepts, and measurements would be more reliable and show better relationships with outcomes like performance if the measurement of job satisfaction separated these two possible elements of job satisfaction.

Dig Deeper

Job Satisfaction in Federal Government Agencies

A 2013 study of job satisfaction in the U.S. federal government found indexes of job satisfaction plummeting compared to the private sector. The largest factor in the decline was satisfaction with pay, followed by training and development opportunities. The Partnership for Public Service, a nonprofit, nonpartisan organization, has conducted research on federal employee job satisfaction since 2003. Its primary goal is to improve the federal government's management. However, the results also provide information to those interested in obtaining employment with the federal government.

Among large agencies, the highest job satisfaction ranking went to NASA, followed by the Department of Commerce and the intelligence community. The lowest scores went to the Department of Homeland Security.

The data used to derive the job satisfaction score come from three questions on the Federal Employee Viewpoint Survey. The questions are:

1. I recommend my organization as a good place to work.

2. Considering everything, how satisfied are you with your job?

3. Considering everything, how satisfied are you with your organization?

The questions have a range of six possible answers, spanning a range of strong agreement or satisfaction to strong disagreement or dissatisfaction. How would you answer these questions with regard to your own job? Would these questions adequately assess your job satisfaction?

You can explore the Best Places to Work in the Federal Government study at their Web site (hawkes.biz/jobsatisfaction). The Office of Personnel Management also produces a report based on their survey (hawkes.biz/jobsatisfactionsurvey).

☑ On Your Own

Which of the following has the lowest impact on job satisfaction?

☐ Role Clarity   ☐ Difficulty   ☐ Salary

Job stress affects job satisfaction. Job stress, or job strain, is caused by specific stressors in an occupation. *Stress* can be an ambiguous term as it is used in common language. Stress is the perception and response of an individual to events judged as overwhelming or threatening to the individual's well-being (Gyllensten & Palmer, 2005). The events themselves are the stressors. Stress is a result of an employee's perception that the demands placed on them exceed their ability to meet them (Gyllensten & Palmer, 2005), such as having to fill multiple roles in a job or life in general, workplace role ambiguity, lack of career progress, lack of job security, lack of control over work outcomes, isolation, work overload, discrimination, harrassment, and bullying (Colligan & Higgins, 2005). The stressors are different for women than men, and these differences are a significant area of research (Gyllensten & Palmer, 2005). Job stress leads to poor employee health, job performance, and family life (Colligan & Higgins, 2005).

As already mentioned, job insecurity contributes significantly to job stress. Two increasing threats to job security are downsizing events and corporate mergers. Businesses typically involve I-O psychologists in planning for, implementing, and managing these types of organizational changes.

Downsizing is an increasingly common response to a business's pronounced failure to achieve profit goals, and it involves laying off a significant percentage of the company's employees. Industrial-organizational psychologists may be involved in all aspects of downsizing: how the news is delivered to employees (both those being let go and those staying), how laid-off employees are supported (e.g., separation packages), and how retained employees are supported. The latter is important for the organization because downsizing events affect the retained employee's intent to quit, organizational commitment, and job insecurity (Ugboro, 2006).

In addition to downsizing as a way of responding to outside strains on a business, corporations often grow larger by combining with other businesses. This can be accomplished through a merger (i.e., the joining of two organizations of equal power and status) or an acquisition (i.e., one organization purchases the other). In an acquisition, the purchasing organization is usually the more powerful or dominant partner. In both cases, there is usually a duplication of services between the two companies, such as two accounting departments and two sales forces. Both departments must be merged, which commonly involves a reduction of staff (Figure 1). This leads to organizational processes and stresses similar to those that occur in downsizing events. Mergers require determining how the organizational culture will change, to which employees also must adjust (van Knippenberg, van Knippenberg, Monden, & de Lima, 2002). There can be additional stress on workers as they lose their connection to the old organization and try to make connections with the new combined group (Amiot, Terry, Jimmieson, & Callan, 2006). Research in this area focuses on understanding employee reactions and making practical recommendations for managing these organizational changes.

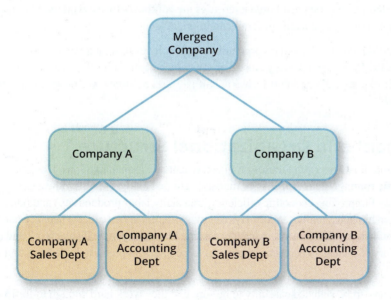

◪ **Figure 1:** When companies are combined through a merger (or acquisition), there are often cuts due to duplication of core functions, like sales and accounting, at each company.

Work-Family Balance

Many people juggle the demands of work life with the demands of their home life, whether it be caring for children or taking care of an elderly parent; this is known as **work-family balance**. We might commonly think about work interfering with family, but it is also the case that family responsibilities may conflict with work obligations (Carlson, Kacmar, & Williams, 2000). Greenhaus and Beutell (1985) first identified three sources of work-family conflicts:

- Time devoted to work makes it difficult to fulfill requirements of family, or vice versa.

- Strain from participation in work makes it difficult to fulfill requirements of family, or vice versa.

- Specific behaviors required by work make it difficult to fulfill the requirements of family, or vice versa.

Women often have greater responsibility for family demands, including home care, child care, and caring for aging parents, yet men in the United States are increasingly assuming a greater share of domestic responsibilities. However, research has documented that women report greater levels of stress from work-family conflict (Gyllensten & Palmer, 2005).

There are many ways to decrease work-family conflict and improve people's job satisfaction (Posig & Kickul, 2004). These include support in the home, which can take various forms: emotional (listening), practical (help with chores), etc. Workplace support can include understanding supervisors, flextime, leave with pay, and telecommuting. Flextime usually involves a requirement of core hours spent in the workplace around which the employee may schedule his arrival and departure from work to meet family demands. **Telecommuting** involves employees working at home and setting their own hours, which allows them to work during different parts of the day and to spend part of the day with their family. Recall that Yahoo! had a policy of allowing employees to telecommute and then rescinded the policy. There are also organizations that have onsite daycare centers, and some companies even have onsite fitness centers and health clinics. In a study of the effectiveness of different coping methods, Lapierre & Allen (2006) found practical support from home more important than emotional support. They also found that immediate-supervisor support for a worker significantly reduced work-family conflict through such mechanisms as allowing an employee the flexibility needed to fulfill family obligations. In contrast, flextime did not help with coping, and telecommuting actually made things worse, perhaps reflecting the fact that being at home intensifies the conflict between work and family because with the employee in the home, the demands of family are more evident.

Posig & Kickul (2004) identify exemplar corporations with policies designed to reduce work-family conflict. Examples include IBM's policy of three years of job-guaranteed leave after the birth of a child, Lucent Technologies offer of one year's childbirth leave at half pay, and SC Johnson's program of concierge services for daytime errands.

Further Resources

Glassdoor (hawkes.biz/jobsatisfaction2) is a website that posts job satisfaction reviews for different careers and organizations. Use this site to research possible careers and/or organizations that interest you.

Management and Organizational Structure

A significant portion of I-O research focuses on management and human relations. Douglas McGregor (1960) combined **scientific management** (a theory of management that analyzes and synthesizes workflows with the main objective of improving economic efficiency, especially labor productivity) and human relations into the notion of leadership behavior. His theory lays out two different styles called Theory X and Theory Y. In the **Theory X** approach to management, managers assume that most people dislike work and are not innately self-directed. Theory X managers perceive employees as people who prefer to be led and told which tasks to perform and when.

Their employees have to be watched carefully to be sure that they work hard enough to fulfill the organization's goals. Theory X workplaces will often have employees punch a clock when arriving and leaving the workplace, and tardiness is punished. Supervisors, not employees, determine whether an employee needs to stay late, and even this decision would require someone higher up in the command chain to approve the extra hours. These supervisors will ignore employees' suggestions for improved efficiency and reprimand employees for speaking out of order. These supervisors blame efficiency failures on individual employees rather than the systems or policies in place. Managerial goals are achieved through a system of punishments and threats rather than enticements and rewards. Managers are suspicious of employees' motivations and always suspect selfish motivations for their behavior at work (e.g., being paid is their sole motivation for working).

In the **Theory Y** approach, on the other hand, managers assume that most people seek inner satisfaction and fulfillment from their work. Employees function better under leadership that allows them to participate in and provide input about setting their personal and work goals. In Theory Y workplaces, employees participate in decisions about prioritizing tasks; they may belong to teams that, once given a goal, decide themselves how it will be accomplished. In such a workplace, employees are able to provide input on matters of efficiency and safety. One example of Theory Y in action is the policy of Toyota production lines that allows any employee to stop the entire line if a defect or other issue appears so that the defect can be fixed and its cause remedied (Toyota Motor Manufacturing, 2013). A Theory Y workplace will also meaningfully consult employees on any changes to the work process or management system. In addition, the organization will encourage employees to contribute their own ideas. McGregor (1960) characterized Theory X as the traditional method of management used in the United States. He argued that a Theory Y approach was needed to improve organizational output and the well-being of individuals. Table 2 summarizes how these two management approaches differ.

Theory X	Theory Y
People dislike work and avoid it.	People enjoy work and find it natural.
People avoid responsibility.	People are more satisified when given responsibility.
People want to be told what to do.	People want to take part in setting their own work goals.
Goals are achieved through rules and punishments.	Goals are achieved through enticements and rewards.

Table 2: Theory X and Theory Y Management Styles

Reflection Questions

Do you agree with McGregor (1960), or do you see a case where Theory X may be more desirable than Theory Y?

Another management style was described by Donald Clifton, who focused his research on how an organization can best use an individual's strengths, an approach he called strengths-based management. He and his colleagues interviewed 8,000 managers and concluded that it is important to focus on a person's strengths, not their weaknesses. A strength is a particular enduring talent possessed by an individual that allows her to provide consistent, near-perfect performance in tasks involving that talent. Clifton argued that our strengths provide the greatest opportunity for growth (Buckingham & Clifton, 2001). An example of a strength is public speaking or the ability to plan a successful event. The strengths-based approach is very popular although its effect on organization performance is not well-studied. However, Kaiser & Overfield (2011) found that managers often neglected improving their weaknesses and overused their strengths, both of which interfered with performance.

Leadership is an important element of management. Leadership styles have been of major interest within I-O research, and researchers have proposed numerous theories of leadership. Bass (1985) popularized and developed the concepts of transactional leadership and transformational leadership styles. In **transactional leadership**, the focus is on supervision and organizational goals, which are achieved through a system of rewards and punishments (i.e., transactions). Transactional leaders maintain the status quo: they are managers. This is in contrast to the transformational leader. People who employ **transformational leadership** possess four attributes to varying degrees: they are charismatic (highly liked role models), inspirational (optimistic about goal attainment), intellectually stimulating (encourage critical thinking and problem solving), and considerate (Bass, Avolio, & Atwater, 1996).

As women increasingly take on leadership roles in corporations, questions have arisen as to whether there are differences in leadership styles between men and women (Eagly, Johannesen-Schmidt, & van Engen, 2003). Eagly & Johnson (1990) conducted a meta-analysis to examine gender and leadership style. They found, to a slight but significant degree, that women tend to practice an interpersonal style of leadership (i.e., focus on the morale and welfare of the employees), and men practice a task-oriented style (i.e., focus on accomplishing tasks). However, the differences were less pronounced when looking only at organizational studies and excluding laboratory experiments or surveys that did not involve actual organizational leaders. Larger differences were observed when leadership style was categorized as democratic or autocratic, and these differences were consistent across all types of studies. The authors suggest that similarities between the sexes in leadership styles are attributable to both sexes needing to conform the organization's culture; additionally, they propose that sex-related differences reflect inherent differences in the strengths each sex brings to leadership practice. In another meta-analysis of leadership style, Eagly, Johannesen-Schmidt, & van Engen (2003) found that women tended to exhibit the characteristics of transformational leaders, while men were more likely to be transactional leaders. However, the differences are not absolute; for example, women were found to use methods of reward for performance more often than men, which is a component of transactional leadership. But overall, the differences they found were relatively small. As Eagly, Johannesen-Schmidt, & van Engen (2003) point out, research shows that transformational leadership approaches are more effective than transactional approaches although individual leaders typically exhibit elements of both approaches.

Goals, Teamwork, and Work Teams

The workplace today is rapidly changing due to a variety of factors, such as shifts in technology, economics, foreign competition, globalization, and workplace demographics. Organizations need to respond quickly to changes in these factors. Many companies are responding to these changes by structuring their organizations so that work can be delegated to **work teams**, which bring together diverse skills, experience, and expertise. This is in contrast to organizational structures that have individuals at their base (Naquin & Tynan, 2003). In the team-based approach, teams are brought together and given a specific task or goal to accomplish. Despite their burgeoning popularity, team structures do not always deliver greater productivity—the work of teams is an active area of research (Naquin & Tynan, 2003).

Why do some teams work well while others do not? There are many contributing factors. For example, teams can mask team members that are not working (i.e., social loafing). Teams can be inefficient due to poor communication; they can have poor decision-making skills due to conformity effects; and they can have conflict within the group. The popularity of teams may result from the team halo effect: teams are given credit for their successes, but individuals within a team are blamed for team failures (Naquin & Tynan, 2003). One aspect of team diversity is their gender mix. Researchers have explored whether gender mix has an effect on team performance. On one hand, diversity can introduce communication and interpersonal-relationship problems that hinder performance, but on the other hand, diversity can also increase the team's skill set, which may include skills that can actually improve team member interactions. Hoogendoorn, Oosterbeek, & van Praag (2013) studied project teams in a university business school in which the gender mix of the teams was manipulated. They found that gender-balanced teams performed better, as measured by sales and profits, than predominantly male teams. The study did not have enough data to determine the relative performance of female dominated teams. It was unsuccessful in identifying which mechanism (interpersonal relationships, learning, or skills mixes) accounted for performance improvement.

Reflection Questions
Why do you think certain teams work well together and certain teams do not?

There are three basic types of teams:

- Problem resolution teams are created for the purpose of solving a particular problem or issue; for example, the diagnostic teams at the Centers for Disease Control.

- Creative teams are used to develop innovative possibilities or solutions; for example, design teams for car manufacturers create new vehicle models.

- Tactical teams are used to execute a well-defined plan or objective, such as a police or FBI SWAT team handling a hostage situation (Larson & LaFasto, 1989).

Reflection Questions

Which team would you like to be a part of—problem resolution, creative, or tactical? Why?

One area of active research involves a fourth kind of team—the virtual team; these studies examine how groups of geographically disparate people brought together using digital communications technology function (Powell, Piccoli, & Ives, 2004). Virtual teams are more common due to the growing globalization of organizations and the use of consulting and partnerships facilitated by digital communication.

Organizational Culture

Each company and organization has an organizational culture. **Organizational culture** encompasses the values, visions, hierarchies, norms, and interactions among its employees. It is how an organization is run, how it operates, and how it makes decisions—the industry in which the organization participates may have an influence. Different departments within one company can develop their own subculture within the organization's culture. Ostroff, Kinicki, & Tamkins (2003) identify three layers in organizational culture: observable artifacts, espoused values, and basic assumptions. Observable artifacts are the symbols, language (jargon, slang, and humor), narratives (stories and legends), and practices (rituals) that represent the underlying cultural assumptions. Espoused values are concepts or beliefs that the management or the entire organization endorse. They are the rules that allow employees to know which actions they should take in different situations and which information they should adhere to. These basic assumptions generally are unobservable and unquestioned. Researchers have developed survey instruments to measure organizational culture.

With the workforce being a global marketplace, your company may have a supplier in Korea and another in Honduras and have employees in the United States, China, and South Africa. You may have coworkers of different religious, ethnic, or racial backgrounds than yourself. Your coworkers may be from different places around the globe. Many workplaces offer diversity training to help everyone involved bridge and understand cultural differences. **Diversity training** educates participants about cultural differences with the goal of improving teamwork. There is always the potential for prejudice between members of two groups, but the evidence suggests that by simply working together, particularly if the conditions of work are set carefully, such prejudice can be reduced or eliminated. Pettigrew and Tropp (2006) conducted a meta-analysis to examine the question of whether contact between groups reduced prejudice between those groups. They found that there was a moderate but significant effect. They also found that, as previously theorized, the effect was enhanced when the two groups met under conditions in which they have equal standing, common goals, cooperation between the groups, and especially support on the part of the institution or authorities for the contact.

Dig Deeper

Managing Generational Differences

Age is an important consideration in managing employees. Workers' expectations and attitudes are developed in part by experience in particular cultural time periods. Generational constructs are somewhat arbitrary, yet they may be helpful in setting broad directions to organizational management as one generation leaves the workforce and another enters it. The baby boomer generation (born between 1946 and 1964) is in the process of leaving the workforce and will continue to depart it for a decade or more. Generation X (born between the early 1960s and the 1980s) are now in the middle of their careers. Millennials (born from 1979 to the early 1994) began to come of age at the turn of the century and are early in their careers.

Today, as these three different generations work side by side in the workplace, employers and managers need to identify their unique characteristics. Each generation has distinctive expectations, habits, attitudes, and motivations (Elmore, 2010). One of the major differences among these generations is knowledge of the use of technology in the workplace. Millennials are technologically sophisticated and believe their use of technology sets them apart from other generations. They have also been characterized as self-centered and overly self-confident. Their attitudinal differences have raised concerns for managers about maintaining their motivation as employees and their ability to integrate into organizational culture created by baby boomers (Myers & Sadaghiani, 2010). For example, millennials may expect to hear that they need to pay their dues in their jobs from baby boomers who believe they paid their dues in their time. Yet millennials may resist doing so because they value life outside of work to a greater degree (Myers & Sadaghiani, 2010). Meister & Willyerd (2010) suggested alternative approaches to training and mentoring that will engage millennials and adapt to their need for feedback from supervisors like reverse mentoring, in which a younger employee educates a senior employee in social media or other digital resources. The senior employee then has the opportunity to provide useful guidance within a less demanding role.

Recruiting and retaining millennials and Generation X employees poses challenges that did not exist in previous generations. The concept of building a career with the company is not relatable to most Generation X employees, who do not expect to stay with one employer for their career. This expectation arises from a reduced sense of loyalty because they do not expect their employer to be loyal to them (Gibson, Greenwood, & Murphy, 2009). Retaining Generation X workers thus relies on motivating them by making their work meaningful (Gibson, Greenwood, & Murphy, 2009). Since millennials lack an inherent loyalty to the company, retaining them also requires effort in the form of nurturing through frequent rewards, praise, and feedback.

Millennials are also interested in having many choices, including options in work scheduling, choice of job duties, and so on. They also expect more training and education from their employers. Companies that offer the best benefit package and brand attract millennials (Myers & Sadaghiani, 2010).

One well-recognized negative aspect of organizational culture is a culture of harassment, including sexual harassment. Most organizations of any size have developed sexual harassment policies that define sexual harassment (or harassment in general) and the procedures the organization has set in place to prevent and address it when it does occur. Thus, in most jobs you have held, you were probably made aware of the company's sexual harassment policy and procedures and may have received training related to the policy. The U.S. Equal Employment Opportunity Commission (n.d.) provides the following description of **sexual harassment**:

> Unwelcome sexual advances, requests for sexual favors, and other verbal or physical conduct of a sexual nature constitute sexual harassment when this conduct explicitly or implicitly affects an individual's employment, unreasonably interferes with an individual's work performance, or creates an intimidating, hostile, or offensive work environment. (par. 2)

There are several forms of sexual harassment, which include the following:

- *Quid pro quo* means you give something to get something, and in this case, it refers to a situation in which organizational rewards are offered in exchange for sexual favors. For example, a supervisor might request an action, such as a kiss or a touch, in exchange for a promotion, a positive performance review, or a pay raise.

- The threat of withholding a reward if a sexual request is refused

- Hostile environment sexual harassment is when an employee experiences conditions in the workplace that are considered hostile or intimidating. For example, a work environment that allows offensive language or jokes or displays sexually explicit images.

Isolated occurrences of these events do not constitute harassment, but a pattern of repeated occurrences does. In addition to violating organizational policies against sexual harassment, these forms of harassment are illegal. It is also important to note that harassment does not have to be sexual; it may be related to any of the protected classes in the statutes regulated by the EEOC: race, national origin, religion, or age.

Violence in the Workplace

In the summer of August 1986, a part-time postal worker with a troubled work history walked into the Edmond, Oklahoma, post office and shot and killed 15 people, including himself. From his action, the term *going postal* was coined, describing a troubled employee who engages in extreme violence.

Workplace violence is one aspect of workplace safety that I-O psychologists study. **Workplace violence** is any act or threat of physical violence, harassment, intimidation, or other threatening, disruptive behavior that occurs at the workplace. It ranges from threats and verbal abuse to physical assaults and even homicide (Occupational Safety & Health Administration, 2014).

There are different targets of workplace violence: a person could commit violence against coworkers, supervisors, or property. Warning signs often precede such actions: intimidating behavior, threats, sabotaging equipment, or radical changes in a coworker's behavior. Often there is intimidation and then escalation that leads to even further escalation. It is important for employees to involve their immediate supervisor if they ever feel intimidated or unsafe.

Reflection Questions

What do you think are some challenges employees face when reporting workplace aggression?

Murder is the second leading cause of death in the workplace. It is also the primary cause of death for women in the workplace. Every year there are nearly two million workers who are physically assaulted or threatened with assault. Many are murdered in domestic violence situations by boyfriends or husbands who chose the woman's workplace to commit their crimes.

Reflection Questions

What is an example of implementing a procedural justice policy in the workplace that may prevent aggression to a supervisor?

There are many triggers for workplace violence. A significant trigger is the feeling of being treated unfairly, unjustly, or disrespectfully. In a research experiment, Greenberg (1993) examined the reactions of students who were given pay for a task. In one group, the students were given extensive explanations for the pay rate. In the second group, the students were given a curt, uninformative explanation. The students were made to believe the supervisor would not know how much money the student withdrew for payment. The rate of stealing (taking more pay than they were told they deserved) was higher in the group who had been given the limited explanation. This is a demonstration of the importance of procedural justice in organizations. **Procedural justice** refers to the fairness of the processes by which outcomes are determined in conflicts with or among employees.

In another study by Greenberg & Barling (1999), they found a history of aggression and amount of alcohol consumed to be accurate predictors of workplace violence against a coworker. Aggression against a supervisor was predicted if a worker felt unfairly treated or untrusted. Job security and alcohol consumption predicted aggression against a subordinate. To understand and predict workplace violence, Greenberg & Barling (1999) emphasize the importance of considering the employee target of aggression or violence and characteristics of both the workplace and the aggressive or violent person.

Summary

Organizational psychology is concerned with the effects of interactions among people in the workplace, on the employees themselves, and on organizational productivity. Job satisfaction and its determinants and outcomes are a major focus of organizational psychology research and practice. Organizational psychologists have also studied the effects of management styles and leadership styles on productivity. In addition to the employees and management, organizational psychology also looks at the organizational culture and how that might affect productivity. One aspect of organizational culture is the prevention and addressing of sexual and other forms of harassment in the workplace. Sexual harassment includes language, behavior, or displays that create a hostile environment; it also includes sexual favors requested in exchange for workplace rewards (i.e., quid pro quo). Industrial-organizational psychology has conducted extensive research on the triggers and causes of workplace violence and safety. This enables the organization to establish procedures that can identify these triggers before they become a problem.

Flash Forward

Ready to dig into the vocabulary? Get some practice with this Hawkes Verified Quizlet set (hawkes.biz/psych12q4)!

12.4 Human Factors Psychology and Workplace Design

Human factors psychology (or *ergonomics*, a term that is favored in Europe) is the third subject area within industrial and organizational psychology. This field is concerned with the integration of the human-machine interface in the workplace through design and specifically with researching and designing machines that fit human requirements.

Human factor professionals help with software design, testing, evaluation, and determining regulations and principles for best design (Howell, 2003). For example, the American National Standards Institute (ANSI, 2000), an independent developer of industrial standards, develops many standards related to ergonomic design, such as the design of control-center workstations that are used for transportation control or industrial process control.

> **Reflection Questions**
> Why do you think psychologists are employed to help address issues related to workplace safety?

Many of the concerns of human factors psychology are related to workplace safety. These concerns can be studied to help prevent work-related injuries of individual workers or those around them. They often assist industry leaders in creating safety **checklists**. The surgical safety checklist shown in Figure 1 was developed by the World Health Organization (WHO) and serves as the basis for many checklists at medical facilities.

✎ On Your Own

Using the following table, provide a safety checklist for cooking food on the stove in your kitchen.

#	Checklist Item
1	
2	
3	

Safety concerns also lead to limits on how long an operator, such as a pilot or truck driver, is allowed to operate the equipment. Recently, the Federal Aviation Administration (FAA) introduced limits for how long a pilot is allowed to fly without an overnight break. For example, Bruno & Abrahão (2012) found that as the number of decisions made per day by the operators climbed (as their cognitive effort increased), the operators made more mistakes in falsely identifying incidents as real security breaches. However, the opposite mistake of identifying real intrusions as false alarms did not increase with increased cognitive demand. Howell (2003) outlines some important areas of research and practice in the field of human factors. These are summarized in Table 1.

Figure 1: Checklists, such as this WHO surgical checklist, help reduce workplace accidents.

Area	Description	I-O Questions
Attention	Includes vigilance and monitoring, recognizing signals in noise, mental resources, and divided attention	How is attention maintained? What about tasks maintains attention? How to design systems to support attention?
Cognitive engineering	Includes human software interactions in complex automated systems, especially the decision-making processes of workers as they are supported by the software system	How do workers use and obtain information provided by software?
Task analysis	Breaking down the elements of a task	How can a task be performed more efficiently? How can a task be performed more safely?
Cognitive task analysis	Breaking down the elements of a cognitive task	How are decisions made?

Table 1: Areas of Study in Human Factors Psychology

✏ On Your Own

Which of the following most closely demonstrates task analysis?

☐ Research on how to safely use a device that assists with tire molds

☐ Identifying which aspects of a software program are going to grab the users' attention

☐ Writing a software program

Summary

Human factors psychology, or ergonomics, studies the interface between workers and their machines and physical environments. Human factors psychologists specifically seek to design machines to better support the workers using them. Psychologists may be involved in design of work tools such as software, displays, or machines from the beginning of the design process or during the testing of an already developed product. Human factor psychologists are also involved in the development of best design recommendations and regulations. One important aspect of human factors psychology is enhancing worker safety. Human factors research involves efforts to understand and improve interactions between technology systems and their human operators.

Chapter 12 Project

Purpose

Industrial and organizational (I-O) psychology is a branch of psychology that studies how human behavior and psychology affect work and how they are affected by work. Organizational psychology specifically focuses on how the relationships between workers impacts business and how organizational culture impacts individual behavior and employee satisfaction. **The purpose of this project is to better understand what organizational psychology is and how it is effectively employed in the business world to maximize success.**

Directions

Imagine you are starting your own small business and want to employ the best practices of organizational psychology to maximize your success. Your business can be anything as long as you have multiple employees and a fixed, physical setting in which they interact, such as an office, store, factory, etc.

Write a mission statement that outlines what your business aims to accomplish and how you plan to go about achieving the optimal work environment to do so. Your mission statement should describe your goals as an organization (beyond making your product/providing your service) and the type of work environment you need to achieve to meet those goals. The mission statement should also tell us what the organizational culture is like and what your organizational values are. Imagine that this mission statement will be how people learn about your company and an important tool for recruiting your new employees.

As you create your mission statement, feel free to be creative! Consider how design elements such as colors, fonts, images, layout, etc. may be employed to "say" something about your company or organizational values. Final submissions should be approximately one page of textual information and should be typed, but otherwise may vary in format.

As you think about what should be included in your mission statement, consider the following themes/questions from organizational psychology. It is not required that you address all of these questions; however, they should serve as guiding principles for what is included in your mission statement.

- What types of employees do you need to be successful, and how will you recruit them?

- What traits should your employees possess?

- What types of training will you provide for your employees (and will they be suited to it)?

- How will employees be evaluated?

- What will the organizational culture of the company be like?

- What is the role of teamwork?

- What are the benefits of working for your organization? What is the role of employee satisfaction in your company?

- How will human factors impact the workplace design/environment?

Materials

None required.

✅ Checklist

- ☐ Mission Statement
    - ☐ Description of the business
        - ☐ Multiple employees
        - ☐ Fixed, physical setting
    - ☐ Outlines what the business aims to accomplish
        - ☐ Goals
            - ☐ Identifies plans for achieving optimal work environment
    - ☐ Description of organizational culture and values
    - ☐ At least one page of textual information, typed
    - ☐ Addresses some of the given concept questions

🏁 Chapter 12 Review

Lesson Summaries

12.1 What Is Industrial and Organizational Psychology?

The field of I-O psychology had its birth in industrial psychology and the use of psychological concepts to aid in personnel selection. However, with research such as the Hawthorne study, it was found that productivity was affected more by human interaction and not physical factors; the field of industrial psychology expanded to include organizational psychology. Both WWI and WWII had a strong influence on the development of an expansion of industrial psychology in the United States and elsewhere. The tasks the psychologists were assigned led to development of tests and research in how the psychological concepts could assist industry and other areas. This movement aided in expanding industrial psychology to include organizational psychology.

12.2 Industrial Psychology: Selecting and Evaluating Employees

Industrial psychology studies the attributes of jobs, applicants of those jobs, and methods for assessing fit to a job. These procedures include job analysis, applicant testing, and interviews. It also studies and puts into place procedures for the orientation of new employees and ongoing training of employees. The process of hiring employees can be vulnerable to bias, which is illegal, and industrial psychologists must develop methods for adhering to the law in hiring. Performance appraisal systems are an active area of research and practice in industrial psychology.

12.3 Organizational Psychology: The Social Dimension of Work

Organizational psychology is concerned with the effects of interactions among people in the workplace, on the employees themselves, and on organizational productivity. Job satisfaction and its determinants and outcomes are a major focus of organizational psychology research and practice. Organizational psychologists have also studied the effects of management styles and leadership styles on productivity. In addition to the employees and management, organizational psychology also looks at the organizational culture and how that might affect productivity. One aspect of organizational culture is the prevention and addressing of sexual and other forms of harassment in the workplace. Sexual harassment includes language, behavior, or displays that create a hostile environment; it also includes sexual favors requested in exchange for workplace rewards (i.e., quid pro quo). Industrial-organizational psychology has conducted extensive research on the triggers and causes of workplace violence and safety. This enables the organization to establish procedures that can identify these triggers before they become a problem.

12.4 Human Factors Psychology and Workplace Design

Human factors psychology, or ergonomics, studies the interface between workers and their machines and physical environments. Human factors psychologists specifically seek to design machines to better support the workers using them. Psychologists may be involved in design of work tools such as software, displays, or machines from the beginning of the design process or during the testing of an already developed product. Human factor psychologists are also involved in the development of best design recommendations and regulations. One important aspect of human factors psychology is enhancing worker safety. Human factors research involves efforts to understand and improve interactions between technology systems and their human operators.

Key Terms

> **Flash Back**
>
> Now that you've worked through the chapter, sharpen your vocabulary with this Hawkes Verified Quizlet set (hawkes.biz/psychch12)!

Americans with Disabilities Act
Employers cannot discriminate against any individual based on a disability

Bona Fide Occupational Qualification (BFOQ)
Requirement of certain occupations for which denying an individual employment would otherwise violate the law, such as requirements concerning religion or sex

Checklist
Method used to reduce workplace accidents

Diversity Training
Training employees about cultural differences with the goal of improving teamwork

Downsizing
Process in which an organization tries to achieve greater overall efficiency by reducing the number of employees

Hawthorne Effect
Increase in performance of individuals who are noticed, watched, and paid attention to by researchers or supervisors

Human Factors Psychology

Branch of psychology that studies how workers interact with the tools of work and how to design those tools to optimize workers' productivity, safety, and health

Immutable Characteristic

Traits that employers cannot use to discriminate in hiring, benefits, promotions, or termination; these traits are fundamental to one's personal identity (e.g. skin color and hair texture)

Industrial and Organizational (I-O) Psychology

Field in psychology that applies scientific principles to the study of work and the workplace

Industrial Psychology

Branch of psychology that studies job characteristics, applicant characteristics, and how to match them; also studies employee training and performance appraisal

Job Analysis

Determining and listing tasks associated with a particular job

Job Satisfaction

Degree of pleasure that employees derive from their job

Organizational Culture

Values, visions, hierarchies, norms, and interactions between its employees; how an organization is run, how it operates, and how it makes decisions

Organizational Psychology

Branch of psychology that studies the interactions between people working in organizations and the effects of those interactions on productivity

Performance Appraisal

Evaluation of an employee's success or lack of success at performing the duties of the job

Procedural Justice

Fairness by which means are used to achieve results in an organization

Scientific Management

Theory of management that analyzes and synthesizes workflows with the main objective of improving economic efficiency, especially labor productivity

Sexual Harassment

Sexually-based behavior that is knowingly unwanted and has an adverse effect of a person's employment status, interferes with a person's job performance, or creates a hostile or intimidating work environment

Telecommuting

Employees' ability to set their own hours allowing them to work from home at different parts of the day

Theory X

Assumes workers are inherently lazy and unproductive; managers must have control and use punishments

Theory Y

Assumes workers are people who seek to work hard and productively; managers and workers can find creative solutions to problems; workers do not need to be controlled and punished

Transactional Leadership Style

Characteristic of leaders who focus on supervision and organizational goals achieved through a system of rewards and punishments; maintenance of the organizational status quo

Transformational Leadership Style

Characteristic of leaders who are charismatic role models, inspirational, intellectually stimulating, and individually considerate and who seek to change the organization

U.S. Equal Employment Opportunity Commission (EEOC)

Responsible for enforcing federal laws that make it illegal to discriminate against a job applicant or an employee because of the person's race, color, religion, sex (including pregnancy), national origin, age (40 or older), disability, or genetic information

Work Team

Group of people within an organization or company given a specific task to achieve together

Work-Family Balance

Occurs when people juggle the demands of work life with the demands of family life

Workplace Violence

Violence or the threat of violence against workers; can occur inside or outside the workplace

Review Questions

1. Who was the first psychologist to use psychology in advertising?

   a. Hugo Münsterberg

   b. Elton Mayo

   c. Walter Dill Scott

   d. Walter Bingham

2. Which test designed for the Army was used for recruits who were not fluent in English?

   a. Army Personality

   b. Army Alpha

   c. Army Beta

   d. Army Intelligence

3. Which area of I-O psychology measures job satisfaction?

   a. Industrial psychology

   b. Organizational psychology

   c. Human factors psychology

   d. Advertising psychology

4. Which statement best describes the Hawthorne effect?

   a. Giving workers rest periods seems like it should decrease productivity, but it actually increases productivity.

   b. Social relations among workers have a greater effect on productivity than physical environment.

   c. Changes in light levels improve working conditions and, therefore, increase productivity.

   d. The attention of researchers on subjects causes the effect the experimenter is looking for.

5. Which of the following questions is illegal to ask in a job interview in the United States?

   a. Which university did you attend?

   b. Which state were you born in?

   c. Do you have a commercial driver's license?

   d. What salary would you expect for this position?

6. Which of the following items is not a part of KSAs?

   a. Aspiration

   b. Knowledge

   c. Skill

   d. Other abilities

7. Who is responsible for enforcing federal laws that make it illegal to discriminate against a job applicant?

   a. Americans with Disabilities Act

   b. Supreme Court of the United States

   c. U.S. Equal Employment Opportunity Commission

   d. Society for Industrial and Organizational Psychology

8. A _____ is an example of a tactical team.

   a. surgical team

   b. car design team

   c. budget committee

   d. sports team

9. Which practice is an example of Theory X management?

   a. Telecommuting

   b. Flextime

   c. Keystroke monitoring

   d. Team meetings

10. Which is one effect of the team halo effect?

    a. Teams appear to work better than they do.

    b. Teams never fail.

    c. Teams lead to greater job satisfaction.

    d. Teams boost productivity.

11. Which is not a job-related factor affecting job satisfaction?

    a. Financial rewards

    b. Personality

    c. Autonomy

    d. Work content

12. What is the name for what occurs when a supervisor offers a work-related reward in exchange for a sexual favor?

    a. Hiring bias

    b. Quid pro quo

    c. Hostile work environment

    d. Immutable characteristics

13. What aspect of an office workstation would a human factors psychologist be concerned about?

    a. Height of the chair

    b. Closeness to the supervisor

    c. Frequency of coworker visits

    d. Presence of an offensive sign

14. A human factors psychologist who studied how a worker interacted with a search engine would be researching in the area of _____.

    a. attention

    b. cognitive engineering

    c. job satisfaction

    d. management

Critical Thinking Questions

15. What societal and management attitudes might have caused organizational psychology to develop later than industrial psychology?

16. Many of the examples of I-O psychology are applications to businesses. Name four different nonbusiness contexts that I-O psychology could impact?

17. Construct a good interview question for a position of your choosing. The question should relate to a specific skill requirement for the position, and you will need to include the criteria for rating the applicant's answer.

18. What might be useful mechanisms for avoiding bias during employment interviews?

19. If you designed an assessment of job satisfaction, what elements would it include?

20. Downsizing has commonly shown to result in a period of lowered productivity for the organizations experiencing it. What might be some of the reasons for this observation?

21. What role could a flight simulator play in the design of a new aircraft?

Chapter 13

Stress, Lifestyle, and Health

Chapter Introduction

🖼 **Figure 1:** Exams are a stressful, but unavoidable, element of college life.

Today's college students are under a lot of pressure. In addition to the many usual stresses of the college experience (e.g., exams, term papers, and the dreaded freshman 15), students today are faced with increased college tuitions, burdensome debt, and difficulty finding employment after graduation. A significant population of non-traditional students may face additional stressors, such as raising children or holding down a full-time job while working toward a degree.

What are your biggest stressors related to college? How do they impact you on a regular basis?

Of course, life is filled with many additional challenges beyond those incurred in college. Some common examples include: Concerns with financial security, difficulties with friends or neighbors, challenges at work, and family responsibilities.

We may not have enough time to do the things we want to do. Even minor hassles—losing things, traffic jams, and loss of internet service—involve pressure and demands that can make life seem like a struggle and that can compromise our sense of well-being.

Scientific interest in stress, including how we adapt and cope, has been longstanding in psychology; after nearly a century of research, much has been learned and many insights have been developed. This chapter examines stress and highlights our current understanding of the phenomenon, including three key aspects:The psychological and physiological natures of stress, causes and consequences of stress, and steps to master stress.

Flash Forward

Ready to dig into the vocabulary? Get some practice with this Hawkes Verified Quizlet set (hawkes.biz/psych13q1)!

Further Resources

Interested in learning how the American Institute of Stress defines the topic and explores its causes and impacts? Check out this link (hawkes.biz/stress) for more information.

Figure 2: The emotion of stress is one that most humans experience in their lives.

Group Activity

With a group, discuss what you feel to be more common: stress as a stimulus or stress as a response. Why do you feel this way?

13.1 What Is Stress?

The term **stress** as it relates to the human condition first emerged in scientific literature in the 1930s, but it did not enter common public discourse until the 1970s (Lyon, 2012). Today, we often use the term loosely in describing a variety of unpleasant feelings; we might say we're stressed out when we feel frustrated, angry, conflicted, overwhelmed, or fatigued. Despite the widespread use of the term, stress is a fairly vague concept that is difficult to define.

Researchers have had a difficult time agreeing on an acceptable definition of stress. Some have conceptualized stress as a demanding or threatening event or situation (e.g., a high-stress job, overcrowding, and long commutes to work). Such conceptualizations are known as stimulus-based definitions because they characterize stress as a stimulus that causes certain reactions. Stimulus-based definitions of stress are problematic, however, because they fail to recognize that people differ in how they view and react to challenging life events and situations. For example, a conscientious student who has studied diligently all semester would likely experience less stress during final exams week than would a less responsible, unprepared student.

✍ On Your Own

Fill in the table below with other examples that show how people might react to the same stimuli differently; one person might see it as stressful, another might not. Use the example just described previously to help get you started.

Stimulus	Reaction 1	Reaction 2

Scenarios that Contradict Stress as a Stimulus

Others have conceptualized stress in ways that emphasize the physiological responses that occur when faced with demanding or threatening situations (e.g., increased arousal). These conceptualizations are referred to as *response-based* definitions because they describe stress as a response to environmental conditions. The endocrinologist Hans Selye, a famous stress researcher, defined stress as the "response of the body to any demand, whether it is caused by, or results in, pleasant or unpleasant conditions" (Selye, 1976, p. 74).

Selye's definition of stress is response-based because it conceptualizes stress in terms of the body's physiological reaction to any demand that is placed on it. Neither stimulus-based nor response-based definitions provide a complete definition of stress. Many of the physiological reactions that occur when faced with demanding situations (e.g., accelerated heart rate) can also occur in response to things that most people would not consider to be stressful, such as receiving unanticipated good news: like an unexpected promotion or raise.

A useful way to conceptualize stress is to view it as a process whereby an individual perceives and responds to events that he appraises as overwhelming or threatening to his well-being (Lazarus & Folkman, 1984). A critical element of this definition is that it emphasizes how we appraise—that is, judge—demanding or threatening events (referred to as **stressors**); these appraisals then influence our reactions to such events.

Two kinds of appraisals of a stressor are especially important:

- Primary Appraisals

- Secondary Appraisals

A **primary appraisal** involves judgment about the degree of potential harm or threat to well-being that a stressor might entail. A stressor would likely be appraised as a threat if one anticipates that it could lead to some kind of harm, loss, or other negative consequence; conversely, a stressor would likely be appraised as a challenge if one believes that it carries the potential for gain or personal growth. Consider the following examples:

> An employee who is promoted to a leadership position would likely perceive the promotion as a much greater threat if she believed the promotion would lead to excessive work demands than if she viewed it as an opportunity to gain new skills and grow professionally.

> A college student on the cusp of graduation may face the change as a threat or a challenge (Figure 3).

The perception of a threat triggers a **secondary appraisal**: judgment of the options available to cope with a stressor, as well as perceptions of how effective such options will be (Lyon, 2012) (Figure 4). An individual's belief in his ability to complete a task is important (Bandura, 1994). A threat tends to be viewed as less catastrophic if one believes something can be done about it (Lazarus & Folkman, 1984). Consider the following example:

Figure 3: Graduating from college and entering the workforce can be viewed as either a threat (loss of financial support) or a challenge (opportunity for independence and growth).

> Imagine that two middle-aged women, Robin and Maria, perform breast self-examinations one morning, and each woman notices a lump on the lower region of her left breast. Although both women view the breast lump as a potential threat (primary appraisal), their secondary appraisals differ considerably. In considering the breast lump, each woman has a different response:

ROBIN	"Oh my God, I could have breast cancer! What if the cancer has spread to the rest of my body? What if I have to go through chemotherapy? What if I have to quit my job? My husband and I won't have enough money to pay the mortgage. Oh, this is horrible…I can't deal with it!"
MARIA	"Hmm, this may not be good. Although most times these things turn out to be benign, I need to have it checked out. If it turns out to be breast cancer, there are doctors who can take care of it because the medical technology today is quite advanced. I'll have a lot of different options, and I'll be just fine."

Clearly, Robin and Maria have different outlooks on what might turn out to be a very serious situation. As such, Robin would clearly experience greater stress than would Maria, at least initially.

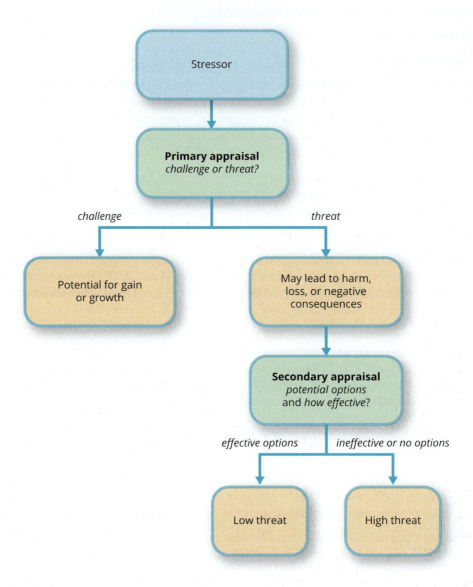

🖼 **Figure 4:** When encountering a stressor, a person judges its potential threat (primary appraisal) and then determines if effective options are available to manage the situation. Stress is likely to result if a stressor is perceived as extremely threatening or threatening with few or no effective coping options available.

Some stressors are inherently more stressful than others because they are more threatening and leave less potential for variation in cognitive appraisals (e.g., objective threats to one's health or safety). Nevertheless, appraisal will play a role in augmenting or diminishing our reactions to such events (Everly & Lating, 2002).

If a person appraises an event as harmful and believes that the demands imposed by the event exceed the available resources to manage or adapt to it, the person will subjectively experience a state of stress. In contrast, if one does not appraise the same event as harmful or threatening, she is unlikely to experience stress. According to this definition, environmental events trigger stress reactions by the way they are interpreted and the meanings they are assigned.

In short, stress is not so much what happens to you as it is how you respond (Selye, 1976).

Reflection Questions

Can you think of a scenario in which you might not feel stressed while most other people do? How about a scenario you find particularly stressful that others might not? What do you think causes these reactions for you?

Good Stress?

Although stress carries a negative connotation, at times it may be of some benefit. Stress can motivate us to do things in our best interests. Some common examples include:

- Studying for exams

- Visiting the doctor regularly

- Exercising

- Performing to the best of our ability at work

Indeed, Selye (1974) pointed out that not all stress is harmful.

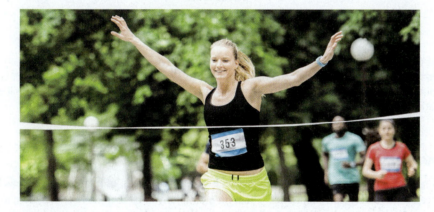

Figure 5: Some levels of stress can help encourage people to meet their goals.

He argued that stress can sometimes be a positive, motivating force that can improve the quality of our lives. This kind of stress, which Selye called **eustress** (from the Greek *eu = good*), is a good kind of stress associated with positive feelings, optimal health, and performance. For example, athletes may be motivated and energized by pregame stress, and students may experience similar beneficial stress before a major exam. Indeed, research shows that moderate stress can enhance both immediate and delayed recall of educational material. Male participants in one study who memorized a scientific text passage showed improved memory of the passage immediately after exposure to a mild stressor, as well as one day following exposure to the stressor (Hupbach & Fieman, 2012).

On Your Own

Discuss an example in your own life of when stress has positively impacted you. Describe what this impact looked like and what, if anything, you learned from the experience.

_____

_____

Increasing one's level of stress will cause performance to change in a predictable way. As shown in Figure 6, as stress increases, so do performance and general well-being (eustress); when stress levels reach an optimal level (the highest point of the curve), performance reaches its peak. A person at this stress level is at the top of her game, meaning she feels fully energized, focused, and can work with minimal effort and maximum efficiency.

But when stress exceeds this optimal level, it is no longer a positive force—it becomes excessive and debilitating, or what Selye termed **distress** (from the Latin *dis = bad*). People who reach this level of stress feel burned out; they are fatigued, exhausted, and their performance begins to decline. If the stress remains excessive, health may begin to erode as well (Everly & Lating, 2002).

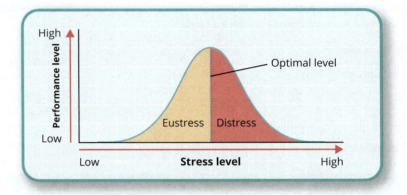

Figure 6: As the stress level increases from low to moderate, so does performance (eustress). At the optimal level (the peak of the curve), performance has reached its peak. If stress exceeds the optimal level, it will reach the distress region, where it will become excessive and debilitating, and performance will decline (Everly & Lating, 2002).

The Prevalence of Stress

As shown in Figure 7, stress has been on the rise over the last several years. In many ways, it feels like a load you just can't carry—a feeling you experience when, for example, you have to drive somewhere in a crippling blizzard, when you wake up late the morning of an important job interview, when you run out of money before your next paycheck, and before taking an important exam for which you realize you are not fully prepared.

Figure 7: Nearly half of U.S. adults indicated that their stress levels have increased over the last five years (Neelakantan, 2013).

Stress evokes a variety of responses that can be classified under the following categories:

Category	Examples
Physiological	Accelerated heart rate Headaches Gastrointestinal problems
Cognitive	Difficulty concentrating Inability to make decisions
Behavioral	Drinking alcohol Smoking Taking actions toward eliminating stress

Responses to Stress

Although stress can be positive at times, it can have harmful health implications, contributing to a variety of physical illnesses and diseases (Cohen & Herbert, 1996).

The scientific study of how stress and other psychological factors impact health falls within the realm of **health psychology**, a subfield of psychology devoted to understanding the importance of psychological influences on three things:

- Health

- Illness

- How people respond when they become ill (Taylor, 1999)

Figure 8: When it goes untreated, stress can have harmful health implications.

Health psychology emerged as a discipline in the 1970s, at a time when there was increasing awareness of the role behavioral and lifestyle factors play in the development of illnesses and diseases (Straub, 2007). Health psychologists investigate issues such as why people make certain lifestyle choices. For example, why do people smoke or eat unhealthy food despite knowing the potential health consequences? Health psychologists also design and investigate the effectiveness of interventions aimed at changing unhealthy behaviors. One of their more fundamental tasks is to identify which groups of people are especially at risk for negative health outcomes based on psychological or behavioral factors. For example, measuring differences in stress levels among demographic groups and how these levels change over time can help identify populations who may have an increased risk for illness or disease.

☑ On Your Own

Which of the following statements are true about health psychology?

- ☐ It is a science exploring stress that emerged in the late 1800s.

- ☐ It is a science exploring stress that emerged in the 1970s.

- ☐ Health psychologists sometimes create interventions to determine behaviors.

- ☐ Health psychologists disregard how interventions might curb behavior.

- ☐ One topic this field primarily focuses on is illness.

- ☐ One topic this field primarily focuses on is the cognitive development of newborns.

Figure 9 depicts the results of three national surveys in which several thousand individuals from different demographic groups completed a brief stress questionnaire; the surveys were administered in 1983, 2006, and 2009 (Cohen & Janicki-Deverts, 2012). They found the following:

- Each one demonstrated higher stress in women than in men.

- Unemployed individuals, those with less education, and those with less income reported high levels of stress.

- From 2006–2009, the greatest *increase* in stress levels occurred in:

  ○ Whites

  ○ people aged 45–64

  ○ college graduates

  ○ those with full-time employment

One interpretation of these findings is that concerns surrounding the 2008–2009 economic downturn (e.g., threat of or actual job loss and substantial loss of retirement savings) may have been especially stressful to White, college-educated, employed men with limited time remaining in their working careers.

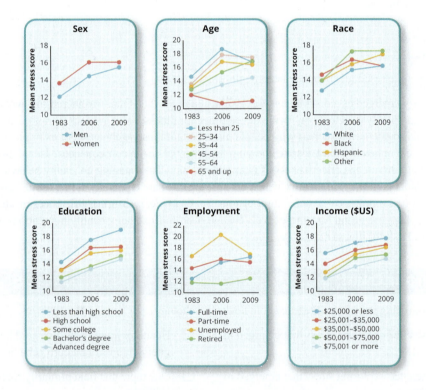

Figure 9: The charts above, adapted from Cohen & Janicki-Deverts (2012), depict the mean stress level scores among different demographic groups during the years 1983, 2006, and 2009. Across categories of sex, age, race, education level, employment status, and income, stress levels generally show a marked increase over this quarter-century time span.

Figure 10: Harvard Medical School is where physiologist Walter Cannon first articulated and named the fight-or-flight response, the nervous system's sympathetic response to a significant stressor.

Early Contributions to the Study of Stress

As previously stated, scientific interest in stress goes back nearly a century. One of the early pioneers in the study of stress was Walter Cannon, a renowned American physiologist at Harvard Medical School (Figure 10). In the early part of the 20th century, Cannon was the first to identify the body's physiological reactions to stress.

Cannon and the Fight-or-Flight Response

Imagine that you are hiking in the beautiful mountains of Colorado on a warm and sunny spring day. As you turn a corner on the trail, a black bear appears and sits about 50 yards from you. The bear notices you, stands up, and begins to lumber in your direction. In addition to thinking, "This is definitely not good," a constellation of physiological reactions begins to take place inside you. Prompted by a deluge of epinephrine (adrenaline) and norepinephrine (noradrenaline) from your adrenal glands, your pupils begin to dilate. Your heart starts to pound, your heartbeat speeds up, you begin to breathe heavily and perspire, you get butterflies in your stomach, and your muscles become tense, preparing you to take some kind of direct action.

Cannon proposed that this reaction, which he called the **fight-or-flight response**, occurs when a person experiences very strong emotions—especially those associated with a perceived threat (Cannon, 1932). The body is rapidly aroused by activation of both the sympathetic nervous system and the endocrine system (Figure 11). This arousal helps prepare the person to either fight or flee from a perceived threat.

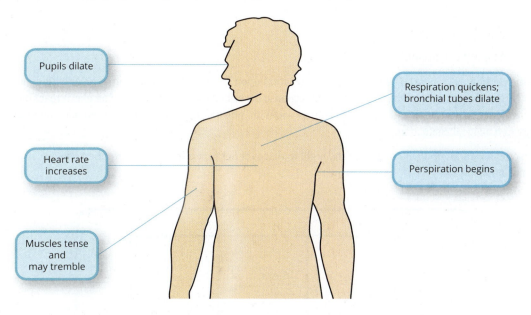

🖼 **Figure 11:** Fight or flight is a physiological response to a stressor.

According to Cannon, the fight-or-flight response is a built-in mechanism that assists in maintaining homeostasis—an internal environment in which physiological variables are stabilized at levels optimal for survival. These variables include:

- Blood pressure
- Respiration
- Digestion
- Temperature

Thus, Cannon viewed the fight-or-flight response as adaptive because it enables us to adjust internally and externally to changes in our surroundings, which is helpful in species survival.

Selye and the General Adaptation Syndrome

Another important early contributor to the stress field was Hans Selye, one of the world's foremost experts in the study of stress (Figure 12). As a young assistant in the biochemistry department at McGill University in the 1930s, Selye was engaged in research involving sex hormones in rats. Although he was unable to find an answer for what he was initially researching, he incidentally discovered that when exposed to prolonged

Further Resources

Interested in reading about one woman's fight-or-flight response that led her Louisiana town to call her a hero? Read the story here. (hawkes.biz/fightorflight)

negative stimulation (stressors)—such as extreme cold, surgical injury, excessive muscular exercise, and shock—the rats showed the following three signs:

- Adrenal enlargement

- Thymus and lymph node shrinkage

- Stomach ulceration

Selye realized that these responses were triggered by a coordinated series of physiological reactions that unfold over time during continued exposure to a stressor. These physiological reactions were nonspecific, which means that regardless of the type of stressor, the same pattern of reactions would occur. What Selye discovered was the **general adaptation syndrome**, the body's nonspecific physiological response to stress.

Figure 12: Hans Selye specialized in research about stress.

The general adaptation syndrome, shown in Figure 13, consists of three stages:

1. Alarm reaction

2. Stage of resistance

3. Stage of exhaustion

Alarm reaction describes the body's immediate reaction upon facing a threatening situation or emergency, and it is roughly analogous to the fight-or-flight response described by Cannon. During an alarm reaction, you are alerted to a stressor, and your body alarms you with physiological reactions that provide you with the energy to manage the situation.

A person who wakes up in the middle of the night to discover her house is on fire is experiencing an alarm reaction.

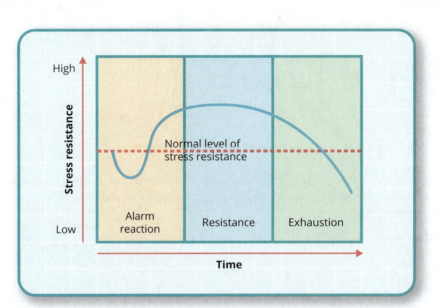

Figure 13: The three stages of Selye's general adaptation syndrome are shown in this graph. Prolonged stress ultimately results in exhaustion (Selye, 1936; 1976).

If exposure to a stressor is prolonged, the organism will enter the **stage of resistance**. During this stage, the initial shock of alarm reaction has worn off, and the body has adapted to the stressor. Nevertheless, the body also remains on alert and is prepared to respond as it did during the alarm reaction although with less intensity.

A child who went missing is still missing 72 hours later. Although the child's family would remain extremely disturbed, the magnitude of physiological reactions would likely have diminished over the 72 intervening hours due to some adaptation.

If exposure to a stressor continues over a longer period of time, the **stage of exhaustion** ensues. At this stage, the person is no longer able to adapt to the stressor: the body's ability to resist becomes depleted as physical wear takes its toll on the body's tissues and organs. As a result, illness, disease, and other permanent damage to the body—even death—may occur.

Figure 14: Extremely stressful circumstances often have intense physical impacts.

If a missing child still remains missing after three months, the long-term stress associated with this situation may cause a family member to faint with exhaustion or to develop a serious and irreversible illness.

In short, Selye's general adaptation syndrome suggests that stressors tax the body via a three-phase process:

1. An initial jolt

2. A subsequent readjustment

3. A later depletion of all physical resources that ultimately lays the groundwork for serious health problems and even death

It should be pointed out, however, that this model is a response-based conceptualization of stress, focusing exclusively on the body's physical responses while largely ignoring psychological factors such as appraisal and interpretation of threats. Nevertheless, Selye's model has had an enormous impact on the field of stress because it offers a general explanation for how stress can lead to physical damage and, thus, disease. As we'll discuss later, prolonged or repeated stress has been implicated in the development of a number of disorders such as hypertension and coronary artery disease.

Reflection Questions

Does it surprise you to learn of the potential serious impacts of stress? Why or why not?

The Physiological Basis of Stress

What goes on inside our bodies when we experience stress? The physiological mechanisms of stress are extremely complex, but they generally involve the work of two systems:

- The sympathetic nervous system

- The hypothalamic-pituitary-adrenal (HPA) axis

When a person first perceives something as stressful, the sympathetic nervous system triggers arousal via the release of adrenaline from the adrenal glands. Release of these hormones activates the fight-or-flight responses to stress, such as accelerated heart rate and respiration. At the same time, the **HPA axis**, which is primarily endocrine in nature, becomes especially active although it works much more slowly than the sympathetic nervous system. In response to stress, the hypothalamus (one of the limbic structures in the brain) releases corticotrophin-releasing factor, a hormone that causes the pituitary gland to release adrenocorticotropic hormone (ACTH) (Figure 15). The ACTH then activates the adrenal glands to secrete a number of hormones into the bloodstream; an important one is cortisol, which can affect virtually every organ within the body. **Cortisol** is commonly known as a stress hormone and helps provide that boost of energy when we first encounter a stressor, preparing us to run away or fight. However, sustained elevated levels of cortisol weaken the immune system.

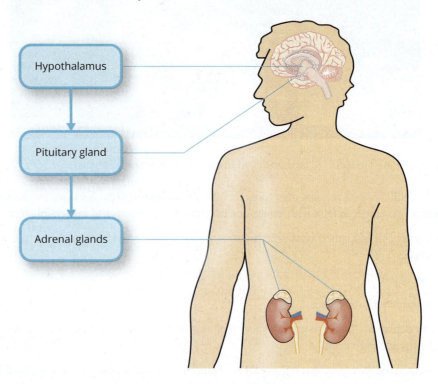

Figure 15: This diagram shows the functioning of the hypothalamic-pituitary-adrenal (HPA) axis. The hypothalamus activates the pituitary gland, which in turn activates the adrenal glands, increasing their secretion of cortisol.

In short bursts, this process can have some favorable effects, such as the following:

- Providing extra energy

- Improving immune system functioning temporarily

- Decreasing pain sensitivity

However, extended release of cortisol—as would happen with prolonged or chronic stress—often comes at a high price. High levels of cortisol have been shown to produce a number of harmful effects. For example, increases in cortisol can significantly weaken our immune system (Glaser & Kiecolt-Glaser, 2005), and high levels are frequently observed among depressed individuals (Geoffroy, Hertzman, Li, & Power, 2013).

In summary, a stressful event causes a variety of physiological reactions that activate the adrenal glands, which in turn release epinephrine, norepinephrine, and cortisol. These hormones affect a number of bodily processes in ways that prepare the stressed person to take direct action, but also in ways that may heighten the potential for illness.

When stress is extreme or chronic, it can have profoundly negative consequences. For example, stress often contributes to the development of certain psychological disorders, including post-traumatic stress disorder, major depressive disorder, and other serious psychiatric conditions. Additionally, stress is linked to the development and progression of a variety of physical illnesses and diseases. Consider these examples:

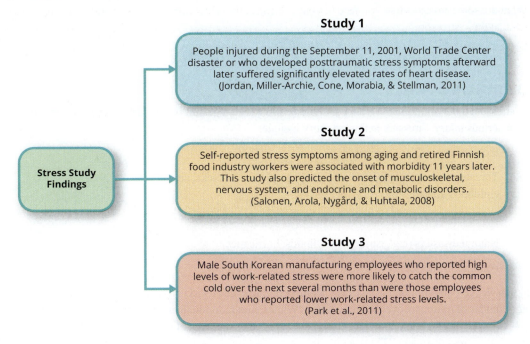

Study 1

People injured during the September 11, 2001, World Trade Center disaster or who developed posttraumatic stress symptoms afterward later suffered significantly elevated rates of heart disease. (Jordan, Miller-Archie, Cone, Morabia, & Stellman, 2011)

Study 2

Self-reported stress symptoms among aging and retired Finnish food industry workers were associated with morbidity 11 years later. This study also predicted the onset of musculoskeletal, nervous system, and endocrine and metabolic disorders. (Salonen, Arola, Nygård, & Huhtala, 2008)

Study 3

Male South Korean manufacturing employees who reported high levels of work-related stress were more likely to catch the common cold over the next several months than were those employees who reported lower work-related stress levels. (Park et al., 2011)

Stress Study Findings

Summary

Stress is a process whereby an individual perceives and responds to events appraised as overwhelming or threatening to one's well-being. The scientific study of how stress and emotional factors impact health and well-being is called health psychology, a field devoted to studying the general impact of psychological factors on health. The body's primary physiological response during stress, the fight-or-flight response, was first identified in the early 20th century by Walter Cannon. The fight-or-flight response involves the coordinated activity of both the sympathetic nervous system and the hypothalamic-pituitary-adrenal (HPA) axis. Hans Selye, a noted endocrinologist, referred to these physiological reactions to stress as part of general adaptation syndrome, which occurs in three stages: alarm reaction (fight-or-flight reactions begin), resistance (the body begins to adapt to continuing stress), and exhaustion (adaptive energy is depleted, and stress begins to take a physical toll).

13.2 Stressors

For an individual to experience stress, he must first encounter a potential stressor. In general, stressors can be placed into one of two broad categories: chronic and acute (Cohen, Janicki-Deverts, & Miller, 2007). They can be understood as follows:

Stressor Type	Examples
Chronic Stressors: persist over an extended period of time	Caring for a parent with dementia Long-term unemployment
Acute Stressors: involve brief focal events that sometimes continue to be experienced	Falling on an icy sidewalk and breaking your leg

Whether chronic or acute, potential stressors come in many shapes and sizes. They can include major traumatic events, significant life changes, daily hassles, and other situations in which a person is regularly exposed to threat, challenge, or danger.

Flash Forward

Ready to dig into the vocabulary? Get some practice with this Hawkes Verified Quizlet set (hawkes.biz/ psych13q2)!

Reflection Questions

What are some stressors that you face in your life currently? How does your mind and body generally react to these stressors?

Figure 1: Both chronic and acute stressors can cause an individual to feel burnt out.

Traumatic Events

Some stressors involve traumatic events or situations in which a person is exposed to actual or threatened death or serious injury. Stressors in this category include:

- Exposure to military combat
- Threatened or actual physical assaults (e.g., physical attacks, sexual assault, robbery, childhood abuse)
- Terrorist attacks
- Natural disasters (e.g., earthquakes, floods, hurricanes)
- Automobile accidents

Men, non-Whites, and individuals in lower socioeconomic status (SES) groups report experiencing a greater number of traumatic events than women, Whites, and individuals in higher SES groups (Hatch & Dohrenwend, 2007). Some individuals who are exposed to stressors of extreme magnitude develop posttraumatic stress disorder (PTSD): a chronic stress reaction characterized by experiences and behaviors that may include intrusive and painful memories of the stressor event, jumpiness, persistent negative emotional states, detachment from others, angry outbursts, and avoidance of reminders of the event (American Psychiatric Association [APA], 2013).

☑ **On Your Own**

In your own words, describe the differences between chronic stressors and acute stressors.

_____

_____

Figure 2: Some fairly typical life events, such as moving, can be significant stressors. Even when the move is intentional and positive, the amount of resulting change in daily life can cause stress.

Life Changes

Most stressors that we encounter are not nearly as intense as the ones described above. Many potential stressors we face involve events or situations that require us to make changes in our ongoing lives and require time as we adjust to those changes. Four common examples include:

1. Death of a close family member
2. Marriage
3. Divorce
4. Moving

In the 1960s, psychiatrists Thomas Holmes and Richard Rahe wanted to examine the link between life stressors and physical illness, based on the hypothesis that life events requiring significant changes in a person's normal routines are stressful, whether these events are desirable or undesirable. They developed the **Social Readjustment Rating Scale (SRRS)**, consisting of 43 life events that require varying degrees of personal readjustment (Holmes & Rahe, 1967). Many life events that most people would consider pleasant (e.g., holidays, retirement, marriage) are among those listed on the SRRS; these are examples of eustress. Holmes and Rahe also proposed that life events can add up over time and that experiencing a cluster of stressful events increases one's risk of developing physical illnesses.

In developing their scale, Holmes and Rahe asked 394 participants to provide a numerical estimate for each of the 43 items; each estimate corresponded to how much readjustment participants felt each event would require. These estimates resulted in mean value scores for each event—often called life change units (LCUs) (Rahe, McKeen, & Arthur, 1967). The numerical scores ranged from 11 to 100, representing the perceived magnitude of life change each event entails. Below is some key information to come out of the research:

- Death of a spouse ranked highest on the scale with 100 LCUs, and divorce ranked second highest with 73 LCUs.

- Personal injury or illness, marriage, and job termination also ranked highly on the scale with 53, 50, and 47 LCUs respectively.

- Conversely, change in residence (20 LCUs), change in eating habits (15 LCUs), and vacation (13 LCUs) ranked low on the scale.

- Minor violations of the law ranked the lowest with 11 LCUs (Table 1).

To complete the scale, participants checked "yes" for events experienced within the last 12 months. LCUs for each checked item are totaled for a score quantifying the amount of life change. Agreement on the amount of adjustment required by the various life events on the SRRS is highly consistent, even cross-culturally (Holmes & Masuda, 1974).

Figure 3: Even pre-planned, pleasant life events, like getting married, can be stressors.

Life event	Life change units
Death of a close family member	63
Personal injury or illness	53
Dismissal from work	47
Change in financial state	38
Change to different line of work	36
Outstanding personal achievement	28
Beginning or ending school	26
Change in living conditions	25
Change in working hours or conditions	20
Change in residence	20
Change in schools	20
Change in social activities	18
Change in sleeping habits	16
Change in eating habits	15
Minor violation of the law	11

Table 1: Some Stressors on the Social Readjustment Rating Scale (Holmes & Rahe, 1967)

Group Activity

As a group, discuss why pleasant events like holidays and marriage are likely to induce stress. How does this make sense? Can you come up with other examples of positive experiences that might cause stress?

Extensive research has demonstrated that accumulating a high number of life change units within a brief period of time (one or two years) is related to a wide range of physical illnesses (even accidents and athletic injuries) and mental health problems (Monat & Lazarus, 1991; Scully, Tosi, & Banning, 2000). In an early demonstration, researchers obtained LCU scores for U.S. and Norwegian Navy personnel who were about to embark on a six-month voyage. A later examination of medical records revealed positive (but small) correlations between LCU scores prior to the voyage and subsequent illness symptoms during the six-month journey (Rahe, 1974).

Further Resources

Are you interested in learning more about the ways in which stress impacts your body? Read this article (hawkes.biz/stressimpacts) from WebMD for the latest research.

Figure 4: Rahe's study involved 2,500 sailors before and after a six-month deployment; there was a positive correlation between stress scores and physical illness.

In addition, people tend to experience more physical symptoms, such as backache, upset stomach, diarrhea, and acne, on specific days in which self-reported LCU values are considerably higher than normal, such as the day of a family member's wedding (Holmes & Holmes, 1970).

Despite its widespread use, the SRRS has been subject to criticism for the following reasons:

- Many of the items on the SRRS are vague; for example, death of a close friend could involve the death of a long-absent childhood friend that requires little social readjustment (Dohrenwend, 2006).

- Some have challenged its assumption that undesirable life events are no more stressful than desirable ones (Derogatis & Coons, 1993). However, most evidence suggests that, as far as mental health is concerned, undesirable or negative events are more strongly associated with poor outcomes, like depression, than are desirable, positive events (Hatch & Dohrenwend, 2007).

Further Resources

Go to this site (hawkes.biz/srrsscale) to complete the SRRS scale and determine the total number of LCUs you have experienced over the last year.

- The scale does not take into consideration respondents' appraisals of life events it contains. As you recall, appraisal of a stressor is a key element in the conceptualization and overall experience of stress. Being fired from work may be devastating to some but a welcome opportunity to obtain a better job for others.

The SRRS remains one of the most well-known instruments in the study of stress, and it is a useful tool for identifying potential stress-related health outcomes (Scully et al., 2000).

♀ Connect the Concepts

Correlational Research

The Holmes and Rahe Social Readjustment Rating Scale uses the **correlational research** method to identify the connection between stress and health. That is, respondents' LCU scores are correlated with the number or frequency of self-reported symptoms indicating health problems. These correlations are typically positive—as LCU scores increase, the number of symptoms increase. Consider all the thousands of studies that have used this scale to correlate stress and illness symptoms: if you were to assign an average correlation coefficient to this body of research, what would be your best guess? How strong do you think the correlation coefficient would be? Why can't the SRRS show a causal relationship between stress and illness? If it were possible to show causation, do you think stress causes illness or illness causes stress?

Hassles

Potential stressors do not always involve major life events. **Daily hassles**—the minor irritations and annoyances that are part of our everyday lives (e.g., rush hour traffic or lost keys)—can build on one another and leave us just as stressed as life change events (Figure 5) (Kanner, Coyne, Schaefer, & Lazarus, 1981).

Figure 5: Daily commutes, whether on the road or via public transportation, can be hassles that contribute to our feelings of everyday stress.

In a well-known study of San Francisco residents, the frequency of daily hassles was found to be more strongly associated with physical health problems than were life change events (DeLongis, Coyne, Dakof, Folkman, & Lazarus, 1982). In addition, daily minor hassles, especially interpersonal conflicts, often lead to negative and distressed mood states (Bolger, DeLongis, Kessler, & Schilling, 1989). Cyber hassles that occur on social media may represent a new source of stress. In one investigation, undergraduates who, over a 10-week period, reported greater Facebook-induced stress experienced increased rates of upper respiratory infections, especially if they had larger social networks (Campisi et al., 2012). Clearly, daily hassles can add up and take a toll on us both emotionally and physically.

Other Stressors

Stressors can include situations in which one is frequently exposed to challenging and unpleasant events, such as difficult, demanding, or unsafe working conditions. Although most jobs and occupations can be demanding, some are clearly more stressful than others (Figure 6). For example, most people would likely agree that a firefighter's work is inherently more stressful than that of a florist. Equally likely, most would agree that jobs containing various unpleasant elements, such as those requiring exposure to loud noise, constant harassment and threats of physical violence (prison guard), perpetual frustration, or those mandating that an employee work alternating day and night shifts are much more stressful than others. Table 2 lists several occupations and some of the specific stressors associated with those occupations (Sulsky & Smith, 2005).

Further Resources

Social media has been a popular and controversial topic in public discourse. Read this article (hawkes. biz/socialmedia) from *Forbes* magazine for specific reasons why these sites can negatively impact us.

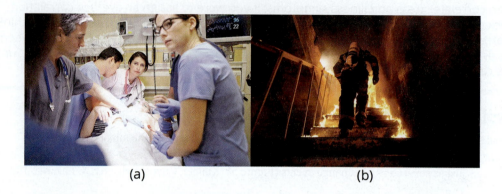

(a)   (b)

Figure 6: (a) Emergency room physicians and (b) firefighters hold high stress occupations.

Occupation	Stressors Specific to Occupation
Police officer	Physical dangers, excessive paperwork, red tape, dealing with court system, coworker and supervisor conflict, lack of support from the public
Firefighter	Uncertainty over whether a serious fire or hazard awaits after an alarm
Social worker	Little positive feedback from jobs or from the public, unsafe work environments, frustration in dealing with bureaucracy, excessive paperwork, sense of personal responsibility for clients, work overload
Teacher	Excessive paperwork, lack of adequate supplies or facilities, work overload, lack of positive feedback, vandalism, threat of physical violence
Nurse	Work overload, heavy physical work, patient concerns (dealing with death and medical concerns), interpersonal problems with other medical staff (especially physicians)
Emergency medical worker	Unpredictable and extreme nature of the job, inexperience
Air traffic controller	Little control over potential crisis situations and workload, fear of causing an accident, peak traffic situations, general work environment
Clerical and secretarial work	Little control over job mobility, unsupportive supervisors, work overload, lack of perceived control
Managerial work	Work overload, conflict and ambiguity in defining the managerial role, difficult work relationships

Table 2: Occupations and Their Related Stressors

Although the specific stressors for these occupations are diverse, they seem to share two common denominators:

- Heavy workload

- Uncertainty about and lack of control over certain aspects of a job

Both of these factors contribute to **job strain**, a work situation that combines excessive job demands and workload with little discretion in decision making or job control (Karasek & Theorell, 1990). Clearly, many occupations involve at least a moderate amount of job strain in that they often involve heavy workloads and little job control. Such jobs are often low-status and include positions like:

- Factory workers
- Postal clerks
- Supermarket cashiers
- Taxi drivers
- Short-order cooks

📷 **Figure 7:** Most occupations involve at least a moderate amount of job strain.

Job strain can have adverse consequences on both physical and mental health; it has been associated with increased risk of hypertension (Schnall & Landsbergis, 1994), heart attacks (Theorell et al., 1998), recurrence of heart disease after a first heart attack (Aboa-Éboulé et al., 2007), significant weight loss or gain (Kivimäki et al., 2006), and major depressive disorder (Stansfeld, Shipley, Head, & Fuhrer, 2012). A longitudinal study of over 10,000 British civil servants reported that workers under 50 years old who earlier had reported high job strain were 68% more likely to later develop heart disease than were those workers under 50 years old who reported little job strain (Chandola et al., 2008).

✏️ On Your Own

Does it surprise you to learn that these types of jobs can create such a negative impact on one's life? What suggestions might you have for someone facing a high level of stress in his or her occupation?

_____

_____

_____

Some people who are exposed to chronically stressful work conditions can experience **job burnout**, which is a general sense of emotional exhaustion and cynicism in relation to one's job (Maslach & Jackson, 1981). Job burnout occurs frequently among those in human service jobs (e.g., social workers, teachers, therapists, and police officers). Job burnout consists of three dimensions.

- Exhaustion—a sense that one's emotional resources are drained or that one has nothing more to give at a psychological level

📷 **Figure 8:** Educators often experience the exhaustion, depersonalization, and feelings of diminished personal accomplishment associated with job burnout.

- Depersonalization—a sense of emotional detachment between the worker and the recipients of his services, often resulting in callous, cynical, or indifferent attitudes toward these individuals

- Diminished Personal Accomplishment—the tendency to evaluate one's work negatively by, for example, experiencing dissatisfaction with one's job-related accomplishments or feeling as though one has categorically failed to influence others' lives through one's work

Job strain appears to be one of the greatest risk factors leading to job burnout, which is most commonly observed in workers who are older (ages 55–64), unmarried, and whose jobs involve manual labor. Heavy alcohol consumption, physical inactivity, being overweight, and having a physical or lifetime mental disorder are also associated with job burnout (Ahola, et al., 2006). In addition, depression often co-occurs with job burnout. One large-scale study of over 3,000 Finnish employees reported that half of the participants with severe job burnout had some form of depressive disorder (Ahola et al., 2005).

Reflection Questions

What career aspirations do you have? Do you think that stress will play a large role in these positions? Why or why not?

Finally, our close relationships with friends and family—particularly the negative aspects of these relationships—can be a potent source of stress. Negative aspects of close relationships can include the following:

- Adverse exchanges and conflicts

- Lack of emotional support or confiding

- Lack of reciprocity

All of these can be overwhelming, threatening to the relationship, and thus stressful. Such stressors can take a toll both emotionally and physically. A longitudinal investigation of over 9,000 British civil servants found that those who at one point had reported the highest levels of negative interactions in their closest relationship were 34% more likely to experience serious heart problems (fatal or nonfatal heart attacks) over a 13–15 year period, compared to those who experienced the lowest levels of negative interaction (De Vogli, Chandola & Marmot, 2007).

Figure 9: Negative aspects of our closest relationships can be sources of stress and dissension.

Summary

Stressors can be chronic (long term) or acute (short term) and can include traumatic events, significant life changes, daily hassles, and situations in which people are frequently exposed to challenging and unpleasant events. Many potential stressors include events or situations that require us to make changes in our lives. Thomas Holmes and Richard Rahe developed the Social Readjustment Rating Scale (SRRS) to measure stress by assigning a number of life change units to life events that typically require some adjustment, including positive events. Although the SRRS has been criticized on a number of grounds, extensive research has shown that the accumulation of many LCUs is associated with increased risk of illness. Many potential stressors also include daily hassles, which are minor irritations and annoyances that can build up over time. In addition, jobs that are especially demanding, offer little control over one's working environment, or involve unfavorable working conditions can lead to job strain, thereby setting the stage for job burnout.

13.3 Stress and Illness

In this section, we will discuss stress and illness. As stress researcher Robert Sapolsky (1998) describes,

stress-related disease emerges, predominantly, out of the fact that we so often activate a physiological system that has evolved for responding to acute physical emergencies, but we turn it on for months on end, worrying about mortgages, relationships, and promotions. (p. 6)

The stress response consists of a coordinated but complex system of physiological reactions that are called upon as needed. These reactions are beneficial at times because they prepare us to deal with potentially dangerous or threatening situations. However, health is affected when stress is ongoing and results in sustained physiological reactions.

Psychophysiological Disorders

If the reactions that compose the stress response are chronic or if they frequently exceed normal ranges, they can lead to cumulative wear and tear on the body, similar to how running your air conditioner on full blast all summer will cause wear and tear on it. Consider these examples:

> The high blood pressure that a person under considerable job strain experiences might eventually take a toll on his heart and set the stage for a heart attack or heart failure.

> Someone exposed to high levels of the stress hormone cortisol might become vulnerable to infection or disease because of weakened immune system functioning (McEwen, 1998).

Physical disorders or diseases whose symptoms are brought about or worsened by stress and emotional factors are called **psychophysiological disorders**. The physical symptoms of psychophysiological disorders are real, and they can be produced or exacerbated by psychological factors. A list of frequently encountered psychophysiological disorders is provided in Table 1.

🖼 **Figure 1:** Robert Sapolsky is a noted Stanford University neurobiologist and professor who has extensively studied stress and its effects.

Type of Psychophysiological Disorder	Examples
Cardiovascular	hypertension, coronary heart disease
Gastrointestinal	irritable bowel syndrome
Respiratory	asthma, allergy
Musculoskeletal	low back pain, tension headaches
Skin	acne, eczema, psoriasis

Table 1: Types of Psychophysiological Disorders
(adapted from Everly & Lating, 2002)

In addition to stress itself, emotional upset and certain stressful personality traits have been proposed as potential contributors to ill health. Franz Alexander (1950), an early-20th-century psychoanalyst and physician, once postulated that various diseases are caused by specific unconscious conflicts. He linked the following together:

Disease	Conflict
Hypertension	Repressed Anger
Asthma	Separation Anxiety
Ulcers	An unconscious desire to "remain in the dependent infantile situation—to be loved and cared for" (Alexander, 1950, p. 102)

Although hypertension does appear to be linked to anger, Alexander's assertions have *not* been supported by research. Years later, after statistically reviewing 101 studies examining the link between personality and illness, Friedman and Booth-Kewley (1987) proposed the existence of disease-prone personality characteristics, including depression, anger/hostility, and anxiety.

Further Resources

Robert Sapolsky (Figure 1), a noted Stanford University neurobiologist and professor, has for over 30 years conducted extensive research on stress, its impact on our bodies, and how psychological tumult can escalate stress—even in baboons. Here is an excellent in-depth documentary (hawkes.biz/stresseffects) from *National Geographic*.

🖼 **Figure 2:** Repressed anger/hostility may be linked to health problems like hypertension.

Indeed, a study of over 61,000 Norwegians identified depression as a risk factor for all major disease-related causes of death (Mykletun et al., 2007). In addition, neuroticism—a personality trait that reflects how anxious, moody, and sad one is—has been identified as a risk factor for chronic health problems and mortality (Ploubidis & Grundy, 2009).

> ### Reflection Questions
> Have you ever experienced a physical effect of stress? If so, what happened? Did you make any attempts to cope with this stress?

We're going to discuss two kinds of psychophysiological disorders about which a great deal is known:

- Cardiovascular disorders

- Asthma

First, however, let's to turn our attention to a discussion of the immune system—one of the major pathways through which stress and emotional factors can lead to illness and disease.

Stress and the Immune System

In a sense, the **immune system** is the body's surveillance system. It consists of a variety of structures, cells, and mechanisms that serve to protect the body from invading toxins and microorganisms that can harm or damage the body's tissues and organs. When the immune system is working as it should, it keeps us healthy and disease free by eliminating bacteria, viruses, and other foreign substances that have entered the body (Everly & Lating, 2002).

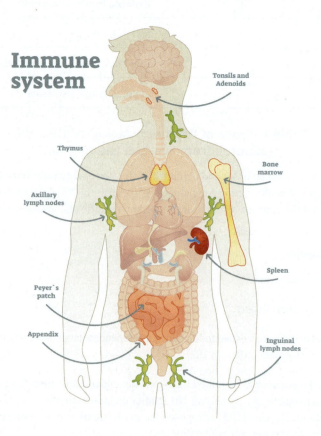

🖼 **Figure 3:** The immune system is a complex set of mechanisms that helps defend our bodies.

Immune System Errors

Sometimes, the immune system will function erroneously. For example, sometimes it can go awry by mistaking your body's own healthy cells for invaders and repeatedly attacking them. When this happens, the person is said to have an autoimmune disease, which can affect almost any part of the body. How an autoimmune disease affects a person depends on what part of the body is targeted. For example:

- Rheumatoid arthritis, an autoimmune disease that affects the joints, results in joint pain, stiffness, and loss of function.

- Systemic lupus erythematosus, an autoimmune disease that affects the skin, can result in rashes and swelling of the skin.

- Graves' disease, an autoimmune disease that affects the thyroid gland, can result in fatigue, weight gain, and muscle aches (National Institute of Arthritis and Musculoskeletal and Skin Diseases [NIAMS], 2012).

In addition, the immune system may sometimes break down and be unable to do its job. This situation is referred to as **immunosuppression**, the decreased effectiveness of the immune system. When people experience immunosuppression, they become susceptible to any number of infections, illness, and diseases. For example:

- Acquired immune deficiency syndrome (AIDS) is a serious and lethal disease that is caused by human immunodeficiency virus (HIV), which greatly weakens the immune system by infecting and destroying antibody-producing cells, thus rendering a person vulnerable to any of a number of opportunistic infections (Powell, 1996).

Figure 4: This is the AIDS Memorial Quilt on display in front of the Washington Memorial. AIDS is a lethal immune disease.

Further Resources

Read one woman's story (hawkes.biz/immunesystem) about living with a suppressed immune system.

Stressors and Immune Function

The question of whether stress and negative emotional states can influence immune function has captivated researchers for over three decades, and discoveries made over that time have dramatically changed the face of health psychology (Kiecolt-Glaser, 2009).

Psychoneuroimmunology is the field that studies how psychological factors such as stress influence the immune system and immune functioning. The term *psychoneuroimmunology* was first coined in 1981, as the title of a book that reviewed available evidence for associations between the brain, endocrine system, and immune system (Zacharie, 2009). This field evolved from the discovery that there is a connection between the central nervous system and the immune system.

Some of the most compelling evidence for a connection between the brain and the immune system comes from studies in which researchers demonstrated that immune responses in animals could be classically conditioned (Everly & Lating, 2002).

Consider this example:

> Ader and Cohen (1975) paired flavored water (the conditioned stimulus) with the presentation of an immunosuppressive drug (the unconditioned stimulus), causing sickness (an unconditioned response). Not surprisingly, rats exposed to this pairing developed a conditioned aversion to the flavored water. However, the taste of the water itself later produced immunosuppression (a conditioned response), indicating that the immune system itself had been conditioned.

Subsequent studies over the years have further demonstrated that immune responses can be classically conditioned in both animals and humans (Ader & Cohen, 2001). So, if classical conditioning can alter immunity, other psychological factors should be capable of altering it as well.

✎ On Your Own

What does Ader and Cohen's research suggest about us as human beings and the impact of stress?

_____

_____

Hundreds of studies involving tens of thousands of participants have tested many kinds of brief and chronic stressors and their effect on the immune system. Examples include:

- public speaking

- medical school examinations

- unemployment

- marital discord

- divorce

- death of spouse

- burnout and job strain

- caring for a relative with Alzheimer's disease

- exposure to the harsh climate of Antarctica

🖼 **Figure 5:** Public speaking is one stressor that may be associated with poor immune function.

It has been repeatedly demonstrated that many kinds of stressors are associated with poor or weakened immune functioning (Glaser & Kiecolt-Glaser, 2005; Kiecolt-Glaser, McGuire, Robles, & Glaser, 2002; Segerstrom & Miller, 2004).

There is a tangible physiological connection between the brain and the immune system. For example, the sympathetic nervous system innervates immune organs such as the thymus, bone marrow, spleen, and even lymph nodes (Maier, Watkins, & Fleshner, 1994). Also, we noted earlier that stress hormones released during hypothalamic-pituitary-adrenal (HPA) axis activation can adversely impact immune function. One way they do this is by inhibiting the production of **lymphocytes**, white blood cells that circulate in the body's fluids that are important in the immune response (Everly & Lating, 2002).

Some of the more dramatic examples demonstrating the link between stress and impaired immune function involve studies in which volunteers were exposed to viruses. Because stress weakens the immune system, people with high stress levels should be more likely to develop an illness compared to those under little stress.

In one memorable experiment using this method, researchers interviewed 276 healthy volunteers about recent stressful experiences (Cohen et al., 1998). Following the interview, these participants were given nasal drops containing the cold virus (in case you are wondering why anybody would ever want to participate in a study in which they are subjected to such treatment, the participants were paid $800 for their trouble). What were the results?

When examined later, participants who reported experiencing *chronic stressors* for more than one month—especially enduring difficulties involving work or relationships—were *considerably more likely* to have developed colds than were participants who reported no chronic stressors (Figure 7).

Figure 6: Lymphocytes are key components of the body's immune response.

Figure 7: This graph shows the percentages of participants who developed colds (after receiving the cold virus) after reporting having experienced chronic stressors lasting at least one month, three months, and six months (adapted from Cohen et al., 1998).

In another study, older volunteers were given an influenza virus vaccination. Compared to controls, those who were caring for a spouse with Alzheimer's disease (and thus were under chronic stress) showed poorer antibody response following the vaccination (Kiecolt-Glaser, Glaser, Gravenstein, Malarkey, & Sheridan, 1996).

Other studies have demonstrated that stress slows down wound healing by impairing immune responses important to wound repair (Glaser & Kiecolt-Glaser, 2005). In one study, for example, skin blisters were induced on the forearm. What were the results?

Subjects who reported higher levels of stress produced lower levels of immune proteins necessary for wound healing (Glaser et al., 1999).

Figure 8: Stress can accelerate the biological aging process.

Dig Deeper

Stress and Aging: A Tale of Telomeres

Have you ever wondered why people who are stressed often seem to have a haggard look about them? A pioneering study from 2004 suggests that this is because stress can actually accelerate the cell biology of aging.

Stress, it seems, can shorten telomeres, which are segments of DNA that protect the ends of chromosomes. Shortened telomeres can inhibit or block cell division, which includes growth and proliferation of new cells, thereby leading to more rapid aging (Sapolsky, 2004). Researchers compared telomere lengths in the white blood cells in mothers of chronically ill children to those of presumably less-stressed mothers of healthy children (Epel et al., 2004). The longer a mother had spent caring for her ill child, the shorter her telomeres (the correlation between years of caregiving and telomere length was r=−.40). In addition, higher levels of perceived stress were negatively correlated with telomere size (r=−.31). These researchers also found that the average telomere length of the most stressed mothers, compared to the least stressed, was similar to what you would find in people who were 9–17 years older than they were on average.

Numerous other studies since have continued to find associations between stress and eroded telomeres (Blackburn & Epel, 2012). Some studies have even demonstrated that stress can begin to erode telomeres in childhood and perhaps even before children are born. For example, childhood exposure to violence (e.g., maternal domestic violence, bullying victimization, and physical maltreatment) was found in one study to accelerate telomere erosion from ages 5 to 10 (Shalev et al., 2013). Another study reported that young adults whose mothers had experienced severe stress during their pregnancy had shorter telomeres than did those whose mothers had stress-free and uneventful pregnancies (Entringer et al., 2011). Further, the corrosive effects of childhood stress on telomeres can extend into young adulthood. In an investigation of over 4,000 U.K. women ages 41–80, adverse experiences during childhood (e.g., physical abuse, being sent away from home, and parent divorce) were associated with shortened telomere length (Surtees et al., 2010), and telomere size decreased as the amount of experienced adversity increased (Figure 9).

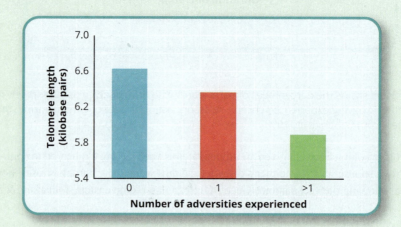

Figure 9: Telomeres are shorter in adults who experienced more trauma as children (adapted from Blackburn & Epel, 2012).

Efforts to dissect the precise cellular and physiological mechanisms linking short telomeres to stress and disease are currently underway. For the time being, telomeres provide us with yet another reminder that stress, especially during early life, can be just as harmful to our health as smoking or fast food (Blackburn & Epel, 2012).

Cardiovascular Disorders

The cardiovascular system is composed of the heart and blood circulation system. For many years, disorders that involve the cardiovascular system—known as **cardiovascular disorders**—have been a major focal point in the study of psychophysiological disorders because of the cardiovascular system's centrality in the stress response (Everly & Lating, 2002). **Heart disease** is one such condition. Each year, heart disease causes approximately one in three deaths in the United States, and it is the leading cause of death in the developed world (Centers for Disease Control and Prevention [CDC], 2011; Shapiro, 2005).

The symptoms of heart disease vary somewhat depending on the specific kind of heart disease one has, but they generally involve angina—chest pains or discomfort that occur when the heart does not receive enough blood (Office on Women's Health, 2009). The pain often feels like the chest is being pressed or squeezed; burning sensations in the chest and shortness of breath are also commonly reported. Such pain and discomfort can spread to the arms, neck, jaws, stomach (as nausea), and back (American Heart Association [AHA], 2012a) (Figure 10).

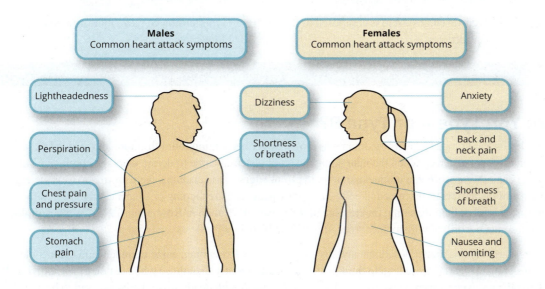

Figure 10: Males and females often experience different symptoms of a heart attack.

A major risk factor for heart disease is **hypertension**, which is high blood pressure. Hypertension forces a person's heart to pump harder, thus putting more physical strain on the heart. If left unchecked, hypertension can lead to of the following:

• Heart attack	• Heart failure	• Blindness
• Stroke	• Kidney failure	

Hypertension is a serious cardiovascular disorder, and it is sometimes called the silent killer because it has no symptoms—one who has high blood pressure may not even be aware of it (AHA, 2012b).

Many risk factors contributing to cardiovascular disorders have been identified. These risk factors include (World Health Organization [WHO], 2013):

• Aging	• Unhealthy diet	• Excessive alcohol consumption
• Income	• Tobacco use	
• Education	• Physical inactivity	• Obesity
• Employment status		• Diabetes

Over the past few decades, there has been much greater recognition and awareness of the importance of stress and other psychological factors in cardiovascular health (Nusair, Al-dadah, & Kumar, 2012). Indeed, exposure

Figure 11: Stress and psychological factors can elevate blood pressure.

to stressors of many kinds has also been linked to cardiovascular problems; in the case of hypertension, some of these stressors include job strain (Trudel, Brisson, & Milot, 2010), natural disasters (Saito, Kim, Maekawa, Ikeda, & Yokoyama, 1997), marital conflict (Nealey-Moore, Smith, Uchino, Hawkins, & Olson-Cerny, 2007), and exposure to high traffic noise levels at one's home (de Kluizenaar, Gansevoort, Miedema, & de Jong, 2007). Perceived discrimination appears to be associated with hypertension among African Americans (Sims et al., 2012). In addition, laboratory-based stress tasks, such as performing mental arithmetic under time pressure, immersing one's hand into ice water (known as the cold pressor test), mirror tracing, and public speaking have all been shown to elevate blood pressure (Phillips, 2011).

✎ On Your Own

Which of the following statements are true about cardiovascular disorders?

☐ The cardiovascular system is composed of the heart and blood circulation systems.

☐ Hypertension can potentially lead to a heart attack or a stroke.

☐ The cardiovascular system is composed of the lungs and arteries.

☐ Hypertension can lead to hearing loss or blood clots.

Are You Type A or Type B?

In the 1950s, cardiologist Meyer Friedman was looking over his waiting room furniture and decided to have these chairs reupholstered. When the man doing the reupholstering came to do the work, he commented on how the chairs were worn in a unique manner—the front edges of the cushions were worn down, as were the front tips of the arm rests. It seemed like the cardiology patients were tapping or squeezing the front of the armrests, as well as literally sitting on the edge of their seats (Friedman & Rosenman, 1974). Were cardiology patients somehow different than other types of patients? If so, how?

After researching this matter, Friedman and his colleague, Ray Rosenman, came to understand that people who are prone to heart disease tend to think, feel, and act differently than those who are not. These individuals tend to be intensively driven workaholics who are preoccupied with deadlines and always seem to be in a rush. According to Friedman and Rosenman, these individuals exhibit **Type A** behavior pattern; those who are more relaxed and laid-back were characterized as **Type B** (Figure 12). In a sample of Type As and Type Bs, Friedman and Rosenman were startled to discover that heart disease was over seven times more frequent among the Type As than the Type Bs (Friedman & Rosenman, 1959).

(a)   (b)

Figure 12: (a) Type A individuals are characterized as intensely driven, (b) while Type B people are characterized as laid-back and relaxed.

The major components of the Type A pattern include:

- An aggressive and chronic struggle to achieve more and more in less and less time (Friedman & Rosenman, 1974)

- An excessive competitive drive

- Chronic sense of time urgency

- Impatience

- Hostility toward others (particularly those who get in the person's way)

Let's consider Jeffrey, a person with a Type A behavioral pattern.

> Even as a child, Jeffrey was intense and driven. He excelled at school, was captain of the swim team, and graduated with honors from an Ivy League college. Jeffrey never seems able to relax; he is always working on something. However, Jeffrey always seems to feel as though there are not enough hours in the day to accomplish all he feels he should. He volunteers to take on extra tasks at work and often brings his work home with him; he goes to bed angry very late at night because he feels that he has not done enough. Jeffrey is quick tempered with his coworkers; he often becomes noticeably agitated when dealing with coworkers he feels work too slowly or whose work does not meet his standards. He reacts with hostility when interrupted at work. He has experienced problems in his marriage over his lack of time spent with family. When caught in traffic during his work commute, Jeffrey incessantly pounds on his horn and swears loudly at other drivers.

> When Jeffrey was 52, he suffered his first heart attack.

A number of early longitudinal investigations demonstrated a link between Type A behavior pattern and later development of heart disease (Rosenman et al., 1975; Haynes, Feinleib, & Kannel, 1980).

Subsequent research examining the association between Type A and heart disease, however, failed to replicate these earlier findings (Glassman, 2007; Myrtek, 2001). Because the Type A theory did not pan out as well as they had hoped, researchers shifted their attention toward determining if any of the specific elements of Type A predict heart disease.

Reflection Questions

Do you feel that you are more of a Type A person or a Type B person? What behaviors do you exude that reflect your thoughts on this?

Extensive research suggests that the anger/hostility dimension of Type A behavior pattern may be one of the most important factors in the development of heart disease. Suppressed hostility was found to substantially elevate the risk of heart disease for both men and women.

One investigation followed over 1,000 male medical students from 32 to 48 years. At the beginning of the study, these men completed a questionnaire assessing how they react to pressure; some indicated that they respond with high levels of anger, whereas others indicated that they respond with less anger. Decades later, researchers found that those who earlier had indicated the highest levels of anger were over 6 times more likely than those who indicated less anger to have had a heart attack by age 55, and they were 3.5 times more likely to have experienced heart disease by the same age (Chang, Ford, Meoni, Wang, & Klag, 2002). From a health standpoint, it clearly does not pay to be an angry young person.

After reviewing and statistically summarizing 35 studies from 1983 to 2006, Chida and Steptoe (2009) concluded that the bulk of the evidence suggests that anger and hostility constitute serious long-term risk factors for adverse cardiovascular outcomes among both healthy individuals and those already suffering from heart disease. In this transactional model, hostility and social strain form a cycle (Figure 13).

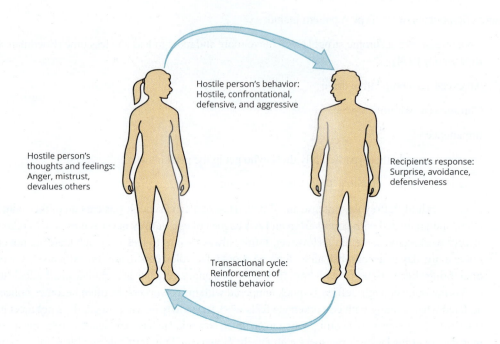

Hostile person's behavior:
Hostile, confrontational,
defensive, and aggressive

Hostile person's
thoughts and feelings:
Anger, mistrust,
devalues others

Recipient's response:
Surprise, avoidance,
defensiveness

Transactional cycle:
Reinforcement of
hostile behavior

Figure 13: According to the transactional model of hostility for predicting social interactions (Vella et al., 2012), the thoughts and feelings of a hostile person promote antagonistic behavior toward others, which in turn reinforces complimentary reactions from others, thereby intensifying ones' hostile disposition and intensifying the cyclical nature of this relationship.

In addition to anger and hostility, a number of other negative emotional states have been linked with heart disease, including negative affectivity and depression (Suls & Bunde, 2005). **Negative affectivity** is a tendency to experience distressed emotional states involving anger, contempt, disgust, guilt, fear, and nervousness (Watson, Clark, & Tellegen, 1988). It has been linked with the development of both hypertension and heart disease.

For example, over 3,000 initially healthy participants in one study were tracked longitudinally, up to 22 years. Those with higher levels of negative affectivity at the time the study began were substantially more likely to develop and be treated for hypertension during the ensuing years than were those with lower levels of negative affectivity (Jonas & Lando, 2000). In addition, a study of over 10,000 middle-aged London-based civil servants who were followed an average of 12.5 years revealed that those who earlier had scored in the upper third on a test of negative affectivity were 32% more likely to have experienced heart disease, heart attack, or angina over a period of years than were those who scored in the lowest third (Nabi, Kivimaki, De Vogli, Marmot, & Singh-Manoux, 2008). Hence, negative affectivity appears to be a potentially vital risk factor for the development of cardiovascular disorders.

Figure 14: Negative affectivity is linked to cardiovascular disorders.

Depression and the Heart

For centuries, poets and folklore have asserted that there is a connection between moods and the heart (Glassman & Shapiro, 1998). You are no doubt familiar with the notion of a broken heart following a disappointing or depressing event and have encountered that notion in songs, films, and literature.

Perhaps the first to recognize the link between depression and heart disease was Benjamin Malzberg (1937), who found that the death rate among institutionalized patients with melancholia (an archaic term for depression) was six times higher than that of the population. A classic study in the late 1970s looked at over 8,000 manic-depressive persons in Denmark, finding a nearly 50% increase in deaths from heart disease among these patients compared with the general Danish population (Weeke, 1979).

📈 **Figure 15:** This graph shows the incidence of heart attacks among men and women by depression score quartile (adapted from Barefoot & Schroll, 1996).

By the early 1990s, evidence began to accumulate showing that depressed individuals who were followed for long periods of time were at increased risk for heart disease and cardiac death (Glassman, 2007). In one investigation of over 700 Denmark residents, those with the highest depression scores were 71% more likely to have experienced a heart attack than were those with lower depression scores (Barefoot & Schroll, 1996). Figure 15 illustrates the gradation in risk of heart attacks for both men and women.

✐ On Your Own

Have you or someone you know well ever suffered from depression? If so, how has that impacted your physical well-being?

_____

_____

After more than two decades of research, it is now clear that a relationship exists. Patients with heart disease have more depression than the general population, and people with depression are more likely to eventually develop heart disease and experience higher mortality than those who do not have depression (Hare, Toukhsati, Johansson, & Jaarsma, 2013); the more severe the depression, the higher the risk (Glassman, 2007).

Consider the following:

- In one study, death rates from cardiovascular problems was substantially higher in depressed people; depressed men were 50% more likely to have died from cardiovascular problems, and depressed women were 70% more likely (Ösby, Brandt, Correia, Ekbom, & Sparén, 2001).

- A statistical review of 10 longitudinal studies involving initially healthy individuals revealed that those with elevated depressive symptoms have, on average, a 64% greater risk of developing heart disease than do those with fewer symptoms (Wulsin & Singal, 2003).

- A study of over 63,000 registered nurses found that those with more depressed symptoms when the study began were 49% more likely to experience fatal heart disease over a 12-year period (Whang et al., 2009).

The American Heart Association, fully aware of the established importance of depression in cardiovascular diseases, several years ago recommended routine depression screening for all heart disease patients (Lichtman

Figure 16: Unhealthy lifestyle habits can have negative impacts on heart health later in life.

et al., 2008). Recently, they have recommended including depression as a risk factor for heart disease patients (AHA, 2014).

Although the exact mechanisms through which depression might produce heart problems have not been fully clarified, a recent investigation examining this connection in early life has shed some light. In an ongoing study of childhood depression, adolescents who had been diagnosed with depression as children were more likely to be obese, smoke, and be physically inactive than were those who had not received this diagnosis (Rottenberg et al., 2014). One implication of this study is that depression, especially if it occurs early in life, may increase the likelihood of living an unhealthy lifestyle, thereby predisposing people to an unfavorable cardiovascular disease risk profile.

When multiple negative psychological attributes were combined into a single variable, this new variable (which researchers called psychological risk factor) predicted heart disease more strongly than any of the individual variables. Thus, rather than examining the predictive power of isolated psychological risk factors, it seems crucial for future researchers to examine the effects of combined and more general negative emotional and psychological traits in the development of cardiovascular illnesses.

Asthma

Asthma is a chronic and serious disease in which the airways of the respiratory system become obstructed, leading to great difficulty expelling air from the lungs. The airway obstruction is caused by inflammation of the airways (leading to thickening of the airway walls) and a tightening of the muscles around them, resulting in a narrowing of the airways (Figure 17) (American Lung Association, 2010). Because airways become obstructed, a person with asthma will sometimes have great difficulty breathing and will experience repeated episodes of wheezing, chest tightness, shortness of breath, and coughing, the latter occurring mostly during the morning and night (CDC, 2006).

Figure 17: In asthma, the airways become inflamed and narrowed.

The Centers for Disease Control and Prevention (CDC) has offered a number of statistics about asthma:

- Around 4,000 people die each year from asthma-related causes.

- It is a contributing factor to another 7,000 deaths each year (CDC, 2013a).

- Asthma affects 18.7 million U.S. adults.

- It is more common among people with lower education and income levels (CDC, 2013b).

- Asthma is on the rise, with rates of asthma increasing 157% between 2000 and 2010 (CDC, 2013b).

Asthma attacks are acute episodes in which an asthma sufferer experiences the full range of symptoms. Asthma exacerbation is often triggered by environmental factors, such as air pollution, allergens (e.g., pollen, mold, and pet hairs), cigarette smoke, airway infections, cold air or a sudden change in temperature, and exercise (CDC, 2013b).

Psychological factors appear to play an important role in asthma (Wright, Rodriguez, & Cohen, 1998) although some believe that psychological factors serve as potential triggers in only a subset of asthma patients (Ritz, Steptoe, Bobb, Harris, & Edwards, 2006). Many studies over the years have demonstrated that some people with asthma will experience asthma-like symptoms if they expect to experience such symptoms, such as when breathing an inert substance that they (falsely) believe will lead to airway obstruction (Sodergren & Hyland, 1999). As stress and emotions directly affect immune and respiratory functions, psychological factors likely serve as one of the most common triggers of asthma exacerbation (Trueba & Ritz, 2013).

People with asthma tend to report and display a high level of negative emotions, and asthma attacks have been linked to periods of high emotionality (Lehrer, Isenberg, & Hochron, 1993). In addition, high levels of emotional distress during both laboratory tasks and daily life have been found to negatively affect airway function and can produce asthma-like symptoms in people with asthma (von Leupoldt, Ehnes, & Dahme, 2006).

In one study, D'Amato, Liccardi, Cecchi, Pellegrino, & D'Amato (2010) described a case study of an 18-year-old man with asthma whose girlfriend had broken up with him, leaving him depressed. She "unfriended" him on Facebook while friending other young males. Eventually, the young man was able to "friend" her once again and could monitor her activity. Subsequently, he would experience asthma symptoms whenever he logged on and accessed her profile. When he later resigned not to use Facebook any longer, the asthma attacks stopped. This case suggests that the use social media may be a triggering factor for asthma attacks, especially in depressed asthmatic individuals.

Figure 18: Asthmatic individuals often experience attacks during periods of high emotionality.

> **Reflection Questions**
>
> Does it surprise you to learn of the ways in which social media has created an unhealthy situation for this man? Why or why not?

Exposure to stressful experiences has been linked to the development of asthma throughout the lifespan. A longitudinal study of 145 children found that parenting difficulties during the first year of life increased the chances that the child developed asthma by 107% (Klinnert et al., 2001). In addition, a cross-sectional study of over 10,000 Finnish college students found that high rates of parent or personal conflicts (e.g., parental divorce, separation from spouse, or severe conflicts in other long-term relationships) increased the risk of asthma onset (Kilpeläinen, Koskenvuo, Helenius, & Terho, 2002).

Tension Headaches

A headache is a continuous pain anywhere in the head and neck region. Migraine headaches are a type of headache thought to be caused by blood vessel swelling and increased blood flow (McIntosh, 2013). Migraines are characterized by severe pain on one or both sides of the head, an upset stomach, and disturbed vision. They are more frequently experienced by women than by men (American Academy of Neurology, 2014). Tension headaches are triggered by tightening/tensing of facial and neck muscles; they are the most commonly experienced kind of headache, accounting for about 42% of all headaches worldwide (Stovner et al., 2007). In the United States, well over one-third of the population experiences tension headaches each year, and 2–3% of the population suffers from chronic tension headaches (Schwartz, Stewart, Simon, & Lipton, 1998).

HEADACHE TYPE

Sinus Tension Migraine Cluster

Figure 19: More than one third of the U.S. population experiences at least one tension headache per year.

A number of factors can contribute to tension headaches, including (MedicineNet, 2013):

- Sleep deprivation
- Eye strain
- Muscular tension caused by poor posture
- Stress
- Skipping meals
- Overexertion

Although there is uncertainty regarding the exact mechanisms through which stress can produce tension headaches, stress has been demonstrated to increase sensitivity to pain (Caceres & Burns, 1997; Logan et al., 2001). In general, tension headache sufferers, compared to non-sufferers, have a lower threshold for and greater sensitivity to pain (Ukestad & Wittrock, 1996), and they report greater levels of subjective stress when faced with a stressor (Myers, Wittrock, & Foreman, 1998). Thus, stress may contribute to tension headaches by increasing pain sensitivity in already-sensitive pain pathways in tension headache sufferers (Cathcart, Petkov, & Pritchard, 2008).

Summary

Psychophysiological disorders are physical diseases that are either brought about or worsened by stress and other emotional factors. One of the mechanisms through which stress and emotional factors can influence the development of these diseases is by adversely affecting the body's immune system. A number of studies have demonstrated that stress weakens the functioning of the immune system. Cardiovascular disorders are serious medical conditions that have been consistently shown to be influenced by stress and negative emotions, such as anger, negative affectivity, and depression. Other psychophysiological disorders that are known to be influenced by stress and emotional factors include asthma and tension headaches.

Flash Forward

Ready to dig into the vocabulary? Get some practice with this Hawkes Verified Quizlet set (hawkes.biz/ psych13q4)!

13.4 Regulation of Stress

As we learned in the previous section, stress takes a toll on our bodies and can have enormously negative health implications. When we experience events in our lives that we appraise as stressful, it is essential that we use effective coping strategies to manage our stress. **Coping** refers to mental and behavioral efforts that we use to deal with problems relating to stress, including its presumed cause and the unpleasant feelings and emotions it produces.

Coping Styles

Lazarus and Folkman (1984) distinguished two fundamental kinds of coping:

- Problem-focused coping
- Emotion-focused coping

Read the following chart to better understand each style's unique qualities.

Problem-Focused Coping

Attempts to *manage or alter the problem* that is causing one to experience stress (i.e., the stressor)

Strategies typically involve identifying the problem, considering possible solutions, weighing the costs and benefits of these solutions, and then selecting an alternative (Lazarus & Folkman, 1984).

Emotional-Focused Coping

Attempts to *change or reduce the negative emotions* associated with stress

Strategies include avoiding, minimizing, or distancing oneself from the problem; positive comparisons with others; seeking something positive in a negative event; and reappraisal, whereby the stressor is construed differently without changing its objective level of threat (Lazarus & Folkman, 1984).

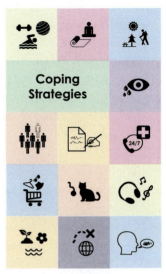

Figure 1: There are a number of ways in which people can cope with their stress.

Consider this example of problem-focused coping:

Bradford receives a midterm notice that he is failing his statistics class.

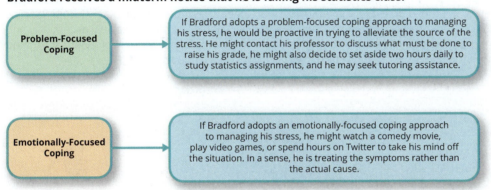

Problem-Focused Coping
If Bradford adopts a problem-focused coping approach to managing his stress, he would be proactive in trying to alleviate the source of the stress. He might contact his professor to discuss what must be done to raise his grade, he might also decide to set aside two hours daily to study statistics assignments, and he may seek tutoring assistance.

Emotionally-Focused Coping
If Bradford adopts an emotionally-focused coping approach to managing his stress, he might watch a comedy movie, play video games, or spend hours on Twitter to take his mind off the situation. In a sense, he is treating the symptoms rather than the actual cause.

While many stressors elicit both kinds of coping strategies, problem-focused coping is more likely to occur when encountering stressors we perceive as controllable, while emotion-focused coping is more likely to predominate when faced with stressors that we believe we are powerless to change (Folkman & Lazarus, 1980). Clearly, emotion-focused coping is more effective in dealing with uncontrollable stressors. For example, if at midnight you are stressing over a 40-page paper due in the morning that you have not yet started, you are probably better off recognizing the hopelessness of the situation and doing something to take your mind off it; taking a problem-focused approach by trying to accomplish this task would only lead to frustration, anxiety, and even more stress.

Fortunately, most stressors we encounter can be modified and are, to varying degrees, controllable. A person who cannot stand her job can quit and look for work elsewhere; a middle-aged divorcee can find another potential partner; the freshman who fails an exam can study harder next time; and a breast lump does not necessarily mean that one is fated to die of breast cancer.

Group Activity

As a group, brainstorm other scenarios in which an emotional-focused coping strategy is more effective than a problem-focused attempt. Do you notice any similarities in the kind of situations you came up with?

Control and Stress

The desire and ability to predict events, make decisions, and affect outcomes—that is, to enact control in our lives—is a basic tenet of human behavior (Everly & Lating, 2002). Albert Bandura (1997) stated that "the intensity and chronicity of human stress is governed largely by perceived control over the demands of one's life" (p. 262). As cogently described in his statement, our reaction to potential stressors depends to a large extent on how much control we feel we have over such things. **Perceived control** is our beliefs about our personal capacity to exert influence over and shape outcomes, and it has major implications for our health and happiness (Infurna & Gerstorf, 2014). Extensive research has demonstrated that perceptions of personal control are associated with a variety of favorable outcomes including:

- Better physical health

- Better mental health

- Greater psychological well-being (Diehl & Hay, 2010)

- Greater personal control

Figure 2: Feeling in control over one's life can have a plethora of positive benefits.

Researchers in one investigation found that higher levels of perceived control at one point in time were later associated with lower emotional and physical reactivity to interpersonal stressors (Neupert, Almeida, & Charles, 2007). Further, a daily diary study with 34 older widows found that their stress and anxiety levels were significantly reduced on days during which the widows felt greater perceived control (Ong, Bergeman, & Bisconti, 2005).

Dig Deeper

Learned Helplessness

When we lack a sense of control over the events in our lives, particularly when those events are threatening, harmful, or noxious, the psychological consequences can be profound. In one of the better illustrations of this concept, psychologist Martin Seligman conducted a series of classic experiments in the 1960s (Seligman & Maier, 1967) in which dogs were placed in a chamber where they received electric shocks from which they could not escape. Later, when these dogs were given the opportunity to escape the shocks by jumping across a partition, most failed to even try; they seemed to just give up and passively accept any shocks the experimenters chose to administer. In comparison, dogs who were previously allowed to escape the shocks tended to jump the partition and escape the pain (Figure 3).

Shock

No shock

🖼 **Figure 3:** Seligman's learned helplessness experiments with dogs used an apparatus that measured when the animals would move from a floor delivering shocks to one without.

Seligman believed that the dogs who failed to try to escape the later shocks were demonstrating learned helplessness: they had acquired a belief that they were powerless to do anything about the negative stimulation they were receiving. Seligman also believed that the passivity these dogs demonstrated was similar to that observed in human depression. Seligman speculated that acquiring learned helplessness might be an important cause of depression in humans: humans who experience negative life events that they believe they are unable to control may become helpless. As a result, they give up trying to control or change the situation, and some may become depressed and show lack of initiative in future situations they can control (Seligman, Maier, & Geer, 1968).

Seligman and colleagues later reformulated the original learned helplessness model of depression (Abramson, Seligman, & Teasdale, 1978). In their reformulation, they emphasized attributions (i.e., a mental explanation for why something occurred) that lead to the perception that one lacks control over negative outcomes are important in fostering a sense of learned helplessness. For example, suppose a coworker shows up late to work; your belief as to what caused the coworker's tardiness would be an attribution (e.g., too much traffic, slept too late, or just doesn't care about being on time).

The reformulated version of Seligman's study holds that the attributions made for negative life events contribute to depression. Consider the example of a student who performs poorly on a midterm exam. This model suggests that the student will make three kinds of attributions for this outcome: internal vs. external (believing the outcome was caused by his own personal inadequacies or by environmental factors), stable vs. unstable (believing the cause can be changed or is permanent), and global vs. specific (believing the outcome is a sign of inadequacy in most everything versus just this area). Assume that the student makes an internal ("I'm just not smart."), stable ("Nothing can be done to change the fact that I'm not smart."), and global ("This is another example of how lousy I am at everything.") attribution for the poor performance. The reformulated theory predicts that the student would perceive a lack of control over this stressful event and thus be especially prone to developing depression. Indeed, research has demonstrated that people who have a tendency to make internal, global, and stable attributions for bad outcomes tend to develop symptoms of depression when faced with negative life experiences (Peterson & Seligman, 1984).

Seligman's learned helplessness model has emerged over the years as a leading theoretical explanation for the onset of major depressive disorder. When you study psychological disorders, you will learn more about the latest reformulation of this model—now called hopelessness theory.

People who report higher levels of perceived control view their health as controllable, thereby making it more likely that they will better manage their health and engage in behaviors conducive to good health (Bandura, 2004). Not surprisingly, greater perceived control has been linked to lower risk of physical health problems, including:

- Declines in physical functioning (Infurna, Gerstorf, Ram, Schupp, & Wagner, 2011)

- Declines in heart attacks (Rosengren et al., 2004)

- Declines in both cardiovascular disease incidence (Stürmer, Hasselbach, & Amelang, 2006) and mortality from cardiac disease (Surtees et al., 2010)

🖼 **Figure 4:** Perceived control over one's circumstances can lead to positive health outcomes.

In addition, longitudinal studies of British civil servants have found that those in low-status jobs (e.g., clerical and office support staff) in which the degree of control over the job is minimal are considerably more likely to develop heart disease than those with high-status jobs or considerable control over their jobs (Marmot, Bosma, Hemingway, & Stansfeld, 1997).

The link between perceived control and health may provide an explanation for the frequently observed relationship between social class and health outcomes (Kraus, Piff, Mendoza-Denton, Rheinschmidt, & Keltner, 2012). In general, research has found that more affluent individuals experience better health mainly because they tend to believe that they can personally control and manage their reactions to life's stressors (Johnson & Krueger, 2006). Perhaps buoyed by the perceived level of control, individuals of higher social class may be prone to overestimating the degree of influence they have over particular outcomes. For example, those of higher social class tend to believe that their votes have greater sway on election outcomes than do those of lower social class, which may explain higher rates of voting in more affluent communities (Krosnick, 1990). Other research has found that a sense of perceived control can protect less affluent individuals from poorer health, depression, and reduced life-satisfaction—all of which tend to accompany lower social standing (Lachman & Weaver, 1998).

> ### Reflection Questions
>
> Why do you think that people in a higher economic status are more likely to believe that their vote actually matters when we live in a system where each vote is counted equally? What larger issues might be at play here?

Taken together, findings from these and many other studies clearly suggest that perceptions of control and coping abilities are important in managing and coping with the stressors we encounter throughout life.

Social Support

The need to form and maintain strong, stable relationships with others is a powerful, pervasive, and fundamental human motive (Baumeister & Leary, 1995). Building strong interpersonal relationships with others helps us establish a network of close, caring individuals who can provide social support in times of distress, sorrow, and fear. **Social support** can be thought of as the soothing impact of friends, family, and acquaintances (Baron & Kerr, 2003). It can take many forms, including:

- Advice
- Guidance
- Encouragement
- Acceptance
- Emotional comfort
- Tangible assistance (such as financial help)

Figure 5: Maintaining a strong social network has countless positive impacts on one's mental health.

Thus, other people can be very comforting to us when we are faced with a wide range of life stressors, and they can be extremely helpful in our efforts to manage these challenges. Even in nonhuman animals, species' mates can offer social support during times of stress. For example, elephants seem to be able to sense when other elephants are stressed and will often comfort them with physical contact—such as a trunk touch—or an empathetic vocal response (Krumboltz, 2014).

✍ **On Your Own**

What does your emotional support system look like? Have you been able to lean on it over the years? Why or why not?

Scientific interest in the importance of social support first emerged in the 1970s when health researchers developed an interest in the health consequences of being socially integrated (Stroebe & Stroebe, 1996). Interest was further fueled by longitudinal studies showing that social connectedness reduced mortality. Consider the below study:

> Nearly 7,000 Alameda County, California, residents were followed over 9 years. Those who had previously indicated that they lacked social and community ties were more likely to die during the follow-up period than those with more extensive social networks.

> Compared to those with the most social contacts, isolated men and women were, respectively, 2.3 and 2.8 times more likely to die. These trends persisted even after controlling for a variety of health-related variables, such as (Berkman & Syme, 1979):

- Smoking

- Alcohol consumption

- Self-reported health at the beginning of the study

- Physical activity

Since the time of that study, social support has emerged as one of the well-documented psychosocial factors affecting health outcomes (Uchino, 2009). A statistical review of 148 studies conducted between 1982 and 2007 involving over 300,000 participants concluded that individuals with stronger social relationships have a 50% greater likelihood of survival compared to those with weak or insufficient social relationships (Holt-Lunstad, Smith, & Layton, 2010). According to the researchers, the magnitude of the effect of social support observed in this study is comparable with quitting smoking and exceeded many well-known risk factors for mortality, such as obesity and physical inactivity (Figure 6).

(a)   (b)

🖼 **Figure 6:** Close relationships with others, whether (a) a group of friends or (b) a family circle, provide more than happiness and fulfillment—they can help foster good health.

A number of large-scale studies have found that individuals with low levels of social support are at greater risk of mortality, especially from cardiovascular disorders (Brummett et al., 2001). Further, higher levels of social support have been linked to better survival rates following breast cancer (Falagas et al., 2007) and infectious diseases, especially HIV infection (Lee & Rotheram-Borus, 2001). *In fact, a person with high levels of social support is less likely to contract a common cold.*

In one study, 334 participants completed questionnaires assessing their sociability; these individuals were subsequently exposed to a virus that causes a common cold and monitored for several weeks to see who became ill. Results showed that increased sociability was linearly associated with a decreased probability of developing a cold (Cohen, Doyle, Turner, Alper, & Skoner, 2003).

Reflection Questions

Does it surprise you to learn of the enormous impact of a social support system? How might this research have implications for the way human beings should treat one another?

For many of us, friends are a vital source of social support, but what if you found yourself in a situation in which you lacked friends or companions? Consider this example:

> A social high school student attends a far-away college, does not know anyone, and has trouble making friends and meaningful connections with others during the first semester. What can be done?

If real life social support is lacking, access to distant friends via social media may help compensate. In a study of college freshmen, those with few face-to-face friends on campus but who communicated electronically with distant friends were less distressed that those who did not (Raney & Troop-Gordon, 2012). Also, for some people, our families—especially our parents—are a major source of social support.

Reflection Questions

Do you use any forms of social media? If so, do you agree that it helps you to feel connected to others? Why or why not?

Figure 7: People suffering from illness have a higher likelihood of recovery if they have a strong social network.

Social support appears to work by boosting the immune system, especially among people who are experiencing stress (Uchino, Vaughn, Carlisle, & Birmingham, 2012). In a pioneering study, spouses of cancer patients who reported high levels of social support showed indications of better immune functioning on two out of three immune functioning measures, compared to spouses who were below the median on reported social support (Baron, Cutrona, Hicklin, Russell, & Lubaroff, 1990). Studies of other populations have produced similar results, including those of spousal caregivers of dementia sufferers, medical students, elderly adults, and cancer patients (Cohen & Herbert, 1996; Kiecolt-Glaser, McGuire, Robles, & Glaser, 2002).

In addition, social support has been shown to reduce blood pressure for people performing stressful tasks, such as giving a speech or performing mental arithmetic (Lepore, 1998). In these kinds of studies, participants are usually asked to perform a stressful task either alone, with a stranger present (who may be either supportive or unsupportive), or with a friend present. Those tested with a friend present generally exhibited lower blood pressure than those tested alone or with a stranger (Fontana, Diegnan, Villeneuve, & Lepore, 1999). In one study, 112 female participants who performed stressful mental arithmetic exhibited lower blood pressure when they received support from a friend rather than a stranger, but only if the friend was a male (Phillips, Gallagher, & Carroll, 2009). Although these findings are somewhat difficult to interpret, the authors mentioned that it is possible that females feel less supported and more evaluated by other females, particularly females whose opinions they value.

Taken together, the findings above suggest one of the reasons social support is connected to favorable health outcomes is because it has several beneficial physiological effects in stressful situations. However, it is also important to consider the possibility that social support may lead to better health behaviors, such as a healthy diet, exercising, smoking cessation, and cooperation with medical regimens (Uchino, 2009).

On Your Own

Which of the following statements about social support systems are true?

☐ Social media can help to make people feel more connected to others.

☐ Social media never helps to make people feel connected.

☐ Social support has been shown not to alter blood pressure for people performing stressful tasks.

☐ Social support can reduce blood pressure for people performing stressful tasks.

Dig Deeper

Coping with Prejudice and Discrimination

While having social support is quite beneficial, being the recipient of prejudicial attitudes and discriminatory behaviors is associated with a number of negative outcomes. In their literature review, Brondolo, Brady, Pencille, Beatty, and Contrada (2009) described how racial prejudice and discrimination serve as unique, significant stressors for those who are the targets of such attitudes and behavior. Being the target of racism is associated with increased rates of depression, lowered self-esteem, hypertension, and cardiovascular disease.

Given the complex and pervasive nature of racism as a stressor, Brondolo et al. (2009) pointed out the importance of coping with this specific stressor. Their review is aimed at determining which coping strategies are most effective at offsetting negative health outcomes associated with racism-related stress. The authors examined the effectiveness of three coping strategies: focusing on racial identity to handle race-related stress, anger expression/suppression, and seeking social support. You've learned a bit about social support, so we'll focus the remainder of this discussion on the potential coping strategies of focusing on racial identity and anger expression/suppression.

Focusing on racial identity refers to the process by which a person comes to feel as if he belongs to a given racial group; this may increase a sense of pride associated with group membership. Brondolo et al. (2009) suggested that a strong sense of racial identity might help an individual who is the target of racism differentiate between prejudicial attitudes/behaviors that are directed toward his group as a whole rather than at him as a person. Furthermore, the sense of belonging to his group might alleviate the distress of being ostracized by others. However, the research literature on the effectiveness of this technique has produced mixed results.

Anger expression/suppression refers to the options available as a function of the anger evoked by racial prejudice and discrimination. Put simply, a target of racist attitudes and behaviors can act upon her anger or suppress her anger. As discussed by Brondolo et al. (2009), there has been very little research on the effectiveness of either approach; the results are quite mixed with some showing anger expression and others showing anger suppression as the healthier option.

In the end, racism-related stress is a complex issue and each of the coping strategies discussed here has strengths and weaknesses. Brondolo et al. (2009) argued that it is imperative that additional research be conducted to ascertain the most effective strategies for coping with the negative outcomes that are experienced by the targets of racism.

Stress Reduction Techniques

Beyond having a sense of control and establishing social support networks, there are numerous other means by which we can manage stress (Figure 9). A common technique people use to combat stress is exercise (Salmon, 2001). It is well-established that exercise, both of long (aerobic) and short (anaerobic) duration, is beneficial for both physical and mental health (Everly & Lating, 2002). There is considerable evidence that physically fit individuals are more resistant to the adverse effects of stress and recover more quickly from stress than less physically fit individuals (Cotton, 1990). In a study of more than 500 Swiss police officers and emergency service personnel, increased physical fitness was associated with reduced stress, and regular exercise was reported to protect against stress-related health problems (Gerber, Kellman, Hartman, & Pühse, 2010).

Figure 8: Exercise has wonderful physical and mental health benefits.

> ### Reflection Questions
>
> How has exercise, or lack thereof, impacted your mental health?

| (a) | (b) | (c) |

Figure 9: Stress reduction techniques may include (a) exercise, (b) meditation and relaxation, or (c) biofeedback.

One reason exercise may be beneficial is because it might buffer some of the deleterious physiological mechanisms of stress. One study found rats that exercised for six weeks showed a decrease in hypothalamic-pituitary-adrenal responsiveness to mild stressors (Campeau et al., 2010). In high-stress humans, exercise has been shown to prevent telomere shortening, which may explain the common observation of a youthful appearance among those who exercise regularly (Puterman et al., 2010). Further, exercise in later adulthood appears to minimize the detrimental effects of stress on the hippocampus and memory (Head, Singh, & Bugg, 2012). Among cancer survivors, exercise has been shown to reduce anxiety (Speck, Courneya, Masse, Duval, & Schmitz, 2010) and depressive symptoms (Craft, VanIterson, Helenowski, Rademaker, & Courneya, 2012). Clearly, exercise is a highly effective tool for regulating stress.

In the 1970s, Herbert Benson, a cardiologist, developed a stress reduction method called the **relaxation response technique** (Greenberg, 2006). The relaxation response technique combines relaxation with transcendental meditation and consists of four components (Stein, 2001):

- sitting upright on a comfortable chair with feet on the ground and body in a relaxed position

- a quiet environment with eyes closed

- repeating a word or a phrase—a mantra—to oneself, such as "alert mind, calm body"

- passively allowing the mind to focus on pleasant thoughts, such as nature or the warmth of your blood nourishing your body

The relaxation response approach is conceptualized as a general approach to stress reduction that reduces sympathetic arousal, and it has been used effectively to treat people with high blood pressure (Benson & Proctor, 1994).

Another technique to combat stress, **biofeedback**, was developed by Gary Schwartz at Harvard University in the early 1970s. Biofeedback is a technique that uses electronic equipment to accurately measure a person's neuromuscular and autonomic activity—feedback is provided in the form of visual or auditory signals. The main assumption of this approach is that providing somebody biofeedback will enable the individual to develop strategies that help gain some level of voluntary control over what are normally involuntary bodily processes (Schwartz & Schwartz, 1995).

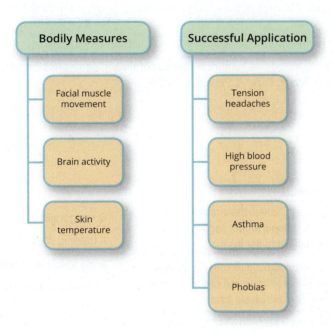

Figure 10: A number of different bodily measures have been used in biofeedback research, including facial muscle movement, brain activity, and skin temperature, and it has been applied successfully with individuals experiencing tension headaches, high blood pressure, asthma, and phobias (Stein, 2001).

Summary

When faced with stress, people should attempt to manage it or cope with it. In general, there are two basic forms of coping: problem-focused coping and emotion-focused coping. Those who use problem-focused coping strategies tend to cope better with stress because these strategies address the source of stress rather than the symptoms. To a large extent, perceived control greatly impacts reaction to stressors and is associated with greater physical and mental well-being.

Social support has been demonstrated to be a highly effective buffer against the adverse effects of stress. Extensive research has shown that social support has beneficial physiological effects for people, and it seems to influence immune functioning. However, the beneficial effects of social support may be related to its influence on promoting healthy behavior.

13.5 The Pursuit of Happiness

Although the study of stress and how it affects us physically and psychologically is fascinating, it isn't exactly the most uplifting thing to think about. Psychology is also interested in the study of a more upbeat and encouraging approach to human affairs—the quest for happiness.

Happiness

America's founders declared that its citizens have an unalienable right to pursue happiness. But what is happiness? When asked to define the term, people emphasize different aspects of this elusive state. Indeed,

Flash Forward

Ready to dig into the vocabulary? Get some practice with this Hawkes Verified Quizlet set (hawkes.biz/psych13q5)!

Figure 1: Many humans strive to feel happiness.

happiness is somewhat ambiguous. Some people, especially those who are highly committed to their religious faith, view happiness in ways that emphasize virtuosity, reverence, and enlightened spirituality. Others see happiness as primarily contentment—the inner peace and joy that come from deep satisfaction with one's surroundings, relationships with others, accomplishments, and oneself. Still others view happiness mainly as pleasurable engagement with their personal environment—having a career and hobbies that are engaging, meaningful, rewarding, and exciting. These differences, of course, are merely differences in emphasis. Many people would probably agree that each of these views, in some respects, captures the essence of happiness.

Elements of Happiness

Some psychologists have suggested that happiness consists of three distinct elements as shown in Figure 2 (Seligman, 2002; Seligman, Steen, Park, & Peterson, 2005):

- The pleasant life
- The good life
- The meaningful life

Distinct Element	Definition	Example
The Pleasant Life	Realized through the attainment of day-to-day pleasures that add fun, joy, and excitement to our lives	Evening walks along the beach A fulfilling sex life
The Good Life	Achieved through identifying our unique skills and abilities and engaging these talents to enrich our lives	Being absorbed in work Frequent participation in recreational pursuits
The Meaningful Life	Involves a deep sense of fulfillment that comes from using our talents in the service of the greater good in ways that benefit the lives of others or that make the world a better place	Contributing to community service Mentoring at-risk students

In general, the happiest people tend to be those who pursue the full life—they orient their pursuits toward all three elements (Seligman et al., 2005).

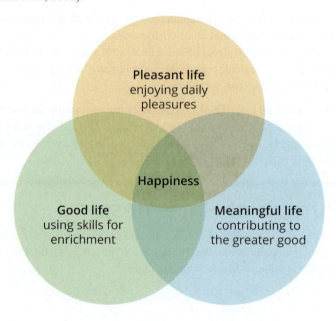

Figure 2: Happiness is an enduring state of well-being involving satisfaction in the pleasant, good, and meaningful aspects of life.

For practical purposes, a precise definition of **happiness** might incorporate each of these elements: an enduring state of mind consisting of joy, contentment, and other positive emotions plus the sense that one's life has meaning and value (Lyubomirsky, 2001). The definition implies that happiness is a long-term state—what is often characterized as subjective well-being—rather than merely a transient positive mood we all experience from time to time. This enduring happiness has captured the interests of psychologists and other social scientists.

The study of happiness has grown dramatically in the last three decades (Diener, 2013). One of the most basic questions that happiness investigators routinely examine is this: *how happy are people in general?*

Reflection Questions

Do you feel that most people you come in contact with are truly happy? Why or why not?

The average person in the world tends to be relatively happy and tends to indicate experiencing more positive feelings than negative feelings (Diener, Ng, Harter, & Arora, 2010). When asked to evaluate their current lives on a scale ranging from 0 to 10 (with 0 representing "worst possible life" and 10 representing "best possible life"), people in more than 150 countries surveyed from 2010–2012 reported an average score of 5.2. People who live in North America, Australia, and New Zealand reported the highest average score at 7.1, whereas those living Sub-Saharan Africa reported the lowest average score at 4.6 (Helliwell, Layard, & Sachs, 2013). Worldwide, the five happiest countries are:

1. Denmark

2. Norway

3. Switzerland

4. The Netherlands

5. Sweden

The United States is ranked 17th happiest (Figure 3) (Helliwell et al., 2013).

Reflection Questions

Does it surprise you to learn that the United States ranked 17th in happiness? Why or why not?

(a)   (b)

Figure 3: (a) Surveys of residents in over 150 countries indicate that Denmark has the happiest citizens in the world. (b) Americans ranked the United States as the 17th happiest country in which to live.

Several years ago, a Gallup survey of over 1,000 U.S. adults found that 52% reported that they were "very happy." However, a recent poll of 2,345 U.S. adults revealed that only one-third reported they are "very happy." The poll also revealed that the happiness levels of certain groups, including minorities, recent college graduates, and the disabled, have trended downward in recent years (Gregoire, 2013). Although it is difficult to explain this apparent decline in happiness, it may be connected to the challenging economic conditions the United States has endured over the last several years. Of course, this presumption would imply that happiness is closely tied to one's finances. But, is it? This question brings us to the next important issue: what factors influence happiness?

Factors Connected to Happiness

What really makes people happy? What factors contribute to sustained joy and contentment? Some common guesses include:

- Money
- Material possessions
- A satisfying relationship
- Attractiveness
- A rewarding occupation

Extensive research over the years has examined this question. One finding is that age is related to happiness: life satisfaction usually increases the older people get, but there do not appear to be gender differences in happiness (Diener, Suh, Lucas, & Smith, 1999).

Family and other social relationships appear to be key factors correlated with happiness. Studies show that married people report being happier than those who are single, divorced, or widowed (Diener et al., 1999). Happy individuals also report that their marriages are fulfilling (Lyubomirsky, King, & Diener, 2005). In fact, some have suggested that satisfaction with marriage and family life is the strongest predictor of happiness (Myers, 2000). Happy people tend to have more friends, more high-quality social relationships, and stronger social support networks than less happy people (Lyubomirsky et al., 2005). Happy people also have a high frequency of contact with friends (Pinquart & Sörensen, 2000).

> **Reflection Questions**
>
> Does it surprise you to learn that so many people gain happiness from their marriage and family relationships? Why or why not?

Figure 4: Does it surprise you to learn that money has such strong correlations with happiness? Can you think of instances when this might not be the case?

Can money buy happiness? In general, extensive research suggests that the answer is "yes" but with several caveats.

While a nation's per capita gross domestic product (GDP) is associated with happiness levels (Helliwell et al., 2013), changes in GDP (which is a less certain index of household income) bear little relationship to changes in happiness (Diener, Tay, & Oishi, 2013). On the whole, residents of affluent countries tend to be happier than residents of poor countries; within countries, wealthy individuals are happier than poor individuals, but the association is much weaker (Diener & Biswas-Diener, 2002). To the extent that it leads to increases in purchasing power, increases in income are associated with increases in happiness (Diener, Oishi, & Ryan, 2013).

However, income within societies appears to correlate with happiness only up to a point. In a study of over 450,000 U.S. residents surveyed by the Gallup Organization, Kahneman and Deaton (2010) found that well-being rises with annual income but only up to $75,000. The average increase in reported well-being for people with incomes greater than $75,000 was null. As implausible as these findings might seem—after all, higher incomes would enable people to indulge in Hawaiian vacations, prime seats as sporting events, expensive automobiles, and expansive new homes—higher incomes may impair people's ability to savor and enjoy the small pleasures of life (Kahneman, 2011).

What about education and employment? Happy people, compared to those who are less happy, are more likely to graduate from college and secure more meaningful and engaging jobs. Once they obtain a job, they are also more likely to succeed (Lyubomirsky et al., 2005). While education shows a positive (but weak) correlation with happiness, intelligence is not appreciably related to happiness (Diener et al., 1999).

Does religiosity correlate with happiness? In general, the answer is "yes" (Hackney & Sanders, 2003). However, the relationship between religiosity and happiness depends on societal circumstances. Nations and states with more difficult living conditions (e.g., widespread hunger and low life expectancy) tend to be more highly religious than societies with more favorable living conditions. Among those who live in nations with difficult living conditions, religiosity is associated with greater well-being; in nations with more favorable living conditions, religious and nonreligious individuals report similar levels of well-being (Diener, Tay, & Myers, 2011).

Reflection Questions

Why do you think less wealthy countries are more religious? What relationship might exist between those two things?

Clearly the living conditions of one's nation can influence factors related to happiness. What about the influence of one's culture? To the extent that people possess characteristics that are highly valued by their culture, they tend to be happier (Diener, 2012). For example, self-esteem is a stronger predictor of life satisfaction in individualistic cultures than in collectivistic cultures (Diener, Diener, & Diener, 1995), and extroverted people tend to be happier in extroverted cultures than in introverted cultures (Fulmer et al., 2010).

What about factors that don't show a correlation to happiness? Researchers have studied both parenthood and physical attractiveness as potential contributors to happiness, but no link has been identified. Although people tend to believe that parenthood is central to a meaningful and fulfilling life, aggregate findings from a range of countries indicate that people who do not have children are generally happier than those who do (Hansen, 2012). And although one's perceived level of attractiveness seems to predict happiness, a person's objective physical attractiveness is only weakly correlated with her happiness (Diener, Wolsic, & Fujita, 1995).

🖼 **Figure 5:** Based on your observations and experiences, do you think adults who have children tend to be happier than those who do not?

Life Events and Happiness

An important point should be considered regarding happiness. People are often poor at affective forecasting: predicting the intensity and duration of their future emotions (Wilson & Gilbert, 2003). In one study, nearly all newlywed spouses predicted their marital satisfaction would remain stable or improve over the following four years; despite this high level of initial optimism, their marital satisfaction actually declined during this period (Lavner, Karner, & Bradbury, 2013). In addition, we are often incorrect when estimating how our long-term happiness would change for the better or worse in response to certain life events. For example, it is easy for many of us to imagine how euphoric we would feel if we won the lottery, were asked on a date by an attractive celebrity, or were offered our dream job. It is also easy to understand how long-suffering fans of the Chicago Cubs baseball team, which had not won a World Series championship since 1908, thought they would feel permanently elated if their team finally won another World Series. Since their win in 2016, it would be interesting to know how their predictions turned out. Likewise, it's easy to predict that we would feel permanently miserable if we suffered a crippling accident or if a romantic relationship ended.

However, when we experience emotional reactions to life events, we eventually adapt to changing emotional circumstances in our lives (Brickman & Campbell, 1971; Helson, 1964). When an event that provokes positive or negative emotions occurs, at first we tend to experience its emotional impact at full intensity. We feel a burst of pleasure following such things as a marriage proposal, birth of a child, acceptance to law school, an inheritance, and the like; as you might imagine, lottery winners experience a surge of happiness after hitting the jackpot (Lutter, 2007). Likewise, we experience a surge of misery following widowhood, a divorce, or a layoff from work. In the long run, however, we eventually adjust to the emotional new normal; the emotional impact of the event tends to erode, and we eventually revert to our original baseline happiness levels. Thus, what was at first a thrilling lottery windfall or World Series championship eventually loses its luster and becomes the status quo (Figure 6). Indeed, dramatic life events have much less long-lasting impact on happiness than might be expected (Brickman, Coats, & Janoff-Bulman, 1978).

(a)   (b)

Figure 6: (a) Long-suffering Chicago Cub fans no doubt predicted feeling elated when their team won a World Series championship, a feat that had not been accomplished by that franchise in over a century. (b) In ways that are similar, those who play the lottery rightfully think that choosing the correct numbers and winning millions would lead to a surge in happiness. However, the initial burst of elation following such elusive events would most likely erode with time.

Recently, some have raised questions concerning the extent to which important life events can permanently alter people's happiness set points (Diener, Lucas, & Scollon, 2006). Evidence from a number of investigations suggests that, in some circumstances, happiness levels do not revert to their original positions. For example, although people generally tend to adapt to marriage so that it no longer makes them happier or unhappier than before, they often do not fully adapt to unemployment or severe disabilities (Diener, 2012).

Figure 7, which is based on longitudinal data from a sample of over 3,000 German respondents, shows life satisfaction scores several years before, during, and after various life events.

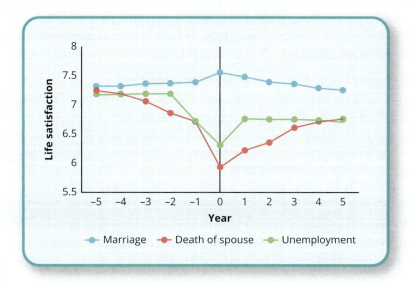

Figure 7: This graphs shows life satisfaction scores several years before and after three significant life events (0 represents the year the event happened) (Diener et al., 2006).

Increasing Happiness

Some recent findings about happiness provide an optimistic picture, suggesting that real changes in happiness are possible. For example, well-being interventions designed to augment people's levels of happiness may increase happiness in ways that are permanent and long-lasting. These changes may be targeted at the following levels (Diener et al., 2006):

- Individual
- Organizational
- Societal

Researchers in one study found that a series of happiness interventions, involving such exercises as writing down three good things that occurred each day, led to increases in happiness that lasted over six months (Seligman et al., 2005).

Measuring happiness and well-being at the societal level over time may assist policy makers in determining if people are generally happy or miserable, as well as when and why they might feel the way they do. Studies show that average national happiness scores (over time and across countries) relate strongly to six key variables (Helliwell et al., 2013):

- Per capita gross domestic product (GDP, which reflects a nation's economic standard of living)
- Social support
- Freedom to make important life choices
- Healthy life expectancy
- Freedom from perceived corruption in government and business
- Generosity

Investigating why people are happy or unhappy might help policymakers develop programs that increase happiness and well-being within a society (Diener et al., 2006). Resolutions about contemporary political and social issues that are frequent topics of debate—such as poverty, taxation, affordable health care and housing, clean air and water, and income inequality—might be best considered with people's happiness in mind.

Positive Psychology

In 1998, Seligman (who conducted the learned helplessness experiments mentioned earlier) was then president of the American Psychological Association. He urged psychologists to focus more on understanding how to build human strength and psychological well-being. In deliberately setting out to create a new direction and new orientation for psychology, Seligman helped establish a growing movement and field of research called

📷 **Figure 8:** Simple tasks like expressing gratitude through writing can help to boost one's level of happiness.

Figure 9: The entire field of positive psychology is dedicated toward studying happiness.

positive psychology (Compton, 2005). **Positive psychology** is the science of happiness; it is an area of study that seeks to identify and promote those qualities that lead to greater fulfillment in our lives. This field looks at people's strengths and what helps individuals lead happy, contented lives, and it moves away from focusing on people's pathology, faults, and problems.

According to Seligman and Csikszentmihalyi (2000), positive psychology

> at the subjective level is about valued subjective experiences: well-being, contentment, and satisfaction (in the past); hope and optimism (for the future); and…happiness (in the present). At the individual level, it is about positive individual traits: the capacity for love and vocation, courage, interpersonal skill, aesthetic sensibility, perseverance, forgiveness, originality, future mindedness, spirituality, high talent, and wisdom. (p. 5)

✍ On Your Own

In your own words, rephrase how Seligman and Csikszentmihalyi classify positive psychology.

_____

_____

Further Resources

Read this article (hawkes.biz/happiness) to learn about psychology's most recent findings related to happiness.

Some of the topics studied by positive psychologists include altruism and empathy, creativity, forgiveness and compassion, the importance of positive emotions, enhancement of immune system functioning, savoring the fleeting moments of life, and strengthening virtues as a way to increase authentic happiness (Compton, 2005). Recent efforts in the field of positive psychology have focused on extending its principles toward peace and well-being at the level of the global community. In a war-torn world in which conflict, hatred, and distrust are common, such an extended "positive peace psychology" could have important implications for understanding how to overcome oppression and work toward global peace (Cohrs, Christie, White, & Das, 2013).

Dig Deeper

The Center for Investigating Healthy Minds

On the campus of the University of Wisconsin—Madison, the Center for Investigating Healthy Minds at the Waisman Center conducts rigorous scientific research on healthy aspects of the mind, such as kindness, forgiveness, compassion, and mindfulness. Established in 2008 and led by renowned neuroscientist Dr. Richard J. Davidson, the Center examines a wide range of ideas, including such things as a kindness curriculum in schools, neural correlates of prosocial behavior, psychological effects of Tai Chi training, digital games to foster prosocial behavior in children, and the effectiveness of yoga and breathing exercises in reducing symptoms of post traumatic stress disorder.

According to its website, the Center was founded after Dr. Davidson was challenged by His Holiness, the 14th Dalai Lama, "to apply the rigors of science to study positive qualities of mind" (Center for Investigating Health Minds, 2013). The Center continues to conduct scientific research with the aim of developing mental health training approaches that help people to live happier, healthier lives.

Positive Affect and Optimism

Taking a cue from positive psychology, extensive research over the last 10–15 years has examined the importance of positive psychological attributes in physical well-being. Qualities that help promote psychological well-being (e.g., having meaning and purpose in life, a sense of autonomy, positive emotions, and satisfaction with life) are linked with a range of favorable health outcomes (especially improved cardiovascular health) mainly through their relationships with biological functions and health behaviors. These include (Boehm & Kubzansky, 2012):

- Diet
- Physical activity
- Sleep quality

📷 **Figure 10:** Better sleep is a health-induced effect of optimism.

The quality that has received attention is **positive affect**, which refers to pleasurable engagement with the environment, such as happiness, joy, enthusiasm, alertness, and excitement (Watson, Clark, & Tellegen, 1988). The characteristics of positive affect, as with negative affect (discussed earlier), can be brief, long-lasting, or trait-like (Pressman & Cohen, 2005). Independent of age, gender, and income, positive affect is associated with (Steptoe, O'Donnell, Marmot, & Wardle, 2008):

- Greater social connectedness
- Emotional and practical support
- Adaptive coping efforts
- Lower depression
- Longevity and favorable physiological functioning

Positive affect also serves as a protective factor against heart disease. In a 10-year study of Nova Scotians, the rate of heart disease was 22% lower for each one-point increase on the measure of positive affect, from 1 (no positive affect expressed) to 5 (extreme positive affect) (Davidson, Mostofsky, & Whang, 2010). In terms of our health, the expression, "don't worry, be happy" is helpful advice indeed. There has also been much work suggesting that **optimism**—the general tendency to look on the bright side of things—is also a significant predictor of positive health outcomes.

Reflection Questions

Do you feel that you are a genuinely happy person? If so, why? If not, what strategies might you employ to boost your happiness (and health)?

Although positive affect and optimism are related in some ways, they are not the same (Pressman & Cohen, 2005). Whereas positive affect is mostly concerned with positive feeling states, optimism has been regarded as a generalized tendency to expect that good things will happen (Chang, 2001). It has also been conceptualized as a tendency to view life's stressors and difficulties as temporary and external to oneself (Peterson & Steen, 2002). Numerous studies over the years have consistently shown that optimism is linked to longevity, healthier behaviors, fewer postsurgical complications, better immune functioning among men with prostate cancer, and better treatment adherence (Rasmussen & Wallio, 2008). Further, optimistic people report fewer physical symptoms, less pain, better physical functioning, and are less likely to be rehospitalized following heart surgery (Rasmussen, Scheier, & Greenhouse, 2009).

Flow

Figure 11: Some people find their flow through artistic expression.

Another factor that seems to be important in fostering a deep sense of well-being is the ability to derive flow from the things we do in life. **Flow** is described as a particular experience that is so engaging and engrossing that it becomes worth doing for its own sake (Csikszentmihalyi, 1997). It is usually related to creative endeavors and leisure activities, but it can also be experienced by workers who like their jobs or students who love studying (Csikszentmihalyi, 1999).

Many of us instantly recognize the notion of flow. In fact, the term was derived from respondents' spontaneous use of the term when asked to describe how it felt when they were doing well. When people experience flow, they become involved in an activity to the point where they feel they lose themselves in the activity. They effortlessly maintain their concentration and focus, they feel as though they have complete control of their actions, and time seems to pass more quickly than usual (Csikszentmihalyi, 1997). Flow is considered a pleasurable experience, and it typically occurs when people are engaged in challenging activities that require skills and knowledge they know they possess. For example, people would be more likely to report flow experiences in relation to their work or hobbies than in relation to eating.

Reflection Questions

Have you ever experienced this state of flow? If so, what were you doing? How did you feel during that time?

When asked the question "do you ever get involved in something so deeply that nothing else seems to matter, and you lose track of time?" about 20% of Americans and Europeans report having these flow-like experiences regularly (Csikszentmihalyi, 1997).

Although wealth and material possessions are nice to have, the notion of flow suggests that neither are prerequisites for a happy and fulfilling life. Finding an activity that you are truly enthusiastic about, something so absorbing that doing it is reward itself (whether it be playing tennis, studying Arabic, writing children's novels, or cooking lavish meals) is perhaps the real key. According to Csikszentmihalyi (1999), creating conditions that make flow experiences possible should be a top social and political priority. How might this goal be achieved? How might flow be promoted in school systems? In the workplace? What potential benefits might be accrued from such efforts?

In an ideal world, scientific research endeavors should inform us on how to bring about a better world for all people. The field of positive psychology promises to be instrumental in helping us understand what truly builds hope, optimism, happiness, healthy relationships, flow, and genuine personal fulfillment.

Summary

Happiness is conceptualized as an enduring state of mind that consists of the capacity to experience pleasure in daily life, as well as the ability to engage one's skills and talents to enrich one's life and the lives of others. Although people around the world generally report that they are happy, there are differences in average happiness levels across nations. Even though people have a tendency to overestimate the extent to which their happiness set points would change for the better or for the worse following certain life events, researchers have identified a number of factors that are consistently related to happiness. In recent years, positive psychology has emerged as an area of study seeking to identify and promote qualities that lead to greater happiness and fulfillment in our lives. These components include positive affect, optimism, and flow.

Chapter 13 Project

Purpose

The physical and emotional impacts of stress are real and meaningful. Both good and bad sources of stress contribute to physiological, emotional, and behavioral outcomes in individuals. **The purpose of this project is to help you better understand how and what environmental events trigger stress reactions, what those reactions look like and why, and how stress impacts health and well-being.**

Directions

Think about a time you have experienced stress. What triggered the stress reaction? What factors contributed to your appraisal of the situation, and what were the consequences of experiencing this stressor? How did you respond and cope? As you think about this stressor, it may be helpful to take notes about the experience, your reactions, and the outcomes.

After identifying your specific stressor and stress situation, think about what psychology says regarding stress reactions and the outcomes of stress. What would psychologists explore to better understand your stress situation? What would they make of your reactions and coping mechanisms?

Using the following guide to analyze your stress situation and reaction.

1. Briefly describe your stressor. What environmental event, hassle, or life challenge caused your stress?

2. Was your stressor chronic or acute? Briefly explain why or why not.

3. What was your initial appraisal of the stressor? In other words, did you appraise the stressor as a challenge and/or a threat? Briefly explain why or why not.

4. Briefly describe your reaction to the stressor as related to each of these categories:

	Description	Did you experience distress? (Yes or No)
Physiological		
Cognitive		
Behavioral		

5. What, if any, individual factors or personal characteristics might have contributed to your initial reaction?

6. What was your secondary appraisal of the stressor? What, if anything, changed?

7. What, if any, type of social support did you receive when coping with this stress?

8. What, if any, additional social supports would have been helpful?

9. What coping mechanisms emerged for handling your stress? Complete the following chart to explore 2 of the coping mechanisms that emerged to deal with your stress.

Coping Mechanism (Briefly describe)	Is this mechanism problem-focused or emotion-focused? (Briefly explain)	Did this coping mechanism address physiological, cognitive, and/or behavioral reactions to the stressor? (Briefly explain)

10. What, if any, impacts did this stressor have on your health and/or lifestyle?

11. What would be the long-term physical and/or mental health consequences of this stressor if it were left unaddressed?

Materials

None required.

☑ Checklist

☐ All questions answered

    ☐ A stressor described

        ☐ Described as chronic or acute

        ☐ Initial appraisal

            ☐ Physiological, cognitive, and behavioral responses to the stressor

            ☐ Contributing factors

        ☐ Secondary appraisal

            ☐ Social support received

            ☐ Social support requested

        ☐ 2 coping mechanisms described

            ☐ Problem-focused or emotion-focused

            ☐ Addressed physiological, cognitive, or behavioral responses

        ☐ Impact on health and/or lifestyle

        ☐ Long-term physical and/or mental health consequences

🏁 Chapter 13 Review

Lesson Summaries

13.1 What Is Stress?

Stress is a process whereby an individual perceives and responds to events appraised as overwhelming or threatening to one's well-being. The scientific study of how stress and emotional factors impact health and well-being is called health psychology, a field devoted to studying the general impact of psychological factors on health. The body's primary physiological response during stress, the fight-or-flight response, was first identified in the early 20th century by Walter Cannon. The fight-or-flight response involves the coordinated activity of both the sympathetic nervous system and the hypothalamic-pituitary-adrenal (HPA) axis. Hans Selye, a noted endocrinologist, referred to these physiological reactions to stress as part of general adaptation syndrome, which occurs in three stages: alarm reaction (fight-or-flight reactions begin), resistance (the body begins to adapt to continuing stress), and exhaustion (adaptive energy is depleted, and stress begins to take a physical toll).

13.2 Stressors

Stressors can be chronic (long term) or acute (short term) and can include traumatic events, significant life changes, daily hassles, and situations in which people are frequently exposed to challenging and unpleasant events. Many potential stressors include events or situations that require us to make changes in our lives. Thomas Holmes and Richard Rahe developed the Social Readjustment Rating Scale (SRRS) to measure stress by assigning a number of life change units to life events that typically require some adjustment, including positive events. Although the SRRS has been criticized on a number of grounds, extensive research has shown that the accumulation of many LCUs is associated with increased risk of illness. Many potential stressors also include daily hassles, which are minor irritations and annoyances that can build up over time. In addition, jobs that are especially demanding, offer little control over one's working environment, or involve unfavorable working conditions can lead to job strain, thereby setting the stage for job burnout.

13.3 Stress and Illness

Psychophysiological disorders are physical diseases that are either brought about or worsened by stress and other emotional factors. One of the mechanisms through which stress and emotional factors can influence the development of these diseases is by adversely affecting the body's immune system. A number of studies have demonstrated that stress weakens the functioning of the immune system. Cardiovascular disorders are serious medical conditions that have been consistently shown to be influenced by stress and negative emotions, such as anger, negative affectivity, and depression. Other psychophysiological disorders that are known to be influenced by stress and emotional factors include asthma and tension headaches.

13.4 Regulation of Stress

When faced with stress, people should attempt to manage it or cope with it. In general, there are two basic forms of coping: problem-focused coping and emotion-focused coping. Those who use problem-focused coping strategies tend to cope better with stress because these strategies address the source of stress rather than the symptoms. To a large extent, perceived control greatly impacts reaction to stressors and is associated with greater physical and mental well-being.

Social support has been demonstrated to be a highly effective buffer against the adverse effects of stress. Extensive research has shown that social support has beneficial physiological effects for people, and it seems to influence immune functioning. However, the beneficial effects of social support may be related to its influence on promoting healthy behavior.

13.5 The Pursuit of Happiness

Happiness is conceptualized as an enduring state of mind that consists of the capacity to experience pleasure in daily life, as well as the ability to engage one's skills and talents to enrich one's life and the lives of others. Although people around the world generally report that they are happy, there are differences in average happiness levels across nations. Even though people have a tendency to overestimate the extent to which their happiness set points would change for the better or for the worse following certain life events, researchers have identified a number of factors that are consistently related to happiness. In recent years, positive psychology has emerged as an area of study seeking to identify and promote qualities that lead to greater happiness and fulfillment in our lives. These components include positive affect, optimism, and flow.

Key Terms

Flash Back

Now that you've worked through the chapter, sharpen your vocabulary with this Hawkes Verified Quizlet set (hawkes.biz/psychch13)!

Alarm Reaction

First stage of the general adaptation syndrome; characterized as the body's immediate physiological reaction to a threatening situation or some other emergency; analogous to the fight-or-flight response

Asthma

Psychophysiological disorder in which the airways of the respiratory system become obstructed, leading to great difficulty expelling air from the lungs

Biofeedback

Stress-reduction technique using electronic equipment to measure a person's involuntary (neuromuscular and autonomic) activity and provide feedback to help the person gain a level of voluntary control over these processes

Cardiovascular Disorders

Disorders that involve the heart and blood circulation system

Coping

Mental or behavioral efforts used to manage problems relating to stress, including its cause and the unpleasant feelings and emotions it produces

Cortisol

Stress hormone released by the adrenal glands when encountering a stressor; helps to provide a boost of energy, thereby preparing the individual to take action

Daily Hassles

Minor irritations and annoyances that are part of our everyday lives and are capable of producing stress

Distress

Bad form of stress; usually high in intensity; often leads to exhaustion, fatigue, feeling burned out; associated with erosions in performance and health

Eustress

Good form of stress; low to moderate in intensity; associated with positive feelings, as well as optimal health and performance

Fight-or-Flight Response

Set of physiological reactions (increases in blood pressure, heart rate, respiration rate, and sweat) that occur when an individual encounters a perceived threat; these reactions are produced by activation of the sympathetic nervous system and the endocrine system

Flow

State involving intense engagement in an activity; usually is experienced when participating in creative, work, and leisure endeavors

General Adaptation Syndrome

Hans Selye's three-stage model of the body's physiological reactions to stress and the process of stress adaptation: alarm reaction, stage of resistance, and stage of exhaustion

Happiness

Enduring state of mind consisting of joy, contentment, and other positive emotions; the sense that one's life has meaning and value

Health Psychology

Subfield of psychology devoted to studying psychological influences on health, illness, and how people respond when they become ill

Heart Disease

Several types of adverse heart conditions, including those that involve the heart's arteries or valves or those involving the inability of the heart to pump enough blood to meet the body's needs; can include heart attack and stroke

Hypertension

High blood pressure

Hypothalamic-Pituitary-Adrenal (HPA) Axis

Set of structures found in both the limbic system (hypothalamus) and the endocrine system (pituitary gland and adrenal glands) that regulate many of the body's physiological reactions to stress through the release of hormones

Immune System

Various structures, cells, and mechanisms that protect the body from foreign substances that can damage the body's tissues and organs

Immunosuppression

Decreased effectiveness of the immune system

Job Burnout

General sense of emotional exhaustion and cynicism in relation to one's job; consists of three dimensions: exhaustion, depersonalization, and sense of diminished personal accomplishment

Job Strain

Work situation involving the combination of excessive job demands and workload with little decision-making latitude or job control

Lymphocytes

White blood cells that circulate in the body's fluids and are especially important in the body's immune response

Negative Affectivity

Tendency to experience distressed emotional states involving anger, contempt, disgust, guilt, fear, and nervousness

Optimism

Tendency toward a positive outlook and positive expectations

Perceived Control

Peoples' beliefs concerning their capacity to influence and shape outcomes in their lives

Positive Affect

State or a trait that involves pleasurable engagement with the environment, the dimensions of which include happiness, joy, enthusiasm, alertness, and excitement

Positive Psychology

Scientific area of study seeking to identify and promote those qualities that lead to happy, fulfilled, and contented lives

Primary Appraisal

Judgment about the degree of potential harm or threat to well-being that a stressor might entail

Psychoneuroimmunology

Field that studies how psychological factors (such as stress) influence the immune system and immune functioning

Psychophysiological Disorders

Physical disorders or diseases in which symptoms are brought about or worsened by stress and emotional factors

Relaxation Response Technique

Stress reduction technique combining elements of relaxation and meditation

Secondary Appraisal

Judgment of options available to cope with a stressor and their potential effectiveness

Social Readjustment Rating Scale (SRRS)

Popular scale designed to measure stress; consists of 43 potentially stressful events, each of which has a numerical value quantifying how much readjustment is associated with the event

Social Support

Soothing and often beneficial support of others; can take different forms, such as advice, guidance, encouragement, acceptance, emotional comfort, and tangible assistance

Stage of Exhaustion

Third stage of the general adaptation syndrome; the body's ability to resist stress becomes depleted; illness, disease, and even death may occur

Stage of Resistance

Second stage of the general adaptation syndrome; the body adapts to a stressor for a period of time

Stress

Process whereby an individual perceives and responds to events that one appraises as overwhelming or threatening to one's well-being

Stressors

Environmental events that may be judged as threatening or demanding; stimuli that initiate the stress process

Type A

Psychological and behavior pattern exhibited by individuals who tend to be extremely competitive, impatient, rushed, and hostile toward others

Type B

Psychological and behavior pattern exhibited by a person who is relaxed and laid back

🔆 Exercises

Review Questions

1. Negative effects of stress are most likely to be experienced when an event is perceived as _____.

   a. negative, but it is likely to affect one's friends rather than oneself

   b. challenging

   c. confusing

   d. threatening, and no clear options for dealing with it are apparent

2. Between 2006 and 2009, the greatest increases in stress levels were found to occur among _____.

   a. Blacks

   b. those aged 45-64

   c. the unemployed

   d. those without college degrees

3. At which stage of Selye's general adaptation syndrome is a person especially vulnerable to illness?

   a. Exhaustion

   b. Alarm reaction

   c. Fight-or-flight

   d. Resistance

4. During an encounter judged as stressful, cortisol is released by the _____.

   a. sympathetic nervous system

   b. hypothalamus

   c. pituitary gland

   d. adrenal glands

5. According to the Holmes and Rahe scale, which life event requires the greatest amount of readjustment?

   a. Marriage

   b. Personal illness

   c. Divorce

   d. Death of spouse

6. While waiting to pay for his weekly groceries at the supermarket, Paul had to wait about 20 minutes in a long line at the checkout because only one cashier was on duty. When he was finally ready to pay, his debit card was declined because he did not have enough money left in his checking account. Because he had left his credit cards at home, he had to place the groceries back into the cart and head home to retrieve a credit card. While driving back to his home, traffic was backed up two miles due to an accident. These events that Paul had to endure are best characterized as _____.

   a. chronic stressors

   b. acute stressors

   c. daily hassles

   d. readjustment occurrences

7. What is one of the major criticisms of the Social Readjustment Rating Scale?

   a. It has too few items.

   b. It was developed using only people from the New England region of the United States.

   c. It does not take into consideration how a person appraises an event.

   d. None of the items included are positive.

8. Which of the following is not a dimension of job burnout?

   a. Depersonalization

   b. Hostility

   c. Exhaustion

   d. Diminished personal accomplishment

9. The white blood cells that attack foreign invaders to the body are called _____.

   a. antibodies

   b. telomeres

   c. lymphocytes

   d. immune cells

10. The risk of heart disease is especially high among individuals with _____.

   a. depression

   b. asthma

   c. telomeres

   d. lymphocytes

11. The most lethal dimension of Type A behavior pattern seems to be _____.

   a. hostility

   b. impatience

   c. time urgency

   d. competitive drive

12. Which of the following statements pertaining to asthma is false?

   a. Parental and interpersonal conflicts have been tied to the development of asthma.

   b. Asthma sufferers can experience asthma-like symptoms simply by believing that an inert substance they breathe will lead to airway obstruction.

   c. Asthma has been shown to be linked to hostility.

   d. Rates of asthma have decreased considerably since 2000.

13. Emotion-focused coping would likely be a better method than problem-focused coping for dealing with which of the following stressors?

   a. Terminal cancer

   b. Poor grades in school

   c. Unemployment

   d. Divorce

14. Studies of British civil servants have found that those in the lowest status jobs are much more likely to develop heart disease than those who have high status jobs. These findings attest to the importance of _____ in dealing with stress.

   a. biofeedback

   b. social support

   c. perceived control

   d. emotion-focused coping

15. Relative to those with low levels of social support, individuals with high levels of social support _____.

   a. are more likely to develop asthma

   b. tend to have less perceived control

   c. are more likely to develop cardiovascular disorders

   d. tend to tolerate stress well

16. The concept of learned helplessness was formulated by Seligman to explain the _____.

   a. inability of dogs to attempt to escape avoidable shocks after having received inescapable shocks

   b. failure of dogs to learn to from prior mistakes

   c. ability of dogs to learn to help other dogs escape situations in which they are receiving uncontrollable shocks

   d. inability of dogs to learn to help other dogs escape situations in which they are receiving uncontrollable electric shocks

17. Which of the following is not one of the presumed components of happiness?

   a. Using our talents to help improve the lives of others

   b. Learning new skills

   c. Regular pleasurable experiences

   d. Identifying and using our talents to enrich our lives

18. Researchers have identified a number of factors that are related to happiness. Which of the following is not one of them?

   a. Age

   b. Annual income up to $75,000

   c. Physical attractiveness

   d. Marriage

19. How does positive affect differ from optimism?

    a. Optimism is more scientific than positive affect.

    b. Positive affect is more scientific than optimism.

    c. Positive affect involves feeling states, whereas optimism involves expectations.

    d. Optimism involves feeling states, whereas positive affect involves expectations.

20. Carson enjoys writing mystery novels and has even managed to publish some of his work. When he's writing, Carson becomes extremely focused on his work; in fact, he becomes so absorbed that that he often loses track of time, staying up well past 3 a.m. Carson's experience best illustrates the concept of _____.

    a. happiness set point

    b. adaptation

    c. positive affect

    d. flow

Critical Thinking Questions

21. Provide an example (other than the one described earlier) of a situation or event that could be appraised as either threatening or challenging.

22. Provide an example of a stressful situation that may cause a person to become seriously ill. How would Selye's general adaptation syndrome explain this occurrence?

23. Review the items on the Social Readjustment Rating Scale. Select one of the items and discuss how it might bring about distress and eustress.

24. Job burnout tends to be high in people who work in human service jobs. Considering the three dimensions of job burnout, explain how various job aspects unique to being a police officer might lead to job burnout in that line of work.

25. Discuss the concept of Type A behavior pattern, its history, and what we now know concerning its role in heart disease.

26. Consider the study in which volunteers were given nasal drops containing the cold virus to examine the relationship between stress and immune function (Cohen et al., 1998). How might this finding explain how people seem to become sick during stressful times in their lives (e.g., final exam week)?

27. Although problem-focused coping seems to be a more effective strategy when dealing with stressors, do you think there are any kinds of stressful situations in which emotion-focused coping might be a better strategy?

28. Describe how social support can affect health both directly and indirectly.

29. In considering the three dimensions of happiness discussed in Lesson 13.5 (the pleasant life, the good life, and the meaningful life), what are some steps you could take to improve your personal level of happiness?

30. The day before the drawing of a $300 million Powerball lottery, you notice that a line of people waiting to buy their Powerball tickets is stretched outside the door of a nearby convenience store. Based on what you've learned, provide some perspective on why these people are doing this, and what would likely happen if one of these individuals happened to pick the right numbers.

Chapter Introduction

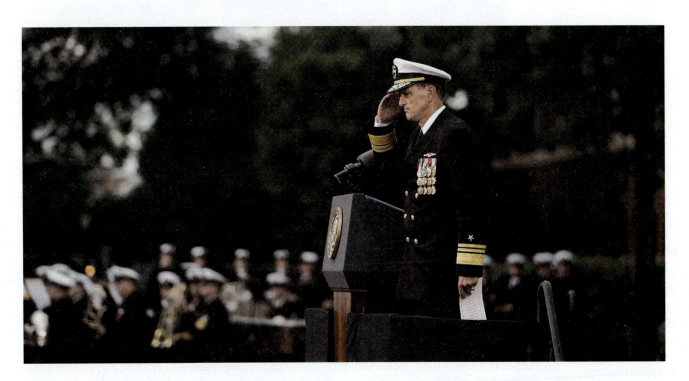

📷 **Figure 1:** Vice Admiral William Hilarides salutes the families of the victims of the Washington Navy Yard shooting.

On Monday, September 16, 2013, a gunman killed 12 people as the workday began at the Washington Navy Yard in Washington, DC. Aaron Alexis, 34, had a troubled history: he thought that he was being controlled by radio waves. He called the police to complain about voices in his head and being under surveillance by "shadowy forces" (Thomas, Levine, Date, & Cloherty, 2013). While Alexis's actions cannot be excused, it is clear that he had some form of mental illness. Mental illness is not necessarily a cause of violence; it is far more likely that the mentally ill will be victims rather than perpetrators of violence (Stuart, 2003). If, however, Alexis had received the help he needed, this tragedy might have been averted.

Flash Forward

Ready to dig into the vocabulary? Get some practice with this Hawkes Verified Quizlet set (hawkes.biz/psych14q1)!

14.1 What Are Psychological Disorders?

A **psychological disorder** is a condition characterized by abnormal thoughts, feelings, and behaviors. **Psychopathology** is the study of psychological disorders, including their symptoms, **etiology** (i.e., their causes), and treatment. The term *psychopathology* can also refer to the manifestation of a psychological disorder. Although consensus can be difficult, it is extremely important for mental health professionals to agree on what kinds of thoughts, feelings, and behaviors are truly abnormal in the sense that they genuinely indicate the presence of psychopathology. Certain patterns of behavior and inner experience can easily be labeled as abnormal and clearly signify some kind of psychological disturbance. The person who washes his hands 40 times per day and the person who claims to hear the voices of demons exhibit behaviors and inner experiences that most would regard as abnormal: beliefs and behaviors that suggest the existence of a psychological disorder. But, consider the nervousness a young man feels when talking to attractive women or the loneliness and longing for home a freshman experiences during her first semester of college—these feelings may not be regularly present, but they fall in the range of normal. So, what kinds of thoughts, feelings, and behaviors represent a true psychological disorder? Psychologists work to distinguish psychological disorders from inner experiences and behaviors that are merely situational, idiosyncratic, or unconventional.

Figure 2: Psychologists work to distinguish thoughts, feelings, and behaviors that represent true psychological disorders.

Group Activity

Individually, write a list of behaviors that you would describe as "abnormal." As a class, write the list on the board.

Looking at the list, is there any situation in which that behavior would be considered normal? What is the difference?

Definition of a Psychological Disorder

Perhaps the simplest approach to conceptualizing psychological disorders is to label behaviors, thoughts, and inner experiences that are atypical, distressful, dysfunctional, and sometimes even dangerous as signs of a disorder. For example, if you ask a classmate on a date and you are rejected, you probably would feel a little dejected. Such feelings would be normal. If you felt extremely depressed—so much so that you lost interest in activities, had difficulty eating or sleeping, felt utterly worthless, and contemplated suicide—your feelings would be **atypical**, would deviate from the norm, and could signify the presence of a psychological disorder. Just because something is atypical, however, does not necessarily mean it is disordered.

For example, only about 4% of people in the United States have red hair, so red hair is considered an atypical characteristic (Figure 3), but it is not considered disordered, just unusual. And it is less unusual in Scotland, where approximately 13% of the population has red hair ("DNA Project Aims," 2012). As you will learn, some disorders, although not exactly typical, are far from atypical, and the rates in which they appear in the population are surprisingly high.

🖼 **Figure 3:** Red hair is considered unusual but not abnormal.

If we can agree that merely being atypical is an insufficient criterion for a having a psychological disorder, is it reasonable to consider behavior or inner experiences that differ from widely expected cultural values or expectations as disordered? Using this criterion, a woman who walks around a subway platform wearing a heavy winter coat in July while screaming obscenities at strangers may be considered as exhibiting symptoms of a psychological disorder. Her actions and clothes violate socially accepted rules governing appropriate dress and behavior; these characteristics are atypical.

Cultural Expectations

Violating cultural expectations is not, in and of itself, a satisfactory means of identifying the presence of a psychological disorder. Since behavior varies from one culture to another, what may be expected and considered appropriate in one culture may not be viewed as such in other cultures. For example, returning a stranger's smile is expected in the United States because a pervasive social norm dictates that we reciprocate friendly gestures. A person who refuses to acknowledge such gestures might be considered socially awkward—perhaps even disordered—for violating this expectation. However, such expectations are not universally shared. Cultural expectations in Japan involve showing reserve, restraint, and a concern for maintaining privacy around strangers. Japanese people are generally unresponsive to smiles from strangers (Patterson et al., 2007). Eye contact provides another example. In the United States and Europe, eye contact with others typically signifies honesty and attention. However, most Latin-American, Asian, and African cultures interpret direct eye contact as rude, confrontational, and aggressive (Pazain, 2010). Thus, someone who makes eye contact with you could be considered appropriate and respectful or brazen and offensive, depending on your culture (Figure 4).

🖼 **Figure 4:** Eye contact is one of many social gestures that vary from culture to culture.

Hallucinations (seeing or hearing things that are not physically present) in Western societies is a violation of cultural expectations, and a person who reports such inner experiences is readily labeled as psychologically disordered. In other cultures, visions that, for example, pertain to future events may be regarded as normal experiences that are positively valued (Bourguignon, 1970). Finally, it is important to recognize that cultural norms change over time: what might be considered typical in a society at one time may no longer be viewed this way later, similar to how fashion trends from one era may elicit quizzical looks decades later—imagine how a headband, legwarmers, and the big hair of the 1980s would go over on your campus today.

Dig Deeper

The Myth of Mental Illness

In the 1950s and 1960s, the concept of mental illness was widely criticized. One of the major criticisms focused on the notion that mental illness was a "myth that justifies psychiatric intervention in socially disapproved behavior" (Wakefield, 1992). Thomas Szasz (1960), a noted psychiatrist, was perhaps the biggest proponent of this view. Szasz argued that the notion of mental illness was invented by society (and the mental health establishment) to stigmatize and subjugate people whose behavior violates accepted social and legal norms. Indeed, Szasz suggested that what appear to be symptoms of mental illness are more appropriately characterized as "problems in living" (Szasz, 1960).

In his 1961 book *The Myth of Mental Illness: Foundations of a Theory of Personal Conduct*, Szasz expressed his disdain for the concept of mental illness and for the field of psychiatry in general (Oliver, 2006). The basis for Szasz's attack was his contention that detectable abnormalities in bodily structures and functions (e.g., infections and organ damage or dysfunction) represent the defining features of genuine illness or disease, and because symptoms of purported mental illness are not accompanied by such detectable abnormalities, so-called psychological disorders are not disorders at all. Szasz (1961/2010) proclaimed that "disease or illness can only affect the body; hence, there can be no mental illness" (p. 267).

Today, we recognize the extreme level of psychological suffering experienced by people with psychological disorders: the painful thoughts and feelings they experience, the disordered behavior they demonstrate, and the levels of distress and impairment they exhibit. This makes it very difficult to deny the reality of mental illness.

However controversial Szasz's views and those of his supporters might have been, they have influenced the mental health community and society in several ways. First, lay people, politicians, and professionals now often refer to mental illness as mental health "problems," implicitly acknowledging the "problems in living" perspective Szasz described (Buchanan-Barker & Barker, 2009). Also influential was Szasz's view of homosexuality. Szasz was perhaps the first psychiatrist to openly challenge the idea that homosexuality represented a form of mental illness or disease (Szasz, 1965). By challenging the idea that homosexuality represented a form a mental illness, Szasz helped pave the way for the social and civil rights that gay and lesbian people now have (Barker, 2010). His work also inspired legal changes that protect the rights of people in psychiatric institutions and allow such individuals a greater degree of influence and responsibility over their lives (Buchanan-Barker & Barker, 2009).

Figure 5: Szasz's controversial views have since influenced the societal shift surrounding mental illness.

Harmful Dysfunction

If none of the criteria discussed so far is adequate by itself to define the presence of a psychological disorder, how can a disorder be conceptualized? Many efforts have been made to identify the specific dimensions of psychological disorders, yet none is entirely satisfactory. No universal definition of psychological disorder exists that can apply to all situations in which a disorder is thought to be present (Zachar & Kendler, 2007). However, one of the more influential conceptualizations was proposed by Wakefield (1992), who defined psychological disorder as a **harmful dysfunction**. Wakefield argued that natural internal mechanisms—that is, psychological processes honed by evolution, such as cognition, perception, and learning—have important functions, such as enabling us to experience the world the way others do and to engage in rational thought, problem solving, and communication. For example, learning allows us to associate a fear with a potential danger in such a way that the intensity of fear is roughly equal to the degree of actual danger. Dysfunction occurs when an internal mechanism breaks down and can no longer perform its normal function. But, the presence of a dysfunction by itself does not determine a disorder. The dysfunction must be harmful in that it leads to negative consequences for the individual or for others, as judged by the standards of the individual's culture. The harm may include significant internal anguish (e.g., high levels of anxiety or depression) or problems in day-to-day living (e.g., in one's social or work life).

Further Resources

What is borderline personality disorder?

Watch this video (hawkes.biz/bpdlife) for some insight on what it's like to live with BPD.

Visit this site (hawkes.biz/bpd) for more information on this disorder.

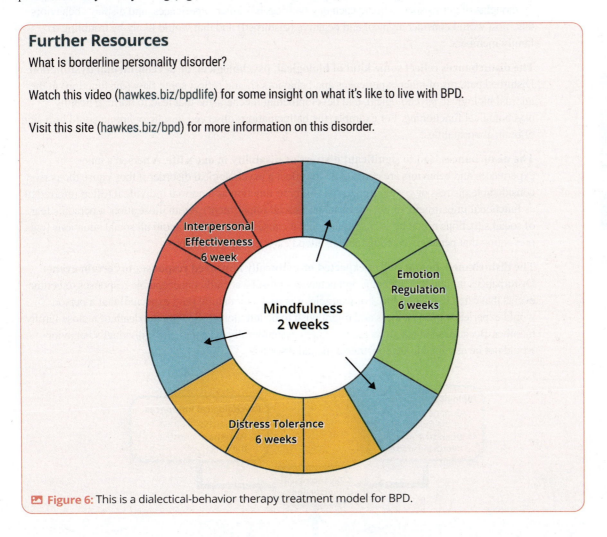

Figure 6: This is a dialectical-behavior therapy treatment model for BPD.

To illustrate, Janet has an extreme fear of spiders. Janet's fear might be considered a dysfunction in that it signals that the internal mechanism of learning is not working correctly (i.e., a faulty process prevents Janet from appropriately associating the magnitude of her fear with the actual threat posed by spiders). Janet's fear of spiders has a significant negative influence on her life: she avoids all situations in which she suspects spiders to be present (e.g., the basement or a friend's home), and she quit her job last month because she saw a spider in the restroom at work and is now unemployed. According to the harmful dysfunction model, Janet's condition would signify a disorder because (a) there is a dysfunction in an internal mechanism, and (b) the dysfunction has resulted in harmful consequences. Similar to how the symptoms of physical illness reflect dysfunctions in biological processes, the symptoms of psychological disorders presumably reflect dysfunctions in mental processes. The internal mechanism component of this model is especially appealing because it implies that disorders may occur through a breakdown of biological functions that govern various psychological processes, thus supporting contemporary neurobiological models of psychological disorders (Fabrega, 2007).

The American Psychiatric Association (APA) Definition

Many of the features of the harmful dysfunction model are incorporated in a formal definition of psychological disorder developed by the American Psychiatric Association (APA). According to the APA (2013), a psychological disorder is a condition that is said to consist of the following:

- **There are significant disturbances in thoughts, feelings, and behaviors**. A person must experience inner states (e.g., thoughts and/or feelings) and exhibit behaviors that are clearly disturbed—that is, unusual but in a negative, self-defeating way. Often, such disturbances are troubling to those around the individual who experiences them. For example, an individual who is uncontrollably preoccupied by thoughts of germs spends hours each day bathing, has inner experiences, and displays behaviors that most would consider atypical and negative (disturbed) and that would likely be troubling to family members.

- **The disturbances reflect some kind of biological, psychological, or developmental dysfunction**. Disturbed patterns of inner experiences and behaviors should reflect some flaw (dysfunction) in the internal biological, psychological, and developmental mechanisms that lead to normal, healthy psychological functioning. For example, the hallucinations observed in schizophrenia could be a sign of brain abnormalities.

- **The disturbances lead to significant distress or disability in one's life**. A person's inner experiences and behaviors are considered to reflect a psychological disorder if they cause the person considerable distress or greatly impair his ability to function as a normal individual (often referred to as functional impairment, or occupational and social impairment). As an illustration, a person's fear of social situations might be so distressing that it causes the person to avoid all social situations (e.g., preventing that person from being able to attend class or apply for a job).

- **The disturbances do not reflect expected or culturally approved responses to certain events**. Disturbances in thoughts, feelings, and behaviors must be socially unacceptable responses to certain events that often happen in life. For example, it is perfectly natural (and expected) that a person would experience great sadness and might wish to be left alone following the death of a close family member. Because such reactions are in some ways culturally expected, the individual's behavior would not be assumed to demonstrate a mental disorder.

Figure 7: Brain abnormalities can be linked to psychological disorders like schizophrenia.

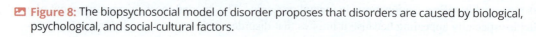

Figure 8: The biopsychosocial model of disorder proposes that disorders are caused by biological, psychological, and social-cultural factors.

Some believe that there is no essential criterion or set of criteria that can definitively distinguish all cases of disorder from nondisorder (Lilienfeld & Marino, 1999). In truth, no single approach to defining a psychological disorder is adequate by itself, nor is there universal agreement on where the boundary is between disordered and not disordered. From time to time we all experience anxiety, unwanted thoughts, and moments of sadness; our behavior at other times may not make much sense to ourselves or to others. These inner experiences and behaviors can vary in their intensity but are only considered disordered when they are highly disturbing to us and/or others, suggest a dysfunction in normal mental functioning, and are associated with significant distress or disability in social or occupational activities.

🖼 **Figure 9:** Feelings of anxiety in social situations can range from normal to significantly disabling.

Summary

Psychological disorders are conditions characterized by abnormal thoughts, feelings, and behaviors. Although challenging, it is essential for psychologists and mental health professionals to agree on what kinds of inner experiences and behaviors constitute the presence of a psychological disorder. Inner experiences and behaviors that are atypical or violate social norms could signify the presence of a disorder; however, each of these criteria alone is inadequate. Harmful dysfunction describes the view that psychological disorders result from the inability of an internal mechanism to perform its natural function. Many of the features of harmful dysfunction conceptualization have been incorporated in the APA's formal definition of psychological disorders. According to this definition, the presence of a psychological disorder is signaled by significant disturbances in thoughts, feelings, and behaviors; these disturbances must reflect some kind of dysfunction (biological, psychological, or developmental), must cause significant impairment in one's life, and must not reflect culturally expected reactions to certain life events.

14.2 Diagnosing and Classifying Psychological Disorders

A first step in the study of psychological disorders is carefully and systematically discerning significant signs and symptoms. How do mental health professionals know whether or not a person's inner states and behaviors truly represent a psychological disorder? Arriving at a proper **diagnosis**—that is, appropriately identifying and labeling a set of defined symptoms—is absolutely crucial. This process enables professionals to use a common language with others in the field and aids in communication about the disorder with the patient, colleagues, and the public. A proper diagnosis is an essential element to guide proper and successful treatment. For these reasons, classification systems that organize psychological disorders systematically are necessary.

Flash Forward

Ready to dig into the vocabulary? Get some practice with this Hawkes Verified Quizlet set (hawkes.biz/psych14q2)!

The Diagnostic and Statistical Manual of Mental Disorders (DSM)

Figure 1: Just as physical health issues are diagnosed, psychological disorders require diagnoses for proper treatment and care.

Although a number of classification systems have been developed over time, the one that is used by most mental health professionals in the United States is ***The Diagnostic and Statistical Manual of Mental Disorders* (DSM-5)**, published by the American Psychiatric Association (2013). (Note that the American Psychiatric Association differs from the American Psychological Association; both are abbreviated APA.) The first edition of the DSM, published in 1952, classified psychological disorders according to a format developed by the U.S. Army during World War II (Clegg, 2012). In the years since, the DSM has undergone numerous revisions and editions. The most recent edition, published in 2013, is the DSM-5 (APA, 2013).

Reflection Questions

Given the prediction that over half of Americans will suffer from mental illness at some point in their lives, do you think we are over-pathologizing? Why is it surprising that most of us might suffer mental illness at some point but not surprising that we will suffer physical illness?

The DSM-5 includes many categories of disorders (e.g., anxiety disorders, depressive disorders, and dissociative disorders). Each disorder is described in detail, including an overview of the disorder (diagnostic features), specific symptoms required for diagnosis (diagnostic criteria), prevalence information (what percent of the population is thought to be afflicted with the disorder), and risk factors associated with the disorder. Figure 2 shows lifetime prevalence rates—the percentage of people in a population who develop a disorder in their lifetime—of various psychological disorders among U.S. adults. These data are based on a national sample of 9,282 U.S. residents (National Comorbidity Survey, 2007).

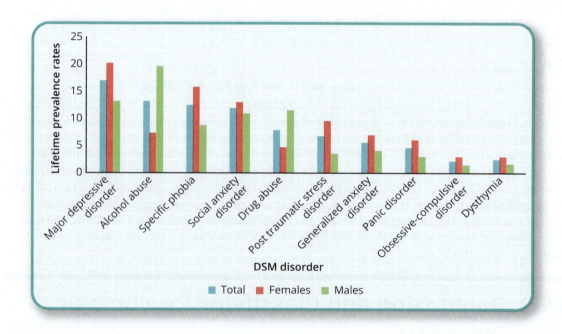

Figure 2: The graph shows the breakdown of psychological disorders, comparing the percentage prevalence among adult males and adult females in the United States. Because the data is from 2007, the categories shown here are from the DSM-IV, which has been supplanted by the DSM-5. Most categories remain the same; however, alcohol abuse now falls under a broader Alcohol Use Disorder category.

The DSM-5 also provides information about **comorbidity**; the co-occurrence of two disorders. For example, the DSM-5 mentions that 41% of people with obsessive-compulsive disorder (OCD) also meet the diagnostic criteria for major depressive disorder (Figure 3). Drug use is highly comorbid with other mental illnesses;

6 out of 10 people who have a substance use disorder also suffer from another form of mental illness (National Institute on Drug Abuse [NIDA], 2007).

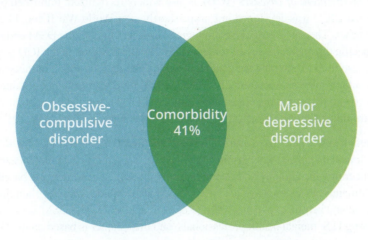

Figure 3: Obsessive-compulsive disorder and major depressive disorder frequently occur in the same person.

🖉 On Your Own

Which of the following individuals has a comorbidity?

☐   An individual who has been diagnosed with an anxiety disorder

☐   An individual who has been diagnosed with Attention Deficit Hyperactivity Disorder and dyslexia

☐   An individual who has been diagnosed with a depressive disorder

---

The DSM has changed considerably in the half century since it was originally published. The first two editions of the DSM, for example, listed homosexuality as a disorder; however, in 1973, the APA voted to remove it from the manual (Silverstein, 2009). Additionally, beginning with the DSM-III in 1980, mental disorders have been described in much greater detail, and the number of diagnosable conditions has grown steadily, as has the size of the manual itself. DSM-I included 106 diagnoses and was 130 total pages, whereas DSM-III included more than 2 times as many diagnoses (265) and was nearly seven times its size (886 total pages) (Mayes & Horowitz, 2005). Although DSM-5 is longer than DSM-IV, the volume includes only 237 disorders, a decrease from the 297 disorders that were listed in DSM-IV. The latest edition, DSM-5, includes revisions in the organization and naming of categories and in the diagnostic criteria for various disorders (Regier, Kuhl, & Kupfer, 2012) while emphasizing careful consideration of the importance of gender and cultural difference in the expression of various symptoms (Fisher, 2010).

Some believe that establishing new diagnoses might overpathologize the human condition by turning common human problems into mental illnesses (The Associated Press, 2013). Indeed, the finding that nearly half of all Americans will meet the criteria for a DSM disorder at some point in their life (Kessler et al., 2005) likely fuels much of this skepticism. The DSM-5 is also criticized on the grounds that its diagnostic criteria have been loosened, thereby threatening to "turn our current diagnostic inflation into diagnostic hyperinflation" (Frances, 2012, para. 22). For example, DSM-IV specified that the symptoms of major depressive disorder must not be attributable to normal bereavement (loss of a loved one). The DSM-5, however, has removed this bereavement exclusion, essentially meaning that grief and sadness after a loved one's death can constitute major depressive disorder.

The International Classification of Diseases

The International Classification of Diseases (**ICD**), is also widely recognized. Published by the World Health Organization (WHO), the ICD was developed in Europe shortly after World War II and, like the DSM, has been revised several times. The categories of psychological disorders in both the DSM and ICD are similar, as are the criteria for specific disorders; however, some differences exist. Although the ICD is used for clinical purposes, this tool is also used to examine the general health of populations and to monitor the prevalence of diseases and other health problems internationally (WHO, 2013). The ICD is in its 10th edition (ICD-10); however, efforts are now underway to develop a new edition (ICD-11) that, in conjunction with the changes in DSM-5, will help harmonize the two classification systems as much as possible (APA, 2013).

Figure 4: A streamlined classification system aims to unify the research and diagnosis process.

A study that compared the use of the two classification systems found that worldwide the ICD is more frequently used for clinical diagnosis, whereas the DSM is more valued for research (Mezzich, 2002). Most research findings concerning the etiology and treatment of psychological disorders are based on criteria set forth in the DSM (Oltmanns & Castonguay, 2013). The DSM also includes more explicit disorder criteria, along with an extensive and helpful explanatory text (Regier et al., 2012). The DSM is the classification system of choice among U.S. mental health professionals, and this chapter is based on the DSM paradigm.

The Compassionate View of Psychological Disorders

As these disorders are outlined, please bear two things in mind. First, remember that psychological disorders represent *extremes* of inner experience and behavior. If, while reading about these disorders, you feel that these descriptions begin to personally characterize you, do not worry—this moment of enlightenment probably means nothing more than you are normal.

> ### Reflection Question
> How do you think labels of psychological disorders can be harmful to individuals who suffer from mental illness?

Each of us experiences episodes of sadness, anxiety, and preoccupation with certain thoughts—times when we do not quite feel ourselves. These episodes should not be considered problematic unless the accompanying thoughts and behaviors become extreme and have a disruptive effect on one's life. Second, understand that people with psychological disorders are far more than just embodiments of their disorders. We do not use terms such as *schizophrenics*, *depressives*, or *phobics* because they are labels that objectify people who suffer from these conditions, thus promoting biased and disparaging assumptions about them. It is important to remember that a psychological disorder is not what a person *is*; it is something that a person *has*—through no fault of his or her own. As is the case with cancer or diabetes, those with psychological disorders suffer debilitating, often painful conditions that are not of their own choosing. These individuals deserve to be viewed and treated with compassion, understanding, and dignity.

Figure 5: A person is not defined by his or her psychological disorder.

Summary

The diagnosis and classification of psychological disorders is essential in studying and treating psychopathology. The classification system used by most U.S. professionals is the DSM-5. The first edition of the DSM was published in 1952 and has undergone numerous revisions. The 5th and most recent edition, the DSM-5, was published in 2013. The diagnostic manual includes a total of 237 specific diagnosable disorders, each described in detail, including its symptoms, prevalence, risk factors, and comorbidity. Over time, the number of diagnosable conditions listed in the DSM has grown steadily, prompting criticism from some. Nevertheless, the diagnostic criteria in the DSM are more explicit than that of any other system, which makes the DSM system highly desirable for both clinical diagnosis and research.

14.3 Perspectives on Psychological Disorders

Scientists and mental health professionals may adopt different perspectives in attempting to understand or explain the underlying mechanisms that contribute to the development of a psychological disorder. The perspective used in explaining a psychological disorder is extremely important, in that it will consist of explicit assumptions regarding how best to study the disorder, its etiology, and what kinds of therapies or treatments are most beneficial. Different perspectives provide alternate ways for how to think about the nature of psychopathology.

Flash Forward

Ready to dig into the vocabulary? Get some practice with this Hawkes Verified Quizlet set (hawkes.biz/psych14q3)!

Supernatural Perspectives of Psychological Disorders

For centuries, psychological disorders were viewed from a **supernatural** perspective: attributed to a force beyond scientific understanding. Those afflicted were thought to be practitioners of black magic or possessed by spirits (Figure 1) (Maher & Maher, 1985). For example, convents throughout Europe in the 16th and 17th centuries reported hundreds of nuns falling into a state of frenzy in which the afflicted foamed at the mouth, screamed and convulsed, sexually propositioned priests, and confessed to having carnal relations with devils or Christ. Although today these cases would suggest serious mental illness, at the time, these events were routinely explained as possession by devilish forces (Waller, 2009a). Similarly, grievous fits by young girls are believed to have precipitated the witch panic in New England late in the 17th century (Demos, 1983). Such beliefs in supernatural causes of mental illness are still held in some societies today; for example, beliefs that supernatural forces cause mental illness are common in some cultures in modern-day Nigeria (Aghukwa, 2012).

Figure 1: In *The Extraction of the Stone of Madness*, a 15th century painting by Hieronymus Bosch, a practitioner is using a tool to extract an object (the supposed "stone of madness") from the head of an afflicted person.

Reflection Question

How do you think the understanding of psychological disorders affected their treatment in the 15th through 17th centuries?

Dig Deeper

Dancing Mania

Between the 11th and 17th centuries, a curious epidemic swept across Western Europe. Groups of people would suddenly begin to dance with wild abandon. This compulsion to dance—referred to as dancing mania—sometimes gripped thousands of people at a time (Figure 2). Historical accounts indicate that those afflicted would sometimes dance with bruised and bloody feet for days or weeks, screaming of terrible visions and begging priests and monks to save their souls (Waller, 2009b). What caused dancing mania is not known, but several explanations have been proposed, including spider venom and ergot poisoning ("Dancing Mania," 2011).

Figure 2: Although the cause of dancing mania, depicted in this painting, was unclear, the behavior was attributed to supernatural forces.

Historian John Waller (2009a, 2009b) has provided a comprehensive and convincing explanation of dancing mania that suggests the phenomenon was attributable to a combination of three factors: psychological distress, social contagion, and belief in supernatural forces. Waller argued that various disasters of the time (such as famine, plagues, and floods) produced high levels of psychological distress that could increase the likelihood of succumbing to an involuntary trance state. Waller indicated that anthropological studies and accounts of possession rituals show that people are more likely to enter a trance state if they expect it to happen and that entranced individuals behave in a ritualistic manner, their thoughts and behavior shaped by the spiritual beliefs of their culture. Thus, during periods of extreme physical and mental distress, all it took were a few people—believing themselves to have been afflicted with a dancing curse—to slip into a spontaneous trance and then act out the part of one who is cursed by dancing for days on end.

Biological Perspectives of Psychological Disorders

The biological perspective views psychological disorders as linked to biological phenomena, such as genetic factors, chemical imbalances, and brain abnormalities; it has gained considerable attention and acceptance in recent decades (Wyatt & Midkiff, 2006). Evidence from many sources indicates that most psychological disorders have a genetic component; in fact, there is little dispute that some disorders are largely due to genetic factors. The graph in Figure 3 shows heritability estimates for schizophrenia.

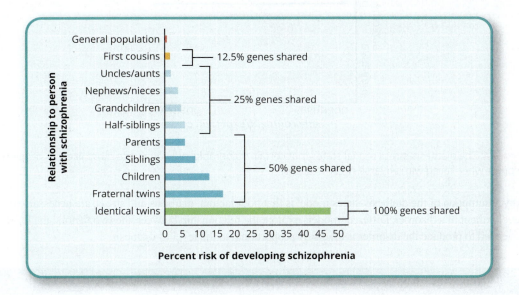

Figure 3: A person's risk of developing schizophrenia increases if a relative has schizophrenia. The closer the genetic relationship, the higher the risk.

Reflection Question

Do you think psychological disorders are mostly explained by genetics? Why or why not?

Findings such as these have led many of today's researchers to search for specific genes and genetic mutations that contribute to mental disorders. Also, sophisticated neural imaging technology in recent decades has revealed how abnormalities in brain structure and function might be directly involved in many disorders, and advances in our understanding of neurotransmitters and hormones have yielded insights into their possible connections. The biological perspective is currently thriving in the study of psychological disorders.

The Diathesis-Stress Model of Psychological Disorders

Despite advances in understanding the biological basis of psychological disorders, the psychosocial perspective is still very important. This perspective emphasizes the importance of learning, stress, faulty and self-defeating thinking patterns, and environmental factors. Perhaps the best way to think about psychological disorders, then, is to view them as originating from a combination of biological and psychological processes. Many develop not from a single cause but from a delicate fusion between partly biological and partly psychosocial factors.

The **diathesis-stress model** (Zuckerman, 1999) integrates biological and psychosocial factors to predict the likelihood of a disorder. This diathesis-stress model suggests that people with an underlying predisposition for a disorder (i.e., a diathesis) are more likely than others to develop a disorder when faced with adverse environmental or psychological events (i.e., stress), such as childhood maltreatment, negative life events, trauma, and so on. A diathesis is not always a biological vulnerability to an illness; some diatheses may be psychological (e.g., a tendency to think about life events in a pessimistic, self-defeating way).

Figure 4: The diathesis-stress model states that certain vulnerable individuals are more likely to develop a disorder when faced with adverse circumstances.

The key assumption of the diathesis-stress model is that both factors, diathesis and stress, are necessary in the development of a disorder. Different models explore the relationship between the two factors: the level of stress needed to produce the disorder is inversely proportional to the level of diathesis.

☑ On Your Own

Using the following table, explain why an individual would have schizophrenia from a supernatural, biological, and diathesis-stress perspective. At the end, explain which perspective you think makes the most sense and why?

Why would an individual have schizophrenia?	Response
Supernatural Perspective	
Biological Perspective	
Diathesis-Stress Model	
Which perspective do you think makes the most sense and why?	

Summary

Psychopathology is very complex, involving a plethora of etiological theories and perspectives. For centuries, psychological disorders were viewed primarily from a supernatural perspective and thought to arise from divine forces or possession from spirits. Some cultures continue to hold this supernatural belief. Today, many who study psychopathology view mental illness from a biological perspective, whereby psychological disorders are thought to result largely from faulty biological processes. Indeed, scientific advances over the last several decades have provided a better understanding of the genetic, neurological, hormonal, and biochemical bases of psychopathology. The psychological perspective, in contrast, emphasizes the importance of psychological factors (e.g., stress and thoughts) and environmental factors in the development of psychological disorders. A contemporary, promising approach is to view disorders as originating from an integration of biological and psychosocial factors. The diathesis-stress model suggests that people with an underlying diathesis, or vulnerability, for a psychological disorder are more likely than those without the diathesis to develop the disorder when faced with stressful events.

14.4 Anxiety Disorders

Everybody experiences anxiety from time to time. Although anxiety is closely related to fear, the two states possess important differences.

Flash Forward

Ready to dig into the vocabulary? Get some practice with this Hawkes Verified Quizlet set (hawkes.biz/psych14q4)!

🖼 **Figure 1:** Fear and anxiety are related but different concepts.

Although anxiety is unpleasant to most people, it is important to our health, safety, and well-being. Anxiety motivates us to take actions—such as preparing for exams, watching our weight, and showing up to work on time—that enable us to avert potential future problems. Anxiety also motivates us to avoid certain things—such as running up debts and engaging in illegal activities—that could lead to future trouble. Most individuals' level and duration of anxiety approximates the magnitude of the potential threat they face. For example, suppose a 38 year old who wants to marry is concerned about the possibility of having to settle for a spouse who is less attractive and educated than desired. This person likely would experience anxiety of greater intensity and duration than would a 21-year-old college junior who is having trouble finding a date for a formal.

✍ On Your Own

What causes you anxiety on a daily basis? Rank these occurrences from most anxiety-inducing to least anxiety-inducing.

Most Anxiety-Inducing Daily Events

Least Anxiety-Inducing Daily Events

Some people, however, experience anxiety that is excessive, persistent, and greatly out of proportion to the actual threat; if one's anxiety has a disruptive influence on one's life, this is a strong indicator that the individual is experiencing an anxiety disorder.

Anxiety disorders are characterized by excessive and persistent fear and anxiety and by related disturbances in behavior (APA, 2013). Although anxiety is universally experienced, anxiety disorders cause considerable distress. As a group, anxiety disorders are common: approximately 25%–30% of the U.S. population meets the criteria for at least one anxiety disorder during their lifetime (Kessler et al., 2005). Also, these disorders appear to be much more common in women than they are in men; within a 12-month period, around 23% of women and 14% of men will experience at least one anxiety disorder (National Comorbidity Survey, 2007). Anxiety disorders are the most frequently occurring class of mental disorders and are often comorbid with each other and with other mental disorders (Kessler, Ruscio, Shear, & Wittchen, 2009).

Specific Phobia

Phobia is a Greek word that means "fear." A person diagnosed with a **specific phobia** (formerly known as simple **phobia**) experiences excessive, distressing, and persistent fear or anxiety about a specific object or situation (such as animals, enclosed spaces, elevators, or flying) (APA, 2013). Even though people realize their level of fear and anxiety in relation to the phobic stimulus is irrational, some people with a specific phobia may go to great lengths to avoid the phobic stimulus (the object or situation that triggers the fear and anxiety). Typically, the fear and anxiety a phobic stimulus elicits is disruptive to the person's life. For example, a man with a phobia of flying might refuse to accept a job that requires frequent air travel, thus negatively affecting his career. Clinicians who have worked with people who have specific phobias have encountered many kinds of phobias, some of which are shown in Table 1.

Phobia	Feared Object or Situation
Acrophobia	heights
Aerophobia	flying
Arachnophobia	spiders
Claustrophobia	enclosed spaces
Cynophobia	dogs
Hematophobia	blood
Ophidiophobia	snakes
Taphophobia	being buried alive
Trypanophobia	injections
Xenophobia	strangers

Table 1: Specific Phobias

Reflection Question

What would your life be like if you had a severe phobia of elevators?

Specific phobias are common; in the United States, around 12.5% of the population will meet the criteria for a specific phobia at some point in their lifetime (Kessler et al., 2005). One type of phobia, **agoraphobia**, is listed in the DSM-5 as a separate anxiety disorder. Agoraphobia, which literally means "fear of the marketplace," is characterized by intense fear, anxiety, and avoidance of situations in which it might be difficult to escape or receive help if one experiences symptoms of a panic attack (a state of extreme anxiety that we will discuss shortly). These situations include public transportation, open spaces (parking lots), enclosed spaces (stores), crowds, or being outside the home alone (APA, 2013). About 1.4% of Americans experience agoraphobia during their lifetime (Kessler et al., 2005).

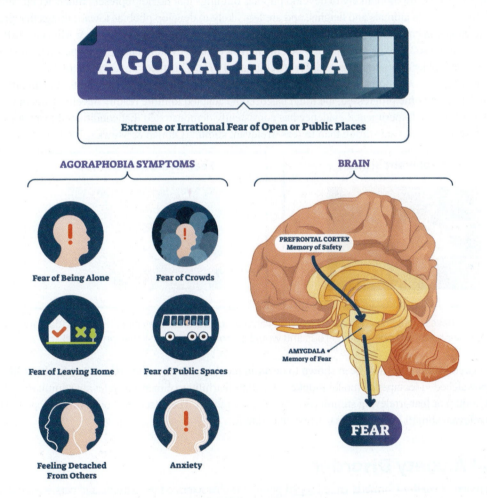

Figure 2: Agoraphobia is the extreme fear of places or situations that might induce panic or helplessness.

Acquisition of Phobias through Learning

Many theories suggest that phobias develop through learning. Rachman (1977) proposed that phobias can be acquired through three major learning pathways. The first pathway is through classical conditioning. Remember that classical conditioning is a form of learning in which a previously neutral stimulus is paired with an unconditioned stimulus (UCS) that reflexively elicits an unconditioned response (UCR), eliciting the same response through its association with the unconditioned stimulus. The response is called a conditioned

Further Resources

Many people have heard of phobias, but they may not realize just how strange some phobias are. Check out this video (hawkes.biz/phobias) about unusual phobias.

response (CR). An example of classical conditioning of a phobia might include a child who has been bitten by a dog; she may come to fear dogs because of her past association with pain. In this case, the dog bite is the UCS, and the fear it elicits is the UCR. Because a dog was associated with the bite, any dog may come to serve as a conditioned stimulus, thereby eliciting fear; the fear the child experiences around dogs then becomes a CR.

Figure 3: Fear is theorized as an evolutionary response to dangerous situations.

The second pathway of phobia acquisition is through vicarious learning, such as modeling. For example, a child who observes his cousin react fearfully to spiders may later express the same fears even though spiders have never presented any danger to him. This phenomenon has been observed in both humans and nonhuman primates (Olsson & Phelps, 2007). A study of laboratory-reared monkeys readily acquired a fear of snakes after observing wild-reared monkeys react fearfully to snakes (Mineka & Cook, 1993).

The third pathway is through verbal transmission or information. For example, a child whose parents, siblings, friends, and classmates constantly tell her how disgusting and dangerous snakes are may come to acquire a fear of snakes.

Interestingly, people are more likely to develop phobias of things that do not represent much actual danger to themselves, such as animals and heights, and are less likely to develop phobias toward things that present legitimate danger in contemporary society, such as motorcycles and weapons (Öhman & Mineka, 2001). Why might this be so? One theory suggests that the human brain is evolutionarily predisposed to more readily associate certain objects or situations with fear (Seligman, 1971). This theory argues that throughout our evolutionary history, our ancestors associated certain stimuli (e.g., snakes, spiders, heights, and thunder) with potential danger. As time progressed, the mind has become adapted to more readily develop fears of these things than of others. Experimental evidence has consistently demonstrated that conditioned fears develop more readily to fear-relevant stimuli than to fear-irrelevant stimuli (Öhman & Mineka, 2001).

Fear-Relevant Stimuli

Fear-Irrelevant Stimuli

Figure 4: Snakes would be considered fear-relevant stimuli because they can pose an actual threat. Flowers, on the other hand, are not as dangerous and would be considered fear-irrelevant stimuli.

Such prepared learning has also been shown to occur in monkeys. In one study (Cook & Mineka, 1989), monkeys watched videotapes of model monkeys reacting fearfully to either fear-relevant stimuli (toy snakes or a toy crocodile) or fear-irrelevant stimuli (flowers or a toy rabbit). The observer monkeys developed fears of the fear-relevant stimuli but not the fear-irrelevant stimuli.

Social Anxiety Disorder

Social anxiety disorder (formerly called social phobia) is characterized by extreme and persistent fear or anxiety and avoidance of social situations in which the person could potentially be evaluated negatively by others (APA, 2013). As with specific phobias, social anxiety disorder is common in the United States; a little over 12% of all Americans experience social anxiety disorder during their lifetime (Kessler et al., 2005).

The heart of the fear and anxiety in social anxiety disorder is the person's concern that he may act in a humiliating or embarrassing way, such as appearing foolish, showing symptoms of anxiety (blushing), or doing or saying something that might lead to rejection (such as offending others).

Group Activity

We all have moments of social anxiety, whether it be fear of an upcoming speaking engagement or jitters about meeting new people. How can you know if your feelings of social anxiety qualify as a disorder? Discuss in a small group with your classmates.

Figure 5: Problematic situations can include public situations, which might elicit fear or panic.

Although many people become anxious in social situations like public speaking, the fear, anxiety, and avoidance experienced in social anxiety disorder are highly distressing and lead to serious impairments in life. Adults with this disorder are more likely to experience lower educational attainment and lower earnings (Katzelnick et al., 2001), perform more poorly at work and are more likely to be unemployed (Moitra, Beard, Weisberg, & Keller, 2011), and report greater dissatisfaction with their family lives, friends, leisure activities, and income (Stein & Kean, 2000).

When people with social anxiety disorder are unable to avoid situations that provoke anxiety, they typically perform **safety behaviors**: mental or behavioral acts that reduce anxiety in social situations by reducing the chance of negative social outcomes.

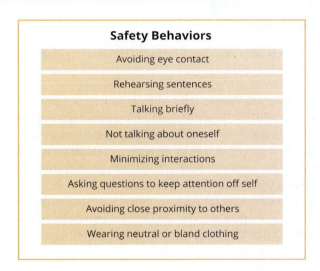

Figure 6: Safety behaviors are behaviors that individuals with social anxiety disorder engage in to lessen the anxiety.

Although these behaviors are intended to prevent the person with social anxiety disorder from doing something awkward that might draw criticism, these actions usually exacerbate the problem because they do not allow the individual to disconfirm his negative beliefs, often eliciting rejection and other negative reactions from others (Alden & Bieling, 1998).

People with social anxiety disorder may resort to self-medication, such as drinking alcohol, as a means to avert the anxiety symptoms they experience in social situations (Battista & Kocovski, 2010). The use of alcohol when faced with such situations may become negatively reinforcing: encouraging individuals with social anxiety disorder to turn to the substance whenever they experience anxiety symptoms. The tendency to use alcohol as a coping mechanism for social anxiety, however, can come with a hefty price tag: a number of large scale studies have reported a high rate of comorbidity between social anxiety disorder and alcohol use disorder (Morris, Stewart, & Ham, 2005).

Figure 7: Substance abuse is not a healthy coping mechanism for social anxiety.

As with specific phobias, it is highly probable that the fears inherent to social anxiety disorder can develop through conditioning experiences. For example, a child who is subjected to early unpleasant social experiences (e.g., bullying at school) may develop negative social images of herself that become activated later in anxiety-provoking situations (Hackmann, Clark, & McManus, 2000).

Figure 8: It seems that severe teasing as a child can lead to conditioning that develops into social anxiety disorder or panic disorder.

One of the most well-established risk factors for developing social anxiety disorder is behavioral inhibition (Clauss & Blackford, 2012). Behavioral inhibition is thought to be an inherited trait, and it is characterized by a consistent tendency to show fear and restraint when presented with unfamiliar people or situations (Kagan, Reznick, & Snidman, 1988). Behavioral inhibition is displayed very early in life; behaviorally inhibited toddlers and children respond with great caution and restraint in unfamiliar situations, and they are often timid, fearful, and shy around unfamiliar people (Fox, Henderson, Marshall, Nichols, & Ghera, 2005). A recent statistical review of studies demonstrated that behavioral inhibition was associated with more than a sevenfold increase in the risk of development of social anxiety disorder, demonstrating that behavioral inhibition is a major risk factor for the disorder (Clauss & Blackford, 2012).

Panic Disorder

Imagine that you are at the mall one day with your friends, and—suddenly and inexplicably—you begin sweating and trembling, your heart starts pounding, you have trouble breathing, and you start to feel dizzy and nauseous. This episode lasts for 10 minutes and is terrifying because you start to think that you are going to die. When you visit your doctor the following morning and describe what happened, she tells you that you have experienced a panic attack (Figure 9). If you experience another one of these episodes two weeks later and worry for a month or more that similar episodes will occur in the future, it is likely that you have developed panic disorder.

Figure 9: Some of the physical manifestations of a panic attack are shown. People may experience sweating, trembling, feelings of faintness, or a fear of losing control, among other symptoms.

People with **panic disorder** experience recurrent (more than one) and unexpected panic attacks, along with at least one month of persistent concern about additional panic attacks, worry over the consequences of the attacks, or self-defeating changes in behavior related to the attacks (e.g., avoidance of exercise or unfamiliar situations) (APA, 2013). As is the case with other anxiety disorders, the panic attacks cannot result from the physiological effects of drugs and other substances, a medical condition, or another mental disorder. A **panic attack** is defined as a period of extreme fear or discomfort that develops abruptly and reaches a peak within 10 minutes. Its symptoms include accelerated heart rate, sweating, trembling, choking sensations, hot flashes or chills, dizziness or lightheadedness, fears of losing control or going crazy, and fears of dying (APA, 2013). Sometimes panic attacks are expected, occurring in response to specific environmental triggers (such as being in a tunnel); other times, these episodes are unexpected and emerge randomly (such as when relaxing). According to the DSM-5, the person must experience unexpected panic attacks to qualify for a diagnosis of panic disorder.

Experiencing a panic attack is often terrifying. Rather than recognizing the symptoms of a panic attack merely as signs of intense anxiety, individuals with panic disorder often misinterpret them as a sign that something is intensely wrong internally (thinking, for example, that the pounding heart represents an impending heart attack). Panic attacks can occasionally precipitate trips to the emergency room because several symptoms of panic attacks are, in fact, similar to those associated with heart problems (Root, 2000).

Components of Emotion

Figure 10: The symptoms of a panic attack and a heart attack are similar.

Unsurprisingly, those with panic disorder fear future attacks and may become preoccupied with modifying their behavior in an effort to avoid future panic attacks. For this reason, panic disorder is often characterized as fear of fear (Goldstein & Chambless, 1978).

Panic attacks themselves are not mental disorders. Indeed, around 23% of Americans experience isolated panic attacks in their lives without meeting the criteria for panic disorder (Kessler et al., 2006), indicating that panic attacks are fairly common. Panic disorder is, of course, much less common, afflicting 4.7% of Americans during their lifetime (Kessler et al., 2005). Many people with panic disorder develop agoraphobia, which is marked by fear and avoidance of situations in which escape might be difficult or help might not be available if one were to develop symptoms of a panic attack. People with panic disorder often experience a comorbid disorder, such as other anxiety disorders or major depressive disorder (APA, 2013).

Researchers are not entirely sure what causes panic disorder. Children are at a higher risk of developing panic disorder if their parents have the disorder (Biederman et al., 2001), and family and twin studies indicate that the heritability of panic disorder is around 43% (Hettema, Neale, & Kendler, 2001). The exact genes and gene functions involved in this disorder, however, are not well-understood (APA, 2013). Neurobiological theories of panic disorder suggest that a region of the brain called the **locus coeruleus** may play a role in this disorder. Located in the brainstem, the locus coeruleus is the brain's major source of norepinephrine, a neurotransmitter that triggers the body's fight-or-flight response. Activation of the locus coeruleus is associated with anxiety and fear, and research with nonhuman primates has shown that stimulating the locus coeruleus either electrically or through drugs produces panic-like symptoms (Charney et al., 1990). Such findings have led to the theory that panic disorder may be caused by abnormal norepinephrine activity in the locus coeruleus (Bremner, Krystal, Southwick, & Charney, 1996).

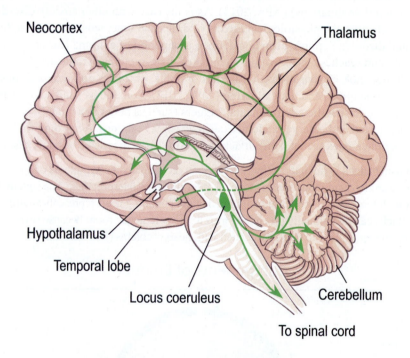

📷 **Figure 11:** The locus coeruleus is the brain's major source of norepinephrine.

Group Activity

In a small group, discuss why it makes sense that the locus coeruleus is known as an "alarm center."

Conditioning theories of panic disorder propose that panic attacks are classical conditioning responses to subtle bodily sensations resembling those normally occurring when one is anxious or frightened (Bouton, Mineka, & Barlow, 2001). For example, consider a child who has asthma. An acute asthma attack produces sensations, such as shortness of breath, coughing, and chest tightness, that typically elicit fear and anxiety. Later, when the child experiences subtle symptoms that resemble the frightening symptoms of earlier asthma attacks (such as shortness of breath after climbing stairs), he may become anxious, fearful, and then experience a panic attack. In this situation, the subtle symptoms would represent a conditioned stimulus, and the panic attack would be a conditioned response. The finding that panic disorder is nearly three times as frequent among people with asthma as it is among people without asthma (Weiser, 2007) supports the possibility that panic disorder has the potential to develop through classical conditioning.

Cognitive factors may play an integral part in panic disorder. Generally, cognitive theories (Clark, 1996) argue that those with panic disorder are prone to interpret ordinary bodily sensations catastrophically, and these fearful interpretations set the stage for panic attacks. For example, a person might detect bodily changes that are routinely triggered by innocuous events such getting up from a seated position (dizziness), exercising (increased heart rate, shortness of breath), or drinking a large cup of coffee (increased heart rate, trembling). The individual interprets these subtle bodily changes catastrophically ("Maybe I'm having a heart attack!"). Such interpretations create fear and anxiety, which trigger additional physical symptoms; subsequently, the person experiences a panic attack. Support of this contention rests with findings that people with more severe catastrophic thoughts about sensations have more frequent and severe panic attacks, and among those with panic disorder, reducing catastrophic cognitions about their sensations is as effective as medication in reducing panic attacks (Good & Hinton, 2009).

🖼 **Figure 12:** There are physical and mental stimulations that can result in a panic attack.

Generalized Anxiety Disorder

Alex was always worried about many things. He worried that his children would drown when they played at the beach. Each time he left the house, he worried that an electrical short circuit would start a fire in his home. He worried that his wife would lose her job at the prestigious law firm. He worried that his daughter's minor staph infection could turn into a massive life-threatening condition. These and other worries constantly weighed heavily on Alex's mind, so much so that they made it difficult for him to make decisions and often left him feeling tense, irritable, and worn out. One night, Alex's wife was to drive their son home from a soccer game. However, his wife stayed after the game and talked with some of the other parents, resulting in her arriving home 45 minutes late. Alex had tried to call her cell phone three or four times, but he could not get through because the soccer field did not have a signal. Extremely worried, Alex eventually called the police, convinced that his wife and son had not arrived home because they had been in a terrible car accident.

Alex suffers from **generalized anxiety disorder**: a relatively continuous state of excessive, uncontrollable, and pointless worry and apprehension. People with generalized anxiety disorder often worry about routine, everyday things even though their concerns are unjustified (Figure 13). For example, an individual may worry about her health and finances, the health of family members, the safety of her children, or minor matters (e.g., being late for an appointment) without having any legitimate reason for doing so (APA, 2013).

Figure 13: Worry is a defining feature of generalized anxiety disorder.

Diagnosis of Generalized Anxiety Disorder

Primary Symptom		Three of the following
Diffuse worrying that happens most days for at least 6 months	**and**	Restlessness
		Difficulty concentrating
		Fatigue easily
		Muscle tension
		Irritability
		Sleep difficulties

📷 **Figure 14:** Worry must occur consistently for a period of six months, and additional symptoms must occur to be diagnosed with a generalized anxiety disorder.

About 5.7% of the U.S. population will develop symptoms of generalized anxiety disorder during their lifetime (Kessler et al., 2005), and females are 2 times as likely as males to experience the disorder (APA, 2013). Generalized anxiety disorder is highly comorbid with mood disorders and other anxiety disorders (Noyes, 2001), and it tends to be chronic. Also, generalized anxiety disorder appears to increase the risk for heart attacks and strokes, especially in people with preexisting heart conditions (Martens et al., 2010).

Although there have been few investigations aimed at determining the heritability of generalized anxiety disorder, a summary of available family and twin studies suggests that genetic factors play a modest role in the disorder (Hettema et al., 2001). Cognitive theories of generalized anxiety disorder suggest that worry represents a mental strategy to avoid more powerful negative emotions (Aikins & Craske, 2001), perhaps stemming from earlier unpleasant or traumatic experiences. Indeed, one longitudinal study found that childhood maltreatment was strongly related to the development of this disorder during adulthood (Moffitt et al., 2007); worrying might distract people from remembering painful childhood experiences.

Summary

Anxiety disorders are a group of disorders in which a person experiences excessive, persistent, and distressing fear and anxiety that interferes with normal functioning. Anxiety disorders include specific phobia (a specific, unrealistic fear), social anxiety disorder (extreme fear and avoidance of social situations), panic disorder (sudden, overwhelming panic even though there is no apparent reason to be frightened), agoraphobia (an intense fear and avoidance of situations in which it might be difficult to escape), and generalized anxiety disorder (a relatively continuous state of tension, apprehension, and dread).

14.5 Obsessive-Compulsive and Related Disorders

Flash Forward

Ready to dig into the vocabulary? Get some practice with this Hawkes Verified Quizlet set (hawkes.biz/psych14q5)!

Obsessive-compulsive and related disorders are a group of overlapping disorders that generally involve intrusive, unpleasant thoughts and repetitive behaviors. Many of us experience unwanted thoughts from time to time (e.g., craving double cheeseburgers when dieting), and many of us engage in repetitive behaviors on occasion (e.g., pacing when nervous). However, obsessive-compulsive and related disorders elevate the unwanted thoughts and repetitive behaviors to a status so intense that these cognitions and activities disrupt daily life. Included in this category are obsessive-compulsive disorder (OCD), body dysmorphic disorder, and hoarding disorder.

Obsessive-Compulsive Disorder

People with **obsessive-compulsive disorder (OCD)** experience thoughts and urges that are intrusive and unwanted (obsessions) and/or the need to engage in repetitive behaviors or mental acts (compulsions). Obsessions are characterized as persistent, unintentional, and unwanted thoughts and urges that are highly intrusive, unpleasant, and distressing (APA, 2013).

Compulsions are repetitive and ritualistic acts that are typically carried out primarily to minimize the distress that obsessions trigger or to reduce the likelihood of a feared event (APA, 2013). Compulsions characteristic of OCD are not performed out of pleasure, nor are they connected in a realistic way to the source of the distress or feared event. The following table outlines some of the most common obsessions and related behaviors or compulsions.

Figure 1: Obsessive-compulsive and related disorders cause more disruption than a typical desire for organization.

Obsessions	Example	Compulsions
Concerns about germs and contamination	"My hands still have germs on them."	Washing hands excessively
Doubts	"Did I turn the water off?"	Checking to see if the sink is on several times
Order and symmetry	"I need the spoons in the tray to be arranged in a certain way."	Taking time to organize things in a certain way
Urges that are aggressive or lustful	"I need to avoid becoming violent."	Hiding everyday objects that might be used to hurt others

✐ On Your Own

Using the following table, identify three obsessions and a related compulsion.

#	Obsession	Compulsion
1		
2		
3		

Figure 2: Repetitive hand washing is one common compulsion among those with obsessive-compulsive disorder.

Approximately 2.3% of the U.S. population will experience OCD in their lifetime (Ruscio, Stein, Chiu, & Kessler, 2010), and if left untreated, OCD tends to be a chronic condition creating lifelong interpersonal and psychological problems (Norberg, Calamari, Cohen, & Riemann, 2008). People with first degree relatives who have OCD are five times more likely to have the same diagnosis than those who do not (Nestadt et al., 2000).

Body Dysmorphic Disorder

Figure 3: Physical flaws are disproportionately magnified or fabricated for people who suffer from body dysmorphic disorder.

An individual with **body dysmorphic disorder** is preoccupied with a perceived flaw in her physical appearance that is either nonexistent or barely noticeable to other people (APA, 2013). These perceived physical defects cause the person to think she is unattractive, ugly, hideous, or deformed. The preoccupation with imagined physical flaws drives the person to engage in repetitive and ritualistic behavioral and mental acts, such as constantly looking in the mirror, trying to hide the offending body part, and, in some extreme cases, cosmetic surgery (Phillips, 2005). An estimated 2.4% of the adults in the United States meet the criteria for body dysmorphic disorder, with slightly higher rates in women than in men (APA, 2013).

> ### Reflection Questions
>
> What do you think is the difference between an individual who has body dysmorphic disorder and someone who is just very concerned with how they look?

Hoarding Disorder

People with **hoarding disorder** cannot bear to part with personal possessions, regardless of how valueless or useless these possessions are. As a result, these individuals accumulate excessive amounts of usually worthless items that clutter their living areas (Figure 4). Often, the quantity of cluttered items is so excessive that the person is unable to use his kitchen or sleep in his bed. People who suffer from this disorder have great difficulty parting with items because they believe the items might be of some later use or because they form sentimental attachments to the items (APA, 2013). Remember, a diagnosis of hoarding disorder is made only if the hoarding is not caused by another medical condition and if the hoarding is not a symptom of another disorder (e.g., schizophrenia) (APA, 2013).

Figure 4: Those who suffer from hoarding disorder have great difficulty in discarding possessions, usually resulting in an accumulation of items that clutter living or work areas.

> **Reflection Questions**
>
> How do you think hoarding disorder relates to OCD?

Causes of OCD

The results of family and twin studies suggest that OCD has a moderate genetic component. The disorder is five times more frequent in the first-degree relatives of people with OCD than in people without the disorder (Nestadt et al., 2000). Additionally, the concordance rate of OCD among identical twins is around 57%; however, the concordance rate for fraternal twins is 22% (Bolton, Rijsdijk, O'Connor, Perrin, & Eley, 2007). Studies have implicated about two dozen potential genes that may be involved in OCD; these genes regulate the function of three neurotransmitters: serotonin, dopamine, and glutamate (Pauls, 2010). Many of these studies included small sample sizes and have yet to be replicated. Thus, additional research needs to be done in this area.

A brain region that is believed to play a critical role in OCD is the **orbitofrontal cortex** (Kopell & Greenberg, 2008), an area of the frontal lobe involved in learning and decision-making (Rushworth, Noonan, Boorman, Walton, & Behrens, 2011) (Figure 5). In people with OCD, the orbitofrontal cortex becomes especially hyperactive when they are provoked with tasks in which, for example, they are asked to look at a photo of a toilet or of pictures hanging crookedly on a wall (Simon, Kaufmann, Müsch, Kischkel, & Kathmann, 2010). The orbitofrontal cortex is part of a series of brain regions that, collectively, is called the OCD circuit; this circuit consists of several interconnected regions that influence the perceived emotional value of stimuli and the selection of both behavioral and cognitive responses (Graybiel & Rauch, 2000). As with the orbitofrontal cortex, other regions of the OCD circuit show heightened activity during symptom provocation (Rotge et al., 2008), which suggests that abnormalities in these regions may produce the symptoms of OCD (Saxena, Bota, & Brody, 2001). Consistent with this explanation, people with OCD show a substantially higher degree of connectivity of the orbitofrontal cortex and other regions of the OCD circuit than do those without OCD (Beucke et al., 2013).

Anterior cingulate cortex
(Hoarding disorder)

Prefrontal cortex
(Body dysmorphic
disorder)

Orbitofrontal cortex
(Obsessive-compulsive
disorder)

Figure 5: Different regions of the brain may be associated with different psychological disorders.

The findings discussed previously were based on imaging studies, and they highlight the potential importance of brain dysfunction in OCD. However, one important limitation of these findings is the inability to explain differences in obsessions and compulsions. Another limitation is that the correlational relationship between neurological abnormalities and OCD symptoms cannot imply causation (Abramowitz & Siqueland, 2013).

♀ Connect the Concepts

Conditioning and OCD

The symptoms of OCD have been theorized to be learned responses, acquired and sustained as the result of a combination of two forms of learning: classical conditioning and operant conditioning (Mowrer, 1960; Steinmetz, Tracy, & Green, 2001). Specifically, the acquisition of OCD may occur first as the result of classical conditioning, whereby a neutral stimulus becomes associated with an unconditioned stimulus that provokes anxiety or distress. When an individual has acquired this association, subsequent encounters with the neutral stimulus trigger anxiety, including obsessive thoughts; the anxiety and obsessive thoughts (which are now a conditioned response) may persist until she identifies some strategy to relieve it. Relief may take the form of a ritualistic behavior or mental activity that, when enacted repeatedly, reduces the anxiety. Such efforts to relieve anxiety constitute an example of negative reinforcement (a form of operant conditioning). Recall from the chapter on learning that negative reinforcement involves the strengthening of behavior through its ability to remove something unpleasant or aversive. Hence, compulsive acts observed in OCD may be sustained because they are negatively reinforcing, in the sense that they reduce anxiety triggered by a conditioned stimulus.

Suppose an individual with OCD experiences obsessive thoughts about germs, contamination, and disease whenever she encounters a doorknob. What might have constituted a viable unconditioned stimulus? Also, what would constitute the conditioned stimulus, unconditioned response, and conditioned response? What kinds of compulsive behaviors might we expect, and how do they reinforce themselves? What is decreased? Additionally, and from the standpoint of learning theory, how might the symptoms of OCD be treated successfully?

🖼 **Figure 6:** Compulsive acts offer a sense of relief for individuals with obsessive-compulsive disorder.

Summary

Obsessive-compulsive and related disorders are a group of DSM-5 disorders that overlap somewhat in that they each involve intrusive thoughts and/or repetitive behaviors. Perhaps the most recognized of these disorders is obsessive-compulsive disorder, in which a person is obsessed with unwanted, unpleasant thoughts and/or compulsively engages in repetitive behaviors or mental acts, perhaps as a way of coping with the obsessions. Body dysmorphic disorder is characterized by the individual becoming excessively preoccupied with one or more perceived flaws in his physical appearance that are either nonexistent or unnoticeable to others. Preoccupation with the perceived physical defects causes the person to experience significant anxiety regarding how he appears to others. Hoarding disorder is characterized by persistent difficulty in discarding or parting with objects, regardless of their actual value, often resulting in the accumulation of items that clutter and congest her living area.

Flash Forward

Ready to dig into the vocabulary? Get some practice with this Hawkes Verified Quizlet set (hawkes.biz/psych14q6)!

14.6 Posttraumatic Stress Disorder

Extremely stressful or traumatic events, such as combat, natural disasters, and terrorist attacks, place the people who experience them at an increased risk for developing psychological disorders such as **posttraumatic stress disorder (PTSD)**. Throughout much of the 20th century, this disorder was called *shell shock* and *combat neurosis* because its symptoms were observed in soldiers who had engaged in wartime combat. By the late 1970s, it had become clear that women who had experienced sexual traumas (e.g., rape, domestic battery, and incest) often experienced the same set of symptoms as did soldiers (Herman, 1997). The term *posttraumatic stress disorder* was developed given that these symptoms could happen to anyone who experienced psychological trauma.

A Broader Definition of PTSD

PTSD was listed among the anxiety disorders in previous DSM editions. In DSM-5, it is now listed among a group called Trauma-and-Stressor-Related Disorders. For a person to be diagnosed with PTSD, she be must exposed to, witness, or experience the details of a traumatic experience (e.g., a first responder), one that involves "actual or threatened death, serious injury, or sexual violence" (APA, 2013, p. 271). These experiences can include such events as combat, threatened or actual physical attack, sexual assault, natural disasters, terrorist attacks, and automobile accidents. This criterion makes PTSD the only disorder listed in the DSM in which a cause (extreme trauma) is explicitly specified.

Symptoms of PTSD include intrusive and distressing memories of the event, **flashbacks** (states that can last from a few seconds to several days, during which the individual relives the event and behaves as if the event were occurring at that moment [APA, 2013]), avoidance of stimuli connected to the event, persistently negative emotional states (e.g., fear, anger, guilt, and shame), feelings of detachment from others, irritability, proneness toward outbursts, and an exaggerated startle response (jumpiness). For PTSD to be diagnosed, these symptoms must occur for at least one month.

Roughly 7% of adults in the United States, including 9.7% of women and 3.6% of men, experience PTSD in their lifetime (National Comorbidity Survey, 2007), with higher rates among people exposed to mass trauma and people whose jobs involve duty-related trauma exposure (e.g., police officers, firefighters, and emergency medical personnel) (APA, 2013). Nearly 21% of residents of areas affected by Hurricane Katrina suffered from PTSD one year following the hurricane (Kessler et al., 2008), and 12.6% of Manhattan residents were observed as having PTSD two to three years after the 9/11 terrorist attacks (DiGrande et al., 2008).

📷 **Figure 1:** Here a NYPD firefighter is shown at Ground Zero after the 9/11 terrorist attacks.

✎ **On Your Own**

Which of the following people meets the diagnostic criteria for PTSD?

☐ A combat veteran who has experienced nightmares about the events

☐ An individual who experienced the 9/11 terrorist attacks and has had difficulty sleeping since then

☐ An individual who was a victim of rape that has become persistently more irritable, avoids places and smells that remind her of the event, is detached from others, and experiences fear and shame persistently since the event, which occurred over a month ago

---

Risk Factors for PTSD

Of course, not everyone who experiences a traumatic event will go on to develop PTSD. The following are some factors that impact one's ability to suffer from PTSD:

- Greater trauma severity

- Lack of immediate social support (comfort, advice, and assistance received from relatives, friends, and neighbors) (Koenen, Stellman, Stellman, & Sommer, 2003)

- More subsequent life stress (Brewin, Andrews, & Valentine, 2000)

- Less involvement in the community (Koenen, Stellman, Stellman, & Sommer, 2003)

- Experience traumatic events that involve harm by others (e.g., combat, rape, and sexual molestation) (Kessler, Sonnega, Bromet, Hughes, & Nelson, 1995)

- Gender (females are more likely to develop PTSD)

- Low socioeconomic status

- Low intelligence

- Personal history of mental disorders

- History of childhood adversity (abuse or other trauma during childhood)

- Family history of mental disorders (Brewin et al., 2000)

> **Reflection Questions**
>
> Why do you think females are more likely to receive a PTSD diagnosis than men?

Support for Sufferers of PTSD

Research has shown that social support following a traumatic event can reduce the likelihood of PTSD (Ozer, Best, Lipsey, & Weiss, 2003). Social support is often defined as the comfort, advice, and assistance received from relatives, friends, and neighbors. Social support can help individuals cope during difficult times by allowing them to discuss feelings and experiences and by providing a sense of being loved and appreciated. A 14-year study of 1,377 American Legionnaires who had served in the Vietnam War found that those who perceived less social support when they came home were more likely to develop PTSD than were those who perceived greater support (Figure 2). In addition, those who became involved in the community were less likely to develop PTSD, and they were more likely to experience a remission of PTSD than were those who were less involved (Koenen, Stellman, Stellman, & Sommer, 2003).

Figure 2: PTSD was first recognized in soldiers who had engaged in combat. Research has shown that strong social support decreases the risk of PTSD. This person stands at the Vietnam Veterans Memorial Wall in Washington, D.C.

Learning and the Development of PTSD

PTSD learning models suggest that some symptoms are developed and maintained through classical conditioning. The traumatic event may act as an unconditioned stimulus that elicits an unconditioned response characterized by extreme fear and anxiety. Cognitive, emotional, physiological, and environmental cues accompanying or related to the event are conditioned stimuli. These traumatic reminders evoke conditioned responses (extreme fear and anxiety) similar to those caused by the event itself (Nader, 2001). A person who was in the vicinity of the Twin Towers during the 9/11 terrorist attacks and who developed PTSD may display excessive hypervigilance and distress when planes fly overhead; this behavior constitutes a conditioned response to the traumatic reminder (conditioned stimulus of the sight and sound of an airplane). Differences in how conditionable individuals are help to explain differences in the development and maintenance of PTSD symptoms (Pittman, 1988). Conditioning studies demonstrate facilitated acquisition of conditioned responses and delayed extinction of conditioned responses in people with PTSD (Orr et al., 2000).

Cognitive factors are important in the development and maintenance of PTSD. One model suggests that two key processes are crucial: disturbances in memory for the event and negative appraisals of the trauma and its aftermath (Ehlers & Clark, 2000). According to this theory, some people who experience traumas do not form coherent memories of the trauma; memories of the traumatic event are poorly encoded and, thus, are fragmented, disorganized, and lacking in detail. Therefore, these individuals are unable to remember the event in a way that gives it meaning and context. A rape victim who cannot coherently remember the event may remember only bits and pieces (e.g., the attacker repeatedly telling her she is stupid); because she was unable to develop a fully integrated memory, the fragmentary memory tends to stand out. Although unable to retrieve a complete memory of the event, she may be haunted by intrusive fragments involuntarily triggered by stimuli associated with the event (e.g., memories of the attacker's comments when encountering a person who resembles the attacker). This interpretation fits previously discussed material concerning PTSD and conditioning. The model also proposes that negative appraisals of the event ("I deserved this because I made stupid choices.") may lead to dysfunctional behavioral strategies (e.g., avoiding social activities where men are likely to be present) that maintain PTSD symptoms by preventing both a change in the nature of the memory and a change in the problematic appraisals.

Figure 3: The paintings are by Marines and sailors who attended art therapy to relieve post-traumatic stress disorder symptoms. During these therapy sessions, participants used a variety of art supplies to express their thoughts, feelings, and memories.

✎ On Your Own

Explain why a combat veteran would get PTSD from the classical conditioning perspective and based on the model that focuses on memory disturbance and negative appraisals of the event.

Conceptualization of PTSD	Response
Classical Conditioning	

Conceptualization of PTSD	Response
Disturbances in Memory/ Negative Appraisals	

Summary

Posttraumatic stress disorder (PTSD) was described through much of the 20th century and was referred to as *shell shock* and *combat neurosis* in the belief that its symptoms were thought to emerge from the stress of active combat. Today, PTSD is defined as a disorder in which the experience of a traumatic or profoundly stressful event, such as combat, sexual assault, or natural disaster, produces a constellation of symptoms that must last for one month or more. These symptoms include intrusive and distressing memories of the event, flashbacks, avoidance of stimuli or situations that are connected to the event, persistently negative emotional states, feeling detached from others, irritability, proneness toward outbursts, and a tendency to be easily startled. Not everyone who experiences a traumatic event will develop PTSD; a variety of risk factors associated with its development have been identified.

Flash Forward

Ready to dig into the vocabulary? Get some practice with this Hawkes Verified Quizlet set (hawkes.biz/psych14q7)!

14.7 Mood Disorders

Blake cries all day and feels that he is worthless, and his life is hopeless. So much so that he cannot get out of bed. Crystal stays up all night, talks very rapidly, and went on a shopping spree in which she spent $3,000 on furniture although she cannot afford it. Maria recently had a baby, and she feels overwhelmed, teary, anxious, and panicked and believes she is a terrible mother—practically every day since the baby was born. All these individuals demonstrate symptoms of a potential mood disorder.

Mood disorders (Figure 1) are characterized by severe disturbances in mood and emotions—most often depression but also mania and elation (Rothschild, 1999).

All of us experience fluctuations in our moods and emotional states, and often these fluctuations are caused by events in our lives. We become elated if our favorite team wins the World Series and dejected if a romantic relationship ends or if we lose our job. At times, we feel fantastic or miserable for no clear reason. People with mood disorders also experience mood fluctuations, but their fluctuations are extreme, distort their outlook on life, and impair their ability to function.

Figure 1: Mood disorders are characterized by massive disruptions in mood. Symptoms can range from the extreme sadness and hopelessness of depression to the extreme elation and irritability of mania.

The DSM-5 lists two general categories of mood disorders. **Depressive disorders** are a group of disorders in which depression is the main feature. *Depression* is a vague term that, in everyday language, refers to an intense and persistent sadness. Depression is a heterogeneous mood state—it consists of a broad spectrum of symptoms that range in severity. Depressed people feel sad, discouraged, and hopeless. These individuals lose interest in activities once enjoyed, often experience a decrease in drives such as hunger and sex, and frequently doubt personal worth. Depressive disorders vary by degree, but this lesson highlights the most well-known: major depressive disorder (sometimes called unipolar depression).

Bipolar and related disorders are a group of disorders in which mania is the defining feature. **Mania** is a state of extreme elation and agitation. When people experience mania, they may become extremely talkative, behave recklessly, or attempt to take on many tasks simultaneously. The most recognized of these disorders is bipolar disorder.

Major Depressive Disorder

According to the DSM-5, the defining symptoms of **major depressive disorder** include "depressed mood most of the day, nearly every day" (feeling sad, empty, hopeless, or appearing tearful to others), and loss of interest and pleasure in usual activities (APA, 2013). In addition to feeling overwhelmingly sad most of each day, people with depression will no longer show interest or enjoyment in activities that previously were gratifying, such as hobbies, sports, sex, social events, time spent with family, and so on. Friends and family members may notice that the person has completely abandoned previously enjoyed hobbies; for example, an avid tennis player who develops major depressive disorder no longer plays tennis (Rothschild, 1999).

To receive a diagnosis of major depressive disorder, one must experience a total of five symptoms for at least a two-week period; these symptoms must cause significant distress or impair normal functioning, and they must not be caused by substances or a medical condition. At least one of the two symptoms mentioned previously must be present, plus any combination of the following symptoms (APA, 2013):

- significant weight loss (when not dieting) or weight gain and/or significant decrease or increase in appetite

- difficulty falling asleep or sleeping too much

- psychomotor agitation (the person is noticeably fidgety and jittery, demonstrated by behaviors like the inability to sit, pacing, hand-wringing, pulling or rubbing of the skin, clothing, or other objects) or psychomotor retardation (the person talks and moves slowly, for example, talking softly, very little, or in a monotone)

- fatigue or loss of energy

- feelings of worthlessness or guilt

- difficulty concentrating and indecisiveness

- **suicidal ideation**: thoughts of death (not just fear of dying), thinking about or planning suicide, or making an actual suicide attempt

📷 **Figure 2:** People who suffer from major depressive disorder may struggle to see a way out.

Major depressive disorder is considered episodic: its symptoms are typically present at their full magnitude for a certain period of time and then gradually abate. Approximately 50%–60% of people who experience an episode of major depressive disorder will have a second episode at some point in the future; those who have had two episodes have a 70% chance of having a third episode, and those who have had three episodes have a 90% chance of having a fourth episode (Rothschild, 1999). Although the episodes can last for months, a majority a people diagnosed with this condition (around 70%) recover within a year. However, a substantial number do not recover; around 12% show serious signs of impairment associated with major depressive disorder after five years (Boland & Keller, 2009). In the long term, many who do recover will still show minor symptoms that fluctuate in their severity (Judd, 2012).

Results of Major Depressive Disorder

Major depressive disorder is a serious and incapacitating condition that can have a devastating effect on the quality of one's life. The person suffering from this disorder lives a profoundly miserable existence that often results in unavailability for work or education, abandonment of promising careers, and lost wages; occasionally, the condition requires hospitalization. The majority of those with major depressive disorder report having faced some kind of discrimination, and many report that having received such treatment has stopped them from initiating close relationships, applying for jobs for which they are qualified, and applying for education or training (Lasalvia et al., 2013). Major depressive disorder also takes a toll on health. Depression is a risk factor for the development of heart disease in healthy patients, as well as adverse cardiovascular outcomes in patients with preexisting heart disease (Whooley, 2006).

📷 **Figure 3:** Major depressive disorder can result in loss of interest and interpersonal relationships.

Risk Factors for Major Depressive Disorder

Major depressive disorder is often referred to as the common cold of psychiatric disorders. Around 6.6% of the U.S. population experiences major depressive disorder each year; 16.9% will experience the disorder during their lifetime (Kessler & Wang, 2009). It is more common among women than among men, affecting approximately 20% of women and 13% of men at some point in their lives (National Comorbidity Survey, 2007). The greater risk among women is not accounted for by a tendency to report symptoms or to seek help more readily, suggesting that gender differences in the rates of major depressive disorder may reflect biological and gender-related environmental experiences (Kessler, 2003).

Lifetime rates of major depressive disorder tend to be highest in North and South America, Europe, and Australia; they are considerably lower in Asian countries (Hasin, Fenton, & Weissman, 2011). The rates of major depressive disorder are higher among younger age cohorts than among older cohorts, perhaps because people in younger age cohorts are more willing to admit depression (Kessler & Wang, 2009).

A number of risk factors are associated with major depressive disorder: unemployment (including homemakers); earning less than $20,000 per year; living in urban areas; or being separated, divorced, or widowed (Hasin et al., 2011). Comorbid disorders include anxiety disorders and substance abuse disorders (Kessler & Wang, 2009).

Subtypes of Depression

The DSM-5 lists several different subtypes of depression. These subtypes—what the DSM-5 refer to as specifiers—are not specific disorders; rather, they are labels used to indicate specific patterns of symptoms or to specify certain periods of time in which the symptoms may be present. One subtype, **seasonal pattern**, applies to situations in which a person experiences the symptoms of major depressive disorder only during a particular time of year (e.g., fall or winter). In everyday language, people often refer to this subtype as the winter blues.

Another subtype, **peripartum onset** (commonly referred to as **postpartum depression**), applies to women who experience major depression during pregnancy or in the four weeks following the birth of their child (APA, 2013). These women often feel very anxious and may even have panic attacks. They may feel guilty, agitated, and be weepy. They may not want to hold or care for their newborn, even in cases in which the pregnancy was desired and intended. In extreme cases, the mother may have feelings of wanting to harm her child or herself. In a horrific illustration, a woman named Andrea Yates, who suffered from extreme peripartum-onset depression (as well as other mental illnesses), drowned her five children in a bathtub (Roche, 2002). Most women with peripartum-onset depression do not physically harm their children, but most do have difficulty being adequate caregivers (Fields, 2010). A surprisingly high number of women experience symptoms of peripartum-onset depression. A study of 10,000 women who had recently given birth found that 14% screened positive for peripartum-onset depression and that nearly 20% reported having thoughts of wanting to harm themselves (Wisner et al., 2013).

People with **persistent depressive disorder** (previously known as dysthymia) experience depressed moods most of the day nearly every day for at least two years, as well as at least two of the other symptoms of major depressive disorder. People with persistent depressive disorder are chronically sad and melancholy but do not meet all the criteria for major depression. However, episodes of full-blown major depressive disorder can occur during persistent depressive disorder (APA, 2013).

🖼 **Figure 4:** Peripartum onset is a surprisingly common experience, and sufferers should not feel marginalized.

🖉 On Your Own

For an individual who has reported feeling hopeless and down for a period of more than two years, which of the following diagnoses could you give them?

☐ Major Depressive Disorder   ☐ Persistent Depressive Disorder   ☐ MDD or PDD

Bipolar Disorder

A person with **bipolar disorder** (commonly known as **manic depression**) often experiences mood states that vacillate between depression and mania; that is, the person's mood is said to alternate from one emotional extreme to the other (in contrast to unipolar, which indicates a persistently sad mood).

> **Reflection Questions**
>
> What do you think might be a challenge in helping a friend or family member with bipolar disorder?

Further Resources

Watch this clip (hawkes.biz/bipolar) from *Jimmy Kimmel Live!* to hear Kanye West discuss his experience with bipolar disorder.

To be diagnosed with bipolar disorder, a person must have experienced a manic episode at least once in his life; although major depressive episodes are common in bipolar disorder, they are not required for a diagnosis (APA, 2013). According to the DSM-5, a **manic episode** is characterized as a "distinct period of abnormally and persistently elevated, expansive, or irritable mood and abnormally and persistently increased activity or energy lasting at least one week," that lasts most of the time each day (APA, 2013, p. 124). During a manic episode, some experience a mood that is almost euphoric and become excessively talkative, sometimes spontaneously starting conversations with strangers; others become excessively irritable and complain or make hostile comments. The person may talk loudly and rapidly, exhibiting **flight of ideas**, abruptly switching from one topic to another. These individuals are easily distracted, which can make a conversation very difficult. They may exhibit grandiosity, in which they experience inflated but unjustified self-esteem and self-confidence. For example, they might quit a job in order to "strike it rich" in the stock market, despite lacking the knowledge, experience, and capital for such an endeavor. They may take on several tasks at the same time (e.g., several time-consuming projects at work) and yet show little, if any, need for sleep; some may go for days without sleep. Patients may also recklessly engage in pleasurable activities that could have harmful consequences, including spending sprees, reckless driving, making foolish investments, excessive gambling, or engaging in sexual encounters with strangers (APA, 2013).

Figure 5: During a manic episode, patients may exhibit reckless behavior.

During a manic episode, individuals usually feel as though they are not ill and do not need treatment. However, the reckless behaviors that often accompany these episodes—which can be antisocial, illegal, or physically threatening to others—may require involuntary hospitalization (APA, 2013). Some patients with bipolar disorder will experience a rapid-cycling subtype, which is characterized by at least four manic episodes (or some combination of at least four manic and major depressive episodes) within one year. People with bipolar disorder usually experience depression following mania. Since people with bipolar disorder can frequently experience depression, suicide rates are extremely high. For example, around 36% of individuals with bipolar disorder attempt suicide once in their life, and approximately 15% to 19% complete it (Novick, Swartz, & Frank, 2010; Newman, 2004).

☑ On Your Own

Which of the following is a behavior that a person in manic state might engage in?

☐ Quitting his job and making a foolish investment trying to "strike it rich"

☐ Not showing up at work because you feel too tired and decide to sleep all day

☐ Having suicidal thoughts

Risk Factors for Bipolar Disorder

Bipolar disorder is considerably less frequent than major depressive disorder. In the United States, 1 out of every 167 people meets the criteria for bipolar disorder each year, and 1 out of 100 meet the criteria within their lifetime (Merikangas et al., 2011). The rates are higher in men than in women, and about half of those with this disorder report onset before the age of 25 (Merikangas et al., 2011). Around 90% of those with bipolar disorder have a comorbid disorder, most often an anxiety disorder or a substance abuse problem. Unfortunately, close to half of the people suffering from bipolar disorder do not receive treatment (Merikangas & Tohen, 2011).

The Biological Basis of Mood Disorders

Mood disorders have been shown to have a strong genetic and biological basis. Relatives of those with major depressive disorder have double the risk of developing major depressive disorder, whereas relatives of patients with bipolar disorder have over nine times the risk (Merikangas et al., 2011). The rate of concordance for major depressive disorder is higher among identical twins than fraternal twins (50% vs. 38%, respectively), as is that of bipolar disorder (67% vs. 16%, respectively), suggesting that genetic factors play a stronger role in bipolar disorder than in major depressive disorder (Merikangas et al. 2011).

People with mood disorders often have imbalances in certain neurotransmitters, particularly norepinephrine and serotonin (Thase, 2009). These neurotransmitters are important regulators of the bodily functions that are disrupted in mood disorders, including appetite, sex drive, sleep, arousal, and mood. Medications that are used to treat major depressive disorder typically boost serotonin and norepinephrine activity, whereas lithium—used in the treatment of bipolar disorder—blocks norepinephrine activity at the synapses (Figure 6).

Synapse   Presynaptic cell

Neurotransmitter released into synapse

Neurotransmitter

Neurotransmitter reuptake inhibitor

Reuptake receptor

Neurotransmitter attached to receptor

Postsynaptic cell

Figure 6: Many medications designed to treat mood disorders work by altering neurotransmitter activity in the neural synapse.

Depression is linked to abnormal activity in several regions of the brain (Fitzgerald, Laird, Maller, & Daskalakis, 2008) including those important in assessing the emotional significance of stimuli and experiencing emotions (amygdala) and in regulating and controlling emotions (like the prefrontal cortex, or PFC) (LeMoult, Castonguay, Joormann, & McAleavey, 2013). Depressed individuals show elevated amygdala activity (Drevets, Bogers, & Raichle, 2002), especially when presented with negative emotional stimuli, such as photos of sad faces (Figure 7) (Surguladze et al., 2005). Interestingly, heightened amygdala activation to negative emotional stimuli among depressed persons occurs even when stimuli are presented outside of conscious awareness (Victor, Furey, Fromm, Öhman, & Drevets, 2010), and it persists even after the negative emotional stimuli are no longer present (Siegle, Thompson, Carter, Steinhauer, & Thase, 2007). Additionally, depressed individuals exhibit less activation in the prefrontal cortex, particularly on the left side (Davidson, Pizzagalli, & Nitschke, 2009). Because the PFC can dampen amygdala activation, thereby enabling one to suppress negative emotions (Phan et al., 2005), decreased activation in certain regions of the PFC may inhibit its ability to override negative emotions that might then lead to more negative mood states (Davidson et al., 2009). These findings suggest that depressed persons are more prone to react to emotionally negative stimuli yet have greater difficulty controlling these reactions.

📷 **Figure 7:** Depressed individuals react to negative emotional stimuli, such as sad faces, with greater amygdala activation than do non-depressed individuals.

Since the 1950s, researchers have noted that depressed individuals have abnormal levels of cortisol, a stress hormone released into the blood by the neuroendocrine system during times of stress (Mackin & Young, 2004). When cortisol is released, the body initiates a fight-or-flight response in reaction to a threat or danger. Many people with depression show elevated cortisol levels (Holsboer & Ising, 2010), especially those reporting a history of early life trauma, such as the loss of a parent or abuse during childhood (Baes, Tofoli, Martins, & Juruena, 2012). Such findings raise the question of whether high cortisol levels are a cause or a consequence of depression. High levels of cortisol are a risk factor for future depression (Halligan, Herbert, Goodyer, & Murray, 2007), and cortisol activates activity in the amygdala while deactivating activity in the PFC (McEwen, 2005)—both brain disturbances are connected to depression. Thus, high cortisol levels may have a causal effect on depression, as well as on its brain function abnormalities (van Praag, 2005). Also, because stress results in increased cortisol release (Michaud, Matheson, Kelly, Anisman, 2008), it is equally reasonable to assume that stress may precipitate depression.

A Diathesis-Stress Model and Major Depressive Disorders

Indeed, it has long been believed that stressful life events can trigger depression, and research has consistently supported this conclusion (Mazure, 1998). Stressful life events include significant losses, such as death of a loved one, divorce or separation, and serious health and money problems; life events such as these often precede the onset of depressive episodes (Brown & Harris, 1989). In particular, exit events—instances in which an important person departs (e.g., a death, divorce or separation, or a family member leaving home)—often occur prior to an episode (Paykel, 2003). Exit events are especially likely to trigger depression if these happenings occur in a way that humiliates or devalues the individual. Consider these findings:

- People who experience the breakup of a relationship initiated by the other person develop major depressive disorder at a rate more than two times that of people who experience the death of a loved one (Kendler, Hettema, Butera, Gardner, & Prescott, 2003).

- People who experienced traumatic stress in childhood are more likely to develop depression at some point in their lives (Kessler, 1997).

- Studies suggest that these stressful events alter the way a specific gene regulates serotonin activity, which may initiate depressive symptoms (Caspi et al., 2003).

Cognitive Theories of Depression

Cognitive theories of depression take the view that depression is triggered by negative thoughts, interpretations, self-evaluations, and expectations (Joormann, 2009). These diathesis-stress models propose that depression is triggered by a "cognitive vulnerability" (negative and maladaptive thinking) and by precipitating stressful life events (Gotlib & Joormann, 2010). Perhaps the most well-known cognitive theory of depression was developed in the 1960s by psychiatrist Aaron Beck, based on clinical observations and supported by research (Beck, 2008). Beck theorized that depression-prone people possess depressive schemas, or mental predispositions to think about most things in a negative way (Beck, 1976). Depressive schemas contain themes of loss, failure, rejection, worthlessness, and inadequacy and may develop early in childhood in response to adverse experiences then remain dormant until they are activated by stressful or negative life events. Depressive schemas prompt dysfunctional and pessimistic thoughts about the self, the world, and the future. Beck believed that this dysfunctional style of thinking is maintained by cognitive biases, or errors in how we process information about ourselves, which lead us to focus on negative aspects of experiences, interpret things negatively, and block positive memories (Beck, 2008).

negative views about the world

negative views about oneself

negative views about the future

Reflection Questions

Have you ever had a negative view about something that may not have been accurate? What was it? Why do you think you didn't look at it positively?

A person whose depressive schema consists of a theme of rejection might be overly attentive to social cues of rejection (more likely to notice another's frown), and he might interpret this cue as a sign of rejection and automatically remember past incidents of rejection. Longitudinal studies have supported Beck's theory, in showing that a preexisting tendency to engage in this negative, self-defeating style of thinking—when combined with life stress—over time predicts the onset of depression (Dozois & Beck, 2008). Cognitive therapies for depression, aimed at changing a depressed person's negative thinking, were developed as an expansion of this theory (Beck, 1976).

Reflection Questions

If you were a therapist, how would you challenge the following statement?

"I am always going to fail, no matter how hard I try."

Figure 8: Hopelessness theory posits that depression can stem from negative thinking.

Another cognitive theory of depression, **hopelessness theory**, postulates that a style of negative thinking leads to a sense of hopelessness, which then leads to depression (Abramson, Metalsky, & Alloy, 1989). According to this theory, hopelessness is an expectation that unpleasant outcomes will occur or that desired outcomes will not occur, and there is nothing one can do to prevent such outcomes. A key assumption of this theory is that hopelessness stems from a tendency to perceive negative life events as having stable ("It's never going to change.") and global ("It's going to affect my whole life.") causes, in contrast to unstable ("It's fixable.") and specific ("It applies only to this particular situation.") causes, especially if these negative life events occur in important life realms, such as relationships, academic achievement, and the like. Suppose a student who wishes to go to law school does poorly on an admissions test. If the student infers negative life events as having stable and global causes, she may believe that her poor performance has a stable and global cause ("I lack intelligence, and it's going to prevent me from ever finding a meaningful career."), as opposed to an unstable and specific cause ("I was sick the day of the exam, so my low score was a fluke."). Hopelessness theory predicts that people who exhibit this cognitive style in response to undesirable life events will view such events as having negative implications for their future and self-worth, thereby increasing the likelihood of hopelessness—the primary cause of depression (Abramson et al., 1989). One study testing hopelessness theory measured the tendency to make negative inferences for bad life effects in participants who were experiencing uncontrollable stressors. Over the ensuing six months, those with scores reflecting high cognitive vulnerability were seven times more likely to develop depression compared to those with lower scores (Kleim, Gonzalo, & Ehlers, 2011).

A third cognitive theory of depression focuses on how people's thoughts about their distressed moods—depressed symptoms in particular—can increase the risk and duration of depression. This theory, which focuses on rumination in the development of depression, was first described in the late 1980s to explain the higher rates of depression in women than in men (Nolen-Hoeksema, 1987). **Rumination** is the repetitive and passive focus on the fact that one is depressed and dwelling on depressed symptoms, rather that distracting one's self from the symptoms or attempting to address them in an active, problem-solving manner (Nolen-Hoeksema, 1991). When people ruminate, they have thoughts such as "Why am I so unmotivated? I just can't get going. I'm never going to get my work done feeling this way" (Nolen-Hoeksema & Hilt, 2009, p. 393). Women are more likely than men to ruminate when they are sad or depressed (Butler & Nolen-Hoeksema, 1994), and the tendency to ruminate is associated with increases in depression symptoms (Nolen-Hoeksema, Larson, & Grayson, 1999), a heightened risk of major depressive episodes (Abela & Hankin, 2011), and chronicity of such episodes (Robinson & Alloy, 2003).

Figure 9: Rumination also refers to some mammals' process of re-chewing stomach contents a second time for digestion. What kind of parallels exist between the two meanings of *rumination*?

☑ On Your Own

Fill in the corresponding terms with the examples provided in the table: *depressive schemas, hopelessness,* and *rumination.*

Example	Term
Michelle believes that she will not be able to get anything done feeling the way she does every day. So, she just decides not to do anything.	
Michelle thinks that no matter what she does, she is going to fail.	
Michelle receives some slight critical feedback from her supervisor on how to improve her report and interprets this as him stating that her paper is terrible, she is bad at her job, and she should quit.	

Suicide

For some people with mood disorders, the extreme emotional pain they experience becomes unendurable. Overwhelmed by hopelessness, devastated by incapacitating feelings of worthlessness, and burdened with the inability to adequately cope with such feelings, they may consider suicide to be a reasonable way out. **Suicide**, defined by the CDC as "death caused by self-directed injurious behavior with any intent to die as the result of the behavior" (CDC, 2013a), in a sense represents an outcome of several things going wrong all at the same time (Crosby, Ortega, & Melanson, 2011). Not only must the person be biologically or psychologically vulnerable, but he must also have the means to perform the suicidal act, and he must lack the necessary protective factors (e.g., social support from friends and family, religion, coping skills, and problem-solving skills) that provide comfort and enable one to cope during times of crisis or great psychological pain (Berman, 2009).

Suicide is not listed as a disorder in the DSM-5; however, suffering from a mental disorder—especially a mood disorder—poses the greatest risk for suicide. Around 90% of those who complete suicides have a diagnosis of at least one mental disorder, with mood disorders being the most frequent (Fleischman, Bertolote, Belfer, & Beautrais, 2005). In fact, the association between major depressive disorder and suicide is so strong that one of the criteria for the disorder is thoughts of suicide, as discussed previously (APA, 2013).

Suicide rates can be difficult to interpret because some deaths that appear to be accidental may in fact be acts of suicide (e.g., automobile crash). Nevertheless, investigations into U.S. suicide rates have uncovered these facts:

📷 **Figure 10:** Men are four times more likely to commit suicide.

- Suicide was the 10th leading cause of death for all ages in 2010 (Centers for Disease Control and Prevention [CDC], 2012).

- There were 38,364 suicides in 2010 in the United States—an average of 105 each day (CDC, 2012).

- Suicide among males is four times higher than among females and accounts for 79% of all suicides; firearms are the most commonly used method of suicide for males, whereas poisoning is the most commonly used method for females (CDC, 2012).

- From 1991 to 2003, suicide rates were consistently higher among those 65 years and older. Since 2001, however, suicide rates among the ages 25–64 have risen consistently, and since 2006, suicide rates have been greater for those ages 65 and older (CDC, 2013b). This increase in suicide rates among middle-aged Americans has prompted concern in some quarters that baby boomers (individuals born between 1946–1964) who face economic worry and easy access to prescription medication may be particularly vulnerable to suicide (Parker-Pope, 2013).

- The highest rates of suicide within the United States are among American Indians/Alaskan natives and non-Hispanic Whites (CDC, 2013b).

- Suicide rates vary across the United States, with the highest rates consistently found in the mountain states of the west (Alaska, Montana, Nevada, Wyoming, Colorado, and Idaho) (Berman, 2009).

Contrary to popular belief, suicide rates peak during the springtime (April and May), not during the holiday season or winter. In fact, suicide rates are generally lowest during the winter months (Postolache et al., 2010).

Reflection Questions

Why do you think males are more likely to commit suicide than females?

Risk Factors for Suicide

Aside from being diagnosed with a mental disorder, there are several risk factors for suicide, which include:

- Substance abuse problems; alcohol dependence is associated with a 10 times increased risk for suicide than the general population (Wilcox, Conner, & Caine, 2004)

- A past suicide attempt; approximately one in five who have made a prior suicide attempt will make another in the next four years (Owens, Horrocks, & House, 2002)

- Access to lethal means in which to act, such as a handgun in the home (Brent & Bridge, 2003)

- Withdrawal from social relationships, feeling like a burden to others, and risk-taking behavior (Berman, 2009)

- A sense of entrapment or feeling unable to escape one's miserable feelings or external circumstances (e.g., an abusive relationship with no perceived way out) predicts suicidal behavior (O'Connor, Smyth, Ferguson, Ryan, & Williams, 2013)

- Victims of bullying or cyberbullying (McCabe, 2010)

- A family member committing suicide increases the risk of suicide for other family members (Agerbo, Nordentoft, & Mortensen, 2002)

Suicides can have a contagious effect on people. For example, another's suicide, especially that of a family member, heightens one's risk of suicide (Agerbo, Nordentoft, & Mortensen, 2002). Additionally, widely-publicized suicides tend to trigger copycat suicides in some individuals. One study examining suicide statistics in the United States from 1947–1967 found that the rates of suicide skyrocketed for the first month after a suicide story was printed on the front page of *The New York Times* (Phillips, 1974). Austrian researchers found a significant increase in the number of suicides by firearms in the three weeks following extensive reports in Austria's largest newspaper of a celebrity suicide by gun (Etzersdorfer, Voracek, & Sonneck, 2004). A review of 42 studies concluded that media coverage of celebrity suicides is more than 14 times more likely to trigger copycat suicides than is coverage of non-celebrity suicides (Stack, 2000). This review also demonstrated that the medium of coverage is important: televised stories are considerably less likely to prompt a surge in suicides than are newspaper stories.

Figure 11: Anthony Bourdain, a well-loved celebrity chef, author, and travel documentarian, was a victim of suicide.

Reflection Questions

Why do you think there is a relationship between media coverage of suicides and suicide rates? Do you think it is a coincidence? Why or why not?

One possible contributing factor in suicide is brain chemistry. Contemporary neurological research shows that disturbances in the functioning of serotonin are linked to suicidal behavior (Pompili et al., 2010). Low levels of serotonin predict future suicide attempts and suicide completions, and low levels have been observed post-mortem among suicide victims (Mann, 2003). Serotonin dysfunction, as noted earlier, is also known to play an important role in depression; low levels of serotonin have also been linked to aggression and impulsivity (Stanley et al., 2000). The combination of these three characteristics constitutes a potential formula for suicide—especially violent suicide. A classic study conducted during the 1970s found that patients with major depressive disorder who had very low levels of serotonin attempted suicide more frequently and more violently than did patients with higher levels (Asberg, Thorén, Träskman, Bertilsson, & Ringberger, 1976; Mann, 2003).

Reflection Questions

What do you think are the most important factors that lead someone who is depressed to consider suicide? What are some things we can do to support someone who may be experiencing those factors?

Suicidal thoughts, plans, and even off-hand remarks ("I might kill myself this afternoon.") should always be taken extremely seriously. People who contemplate terminating their life need immediate help. Here are two excellent websites that contain resources (including hotlines) for people who are struggling with suicidal ideation, have loved ones who may be suicidal, or who have lost loved ones to suicide: the American Foundation for Suicide Prevention (hawkes.biz/afsp) and the American Association of Suicidology (hawkes.biz/suicide).

Summary

Mood disorders are those in which the person experiences severe disturbances in mood and emotion. They include depressive disorders and bipolar and related disorders. Depressive disorders include major depressive disorder, which is characterized by episodes of profound sadness and loss of interest or pleasure in usual activities and other associated features, and persistent depressive disorder, which is marked by a chronic state of sadness. Bipolar disorder is characterized by mood states that vacillate between sadness and euphoria; a diagnosis of bipolar disorder requires experiencing at least one manic episode, which is defined as a period of extreme euphoria, irritability, and increased activity. Mood disorders appear to have a genetic component, with genetic factors playing a more prominent role in bipolar disorder than in depression. Both biological and psychological factors are important in the development of depression. People who suffer from mental health problems, especially mood disorders, are at heightened risk for suicide.

Flash Forward

Ready to dig into the vocabulary? Get some practice with this Hawkes Verified Quizlet set (hawkes.biz/psych14q8)!

Figure 1: Researchers have long been studying potential connections between schizophrenia and creativity, as art can be a form of therapy and self-expression for those with schizophrenia.

14.8 Schizophrenia

What is schizophrenia? First, schizophrenia is *not* a condition involving a split personality; that is, schizophrenia is not the same thing as dissociative identity disorder (better known as multiple personality disorder). These disorders are sometimes confused because the word *schizophrenia* first coined by the Swiss psychiatrist Eugen Bleuler in 1911, derives from Greek words that refer to a "splitting" (*schizo*) of psychic functions (*phrene*) (Green, 2001).

Schizophrenia is a devastating psychological disorder that is characterized by major disturbances in thought, perception, emotion, and behavior.

About 1% of the population experiences schizophrenia in their lifetime, and usually the disorder is first diagnosed during early adulthood (early to mid-20s). Most people with schizophrenia experience significant difficulties in many day-to-day activities, such as holding a job, paying bills, caring for oneself (grooming and hygiene), and maintaining relationships with others. Frequent hospitalizations are more often the rule rather than the exception with schizophrenia. Even when they receive the best treatments available, many with schizophrenia will continue to experience serious social and occupational impairment throughout their lives.

Schizophrenia is considered a psychotic disorder, or one in which the person's thoughts, perceptions, and behaviors are impaired to the point where she is not able to function normally in life. In informal terms, one who suffers from a psychotic disorder (that is, has a psychosis) is disconnected from the world in which most of us live.

Symptoms of Schizophrenia

The main symptoms of schizophrenia include hallucinations, delusions, disorganized thinking, disorganized or abnormal motor behavior, and negative symptoms (APA, 2013). A **hallucination** is a perceptual experience that occurs in the absence of external stimulation. Auditory hallucinations (hearing voices) occur in roughly two-thirds of patients with schizophrenia and are by far the most common form of hallucination (Andreasen, 1987). The voices may be familiar or unfamiliar, they may have a conversation or argue, or the voices may provide a running commentary on the person's behavior (Tsuang, Farone, & Green, 1999).

Less common are visual hallucinations (seeing things that are not there) and olfactory hallucinations (smelling odors that are not actually present).

Delusions are beliefs that are contrary to reality and are firmly held even in the face of contradictory evidence. Many of us hold beliefs that some would consider odd, but a delusion is easily identified because it is clearly absurd. A person with schizophrenia may believe that his mother is plotting with the FBI to poison his coffee, or that his neighbor is an enemy spy who wants to kill him. These kinds of delusions are known as **paranoid delusions**, which involve the (false) belief that other people or agencies are plotting to harm the person. People with schizophrenia also may hold **grandiose delusions**, beliefs that one holds special power, unique knowledge, or is extremely important. For example, someone who claims to be Jesus Christ who is not, or who claims to have specific knowledge going back 5,000 years, or who claims to be the great philosopher Socrates is most likely experiencing grandiose delusions. Other delusions include the belief that one's thoughts are being removed (thought withdrawal) or thoughts have been placed inside one's head (thought insertion). Another type of delusion is **somatic delusion**, which is the belief that something highly abnormal is happening to one's body (e.g., that one's kidneys are being eaten by cockroaches).

Figure 2: Delusions of grandeur falsely distort one's self-perception.

✐ **On Your Own**

Which of the following is an example of a paranoid delusion?

☐ Hearing voices that other people do not hear   ☐ "I am a god."   ☐ "The FBI wants to kill me."

Disorganized thinking refers to disjointed and incoherent thought processes—usually detected by what a person says. The person might ramble, exhibit loose associations (jump from topic to topic), or talk in a way that is so disorganized and incomprehensible that it seems as though the person is randomly combining words. Disorganized thinking is also exhibited by blatantly illogical remarks (e.g., "Fenway Park is in Boston. I live in Boston. Therefore, I live at Fenway Park.") and by tangentiality: responding to others' statements or questions by remarks that are either barely related or unrelated to what was said or asked. For example, if a person diagnosed with schizophrenia is asked if she is interested in receiving special job training, she might state that she once rode on a train somewhere. To a person with schizophrenia, the tangential (slightly related) connection between job *training* and riding a *train* are sufficient enough to cause such a response.

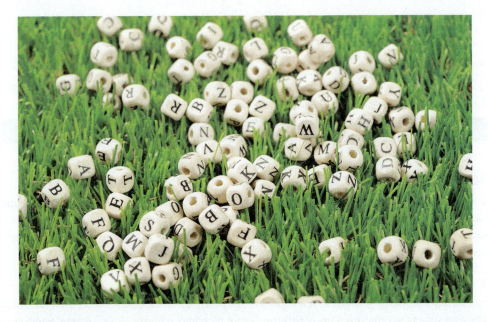

🖼 **Figure 3:** Disjointed thoughts, remarks, speech, and motor behavior can be symptoms of schizophrenia.

Disorganized or abnormal motor behavior refers to unusual behaviors and movements: becoming unusually active, exhibiting silly child-like behaviors (giggling and self-absorbed smiling), engaging in repeated and purposeless movements, or displaying odd facial expressions and gestures. In some cases, the person will exhibit **catatonic behaviors**, which show decreased reactivity to the environment, such as posturing, in which the person maintains a rigid and bizarre posture for long periods of time, or catatonic stupor, a complete lack of movement and verbal behavior.

✐ **On Your Own**

Which of the following is *not* an example of disorganized movements?

☐ Smiling when other people smile   ☐ Maintaining a rigid or bizarre posture for long periods of time

☐ Hyperactivity

Negative symptoms are those that reflect noticeable decreases and absences in certain behaviors, emotions, or drives (Green, 2001). A person who exhibits diminished emotional expression shows no emotion in his facial expressions, speech, or movements, even when such expressions are normal or expected. People with schizophrenia may experience avolition, which is a lack of motivation to engage in self-initiated meaningful activity or asociality, which is social withdrawal and lack of interest in engaging with others. A final negative symptom, anhedonia, refers to an inability to experience pleasure.

Further Resources

Watch this video (hawkes. biz/schizophrenia) and try to identify which classic symptoms of schizophrenia are shown.

✎ On Your Own

Imagine you are a clinical psychologist who was referred a patient whose mother thinks he may have schizophrenia. Using the following table, write five questions you would ask the mother about her son's behavior and indicate why you would ask that question.

#	Question	Why?
1		
2		
3		
4		
5		

Causes of Schizophrenia

There is considerable evidence suggesting that schizophrenia has a genetic basis. The risk of developing schizophrenia is nearly 6 times greater if one has a parent with schizophrenia than if one does not (Goldstein, Buka, Seidman, & Tsuang, 2010). Additionally, one's risk of developing schizophrenia increases as genetic relatedness to family members diagnosed with schizophrenia increases (Gottesman, 2001).

Genes

When considering the role of genetics in schizophrenia, as in any disorder, conclusions based on family and twin studies are subject to criticism. This is because family members who are closely related (such as siblings) are more likely to share similar environments than are family members who are less closely related (such as cousins); further, identical twins may be more likely to be treated similarly by others than might fraternal twins. Thus, family and twin studies cannot completely rule out the possible effects of shared environments and experiences. Such problems can be corrected by using adoption studies, in which children are separated from their parents at an early age. One of the first adoption studies of schizophrenia conducted by Heston (1966) followed 97 adoptees, including 47 who were born to mothers with schizophrenia, over a 36-year period. Five of the 47 adoptees (11%) whose mothers had schizophrenia were later diagnosed with schizophrenia, compared to none of the 50 control adoptees. Other adoption studies have consistently reported that for adoptees who are later diagnosed with schizophrenia, their biological relatives have a higher risk of schizophrenia than do adoptive relatives (Shih, Belmonte, & Zandi, 2004).

Although adoption studies have supported the hypothesis that genetic factors contribute to schizophrenia, they have also demonstrated that the disorder most likely arises from a combination of genetic and environmental factors, rather than just genes themselves. For example, investigators in one study examined the rates of schizophrenia among 303 adoptees (Tienari et al., 2004). A total of 145 of the adoptees had biological mothers with schizophrenia; these adoptees constituted the high genetic risk group. The other 158 adoptees had mothers with no psychiatric history; these adoptees composed the low genetic risk group. The researchers managed to determine whether the adoptees' families were either healthy or disturbed. For example, the

📷 **Figure 4:** Both genetics and environmental factors contribute to a schizophrenia diagnosis.

adoptees were considered to be raised in a disturbed family environment if the family exhibited a lot of criticism, conflict, and a lack of problem-solving skills. The findings revealed that adoptees whose mothers had schizophrenia (high genetic risk) *and* who had been raised in a disturbed family environment were much more likely to develop schizophrenia or another psychotic disorder (36.8%) than were adoptees whose biological mothers had schizophrenia but who had been raised in a healthy environment (5.8%), or than adoptees with a low genetic risk who were raised in either a disturbed (5.3%) or healthy (4.8%) environment. Because the adoptees who were at high genetic risk were likely to develop schizophrenia *only* if they were raised in a disturbed home environment, this study supports a diathesis-stress interpretation of schizophrenia—both genetic vulnerability and environmental stress are necessary for schizophrenia to develop; genes alone do not show the complete picture.

Neurotransmitters

If we accept that schizophrenia is at least partly genetic in origin, as it seems to be, it makes sense that the next step should be to identify biological abnormalities commonly found in people with the disorder. Perhaps not surprisingly, a number of neurobiological factors have indeed been found to be related to schizophrenia. One such factor that has received considerable attention for many years is the neurotransmitter dopamine. Interest in the role of dopamine in schizophrenia was stimulated by two sets of findings: drugs that increase dopamine levels can produce schizophrenia-like symptoms, and medications that block dopamine activity reduce the symptoms (Howes & Kapur, 2009). The **dopamine hypothesis** of schizophrenia proposed that an overabundance of dopamine or too many dopamine receptors are responsible for the onset and maintenance of schizophrenia (Snyder, 1976). More recent work in this area suggests that abnormalities in dopamine vary by brain region and thus contribute to symptoms in unique ways. In general, this research has suggested that an overabundance of dopamine in the limbic system may be responsible for some symptoms, such as hallucinations and delusions, whereas low levels of dopamine in the prefrontal cortex might be responsible primarily for the negative symptoms (avolition, alogia, asociality, and anhedonia) (Davis, Kahn, Ko, & Davidson, 1991). In recent years, serotonin has received attention, and newer antipsychotic medications used to treat the disorder work by blocking serotonin receptors (Baumeister & Hawkins, 2004).

✐ On Your Own

The dysregulation of what neurotransmitter is associated with schizophrenia?

☐ GABA   ☐ Norepinephrine

☐ Glutamate   ☐ Dopamine

DOPAMINE
DOPAMINERGIC NEURONS
(dopamine-producing nerve cells)

Synaptic vesicle

Dopamine

Synaptic cleft

Dopamine metabolites

Dopamine receptor

Signal

DOPAMINE-RECEIVING NERVE CELLS

Figure 5: An overabundance of dopamine is a possible factor that influences schizophrenia onset and maintenance.

Brain Anatomy

Brain imaging studies reveal that people with schizophrenia have enlarged **ventricles**, the cavities within the brain that contain cerebral spinal fluid (Green, 2001). The enlarged ventricles suggest various brain regions are reduced in size, which can be associated with a loss in brain tissue. In addition, many people with schizophrenia display a reduction in gray matter (cell bodies of neurons) in the frontal lobes (Lawrie & Abukmeil, 1998), and many show less frontal lobe activity when performing cognitive tasks (Buchsbaum et al., 1990). The frontal lobes are important in a variety of complex cognitive functions, such as planning and executing behavior, attention, speech, movement, and problem solving. Hence, abnormalities in this region provide merit in explaining why people with schizophrenia experience deficits in these areas.

Events During Pregnancy

High rates of obstetric complications in the births of children who later developed schizophrenia have been reported (Cannon, Jones, & Murray, 2002). In addition, people are at an increased risk for developing schizophrenia if their mother was exposed to influenza during the first trimester of pregnancy (Brown et al., 2004). Research has also suggested that a mother's emotional stress during pregnancy may increase the risk of schizophrenia in offspring. For example, one study reported that the risk of schizophrenia is elevated substantially in offspring whose mothers experienced the death of a relative during the first trimester of pregnancy (Khashan et al., 2008).

Reflection Questions

Based on what you know about pregnancy and schizophrenia, what can mothers do to reduce their child's risk of developing schizophrenia?

Marijuana

A number of longitudinal studies have suggested that marijuana use is, in fact, a risk factor for schizophrenia. A review of 35 longitudinal studies found a substantially increased risk of schizophrenia and other psychotic disorders in people who had used marijuana, with the greatest risk in the most frequent users (Moore et al., 2007). However, not all people with schizophrenia have used marijuana and the majority of marijuana users do not develop schizophrenia (Casadio, Fernandes, Murray, & Di Forti, 2011). Researchers have hypothesized that early marijuana use may disrupt normal brain development during important early maturation periods in adolescence (Trezza, Cuomo, & Vanderschuren, 2008). So far, there is not enough evidence to imply causation, but the correlation between marijuana use and schizophrenia has led to calls for more research on the potential relationship.

Further Resources

Read this January 2019 *New York Times* article (hawkes.biz/schizophreniamarijuana) for more on what scientists do know about marijuana and schizophrenia.

Reflection Questions

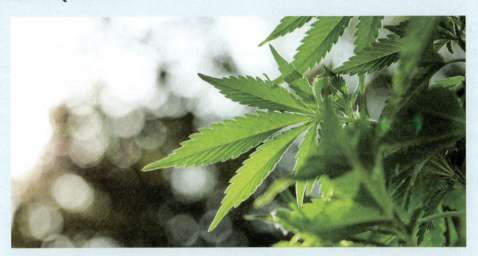

Figure 6: Do you think the link between marijuana use and schizophrenia should be considered by legislators who are considering legalizing marijuana? Why or why not?

Schizophrenia: Early Warning Signs

Early detection and treatment of conditions such as heart disease and cancer have improved survival rates and quality of life for people who suffer from these conditions. A new approach involves identifying people who show minor symptoms of psychosis, such as unusual thought content, paranoia, odd communication, delusions, problems at school or work, and a decline in social functioning—which are coined **prodromal symptoms**—and following these individuals over time to determine which of them develop a psychotic disorder and which factors best predict such a disorder. A number of factors have been identified that predict a greater likelihood that prodromal individuals will develop a psychotic disorder: genetic risk (a family history of psychosis), recent deterioration in functioning, high levels of unusual thought content, high levels of suspicion or paranoia, poor social functioning, and a history of substance abuse (Fusar-Poli et al., 2013). Further research will enable a more accurate prediction of those at greatest risk for developing schizophrenia, and thus to whom early intervention efforts should be directed.

Summary

Schizophrenia is a severe disorder characterized by a complete breakdown in one's ability to function in life; it often requires hospitalization. People with schizophrenia experience hallucinations and delusions, and they have extreme difficulty regulating their emotions and behavior. Thinking is incoherent and disorganized, behavior is extremely bizarre, emotions are flat, and motivation to engage in most basic life activities is lacking. Considerable evidence shows that genetic factors play a central role in schizophrenia; however, adoption studies have highlighted the additional importance of environmental factors. Neurotransmitter and brain abnormalities, which may be linked to environmental factors such as obstetric complications or exposure to influenza during the gestational period, have also been implicated. A promising new area of schizophrenia research involves identifying individuals who show prodromal symptoms and following them over time to determine which factors best predict the development of schizophrenia. Future research may enable us to pinpoint those especially at risk for developing schizophrenia and who may benefit from early intervention.

14.9 Dissociative Disorders

Flash Forward

Ready to dig into the vocabulary? Get some practice with this Hawkes Verified Quizlet set (hawkes.biz/psych14q9)!

📷 **Figure 1:** Dissociation disturbs memory or identity.

Dissociative disorders are characterized by an individual's memory or identity becoming disturbed, which could have psychological rather than physical consequences. Dissociative disorders listed in the DSM-5 include dissociative amnesia, depersonalization/derealization disorder, and dissociative identity disorder.

Dissociative Amnesia

Dissociative amnesia, is a symptom of dissociative disorders where an individual is unable to recall important personal information, usually following an extremely stressful or traumatic experience such as combat, natural disasters, or being the victim of violence. A **dissociative fugue** (from the word "to flee" in French) is when an individual wanders away from their home due to experiencing confusion about their identity and may result in adopting a new identity (Cardeña & Gleaves, 2006). Most fugue episodes last only a few hours or days, but some can last longer.

> **Reflection Question**
>
> Why do you think people have dissociative amnesia?

Depersonalization/Derealization Disorder

Depersonalization/derealization disorder is characterized by recurring episodes of depersonalization, derealization, or both. Depersonalization is defined as feelings of "unreality or detachment from, or unfamiliarity with, one's whole self or from aspects of the self" (APA, 2013, p. 302). Individuals who experience depersonalization might believe their thoughts and feelings are not their own; they may feel robotic as though they lack control over their movements and speech; they may experience a distorted sense of time, and in extreme cases, they may sense an "out-of-body" experience in which they see themselves from the vantage point of another person. Derealization is conceptualized as a sense of "unreality or detachment from, or unfamiliarity with, the world, be it individuals, inanimate objects, or all surroundings" (APA, 2013, p. 303). A person who experiences derealization might feel as though he is in a fog or a dream or that the surrounding world is somehow artificial and unreal. Individuals with depersonalization/derealization disorder often have difficulty describing their symptoms and may think they are going crazy (APA, 2013).

Dissociative Identity Disorder

People with **dissociative identity disorder** (formerly known as multiple personality disorder) exhibit two or more separate personalities or identities, each well-defined and distinct from one another. They also experience memory gaps for the times during which another identity is in charge (e.g., one might find unfamiliar items in her shopping bags or among her possessions), and in some cases, they may report hearing voices, such as a child's voice or the sound of somebody crying (APA, 2013). Ross et al., (1990) estimated that 95% of people diagnosed with DID were physically and/or sexually abused as children.

Dissociative identity disorder (DID) is a highly controversial diagnosis because of its portrayal in the media. For example, Kenneth Bianchi, a serial killer, pleaded not guilty due to insanity, claiming he had a different personality that committed the murders. Prosecutors were able to show that he was faking the symptoms and found him guilty (Schwartz, 1981). The movie and book *Sybil*, portraying a women with 16 different personalities, may have prompted a clinicians' increase of diagnoses for the disorder (Piper & Merskey, 2004). However, despite the controversial nature of DID, it is accepted in the psychological community as a legitimate disorder.

🖼 **Figure 2:** Robert Lewis Stevenson's classic novella portrays a man suffering with what we know today as DID.

Reflection Questions

Do you believe that dissociative identity disorder (DID) is a legitimate diagnosis? Why or why not?

Summary

The main characteristic of dissociative disorders is that people become dissociated from their sense of self, resulting in memory and identity disturbances. Dissociative disorders listed in the DSM-5 include dissociative amnesia, depersonalization/derealization disorder, and dissociative identity disorder. A person with dissociative amnesia is unable to recall important personal information, often after a stressful or traumatic experience.

Depersonalization/derealization disorder is characterized by recurring episodes of depersonalization (i.e., detachment from or unfamiliarity with the self) and/or derealization (i.e., detachment from or unfamiliarity with the world). A person with dissociative identity disorder exhibits two or more well-defined and distinct personalities or identities, as well as memory gaps for the times during which another identity was present.

Dissociative identity disorder has generated controversy, mainly because some believe its symptoms can be faked by patients if presenting its symptoms somehow benefits the patient in avoiding negative consequences or taking responsibility for one's actions. The diagnostic rates of this disorder have increased dramatically following its portrayal in popular culture. However, many people legitimately suffer with this disorder over the course of their lives.

Flash Forward

Ready to dig into the vocabulary? Get some practice with this Hawkes Verified Quizlet set (hawkes.biz/psych14q10)!

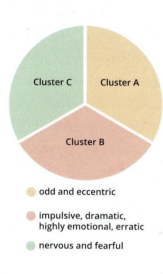

- odd and eccentric

- impulsive, dramatic, highly emotional, erratic

- nervous and fearful

14.10 Personality Disorders

The term *personality* refers loosely to one's stable, consistent, and distinctive way of thinking about, feeling, acting, and relating to the world. People with **personality disorders**, however, have a personality style that meets the following criteria (APA, 2013):

- differs markedly from the expectations of their culture

- is pervasive and inflexible

- begins in adolescence or early adulthood

- causes distress or impairment

Generally, individuals with these disorders exhibit enduring personality styles that are extremely troubling and often create problems for them and those with whom they come into contact. Their maladaptive personality styles frequently bring them into conflict with others, disrupt their ability to develop and maintain social relationships, and prevent them from accomplishing realistic life goals.

The DSM-5 recognizes 10 personality disorders, organized into 3 different clusters. Cluster A characterizes personality styles that are odd and eccentric. Cluster B includes personality styles that are impulsive, dramatic, highly emotional, and erratic, and those in Cluster C include nervous and fearful personality styles.

DSM-5 Personality Disorder	Description	Cluster
Paranoid	harbors a pervasive and unjustifiable suspiciousness and mistrust of others; reluctant to confide in or become close to others; reads hidden demeaning or threatening meaning into benign remarks or events; takes offense easily and bears grudges; not due to schizophrenia or other psychotic disorders	A
Schizoid	lacks interest and desire to form relationships with others; aloof and shows emotional coldness and detachment; indifferent to approval or criticism of others; lacks close friends or confidants; not due to schizophrenia or other psychotic disorders, not an autism spectrum disorder	A
Schizotypal	exhibits eccentricities in thought, perception, emotion, speech, and behavior; shows suspiciousness or paranoia; has unusual perceptual experiences; speech is often idiosyncratic; displays inappropriate emotions; lacks friends or confidants; not due to schizophrenia or other psychotic disorder, or to autism spectrum disorder	A
Antisocial	continuously violates the rights of others; history of antisocial tendencies prior to age 15; often lies, fights, and has problems with the law; impulsive and fails to think ahead; can be deceitful and manipulative in order to gain profit or pleasure; irresponsible and often fails to hold down a job or pay financial debts; lacks feelings for others and remorse over misdeeds	B

DSM-5 Personality Disorder	Description	Cluster
Histrionic	excessively overdramatic, emotional, and theatrical; feels uncomfortable when not the center of others' attention; behavior is often inappropriately seductive or provocative; speech is highly emotional but often vague and diffuse; emotions are shallow and often shift rapidly; may alienate friends with demands for constant attention	B
Narcissistic	overinflated and unjustified sense of self-importance and preoccupied with fantasies of success; believes he is entitled to special treatment from others; shows arrogant attitudes and behaviors; takes advantage of others; lacks empathy	B
Borderline	unstable in self-image, mood, and behavior; cannot tolerate being alone and experiences chronic feelings of emptiness; unstable and intense relationships with others; behavior is impulsive, unpredictable, and sometimes self-damaging; shows inappropriate and intense anger; makes suicidal gestures	B
Avoidant	socially inhibited and oversensitive to negative evaluation; avoids occupations that involve interpersonal contact because of fears of criticism or rejection; avoids relationships with others unless guaranteed to be accepted unconditionally; feels inadequate and views self as socially inept and unappealing; unwilling to take risks or engage in new activities if they may prove embarrassing	C
Dependent	allows others to take over and run her life; is submissive, clingy, and fears separation; cannot make decisions without advice and reassurance from others; lacks self-confidence; cannot do things on her own; feels uncomfortable or helpless when alone	C
Obsessive-Compulsive	pervasive need for perfectionism that interferes with the ability to complete tasks; preoccupied with details, rules, order, and schedules; excessively devoted to work at the expense of leisure and friendships; rigid, inflexible, and stubborn; insists things be done his way; miserly with money	C

Table 1: DSM-5 Personality Disorders

Slightly over 9% of the U.S. population suffers from a personality disorder, with avoidant and schizoid personality disorders most frequent (Lezenweger, Lane, Loranger, & Kessler, 2007). Two of these personality disorders, borderline personality disorder and antisocial personality disorder, are regarded by many as especially problematic.

✎ On Your Own

Which personality disorder is best represented in the following example?

Shauntey is often impulsive and engages in activities without regard for others. The only thing important is her and her interests; in fact, she often feels that the world "owes" her and expects everyone to cater to her wishes.

☐ Histrionic   ☐ Narcissistic   ☐ Borderline

Borderline Personality Disorder

The *borderline* in borderline personality disorder was originally coined in the late 1930s in an effort to describe patients who appeared anxious but were prone to brief psychotic experiences—that is, patients who were thought to be literally on the borderline between anxiety and psychosis (Freeman, Stone, Martin, & Reinecke, 2005). Today, borderline personality disorder has a completely different meaning. **Borderline personality disorder** is characterized by the following (APA, 2013):

- instability in interpersonal relationships, self-image, and mood

- marked impulsivity

- inability to be alone

- frantic efforts to avoid real or imagined abandonment

- intense and unstable relationships

- reckless and self-destructive behaviors

Figure 1: Self-destructive behavior can be one symptom of BPD.

These individuals have an unstable view of self and, thus, might suddenly display a shift in personal attitudes, interests, career plans, and choice of friends. For example, a law school student may, despite having invested tens of thousands of dollars toward earning a law degree and despite having performed well in the program, consider dropping out and pursuing a career in another field. People with borderline personality disorder may be highly impulsive and may engage in reckless and self-destructive behaviors.

Self-Destructive Behaviors

Excessive gambling

Irresponsible spending

Substance abuse

Unsafe sexual practices

Reckless driving

They sometimes show intense and inappropriate anger that they have difficulty controlling, and they can be moody, sarcastic, bitter, and verbally abusive.

The prevalence of borderline personality disorder in the U.S. population is estimated to be around 1.4% (Lezenweger et al., 2007), but the rates are higher among those who use mental health services; approximately 10% of mental health outpatients and 20% of psychiatric inpatients meet the criteria for diagnosis (APA, 2013). Additionally, borderline personality disorder is comorbid with anxiety, mood, and substance use disorders (Lezenweger et al., 2007).

Biological Basis for Borderline Personality Disorder

Genetic factors appear to be important in the development of borderline personality disorder. For example, core personality traits that characterize this disorder, such as impulsivity and emotional instability, show a high degree of heritability (Livesley, 2008). Also, the rates of borderline personality disorder among relatives of people with this disorder have been found to be as high as 24.9% (White, Gunderson, Zanarani, & Hudson, 2003). Individuals with borderline personality disorder report experiencing childhood physical, sexual, and/or emotional abuse at rates far greater than those observed in the general population (Afifi et al., 2010), indicating that environmental factors are also crucial. These findings would suggest that borderline personality disorder may be determined by an interaction between genetic factors and adverse environmental experiences. Consistent with this hypothesis, one study found that the highest rates of borderline personality disorder were among individuals with a borderline temperament (characterized by high novelty seeking and high harm-avoidance) and those who experienced childhood abuse and/or neglect (Joyce et al., 2003).

Figure 2: Negative environmental factors during the developmental years can have lasting impacts into adulthood.

Antisocial Personality Disorder

Most human beings live in accordance with a moral compass, a sense of right and wrong. Most individuals learn at a very young age that there are certain things that should not be done. We learn that we should not lie or cheat. We are taught that it is wrong to take things that do not belong to us and that it is wrong to exploit others for personal gain. We also learn the importance of living up to our responsibilities, of doing what we say we will do. People with antisocial personality disorder, however, do not seem to have a moral compass. These individuals act as though they neither have a sense of nor care about right or wrong. Not surprisingly, these people represent a serious problem for others and for society in general.

According to the DSM-5, the individual with **antisocial personality disorder** (sometimes referred to as *psychopathy*) shows no regard at all for other people's rights or feelings. This lack of regard is exhibited a number of ways including (APA, 2013):

- repeatedly performing illegal acts

- lying to or conning others

- impulsivity and recklessness

- irritability and aggressiveness toward others

- failure to act in a responsible way

The worst part about antisocial personality disorder, however, is that people with this disorder have no remorse over one's misdeeds; these people will hurt, manipulate, exploit, and abuse others and not feel any guilt. Signs of this disorder can emerge early in life; however, a person must be at least 18 years old to be diagnosed with antisocial personality disorder.

Reflection Questions

How would your life differ if you had antisocial personality disorder? What rules and regulations do you follow on a daily basis that may mean less to you with this disorder?

People with antisocial personality disorder seem to view the world as self-serving and unkind. They seem to think that they should use whatever means necessary to get by in life. They tend to view others not as living, thinking, feeling beings but rather as pawns to be used or abused for a specific purpose. They often have an over-inflated sense of themselves and can appear extremely arrogant. They frequently display superficial charm; for example, without really meaning it, they might say exactly what they think another person wants to hear. They lack empathy: they are incapable of understanding the emotional point-of-view of others.

Possible Behavioral Outcomes

Getting involved in illegal enterprises

Showing cruelty towards others

Leaving jobs with no plans for a new one

Having multiple sexual partners

Repeatedly getting into fights

Having a reckless disregard for self and others

A useful way to conceptualize antisocial personality disorder is boiling the diagnosis down to three major concepts: disinhibition, boldness, and meanness (Patrick, Fowles, & Krueger, 2009). *Disinhibition* is a propensity toward impulse control problems, lack of planning and forethought, insistence on immediate gratification, and inability to restrain behavior. *Boldness* describes a tendency to remain calm in threatening situations, high self-assurance, a sense of dominance, and a tendency toward thrill-seeking. *Meanness* is defined as "aggressive resource seeking without regard for others" and is signaled by a lack of empathy, disdain for and lack of close relationships with others, and a tendency to accomplish goals through cruelty (Patrick et al., 2009, p. 913).

Figure 3: Blatant disregard for self and others is characteristic of antisocial personality disorder.

Reflection Questions

If a person with antisocial personality disorder commits a crime, do you feel the person is less responsible for the crime?

Risk Factors for Antisocial Personality Disorder

Antisocial personality disorder is observed in about 3.6% of the population; the disorder is much more common among males, with a 3 to 1 ratio of men to women, and it is more likely to occur in men who are younger, widowed, separated, divorced, of lower socioeconomic status, or live in urban areas and the western United States (Compton, Conway, Stinson, Colliver, & Grant, 2005). Compared to men with antisocial personality disorder, women with the disorder are more likely to have experienced emotional neglect and sexual abuse during childhood, and they are more likely to have had parents who abused substances and who engaged in antisocial behaviors themselves (Alegria et al., 2013).

Table 2 shows some of the differences in the specific types of antisocial behaviors that men and women with antisocial personality disorder exhibit (Alegria et al., 2013).

Men with antisocial personality disorder are more likely than women with antisocial personality disorder to:	Women with antisocial personality disorder are more likely than men with antisocial personality to:
• do things that could easily hurt themselves or others	• run away from home overnight
• receive three or more traffic tickets for reckless driving	• frequently miss school or work
• have their driver's license suspended	• lie frequently
• destroy others' property	• forge someone's signature
• start a fire on purpose	• get into a fight that comes to blows with an intimate partner
• make money illegally	• live with others besides their family for at least one month
• do anything that could lead to arrest	• harass, threaten, or blackmail someone
• hit someone hard enough to injure them	
• hurt an animal on purpose	

Table 2: Gender Differences in Antisocial Personality Disorder

Family, twin, and adoption studies suggest that both genetic and environmental factors influence the development of antisocial personality disorder, as well as general antisocial behavior (criminality, violence, aggressiveness) (Baker, Bezdjian, & Raine, 2006). Personality and temperament dimensions that are related to this disorder, including fearlessness, impulsive antisociality, and callousness, have a substantial genetic influence (Livesley & Jang, 2008). Adoption studies clearly demonstrate that the development of antisocial behavior is determined by the interaction of genetic factors and adverse environmental circumstances (Rhee & Waldman, 2002). For example, one investigation found that adoptees of biological parents with antisocial personality disorder were more likely to exhibit adolescent and adult antisocial behaviors if they were raised in adverse adoptive family environments (e.g., adoptive parents had marital problems, were divorced, used drugs, and had legal problems) than if they were raised in a more normal adoptive environment (Cadoret, Yates, Ed, Woodworth, & Stewart, 1995).

Researchers who are interested in the importance of environment in the development of antisocial personality disorder have directed their attention to such factors as the community, the structure and functioning of the family, and peer groups. Each of these factors influences the likelihood of antisocial behavior. One longitudinal investigation of more than 800 Seattle-area youth measured risk factors for violence at 10, 14, 16, and 18 years of age (Herrenkohl et al., 2000). The risk factors examined included those involving the family, peers, and community. A portion of the findings from this study are provided in Figure 4.

Risk Factors During Adolescence That Predict Later Violence

Risk factor	Age 10 predictor (elementary school)	Age 14 predictor (middle school)	Age 16 predictor (high school)
Family			
Parental violence		✗	
Parental criminality		✗	✗
Poor family management		✗	✗
Family conflict		✗	✗
Parental attitudes favorable to violence	✗		
Frequent moves			✗
Peer			
Peer delinquency	✗	✗	✗
Gang membership		✗	✗
Community			
Economic deprivation	✗		✗
Community disorganization		✗	✗
Availability of drugs	✗	✗	✗
Neighborhood adults involved in crime		✗	✗

Figure 4: Longitudinal studies have helped to identify risk factors for predicting violent behavior.

Those with antisocial tendencies do not seem to experience emotions the way most other people do. These individuals fail to show fear in response to environment cues that signal punishment, pain, or noxious stimulation. For instance, they show less skin conductance (sweatiness on hands) in anticipation of electric shock than do people without antisocial tendencies (Hare, 1965). Skin conductance is controlled by the sympathetic nervous system and is used to assess autonomic nervous system functioning. When the sympathetic nervous system is active, people become aroused and anxious, and sweat gland activity increases. Thus, increased sweat gland activity, as assessed through skin conductance, is taken as a sign of arousal or anxiety. For those with antisocial personality disorder, a lack of skin conductance may indicate the presence of characteristics such as emotional deficits and impulsivity that underlie the propensity for antisocial behavior and negative social relationships (Fung et al., 2005).

While emotional deficits may contribute to antisocial personality disorder, so too might an inability to relate to others' pain. In a recent study, 80 prisoners were shown photos of people being intentionally hurt by others (e.g., someone crushing a person's hand in an automobile door) while undergoing brain imaging (Decety, Skelly, & Kiehl, 2013). Prisoners who scored high on a test of antisocial tendencies showed significantly less activation in brain regions involved in the experience of empathy and feeling concerned for others than did prisoners with low scores on the antisocial test. Notably, the prisoners who scored high on the antisocial test showed greater activation in a brain area involved in self-awareness, cognitive function, and interpersonal experience. The investigators suggested that the heightened activation in this region when watching social interactions involving one person harming another may reflect a propensity or desire for this kind of behavior.

☑ On Your Own

Answer the following questions in the space provided.

1. Which personality disorders fall into Cluster B?

2. Which two personality disorders are most common?

3. Which two personality disorders are considered most problematic?

Summary

Individuals with personality disorders exhibit a personality style that is inflexible, causes distress and impairment, and creates problems for themselves and others. The DSM-5 recognizes 10 personality disorders, organized into three clusters. The disorders in Cluster A include those characterized by a personality style that is odd and eccentric. Cluster B includes personality disorders characterized chiefly by a personality style that is impulsive, dramatic, highly emotional, and erratic, and those in Cluster C are characterized by a nervous and fearful personality style. Two Cluster B personality disorders, borderline personality disorder and antisocial personality disorder, are especially problematic. People with borderline personality disorder show marked instability in mood, behavior, and self-image, as well as impulsivity. They cannot stand to be alone, are unpredictable, have a history of stormy relationships, and frequently display intense and inappropriate anger. Genetic factors and adverse childhood experiences (e.g., sexual abuse) appear to be important in its development. People with antisocial personality display a lack of regard for the rights of others; they are impulsive, deceitful, irresponsible, and unburdened by any sense of guilt. Genetic factors and socialization both appear to be important in the origin of antisocial personality disorder. Research has also shown that those with this disorder do not experience emotions the way most other people do.

14.11 Disorders in Childhood

Most of the disorders we have discussed so far are typically diagnosed in adulthood although they can and sometimes do occur during childhood. However, there are a group of conditions that, when present, are diagnosed early in childhood, often before the time a child enters school. These conditions are listed in the DSM-5 as **neurodevelopmental disorders**, and they involve developmental problems in personal, social, academic, and intellectual functioning (APA, 2013). In this lesson, we will discuss two such disorders: attention deficit/hyperactivity disorder and autism.

Flash Forward

Ready to dig into the vocabulary? Get some practice with this Hawkes Verified Quizlet set (hawkes.biz/psych14q11)!

Attention Deficit/Hyperactivity Disorder

Diego is always active, from the time he wakes up in the morning until the time he goes to bed at night. His mother reports that he came out the womb kicking and screaming, and he has not stopped moving since. He has a sweet disposition but always seems to be in trouble with his teachers, parents, and after-school program counselors. He accidently breaks things; he lost his jacket three times last winter, and he never seems to sit still. His teachers believe he is a smart child, but he never finishes anything he starts and is so impulsive that he does not seem to learn much in school.

Diego likely has **attention deficit/hyperactivity disorder (ADHD)**. The symptoms of this disorder were first described by Hans Hoffman in the 1920s. While taking care of his son while his wife was in the hospital giving birth to a second child, Hoffman noticed that the boy had (Jellinek & Herzog, 1999):

- trouble concentrating on his homework

- a short attention span

- a need to repeatedly go over easy homework to learn the material

Later, it was discovered that many hyperactive children—those who are fidgety, restless, socially disruptive, and have trouble with impulse control—also display short attention spans, problems with concentration, and distractibility. By the 1970s, it had become clear that many children who display attention problems often also exhibit signs of hyperactivity. In recognition of such findings, the DSM-III (published in 1980) included a new disorder: attention deficit disorder with and without hyperactivity, now known as attention deficit/hyperactivity disorder (ADHD).

Figure 1: Many hyperactive children also display attention problems.

A child with ADHD shows a constant pattern of inattention and/or hyperactive and impulsive behavior that interferes with normal functioning (APA, 2013).

Some Signs of Inattention	Some Signs of Hyperactivity
Difficulty with sustained attention	Excessive movement
Failure to follow instructions	Blurting out responses
Disorganization	Difficulty waiting

Some Signs of Inattention

Lack of attention to detail

Becoming easily distracted

Forgetfulness

Some Signs of Hyperactivity

Interrupting others

Hasty, impulsive

Frequently, the hyperactive child comes across as noisy and boisterous. The child's behavior is hasty, impulsive, and seems to occur without much forethought; these characteristics may explain why adolescents and young adults diagnosed with ADHD receive more traffic tickets and have more automobile accidents than do others (Thompson, Molina, Pelham, & Gnagy, 2007).

✎ On Your Own

Which of the previous symptoms of inattention and hyperactivity do you have (even if only on occasion)? List them in the table below.

Inattention	Hyperactivity

ADHD occurs in about 5% of children (APA, 2013). On the average, boys are 3 times more likely to have ADHD than are girls; however, such findings might reflect the greater propensity of boys to engage in aggressive and antisocial behavior and thus incur a greater likelihood of being referred to psychological clinics (Barkley, 2006). Children with ADHD face severe academic and social challenges.

Impacts of ADHD

Lower grades

Lower standardized scores

More expulsions

Being held back in school

Dropping out of school

Rejection from peers

Previously, ADHD was thought to fade away by adolescence. However, longitudinal studies have suggested that ADHD is a chronic problem, one that can persist into adolescence and adulthood (Barkley, Fischer, Smallish, & Fletcher, 2002). A recent study found that 29.3% of adults who had been diagnosed with ADHD decades earlier still showed symptoms (Barbaresi et al., 2013). Somewhat troubling, this study also reported that nearly 81% of those whose ADHD persisted into adulthood had experienced at least one other comorbid disorder, compared to 47% of those whose ADHD did not persist.

✎ On Your Own

Do the following symptoms fit into the category of inattention or hyperactivity?

1. Carson fidgets constantly, always bouncing his leg up and down to the point that his desk seems to vibrate.

☐ Inattention   ☐ Hyperactivity

📷 **Figure 2:** ADHD symptoms carrying over into adulthood are not uncommon.

2. Bella's desk is in such a state of disarray that she often cannot find her homework in order to bring it home for the evening.

☐ Inattention   ☐ Hyperactivity

3. Kacey cannot sit through an hour long exam without mentally drifting off, thinking about anything and everything except the exam questions in front of him.

☐ Inattention   ☐ Hyperactivity

Life Problems from ADHD

Children diagnosed with ADHD sometimes face considerably worse long-term outcomes than do those children who do not receive such a diagnosis. In one investigation, 135 adults who had been identified as having ADHD symptoms in the 1970s were contacted decades later and interviewed (Klein et al., 2012). Compared to a control sample of 136 participants who had never been diagnosed with ADHD, those who were diagnosed as children suffered the following long-term effects:

Long-Term Effects

Worse educational attainment

Lower socioeconomic status

Held less prestigious occupational positions

More likely to be unemployed

Made less in salary

Scored worse on measure of occupational and social functioning

More likely to be divorced

More likely to have non-alcohol substance abuse

Figure 3: A childhood ADHD diagnosis can result in long-term disadvantages.

Longitudinal studies also show that children diagnosed with ADHD are at higher risk for substance abuse problems. One study reported that childhood ADHD predicted later drinking problems, daily smoking, use of marijuana, and use of illicit drugs (Molina & Pelham, 2003). The risk of substance abuse problems appears to be even greater for those with ADHD who also exhibit antisocial tendencies (Marshal & Molina, 2006).

Causes of ADHD

Family and twin studies indicate that genetics play a significant role in the development of ADHD. Burt (2009), in a review of 26 studies, reported that the median rate of concordance for identical twins was .66 (one study reported a rate of .90), whereas the median concordance rate for fraternal twins was .20. This study also found that the median concordance rate for unrelated (adoptive) siblings was .09; although this number is small, it is greater than 0, thus suggesting that the environment may have at least some influence. Another review of studies concluded that the heritability of inattention and hyperactivity were 71% and 73%, respectively (Nikolas & Burt, 2010).

The specific genes involved in ADHD are thought to include at least two that are important in the regulation of the neurotransmitter dopamine (Gizer, Ficks, & Waldman, 2009), suggesting that dopamine may be important in ADHD. Indeed, medications used in the treatment of ADHD, such as methylphenidate (Ritalin) and amphetamine with dextroamphetamine (Adderall), have stimulant qualities and elevate dopamine activity. People with ADHD show less dopamine activity in key regions of the brain, especially those associated with motivation and reward (Volkow et al., 2009), which provides support to the theory that dopamine deficits may be a vital factor in the development of this disorder (Swanson et al., 2007).

🖼 **Figure 4:** Children with ADHD have shown abnormalities in their frontal lobes.

Brain imaging studies have shown that children with ADHD exhibit abnormalities in their frontal lobes, an area in which dopamine is in abundance. Compared to children without ADHD, those with ADHD appear to have smaller frontal lobe volume, and they show less frontal lobe activation when performing mental tasks. Recall that one of the functions of the frontal lobes is to inhibit our behavior. Thus, abnormalities in this region may go a long way toward explaining the hyperactive, uncontrolled behavior of ADHD.

By the 1970s, many had become aware of the connection between nutritional factors and childhood behavior. At the time, much of the public believed that hyperactivity was caused by sugar and food additives, such as artificial coloring and flavoring. Undoubtedly, part of the appeal of this hypothesis was that it provided a simple explanation of (and treatment for) behavioral problems in children. A statistical review of 16 studies, however, concluded that sugar consumption has no effect at all on the behavioral and cognitive performance of children (Wolraich, Wilson, & White, 1995). Additionally, although food additives have been shown to increase hyperactivity in non-ADHD children, the effect is rather small (McCann et al., 2007). Numerous studies, however, have shown a significant relationship between exposure to nicotine in cigarette smoke during the prenatal period and ADHD (Linnet et al., 2003). Maternal smoking during pregnancy is associated with the development of more severe symptoms of the disorder (Thakur et al., 2013).

Reflection Questions

Why do you suppose the idea that ADHD is caused by sugar consumption persists?

Is ADHD caused by poor parenting? Not likely. Remember, the genetics studies discussed previously suggested that the family environment does not seem to play much of a role in the development of this disorder; if it did, we would expect the concordance rates to be higher for fraternal twins and adoptive siblings than has been demonstrated. All things considered, the evidence seems to point to the conclusion that ADHD is triggered more by genetic and neurological factors and less by social or environmental ones.

Dig Deeper

Why Is the Prevalence Rate of ADHD Increasing?

Many people believe that the rates of ADHD have increased in recent years, and there is evidence to support this contention. In a recent study, investigators found that the parent-reported prevalence of ADHD among children (4–17 years old) in the United States increased by 22% during a 4-year period, from 7.8% in 2003 to 9.5% in 2007 (CDC, 2010). Over time, this increase in parent-reported ADHD was observed in all sociodemographic groups and was reflected by substantial increases in 12 states (Indiana, North Carolina, and Colorado were the top three). The increases were greatest for older teens (ages 15–17), multiracial and Hispanic children, and children with a primary language other than English. Another investigation found that from 1998–2000 through 2007–2009 the parent-reported prevalence of ADHD increased among U.S. children between the ages of 5–17 years old, from 6.9% to 9.0% (Akinbami, Liu, Pastor, & Reuben, 2011).

A major weakness of both studies was that children were not actually given a formal diagnosis. Instead, parents were simply asked whether or not a doctor or other health-care provider had ever told them their child had ADHD; the reported prevalence rates thus may have been affected by the accuracy of parental memory. Nevertheless, the findings from these studies raise important questions concerning what appears to be a demonstrable rise in the prevalence of ADHD. Although the reasons underlying this apparent increase in the rates of ADHD over time are poorly understood and, at best, speculative, several explanations are viable:

- ADHD may be over-diagnosed by doctors who are too quick to medicate children as a behavior treatment.

- There is greater awareness of ADHD now than in the past. Nearly everyone has heard of ADHD, and most parents and teachers are aware of its key symptoms. Thus, parents may be quick to take their children to a doctor if they believe their child possesses these symptoms, or teachers may be more likely now than in the past to notice the symptoms and refer the child for evaluation.

- The use of computers, video games, iPhones, and other electronic devices has become pervasive among children in the early 21st century, and these devices could potentially shorten children's attention spans. Thus, what might seem like inattention to some parents and teachers could simply reflect exposure to too much technology.

- ADHD diagnostic criteria have changed over time.

Figure 5: The recent prevalence of technology in childhood could be resulting in shortened attention spans.

Autism Spectrum Disorder

A seminal paper published in 1943 by psychiatrist Leo Kanner described an unusual neurodevelopmental condition he observed in a group of children. He called this condition early infantile autism, and it was characterized mainly by an inability to form close emotional ties with others, speech and language abnormalities, repetitive behaviors, and an intolerance of minor changes in the environment and in normal routines (Bregman, 2005). What the DSM-5 refers to as **autism spectrum disorder** today, is a direct extension of Kanner's work.

Autism spectrum disorder is probably the most misunderstood and puzzling of the neurodevelopmental disorders. Children with this disorder show signs of significant disturbances in three main areas.

🖼 **Figure 6:** The types and severities of autism fall on a spectrum, not within a black-and-white classification system.

These disturbances appear early in life and cause serious impairments in functioning (APA, 2013). The child with autism spectrum disorder might exhibit deficits in social interaction by not initiating conversations with other children or turning their head away when spoken to. These children do not make eye contact with others and seem to prefer playing alone rather than with others. In a certain sense, it is almost as though these individuals live in a personal and isolated social world others are simply not privy to or able to penetrate. Communication deficits can range from a complete lack of speech, to one word responses (e.g., saying "Yes" or "No" when replying to questions or statements that require additional elaboration), to echoed speech (e.g., parroting what another person says, either immediately or several hours or even days later), to difficulty maintaining a conversation because of an inability to reciprocate others' comments. These deficits can also include problems in using and understanding nonverbal cues (e.g., facial expressions, gestures, and postures) that facilitate normal communication.

Repetitive patterns of behavior or interests can be exhibited a number of ways. The child might engage in stereotyped, repetitive movements (rocking, head-banging, or repeatedly dropping an object and then picking it up), or she might show great distress at small changes in routine or the environment. For example, the child might throw a temper tantrum if an object is not in its proper place or if a regularly-scheduled activity is rescheduled. In some cases, the person with autism spectrum disorder might show highly restricted and fixated interests that appear to be abnormal in their intensity. For instance, the person might learn and memorize every detail about something even though doing so serves no apparent purpose. Importantly, autism spectrum disorder is not the same thing as intellectual disability although these two conditions are often comorbid. The DSM-5 specifies that the symptoms of autism spectrum disorder are not caused or explained by intellectual disability.

Life Problems from Autism Spectrum Disorder

Autism spectrum disorder is referred to in everyday language as autism; in fact, the disorder was termed *autistic disorder* in earlier editions of the DSM, and its diagnostic criteria were much narrower than those of autism spectrum disorder. The qualifier *spectrum* in autism spectrum disorder is used to indicate that individuals with the disorder can show a range, or spectrum, of symptoms that vary in their magnitude and severity: some severe, others less severe. The previous edition of the DSM included a diagnosis of Asperger's disorder, generally recognized as a less severe form of autistic disorder; individuals diagnosed with Asperger's disorder were described as having average or high intelligence and a strong vocabulary but exhibiting impairments in social interaction and social communication, such as talking only about their special interests (Wing, Gould, & Gillberg, 2011). However, because research has failed to demonstrate that Asperger's disorder differs qualitatively from autistic disorder, the DSM-5 does not include it, which is prompting concerns among some parents that their children may no longer be eligible for special services ("Asperger's Syndrome Dropped," 2012). Some individuals with autism spectrum disorder, particularly those with better language and intellectual skills, can live and work independently as adults. However, most do not because the symptoms remain sufficient to cause serious impairment in many realms of life (APA, 2013).

Further Resources

Watch this excerpt (hawkes. biz/autism) from the movie *Rainman* (1988).

How does the movie depict autism spectrum disorder? What do you think a depiction like this does for our understanding of the disorder?

Further Resources

Watch this instructive and poignant video (hawkes.biz/ autisminfo) to learn more about severe autism.

Currently, estimates indicate that nearly 1 in 59 children in the United States has autism spectrum disorder; the disorder is 4 times more common in boys (1 out of 37) than girls (1 out of 151) (CDC, 2018). Rates of autistic spectrum disorder have increased dramatically since the 1980s. For example, California saw an increase of 273% in reported cases from 1987 through 1998 (Byrd, 2002); between 2000 and 2008, the rate of autism diagnoses in the United States increased 78% (CDC, 2012). Although it is difficult to interpret this increase, it is possible that the rise in prevalence is the result of the broadening of the diagnosis, increased efforts to identify cases in the community, and greater awareness and acceptance of the diagnosis. In addition, mental health professionals are now more knowledgeable about autism spectrum disorder and are better equipped to make the diagnosis, even in subtle cases (Novella, 2008).

Causes of Autism Spectrum Disorder

Early theories of autism placed the blame squarely on the shoulders of the child's parents, particularly the mother. Bruno Bettelheim (an Austrian-born American child psychologist who was heavily influenced by Sigmund Freud's ideas) suggested that a mother's ambivalent attitudes and her frozen and rigid emotions toward her child were the main causal factors in childhood autism. In what must certainly stand as one of the more controversial assertions in psychology over the last 50 years, he wrote, "I state my belief that the precipitating factor in infantile autism is the parent's wish that his child should not exist" (Bettelheim, 1967, p. 125). As you might imagine, Bettelheim did not endear himself to a lot of people with this position; incidentally, no scientific evidence exists supporting his claims.

Figure 7: April is World Autism Awareness Month.

The exact causes of autism spectrum disorder remain unknown despite massive research efforts over the last two decades (Meek, Lemery-Chalfant, Jahromi, & Valiente, 2013). Autism appears to be strongly influenced by genetics, as identical twins show concordance rates of 60%–90%, whereas concordance rates for fraternal twins and siblings are 5%–10% (Autism Genome Project Consortium, 2007). Many different genes and gene mutations have been implicated in autism (Meek et al., 2013). Among the genes involved are those important in the formation of synaptic circuits that facilitate communication between different areas of the brain (Gauthier et al., 2011). A number of environmental factors are also thought to be associated with an increased risk for autism spectrum disorder, at least in part, because they contribute to new mutations. These factors include exposure to pollutants, such as plant emissions and mercury, urban versus rural residence, and vitamin D deficiency (Kinney, Barch, Chayka, Napoleon, & Munir, 2009).

Child Vaccinations and Autism Spectrum Disorder

In the late 1990s, a prestigious medical journal published an article purportedly showing that autism is triggered by the MMR (measles, mumps, and rubella) vaccine. These findings were very controversial and drew a great deal of attention, sparking an international forum on whether children should be vaccinated. In a shocking turn of events, some years later the article was retracted by the journal that had published it after accusations of fraud on the part of the lead researcher. Despite the retraction, the reporting in popular media led to concerns about a possible link between vaccines and autism persisting. A recent survey of parents, for example, found that roughly a third of respondents expressed such a concern (Kennedy, LaVail, Nowak, Basket, & Landry, 2011); and perhaps fearing that their children would develop autism, more than 10% of parents of young children refuse or delay vaccinations (Dempsey et al., 2011). Some parents of children with autism mounted a campaign against scientists who refuted the vaccine-autism link. Even politicians and several well-known celebrities weighed in; for example, actress Jenny McCarthy (who believed that a vaccination caused her son's autism) co-authored a book on the matter. However, there is no scientific evidence that a link exists between autism and vaccinations (Hughes, 2007). Indeed, a recent study compared the vaccination histories of 256 children with autism spectrum disorder with that of 752 control children across three time periods during their

Figure 8: The purported link between MMR vaccines and autism was later redacted by the medical journal that published the controversial article.

Group Activity

With 2 or 3 classmates, discuss ways in which you could help change public opinion about the false relationship between vaccinations and autism.

first two years of life (birth to 3 months, birth to 7 months, and birth to 2 years) (DeStefano, Price, & Weintraub, 2013). At the time of the study, the children were between 6 and 13 years old, and their prior vaccination records were obtained. Because vaccines contain immunogens (substances that fight infections), the investigators examined medical records to see how many immunogens children received to determine if those children who received more immunogens were at greater risk for developing autism spectrum disorder. The results of this study, a portion of which are shown in Figure 9, clearly demonstrate that the quantity of immunogens from vaccines received during the first two years of life were not at all related to the development of autism spectrum disorder.

There is no relationship between vaccinations and autism spectrum disorder.

Figure 9: In terms of their exposure to immunogens in vaccines, overall, there is not a significant difference between children with autism spectrum disorder and their age-matched controls without the disorder (DeStefano et al., 2013).

Why does concern over vaccines and autism spectrum disorder persist? Since the proliferation of the Internet in the 1990s, parents have been constantly bombarded with online information that can become magnified and take on a life of its own. The enormous volume of electronic information pertaining to autism spectrum disorder, combined with how difficult it can be to grasp complex scientific concepts, can make separating good research from bad challenging (Downs, 2008). Notably, the study that fueled the controversy reported that 8 out of 12 children—according to their parents—developed symptoms consistent with autism spectrum disorder shortly after receiving a vaccination. To conclude that vaccines cause autism spectrum disorder on this basis, as many did, is clearly incorrect for a number of reasons, not the least of which is because correlation does not imply causation, as you've learned.

Group Activity

The previous statement reads that "to conclude that vaccines cause autism spectrum disorder on this basis... was clearly incorrect for a number of reasons." Discuss those reasons with 2 or 3 classmates.

Additionally, as was the case with diet and ADHD in the 1970s, the notion that autism spectrum disorder is caused by vaccinations is appealing to some because it provides a simple explanation for this condition. Like all disorders, however, there are no simple explanations for autism spectrum disorder. Although the research discussed previously has shed some light on its causes, science is still a long way from complete understanding of the disorder.

Summary

Neurodevelopmental disorders are a group of disorders that are typically diagnosed during childhood and are characterized by developmental deficits in personal, social, academic, and intellectual realms; these disorders include attention deficit/hyperactivity disorder (ADHD) and autism spectrum disorder. ADHD is characterized by a pervasive pattern of inattention and/or hyperactive and impulsive behavior that interferes with normal functioning. Genetic and neurobiological factors contribute to the development of ADHD, which can persist well into adulthood and can be associated with poor long-term outcomes. The major features of autism spectrum disorder include deficits in social interaction and communication and repetitive movements or interests. As with ADHD, genetic factors appear to play a prominent role in the development of autism spectrum disorder; exposure to environmental pollutants such as mercury has also been linked to the development of this disorder. Although it is believed by some that autism is triggered by the MMR vaccination, evidence does not support this claim.

Chapter 14 Project

Purpose

In this chapter, you have learned about a variety of psychological disorders. Many of the disorders share similar features or symptoms, while others are significantly different. **The purpose of this project is to explore the complexities of the human condition through application of the knowledge you have gained in this chapter.** You are going to be creating your own version of the DSM-5 to organize the various mental health conditions you have been exposed to in this chapter.

Directions

For this project, imagine that you are the author of the DSM-5 and have been approached by a psychiatrist's office to create a simplified version of the manual. You will use a word processor, like Microsoft Word, and create a "book." Each page will contain a major disorder category noted in this chapter (i.e., anxiety, mood, etc.) and applicable information pertaining to that category of disorders.

Please use the following template for each class or category:

1. Class or Category

    A. Five or more pieces of pertinent information pertaining to the class or category of disorders (i.e., concepts and or ideas)

    B. Symptoms common to all disorders within the category

    C. Therapy common to all disorders within the category

    D. Specific conditions under the class or category of mental health disorders

        i. For each condition, list unique symptoms, treatments, and famous people who have suffered from the condition.

FOR EXAMPLE:

1. Anxiety Disorders

    A. Fact 1

    B. Fact 2

    C. Fact 3

    D. Fact 4

    E. Fact 5

    F. Shared Symptoms

        i. Symptom 1

        ii. Symptom 2

        iii. Symptom 3

    G. Shared Therapy

        i. Therapy 1

        ii. Therapy 2

        iii. Therapy 3

    H. Types of Anxiety Disorders

        i. Specific Phobia

            a. Symptoms

            b. Treatments

            c. Famous examples

        ii. Social Anxiety Disorder

            a. Symptoms

            b. Treatments

            c. Famous examples

Materials

Word processing application, like Microsoft Word

✔ Checklist

☐ All classes or categories in the chapter are addressed

☐ Each class or category has:

☐ 5 or more facts/examples of pertinent information

☐ Symptoms common to all disorders in the category

☐ Therapy common to all disorders in the category

☐ Specific conditions under this class or category of disorder

☐ List of symptoms, treatments, and examples of famous people with the disorder

🏁 Chapter 14 Review

Lesson Summaries

14.1 What Are Psychological Disorders?

Psychological disorders are conditions characterized by abnormal thoughts, feelings, and behaviors. Although challenging, it is essential for psychologists and mental health professionals to agree on what kinds of inner experiences and behaviors constitute the presence of a psychological disorder. Inner experiences and behaviors that are atypical or violate social norms could signify the presence of a disorder; however, each of these criteria alone is inadequate. Harmful dysfunction describes the view that psychological disorders result from the inability of an internal mechanism to perform its natural function. Many of the features of harmful dysfunction conceptualization have been incorporated in the APA's formal definition of psychological disorders. According to this definition, the presence of a psychological disorder is signaled by significant disturbances in thoughts, feelings, and behaviors; these disturbances must reflect some kind of dysfunction (biological, psychological, or developmental), must cause significant impairment in one's life, and must not reflect culturally expected reactions to certain life events.

14.2 Diagnosing and Classifying Psychological Disorders

The diagnosis and classification of psychological disorders is essential in studying and treating psychopathology. The classification system used by most U.S. professionals is the DSM-5. The first edition of the DSM was published in 1952 and has undergone numerous revisions. The 5th and most recent edition, the DSM-5, was published in

2013. The diagnostic manual includes a total of 237 specific diagnosable disorders, each described in detail, including its symptoms, prevalence, risk factors, and comorbidity. Over time, the number of diagnosable conditions listed in the DSM has grown steadily, prompting criticism from some. Nevertheless, the diagnostic criteria in the DSM are more explicit than that of any other system, which makes the DSM system highly desirable for both clinical diagnosis and research.

14.3 Perspectives on Psychological Disorders

Psychopathology is very complex, involving a plethora of etiological theories and perspectives. For centuries, psychological disorders were viewed primarily from a supernatural perspective and thought to arise from divine forces or possession from spirits. Some cultures continue to hold this supernatural belief. Today, many who study psychopathology view mental illness from a biological perspective, whereby psychological disorders are thought to result largely from faulty biological processes. Indeed, scientific advances over the last several decades have provided a better understanding of the genetic, neurological, hormonal, and biochemical bases of psychopathology. The psychological perspective, in contrast, emphasizes the importance of psychological factors (e.g., stress and thoughts) and environmental factors in the development of psychological disorders. A contemporary, promising approach is to view disorders as originating from an integration of biological and psychosocial factors. The diathesis-stress model suggests that people with an underlying diathesis, or vulnerability, for a psychological disorder are more likely than those

without the diathesis to develop the disorder when faced with stressful events.

14.4 Anxiety Disorders

Anxiety disorders are a group of disorders in which a person experiences excessive, persistent, and distressing fear and anxiety that interferes with normal functioning. Anxiety disorders include specific phobia (a specific, unrealistic fear), social anxiety disorder (extreme fear and avoidance of social situations), panic disorder (sudden, overwhelming panic even though there is no apparent reason to be frightened), agoraphobia (an intense fear and avoidance of situations in which it might be difficult to escape), and generalized anxiety disorder (a relatively continuous state of tension, apprehension, and dread).

14.5 Obsessive-Compulsive and Related Disorders

Obsessive-compulsive and related disorders are a group of DSM-5 disorders that overlap somewhat in that they each involve intrusive thoughts and/or repetitive behaviors. Perhaps the most recognized of these disorders is obsessive-compulsive disorder, in which a person is obsessed with unwanted, unpleasant thoughts and/or compulsively engages in repetitive behaviors or mental acts, perhaps as a way of coping with the obsessions. Body dysmorphic disorder is characterized by the individual becoming excessively preoccupied with one or more perceived flaws in his physical appearance that are either nonexistent or unnoticeable to others. Preoccupation with the perceived physical defects causes the person to experience significant anxiety regarding how he appears to others. Hoarding disorder is characterized by persistent difficulty in discarding or parting with objects, regardless of their actual value, often resulting in the accumulation of items that clutter and congest her living area.

14.6 Posttraumatic Stress Disorder

Posttraumatic stress disorder (PTSD) was described through much of the 20th century and was referred to as *shell shock* and *combat neurosis* in the belief that its symptoms were thought to emerge from the stress of active combat. Today, PTSD is defined as a disorder in which the experience of a traumatic or profoundly stressful event, such as combat, sexual assault, or natural disaster, produces a constellation of symptoms that must last for one month or more. These symptoms include intrusive and distressing memories of the event, flashbacks, avoidance of stimuli or situations that are connected to the event, persistently negative emotional states, feeling detached from others, irritability, proneness toward outbursts, and a tendency to be easily startled. Not everyone who experiences a traumatic event will develop PTSD; a variety of risk factors associated with its development have been identified.

14.7 Mood Disorders

Mood disorders are those in which the person experiences severe disturbances in mood and emotion. They include depressive disorders and bipolar and related disorders. Depressive disorders include major depressive disorder, which is characterized by episodes of profound sadness and loss of interest or pleasure in usual activities and other associated features, and persistent depressive disorder, which is marked by a chronic state of sadness. Bipolar disorder is characterized by mood states that vacillate between sadness and euphoria; a diagnosis of bipolar disorder

requires experiencing at least one manic episode, which is defined as a period of extreme euphoria, irritability, and increased activity. Mood disorders appear to have a genetic component, with genetic factors playing a more prominent role in bipolar disorder than in depression. Both biological and psychological factors are important in the development of depression. People who suffer from mental health problems, especially mood disorders, are at heightened risk for suicide.

14.8 Schizophrenia

Schizophrenia is a severe disorder characterized by a complete breakdown in one's ability to function in life; it often requires hospitalization. People with schizophrenia experience hallucinations and delusions, and they have extreme difficulty regulating their emotions and behavior. Thinking is incoherent and disorganized, behavior is extremely bizarre, emotions are flat, and motivation to engage in most basic life activities is lacking. Considerable evidence shows that genetic factors play a central role in schizophrenia; however, adoption studies have highlighted the additional importance of environmental factors. Neurotransmitter and brain abnormalities, which may be linked to environmental factors such as obstetric complications or exposure to influenza during the gestational period, have also been implicated. A promising new area of schizophrenia research involves identifying individuals who show prodromal symptoms and following them over time to determine which factors best predict the development of schizophrenia. Future research may enable us to pinpoint those especially at risk for developing schizophrenia and who may benefit from early intervention.

14.9 Dissociative Disorders

The main characteristic of dissociative disorders is that people become dissociated from their sense of self,

resulting in memory and identity disturbances. Dissociative disorders listed in the DSM-5 include dissociative amnesia, depersonalization/derealization disorder, and dissociative identity disorder. A person with dissociative amnesia is unable to recall important personal information, often after a stressful or traumatic experience.

Depersonalization/derealization disorder is characterized by recurring episodes of depersonalization (i.e., detachment from or unfamiliarity with the self) and/or derealization (i.e., detachment from or unfamiliarity with the world). A person with dissociative identity disorder exhibits two or more well-defined and distinct personalities or identities, as well as memory gaps for the times during which another identity was present.

Dissociative identity disorder has generated controversy, mainly because some believe its symptoms can be faked by patients if presenting its symptoms somehow benefits the patient in avoiding negative consequences or taking responsibility for one's actions. The diagnostic rates of this disorder have increased dramatically following its portrayal in popular culture. However, many people legitimately suffer with this disorder over the course of their lives.

14.10 Personality Disorders

Individuals with personality disorders exhibit a personality style that is inflexible, causes distress and impairment, and creates problems for themselves and others. The DSM-5 recognizes 10 personality disorders, organized into three clusters. The disorders in Cluster A include those characterized by a personality style that is odd and eccentric. Cluster B includes personality disorders characterized chiefly by a personality style that is impulsive, dramatic, highly emotional, and erratic, and those in Cluster C are characterized by a nervous and fearful personality style. Two Cluster

B personality disorders, borderline personality disorder and antisocial personality disorder, are especially problematic. People with borderline personality disorder show marked instability in mood, behavior, and self-image, as well as impulsivity. They cannot stand to be alone, are unpredictable, have a history of stormy relationships, and frequently display intense and inappropriate anger. Genetic factors and adverse childhood experiences (e.g., sexual abuse) appear to be important in its development. People with antisocial personality display a lack of regard for the rights of others; they are impulsive, deceitful, irresponsible, and unburdened by any sense of guilt. Genetic factors and socialization both appear to be important in the origin of antisocial personality disorder. Research has also shown that those with this disorder do not experience emotions the way most other people do.

14.11 Disorders in Childhood

Neurodevelopmental disorders are a group of disorders that are typically diagnosed during childhood and are characterized by developmental deficits in personal, social, academic, and intellectual realms; these disorders include attention deficit/hyperactivity disorder (ADHD) and autism spectrum disorder. ADHD is characterized by a pervasive pattern of inattention and/or hyperactive and impulsive behavior that interferes with normal functioning. Genetic and neurobiological factors contribute to the development of ADHD, which can persist well into adulthood and can be associated with poor long-term outcomes. The major features of autism spectrum disorder include deficits in social interaction and communication and repetitive movements or interests. As with ADHD, genetic factors appear to play a prominent role in the development of autism spectrum disorder; exposure to environmental pollutants such as

mercury has also been linked to the development of this disorder. Although it is believed by some that autism is triggered by the MMR vaccination, evidence does not support this claim.

Key Terms

Flash Back

Now that you've worked through the chapter, sharpen your vocabulary with this Hawkes Verified Quizlet set (hawkes.biz/psychch14)!

Agoraphobia

Anxiety disorder characterized by intense fear, anxiety, and avoidance of situations in which it might be difficult to escape if one experiences symptoms of a panic attack

Antisocial Personality Disorder

Characterized by a lack of regard for others' rights, impulsivity, deceitfulness, irresponsibility, and lack of remorse over misdeeds

Anxiety Disorder

Characterized by excessive and persistent fear and anxiety, and by related disturbances in behavior

Attention Deficit/Hyperactivity Disorder

Childhood disorder characterized by inattentiveness and/or hyperactive, impulsive behavior

Atypical

Describes behaviors or feelings that deviate from the norm

Autism Spectrum Disorder

Childhood disorder characterized by deficits in social interaction and communication and repetitive patterns of behavior or interests

Bipolar and Related Disorders

Group of mood disorders in which mania is the defining feature

Bipolar Disorder

Mood disorder characterized by mood states that vacillate between depression and mania

Body Dysmorphic Disorder

Involves excessive preoccupation with an imagined defect in physical appearance

Borderline Personality Disorder

Instability in interpersonal relationships, self-image, and mood, as well as impulsivity; key features include intolerance of being alone and fear of abandonment, unstable relationships, unpredictable behavior and moods, and intense and inappropriate anger

Catatonic Behavior

Decreased reactivity to the environment; includes posturing and catatonic stupor

Comorbidity

Co-occurrence of two disorders in the same individual

Delusion

Belief that is contrary to reality and is firmly held, despite contradictory evidence

Depersonalization/Derealization Disorder

Dissociative disorder in which people feel detached from the self (depersonalization), and the world feels artificial and unreal (derealization)

Depressive Disorder

One of a group of mood disorders in which depression is the defining feature

Diagnosis

Determination of which disorder a set of symptoms represents

Diagnostic and Statistical Manual of Mental Disorders, Fifth Edition (DSM-5)

Authoritative index of mental disorders and the criteria for their diagnosis; published by the American Psychiatric Association (APA)

Diathesis-Stress Model

Suggests that people with a predisposition for a disorder (a diathesis) are more likely to develop the disorder when faced with stress; model of psychopathology

Disorganized Thinking

Disjointed and incoherent thought processes, usually detected by what a person says

Disorganized/Abnormal Motor Behavior

Highly unusual behaviors and movements (such as child-like behaviors), repeated and purposeless movements, and displaying odd facial expressions and gestures

Dissociative Amnesia

Dissociative disorder characterized by an inability to recall important personal information, usually following an extremely stressful or traumatic experience

Dissociative Disorders

Group of DSM-5 disorders in which the primary feature is that a person becomes dissociated, or split off, from his or her core sense of self, resulting in disturbances in identity and memory

Dissociative Fugue

Symptom of dissociative amnesia in which a person suddenly wanders away from one's home and experiences confusion about his or her identity

Dissociative Identity Disorder

Dissociative disorder (formerly known as *multiple personality disorder*) in which a person exhibits two or more distinct, well-defined personalities or identities and experiences memory gaps for the time during which another identity emerged

Dopamine Hypothesis

Theory of schizophrenia that proposes that an overabundance of dopamine or dopamine receptors is responsible for the onset and maintenance of schizophrenia

Etiology

Cause or causes of a psychological disorder

Flashback

Psychological state lasting from a few seconds to several days, during which one relives a traumatic event and behaves as though the event were occurring at that moment

Flight of Ideas

Symptom of mania that involves an abrupt switch in conversation from one topic to another

Generalized Anxiety Disorder

Characterized by a continuous state of excessive, uncontrollable, and pointless worry and apprehension

Grandiose Delusion

Characterized by beliefs that one holds special power, unique knowledge, or is extremely important

Hallucination

Perceptual experience that occurs in the absence of external stimulation, such as the auditory hallucinations (hearing voices) common to schizophrenia

Harmful Dysfunction

Model of psychological disorders resulting from the inability of an internal mechanism to perform its natural function

Hoarding Disorder

Characterized by persistent difficulty in parting with possessions, regardless of their actual value or usefulness

Hopelessness Theory

Cognitive theory of depression proposing that a style of thinking that perceives negative life events as having stable and global causes leads to a sense of hopelessness and then to depression

International Classification of Diseases (ICD)

Authoritative index of mental and physical diseases, including infectious diseases, and the criteria for their diagnosis; published by the World Health Organization (WHO)

Locus Coeruleus

Area of the brainstem that contains norepinephrine, a neurotransmitter that triggers the body's fight-or-flight response; has been implicated in panic disorderr

Major Depressive Disorder

Commonly referred to as *depression* or *major depression,* characterized by sadness or loss of pleasure in usual activities, as well other symptoms

Mania

State of extreme elation and agitation

Manic Episode

Period in which an individual experiences mania, characterized by extremely cheerful and euphoric mood, excessive talkativeness, irritability, increased activity levels, and other symptoms

Mood Disorder

One of a group of disorders characterized by severe disturbances in mood and emotions; the categories of mood disorders listed in the DSM-5 are bipolar and related disorders and depressive disorders

Negative Symptom

Characterized by decreases and absences in certain normal behaviors, emotions, or drives, such as an expressionless face, lack of motivation to engage in activities, reduced speech, lack of social engagement, and inability to experience pleasure

Neurodevelopmental Disorder

One of the disorders that are first diagnosed in childhood and involve developmental problems in academic, intellectual, and social functioning

Obsessive-Compulsive and Related Disorders

Group of overlapping disorders listed in the DSM-5 that involves intrusive, unpleasant thoughts and/or repetitive behaviors

Obsessive-Compulsive Disorder (OCD)

Characterized by the tendency to experience intrusive and unwanted thoughts and urges (obsession) and/or the need to engage in repetitive behaviors or mental acts (compulsions) in response to the unwanted thoughts and urges

Orbitofrontal Cortex

Area of the frontal lobe involved in learning and decision-making

Panic Attack

Period of extreme fear or discomfort that develops abruptly; symptoms of panic attacks are both physiological and psychological

Panic Disorder

Anxiety disorder characterized by unexpected panic attacks, along with at least one month of worry about panic attacks or self-defeating behavior related to the attacks

Paranoid Delusion

Characterized by beliefs that others are out to harm them

Peripartum Onset

Subtype of depression that applies to women who experience an episode of major depression either during pregnancy or in the four weeks following childbirth

Persistent Depressive Disorder

Depressive disorder characterized by a chronically sad and melancholy mood

Personality Disorder

Group of DSM-5 disorders characterized by an inflexible and pervasive personality style that differs markedly from the expectations of one's culture and causes distress and impairment; people with these disorders have a personality style that frequently brings them into conflict with others and disrupts their ability to develop and maintain social relationships

Posttraumatic Stress Disorder (PTSD)

Experiencing a profoundly traumatic event leads to a constellation of symptoms that includes intrusive and distressing memories of the event, avoidance of stimuli connected to the event, negative emotional states, feelings of detachment from others, irritability, proneness toward outbursts, hypervigilance, and a tendency to startle easily; these symptoms must occur for at least one month

Prodromal Symptom

In schizophrenia, one of the early minor symptoms of psychosis

Psychological Disorder

Condition characterized by abnormal thoughts, feelings, and behaviors

Psychopathology

Study of psychological disorders, including their symptoms, causes, and treatment; manifestation of a psychological disorder

Rumination

In depression, tendency to repetitively and passively dwell on one's depressed symptoms, their meanings, and their consequences

Safety Behavior

Mental and behavior acts designed to reduce anxiety in social situations by reducing the chance of negative social outcomes; common in social anxiety disorder

Schizophrenia

Severe disorder characterized by major disturbances in thought, perception, emotion, and behavior with symptoms that include hallucinations, delusions, disorganized thinking and behavior, and negative symptoms

Seasonal Pattern

Subtype of depression in which a person experiences the symptoms of major depressive disorder only during a particular time of year

Social Anxiety Disorder

Characterized by extreme and persistent fear or anxiety and avoidance of social situations in which one could potentially be evaluated negatively by others

Somatic Delusion

Belief that something highly unusual is happening to one's body or internal organs

Specific Phobia

Anxiety disorder characterized by excessive, distressing, and persistent fear or anxiety about a specific object or situation

Suicidal Ideation

Thoughts of death by suicide, thinking about or planning suicide, or making a suicide attempt

Suicide

Death caused by intentional, self-directed injurious behavior

Supernatural

Describes a force beyond scientific understanding

Ventricle

One of the fluid-filled cavities within the brain

Exercises

Review Questions

1. In the harmful dysfunction definition of psychological disorders, dysfunction involves _____.

   a. the inability of a psychological mechanism to perform its function

   b. the breakdown of social order in one's community

   c. communication problems in one's immediate family

   d. all the above

2. Patterns of inner experience and behavior are thought to reflect the presence of a psychological disorder if they _____.

   a. are highly atypical

   b. lead to significant distress and impairment in one's life

   c. embarrass one's friends and/or family

   d. violate the norms of one's culture

3. The letters in the abbreviation DSM-5 stand for _____.

   a. Diseases and Statistics Manual of Medicine

   b. Diagnosable Standards Manual of Mental Disorders

   c. Diseases and Symptoms Manual of Mental Disorders

   d. Diagnostic and Statistical Manual of Mental Disorders

4. A study based on over 9,000 U.S. residents found that the most prevalent disorder was _____.

   a. major depressive disorder

   b. social anxiety disorder

   c. obsessive-compulsive disorder

   d. specific phobia

5. The diathesis-stress model presumes that psychopathology results from _____.

   a. vulnerability and adverse experiences

   b. biochemical factors

   c. chemical imbalances and structural abnormalities in the brain

   d. adverse childhood experiences

6. Dr. Anastasia believes that major depressive disorder is caused by an over-secretion of cortisol. His view on the cause of major depressive disorder reflects a _____ perspective.

   a. psychological

   b. supernatural

   c. biological

   d. diathesis-stress

7. In which of the following anxiety disorders is the person in a continuous state of excessive, pointless worry and apprehension?

   a. Panic disorder

   b. Generalized anxiety disorder

   c. Agoraphobia

   d. Social anxiety disorder

8. Which of the following would constitute a safety behavior?

   a. Encountering a phobic stimulus in the company of other people

   b. Avoiding a field where snakes are likely to be present

   c. Avoiding eye contact

   d. Worrying as a distraction from painful memories

9. Which of the following best illustrates a compulsion?

   a. Mentally counting backward from 1,000

   b. Persistent fear of germs

   c. Thoughts of harming a neighbor

   d. Falsely believing that a spouse has been cheating

10. Research indicates that the symptoms of OCD _____.

   a. are similar to the symptoms of panic disorder

   b. are triggered by low levels of stress hormones

   c. are related to hyperactivity in the orbitofrontal cortex

   d. are reduced if people are asked to view photos of stimuli that trigger the symptoms

11. Symptoms of PTSD include all of the following *except* _____.

   a. intrusive thoughts or memories of a traumatic event

   b. avoidance of things that remind one of a traumatic event

   c. jumpiness

   d. physical complaints that cannot be explained medically

12. Which of the following elevates the risk for developing PTSD?

   a. Severity of the trauma

   b. Frequency of the trauma

   c. High levels of intelligence

   d. Social support

13. Common symptoms of major depressive disorder include all of the following *except* _____.

   a. periods of extreme elation and euphoria

   b. difficulty concentrating and making decisions

   c. loss of interest or pleasure in usual activities

   d. psychomotor agitation and retardation

14. Suicide rates are _____ among men than among women, and they are _____ during the winter holiday season than during the spring months.

   a. higher; higher

   b. lower; lower

   c. higher; lower

   d. lower; higher

15. Clifford falsely believes that the police have planted secret cameras in his home to monitor his every movement. Clifford's belief is an example of _____.

   a. a delusion

   b. a hallucination

   c. tangentiality

   d. a negative symptom

16. A study of adoptees whose biological mothers had schizophrenia found that the adoptees were most likely to develop schizophrenia _____.

   a. if their childhood friends later developed schizophrenia

   b. if they abused drugs during adolescence

   c. if they were raised in a disturbed adoptive home environment

   d. regardless of whether they were raised in a healthy or disturbed home environment

17. Dissociative amnesia involves _____.

   a. memory loss following head trauma

   b. memory loss following stress

   c. feeling detached from the self

   d. feeling detached from the world

18. Dissociative identity disorder mainly involves _____.

   a. depersonalization

   b. derealization

   c. schizophrenia

   d. different personalities

19. People with borderline personality disorder often _____.

    a.   try to be the center of attention

    b.   are shy and withdrawn

    c.   are impulsive and unpredictable

    d.   tend to accomplish goals through cruelty

20. Antisocial personality disorder is associated with _____.

    a.   emotional deficits

    b.   memory deficits

    c.   parental overprotection

    d.   increased empathy

21. Which of the following is not a primary characteristic of ADHD?

    a.   Short attention span

    b.   Difficulty concentrating and distractibility

    c.   Restricted and fixated interest

    d.   Excessive fidgeting and squirming

22. One of the primary characteristics of autism spectrum disorder is _____.

    a.   bed-wetting

    b.   difficulty relating to others

    c.   short attention span

    d.   intense and inappropriate interest in others

Critical Thinking Questions

23. Discuss why thoughts, feelings, or behaviors that are merely atypical or unusual would not necessarily signify the presence of a psychological disorder. Provide an example.

24. Describe the DSM-5. What is it, what kind of information does it contain, and why is it important to the study and treatment of psychological disorders?

25. *The International Classification of Diseases* (ICD) and the DSM differ in various ways. What are some of the differences in these two classification systems?

26. Why is the perspective one uses in explaining a psychological disorder important?

27. Describe how cognitive theories of the etiology of anxiety disorders differ from learning theories.

28. Discuss the common elements of each of the three disorders covered in Lesson 14.5: obsessive-compulsive disorder, body dysmorphic disorder, and hoarding disorder.

29. List some of the risk factors associated with the development of PTSD following a traumatic event.

30. Describe several of the factors associated with suicide.

31. Why is research following individuals who show prodromal symptoms of schizophrenia so important?

32. The prevalence of most psychological disorders has increased since the 1980s. However, as discussed in Lesson 14.9, scientific publications regarding dissociative amnesia peaked in the mid-1990s but then declined steeply through 2003. In addition, no fictional or nonfictional description of individuals showing dissociative amnesia following a trauma exists prior to 1800. How would you explain this phenomenon?

33. Imagine that a child has a genetic vulnerability to antisocial personality disorder. How might this child's environment shape the likelihood of developing this personality disorder?

34. Compare the factors that are important in the development of ADHD with those that are important in the development of autism spectrum disorder.

Chapter 15

Therapy and Treatment

Chapter Introduction

🖼 **Figure 1:** Many forms of therapy have been developed to treat a wide array of problems. Jo Newton and Donna Otabachian of the Star Healing with Horses ranch get some attention from one of their therapists, June 17, 2014. SHWH, located on the sprawling Parrie Haynes Ranch south of Fort Hood, is an organization dedicated to healing all who have experienced trauma, PTSD, and secondary PTSD.

What comes to mind when you think about therapy for psychological problems? You might picture someone lying on a couch talking about his childhood while the therapist sits and takes notes, à la Sigmund Freud. But can you envision a therapy session in which someone is wearing virtual reality headgear to conquer a fear of snakes?

In this chapter, you will see that approaches to therapy include both psychological and biological interventions, all with the goal of alleviating distress. Because psychological problems can originate from various sources—biology, genetics, childhood experiences, conditioning, and sociocultural influences—psychologists have developed many different therapeutic techniques and approaches. The Star Healing with Horses program shown in Figure 1 uses horses to support the mental health of those struggling with PTSD.

Flash Forward

Ready to dig into the vocabulary? Get some practice with this Hawkes Verified Quizlet set (hawkes.biz/psych15q1)!

15.1 Mental Health Treatment: Past and Present

Before we explore the various approaches to therapy used today, let's begin our study by looking at how many people experience mental illness and how many receive treatment. According to the U.S. Department of Health and Human Services (2013), prevalence of mental illness in 2012 included:

- 19% of U.S. adults

- Similar rates as adults for teens (ages 13–18)

- 13% for children (8–13 years)

With many different treatment options available, approximately how many people receive mental health treatment per year? According to the Substance Abuse and Mental Health Services Administration (SAMHSA), in 2008, 13.4% of adults received treatment for a mental health issue (NIMH, n.d.-b). These percentages, shown in Figure 2, reflect the number of adults who received care in inpatient and outpatient settings and/or used prescription medication for psychological disorders.

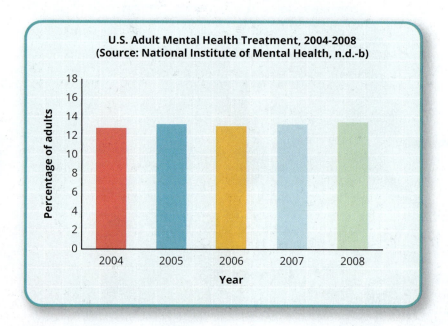

Figure 2: The percentage of adults who received mental health treatment in 2004–2008 is shown. Adults seeking treatment increased slightly during these years.

Children and adolescents also receive mental health services. The Centers for Disease Control and Prevention's National Health and Nutrition Examination Survey (NHANES) found that approximately half (50.6%) of children with mental disorders had received treatment for their disorder within the past year (NIMH, n.d.-c). However, there were some differences between treatment rates by category of disorder (Figure 3). For example, children with anxiety disorders were least likely to have received treatment in the past year while children with ADHD or a conduct disorder were more likely to receive treatment.

Reflection Questions

Can you think of some possible reasons for the differences in treatment rates between anxiety disorders and ADHD/conduct disorders? What other disorders among children may have a higher rate of treatment?

Figure 3: About one-third to one-half of U.S. adolescents (ages 8–15) with mental disorders receive treatment, with behavior-related disorders more likely to be treated.

Considering the many forms of treatment for mental health disorders available today, how did these forms of treatment emerge? Let's take a look at the history of mental health treatment from the past (with some questionable approaches in light of modern understanding of mental illness) to where we are today.

Treatment in the Past

For much of history, the mentally ill have been treated very poorly. It was believed that mental illness was caused by demonic possession, witchcraft, or an angry god (Szasz, 1960). For example, in medieval times, abnormal behaviors were viewed as a sign that a person was possessed by demons. If someone was considered to be possessed, there were several forms of treatment to release spirits from the individual. The most common treatment was exorcism, often conducted by priests or other religious figures: incantations and prayers were said over the person's body, and she may have been given some medicinal drinks. Another form of treatment for extreme cases of mental illness was trephining: a small hole was made in the afflicted individual's skull to release spirits from the body. Most people treated in this manner died. In addition to exorcism and trephining, other practices involved execution or imprisonment of people with psychological disorders. Still others were left to be homeless beggars.

Medieval Treatment Methods

Exorcism

Trephination

Execution

Imprisonment

From the late 1400s to the late 1600s, a common belief perpetuated by some religious organizations was that some people made pacts with the devil and committed horrible acts, such as eating babies (Blumberg, 2007). These people were considered to be witches and were tried and condemned by courts—they were often burned at the stake. Worldwide, it is estimated that tens of thousands of mentally ill people were killed after being accused of being witches or under the influence of witchcraft (Hemphill, 1966).

By the 18th century, people who were considered odd and unusual were placed in asylums (Figure 4). **Asylums** were the first institutions created for the specific purpose of housing people with psychological disorders, but the focus was ostracizing them from society rather than treating their disorders. Often these people were kept in windowless dungeons, beaten, chained to their beds, and had little to no contact with caregivers.

🖼 **Figure 4:** This painting by Francisco Goya, called *The Madhouse*, depicts a mental asylum and its inhabitants in the early 1800s. It portrays those with psychological disorders as victims.

In the late 1700s, a French physician, Philippe Pinel, argued for more humane treatment of the mentally ill. He suggested that they be unchained and talked to, and that's just what he did for patients at La Salpêtrière in Paris in 1795 (Figure 5). Patients benefited from this more humane treatment, and many were able to leave the hospital.

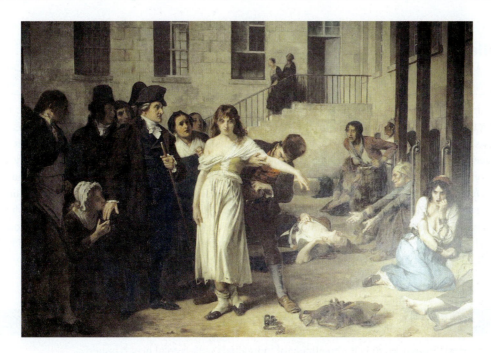

Figure 5: This painting by Tony Robert-Fleury depicts French psychiatrist Philippe Pinel (1745-1826) releasing "lunatics" from their chains at the Salpêtrière asylum in Paris in 1795.

In the 19th century, Dorothea Dix led reform efforts for mental health care in the United States (Figure 6). She investigated how those who were mentally ill and poor were cared for, and she discovered an underfunded and unregulated system that perpetuated abuse of this population (Tiffany, 1891). Horrified by her findings, Dix began lobbying various state legislatures and the U.S. Congress for change (Tiffany, 1891). Her efforts led to the creation of the first mental asylums in the United States.

Despite reformers' efforts, however, a typical asylum was:

- filthy

- offered little treatment

- often kept people for decades

🖉 On Your Own

Who first argued that people who are mentally ill should be treated humanely?

☐ Dorothea Dix

☐ William Wundt

☐ Philippe Pinel

Figure 6: Dorothea Dix was a social reformer who became an advocate for the indigent insane and was instrumental in creating the first American mental asylum. She did this by relentlessly lobbying state legislatures and Congress to set up and fund such institutions.

At Willard Psychiatric Center in upstate New York, for example, one treatment was to submerge patients in cold baths for long periods of time. Electroshock treatment was also used, and the way the treatment was administered often broke patients' backs; in 1943, doctors at Willard administered 1,443 shock treatments (Willard Psychiatric Center, 2009). (Electroshock is now called electroconvulsive treatment, and the therapy is still used, but with safeguards and under anesthesia. A brief application of electric stimulus is used to produce a generalized seizure. Controversy continues over its effectiveness versus the side effects.) Many of the wards and rooms were so cold that a glass of water would be frozen by morning (Willard Psychiatric Center, 2009). Despite all of this, Willard's doors were not closed until 1995. Conditions like these remained commonplace until well into the 20th century.

Reflection Questions

Why do you suppose that places like the Willard Psychiatric Center remained open into the 1990s?

Figure 7: John F. Kennedy signs the Community Mental Health Act in 1963.

Starting in 1954 and gaining popularity in the 1960s, antipsychotic medications were introduced. These proved a tremendous help in controlling the symptoms of certain psychological disorders, such as psychosis. Psychosis was a common diagnosis of individuals in mental hospitals, and it was often evidenced by symptoms like hallucinations and delusions, indicating a loss of contact with reality. Then in 1963, Congress passed and John F. Kennedy signed the Mental Retardation Facilities and Community Mental Health Centers Construction Act, which provided federal support and funding for community mental health centers (National Institutes of Health, 2013). This legislation changed how mental health services were delivered in the United States. It started the process of **deinstitutionalization**, the closing of large asylums, by providing for people to stay in their communities and be treated locally. In 1955, there were 558,239 severely mentally ill patients institutionalized at public hospitals (Torrey, 1997). By 1994, by percentage of the population, there were 92% fewer hospitalized individuals (Torrey, 1997).

On Your Own

What new breakthrough led to better treatment of individuals with mental health issues?

- ☐ Asylums
- ☐ Antipsychotic medications
- ☐ Public hospitals for mental illness

Mental Health Treatment Today

Today, there are community mental health centers across the nation. They are located in neighborhoods near the homes of clients, and they provide large numbers of people with mental health services of various kinds and for many kinds of problems. Unfortunately, part of what occurred with deinstitutionalization was that those released from institutions were supposed to go to newly created centers, but the system was not set up effectively.

Problems with Mental Health Centers

Underfunded

Staff not trained to handle severe illnesses

High staff burnout

No provisions made for the other services people needed

Without these supports, those people released under deinstitutionalization often ended up homeless. Even today, a large portion of the homeless population is considered to be mentally ill (Figure 8). Statistics show that 26% of homeless adults living in shelters experience mental illness (U.S. Department of Housing and Urban Development [HUD], 2011).

📷 **Figure 8:** Of the homeless individuals in U.S. shelters, about one-quarter are said to have a severe mental illness (HUD, 2011).

Another group of the mentally ill population is involved in the corrections system. According to a 2006 special report by the Bureau of Justice Statistics (BJS), approximately 705,600 mentally ill adults were incarcerated in the state prison system, and another 78,800 were incarcerated in the federal prison system. A further 479,000 were in local jails. According to the study, "people with mental illnesses are overrepresented in probation and parole populations at estimated rates ranging from two to four times the general population" (Prins & Draper, 2009, p. 23). The Treatment Advocacy Center reported that the growing number of mentally ill inmates has placed a burden on the correctional system (Torrey et al., 2014).

Today, instead of asylums, there are psychiatric hospitals run by state governments and local community hospitals focused on short-term care. In all types of hospitals, the emphasis is on short-term stays, with the average length of stay being less than two weeks and often only several days. This is partly due to the very high cost of psychiatric hospitalization, which can be about $800 to $1,000 per night (Stensland, Watson, & Grazier, 2012). Therefore, insurance coverage often limits the length of time a person can be hospitalized for treatment. Usually, individuals are hospitalized only if they are an imminent threat to themselves or others.

Most people suffering from mental illnesses are not hospitalized. If someone is feeling depressed, complains of hearing voices, or feels anxious all the time, he or she might seek psychological treatment. A friend, spouse, or parent might refer someone for treatment. The individual might go see his primary care physician first and then be referred to a mental health practitioner.

Some people seek treatment because they are involved with the state's child protective services—that is, their children have been removed from their care due to abuse or neglect. The parents might be referred to psychiatric or substance abuse facilities, and the children would likely receive treatment for trauma. If the parents are interested in and capable of becoming better parents, the goal of treatment might be family reunification. For other children whose parents are unable to change—for example, the parent or parents who are heavily addicted to drugs and refuse to enter treatment—the goal of therapy might be to help the children adjust to foster care and/or adoption (Figure 9).

Group Activity

Brainstorm some ways in which the current population of homeless individuals with mental illness could be reduced.

Further Resources

For some people today, a struggle with something like substance abuse can land them in prison, rather than in treatment. Read this article (hawkes.biz/subabusediscrimination)about discriminatory treatment of men with substance abuse issues in Massachusetts. Do you think proposed changes will make a difference?

Further Resources

View this timeline (hawkes.biz/mentalinstitutions) showing the history of mental institutions in the United States.

📷 **Figure 9:** Therapy with children may involve play.

Some people seek therapy because the criminal justice system referred them or required them to go. For some individuals, for example, attending weekly counseling sessions might be a condition of parole. If an individual is mandated to attend therapy, she is seeking services involuntarily. **Involuntary treatment** refers to therapy that is not the individual's choice. Other individuals might voluntarily seek treatment. **Voluntary treatment** means the person chooses to attend therapy to obtain relief from symptoms.

Reflection Questions

Do you imagine that treatment success is influenced by whether the individual is there voluntarily or involuntarily? If so, how might success rates be increased for involuntary treatment?

Psychological treatment can occur in a variety of places. An individual might go to a community mental health center or a practitioner in a private or community practice. A child might see a school counselor, school psychologist, or school social worker. An incarcerated person might receive group therapy in prison. There are many different types of treatment providers, and licensing requirements vary from state to state. Besides psychologists and psychiatrists, there are clinical social workers, marriage and family therapists, and trained religious personnel who also perform counseling and therapy.

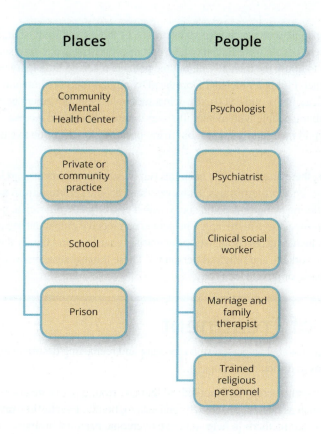

📖 **Figure 10:** There are several different places people can go and several different kinds of professionals people can see to seek mental health treatment.

A range of funding sources pay for mental health treatment: health insurance, government, and private pay. In the past, even when people had health insurance, the coverage would not always pay for mental health services. This changed with the Mental Health Parity and Addiction Equity Act of 2008, which requires group health plans and insurers to make sure there is parity of mental health services (U.S. Department of Labor, n.d.). This means that co-pays, total number of visits, and deductibles for mental health and substance abuse treatment need to be equal to and cannot be more restrictive or harsher than those for physical illnesses and medical/surgical problems.

Finding treatment sources is also not always easy for a variety of reasons, such as:

- limited options, especially in rural and low-income urban areas

- waiting lists

- poor quality of care available for indigent patients

- financial obstacles such as co-pays, deductibles, and time off work

Over 85% of the 1,669 federally designated mental health professional shortage areas are rural; often primary care physicians and law enforcement are the first-line of mental health providers (Ivey, Scheffler, & Zazzali, 1998) although they do not have the specialized training of a mental health professional, who often would be better equipped to provide care. Availability, accessibility, and acceptability (the stigma attached to mental illness) are all problems in rural areas.

Approximately two-thirds of those with symptoms receive no care at all (U.S. Department of Health and Human Services, 2005; Wagenfeld, Murray, Mohatt, & DeBruiynb, 1994). At the end of 2013, the U.S. Department of Agriculture announced an investment of $50 million to help improve access and treatment for mental health problems as part of the Obama administration's effort to strengthen rural communities.

Summary

It was once believed that people with psychological disorders, or those exhibiting strange behavior, were possessed by demons. These people were forced to take part in exorcisms, were imprisoned, or executed. Later, asylums were built to house the mentally ill, but the patients received little to no treatment, and many of the methods used were cruel. Philippe Pinel and Dorothea Dix argued for more humane treatment of people with psychological disorders. In the mid-1960s, the deinstitutionalization movement gained support and asylums were closed, enabling people with mental illnesses to return home and receive treatment in their own communities. Some did go to their family homes, but many became homeless due to a lack of resources and support mechanisms.

Today, instead of asylums, there are psychiatric hospitals run by state governments and local community hospitals, with an emphasis on short-term stays. However, most people suffering from mental illness are not hospitalized. A person suffering symptoms could speak with a primary care physician, who most likely would refer him to someone who specializes in therapy. The person can receive outpatient mental health services from a variety of sources, including psychologists, psychiatrists, marriage and family therapists, school counselors, clinical social workers, and religious personnel. These therapy sessions would be covered through insurance, government funds, or private (self) pay.

Flash Forward

Ready to dig into the vocabulary? Get some practice with this Hawkes Verified Quizlet set (hawkes.biz/psych15q2)!

15.2 Types of Treatment

One of the goals of therapy is to help a person stop repeating and reenacting destructive patterns and to start looking for better solutions to difficult situations.

Two types of therapy are psychotherapy and biomedical therapy. Both types of treatment help people with psychological disorders, such as depression, anxiety, and schizophrenia. **Psychotherapy** is a psychological treatment that employs various methods to help someone overcome personal problems, or to attain personal growth. In modern practice, it has evolved into what is known as psychodynamic therapy, which will be discussed later. **Biomedical therapy** involves medication and/or medical procedures to treat psychological disorders. First, we will explore the various psychotherapeutic orientations outlined in Table 1.

Type	Description	Example
Psychodynamic Psychotherapy	Talk therapy based on belief that the unconscious and childhood conflicts impact behavior	Patient talks about his past
Play Therapy	Psychoanalytical therapy wherein interaction with toys is used instead of talk; used in child therapy	Patient (child) acts out family scenes with dolls
Behavior Therapy	Principles of learning applied to change undesirable behaviors	Patient learns to overcome fear of elevators through several stages of relaxation techniques
Cognitive Therapy	Awareness of cognitive processes helps patients eliminate thought patterns that lead to distress	Patient learns not to overgeneralize failure based on single failure
Cognitive-Behavioral Therapy	Work to change cognitive distortions and self-defeating behaviors	Patient learns to identify self-defeating behaviors to overcome an eating disorder
Humanistic Therapy	Increase self-awareness and acceptance through focus on conscious thoughts	Patient learns to articulate thoughts that keep her from achieving her goals

Table 1: Various Psychotherapy Techniques

Psychotherapy Techniques: Psychoanalysis

Psychoanalysis was developed by Sigmund Freud and was the first form of psychotherapy. It was the dominant therapeutic technique in the early 20th century, but it has since waned significantly in popularity. Freud believed most of our psychological problems are the result of repressed impulses and trauma experienced in childhood, and he believed psychoanalysis would help uncover long-buried feelings. In a psychoanalyst's office, you might see a patient lying on a couch speaking of dreams or childhood memories, and the therapist using various Freudian methods such as free association and dream analysis (Figure 2). In **free association**, the patient relaxes and then says whatever comes to mind at the moment. However, Freud felt that the ego would at times try to block, or repress, unacceptable urges or painful conflicts during free association. Consequently, a patient would demonstrate resistance to recalling these thoughts or situations. In **dream analysis**, a therapist interprets the underlying meaning of dreams.

Psychoanalysis is a therapy approach that typically takes years. Over the course of time, the patient reveals a great deal about himself to the therapist. Freud suggested that during this patient-therapist relationship, the patient comes to develop strong feelings for the therapist—maybe positive feelings, maybe negative feelings. Freud called this **transference**: the patient transfers all the positive or negative emotions associated with the patient's other relationships to the psychoanalyst. For example, Crystal is seeing a psychoanalyst. During the years of therapy, she comes to see her therapist as a father figure. She transfers her feelings about her father onto her therapist, perhaps in an effort to gain the love and attention she did not receive from her own father.

Figure 1: Thanks to Freud's famous couch, we typically think of psychoanalysis as a patient lying down while a therapist takes notes.

Figure 2: Today, a psychotherapy patient is more likely to sit facing the therapist than lie on a couch.

✎ On Your Own

Gerald did not grow up with a father, so he is afraid that male figures in his life are going to leave him. He seems anxious that his male therapist will discontinue sessions with him. Freud would call this:

- ☐ Free association
- ☐ Dream analysis
- ☐ Transference

Today, Freud's psychoanalytical perspective, expanded upon by the developments of subsequent theories and methodologies, is called the psychodynamic perspective. This approach to therapy remains centered on the role of people's internal drives and forces, but treatment is less intensive than Freud's original model.

Psychotherapy: Play Therapy

Play therapy is often used with children since they are not likely to sit on a couch and recall their dreams or engage in traditional talk therapy. This technique uses a therapeutic process of play to "help clients prevent or resolve psychosocial difficulties and achieve optimal growth" (O'Connor, 2000, p. 7). The idea is that children play out their hopes, fantasies, and traumas while using dolls, stuffed animals, and sandbox figurines (Figure 3). Play therapy can also be used to help a therapist make a diagnosis. The therapist observes how the child interacts with toys (e.g., dolls, animals, and home settings) in an effort to understand the roots of the child's disturbed behavior. Play therapy can be nondirective or directive. In nondirective play therapy, children are encouraged to work through their problems by playing freely while the therapist observes (LeBlanc & Ritchie, 2001). In directive play therapy, the therapist provides more structure and guidance in the play session by suggesting topics, asking questions, and even playing with the child (Harter, 1977).

Figure 3: Therapy with children may involve play, such as sandplay that involves sand and miniature figures to reflect a child's inner thoughts, concerns, and struggles.

✏ On Your Own

The therapist lets a child play and interact with toys without providing any directions or structure. This best describes which of the following intervention strategies?

- ☐ Free association
- ☐ Directive play therapy
- ☐ Non-directive play therapy

Psychotherapy: Behavior Therapy

In **psychoanalysis**, therapists help their patients look into their past to uncover repressed feelings. In **behavior therapy**, a therapist employs principles of learning to help clients change undesirable behaviors—rather than digging deeply into one's unconscious. Therapists with this orientation believe that dysfunctional behaviors, like phobias and bedwetting, can be changed by teaching clients new, more constructive behaviors. Behavior therapy employs both classical and operant conditioning techniques to change behavior.

One type of behavior therapy utilizes classical conditioning techniques. Therapists using these techniques believe that dysfunctional behaviors are conditioned responses. Applying the conditioning principles developed by Ivan Pavlov, these therapists seek to recondition their clients and thus change their behavior.

Emmie is eight years old and frequently wets her bed at night. She's been invited to several sleepovers, but she won't go because of her problem. Using a type of conditioning therapy, Emmie begins to sleep on a liquid-sensitive bed pad that is hooked to an alarm. When moisture touches the pad, it sets off the alarm, waking up Emmie. When this process is repeated enough times, Emmie develops an association between urinary relaxation and waking up, and this stops the bedwetting. Emmie has now gone three weeks without wetting her bed and is looking forward to her first sleepover this weekend.

One commonly used classical conditioning therapeutic technique is **counterconditioning**: a client learns a new response to a stimulus that has previously elicited an undesirable behavior. Two counterconditioning techniques are aversive conditioning and exposure therapy. **Aversive conditioning** uses an unpleasant stimulus to stop an undesirable behavior. Therapists apply this technique to eliminate addictive behaviors, such as smoking, nail biting, and drinking. In aversion therapy, clients will typically engage in a specific behavior (such as nail biting) and at the same time are exposed to something unpleasant, such as a mild electric shock or a bad taste. After repeated associations between the unpleasant stimulus and the behavior, the client can learn to stop the unwanted behavior.

Figure 4: Bitter-tasting varnish acts as an unpleasant stimulus to stop nail biting.

Aversion therapy has been used effectively for years in the treatment of alcoholism (Davidson, 1974; Elkins, 1991; Streeton & Whelan, 2001). One common way this occurs is through a chemically based substance known as Antabuse. When a person takes Antabuse and then consumes alcohol, uncomfortable side effects result including nausea, vomiting, increased heart rate, heart palpitations, severe headache, and shortness of breath. Antabuse is repeatedly paired with alcohol until the client associates alcohol with unpleasant feelings, which decreases the client's desire to consume alcohol. Antabuse creates a conditioned aversion to alcohol because it replaces the original pleasure response with an unpleasant one.

Reflection Questions

Do you, a friend, or a family member have an unhealthy habit that you would like to stop? How do you think aversive conditioning would work to eliminate the behavior in question? Do you think this strategy would be effective? Why or why not?

In **exposure therapy**, a therapist seeks to treat clients' fears or anxiety by presenting them with the object or situation that causes their problem, with the idea that they will eventually get used to it. This can be done via reality, imagination, or virtual reality. Exposure therapy was first reported in 1924 by Mary Cover Jones, who is considered the mother of behavior therapy. Jones worked with a boy named Peter who was afraid of rabbits. Her goal was to replace Peter's fear of rabbits with a conditioned response of relaxation, which is a response that is incompatible with fear (Figure 5). How did she do it? Jones began by placing a caged rabbit on the other side of a room with Peter while he ate his afternoon snack. Over the course of several days, Jones moved the rabbit closer and closer to where Peter was seated with his snack. After two months of being exposed to the rabbit while relaxing with his snack, Peter was able to hold the rabbit and pet it while eating (Jones, 1924).

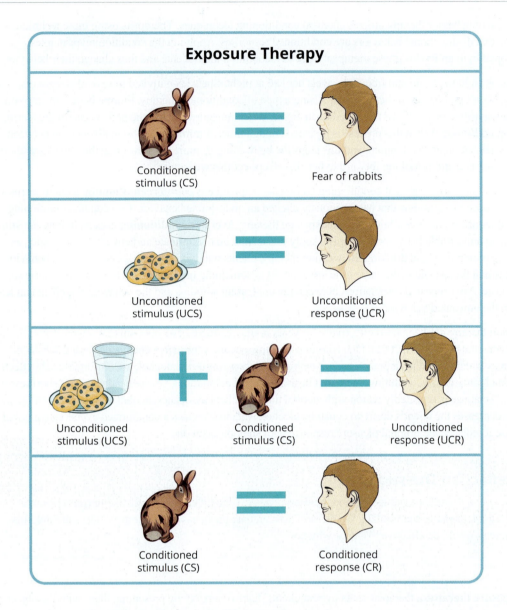

Exposure Therapy

Conditioned stimulus (CS) = Fear of rabbits

Unconditioned stimulus (UCS) = Unconditioned response (UCR)

Unconditioned stimulus (UCS) + Conditioned stimulus (CS) = Unconditioned response (UCR)

Conditioned stimulus (CS) = Conditioned response (CR)

Figure 5: Exposure therapy seeks to change the response to a conditioned stimulus (CS). An unconditioned stimulus is presented over and over just after the presentation of the conditioned stimulus. This figure shows conditioning as conducted in Mary Cover Jones's 1924 study.

Thirty years later, Joseph Wolpe (1958) refined Jones's techniques, giving us the behavior therapy technique of exposure therapy that is used today. A popular form of exposure therapy is **systematic desensitization**, wherein a calm and pleasant state is gradually associated with increasing levels of anxiety-inducing stimuli.

Jayden is terrified of elevators. Jayden knows he can't climb twenty-nine flights of stairs to get to work each day, so he decided to see a behavior therapist for help. The therapist asks Jayden to first construct a hierarchy of elevator-related situations that elicit fear and anxiety. They range from situations of mild anxiety, such as being nervous around the other people in the elevator, to the fear of getting an arm caught in the door, to panic-provoking situations such as getting trapped or the cable snapping. Next, the therapist uses progressive relaxation. She teaches Jayden how to relax each of his muscle groups so that he achieves a drowsy, relaxed, and comfortable state of mind. Once he's in this state, she asks Jayden to imagine a mildly anxiety-provoking situation. Jayden is standing in front of the elevator thinking about pressing the call button. Eventually, Jayden will work in steps until he is able to take the elevator all the way up to the 29th floor of his office without feeling anxiety.

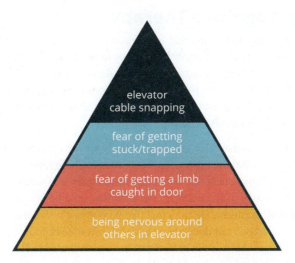

elevator
cable snapping

fear of getting
stuck/trapped

fear of getting a limb
caught in door

being nervous around
others in elevator

Reflection Questions

Do you have any irrational fears that impact your daily life? How do you think they started? Do you think exposure therapy and systematic desensitization would work for you? Why or why not?

Further Resources

Check out this story (hawkes.biz/virtualreality) from NBC News to see how virtual reality is being used to help soldiers with PTSD.

Sometimes, it's too impractical, expensive, or embarrassing to re-create anxiety-producing situations, so a therapist might employ **virtual reality exposure therapy** by using a simulation to help conquer fears. Virtual reality exposure therapy has been used effectively to treat numerous anxiety disorders such as the fear of public speaking, claustrophobia (fear of enclosed spaces), aviophobia (fear of flying), and posttraumatic stress disorder (PTSD), a trauma-and-stressor-related disorder (Gerardi, Cukor, Difede, Rizzo, & Rothbaum, 2010).

Operant conditioning interventions reinforce desirable behavior and punish undesirable behavior. For example, Applied Behavior Analysis (ABA) is a treatment that uses reinforcement (stickers, praise, candy, etc.) to reward and motivate autistic children when they demonstrate desired behaviors such as sitting on a chair when requested, verbalizing a greeting, or making eye contact. Punishment such as a timeout or a sharp "No!" from the therapist or parent might be used to discourage undesirable behaviors, such as pinching, scratching, and pulling hair.

One popular operant conditioning intervention is called the **token economy**. This involves a controlled setting where individuals are reinforced for desirable behaviors with tokens, such as poker chips, that can be exchanged for items or privileges. Patients are rewarded with tokens when they engage in positive behaviors (e.g., making their beds, brushing their teeth, coming to the cafeteria on time, and socializing with other patients). They can later exchange the tokens for extra TV time, private rooms, visits to the canteen, and so on (Dickerson, Tenhula, & Green-Paden, 2005).

Figure 6: U.S. Navy parachutists virtually practice parachuting with head-mounted displays. VR simulations are a practical alternative to re-creating anxiety producing scenarios.

✎ On Your Own

Which of the following best relates to the theory behind applied behavioral analysis?

☐   A child gets cookies for sharing a truck with his brother.

☐   A child is put in the room with a dog to overcome his fear of dogs.

☐   A child is asked to say everything that comes into his head at the given moment.

Figure 7: Token economies will use stickers, candy, or poker chips to reward and encourage good behavior.

Psychotherapy: Cognitive Therapy

Cognitive therapy is a form of psychotherapy that focuses on how a person's thoughts lead to feelings of distress. Psychiatrist Aaron Beck developed cognitive therapy in the 1960s. His initial focus was on depression and how a client's self-defeating attitude served to maintain a depression despite positive factors in her life (Beck, Rush, Shaw, & Emery, 1979) (Figure 8). Through questioning, a cognitive therapist can help a client recognize dysfunctional ideas, challenge catastrophizing thoughts about themselves and their situations, and find a more positive way to view things (Beck, 2011).

The idea behind cognitive therapy is that how you think determines how you feel and act. Cognitive therapists help their clients change dysfunctional thoughts about themselves to help relieve stress and improve success toward their future goals. They help a client see how they misinterpret a situation, which is called a cognitive distortion. For example, a client may overgeneralize. Because Ray failed one test in his Psychology 101 course, he feels he is stupid and worthless. He may feel like he is going to fail the entire course and flunk out of school. Just because Ray failed one test does not necessarily mean he is going to fail the course let alone cause him to flunk out of college. These errors in thinking have contributed to Ray's feelings of distress. His therapist will help him challenge these irrational beliefs, focus on their illogical basis, and correct them with more logical and rational thoughts and beliefs.

Figure 8: Your emotional reactions are the result of your thoughts about the situation rather than the situation itself. For instance, if you consistently interpret events and emotions around the themes of loss and defeat, then you are likely to be depressed. Through therapy, you can learn more logical ways to interpret situations.

Psychotherapy: Cognitive-Behavioral Therapy

Cognitive-behavioral therapists focus much more on present issues than on a patient's childhood or past, as in other forms of psychotherapy. One of the first forms of cognitive-behavioral therapy was **rational emotive therapy (RET)**, which was founded by Albert Ellis and grew out of his dislike of Freudian psychoanalysis (Daniel, n.d.). Behaviorists such as Joseph Wolpe also influenced Ellis's therapeutic approach (National Association of Cognitive-Behavioral Therapists, 2009).

Cognitive-behavioral therapy (CBT) helps clients examine how their thoughts affect their behavior. It aims to change cognitive distortions and self-defeating behaviors. In essence, this approach is designed to change the way people think as well as how they act. It is similar to cognitive therapy in that CBT attempts to make individuals aware of their irrational and negative thoughts and helps people replace them with new, more positive ways of thinking. It is also similar to behavior therapies in that CBT teaches people how to practice and engage in more positive and healthy approaches to daily situations. In total, hundreds of studies have shown the effectiveness of cognitive-behavioral therapy in the treatment of numerous psychological disorders, such as depression, PTSD, anxiety disorders, eating disorders, bipolar disorder, and substance abuse (Beck Institute for Cognitive Behavior Therapy, n.d.). For example, CBT is effective in decreasing levels of hopelessness and suicidal thoughts in previously suicidal teenagers (Alavi, Sharifi, Ghanizadeh,

& Dehbozorgi, 2013). Cognitive-behavioral therapy has also been effective in reducing PTSD in specific populations, such as transit workers (Lowinger & Rombom, 2012).

Cognitive-behavioral therapy aims to change cognitive distortions and self-defeating behaviors using techniques like the ABC model. With this model, there is an **A**ction (sometimes called an activating event), the **B**elief about the event, and the **C**onsequences of this belief. Let's say Jon and Joe both go to a party. Jon and Joe each have met a young woman at the party: Jon is talking with Megan most of the party, and Joe is talking with Amanda. At the end of the party, Jon asks Megan for her phone number, and Joe asks Amanda. Megan tells Jon she would rather not give him her number, and Amanda tells Joe the same thing. Both Jon and Joe are surprised, as they thought things were going well. What can Jon and Joe tell themselves about why the women were not interested? Jon tells himself he is a loser, or is ugly, or "has no game." Jon then gets depressed and decides not to go to another party, which starts a cycle that keeps him depressed. Joe tells himself that he had bad breath, goes out and buys a new toothbrush, goes to another party, and meets someone new.

Figure 9: CBT examines how thoughts affect behavior.

Jon's belief about what happened results in a consequence of further depression, whereas Joe's belief does not. Jon is internalizing the attribution or reason for the rebuffs, which triggers his depression. On the other hand, Joe is externalizing the cause, so his thinking does not contribute to feelings of depression. Cognitive-behavioral therapy examines specific maladaptive and automatic thoughts and cognitive distortions. Some examples of cognitive distortions are all-or-nothing thinking, overgeneralization, and jumping to conclusions. In overgeneralization, someone takes a small situation and makes it huge—for example, instead of saying, "This particular woman was not interested in me," the man says, "I am ugly, a loser, and no one is ever going to be interested in me."

All-or-nothing thinking, which is a common type of cognitive distortion for people suffering from depression, reflects extremes. In other words, everything is black or white. After being turned down for a date, Jon begins to think, "No woman will ever go out with me. I'm going to be alone forever." He begins to feel anxious and sad as he contemplates his future.

The third kind of distortion involves jumping to conclusions—assuming that people are thinking negatively about you or reacting negatively to you even though there is no evidence. Consider the example of Savannah and Hillaire, who recently met at a party. They have a lot in common, and Savannah thinks they could become friends. She calls Hillaire to invite her for coffee. Since Hillaire doesn't answer, Savannah leaves her a message. Several days go by and Savannah never hears back. Maybe Hillaire never received the message because she lost her phone or she is too busy to return the phone call. But if Savannah believes that Hillaire didn't like her or didn't want to be her friend, she is demonstrating the cognitive distortion of jumping to conclusions.

Figure 10: All-or-nothing thinking reflects the extremes of a given scenario.

✏ On Your Own

Think about an event where something negative happened to you, which led to a cognitive distortion. Explain this event, your belief, and the consequence of your belief on your behavior.

Event	Belief	Consequence

How effective is CBT? One client said this about his cognitive-behavioral therapy:

> I have had many painful episodes of depression in my life, and this has had a negative effect on my career and has put considerable strain on my friends and family. The treatments I have received, such

as taking antidepressants and psychodynamic counseling, have helped [me] to cope with the symptoms and to get some insights into the roots of my problems. CBT has been by far the most useful approach I have found in tackling these mood problems. It has raised my awareness of how my thoughts impact on my moods. How the way I think about myself, about others, and about the world can lead me into depression. It is a practical approach, which does not dwell so much on childhood experiences, whilst acknowledging that it was then that these patterns were learned. It looks at what is happening now and gives tools to manage these moods on a daily basis. (Martin, 2007, n.p.)

Psychotherapy: Humanistic Therapy

Humanistic psychology focuses on helping people achieve their potential, so it makes sense that the goal of **humanistic therapy** is to help people become more self-aware and accepting of themselves. In contrast to psychoanalysis, humanistic therapists focus on conscious rather than unconscious thoughts. They also emphasize the patient's present and future, as opposed to exploring the patient's past.

Psychologist Carl Rogers developed a therapeutic orientation known as **Rogerian**, or **client-centered therapy**. Note the change from *patients* to *clients*. Rogers (1951) felt that the term *patient* suggested the person seeking help was sick and looking for a cure. Since this is a form of **nondirective therapy**, a therapeutic approach in which the therapist does not give advice or provide interpretations but helps the person to identify conflicts and understand feelings, Rogers (1951) emphasized the importance of the person taking control of his own life to overcome life's challenges.

In client-centered therapy, the therapist uses the technique of active listening. In active listening, the therapist acknowledges, restates, and clarifies what the client expresses. Therapists also practice what Rogers called **unconditional positive regard**, which involves not judging clients and simply accepting them for who they are. Rogers (1951) also felt that therapists should demonstrate genuineness, empathy, and acceptance toward their clients because this helps people become more accepting of themselves, which results in personal growth.

Figure 11: Client-centered therapy focuses on conscious thoughts, present and future experiences, and self-identification.

✎ On Your Own

Complete the table by identifying the type of psychotherapy that matches the description and example.

Type	Description	Example
	Talk therapy based on belief that the unconscious and childhood conflicts impact behavior	Patient talks about his past
	Psychoanalytical therapy wherein interaction with toys is used instead of talk; used in child therapy	Patient (child) acts out family scenes with dolls
	Principles of learning applied to change undesirable behaviors	Patient learns to overcome fear of elevators through several stages of relaxation techniques
	Awareness of cognitive processes helps patients eliminate thought patterns that lead to distress	Patient learns not to overgeneralize failure based on single failure
	Work to change cognitive distortions and self-defeating behaviors	Patient learns to identify self-defeating behaviors to overcome an eating disorder
	Increase self-awareness and acceptance through focus on conscious thoughts	Patient learns to articulate thoughts that keep her from achieving her goals

Evaluating Various Forms of Psychotherapy

According to the American Psychological Association, three factors work together to produce successful treatment. The first is the use of evidence-based treatment that is deemed appropriate for the client's problem. The second important factor is the clinical expertise of the psychologist or therapist. The third factor is your own characteristics, values, preferences, and culture. Many people begin psychotherapy feeling like their problem will never be resolved; however, psychotherapy helps people see that they can do things to improve their situation.

Many studies have explored the effectiveness of psychotherapy. For example, one large-scale study that examined sixteen meta-analyses of CBT reported that it was equally effective or more effective than other therapies in treating PTSD, generalized anxiety disorder, depression, and social phobia (Butlera, Chapmanb, Formanc, & Becka, 2006). Another study found that CBT was as effective at treating depression (43% success rate) as prescription medication (50% success rate) compared to the placebo rate of 25% (DeRubeis et al., 2005). Another meta-analysis found that psychodynamic therapy was also as effective at treating these types of psychological issues as CBT (Shedler, 2010). However, no studies have found one psychotherapeutic approach more effective than another (Abbass, Kisely, & Kroenke, 2006; Chorpita et al., 2011), nor have they shown any relationship between a client's treatment outcome and the level of the clinician's training or experience (Wampold, 2007). Regardless of which type of psychotherapy an individual chooses, one critical factor that determines the success of treatment is the person's relationship with the psychologist or therapist.

> ### Reflection Question
> Which type of therapy discussed in this lesson most appeals to you, and why?

Biomedical Therapies

Individuals can be prescribed biologically based treatments or psychotropic medications that are used to treat mental disorders. While these are often used in combination with psychotherapy, they also are taken by individuals not in therapy. This is known as biomedical therapy. Medications used to treat psychological disorders are called psychotropic medications and are prescribed by medical doctors, including psychiatrists. In Louisiana and New Mexico, psychologists are able to prescribe some types of these medications (American Psychological Association, 2014).

Different types and classes of medications are prescribed for different disorders. A depressed person might be given an antidepressant, a bipolar individual might be given a mood stabilizer, and a schizophrenic individual might be given an antipsychotic. These medications treat the symptoms of a psychological disorder. They can help people feel better so that they can function, but they do not cure the disorder. Some people may only need to take a psychotropic medication for a short period of time. Others with severe disorders like bipolar disorder or schizophrenia may need to take psychotropic medication for a long time. Table 2 shows the types of medication and how they are used.

Figure 12: Psychotropic medications can treat symptoms of various psychological disorders.

Type of Medication	Used to Treat	Brand Names of Commonly Prescribed Medications	How They Work	Side Effects
Antipsychotics (developed in the 1950s)	Schizophrenia and other types of severe thought disorders	Haldol, Mellaril, Prolixin, Thorazine	Treat positive psychotic symptoms such as auditory and visual hallucinations, delusions, and paranoia by blocking the neurotransmitter dopamine	Long-term use can lead to tardive dyskinesia, involuntary movements of the arms, legs, tongue, and facial muscles, resulting in Parkinson's-like tremors
Atypical Antipsychotics (developed in the late 1980s)	Schizophrenia and other types of severe thought disorders	Abilify, Risperdal, Clozaril	Treat the negative symptoms of schizophrenia, such as withdrawal and apathy, by targeting both dopamine and serotonin receptors; newer medications may treat both positive and negative symptoms	Can increase the risk of obesity and diabetes as well as elevate cholesterol levels; constipation, dry mouth, blurred vision, drowsiness, and dizziness
Anti-depressants	Depression and increasingly for anxiety	Paxil, Prozac, Zoloft (selective serotonin reuptake inhibitors, [SSRIs]); Tofranil and Elavil (tricyclics)	Alter levels of neurotransmitters such as serotonin and norepinephrine	SSRIs: headache, nausea, weight gain, drowsiness, reduced sex drive

Tricyclics: dry mouth, constipation, blurred vision, drowsiness, reduced sex drive, increased risk of suicide |
Anti-anxiety agents	Anxiety and agitation that occur in OCD, PTSD, panic disorder, and social phobia	Xanax, Valium, Ativan	Depress central nervous system activity	Drowsiness, dizziness, headache, fatigue, lightheadedness
Mood Stabilizers	Bipolar disorder	Lithium, Depakote, Lamictal, Tegretol	Treat episodes of mania as well as depression	Excessive thirst, irregular heartbeat, itching/rash, swelling (face, mouth, and extremities), nausea, loss of appetite
Stimulants	ADHD	Adderall, Ritalin	Improve ability to focus on a task and maintain attention	Decreased appetite, difficulty sleeping, stomachache, headache

Table 2: Commonly Prescribed Psychotropic Medications

> ### Reflection Question
>
> Do you think biomedical therapies are preferable to psychotherapies? Why or why not?

Figure 13: This is an ECT machine from the 1960s.

Another biologically based treatment that continues to be used, although infrequently, is **electroconvulsive therapy (ECT)** (formerly known by its unscientific name *electroshock therapy*). It involves using an electrical current to induce seizures to help alleviate the effects of severe depression. The exact mechanism is unknown although it does help alleviate symptoms for people with severe depression who have not responded to traditional drug therapy (Pagnin, de Queiroz, Pini, & Cassano, 2004). About 85% of people treated with ECT improve (Reti, n.d.). However, the memory loss associated with repeated administrations has led to it being implemented as a last resort (Donahue, 2000; Prudic, Peyser, & Sackeim, 2000). A more recent alternative is transcranial magnetic stimulation (TMS), a procedure approved by the FDA in 2008 that uses magnetic fields to stimulate nerve cells in the brain to improve depression symptoms; it is used when other treatments have not worked (Mayo Clinic, 2012).

Dig Deeper

Evidence-Based Practice

A buzzword in therapy today is evidence-based practice. It's not a novel concept but one that has been used in medicine for at least two decades. Evidence-based practice is used to reduce errors in treatment selection by making clinical decisions based on research (Sackett & Rosenberg, 1995). In any case, evidence-based treatment is on the rise in the field of psychology. So what is it, and why does it matter? In an effort to determine which treatment methodologies are evidence-based, professional organizations such as the American Psychological Association (APA) have recommended that specific psychological treatments be used to treat certain psychological disorders (Chambless & Ollendick, 2001). According to the APA (2005), "Evidence-based practice in psychology (EBPP) is the integration of the best available research with clinical expertise in the context of patient characteristics, culture, and preferences" (p. 1).

The foundational idea behind evidence-based treatment is that best practices are determined by research evidence that has been compiled by comparing various forms of treatment (Charman & Barkham, 2005). These treatments are then operationalized and placed in treatment manuals—trained therapists follow these manuals. The benefits are that evidence-based treatment can reduce variability between therapists to ensure that a specific approach is delivered with integrity (Charman & Barkham, 2005). Therefore, clients have a higher chance of receiving therapeutic interventions that are effective at treating their specific disorder. While EBPP is based on randomized control trials, critics of EBPP reject it stating that the results of trials cannot be applied to individuals, and instead, determinations regarding treatment should be based on a therapist's judgment (Mullen & Streiner, 2004).

Summary

Psychoanalysis was developed by Sigmund Freud. Freud's theory is that a person's psychological problems are the result of repressed impulses or childhood trauma. The goal of the therapist is to help a person uncover buried feelings by using techniques such as free association and dream analysis.

Play therapy is a psychodynamic therapy technique often used with children. The idea is that children play out their hopes, fantasies, and traumas using dolls, stuffed animals, and sandbox figurines.

In behavior therapy, a therapist employs principles of learning from classical and operant conditioning to help clients change undesirable behaviors. Counterconditioning is a commonly used therapeutic technique in which a client learns a new response to a stimulus that has previously elicited an undesirable behavior via classical conditioning. Principles of operant conditioning can be applied to help people deal with a wide range of psychological problems. Token economy is an example of a popular operant conditioning technique.

Cognitive therapy is a technique that focuses on how thoughts lead to feelings of distress. The idea behind cognitive therapy is that how you think determines how you feel and act. Cognitive therapists help clients change dysfunctional thoughts in order to relieve distress. Cognitive-behavioral therapy explores how our thoughts affect our behavior. Cognitive-behavioral therapy aims to change cognitive distortions and self-defeating behaviors.

Humanistic therapy focuses on helping people achieve their potential. One form of humanistic therapy developed by Carl Rogers is known as client-centered or Rogerian therapy. Client-centered therapists use the techniques of active listening, unconditional positive regard, genuineness, and empathy to help clients become more accepting of themselves.

Often in combination with psychotherapy, people can be prescribed biologically based treatments, such as psychotropic medications, and/or other medical procedures, such as electro-convulsive therapy.

Flash Forward

Ready to dig into the vocabulary? Get some practice with this Hawkes Verified Quizlet set (hawkes.biz/psych15q3)!

15.3 Treatment Modalities

Once a person seeks treatment, whether voluntarily or involuntarily, he has an intake done to assess his clinical needs. An **intake** is the therapist's first meeting with the client. The therapist gathers specific information to address the client's immediate needs, such as the presenting problem, the client's support system, and insurance status. The therapist informs the client about confidentiality, fees, and what to expect in treatment. **Confidentiality** means the therapist cannot disclose confidential communications to any third party unless mandated or permitted by law to do so. During the intake, the therapist and client will work together to discuss treatment goals. Then a treatment plan will be formulated, usually with specific measurable objectives. Also, the therapist and client will discuss how treatment success will be measured and the estimated length of treatment. There are several different modalities of treatment (Figure 1): individual therapy, family therapy, couples therapy, and group therapy are the most common.

🖼 **Figure 1:** Therapy may occur one-on-one between a therapist and client or in a group setting, as shown here.

Individual Therapy

In **individual therapy**, also known as individual psychotherapy or individual counseling, the client and clinician meet one-on-one (usually from 45 minutes to 1 hour). These meetings typically occur weekly or every other week, and sessions are conducted in a confidential and caring environment (Figure 2).

Work with Clients

Help explore feelings

Work through life challenges

Identify aspects of self they wish to change

Set goals to work towards change

A client might see a clinician for only a few sessions, or the client may attend individual therapy sessions for a year or longer. The amount of time spent in therapy depends on the needs of the client as well as her personal goals.

Reflection Questions

If a client has issues with angry outbursts with his family and friends, what goals might he and his therapist set for his improvement?

📷 **Figure 2:** In an individual therapy session, a client works one-on-one with a trained therapist.

Group Therapy

In **group therapy**, a clinician meets together with several clients with similar problems (Figure 3). When children are placed in group therapy, it is particularly important to match clients for age and problems. One benefit of group therapy is that it can help decrease a client's shame and isolation about a problem while offering needed support, both from the therapist and other members of the group (American Psychological Association, 2014). Consider the following examples:

- A nine-year-old sexual abuse victim feels embarrassed and ashamed. Placed in a group with other sexually abused boys, however, he realizes he is not alone.

- A child struggling with poor social skills benefits from a group with a specific curriculum to foster these skills.

- A woman suffering from post-partum depression feels less guilty and more supported by being in a group with similar women.

Group therapy also has some specific limitations. Members of the group may be afraid to speak in front of other people because sharing secrets and problems with complete strangers can be stressful and overwhelming. There may be personality clashes and arguments among group members. There could also be concerns about confidentiality: someone from the group might share what another participant said to people outside of the group.

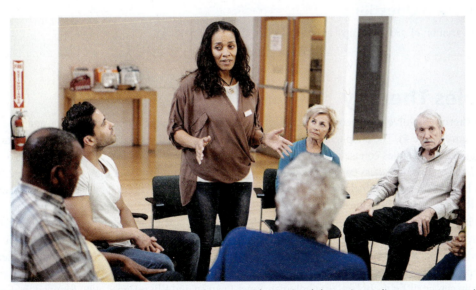

📷 **Figure 3:** In group therapy, usually 5–10 people meet with a trained therapist to discuss a common issue such as divorce, grief, an eating disorder, substance abuse, or anger management.

Another benefit of group therapy is that members can confront each other about their patterns. For those with some types of problems, such as sexual abusers, group therapy is the recommended treatment. Group treatment for this population is considered to have several benefits:

> Group treatment is more economical than individual, couples, or family therapy. Sexual abusers often feel more comfortable admitting and discussing their offenses in a treatment group where others are modeling openness. Clients often accept feedback about their behavior more willingly from other group members than from therapists. Finally, clients can practice social skills in group treatment settings. (McGrath, Cumming, Burchard, Zeoli, & Ellerby, 2009)

Groups that have a strong educational component are called psycho-educational groups. For example, a group for children whose parents have cancer might discuss what cancer is, types of treatment for cancer, and the side effects of treatments. Often, group therapy sessions with children take place in school. They are led by a school counselor, a school psychologist, or a school social worker.

The Focus of School Groups

Test anxiety

Social isolation

Self esteem

Bullying

School failure

Whether the group is held in school or in a clinician's office, group therapy has been found to be effective with children facing numerous kinds of challenges (Shechtman, 2002).

During a group session, the entire group could reflect on an individual's problems or difficulties, and others might disclose what they have done in that situation. When a clinician is facilitating a group, the focus is always on making sure that everyone benefits and participates in the group and that no one person is the focus of the entire session. Groups can be organized in various ways: some have an overarching theme or purpose, some are time-limited, some have open membership that allows people to come and go, and some are closed. Some groups are structured with planned activities and goals, while others are unstructured: there is no specific plan, and group members themselves decide how the group will spend its time and on what goals it will focus. This can become a complex and emotionally charged process, but it is also an opportunity for personal growth (Page & Berkow, 1994).

> **Reflection Questions**
> What variation of group therapy would you personally find helpful?

Couples Therapy

Couples therapy involves two people in an intimate relationship who are having difficulties and are trying to resolve them (Figure 4). The couple may be dating, partnered, engaged, or married. The primary therapeutic orientation used in couples counseling is cognitive-behavioral therapy (Rathus & Sanderson, 1999). Couples meet with a therapist to discuss conflicts and/or aspects of their relationship that they want to change. The therapist helps them see how their individual backgrounds, beliefs, and actions are affecting their relationship. Often, a therapist tries to help the couple resolve these problems, as well as implement strategies that will lead to a healthier and happier relationship, such as how to listen, how to argue, and how to express feelings. However, sometimes, after working with a therapist, a couple will realize that they are too incompatible and will decide to separate. Some couples seek therapy to work out their problems, while others attend therapy to determine whether staying together is the best solution. Counseling couples in a high-conflict and volatile relationship can be difficult. In fact, psychologists Peter Pearson and Ellyn Bader, who founded the Couples Institute in Palo Alto, California, have compared the experience of being the clinician in couples' therapy to be like "piloting a helicopter in a hurricane" (Weil, 2012, para. 7).

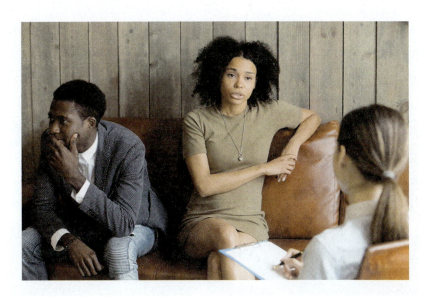

Figure 4: In couples counseling, a therapist helps people work on their relationship.

Family Therapy

Family therapy is a special form of group therapy, consisting of one or more families. Although there are many theoretical orientations in family therapy, one of the most predominant is the systems approach. The family is viewed as an organized system, and each individual within the family is a contributing member who creates and maintains processes within the system that shape behavior (Minuchin, 1985). Each member of the family influences and is influenced by the others. The goal of this approach is to enhance the growth of each family member as well as that of the family as a whole.

Often, dysfunctional patterns of communication that develop between family members can lead to conflict. A family with this dynamic might wish to attend therapy together rather than individually. In many cases, one member of the family has problems that detrimentally affect everyone. Consider the following examples:

- A mother's depression impacts other family members because they are unable to help the mother feel better or cope.

- A teen daughter's eating disorder may cause behavioral issues or may cause general rifts between family members.

- A father's alcohol dependence may impact all members of the family. In fact, most addictions are considered "family affairs" as they impact all members of the household.

Goals of Family Therapy

Help each family member cope with the issue

Encourage resolution and growth for individual family members

Encourage resolution and growth for the family as a whole

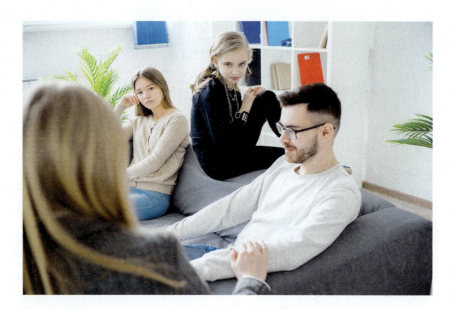

📷 **Figure 5:** The goal of family therapy is to encourage growth of each individual member and the family dynamic as a whole.

With family therapy, the nuclear family (i.e., parents and children) or the nuclear family plus whoever lives in the household (e.g., grandparent) come into treatment. Family therapists work with the whole family unit to heal the family. There are several different types of family therapy. In **structural family therapy**, the therapist examines and discusses the boundaries and structure of the family: who makes the rules, who sleeps in the bed with whom, how decisions are made, and what are the boundaries within the family. In some families, the parents do not work together to make rules, or one parent may undermine the other, leading the children to act out. The therapist helps them resolve these issues and learn to communicate more effectively.

In **strategic family therapy**, the goal is to address specific problems within the family that can be dealt with in a relatively short amount of time. Typically, the therapist would guide what happens in the therapy session and design a detailed approach to resolving each member's problem (Madanes, 1991).

> **Further Resources**
>
> Watch this video (hawkes. biz/familytherapy) to view a structural family session.

✍ On Your Own

Answer the following questions about couples and family therapy.

1. When it comes to couples therapy, what is the primary therapeutic orientation?

   ☐ Cognitive-behavioral therapy

   ☐ Aversion therapy

2. When it comes to family therapy, what is the predominant theoretical orientation?

   ☐ Systems approach

   ☐ Psychodynamic approach

Summary

There are several modalities of treatment; individual therapy, group therapy, couples therapy, and family therapy are the most common. In an individual therapy session, a client works one-on-one with a trained therapist. In group therapy, usually 5–10 people meet with a trained group therapist to discuss a common issue (e.g., divorce, grief, eating disorders, substance abuse, or anger management). Couples therapy involves two people in an intimate relationship who are having difficulties and are trying to resolve them. The couple may be dating, partnered, engaged, or married. The therapist helps them resolve their problems as well as implement strategies that will lead to a healthier and happier relationship. Family therapy is a special form of group therapy. The therapy group is made up of one or more families. The goal of this approach is to enhance the growth of each individual family member and the family as a whole.

15.4 Substance-Related and Addictive Disorders: A Special Case

Addiction is often viewed as a chronic disease (Figure 1). The choice to use a substance is initially voluntary; however, because chronic substance use can permanently alter the neural structure in the prefrontal cortex, an area of the brain associated with decision-making and judgment, a person becomes driven to use drugs and/or alcohol (Muñoz-Cuevas, Athilingam, Piscopo, & Wilbrecht, 2013). This helps explain why relapse rates tend to be high. About 40%–60% of individuals **relapse**, which means they return to abusing drugs and/or alcohol after a period of improvement (National Institute on Drug Abuse [NIDA], 2008).

Flash Forward

Ready to dig into the vocabulary? Get some practice with this Hawkes Verified Quizlet set (hawkes.biz/psych15q4)!

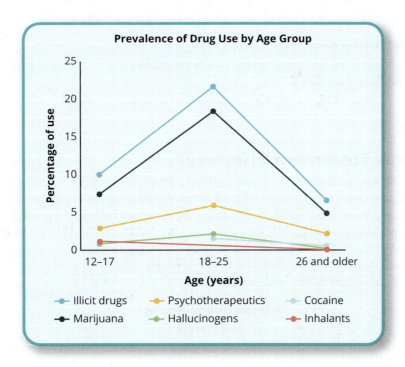

📊 **Figure 1:** The National Survey on Drug Use and Health shows trends in prevalence of various drugs for ages 12–17, 18–25, and 26 or older.

The goal of substance-related treatment is to help an addicted person stop compulsive drug-seeking behaviors (NIDA, 2012). This means an addicted person will need long-term treatment, similar to a person battling a chronic physical disease such as hypertension or diabetes. Treatment usually includes behavioral therapy and/or medication, depending on the individual (NIDA, 2012). Specialized therapies have also been developed for specific types of substance-related disorders, including alcohol, cocaine, and opioids (McGovern & Carroll, 2003). Substance-related treatment is considered much more cost-effective than incarceration or not treating those with addictions (NIDA, 2012) (Figure 2).

Further Resources

One approach to America's current opioid crisis is called harm reduction. Some people want to make drug use less dangerous in order to save lives, while others want to continue criminalizing drug use. There is some evidence (hawkes.biz/safeinjection) that safe injection sites reduce the costs of drug use, both in terms of overdose deaths and the burden on taxpayers. Read this article (hawkes.biz/safeinjection2) for more on safe injection sites.

Why do you think these sites have been so effective?

Figure 2: Substance use and abuse costs the United States over $600 billion a year (NIDA, 2012).

Reflection Questions

What is your reaction to the idea that treatment for substance abuse is actually more cost effective than incarceration for these individuals?

What Makes Treatment Effective?

Specific factors make substance-related treatment much more effective. One factor is duration of treatment. Generally, the addict needs to be in treatment for at least three months to achieve a positive outcome (Simpson, 1981; Simpson, Joe, & Bracy, 1982; NIDA, 2012). This is due to the psychological, physiological, behavioral, and social aspects of abuse (Simpson, 1981; Simpson et al., 1982; NIDA, 2012). While in treatment, an addict might receive behavior therapy, which can help motivate the addict to participate in the treatment program and teach strategies for dealing with cravings and how to prevent relapse. Also, treatment needs to be holistic and address multiple needs, not just the drug addiction.

Aspects of Holistic Treatment

Drug addiction

Communication

Stress management

Relationship issues

Parenting

Vocational concerns

Legal concerns

While individual therapy is used in the treatment of substance-related disorders, group therapy is the most widespread treatment modality (Weiss, Jaffee, de Menil, & Cogley, 2004). The rationale behind using group therapy for addiction treatment is that addicts are much more likely to maintain sobriety in a group format. It has been suggested that this is due to the rewarding and therapeutic benefits of the group, such as support, affiliation, identification, and even confrontation (Center for Substance Abuse Treatment, 2005). For teenagers, the whole family often needs to participate in treatment to address issues such as family dynamics, communication, and relapse prevention. Family involvement in teen drug addiction is vital. Research suggests that greater parental involvement is correlated with a greater reduction in use by teen substance abusers. Also, mothers who participated in treatment displayed better mental health and greater warmth toward their children

(Bertrand et al., 2013). However, neither individual nor group therapy has been found to be more effective than the other (Weiss et al., 2004). Regardless of the type of treatment service, the primary focus is on abstinence or at the very least a significant reduction in use (McGovern & Carroll, 2003).

Treatment also usually involves medications; medications may be used in the following ways:

- to detox the addict safely after an overdose

- to prevent seizures and agitation that often occur in detox

- to prevent reuse of the drug

- to manage withdrawal symptoms

Getting off drugs often involves the use of drugs—some of which can be just as addictive. Detox can be difficult and dangerous.

Further Resources

Watch this video (hawkes.biz/treatingsubabuse) to find out more about treating substance-related disorders using the biological, behavioral, and psychodynamic approaches.

Comorbid Disorders

Frequently, a person who is addicted to drugs and/or alcohol has an additional psychological disorder. Saying a person has **comorbid disorders** means the individual has two or more diagnoses. This can often be a substance-related diagnosis and another psychiatric diagnosis, such as depression, bipolar disorder, or schizophrenia. These individuals fall into the category of mentally ill and chemically addicted (MICA)—their problems are often chronic and expensive to treat, with limited success. Compared with the overall population, substance abusers are twice as likely to have a mood or anxiety disorder. Drug abuse can cause symptoms of mood and anxiety disorders, and the reverse is also true—people with debilitating symptoms of a psychiatric disorder may self-medicate and abuse substances.

Reflection Questions

What additional challenges would be present in treating a person who has both a mental disorder and is addicted to heroin?

In cases of comorbidity, the best treatment addresses both (or multiple) disorders simultaneously (NIDA, 2012). Behavior therapies are used to treat comorbid conditions, and in many cases, psychotropic medications are used along with psychotherapy. For example, evidence suggests that bupropion (trade names: Wellbutrin and Zyban), approved for treating depression and nicotine dependence, might also help reduce craving and use of the drug methamphetamine (NIDA, 2011). However, more research is needed to better understand how these medications work—particularly when combined in patients with comorbidities.

Figure 3: Wellbutrin, a drug used to treat depression, may also address nicotine and methamphetamine cravings.

✎ On Your Own

Answer the following questions about substance abuse.

1. How long (at a minimum) should an addict be in treatment?

☐ 2 weeks

☐ 3 months

2. How much greater is the likelihood of a substance abuser having a comorbid mood or anxiety disorder?

☐ Twice as likely

☐ Five times as likely

Summary

Addiction is often viewed as a chronic disease that rewires the brain. This helps explain why relapse rates tend to be high, around 40%–60% (McLellan, Lewis, & O'Brien, & Kleber, 2000). The goal of treatment is to help an addict stop compulsive drug-seeking behaviors. Treatment usually includes behavioral therapy, which can take place individually or in a group setting. Treatment may also include medication. Sometimes a person has comorbid disorders, which usually means that they have a substance-related disorder diagnosis and another psychiatric diagnosis, such as depression, bipolar disorder, or schizophrenia. The best treatment would address both problems simultaneously.

> **Flash Forward**
>
> Ready to dig into the vocabulary? Get some practice with this Hawkes Verified Quizlet set (hawkes.biz/ psych15q5)!

15.5 The Sociocultural Model and Therapy Utilization

The sociocultural perspective looks at you, your behaviors, and your symptoms in the context of your culture and background. For example, Mateo is an 18-year-old Hispanic male from a traditional family. Mateo comes to treatment because of depression. During the intake session, he reveals that he is gay and is nervous about telling his family. He also discloses that he is concerned because his religious background has taught him that homosexuality is wrong. How does his religious and cultural background affect him? How might his cultural background affect how his family reacts if Mateo were to tell them he is gay?

As our society becomes increasingly multiethnic and multiracial, mental health professionals must develop **cultural competence**, which means they must understand and address issues of race, culture, and ethnicity. They must also develop strategies to effectively address the needs of various populations for which Eurocentric therapies have limited application (Sue, 2004). For example, a counselor whose treatment focuses on individual decision making may be ineffective at helping a Chinese client with a collectivist approach to problem solving (Sue, 2004).

> **Reflection Questions**
>
> How culturally competent are you? Which diverse groups do you have knowledge about?

Multicultural counseling and therapy aim to:

- offer a helping role

- offer a process that uses modalities and defines goals consistent with the life experiences and cultural values of clients

- recognize client identities to include individual, group, and universal dimensions

- advocate the use of universal and culture-specific strategies and roles in the healing process

- balance the importance of individualism and collectivism in the assessment, diagnosis, and treatment of the client and client systems (Sue, 2001)

This therapeutic perspective integrates the impact of cultural and social norms, starting at the beginning of treatment. Therapists who use this perspective work with clients to obtain and integrate information about their cultural patterns into a unique treatment approach based on their particular situation (Stewart, Simmons, & Habibpour, 2012). Sociocultural therapy can include individual, group, family, and couples treatment modalities.

Figure 1: How do your cultural and religious beliefs affect your attitude toward mental health treatment?

Further Resources

Watch this short video (hawkes.biz/culturalcompetence) to learn more about cultural competence and sociocultural treatments.

Barriers to Treatment

Statistically, ethnic minorities tend to utilize mental health services less frequently than White, middle-class Americans (Alegría et al., 2008; Richman, Kohn-Wood, & Williams, 2007).

Perhaps the reason has to do with access and availability of mental health services. Ethnic minorities and individuals of low socioeconomic status (SES) report that barriers to services include lack of:

- insurance

- transportation

- time (Thomas & Snowden, 2002)

However, researchers have found that even when income levels and insurance variables are taken into account, ethnic minorities are far less likely to seek out and utilize mental health services. And when access to mental health services is comparable across ethnic and racial groups, differences in service utilization remain (Richman et al., 2007).

In a study involving thousands of women, it was found that the prevalence rate of anorexia was similar across different races, but that bulimia nervosa was more prevalent among Hispanic and African-American women when compared with non-Hispanic whites (Marques et al., 2011). Although they have similar or higher rates of eating disorders, Hispanic and African-American women with these disorders tend to seek and engage in treatment far less than Caucasian women. These findings suggest ethnic disparities in access to care, as well as clinical and referral practices that may prevent Hispanic and African-American women from receiving care.

Reasons Hispanic and African-American Women May Not Receive Care

Lack of bilingual treatment

Stigma

Fear of not being understood

Family privacy

Lack of education about eating disorders

Perceptions and attitudes toward mental health services may also contribute to this imbalance. A recent study at King's College, London, found many complex reasons why people do not seek treatment:

- self-sufficiency and not seeing the need for help

- not seeing therapy as effective

- concerns about confidentiality

- the many effects of stigma and shame (Clement et al., 2014)

Group Activity

In small groups, brainstorm some reasons why ethnic minorities are less likely to utilize mental health services.

Figure 2: Here are worshippers at Holy Angel Catholic Church in Chicago, IL; it is the city's largest Black Catholic Church.

And in another study, African Americans exhibiting depression were less willing to seek treatment due to fear of possible psychiatric hospitalization as well as fear of the treatment itself (Sussman, Robins, & Earls, 1987). Instead of mental health treatment, many African Americans prefer to be self-reliant or use spiritual practices (Snowden, 2001; Belgrave & Allison, 2010). For example, it has been found that predominately Black churches play a significant role as an alternative to mental health services by providing prevention and treatment-type programs designed to enhance the psychological and physical well-being of their members (Blank, Mahmood, Fox, & Guterbock, 2002).

Additionally, people belonging to ethnic groups that already report concerns about prejudice and discrimination are less likely to seek services for a mental illness because they view it as an additional stigma (Gary, 2005; Townes, Cunningham, & Chavez-Korell, 2009; Scott, McCoy, Munson, Snowden, & McMillen, 2011). For example, in one recent study of 462 older Korean Americans (over the age of 60), many participants reported suffering from depressive symptoms. However, 71% indicated they thought depression was a sign of personal weakness, and 14% reported that having a mentally ill family member would bring shame to the family (Jang, Chiriboga, & Okazaki, 2009).

Reflection Questions

How can we change the belief that having a mental illness means the individual is weak?

Language differences are a further barrier to treatment. In the previous study on Korean-Americans' attitudes toward mental health services, it was found that there were no Korean-speaking mental health professionals where the study was conducted (Orlando and Tampa, Florida Jang et al., 2009). Because of the growing number of people from ethnically diverse backgrounds, there is a need for therapists and psychologists to develop knowledge and skills to become culturally competent (Ahmed, Wilson, Henriksen, & Jones, 2011). Those providing therapy must approach the process from the context of the unique culture of each client (Sue & Sue, 2007).

Figure 3: Mental health professionals should pursue continuous growth in cultural competency.

Dig Deeper

Treatment Perceptions

By the time a child is a senior in high school, 20% of his classmates—that is one in five—will have experienced a mental health problem (U.S. Department of Health and Human Services, 1999), and 8%—about one in twelve—will have attempted suicide (Centers for Disease Control and Prevention, 2014). Of those classmates experiencing mental disorders, only 20% will receive professional help (U.S. Public Health Service, 2000). Why?

It seems that the public has a negative perception of children and teens with mental health disorders. According to researchers from Indiana University, the University of Virginia, and Columbia University, interviews with over 1,300 U.S. adults show that they believe children with depression are prone to violence and that if a child receives treatment for a psychological disorder, then that child is more likely to be rejected by peers at school.

Bernice Pescosolido, author of the study, asserted that this is a misconception. However, stigmatization of psychological disorders is one of the main reasons why young people do not get the help they need when they are having difficulties. Pescosolido and her colleagues cautioned that this stigma surrounding mental illness, based on misconceptions rather than facts, can be devastating to the emotional and social well-being of our nation's children.

This warning played out as a national tragedy in the 2012 shootings at Sandy Hook Elementary. In her blog, Suzy DeYoung (2013), co-founder of Sandy Hook Promise (the organization that parents and concerned others set up in the wake of the school massacre) spoke to treatment perceptions and what happens when children do not receive the mental health treatment they desperately need.

I've become accustomed to the reaction when I tell people where I'm from.

Eleven months later, it's as consistent as it was back in January.

Just yesterday, inquiring as to the availability of a rental house this holiday season, the gentleman taking my information paused to ask, "Newtown, CT? Isn't that where that... that *thing* happened?"

A recent encounter in the Massachusetts Berkshires, however, took me by surprise.

It was in a small, charming art gallery. The proprietor, a woman who looked to be in her 60s, asked where we were from. My response usually depends on my present mood and readiness for the inevitable dialogue. Sometimes it's simply, Connecticut. This time, I replied, Newtown, CT.

The woman's demeanor abruptly shifted from one of amiable graciousness to one of visible agitation.

"Oh my God," she said wide eyed and open mouthed. "Did you know her?"

...

"Her?" I inquired.

"That woman," she replied with disdain, "that woman that raised that monster."

That woman's name was Nancy Lanza. Her son, Adam, killed her with a rifle blast to the head before heading out to kill 20 children and six educators at Sandy Hook Elementary School in Newtown, CT, last December 14th.

When Nelba Marquez Greene, whose beautiful 6-year-old daughter, Ana, was killed by Adam Lanza, was recently asked how she felt about "that woman," this was her reply:

"She's a victim herself. And it's time in America that we start looking at mental illness with compassion and helping people who need it.

"This was a family that needed help, an individual that needed help and didn't get it. And what better can come of this, of this time in America, than if we can get help to people who really need it?" (pars. 1–7, 10–15)

Fortunately, we are starting to see campaigns related to the destigmatization of mental illness and an increase in public education and awareness. Join the effort by encouraging and supporting those around you to seek help if they need it. To learn more, visit the National Alliance on Mental Illness (NAMI) website (hawkes.biz/nami). NAMI is the nation's largest nonprofit mental health advocacy and support organization.

Summary

The sociocultural perspective looks at you, your behaviors, and your symptoms in the context of your culture and background. Clinicians using this approach integrate cultural and religious beliefs into the therapeutic process. Research has shown that ethnic minorities are less likely to access mental health services than their White middle-class American counterparts. Barriers to treatment include lack of insurance, transportation, and time; cultural views that mental illness is a stigma; fears about treatment; and language barriers.

Chapter 15 Project

Purpose

A 2013 survey by the Association for University and College Counseling Center Directors (AUCCCD) stated that around half of college students reported having "overwhelming anxiety," and nearly one-third of students reported depression so severe that it made it difficult to function. The good news is that most college campuses offer mental health services to students and often for free. **The purpose of this project is to help you to determine where college students can get mental health support, and what mental health treatment might be like for them.**

Directions

This project has two parts:

Part 1 - College Counseling Services

Part 2 - Therapeutic Perspectives

Part 1 - College Counseling Services

Investigate where counseling services are and types of services that are offered on your campus. If your counseling center has a website, that is a great place to start. However, you should also physically visit the counseling center. Walk around, observe the space, look through the available materials, chat with someone who is at the front desk, etc. Then, in two-to-three paragraphs, write a letter to your friend Ivan who is experiencing anxiety about his college performance, his relationships, and his future. Your letter should answer the question, "what would it be like to go to counseling?" Be sure to write in a way that Ivan can understand. That is, avoid jargon.

If your college does not have a counseling center, find a counseling center near your college campus.

Part 2 - Therapeutic Perspectives

Imagine that a friend of yours, Michelle, is having depression that makes it difficult for her to get to class, to keep up with schoolwork, or to spend time with friends. She has very little energy, she is often sad and tearful, and she feels guilty for not doing what she is supposed to be doing in school.

She has recently begun to see a psychologist for her depression. For each of the following therapeutic perspectives, describe how a psychologist might a) explain the origins of this depression, and b) treat the depression that Michelle is experiencing. It is okay to speculate within these answers, though they should communicate a clear understanding of each particular therapeutic perspective, and they should be specific to Michelle.

- Psychodynamic
- Cognitive
- Behavioral
- Humanistic
- Biological

Finally include a paragraph that describes when and why you think Michelle should conclude therapy for her depression, regardless of therapeutic perspective. That is, when will she and her psychologist know she is finished? Discuss her original symptoms, what has taken place in therapy, and her current experiences. Once again, it is okay to speculate.

Materials

None required.

✅ Checklist

- ☐ College Counseling Services section completed
  - ☐ Two-to-three paragraph letter to Ivan explaining what it would be like to go to counseling
- ☐ Therapeutic Perspectives section completed
  - ☐ All therapeutic perspectives included:
    - ☐ Psychodynamic
      - ☐ Explain the origins of depression from this perspective
      - ☐ Treat depression from this perspective
    - ☐ Cognitive
      - ☐ Explain the origins of depression from this perspective
      - ☐ Treat depression from this perspective
    - ☐ Behavioral
      - ☐ Explain the origins of depression from this perspective
      - ☐ Treat depression from this perspective
    - ☐ Humanistic
      - ☐ Explain the origins of depression from this perspective
      - ☐ Treat depression from this perspective
    - ☐ Biological
      - ☐ Explain the origins of depression from this perspective
      - ☐ Treat depression from this perspective
- ☐ Paragraph describing when and why Michelle should conclude therapy
  - ☐ Discusses her original symptoms
  - ☐ What has taken place in therapy
  - ☐ Her current experiences

Lesson Summaries

15.1 Mental Health Treatment: Past and Present

It was once believed that people with psychological disorders, or those exhibiting strange behavior, were possessed by demons. These people were forced to take part in exorcisms, were imprisoned, or executed. Later, asylums were built to house the mentally ill, but the patients received little to no treatment, and many of the methods used were cruel. Philippe Pinel and Dorothea Dix argued for more humane treatment of people with psychological disorders. In the mid-1960s, the deinstitutionalization movement gained support and asylums were closed, enabling people with mental illnesses to return home and receive treatment in their own communities. Some did go to their family homes, but many became homeless due to a lack of resources and support mechanisms.

Today, instead of asylums, there are psychiatric hospitals run by state governments and local community hospitals, with an emphasis on short-term stays. However, most people suffering from mental illness are not hospitalized. A person suffering symptoms could speak with a primary care physician, who most likely would refer him to someone who specializes in therapy. The person can receive outpatient mental health services from a variety of sources, including psychologists, psychiatrists, marriage and family therapists, school counselors, clinical social workers, and religious personnel. These therapy sessions would be covered through insurance, government funds, or private (self) pay.

15.2 Types of Treatment

Psychoanalysis was developed by Sigmund Freud. Freud's theory is that a person's psychological problems are the result of repressed impulses or childhood trauma. The goal of the therapist is to help a person uncover buried feelings by using techniques such as free association and dream analysis.

Play therapy is a psychodynamic therapy technique often used with children. The idea is that children play out their hopes, fantasies, and traumas using dolls, stuffed animals, and sandbox figurines.

In behavior therapy, a therapist employs principles of learning from classical and operant conditioning to help clients change undesirable behaviors. Counterconditioning is a commonly used therapeutic technique in which a client learns a new response to a stimulus that has previously elicited an undesirable behavior via classical conditioning. Principles of operant conditioning can be applied to help people deal with a wide range of psychological problems. Token economy is an example of a popular operant conditioning technique.

Cognitive therapy is a technique that focuses on how thoughts lead to feelings of distress. The idea behind cognitive therapy is that how you think determines how you feel and act. Cognitive therapists help clients change dysfunctional thoughts in order to relieve distress. Cognitive-behavioral therapy explores how our thoughts affect our behavior. Cognitive-behavioral therapy aims to change cognitive distortions and self-defeating behaviors.

Humanistic therapy focuses on helping people achieve their potential. One form of humanistic therapy developed by Carl Rogers is known as client-centered or Rogerian therapy. Client-centered therapists use the techniques of active listening, unconditional positive regard, genuineness, and empathy to help clients become more accepting of themselves.

Often in combination with psychotherapy, people can be prescribed biologically based treatments, such as psychotropic medications, and/or other medical procedures, such as electro-convulsive therapy.

15.3 Treatment Modalities

There are several modalities of treatment; individual therapy, group therapy, couples therapy, and family therapy are the most common. In an individual therapy session, a client works one-on-one with a trained therapist. In group therapy, usually 5–10 people meet with a trained group therapist to discuss a common issue (e.g., divorce, grief, eating disorders, substance abuse, or anger management). Couples therapy involves two people in an intimate relationship who are having difficulties and are trying to resolve them. The couple may be dating, partnered, engaged, or married. The therapist helps them resolve their problems as well as implement strategies that will lead to a healthier and happier relationship. Family therapy is a special form of group therapy. The therapy group is made up of one or more families. The goal of this approach is to enhance the growth of each individual family member and the family as a whole.

15.4 Substance-Related and Addictive Disorders: A Special Case

Addiction is often viewed as a chronic disease that rewires the brain. This helps explain why relapse rates tend to be high, around 40%–60% (McLellan, Lewis, & O'Brien, & Kleber, 2000). The goal of treatment is to help an addict stop compulsive drug-seeking behaviors. Treatment usually includes behavioral therapy, which can take place individually or in a group setting. Treatment may also include medication. Sometimes a person has comorbid disorders, which usually means that they have a substance-related disorder diagnosis and another psychiatric diagnosis, such as depression, bipolar disorder, or schizophrenia. The best treatment would address both problems simultaneously.

15.5 The Sociocultural Model and Therapy Utilization

The sociocultural perspective looks at you, your behaviors, and your symptoms in the context of your culture and background. Clinicians using this approach integrate cultural and religious beliefs into the therapeutic process. Research has shown that ethnic minorities are less likely to access mental health services than their White middle-class American counterparts. Barriers to treatment include lack of insurance, transportation, and time; cultural views that mental illness is a stigma; fears about treatment; and language barriers.

Key Terms

Flash Back

Now that you've worked through the chapter, sharpen your vocabulary with this Hawkes Verified Quizlet set (hawkes.biz/psychch15)!

Asylum
Institution created for the specific purpose of housing people with psychological disorders

Aversive Conditioning
Counterconditioning technique that pairs an unpleasant stimulant with an undesirable behavior

Behavior Therapy
Therapeutic orientation that employs principles of learning to help clients change undesirable behaviors

Biomedical Therapy
Treatment that involves medication and/or medical procedures to treat psychological disorders

Cognitive Therapy
Form of psychotherapy that focuses on how a person's thoughts lead to feelings of distress, with the aim of helping them change these irrational thoughts

Cognitive-Behavioral Therapy (CBT)
Form of psychotherapy that aims to change cognitive distortions and self-defeating behaviors

Comorbid Disorder
Individual who has two or more diagnoses, which often includes a substance abuse diagnosis and another psychiatric diagnosis, such as depression, bipolar disorder, or schizophrenia

Confidentiality
Therapist cannot disclose confidential communications to any third party, unless mandated or permitted by law

Counterconditioning
Classical conditioning therapeutic technique in which a client learns a new response to a stimulus that has previously elicited an undesirable behavior

Couples Therapy
Two people in an intimate relationship, such as husband and wife, who are having difficulties and are trying to resolve them with therapy

Cultural Competence
Therapist's understanding and attention to issues of race, culture, and ethnicity in providing treatment

Deinstitutionalization
Process of closing large asylums and integrating people back into the community where they can be treated locally

Dream Analysis
Technique in psychoanalysis in which patients recall their dreams and the psychoanalyst interprets them to reveal unconscious desires or struggles

Electroconvulsive Therapy (ECT)
Type of biomedical therapy that involves using an electrical current to induce seizures in a person to help alleviate the effects of severe depression

Exposure Therapy
Counterconditioning technique in which a therapist seeks to treat a client's fear or anxiety by presenting the feared object or situation with the idea that the person will eventually get used to it

Family Therapy
Special form of group therapy consisting of one or more families

Free Association
Technique in psychoanalysis in which the patient says whatever comes to mind at the moment

Group Therapy
Treatment modality in which 5–10 people with the same issue or concern meet together with a trained clinician

Humanistic Therapy
Therapeutic orientation aimed at helping people become more self-aware and accepting of themselves

Individual Therapy
Treatment modality in which the client and clinician meet one-on-one

Intake

Therapist's first meeting with the client in which the therapist gathers specific information to address the client's immediate needs

Involuntary Treatment

Therapy that is mandated by the courts or other systems

Nondirective Therapy

Therapeutic approach in which the therapist does not give advice or provide interpretations but helps the person identify conflicts and understand feelings

Play Therapy

Therapeutic process, often used with children, that employs toys to help them resolve psychological problems

Psychoanalysis

Therapeutic orientation developed by Sigmund Freud that employs free association, dream analysis, and transference to uncover repressed feelings

Psychotherapy

(Also, *psychodynamic psychotherapy*) psychological treatment that employs various methods to help someone overcome personal problems, or to attain personal growth

Rational Emotive Therapy (RET)

Form of cognitive-behavioral therapy

Relapse

Repeated drug use and/or alcohol use after a period of improvement from substance abuse

Rogerian (Client-Centered) Therapy

Non-directive form of humanistic psychotherapy developed by Carl Rogers that emphasizes unconditional positive regard and self-acceptance

Strategic Family Therapy

Therapist guides the therapy sessions and develops treatment plans for each family member for specific problems that can be addressed in a short amount of time

Structural Family Therapy

Therapist examines and discusses with the family the boundaries and structure of the family: who makes the rules, who sleeps in the bed with whom, how decisions are made, and what are the boundaries within the family

Systematic Desensitization

Form of exposure therapy used to treat phobias and anxiety disorders by exposing a person to the feared object or situation through a stimulus hierarchy

Token Economy

Controlled setting where individuals are reinforced for desirable behaviors with tokens (e.g., poker chips) that be exchanged for items or privileges

Transference

Process in psychoanalysis in which the patient transfers all of the positive or negative emotions associated with the patient's other relationships to the psychoanalyst

Unconditional Positive Regard

Fundamental acceptance of a person regardless of what they say or do; term associated with humanistic psychology

Virtual Reality Exposure Therapy

Uses a simulation rather than the actual feared object or situation to help people conquer their fears

Voluntary Treatment

Therapy that a person chooses to attend in order to obtain relief from her symptoms

Exercises

Review Questions

1. Who of the following does not support the humane and improved treatment of mentally ill persons?

    a. Philippe Pinel

    b. Medieval priests

    c. Dorothea Dix

    d. All of the above

2. The process of closing large asylums and providing for people to stay in the community to be treated locally is known as _____.

    a. deinstitutionalization

    b. exorcism

    c. deactivation

    d. decentralization

3. Joey was convicted of domestic violence. As part of his sentence, the judge has ordered that he attend therapy for anger management. This is considered _____ treatment.

    a. involuntary

    b. voluntary

    c. forced

    d. mandatory

4. Today, most people with psychological problems are not hospitalized. Typically, they are only hospitalized if they _____.

    a. have schizophrenia

    b. have insurance

    c. are an imminent threat to themselves or others

    d. require therapy

5. The idea behind _____ is that how you think determines how you feel and act.

    a. cognitive therapy

    b. cognitive-behavioral therapy

    c. behavior therapy

    d. client-centered therapy

6. Mood stabilizers, such as lithium, are used to treat _____.

    a. anxiety disorders

    b. depression

    c. bipolar disorder

    d. ADHD

7. Clay is in a therapy session. The therapist asks him to relax and say whatever comes to his mind at the moment. This therapist is using _____, which is a technique of _____.

    a. active listening; client-centered therapy

    b. systematic desensitization; behavior therapy

    c. transference; psychoanalysis

    d. free association; psychoanalysis

8. A treatment modality in which 5–10 people with the same issue or concern meet together with a trained clinician is known as _____.

    a. family therapy

    b. couples therapy

    c. group therapy

    d. self-help group

9. What happens during an intake?

    a. The therapist gathers specific information to address the client's immediate needs such as the presenting problem, the client's support system, and insurance status. The therapist informs the client about confidentiality, fees, and what to expect in a therapy session.

    b. The therapist guides what happens in the therapy session and designs a detailed approach to resolving each member's presenting problem.

    c. The therapist meets with a couple to help them see how their individual backgrounds, beliefs, and actions are affecting their relationship.

    d. The therapist examines and discusses with the family the boundaries and structure of the family like who makes the rules, who sleeps in the bed with whom, and how decisions are made.

10. What is the minimum amount of time addicts should receive treatment if they are to achieve a desired outcome?

    a. 3 months

    b. 6 months

    c. 9 months

    d. 12 months

11. When an individual has two or more diagnoses, which often includes a substance-related diagnosis and another psychiatric diagnosis, this is known as _____.

    a. bipolar disorder

    b. comorbid disorder

    c. codependency

    d. bi-morbid disorder

12. John was drug-free for almost six months. Then he started hanging out with his addict friends, and he has now started abusing drugs again. This is an example of _____.

    a. release

    b. reversion

    c. re-addiction

    d. relapse

13. The sociocultural perspective looks at you, your behaviors, and your symptoms in the context of your _____.

    a. education

    b. socioeconomic status

    c. culture and background

    d. age

14. Which of the following was not listed as a barrier to mental health treatment?

    a. Fears about treatment

    b. Language

    c. Transportation

    d. Being a member of the ethnic majority

Critical Thinking Questions

15. People with psychological disorders have been treated poorly throughout history. Describe some efforts to improve treatment, include explanations for the success or lack thereof.

16. Usually someone is hospitalized only if they are an imminent threat to themselves or others. Describe a situation that might meet these criteria.

17. Imagine that you are a psychiatrist. Your patient, Pat, comes to you with anxiety and feelings of sadness. Which therapeutic approach would you recommend and why?

18. Compare and contrast individual and group therapies.

19. You are conducting an intake assessment. Your client is a 45-year-old single, employed male with cocaine dependence. He failed a drug screening at work and has been mandated to treatment by his employer if he wants to keep his job. Your client admits that he needs help. Why would you recommend group therapy for him?

20. Deja is a 24-year-old African-American female. For years she has been struggling with bulimia. She knows she has a problem, but she is not willing to seek mental health services. What are some reasons why she may be hesitant to get help?

Answer Key

Chapter 1

1. **d.** All of the above
3. **c.** philosophy
5. **b.** Max Wertheimer
7. **d.** unconditional positive regard
9. **a.** biological
11. **b.** $\frac{2}{3}$
13. **d.** PhD
15. **d.** Bachelor's degree
17. **d.** testable
19. **b.** empirical
21. **b.** case study
23. **c.** the inability to generalize the findings from this approach to the larger population
25. **d.** archival research
27. **d.** survey
29. **d.** increases; increases
31. **d.** Students who watch more television perform more poorly on their exams.
33. **d.** Random sampling
35. **c.** operationalize
37. **b.** IACUC; IRB
39. **c.** voluntary
41. Psychology courses deal with a number of issues that are helpful in a variety of settings. The text made mention of the types of skills as well as the knowledge base with which students of psychology become familiar. As mentioned in the further resources, psychology is often helpful/valued in fields in which interacting with others is a major part of the job.
43. In its early days, psychology could be defined as the scientific study of mind or mental processes. Over time, psychology began to shift more towards the scientific study of behavior. However, as the cognitive revolution took hold, psychology once again began to focus on mental processes as necessary to the understanding of behavior.
45. Although the different perspectives all operate on different levels of analyses, have different foci of interests, and different methodological approaches, all of these areas share a focus on understanding and/or correcting patterns of thought and/or behavior.
47. An undergraduate education in psychology hones critical thinking skills. These skills are useful in many different work settings.
49. There is probably tremendous political pressure to appear to be hard on drugs. Therefore, even though D.A.R.E. might be ineffective, it is a well-known program with which voters are familiar.
51. Case studies might prove especially helpful using individuals who have rare conditions. For instance, if one wanted to study multiple personality disorder then the case study approach with individuals diagnosed with multiple personality disorder would be helpful.
53. Longitudinal research would be an excellent approach in studying the effectiveness of this program because it would follow students as they aged to determine if their choices regarding alcohol and drugs were affected by their participation in the program.
55. The cereal companies are trying to make a profit, so framing the research findings in this way would improve their bottom line. However, it could be that people who eat cereal for breakfast are health conscious and engage in a variety of other behaviors that help them maintain a healthy weight.
57. If research is limited to students enrolled in Introduction to Psychology courses, then our ability to generalize to the larger population would be dramatically reduced. One could also argue that students enrolled in Introduction to Psychology courses may not be representative of the larger population of college students at their school, much less the larger general population.
59. In general, the fact that consent cannot be obtained from animal research subjects places extra responsibility on the researcher to ensure that the animal is treated as humanely as possible and to respect the sacrifice that the animal is making for the advancement of science. Like human research, the animals themselves should also receive some of the benefits of the research, and they do in the form of advanced veterinary medicine, and so on.

Chapter 2

1. **d.** mutation
3. **c.** Epigenetics
5. **d.** dendrites
7. **b.** myelin sheath
9. **b.** somatic
11. **d.** the brain and spinal cord
13. **d.** thalamus
15. **b.** MRI
17. **d.** glucagon and insulin
19. **a.** adrenal
21. Variability is essential for natural selection to work. If all individuals are the same on a given trait, there will be no relative difference in their reproductive success because everyone will be equally adapted to their environments on that trait. Mutations are one source of variability, but sexual reproduction is

another important source of variation given that individuals inherit half of their genetic makeup from each of their parents.

23. The action potential is initiated by an influx of Na⁺ into the neuron. If this process is prevented, then no action potentials in neurons in a given area will occur. Therefore, any painful stimuli would not result in action potentials carrying that information to the brain.

25. Most of these effects directly impact energy availability and redistribution of key resources and heightened sensory capacity. The individual experiencing these effects would be better prepared to fight or flee.

27. The most viable techniques are MRI and PET because of their ability to provide information about brain activity and structure simultaneously.

29. Both systems involve chemical messengers that must interact with receptors in order to have an effect. The relative proximity of the release site and target tissue varies dramatically between the two systems. In neurotransmission, reuptake and enzymatic breakdown immediately clear the synapse. Metabolism of hormones must occur in the liver. Therefore, while neurotransmission is much more rapid in signaling information, hormonal signaling can persist for quite some time as the concentrations of the hormone in the bloodstream vary gradually over time.

Chapter 3

1. **c.** hypothalamus

3. **b.** Circadian

5. **c.** pituitary gland

7. **b.** Melatonin

9. **c.** Stage 3 and stage 4

11. **c.** depression

13. **c.** Cataplexy

15. **d.** narcolepsy

17. **c.** Tolerance

19. **a.** Psychological dependence

21. **a.** Hypnosis

23. **d.** both a and b

25. Given that rotating shift work can lead to exhaustion and decreased mental efficiency, individuals working under these conditions are more likely to make mistakes on the job. The implications for this in the health care professions are obvious. Those in health care professions could be educated about the benefits of light-dark exposure to help alleviate such problems.

27. Those individuals (or species) that expend the greatest amounts of energy would require the longest periods of sleep.

29. One evolutionary theory of sleep holds that sleep is essential for restoration of resources that are expended during the demands of day-to-day life. A second theory proposes that our sleep patterns evolved as an adaptive response to predatory risks, which increase in darkness. The first theory has little or no empirical support, and the second theory is supported by some, though not all, research.

31. Dreaming occurs during REM sleep. One of the hallmarks of this particular stage of sleep is the paralysis of the voluntary musculature which would make acting out dreams improbable.

33. Similarities include muscle atony and the hypnagogic hallucinations associated with narcoleptic episodes. The differences involve the uncontrollable nature of narcoleptic attacks and the fact that these come on in situations that would normally not be associated with sleep of any kind (e.g., instances of heightened arousal or emotionality).

35. Given that currently available programs designed to help people quit using tobacco products are not necessarily effective in the long term, programs designed to prevent people

from using these products in the first place may be the best hope for dealing with the enormous public health concerns associated with tobacco use.

37. Ideally, double-blind experimental trials would be best suited to speak to the effectiveness of meditation. At the very least, some sort of randomized control trial would be very informative.

Chapter 4

1. **a.** Absolute threshold

3. **d.** Transduction

5. **b.** Yellow to orange to red

7. **d.** all of the above

9. **d.** timbre

11. **a.** Cones

13. **d.** red

15. **d.** both a and b (malleus, incus, and stapes and hammer, anvil, and stirrup)

17. **d.** binaural

19. **c.** Umami

21. **d.** Vestibular system

23. **a.** closure

25. **d.** figure

27. There are many potential examples. One example involves the detection of weight differences. If two people are holding standard envelopes and one contains a quarter while the other is empty, the difference in weight between the two is easy to detect. However, if those envelopes are placed inside two textbooks of equal weight, the ability to discriminate which is heavier is much more difficult.

29. Once again, one could make an evolutionary argument here. Given that the human voice falls in this middle range and the importance of communication among humans, one

could argue that it is quite adaptive to have an audible range that centers on this particular type of stimulus.

31. Color vision probably serves multiple adaptive purposes. One popular hypothesis suggests that seeing in color allowed our ancestors to differentiate ripened fruits and vegetables more easily.

33. Pitch of sounds below this threshold could be encoded by the combination of the place and firing rate of stimulated hair cells. So, in general, hair cells located near the tip of the basilar membrane would signal that we're dealing with a lower-pitched sound. However, differences in firing rates of hair cells within this location could allow for fine discrimination between low-, medium-, and high-pitch sounds within the larger low-pitch context.

35. Pain serves important functions that are critical to our survival. As noxious as pain stimuli may be, the experiences of individuals who suffer from congenital insensitivity to pain makes the consequences of a lack of pain all too apparent.

37. This means that perception cannot be understood completely simply by combining the parts. Rather, the relationship that exists among those parts (which would be established according to the principles described in this chapter) is important in organizing and interpreting sensory information into a perceptual set.

Chapter 5

1. **c.** Infant sucking on a nipple

3. **a.** classical conditioning; operant conditioning

5. **b.** neutral stimulus

7. **a.** the conditioned stimulus is presented repeatedly without being paired with an unconditioned stimulus

9. **d.** Negative punishment

11. **a.** shaping

13. **b.** model

15. **a.** Attention, retention, reproduction, motivation

17. Both classical and operant conditioning involve learning by association. In classical conditioning, responses are involuntary and automatic; however, responses are voluntary and learned in operant conditioning. In classical conditioning, the event that drives the behavior (the stimulus) comes before the behavior; in operant conditioning, the event that drives the behavior (the consequence) comes after the behavior. Also, whereas classical conditioning involves an organism forming an association between an involuntary (reflexive) response and a stimulus, operant conditioning involves an organism forming an association between a voluntary behavior and a consequence.

19. The food being toasted is the UCS; the sound of the toaster popping up is the CS; salivating to the sound of the toaster is the CR.

21. This occurs through the process of acquisition. A human or an animal learns to connect a neutral stimulus and an unconditioned stimulus. During the acquisition phase, the neutral stimulus begins to elicit the conditioned response. The neutral stimulus is becoming the conditioned stimulus. At the end of the acquisition phase, learning has occurred and the neutral stimulus becomes a conditioned stimulus capable of eliciting the conditioned response by itself.

23. In negative reinforcement you are taking away an undesirable stimulus in order to increase the frequency of a certain behavior (e.g., buckling your seat belt stops the annoying beeping sound in your car and increases the likelihood that you will wear your seatbelt). Punishment is designed to

reduce a behavior (e.g., you scold your child for running into the street in order to decrease the unsafe behavior).

25. Prosocial modeling can prompt others to engage in helpful and healthy behaviors, while antisocial modeling can prompt others to engage in violent, aggressive, and unhealthy behaviors.

Chapter 6

1. **b.** human thinking

3. **b.** A triangle's area

5. **d.** Syntax

7. **d.** semantics

9. **a.** an algorithm

11. **a.** Anchoring bias

13. **d.** being able to see complex relationships and solve problems

15. **c.** Sternberg

17. **b.** a representative sample

19. **d.** David Wechsler

21. **c.** Both A and B

23. **b.** A neurological disorder

25. Answers will vary. When attending a basketball game, it is typical to support your team by wearing the team colors and sitting behind their bench.

27. People tend to talk about the things that are important to them or the things they think about the most. What we talk about, therefore, is a reflection of our values.

29. Functional fixedness occurs when you cannot see a use for an object other than the use for which it was intended. For example, if you need something to hold up a tarp in the rain, but only have a pitchfork, you must overcome your expectation that a pitchfork can only be used for garden chores before you realize that you could stick it in the ground and drape the tarp on top of it to hold it up.

31. You are out with friends, and it is getting late. You need to make it home before your curfew, but you don't have a ride home. You need to get in touch with your parents, but your cell phone is dead. So, you enter a nearby convenience store and explain your situation to the clerk. He allows you to use the store's phone to call your parents, and they come and pick you and your friends up and take all of you home.

33. Since cognitive processes are complex, ascertaining them in a measurable way is challenging. Researchers have taken different approaches to define intelligence in an attempt to comprehensively describe and measure it.

35. Twin studies are one strong indication that IQ has a genetic component. Another indication is anecdotal evidence in the form of stories about highly intelligent individuals who come from difficult backgrounds yet still become highly successful adults.

Chapter 7

1. **c.** Working memory

3. **d.** encoding, storage, and retrieval

5. **c.** flashbulb memory

7. **d.** blocking

9. **c.** acrostic

11. **a.** making the material you are trying to memorize personally meaningful to you

13. Both are types of long-term memory. Explicit memories are memories we consciously try to remember and recall. Explicit memory is also called declarative memory and is subdivided into episodic memory (life events) and semantic memory (words, ideas, and concepts). Implicit memories are memories that are not part of our consciousness; they are memories formed from behaviors. Implicit memory is also called non-declarative memory and includes procedural memory as well as things learned through classical conditioning.

15. Information is encoded through automatic or effortful processing. Automatic processing refers to all information that enters long-term memory without conscious effort. This includes things such as time, space, and frequency—for example, your ability to remember what you ate for breakfast today or the fact that you remember that you ran into your best friend in the supermarket twice this week. Effortful processing refers to encoding information through conscious attention and effort. Material that you study for a test requires effortful processing.

17. There are two types of interference: retroactive and proactive. Both are types of forgetting caused by a failure to retrieve information. With retroactive interference, new information hinders the ability to recall older information. With proactive interference, it's the opposite: old information hinders the recall of newly learned information.

19. The self-reference effect is the tendency for an individual to have better memory for information that relates to oneself than information that is not personally relevant. You can use the self-reference effect to relate the material to something you have already learned for another class, or think how you can apply the concepts to your life. When you do this, you are building a web of retrieval cues that will help you access the material when you want to remember it.

Chapter 8

1. **c.** continuous development

3. **a.** The study of how we grow and change from conception to death.

5. **d.** Lawrence Kohlberg

7. **d.** Zygote, embryo, fetus

9. **c.** Zygote

11. **a.** Secure

13. **b.** Cicely Saunders

15. The nature versus nurture controversy seeks to understand whether our personalities and traits are the product of our genetic makeup and biological factors, or whether they are shaped by our environment, which includes such things as our parents, peers, and culture. Today, psychologists agree that both nature and nurture interact to shape who we become, but the debate over the relative contributions of each continues. An example would be a child learning to walk: nature influences when the physical ability occurs, but culture can influence when a child masters this skill, as in Aché culture.

17. Children develop at different rates. For example, some children may walk and talk as early as 8 months old, while others may not do so until well after their first birthday. Each child's unique contexts will influence when he reaches these milestones.

19. Gilligan criticized Kohlberg because his theory was based on the responses of upper-class White men and boys, arguing that it was biased against women. While Kohlberg concluded that women must be deficient in their moral reasoning abilities, Gilligan disagreed, suggesting that female moral reasoning is not deficient, just different.

21. Alcohol is a teratogen. Excessive drinking can cause intellectual disabilities in children. The child can also have a small head and abnormal facial features, which are characteristic of fetal alcohol syndrome (FAS). Another teratogen is nicotine. Smoking while pregnant can lead to low-birth weight, premature birth, stillbirth, and SIDS.

23. In the embryonic stage, basic structures of the embryo start to develop into areas that will become the head, chest, and abdomen. The heart begins to beat and organs form and begin to function. The neural tube forms along the back of the embryo, developing into the spinal cord and brain. In the fetal stage, the brain and body continue to develop. Fingers and toes develop along with hearing, and internal organs form.

25. The sucking reflex is the automatic, unlearned sucking motions that infants do with their mouths. It may help promote survival because this action helps the baby take in nourishment. The rooting reflex is the newborn's response to anything that touches her cheek. When you stroke a baby's cheek, she will naturally turn her head that way and begin to suck. This may aid survival because it helps the newborn locate a source of food.

27. Emerging adulthood is a relatively new period of lifespan development from 18 years old to the mid-20s, characterized as a transitional time in which identity exploration focuses on work and love. According to Arnett, changing cultural expectations facilitate the delay to full adulthood. People are spending more time exploring their options, so they are delaying marriage and work as they change majors and jobs multiple times, putting them on a much later timetable than their parents.

29. Hospice is a program of services that provide medical, social, and spiritual support for dying people and their families.

Chapter 9

1. **b.** affiliation

3. **d.** Self-efficacy

5. **b.** one third

7. **d.** Bulimia nervosa

9. **c.** medial preoptic area of the hypothalamus

11. **a.** Sexual desire and sexual ability can be separate functions.

13. **b.** hippocampus

15. **c.** Melancholy

17. The idea of optimal levels of arousal is similar to a drive theory of motivation. Presumably, we all seek to maintain some intermediate level of arousal. If we are underaroused, we are bored. If we are overaroused, we experience stress. The rides at an amusement park would provide higher arousal (however, we would hope that these rides don't actually pose significant threats to personal safety that would lead to a state of panic) to push us toward our own optimal level of arousal. Individuals at the park would choose different rides based on their specific arousal thresholds; for example, one person might find a simple water ride optimally arousing and an extreme roller coaster overarousing, while others would find the extreme roller coaster optimally arousing.

19. Using BMI as a sole metric can actually be misleading because people who have large amounts of lean muscle mass can actually be characterized as being overweight or obese based on their height and weight. Weight versus height is a somewhat crude measurement as it doesn't distinguish the amount of body weight that comes from lean versus fatty tissue.

21. Given the stigma associated with being non-heterosexual, participants who openly identify as homosexual or bisexual in research projects may not be entirely representative of the non-heterosexual population as a whole.

23. The James-Lange theory would predict that I would not feel fear because I haven't had the physiological arousal necessary to induce that emotional state.

Chapter 10

1. **d.** long term, stable, and not easily changed

3. **d.** Freud

5. **b.** pleasure

7. **c.** phallic

9. **b.** will power

11. **b.** external

13. **d.** congruence

15. **b.** a difficult baby

17. **a.** inborn, genetically based personality differences

19. **b.** individualist

21. **a.** Minnesota Multiphasic Personality Inventory (MMPI)

23. **a.** Minnesota Multiphasic Personality Inventory (MMPI)

25. Since the idea behind the Electra complex is that the daughter competes with her same-sex parent for the attention of her opposite-sex parent, the term "daddy's girl" might suggest that the daughter has an overly close relationship with her father and a more distant—or even antagonistic—relationship with her mother.

27. Extroverts are energized by social engagement. Introverts are recharged by solitary time.

29. People who have high self-efficacy believe that their efforts matter. They perceive their goals as being within reach; have a positive view of challenges, seeing them as tasks to be mastered; develop a deep interest in and strong commitment to the activities in which they are involved; and quickly recover from setbacks. Conversely, people with low self-efficacy believe their efforts have little or no effect, and that outcomes are beyond their control. They avoid challenging tasks because they doubt their abilities to be successful; tend to focus on failure and negative outcomes; and lose confidence in their abilities if they experience setbacks.

31. An easygoing parent may be irritated by a difficult child. If both parent and child have difficult temperaments, then conflicts in the parent-child relationship might result quite often.

33. A person with a high score on agreeableness is typically pleasant, cooperative, trustworthy and good-natured. People who score low on agreeableness tend to be described as rude and uncooperative. They may be difficult with which to work.

35. They can help an employer predict a candidate's reactions and attitudes to various situations they might encounter on the job, thus helping choose the right person for the job. This is particularly important in hiring for a high-risk job, such as law enforcement. Personality tests can also reveal a potential employee's desirable qualities, such as honesty, motivation, and conscientiousness.

Chapter 11

1. **d.** situational factors

3. **b.** situational; dispositional

5. **b.** social norm

7. **c.** fitting in

9. **b.** evaluations

11. **a.** analytical; motivated

13. **b.** normative

15. **c.** both a and b

17. **a.** feelings; behaviors

19. **c.** Scapegoating

21. **b.** physical harm; emotional harm

23. **c.** diffusion of responsibility

25. **a.** his next door neighbor

27. **c.** Romantic love

29. A situationism view is that our behaviors are determined by the situation—for example, a person who is late for work claims that heavy traffic caused the delay. A dispositional view is that our behaviors are determined by personality traits—for example, a driver in a road rage incident claims the driver who cut her off is an aggressive person. Thus, a situational view tends to provide an excuse for inappropriate behavior, and a dispositional view tends to lay blame for inappropriate behavior.

31. The "good" guards were fulfilling their social roles, and they did not object to other guards' abusive behavior because of the power of the situation. In addition, the prison supervisor's behavior sanctioned the guards' negative treatment of prisoners. The prisoners were not weak people; they were recruited because they were healthy, mentally stable adults. The power of their social role influenced them to engage in subservient prisoner behavior. The script for prisoners is to accept abusive behavior from authority figures, especially for punishment, when they do not follow the rules.

33. One example is choosing which college to attend—the public school close to home or the Ivy League school out of state. Since both schools are desirable, the student is likely to experience cognitive dissonance in making this decision. In order to justify choosing the public school close to home, the student could change her cognition about the Ivy League school, asserting that it is too expensive and the quality of education at the public school is just as good. She could change her attitude toward the Ivy League school and determine that the students there are too stuffy and wouldn't make good classmates.

35. Outsiders can serve as a quality control by offering diverse views and views that may differ from the leader's opinion. The outsider can also remove the illusion of invincibility by having the group's action held up to outside scrutiny. An outsider may offer additional information and uncover information that group members withheld.

37. In the United States, many people believe that sexual orientation is a choice, and there is some debate in the research literature as to the extent sexual orientation is biological or influenced by social factors. Because race and gender are not chosen, many Americans believe it is unfair to negatively judge women or racial minority groups for a characteristic that is determined by genetics. In addition, many people in the United States practice religions that believe homosexuality is wrong.

39. Hostile aggression is intentional with the purpose to inflict pain. Hostile aggression is often motivated by anger. In contrast, instrumental aggression is not motivated by anger or the intention to cause pain. Instrumental aggression serves as a means to reach a goal. In a sense it is a more practical or functional form of aggression, whereas hostile aggression is more emotion-driven and less functional and rational.

41. Proximity is a major situational factor in relationship formation; people who have frequent contact are more likely to form relationships. Whether or not individuals will form a relationship is based on non-situational factors such as similarity, reciprocity, self-disclosure, and physical attractiveness. In relationships, people seek reciprocity (i.e., a give and take in costs and benefits), self-disclosure of intimate information, and physically attractive partners.

Chapter 12

1. **c.** Walter Dill Scott

3. **b.** Organizational psychology

5. **b.** Which state were you born in?

7. **c.** U.S. Equal Employment Opportunity Commission

9. **c.** Keystroke monitoring

11. **d.** Personality

13. **a.** Height of the chair

15. Answers will vary. Organizational psychology finds social relations of employees important and that

historically workers were thought of more as individual machines rather than a social group.

17. Answers will vary depending on the occupation and question. The question should relate to a specific skill for the job and the rating should relate to how the answer demonstrates the skill.

19. Answers may vary, but they should include that the assessment would include more than one question to try to understand the reasons for the level of job satisfaction. It may also include questions that assess the importance of emotional and cognitive job satisfaction factors.

21. Answers will vary, but they should include that the simulator would be used to determine how pilots interact with the controls and displays within the cockpit, including under conditions of simulated emergencies.

Chapter 13

1. **d.** threatening, and no clear options for dealing with it are apparent
3. **a.** Exhaustion
5. **d.** Death of spouse
7. **c.** It does not take into consideration how a person appraises an event.
9. **c.** lymphocytes
11. **a.** hostility
13. **a.** Terminal cancer
15. **d.** tend to tolerate stress well
17. **b.** Learning new skills
19. **c.** Positive affect involves feeling states, whereas optimism involves expectations.
21. Answers will vary. One example is divorce. People may perceive a divorce as a threat if they believe it will result in loneliness, change of lifestyle (due to loss of additional income), or humiliation in the eyes of their family. However, divorce may be perceived as a challenge if they view it as an opportunity to find somebody

more compatible, and if they consider the process of finding a new partner a pleasant one, perhaps involving mystery and excitement.

23. Answers will vary. For example, many people look forward to celebrating the Christmas holiday, but it can be stressful in that it requires some degree of readjustment. Getting together with family may bring eustress, while the schedule and travel demands of may bring distress. Giving gifts to others and seeing their enjoyment may bring eustress, but the financial burden associated with buying presents could produce distress. Each of these things requires making some minor adjustments to one's life, and, thus, is considered somewhat stressful.

25. Type A was conceptualized as a behavioral style characterized by competitiveness, time urgency, impatience, and anger/hostility. It was later discovered, however, that anger/hostility seems to be the dimension that most clearly predicts heart disease.

27. Emotion-focused coping would likely be a better coping strategy in situations in which a stressor is uncontrollable, or in which nothing could otherwise be done about it, such as a fatal illness.

29. Answers will vary but may include mentioning things that boost positive emotions (the pleasant life), developing and using skills and talents (the good life), and using one's talents to help others (the meaningful life).

Chapter 14

1. **a.** the inability of an psychological mechanism to perform its function
3. **d.** Diagnostic and Statistical Manual of Mental Disorders
5. **a.** vulnerability and adverse experiences
7. **b.** Generalized anxiety disorder

9. **a.** Mentally counting backward from 1,000
11. **d.** physical complaints that cannot be explained medically
13. **a.** periods of extreme elation and euphoria
15. **a.** a delusion
17. **b.** memory loss following stress
19. **c.** are impulsive and unpredictable
21. **c.** Restricted and fixated interest
23. Just because something is atypical or unusual does not mean it is disordered. A person may experience atypical inner experiences or exhibit unusual behaviors, but she would not be considered disordered if they are not distressing, disturbing, or reflecting a dysfunction. For example, a classmate might stay up all night studying before exams; although atypical, this behavior is unlikely to possess any of the other criteria for psychological disorder mentioned previously.

25. The ICD is used primarily for making clinical diagnoses and more broadly for examining the general health of populations and monitoring the international prevalence of diseases and other health problems. While the DSM is also used for diagnostic purposes, it is also highly valued as a research tool.

27. Learning theories suggest that some anxiety disorders, especially specific phobia, can develop through a number of learning mechanisms. These mechanisms can include classical and operant conditioning, modeling, or vicarious learning. Cognitive theories, in contrast, assume that some anxiety disorders, especially panic disorder, develop through cognitive misinterpretations of anxiety and other symptoms.

29. Risk factors associated with PTSD include gender (female), low socioeconomic status, low intelligence, personal and family history of mental illness, and childhood abuse or trauma.

Personality factors, including neuroticism and somatization, may also serve as risk factors. Also, certain versions of a gene that regulates serotonin may constitute a diathesis.

31. This research enables researchers to identify potential warning signs that predict the onset of schizophrenia.

33. The environment is likely to be very instrumental in determining the likelihood of developing antisocial personality disorder. Research has shown that adverse family environments are connected to antisocial personality disorder, particularly if one is genetically vulnerable. Beyond one's family environment, peer group delinquency and community variables heighten the risk of violent behavior.

Chapter 15

1. **b.** Medieval priests

3. **a.** involuntary

5. **a.** cognitive therapy

7. **d.** free association; psychoanalysis

9. **a.** The therapist gathers specific information to address the client's immediate needs such as the presenting problem, the client's support system, and insurance status. The therapist informs the client about confidentiality, fees, and what to expect in a therapy session.

11. **b.** comorbid disorder

13. **c.** culture and background

15. Beginning in the Middle Ages and up until the mid-20th century, the mentally ill were misunderstood and treated cruelly. In the 1700s, Philippe Pinel advocated for patients to be unchained, and he was able to affect this in a Paris hospital. In the 1800s, Dorothea Dix urged the government to provide better funded and regulated care, which led to the creation of asylums, but treatment generally remained quite poor. Federally

mandated deinstitutionalization in the 1960s began the elimination of asylums, but it was often inadequate in providing the infrastructure for replacement treatment.

17. I would recommend psychodynamic talk therapy or cognitive therapy to help the person see how her thoughts and behaviors are having negative effects.

19. The rationale behind using group therapy for addiction treatment is that addicts are much more likely to maintain sobriety when treatment is in a group format. It has been suggested that it's due to the rewarding and therapeutic benefits of the group, such as support, affiliation, identification, and even confrontation. Because this client is single, he may not have family support, so support from the group may be even more important in his ability to recover and maintain his sobriety.

Glossary

Absentmindedness

Lapses in memory that are caused by breaks in attention or our focus being somewhere else

Absolute Threshold

Minimum amount of stimulus energy that must be present for the stimulus to be detected 50% of the time

Accommodation

Adjustment of a schema by changing a scheme to accommodate new information different from what was already known

Acoustic Encoding

Input of sounds, words, and music

Acquisition

Period of initial learning in classical conditioning in which a human or an animal begins to connect a neutral stimulus and an unconditioned stimulus so that the neutral stimulus will begin to elicit the conditioned response

Action Potential

Electrical signal that moves down the neuron's axon

Actor-Observer Bias

Phenomenon of explaining other people's behaviors are due to internal factors and our own behaviors are due to situational forces

Adolescence

Period of development that begins at puberty and ends at early adulthood

Adrenal Gland

Sits atop our kidneys and secretes hormones involved in the stress response

Adrenarche

Maturing of the adrenal glands

Afterimage

Continuation of a visual sensation after removal of the stimulus

Ageism

Prejudice and discrimination toward individuals based solely on their age

Aggression

Seeking to cause harm or pain to another person

Agonist

Drug that mimics or strengthens the effects of a neurotransmitter

Agoraphobia

Anxiety disorder characterized by intense fear, anxiety, and avoidance of situations in which it might be difficult to escape if one experiences symptoms of a panic attack

Alarm Reaction

First stage of the general adaptation syndrome; characterized as the body's immediate physiological reaction to a threatening situation or some other emergency; analogous to the fight-or-flight response

Algorithm

Problem-solving strategy characterized by a specific set of instructions

All-or-None

Phenomenon that the incoming signal from another neuron is either sufficient or insufficient to reach the threshold of excitation

Allele

Specific version of a gene

Alpha Wave

Type of relatively low frequency, relatively high amplitude brain wave that becomes synchronized; characteristic of the beginning of stage 1 sleep

Altruism

Humans' desire to help others even if the costs outweigh the benefits of helping

American Psychological Association

Professional organization representing psychologists in the United States

Americans with Disabilities Act

Employers cannot discriminate against any individual based on a disability

Amnesia

Loss of long-term memory that occurs as the result of disease, physical trauma, or psychological trauma

Amplitude

Height of a wave

Amygdala

Structure in the limbic system involved in our experience of emotion and tying emotional meaning to our memories

Anal Stage

Psychosexual stage in which children experience pleasure in their bowel and bladder movements

Analytical Intelligence

Aligned with academic problem solving and computations

Analytical Psychology

Jung's theory focusing on the balance of opposing forces within one's personality and the significance of the collective unconscious

Anchoring Bias

Faulty heuristic in which you fixate on a single aspect of a problem to find a solution

Anorexia Nervosa

Eating disorder characterized by an individual maintaining body weight that is well below average through starvation and/or excessive exercise

Antagonist

Drug that blocks or impedes the normal activity of a given neurotransmitter

Anterograde Amnesia

Loss of memory for events that occur after the brain trauma

Antisocial Personality Disorder

Characterized by a lack of regard for others' rights, impulsivity, deceitfulness, irresponsibility, and lack of remorse over misdeeds

Anxiety Disorder

Characterized by excessive and persistent fear and anxiety, and by related disturbances in behavior

Archetype

Pattern that exists in our collective unconscious across cultures and societies

Archival Research

Method of research using past records or data sets to answer various research questions, or to search for interesting patterns or relationships

Arousal Theory

Strong emotions trigger the formation of strong memories and weaker emotional experiences form weaker memories

Artificial Concept

Concept that is defined by a very specific set of characteristics

Asch Effect

Group majority influences an individual's judgment, even when that judgment is inaccurate

Assimilation

Adjustment of a schema by adding information similar to what is already known

Associative Learning

Form of learning that involves connecting certain stimuli or events that occur together in the environment (classical and operant conditioning)

Asthma

Psychophysiological disorder in which the airways of the respiratory system become obstructed, leading to great difficulty expelling air from the lungs

Asylum

Institution created for the specific purpose of housing people with psychological disorders

Atkinson-Shiffrin Model (A-S)

Memory model that states we process information through three systems: sensory memory, short-term memory, and long-term memory

Attachment

Long-standing connection or bond with others

Attention Deficit/Hyperactivity Disorder

Childhood disorder characterized by inattentiveness and/or hyperactive, impulsive behavior

Attitude

Evaluations of or feelings toward a person, idea, or object that are typically positive or negative

Attribution

Explanation for the behavior of other people

Attrition

Reduction in number of research participants as some drop out of the study over time

Atypical

Describes behaviors or feelings that deviate from the norm

Auditory Cortex

Strip of cortex in the temporal lobe that is responsible for processing auditory information

Authoritarian Parenting Style

Parents place a high value on conformity and obedience, are often rigid, and express little warmth to the child

Authoritative Parenting Style

Parents give children reasonable demands and consistent limits, express warmth and affection, and listen to the child's point of view

Autism Spectrum Disorder

Childhood disorder characterized by deficits in social interaction and communication, and repetitive patterns of behavior or interests

Automatic Processing

Encoding of informational details like time, space, frequency, and the meaning of words

Autonomic Nervous System

Controls our internal organs and glands

Availability Heuristic

Faulty heuristic in which you make a decision based on information readily available to you

Aversive Conditioning

Counterconditioning technique that pairs an unpleasant stimulant with an undesirable behavior

Avoidant Attachment

Characterized by child's unresponsiveness to parent, does not use the parent as a secure base, and does not care if parent leaves

Axon

Major extension of the soma

Bariatric Surgery

Type of surgery that modifies the gastrointestinal system to reduce the amount of food that can be eaten and/or limiting how much of the digested food can be absorbed

Basilar Membrane

Thin strip of tissue within the cochlea that contains the hair cells which serve as the sensory receptors for the auditory system

Basolateral Complex

Part of the brain with dense connections with a variety of sensory areas of the brain; it is critical for classical conditioning and attaching emotional value to memory

Behavior Therapy

Therapeutic orientation that employs principles of learning to help clients change undesirable behaviors

Behaviorism

Focus on observing and controlling behavior

Bias

How feelings and view of the world distort memory of past events

Binaural Cue

Two-eared cue to localize sound

Binge Eating Disorder

Type of eating disorder characterized by binge eating and associated distress

Binocular Cue

Cue that relies on the use of both eyes

Binocular Disparity

Slightly different view of the world that each eye receives

Biofeedback

Stress-reduction technique using electronic equipment to measure a person's involuntary (neuromuscular and autonomic) activity and provide feedback to help the person gain a level of voluntary control over these processes

Biological Perspective

View that psychological disorders like depression and schizophrenia are associated with imbalances in one or more neurotransmitter systems

Biological Rhythm

Internal cycle of biological activity

Biomedical Therapy

Treatment that involves medication and/or medical procedures to treat psychological disorders

Biopsychosocial Model

Perspective that asserts that biology, psychology, and social factors interact to determine an individual's health

Biopsychology

Study of how biology influences behavior

Bipolar and Related Disorders

Group of mood disorders in which mania is the defining feature

Bipolar Disorder

Mood disorder characterized by mood states that vacillate between depression and mania

Bisexual

Emotional and erotic attractions to both same-sexed individuals and opposite-sexed individuals

Blind Spot

Point where we cannot respond to visual information in that portion of the visual field

Blocking

Memory error in which you cannot access stored information

Body Dysmorphic Disorder

Involves excessive preoccupation with an imagined defect in physical appearance

Body Language

Emotional expression through body position or movement

Bona Fide Occupational Qualification (BFOQ)

Requirement of certain occupations for which denying an individual employment would otherwise violate the law, such as requirements concerning religion or sex

Borderline Personality Disorder

Instability in interpersonal relationships, self-image, and mood, as well as impulsivity; key features include intolerance of being alone and fear of abandonment, unstable relationships, unpredictable behavior and moods, and intense and inappropriate anger

Bottom-Up Processing

System in which perceptions are built from sensory input

Broca's Area

Region in the left hemisphere that is essential for language production

Bulimia Nervosa

Type of eating disorder characterized by binge eating followed by purging

Bullying

A person, often an adolescent, being treated negatively repeatedly and over time

Bystander Effect

Situation in which a witness or bystander does not volunteer to help a victim or person in distress

Cannon-Bard Theory of Emotion

Physiological arousal and emotional experience occur at the same time

Cardiovascular Disorders

Disorders that involve the heart and blood circulation system

Cataplexy

Lack of muscle tone or muscle weakness, and in some cases complete paralysis of the voluntary muscles

Catatonic Behavior

Decreased reactivity to the environment; includes posturing and catatonic stupor

Cause-and-Effect Relationship

Changes in one variable cause the changes in the other variable; can be determined only through an experimental research design

Central Nervous System (CNS)

Brain and spinal cord

Central Nucleus

Part of the brain involved in attention and has connections with the hypothalamus and various brainstem areas to regulate the autonomic nervous and endocrine systems' activity

Central Route Persuasion

Logic-driven arguments using data and facts to convince people of an argument's worthiness

Central Sleep Apnea

Sleep disorder with periods of interrupted breathing due to a disruption in signals sent from the brain that regulate breathing

Cerebellum

Hindbrain structure that controls our balance, coordination, movement, and motor skills, and it is thought to be important in processing some types of memory

Cerebral Cortex

Surface of the brain that is associated with our highest mental capabilities

Checklist

Method used to reduce workplace accidents

Chromosome

Long strand of genetic information

Chunking

Organizing information into manageable bits or chunks

Circadian Rhythm

Biological rhythm that occurs over approximately 24 hours

Classical Conditioning

Learning in which the stimulus or experience occurs before the behavior and then gets paired or associated with the behavior

Clinical or Case Study

Observational research study focusing on one or a few people

Clinical Psychology

Area of psychology that focuses on the diagnosis and treatment of psychological disorders and other problematic patterns of behavior

Closure

Organizing our perceptions into complete objects rather than as a series of parts

Cochlea

Fluid-filled, snail-shaped structure that contains the sensory receptor cells of the auditory system

Cochlear Implant

Electronic device that consists of a microphone, a speech processor, and an electrode array to directly stimulate the auditory nerve to transmit information to the brain

Codeine

Opiate with relatively low potency often prescribed for minor pain

Cognition

Thinking, including perception, learning, problem solving, judgment, and memory

Cognitive Development

Domain of lifespan development that examines learning, attention, memory, language, thinking, reasoning, and creativity

Cognitive Dissonance

Psychological discomfort that arises from a conflict in a person's behaviors, attitudes, or beliefs that runs counter to one's positive self-perception

Cognitive Empathy

Ability to take the perspective of others and to feel concern for others

Cognitive Map

Mental picture of the layout of the environment

Cognitive Psychology

Field of psychology dedicated to studying every aspect of how people think

Cognitive Script

Set of behaviors that are performed the same way each time; also referred to as an *event schema*

Cognitive Therapy

Form of psychotherapy that focuses on how a person's thoughts lead to feelings of distress, with the aim of helping them change these irrational thoughts

Cognitive-Behavioral Therapy (CBT)

Psychotherapy that focuses on cognitive processes and problem behaviors that is sometimes used to treat sleep disorders such as insomnia

Cognitive-Mediational Theory

Our emotions are determined by our appraisal of the stimulus

Collective Unconscious

Theoretical repository of information shared by all people across cultures, as described by Carl Jung; common psychological tendencies that have been passed down from one generation to the next

Collectivistic Culture

Culture that focuses on communal relationships with others such as family, friends, and community

Comorbid Disorder

Individual who has two or more diagnoses, which often includes a substance abuse diagnosis and another psychiatric diagnosis, such as depression, bipolar disorder, or schizophrenia

Comorbidity

Co-occurrence of two disorders in the same individual

Companionate Love

Type of love consisting of intimacy and commitment, but not passion; associated with close friendships and family relationships

Components of Emotion

Physiological arousal, psychological appraisal, and subjective experience

Computerized Tomography (CT) Scan

Imaging technique in which a computer coordinates and integrates multiple x-rays of a given area

Concept

Category or grouping of linguistic information, objects, ideas, or life experiences

Conception

When a sperm fertilizes an egg and forms a zygote

Concrete Operational Stage

Third stage in Piaget's theory of cognitive development; from about 7 to 11 years old, children can think logically about real (concrete) events

Conditioned Response (CR)

Response caused by the conditioned stimulus

Conditioned Stimulus (CS)

Stimulus that elicits a response due to its being paired with an unconditioned stimulus

Conductive Hearing Loss

Failure in the vibration of the eardrum and/or movement of the ossicles

Cone

Specialized photoreceptor that works best in bright light conditions and detects color

Confederate

Person who works for a researcher and is aware of the experiment, but who acts as a participant; used to manipulate social situations as part of the research design

Confidentiality

Therapist cannot disclose confidential communications to any third party, unless mandated or permitted by law

Confirmation Bias

Tendency to ignore evidence that disproves ideas or beliefs

Conformity

When individuals change their behavior to go along with the group even if they do not agree with the group

Confounding Variable

Unanticipated outside factor that affects both variables of interest, often giving the false impression that changes in one variable causes changes in the other variable, when, in actuality, the outside factor causes changes in both variables

Congenital Deafness

Deafness from birth

Congenital Insensitivity to Pain (Congenital Analgesia)

Genetic disorder that results in the inability to experience pain

Congruence

State of being in which our thoughts about our real and ideal selves are very similar

Conscious

Mental activity (thoughts, feelings, and memories) that we can access at any time

Consciousness

Awareness of internal and external stimuli

Conservation

Idea that even if you change the appearance of something, it is still equal in size, volume, or number as long as nothing is added or removed

Construction

Formulation of new memories

Consummate Love

Type of love occurring when intimacy, passion, and commitment are all present

Contemporized-Themes Concerning Blacks Test (C-TCB)

Projective test designed to be culturally relevant to African Americans, using images that relate to African-American culture

Continuous Development

View that development is a cumulative process: gradually improving on existing skills

Continuous Positive Airway Pressure (CPAP)

Device used to treat sleep apnea; includes a mask that fits over the sleeper's nose and mouth, which is connected to a pump that pumps air into the person's airways, forcing them to remain open

Continuous Reinforcement

Rewarding a behavior every time it occurs

Control Group

Serves as a basis for comparison and controls for chance factors that might influence the results of the study—by holding such factors constant across groups so that the experimental manipulation is the only difference between groups

Convergent Thinking

Providing correct or established answers to problems

Coping

Mental or behavioral efforts used to manage problems relating to stress, including its cause and the unpleasant feelings and emotions it produces

Cornea

Transparent covering over the eye

Corpus Callosum

Thick band of neural fibers connecting the brain's two hemispheres

Correlation

Relationship between two or more variables; when two variables are correlated, one variable changes as the other does

Correlation Coefficient

Number from −1 to +1, indicating the strength and direction of the relationship between variables, and usually represented by *r*

Cortisol

Stress hormone released by the adrenal glands when encountering a stressor; helps to provide a boost of energy, thereby preparing the individual to take action

Counseling Psychology

Area of psychology that focuses on improving emotional, social, vocational, and other aspects of the lives of psychologically healthy individuals

Counterconditioning

Classical conditioning therapeutic technique in which a client learns a new response to a stimulus that has previously elicited an undesirable behavior

Couples Therapy

Two people in an intimate relationship, such as husband and wife, who are having difficulties and are trying to resolve them with therapy

Creative Intelligence

Ability to produce new products, ideas, or inventing a new, novel solution to a problem

Creativity

Ability to generate, create, or discover new ideas, solutions, and possibilities

Critical (Sensitive) Period

Time during fetal growth when specific parts or organs develop

Cross-Sectional Research

Compares multiple segments of a population at a single time

Crystallized Intelligence

Characterized by acquired knowledge and the ability to retrieve it

Cultural Competence

Therapist's understanding and attention to issues of race, culture, and ethnicity in providing treatment

Cultural Display Rule

One of the culturally specific standards that govern the types and frequencies of emotions that are acceptable

Cultural Intelligence

Ability with which people can understand and relate to those in another culture

Culture

All of the beliefs, customs, art, and traditions of a particular society

Cyberbullying

Repeated behavior that is intended to cause psychological or emotional harm to another person and that takes place online

Daily Hassles

Minor irritations and annoyances that are part of our everyday lives and are capable of producing stress

Deafness

Partial or complete inability to hear

Debriefing

When an experiment involved deception, participants are told complete and truthful information about the experiment at its conclusion

Deception

Purposely misleading experiment participants in order to maintain the integrity of the experiment

Decibel (dB)

Logarithmic unit of sound intensity

Declarative Memory

Type of long-term memory of facts and events we personally experience

Deductive Reasoning

Results are predicted based on a general premise

Defense Mechanism

Unconscious protective behaviors designed to reduce ego anxiety

Deinstitutionalization

Process of closing large asylums and integrating people back into the community where they can be treated locally

Delta Wave

Type of low frequency, high amplitude brain wave characteristic of stage 3 and stage 4 sleep

Delusion

Belief that is contrary to reality and is firmly held, despite contradictory evidence

Dendrite

Branch-like extension of the soma that receives incoming signals from other neurons

Deoxyribonucleic Acid (DNA)

Helix-shaped molecule made of nucleotide base pairs

Dependent Variable

Variable that the researcher measures to see how much effect the independent variable had

Depersonalization/Derealization Disorder

Dissociative disorder in which people feel detached from the self (depersonalization), and the world feels artificial and unreal (derealization)

Depressant

Drug that tends to suppress central nervous system activity

Depressive Disorder

One of a group of mood disorders in which depression is the defining feature

Depth Perception

Ability to perceive depth

Developmental Milestone

Approximate ages at which children reach specific normative events

Developmental Psychology

Scientific study of development across a lifespan

Diabetes

Disease related to insufficient insulin production

Diagnosis

Determination of which disorder a set of symptoms represents

***Diagnostic and Statistical Manual of Mental Disorders, Fifth Edition* (DSM-5)**

Authoritative index of mental disorders and the criteria for their diagnosis; published by the American Psychiatric Association (APA)

Diathesis-Stress Model

Suggests that people with a predisposition for a disorder (a diathesis) are more likely to develop the disorder when faced with stress; model of psychopathology

Diffusion of Resonsibility

Tendency for no one in a group to help because the responsibility to help is spread throughout the group

Discontinuous Development

View that development takes place in unique stages, which happen at specific times or ages

Discrimination

Negative actions toward individuals as a result of their membership in a particular group

Disorganized Attachment

Characterized by the child's odd behavior when faced with the parent; type of attachment seen most often with kids that are abused

Disorganized Thinking

Disjointed and incoherent thought processes, usually detected by what a person says

Disorganized/Abnormal Motor Behavior

Highly unusual behaviors and movements (such as child-like behaviors), repeated and purposeless movements, and displaying odd facial expressions and gestures

Displacement

Ego defense mechanism in which a person transfers inappropriate urges or behaviors toward a more acceptable or less threatening target

Dispositionism

Describes a perspective common to personality psychologists, which asserts that our behavior is determined by internal factors, such as personality traits and temperament

Dissertation

Long paper on research that was conducted as a part of the candidate's doctoral training

Dissociative Amnesia

Dissociative disorder characterized by an inability to recall important personal information, usually following an extremely stressful or traumatic experience

Dissociative Disorders

Group of DSM-5 disorders in which the primary feature is that a person becomes dissociated, or split off, from his or her core sense of self, resulting in disturbances in identity and memory

Dissociative Fugue

Symptom of dissociative amnesia in which a person suddenly wanders away from one's home and experiences confusion about his or her identity

Dissociative Identity Disorder

Dissociative disorder (formerly known as *multiple personality disorder*) in which a person exhibits two or more distinct, well-defined personalities or identities and experiences memory gaps for the time during which another identity emerged

Distorted Body Image

Individuals view themselves as overweight even though they are not

Distress

Bad form of stress; usually high in intensity; often leads to exhaustion, fatigue, feeling burned out; associated with erosions in performance and health

Divergent Thinking

Ability to think "outside the box" to arrive at novel solutions to a problem

Diversity Training

Training employees about cultural differences with the goal of improving teamwork

Dominant Allele

Allele whose phenotype will be expressed in an individual that possesses that allele

Dopamine Hypothesis

Theory of schizophrenia that proposes that an overabundance of dopamine or dopamine receptors is responsible for the onset and maintenance of schizophrenia

Double-Blind Study

Experiment in which both the researchers and the participants are blind to group assignments

Downsizing

Process in which an organization tries to achieve greater overall efficiency by reducing the number of employees

Dream Analysis

Technique in psychoanalysis in which patients recall their dreams and the psychoanalyst interprets them to reveal unconscious desires or struggles

Drive Theory

Deviations from homeostasis create physiological needs that result in psychological drive states that direct behavior to meet the need and ultimately bring the system back to homeostasis

Dysgraphia

Learning disability that causes extreme difficulty in writing legibly

Dyslexia

Common learning disability in which letters are not processed properly by the brain

Effortful Processing

Encoding of information that takes effort and attention

Ego

Aspect of personality that represents the self, or the part of one's personality that is visible to others

Egocentrism

Preoperational child's difficulty in taking the perspective of others

Elaborative Rehearsal

Thinking about the meaning of the new information and its relation to knowledge already stored in your memory

Electroconvulsive Therapy (ECT)

Type of biomedical therapy that involves using an electrical current to induce seizures in a person to help alleviate the effects of severe depression

Electroencephalography (EEG)

Recording the electrical activity of the brain via electrodes on the scalp

Electromagnetic Spectrum

All the electromagnetic radiation that occurs in our environment

Embryo

Multi-cellular organism in its early stages of development

Emerging Adulthood

Newly defined period of lifespan development from 18 years old to the mid-20s; young people are taking longer to complete college, get a job, get married, and start a family

Emotion

Subjective state of being often described as feelings

Emotional Intelligence

Ability to understand emotions and motivations in yourself and others

Empathy

Capacity to understand another person's perspective—to feel what he or she feels

Empirical

Grounded in objective, tangible evidence that can be observed time and time again, regardless of who is observing

Empirical Method

Method for acquiring knowledge based on observation, including experimentation, rather than a method based only on forms of logical argument or previous authorities

Encoding

Input of information into the memory system

Endocrine System

Series of glands that produce chemical substances known as hormones

Engram

Physical trace of memory

Epigenetics

Study of gene-environment interactions, such as how the same genotype leads to different phenotypes

Episodic Memory

Type of declarative memory that contains information about events we have personally experienced, also known as *autobiographical memory*

Equipotentiality Hypothesis

Some parts of the brain can take over for damaged parts in forming and storing memories

Etiology

Cause or causes of a psychological disorder

Euphoric High

Feelings of intense elation and pleasure from drug use

Eustress

Good form of stress; low to moderate in intensity; associated with positive feelings, as well as optimal health and performance

Event Schema

Set of behaviors that are performed the same way each time; also referred to as a *cognitive script*

Evolutionary Psychology

Discipline that studies how universal patterns of behavior and cognitive processes have evolved over time as a result of natural selection

Excitement

Phase of the sexual response cycle that involves sexual arousal

Experimental Group

Group designed to answer the research question; experimental manipulation is the only difference between the experimental and control groups, so any differences between the two are due to experimental manipulation rather than chance

Experimenter Bias

Researcher expectations skew the results of the study

Explicit Memory

Memories we consciously try to remember and recall

Exposure Therapy

Counterconditioning technique in which a therapist seeks to treat a client's fear or anxiety by presenting the feared object or situation with the idea that the person will eventually get used to it

Extinction

Decrease in the conditioned response when the unconditioned stimulus is no longer paired with the conditioned stimulus

Extrinsic Motivation

Motivation that arises from external factors or rewards

Facial Feedback Hypothesis

Facial expressions are capable of influencing our emotions

Fact

Objective and verifiable observation, established using evidence collected through empirical research

False Memory Syndrome

Recall of false autobiographical memories

Falsifiable

Able to be disproven by experimental results

Family Therapy

Special form of group therapy consisting of one or more families

Fight-or-Flight Response

Set of physiological reactions (increases in blood pressure, heart rate, respiration rate, and sweat) that occur when an individual encounters a perceived threat; these reactions are produced by activation of the sympathetic nervous system and the endocrine system, allowing access to energy reserves and heightened sensory capacity

Figure-Ground Relationship

Segmenting our visual world into figure and ground

Fine Motor Skills

Use of muscles in fingers, toes, and eyes to coordinate small actions

Five Factor Model

Theory that personality is composed of five factors or traits, including openness, conscientiousness, extroversion, agreeableness, and neuroticism

Fixed Interval Reinforcement Schedule

Behavior is rewarded after a set amount of time

Fixed Ratio Reinforcement Schedule

Set number of responses must occur before a behavior is rewarded

Flashback

Psychological state lasting from a few seconds to several days, during which one relives a traumatic event and behaves as though the event were occurring at that moment

Flashbulb Memory

Exceptionally clear recollection of an important event

Flight of Ideas

Symptom of mania that involves an abrupt switch in conversation from one topic to another

Flow

State involving intense engagement in an activity; usually is experienced when participating in creative, work, and leisure endeavors

Fluid Intelligence

Ability to see complex relationships and solve problems

Flynn Effect

Observation that each generation has a significantly higher IQ than the previous generation

Foot-in-the-Door Technique

Persuasion of one person by another person, encouraging a person to agree to a small favor, or to buy a small item, only to later request a larger favor or purchase of a larger item

Forebrain

Largest part of the brain, containing the cerebral cortex, the thalamus, and the limbic system, among other structures

Forensic Psychology

Area of psychology that applies the science and practice of psychology to issues within and related to the justice system

Forgetting

Loss of information from long-term memory

Formal Operational Stage

Final stage in Piaget's theory of cognitive development; from age 11 and up, children are able to deal with abstract ideas and hypothetical situations

Fovea

Small indentation in the retina that contains cones

Fraternal Twins

Twins who develop from two different eggs fertilized by different sperm, so their genetic material varies the same as in non-twin siblings

Free Association

Technique in psychoanalysis in which the patient says whatever comes to mind at the moment

Frequency

Number of waves that pass a given point in a given time period

Frontal Lobe

Part of the cerebral cortex involved in reasoning, motor control, emotion, and language; contains motor cortex

Functional Fixedness

Inability to see an object as useful for any other use other than the one for which it was intended

Functional Magnetic Resonance Imaging (fMRI)

MRI that shows changes in metabolic activity over time

Functionalism

Focuses on how mental activities help an organism adapt to its environment

Fundamental Attribution Error

Tendency to overemphasize internal factors as attributions for behavior and underestimate the power of the situation

Gender Dysphoria

Diagnostic category in DSM-5 for individuals who do not identify as the gender associated with their biological sex

Gender Identity

Individual's sense of being male or female

Gene

Sequence of DNA that controls or partially controls physical characteristics

General Adaptation Syndrome

Hans Selye's three-stage model of the body's physiological reactions to stress and the process of stress adaptation: alarm reaction, stage of resistance, and stage of exhaustion

Generalize

Inferring that the results for a sample apply to the larger population

Generalized Anxiety Disorder

Characterized by a continuous state of excessive, uncontrollable, and pointless worry and apprehension

Genetic Environmental Correlation

View of gene-environment interaction that asserts our genes affect our environment, and our environment influences the expression of our genes

Genital Stage

Psychosexual stage in which the focus is on mature sexual interests

Genotype

Genetic makeup of an individual

Gestalt Psychology

Field of psychology based on the idea that the whole is different from the sum of its parts

Glial Cell

Nervous system cell that provides physical and metabolic support to neurons, including neuronal insulation and communication, and nutrient and waste transport

Gonad

Secretes sexual hormones, which are important for successful reproduction, and mediates both sexual motivation and behavior

Gonadarche

Maturing of the sex glands

Good Continuation

(Also, *continuity*) we are more likely to perceive continuous, smooth flowing lines rather than jagged, broken lines

Grammar

Set of rules that are used to convey meaning through the use of a lexicon

Grandiose Delusion

Characterized by beliefs that one holds special power, unique knowledge, or is extremely important

Gross Motor Skills

Use of large muscle groups to control arms and legs for large body movements

Group Polarization

Strengthening of the original group attitude after discussing views within the group

Group Therapy

Treatment modality in which 5–10 people with the same issue or concern meet together with a trained clinician

Groupthink

Group members modify their opinions to match what they believe is the group consensus

Gyrus

(Plural: *gyri*) bump or ridge on the cerebral cortex

Habit

Pattern of behavior in which we regularly engage

Habituation

When we learn not to respond to a stimulus that is presented repeatedly without change

Hair Cell

Auditory receptor cell of the inner ear

Hallucination

Perceptual experience that occurs in the absence of external stimulation, such as the auditory hallucinations (hearing voices) common to schizophrenia

Hallucinogen

One of a class of drugs that results in profound alterations in sensory and perceptual experiences, often with vivid hallucinations

Happiness

Enduring state of mind consisting of joy, contentment, and other positive emotions; the sense that one's life has meaning and value

Harmful Dysfunction

Model of psychological disorders resulting from the inability of an internal mechanism to perform its natural function

Hawthorne Effect

Increase in performance of individuals who are noticed, watched, and paid attention to by researchers or supervisors

Health Psychology

Subfield of psychology devoted to studying psychological influences on health, illness, and how people respond when they become ill

Heart Disease

Several types of adverse heart conditions, including those that involve the heart's arteries or valves or those involving the inability of the heart to pump enough blood to meet the body's needs; can include heart attack and stroke

Hemisphere

Left or right half of the brain

Heritability

Proportion of difference among people that is attributed to genetics

Hertz (Hz)

Cycles per second; measure of frequency

Heterosexual

Emotional and erotic attractions to opposite-sexed individuals

Heterozygous

Consisting of two different alleles

Heuristic

Mental shortcut that saves time when solving a problem

Hierarchy of Needs

Spectrum of needs ranging from basic biological needs to social needs to self-actualization

Higher-Order Conditioning

(Also, *second-order conditioning*) using a conditioned stimulus to condition a neutral stimulus

Hindbrain

Division of the brain containing the medulla, pons, and cerebellum

Hindsight Bias

Belief that the event just experienced was predictable even though it really wasn't

Hippocampus

Structure in the temporal lobe associated with learning and memory

Hoarding Disorder

Characterized by persistent difficulty in parting with possessions, regardless of their actual value or usefulness

Homeostasis

State of equilibrium—biological conditions, such as body temperature, are maintained at optimal levels

Homophily

Tendency for people to form social networks, including friendships, marriages, business relationships, and many other types of relationships, with others who are similar

Homophobia

Prejudice and discrimination against individuals based solely on their sexual orientation

Homosexual

Emotional and erotic attractions to same-sexed individuals

Homozygous

Consisting of two identical alleles

Hopelessness Theory

Cognitive theory of depression proposing that a style of thinking that perceives negative life events as having stable and global causes leads to a sense of hopelessness and then to depression

Hormone

Chemical messenger released by endocrine glands

Hospice

Service that provides a death with dignity; pain management in a humane and comfortable environment; usually outside of a hospital setting

Hostile Aggression

Aggression motivated by feelings of anger with intent to cause pain

Human Factors Psychology

Branch of psychology that studies how workers interact with the tools of work and how to design those tools to optimize workers' productivity, safety, and health

Humanism

Perspective within psychology that emphasizes the potential for good that is innate to all humans

Humanistic Therapy

Therapeutic orientation aimed at helping people become more self-aware and accepting of themselves

Hypertension

High blood pressure

Hypnosis

State of extreme self-focus and attention in which minimal attention is given to external stimuli

Hypothalamic-Pituitary-Adrenal (HPA) Axis

Set of structures found in both the limbic system (hypothalamus) and the endocrine system (pituitary gland and adrenal glands) that regulate many of the body's physiological reactions to stress through the release of hormones

Hypothalamus

Forebrain structure that regulates sexual motivation and behavior and a number of homeostatic processes; serves as an interface between the nervous system and the endocrine system

Hypothesis

(Plural: *hypotheses*) tentative and testable statement about the relationship between two or more variables

Id

Aspect of personality that consists of our most primitive drives or urges, including impulses for hunger, thirst, and sex

Ideal Self

Person we would like to be

Identical Twins

Twins that develop from the same sperm and egg

Illusory Correlation

Seeing relationships between two things when in reality no such relationship exists

Immune System

Various structures, cells, and mechanisms that protect the body from foreign substances that can damage the body's tissues and organs

Immunosuppression

Decreased effectiveness of the immune system

Immutable Characteristic

Traits that employers cannot use to discriminate in hiring, benefits, promotions, or termination; these traits are fundamental to one's personal identity (e.g. skin color and hair texture)

Implicit Memory

Memories that are not part of our consciousness

In-Group

Group that we identify with or see ourselves as belonging to

In-Group Bias

Preference for our own group over other groups

Inattentional Blindness

Failure to notice something that is completely visible because of a lack of attention

Incongruence

State of being in which there is a great discrepancy between our real and ideal selves

Incus

Middle ear ossicle; also known as the *anvil*

Independent Variable

Variable that is influenced or controlled by the experimenter; in a sound experimental study, the independent variable is the only important difference between the experimental and control group

Individual Psychology

School of psychology proposed by Adler that focuses on our drive to compensate for feelings of inferiority

Individual Therapy

Treatment modality in which the client and clinician meet one-on-one

Individualistic Culture

Culture that focuses on individual achievement and autonomy

Inductive Reasoning

Conclusions are drawn from observations

Industrial and Organizational (I-O) Psychology

Field in psychology that applies scientific principles to the study of work and the workplace

Industrial Psychology

Branch of psychology that studies job characteristics, applicant characteristics, and how to match them; also studies employee training and performance appraisal

Inferiority Complex

Refers to a person's feelings that they lack worth and don't measure up to others' or to society's standards

Inflammatory Pain

Signal that some type of tissue damage has occurred

Informational Social Influence

Conformity to a group norm prompted by the belief that the group is competent and has the correct information

Informed Consent

Process of informing a research participant about what to expect during an experiment, any risks involved, and the implications of the research, and then obtaining the person's consent to participate

Insomnia

Consistent difficulty in falling or staying asleep for at least three nights a week over a month's time

Instinct

Unlearned knowledge, involving complex patterns of behavior; instincts are thought to be more prevalent in lower animals than in humans

Institutional Animal Care and Use Committee (IACUC)

Committee of administrators, scientists, veterinarians, and community members that reviews proposals for research involving non-human animals

Institutional Review Board (IRB)

Committee of administrators, scientists, and community members that reviews proposals for research involving human participants

Instrumental Aggression

Aggression motivated by achieving a goal and does not necessarily involve intent to cause pain

Intake

Therapist's first meeting with the client in which the therapist gathers specific information to address the client's immediate needs

Intelligence Quotient

(Also, *IQ*) score on a test designed to measure intelligence

Inter-rater Reliability

Measure of agreement among observers on how they record and classify a particular event

Interaural Level Difference

Sound coming from one side of the body is more intense at the closest ear because of the attenuation of the sound wave as it passes through the head

Interaural Timing Difference

Small difference in the time at which a given sound wave arrives at each ear

Internal Factor

Internal attribute of a person, such as personality traits or temperament

International Classification of Diseases (ICD)

Authoritative index of mental and physical diseases, including infectious diseases, and the criteria for their diagnosis; published by the World Health Organization (WHO)

Intrinsic Motivation

Motivation based on internal feelings rather than external rewards

Introspection

Process by which someone examines their own conscious experience in an attempt to break it into its component parts

Involuntary Treatment

Therapy that is mandated by the courts or other systems

Iris

Colored portion of the eye

James-Lange Theory of Emotion

Emotions arise from physiological arousal

Jet Lag

Collection of symptoms brought on by travel from one time zone to another that results from the mismatch between our internal circadian cycles and our environment

Job Analysis

Determining and listing tasks associated with a particular job

Job Burnout

General sense of emotional exhaustion and cynicism in relation to one's job; consists of three dimensions: exhaustion, depersonalization, and sense of diminished personal accomplishment

Job Satisfaction

Degree of pleasure that employees derive from their job

Job Strain

Work situation involving the combination of excessive job demands and workload with little decision-making latitude or job control

Just Noticeable Difference

Difference in stimuli required to detect a difference between the stimuli

Just-World Hypothesis

Ideology common in the United States that people get the outcomes they deserve

K-Complex

Very high amplitude pattern of brain activity associated with stage 2 sleep that may occur in response to environmental stimuli

Kinesthesia

Perception of the body's movement through space

Language

Communication system that involves using words to transmit information from one individual to another

Latency Period

Psychosexual stage in which sexual feelings are dormant

Latent Content

Hidden meaning of a dream, per Sigmund Freud's view of the function of dreams

Latent Learning

Learning that occurs, but it may not be evident until there is a reason to demonstrate it

Lateralization

Concept that each hemisphere of the brain is associated with specialized functions

Law of Effect

Behavior that is followed by consequences satisfying to the organism will be repeated and behaviors that are followed by unpleasant consequences will be discouraged

Learning

Change in behavior or knowledge that is the result of experience

Lens

Curved, transparent structure that provides additional focus for light entering the eye

Leptin

Satiety hormone

Levels of Processing

Information that is thought of more deeply becomes more meaningful and thus better committed to memory

Lexicon

The words of a given language

Limbic System

Collection of structures involved in processing emotion and memory

Linear Perspective

Perceive depth in an image when two parallel lines seem to converge

Locus Coeruleus

Area of the brainstem that contains norepinephrine, a neurotransmitter that triggers the body's fight-or-flight response; has been implicated in panic disorder

Locus of Control

Beliefs about the power we have over our lives; an external locus of control is the belief that our outcomes are outside of our control; an internal locus of control is the belief that we control our own outcomes

Long-Term Memory (LTM)

Continuous storage of information

Longitudinal Fissure

Deep groove in the brain's cortex

Longitudinal Research

Studies in which the same group of individuals is surveyed or measured repeatedly over an extended period of time

Lucid Dream

People become aware that they are dreaming and can control the dream's content

Lymphocytes

White blood cells that circulate in the body's fluids and are especially important in the body's immune response

Magnetic Resonance Imaging (MRI)

Magnetic fields used to produce a picture of the tissue being imaged

Major Depressive Disorder

Commonly referred to as *depression* or *major depression*, characterized by sadness or loss of pleasure in usual activities, as well other symptoms

Malleus

Middle ear ossicle; also known as the *hammer*

Mania

State of extreme elation and agitation

Manic Episode

Period in which an individual experiences mania, characterized by extremely cheerful and euphoric mood, excessive talkativeness, irritability, increased activity levels, and other symptoms

Manifest Content

Storyline of events that occur during a dream, per Sigmund Freud's view of the function of dreams

Meditation

Clearing the mind in order to achieve a state of relaxed awareness and focus

Medulla

Hindbrain structure that controls automated processes like breathing, blood pressure, and heart rate

Meissner's Corpuscle

Touch receptor that responds to pressure and lower frequency vibrations

Melatonin

Hormone secreted by the endocrine gland that serves as an important regulator of the sleep-wake cycle

Membrane Potential

Difference in charge across the neuronal membrane

Memory

System or process that stores what we learn for future use

Memory Consolidation

Active rehearsal to move information from short-term memory into long-term memory

Memory-Enhancing Strategy

Technique to help make sure information goes from short-term memory to long-term memory

Menarche

Beginning of menstrual period; around 12–13 years old

Ménière's Disease

Results in a degeneration of inner ear structures that can lead to hearing loss, tinnitus, vertigo, and an increase in pressure within the inner ear

Mental Set

Continually using an old solution to a problem without results

Merkel's Disk

Touch receptor that responds to light touch

Meta-Analysis

Study that combines the results of several related studies

Metabolic Rate

Amount of energy that is expended in a given period of time

Methadone

Synthetic opioid that is less euphorogenic than heroin and similar drugs; used to manage withdrawal symptoms in opiate users

Methadone Clinic

Uses methadone to treat withdrawal symptoms in opiate users

Methamphetamine

Type of amphetamine that can be made from pseudoephedrine, an over-the-counter drug; widely manufactured and abused

Midbrain

Division of the brain located between the forebrain and the hindbrain; contains the reticular formation

Minnesota Multiphasic Personality Inventory (MMPI)

Personality test composed of a series of true/false questions in order to establish a clinical profile of an individual

Misattribution

Memory error in which you confuse the source of your information

Misinformation Effect Paradigm

After exposure to incorrect information, a person may misremember the original event

Mitosis

Process of cell division

Mnemonic Device

Memory aids that help organize information for encoding

Model

Person who performs a behavior that serves as an example (in observational learning)

Monaural Cue

One-eared cue to localize sound

Monocular Cue

Cue that requires only one eye

Mood Disorder

One of a group of disorders characterized by severe disturbances in mood and emotions; the categories of mood disorders listed in the DSM-5 are bipolar and related disorders and depressive disorders

Morbid Obesity

Adult with a BMI over 40

Morpheme

Smallest unit of language that conveys some type of meaning

Motivation

Wants or needs that direct behavior toward some goal

Motor Cortex

Strip of cortex involved in planning and coordinating movement

Motor Skills

Ability to move our body and manipulate objects

Multiple Intelligences Theory

Gardner's theory that each person possesses at least eight types of intelligence

Mutation

Sudden, permanent change in a gene

Myelin Sheath

Fatty substance that insulates axons

Narcolepsy

Sleep disorder in which the sufferer cannot resist falling to sleep at inopportune times

Natural Concept

Mental groupings that are created "naturally" through your experiences

Naturalistic Observation

Observation of behavior in its natural setting

Nature

Genes and biology

Negative Affectivity

Tendency to experience distressed emotional states involving anger, contempt, disgust, guilt, fear, and nervousness

Negative Correlation

Two variables change in different directions, with one becoming larger as the other becomes smaller; a negative correlation is not the same thing as no correlation

Negative Punishment

Taking away a pleasant stimulus to decrease or stop a behavior

Negative Reinforcement

Taking away an undesirable stimulus to increase a behavior

Negative Symptom

Characterized by decreases and absences in certain normal behaviors, emotions, or drives, such as an expressionless face, lack of motivation to engage in activities, reduced speech, lack of social engagement, and inability to experience pleasure

Neurodevelopmental Disorder

One of the disorders that are first diagnosed in childhood and involve developmental problems in academic, intellectual, and social functioning

Neuron

Cells in the nervous system that act as interconnected information processors, which are essential for all of the tasks of the nervous system

Neuropathic Pain

Pain from damage to neurons of either the peripheral or central nervous system

Neurosis

Tendency to experience negative emotions

Neurotransmitter

Chemical messenger of the nervous system

Neutral Stimulus (NS)

Stimulus that does not initially elicit a response

Newborn Reflexes

Inborn automatic response to a particular form of stimulation that all healthy babies are born with

Night Terror

Sleep disorder in which the sleeper experiences a sense of panic and may scream or attempt to escape from the immediate environment

Nociception

Sensory signal indicating potential harm and maybe pain

Non-REM (NREM) Sleep

Period of sleep outside periods of rapid eye movement (REM) sleep

Nondirective Therapy

Therapeutic approach in which the therapist does not give advice or provide interpretations but helps the person identify conflicts and understand feelings

Normative Approach

Study of development using norms, or average ages, when most children reach specific developmental milestones

Normative Social Influence

Conformity to a group norm to fit in, feel good, and be accepted by the group

Norming

Administering a test to a large population so data can be collected to reference the normal scores for a population and its groups

Nurture

Environment and culture

Obedience

Change of behavior to please an authority figure or to avoid aversive consequences

Obese

Adult with a BMI of 30 or higher

Object Permanence

Idea that even if something is out of sight, it still exists

Observational Learning

Type of learning that occurs by watching others

Observer Bias

When observations may be skewed to align with observer expectations

Obsessive-Compulsive and Related Disorders

Group of overlapping disorders listed in the DSM-5 that involves intrusive, unpleasant thoughts and/or repetitive behaviors

Obsessive-Compulsive Disorder (OCD)

Characterized by the tendency to experience intrusive and unwanted thoughts and urges (obsession) and/or the need to engage in repetitive behaviors or mental acts (compulsions) in response to the unwanted thoughts and urges

Obstructive Sleep Apnea

Sleep disorder defined by episodes when breathing stops during sleep as a result of blockage of the airway

Occipital Lobe

Part of the cerebral cortex associated with visual processing; contains the primary visual cortex

Olfactory Bulb

Bulb-like structure at the tip of the frontal lobe, where the olfactory nerves begin

Olfactory Receptor

Sensory cell for the olfactory system

-ology

Suffix that denotes "scientific study of"

Operant Conditioning

Form of learning in which the stimulus/experience happens after the behavior is demonstrated

Operational Definition

Description of what actions and operations will be used to measure the dependent variables and manipulate the independent variables

Opiate/Opioid

One of a category of drugs that has strong analgesic properties; opiates are produced from the resin of the opium poppy; includes heroin, morphine, methadone, and codeine

Opinion

Personal judgments, conclusions, or attitudes that may or may not be accurate

Opponent-Process Theory of Color Perception

Color is coded in opponent pairs: black-white, yellow-blue, and red-green

Optic Chiasm

X-shaped structure that sits just below the brain's ventral surface; represents the merging of the optic nerves from the two eyes and the separation of information from the two sides of the visual field to the opposite side of the brain

Optic Nerve

Carries visual information from the retina to the brain

Optimism

Tendency toward a positive outlook and positive expectations

Oral Stage

Psychosexual stage in which an infant's pleasure is focused on the mouth

Orbitofrontal Cortex

Area of the frontal lobe involved in learning and decision making

Organizational Culture

Values, visions, hierarchies, norms, and interactions between its employees; how an organization is run, how it operates, and how it makes decisions

Organizational Psychology

Branch of psychology that studies the interactions between people working in organizations and the effects of those interactions on productivity

Orgasm

Peak phase of the sexual response cycle associated with rhythmic muscle contractions (and ejaculation)

Out-Group

Group that we don't belong to—one that we view as fundamentally different from us

Overgeneralization

Extension of a rule that exists in a given language to an exception to the rule

Overweight

Adult with a BMI between 25 and 29.9

Pacinian Corpuscle

Touch receptor that detects transient pressure and higher frequency vibrations

Pancreas

Secretes hormones that regulate blood sugar

Panic Attack

Period of extreme fear or discomfort that develops abruptly; symptoms of panic attacks are both physiological and psychological

Panic Disorder

Anxiety disorder characterized by unexpected panic attacks, along with at least one month of worry about panic attacks or self-defeating behavior related to the attacks

Paranoid Delusion

Characterized by beliefs that others are out to harm them

Parasomnia

One of a group of sleep disorders characterized by unwanted, disruptive motor activity and/or experiences during sleep

Parasympathetic Nervous System

Associated with routine, day-to-day operations of the body

Parietal Lobe

Part of the cerebral cortex involved in processing various sensory and perceptual information; contains the primary somatosensory cortex

Partial Reinforcement

Rewarding behavior only some of the time

Participants

Subjects of psychological research

Pattern Perception

Ability to discriminate among different figures and shapes

Peak

(Also, *crest*) highest point of a wave

Peer-Reviewed Journal Article

Article read by several other scientists (usually anonymously) with expertise in the subject matter, who provide feedback regarding the quality of the manuscript before it is accepted for publication

Perceived Control

Peoples' beliefs concerning their capacity to influence and shape outcomes in their lives

Perception

Way that sensory information is interpreted and consciously experienced

Perceptual Hypothesis

Educated guess used to interpret sensory information

Performance Appraisal

Evaluation of an employee's success or lack of success at performing the duties of the job

Peripartum Onset

Subtype of depression that applies to women who experience an episode of major depression either during pregnancy or in the four weeks following childbirth

Peripheral Nervous System (PNS)

Connects the brain and spinal cord to the muscles, organs, and senses in the periphery of the body

Peripheral Route Persuasion

One person persuades another person; an indirect route that relies on association of peripheral cues (such as positive emotions and celebrity endorsement) to associate positivity with a message

Permissive Parenting Style

Parents make few demands and rarely use punishment

Persistence

Failure of the memory system that involves the involuntary recall of unwanted memories, particularly unpleasant ones

Persistent Depressive Disorder

Depressive disorder characterized by a chronically sad and melancholy mood

Personality

Long-standing traits and patterns that propel individuals to consistently think, feel, and behave in specific ways

Personality Disorder

Group of DSM-5 disorders characterized by an inflexible and pervasive personality style that differs markedly from the expectations of one's culture and causes distress and impairment; people with these disorders have a personality style that frequently brings them into conflict with others and disrupts their ability to develop and maintain social relationships

Personality Psychology

Study of patterns of thoughts and behaviors that make each individual unique

Personality Trait

Consistent pattern of thought and behavior

Persuasion

Process of changing our attitude toward something based on some form of communication

Phallic Stage

Psychosexual stage in which the focus is on the genitals

PhD

(Doctor of philosophy) doctoral degree conferred in many disciplinary perspectives housed in a traditional college of liberal arts and sciences

Phenotype

Individual's inheritable physical characteristics

Pheromone

Chemical message sent by another individual

Phoneme

Basic sound unit of a given language

Photoreceptor

Light-detecting cell

Physical Dependence

Changes in normal bodily functions that cause a drug user to experience withdrawal symptoms upon cessation of use

Physical Development

Domain of lifespan development that examines growth and changes in the body and brain, the senses, motor skills, and health and wellness

Pineal Gland

Endocrine structure located inside the brain that releases melatonin

Pinna

Visible part of the ear that protrudes from the head

Pitch

Perception of a sound's frequency

Pituitary Gland

Secretes a number of key hormones, which regulate fluid levels in the body, and a number of messenger hormones, which direct the activity of other glands in the endocrine system

Place Theory of Pitch Perception

Different portions of the basilar membrane are sensitive to sounds of different frequencies

Placebo Effect

People's expectations or beliefs influencing or determining their experience in a given situation

Placenta

Structure connected to the uterus that provides nourishment and oxygen to the developing baby

Plateau

Phase of the sexual response cycle that falls between excitement and orgasm

Play Therapy

Therapeutic process, often used with children, that employs toys to help them resolve psychological problems

Polygenic

Multiple genes affecting a given trait

Polygraph

Lie detector test that measures physiological arousal of individuals as they answer a series of questions

Pons

Hindbrain structure that connects the brain and spinal cord; involved in regulating brain activity during sleep

Population

Overall group of individuals that the researchers are interested in

Positive Affect

State or a trait that involves pleasurable engagement with the environment, the dimensions of which include happiness, joy, enthusiasm, alertness, and excitement

Positive Correlation

Two variables change in the same direction, both becoming either larger or smaller

Positive Psychology

Scientific area of study seeking to identify and promote those qualities that lead to happy, fulfilled, and contented lives

Positive Punishment

Adding an undesirable stimulus to stop or decrease a behavior

Positive Reinforcement

Adding a desirable stimulus to increase a behavior

Positron Emission Tomography (PET) Scan

Involves injecting individuals with a mildly radioactive substance and monitoring changes in blood flow to different regions of the brain

Postdoctoral Training Program

Allows young scientists to further develop their research programs and broaden their research skills under the supervision of other professionals in the field

Posttraumatic Stress Disorder (PTSD)

Experiencing a profoundly traumatic event leads to a constellation of symptoms that includes intrusive and distressing memories of the event, avoidance of stimuli connected to the event, negative emotional states, feelings of detachment from others, irritability, proneness toward outbursts, hypervigilance, and a tendency to startle easily; these symptoms must occur for at least one month

Practical Intelligence

Also known as "street smarts"

Prefrontal Cortex

Area in the frontal lobe responsible for higher-level cognitive functioning

Prejudice

Negative attitudes and feelings toward individuals based solely on their membership in a particular group

Prenatal Care

Medical care during pregnancy that monitors the health of both the mother and the fetus

Preoperational Stage

Second stage in Piaget's theory of cognitive development; from ages 2 to 7, children learn to use symbols and language but do not understand mental operations and often think illogically

Primary Appraisal

Judgment about the degree of potential harm or threat to well-being that a stressor might entail

Primary Reinforcer

Has innate reinforcing qualities (e.g., food, water, shelter, sex)

Primary Sexual Characteristics

Organs specifically needed for reproduction

Proactive Interference

Old information hinders the recall of newly learned information

Problem-Solving Strategy

Method for solving problems

Procedural Justice

Fairness by which means are used to achieve results in an organization

Procedural Memory

Type of long-term memory for making skilled actions, such as how to brush your teeth, how to drive a car, and how to swim

Prodromal Symptom

In schizophrenia, one of the early minor symptoms of psychosis

Projection

Ego defense mechanism in which a person confronted with anxiety disguises their unacceptable urges or behaviors by attributing them to other people

Projective Test

Personality assessment in which a person responds to ambiguous stimuli, revealing hidden feelings, impulses, and desires

Proprioception

Perception of body position

Prosocial Behavior

Voluntary behavior with the intent to help other people

Prototype

Best representation of a concept

Proximity

Things that are close to one another tend to be grouped together

Psyche

Greek word for *soul*

Psychoanalysis

Therapeutic orientation developed by Sigmund Freud that employs free association, dream analysis, and transference to uncover repressed feelings

Psychoanalytic Theory

Focus on the role of the unconscious in affecting conscious behavior

Psychological Dependence

Emotional, rather than a physical, need for a drug which may be used to relieve psychological distress

Psychological Disorder

Condition characterized by abnormal thoughts, feelings, and behaviors

Psychology

Scientific study of the mind and behavior

Psychoneuroimmunology

Field that studies how psychological factors (such as stress) influence the immune system and immune functioning

Psychopathology

Study of psychological disorders, including their symptoms, causes, and treatment; manifestation of a psychological disorder

Psychophysiological Disorders

Physical disorders or diseases in which symptoms are brought about or worsened by stress and emotional factors

Psychosexual Development

Process proposed by Freud in which pleasure-seeking urges focus on different erogenous zones of the body as humans move through five stages of life

Psychosexual Stages of Development

Stages of child development in which a child's pleasure-seeking urges are focused on specific areas of the body called erogenous zones

Psychosocial Development

Process proposed by Erikson in which social tasks are mastered as humans move through eight stages of life from infancy to adulthood

Psychotherapy

(Also, *psychodynamic psychotherapy*) psychological treatment that employs various methods to help someone overcome personal problems, or to attain personal growth

Psychotropic Medication

Drugs that treat psychiatric symptoms by restoring neurotransmitter balance

PsyD

(Doctor of psychology) doctoral degree that places less emphasis on research-oriented skills and focuses more on application of psychological principles in the clinical context

Punishment

Implementation of a consequence in order to decrease a behavior

Pupil

Small opening in the eye through which light passes

Racism

Prejudice and discrimination toward individuals based solely on their race

Random Assignment

Method of experimental group assignment in which all participants have an equal chance of being assigned to either group

Random Sample

Subset of a larger population in which every member of the population has an equal chance of being selected

Range of Reaction

Asserts our genes set the boundaries within which we can operate, and our environment interacts with the genes to determine where in that range we will fall

Rapid Eye Movement (REM) Sleep

Period of sleep characterized by brain waves very similar to those during wakefulness and by darting movements of the eyes under closed eyelids

Rational Emotive Therapy (RET)

Form of cognitive-behavioral therapy

Rationalization

Ego defense mechanism in which a person confronted with anxiety makes excuses to justify behavior

Reaction Formation

Ego defense mechanism in which a person confronted with anxiety swaps unacceptable urges or behaviors for their opposites

Real Self

Person we actually are

Recall

Accessing information without cues

Receptor

Protein on the cell surface where neurotransmitters attach

Recessive Allele

Allele whose phenotype will be expressed only if an individual is homozygous for that allele

Reciprocal Determinism

Belief that one's environment can determine behavior, but at the same time, people can influence the environment with both their thoughts and behaviors

Reciprocity

Give and take in relationships

Recognition

Identifying previously learned information after encountering it again, usually in response to a cue

Reconstruction

Process of bringing up old memories that might be distorted by new information

Reflex

Unlearned, automatic response by an organism to a stimulus in the environment

Refractory Period

Time immediately following an orgasm during which an individual is incapable of experiencing another orgasm

Regression

Ego defense mechanism in which a person confronted with anxiety returns to a more immature behavioral state

Rehearsal

Conscious repetition of information to be remembered

Reinforcement

Implementation of a consequence in order to increase a behavior

Relapse

Repeated drug use and/or alcohol use after a period of improvement from substance abuse

Relaxation Response Technique

Stress reduction technique combining elements of relaxation and meditation

Relearning

Learning information that was previously learned

Reliability

Consistency and reproducibility of a given result

REM Sleep Behavior Disorder (RBD)

Sleep disorder in which the muscle paralysis associated with the REM sleep phase does not occur; sleepers have high levels of physical activity during REM sleep, especially during disturbing dreams

Replicate

Repeating an experiment using different samples to determine the research's reliability

Representative Bias

Faulty heuristic in which you stereotype someone or something without a valid basis for your judgment

Representative Sample

Subset of the population that accurately represents the general population

Repression

Ego defense mechanism in which anxiety-related thoughts and memories are kept in the unconscious

Resistant Attachment

Characterized by the child's tendency to show clingy behavior and rejection of the parent when she attempts to interact with the child

Resolution

Phase of the sexual response cycle following orgasm during which the body returns to its unaroused state

Resting Potential

The state of readiness of a neuron membrane's potential between signals

Restless Leg Syndrome

Sleep disorder in which the sufferer has uncomfortable sensations in the legs when trying to fall asleep that are relieved by moving the legs

Reticular Formation

Midbrain structure important in regulating the sleep/wake cycle, arousal, alertness, and motor activity

Retina

Light-sensitive lining of the eye

Retrieval

Act of getting information out of long-term memory storage and back into conscious awareness

Retroactive Interference

Information learned more recently hinders the recall of older information

Retrograde Amnesia

Loss of memory for events that occurred prior to brain trauma

Reuptake

Neurotransmitter is pumped back into the neuron that released it

Reversibility

Principle that objects can be changed, but then returned back to their original form or condition

Rod

Specialized photoreceptor that works well in low light conditions

Rogerian (Client-Centered) Therapy

Non-directive form of humanistic psychotherapy developed by Carl Rogers that emphasizes unconditional positive regard and self-acceptance

Role Schema

Set of expectations that define the behaviors of a person occupying a particular role

Romantic Love

Type of love consisting of intimacy and passion, but no commitment

Rorschach Inkblot Test

Projective test that employs a series of symmetrical inkblot cards that are presented to a client by a psychologist in an effort to reveal the person's unconscious desires, fears, and struggles

Rotating Shift Work

Work schedule that changes from early to late on a daily or weekly basis

Rotter Incomplete Sentence Blank (RISB)

Projective test that is similar to a word association test in which a person completes sentences in order to reveal their unconscious desires, fears, and struggles

Ruffini Corpuscle

Touch receptor that detects stretch

Rumination

In depression, tendency to repetitively and passively dwell on one's depressed symptoms, their meanings, and their consequences

Safety Behavior

Mental and behavior acts designed to reduce anxiety in social situations by reducing the chance of negative social outcomes; common in social anxiety disorder

Sample

Subset of individuals selected from the larger population

Satiation

Fullness; satisfaction

Scapegoating

Act of blaming an out-group when the in-group experiences frustration or is blocked from obtaining a goal

Schachter-Singer Two-Factor Theory of Emotion

Emotions consist of two factors: physiological and cognitive

Schema

(Plural: *schemata*) mental construct consisting of a cluster or collection of related concepts

Schizophrenia

Severe disorder characterized by major disturbances in thought, perception, emotion, and behavior with symptoms that include hallucinations, delusions, disorganized thinking and behavior, and negative symptoms

Scientific Management

Theory of management that analyzes and synthesizes workflows with the main objective of improving economic efficiency, especially labor productivity

Script

Person's knowledge about the sequence of events in a specific setting

Seasonal Pattern

Subtype of depression in which a person experiences the symptoms of major depressive disorder only during a particular time of year

Secondary Appraisal

Judgment of options available to cope with a stressor and their potential effectiveness

Secondary Reinforcer

Has no inherent value unto itself and only has reinforcing qualities when linked with something else (e.g., money, gold stars, poker chips)

Secondary Sexual Characteristics

Physical signs of sexual maturation that do not directly involve sex organs

Secure Attachment

Characterized by the child using the parent as a secure base from which to explore

Secure Base

Parental presence that gives the infant/toddler a sense of safety as he explores his surroundings

Selective Migration

Concept that people choose to move to places that are compatible with their personalities and needs

Self-Concept

Our thoughts and feelings about ourselves

Self-Disclosure

Sharing personal information in relationships

Self-Efficacy

An individual's belief in his own capabilities or capacities to complete a task

Self-Fulfilling Prophecy

Treating stereotyped group members according to our biased expectations only to have this treatment influence the individual to act according to our stereotypic expectations, thus confirming our stereotypic beliefs

Self-Reference Effect

Tendency for an individual to have better memory for information that relates to oneself in comparison to material that has less personal relevance

Self-Serving Bias

Tendency for individuals to take credit by making dispositional or internal attributions for positive outcomes and situational or external attributions for negative outcomes

Semantic Encoding

Input of words and their meaning

Semantic Memory

Type of declarative memory about words, concepts, and language-based knowledge and facts

Semantics

Process by which we derive meaning from morphemes and words

Semipermeable Membrane

Cell membrane that allows smaller molecules or molecules without an electrical charge to pass through it while stopping larger or highly charged molecules

Sensation

What happens when sensory information is detected by a sensory receptor

Sensorimotor Stage

First stage in Piaget's theory of cognitive development; from birth through age 2, a child learns about the world through senses and motor behavior

Sensorineural Hearing Loss

Failure to transmit neural signals from the cochlea to the brain

Sensory Adaptation

Not perceiving stimuli that remain relatively constant over prolonged periods of time

Sensory Memory

Storage of brief sensory events, such as sights, sounds, and tastes

Set-Point Theory

Assertion that each individual has an ideal body weight, or set point, that is resistant to change

Sexism

Prejudice and discrimination toward individuals based on their sex

Sexual Harassment

Sexually-based behavior that is knowingly unwanted and has an adverse effect on a person's employment status, interferes with a person's job performance, or creates a hostile or intimidating work environment

Sexual Orientation

Emotional and erotic attraction to same-sexed individuals, opposite-sexed individuals, or both

Sexual Response Cycle

Divided into four phases including excitement, plateau, orgasm, and resolution

Shaping

Rewarding successive approximations toward a target behavior

Short-Term Memory (STM)

(Also, *working memory*) holds about seven bits of information before it is forgotten or stored, as well as information that has been retrieved and is being used

Signal Detection Theory

Change in stimulus detection as a function of current mental state

Similarity

Things that are alike tend to be grouped together

Single-Blind Study

Experiment in which the researcher knows which participants are in the experimental group and which are in the control group

Situationism

Describes a perspective that behavior and actions are determined by the immediate environment and surroundings; a view promoted by social psychologists

Sleep

State marked by relatively low levels of physical activity and reduced sensory awareness that is distinct from periods of rest that occur during wakefulness

Sleep Apnea

Sleep disorder defined by episodes during which breathing stops during sleep

Sleep Debt

Result of insufficient sleep on a chronic basis

Sleep Rebound

Sleep-deprived individuals will experience shorter sleep latencies during subsequent opportunities for sleep

Sleep Regulation

Brain's control of switching between sleep and wakefulness as well as coordinating this cycle with the outside world

Sleep Spindle

Rapid burst of high frequency brain waves during stage 2 sleep that may be important for learning and memory

Sleepwalking

(Also, *somnambulism*) sleep disorder in which the sleeper engages in relatively complex behaviors

Social Anxiety Disorder

Characterized by extreme and persistent fear or anxiety and avoidance of social situations in which one could potentially be evaluated negatively by others

Social Exchange Theory

Humans act as naïve economists in keeping a tally of the ratio of costs and benefits of forming and maintain a relationship, with the goal to maximize benefits and minimize costs

Social Facilitation

Improved performance when an audience is watching versus when the individual performs the behavior alone

Social Loafing

Exertion of less effort by a person working in a group because individual performance cannot be evaluated separately from the group, thus causing performance decline on easy tasks

Social Norm

Group's expectations regarding what is appropriate and acceptable for the thoughts and behavior of its members

Social Psychology

Field of psychology that examines how people impact or affect each other, with particular focus on the power of the situation

Social Readjustment Rating Scale (SRRS)

Popular scale designed to measure stress; consists of 43 potentially stressful events, each of which has a numerical value quantifying how much readjustment is associated with the event

Social Role

Socially defined pattern of behavior that is expected of a person in a given setting or group

Social Support

Soothing and often beneficial support of others; can take different forms, such as advice, guidance, encouragement, acceptance, emotional comfort, and tangible assistance

Social-Cognitive Theory

Bandura's theory of personality that emphasizes both cognition and learning as sources of individual differences in personality

Socioemotional Selectivity Theory

Social support/friendships dwindle in number, but remain as close, if not more close than in earlier years

Soma

Cell body

Somatic Delusion

Belief that something highly unusual is happening to one's body or internal organs

Somatic Nervous System

Relays sensory and motor information to and from the CNS

Somatosensory Cortex

Essential for processing sensory information from across the body, such as touch, temperature, and pain

Specific Phobia

Anxiety disorder characterized by excessive, distressing, and persistent fear or anxiety about a specific object or situation

Spermarche

First male ejaculation

Spontaneous Recovery

Return of a previously extinguished conditioned response

Sport and Exercise Psychology

Area of psychology that focuses on the interactions between mental and emotional factors and physical performance in sports, exercise, and other activities

Stage 1 Sleep

First stage of sleep; transitional phase that occurs between wakefulness and sleep; the period during which a person drifts off to sleep

Stage 2 Sleep

Second stage of sleep; the body goes into deep relaxation; characterized by the appearance of sleep spindles

Stage 3 Sleep

Third stage of sleep; deep sleep characterized by low frequency, high amplitude delta waves

Stage 4 Sleep

Fourth stage of sleep; deep sleep characterized by low frequency, high amplitude delta waves

Stage of Exhaustion

Third stage of the general adaptation syndrome; the body's ability to resist stress becomes depleted; illness, disease, and even death may occur

Stage of Moral Reasoning

Process proposed by Kohlberg; humans move through three stages of moral development

Stage of Resistance

Second stage of the general adaptation syndrome; the body adapts to a stressor for a period of time

Standard Deviation

Measure of variability that describes the difference between a set of scores and their mean

Standardization

Method of testing in which administration, scoring, and interpretation of results are consistent

Stanford Prison Experiment

Stanford University conducted an experiment in a mock prison that demonstrated the power of social roles, social norms, and scripts

Stapes

Middle ear ossicle; also known as the *stirrup*

Statistical Analysis

Determines how likely any difference between experimental groups is due to chance

Stereotype

Specific beliefs or assumptions about individuals based solely on their membership in a group, regardless of their individual characteristics

Stimulant

Drug that tends to increase overall levels of neural activity; includes caffeine, nicotine, amphetamines, and cocaine

Stimulus Discrimination

Ability to respond differently to similar stimuli

Stimulus Generalization

Demonstrating the conditioned response to stimuli that are similar to the conditioned stimulus

Storage

Creation of a permanent record of information

Strategic Family Therapy

Therapist guides the therapy sessions and develops treatment plans for each family member for specific problems that can be addressed in a short amount of time

Stress

Process whereby an individual perceives and responds to events that one appraises as overwhelming or threatening to one's well-being

Stressors

Environmental events that may be judged as threatening or demanding; stimuli that initiate the stress process

Structural Family Therapy

Therapist examines and discusses with the family the boundaries and structure of the family: who makes the rules, who sleeps in the bed with whom, how decisions are made, and what are the boundaries within the family

Structuralism

Understanding the conscious experience through introspection

Sublimation

Ego defense mechanism in which unacceptable urges are channeled into more appropriate activities

Subliminal Message

Message presented below the threshold of conscious awareness

Substantia Nigra

Midbrain structure where dopamine is produced; involved in control of movement

Sudden Infant Death Syndrome (SIDS)

Infant (one year old or younger) with no apparent medical condition suddenly dies during sleep

Suggestibility

Effects of misinformation from external sources that leads to the creation of false memories

Suicidal Ideation

Thoughts of death by suicide, thinking about or planning suicide, or making a suicide attempt

Suicide

Death caused by intentional, self-directed injurious behavior

Sulcus

(Plural: *sulci*) depressions or grooves in the cerebral cortex

Superego

Aspect of the personality that serves as one's moral compass, or conscience

Supernatural

Describes a force beyond scientific understanding

Suprachiasmatic Nucleus (SCN)

Area of the hypothalamus in which the body's biological clock is located

Survey

List of questions to be answered by research participants—given as paper-and-pencil questionnaires, administered electronically, or conducted verbally—allowing researchers to collect data from a large number of people

Sympathetic Nervous System

Involved in stress-related activities and functions

Synapse

Small gap between two neurons where communication occurs

Synaptic Vesicle

Storage site for neurotransmitters

Syntax

Manner by which words are organized into sentences

Systematic Desensitization

Form of exposure therapy used to treat phobias and anxiety disorders by exposing a person to the feared object or situation through a stimulus hierarchy

Taste Bud

Grouping of taste receptor cells with hair-like extensions that protrude into the central pore of the taste bud

Telecommuting

Employees' ability to set their own hours allowing them to work from home at different parts of the day

TEMAS Multicultural Thematic Apperception Test

Projective test designed to be culturally relevant to minority groups, especially Hispanic youths, using images and storytelling that relate to minority culture

Temperament

Innate traits that influence how one thinks, behaves, and reacts with the environment

Temporal Lobe

Part of cerebral cortex associated with hearing, memory, emotion, and some aspects of language; contains primary auditory cortex

Temporal Theory of Pitch Perception

Sound's frequency is coded by the activity level of a sensory neuron

Teratogen

Biological, chemical, or physical environmental agent that causes damage to the developing embryo or fetus

Terminal Button

Axon terminal containing synaptic vesicles

Thalamus

Sensory relay for the brain

Thematic Apperception Test (TAT)

Projective test in which people are presented with ambiguous images, and they then make up stories to go with the images in an effort to uncover their unconscious desires, fears, and struggles

Theory

Well-developed set of ideas that propose an explanation for observed phenomena

Theory of Evolution by Natural Selection

States that organisms that are better suited for their environments will survive and reproduce compared to those that are poorly suited for their environments

Theory X

Assumes workers are inherently lazy and unproductive; managers must have control and use punishments

Theory Y

Assumes workers are people who seek to work hard and productively; managers and workers can find creative solutions to problems; workers do not need to be controlled and punished

Thermoception

Temperature perception

Theta Wave

Type of low frequency, high amplitude brain wave characteristic of stage 1 and stage 2 sleep

Threshold of Excitation

Level of charge in the membrane that causes the neuron to become active

Thyroid

Secretes hormones that regulate growth, metabolism, and appetite

Timbre

Sound's purity

Token Economy

Controlled setting where individuals are reinforced for desirable behaviors with tokens (e.g., poker chips) that can be exchanged for items or privileges

Tolerance

State of requiring increasing quantities of the drug to gain the desired effect

Top-Down Processing

Interpretation of sensations is influenced by available knowledge, experiences, and thoughts

Traits

Characteristic ways of behaving

Transactional Leadership Style

Characteristic of leaders who focus on supervision and organizational goals achieved through a system of rewards and punishments; maintenance of the organizational status quo

Transduction

Conversion from sensory stimulus energy to action potential

Transference

Process in psychoanalysis in which the patient transfers all of the positive or negative emotions associated with the patient's other relationships to the psychoanalyst

Transformational Leadership Style

Characteristic of leaders who are charismatic role models, inspirational, intellectually stimulating, and individually considerate and who seek to change the organization

Transgender Hormone Therapy

Use of hormones to make one's body look more like the opposite-sex

Transience

Memory error in which unused memories fade with the passage of time

Trial and Error

Problem-solving strategy in which multiple solutions are attempted until the correct one is found

Triangular Theory of Love

Model of love based on three components: intimacy, passion, and commitment; several types of love exist, depending on the presence or absence of each of these components

Triarchic Theory of Intelligence

Sternberg's theory of intelligence; three facets of intelligence: practical, creative, and analytical

Trichromatic Theory of Color Perception

Color vision is mediated by the activity across the three groups of cones

Trough

Lowest point of a wave

Tympanic Membrane

Eardrum

Type A

Psychological and behavior pattern exhibited by individuals who tend to be extremely competitive, impatient, rushed, and hostile toward others

Type B

Psychological and behavior pattern exhibited by a person who is relaxed and laid back

U.S. Equal Employment Opportunity Commission (EEOC)

Responsible for enforcing federal laws that make it illegal to discriminate against a job applicant or an employee because of the person's race, color, religion, sex (including pregnancy), national origin, age (40 or older), disability, or genetic information

Umami

Taste for monosodium glutamate

Unconditional Positive Regard

Fundamental acceptance of a person regardless of what they say or do; term associated with humanistic psychology

Unconditioned Response (UCR)

Natural (unlearned) behavior to a given stimulus

Unconditioned Stimulus (UCS)

Stimulus that elicits a reflexive response

Unconscious

Mental activity of which we are unaware and unable to access

Uninvolved Parenting Style

Parents are indifferent, uninvolved, and sometimes referred to as neglectful; they don't respond to the child's needs and make relatively few demands

Validity

Accuracy of a given result in measuring what it is designed to measure

Variable Interval Reinforcement Schedule

Behavior is rewarded after unpredictable amounts of time have passed

Variable Ratio Reinforcement Schedule

Number of responses differ before a behavior is rewarded

Ventral Tegmental Area (VTA)

Midbrain structure where dopamine is produced; associated with mood, reward, and addiction

Ventricle

One of the fluid-filled cavities within the brain

Vertigo

Spinning sensation

Vestibular Sense

Contributes to our ability to maintain balance and body posture

Vicarious Punishment

Process where the observer sees the model punished, making the observer less likely to imitate the model's behavior

Vicarious Reinforcement

Process where the observer sees the model rewarded, making the observer more likely to imitate the model's behavior

Virtual Reality Exposure Therapy

Uses a simulation rather than the actual feared object or situation to help people conquer their fears

Visible Spectrum

Portion of the electromagnetic spectrum that we can see

Visual Encoding

Input of images

Voluntary Treatment

Therapy that a person chooses to attend in order to obtain relief from her symptoms

Wakefulness

Characterized by high levels of sensory awareness, thought, and behavior

Wavelength

Length of a wave from one peak to the next peak

Wernicke's Area

Important for speech comprehension

Withdrawal

Variety of negative symptoms experienced when drug use is discontinued

Work Team

Group of people within an organization or company given a specific task to achieve together

Work-Family Balance

Occurs when people juggle the demands of work life with the demands of family life

Working Backwards

Heuristic in which you begin to solve a problem by focusing on the end result

Workplace Violence

Violence or the threat of violence against workers; can occur inside or outside the workplace

Yerkes-Dodson Law

Simple tasks are performed best when arousal levels are relatively high, while complex tasks are best performed when arousal is lower

Zygote

Structure created when a sperm and egg merge at conception; begins as a single cell and rapidly divides to form the embryo and placenta

Index

References

Chapter 1

American Academy of Pediatrics, American Academy of Child & Adolescent Psychiatry, American Psychological Association, American Medical Association, American Academy of Family Physicians, American Psychiatric Association. (2000). *Joint statement on the impact of entertainment violence on children*. http://www2.aap.org/advocacy/releases/jstmtevc.htm.

American Board of Forensic Psychology. (2014). *Brochure*. http://www.abfp.com/brochure.asp

American Cancer Society. (n.d.). History of the cancer prevention studies. http://www.cancer.org/research/researchtopreventcancer/history-cancer-prevention-study

American Psychological Association. (2009). *Publication Manual of the American Psychological Association* (6th ed.). Author.

American Psychological Association. (2014). http://www.apa.org

American Psychological Association. (2014). *Graduate training and career possibilities in exercise and sport psychology*. http://www.apadivisions.org/division-47/about/resources/training.aspx?item=1

American Psychological Association. (2011). *Psychology as a career*. http://www.apa.org/education/undergrad/psych-career.aspx

American Psychological Association. (n.d.). *Research with animals in psychology*. https://www.apa.org/research/responsible/research-animals.pdf

Arnett, J. (2008). The neglected 95%: Why American psychology needs to become less American. *American Psychologist*, *63*(7), 602–614.

Ashliman, D.L. (2001). Cupid and Psyche. In *Folktexts: A library of folktales, folklore, fairy tales, and mythology*. http://www.pitt.edu/~dash/cupid.html

Barton, B.A., Eldridge, A.L., Thompson, D., Affenito, S.G., Striegel-Moore, R.H., Franko, D.L.,…Crockett, S.J. (2005). The relationship of breakfast and cereal consumption to nutrient intake and body mass index: The national heart, lung, and blood institute growth and health study. *Journal of the American Dietetic Association*, *105*(9), 1383–1389. http://dx.doi.org/10.1016/j.jada.2005.06.003

Betancourt, H., & López, S.R. (1993). The study of culture, ethnicity, and race in American psychology. *American Psychologist*, *48*, 629–637.

Black, S.R., Spence, S.A., & Omari, S.R. (2004). Contributions of African Americans to the field of psychology. *Journal of Black Studies*, *35*, 40–64.

Bulfinch, T. (1855). *The age of fable: Or, stories of gods and heroes*. Chase, Nichols and Hill.

Buss, D.M. (1989). Sex differences in human mate preferences: Evolutionary hypotheses tested in 37 cultures. *Behavioral and Brain Sciences*, *12*, 1–49.

Carlson, N.R. (2013). *Physiology of Behavior* (11th ed.). Pearson.

Chwalisz, K., Diener, E., & Gallagher, D. (1988). Autonomic arousal feedback and emotional experience: Evidence from the spinal cord injured. *Journal of Personality and Social Psychology*, *54*, 820–828.

Clayton, R.R., Cattarello, A.M., & Johnstone, B.M. (1996). The effectiveness of Drug Abuse Resistance Education (Project DARE): 5-year follow-up results. *Preventive Medicine: An International Journal Devoted to Practice and Theory*, *25*(3), 307–318. https://doi.org/10.1006/pmed.1996.0061

Confer, J.C., Easton, J.A., Fleischman, D.S., Goetz, C.D., Lewis, D.M.G., Perilloux, C., & Buss, D.M. (2010). Evolutionary psychology. Controversies, questions, prospects, and limitations. *American Psychologist*, *65*, 100–126.

Crawford, M., & Marecek, J. (1989). Psychology reconstructs the female 1968–1988. *Psychology of Women Quarterly*, *13*, 147–165.

Danziger, K. (1980). The history of introspection reconsidered. *Journal of the History of the Behavioral Sciences*, *16*, 241–262.

D.A.R.E. (n.d.). D.A.R.E. is substance abuse prevention education and much more! [About page] http://www.dare.org/about-d-a-r-e/

Darwin, C. (1871). *The descent of man and selection in relation to sex*. John Murray.

Darwin, C. (1872). *The expression of the emotions in man and animals*. John Murray.

DeAngelis, T. (2010). Fear not. *gradPSYCH Magazine*, *8*, 38.

Department of Health and Human Services. (n.d.). Projected future growth of the older population. http://www.aoa.gov/Aging_Statistics/future_growth/future_growth.aspx#age

Dominus, S. (2011, May 25). Could conjoined twins share a mind? *New York Times Sunday Magazine*. http://www.nytimes.com/2011/05/29/magazine/could-conjoined-twins-share-a-mind.html?_r=5&hp&

Endler, J.A. (1986). *Natural Selection in the Wild*. Princeton University Press.

Ennett, S.T., Tobler, N.S., Ringwalt, C.L., & Flewelling, R.L. (1994). How effective is drug abuse resistance education? A meta-analysis of Project DARE outcome evaluations. *American Journal of Public Health*, *84*(9), 1394–1401. https://doi.org/10.2105/AJPH.84.9.1394

Fanger, S.M., Frankel, L.A., & Hazen, N. (2012). Peer exclusion in preschool children's play: Naturalistic observations in a playground setting. *Merrill-Palmer Quarterly*, *58*, 224–254.

Fiedler, K. (2004). Illusory correlation. In R. F. Pohl (Ed.), *Cognitive illusions: A handbook on fallacies and biases in thinking, judgment and memory* (pp. 97–114). Psychology Press.

Fogg, N.P., Harrington, P.E., Harrington, T.F., & Shatkin, L. (2012). *College majors handbook with real career paths and payoffs* (3rd ed.). JIST Publishing.

Franko, D.L., et al. (2012). Racial/ethnic differences in adults in randomized clinical trials of binge eating disorder. *Journal of Consulting and Clinical Psychology*, *80*, 186–195.

Frantzen, L.B., Treviño, R.P., Echon, R.M., Garcia-Dominic, O., & DiMarco, N. (2013). Association between frequency of ready-to-eat cereal consumption, nutrient intakes, and body mass index in fourth- to sixth-grade low-income minority children. *Journal of the Academy of Nutrition and Dietetics*, *113*(4), 511–519.

Friedman, H. (2008), Humanistic and positive psychology: The methodological and epistemological divide. *The Humanistic Psychologist*, *36*, 113–126.

Gordon, O.E. (1995). *A brief history of psychology*. http://www.psych.utah.edu/gordon/Classes/Psy4905Docs/PsychHistory/index.html#maptop

Greek Myths & Greek Mythology. (2014). *The myth of Psyche and Eros*. http://www.greekmyths-greekmythology.com/psyche-and-eros-myth/

Green, C.D. (2001). Classics in the history of psychology. http://psychclassics.yorku.ca/Krstic/marulic.htm

Greengrass, M. (2004). 100 years of B.F. Skinner. *Monitor on Psychology*, *35*, 80.

Halonen, J.S. (2011). *White paper: Are there too many psychology majors?* Prepared for the Staff of the State University System of Florida Board of Governors. http://www.cogdop.org/page_attachments/0000/0200/FLA_White_Paper_for_cogop_posting.pdf

Harper, J. (2013, July 5). Ice cream and crime: Where cold cuisine and hot disputes intersect. *The Times-Picaune*. http://www.nola.com/crime/index.ssf/2013/07/ice_cream_and_crime_where_hot.html

Hock, R.R. (2009). Social psychology. *Forty studies that changed psychology: Explorations into the history of psychological research* (pp. 308–317). Pearson.

Hoffman, C. (2012). *Careers in clinical, counseling, or school psychology; mental health counseling; clinical social work; marriage & family therapy and related professions*. http://www.indiana.edu/~psyugrad/advising/docs/Careers%20in%20Mental%20Health%20Counseling.pdf

Jang, K.L., Lively, W.J., & Vernon, P.A. (1996). Heritability of the Big Five personality dimensions and their facets: A twin study. *Journal of Personality*, 64, 577–591.

Jenkins, W.J., Ruppel, S.E., Kizer, J.B., Yehl, J.L., & Griffin, J.L. (2012). An examination of post 9-11 attitudes towards Arab Americans. *North American Journal of Psychology*, 14, 77–84.

Johnson, R., & Lubin, G. (2011). College exposed: What majors are most popular, highest paying and most likely to get you a job. *Business Insider.com*. http://www.businessinsider.com/best-college-majors-highest-income-most-employed-georgetwon-study-2011-6?op=1

Jones, J.M. (2013, May 13). Same-sex marriage support solidifies above 50% in U.S. *Gallup Politics*. http://www.gallup.com/poll/162398/sex-marriage-support-solidifies-above.aspx

Knekt, P.P., et al. (2008). Randomized trial on the effectiveness of long- and short-term psychodynamic psychotherapy and solution-focused therapy on psychiatric symptoms during a 3-year follow-up. *Psychological Medicine: A Journal of Research In Psychiatry And The Allied Sciences*, 38, 689–703.

Kobrin, J.L., Patterson, B.F., Shaw, E.J., Mattern, K.D., & Barbuti, S.M. (2008). *Validity of the SAT for predicting first-year college grade point average* (Research Report No. 2008-5). https://research.collegeboard.org/sites/default/files/publications/2012/7/researchreport-2008-5-validity-sat-predicting-first-year-college-grade-point-average.pdf

Landers, R.N. (2011, June 14). Grad school: Should I get a PhD or Master's in I/O psychology? [Web log post]. http://neoacademic.com/2011/06/14/grad-school-should-i-get-a-ph-d-or-masters-in-io-psychology/#.UuKKLftOnGg

Lewin, T. (2014, March 5). A new SAT aims to realign with schoolwork. *New York Times*. Retreived from http://www.nytimes.com/2014/03/06/education/major-changes-in-sat-announced-by-college-board.html.

Lowcock, E.C., Cotterchio, M., Anderson, L.N., Boucher, B.A., & El-Sohemy, A. (2013). High coffee intake, but not caffeine, is associated with reduced estrogen receptor negative and postmenopausal breast cancer risk with no effect modification by CYP1A2 genotype. *Nutrition and Cancer*, 65(3), 398–409. https://doi.org/10.1080/01635581.2013.768348

Lowry, M., Dean, K., & Manders, K. (2010). The link between sleep quantity and academic performance for the college student. *Sentience: The University of Minnesota Undergraduate Journal of Psychology*, 3(Spring), 16–19. http://www.psych.umn.edu/sentience/files/SENTIENCE_Vol3.pdf

Lynam, D.R., Milich, R., Zimmerman, R., Novak, S.P., Logan, T.K., Martin, C.,... Clayton, R. (1999). Project DARE: No effects at 10-year follow-up. *Journal of Consulting and Clinical Psychology*, 67(4), 590–593. https://doi.org/10.1037/0022-006X.67.4.590

Macdonald, C. (2013). *Health psychology center presents: What is health psychology?* http://healthpsychology.org/what-is-health-psychology/

McCrae, R.R. & Costa, P.T. (2008). Empirical and theoretical status of the five-factor model of personality traits. In G. J. Boyle, G. Matthews, & D. H. Saklofske (Eds.), *The Sage handbook of personality theory and assessment. Vol. 1 Personality theories and models*. Sage.

McKie, R. (2010, June 26). Chimps with everything: Jane Goodall's 50 years in the jungle. *The Guardian*. http://www.theguardian.com/science/2010/jun/27/jane-goodall-chimps-africa-interview

Michalski, D., Kohout, J., Wicherski, M., & Hart, B. (2011). *2009 Doctorate Employment Survey*. APA Center for Workforce Studies. http://www.apa.org/workforce/publications/09-doc-empl/index.aspx

Miller, G.A. (2003). The cognitive revolution: A historical perspective. *Trends in Cognitive Sciences*, 7, 141–144.

Munakata, Y., McClelland, J.L., Johnson, M.H., & Siegler, R.S. (1997). Rethinking infant knowledge: Toward an adaptive process account of successes and failures in object permanence tasks. *Psychological Review*, 104, 689–713.

Mundasad, S. (2013). *Word-taste synaesthesia: Tasting names, places, and Anne Boleyn*. http://www.bbc.co.uk/news/health-21060207

Munsey, C. (2009). More states forgo a postdoc requirement. *Monitor on Psychology*, 40, 10.

National Association of School Psychologists. (n.d.). *Becoming a nationally certified school psychologist (NCSP)*. http://www.nasponline.org/CERTIFICATION/becomeNCSP.aspx

Nicolas, S., & Ferrand, L. (1999). Wundt's laboratory at Leipzig in 1891. *History of Psychology*, 2, 194–203.

Norcross, J.C. (n.d.) Clinical versus counseling psychology: What's the diff? Available at http://www.csun.edu/~hcpsy002/Clinical%20Versus%20Counseling%20Psychology.pdf

Norcross, J.C., & Castle, P.H. (2002). Appreciating the PsyD: The facts. *Eye on Psi Chi*, 7, 22–26.

O'Connor, J.J., & Robertson, E.F. (2002). *John Forbes Nash*. http://www-groups.dcs.st-and.ac.uk/~history/Biographies/Nash.html

O'Hara, M. (n.d.). Historic review of humanistic psychology. http://www.ahpweb.org/index.php?option=com_k2&view=item&layout=item&id=14&Itemid=24

Offit, P. (2008). *Autism's false prophets: Bad science, risky medicine, and the search for a cure*. Columbia University Press.

Perkins, H.W., Haines, M.P., & Rice, R. (2005). Misperceiving the college drinking norm and related problems: A nationwide study of exposure to prevention information, perceived norms and student alcohol misuse. *J. Stud. Alcohol*, 66(4), 470–478.

Person, E.S. (1980). Sexuality as the mainstay of identity: Psychoanalytic perspectives. *Signs*, 5, 605–630.

Rantanen, J., Metsäpelto, R.L., Feldt, T., Pulkkinen, L., & Kokko, K. (2007). Long-term stability in the Big Five personality traits in adulthood. *Scandinavian Journal of Psychology*, 48, 511 & 518.

Riggio, R.E. (2013). What is industrial/organizational psychology? *Psychology Today*. http://www.psychologytoday.com/blog/cutting-edge-leadership/201303/what-is-industrialorganizational-psychology

Rimer, S. (2008, September 21). College panel calls for less focus on SATs. *The New York Times.* http://www.nytimes.com/2008/09/22/education/22admissions.html?_r=0

Ringwalt, C., Ennett, S.T., & Holt, K.D. (1991). An outcome evaluation of Project DARE (Drug Abuse Resistance Education). *Health Education Research*, 6(3), 327–337. https://doi.org/10.1093/her/6.3.327

Rothstein, J.M. (2004). College performance predictions and the SAT. *Journal of Econometrics*, 121, 297–317.

Rotton, J., & Kelly, I.W. (1985). Much ado about the full moon: A meta-analysis of lunar-lunacy research. *Psychological Bulletin*, 97(2), 286–306. https://doi.org/10.1037/0033-2909.97.2.286

Sacks, O. (2007). A neurologists notebook: The abyss, music and amnesia. *The New Yorker.* http://www.newyorker.com/reporting/2007/09/24/070924fa_fact_sacks?currentPage=all

Santelices, M.V., & Wilson, M. (2010). Unfair treatment? The case of Freedle, the SAT, and the standardization approach to differential item functioning. *Harvard Education Review*, 80, 106–134.

Sears, D.O. (1986). College sophomores in the laboratory: Influences of a narrow data base on social psychology's view of human nature. *Journal of Personality and Social Psychology*, 51, 515–530.

Shedler, J. (2010). The efficacy of psychodynamic psychotherapy. *American Psychologist*, 65(2), 98–109.

Soldz, S., & Vaillant, G.E. (1999). The Big Five personality traits and the life course: A 45-year longitudinal study. *Journal of Research in Personality*, 33, 208–232.

Thorne, B.M., & Henley, T.B. (2005). *Connections in the history and systems of psychology* (3rd ed.). Houghton Mifflin Company.

Tolman, E.C. (1938). The determiners of behavior at a choice point. *Psychological Review*, 45, 1–41.

Tuskegee University. (n.d.). *About the USPHS Syphilis Study.* http://www.tuskegee.edu/about_us/centers_of_excellence/bioethics_center/about_the_usphs_syphilis_study.aspx.

U.S. Department of Education, National Center for Education Statistics. (2013). *Digest of Education Statistics*, 2012 (NCES 2014-015).

Weisstein, N. (1993). Psychology constructs the female: Or, the fantasy life of the male psychologist (with some attention to the fantasies of his friends, the male biologist and the male anthropologist). *Feminism and Psychology*, 3, 195–210.

Westen, D. (1998). The scientific legacy of Sigmund Freud, toward a psychodynamically informed psychological science. *Psychological Bulletin*, 124, 333–371.

Chapter 2

Arnst, C. (2003, November). Commentary: Getting rational about health-care rationing. *Bloomberg Businessweek Magazine.* http://www.businessweek.com/stories/2003-11-16/commentary-getting-rational-about-health-care-rationing

Berridge, K.C., & Robinson, T.E. (1998). What is the role of dopamine in reward: Hedonic impact, reward learning, or incentive salience? *Brain Research Reviews*, 28, 309–369.

Chandola, T., Brunner, E., & Marmot, M. (2006). Chronic stress at work and the metabolic syndrome: A prospective study. *BMJ*, 332, 521–524.

Comings, D.E., Gonzales, N., Saucier, G., Johnson, J.P., & MacMurray, J.P. (2000). The DRD4 gene and the spiritual transcendence scale of the character temperament index. *Psychiatric Genetics*, 10, 185–189.

Confer, J.C., Easton, J.A., Fleischman, D.S., Goetz, C.D., Lewis, D.M.G, Perilloux, C., & Buss, D.M. (2010). Evolutionary psychology: Controversies, questions, prospects, and limitations. *American Psychologist*, 65, 110–126.

Gaines, C. (2013, August). An A-Rod suspension would save the Yankees as much as $37.5 million in 2014 alone. *Business Insider.* http://www.businessinsider.com/an-a-rod-suspension-would-save-the-yankees-as-much-as-375-million-in-2014-2013-8

Gardner, E.L. (2011). Addiction and brain reward and antireward pathways. *Advances in Psychosomatic Medicine*, 30, 22–60.

George, O., Le Moal, M., & Koob, G.F. (2012). Allostasis and addiction: Role of the dopamine and corticotropin-releasing factor systems. *Physiology & Behavior*, 106, 58–64.

Glaser, R., & Kiecolt-Glaser, J.K. (2005). Stress-induced immune dysfunction: Implications for health. *Nature Reviews Immunology*, 5, 243–251.

Gong, L., Parikh, S., Rosenthal, P.J., & Greenhouse, B. (2013). Biochemical and immunological mechanisms by which sickle cell trait protects against malaria. *Malaria Journal.* Advance online publication. https://doi.org/10.1186/1475-2875-12-317

Hardt, O., Einarsson, E.Ö., & Nader, K. (2010). A bridge over troubled water: Reconsolidation as a link between cognitive and neuroscientific memory research traditions. *Annual Review of Psychology*, 61, 141–167.

Macmillan, M. (1999). The Phineas Gage Information Page. http://www.uakron.edu/gage

March, J.S., Silva, S., Petrycki, S., Curry, J., Wells, K., Fairbank, J.,...Severe, J. (2007). The treatment for adolescents with depression study (TADS): Long-term effectiveness and safety outcomes. *Arch Gen Psychiatry*, 64, 1132–1143.

Mustanski, B.S., DuPree, M.G., Nievergelt, C.M., Bocklandt, S., Schork, N.J., & Hamer, D.H. (2005). A genome wide scan of male sexual orientation. *Human Genetics*, 116, 272–278.

National Institute on Drug Abuse. (2001, July). Anabolic steroid abuse: What are the health consequences of steroid abuse? *National Institutes of Health.* http://www.drugabuse.gov/publications/research-reports/anabolic-steroid-abuse/what-are-health-consequences-steroid-abuse

Squire, L.R. (2009). The legacy of patient H. M. for neuroscience. *Neuron*, 61, 6–9.

Tienari, P., Wynne, L.C., Sorri, A., et al. (2004). Genotype–environment interaction in schizophrenia spectrum disorder: long-term follow-up study of Finnish adoptees. *British Journal of Psychiatry*, 184, 216–222.

University of Utah Genetic Science Learning Center. (n.d.). What are genetic disorders? http://learn.genetics.utah.edu/content/disorders/whataregd/

Chapter 3

Aggarwal, S.K., Carter, G.T., Sullivan, M.D., ZumBrunnen, C., Morrill, R., & Mayer, J.D. (2009). Medicinal use of cannabis in the United States: Historical perspectives, current trends, and future directions. *Journal of Opioid Management*, 5, 153–168.

Alhola, P. & Polo-Kantola, P. (2007). Sleep Deprivation: Impact on cognitive performance. *Neuropsychiatric Disease and Treatment*, 3, 553–557.

Alladin, A. (2012). Cognitive hypnotherapy for major depressive disorder. *The American Journal of Clinical Hypnosis*, 54, 275–293.

American Psychiatric Association. (2013). *Diagnostic and statistical manual of mental disorders* (5th ed.). Author.

Aquina, C.T., Marques-Baptista, A., Bridgeman, P., & Merlin, M.A. (2009). Oxycontin abuse and overdose. *Postgraduate Medicine*, 121, 163–167.

Arnulf, I. (2012). REM sleep behavior disorder: Motor manifestations and pathophysiology. *Movement Disorders*, 27, 677–689.

Augustinova, M., & Ferrand, L. (2012). Suggestion does not de-automatize word reading: Evidence from the semantically based Stroop task. *Psychonomic Bulletin & Review*, 19, 521–527.

Banks, S., & Dinges, D.F. (2007). Behavioral and physiological consequences of sleep restriction. *Journal of Clinical Sleep Medicine*, 3, 519–528.

Bartke, A., Sun, L.Y., & Longo, V. (2013). Somatotropic signaling: Trade-offs between growth, reproductive development, and longevity. *Physiological Reviews*, 93, 571–598.

Berkowitz, C.D. (2012). Sudden infant death syndrome, sudden unexpected infant death, and apparent life-threatening events. *Advances in Pediatrics*, 59, 183–208.

Berry, R.B., Kryger, M.H., & Massie, C.A. (2011). A novel nasal excitatory positive airway pressure (EPAP) device for the treatment of obstructive sleep apnea: A randomized controlled trial. *Sleep*, 34, 479–485.

Bixler, E.O., Kales, A., Soldatos, C.R., Kales, J.D., & Healey, S. (1979). Prevalence of sleep disorders in the Los Angeles metropolitan area. *American Journal of Psychiatry*, 136, 1257–1262.

Bostwick, J.M. (2012). Blurred boundaries: The therapeutics and politics of medical marijuana. *Mayo Clinic Proceedings*, 87, 172–186.

Brook, R.D., Appel, L.J., Rubenfire, M., Ogedegbe, G., Bisognano, J.D., Elliott, W.K.,…Rajagopalan, S. (2013). Beyond medications and diet: Alternative approaches to lowering blood pressure: A scientific statement from the American Heart Association. *Hypertension*, 61, 1360–1383.

Broughton, R., Billings, R., Cartwright, R., Doucette, D., Edmeads, J., Edwardh, M.,…Turrell, G. (1994). Homicidal somnambulism: A case report. *Sleep*, 17, 253–264.

Brown, L.K. (2012). Can sleep deprivation studies explain why human adults sleep? *Current Opinion in Pulmonary Medicine*, 18, 541–545.

Burgess, C.R., & Scammell, T.E. (2012). Narcolepsy: Neural mechanisms of sleepiness and cataplexy. *Journal of Neuroscience*, 32, 12305–12311.

Cai, D.J., Mednick, S.A., Harrison, E.M., Kanady, J.C., & Mednick, S.C. (2009). REM, not incubation, improves creativity by priming associative networks. *Proceedings of the National Academy of Sciences, USA*, 106, 10130–10134.

Caldwell, K., Harrison, M., Adams, M., Quin, R.H., & Greeson, J. (2010). Developing mindfulness in college students through movement based courses: Effects on self-regulatory self-efficacy, mood, stress, and sleep quality. *Journal of American College Health*, 58, 433–442.

Capellini, I., Barton, R.A., McNamara, P., Preston, B.T., & Nunn, C.L. (2008). Phylogenetic analysis of the ecology and evolution of mammalian sleep. *Evolution*, 62, 1764–1776.

Cartwright, R. (2004). Sleepwalking violence: A sleep disorder, a legal dilemma, and a psychological challenge. *American Journal of Psychiatry*, 161, 1149–1158.

Cartwright, R., Agargun, M.Y., Kirkby, J., & Friedman, J.K. (2006). Relation of dreams to waking concerns. *Psychiatry Research*, 141, 261–270.

Casati, A., Sedefov, R., & Pfeiffer-Gerschel, T. (2012). Misuse of medications in the European Union: A systematic review of the literature. *European Addiction Research*, 18, 228–245.

Chen, K.W., Berger, C.C., Manheimer, E., Forde, D., Magidson, J., Dachman, L., & Lejuez, C.W. (2013). Meditative therapies for reducing anxiety: A systematic review and meta-analysis of randomized controlled trials. *Depression and Anxiety*, 29, 545–562.

Chokroverty, S. (2010). Overview of sleep & sleep disorders. *Indian Journal of Medical Research*, 131, 126–140.

Christensen, A., Bentley, G.E., Cabrera, R., Ortega, H.H., Perfito, N., Wu, T.J., & Micevych, P. (2012). Hormonal regulation of female reproduction. *Hormone and Metabolic Research*, 44, 587–591.

CNN. (1999, June 25). 'Sleepwalker' convicted of murder. http://www.cnn.com/US/9906/25/sleepwalker.01/

Cropley, M., Theadom, A., Pravettoni, G., & Webb, G. (2008). The effectiveness of smoking cessation interventions prior to surgery: A systematic review. *Nicotine and Tobacco Research*, 10, 407–412.

De la Herrán-Arita, A.K., & Drucker-Colín, R. (2012). Models for narcolepsy with cataplexy drug discovery. *Expert Opinion on Drug Discovery*, 7, 155–164.

Del Casale, A., Ferracuti, S., Rapinesi, C., Serata, D., Sani, G., Savoja, V.,…Girardi, P. (2012). Neurocognition under hypnosis: Findings from recent functional neuroimaging studies. *International Journal of Clinical and Experimental Hypnosis*, 60, 286–317.

Elkins, G., Johnson, A., & Fisher, W. (2012). Cognitive hypnotherapy for pain management. *The American Journal of Clinical Hypnosis*, 54, 294–310.

Ellenbogen, J.M., Hu, P.T., Payne, J.D., Titone, D., & Walker, M.P. (2007). Human relational memory requires time and sleep. *Proceedings of the National Academy of Sciences, USA*, 104, 7723–7728.

Fell, J., Axmacher, N., & Haupt, S. (2010). From alpha to gamma: Electrophysiological correlates meditation-related states of consciousness. *Medical Hypotheses*, 75, 218–224.

Fenn, K.M., Nusbaum, H.C., & Margoliash, D. (2003). Consolidation during sleep of perceptual learning of spoken language. *Nature*, 425, 614–616.

Ferini-Strambi, L. (2011). Does idiopathic REM sleep behavior disorder (iRBD) really exist? What are the potential markers of neurodegeneration in iRBD [Supplemental material]? *Sleep Medicine*, 12(2 Suppl.), S43–S49.

Fiorentini, A., Volonteri, L.S., Dragogna, F., Rovera, C., Maffini, M., Mauri, M.C., & Altamura, C.A. (2011). Substance-induced psychoses: A critical review of the literature. *Current Drug Abuse Reviews*, 4, 228–240.

Fogel, S.M., & Smith, C.T. (2011). The function of the sleep spindle: A physiological index of intelligence and a mechanism for sleep-dependent memory consolidation. *Neuroscience and Biobehavioral Reviews*, 35, 1154–1165.

Frank, M.G. (2006). The mystery of sleep function: Current perspectives and future directions. *Reviews in the Neurosciences*, 17, 375–392.

Freeman, M.P., Fava, M., Lake, J., Trivedi, M.H., Wisner, K.L., & Mischoulon, D. (2010). Complementary and alternative medicine in major depressive disorder: The American Psychiatric Association task force report. *The Journal of Clinical Psychiatry*, 71, 669–681.

Giedke, H., & Schwärzler, F. (2002). Therapeutic use of sleep deprivation in depression. *Sleep Medicine Reviews*, 6, 361–377.

Gold, D.R., Rogacz, S.R., Bock, N., Tosteson, T.D., Baum, T.M., Speizer, F.M., & Czeisler, C.A. (1992). Rotating shift work, sleep, and accidents related to sleepiness in hospital nurses. *American Journal of Public Health*, 82, 1011–1014.

Golden, W.L. (2012). Cognitive hypnotherapy for anxiety disorders. *The American Journal of Clinical Hypnosis*, 54, 263–274.

Gómez, R.L., Bootzin, R.R., & Nadel, L. (2006). Naps promote abstraction in language-learning infants. *Psychological Science*, 17, 670–674.

Guilleminault, C., Kirisoglu, C., Bao, G., Arias, V., Chan, A., & Li, K.K. (2005). Adult chronic sleepwalking and its treatment based on polysomnography. *Brain*, 128, 1062–1069.

Gujar, N., Yoo, S., Hu, P., & Walker, M.P. (2011). Sleep deprivation amplifies reactivity of brain reward networks, biasing the appraisal of positive emotional experiences. *The Journal of Neuroscience*, 31, 4466–4474.

Guldenmund, P., Vanhaudenhuyse, A., Boly, M., Laureys, S., & Soddu, A. (2012). A default mode of brain function in altered states of consciousness. *Archives Italiennes de Biologie*, 150, 107–121.

Haasen, C., & Krausz, M. (2001). Myths versus experience with respect to cocaine and crack: Learning from the US experience. *European Addiction Research*, 7, 159–160.

Halász, P. (1993). Arousals without awakening—Dynamic aspect of sleep. *Physiology and Behavior*, 54, 795–802.

Han, F. (2012). Sleepiness that cannot be overcome: Narcolepsy and cataplexy. *Respirology*, 17, 1157–1165.

Hardeland, R., Pandi-Perumal, S.R., & Cardinali, D.P. (2006). Melatonin. *International Journal of Biochemistry & Cell Biology*, 38, 313–316.

Henry, D., & Rosenthal, L. (2013). "Listening for his breath:" The significance of gender and partner reporting on the diagnosis, management, and treatment of obstructive sleep apnea. *Social Science & Medicine*, 79, 48–56.

Hicks, R.A., Fernandez, C., & Pelligrini, R.J. (2001). The changing sleep habits of university students: An update. *Perceptual and Motor Skills*, 93, 648.

Hicks, R.A., Johnson, C., & Pelligrini, R.J. (1992). Changes in the self-reported consistency of normal habitual sleep duration of college students (1978 and 1992). *Perceptual and Motor Skills*, 75, 1168–1170.

Hilgard, E.R., & Hilgard, J.R. (1994). *Hypnosis in the Relief of Pain*. Brunner/Mazel.

Hishikawa, Y., & Shimizu, T. (1995). Physiology of REM sleep, cataplexy, and sleep paralysis. *Advances in Neurology*, 67, 245–271.

Herman, A., & Herman, A.P. (2013). Caffeine's mechanism of action and its cosmetic use. *Skin Pharmacology and Physiology*, 26, 8–14.

Hobson, J.A. (2009). REM sleep and dreaming: Towards a theory of protoconsciousness. *Nature Reviews Neuroscience*, 10, 803–814.

Horikawa, T., Tamaki, M., Miyawaki, Y. & Kamitani, Y. (2013). Neural Decoding of Visual Imagery During Sleep. *Science*, 340(6132), 639–642. https://doi.org/10.1126/science.1234330

Hossain, J.L., & Shapiro, C.M. (2002). The prevalence, cost implications, and management of sleep disorders: An overview. *Sleep and Breathing*, 6, 85–102.

Huang, L.B., Tsai, M.C., Chen, C.Y., & Hsu, S.C. (2013). The effectiveness of light/dark exposure to treat insomnia in female nurses undertaking shift work during the evening/night shift. *Journal of Clinical Sleep Medicine*, 9, 641–646.

Huber, R., Ghilardi, M.F., Massimini, M., & Tononi, G. (2004). Local sleep and learning. *Nature*, 430, 78–81.

Jayanthi, L.D., & Ramamoorthy, S. (2005). Regulation of monoamine transporters: Influence of psychostimulants and therapeutic antidepressants. *The AAPS Journal*, 7, E728–738.

Julien, R.M. (2005). Opioid analgesics. In *A primer of drug action: A comprehensive guide to the actions, uses, and side effects of psychoactive drugs* (pp. 461–500). Worth.

Kihlstrom, J.F. (2013). Neuro-hypnotism: Prospects for hypnosis and neuroscience. *Cortex*, 49, 365–374.

Klein, D.C., Moore, R.Y., & Reppert, S.M. (Eds.). (1991). *Suprachiasmatic nucleus: The mind's clock*. Oxford University Press.

Kogan, N.M., & Mechoulam, R. (2007). Cannabinoids in health and disease. *Dialogues in Clinical Neuroscience*, 9, 413–430.

Kromann, C.B., & Nielson, C.T. (2012). A case of cola dependency in a woman with recurrent depression. *BMC Research Notes*, 5, 692.

LaBerge, S. (1990). Lucid dreaming: Psychophysiological studies of consciousness during REM sleep. In R. R. Bootzen, J.F. Kihlstrom, & D. L. Schacter (Eds.), *Sleep and cognition* (pp. 109–126). American Psychological Association.

Lang, A.J., Strauss, J.L., Bomeya, J., Bormann, J.E., Hickman, S.D., Good, R.C., & Essex, M. (2012). The theoretical and empirical basis for meditation as an intervention for PTSD. *Behavior Modification*, 36, 759–786.

Lesku, J.A., Roth, T.C., 2nd, Amlaner, C.J., & Lima, S.L. (2006). A phylogenetic analysis of sleep architecture in mammals: The integration of anatomy, physiology, and ecology. *The American Naturalist*, 168, 441–453.

Levitt, C., Shaw, E., Wong, S., & Kaczorowski, J. (2007). Systematic review of the literature on postpartum care: Effectiveness of interventions for smoking relapse prevention, cessation, and reduction in postpartum women. *Birth*, 34, 341–347.

Lifshitz, M., Aubert Bonn, N., Fischer, A., Kashem, I.F., & Raz, A. (2013). Using suggestion to modulate automatic processes: From Stroop to McGurk and beyond. *Cortex*, 49, 463–473.

Luppi, P.H., Clément, O., Sapin, E., Gervasoni, D., Peyron, C., Léger, L.,...Fort, P. (2011). The neuronal network responsible for paradoxical sleep and its dysfunctions causing narcolepsy and rapid eye movement (REM) behavior disorder. *Sleep Medicine Reviews*, 15, 153–163.

Mage, D.T., & Donner, M. (2006). Female resistance to hypoxia: Does it explain the sex difference in mortality rates? *Journal of Women's Health*, 15, 786–794.

Mahowald, M.W., & Schenck, C.H. (2000). Diagnosis and management of parasomnias. *Clinical Cornerstone*, 2, 48–54.

Mahowald, M.W., Schenck, C.H., & Cramer Bornemann, M.A. (2005). Sleep-related violence. *Current Neurology and Neuroscience Reports*, 5, 153–158.

Mather, L.E., Rauwendaal, E.R., Moxham-Hall, V.L., & Wodak, A.D. (2013). (Re) introducing medical cannabis. *The Medical Journal of Australia*, 199, 759–761.

Maxwell, J.C. (2006). *Trends in the abuse of prescription drugs. Gulf Coast Addiction Technology Transfer Center*. http://asi.nattc.org/userfiles/file/GulfCoast/PrescriptionTrends_Web.pdf

Mayo Clinic. (n.d.). *Sleep terrors (night terrors)*. http://www.mayoclinic.org/diseases-conditions/night-terrors/basics/treatment/con-20032552

McCarty, D.E. (2010). A case of narcolepsy with strictly unilateral cataplexy. *Journal of Clinical Sleep Medicine*, 15, 75–76.

McDaid, C., Durée, K.H., Griffin, S.C., Weatherly, H.L., Stradling, J.R., Davies, R.J.,... Westwood, M.E. (2009). A systematic review of continuous positive airway pressure for obstructive sleep apnoea-hypopnoea syndrome. *Sleep Medicine Reviews*, 13, 427–436.

McKim, W.A., & Hancock, S.D. (2013). *Drugs and behavior: An introduction to behavioral pharmacology, 7th edition*. Pearson.

Mignot, E.J.M. (2012). A practical guide to the therapy of narcolepsy and hypersomnia syndromes. *Neurotherapeutics*, 9, 739–752.

Miller, N.L., Shattuck, L.G., & Matsangas, P. (2010). Longitudinal study of sleep patterns of United States Military Academy cadets. *Sleep, 33,* 1623–1631.

Mitchell, E.A. (2009). SIDS: Past, present and future. *Acta Paediatrica, 98,* 1712–1719.

Montgomery, G.H., Schnur, J.B., & Kravits, K. (2012). Hypnosis for cancer care: Over 200 years young. *CA: A Cancer Journal for Clinicians, 63,* 31–44.

National Institutes of Health. (n.d.). *Information about sleep.* http://science.education.nih.gov/supplements/nih3/sleep/guide/info-sleep.htm

National Research Council. (1994). *Learning, remembering, believing: Enhancing human performance.* The National Academies Press.

National Sleep Foundation. (n.d.). *How much sleep do we really need?* http://sleepfoundation.org/how-sleep-works/how-much-sleep-do-we-really-need

Ohayon, M.M. (1997). Prevalence of DSM-IV diagnostic criteria of insomnia: Distinguishing insomnia related to mental disorders from sleep disorders. *Journal of Psychiatric Research, 31,* 333–346.

Ohayon, M.M. (2002). Epidemiology of insomnia: What we know and what we still need to learn. *Sleep Medicine Reviews, 6,* 97–111.

Ohayon, M.M., Carskadon, M.A., Guilleminault, C., & Vitiello, M.V. (2004). Meta-analysis of quantitative sleep parameters from childhood to old age in healthy individuals: Developing normative sleep values across the human lifespan. *Sleep, 27,* 1255–1273.

Ohayon, M.M., & Roth, T. (2002). Prevalence of restless legs syndrome and periodic limb movement disorder in the general population. *Journal of Psychosomatic Research, 53,* 547–554.

Poe, G.R., Walsh, C.M., & Bjorness, T.E. (2010). Cognitive neuroscience of sleep. *Progress in Brain Research, 185,* 1–19.

Porkka-Heiskanen, T. (2011). Methylxanthines and sleep. *Handbook of Experimental Pharmacology, 200,* 331–348.

Presser, H.B. (1995). Job, family, and gender: Determinants of nonstandard work schedules among employed Americans in 1991. *Demography, 32,* 577–598.

Pressman, M.R. (2007). Disorders of arousal from sleep and violent behavior: The role of physical contact and proximity. *Sleep, 30,* 1039–1047.

Provini, F., Tinuper, P., Bisulli, F., & Lagaresi, E. (2011). Arousal disorders [Supplemental material]. *Sleep Medicine, 12*(2 Suppl.), S22–S26.

Rattenborg, N.C., Lesku, J.A., Martinez-Gonzalez, D., & Lima, S.L. (2007). The non-trivial functions of sleep. *Sleep Medicine Reviews, 11,* 405–409.

Raz, A. (2011). Hypnosis: A twilight zone of the top-down variety: Few have never heard of hypnosis but most know little about the potential of this mind-body regulation technique for advancing science. *Trends in Cognitive Sciences, 15,* 555–557.

Raz, A., Shapiro, T., Fan, J., & Posner, M.I. (2002). Hypnotic suggestion and the modulation of Stroop interference. *Archives of General Psychiatry, 59,* 1151–1161.

Reiner, K., Tibi, L., & Lipsitz, J.D. (2013). Do mindfulness-based interventions reduce pain intensity? A critical review of the literature. *Pain Medicine, 14,* 230–242.

Restless Legs Syndrome Foundation. (n.d.). *Restless legs syndrome: Causes, diagnosis, and treatment for the patient living with Restless legs syndrome (RSL).* www.rls.org

Rial, R.V., Nicolau, M.C., Gamundí, A., Akaârir, M., Aparicio, S., Garau, C.,…Esteban, S. (2007). The trivial function of sleep. *Sleep Medicine Reviews, 11,* 311–325.

Riemann, D., Berger, M., & Volderholzer, U. (2001). Sleep and depression—Results from psychobiological studies: An overview. *Biological Psychology, 57,* 67–103.

Reinerman, C. (2007, October 14). 5 myths about that demon crack. *Washington Post.* http://www.washingtonpost.com/wp-dyn/content/article/2007/10/09/AR2007100900751.html

Reissig, C.J., Strain, E.C., & Griffiths, R.R. (2009). Caffeinated energy drinks—A growing problem. *Drug and Alcohol Dependence, 99,* 1–10.

Robson, P.J. (2014). Therapeutic potential of cannabinoid medicines. *Drug Testing and Analysis, 6,* 24–30.

Roth, T. (2007). Insomnia: Definition, prevalence, etiology, and consequences [Supplemental material]. *Journal of Clinical Sleep Medicine, 3*(5 Suppl.), S7–S10.

Rothman, R.B., Blough, B.E., & Baumann, M.H. (2007). Dual dopamine/serotonin releasers as potential medications for stimulant and alcohol addictions. *The AAPS Journal, 9,* E1–10.

Sánchez-de-la-Torre, M., Campos-Rodriguez, F., & Barbé, F. (2012). Obstructive sleep apnoea and cardiovascular disease. *The Lancet Respiratory Medicine, 1,* 31–72.

Savard, J., Simard, S., Ivers, H., & Morin, C.M. (2005). Randomized study on the efficacy of cognitive-behavioral therapy for insomnia secondary to breast cancer, part I: Sleep and psychological effects. *Journal of Clinical Oncology, 23,* 6083–6096.

Schicho, R., & Storr, M. (2014). Cannabis finds its way into treatment of Crohn's disease. *Pharmacology, 93,* 1–3.

Shukla, R. K, Crump, J.L., & Chrisco, E.S. (2012). An evolving problem: Methamphetamine production and trafficking in the United States. *International Journal of Drug Policy, 23,* 426–435.

Siegel, J.M. (2008). Do all animals sleep? *Trends in Neuroscience, 31,* 208–213.

Siegel, J.M. (2001). The REM sleep-memory consolidation hypothesis. *Science, 294,* 1058–1063.

Singh, G.K., & Siahpush, M. (2006). Widening socioeconomic inequalities in US life expectancy, 1980–2000. *International Journal of Epidemiology, 35,* 969–979.

Smedslund, G., Fisher, K.J., Boles, S.M., & Lichtenstein, E. (2004). The effectiveness of workplace smoking cessation programmes: A meta-analysis of recent studies. *Tobacco Control, 13,* 197–204.

Sofikitis, N., Giotitsas, N., Tsounapi, P., Baltogiannis, D., Giannakis, D., & Pardalidis, N. (2008). Hormonal regulation of spermatogenesis and spermiogenesis. *Journal of Steroid Biochemistry and Molecular Biology, 109,* 323–330.

Steriade, M., & Amzica, F. (1998). Slow sleep oscillation, rhythmic K-complexes, and their paroxysmal developments [Supplemental material]. *Journal of Sleep Research, 7*(1 Suppl.), 30–35.

Stickgold, R. (2005). Sleep-dependent memory consolidation. *Nature, 437,* 1272–1278.

Stone, K.C., Taylor, D.J., McCrae, C.S., Kalsekar, A., & Lichstein, K.L. (2008). Nonrestorative sleep. *Sleep Medicine Reviews, 12,* 275–288.

Suchecki, D., Tiba, P.A., & Machado, R.B. (2012). REM sleep rebound as an adaptive response to stressful situations. *Frontiers in Neuroscience, 3.* https://doi.org/ 10.3389/fneur.2012.00041

Taillard, J., Philip, P., Coste, O., Sagaspe, P., & Bioulac, B. (2003). The circadian and homeostatic modulation of sleep pressure during wakefulness differs between morning and evening chronotypes. *Journal of Sleep Research, 12,* 275–282.

Task Force on Sudden Infant Death Syndrome. (2011). SIDS and other sleep-related infant deaths: Expansion of recommendations for a safe infant sleeping environment. *Pediatrics*, 128, 1030–1039.

Thach, B.T. (2005). The role of respiratory control disorders in SIDS. *Respiratory Physiology & Neurobiology*, 149, 343–353.

U.S. Food and Drug Administration. (2013, October 24). *Statement on Proposed Hydrocodone Reclassification from Janet Woodcock, M.D., Director, Center for Drug Evaluation and Research.* http://www.fda.gov/drugs/drugsafety/ucm372089.htm

Vogel, G.W. (1975). A review of REM sleep deprivation. *Archives of General Psychiatry*, 32, 749–761.

Vøllestad, J., Nielsen, M.B., & Nielsen, G.H. (2012). Mindfulness- and acceptance-based interventions for anxiety disorders: A systematic review and meta-analysis. *The British Journal of Clinical Psychology*, 51, 239–260.

Wagner, U., Gais, S., & Born, J. (2001). Emotional memory formation is enhanced across sleep intervals with high amounts of rapid eye movement sleep. *Learning & Memory*, 8, 112–119.

Wagner, U., Gais, S., Haider, H., Verleger, R., & Born, J. (2004). Sleep improves insight. *Nature*, 427, 352–355.

Walker, M.P. (2009). The role of sleep in cognition and emotion. *Annals of the New York Academy of Sciences*, 1156, 168–197.

Wark, D.M. (2011). Traditional and alert hypnosis for education: A literature review. *The American Journal of Clinical Hypnosis*, 54(2), 96–106.

Waterhouse, J., Fukuda, Y., & Morita, T. (2012). Daily rhythms of the sleep-wake cycle [Special issue]. *Journal of Physiological Anthropology*, 31(5). https://doi.org/10.1186/1880-6805-31-5

Welsh, D.K. Takahashi, J.S., & Kay, S.A. (2010). Suprachiasmatic nucleus: Cell autonomy and network properties. *Annual Review of Physiology*, 72, 551–577.

West, S., Boughton, M., & Byrnes, M. (2009). Juggling multiple temporalities: The shift work story of mid-life nurses. *Journal of Nursing Management*, 17, 110–119.

White, D.P. (2005). Pathogenesis of obstructive and central sleep apnea. *American Journal of Respiratory and Critical Care Medicine*, 172, 1363–1370.

Williams, J., Roth, A., Vatthauer, K., & McCrae, C.S. (2013). Cognitive behavioral treatment of insomnia. *Chest*, 143, 554–565.

Williamson, A.M., & Feyer, A.M. (2000). Moderate sleep deprivation produces impairments in cognitive and motor performance equivalent to legally prescribed levels of alcohol intoxication. *Occupational and Environmental Medicine*, 57, 649–655.

Wolt, B.J., Ganetsky, M., & Babu, K.M. (2012). Toxicity of energy drinks. *Current Opinion in Pediatrics*, 24, 243–251.

Zangini, S., Calandra-Buonaura, G., Grimaldi, D., & Cortelli, P. (2011). REM behaviour disorder and neurodegenerative diseases [Supplemental material]. *Sleep Medicine*, 12(2 Suppl.), S54–S58.

Zeidan, F., Grant, J.A., Brown, C.A., McHaffie, J.G., & Coghill, R.C. (2012). Mindfulness meditation-related pain relief: Evidence for unique brain mechanisms in the regulation of pain. *Neuroscience Letters*, 520, 165–173.

Chapter 4

Aaron, J.I., Mela, D.J., & Evans, R.E. (1994). The influences of attitudes, beliefs, and label information on perceptions of reduced-fat spread. *Appetite*, 22, 25–37.

Abraira, V.E., & Ginty, D.D. (2013). The sensory neurons of touch. *Neuron*, 79, 618–639.

Ayabe-Kanamura, S., Saito, S., Distel, H., Martínez-Gómez, M., & Hudson, R. (1998). Differences and similarities in the perception of everyday odors: A Japanese-German cross-cultural study. *Annals of the New York Academy of Sciences*, 855, 694–700.

Chen, Q., Deng, H., Brauth, S.E., Ding, L., & Tang, Y. (2012). Reduced performance of prey targeting in pit vipers with contralaterally occluded infrared and visual senses. *PloS ONE*, 7(5), e34989. https://doi.org/10.1371/journal.pone.0034989

Comfort, A. (1971). Likelihood of human pheromones. *Nature*, 230, 432–479.

Correll, J., Park, B., Judd, C.M., & Wittenbrink, B. (2002). The police officer's dilemma: Using ethnicity to disambiguate potentially threatening individuals. *Journal of Personality and Social Psychology*, 83, 1314–1329.

Correll, J., Urland, G.R., & Ito, T.A. (2006). Event-related potentials and the decision to shoot: The role of threat perception and cognitive control. *The Journal of Experimental Social Psychology*, 42, 120–128.

Dunkle T. (1982). The sound of silence. *Science*, 82, 30–33.

Fawcett, S.L., Wang, Y., & Birch, E.E. (2005). The critical period for susceptibility of human stereopsis. *Investigative Ophthalmology and Visual Science*, 46, 521–525.

Furlow, F.B. (1996, 2012). The smell of love. http://www.psychologytoday.com/articles/200910/the-smell-love

Galanter, E. (1962). Contemporary Psychophysics. In R. Brown, E. Galanter, E.H. Hess, & G. Mandler (Eds.), New directions in psychology. Holt, Rinehart & Winston.

Garland, E.L. (2012). Pain processing in the human nervous system: A selective review of nociceptive and biobehavioral pathways. *Primary Care*, 39, 561–571.

Goolkasian, P. & Woodbury, C. (2010). Priming effects with ambiguous figures. *Attention, Perception & Psychophysics*, 72, 168–178.

Grothe, B., Pecka, M., & McAlpine, D. (2010). Mechanisms of sound localization in mammals. *Physiological Reviews*, 90, 983–1012.

Hartline, P.H., Kass, L., & Loop, M.S. (1978). Merging of modalities in the optic tectum: Infrared and visual integration in rattlesnakes. *Science*, 199, 1225–1229.

Kaiser, P.K. (1997). *The joy of visual perception: A web book.* http://www.yorku.ca/eye/noframes.htm

Khan, S., & Chang, R. (2013). Anatomy of the vestibular system: A review. *NeuroRehabilitation*, 32, 437–443.

Kinnamon, S.C., & Vandenbeuch, A. (2009). Receptors and transduction of umami taste stimuli. *Annals of the New York Academy of Sciences*, 1170, 55–59.

Kunst-Wilson, W.R., & Zajonc, R.B. (1980). Affective discrimination of stimuli that cannot be recognized. *Science*, 207, 557–558.

Lackner, J.R., & DiZio, P. (2005). Vestibular, proprioceptive, and haptic contributions to spatial orientation. *Annual Review of Psychology*, 56, 115–147.

Land, E.H. (1959). Color vision and the natural image. Part 1. *Proceedings of the National Academy of Science*, 45(1), 115–129.

Liem, D.G., Westerbeek, A., Wolterink, S., Kok, F.J., & de Graaf, C. (2004). Sour taste preferences of children relate to preference for novel and intense stimuli. *Chemical Senses*, 29, 713–720.

Lodovichi, C., & Belluscio, L. (2012). Odorant receptors in the formation of olfactory bulb circuitry. *Physiology*, 27, 200–212.

Loersch, C., Durso, G.R. O., & Petty, R.E. (2013). Vicissitudes of desire: A matching mechanism for subliminal persuasion. *Social Psychological and Personality Science, 4*(5), 624–631.

Maffei, A., Haley, M., & Fontanini, A. (2012). Neural processing of gustatory information in insular circuits. *Current Opinion in Neurobiology, 22,* 709–716.

Milner, A.D., & Goodale, M.A. (2008). Two visual systems re-viewed. *Neuropsychological, 46,* 774–785.

Mizushige, T., Inoue, K., Fushiki, T. (2007). Why is fat so tasty? Chemical reception of fatty acid on the tongue. *Journal of Nutritional Science and Vitaminology, 53,* 1–4.

Most, S.B., Simons, D.J., Scholl, B.J., & Chabris, C.F. (2000). Sustained inattentional blindness: The role of location in the detection of unexpected dynamic events. *PSYCHE, 6*(14).

Nelson, M.R. (2008). The hidden persuaders: Then and now. *Journal of Advertising, 37*(1), 113–126.

Niimura, Y., & Nei, M. (2007). Extensive gains and losses of olfactory receptor genes in mammalian evolution. *PLoS ONE, 2,* e708.

Okawa, H., & Sampath, A.P. (2007). Optimization of single-photon response transmission at the rod-to-rod bipolar synapse. *Physiology, 22,* 279–286.

Payne, B.K. (2001). Prejudice and perception: The role of automatic and controlled processes in misperceiving a weapon. *Journal of Personality and Social Psychology, 81,* 181–192.

Payne, B.K., Shimizu, Y., & Jacoby, L.L. (2005). Mental control and visual illusions: Toward explaining race-biased weapon misidentifications. *Journal of Experimental Social Psychology, 41,* 36–47.

Peck, M. (2012, July 19). *How a movie changed one man's vision forever.* http://www.bbc.com/future/story/20120719-awoken-from-a-2d-world

Peterson, M.A., & Gibson, B.S. (1994). Must figure-ground organization precede object recognition? An assumption in peril. *Psychological Science, 5,* 253–259.

Petho, G., & Reeh, P.W. (2012). Sensory and signaling mechanisms of bradykinin, eicosanoids, platelet-activating factor, and nitric oxide in peripheral nociceptors. *Physiological Reviews, 92,* 1699–1775.

Proske, U. (2006). Kinesthesia: The role of muscle receptors. *Muscle & Nerve, 34,* 545–558.

Proske, U., & Gandevia, S.C. (2012). The proprioceptive senses: Their roles in signaling body shape, body position and movement, and muscle force. *Physiological Reviews, 92,* 1651–1697.

Purvis, K., & Haynes, N.B. (1972). The effect of female rat proximity on the reproductive system of male rats. *Physiology & Behavior, 9,* 401–407.

Radel, R., Sarrazin, P., Legrain, P., & Gobancé, L. (2009). Subliminal priming of motivational orientation in educational settings: Effect on academic performance moderated by mindfulness. *Journal of Research in Personality, 43*(4), 1–18.

Rauschecker, J.P., & Tian, B. (2000). Mechanisms and streams for processing "what" and "where" in auditory cortex. *Proceedings of the National Academy of Sciences, USA, 97,* 11800–11806.

Renier, L.A., Anurova, I., De Volder, A.G., Carlson, S., VanMeter, J., & Rauschecker, J.P. (2009). Multisensory integration of sounds and vibrotactile stimuli in processing streams for "what" and "where." *Journal of Neuroscience, 29,* 10950–10960.

Rensink, R.A. (2004). Visual sensing without seeing. *Psychological Science, 15,* 27–32.

Rock, I., & Palmer, S. (1990). The legacy of Gestalt psychology. *Scientific American, 262,* 84–90.

Roper, S.D. (2013). Taste buds as peripheral chemosensory receptors. *Seminars in Cell & Developmental Biology, 24,* 71–79.

Russell, M.J. (1976). Human olfactory communication. *Nature, 260,* 520–522.

Sachs, B.D. (1997). Erection evoked in male rats by airborne scent from estrous females. *Physiology & Behavior, 62,* 921–924.

Segall, M.H., Campbell, D.T., & Herskovits, M.J. (1963). Cultural differences in the perception of geometric illusions. *Science, 139,* 769–771.

Segall, M.H., Campbell, D.T., & Herskovits, M.J. (1966). *The influence of culture on visual perception.* Bobbs-Merrill.

Segall, M.H., Dasen, P.P., Berry, J.W., & Poortinga, Y.H. (1999). *Human behavior in global perspective* (2nd ed.). Allyn & Bacon.

Semaan, M.T., & Megerian, C.A. (2010). Contemporary perspectives on the pathophysiology of Meniere's disease: implications for treatment. *Current opinion in Otolaryngology & Head and Neck Surgery, 18*(5), 392–398.

Shamma, S. (2001). On the role of space and time in auditory processing. *Trends in Cognitive Sciences, 5,* 340–348.

Simons, D.J., & Chabris, C.F. (1999). Gorillas in our midst: Sustained inattentional blindness for dynamic events. *Perception, 28,* 1059–1074.

Spors, H., Albeanu, D.F., Murthy, V.N., Rinberg, D., Uchida, N., Wachowiak, M., & Friedrich, R.W. (2013). Illuminating vertebrate olfactory processing. *Journal of Neuroscience, 32,* 14102–14108.

Spray, D.C. (1986). Cutaneous temperature receptors. *Annual Review of Physiology, 48,* 625–638.

Strain, G.M. (2003). *How well do dogs and other animals hear?* http://www.lsu.edu/deafness/HearingRange.html

Swets, J.A. (1964). Signal detection and recognition by human observers. *Psychological Bulletin, 60,* 429–441.

Ungerleider, L.G., & Haxby, J.V. (1994). 'What' and 'where' in the human brain. *Current Opinion in Neurobiology, 4,* 157–165.

U.S. National Library of Medicine. (2013). Genetics home reference: Congenital insensitivity to pain. http://ghr.nlm.nih.gov/condition/congenital-insensitivity-to-pain

Vecera, S.P., & O'Reilly, R.C. (1998). Figure-ground organization and object recognition processes: An interactive account. *Journal of Experimental Psychology-Human Perception and Performance, 24,* 441–462.

Wakakuwa, M., Stavenga, D.G., & Arikawa, K. (2007). Spectral organization of ommatidia in flower-visiting insects. *Photochemistry and Photobiology, 83,* 27–34.

Weller, A. (1998). Human pheromones: Communication through body odour. *Nature, 392,* 126–127.

Wells, D.L. (2010). Domestic dogs and human health: An overview. *British Journal of Health Psychology, 12,* 145–156.

Wolfgang-Kimball, D. (1992). Pheromones in humans: myth or reality?. http://www.anapsid.org/pheromones.html

Wysocki, C.J., & Preti, G. (2004). Facts, fallacies, fears, and frustrations with human pheromones. *The Anatomical Record Part A: Discoveries in Molecular, Cellular, and Evolutionary Biology, 281,* 1201–1211.

Chapter 5

Anderson, C.A., & Gentile, D.A. (2008). Media violence, aggression, and public policy. In E. Borgida & S. Fiske (Eds.), *Beyond common sense: Psychological science in the courtroom* (p. 322). Blackwell.

Bandura, A., Ross, D., & Ross, S.A. (1961). Transmission of aggression through imitation of aggressive models. *Journal of Abnormal and Social Psychology, 63,* 575–582.

Cangi, K., & Daly, M. (2013). The effects of token economies on the occurrence of appropriate and inappropriate behaviors by children with autism in a social skills setting. *West Chester University: Journal of Undergraduate Research*. http://www.wcupa.edu/UndergraduateResearch/journal/documents/cangi_S2012.pdf

Carlson, L., Holscher, C., Shipley, T., & Conroy Dalton, R. (2010). Getting lost in buildings. *Current Directions in Psychological Science, 19*(5), 284–289.

Cialdini, R.B. (2008). *Influence: Science and practice* (5th ed.). Pearson Education.

Chance, P. (2009). *Learning and behavior* (6th ed.). Wadsworth, Cengage Learning.

DeAngelis, T. (2010). 'Little Albert' regains his identity. *Monitor on Psychology, 41*(1), 10.

Franzen, H. (2001, May 24). Gambling, like food and drugs, produces feelings of reward in the brain. Scientific American [online]. http://www.scientificamerican.com/article.cfm?id=gamblinglike-food-and-dru

Fryer, R.G., Jr. (2010, April). Financial incentives and student achievement: Evidence from randomized trials. *National Bureau of Economic Research [NBER] Working Paper, No. 15898*. http://www.nber.org/papers/w15898

Garcia, J., & Koelling, R.A. (1966). Relation of cue to consequence in avoidance learning. *Psychonomic Science, 4*, 123–124.

Garcia, J., & Rusiniak, K.W. (1980). What the nose learns from the mouth. In D. Müller-Schwarze & R. M. Silverstein (Eds.), *Chemical signals: Vertebrates and aquatic invertebrates* (pp. 141–156). Plenum Press.

Gershoff, E.T. (2002). Corporal punishment by parents and associated child behaviors and experiences: A meta-analytic and theoretical review. *Psychological Bulletin, 128*(4), 539–579. https://doi.org/10.1037//0033-2909.128.4.539

Gershoff, E.T., Grogan-Kaylor, A., Lansford, J.E., Chang, L., Zelli, A., Deater-Deckard, K., & Dodge, K.A. (2010). Parent discipline practices in an international sample: Associations with child behaviors and moderation by perceived normativeness. *Child Development, 81*(2), 487–502.

Hickock, G. (2010). The role of mirror neurons in speech and language processing. *Brain and Language*, 112, 1–2.

Holmes, S. (1993). Food avoidance in patients undergoing cancer chemotherapy. *Support Care Cancer, 1*(6), 326–330.

Hunt, M. (2007). *The story of psychology*. Doubleday.

Huston, A.C., Donnerstein, E., Fairchild, H., Feshbach, N.D., Katz, P.A., Murray, J.P.,…Zuckerman, D. (1992). *Big world, small screen: The role of television in American society*. University of Nebraska Press.

Hutton, J.L., Baracos, V.E., & Wismer, W.V. (2007). Chemosensory dysfunction is a primary factor in the evolution of declining nutritional status and quality of life with patients with advanced cancer. *Journal of Pain Symptom Management, 33*(2), 156–165.

Illinois Institute for Addiction Recovery. (n.d.). *WTVP on gambling*. http://www.addictionrecov.org/InTheNews/Gambling/

Jacobsen, P.B., Bovbjerg, D.H., Schwartz, M.D., Andrykowski, M.A., Futterman, A.D., Gilewski, T.,…Redd, W.H. (1993). Formation of food aversions in cancer patients receiving repeated infusions of chemotherapy. *Behaviour Research and Therapy, 31*(8), 739–748.

Kirsch, SJ (2010). Media and youth: A developmental perspective. Wiley Blackwell.

Lefrançois, G.R. (2012). *Theories of human learning: What the professors said* (6th ed.). Wadsworth, Cengage Learning.

Miller, L.E., Grabell, A., Thomas, A., Bermann, E., & Graham-Bermann, S.A. (2012). The associations between community violence, television violence, intimate partner violence, parent-child aggression, and aggression in sibling relationships of a sample of preschoolers. *Psychology of Violence, 2*(2), 165–78. https://doi.org/10.1037/a0027254

Murrell, A., Christoff, K. & Henning, K. (2007) Characteristics of domestic violence offenders: associations with childhood exposure to violence. *Journal of Family Violence, 22*(7), 523-532.

Pavlov, I.P. (1927). *Conditioned reflexes: An investigation of the physiological activity of the cerebral cortex* (G. V. Anrep, Ed. & Trans.). Oxford University Press.

Rizzolatti, G., Fadiga, L., Fogassi, L., & Gallese, V. (2002). From mirror neurons to imitation: Facts and speculations. In A. N. Meltzoff & W. Prinz (Eds.), *The imitative mind: Development, evolution, and brain bases* (pp. 247–66). Cambridge University Press.

Rizzolatti, G., Fogassi, L., & Gallese, V. (2006, November). Mirrors in the mind. *Scientific American* [online], pp. 54–61.

Roy, A., Adinoff, B., Roehrich, L., Lamparski, D., Custer, R., Lorenz, V.,…Linnoila, M. (1988). Pathological gambling: A psychobiological study. *Archives of General Psychiatry, 45*(4), 369–373. https://doi.org/10.1001/archpsyc.1988.01800280085011

Skinner, B.F. (1938). *The behavior of organisms: An experimental analysis*. Appleton-Century-Crofts.

Skinner, B.F. (1953). *Science and human behavior*. Macmillan.

Skinner, B.F. (1961). *Cumulative record: A selection of papers*. Appleton-Century-Crofts.

Skinner's utopia: Panacea, or path to hell? (1971, September 20). *Time* [online]. http://www.wou.edu/~girodm/611/Skinner%27s_utopia.pdf

Skolin, I., Wahlin, Y.B., Broman, D.A., Hursti, U-K. K., Larsson, M.V., & Hernell, O. (2006). Altered food intake and taste perception in children with cancer after start of chemotherapy: Perspectives of children, parents and nurses. *Supportive Care in Cancer*, 14, 369–78.

Thorndike, E.L. (1911). Animal intelligence: An experimental study of the associative processes in animals. *Psychological Monographs*, 8.

Tolman, E.C., & Honzik, C.H. (1930). Degrees of hunger, reward, and non-reward, and maze performance in rats. *University of California Publications in Psychology*, 4, 241–256.

Tolman, E.C., Ritchie, B.F., & Kalish, D. (1946). Studies in spatial learning: II. Place learning versus response learning. *Journal of Experimental Psychology*, 36, 221–229. https://doi.org/10.1037/h0060262

Watson, J.B. (1919). *Psychology from the standpoint of a behaviorist*. J. B. Lippincott.

Watson, J.B. & Rayner, R. (1920). Conditioned emotional reactions. *Journal of Experimental Psychology*, 3, 1–14.

Yamamoto, S., Humle, T., & Tanaka, M. (2013). Basis for cumulative cultural evolution in chimpanzees: Social learning of a more efficient tool-use technique. *PLoS ONE, 8*(1): e55768. https://doi.org/10.1371/journal.pone.0055768

Chapter 6

Abler, W. (2013). Sapir, Harris, and Chomsky in the twentieth century. *Cognitive Critique*, 7, 29–48.

American Association on Intellectual and Developmental Disabilities. (2013). *Definition of intellectual disability*. http://aaidd.org/intellectual-disability/definition#.UmkR2xD2Bh4

American Psychological Association. (2013). In *Diagnostic and statistical manual of psychological disorders* (5th ed., pp. 34–36). American Psychological Association.

Aronson, E. (Ed.). (1995). Social cognition. In *The social animal* (p. 151). W.H. Freeman and Company.

Atkins v. Virginia, 00-8452 (2002).

Bartels, M., Rietveld, M., Van Baal, G., & Boomsma, D.I. (2002). Genetic and environmental influences on the development of intelligence. *Behavior Genetics*, *32*(4), 237–238.

Bartlett, F.C. (1932). Remembering: A study in experimental and social psychology. Cambridge University Press.

Barton, S.M. (2003). Classroom accommodations for students with dyslexia. *Learning Disabilities Journal*, 13, 10–14.

Bayer, J.B., & Campbell, S.W. (2012). Texting while driving on automatic: Considering the frequency-independent side of habit. *Computers in Human Behavior*, 28, 2083–2090.

Berlin, B., & Kay, P. (1969). *Basic color terms: Their universality and evolution*. University of California Press.

Berninger, V.W. (2008). Defining and differentiating dysgraphia, dyslexia, and language learning disability within a working memory model. In M. Mody & E. R. Silliman (Eds.), *Brain, behavior, and learning in language and reading disorders* (pp. 103–134). The Guilford Press.

Blossom, M., & Morgan, J.L. (2006). Does the face say what the mouth says? A study of infants' sensitivity to visual prosody. In the 30th annual Boston University Conference on Language Development, Somerville, MA.

Boake, C. (2002, May 24). From the Binet-Simon to the Wechsler-Bellevue: Tracing the history of intelligence testing. *Journal of Clinical and Experimental Neuropsychology*, *24*(3), 383–405.

Boroditsky, L. (2001). Does language shape thought? Mandarin and English speakers' conceptions of time. *Cognitive Psychology*, 43, 1–22.

Boroditsky, L. (2011, February). How language shapes thought. *Scientific American*, 63–65. Chomsky, N. (1965). Aspects of the theory of syntax. MIT Press

Bouchard, T.J., Lykken, D.T., McGue, M., Segal, N.L., & Tellegen, A. (1990). Sources of human psychological differences: The Minnesota Study of Twins Reared Apart. *Science*, 250, 223–228.

Cairns Regional Council. (n.d.). Cultural greetings. http://www.cairns.qld.gov.au/__data/assets/pdf_file/0007/8953/CulturalGreetingExercise.pdf

Callero, P.L. (1994). From role-playing to role-using: Understanding role as resource. *Social Psychology Quarterly*, 57, 228–243.

Cattell, R. (1963). Theory of fluid and crystallized intelligence: A critical experiment. *Journal of Educational Psychology*, *54*(1), 1–22.

Cianciolo, A.T., & Sternberg, R.J. (2004). *Intelligence: A brief history*. Blackwell Publishing.

Chomsky, N. (1965). Aspects of the theory of syntax. MIT Press

Corballis, M.C., & Suddendorf, T. (2007). Memory, time, and language. In C. Pasternak (Ed.), *What makes us human* (pp. 17–36). Oneworld Publications.

Constitutional Rights Foundation. (2013). Gandhi and civil disobedience. http://www.crf-usa.org/black-history-month/gandhi-and-civil-disobedience

Cropley, A. (2006). In praise of convergent thinking. *Creativity Research Journal*, *18*(3), 391–404.

Csikszentmihalyi, M., & Csikszentmihalyi, I. (1993). Family influences on the development of giftedness. *Ciba Foundation Symposium*, 178, 187–206.

Curtiss, S. (1981). Dissociations between language and cognition: Cases and implications. *Journal of Autism and Developmental Disorders*, *11*(1), 15–30.

Cyclopedia of Puzzles. (n.d.) http://www.mathpuzzle.com/loyd/

Dates and Events. (n.d.). *Oprah Winfrey timeline*. http://www.datesandevents.org/people-timelines/05-oprah-winfrey-timeline.htm

Fernández, E.M., & Cairns, H.S. (2011). *Fundamentals of psycholinguistics*. Wiley-Blackwell.

Flanagan, D., & Kaufman, A. (2004). *Essentials of WISC-IV assessment*. John Wiley and Sons, Inc.

Flynn, J., Shaughnessy, M.F., & Fulgham, S.W. (2012) Interview with Jim Flynn about the Flynn effect. *North American Journal of Psychology*, *14*(1), 25–38.

Fox, M. (2012, November 1). Arthur R. Jensen dies at 89; Set off debate about I.Q. *New York Times*, p. B15.

Fromkin, V., Krashen, S., Curtiss, S., Rigler, D., & Rigler, M. (1974). The development of language in Genie: A case of language acquisition beyond the critical period. *Brain and Language*, 1, 81–107.

Furnham, A. (2009). The validity of a new, self-report measure of multiple intelligence. *Current Psychology: A Journal for Diverse Perspectives on Diverse Psychological Issues*, 28, 225–239.

Gardner, H. (1983). *Frames of mind: The theory of multiple intelligences*. Basic Books.

Gardner, H., & Moran, S. (2006). The science of multiple intelligences theory: A response to Lynn Waterhouse. *Educational Psychologist*, 41, 227–232.

German, T.P., & Barrett, H.C. (2005). Functional fixedness in a technologically sparse culture. *Psychological Science*, 16, 1–5.

Goad, B. (2013, January 25). *SSA wants to stop calling people 'mentally retarded.'* http://thehill.com/blogs/regwatch/pending-regs/279399-ssa-wants-to-stop-calling-people-mentally-retarded

Goldstone, R.L., & Kersten, A. (2003). Concepts and categorization. In A.F. Healy, R.W. Proctor, & I.B. Weiner (Eds.), *Handbook of psychology* (Vol. 4, pp. 599–622). John Wiley & Sons, Inc.

Goleman, D. (1995). *Emotional intelligence; Why it can matter more than IQ*. Bantam Books.

Gordon, O.E. (1995). *Francis Galton (1822–1911)*. http://www.psych.utah.edu/gordon/Classes/Psy4905Docs/PsychHistory/Cards/Galton.html

Gresham, F.M., & Witt, J.C. (1997). Utility of intelligence tests for treatment planning, classification, and placement decisions: Recent empirical findings and future directions. *School Psychology Quarterly*, *12*(3), 249–267.

Guilford, J.P. (1967). *The nature of human intelligence*. McGraw Hill.

Heaton, S. (2004). Making the switch: Unlocking the mystery of the WISC-IV. *Case Conference*. University of Florida.

Jensen, J. (2011). Phoneme acquisition: Infants and second language learners. *The Language Teacher*, *35*(6), 24–28.

Johnson, J.S., & Newport, E.L. (1989). Critical period effects in second language learning: The influence of maturational state on the acquisition of English as a second language. *Cognitive Psychology*, 21, 60–99.

Kahneman, D. (2011). Thinking, fast and slow. Farrar, Straus, and Giroux.

Kishyama, M.M., Boyce, W.T., Jimenez, A.M., Perry, L.M., & Knight, R.T. (2009). Socioeconomic disparities affect prefrontal function in children. *Journal of Cognitive Neuroscience*, *21*(6), 1106–1115.

Klein, P.D. (1997). Multiplying the problems of intelligence by eight: A critique of Gardner's theory. *Canadian Journal of Education*, 22, 377-94.

Larry P v. Riles, C-71-2270 RFP. (1979).

Lenneberg, E. (1967). Biological foundations of language. Wiley.

Liptak, A. (2008, January 19). Lawyer reveals secret, toppling death sentence. *New York Times*. http://www.nytimes.com/2008/01/19/us/19death.html?_r=0

Locke, E.A. (2005, April 14). Why emotional intelligence is an invalid concept. *Journal of Organizational Behavior*, 26, 425–431.

Mayer, J.D., Salovey, P., & Caruso, D. (2004). Emotional intelligence: Theory, findings, and implications, *Psychological Inquiry*, 15(3), 197–215.

Modgil, S., & Routledge, C.M. (Eds.). (1987). *Arthur Jensen: Consensus and controversy*. Falmer Press.

Morgan, H. (1996). An analysis of Gardner's theory of multiple intelligence. *Roeper Review: A Journal on Gifted Education*, 18, 263–269.

Moskowitz, B.A. (1978). The acquisition of language. *Scientific American*, 239, 92–108.

Neyfakh, L. (2013, October 7). "Why you can't stop checking your phone." http://www.bostonglobe.com/ideas/2013/10/06/why-you-can-stop-checking-your-phone/rrBJzyBGDAr1YlEH5JQDcM/story.html

Parker, J.D., Saklofske, D.H., & Stough, C. (Eds.). (2009). *Assessing emotional intelligence: Theory, research, and applications*. New York: Springer.

Petitto, L.A., Holowka, S., Sergio, L.E., Levy, B., & Ostry, D.J. (2004). Baby hands that move to the rhythm of language: Hearing babies acquiring sign languages babble silently on the hands. Cognition, 93, 43–73.

Pickens, J. (1994). Full-term and preterm infants' perception of face-voice synchrony. *Infant Behavior and Development*, 17, 447–455.

Pratkanis, A. (1989). The cognitive representation of attitudes. In A. R. Pratkanis, S.J. Breckler, & A. G. Greenwald (Eds.), *Attitude structure and function* (pp. 71–98). Erlbaum.

Regier, T., & Kay, P. (2009). Language, thought, and color: Whorf was half right. *Trends in Cognitive Sciences*, 13(10), 439–446.

Riccio, C.A., Gonzales, J.J., & Hynd, G.W. (1994). Attention-deficit Hyperactivity Disorder (ADHD) and learning disabilities. *Learning Disability Quarterly*, 17, 311–322.

Richardson, K. (2002). What IQ tests test. *Theory & Psychology*, 12(3), 283–314.

Roberts, D. (2014, May 27). U.S. Supreme Court bars Florida from using IQ score cutoff for executions. *The Guardian*. http://www.theguardian.com/world/2014/may/27/us-supreme-court-iq-score-cutoff-florida-execution

Rushton, J.P., & Jensen, A.R. (2005). Thirty years of research on race differences in cognitive ability. *Psychology, public policy, and law*, 11(2), 235–294.

Rymer, R. (1993). *Genie: A Scientific Tragedy*. Harper Collins.

Sapir, E. (1964). *Culture, language, and personality*. University of California Press. (Original work published 1941)

Schlinger, H.D. (2003). The myth of intelligence. *The Psychological Record*, 53(1), 15–32.

Severson, K. (2011, December 9). Thousands sterilized, a state weighs restitution. *The New York Times*. http://www.nytimes.com/2011/12/10/us/redress-weighed-for-forced-sterilizations-in-north-carolina.html?pagewanted=all&_r=0

Singleton, D.M. (1995). Introduction: A critical look at the critical period hypothesis in second language acquisition research. In D.M. Singleton & Z. Lengyel (Eds.), *The age factor in second language acquisition: A critical look at the critical period hypothesis in second language acquisition research* (pp. 1–29). Multilingual Matters Ltd.

Skinner, B.F. (1957). *Verbal behavior*. Copley Publishing Group.

Smits-Engelsman, B.C.M., & Van Galen, G.P. (1997). Dysgraphia in children: Lasting psychomotor deficiency or transient developmental delay? *Journal of Experimental Child Psychology*, 67, 164–184.

Spelke, E.S., & Cortelyou, A. (1981). Perceptual aspects of social knowing: Looking and listening in infancy. In M.E. Lamb & L.R. Sherrod (Eds.), *Infant social cognition: Empirical and theoretical considerations* (pp. 61–83). Erlbaum.

Steitz, T. (2010). *Thomas A. Steitz – Biographical*. (K. Grandin, Ed.) http://www.nobelprize.org/nobel_prizes/chemistry/laureates/2009/steitz-bio.html

Sternberg, R.J. (1988). *The triarchic mind: A new theory of intelligence*. Viking-Penguin.

Terman, L.M. (1925). *Mental and physical traits of a thousand gifted children (I)*. Stanford University Press.

Terman, L.M., & Oden, M.H. (1947). *The gifted child grows up: 25 years' follow-up of a superior group: Genetic studies of genius (Vol. 4)*. Stanford University Press.

Terman, L.M. (1916). *The measurement of intelligence*. Houghton-Mifflin.

Tomasello, M., & Rakoczy, H. (2003). What makes human cognition unique? From individual to shared to collective intentionality. *Mind & Language*, 18(2), 121–147.

Tversky, A., & Kahneman, D. (1974). Judgment under uncertainty: Heuristics and biases. *Science*, 185(4157), 1124–1131.

van Troyer, G. (1994). Linguistic determinism and mutability: The Sapir-Whorf "hypothesis" and intercultural communication. *JALT Journal*, 2, 163–178.

Wechsler, D. (1958). *The measurement of adult intelligence*. Williams & Wilkins.

Wechsler, D. (1981). *Manual for the Wechsler Adult Intelligence Scale–revised*. Psychological Corporation.

Wechsler, D. (2002). *WPPSI-R manual*. Psychological Corporation.

Werker, J.F., & Lalonde, C.E. (1988). Cross-language speech perception: Initial capabilities and developmental change. *Developmental Psychology*, 24, 672–683.

Werker, J.F., & Tees, R.C. (1984). Cross-language speech perception: Evidence for perceptual reorganization during the first year of life. *Infant Behavior and Development*, 7, 49–63.

Whorf, B.L. (1956). *Language, thought and relativity*. MIT Press.

Williams, R.L., (1970). Danger: Testing and dehumanizing black children. *Clinical Child Psychology Newsletter*, 9(1), 5–6.

Zwicker, J.G. (2005). *Effectiveness of occupational therapy in remediating handwriting difficulties in primary students: Cognitive versus multisensory interventions*. Unpublished master's thesis, University of Victoria, Victoria, British Columbia, Canada). http://dspace.library.uvic.ca:8080/bitstream/handle/1828/49/Zwicker%20thesis.pdf?sequence=1

Chapter 7

Abel, M., & Bäuml, K.-H. T. (2013). Sleep can reduce proactive interference. *Memory*, 22(4), 332–339. https://doi.org/10.1080/09658211.2013.785570. http://www.psychologie.uni-regensburg.de/Baeuml/papers_in_press/sleepPI.pdf

Anderson, N.S. (1969). The influence of acoustic similarity on serial recall of letter sequences. *Quarterly Journal of Experimental Psychology*, 21(3), 248–255.

Anderson, R.C. (1984). Role of the reader's schema in comprehension, learning, and memory. In R. C. Anderson, J. Osborn, & R. J. Tierney (Eds.), *Learning to read in American schools: Basal Readers and Content Texts* (pp. 243–257). Erlbaum.

Atkinson, R.C., & Shiffrin, R.M. (1968). Human memory: A proposed system and its control processes. In K. W. Spence & J. T. Spence (Eds.), *The psychology of learning and motivation* (Vol. 2, pp. 89–195). Academic Press.

Baddeley, A. (2004). *Your memory: A user's guide*. Firefly Books.

Baddeley, A.D., & Hitch, G. (1974). Working memory. In G. H. Bower (Ed.), *The psychology of learning and motivation: Advances in research and theory* (Vol. 8, pp. 47–89). Academic Press.

Bayley, P.J., & Squire, L.R. (2002). Medial temporal lobe amnesia: Gradual acquisition of factual information by nondeclarative memory. *Journal of Neuroscience, 22,* 5741–5748.

Bellezza, F.S. (1981). Mnemonic devices: Classification, characteristics and criteria. *Review of Educational Research, 51,* 247–275.

Benjamin N. Cardozo School of Law, Yeshiva University. (2009). Reevaluating lineups: Why witnesses make mistakes and how to reduce the chance of a misidentification. The Innocence Project website: http://www.innocenceproject.org/docs/Eyewitness_ID_Report.pdf

Blockland, A. (1996). Acetylcholine: A neurotransmitter for learning and memory? *Brain Research Reviews, 21,* 285–300.

Bodie, G.D., Powers, W.G., & Fitch-Hauser, M. (2006). Chunking, priming, and active learning: Toward an innovative approach to teaching communication-related skills. *Interactive Learning Environment, 14*(2), 119–135.

Bousfield, W. (1935). The occurrence of clustering in the recall of randomly arranged associates. *Journal of General Psychology, 49,* 229–240.

Bransford, J.D., & McCarrell, N.S. (1974). A sketch of a cognitive approach to comprehension. In W. B. Weimer & D. J. Palermo (Eds.), *Cognition and the symbolic processes* (pp. 189–229). Lawrence Erlbaum Associates.

Briere, J., & Conte, J. (1993). Self-reported amnesia for abuse in adults molested as children. *Journal of Traumatic Stress, 6,* 21–31.

Carli, L. (1999). Cognitive reconstruction, hindsight, and reactions to victims and perpetrators. *Personality and Social Psychology Bulletin, 25*(8), 966–979. https://doi.org/10.1177/01461672992511005

Ceci, S.J., & Bruck, M. (1993). Child witness: Translating research into policy. *Social Policy Report, 7*(3), 1–30.

Ceci, S.J., & Bruck, M. (1995). *Jeopardy in the courtroom: A scientific analysis of children's testimony.* American Psychological Association.

Cheit, R.E. (2007). *The recovered memory project.* http://blogs.brown.edu/recoveredmemory/.

Christianson, S.A. (1992). *The handbook of emotion and memory: Research and theory.* Erlbaum.

Clark, R.E., Zola, S.M., & Squire, L.R. (2000). Impaired recognition memory in rats after damage to the hippocampus. *The Journal of Neuroscience, 20*(23), 8853–8860.

Corkin, S. (1965). Tactually-guided maze learning in man: Effects of unilateral cortical excisions and bilateral hippocampal lesions. *Neuropsychologia, 3,* 339–351.

Corkin, S. (1968). Acquisition of motor skill after bilateral medial temporal-lobe excision. *Neuropsychologia, 6,* 255–264.

Corkin, S., Amaral D. G., González, R.G., Johnson, K.A., & Hyman, B.T. (1997). H. M.'s medial temporal lobe lesion: Findings from magnetic resonance imaging. *Journal of Neuroscience, 17*(10), 3964–3979.

Craik, F.I.M., & Lockhart, R.S. (1972). Levels of processing: A framework for memory research. *Journal of Verbal Learning and Verbal Behavior, 11,* 671–684.

Craik, F.I. M., Moroz, T.M., Moscovitch, M., Stuss, D.T., Winocur, G., Tulving, E., & Kapur, S. (1999). In search of the self: A positron emission tomography study. *Psychological Science, 10*(1), 26–34.

Craik, F.I. M., & Tulving, E. (1975). Depth of processing and the retention of words in episodic memory. *Journal of Experimental Psychology, 104*(3), 268–294.

Craik, F.I. M., & Watkins, M.J. (1973). The role of rehearsal in short-term memory. *Journal of Verbal Learning and Verbal Behavior, 12,* 599–607.

Devilly, G.J. (2007). If nothing happened why do I still hurt? An update on the memory wars. *InPsych, 29*(2), 16–18.

Ebbinghaus, H. (1964). *Memory: A contribution to experimental psychology* (H. A. Ruger & C. E. Bussenius, Trans.). Dover. (Original work published 1885)

Goodman, G.S. (2006). Children's eyewitness memory: A modern history and contemporary commentary. *Journal of Social Issues, 62,* 811–832.

Green, J.T., & Woodruff-Pak, D.S. (2000). Eyeblink classical conditioning in aging animals. In D. S. Woodruff-Pak & J. E. Steinmetz (Eds.), *Eyeblink classical conditioning: Animal models* (Vol. 2, pp.155–178). Kluwer Academic.

Greenberg, D.L. (2004). President Bush's false [flashbulb] memory of 9/11/01. *Applied. Cognitive Psychology, 18*(3), 363–370. https://doi.org/10.1002/acp.1016

Hassabis D., & Maguire E. A. (2007). Deconstructing episodic memory with construction. *Trends in Cognitive Sciences, 11*(7), 299–306.

Jacobs, J. (1887). Experiments on "prehension." *Mind, 12,* 75–79.

Josselyn, J.A. (2010). Continuing the search for the engram: Examining the mechanism of fear memories. *Journal of Psychiatry Neuroscience, 35*(4), 221–228.

Kapur, S., Craik, F.I. M., Tulving, E., Wilson, A.A., Houle, S., & Brown, G.M. (1994). Neuroanatomical correlates of encoding in episodic memory: Levels of processing effect. *Proceedings of the National Academy of Sciences of the United States of America, 91*(6), 208–2011.

Lashley K. S. (1950). In search of the engram. *Society of Experimental Biology Symposium, 4: Psychological Mechanisms in Animal Behavior.* Cambridge University Press.

Loftus, E.F., & Palmer, J.C. (1974). Reconstruction of auto-mobile destruction: An example of the interaction between language and memory. *Journal of Verbal Learning and Verbal Behavior, 13,* 585–589.

MacLeod, C.M., Gopie, N., Hourihan, K.L., Neary, K.R., & Ozubko, J.D. (2010). The production effect: Delineation of a phenomenon. *Journal of Experimental Psychology: Learning, Memory, and Cognition, 36*(3), 671–685.

Mayford, M., Siegelbaum, S.A., & Kandel, E.R. (2012). *Synapses and memory storage.* Cold Spring Harbor Perspectives in Biology, Cold Spring Harbor Laboratory Press.

McGaugh, J.L. (2003). *Memory and emotion: The making of lasting memories.* Columbia University Press.

McLeod, S.A. (2011). Anterograde amnesia [Web log post]. http://www.simplypsychology.org/anterograde-amnesia.html

Miller, G.A. (1956). The magical number seven, plus or minus two: Some limits on our capacity for processing information. *Psychological Review, 68,* 81–87.

Myhrer, T. (2003). Neurotransmitter systems involved in learning and memory in the rat: A meta-analysis based on studies of four behavioral tasks. *Brain Research Reviews, 41*(2–3), 268–287.

Newseum. (n.d.). G-men and journalists: D. C. sniper [Web log post]. http://www.newseum.org/exhibits-and-theaters/temporary-exhibits/g-men-and-journalists/sniper/

Nickerson, R.S., & Adams, M.J. (1979). Long-term memory for a common object. *Cognitive Psychology, 11*(3), 287–307.

Paivio, A. (1986). *Mental representations: A dual coding approach.* Oxford University Press.

Parker, E.S., Cahill, L., & McGaugh, J.L. (2006). A case of unusual autobiographical remembering. *Neurocase, 12,* 35–49.

Payne, B.K., Jacoby, L.L., & Lambert, A.J. (2004). Memory monitoring and the control of stereotype distortion. *Journal of Experimental Social Psychology, 40,* 52–64.

Pew Research Center (2011, September 1). *Ten years after 9/11: United in remembrance, divided over policies*. People Press.

Pipe, M.-E. (1996). Children's eyewitness memory. *New Zealand Journal of Psychology, 25*(2), 36–43.

Pipe, M.-E., Lamb, M., Orbach, Y., & Esplin, P.W. (2004). Recent research on children's testimony about experienced and witnessed events. *Developmental Review, 24,* 440–468.

Roediger, H.L., & DeSoto, K.A. (in press). The psychology of reconstructive memory. In J. Wright (Ed.), *International Encyclopedia of the Social and Behavioral sciences,* 2e. Elsevier.

Roediger, H.L., III, & McDermott, K.B. (2000). Tricks of memory. *Current Directions in Psychological Science, 9,* 123–127.

Rogers, T.B., Kuiper, N.A., & Kirker, W.S. (1977). Self-reference and the encoding of personal information. *Journal of Personal Social Psychology, 35*(9), 677–688.

Schacter, D. (2001). *The seven sins of memory: How the mind forgets and remembers.* Houghton Mifflin.

Steinmetz, J.E. (1999). A renewed interest in human classical eyeblink conditioning. *Psychological Science, 10,* 24–25.

Tigner, R.B. (1999). Putting memory research to good use. *College Teaching, 47*(4), 149–152.

Tulving, E. (1972). Episodic and semantic memory. In E. Tulving & W. Dolandson (Eds.), *Organization of memory* (pp. 381–403). Academic Press.

Tulving, E. (2002, February). Episodic memory: From mind to brain. *Annual Review of Psychology, 53,* 1–25. https://doi.org/10.1146/annurev. psych.53.100901.135114

van Praag, H. (2008). Neurogenesis and exercise: Past and future directions. *NeuroMolecular Medicine, 10*(2), 128–140.

Wells, G.L., & Quinlivan, D.S. (2009). Suggestive eyewitness identification procedures and the Supreme Court's reliability test in light of eyewitness science: 30 years later. *Law and Human Behavior, 33,* 1–24. https://doi. org/10.1007/s10979-008-9130-3

Wrubel, B. (Writer), & Spiller, M. (Director). (2010). The Old Wagon [Television series episode]. In S. Levitan & C. Lloyd (Executive producers), *Modern Family.* 20th Century Fox Television.

Yogo, M., & Fujihara, S. (2008). Working memory capacity can be improved by expressive writing: A randomized experiment in a Japanese sample. *British Journal of Health Psychology, 13*(1), 77–80. https://doi. org/10.1348/135910707X252440

Chapter 8

Ainsworth, M.D. S., & Bell, S.M. (1970). Attachment, exploration, and separation: Illustrated by the behavior of one-year-olds in a strange situation. *Child Development, 41,* 49–67.

Ainsworth, M.D. S., Blehar, M.C., Waters, E., & Wall, S. (1978). *Patterns of attachment: A psychological study of the strange situation.* Erlbaum.

American Academy of Pediatrics. (2007). The importance of play in promoting healthy child development and maintaining strong parent-child bonds. *Pediatrics, 199*(1), 182–191.

Amsterdam, B. (1972). Mirror image reactions before age two. *Developmental Psychobiology, 5,* 297–305.

Archer, J. (1992). *Ethology and human development.* Harvester Wheatsheaf.

Arnett, J. (2000). Emerging adulthood: A theory of development from the late teens through the twenties. *American Psychologist, 55*(5), 469–480.

Ashley, S.J., Magnuson, S.I., Omnell, L.M., & Clarren, S.K. (1999). Fetal alcohol syndrome: Changes in craniofacial form with age, cognition, and timing of ethanol exposure in the macaque. *Teratology, 59*(3), 163–172.

Bahr, S.J., & Hoffman, J.P. (2010). Parenting style, religiosity, peers, and adolescent heavy drinking. *Journal of Studies on Alcohol and Drugs, 71,* 539–543.

Baillargeon, R. (1987). Young infants' reasoning about the physical and spatial properties of a hidden object. *Cognitive Development, 2*(3), 179–200.

Baillargeon, R. (2004). Infants' reasoning about hidden objects: Evidence for event-general and event-specific expectations. *Developmental Science, 7*(4), 391–424.

Baillargeon, R., Li, J., Gertner, Y., & Wu, D. (2011). How do infants reason about physical events. *The Wiley-Blackwell handbook of childhood cognitive development, 2,* 11–48.

Barber, B.K. (1994). Cultural, family, and person contexts of parent-adolescent conflict. *Journal of Marriage and the Family, 56,* 375–386.

Basseches, M. (1984). Dialectical thinking as metasystematic form of cognitive organization. In M. L. Commons, F.A. Richards, & C. Armon (Eds.), *Beyond formal operations: Late adolescent and adult cognitive development* (pp. 216–238). Praeger.

Baumrind, D. (1971). Current patterns of parental authority. *Developmental Psychology, 4*(1, Pt. 2), 1–103. https:// doi.org/10.1037/h0030372

Baumrind, D. (1991). The influence of parenting style on adolescent competence and substance use. *Journal of Early Adolescence, 11*(1), 56–95.

Bayley, N., & Oden, M.H. (1955). The maintenance of intellectual ability in gifted adults. *Journal of Gerontology, 10,* 91–107.

Bjorklund, D.F. (1987). A note on neonatal imitation. *Developmental Review, 7,* 86–92.

Blossom, M., & Morgan, J.L. (2006). Does the face say what the mouth says? A study of infants' sensitivity to visual prosody. In *30th anuual Boston University conference on language development, Somerville, MA.*

Bogartz, R.S., Shinskey, J.L., & Schilling, T. (2000). *Infancy, 1*(4), 403–428.

Bowlby, J. (1969). *Attachment and loss: Attachment* (Vol. 1). Basic Books.

Bowlby, J. (1988). *A secure base: Parent-child attachment and health human development.* Basic Books.

Brumley, R., Enquidanos, S., Jamison, P., Seitz, R., Morgenstern, N., Saito, S.,…Gonzalez, J. (2007). Increased satisfaction with care and lower costs: Results of a randomized trial of in-home palliative care. *Journal of the American Geriatric Society, 55*(7), 993–1000.

Brumley, R.D., Enquidanos, S., & Cherin, D.A. (2003). Effectiveness of a home-based palliative care program for end-of-life. *Journal of Palliative Medicine, 6*(5), 715–724.

Callaghan, T.C., Rochat, P., Lillard, A., Claux, M.L., Odden, H., Itakura, S.,…Singh, S. (2005). Synchrony in the onset of mental-state reasoning. *Psychological Science, 16,* 378–384.

Carel, J-C., Lahlou, N., Roger, M., & Chaussain, J.L. (2004). Precocious puberty and statural growth. *Human Reproduction Update, 10*(2), 135–147.

Carstensen, L.L. (1992). Social and emotional patterns in adulthood: Support for socioemotional selectivity. *Psychology and Aging, 7*(3), 331–338.

Case, R. (1985). *Intellectual development: Birth to Adulthood.* Academic.

Casey, B.J., Tottenham, N., Liston, C., & Durston, S. (2005). Imaging the developing brain: What have we learned about cognitive development? *TRENDS in Cognitive Sciences, 19*(3), 104–110.

Centers for Disease Control and Prevention. (2013). *Smoking during pregnancy.* http://www.cdc.gov/tobacco/basic_ information/health_effects/pregnancy/

Chick, K., Heilman-Houser, R., & Hunter, M. (2002). The impact of child care on gender role development and gender stereotypes. *Early Childhood Education Journal, 29*(3), 149–154.

Chomsky, N. (1957). *Syntactic structures*. Mouton.

Clements, R. (2004). An investigation of the status of outdoor play. *Contemporary Issues in Early Childhood, 5*(1), 68–80.

Commons, M.L., & Bresette, L.M. (2006). Illuminating major creative scientific innovators with postformal stages. In C. Hoare (Ed.), *Handbook of adult development and learning* (pp. 255–280). New York, NY: Oxford University Press.

Connor, S.R., Pyenson, B., Fitch, K., Spence, C., & Iwasaki, K. (2007). Comparing hospice and nonhospice patient survival among patients who die within a three-year window. *Journal of Pain and Symptom Management, 33*(3), 238–246.

Courage, M.L., & Howe, M.L. (2002). From infant to child: The dynamics of cognitive change in the second year of life. *Psychological Bulletin, 128*, 250–277.

Curtiss, S. (1981). Dissociations between language and cognition: Cases and implications. *Journal of Autism and Developmental Disorders, 11*(1), 15–30.

Darling, N. (1999). *Parenting style and its correlates*. ERIC database (EDO-PS-99-3) http://ecap.crc.illinois.edu/eecearchive/digests/1999/darlin99.pdf

de Hevia, M.D., & Spelke, E.S. (2010). Number-space mapping in human infants. *Psychological Science, 21*(5), 653–660.

Dennett, D. (1987). *The intentional stance*. MIT Press.

Diamond, A. (2009). The interplay of biology and the environment broadly defined. *Developmental Psychology, 45*(1), 1–8.

Donenberg, G.R., Wilson, H.W., Emerson, E., Bryant, F.B. (2002). Holding the line with a watchful eye: The impact of perceived parental permissiveness and parental monitoring on risky sexual behavior among adolescents in psychiatric care. *AIDS Education Prevention, 14*(2), 138–157.

Dornbusch, S.M., Ritter, P.L., Leiderman, P.H., Roberts, D.F., & Fraleigh, M.J. (1987). The relation of parenting style to adolescent school performance. *Child Development, 58*(5), 1244–1257.

Duncan, G.J., & Magnuson, K.A. (2005). Can family socioeconomic resources account for racial and ethnic test score gaps? *The Future of Children, 15*(1), 35–54.

Erikson, E.H. (1963). *Childhood and Society* (2nd ed.). Norton.

Erikson, E.H. (1968). *Identity: Youth and crisis*. Norton.

Ferrer, M., & Fugate, A. (2003). *Helping your school-age child develop a healthy self-concept*. http://edis.ifas.ufl.edu/fy570#FOOTNOTE_2

Figdor, E., & Kaeser, L. (1998). Concerns mount over punitive approaches to substance abuse among pregnant women. *The Guttmacher Report on Public Policy 1*(5), 3–5.

Fischer, K.W., Yan, Z., & Stewart, J. (2003). Adult cognitive development: Dynamics in the developmental web. In J. Valsiner & K Connolly (Eds.), *Handbook of developmental psychology* (pp. 491–516). Sage Publications.

Flannery, D.J., Rowe, D.C., & Gulley, B.L. (1993). Impact of pubertal status, timing, and age on adolescent sexual experience and delinquency. *Journal of Adolescent Research, 8*, 21–40.

Freud, S. (1909). Analysis of a phobia in a five-year-old boy. In *Collected Papers: Volume 111, Case Histories* (1949) (pp. 149–289). London.

Fromkin, V., Krashen, S., Curtiss, S., Rigler, D., & Rigler, M. (1974). The development of language in Genie: A case of language acquisition beyond the critical period. *Brain and Language, 1*, 81–107.

Galambos, N.L., & Almeida, D.M. (1992). Does parent-adolescent conflict increase in early adolescence? *Journal of Marriage and the Family, 54*, 737–747.

Ganger, J., & Brent, M.R. (2004). Reexamining the vocabulary spurt. *Developmental Psychology, 40*(4), 621–632.

Ge, X., Conger, R.D., & Elder, G.H. (2001). Pubertal transition, stressful life events, and the emergence of gender differences in adolescent depressive symptoms. *Developmental Psychology, 37*, 404–417.

Gervai, J. (2009). Environmental and genetic influences on early attachment. *Child and Adolescent Psychiatry and Mental Health, 3*, 25.

Gesell, A. (1933). Maturation and the patterning of behavior. In C. Murchison (Ed.), *A handbook of child psychology* (2nd ed., pp. 209–235). Clark University Press.

Gesell, A. (1939). *Biographies of child development*. Paul B. Hoeber.

Gesell, A. (1940). *The first five years of life*. Harper.

Gesell, A., & Ilg, F.L. (1946). *The child from five to ten*. Harper.

Gilligan, C. (1982). *In a different voice: Psychological theory and women's development*. Harvard University Press.

Gleitman, L.R., & Newport, E.L. (1995). The invention of language by children: Environmental and biological influences on the acquisition of language. In D.N. Osherson, L.R. Gleitman, & M. Liberman (Eds.), *An invitation to cognitive science: Language* (pp. 1–24). The MIT Press.

Godkin, M., Krant, M., & Doster, N. (1984). The impact of hospice care on families. *International Journal of Psychiatry in Medicine, 13*, 153–165.

Graber, J.A., Lewinsohn, P.M., Seeley, J.R., & Brooks-Gunn, J. (1997). Is psychopathology associated with the timing of pubertal development? *Journal of the Academy of Child and Adolescent Psychiatry, 36*, 1768–1776.

Hair, E.C., Moore, K.A., Garrett, S.B., Kinukawa, A., Lippman, L., & Michelson, E. (2005). The parent-adolescent relationship scale. In L. Lippman (Ed.), *Conceptualizing and Measuring Indicators of Positive Development: What Do Children Need to Fluorish?* (pp. 183–202). Kluwer Academic/Plenum Press.

Harlow, H. (1958). The nature of love. *American Psychologist, 13*, 673–685.

Hall, S.S. (2004, May). The good egg. *Discover*, 30–39.

Hall, G.S. (1904). *Adolescence*. Appleton.

Harris, J.R. (2009). *The nurture assumption: Why children turn out the way they do* (2nd ed.). Free Press.

Hart, B., & Risley, T.R. (2003). The early catastrophe: The 30 million word gap. *American Educator, 27*(1), 4–9.

Hatch, E. (1983). *Psycholinguistics: A second language perspective*. Newbury House.

Hertzog, C., Kramer, A.F., Wilson, R.S., & Lindenberger, U. (2009). Enrichment effects on adult cognitive development. *Psychological Science in the Public Interest, 9*(1), 1–65.

Hood, R.W., Jr., Spilka, B., Hunsberger, B., & Corsuch, R. (1996). *The psychology of religion: An empirical approach* (2nd ed.). Guilford.

Huebler, F. (2005, December 14). International education statistics [Web log post]. http://huebler.blogspot.com/2005/12/age-and-level-of-education-in-nigeria.html

Hutchinson, N. (2011). A geographically informed vision of skills development. *Geographical Education, 24*, 15.

Huttenlocher, P.R., & Dabholkar, A.S. (1997). Regional differences in synaptogenesis in human cerebral cortex. *Journal of Comparative Neurology, 387*(2), 167–178.

Iverson, J.M., & Goldin-Meadow, S. (2005). Gesture paves the way for language development. *Psychological Science, 16*(5), 367–71.

Iyengar, S.S., Wells, R.E., & Schwartz, B. (2006). Doing better but feeling worse: Looking for the best job undermines satisfaction. *Psychological Science, 17,* 143–150.

Jos, P.H., Marshall, M.F., & Perlmutter, M. (1995). The Charleston policy on cocaine use during pregnancy: A cautionary tale. *The Journal of Law, Medicine & Ethics, 23*(2), 120–128.

Kaltiala-Heino, R.A., Rimpela, M., Rissanen, A., & Rantanen, P. (2001). Early puberty and early sexual activity are associated with bulimic-type eating pathology in middle adolescence. *Journal of Adolescent Health, 28,* 346–352.

Kaplan, H., & Dove, H. (1987). Infant development among the Aché of Eastern Paraguay. *Developmental Psychology, 23,* 190–198.

Karasik, L.B., Adolph, K.E., Tamis-LeMonda, C.S., & Bornstein, M.H. (2010). WEIRD Walking: Cross-cultural research on motor development. *Behavioral & Brain Sciences, 33*(2-3), 95–96.

Karnik, S., & Kanekar, A. (2012). Childhood obesity: A global public health crisis. *International Journal of Preventive Medicine, 3*(1), 1–7.

Kohlberg, L. (1969). Stage and sequence: The cognitive-developmental approach to socialization. In D. A. Goslin (Ed.), *Handbook of socialization theory and research* (p. 379). Rand McNally.

Kolb, B., & Whishaw, I.Q. (2009). *Fundamentals of human neuropsychology.* Worth.

Kübler-Ross, E. (1969). *On death and dying.* Macmillan.

Labouvie-Vief, G., & Diehl, M. (1999). Self and personality development. In J. C. Cavanaugh & S. K. Whitbourne (Eds.), *Gerontology: An interdisciplinary perspective* (pp. 238–268). Oxford University Press.

Larson, E.B., Wang, L., Bowen, J.D., McCormick, W.C., Teri, L., Crane, P., & Kukull, W. (2006). Exercise is associated with reduced risk for incident dementia among persons 65 years of age or older. *Annals of Internal Medicine, 144,* 73–81.

Lee, V.E., & Burkam, D.T. (2002). *Inequality at the starting gate: Social background differences in achievement as children begin school.* Economic Policy Institute.

Lobo, I. (2008) Environmental influences on gene expression. *Nature Education 1*(1), 39.

Loop, E. (2013). *Major milestones in cognitive development in early childhood.* http://everydaylife.globalpost.com/major-milestones-cognitive-development-early-childhood-4625.html

Maccoby, E. (1980). *Social development: Psychological growth and the parent-child relationship.* Harcourt Brace Jovanovich.

MacFarlane, A. (1978, February). What a baby knows. *Human Nature,* 74–81.

Maier, S.E., & West, J.R. (2001). Drinking patterns and alcohol-related birth defects. *Alcohol Research & Health, 25*(3), 168–174.

Main, M., & Solomon, J. (1990). Procedures for identifying infants as disorganized/disoriented during the Ainsworth Strange Situation. In M. T. Greenberg, D. Cicchetti, & E. M. Cummings (Eds.), *Attachment in the Preschool Years* (pp. 121–160). University of Chicago Press.

Markus, H.R., Ryff, C.D., Curan, K., & Palmersheim, K.A. (2004). In their own words: Well-being at midlife among high school-educated and college-educated adults. In O. G. Brim, C.D. Ryff, & R. C. Kessler (Eds.), *How healthy are we? A national study of well-being at midlife* (pp. 273–319). University of Chicago Press.

McIntosh, D.N., Silver, R.C., & Wortman, C.B. (1993). Religion's role in adjustment to a negative life event: Coping with the loss of a child. *Journal of Personality and Social Psychology, 65,* 812–821.

McMillan, S.C., Small, B.J., Weitzner, M., Schonwetter, R., Tittle, M., Moody, L., & Haley, W.E. (2006). Impact of coping skills intervention with family caregivers of hospice patients with cancer. *Cancer, 106*(1), 214-222.

Miklikowska, M., Duriez, B., & Soenens, B. (2011). Family roots of empathy-related characteristics: The role of perceived maternal and paternal need support in adolescence. *Developmental Psychology, 47*(5), 1342–1352.

Mills, M., & Melhuish, E. (1974). Recognition of mother's voice in early infancy. *Nature, 252,* 123–124.

Mohr, R.D., & Zoghi, C. (2006). Is job enrichment really enriching? (U.S. Bureau of Labor Statistics Working Paper 389). Washington, DC: U.S. Bureau of Labor Statistics. http://www.bls.gov/ore/pdf/ec060010.pdf

Moore, K.A., Guzman, L., Hair, E.C., Lippman, L., & Garrett, S.B. (2004). Parent-teen relationships and interactions: Far more positive than not. *Child Trends Research Brief, 2004-25.* Child Trends.

National Institutes of Health. (2013). *What is prenatal care and why is it important?* http://www.nichd.nih.gov/health/topics/pregnancy/conditioninfo/Pages/prenatal-care.aspx

Nolen-Hoeksema, S., & Larson, J. (1999). *Coping with loss.* Erlbaum.

Overman, W.H., Bachevalier, J., Turner, M., & Peuster, A. (1992). Object recognition versus object discrimination: Comparison between human infants and infant monkeys. *Behavioral Neuroscience, 106,* 15–29.

Paloutzian, R.F. (1996). *Invitation to the psychology of religion.* Allyn & Bacon.

Parent, J., Forehand, R., Merchant, M.J., Edwards, M.C., Conners-Burrow, N.A., Long, N., & Jones, D.J. (2011). The relation of harsh and permissive discipline with child disruptive behaviors: Does child gender make a difference in an at-risk sample? *Journal of Family Violence, 26,* 527–533.

Piaget, J. (1930). *The child's conception of the world.* Harcourt, Brace & World.

Piaget, J. (1932). *The moral judgment of the child.* Harcourt, Brace & World.

Piaget, J. (1954). *The construction of reality in the child.* Basic Books.

Pickens, J. (1994). Full-term and preterm infants' perception of face-voice synchrony. *Infant Behavior and Development, 17,* 447–455.

Podewils, L.J., Guallar, E., Kuller, L.H., Fried, L.P., Lopez, O.L., Carlson, M., & Lyketsos, C.G. (2005). Physical activity, APOE genotype, and dementia risk: Findings from the Cardiovascular Health Cognition Study. *American Journal of Epidemiology, 161,* 639–651.

Pollack, W., & Shuster, T. (2000). *Real boys' voices.* Random House.

Rhodes, R.L., Mitchell, S.L., Miller, S.C., Connor, S.R., & Teno, J.M. (2008). Bereaved family members' evaluation of hospice care: What factors influence overall satisfaction with services? *Journal of Pain and Symptom Management, 35,* 365–371.

Risley, T.R., & Hart, B. (2006). Promoting early language development. In N. F. Watt, C. Ayoub, R.H. Bradley, J.E. Puma, & W. A. LeBoeuf (Eds.), *The crisis in youth mental health: Early intervention programs and policies* (Vol. 4, pp. 83–88). Praeger.

Rothbaum, R., Weisz, J., Pott, M., Miyake, K., & Morelli, G. (2000). Attachment and culture: Security in the United States and Japan. *American Psychologist, 55,* 1093–1104.

Russell, S.T., Crockett, L.J., & Chao, R. (Eds.). (2010). Asian American parenting and parent-adolescent relationships. In R. Levesque (Series Ed.), *Advancing responsible adolescent development.* Springer.

Ryff, C.D., & Singer, B. (2009). Understanding healthy aging: Key components and their integration. In V. L. Bengtson, D. Gans., N. M. Putney, & M. Silverstein. (Eds.), *Handbook of theories of aging* (2nd ed., pp. 117–144). Springer.

Samarel, N. (1991). *Caring for life after death*. Hemisphere.

Sanson, A., & Rothbart, M.K. (1995). Child temperament and parenting. In M. Bornstein (Ed.), *Applied and practical parenting* (Vol. 4, pp. 299–321). Lawrence Erlbaum.

Schechter, C., & Byeb, B. (2007). Preliminary evidence for the impact of mixed-income preschools on low-income children's language growth. *Early Childhood Research Quarterly, 22*, 137–146.

Shamay-Tsoory, S.G., Tomer, R., & Aharon-Peretz, J. (2005). The neuroanatomical basis of understanding sarcasm and its relationship to social cognition. *Neuropsychology, 19*(3), 288–300.

Shanahan, L., McHale, S.M., Osgood, D.W., & Crouter, A.C. (2007). Conflict frequency with mothers and fathers from middle childhood to late adolescence: Within and between family comparisons. *Developmental Psychology, 43*, 539–550.

Siegler, R.S. (2005). *Children's thinking* (4th ed). Erlbaum.

Siegler, R.S. (2006). Microgenetic analyses of learning. In D. Kuhn & R. S. Siegler (Eds.), *Handbook of child psychology: Cognition, perception, and language* (6th ed., Vol. 2). Wiley.

Sinnott, J.D. (1998). *The development of logic in adulthood: Postformal thought and its applications*. Springer.

Small, M.F. (1999). *Our babies, ourselves: How biology and culture shape the way we parent*. Anchor Books.

Spelke, E.S., & Cortelyou, A. (1981). Perceptual aspects of social knowing: Looking and listening in infancy. In M.E. Lamb & L.R. Sherrod (Eds.), *Infant social cognition: Empirical and theoretical considerations* (pp. 61–83). Erlbaum.

Steinberg, L., & Morris, A.S. (2001). Adolescent development. *Annual Review of Psychology, 52*, 83–110.

Sterns, H.L., & Huyck, M.H. (2001). The role of work in midlife. In M. Lachman (Ed.), *The handbook of midlife development* (pp. 447–486). Wiley.

Steven L. Youngentob, et. al. (2007). Experience-induced fetal plasticity: The effect of gestational ethanol exposure on the behavioral and neurophysiologic olfactory response to ethanol odor in early postnatal and adult rats. *Behavioral Neuroscience, 121*(6), 1293–1305.

Stork, F.C., & Widdowson, D.A. (1974). *Learning about linguistics*. Hutchinson Ltd.

Streissguth, A.P., Bookstein, F.L., Barr, H.M., Sampson, P.D., O'Malley, K., & Young, J.K. (2004). Risk factors for adverse life outcomes in fetal alcohol syndrome and fetal alcohol effects. *Developmental and Behavioral Pediatrics, 25*(4), 228–238.

Striegel-Moore, R.H., & Cachelin, F.M. (1999). Body image concerns and disordered eating in adolescent girls: Risk and protective factors. In N. G. Johnson, M.C. Roberts, & J. Worell (Eds.), *Beyond appearance: A new look at adolescent girls*. Washington, DC: American Psychological Association

Tanner, J.M. (1978). *Fetus into man: Physical growth from conception to maturity*. Harvard University Press.

Temel, J.S., Greer, J.A., Muzikansky, A., Gallagher, E.R., Admane, S., Jackson, V.A.…Lynch, T.J. (2010). Early palliative care for patients with metastic non-small-cell lung cancer. *New England Journal of Medicine, 363*, 733–742.

Thomas, A. (1984). Temperament research: Where we are, where we are going. *Merrill-Palmer Quarterly, 30*(2), 103–109.

Tran, T.D., & Kelly, S.J. (2003). Critical periods for ethanol-induced cell loss in the hippocampal formation. *Neurotoxicology and Teratology, 25*(5), 519–528.

Umberson, D., Pudrovska, T., & Reczek, C. (2010). Parenthood, childlessness, and well-being: A life course perspective. *Journal of Marriage and the Family, 72*(3), 612–629.

United Nations Educational, Scientific and Cultural Organization. (2013, June). *UIS Fact Sheet: Schooling for millions of children jeopardized by reductions in aid*. Montreal, Canada: UNESCO Institute for Statistics.

Vaillant, G.E. (2002). *Aging well*. Little Brown & Co.

Van der Graaff, J., Branje, S., De Wied, M., Hawk, S., Van Lier, P., & Meeus, W. (2013). Perspective taking and empathetic concern in adolescence: Gender differences in developmental changes. *Developmental Psychology, 50*(3), 881.

van Ijzendoorn, M.H., & Sagi-Schwartz, A. (2008). Cross-cultural patterns of attachment: Universal and contextual dimensions. In J. Cassidy & P. R. Shaver (Eds.), *Handbook of attachment*. Guilford.

Vouloumanos, A., & Werker, J.F. (2004). Tuned to the signal: The privileged status of speech for young infants. *Developmental Science, 7*, 270–276.

WHO Multicentre Growth Reference Study Group. (2006). *WHO Child growth standards: Methods and development: Length/height-for-age, weight-for-age, weight-for-length, weight-for-height and body mass index-for-age*. Geneva, Switzerland: World Health Organization.

Winerman, L. (2011). Closing the achievement gap. *Monitor of Psychology, 42*(8), 36.

Wortman, J.H., & Park, C.L. (2008). Religion and spirituality in adjustment following bereavement: An integrative review. *Death Studies*

Chapter 9

Ahima, R.S., & Antwi, D.A. (2008). Brain regulation of appetite and satiety. *Endocrinology and Metabolism Clinics of North America, 37*, 811–823.

Allen, L.S., & Gorski, R.A. (1992). Sexual orientation and the size of the anterior commissure in the human brain. *Proceedings of the National Academy of Sciences, USA, 89*, 7199–7202.

American Psychiatric Association. (2013). *Feeding and eating disorders*. http://www.dsm5.org/documents/eating%20disorders%20fact%20sheet.pdf

Arnold, H.J. (1976). Effects of performance feedback and extrinsic reward upon high intrinsic motivation. *Organizational Behavior and Human Performance, 17*, 275–288.

Bailey, M.J., & Pillard, R.C. (1991). A genetic study of male sexual orientation. *Archives of General Psychiatry, 48*, 1089–1096.

Baldwin, J.D., & Baldwin, J.I. (1989). The socialization of homosexuality and heterosexuality in a non-western society. *Archives of Sexual Behavior, 18*, 13–29.

Bancroft, J. (2004). Alfred C. Kinsey and the politics of sex research. *Annual Review of Sex Research, 15*, 1–39.

Bandura, A. (1994). Self-efficacy. In V. S. Ramachandran (Ed.), *Encyclopedia of human behavior* (Vol. 4, pp. 71–81). New York, NY: Academic Press.

Bauminger, N. (2002). The facilitation of social-emotional understanding and social interaction in high-functioning children with autism: Intervention outcomes. *Journal of Autism and Developmental Disorders, 32*, 283–298.

Becker, J.B., Rudick, C.N., & Jenkins, W.J. (2001). The role of dopamine in the nucleus accumbens and striatum during sexual behavior in the female rat. *Journal of Neuroscience, 21*, 3236–3241.

Becker, J.M. (2012, April 25). Dr. Robert Spitzer apologizes to gay community for infamous "ex-gay" study [Web log post]. http://www.truthwinsout.org/news/2012/04/24542/

Beedie, C.J., Terry, P.C., Lane, A.M., & Devonport, T.J. (2011). Differential assessment of emotions and moods: Development and validation of the emotion and mood components of anxiety questionnaire. *Personality and Individual Differences*, 50, 228–233.

Bell, A.P., Weinberg, M.S., & Hammersmith, S.K. (1981). *Sexual preferences: Its development in men and women*. Indiana University Press.

Berlyne, D.E. (1960). Toward a theory of exploratory behavior: II. Arousal potential, perceptual curiosity, and learning. In (Series Ed.), *Conflict, arousal, and curiosity* (pp. 193–227). McGraw-Hill Book Company.

Bhasin, S., Enzlin, P., Coviello, A., & Basson, R. (2007). Sexual dysfunction in men and women with endocrine disorders. *The Lancet*, 369, 597–611.

Blackford, J.U., & Pine, D.S. (2012). Neural substrates of childhood anxiety disorders: A review of neuroimaging findings. *Child and Adolescent Psychiatric Clinics of North America*, 21, 501–525.

Bremner, J.D., & Vermetten, E. (2004). Neuroanatomical changes associated with pharmacotherapy in posttraumatic stress disorder. *Annals of the New York Academy of Sciences*, 1032, 154–157.

Buck, R. (1980). Nonverbal behavior and the theory of emotion: The facial feedback hypothesis. *Journal of Personality and Social Psychology*, 38, 811–824.

Bullough, V.L. (1998). Alfred Kinsey and the Kinsey report: Historical overview and lasting contributions. *The Journal of Sex Research*, 35, 127–131.

Byne, W., Tobet, S., Mattiace, L.A., Lasco, M.S., Kemether, E., Edgar, M.A.,...Jones, L.B. (2001). The interstitial nuclei of the human anterior hypothalamus: An investigation of variation with sex, sexual orientation, and HIV status. *Hormones and Behavior*, 40, 86–92.

Cameron, J., & Pierce, W.D. (1994). Reinforcement, reward, and intrinsic motivation: A meta-analysis. *Review of Educational Research*, 64, 363–423.

Carey, B. (2012, May 18). Psychiatry giant sorry for backing gay 'cure.' *The New York Times*. http://www.nytimes.com/2012/05/19/health/dr-robert-l-spitzer-noted-psychiatrist-apologizes-for-study-on-gay-cure.html?_r=0

Carter, C.S. (1992). Hormonal influences on human sexual behavior. In J. B. Becker, S.M. Breedlove, & D. Crews (Eds.), *Behavioral Endocrinology* (pp.131–142). MIT Press.

Cassidy, S.B., & Driscoll, D.J. (2009). Prader-Willi syndrome. *European Journal of Human Genetics*, 17, 3–13.

Centers for Disease Control and Prevention. (2012). *Overweight and obesity*. http://www.cdc.gov/obesity/index.html

Chwalisz, K., Diener, E., & Gallagher, D. (1988). Autonomic arousal feedback and emotional experience: Evidence from the spinal cord injured. *Journal of Personality and Social Psychology*, 54, 820–828.

Colapinto, J. (2000). *As nature made him: The boy who was raised as a girl*. Harper Collins.

Collier, D.A., & Treasure, J.L. (2004). The aetiology of eating disorders. *The British Journal of Psychiatry*, 185, 363–365.

Conrad, P. (2005). The shifting engines of medicalization. *Journal of Health and Social Behavior*, 46, 3–14.

Cunha, C., Monfils, M.H., & LeDoux, J.E. (2010). GABA(C) receptors in the lateral amygdala: A possible novel target for the treatment of fear and anxiety disorders? *Frontiers in Behavioral Neuroscience*, 4, 6.

Daniel, T.L., & Esser, J.K. (1980). Intrinsic motivation as influenced by rewards, task interest, and task structure. *Journal of Applied Psychology*, 65, 566–573.

Darwin, C. (1872). *The expression of emotions in man and animals*. Appleton.

Davis, J.I., Senghas, A., & Ochsner, K.N. (2009). How does facial feedback modulate emotional experience? *Journal of Research in Personality*, 43, 822–829.

Deci, E.L. (1972). Intrinsic motivation, extrinsic reinforcement, and inequity. *Journal of Personality and Social Psychology*, 22, 113–120.

Deci, E.L., Koestner, R., & Ryan, R.M. (1999). A meta-analytic review of experiments examining the effects of extrinsic rewards on intrinsic motivation. *Psychological Bulletin*, 125, 627–668.

de Gelder, B. (2006). Towards the neurobiology of emotional body language. *Nature Reviews Neuroscience*, 7, 242–249.

Drazen, D.L., & Woods, S.C. (2003). Peripheral signals in the control of satiety and hunger. *Current Opinion in Clinical Nutrition and Metabolic Care*, 5, 621–629.

Druce, M.R., Small, C.J., & Bloom, S.R. (2004). Minireview: Gut peptides regulating satiety. *Endocrinology*, 145, 2660–2665.

Ekman, P., & Keltner, D. (1997). Universal facial expressions of emotion: An old controversy and new findings. In U. Segerstråle & P. Molnár (Eds.), *Nonverbal communication: Where nature meets culture* (pp. 27–46). Lawrence Erlbaum.

Everett, B.J. (1990). Sexual motivation: A neural and behavioural analysis of the mechanisms underlying appetitive and copulatory responses of male rats. *Neuroscience and Biobehavioral Reviews*, 14, 217–232.

Faris, E. (1921). Are instincts data or hypotheses? *American Journal of Sociology*, 27, 184–196.

Femenía, T., Gómez-Galán, M., Lindskog, M., & Magara, S. (2012). Dysfunctional hippocampal activity affects emotion and cognition in mood disorders. *Brain Research*, 1476, 58–70.

Fossati, P. (2012). Neural correlates of emotion processing: From emotional to social brain. *European Neuropsychopharmacology*, 22, S487–S491.

Fournier, J.C., Keener, M.T., Almeida, J., Kronhaus, D.M., & Phillips, M.L. (2013). Amygdala and whole-brain activity to emotional faces distinguishes major depressive disorder and bipolar disorder. *Bipolar Disorders*. Advance online publication. https://doi.org/10.1111/bdi.12106

Francis, N.H., & Kritsonis, W.A. (2006). A brief analysis of Abraham Maslow's original writing of *Self-Actualizing People: A Study of Psychological Health*. *Doctoral Forum National Journal of Publishing and Mentoring Doctoral Student Research*, 3, 1–7.

Gloy, V.L., Briel, M., Bhatt, D.L., Kashyap, S.R., Schauer, P.R., Mingrone, G.,...Nordmann, A.J. (2013, October 22). Bariatric surgery versus non-surgical treatment for obesity: A systematic review and meta-analysis of randomized controlled trials. *BMJ*, 347. https://doi.org/10.1136/bmj.f5934

Golan, O., & Baron-Cohen, S. (2006). Systemizing empathy: Teaching adults with Asperger syndrome or high-functioning autism to recognize complex emotions using interactive multimedia. *Development and Psychopathology*, 18, 591–617.

Goosens, K.A., & Maren, S. (2002). Long-term potentiation as a substrate for memory: Evidence from studies of amygdaloid plasticity and Pavlovian fear conditioning. *Hippocampus*, 12, 592–599.

Graham, S., & Weiner, B. (1996). Theories and principles of motivation. In D. C. Berliner & R. C. Calfee (Eds.), *Handbook of educational psychology* (pp. 63–84). Routledge.

Greary, N. (1990). Pancreatic glucagon signals postprandial satiety. *Neuroscience and Biobehavioral Reviews*, 14, 323–328.

Guastella, A.J., Einfeld, S.L., Gray, K.M., Rinehart, N.J., Tonge, B.J., Lambert, T.J., & Hickie, I.B. (2010). Intranasal oxytocin improves emotion recognition for youth with autism spectrum disorders. *Biological Psychiatry*, 67, 692–694.

Hall, J.A., & Kimura, D. (1994). Dermatoglyphic asymmetry and sexual orientation in men. *Behavioral Neuroscience*, 108(6), 1203–1206.

Hamer, D.H., Hu. S., Magnuson, V.L., Hu, N., & Pattatucci, A.M. (1993). A linkage between DNA markers on the X chromosome and male sexual orientation. *Science*, 261, 321-327.

Havas, D.A., Glenberg, A.M., Gutowski, K.A., Lucarelli, M.J., & Davidson, R.J. (2010). Cosmetic use of botulinum toxin-A affects processing of emotional language. *Psychological Science*, 21, 895–900.

Hobson, R.P. (1986). The autistic child's appraisal of expressions of emotion. *The Journal of Child Psychology and Psychiatry*, 27, 321–342.

Hock, R.R. (2008). Emotion and Motivation. In *Forty studies that changed psychology: Explorations into the history of psychological research* (6th ed.) (pp. 158–168). Pearson.

Hu, S.H., Wei, N., Wang, Q.D., Yan, L.Q., Wei, E.Q., Zhang, M.M.,...Xu, Y. (2008). Patterns of brain activation during visually evoked sexual arousal differ between homosexual and heterosexual men. *American Journal of Neuroradiology*, 29, 1890–1896.

Human Rights Campaign. (n.d.). *The lies and dangers of efforts to change sexual orientation or gender identity*. http://www.hrc.org/resources/entry/the-lies-and-dangers-of-reparative-therapy

Jenkins, W.J. (2010). Can anyone tell me why I'm gay? What research suggests regarding the origins of sexual orientation. *North American Journal of Psychology*, 12, 279–296.

Jenkins, W.J., & Becker, J.B. (2001). Role of the striatum and nucleus accumbens in paced copulatory behavior in the female rat. *Behavioural Brain Research*, 121, 19–28.

Kinsey, A.C., Pomeroy, W.B., & Martin, C.E. (1948). *Sexual behavior in the human male*. W.B. Saunders Company.

Koltko-Rivera, M.E. (2006). Rediscovering the later version of Maslow's hierarchy of needs: Self-transcendence and opportunities for theory, research, and unification. *Review of General Psychology*, 10, 302–317.

Konturek, S.J., Pepera, J., Zabielski, K., Konturek, P.C., Pawlick, T., Szlachcic, A., & Hahn. (2003). Brain-gut axis in pancreatic secretion and appetite control. *Journal of Physiology and Pharmacology*, 54, 293–317.

Lang, P.J. (1994). The varieties of emotional experience: A meditation on James-Lange theory. *Psychological Review*, 101, 211–221.

Lazarus, R.S. (1991). *Emotion and adaptation*. Oxford University Press.

LeDoux, J.E. (1996). *The Emotional Brain: The Mysterious Underpinnings of Emotional Life*. Simon & Schuster.

LeDoux, J.E. (2002). *The synaptic self*. Macmillan.

Leonard, G. (1982). The failure of self-actualization theory: A critique of Carl Rogers and Abraham Maslow. *Journal of Humanistic Psychology*, 22, 56–73.

LeVay, S. (1991). A difference in the hypothalamic structure between heterosexual and homosexual men. *Science*, 253, 1034–1037.

LeVay, S. (1996). *Queer science: The use and abuse of research into homosexuality*. The MIT Press.

Levy-Gigi, E., Szabó, C., Kelemen, O., & Kéri, S. (2013). Association among clinical response, hippocampal volume, and FKBP5 gene expression in individuals with posttraumatic stress disorder receiving cognitive behavioral therapy. *Biological Psychiatry*, 74, 793–800.

Lippa, R.A. (2003). Handedness, sexual orientation, and gender-related personality traits in men and women. *Archives of Sexual Behavior*, 32, 103–114.

Loehlin, J.C., & McFadden, D. (2003). Otoacoustic emissions, auditory evoked potentials, and traits related to sex and sexual orientation. *Archives of Sexual Behavior*, 32, 115–127.

Macdonald, H., Rutter, M., Howlin, P., Rios, P., Conteur, A.L., Evered, C., & Folstein, S. (1989). Recognition and expression of emotional cues by autistic and normal adults. *Journal of Child Psychology and Psychiatry*, 30, 865–877.

Malatesta, C.Z., & Haviland, J.M. (1982). Learning display rules: The socialization of emotion expression in infancy. *Child Development*, 53, 991–1003.

Maren, S., Phan, K.L., & Liberzon, I. (2013). The contextual brain: Implications for fear conditioning, extinction and psychopathology. *Nature Reviews Neuroscience*, 14, 417–428.

Martin-Gronert, M.S., & Ozanne, S.E. (2013). Early life programming of obesity. *Developmental Period Medicine*, 17, 7–12.

Maslow, A.H. (1943). A theory of human motivation. *Psychological Review*, 50, 370–396.

Matsumoto, D. (1990). Cultural similarities and differences in display rules. *Motivation and Emotion*, 14, 195–214.

Matsumoto, D., Yoo, S.H., & Nakagawa, S. (2008). Culture, emotion regulation, and adjustment. *Journal of Personality and Social Psychology*, 94, 925–937.

Mayo Clinic. (2012a). *Anorexia nervosa*. http://www.mayoclinic.com/health/anorexia/DS00606

Mayo Clinic. (2012b). *Bulimia nervosa*. http://www.mayoclinic.com/health/bulimia/DS00607

Mayo Clinic. (2013). *Gastric bypass surgery*. http://www.mayoclinic.com/health/gastric-bypass/MY00825

McAdams, D.P., & Constantian, C.A. (1983). Intimacy and affiliation motives in daily living: An experience sampling analysis. *Journal of Personality and Social Psychology*, 45, 851–861.

McClelland, D.C., & Liberman, A.M. (1949). The effect of need for achievement on recognition of need-related words. *Journal of Personality*, 18, 236–251.

McFadden, D., & Champlin, C.A. (2000). Comparisons of auditory evoked potentials in heterosexual, homosexual, and bisexual males and females. *Journal of the Association for Research in Otolaryngology*, 1, 89–99.

McFadden, D., & Pasanen, E.G. (1998). Comparisons of the auditory systems of heterosexuals and homosexuals: Clicked-evoked otoacoustic emissions. *Proceedings of the National Academy of Sciences, USA*, 95, 2709–2713.

McRae, K., Ochsner, K.N., Mauss, I.B., Gabrieli, J.J. D., & Gross, J.J. (2008). Gender differences in emotion regulation: An fMRI study of cognitive reappraisal. *Group Processes and Intergroup Relations*, 11, 143–162.

Miguel-Hidalgo, J.J. (2013). Brain structural and functional changes in adolescents with psychiatric disorders. *International Journal of Adolescent Medicine and Health*, 25, 245–256.

Money, J. (1962). *Cytogenic and psychosexual incongruities with a note on space-form blindness*. Paper presented at the 118th meeting of the American Psychiatric Association, Toronto, Canada.

Money, J. (1975). Ablatio penis: Normal male infant sex-reassigned as a girl. *Archives of Sexual Behavior*, 4, 65–71.

Moriceau, S., & Sullivan, R.M. (2006). Maternal presence serves as a switch between learning fear and attraction in infancy. *Nature Neuroscience*, 9, 1004–1006.

Murray, H.A., Barrett, W.G., Homburger, E., Langer, W.C., Mekeel, H.S., Morgan, C.D.,...Wolf, R.E. (1938). *Explorations in personality: A clinical and experimental study of fifty men of college age*. Oxford University Press.

Niemiec, C.P., & Ryan, R.M. (2009). Autonomy, competence, and relatedness in the classroom: Applying self-determination theory to educational practice. *Theory and Research in Education*, 7, 133–144.

Novin, D., Robinson, K., Culbreth, L.A., & Tordoff, M.G. (1985). Is there a role for the liver in the control of food intake? *The American Journal of Clinical Nutrition*, 42, 1050–1062.

O'Connell, S. (Writer/Producer). (2004). Dr. Money and the boy with no penis. [Television documentary series episode]. In *Horizon*. BBC.

Paramaguru, K. (2013, November). Boy, girl, or intersex? Germany adjusts to a third option at birth. *Time*. http://world.time.com/2013/11/12/boy-girl-or-intersex/

Pessoa, L. (2010). Emotion and cognition and the amygdala: From "what is it?" to "what's to be done?" *Neuropsychologia*, 48, 3416–3429.

Pillard, R.C., & Bailey, M.J. (1995). A biologic perspective on sexual orientation. *The Psychiatric Clinics of North America*, 18(1), 71–84.

Pillard, R.C., & Bailey, M.J. (1998). Sexual orientation has a heritable component. *Human Biology*, 70, 347–365.

Ponseti, J., Bosinski, H.A., Wolff, S., Peller, M., Jansen, O., Mehdorn, H.M.,…Siebner, H.R. (2006). A functional endophenotype for sexual orientation in humans. *Neuroimage*, 33(3), 825–833.

Prader-Willi Syndrome Association. (2012). *What is Prader-Willi Syndrome?* http://www.pwsausa.org/syndrome/index.htm

Qin, S., Young, C.B., Duan, X., Chen, T., Supekar, K., & Menon, V. (2013). Amygdala subregional structure and intrinsic functional connectivity predicts individual differences in anxiety during early childhood. *Biological Psychiatry*. Advance online publication. https://doi.org/10.1016/j.biopsych.2013.10.006

Rahman, Q., & Wilson, G.D. (2003a). Large sexual-orientation-related differences in performance on mental rotation and judgment of line orientation tasks. *Neuropsychology*, 17, 25–31.

Rahman, Q., & Wilson, G.D. (2003b). Sexual orientation and the 2nd to 4th finger length ratio: Evidence for organising effects of sex hormones or developmental instability? *Psychoneuroendocrinology*, 28, 288–303.

Raineki, C., Cortés, M.R., Belnoue, L., & Sullivan, R.M. (2012). Effects of early-life abuse differ across development: Infant social behavior deficits are followed by adolescent depressive-like behaviors mediated by the amygdala. *The Journal of Neuroscience*, 32, 7758–7765.

Rodriguez-Larralde, A., & Paradisi, I. (2009). Influence of genetic factors on human sexual orientation. *Investigacion Clinica*, 50, 377–391.

Ross, M.W., & Arrindell, W.A. (1988). Perceived parental rearing patterns of homosexual and heterosexual men. *The Journal of Sex Research*, 24, 275–281.

Saxe, L., & Ben-Shakhar, G. (1999). Admissibility of polygraph tests: The application of scientific standards post-Daubert. *Psychology, Public Policy, and Law*, 5, 203–223.

Schachter, S., & Singer, J.E. (1962). Cognitive, social, and physiological determinants of emotional state. *Psychological Review*, 69, 379–399.

Sherwin, B.B. (1988). A comparative analysis of the role of androgen in human male and female sexual behavior: Behavioral specificity, critical thresholds, and sensitivity. *Psychobiology*, 16, 416–425.

Smink, F.R.E., van Hoeken, D., & Hoek, H.W. (2012). Epidemiology of eating disorders: Incidence, prevalence, and mortality rates. *Current Psychiatry Reports*, 14, 406–414.

Soussignan, R. (2001). Duchenne smile, emotional experience, and autonomic reactivity: A test of the facial feedback hypothesis. *Emotion*, 2, 52–74.

Speakman, J.R., Levitsky, D.A., Allison, D.B., Bray, M.S., de Castro, J.M., Clegg, D.J.,…Westerterp-Plantenga, M.S. (2011). Set points, settling points and some alternative models: Theoretical options to understand how genes and environment combine to regulate body adiposity. *Disease Models & Mechanisms*, 4, 733–745.

Strack, F., Martin, L. & Stepper, S. (1988). Inhibiting and facilitating conditions of the human smile: A nonobtrusive test of the facial feedback hypothesis. *Journal of Personality and Social Psychology*, 54, 768–777.

Swaab, D.F., & Hofman, M.A. (1990). An enlarged suprachiasmatic nucleus in homosexual men. *Brain Research*, 537, 141–148.

Tamietto, M., Castelli, L., Vighetti, S., Perozzo, P., Geminiani, G., Weiskrantz, L., & de Gelder, B. (2009). Unseen facial and bodily expressions trigger fast emotional reactions. *Proceedings of the National Academy of Sciences, USA*, 106, 17661–17666.

Tangmunkongvorakul, A., Banwell, C., Carmichael, G., Utomo, I.D., & Sleigh, A. (2010). Sexual identities and lifestyles among non-heterosexual urban Chiang Mai youth: Implications for health. *Culture, Health, and Sexuality*, 12, 827–841.

Wang, Z., Neylan, T.C., Mueller, S.G., Lenoci, M., Truran, D., Marmar, C.R.,…Schuff, N. (2010). Magnetic resonance imaging of hippocampal subfields in posttraumatic stress disorder. *Arch Gen Psychiatry*, 67(3), 296–303. https://doi.org/10.1001/archgenpsychiatry.2009.205

Weinsier, R.L., Nagy, T.R., Hunter, G.R., Darnell, B.E., Hensrud, D.D., & Weiss, H.L. (2000). Do adaptive changes in metabolic rate favor weight regain in weight-reduced individuals? An examination of the set-point theory. *The American Journal of Clinical Nutrition*, 72, 1088–1094.

Woods, S.C. (2004). Gastrointestinal satiety signals I. An overview of gastrointestinal signals that influence food intake. *American Journal of Physiology: Gastrointestinal and Liver Physiology*, 286, G7–G13.

Woods, S.C., & D'Alessio, D.A. (2008). Central control of body weight and appetite. *Journal of Clinical Endocrinology and Metabolism*, 93, S37–S50.

Yerkes, R.M., & Dodson, J.D. (1908). The relation of strength of stimulus to rapidity of habit-formation. *Journal of Comparative Neurology and Psychology*, 18, 459–482. https://doi.org/10.1002/cne.920180503

Zajonc, R.B. (1980). Feeling and thinking: Preferences need no inferences. *American Psychologist*, 35(2), 151–175.

Zajonc, R.B. (1998). Emotions. In D. T. Gilbert & S. T. Fiske (Eds.), *Handbook of social psychology* (4th ed., Vol. 1, pp. 591–632). McGraw-Hill.

Chapter 10

Adler, A. (1930). Individual psychology. In C. Murchison (Ed.), *Psychologies of 1930* (pp. 395–405). Clark University Press.

Adler, A. (1937). A school girl's exaggeration of her own importance. *International Journal of Individual Psychology*, 3(1), 3–12.

Adler, A. (1956). *The individual psychology of Alfred Adler: A systematic presentation in selections from his writings.* (C. H. Ansbacher & R. Ansbacher, Eds.). Harper.

Adler, A. (1961). The practice and theory of individual psychology. In T. Shipley (Ed.), *Classics in psychology* (pp. 687–714). Philosophical Library

Adler, A. (1964). *Superiority and social interest*. Norton.

Akomolafe, M.J. (2013). Personality characteristics as predictors of academic performance of secondary school students. *Mediterranean Journal of Social Sciences*, 4(2), 657–664.

Allport, G.W. & Odbert, H.S. (1936). Trait-names: A psycho-lexical study. Psychological Review Company.

Aronow, E., Weiss, K.A., & Rezinkoff, M. (2001). *A practical guide to the Thematic Apperception Test*. Brunner Routledge.

Bandura, A. (1977). Self-efficacy: Toward a unifying theory of behavioral change. *Psychological Review*, 84, 191–215.

Bandura, A. (1986). *Social foundations of thought and action: A social cognitive theory*. Prentice Hall.

Bandura, A. (1995). *Self-efficacy in changing societies*. Cambridge University Press.

Benassi, V.A., Sweeney, P.D., & Dufour, C.L. (1988). Is there a relation between locus of control orientation and depression? *Journal of Abnormal Psychology, 97*(3), 357.

Ben-Porath, Y., & Tellegen, A. (2008). *Minnesota Multiphasic Personality Inventory-2-RF*. University of Minnesota Press.

Benet-Martínez, V. & Karakitapoglu-Aygun, Z. (2003). The interplay of cultural values and personality in predicting life-satisfaction: Comparing Asian- and European-Americans. *Journal of Cross-Cultural Psychology*, 34, 38–61.

Benet-Martínez, V., & Oishi, S. (2008). Culture and personality. In O. P. John, R.W. Robins, L.A. Pervin (Eds.), *Handbook of personality: Theory and research*. Guildford Press.

Beutler, L.E., Nussbaum, P.D., & Meredith, K.E. (1988). Changing personality patterns of police officers. *Professional Psychology: Research and Practice, 19*(5), 503–507.

Bouchard, T., Jr. (1994). Genes, environment, and personality. *Science*, 264, 1700–1701.

Bouchard, T., Jr., Lykken, D.T., McGue, M., Segal, N.L., & Tellegen, A. (1990). Sources of human psychological differences: The Minnesota Study of Twins Reared Apart. *Science*, 250, 223–228.

Burger, J. (2008). *Personality* (7th ed.). Thompson Higher Education.

Carter, J.E., and Heath, B.H. (1990). *Somatotyping: Development and applications*. Cambridge University Press.

Carter, S., Champagne, F., Coates, S., Nercessian, E., Pfaff, D., Schecter, D., & Stern, N.B. (2008). *Development of temperament symposium*. Philoctetes Center, New York.

Cattell, R.B. (1946). *The description and measurement of personality*. Harcourt, Brace, & World.

Cattell, R.B. (1957). *Personality and motivation structure and measurement*. World Book.

Chamorro-Premuzic, T., & Furnham, A. (2008). Personality, intelligence, and approaches to learning as predictors of academic performance. *Personality and Individual Differences*, 44, 1596–1603.

Cheung, F.M., van de Vijver, F.J. R., & Leong, F.T. L. (2011). Toward a new approach to the study of personality in culture. *American Psychologist, 66*(7), 593–603.

Clark, A.L., & Watson, D. (2008). Temperament: An organizing paradigm for trait psychology. In O. P. John, R.W. Robins, & L. A. Previn (Eds.), *Handbook of personality: Theory and research* (3rd ed., pp. 265–286). Guilford Press.

Conrad, N. & Party, M.W. (2012). Conscientiousness and academic performance: A Mediational Analysis. International *Journal for the Scholarship of Teaching and Learning, 6*(1), 1–14.

Cortés, J., & Gatti, F. (1972). Delinquency and crime: A biopsychological approach. Seminar Press.

Costantino, G. (1982). TEMAS: A new technique for personality research assessment of Hispanic children. Hispanic Research Center, Fordham University *Research Bulletin*, 5, 3–7.

Cramer, P. (2004). *Storytelling, narrative, and the Thematic Apperception Test*. Guilford Press.

Damon, S. (1955). Physique and success in military flying. *American Journal of Physical Anthropology, 13*(2), 217–252.

Donnellan, M.B., & Lucas, R.E. (2008). Age differences in the big five across the life span: Evidence from two national samples. *Psychology and Aging, 23*(3), 558–566.

Duzant, R. (2005). *Differences of emotional tone and story length of African American respondents when administered the Contemporized Themes Concerning Blacks test versus the Thematic Apperception Test*. Unpublished doctoral dissertation, The Chicago School of Professional Psychology, Chicago, IL.

Exner, J.E. (2002). *The Rorschach: Basic foundations and principles of interpretation* (Vol. 1). Wiley.

Eysenck, H.J. (1970). *The structure of human personality*. Methuen.

Eysenck, H.J. (1990). An improvement on personality inventory. *Current Contents: Social and Behavioral Sciences, 22*(18), 20.

Eysenck, H.J. (1992). Four ways five factors are *not* basic. *Personality and Individual Differences*, 13, 667–673.

Eysenck, H.J. (2009). *The biological basis of personality* (3rd ed.). Transaction Publishers.

Eysenck, H.J., & Eysenck, M.W. (1985). *Personality and individual differences: A natural science approach*. Plenum Press.

Eysenck, S.B.G., & Eysenck, H.J. (1963). The validity of questionnaire and rating assessments of extroversion and neuroticism, and their factorial stability. *British Journal of Psychology*, 54, 51–62.

Eysenck, S.B.G., Eysenck, H.J., & Barrett, P. (1985). A revised version of the psychoticism scale. *Personality and Individual Differences, 6*(1), 21–29.

Fancher, R.W. (1979). *Pioneers of psychology*. Norton.

Fazeli, S.H. (2012). The exploring nature of the assessment instrument of five factors of personality traits in the current studies of personality. *Asian Social Science, 8*(2), 264–275.

Freud, S. (1920). Resistance and suppression. *A general introduction to psychoanalysis* (pp. 248–261). Horace Liveright.

Freud, S. (1923/1949). The ego and the id. Hogarth.

Freud, S. (1931/1968). Female sexuality. In J. Strachey (Ed. &Trans.), *The standard edition of the complete psychological works of Sigmund Freud* (Vol. 21). Hogarth Press.

Funder, D.C. (2001). Personality. *Annual Review of Psychology*, 52, 197–221.

Genovese, J.E. C. (2008). Physique correlates with reproductive success in an archival sample of delinquent youth. *Evolutionary Psychology, 6*(3), 369-385.

Hofstede, G. (2001). *Culture's consequences: Comparing values, behaviors, institutions, and organizations across nations* (2nd ed.). Sage.

Holaday, D., Smith, D.A., & Sherry, Alissa. (2010). Sentence completion tests: A review of the literature and results of a survey of members of the society for personality assessment. *Journal of Personality Assessment, 74*(3), 371–383.

Hothersall, D. (1995). *History of psychology*. McGraw-Hill.

Hoy, M. (1997). *Contemporizing of the Themes Concerning Blacks test (C-TCB)*. California School of Professional Psychology.

Hoy-Watkins, M., & Jenkins-Moore, V. (2008). The Contemporized-Themes Concerning Blacks Test (C-TCB). In S. R. Jenkins (Ed.), *A Handbook of Clinical Scoring Systems for Thematic Apperceptive Techniques* (pp. 659–698). Lawrence Erlbaum Associates.

Jang, K.L., Livesley, W.J., & Vernon, P.A. (1996). Heritability of the big five personality dimensions and their facts: A twin study. *Journal of Personality, 64*(3), 577–591.

Jang, K.L., Livesley, W.J., Ando, J., Yamagata, S., Suzuki, A., Angleitner, A., et al. (2006). Behavioral genetics of the higher-order factors of the Big Five. *Personality and Individual Differences*, 41, 261–272.

Judge, T.A., Livingston, B.A., & Hurst, C. (2012). Do nice guys-and gals- really finish last? The joint effects of sex and agreeableness on income. *Journal of Personality and Social Psychology, 102*(2), 390–407.

Jung, C.G. (1923). *Psychological types*. Harcourt Brace.

Jung, C.G. (1928). *Contributions to analytical psychology*. Harcourt Brace Jovanovich.

Jung, C.G. (1964). *Man and his symbols*. Doubleday and Company.

Jung, C., & Kerenyi, C. (1963). Science of mythology. In R. F. C. Hull (Ed. & Trans.), *Essays on the myth of the divine child and the mysteries of Eleusis*. Harper & Row.

Launer, J. (2005). Anna O. and the 'talking cure.' *QJM: An International Journal of Medicine, 98*(6), 465–466.

Lecci, L.B. & Magnavita, J.J. (2013). *Personality theories: A scientific approach*. Bridgepoint Education.

Lefcourt, H.M. (1982). *Locus of control: Current trends in theory and research* (2nd ed.). Erlbaum.

Likert, R. (1932). A technique for the measurement of attitudes. *Archives of Psychology*, 140, 1–55.

Lilienfeld, S.O., Wood, J.M., & Garb, H.N. (2000). The scientific status of projective techniques. *Psychological Science in the Public Interest, 1*(2), 27–66.

Maltby, J., Day, L., & Macaskill, A. (2007). *Personality, individual differences and intelligence* (3rd ed.). Pearson.

Maslow, A.H. (1950). Self-actualizing people: A study of psychological health. In W. Wolff (Ed.), *Personality Symposia: Symposium 1 on Values* (pp. 11–34). Grune & Stratton.

Maslow, A.H. (1970). *Motivation and personality*. Harper & Row.

McCrae, R.R., & Costa, P.T. (1997). Personality trait structure as a human universal. *American Psychologist, 52*(5), 509–516.

McCrae, R.R., et al. (2005). Universal features of personality traits from the observer's perspective: Data from 50 cultures. *Journal of Personality and Social Psychology, 88*, 547–561.

Mischel, W. (1993). *Introduction to personality* (5th ed.). Harcourt Brace Jovanovich.

Mischel, W., Ayduk, O., Berman, M.G., Casey, B.J., Gotlib, I.H., Jonides, J., et al. (2010). 'Willpower' over the life span: Decomposing self-regulation. *Social Cognitive and Affective Neuroscience, 6*(2), 252–256.

Mischel, W., Ebbesen, E.B., & Raskoff Zeiss, A. (1972). Cognitive and attentional mechanisms of delay in gratification. *Journal of Personality and Social Psychology, 21*(2), 204–218.

Mischel, W., Shoda, Y., & Rodriguez, M.L. (1989, May 26). Delay of gratification in children. *Science*, 244, 933-938.

Mischel, W., & Shoda, Y. (1995). A cognitive-affective system theory of personality: Reconceptualizing situations, dispositions, dynamics, and invariance in personality structure. *Psychological Review, 102*(2), 246–268.

Motley, M.T. (2002). Theory of slips. In E. Erwin (Ed.), *The Freud encyclopedia: Theory, therapy, and culture* (pp. 530–534). Routledge.

Noftle, E.E., & Robins, R.W. (2007). Personality predictors of academic outcomes: Big Five correlates of GPA and SAT scores. *Personality Processes and Individual Differences*, 93, 116–130.

Noga, A. (2007). *Passions and tempers: A history of the humors*. Harper Collins.

Oyserman, D., Coon, H., & Kemmelmier, M. (2002). Rethinking individualism and collectivism: Evaluation of theoretical assumptions and meta-analyses. *Psychological Bulletin*, 128, 3–72.

Parnell, R.W. (1958). *Behavior and physique: An introduction to practical somatometry*. Edward Arnold Publishers LTD.

Peterson, J., Liivamagi, J., & Koskel, S. (2006). Associations between temperament types and body build in 17–22 year-old Estonian female students. *Papers on Anthropology*, 25, 142–149.

Piotrowski, Z.A. (1987). *Perceptanalysis: The Rorschach method fundamentally reworked, expanded and systematized*. Routledge.

Rafter, N. (2007). Somatotyping, antimodernism, and the production of criminological knowledge. *Criminology*, 45, 805–833.

Rentfrow, P.J., Gosling, S.D., Jokela, M., Stillwell, D.J., Kosinski, M., & Potter, J. (2013, October 14). Divided we stand: Three psychological regions of the United States and their political, economic, social, and health correlates. *Journal of Personality and Social Psychology, 105*(6), 996–1012.

Roesler, C. (2012). Are archetypes transmitted more by culture than biology? Questions arising from conceptualizations of the archetype. *Journal of Analytical Psychology, 57*(2), 223–246.

Rogers, C. (1980). *A way of being*. Houghton Mifflin.

Rosenbaum, R. (1995, January 15). The great Ivy League posture photo scandal. *The New York Times*, pp. A26.

Rothbart, M.K. (2011). *Becoming who we are: Temperament and personality in development*. Guilford Press.

Rothbart, M.K., & Derryberry, D. (1981). Development of individual differences in temperament. In M. E. Lamb & A. L. Brown (Eds.), *Advances in developmental psychology* (Vol. 1, pp. 37–86). Erlbaum.

Rothbart, M.K., Ahadi, S.A., & Evans, D.E. (2000). Temperament and personality: Origins and outcomes. *Journal of Personality and Social Psychology, 78*(1), 122–135.

Rothbart, M.K., Sheese, B.E., Rueda, M.R., & Posner, M.I. (2011). Developing mechanisms of self-regulation in early life. *Emotion Review, 3*(2), 207–213.

Rotter, J. (1966). Generalized expectancies for internal versus external control of reinforcements. *Psychological Monographs*, 80, 609.

Rotter, J.B., & Rafferty, J.E. (1950). *Manual the Rotter Incomplete Sentences Blank College Form*. The Psychological Corporation.

Sanford, R.N., Adkins, M.M., Miller, R.B., & Cobb, E.A. (1943). Physique, personality, and scholarship: A cooperative study of school children. *Monographs of the Society for Research in Child Development, 8*(1), 705.

Schmitt, D.P., Allik, J., McCrae, R.R., & Benet-Martinez, V. (2007). The geographic distribution of Big Five personality traits: Patterns and profiles of human self-description across 56 nations. *Journal of Cross-Cultural Psychology*, 38, 173–212.

Scott, J. (2005). *Electra after Freud: Myth and culture*. Cornell University Press.

Segal, N.L. (2012). *Born together-reared apart: The landmark Minnesota Twin Study*. Harvard University Press.

Sheldon, W.H. (1940). *The varieties of human physique: An introduction to constitutional psychology*. Harper and Row.

Sheldon, W.H. (1942). *The varieties of temperament: A psychology of constitutional differences*. Harper and Row.

Sheldon, W.H. (1949). Varieties of delinquent youth: An introduction to constitutional psychology. Harper and Brothers.

Skinner, B.F. (1953). *Science and human behavior*. The Free Press.

Sotirova-Kohli, M., Opwis, K., Roesler, C., Smith, S.M., Rosen, D.H., Vaid, J., & Djnov, V. (2013). Symbol/meaning paired-associate recall: An "archetypal memory" advantage? *Behavioral Sciences*, 3, 541–561. http://www2.cnr.edu/home/araia/Myth_%20Body.pdf

Stelmack, R.M., & Stalikas, A. (1991). Galen and the humour theory of temperament. *Personal Individual Difference, 12*(3), 255–263.

Terracciano A., McCrae R. R., Brant L. J., Costa P. T., Jr. (2005). Hierarchical linear modeling analyses of the NEO-PI-R scales in the Baltimore Longitudinal Study of Aging. *Psychology and Aging*, 20, 493–506.

Thomas, A., & Chess, S. (1977). *Temperament and development*. Brunner/Mazel.

Tok, S. (2011). The big five personality traits and risky sport participation. *Social Behavior and Personality: An International Journal, 39*(8), 1105–1111.

Triandis, H.C. (1995). *Individualism and collectivism*. Westview.

Triandis, H.C., & Suh, E.M. (2002). Cultural influences on personality. *Annual Review of Psychology*, 53, 133–160.

Wagerman, S.A., & Funder, D.C. (2007). Acquaintance reports of personality and academic achievement: A case for conscientiousness. *Journal of Research in Personality*, 41, 221–229.

Watson, D., & Clark, L.A. (1984). Negative affectivity: The disposition to experience aversive emotional states. *Psychological Bulletin*, 96, 465–490.

Weiner, I.B. (2003). *Principles of Rorschach interpretation*. Lawrence Erlbaum.

Whyte, C. (1978). Effective counseling methods for high-risk college freshmen. *Measurement and Evaluation in Guidance, 6*(4), 198–200.

Whyte, C. (1980). An integrated counseling and learning center. In K. V. Lauridsen (Ed.), *Examining the scope of learning centers* (pp. 33–43). Jossey-Bass.

Whyte, C.B. (1977). High-risk college freshman and locus of control. *The Humanist Educator, 16*(1), 2–5.

Williams, R.L. (1972). Themes Concerning Blacks: Manual. Williams.

Wundt, W. (1874/1886). *Elements du psychologie, physiologique* (2ieme tome). [Elements of physiological psychology, Vol. 2]. (E. Rouvier, Trans.). Paris: Ancienne Librairie Germer Bailliere et Cie.

Yang, K.S. (2006). Indigenous personality research: The Chinese case. In U. Kim, K.-S. Yang, & K.-K. Hwang (Eds.), *Indigenous and cultural psychology: Understanding people in context* (pp. 285–314). Springer.

Young-Eisendrath, P. (1995). *Myth and body: Pandora's legacy in a post-modern world*. http://www2.cnr.edu/home/araia/Myth_%20Body.pdf

Chapter 11

Adams, H.E., Wright, L.W., Jr., & Lohr, B.A. (1996). Is homophobia associated with homosexual arousal? *Journal of Abnormal Psychology*, 105, 440–445.

Albarracín, D., & Wyer, R.S. (2001). Elaborative and nonelaborative processing of a behavior-related communication. *Personality and Social Psychology Bulletin*, 27, 691–705.

Alexander, M. (2001, August 22). Thirty years later, Stanford prison experiment lives on. *Stanford Report*. http://news.stanford.edu/news/2001/august22/prison2-822.html.

Allport, G.W. (1954). *The Nature of Human Prejudice*. Addison-Wesley.

American Psychological Association (2010). Bullying: What parents, teachers can do to stop it. http://www.apa.org/news/press/releases/2010/04/bullying.aspx.

Aronson, E., & Mills, J. (1959). The effect of severity of initiation on liking for a group, *Journal of Abnormal and Social Psychology*, 59, 177–181.

Asch, S.E. (1955). Opinions and social pressure. *Scientific American*, 193, 31–35.

Bandura, A. (1999). Moral disengagement in the perpetration of inhumanities. *Personality and Social Psychology Review, 3*(3), 193–209. https://doi.org/10.1207/s15327957pspr0303_3.

Baron, R.M., Albright, L., & Malloy, T.E. (1995). Effects of behavioral and social class information on social judgment. *Personality and Social Psychology Bulletin*, 21, 308–315.

Batson, C.D. (1991). *The altruism question: Toward a social-psychological answer*. Erlbaum.

Berkowitz, A.D. (2004). *The social norms approach: Theory, research and annotated bibliography*. http://www.alanberkowitz.com/articles/social_norms.pdf.

Berkowitz, L. (1993). *Aggression: Its causes, consequences, and control*. McGraw-Hill.

Betz, N.E. (2008). Women's career development. In F. Denmark & M. Paludi (Eds.), *Psychology of women: Handbook of issues and theories* (2nd ed., pp. 717–752). Praeger.

Blau, F.D., Ferber, M.A., & Winkler, A.E. (2010). *The economics of women, men, and work* (6th ed.). Prentice Hall.

Bond, C.F., & Titus, L.J. (1983). Social facilitation: A meta-analysis of 241 studies. *Psychological Bulletin*, 94, 265–292.

Bond, R., & Smith, P.B. (1996). Culture and conformity: A meta-analysis of studies using Asch's (1952b, 1956) line judgment task. *Psychological Bulletin, 119*(1), 111–137.

Bowen, L. (2011). Bullying may contribute to lower test scores. *Monitor on Psychology, 42*(9), 19.

Brown, R. (2010). *Prejudice: Its social psychology* (2nd ed.). Wiley-Blackwell.

Buss, D.M. (1989). Sex differences in human mate preferences: Evolutionary hypotheses tested in 37 cultures. *Behavioral and Brain Sciences*, 12, 1–49.

Buss, D.M. (2004). *Evolutionary psychology: The new science of the mind* (2nd ed.). Allyn and Bacon.

Ceci, S.J., & Williams, W.M. (2011). Understanding current causes of women's underrepresentation in science. *Proceedings of the National Academy of Sciences*, 108, 3157–3162.

Choi, I., & Nisbett R. E. (1998). Situational salience and cultural differences in the correspondence bias and actor-observer bias. *Personality and Social Psychology Bulletin, 24*(9), 949–960. https://doi.org/10.1177/0146167298249003.

Cialdini, R.B. (2001). Harnessing the science of persuasion. *Harvard Business Review*, 79, 72–81.

Cialdini, R.B., Brown, S.L., Lewis, B.P., Luce, C., & Neuberg, S.L. (1997). Reinterpreting the empathy-altruism relationship: When one into one equals oneness. *Journal of Personality and Social Psychology*, 73, 481–494.

Colin Powell regrets Iraq war intelligence. (2011). Retrieved March 23, 2014, from http://www.aljazeera.com/news/americas/2011/09/20119116916873488.html.

Cozby, P.C. (1973). Self-disclosure: A literature review. *Psychological Bulletin*, 79, 73–91.

Crisp, R.J., & Turner, R.N. (2009). Can imagined interactions produce positive perceptions? Reducing prejudice through simulated social contact. *American Psychologist*, 64, 231–240.

Crowley, A.E., & Hoyer, W.D. (1994). An integrative framework for understanding two-sided persuasion. *Journal of Consumer Research, 20*(4), 561–574.

Croyle, R.T., & Cooper, J. (1983). Dissonance arousal: Physiological evidence. *Journal of Personality and Social Psychology*, 45, 782–791.

Cuddy, A.J., Norton, M.I., & Fiske, S.T. (2005). This old stereotype: The pervasiveness and persistence of the elderly stereotype. *Journal of Social Issues*, 61, 267–285.

Deutsch, M., & Gerard, H. (1955). A study of normative and informational social influences upon individual judgment. *Journal of Abnormal and Social Psychology*, 51, 629–636.

Devine, P.G. (1989). Stereotypes and prejudice: Their automatic and controlled components. *Journal of Personality and Social Psychology*, 56, 5–18.

Devine, P.G., & Elliot, A.J. (1995). Are racial stereotypes really fading? The Princeton trilogy revisited. *Personality and Social Psychology Bulletin*, 21, 1139–1150.

Dixon, T.L., & Linz D. (2000). Overrepresentation and underrepresentation of African Americans and Latinos as lawbreakers on television news. *Journal of Communication*, *50*(2), 131–154.

Dodge, K.A., & Schwartz, D. (1997). Social information processing mechanisms in aggressive behavior. In D. M. Stoff and J. Breiling (Eds.), *Handbook of Antisocial Behavior* (pp. 171–180). John Wiley and Sons.

Dollard, J., Miller, N.E., Doob, L.W., Mowrer, O.H., & Sears, R.R. (1939). *Frustration and aggression*. Yale University Press.

Dovidio, J.F., & Gaertner, S.L. (2004). On the nature of contemporary prejudice. In P. S. Rothenberg, (Ed.), *Race, class, and gender in the United States: An integrated study* (6th ed., pp. 132–142). Worth.

Dovidio, J.F., Gluszek, A., John, M.S., Ditlmann, R., & Lagunes, P. (2010). Understanding bias toward Latinos: Discrimination, dimensions of difference, and experience of exclusion. *Journal of Social Issues*, 66, 59–78.

Eagly, A.H., & Chaiken, S. (1975). An attribution analysis of the effect of communicator characteristics on opinion change: The case of communicator attractiveness. *Journal of Personality and Social Psychology*, 32, 136–144.

Eagly, A.H., & Chaiken, S. (1993). *The psychology of attitudes*. Harcourt Brace Jovanovich College.

East Haven mayor suggests "he might have tacos" to repair relations with Latinos. (2012). Retrieved April 27, 2014, from https://www.youtube.com/watch?v=PCUwtfqF4wU.

Ehrlinger, J., Gilovich, T., & Ross, L. (2005). Peering into the bias blind spot: People's assessments of bias in themselves and others. *Personality and Social Psychology Bulletin*, 31, 680–692.

Festinger, L. (1957). *A theory of cognitive dissonance*. Stanford University Press.

Festinger, L., & Maccoby, N. (1964). On resistance to persuasive communications. *The Journal of Abnormal and Social Psychology*, 68, 359–366.

Festinger, L., Schachler, S., & Back, K.W. (1950). *Social pressures in informal groups: A study of human factors in housing*. Harper.

Fink, B., Neave, N., Manning, J.T., & Grammer, K. (2006). Facial symmetry and judgments of attractiveness, health and personality. *Personality and Individual Differences*, 41, 491–499.

Fiske, S.T., Cuddy, A.J., Glick, P., & Xu, J. (2002). A model of (often mixed) stereotype content: Competence and warmth respectively follow from perceived status and competition. *Journal of Personality and Social Psychology*, *82*(6), 878–902.

Fiske, S.T., Gilbert, D.T., & Lindzey, G. (2010). *Handbook of social psychology* (5th ed.). Wiley.

Freedman, J.L., & Fraser, S.C. (1966). Compliance without pressure: The foot-in-the-door technique. *Journal of Personality and Social Psychology*, 4, 195–202.

Geen, R.G. (1989). Alternative conceptions of social facilitation. In P. B. Paulus (Ed.), *Psychology of group influence* (2nd ed., pp. 15–51). Hillsdale, NJ: Lawrence Erlbaum.

Greenberg, J., Schimel, J., & Martens, A. (2002). Ageism: Denying the face of the future. In T. D. Nelson (Ed.), *Ageism: Stereotyping and prejudice against older persons* (pp. 27–48). Cambridge, MA: MIT Press.

Greenwald, A.G., McGhee, D.E., & Schwartz, J.L. (1998). Measuring individual differences in implicit cognition: The implicit association test. *Journal of Personality and Social Psychology*, 74, 1464–1480.

Greenwald, A.G., & Ronis, D.L. (1978). Twenty years of cognitive dissonance: Case study of the evolution of a theory. *Psychological Review*, 85, 53–57.

Grove, J.R., Hanrahan, S.J., & McInman, A. (1991). Success/failure bias in attributions across involvement categories in sport. *Personality and Social Psychology Bulletin*, *17*(1), 93–97.

Gupta, P.B., & Lord, K.R. (1998). Product placement in movies: The effect of prominence and mode on recall. *Journal of Current Issues and Research in Advertising*, 20, 47–59.

Hare, A.P. (2003). Roles, relationships, and groups in organizations: Some conclusions and recommendations. *Small Group Research*, 34, 123–154.

Haugtvedt, C.P., & Wegener, D.T. (1994). Message order effects in persuasion: An attitude strength perspective. *Journal of Consumer Research*, 21, 205–218.

Hebl, M.R., Foster, J.B., Mannix, L.M., & Dovidio, J.F. (2002). Formal and interpersonal discrimination: A field study of bias toward homosexual applicants. *Personality and Social Psychology Bulletin*, *28*(6), 815–825.

Heckert, T.M., Latier, A., Ringwald-Burton, A., & Drazen, C. (2006). Relations among student effort, perceived class difficulty appropriateness, and student evaluations of teaching: Is it possible to "buy" better evaluations through lenient grading? *College Student Journal*, *40*(3), 588.

Heider, F. (1958). *The psychology of interpersonal relations*. New York: Wiley.

Herek, G.M., & McLemore, K.A. (2013). Sexual prejudice. *Annual Review of Psychology*, 64, 309–33. https://doi.org/10.1146/annurev-psych-113011-143826.

Hinduja, S., & Patchin, J.W. (2010). Bullying, cyberbullying, and suicide. *Archives of Suicide Research*, *14*(3), 206–221.

Hinduja, S., & Patchin, J.W. (2011). Cyberbullying research summary: Bullying, cyberbullying, and sexual orientation. Cyberbullying Research Center. Retrieved April 27, 2014, from http://www.cyberbullying.us/cyberbullying_sexual_orientation_fact_sheet.pdf.

Hodge, S.R., Burden, J.W., Jr., Robinson, L.E., & Bennett, R.A., III. (2008). Theorizing on the stereotyping of black male student-athletes. *Journal for the Study of Sports and Athletes in Education*, 2, 203–226.

Hoff, D.L., & Mitchell, S.N. (2009). Cyberbullying: Causes, effects, and remedies. *Journal of Education*, 47, 652–665.

Hovland, C.I., Janis, I.L. and Kelley, H.H. (1953). *Communications and persuasion: Psychological studies in opinion change*. New Haven, CT: Yale University Press.

Hovland, C.I., Weiss, W. (1951, Winter). The influence of source credibility on communication effectiveness. *Public Opinion Quarterly*, *15*(4), 635–650.

Igou, E.R., & Bless, H. (2003). Inferring the importance of arguments: Order effects and conversational rules. *Journal of Experimental Social Psychology*, 39, 91–99.

Ito, T.A., & Urland, G.R., (2003). Race and gender on the brain: Electrocortical measures of attention to race and gender of multiply categorizable individuals. *Journal of Personality & Social Psychology*, 85, 616–626.

Jackson, J.M., & Williams, K.D. (1985). Social loafing on difficult tasks: Working collectively can improve performance. *Journal of Personality and Social Psychology, 49*, 937–942.

Janis, I.L. (1972). *Victims of groupthink*. Boston, MA: Houghton Mifflin.

Jones, E.E., & Nisbett, R.E. (1971). *The actor and the observer: Divergent perceptions of the causes of behavior*. New York: General Learning Press.

Jost, J.T., Banaji, M.R., & Nosek, B.A. (2004). A decade of system justification theory: Accumulated evidence of conscious and unconscious bolstering of the status quo. *Political Psychology, 25*, 881–919.

Jost, J.T., & Major, B. (Eds.). (2001). *The psychology of legitimacy: Emerging perspectives on ideology, justice, and intergroup relations*. New York, NY: Cambridge University Press.

Karau, S.J., & Williams, K.D. (1993). Social loafing: A meta-analytic review and theoretical integration. *Journal of Personality and Social Psychology, 65*, 681–706.

Krosnick, J.A., & Alwin, D.F. (1989). Aging and susceptibility to attitude change. *Journal of Personality and Social Psychology, 57*, 416–425.

Kumkale, G.T., & Albarracín, D. (2004). The sleeper effect in persuasion: A meta-analytic review. *Psychological Bulletin, 130*(1), 143–172. https://doi.org/10.1037/0033-2909.130.1.143.

Larsen, K.S. (1990). The Asch conformity experiment: Replication and transhistorical comparisons. *Journal of Social Behavior & Personality, 5*(4), 163–168.

Latané, B., & Darley, J.M. (1968). Group inhibition of bystander intervention in emergencies. *Journal of Personality and Social Psychology, 10*, 215–221.

Latané, B., Williams, K. and Harkins, S.G. (1979). Many hands make light the work: The causes and consequences of social loafing. *Journal of Personality and Social Psychology, 37*, 822–832.

Laurenceau, J.-P., Barrett, L.F., & Pietromonaco, P.R. (1998). Intimacy as an interpersonal process: The importance of self-disclosure, partner disclosure, and perceived partner responsiveness in interpersonal exchanges. *Journal of Personality and Social Psychology, 74*(5), 1238–1251. https://doi.org/10.1037/0022-3514.74.5.1238.

Lerner, M.J., & Miller, D.T. (1978). Just world research and the attribution process: Looking back and ahead. *Psychological Bulletin, 85*, 1030–1051.

Lumsdaine, A.A., & Janis, I.L. (1953). Resistance to "counterpropaganda" produced by one-sided and two-sided "propaganda" presentations. *Public Opinion Quarterly, 17*, 311–318.

Malle, B.F. (2006). The actor-observer asymmetry in attribution: A (surprising) meta-analysis [Supplemental material]. *Psychological Bulletin, 132*(6), 895–919. https://doi.org/10.1037/0033-2909.132.6.895.

Malloy, T.E., Albright, L., Kenny, D.A., Agatstein, F., & Winquist, L. (1997). Interpersonal perception and metaperception in non-overlapping social groups. *Journal of Personality and Social Psychology, 72*, 390–398.

Markus, H.R., & Kitayama, S. (1991). Culture and the self: Implications for cognition, emotion, and motivation. *Psychological Review, 98*, 224–253.

Martin, C.H., & Bull, P. (2008). Obedience and conformity in clinical practice. *British Journal of Midwifery, 16*(8), 504–509.

McPherson, M., Smith-Lovin, L., & Cook, J.M. (2001). Birds of a feather: Homophily in social networks. *Annual Review of Sociology, 27*, pp. 415–444. https://doi.org/10.1146/annurev.soc.27.1.415.

Milgram, S. (1963). Behavioral study of obedience. *Journal of Abnormal and Social Psychology, 67*, 371–378.

Milgram, S. (1965). Some conditions of obedience and disobedience to authority. *Human Relations, 18*, 57–76.

Miller, D.T., & Ross, M. (1975). Self-serving biases in the attribution of causality: Fact or fiction? *Psychological Bulletin, 82*, 213–225.

Miller, N., & Campbell, D.T. (1959). Recency and primacy in persuasion as a function of the timing of speeches and measurements. *The Journal of Abnormal and Social Psychology, 59*, 1–9.

Mischel, W. (1977). The interaction of person and situation. *Personality at the crossroads: Current issues in interactional psychology, 333*, 352.

Mitchell, D.H., & Eckstein, D. (2009). Jury dynamics and decision-making: A prescription for groupthink. *International Journal of Academic Research, 1*(1), 163–169.

Nelson, T. (Ed.). (2004). *Ageism: Stereotyping and prejudice against older persons*. The MIT Press.

Nisbett, R.E., Caputo, C., Legant, P., & Marecek, J. (1973). Behavior as seen by the actor and as seen by the observer. *Journal of Personality and Social Psychology, 27*, 154–164.

Nisbett, R.E., Peng, K., Choi, I., & Norenzayan, A. (2001). Culture and systems of thought: Holistic versus analytic cognition. *Psychological Review, 108*, 291–310.

Nosek, B.A. (2005). Moderators of the relationship between implicit and explicit evaluation. *Journal of Experimental Psychology: General, 134*(4), 565–584.

O'Keeffe, G.S., & Clarke-Pearson, K. (2011). The impact of social media on children, adolescents, and families. *Pediatrics, 127*(4), 800–804. https://doi.org/10.1542/peds.2011-0054.

Olson, M.A., & Fazio, R.H. (2003). Relations between implicit measures of prejudice what are we measuring? *Psychological Science, 14*, 636–639.

Olweus, D. (1993). *Bullying at school: What we know and what we can do*. Wiley-Blackwell.

Penton-Voak, I.S., Jones, B.C., Little, A.C., Baker, S., Tiddeman, B., Burt, D.M., & Perrett, D.I. (2001). Symmetry, sexual dimorphism in facial proportions and male facial attractiveness. *Proceedings of the Royal Society B: Biological Sciences, 268*, 1617–1623.

Petty, R.E., & Cacioppo, J.T. (1986). The elaboration likelihood model of persuasion. In *Communication and persuasion: Central and peripheral routes to attitude change* (pp. 1–24). New York, NY: Springer. https://doi.org/10.1007/978-1-4612-4964-1.

Petty, R.E., Wegener, D.T., & Fabrigar, L.R. (1997). Attitudes and attitude change. *Annual Review of Psychology, 48*, 609–647.

Plant, E.A., & Devine, P.G. (1998). Internal and external motivation to respond without prejudice. *Journal of Personality and Social Psychology, 75*, 811–832.

Pliner, P., Hart, H., Kohl, J., & Saari, D. (1974). Compliance without pressure: Some further data on the foot-in-the-door technique. *Journal of Experimental Social Psychology, 10*, 17–22.

Regan, P.C., & Berscheid, E. (1997). Gender differences in characteristics desired in a potential sexual and marriage partner. *Journal of Psychology & Human Sexuality, 9*, 25–37.

Rhodes, N., & Wood, W. (1992). Self-esteem and intelligence affect influenceability: The mediating role of message reception. *Psychological Bulletin, 111*, 156–171.

Richard, F.D., Bond, C.F., Jr., & Stokes-Zoota, J.J. (2003). One hundred years of social psychology quantitatively described. *Review of General Psychology, 7*(4), 331–363. https://doi.org/10.1037/1089-2680.7.4.331.

Riggio, H.R., & Garcia, A.L. (2009). The power of situations: Jonestown and the fundamental attribution error. *Teaching of Psychology, 36*(2), 108–112. https://doi.org/10.1080/00986280902739636.

Rikowski, A., & Grammer, K. (1999). Human body odour, symmetry and attractiveness. *Proceedings of the Royal Society B: Biological Sciences, 266*(1422), 869–874. https://doi.org/10.1098/rspb.1999.0717.

Roesch, S.C., & Amirkham, J.H. (1997). Boundary conditions for self-serving attributions: Another look at the sports pages. *Journal of Applied Social Psychology, 27*, 245–261.

Rojek, J., Rosenfeld, R., & Decker, S. (2012). Policing race: The racial stratification of searches in police traffic stops. *Criminology, 50*, 993–1024.

Rosenberg, M.J., & Hovland, C.I. (1960). Cognitive, affective and behavioral components of attitudes. In *Attitude organization and change: An analysis of consistency among attitude components* (pp. 1–14). Yale University Press.

Rosenthal, R., & Jacobson, L.F. (1968). Teacher expectations for the disadvantaged. *Scientific American, 218*, 19–23.

Ross, L. (1977). The intuitive psychologist and his shortcomings: Distortions in the attribution process. *Advances in Experimental Social Psychology, 10*, 173–220.

Ross, L., Amabile, T.M., & Steinmetz, J.L. (1977). Social roles, social control, and biases in social-perception processes. *Journal of Personality and Social Psychology, 35*, 485–494.

Ross, L., & Nisbett, R.E. (1991). *The person and the situation: Perspectives of social psychology.* McGraw-Hill.

Rudman, L.A. (1998). Self-promotion as a risk factor for women: The costs and benefits of counterstereotypical impression management. *Journal of Personality and Social Psychology, 74*(3), 629–645.

Rusbult, C.E., & Van Lange, P.A. (2003). Interdependence, interaction, and relationships. *Annual Review of Psychology, 54*, 351–575.

Schank, R.C., Abelson, R. (1977). *Scripts, plans, goals, and understanding: An inquiry into human knowledge.* Lawrence Erlbaum Associates.

Shepperd, J.A., & Taylor, K.M. (1999). Social loafing and expectancy-value theory. *Personality and Social Psychology Bulletin, 25*, 1147–1158.

Singh, D. (1993). Adaptive significance of female physical attractiveness: Role of waist-to-hip ratio. *Journal of Personality and Social Psychology, 65*, 293–307.

Sommers, S.R., & Ellsworth, P.C. (2000). Race in the courtroom: Perceptions of guilt and dispositional attributions. *Personality and Social Psychology Bulletin, 26*, 1367–1379.

Spears, B., Slee, P., Owens, L., & Johnson, B. (2009). Behind the scenes and screens: Insights into the human dimension of covert and cyberbullying. *Journal of Psychology, 217*(4), 189–196. https://doi.org/10.1027/0044-3409.217.4.189.

Sternberg, R.J. (1986). A triangular theory of love. *Psychological Review, 93*, 119–135.

Stewart, J.B. (2002). *Heart of a soldier.* Simon and Schuster.

Sutton, R.M. and Douglas, K.M. (2005). Justice for all, or just for me? More support for self-other differences in just world beliefs. Personality and Individual Differences, *9*(3). pp. 637-645. ISSN 0191-8869.

Tajfel, H. (1974). Social identity and intergroup behaviour. *Social Science Information, 13*(2), 65–93.

Tajfel, H., & Turner, J.C. (1979). An integrative theory of intergroup conflict. In W. G. Austin & S. Worchel (Eds.), *The social psychology of intergroup relations* (pp. 33–48). Brooks-Cole.

Tavris, C., & Aronson, E. (2008). *Mistakes were made (but not by me): Why we justify foolish beliefs, bad decisions, and hurtful acts.* Houghton Mifflin Harcourt.

Taylor, L.S., Fiore, A.T., Mendelsohn, G.A., & Cheshire, C. (2011). "Out of my league": A real-world test of the matching hypothesis. *Personality and Social Psychology Bulletin, 37*(7), 942–954. https://doi.org/10.1177/0146167211409947.

Teger, A.I., & Pruitt, D.G. (1967). Components of group risk taking. *Journal of Experimental Social Psychology, 3*, 189–205.

Triandis, H.C. (2001). Individualism-collectivism and personality. *Journal of Personality, 69*, 907–924.

van Veen, V., Krug, M.K., Schooler, J.W., & Carter, C.S. (2009). Neural activity predicts attitude change in cognitive dissonance. *Nature Neuroscience, 12*, 1469–1474.

Vandebosch, H., & Van Cleemput, K. (2009). Cyberbullying among youngsters: Profiles of bullies and victims. *New media & Society, 11*(8), 1349–1371. https://doi.org/10.1177/1461444809341263.

Walker, M.B., & Andrade, M.G. (1996). Conformity in the Asch task as a function of age. *The Journal of Social Psychology, 136*, 367–372.

Walster, E., & Festinger, L. (1962). The effectiveness of "overheard" persuasive communications. *Journal of Abnormal and Social Psychology, 65*, 395–402.

Wason, P.C., & Johnson-Laird, P.N. (1972). *The psychology of deduction: Structure and content.* Harvard University Press.

Weiner, B. (1979). A theory of motivation for some classroom experiences. *Journal of Educational Psychology, 71*(1), 3–25.

Wilson, M., & Daly, M. (1985). Competitiveness, risk taking, and violence: The young male syndrome. *Ethology and Sociobiology, 6*, 59–73.

Wilson, T.D., Lindsey, S., & Schooler, T.Y. (2000). A model of dual attitudes. *Psychological Review, 107*, 101–126.

Zajonc, R.B. (1965). Social facilitation. *Science, 149*(3681), 269–274. https://doi.org/10.1126/science.149.3681.269

Zimbardo, P.G. (2013). An end to the experiment [Slide show of the Stanford prison experiment]. http://www.prisonexp.org/psychology/37.

Chapter 12

ABC News. (2000, September 8). *Court OKs barring high IQs for Cops.* Retrieved from http://abcnews.go.com/US/court-oks-barring-high-iqs-cops/story?id=95836

Agerström, J., & Rooth, D.-O. (2011). The role of automatic obesity stereotypes in real hiring discrimination. *Journal of Applied Psychology, 96*, 790–805.

Allen, T.D., Eby, L.T., Poteet, M.L., Lentz, E., & Lima, L. (2004). Career benefits associated with mentoring for protégés: A meta-analysis. *Journal of Applied Psychology, 89*, 127–136.

Allen, T.D., Lentz, E., & Day, R. (2006). Career success outcomes associated with mentoring others: A comparison of mentors and nonmentors. *Journal of Career Development, 32*, 272–285.

American Civil Liberties Union. (n.d.). *Non-Discrimination Laws: State by State Information—Map.* https://www.aclu.org/maps/non-discrimination-laws-state-state-information-map

American National Standards Institute. (2000). *Control center ergonomic standards.* http://webstore.ansi.org/ergonomics/control_centre_ergonomics.aspx

Amiot, C.E., Terry, D.J., Jimmieson, N.L., & Callan, V.J. (2006). A longitudinal investigation of coping processes during a merger: Implications for job satisfaction and organizational identification. *Journal of Management, 32*, 552–574.

Arthur, W., Bennett, W., Edens, P.S., & Bell, S.T. (2003). Effectiveness of training in organizations: A meta-analysis of design and evaluation features. *Journal of Applied Psychology*, 88, 234–245.

Arthur, W., Woehr, D.J., & Graziano, W.G. (2001). Personality testing in employment settings: Problems and issues in the application of typical selection practices. *Personnel Review*, 30, 657–676.

Atkins, P.W. B., & Wood, R.E. (2002). Self-versus others' ratings as predictors of assessment center ratings: Validation evidence for 360-degree feedback programs. *Personnel Psychology*, 55, 871–904.

Badgett, M.V. L., Sears, B., Lau, H., & Ho, D. (2009). Bias in the workplace: Consistent evidence of sexual orientation and gender identity discrimination 1998–2008. *Chicago-Kent Law Review*, 84, 559–595.

Barrick, M.R., Swider, B.W., & Stewart, G.L. (2010). Initial evaluations in the interview: Relationships with subsequent interviewer evaluations and employment offers. *Journal of Applied Psychology*, 95, 1163–1172.

Bass, B.M. (1985). *Leadership and performance beyond expectations*. Free Press.

Bass, B.M., Avolio, B.J., & Atwater, L. (1996). The transformational and transactional leadership of men and women. *Applied Psychology: An International Review*, 45, 5–34.

Bruno, T., & Abrahão, J. (2012). False alarms and incorrect rejections in an information security center: Correlation with the frequency of incidents. *Work*, 41, 2902–2907.

Buckingham, M., & Clifton, D.O. (2001). *Now, discover your strengths*. Free Press.

Bureau of Labor Statistics—U.S. Department of Labor. (2013). American Time Use Survey—2013 Results [Press release: USDL-14-1137]. Available at http://www.bls.gov/news.release/pdf/atus.pdf

Bye, H.H., Horverak, J.G., Sandal, G.M., Sam, D.L., & Vijver, F.J. R. van de (2014). Cultural fit and ethnic background in the job interview. *International Journal of Cross Cultural Management*, 14, 7–26.

Carlson, D.S., Kacmar, K.M., & Williams, L.J. (2000). Construction and initial validation of a multidimensional measure of work–family conflict. *Journal of Vocational Behavior*, 56, 249–276.

Colligan, T.W., & Higgins, E.M. (2005). Workplace stress: Etiology and consequences. *Journal of Workplace Behavioral Health*, 21, 89–97.

Corbett, C., & Hill, C. (2012) *Graduating to a pay gap: The earnings of women and men one year after college graduation*. American Association of University Women.

DeGroot, T., & Gooty, J. (2009). Can nonverbal cues be used to make meaningful personality attributions in employment interviews? *Journal of Business Psychology*, 24, 179–192.

DeNisi, A.S., & Kluger, A.N. (2000). Feedback effectiveness: Can 360-degree appraisals be improved? *Academy of Management Executive*, 14, 129–139.

Dierdorff, E.C., & Wilson, M.A. (2003). A meta-analysis of job analysis reliability. *Journal of Applied Psychology*, 88, 635–646.

Eagly, A.H., Johannesen-Schmidt, M.C., & van Engen, M.L. (2003). Transformational, transactional, and laissez-faire leadership styles: A meta-analysis comparing women and men. *Psychological Bulletin*, 129, 569–591.

Eagly, A.H., & Johnson, B.T. (1990). Gender and leadership style: A meta-analysis. *Psychological Bulletin*, 108, 233–256.

Eby, L.T., Allen, T.D., Evans, S.C., Ng, T., & DuBois, D. (2008). Does mentoring matter? A multidisciplinary meta-analysis comparing mentored and non-mentored individuals. *Journal of Vocational Behavior*, 72, 254–267.

Eby, L.T., Durley, J.R., Evans, S.C., & Ragins, B.R. (2006). The relationship between short-term mentoring benefits and long-term mentor outcomes. *Journal of Vocational Behavior*, 69, 424–444.

Elmore, L. (2010, June). The workplace generation gaps. *Women in Business*, 62(2), 8–11.

Fletcher, C. (2001). Performance appraisal and management: The developing research agenda. *Journal of Occupational and Organizational Psychology*, 74, 473–487.

Gentry, W.A., Weber, T.J., & Sadri, G. (2008). Examining career-related mentoring and managerial performance across cultures: A multilevel analysis. *Journal of Vocational Behavior*, 72, 241–253.

Gibson, J.W., Greenwood, R.A., & Murphy, E.F. (2009). Generational differences in the workplace: Personal values, behaviors, and popular beliefs. *Journal of Diversity Management*, 4, 1–7.

Gilbreth, L.M. (1914). *The psychology of management: The function of the mind in determining, teaching, and installing methods of least waste*. Sturgis and Walton.

Gilbreth, L.M. (1998). *As I remember: An autobiography of Lillian Gilbreth*. Industrial Engineering and Management Press.

Gilmore, D.C., & Ferris, G.R. (1989). The effects of applicant impression management tactics on interviewer judgments. *Journal of Management*, 15, 557–564.

Greenberg, J. (1993). Stealing in the name of justice: Informational and interpersonal moderators of theft reactions to underpayment inequity. *Organizational Behavior and Human Decision Processes*, 54, 81–103.

Greenberg, L., & Barling, J. (1999). Predicting employee agression against coworkers, subordinates and supervisors: The roles of person behaviors and perceived workplace factors. *Journal of Organizational Behavior*, 20, 897–913.

Greenhaus, J.H., & Beutell, N.J. (1985). Sources of conflict between work and family roles. *Academy of Management Review*, 10, 76–88.

Gyllensten, K., & Palmer, S. (2005). The role of gender in workplace stress: A critical literature review. *Health Education Journal*, 64, 271–288.

Hoogendoorn, S., Oosterbeek, H., & van Praag, M. (2013). The impact of gender diversity on the performance of business teams: Evidence from a field experiment. *Management Science*, 59, 1514–1528.

Hosoda, M., Stone-Romero, E., & Coats, G. (2003). The effects of physical attractiveness on job-related outcomes: A meta-analysis of experimental studies. *Personnel Psychology*, 56, 431–462.

Howard, J.L., & Ferris, G.R. (1996). The employment interview context: Social and situational influences on interviewer decisions. *Journal of Applied Social Psychology*, 26, 112–136.

Howell, W.C. (2003). Human factors and ergonomics. In W. C. Borman, D.R. Ilgen, R.J. Limoski, & I. B. Weiner (Eds.), *Handbook of psychology: Vol. 12: Industrial and organizational psychology* (pp. 565–593). Wiley.

Human Rights Campaign. (2013a). *Cities and counties with non-discrimination ordinances that include gender identity*. http://www.hrc.org/resources/entry/cities-and-counties-with-non-discrimination-ordinances-that-include-gender

Human Rights Campaign. (2013b). *Corporate equality index 2014: Rating American workplaces on lesbian, gay, bisexual and transgender equality*. http://www.hrc.org/campaigns/corporate-equality-index

Jordan v. New London, No. 99-9188, 2000 U.S. App. LEXIS 22195 (2d Cir. 2000) (unpublished). http://www.aele.org/apa/jordan-newlondon.html

Judge, T.A., & Kammeyer-Mueller, J.D. (2012). Job attitudes. *Annual Reviews of Psychology*, 63, 341–367.

Judge, T.A., Piccolo, R.F., Podsakoff, N.P., Shaw, J.C., & Rich, B. (2010). The relationship between pay and job satisfaction: A meta-analysis of the literature. *Journal of Vocational Behavior*, 77, 157–167.

Judge, T.A., & Watanabe, S. (1993). Another look at the job satisfaction–life satisfaction relationship. *Journal of Applied Psychology*, 78, 939–948.

Kaiser, R.B., & Overfield, D.V. (2011). Strengths, strengths overused, and lopsided leadership. *Consulting Psychology*, 63, 89–109.

Katzell, R.A., & Austin, J.T. (1992). From then to now: The development of industrial–organizational psychology in the United States. *Journal of Applied Psychology*, 77, 803–835.

Khanna, C., Medsker, G.J., & Ginter, R. (2012). 2012 income and employment survey results for the Society for Industrial and Organizational Psychology. http://www.siop.org/2012SIOPIncomeSurvey.pdf

Koppes, L.L. (1997). American female pioneers of industrial and organizational psychology during the early years. *Journal of Applied Psychology*, 82, 500–515.

Lancaster, J. (2004). *Making time: Lillian Moller Gilbreth—A life beyond "Cheaper by the Dozen."* Northeastern University Press.

Lapierre, L.M., & Allen, T.D. (2006). Work-supportive family, family-supportive supervision, use of organizational benefits, and problem-focused coping: Implications for work-family conflict and employee well-being. *Journal of Occupational Health Psychology*, 11, 169–181.

Larson, C., & LaFasto, F. (1989). *Teamwork: What must go right / What can go wrong.* Sage.

Levine, S.P., & Feldman, R.S. (2002). Women and men's nonverbal behavior and self-monitoring in a job interview setting. *Applied Human Resources Management Research*, 7, 1–14.

Lewin, K., Lippitt, R., & White, R.K. (1939). Patterns of aggressive behavior in experimentally created "social climates." *Journal of Social Psychology*, 10, 271–301.

Liden, R.C., Martin, C.L., & Parsons, C.K. (1993). Interviewer and applicant behaviors in employment interviews. *Academy of Management Journal*, 36, 373–386.

Lips, H. (2013). The gender pay gap: Challenging the rationalizations. Perceived equity, discrimination, and the limits of human capital models. *Sex Roles*, 68, 169–185.

Locke, E.A. (1976). The nature and causes of job satisfaction. In M. D. Dunnette (Ed.), *Handbook of industrial and organizational psychology* (pp. 1297–1349). Rand McNally.

Manley, K. (2009). The BFOQ defense: Title VII's concession to gender discrimination. *Duke Journal of Gender Law & Policy*, 16, 169–210.

McCarney, R., Warner, J., Iliffe, S., van Haselen, R., Griffin, M., & Fisher, P. (2007). The Hawthorne effect: A randomised, controlled trial. *BMC Medical Research Methodology*, 7, 30.

McDaniel, M.A., Whetzel, D.L., Schmidt, F.L., & Maurer, S.D. (1994). The validity of employment interviews: A comprehensive review and meta-analysis. *Journal of Applied Psychology*, 79, 599–616.

McGregor, D. (1960). *The human side of enterprise*. McGraw Hill.

McKeen, C., & Bujaki, M. (2007). Gender and mentoring. In B. R. Ragins & K. E. Kram (Eds.), *The handbook of mentoring at work: Theory, research and practice* (pp. 197–222). Sage Publications.

McMillan, S.K., Stevens, S., & Kelloway, E.K. (2009). History and development of industrial/organizational psychology in the Canadian forces personnel selection branch: 1938–2009. *Canadian Psychology*, 50, 283–291.

Meister, J.C., & Willyerd, K. (2010, May). Mentoring millennials. *Harvard Business Review*, 1–4.

Münsterberg, H. (1913). *Psychology and industrial efficiency*. Houghton Mifflin Company.

Myers, K.K., & Sadaghiani, K. (2010). Millennials in the workplace: A communication pespective on millennials organizational relationships and performance. *Journal of Business Psychology*, 25, 225–238.

Naquin, C., & Tynan, R. (2003). The team halo effect: Why teams are not blamed for their failures. *Journal of Applied Psychology*, 88, 332–340.

Occupational Safety & Health Administration. (2014). *Workplace violence*. United States Department of Labor website: https://www.osha.gov/SLTC/workplaceviolence/

O'Keefe, J., & Bruyere, S. (1994). *Implications of the Americans with Disabilities Act for psychology*. Springer.

Ostroff, C., Kinicki, A.J., & Tamkins, M.M. (2003). Organizational culture and climate. In W. C. Borman, D.R. Ilgen, R.J. Klimoski, & I. B. Weiner (Eds.), *Handbook of psychology: Vol. 12: Industrial and organizational psychology* (pp. 145–158). Wiley.

Pettigrew, T.F., & Tropp, L.R. (2006). A meta-analytic test of intergroup contact theory. *Journal of Personality and Social Psychology*, 90, 751–783.

Posig, M., & Kickul, J. (2004). Work-role expectation and work family conflict: Gender differences in emotional exhaustion. *Women in Management Review*, 19, 373–386.

Powell, A., Piccoli, G., & Ives, B. (2004). Virtual teams: A review of current literature and directions for future research. *The DATA BASE for Advances in Information Systems*, 35, 6–36.

Ragins, B.R., & Cotton, J.L. (1999). Mentor functions and outcomes: A comparison of men and women in formal and informal mentoring relationships. *Journal of Applied Psychology*, 84, 529–550.

Rakic, T., Steffens, M.C., & Mummendey, A. (2011). When it matters how you pronounce it: The influence of regional accents on job interview outcome. *British Journal of Psychology*, 102, 868–883.

Riley, M., Elgin, B., Lawrence, D., & Matlack, C. (2014, March 13). Missed alarms and 40 million stolen credit card numbers: How Target blew it. *Bloomberg Businessweek*. http://www.businessweek.com/articles/2014-03-13/target-missed-alarms-in-epic-hack-of-credit-card-data

Roethlisberg, F., & Dickson, W. (1939). *Management and the worker*. Harvard University Press.

Saad, L. (2012). U.S. workers least happy with their work stress and pay: Satisfaction is highest for safety conditions and relations with coworkers. Gallup Economy website: http://www.gallup.com/poll/158723/workers-least-happy-work-stress-pay.aspx

Saari, L.M., & Judge, T.A. (2004). Employee attitudes and job satisfaction. *Human Resouce Management*, 43, 395–407.

Schraeder, M., Becton, J.B., & Portis, R. (2007). A critical examination of performance appraisals: An organization's friend or foe? *The Journal for Quality and Participation*, 30, 20–25.

Society for Industrial and Organizational Psychology (SIOP). (2014). What value does SIOP membership provide? http://www.siop.org/benefits/

Taylor, F.W. (1911). *The principles of scientific management*. Harper & Brothers.

Tkaczyk, C. (2013, April 19). Marissa Mayer breaks her silence on Yahoo's telecommuting policy. *Fortune*. http://tech.fortune.cnn.com/2013/04/19/marissa-mayer-telecommuting/

The New York Times. (1999, Sept. 9). *Metro news briefs: Connecticut—Judge rules that police can bar high IQ scores*. http://www.nytimes.com/1999/09/09/nyregion/metro-news-briefs-connecticut-judge-rules-that-police-can-bar-high-iq-scores.html

Tornow, W.W. (1993a). Editor's note: Introduction to special issue on 360-degree feedback. *Human Resource Management*, 32, 211–219.

Tornow, W.W. (1993b). Perceptions or reality: Is multi-perspective measurement a means or an end? *Human Resource Management*, 32, 221–229.

Toyota Motor Manufacturing. (2013). *Toyota production system terms*. http://www.toyotageorgetown.com/terms.asp

Ugboro, I.O. (2006). Organizational commitment, job redesign, employee empowerment and intent to quit among survivors of restructuring and downsizing. *Journal of Behavioral and Applied Management*, 7, 232–257.

United States Nuclear Regulatory Commission. (2013). *Backgrounder on the Three Mile Island accident*. http://www.nrc.gov/reading-rm/doc-collections/fact-sheets/3mile-isle.html

U.S. Equal Employment Opportunity Commission. (2014). *EEOC charge receipts by state (includes U.S. territories) and basis for 2013*. http://www1.eeoc.gov/eeoc/statistics/enforcement/state_13.cfm

U.S. Equal Employment Opportunity Commission. (n.d.). *Facts about sexual harassment*. http://www.eeoc.gov/eeoc/publications/fs-sex.cfm

Van De Water, T. (1997). Psychology's entrepreneurs and the marketing of industrial psychology. *Journal of Applied Psychology*, 82, 486–499.

van Knippenberg, D., van Knippenberg, B., Monden, L., & de Lima, F. (2002). Organizational identification after a merger: A social identity perspective. *British Journal of Social Psychology*, 41, 233–252.

Vinchur, A.J., & Koppes, L.L. (2014). Early contributors to the science and practice of industrial psychology. In L. L. Koppes, (Ed.), *Historical perspectives in industrial and organizational psychology* (pp. 37–58). Erlbaum.

Weiss, H.M. (2002). Deconstructing job satisfaction: Separating evaluations, beliefs and affective experiences. *Human Resouces Management Review*, 12, 173–194.

Chapter 13

Aboa-Éboulé, C., Brisson, C., Maunsell, E., Mâsse, B., Bourbonnais, R., Vézina, M.,… Dagenais, G.R. (2007). Job strain and risk for acute recurrent coronary heart disease events. *Journal of the American Medical Association*, 298, 1652–1660.

Abramson, L.Y., Seligman, M.E.P., & Teasdale, J.D. (1978). Learned helplessness in humans: Critique and reformulation. *Journal of Abnormal Psychology*, 87, 49–74.

Ader, R., & Cohen, N. (1975). Behaviorally conditioned immunosuppression. *Psychosomatic Medicine*, 37, 333–340.

Ader, R., & Cohen, N. (2001). Conditioning and immunity. In R. Ader, D.L. Felten & N. Cohen (Eds.), *Psychoneuroimmunology* (3rd ed., pp. 3–34). New York, NY: Academic Press.

Ahola, K., Honkonen, T., Isometsä, E., Kalimo, R., Nykyri, E., Aromaa, A., & Lönnqvist, J. (2005). The relationship between job-related burnout and depressive disorders—Results from the Finnish Health 2000 study. *Journal of Affective Disorders*, 88, 55–62.

Ahola, K., Honkonen, T., Kivimäki, M., Virtanen, M., Isometsä, E., Aromaa, A., & Lönnqvist, J. (2006). Contribution of burnout to the association between job strain and depression: The Health 2000 study. *Journal of Occupational and Environmental Medicine*, 48, 1023–1030.

Alexander, F. (1950). *Psychosomatic medicine*. Norton.

American Academy of Neurology. (2014). *Headache*. https://patients.aan.com/disorders/index.cfm?event=view&disorder_id=936

American Heart Association. (2012a). *What is angina?* http://www.heart.org/idc/groups/heart-public/@wcm/@hcm/documents/downloadable/ucm_300287.pdf

American Heart Association. (2012b). *Why blood pressure matters*. http://www.heart.org/HEARTORG/Conditions/HighBloodPressure/WhyBloodPressureMatters/Why-Blood-Pressure-Matters_UCM_002051_Article.jsp

American Heart Association. (2014, February 24). Depression as a risk factor for poor prognosis among patients with acute coronary syndrome: Systematic review and recommendations: A scientific statement from the American Heart Association. *Circulation*. http://circ.ahajournals.org/content/early/2014/02/24/CIR.0000000000000019.full.pdf+html

American Lung Association. (2010). *Asthma*. http://www.lung.org/assets/documents/publications/solddc-chapters/asthma.pdf

American Psychiatric Association. (2013). *Diagnostic and statistical manual of mental disorders* (5th ed.). Author.

Bandura, A. (1994). Self-efficacy. In V. S. Ramachandran (Ed.), *Encyclopedia of human behavior* (Vol. 4, pp. 71–81). Academic Press.

Bandura, A. (1997). *Self-efficacy: The exercise of control*. Freeman.

Bandura, A. (2004). Health promotion by social cognitive means. *Health Education & Behavior*, 31, 143–164.

Barefoot, J.C., & Schroll, M.S. (1996). Symptoms of depression, acute myocardial infarction, and total mortality in a community sample. *Circulation*, 93, 1976–1980.

Baron, R.S., & Kerr, N.L. (2003). *Group process, group decision, group action* (2nd ed.). Open University Press.

Baron, R.S., Cutrona, C.E., Hicklin, D., Russell, D.W., & Lubaroff, D.M. (1990). Social support and immune function among spouses of cancer patients. *Journal of Personality and Social Psychology*, 59, 344–352.

Baumeister, R.F., & Leary, M.R. (1995). The need to belong: Desire for interpersonal attachments as a fundamental human motivation. *Psychological Bulletin*, 117, 497–529.

Benson, H., & Proctor, W. (1994). *Beyond the relaxation response: How to harness the healing power of your personal beliefs*. Berkley Publishing Group.

Berkman, L.F., & Syme, L. (1979). Social networks, host resistance, and mortality: A nine-year follow-up study of Alameda County residents. *American Journal of Epidemiology*, 109, 186–204.

Blackburn, E.H., & Epel, E.S. (2012). Telomeres and adversity: Too toxic to ignore. *Nature*, 490(7419), 169–171.

Boehm, J.K., & Kubzansky, L.D. (2012). The heart's content: The association between positive psychological well-being and cardiovascular health. *Psychological Bulletin*, 138, 655–691.

Bolger, N., DeLongis, A., Kessler, R.C., & Schilling, E.A. (1989). Effects of daily stress on negative mood. *Journal of Personality and Social Psychology*, 57, 808–818.

Boyle, S.H., Michalek, J.E., & Suarez, E.C. (2006). Covariation of psychological attributes and incident coronary heart disease in U.S. Air Force veterans of the Vietnam War. *Psychosomatic Medicine*, 68, 844–850.

Brickman, P., & Campbell, D.T. (1971). Hedonic relativism and planning the good society. In M. H. Appley (Ed.), *Adaptation level theory: A symposium* (pp. 287–302). Academic Press.

Brickman, P., Coats, D., & Janoff-Bulman, R. (1978). Lottery winners and accident victims: Is happiness relative? *Journal of Personality and Social Psychology*, 36, 917–927.

Brondolo, E., Brady, N., Pencille, M., Beatty, D., & Contrada, R.J. (2009). Coping with racism: A selective review of the literature and a theoretical and methodological critique. *Journal of Behavioral Medicine*, 32(1), 64–88.

Brummett, B.H., Barefoot, J.C., Siegler, I.C., Clapp-Channing, N.E., Lytle, B.L., Bosworth, H.B.,…Mark, D.B. (2001). Characteristics of socially isolated patients with coronary artery disease who are at elevated risk for mortality. *Psychosomatic Medicine*, 63, 267–272.

Caceres, C., & Burns, J.W. (1997). Cardiovascular reactivity to psychological stress may enhance subsequent pain sensitivity. *Pain*, 69, 237–244.

Campeau, S., Nyhuis, T.J., Sasse, S.K., Kryskow, E.M., Herlihy, L., Masini, C.V.,… Day, H.E. W. (2010). Hypothalamic pituitary adrenal axis responses to low-intensity stressors are reduced after voluntary wheel running in rats. *Journal of Neuroendocrinology*, 22, 872–888.

Campisi, J., Bynog, P., McGehee, H., Oakland, J.C., Quirk, S., Taga, C., & Taylor, M. (2012). Facebook, stress, and incidence of upper respiratory infection in undergraduate college students. *Cyberpsychology, Behavior, and Social Networking*, 15, 675–681.

Cannon, W.B. (1932). *The wisdom of the body*. W. W. Norton.

Carroll, J. (2007). *Most Americans "very satisfied" with their personal lives.* Gallup website: http://www.gallup.com/poll/103483/Most-Americans-Very-Satisfied-Their-Personal-Lives.aspx

Cathcart, S., Petkov, J., & Pritchard, D. (2008). Effects of induced stress on experimental pain sensitivity in chronic tension-type headache sufferers. *European Journal of Neurology*, 15, 552–558.

Centers for Disease Control and Prevention (CDC). (2006). *You can control your asthma: A guide to understanding asthma and its triggers.* http://www.cdc.gov/asthma/pdfs/asthma_brochure.pdf

Centers for Disease Control and Prevention (CDC). (2011). Million hearts: Strategies to reduce the prevalence of leading cardiovascular disease risk factors—United States, 2011. *Morbidity and Mortality Weekly Report [MMWR]*, 60(36), 1248–1251. http://www.cdc.gov/mmwr/pdf/wk/mm6036.pdf

Centers for Disease Control and Prevention (CDC). (2013a). *Asthma's impact on the nation: Data from the CDC National Asthma Control Program.* http://www.cdc.gov/asthma/impacts_nation/AsthmaFactSheet.pdf

Centers for Disease Control and Prevention (CDC). (2013b). *Breathing easier.* http://www.cdc.gov/asthma/pdfs/breathing_easier_brochure.pdf

Center for Investigating Health Minds. (2013). *About.* http://www.investigatinghealthyminds.org/cihmCenter.html

Chandola, T., Britton, A., Brunner, E., Hemingway, H., Malik, M., Kumari, M.,… Marmot, M. (2008). Work stress and coronary heart disease: What are the mechanisms? *European Heart Journal*, 29, 640–648.

Chang, E.C. (2001). Introduction: Optimism and pessimism and moving beyond the most fundamental questions. In E. C. Chang (Ed.), *Optimism and pessimism: Implications for theory, research, and practice* (pp. 3–12). American Psychological Association.

Chang, P.P., Ford, D.E., Meoni, L.A., Wang, N.Y., & Klag, M.J. (2002). Anger in young and subsequent premature cardiovascular disease. *Archives of Internal Medicine*, 162, 901–906.

Chida, Y., & Steptoe, A. (2009). The association of anger and hostility with future coronary heart disease: A meta-analytic review or prospective evidence. *Journal of the American College of Cardiology*, 53, 936–946.

Cohen, S., Doyle, W.J., Turner, R., Alper, C.M., & Skoner, D.P. (2003). Sociability and susceptibility to the common cold. *Psychological Science*, 14, 389–395.

Cohen, S., Frank, E., Doyle, W.J., Skoner, D.P., Rabin, B.S., & Gwaltney, J.M. J. (1998). Types of stressors that increase susceptibility to the common cold in healthy adults. *Health Psychology*, 17, 214–223.

Cohen, S., & Herbert, T.B. (1996). Health psychology: Psychological factors and physical disease from the perspective of human psychoneuroimmunology. *Annual Review of Psychology*, 47, 113–142.

Cohen, S., & Janicki-Deverts, D. (2012). Who's stressed? Distributions of psychological stress in the United States in probability samples in 1993, 2006, and 2009. *Journal of Applied Social Psychology*, 42, 1320–1334.

Cohen, S., Janicki-Deverts, D., & Miller, G.E. (2007). Psychological distress and disease. *Journal of the American Medical Association*, 98, 1685–1687.

Cohrs, J.C., Christie, D.J., White, M.P., & Das, C. (2013). Contributions of positive psychology to peace: Toward global well-being and resilience. *American Psychologist*, 68, 590–600.

Compton, W.C. (2005). *An introduction to positive psychology*. Thomson Wadsworth.

Cotton, D.H.G. (1990). *Stress management: An integrated approach to therapy*. Brunner/Mazel.

Craft, L.L., VanIterson, E.H., Helenowski, I.B., Rademaker, A.W., & Courneya, K.S. (2012). Exercise effects on depressive symptoms in cancer survivors: A systematic review and meta-analysis. *Cancer Epidemiology, Biomarkers & Prevention*, 21, 3–19.

Csikszentmihalyi, M. (1997). *Finding flow*. Basic Books.

Csikszentmihalyi, M. (1999). If we are so rich, why aren't we happy? *American Psychologist*, 54, 821–827.

D'Amato, G., Liccardi, G., Cecchi, L., Pellegrino, F., & D'Amato, M. (2010). Facebook: A new trigger for asthma? *The Lancet*, 376, 1740.

Davidson, K.W., Mostofsky, E., & Whang, W. (2010). Don't worry: be happy: Positive affect and reduced 10-year incident coronary heart disease: The Canadian Nova Scotia Health Survey. *European Heart Journal*, 31, 1065–1070.

de Kluizenaar, Y., Gansevoort, R.T., Miedema, H.M.E., & de Jong, P.E. (2007). Hypertension and road traffic noise exposure. *Journal of Occupational and Environmental Medicine*, 49, 484–492.

De Vogli, R., Chandola, T., & Marmot, M.G. (2007). Negative aspects of close relationships and heart disease. *Archives of Internal Medicine*, 167, 1951–1957.

DeLongis, A., Coyne, J.C., Dakof, G., Folkman, S., & Lazarus, R.S. (1982). Relationship of daily hassles, uplifts, and major life events to health status. *Health Psychology*, 1, 119–136.

Derogatis, L.R., & Coons, H.L. (1993). Self-report measures of stress. In L. Goldberger & S. Breznitz (Eds.), *Handbook of stress: Theoretical and clinical aspects* (2nd ed., pp. 200–233). Free Press.

Diehl, M., & Hay, E.L. (2010). Risk and resilience factors in coping with daily stress in adulthood: The role of age, self-concept incoherence, and personal control. *Developmental Psychology*, 46, 1132–1146.

Diener, E. (2012). New findings and future directions for subjective well-being research. *American Psychologist*, 67, 590–597.

Diener, E. (2013). The remarkable changes in the science of subjective well-being. *Perspectives on Psychological Science*, 8, 663–666.

Diener, E., & Biswas-Diener, R. (2002). Will money increase subjective well-being? A literature review and guide to needed research. *Social Indicators Research*, 57, 119–169.

Diener, E., Diener, M., & Diener, C. (1995). Factors predicting the subjective well-being of nations. *Journal of Personality and Social Psychology*, 69, 851–864.

Diener, E., Lucas, R., & Scollon, C.N. (2006). Beyond the hedonic treadmill: Revising the adaptation theory of well-being. *American Psychologist*, 61, 305–314.

Diener, E., Ng, W., Harter, J., & Arora, R. (2010). Wealth and happiness across the world: Material prosperity predicts life evaluation, whereas psychosocial prosperity predicts positive feelings. *Journal of Personality and Social Psychology*, 99, 52–61.

Diener, E., Oishi, S., & Ryan, K.L. (2013). Universals and cultural differences in the causes and structure of happiness: A multilevel review. In *Mental Well-Being* (pp. 153–176). Springer Netherlands.

Diener, E., Suh, E.M., Lucas, R.E., & Smith, H.L. (1999). Subjective well-being: Three decades of progress. *Psychological Bulletin*, 125, 276–302.

Diener, E., Tay, L., & Myers, D. (2011). The religion paradox: If religion makes people happy, why are so many dropping out? *Journal of Personality and Social Psychology*, 101, 1278–1290.

Diener, E., Tay, L., & Oishi, S. (2013). Rising income and the subjective well-being of nations. *Journal of Personality and Social Psychology*, 104, 267–276.

Diener, E., Wolsic, B., & Fujita, F. (1995). Physical attractiveness and subjective well-being. *Journal of Personality and Social Psychology*, 69, 120–129.

Dohrenwend, B.P. (2006). Inventorying stressful life events as risk factors for psychopathology: Toward resolution of the problem of intracategory variability. *Psychological Bulletin*, 132, 477–495.

Entringer, S., Epel, E.S., Kumsta, R., Lin, J., Hellhammer, D.H., Blackburn, E., Wüst, S., & Wadhwa, P.D. (2011). Stress exposure in intrauterine life is associated with shorter telomere length in young adulthood. *Proceedings of the National Academy of Sciences, USA*, 108, E513–E518.

Epel, E.S., Blackburn, E.H., Lin, J., Dhabhar, F.S., Adler, N.E., Morrow, J.D., & Cawthon, R.M. (2004). Accelerated telomere shortening in response to life stress. *Proceedings of the National Academy of Sciences, USA*, 101, 17312–17315.

Everly, G.S., & Lating, J.M. (2002). *A clinical guide to the treatment of the human stress response* (2nd ed.). Kluwer Academic/Plenum Publishing.

Falagas, M.E., Zarkadoulia, E.A., Ioannidou, E.N., Peppas, G., Christodoulou, C., & Rafailidis, P.I. (2007). The effect of psychosocial factors on breast cancer outcome: A systematic review. *Breast Cancer Research, 9:R44*. http://breast-cancer-research.com/content/pdf/bcr1744.pdf

Folkman, S., & Lazarus, R.S. (1980). An analysis of coping in a middle-aged community sample. *Journal of Health and Social Behavior*, 21, 219–239.

Fontana, A.M., Diegnan, T., Villeneuve, A., & Lepore, S.J. (1999). Nonevaluative social support reduces cardiovascular reactivity in young women during acutely stressful performance situations. *Journal of Behavioral Medicine*, 22, 75–91.

Friedman, H.S., & Booth-Kewley, S. (1987). The "disease-prone personality": A meta-analytic view of the construct. *American Psychologist*, 42, 539–555.

Friedman, M. (1977). Type A behavior pattern: Some of its pathophysiological components. *Bulletin of the New York Academy of Medicine*, 53, 593–604.

Friedman, M., & Rosenman, R. (1974). *Type A behavior and your heart*. Alfred A. Knopf.

Friedman, M., & Rosenman, R.H. (1959). Association of specific overt behavior pattern with blood and cardiovascular findings blood cholesterol level, blood clotting time, incidence of arcus senilis, and clinical coronary artery disease. *Journal of the American Medical Association*, 169(12), 1286–1296.

Fujita, F., & Diener, E. (2005). Life satisfaction set point: Stability and change. *Journal of Personality and Social Psychology*, 88, 158–164.

Fulmer, C.A., Gelfand, M.J., Kruglanski, A., Kim-Prieto, C., Diener, E., Pierro, A., & Higgins, E.T. (2010). On "feeling right" in cultural contexts: How person-culture match affects self-esteem and subjective well-being. *Psychological Science*, 21, 1563–1569.

Geoffroy, M.C., Hertzman, C., Li, L., & Power, C. (2013). Prospective association of morning salivary cortisol with depressive symptoms in mid-life: A life-course study. *PLoS ONE, 8*(11), 1–9.

Gerber, M., Kellman, M., Hartman, T., & Pühse, U. (2010). Do exercise and fitness buffer against stress among Swiss police and emergency response service officers? *Psychology of Sport and Exercise*, 11, 286–294.

Glaser, R., & Kiecolt-Glaser, J.K. (2005). Stress-induced immune dysfunction: Implications for health. *Nature Reviews Immunology*, 5, 243–251.

Glaser, R., Kiecolt-Glaser, J.K., Marucha, P.T., MacCallum, R.C., Laskowski, B.F., & Malarkey, W.B. (1999). Stress-related changes in proinflammatory cytokine production in wounds. *Archives of General Psychiatry*, 56, 450–456.

Glassman, A.H. (2007). Depression and cardiovascular comorbidity. *Dialogues in Clinical Neuroscience*, 9, 9–17.

Glassman, A.H., & Shapiro, P.A. (1998). Depression and the course of coronary artery disease. *American Journal of Psychiatry*, 155, 4–11.

Greenberg, J.S. (2006). *Comprehensive stress management* (9th ed.). McGraw-Hill.

Gregoire, C. (2013, June 5). Happiness index: Only 1 in 3 Americans are very happy, according to Harris Poll. *The Huffington Post*. http://www.huffingtonpost.com/2013/06/01/happiness-index-only-1-in_n_3354524.html

Hackney, C.H., & Sanders, G.S. (2003). Religiosity and mental health: A meta-analysis of recent studies. *Journal for the Scientific Study of Religion*, 42, 43–55.

Hansen, T. (2012). Parenthood and happiness: A review of folk theories versus empirical evidence. *Social Indicators Research*, 108, 29–64.

Hare, D.L., Toukhsati, S.R., Johansson, P., & Jaarsma, T. (2013). Depression and cardiovascular disease: A clinical review. *European Heart Journal*. Advance online publication. https://doi.org/10.1093/eurheartj/eht462

Hatch, S.L., & Dohrenwend, B.P. (2007). Distribution of traumatic and other stressful life events by race/ethnicity, gender, SES, and age: A review of the research. *American Journal of Community Psychology*, 40, 313–332.

Haynes, S.G., Feinleib, M., & Kannel, W.B. (1980). The relationship of psychosocial factors to coronary disease in the Framingham study: III. Eight-year incidence of coronary heart disease. *American Journal of Epidemiology*, 111, 37–58.

Head, D., Singh, T., & Bugg, J.M. (2012). The moderating role of exercise on stress-related effects on the hippocampus and memory in later adulthood. *Neuropsychology*, 26, 133–143.

Helliwell, J., Layard, R., & Sachs, J. (Eds.). (2013). *World happiness report 2013*. United Nations Sustainable Development Solutions Network: http://unsdsn. org/wp-content/uploads/2014/02/ WorldHappinessReport2013_online.pdf

Helson, H. (1964). Current trends and issues in adaptation-level theory. *American Psychologist*, 19, 26–38.

Holmes, T.H., & Masuda, M. (1974). Life change and illness susceptibility. In B. S. Dohrenwend & B. P. Dohrenwend (Eds.), *Stressful life events: Their nature and effects* (pp. 45–72). John Wiley & Sons.

Holmes, T.H., & Rahe, R.H. (1967). The social readjustment rating scale. *Journal of Psychosomatic Research*, 11, 213–218.

Holmes, T.S., & Holmes, T.H. (1970). Short-term intrusions into the life style routine. *Journal of Psychosomatic Research*, 14, 121–132.

Holt-Lunstad, J., Smith, T.B., & Layton, J.B. (2010). Social relationships and mortality risk: A meta-analytic review. *PLoS Medicine*, 7(7), e1000316.

Hupbach, A., & Fieman, R. (2012). Moderate stress enhances immediate and delayed retrieval of educationally relevant material in healthy young men. *Behavioral Neuroscience*, 126, 819–825.

Infurna, F.J., & Gerstorf, D. (2014). Perceived control relates to better functional health and lower cardio-metabolic risk: The mediating role of physical activity. *Health Psychology*, 33, 85–94.

Infurna, F.J., Gerstorf, D., Ram, N., Schupp, J., & Wagner, G.G. (2011). Long-term antecedents and outcomes of perceived control. *Psychology and Aging*, 26, 559–575.

Johnson, W., & Krueger, R.F. (2006). How money buys happiness: Genetic and environmental processes linking finances and life satisfaction. *Journal of Personality and Social Psychology*, 90, 680–691.

Jonas, B.S., & Lando, J.F. (2000). Negative affect as a prospective risk factor for hypertension. *Psychosomatic Medicine*, 62, 188–196.

Jordan, H.T., Miller-Archie, S.A., Cone, J.E., Morabia, A., & Stellman, S.D. (2011). Heart disease among those exposed to the September 11, 2001 World Trade Center disaster: Results from the World Trade Center Health Registry. *Preventive Medicine: An International Journal Devoted to Practice and Theory*, 53, 370–376.

Kahneman, D. (2011). *Thinking fast and slow*. Farrar, Straus, & Giroux.

Kahneman, D., & Deaton, A. (2010). High income improves evaluation of life, but not emotional well-being. *Proceedings of the National Academy of Sciences, USA*, 107, 16489–16493.

Kanner, A.D., Coyne, J.C., Schaefer, C., & Lazarus, R.S. (1981). Comparison of two modes of stress measurement: Daily hassles and uplifts versus major life events. *Journal of Behavioral Medicine*, 4, 1–39.

Karasek, R., & Theorell, T. (1990). *Healthy work: Stress, productivity, and the reconstruction of working life*. Basic Books.

Kiecolt-Glaser, J.K. (2009). Psychoneuroimmunology: Psychology's gateway to the biomedical future. *Perspectives on Psychological Science*, 4, 367–369.

Kiecolt-Glaser, J.K., Glaser, R., Gravenstein, S., Malarkey, W.B., & Sheridan, J., (1996). Chronic stress alters the immune response to influenza virus vaccine in older adults. *Proceedings of the National Academy of Sciences, USA*, 93, 3043–3047.

Kiecolt-Glaser, J.K., McGuire, L., Robles, T.F., & Glaser, R. (2002). Psychoneuroimmunology and psychosomatic medicine: Back to the future. *Psychosomatic Medicine*, 64, 15–28.

Kiecolt-Glaser, J.K., McGuire, L., Robles, T.F., & Glaser, R. (2002). Psychoneuroimmunology: Psychological influences on immune function and health. *Journal of Consulting and Clinical Psychology*, 70, 537–547.

Kilpeläinen, M., Koskenvuo, M., Helenius, H., & Terho, E.O. (2002). Stressful life events promote the manifestation of asthma and atopic diseases. *Clinical and Experimental Allergy*, 32, 256–263.

Kivimäki, M., Head, J., Ferrie, J.E., Shipley, M.J., Brunner, E., Vahtera, J., & Marmot, M.G. (2006). Work stress, weight gain and weight loss. Evidence for bidirectional effects of body mass index in the Whitehall II study. *International Journal of Obesity*, 30, 982–987.

Klinnert, M.D., Nelson, H.S., Price, M.R., Adinoff, A.D., Leung, M., & Mrazek, D.A. (2001). Onset and persistence of childhood asthma: Predictors from infancy. *Pediatrics*, 108, E69.

Kraus, M.W., Piff, P.K., Mendoza-Denton, R., Rheinschmidt, M.L., & Keltner, D. (2012). Social class, solipsism, and contextualism: How the rich are different from the poor. *Psychological Review*, 119, 546–572.

Krosnick, J.A. (1990). *Thinking about politics: Comparisons of experts and novices*. Guilford.

Krumboltz, M. (2014, February 18). Just like us? Elephants comfort each other when they're stressed out. *Yahoo News*. http:// news.yahoo.com/elephants-know-a-thing-or-two-about-empathy-202224477.html

Lachman, M.E., & Weaver, S.L. (1998). The sense of control as a moderator of social class differences in health and well-being. *Journal of Personality and Social Psychology*, 74, 763–773.

Lavner, J.A., Karney, B.R., & Bradbury, T.N. (2013). Newlyweds' optimistic forecasts of their marriage: For better or for worse? *Journal of Family Psychology*, 27, 531–540.

Lazarus, R.P., & Folkman, S. (1984). *Stress, appraisal, and coping*. Springer.

Lee, M., & Rotheram-Borus, M.J. (2001). Challenges associated with increased survival among parents living with HIV. *American Journal of Public Health*, 91, 1303–1309.

Lehrer, P.M., Isenberg, S., & Hochron, S.M. (1993). Asthma and emotion: A review. *Journal of Asthma*, 30, 5–21.

Lepore, S.J. (1998). Problems and prospects for the social support-reactivity hypothesis. *Annals of Behavioral Medicine*, 20, 257–269.

Lichtman, J.H., Bigger, T., Blumenthal, J.A., Frasure-Smith, N., Kaufmann, P.G., Lespérance, F.,...Froelicher, E.S. (2008). Depression and coronary heart disease: Recommendations for screening, referral, and treatment: A science advisory from the American Heart Association Prevention Committee of the Council on Cardiovascular Nursing, Council on Clinical Cardiology, Council on Epidemiology and Prevention, and Interdisciplinary Council on Quality of Care and Outcomes Research. *Circulation*, 118, 1768–1775.

Loerbroks, A., Apfelbacher, C.J., Thayer, J.F., Debling, D., & Stürmer, T. (2009). Neuroticism, extraversion, stressful life events and asthma: A cohort study of middle-aged adults. *Allergy*, 64, 1444–1450.

Logan H., Lutgendorf, S., Rainville, P., Sheffield, D., Iverson, K., & Lubaroff, D. (2001). Effects of stress and relaxation on capsaicin-induced pain. *The Journal of Pain*, 2, 160–170.

Lutter, M. (2007). Book review: Winning a lottery brings no happiness. *Journal of Happiness Studies*, 8, 155–160.

Lyon, B.L. (2012). Stress, coping, and health. In V. H. Rice (Ed.), *Handbook of stress, coping, and health: Implications for nursing research, theory, and practice* (2nd ed., pp. 2–20). Sage.

Lyubomirsky, S. (2001). Why are some people happier than others? The role of cognitive and motivational processes in well-being. *American Psychologist*, 56, 239–249.

Lyubomirsky, S., King, L., & Diener, E. (2005). The benefits of frequent positive affect: Does happiness lead to success? *Psychological Bulletin*, 131, 803–855.

Maier, S.F., Watkins, L.R., & Fleshner, M. (1994). Psychoneuroimmunology: The interface between behavior, brain, and immunity. *American Journal of Psychology* 49(12), 1004–1017.

Malzberg, B. (1937). Mortality among patients with involution melancholia. *American Journal of Psychiatry*, 93, 1231–1238.

Marmot, M.G., Bosma, H., Hemingway, H., & Stansfeld, S. (1997). Contribution of job control and other risk factors to social variations in coronary heart disease incidence. *The Lancet*, 350, 235–239.

Martin, M.W. (2012). *Happiness and the good life*. Oxford University Press.

Maslach, C., & Jackson, S.E. (1981). The measurement of experienced burnout. *Journal of Occupational Behavior*, 2, 99–113.

McEwan, B. (1998). Protective and damaging effects of stress mediators. *New England Journal of Medicine*, 338(3), 171–179.

McIntosh, J. (2014, July 28) What are headaches? What causes headaches? *Medical News Today*. http://www.medicalnewstoday.com/articles/73936.php

MedicineNet. (2013). *Headaches*. http://www.medicinenet.com/tension_headache/article.htm#what_causes_tension_headaches

Monat, A., & Lazarus, R.S. (1991). *Stress and coping: An anthology* (3rd ed.). Columbia University Press.

Myers, D.G. (2000). The funds, friends, and faith of happy people. *American Psychologist*, 55, 56–67.

Myers, T.C., Wittrock, D.A., & Foreman, G.W., (1998). Appraisal of subjective stress in individuals with tension-type headache: The influence of baseline measures. *Journal of Behavioral Medicine*, 21, 469–484.

Mykletun, A., Bjerkeset, O., Dewey, M., Prince, M., Overland, S., & Stewart, R. (2007). Anxiety, depression, and cause-specific mortality: The HUNT study. *Psychosomatic Medicine*, 69, 323–331.

Myrtek, M. (2001). Meta-analyses of prospective studies on coronary heart disease, type A personality, and hostility. *International Journal of Cardiology*, 79, 245–251.

Nabi, H., Kivimaki, M., De Vogli, R., Marmot, M.G., & Singh-Manoux, A. (2008). Positive and negative affect and risk of coronary heart disease: Whitehall II prospective cohort study. *British Medical Journal*, 337, a118.

National Institute of Arthritis and Musculoskeletal and Skin Diseases (NIAMS). (2012). *Understanding autoimmune diseases*. http://www.niams.nih.gov/Health_Info/Autoimmune/understanding_autoimmune.pdf

Nealey-Moore, J.B., Smith, T.W., Uchino, B.N., Hawkins, M.W., & Olson-Cerny, C. (2007). Cardiovascular reactivity during positive and negative marital interactions. *Journal of Behavioral Medicine*, 30, 505–519.

Neelakantan, S. (2013). Mind over myocardium. *Nature*, 493, S16–S17.

Neupert, S.D., Almeida, D.M., & Charles, S.T. (2007). Age differences in reactivity to daily stressors: The role of personal control. *Journal of Gerontology: Psychological Sciences*, 62B, P216–P225.

Nusair, M., Al-dadah, A., & Kumar, A. (2012). The tale of mind and heart: Psychiatric disorders and coronary heart disease. *Missouri Medicine*, 109, 199–203.

Office on Women's Health, U.S. Department of Health and Human Services. (2009). *Heart disease: Frequently asked questions*. http://www.womenshealth.gov/publications/our-publications/fact-sheet/heart-disease.pdf

Ong, A.D., Bergeman, C.S., & Bisconti, T.L. (2005). Unique effects of daily perceived control on anxiety symptomatology during conjugal bereavement. *Personality and Individual Differences*, 38, 1057–1067.

Ösby, U., Brandt, L., Correia, N., Ekbom, A., & Sparén, P. (2001). Excess mortality in bipolar and unipolar depression in Sweden. *Archives of General Psychiatry*, 58, 844–850.

Park, S.G., Kim, H.C., Min, J.Y., Hwang, S.H., Park, Y.S., & Min, K.B. (2011). A prospective study of work stressors and the common cold. *Occupational Medicine*, 61, 53–56.

Peterson, C., & Seligman, M.E. P. (1984). Causal explanations as a risk factor for depression: Theory and evidence. *Psychological Review*, 91, 347–374.

Peterson, C., & Steen, T.A. (2002). Optimistic explanatory style. In C. R. Snyder & S. J. Lopez (Eds.), *Handbook of positive psychology* (pp. 244–256). Oxford University Press.

Phillips, A.C. (2011). Blunted as well as exaggerated cardiovascular reactivity to stress is associated with negative health outcomes. *Japanese Psychological Research*, 53, 177–192.

Phillips, A.C., Gallagher, S., & Carroll, D. (2009). Social support, social intimacy, and cardiovascular reactions to acute psychological stress. *Annals of Behavioral Medicine*, 37, 38–45.

Pinquart, M., & Sörensen, S. (2000). Influence of socioeconomic status, social network, and competence on subjective well-being in later life. A meta-analysis. *Psychology and Aging*, 15, 187–224.

Ploubidis, G.B., & Grundy, E. (2009). Personality and all cause mortality: Evidence for indirect links. *Personality and Individual differences*, 47, 203–208.

Powell, J. (1996). *AIDS and HIV-related diseases: An educational guide for professionals and the public*. Insight Books.

Pressman, S.D., & Cohen, S. (2005). Does positive affect influence health? *Psychological Bulletin*, 131, 925–971.

Puterman, E., Lin, J., Blackburn, E., O'Donovan, A., Adler, N., & Epel, E. (2010). The power of exercise: Buffering the effect of chronic stress on telomere length. *PLoS ONE*, 5(5), e10837.

Quoidbach, J., Dunn, E.W., Petrides, K.V., & Mikolajczak, M. (2010). Money giveth, money taketh away: The dual effect of wealth on happiness. *Psychological Science*, 21, 759–763.

Rahe, R.H. (1974). The pathway between subjects' recent life changes and their near-future illness reports: Representative results and methodological issues. In B. S. Dohrenwend & B. P. Dohrenwend (Eds.), *Stressful life events: Their nature and effects* (pp. 73–86). Wiley & Sons.

Rahe, R.H., McKeen, J.D., & Arthur, R.J. (1967). A longitudinal study of life change and illness patterns. *Journal of Psychosomatic Research*, 10, 355–366.

Raney, J.D., & Troop-Gordon, W. (2012). Computer-mediated communication with distant friends: Relations with adjustment during students' first semester in college. *Journal of Educational Psychology*, 104, 848–861.

Rasmussen, H.N., & Wallio, S.C. (2008). The health benefits of optimism. In S. J. Lopez (Ed.), *Positive psychology: Exploring the best in people* (pp. 131–149). Praeger Publishers.

Rasmussen, H.N., Scheier, M.F., & Greenhouse, J.B. (2009). Optimism and physical health: A meta-analytic review. *Annals of Behavioral Medicine*, 37, 239–256.

Ritz, T., Steptoe, A., Bobb, C., Harris, A.H. S., & Edwards, M. (2006). The asthma trigger inventory: Validation of a questionnaire for perceived triggers of asthma. *Psychosomatic Medicine*, 68, 956–965.

Rosengren, A., Hawken, S., Ounpuu, S., Sliwa, K., Zubaid, M., Almahmeed, W.A.,…Yusuf, S. (2004). Association of psychosocial risk factors with risk of acute myocardial infarction in 11,119 cases and 13,648 controls from 52 countries (the INTERHEART study): Case-control study. *The Lancet*, 364, 953–962.

Rosenman, R.H., Brand, R.J., Jenkins, C.D., Friedman, M., Straus, R., & Wurm, M. (1975). Coronary heart disease in the Western Collaborative Group Study: Final follow-up experience of 8.5 years. *Journal of the American Medical Association*, 223, 872–877.

Rottenberg, J., Yaroslavsky, I., Carney, R.M., Freedland, K.E., George, C.J., Baki, I., Kovacs, M. (2014). The association between major depressive disorder and risk factors for cardiovascular disease in adolescence. *Psychosomatic Medicine*, 76, 122–127.

Saito, K., Kim, J.I., Maekawa, K., Ikeda, Y., & Yokoyama, M. (1997). The great Hanshin-Awaji earthquake aggravates blood pressure control in treated hypertensive patients. *American Journal of Hypertension*, 10, 217–221.

Salmon, P. (2001). Effects of physical exercise on anxiety, depression, and sensitivity to stress: A unifying theory. *Clinical Psychology Review*, 21, 33–61.

Salonen, P., Arola, H., Nygård, C., & Huhtala, H. (2008). Long-term associations of stress and chronic diseases in ageing and retired employees. *Psychology, Health, and Medicine*, 13, 55–62.

Sapolsky, R.M. (1998). *Why zebras don't get ulcers: An updated guide to stress, stress-related disease, and coping*. Freeman.

Sapolsky, R.M. (2004). Organismal stress and telomeric aging. An unexpected connection. *Proceedings of the National Academy of Sciences, USA*, 101, 17323–17324.

Schnall, P.L., & Landsbergis, P.A. (1994). Job strain and cardiovascular disease. *Annual Review of Public Health*, 15, 381–411.

Schwartz, B.S., Stewart, W.F., Simon, D., & Lipton, R.B. (1998). Epidemiology of tension-type headache. *Journal of the American Medical Association*, 279, 381–383.

Schwartz, N.M., & Schwartz, M.S. (1995). Definitions of biofeedback and applied physiology. In M. S. Schwartz & F. Andrasik (Eds.), *Biofeedback: A practitioners guide* (pp. 32–42). Guilford.

Scully, J.A., Tosi, H., & Banning, K. (2000). Life event checklists: Revisiting the Social Readjustment Rating Scale after 30 years. *Educational and Psychological Measurement*, 60, 864–876.

Segerstrom, S.C., & Miller, G.E. (2004). Psychological stress and the human immune system: A meta-analytic study of 30 years of inquiry. *Psychological Bulletin*, 130, 601–630.

Seligman, M.E., & Maier, S.F. (1967). Failure to escape traumatic shock. *Journal of Experimental Psychology*, 74, 1–9.

Seligman, M.E., Maier, S.F., & Geer, J.H. (1968). Alleviation of learned helplessness in the dog. *Journal of Abnormal Psychology*, 3, 256–262.

Seligman, M.E. P. (2002). *Authentic happiness: Using the new positive psychology to realize your potential for lasting fulfillment*. Free Press.

Seligman, M.E. P., Steen, T.A., Park, N., & Peterson, C. (2005). Positive psychology progress: Empirical validation of interventions. *American Psychologist*, 60, 410–421.

Seligman, M.P., & Csikszentmihalyi, M. (2000). Positive psychology: An introduction. *American Psychologist*, 55, 5–14.

Selye, H. (1936). A syndrome produced by diverse nocuous agents. *Nature*, 138, 32–33.

Selye, H. (1974). *Stress without distress*. Lippencott.

Selye, H. (1976). *The stress of life* (Rev. ed.). McGraw-Hill.

Shalev, I., Moffitt, T.E., Sugden, K., Williams, B., Houts, R.M., Danese, A.,…Caspi, A. (2013). Exposure to violence during childhood is associated with telomere erosion from 5 to 10 years of age: A longitudinal study. *Molecular Psychiatry*, 18, 576–581.

Shapiro, P.A. (2005). Heart disease. In J. L. Levenson (Ed.), *Textbook of psychosomatic medicine* (pp. 423–444). American Psychiatric Publishing.

Sims, M., Diez-Roux, A.V., Dudley, A., Gebreab, S., Wyatt, S.B., Bruce, M.A.,…Taylor, H.A. (2012). Perceived discrimination and hypertension among African Americans in the Jackson Heart Study [Supplemental material]. *American Journal of Public Health*, 102(2 Suppl.), S258–S265.

Smyth, J.M., Soefer, M.H., Hurewitz, A., Kliment, A., & Stone, A.A. (1999). Daily psychosocial factors predict levels and diurnal cycles of asthma symptomatology and peak flow. *Journal of Behavioral Medicine*, 22, 179–193.

Sodergren, S.C., & Hyland, M.H. (1999). Expectancy and asthma. In I. Kirsch (Ed.), *How expectancies shape experience* (pp. 197–212). American Psychological Association.

Speck, R.M., Courneya, K.S., Masse, L.C., Duval, S., & Schmitz, K.H. (2010). An update of controlled physical activity trials in cancer survivors: A systematic review and meta-analysis. *Journal of Cancer Survivorship*, 4, 87–100.

Stansfeld, S.A., Shipley, M.J., Head, J., & Fuhrer, R. (2012). Repeated job strain and the risk of depression: Longitudinal analyses from the Whitehall II study. *American Journal of Public Health*, 102, 2360–2366.

Stein, F. (2001). Occupational stress, relaxation therapies, exercise, and biofeedback. *Work: Journal of Prevention, Assessment, and Rehabilitation*, 17, 235–246.

Steptoe, A., O'Donnell, K., Marmot, M., & Wardle, J. (2008). Positive affect and psychosocial processes related to health. *British Journal of Psychology*, 99, 211–227.

Stovner, L.J., Hagen, K., Jensen, R., Katsarava, Z., Lipson, R., Scher, A.,…Zwart, J. (2007). The global burden of headache: A documentation of headache prevalence and disability worldwide. *Cephalalgia*, 27, 193–210.

Straub, R.O. (2007). *Health psychology: A biopsychosocial approach* (2nd ed.). Worth.

Stroebe, W., & Stroebe, M. (1996). The social psychology of social support. In E. T. Higgins & A. W. Kruglanski (Eds.), *Social psychology: Handbook of basic principles* (pp. 597–621). Guilford.

Stürmer, T., Hasselbach, P., & Amelang, M. (2006). Personality, lifestyle, and risk of cardiovascular disease and cancer: Follow-up of population based cohort. *British Medical Journal*, 332, 1359–1362.

Suls, J., & Bunde, J. (2005). Anger, anxiety, and depression as risk factors for cardiovascular disease: The problems and implications of overlapping affective dispositions. *Psychological Bulletin*, 131, 260–300.

Sulsky, L., & Smith, C. (2005). *Work stress*. Thomson Wadsworth.

Surtees, P.G., Wainwright, N.W. J., Luben, R., Wareham, N.J., Bingham, S.A., & Khaw, K.-T. (2010). Mastery is associated with cardiovascular disease mortality in men and women at apparently low risk. *Health Psychology*, 29, 412–420.

Tatris, T.W., Peeters, M.C. W., Le Blanc, P.M., Schreurs, P.J.G., & Schaufeli, W.B. (2001). From inequity to burnout: The role of job stress. *Journal of Occupational Health Psychology*, 6, 303–323.

Taylor, S.E. (1999). *Health psychology* (4th ed.). McGraw-Hill.

Theorell, T., Tsutsumi, A., Hallquist, J., Reuterwall, C., Hogstedt, C., Fredlund, P.,... Johnson, J.V. (1998). Decision latitude, job strain, and myocardial infarction: A study of working men in Stockholm. *American Journal of Public Health*, 88, 382–388.

Thoits, P.A. (2010). Stress and health: Major findings and policy implications [Supplemental material]. *Journal of Health and Social Behavior*, 51(1 Suppl.), S41–S53.

Trudel, X., Brisson, C., & Milot, A. (2010). Job strain and masked hypertension. *Psychosomatic Medicine*, 72, 786–793.

Trueba, A.F., & Ritz, T. (2013). Stress, asthma, and respiratory infections: Pathways involving airway immunology and microbal endocrinology. *Brain, Behavior and Immunity*, 29, 11–27.

Uchino, B.N. (2009). Understanding the links between social support and physical health: A life-span perspective with emphasis on the separability of perceived and received support. *Perspectives on Psychological Science*, 4, 236–255.

Uchino, B.N., Vaughn, A.A., Carlisle, M., & Birmingham, W. (2012). Social support and immunity. In S. C. Segerstrom (Ed.), *The Oxford handbook of psychoneuroimmunology* (pp. 214–233). Oxford University Press.

Ukestad, L.K., and Wittrock, D.A. (1996). Pain perception and coping in recurrent headache. *Health Psychology*, 15, 65–68.

Vella, E.J., Kamarck, T.W., Flory, J.D., & Manuck, S. (2012). Hostile mood and social strain during daily life: A test of the transactional model. *Annals of Behavioral Medicine*, 44, 341–352.

von Leupoldt, A., Ehnes, F., & Dahme, B. (2006). Emotions and respiratory function in asthma: A comparison of findings in everyday life and laboratory. *British Journal of Health Psychology*, 11, 185–198.

Watson, D., Clark, L.A., & Tellegen, A. (1988). Development and validation of brief measures of positive and negative affect: The PANAS scales. *Journal of Personality and Social Psychology*, 54, 1063–1070.

Weeke, A. (1979). Causes of death in manic-depressive. In M. Shou & M. Stromgren (Eds.), *Origin, prevention, and treatment of affective disorders* (pp. 289–299). Academic Press.

Whang, W., Kubzansky, L.D., Kawachi, I., Rexrod, K.M., Kroenke, C.H., Glynn, R.J.,... Albert, C.M. (2009). Depression and risk of sudden cardiac death and coronary heart disease in women: Results from the Nurses' Health Study. *Journal of the American College of Cardiology*, 53, 950–958.

Wilson, T.D., & Gilbert, D.T. (2003). Affective forecasting. *Advances in Experimental Social Psychology*, 35, 345–411.

World Health Organization (WHO). (2013). *A global brief on hypertension: Silent killer, global public health crisis*. http://apps.who.int/iris/bitstream/10665/79059/1/WHO_DCO_WHD_2013.2_eng.pdf?ua=1

Wright, R.J., Rodriguez, M., & Cohen, S. (1998). Review of psychosocial stress and asthma: An integrated biopsychosocial approach. *Thorax*, 53, 1066–1074.

Wulsin, L.R., & Singal, B.M. (2003). Do depressive symptoms increase the risk for the onset of coronary disease? A systematic quantitative review. *Psychosomatic Medicine*, 65, 201–210.

Zacharie, R. (2009). Psychoneuroimmunology: A bio-psycho-social approach to health and disease. *Scandinavian Journal of Psychology*, 50, 645–651.

Chapter 14

Abela, J.R., & Hankin, B.L. (2011). Rumination as a vulnerability factor to depression during the transition from early to middle adolescence: A multiwave longitudinal study. *Journal of Abnormal Psychology*, 120, 259–271.

Abramowitz, J.S., & Siqueland, L. (2013). Obsessive-compulsive disorder. In L. G. Castonguay & T. F. Oltmanns (Eds.), *Psychopathology: From science to clinical practice* (pp. 143–171). Guilford Press.

Abramson, L.Y., Metalsky, G.I., & Alloy, L.B. (1989). Hopelessness depression: A theory-based subtype of depression. *Psychological Review*, 96, 358–372.

Afifi, T.O., Mather, A., Boman, J., Fleisher, W., Enns, M.W., MacMillan, H., & Sareen, J. (2010). Childhood adversity and personality disorder: Results from a nationally representative population-based survey. *Journal of Psychiatric Research*, 45, 814–822.

Agerbo, E., Nordentoft, M., & Mortensen, P.B. (2002). Familial, psychiatric, and socioeconomic risk factors for suicide in young people: Nested case-control study. *British Medical Journal*, 325, 74–77.

Aghukwa, C.N. (2012). Care seeking and beliefs about the cause of mental illness among Nigerian psychiatric patients and their families. *Psychiatric Services*, 63, 616–618.

Aikins, D.E., & Craske, M.G. (2001). Cognitive theories of generalized anxiety disorder. *Psychiatric Clinics of North America*, 24, 57–74.

Akinbami, L.J., Liu, X., Pastor, P., & Reuben, C.A. (2011, August). Attention deficit hyperactivity disorder among children aged 5–17 years in the United States, 1998–2009 (NCHS data brief No. 70). Hyattsville, MD: National Center for Health Statistics. http://www.cdc.gov/nchs/data/databriefs/db70.pdf

Alden, L.E., & Bieling, P. (1998). Interpersonal consequences in the pursuit of safety. *Behaviour Research and Therapy*, 36, 53–64.

Alegria, A.A., Blanco, C., Petry, N.M., Skodol, A.E., Liu, S.M., & Grant, B. (2013). Sex differences in antisocial personality disorder: Results from the National Epidemiological Survey on Alcohol and Related Conditions. *Personality Disorders: Theory, Research, and Treatment*, 4, 214–222.

American Psychiatric Association. (2013). *Diagnostic and statistical manual of mental disorders* (5th ed.). Author.

Andreasen, N.C. (1987). The diagnosis of schizophrenia. *Schizophrenia Bulletin*, 13, 9–22.

Andréasson, S., Allbeck, P., Engström, A., & Rydberg, U. (1987). Cannabis and schizophrenia: A longitudinal study of Swedish conscripts. *Lancet*, 330, 1483–1486.

Asberg, M., Thorén, P., Träskman, L., Bertilsson, L., & Ringberger, V. (1976). "Serotonin depression"—a biochemical subgroup within the affective disorders? *Science*, 191(4226), 478–480. https://doi.org/10.1126/science.1246632

Asperger's syndrome dropped from psychiatrists' handbook the DSM: DSM-5, latest revision of Diagnostic and Statistical Manual, merges Asperger's with autism and widens dyslexia category. (2012, December 1). *The Guardian*. http://www.theguardian.com/society/2012/dec/02/aspergers-syndrome-dropped-psychiatric-dsm

Autism Genome Project Consortium. (2007). Mapping autism risk loci using genetic linkage and chromosomal rearrangements. *Nature Genetics*, 39, 319–328.

Baes, C.V. W., Tofoli, S.M. C., Martins, C.M. S., & Juruena, M.F. (2012). Assessment of the hypothalamic–pituitary–adrenal axis activity: Glucocorticoid receptor and mineralocorticoid receptor function in depression with early life stress—a systematic review. *Acta Neuropsychiatrica*, 24, 4–15.

Baker, L.A., Bezdjian, S., & Raine, A. (2006). Behavioral genetics: The science of antisocial behavior. *Law and Contemporary Problems*, 69, 7–46.

Barbaresi, W.J., Colligan, R.C., Weaver, A.L., Voigt, R.G., Killian, J.M., & Katusic, S.K. (2013). Mortality, ADHD, and psychosocial adversity in adults with childhood ADHD: A prospective study. *Pediatrics*, 131, 637–644.

Barker, P. (2010). *The legacy of Thomas Szasz*. http://www.centerforindependentthought.org/SzaszLegacy.html

Barkley, R.A. (2006). *Attention-deficit hyperactivity disorder: A handbook for diagnosis and treatment*. Guilford Press.

Barkley, R.A., Fischer, M., Smallish, L., & Fletcher, K. (2002). The persistence of attention-deficit/hyperactivity disorder into young adulthood as a function of reporting source and definition of disorder. *Journal of Abnormal Psychology*, 111, 279–289.

Battista, S.R., & Kocovski, N.L. (2010). Exploring the effect of alcohol on post-event processing specific to a social event. *Cognitive Behaviour Therapy*, 39, 1–10.

Baumeister, A.A., & Hawkins, M.F. (2004). The serotonin hypothesis of schizophrenia: A historical case study on the heuristic value of theory in clinical neuroscience. *Journal of the History of the Neurosciences*, 13, 277–291.

Beck, A.T. (1976). *Cognitive therapy and the emotional disorders*. International Universities Press.

Beck, A.T. (2008). The evolution of the cognitive model of depression and its neurobiological correlates. *American Journal of Psychiatry*, 165, 969–977.

Berman, A.L. (2009). School-based suicide prevention: Research advances and practice implications [Commentary]. *School Psychology Review*, 38, 233–238.

Bettelheim, B. (1967). *The empty fortress: Infantile autism and the birth of the self*. Free Press.

Beucke, J.C., Sepulcre, J., Talukdar, T., Linnman, C., Zschenderlein, K., Endrass, T.,...Kathman, N. (2013). Abnormally high degree connectivity of the orbitofrontal cortex in obsessive-compulsive disorder. *JAMA Psychiatry*, 70, 619–629.

Biederman, J., Faraone, S.V., Hirshfeld-Becker, D.R., Friedman, D., Robin, J.A., & Rosenbaum, J.F. (2001). Patterns of psychopathology and dysfunction in high-risk children of parents with panic disorder and major depression. *American Journal of Psychiatry*, 158, 49–57.

Boland, R.J., & Keller, M.B. (2009). Course and outcome of depression. In I. H. Gotlib & C. L. Hammen (Eds.), *Handbook of depression* (pp. 23–43). Guilford Press.

Bolton, D., Rijsdijk, F., O'Connor, T.G., Perrin, S., & Eley, T.C. (2007). Obsessive-compulsive disorder, tics and anxiety in 6-year-old twins. *Psychological Medicine*, 37, 39–48.

Bourguignon, E. (1970). Hallucinations and trance: An anthropologist's perspective. In W. Keup (Ed.), *Origins and mechanisms of hallucination* (pp. 183–190). Plenum Press.

Bouton, M.E., Mineka, S., & Barlow, D.H. (2001). A modern learning theory perspective on the etiology of panic disorder. *Psychological Review*, 108, 4–32.

Bramsen, I., Dirkzwager, A.J.E., & van der Ploeg, H.M. (2000). Predeployment personality traits and exposure to trauma as predictors of posttraumatic stress symptoms: A prospective study of former peacekeepers. *American Journal of Psychiatry*, 157, 1115–1119.

Bregman, J.D. (2005). Definitions and characteristics of the spectrum. In D. Zager (Ed.), *Autism spectrum disorders: Identification, education, and treatment* (3rd ed., pp. 3–46). Erlbaum.

Bremner, J.D., Krystal, J.H., Southwick, S.M., & Charney, D.S. (1996). Noradrenergic mechanisms in stress and anxiety: I. preclinical studies. *Synapse*, 23, 28–38.

Brent, D.A., & Bridge, J. (2003). Firearms availability and suicide: A review of the literature. *American Behavioral Scientist*, 46, 1192–1210.

Brewin, C.R., Andrews, B., & Valentine, J.D. (2000). Meta-analysis of risk factors for posttraumatic stress disorder in trauma-exposed adults. *Journal of Consulting and Clinical Psychology*, 68, 748–756.

Brown, A.S., Begg, M.D., Gravenstein, S., Schaefer, C.A., Wyatt, R.J., Breshnahan, M.,...Susser, E.S. (2004). Serologic evidence of prenatal influenza in the etiology of schizophrenia. *Archives of General Psychiatry*, 61, 774–780.

Brown, G.W., Ban, M., Craig, T.J. K., Harris, T.O., Herbert, J., & Uher, R. (2013). Serotonin transporter length polymorphism, childhood maltreatment, and chronic depression: A specific gene-environment interaction. *Depression and Anxiety*, 30, 5–13.

Brown, G.W., & Harris, T.O. (1989). Depression. In G. W. Brown and T. O. Harris (Eds.), *Life events and illness* (pp. 49–93). Guilford Press.

Buchanan-Barker, P., Barker, P. (2009, February). The convenient myth of Thomas Szasz. *Journal of Psychiatric and Mental Health Nursing*, 16(1): 87–95. https://doi.org/10.1111/j.1365-2850.2008.01310.x

Buchsbaum, M.S., Nuechterlein, K.H., Haier, R.J., Wu, J., Sicotte, N., Hazlett, E.,...Guich, S. (1990). Glucose metabolic rate in normal and schizophrenics during the continuous performance test assessed by positron emission tomography. *British Journal of Psychiatry*, 156, 216–227.

Burt, S.A. (2009). Rethinking environmental contributions to child and adolescent psychopathology: A meta-analysis of shared environmental influences. *Psychological Bulletin*, 135, 608–637.

Butler, L.D., & Nolen-Hoeksema, S. (1994). Gender differences in responses to depressed mood in a college sample. *Sex Roles*, 30, 331–346.

Byrd, R. (2002, October 17). Report to the legislature on the principal findings from the epidemiology of autism in California: A comprehensive pilot study. http://www.dds.ca.gov/Autism/MindReport.cfm

Cadoret, R., Yates, W., Ed., T., Woodworth, G., & Stewart, M. (1995). Genetic environmental interactions in the genesis of aggressivity and conduct disorders. *Archives of General Psychiatry*, 52, 916–924.

Cannon, M., Jones, P.B., & Murray, R.M. (2002). Obstetric complications and schizophrenia: Historical and meta-analytic review. *American Journal of Psychiatry*, 159, 1080–1092.

Cardeña, E., & Gleaves, D.H. (2006). Dissociative disorders. In M. Hersen, S.M. Turner, & D. C. Beidel (Eds.), *Adult psychopathology and diagnosis* (pp. 473–503). John Wiley & Sons.

Casadio, P., Fernandes, C., Murray, R.M., & Di Forti, M. (2011). Cannabis use in young people: The risk for schizophrenia. *Neuroscience and Biobehavioral Reviews*, 35, 1779–1787.

Caspi, A., Sugden, K., Moffitt, T.E., Taylor, A., Craig, I.W., Harrington, H., Poulton, R. (2003). Influence of life stress on depression: Moderation by a polymorphism in the 5-HTT gene. *Science*, 301(5631), 386–389.

Centers for Disease Control and Prevention. (2010, November 12). Increasing prevalence of parent-reported attention-deficit/hyperactivity disorder among children, United States, 2003–2007. *Morbidity and Mortality Weekly Report*, 59(44), 1439–1443.

Centers for Disease Control and Prevention. (2012). Suicide: Facts at a glance. http://www.cdc.gov/ViolencePrevention/pdf/Suicide_DataSheet-a.pdf

Centers for Disease Control and Prevention. (2012, March 30). Prevalence of autism spectrum disorders—autism and developmental disabilities monitoring network, 14 sites, United States, 2008. *Morbidity and Mortality Weekly Report: Surveillance Summaries*, 61(3), 1–19. http://www.cdc.gov/mmwr/pdf/ss/ss6103.pdf

Centers for Disease Control and Prevention. (2013a). *Definitions: Self-directed violence*. http://www.cdc.gov/violenceprevention/suicide/definitions.html.

Centers for Disease Control and Prevention. (2013b). *National suicide statistics at a glance: Trends in suicide rates among both sexes, by age group, United States, 1991–2009*. http://www.cdc.gov/violenceprevention/suicide/statistics/trends02.html

Centers for Disease Control and Prevention. (2018, April 27). Prevalence of Autism Spectrum Disorder Among Children Aged 8 Years—Autism and Developmental Disabilities Monitoring Network, 11 Sites, United States, 2014. Morbidity and Mortality Weekly Reports. https://www.cdc.gov/mmwr/volumes/67/ss/pdfs/ss6706a1-H.pdf

Charney, D.S., Woods, S.W., Nagy, L.M., Southwick, S.M., Krystal, J.H., & Heninger, G.R. (1990). Noradrenergic function in panic disorder [Supplemental material]. *Journal of Clinical Psychiatry*, 51, 5–11.

Clark, D.M. (1996). Panic disorder: From theory to therapy. In R. M. Rapee (Ed.), *Current controversies in the anxiety disorders* (pp. 318–344). Guilford Press.

Clauss, J.A., & Blackford, J.U. (2012). Behavioral inhibition and risk for developing social anxiety disorder: A meta-analytic study. *Journal of the American Academy of Child and Adolescent Psychiatry*, 51(10), 1066–1075.

Clegg, J.W. (2012). Teaching about mental health and illness through the history of the DSM. *History of Psychology*, 15, 364–370.

Compton, W.M., Conway, K.P., Stinson, F.S., Colliver, J.D., & Grant, B.F. (2005). Prevalence, correlates, and comorbidity of DSM-IV antisocial personality syndromes and alcohol and specific drug use disorders in the United States: Results from the national epidemiologic survey on alcohol and related conditions. *Journal of Clinical Psychiatry*, 66, 677–685.

Cook, M., & Mineka, S. (1989). Observational conditioning of fear to fear-relevant versus fear-irrelevant stimuli in rhesus monkeys. *Journal of Abnormal Psychology*, 98, 448–459.

Craske, M.G. (1999). *Anxiety disorders: Psychological approaches to theory and treatment*. Westview Press.

Crosby, A.E., Ortega, L., & Melanson, C. (2011). *Self-directed violence surveillance: Uniform definitions and recommended data elements, version 1.0*. http://www.cdc.gov/violenceprevention/pdf/self-directed-violence-a.pdf

Dalenberg, C.J., Brand, B.L., Gleaves, D.H., Dorahy, M.J., Loewenstein, R.J., Cardeña, E.,…Spiegel, D. (2012). Evaluation of the evidence for the trauma and fantasy models of dissociation. *Psychological Bulletin*, 138, 550–588.

Davidson, R.J., Pizzagalli, D.A., & Nitschke, J.B. (2009). Representation and regulation of emotional depression: Perspectives from cognitive neuroscience. In I. H. Gotlib & C. L. Hammen (Eds.), *Handbook of depression* (pp. 218–248). Guilford Press.

Davis, K.L., Kahn, R.S., Ko., G., & Davidson, M. (1991). Dopamine in schizophrenia: A review and reconceptualization. *American Journal of Psychiatry*, 148, 1474–1486.

Decety, J., Skelly, L.R., & Kiehl, K.A. (2013). Brain response to empathy-eliciting scenarios involving pain in incarcerated individuals with psychopathy. *JAMA Psychiatry*, 70, 638–645.

Demos, J. (1983). *Entertaining Satan: Witchcraft and the culture of early New England*. Oxford University Press.

Dempsey, A.F., Schaffer, S., Singer, D., Butchart, A., Davis, M., & Freed, G.L. (2011). Alternative vaccination schedule preferences among parents of young children. *Pediatrics*, 128, 848–856.

DeStefano, F., Price, C.S., & Weintraub, E.S. (2013). Increasing exposures to antibody-stimulating proteins and polysaccharides in vaccines is not associated with risk of autism. *The Journal of Pediatrics*, 163, 561–567.

DiGrande, L., Perrin, M.A., Thorpe, L.E., Thalji, L., Murphy, J., Wu, D.,…Brackbill, R.M. (2008). Posttraumatic stress symptoms, PTSD, and risk factors among lower Manhattan residents 2–3 years after the September 11, 2001 terrorist attacks. *Journal of Traumatic Stress*, 21, 264–273.

DNA project aims to count Scots redheads. (2012, November 7). *British Broadcast Corporation [BBC]*. http://www.bbc.com/news/uk-scotland-20237511

Downs, M. (2008, March 31). Autism-vaccine link: Evidence doesn't dispel doubts [Web log post]. www.webmd.com/brain/autism/searching-for-answers/vaccines-autism

Dozois, D.J. A., & Beck, A.T. (2008). Cognitive schemas, beliefs and assumptions. In K. S. Dobson & D. J. A. Dozois (Eds.), *Risk factors in depression* (pp. 121–143). Academic Press.

Drevets, W.C., Bogers, W.U., & Raichle, M.E. (2002). Functional anatomical correlates of antidepressant drug treatment assessed using PET measures of regional glucose metabolism. *European Neuropsychopharmacology*, 12, 527–544.

Ehlers, A., & Clark, D.M. (2000). A cognitive model of posttraumatic stress disorder. *Behaviour Research and Therapy*, 38, 319–345.

Etzersdorfer, E., Voracek, M., & Sonneck, G. (2004). A dose-response relationship between imitational suicides and newspaper distribution. *Archives of Suicide Research*, 8, 137–145.

Fabrega, H. (2007). How psychiatric conditions were made. *Psychiatry*, 70, 130–153.

Fields, T. (2010). Postpartum depression effects on early interactions, parenting, and safety practices: A review. *Infant Behavior and Development*, 33, 1–6.

Fisher, C. (2010, February 11). DSM-5 development process included emphasis on gender and cultural sensitivity [Web log post]. http://www.bmedreport.com/archives/9359

Fitzgerald, P.B., Laird, A.R., Maller, J., & Daskalakis, Z.J. (2008). A meta-analytic study of changes in brain activation in depression. *Human Brain Mapping*, 29, 683–695.

Fleischman, A., Bertolote, J.M., Belfer, M., & Beautrais, A. (2005). Completed suicide and psychiatric diagnoses in young people: A critical examination of the evidence. *American Journal of Orthopsychiatry*, 75, 676–683.

Foote, B., Smolin, Y., Kaplan, M., Legatt, M.E., & Lipschitz, D. (2006). Prevalence of dissociative disorders in psychiatric outpatients. *American Journal of Psychiatry*, 163, 623–629.

Fox, N.A., Henderson, H.A., Marshall, P.J., Nichols, K.E., & Ghera, M.M. (2005). Behavioral inhibition: Linking biology and behavior within a developmental framework. *Annual Review of Psychology*, 56, 235–262.

Frances, A. (2012, December 2). DSM 5 is guide not bible—ignore its ten worst changes [Web log post]. http://www.psychologytoday.com/blog/dsm5-in-distress/201212/dsm-5-is-guide-not-bible-ignore-its-ten-worst-changes

Freeman, A., Stone, M., Martin, D., & Reinecke, M. (2005). A review of borderline personality disorder. In A. Freeman, M. Stone, D. Martin, & M. Reinecke (Eds.), *Comparative treatments for borderline personality disorder* (pp. 1–20). Springer.

Fung, M.T., Raine, A., Loeber, R., Lynam, D.R., Steinhauer, S.R., Venables, P.H., & Stouthamer-Loeber, M. (2005). Reduced electrodermal activity in psychopathy-prone adolescents. *Journal of Abnormal Psychology*, 114, 187–196.

Fusar-Poli, P., Borgwardt, S., Bechdolf, A., Addington, J., Riecher-Rössler, A., Schultze-Lutter, F.,…Yung, A. (2013). The psychosis high-risk state: A comprehensive state-of-the-art review. *Archives of General Psychiatry*, 70, 107–120.

Gauthier, J., Siddiqui, T.J., Huashan, P., Yokomaku, D., Hamdan, F.F., Champagne, N.,…Rouleau, G.A. (2011). Truncating mutations in NRXN2 and NRXN1 in autism spectrum disorders and schizophrenia. *Human Genetics*, 130, 563–573.

Gizer, I.R., Ficks, C., & Waldman, I.D. (2009). Candidate gene studies of ADHD: A meta-analytic review. *Human Genetics*, 126, 51–90.

Goldstein, A.J., & Chambless, D.L. (1978). A reanalysis of agoraphobia. *Behavior Therapy*, 9, 47–59.

Goldstein, J.M., Buka, S.L., Seidman, L.J., & Tsuang, M.T. (2010). Specificity of familial transmission of schizophrenia psychosis spectrum and affective psychoses in the New England family study's high-risk design. *Archives of General Psychiatry*, 67, 458–467.

Good, B.J., & Hinton, D.E. (2009). Panic disorder in cross-cultural and historical perspective. In D. E. Hinton & B. J. Good (Eds.), *Culture and panic disorder* (pp. 1–28). Stanford University Press.

Goodman, S.H., & Brand, S.R. (2009). Depression and early adverse experiences. In I. H. Gotlib & C. L. Hammen (Eds.), *Handbook of depression* (pp. 249–274). Guilford Press.

Gotlib, I.H., & Joormann, J. (2010). Cognition and depression: Current status and future directions. *Annual Review of Clinical Psychology*, 6, 285–312.

Gottesman, I.I. (2001). Psychopathology through a life span-genetic prism. *American Psychologist*, 56, 867–878.

Graybiel, A.N., & Rauch, S.L. (2000). Toward a neurobiology of obsessive-compulsive disorder. *Neuron*, 28, 343–347.

Green, M.F. (2001). *Schizophrenia revealed: From neurons to social interactions*. W. W. Norton.

Hackmann, A., Clark, D.M., & McManus, F. (2000). Recurrent images and early memories in social phobia. *Behaviour Research and Therapy*, 38, 601–610.

Halligan, S.L., Herbert, J., Goodyer, I., & Murray, L. (2007). Disturbances in morning cortisol secretion in association with maternal postnatal depression predict subsequent depressive symptomatology in adolescents. *Biological Psychiatry*, 62, 40–46.

Hare, R.D. (1965). Temporal gradient of fear arousal in psychopaths. *Journal of Abnormal Psychology*, 70, 442–445.

Hasin, D.S., Fenton, M.C., & Weissman, M.M. (2011). Epidemiology of depressive disorders. In M. T. Tsuang, M. Tohen, & P. Jones (Eds.), *Textbook of psychiatric epidemiology* (pp. 289–309). John Wiley & Sons.

Herman, J. (1997). *Trauma and recovery: The aftermath of violence—from domestic abuse to political terror*. Basic Books.

Herrenkohl, T.I., Maguin, E., Hill, K.G., Hawkins, J.D., Abbott, R.D., & Catalano, R. (2000). Developmental risk factors for youth violence. *Journal of Adolescent Health*, 26, 176–186.

Heston, L.L. (1966). Psychiatric disorders in foster home reared children of schizophrenic mothers. *British Journal of Psychiatry*, 112, 819–825.

Hettema, J.M., Neale, M.C., & Kendler, K.S. (2001). A review and meta-analysis of the genetic epidemiology of anxiety disorders. *The American Journal of Psychiatry*, 158, 1568–1578.

Holsboer, F., & Ising, M. (2010). Stress hormone regulation: Biological role and translation into therapy. *Annual Review of Psychology*, 61, 81–109.

Howes, O.D., & Kapur, S. (2009). The dopamine hypothesis of schizophrenia: Version III—The final common pathway. *Schizophrenia Bulletin*, 35, 549–562.

Hoza, B., Mrug, S., Gerdes, A.C., Hinshaw, S.P., Bukowski, W.M., Gold, J.A.,…Arnold, L.E. (2005). What aspects of peer relationships are impaired in children with ADHD? *Journal of Consulting and Clinical Psychology*, 73, 411–423.

Hughes, V. (2007). Mercury rising. *Nature Medicine*, 13, 896–897.

Jellinek, M.S., & Herzog, D.B. (1999). The child. In A. M. Nicholi, Jr. (Ed.), *The Harvard guide to psychiatry* (pp. 585–610). The Belknap Press of Harvard University.

Johnson, J.G., Cohen, P., Kasen, S., & Brook, J.S. (2006). Dissociative disorders among adults in the community, impaired functioning, and axis I and II comorbidity. *Journal of Psychiatric Research*, 40, 131–140.

Joormann, J. (2009). Cognitive aspects of depression. In I. H. Gotlib & C. L. Hammen (Eds.), *Handbook of depression* (pp. 298–321). Guilford Press.

Joyce, P.R., McKenzie, J.M., Luty, S.E., Mulder, R.T., Carter, J.D., Sullivan, P.F., & Cloninger, C.R. (2003). Temperament, childhood environment, and psychopathology as risk factors for avoidant and borderline personality disorders. *Australian and New Zealand Journal of Psychiatry*, 37, 756–764.

Judd, L.L. (2012). Dimensional paradigm of the long-term course of unipolar major depressive disorder. *Depression and Anxiety*, 29, 167–171.

Kagan, J., Reznick, J.S., & Snidman, N. (1988). Biological bases of childhood shyness. *Science*, 240, 167–171.

Katzelnick, D.J., Kobak, K.A., DeLeire, T., Henk, H.J., Greist, J.H., Davidson, J.R. T.,…Helstad, C.P. (2001). Impact of generalized social anxiety disorder in managed care. *The American Journal of Psychiatry*, 158, 1999–2007.

Kendler, K.S., Hettema, J.M., Butera, F., Gardner, C.O., & Prescott, C.A. (2003). Life event dimensions of loss, humiliation, entrapment, and danger in the prediction of onsets of major depression and generalized anxiety. *Archives of General Psychiatry*, 60, 789–796.

Kennedy, A., LaVail, K., Nowak, G., Basket, M., & Landry, S. (2011). Confidence about vaccines in the United States: Understanding parents' perceptions. *Health Affairs*, 30, 1151–1159.

Kessler, R.C. (1997). The effects of stressful life events on depression. *Annual Review of Psychology*, 48, 191–214.

Kessler, R.C. (2003). Epidemiology of women and depression. *Journal of Affective Disorders*, 74, 5–13.

Kessler, R.C., Berglund, P., Demler, O., Jin, R., Merikangas, K.P., & Walters, E.F. (2005). Lifetime prevalence and age-of-onset distributions of DSM-IV disorders in the National Comorbidity Survey Replication. *Archives of General Psychiatry*, 62, 593–602.

Kessler, R.C., Chiu, W.T., Jin, R., Ruscio, A.M., Shear, K., & Walters, E. (2006). The epidemiology of panic attacks, panic disorder, and agoraphobia in the National Comorbidity Survey Replication. *Archives of General Psychiatry*, 63, 415–424.

Kessler, R.C., Galea, S., Gruber, M.J., Sampson, N.A., Ursano, R.J., & Wessely, S. (2008). Trends in mental illness and suicidality after Hurricane Katrina. *Molecular Psychiatry*, 13, 374–384.

Kessler, R.C., Ruscio, A.M., Shear, K., & Wittchen, H.U. (2009). Epidemiology of anxiety disorders. In M. B. Stein & T. Steckler (Eds.), *Behavioral neurobiology of anxiety and its treatment* (pp. 21–35). Springer.

Kessler, R.C. Sonnega, A., Bromet, E., Hughes, M., & Nelson, C.B. (1995). Posttraumatic stress disorder in the National Comorbidity Survey. *Archives of General Psychiatry*, 52, 1048–1060.

Kessler, R.C., & Wang, P.S. (2009). Epidemiology of depression. In I. H. Gotlib & C. L. Hammen (Eds.), *Handbook of depression* (pp. 5–22). Guilford Press.

Khashan, A.S., Abel, K.M., McNamee, R., Pedersen, M.G., Webb, R., Baker, P.,… Mortensen, P.B. (2008). Higher risk of offspring schizophrenia following antenatal maternal exposure to severe adverse life events. *Archives of General Psychiatry*, 65, 146–152.

Kinney, D.K., Barch, D.H., Chayka, B., Napoleon, S., & Munir, K.M. (2009). Environmental risk factors for autism: Do they help or cause de novo genetic mutations that contribute to the disorder? *Medical Hypotheses*, 74, 102–106.

Kleim, B., Gonzalo, D., & Ehlers, A. (2011). The Depressive Attributions Questionnaire (DAQ): Development of a short self-report measure of depressogenic attributions. *Journal of Psychopathology and Behavioral Assessment*, 33, 375–385.

Klein, R.G., Mannuzza, S., Olazagasti, M.A. R., Roizen, E., Hutchison, J.A., Lashua, E.C., & Castellanos, F.X. (2012). Clinical and functional outcome of childhood attention-deficit/hyperactivity disorder 33 years later. *Archives of General Psychiatry*, 69, 1295–1303.

Koenen, K.C., Stellman, J.M., Stellman, S.D., & Sommer, J.F. (2003). Risk factors for course of posttraumatic stress disorder among Vietnam veterans: A 14-year follow-up of American Legionnaires. *Journal of Consulting and Clinical Psychology*, 71, 980–986.

Kopell, B.H., & Greenberg, B.D. (2008). Anatomy and physiology of the basal ganglia: Implications for DBS in psychiatry. *Neuroscience and Biobehavioral Reviews*, 32, 408–422.

Large, M., Sharma, S., Compton, M.T., Slade, T., & Nielssen, O. (2011). Cannabis use and earlier onset of psychosis: A systematic meta-analysis. *Archives of General Psychiatry*, 68, 555–561.

Lasalvia, A., Zoppei, S., Van Bortel, T., Bonetto, C., Cristofalo, D., Wahlbeck, K., Thornicroft, G. (2013). Global pattern of experienced and anticipated discrimination reported by people with major depressive disorder: A cross-sectional survey. *The Lancet*, 381, 55–62.

Lawrie, S.M., & Abukmeil, S.S. (1998). Brain abnormality in schizophrenia: A systematic and quantitative review of volumetric magnetic resonance imaging studies. *British Journal of Psychiatry*, 172, 110–120.

LeMoult, J., Castonguay, L.G., Joormann, J., & McAleavey, A. (2013). Depression. In L. G. Castonguay & T. F. Oltmanns (Eds.), *Psychopathology: From science to clinical practice* (pp. 17–61). Guilford Press.

Lezenweger, M.F., Lane, M.C., Loranger, A.W., & Kessler, R.C. (2007). DSM-IV personality disorders in the National Comorbidity Survey Replication. *Biological Psychiatry*, 62, 553–564.

Lilienfeld, S.O., & Marino, L. (1999). Essentialism revisited: Evolutionary theory and the concept of mental disorder. *Journal of Abnormal Psychology*, 108, 400–411.

Linnet, K.M., Dalsgaard, S., Obel, C., Wisborg, K., Henriksen, T.B., Rodriquez, A.,… Jarvelin, M.R. (2003). Maternal lifestyle factors in pregnancy risk of attention deficit hyperactivity disorder and associated behaviors: A review of current evidence. *The American Journal of Psychiatry*, 160, 1028–1040.

Livesley, J. (2008). Toward a genetically-informed model of borderline personality disorder. *Journal of Personality Disorders*, 22, 42–71.

Livesley, J., & Jang, K.L. (2008). The behavioral genetics of personality disorders. *Annual Review of Clinical Psychology*, 4, 247–274.

Loe, I.M., & Feldman, H.M. (2007). Academic and educational outcomes of children with ADHD. *Journal of Pediatric Psychology*, 32, 643–654.

Luxton, D.D., June, J.D., & Fairall, J.M. (2012, May). Social media and suicide: A public health perspective [Supplement 2]. *American Journal of Public Health*, 102(S2), S195–S200. https://doi.org/10.2105/AJPH.2011.300608

Mackin, P., & Young, A.H. (2004, May 1). The role of cortisol and depression: Exploring new opportunities for treatments. *Psychiatric Times*. http://www.psychiatrictimes.com/articles/role-cortisol-and-depression-exploring-new-opportunities-treatments

Maher, W.B., & Maher, B.A. (1985). Psychopathology: I. from ancient times to the eighteenth century. In G. A. Kimble & K. Schlesinger (Eds.), *Topics in the history of psychology: Volume 2* (pp. 251–294). Erlbaum.

Mann, J.J., (2003). Neurobiology of suicidal behavior. *Nature Reviews Neuroscience*, 4, 819–828.

Marker, C.D. (2013, March 3). Safety behaviors in social anxiety: Playing it safe in social anxiety [Web log post]. http://www.psychologytoday.com/blog/face-your-fear/201303/safety-behaviors-in-social-anxiety

Marshal, M.P., & Molina, B.S.G. (2006). Antisocial behaviors moderate the deviant peer pathway to substance use in children with ADHD. *Journal of Clinical Child and Adolescent Psychology*, 35, 216–226.

Martens, E.J., de Jonge, P., Na, B., Cohen, B.E., Lett, H., & Whooley, M.A. (2010). Scared to death? Generalized anxiety disorder and cardiovascular events in patients with stable coronary heart disease. *Archives of General Psychiatry*, 67, 750–758.

Mataix-Cols, D., Frost, R.O., Pertusa, A., Clark, L.A., Saxena, S., Leckman, J.F.,…Wilhelm, S. (2010). Hoarding disorder: A new diagnosis for DSM-V? *Depression and Anxiety*, 27, 556–572.

Mayes, R., & Horowitz, A.V. (2005). DSM-III and the revolution in the classification of mental illness. *Journal of the History of the Behavioral Sciences*, 41, 249–267.

Mazure, C.M. (1998). Life stressors as risk factors in depression. *Clinical Psychology: Science and Practice*, 5, 291–313.

McCabe, K. (2010, January 24). Teen's suicide prompts a look at bullying. *Boston Globe*. http://www.boston.com

McCabe, R.E., Antony, M.M., Summerfeldt, L.J., Liss, A., & Swinson, R.P. (2003). Preliminary examination of the relationship between anxiety disorders in adults and self-reported history of teasing or bullying experiences. *Cognitive Behaviour Therapy*, 32, 187–193.

McCann, D., Barrett, A., Cooper, A., Crumpler, D., Dalen, L., Grimshaw, K.,…Stevenson, J. (2007). Food additives and hyperactive behaviour in 3-year-old and 8/9-year-old children in the community: A randomised, double-blinded, placebo-controlled trial. *The Lancet*, 370(9598), 1560–1567.

McEwen, B.S. (2005). Glucocorticoids, depression, and mood disorders: Structural remodeling in the brain. *Metabolism: Clinical and Experimental*, 54, 20–23.

McNally, R.J. (2003). *Remembering trauma*. Harvard University Press.

Meek, S.E., Lemery-Chalfant, K., Jahromi, L.D., & Valiente, C. (2013). A review of gene-environment correlations and their implications for autism: A conceptual model. *Psychological Review*, 120, 497–521.

Merikangas, K.R., & Tohen, M. (2011). Epidemiology of bipolar disorder in adults and children. In M. T. Tsuang, M. Tohen, & P. Jones (Eds.), *Textbook of psychiatric epidemiology* (pp. 329–342). John Wiley & Sons.

Merikangas, K.R., Jin, R., He, J.P., Kessler, R.C., Lee, S., Sampson, N.A., Zarkov, Z. (2011). Prevalence and correlates of bipolar spectrum disorder in the World Mental Health Survey Initiative. *Archives of General Psychiatry*, 68, 241–251.

Mezzich, J.E. (2002). International surveys on the use of ICD-10 and related diagnostic systems. *Psychopathology*, 35, 72–75.

Michaud, K., Matheson, K., Kelly, O., & Anisman, H. (2008). Impact of stressors in a natural context on release of cortisol in healthy adult humans: A meta-analysis. *Stress*, 11, 177–197.

Mineka, S., & Cook, M. (1993). Mechanisms involved in the observational conditioning of fear. *Journal of Experimental Psychology: General*, 122, 23–38.

Moffitt, T.E., Caspi, A., Harrington, H., Milne, B.J., Melchior, M., Goldberg, D., & Poulton, R. (2007). Generalized anxiety disorder and depression: Childhood risk factors in a birth cohort followed to age 32. *Psychological Medicine*, 37, 441–452.

Moitra, E., Beard, C., Weisberg, R.B., & Keller, M.B. (2011). Occupational impairment and social anxiety disorder in a sample of primary care patients. *Journal of Affective Disorders*, 130, 209–212.

Molina, B.S.G., & Pelham, W.E. (2003). Childhood predictors of adolescent substance abuse in a longitudinal study of children with ADHD. *Journal of Abnormal Psychology*, 112, 497–507.

Moore, T.H., Zammit, S., Lingford-Hughes, A., Barnes, T.R., Jones, P.B., Burke, M., & Lewis, G. (2007). Cannabis use and risk of psychotic or affective mental health outcomes. *Lancet*, 370, 319–328.

Morris, E.P., Stewart, S.H., & Ham, L.S. (2005). The relationship between social anxiety disorder and alcohol use disorders: A critical review. *Clinical Psychology Review*, 25, 734–760.

Mowrer, O.H. (1960). *Learning theory and behavior*. John Wiley & Sons.

Nader, K. (2001). Treatment methods for childhood trauma. In J. P. Wilson, M.J. Friedman, & J. D. Lindy (Eds.), *Treating psychological trauma and PTSD* (pp. 278–334). Guilford Press.

Nanni, V., Uher, R., & Danese, A. (2012). Childhood maltreatment predicts unfavorable course of illness and treatment outcome in depression: A meta-analysis. *American Journal of Psychiatry*, 169, 141–151.

Nathan, D. (2011). *Sybil exposed: The extraordinary story behind the famous multiple personality case*. Free Press.

National Comorbidity Survey. (2007). *NCS-R lifetime prevalence estimates* [Data file]. http://www.hcp.med.harvard.edu/ncs/index.php

National Institute on Drug Abuse (NIDA). (2007, October). *Comorbid drug use and mental illness: A research update from the National Institute on Drug Abuse*. http://www.drugabuse.gov/sites/default/files/comorbid.pdf

Nestadt, G., Samuels, J., Riddle, M., Bienvenu, J., Liang, K.Y., LaBuda, M.,…Hoehn-Saric, R. (2000). A family study of obsessive-compulsive disorder. *Archives of General Psychiatry*, 57, 358–363.

Newman, C.F. (2004). Suicidality. In S. L. Johnson & R. L. Leahy (Eds.), *Psychological treatment of bipolar disorder* (pp. 265–285). Guilford Press.

Nikolas, M.A., & Burt, S.A. (2010). Genetic and environmental influences on ADHD symptom dimensions of inattention and hyperactivity: A meta-analysis. *Journal of Abnormal Psychology*, 119, 1–17.

Nolen-Hoeksema, S. (1987). Sex differences in unipolar depression: Evidence and theory. *Psychological Bulletin*, 101, 259–282.

Nolen-Hoeksema, S. (1991). Responses to depression and their effects on the duration of depressive episodes. *Journal of Abnormal Psychology*, 100, 569–582.

Nolen-Hoeksema, S. & Hilt, L.M. (2009). Gender differences in depression. In I. H. Gotlib & C. L. Hammen (Eds.), *Handbook of depression* (pp. 386–404). Guilford Press.

Nolen-Hoeksema, S., Larson, J., & Grayson, C. (1999). Explaining the gender difference in depressive symptoms. *Journal of Personality and Social Psychology*, 77, 1061–1072.

Norberg, M.M., Calamari, J.E., Cohen, R.J., & Riemann, B.C. (2008). Quality of life in obsessive-compulsive disorder: An evaluation of impairment and a preliminary analysis of the ameliorating effects of treatment. *Depression and Anxiety*, 25, 248–259.

Novella, S. (2008, April 16). The increase in autism diagnoses: Two hypotheses [Web log post]. http://www.sciencebasedmedicine.org/the-increase-in-autism-diagnoses-two-hypotheses/

Novick, D.M., Swartz, H.A., & Frank, E. (2010). Suicide attempts in bipolar I and bipolar II disorder: A review and meta-analysis of the evidence. *Bipolar Disorders*, 12, 1–9.

Noyes, R. (2001). Comorbidity in generalized anxiety disorder. *Psychiatric Clinics of North America*, 24, 41–55.

O'Connor, R.C., Smyth, R., Ferguson, E., Ryan, C., & Williams, J.M.G. (2013). Psychological processes and repeat suicidal behavior: A four-year prospective study. *Journal of Consulting and Clinical Psychology*. Advance online publication. https://doi.org/10.1037/a0033751

Öhman, A., & Mineka, S. (2001). Fears, phobias, and preparedness: Toward an evolved module of fear and fear learning. *Psychological Review*, 108, 483–552.

Oliver, J. (2006, Summer). The myth of Thomas Szasz. *The New Atlantis*, 13. http://www.thenewatlantis.com/docLib/TNA13-Oliver.pdf

Olsson, A., & Phelps, E.A. (2007). Social learning of fear. *Nature Neuroscience*, 10, 1095–1102.

Oltmanns, T.F., & Castonguay, L.G. (2013). General issues in understanding and treating psychopathology. In L. G. Castonguay & T. F. Oltmanns (Eds.), *Psychopathology: From science to clinical practice* (pp. 1–16). Guilford Press.

Orr, S.P., Metzger, L.J., Lasko, N.B., Macklin, M.L., Peri, T., & Pitman, R.K. (2000). De novo conditioning in trauma-exposed individuals with and without posttraumatic stress disorder. *Journal of Abnormal Psychology*, 109, 290–298.

Owens, D., Horrocks, J., & House, A. (2002). Fatal and non-fatal repetition of self-harm: Systematic review. *British Journal of Psychiatry*, 181, 193–199.

Ozer, E.J., Best, S.R., Lipsey, T.L., & Weiss, D.S. (2003). Predictors of posttraumatic stress disorder and symptoms in adults: A meta-analysis. *Psychological Bulletin*, 129, 52–73.

Parker-Pope, T. (2013, May 2). Suicide rates rise sharply in U.S. *The New York Times*. http://www.nytimes.com.

Patrick, C.J., Fowles, D.C., & Krueger, R.F. (2009). Triarchic conceptualization of psychopathy: Developmental origins of disinhibition, boldness, and meanness. *Development and Psychopathology*, 21, 913–938.

Patterson, M.L., Iizuka, Y., Tubbs, M.E., Ansel, J., Tsutsumi, M., & Anson, J. (2007). Passing encounters east and west: Comparing Japanese and American pedestrian interactions. *Journal of Nonverbal Behavior*, 31, 155–166.

Pauls, D.L. (2010). The genetics of obsessive-compulsive disorder: A review. *Dialogues in Clinical Neuroscience*, 12, 149–163.

Paykel, E.S. (2003). Life events and affective disorders [Supplemental material]. *Acta Psychiatrica Scandinavica*, 108(S418), 61–66.

Pazain, M. (2010, December 2). To look or not to look? Eye contact differences in different cultures [Web log post]. http://www.examiner.com/article/to-look-or-not-to-look-eye-contact-differences-different-cultures

Phan, K.L., Fitzgerald, D.A., Nathan, P.J., Moore, G.J., Uhde, T.W., & Tancer, M.E. (2005). Neural substrates for voluntary suppression of negative affect: A functional magnetic resonance imaging study. *Biological Psychiatry*, 57, 210–219.

Phillips, D.P. (1974). The influence of suggestion on suicide: Substantive and theoretical implications of the Werther Effect. *American Sociological Review*, 39, 340–354.

Phillips, K. (2005). *The broken mirror: Understanding and treating body dysmorphic disorder*. Oxford University Press.

Piper, A., & Merskey, H. (2004). The persistence of folly: A critical examination of dissociative identity disorder: Part I: The excesses of an improbable concept. *Canadian Journal of Psychiatry*, 49, 592–600.

Pittman, R.K. (1988). Post-traumatic stress disorder, conditioning, and network theory. *Psychiatric Annals*, 18, 182–189.

Pompili, M., Serafini, G., Innamorati, M., Möller-Leimkühler, A.M., Gupponi, G., Girardi, P., Tatarelli, R., & Lester, D. (2010). The hypothalamic-pituitary-adrenal axis and serotonin abnormalities: A selective overview of the implications of suicide prevention. *European Archives of Psychiatry and Clinical Neuroscience*, 260, 583–600.

Pope, H.G., Jr., Barry, S.B., Bodkin, A., & Hudson, J.I. (2006). Tracking scientific interest in the dissociative disorders: A study of scientific publication output 1984–2003. *Psychotherapy and Psychosomatics*, 75, 19–24.

Pope, H.G., Jr., Hudson, J.I., Bodkin, J.A., & Oliva, P.S. (1998). Questionable validity of 'dissociative amnesia' in trauma victims: Evidence from prospective studies. *British Journal of Psychiatry*, 172, 210–215.

Pope, H.G., Jr., Poliakoff, M.B., Parker, M.P., Boynes, M., & Hudson, J.I. (2006). Is dissociative amnesia a culture-bound syndrome? Findings from a survey of historical literature. *Psychological Medicine*, 37, 225–233.

Postolache, T.T., Mortensen, P.B., Tonelli, L.H., Jiao, X., Frangakis, C., Soriano, J.J., & Qin, P. (2010). Seasonal spring peaks of suicide in victims with and without prior history of hospitalization for mood disorders. *Journal of Affective Disorders*, 121, 88–93.

Putnam, F.W., Guroff, J.J., Silberman, E.K., Barban, L., & Post, R.M. (1986). The clinical phenomenology of multiple personality disorder: A review of 100 recent cases. *Journal of Clinical Psychiatry*, 47, 285–293.

Rachman, S. (1977). The conditioning theory of fear acquisition: A critical examination. *Behaviour Theory and Research*, 15, 375–387.

Regier, D.A., Kuhl, E.A., & Kupfer, D.A. (2012). DSM-5: Classification and criteria changes. *World Psychiatry*, 12, 92–98.

Rhee, S.H., & Waldman, I.D. (2002). Genetic and environmental influences on antisocial behavior: A meta-analysis of twin and adoption studies. *Psychological Bulletin*, 128, 490–529.

Robinson, M.S., & Alloy, L.B. (2003). Negative cognitive styles and stress-reactive rumination interact to predict depression: A prospective study. *Cognitive Therapy and Research*, 27, 275–292.

Roche, T. (2002, March 18). Andrea Yates: More to the story. *Time*. http://content.time.com/time/nation/article/0,8599,218445,00.html.

Root, B.A. (2000). *Understanding panic and other anxiety disorders*. University Press of Mississippi.

Ross, C.A., Miller, S.D., Reagor, P., Bjornson, L., Fraser, G.A., & Anderson, G. (1990). Structured interview data on 102 cases of multiple personality disorder from four centers. The *American Journal of Psychiatry*, 147, 596–601.

Rotge, J.Y., Guehl, D., Dilharreguy, B., Cuny, E., Tignol, J., Biolac, B.,…Aouizerate, B. (2008). Provocation of obsessive-compulsive symptoms: A quantitative voxel-based meta-analysis of functional neuroimaging studies. *Journal of Psychiatry and Neuroscience*, 33, 405–412.

Rothschild, A.J. (1999). Mood disorders. In A. M. Nicholi, Jr. (Ed.), *The Harvard guide to psychiatry* (pp. 281–307). The Belknap Press of Harvard University.

Ruder, T.D., Hatch, G.M., Ampanozi, G., Thali, M.J., & Fischer, N. (2011). Suicide announcement on Facebook. *Crisis*, 35, 280–282.

Ruscio, A.M., Stein, D.J., Chiu, W.T., & Kessler, R.C. (2010). The epidemiology of obsessive-compulsive disorder in the National Comorbidity Survey Replication. *Molecular Psychiatry*, 15, 53–63.

Rushworth, M.F., Noonan, M.P., Boorman, E.D., Walton, M.E., & Behrens, T.E. (2011). Frontal cortex and reward-guided learning and decision-making. *Neuron*, 70, 1054–1069.

Saxena, S., Bota, R.G., & Brody, A.L. (2001). Brain-behavior relationships in obsessive-compulsive disorder. *Seminars in Clinical Neuropsychiatry*, 6, 82–101.

Schwartz, T. (1981). *The hillside strangler: A murderer's mind*. New American Library.

Seligman, M.E. P. (1971). Phobias and preparedness. *Behavioral Therapy*, 2, 307–320.

Shih, R.A., Belmonte, P.L., & Zandi, P.P. (2004). A review of the evidence from family, twin, and adoption studies for a genetic contribution to adult psychiatric disorders. *International Review of Psychiatry*, 16, 260–283.

Siegle, G.J., Thompson, W., Carter, C.S., Steinhauer, S.R., & Thase, M.E. (2007). Increased amygdala and decreased dorsolateral prefrontal BOLD responses in unipolar depression: Related and independent features. *Biological Psychiatry*, 61, 198–209.

Silverstein, C. (2009). The implications of removing homosexuality from the DSM as a mental disorder. *Archives of Sexual Behavior*, 38, 161–163.

Simon, D., Kaufmann, C., Müsch, K., Kischkel, E., & Kathmann, N. (2010). Fronto-striato-limbic hyperactivation in obsessive-compulsive disorder during individually tailored symptom provocation. *Psychophysiology*, 47(4), 728–738. https://doi.org/10.1111/j.1469-8986.2010.00980.x

Snyder, S.H. (1976). The dopamine hypothesis of schizophrenia: Focus on the dopamine receptor. *The American Journal of Psychiatry*, 133, 197–202.

Sometimes Interesting: Weird, Forgotten, and Sometimes Interesting Things. (2011, July 2). Dancing mania [Web log post]. http://sometimes-interesting.com/2011/07/02/dancing-mania/

Stack, S. (2000). Media impacts on suicide: A quantitative review of 243 findings. *Social Science Quarterly*, 81, 957–971.

Stanley, B., Molcho, A., Stanley, M., Winchel, R., Gameroff, M.J., Parson, B., & Mann, J.J. (2000). Association of aggressive behavior with altered serotonergic function in patients who are not suicidal. *American Journal of Psychiatry*, 157, 609–614.

Stein, M.B., & Kean, Y.M. (2000). Disability and quality of life in social phobia: Epidemiological findings. *The American Journal of Psychiatry*, 157, 1606–1613.

Steinmetz, J.E., Tracy, J.A., & Green, J.T. (2001). Classical eyeblink conditioning: Clinical models and applications. *Integrative Physiological and Behavioral Science*, 36, 220–238.

Surguladze, S., Brammer, M.J., Keedwell, P., Giampietro, V., Young, A.W., Travis, M.J.,…Phillips, M.L. (2005). A differential pattern of neural response toward sad versus happy facial expressions in major depressive disorder. *Biological Psychiatry*, 57, 201–209.

Swanson, J.M., Kinsbourne, M., Nigg, J., Lanphear, B., Stephanatos, G., Volkow, N.,…Wadhwa, P.D. (2007). Etiologic subtypes of attention-deficit/hyperactivity disorder: Brain imaging, molecular genetic and environmental factors and the dopamine hypothesis. *Neuropsychology Review*, 17, 39–59.

Szasz, T.S. (1960). The myth of mental illness. *American Psychologist*, 15, 113–118.

Szasz, T.S. (1965). Legal and moral aspects of homosexuality. In J. Marmor (Ed.), *Sexual inversion: The multiple roots of homosexuality* (pp. 124–139). Basic Books.

Szasz, T.S. (2010). *The myth of mental illness: Foundations of a theory of personal conduct*. HarperCollins (Original work published 1961)

Thakur, G.A., Sengupta, S.M., Grizenko, N., Schmitz, N., Pagé, V., & Joober, R. (2013). Maternal smoking during pregnancy and ADHD: A comprehensive clinical and neurocognitive characterization. *Nicotine and Tobacco Research*, 15, 149–157.

Thase, M.E. (2009). Neurobiological aspects of depression. In I. H. Gotlib & C. L. Hammen (Eds.), *Handbook of depression* (pp. 187–217). Guilford Press.

The Associated Press. (2013, May 15). New psychiatric manual, DSM-5, faces criticism for turning "normal" human problems into mental illness [Web log post]. http://www.nydailynews.com/life-style/health/shrinks-critics-face-new-psychiatric-manual-article-1.1344935

Thompson, A., Molina, B.S.G., Pelham, W., & Gnagy, E.M. (2007). Risky driving in adolescents and young adults with childhood ADHD. *Journal of Pediatric Psychology*, 32, 745–759.

Thornicroft, G. (1990). Cannabis and psychosis: Is there epidemiological evidence for an association? *British Journal of Psychiatry*, 157, 25–33.

Tienari, P., Wynne, L.C., Sorri, A., Lahti, I., Lasky, K., Moring, J.,…Wahlberg, K. (2004). Genotype-environment interaction in schizophrenia spectrum disorder. *British Journal of Psychiatry*, 184, 216–222.

Trezza V., Cuomo, V., & Vanderschuren, L.J. (2008). Cannabis and the developing brain: Insights from behavior. *European Journal of Pharmacology*, 585, 441–452.

Tsuang, M.T., Farone, S.V., & Green, A.I. (1999). Schizophrenia and other psychotic disorders. In A. M. Nicholi, Jr. (Ed.), *The Harvard guide to psychiatry* (pp. 240–280). The Belknap Press of Harvard University Press.

van Praag, H.M. (2005). Can stress cause depression? [Supplemental material]. *The World Journal of Biological Psychiatry*, 6(S2), 5–22.

Victor, T.A., Furey, M.L., Fromm, S.J., Öhman, A., & Drevets, W.C. (2010). Relationship between amygdala responses to masked faces and mood state and treatment in major depressive disorder. *Archives of General Psychiatry*, 67, 1128–1138.

Volkow N. D., Fowler J. S., Logan J., Alexoff D., Zhu W., Telang F.,…Apelskog-Torres K. (2009). Effects of modafinil on dopamine and dopamine transporters in the male human brain: clinical implications. *Journal of the American Medical Association*, 301, 1148–1154.

Wakefield, J.C. (1992). The concept of mental disorder: On the boundary between biological facts and social values. *American Psychologist*, 47, 373–388.

Waller, J. (2009a). Looking back: Dancing plagues and mass hysteria. *The Psychologist, 22*(7), 644–647.

Waller, J. (2009b, February 21). A forgotten plague: Making sense of dancing mania. *The Lancet, 373*(9664), 624–625. https://doi.org/10.1016/S0140-6736(09)60386-X

Weiser, E.B. (2007). The prevalence of anxiety disorders among adults with Asthma: A meta-analytic review. *Journal of Clinical Psychology in Medical Settings*, 14, 297–307.

White, C.N., Gunderson, J.G., Zanarani, M.C., & Hudson, J.I. (2003). Family studies of borderline personality disorder: A review. *Harvard Review of Psychiatry*, 11, 8–19.

Whooley, M.A. (2006). Depression and cardiovascular disease: Healing the broken-hearted. *Journal of the American Medical Association*, 295, 2874–2881.

Wilcox, H.C., Conner, K.R., & Caine, E.D. (2004). Association of alcohol and drug use disorders and completed suicide: An empirical review of cohort studies [Supplemental material]. *Drug and Alcohol Dependence*, 76, S11–S19.

Wing, L., Gould, J., & Gillberg, C. (2011). Autism spectrum disorders in the DSM-V: Better or worse than the DSM IV? *Research in Developmental Disabilities*, 32, 768–773.

Wisner, K.L., Sit, D.K. Y., McShea, M.C., Rizzo, D.M., Zoretich, R.A., Hughes, C.L., Hanusa, B.H. (2013). Onset timing, thoughts of self-harm, and diagnoses in postpartum women with screen-positive depression findings. *JAMA Psychiatry*, 70, 490–498.

Wolraich, M.L., Wilson, D.B., & White, J.W. (1995). The effect of sugar on behavior or cognition in children. *Journal of the American Medical Association*, 274, 1617–1621.

World Health Organization (WHO). (2013). *International classification of diseases (ICD)*. http://www.who.int/classifications/icd/en/

Wyatt, W.J., & Midkiff, D.M. (2006). Biological psychiatry: A practice in search of a science. *Behavior and Social Issues*, 15, 132–151.

Xie, P., Kranzler, H.R., Poling, J., Stein, M.B., Anton, R.F., Brady, K., Gelernter, J. (2009). Interactive effect of stressful life events and the serotonin transporter 5-HTTLPR genotype on posttraumatic stress disorder diagnosis in 2 independent populations. *Archives of General Psychology*, 66, 1201–1209.

Zachar, P., & Kendler, K.S. (2007). Psychiatric disorders: A conceptual taxonomy. *The American Journal of Psychiatry*, 16, 557–565.

Zuckerman, M. (1999). *Vulnerability to psychopathology: A biosocial model*. American Psychological Association.

Chapter 15

Abbass, A., Kisely, S., & Kroenke, K. (2006). Short-term psychodynamic psychotherapy for somatic disorders: Systematic review and meta-analysis of clinical trials. *Psychotherapy and Psychosomatics*, 78, 265–274.

Ahmed, S., Wilson, K.B., Henriksen, R.C., & Jones, J.W. (2011). What does it mean to be a culturally competent counselor? *Journal for Social Action in Counseling and Psychology*, 3(1), 17–28.

Alavi, A., Sharifi, B., Ghanizadeh, A., & Dehbozorgi, G. (2013). Effectiveness of cognitive-behavioral therapy in decreasing suicidal ideation and hopelessness of the adolescents with previous suicidal attempts. *Iranian Journal of Pediatrics*, 23(4), 467–472.

Alegría, M., Chatterji, P., Wells, K., Cao, Z., Chen, C.N., Takeuchi, D.,…Meng, X.L. (2008). Disparity in depression treatment among racial and ethnic minority populations in the United States. *Psychiatric Services*, 59(11), 1264–1272.

American Psychological Association. (2005). *Policy statement on evidence-based practice in psychology.* http://www.apapracticecentral.org/ce/courses/ebpstatement.pdf

American Psychological Association. (2014). *Can psychologists prescribe medications for their patients?* http://www.apa.org/news/press/releases/2004/05/louisiana-rx.aspx

American Psychological Association. (2014). *Psychotherapy: Understanding group therapy.* http://www.apa.org/helpcenter/group-therapy.aspx

Beck, A.T., Rush, A.J., Shaw, B.F., & Emery, G. (1979). *Cognitive therapy of depression.* New York, NY: The Guilford Press.

Beck, J.S. (2011). *Cognitive behavior therapy: Basics and beyond* (2nd ed.). The Guilford Press.

Beck Institute for Cognitive Behavior Therapy. (n.d.). *History of cognitive therapy.* http://www.beckinstitute.org/history-of-cbt/

Belgrave, F., & Allison, K. (2010). *African-American psychology: From Africa to America* (2nd ed.). Sage Publications.

Bertrand, K., Richer, I., Brunelle, N., Beaudoin, I., Lemieux, A., & Ménard, J-M. (2013). Substance abuse treatment for adolescents: How are family factors related to substance use change? *Journal of Psychoactive Drugs, 45*(1), 28–38.

Blank, M.B., Mahmood, M., Fox, J.C., & Guterbock, T. (2002). Alternative mental health services: The role of the black church in the South. *American Journal of Public Health, 92,* 1668–1672.

Blumberg, J. (2007, October 24). A brief history of the Salem witch trials. *Smithsonian.com.* http://www.smithsonianmag.com/history-archaeology/brief-salem.html?c=y&page=2

Butlera, A.C., Chapmanb, J.E., Formanc, E.M., & Becka, A.T. (2006). The empirical status of cognitive-behavioral therapy: A review of meta-analyses. *Clinical Psychology Review, 26,* 17–31.

Center for Substance Abuse Treatment. (2005). *Substance Abuse Treatment: Group Therapy.* Treatment Improvement Protocol (TIP) Series 41. DHHS Publication No. (SMA) 05-3991. Substance Abuse and Mental Health Services Administration.

Centers for Disease Control and Prevention. (2014). *Suicide prevention: Youth suicide.* http://www.cdc.gov/violenceprevention/pub/youth_suicide.html

Chambless, D.L., & Ollendick, T.H. (2001). Empirically supported psychological interventions: Controversies and evidence. *Annual Review of Psychology, 52,* 685–716.

Charman, D., & Barkham, M. (2005). Psychological treatments: Evidence-based practice and practice-based evidence. *InPsych Highlights.* www.psychology.org.au/publications/inpsych/treatments

Chorpita, B.F., Daleiden, E.L., Ebesutani, C., Young, J., Becker, K.D., Nakamura, B.J.,…Starace, N. (2011), Evidence-based treatments for children and adolescents: An updated review of indicators of efficacy and effectiveness. *Clinical Psychology: Science and Practice,* 18, 154–172.

Clement, S., Schauman, O., Graham, T., Maggioni, F., Evans-Lacko, S., Bezborodovs, N.,…Thornicroft, G. (2014, February 25). What is the impact of mental health-related stigma on help-seeking? A systematic review of quantitative and qualitative studies. *Psychological Medicine,* 1–17.

Daniel, D. (n.d.). *Rational emotive in behavior therapy the context of modern psychological research.* albertellis.org/rebt-in-the-context-of-modern-psychological-research

Davidson, W.S. (1974). Studies of aversive conditioning for alcoholics: A critical review of theory and research methodology. *Psychological Bulletin, 81*(9), 571–581.

DeRubeis, R.J., Hollon, S.D., Amsterdam, J.D., Shelton, R.C., Young, P.R., Salomon, R.M.,…Gallop, R. (2005). Cognitive Therapy vs medications in the treatment of moderate to severe depression. *Archives of General Psychiatry, 62*(4), 409–416.

DeYoung, S.H. (2013, November 14). The woman who raised that monster [Web log post]. http://www.huffingtonpost.com/suzy-hayman-deyoung/the-woman-who-raised-that_b_4266621.html

Dickerson, F.B., Tenhula, W.N., & Green-Paden, L.D. (2005). The token economy for schizophrenia: Review of the literature and recommendations for future research. *Schizophrenia Research, 75*(2), 405–416.

Donahue, A.B. (2000). Electroconvulsive therapy and memory loss: A personal journey. *The Journal of ECT, 162,* 133–143.

Elkins, R.L. (1991). An appraisal of chemical aversion (emetic therapy) approaches to alcoholism treatment. *Behavior Research and Therapy, 29*(5), 387–413.

Gary, F.A. (2005). Stigma: Barrier to mental health care among ethnic minorities. *Issues in Mental Health Nursing, 26*(10), 979–999.

Gerardi, M., Cukor, J., Difede, J., Rizzo, A., & Rothbaum, B.O. (2010). Virtual reality exposure therapy for post-traumatic stress disorder and other anxiety disorders. *Current Psychiatry Reports, 12*(298), 299–305.

Harter, S. (1977). A cognitive-developmental approach to children's expression of conflicting feelings and a technique to facilitate such expression in play therapy. *Journal of Consulting and Clinical Psychology, 45*(3), 417–432.

Hemphill, R.E. (1966). Historical witchcraft and psychiatric illness in Western Europe. *Proceedings of the Royal Society of Medicine, 59*(9), 891–902.

Ivey, S.L., Scheffler, R., & Zazzali, J.L. (1998). Supply dynamics of the mental health workforce: Implications for health policy. *Milbank Quarterly, 76*(1), 25–58.

Jang, Y., Chiriboga, D.A., & Okazaki, S. (2009). Attitudes toward mental health services: Age group differences in Korean American adults. *Aging & Mental Health, 13*(1), 127–134.

Jones, M.C. (1924). A laboratory study of fear: The case of Peter. *Pedagogical Seminary, 31,* 308–315.

Kalff, D.M. (1991). Introduction to sandplay therapy. *Journal of Sandplay Therapy, 1*(1), 9.

Leblanc, M., & Ritchie, M. (2001). A meta-analysis of play therapy outcomes. *Counselling Psychology Quarterly, 14*(2), 149–163.

Lovaas, O.I. (1987). Behavioral treatment and normal educational and intellectual functioning in young autistic children. *Journal of Consulting & Clinical Psychology, 55,* 3–9.

Lovaas, O.I. (2003). *Teaching individuals with developmental delays: Basic intervention techniques.* Pro-Ed.

Lowinger, R.J., & Rombom, H. (2012). The effectiveness of cognitive behavioral therapy for PTSD in New York City Transit Workers. *North American Journal of Psychology, 14*(3), 471–484.

Madanes, C. (1991). Strategic family therapy. In A. S. Gurman and D. P. Kniskern (Eds.), *Handbook of Family Therapy, Vol. 2.* (pp. 396–416). Brunner/Mazel.

Marques, L., Alegría, M., Becker, A.E., Chen, C.N., Fang, A., Chosak, A., & Diniz, J.B. (2011). Comparative prevalence, correlates of impairment, and service utilization for eating disorders across US ethnic groups: Implications for reducing ethnic disparities in health care access for eating disorders. *International Journal of Eating Disorders, 44*(5), 412–420.

Martin, B. (2007). *In-Depth: Cognitive behavioral therapy*. http://psychcentral.com/lib/in-depth-cognitive-behavioral-therapy/000907

Mayo Clinic. (2012). *Tests and procedures: Transcranial magnetic stimulation*. http://www.mayoclinic.org/tests-procedures/transcranial-magnetic-stimulation/basics/definition/PRC-20020555

McGovern, M.P., & Carroll, K.M. (2003). Evidence-based practices for substance use disorders. *Psychiatric Clinics of North America, 26*, 991–1010.

McGrath, R.J., Cumming, G.F., Burchard, B.L., Zeoli, S., & Ellerby, L. (2009). *Current practices and emerging trends in sexual abuser management: The safer society North American survey*. The SaferSociety Press.

McLellan, A.T., Lewis, D.C., O'Brien, C.P., & Kleber, H.D. (2000). Drug dependence, a chronic medical illness: Implications for treatment, insurance, and outcomes evaluation. *JAMA, 284*(13), 1689–1695.

Minuchin, P. (1985). Families and individual development: Provocations from the field of family therapy. *Child Development, 56*(2), 289–302.

Mullen, E.J., & Streiner, D.L. (2004). The evidence for and against evidence-based practice. *Brief Treatment and Crisis Intervention, 4*(2), 111–121.

Muñoz-Cuevas, F.J., Athilingam, J., Piscopo, D., & Wilbrecht, L. (2013). Cocaine-induced structural plasticity in frontal cortex correlates with conditioned place preference. *Nature Neuroscience, 16*, 1367–1369.

National Association of Cognitive-Behavioral Therapists. (2009). History of cognitive behavioral therapy. Retrieved from: http://nacbt.org/historyofcbt.htm.

National Institute of Mental Health. (n.d.-a) *Any disorder among children*. http://www.nimh.nih.gov/statistics/1ANYDIS_CHILD.shtml

National Institute of Mental Health. (n.d.-b) *Use of mental health services and treatment among adults*. http://www.nimh.nih.gov/statistics/3use_mt_adult.shtml

National Institute of Mental Health. (n.d.-c). *Use of mental health services and treatment among children*. http://www.nimh.nih.gov/statistics/1NHANES.shtml

National Institute on Drug Abuse. (2008). *Addiction science: From Molecules to managed care*. http://www.drugabuse.gov/publications/addiction-science/relapse

National Institute on Drug Abuse. (2011). *Drug facts: Comorbidity: Addiction and other mental disorders*. http://www.drugabuse.gov/publications/drugfacts/comorbidity-addiction-other-mental-disorders

National Institute on Drug Abuse. (2012). *Principles of drug addiction treatment: A research-based guide* (3rd ed.). http://www.drugabuse.gov/publications/principles-drug-addiction-treatment-research-based-guide-third-edition/principles-effective-treatment

National Institutes of Health. (2013, August 6). *Important events in NIMH history*. http://www.nih.gov/about/almanac/organization/NIMH.htm

Nelson, P. (1993). Autobiography in Five Short Chapters. In *There's a Hole in my Sidewalk: The Romance of Self-Discovery*. Beyond Words Publishing.

O'Connor, K.J. (2000). *The play therapy primer* (2nd ed.). Wiley.

Page, R.C., & Berkow, D.N. (1994). *Unstructured group therapy: Creating contact, choosing relationship*. Jossey Bass.

Pagnin, D., de Queiroz, V., Pini, S., & Cassano, G.B. (2004). Efficacy of ECT in depression: A meta-analytic review. *Journal of ECT, 20*, 13–20.

Prins, S.J., & Draper, L. (2009). *Improving outcomes for people with mental illnesses under community corrections supervision: A guide to research-informed policy and practice*. Council of State Governments Justice Center.

Prochaska, J.O., & Norcross, J.C. (2010). *Systems of psychotherapy* (7th ed.). Wadsworth.

Prudic, J., Peyser, S., & Sackeim, H.A. (2000). Subjective memory complaints: A review of patient self-assessment of memory after electroconvulsive therapy. *The Journal of ECT, 16*(2), 121–132.

Rathus, J.H., & Sanderson, W.C. (1999). *Marital distress: Cognitive behavioral treatments for couples*. Jason Aronson.

Reti, I.R. (n.d.). *Electroconvulsive therapy today*. Johns Hopkins Medicine: http://www.hopkinsmedicine.org/psychiatry/specialty_areas/brain_stimulation/docs/DepBulletin407_ECT_extract.pdf

Richman, L.S., Kohn-Wood, L.P., & Williams, D.R. (2007). The role of discrimination and racial identity for mental health service utilization. *Journal of Social and Clinical Psychology, 26*(8), 960–981.

Rizzo, A., Newman, B., Parsons, T., Difede, J., Reger, G., Holloway, K.,...Bordnick, P. (2010). Development and clinical results from the Virtual Iraq exposure therapy application for PTSD. *Annals of the New York Academy of Sciences, 1208*, 114–125.

Rogers, C. (1951). *Client-centered psychotherapy*. Houghton-Mifflin.

Sackett, D.L., & Rosenberg, W.M. (1995). On the need for evidence-based medicine. *Journal of Public Health, 17*, 330–334.

Sallows, G.O., & Graupner, T.D. (2005). Intensive behavioral treatment for children with autism: Four-year outcome and predictors. *American Journal of Mental Retardation, 110*(6), 417–438.

Scott, L.D., McCoy, H., Munson, M.R., Snowden, L.R., & McMillen, J.C. (2011). Cultural mistrust of mental health professionals among Black males transitioning from foster care. *Journal of Child and Family Studies, 20*, 605–613.

Shechtman, Z. (2002). Child group psychotherapy in the school at the threshold of a new millennium. *Journal of Counseling and Development, 80*(3), 293–299.

Shedler, J. (2010). The efficacy of psychodynamic psychotherapy. *American Psychologist, 65*, 98–109.

Simpson D. D. (1981). Treatment for drug abuse. *Archives of General Psychiatry, 38*, 875–880.

Simpson D. D, Joe, G. W, & Bracy, S.A. (1982). Six-year follow-up of opioid addicts after admission to treatment. *Archives General Psychiatry, 39*, 1318–1323.

Snowden, L.R. (2001). Barriers to effective mental health services for African Americans. *Mental Health Services Research, 3*, 181–187.

Stensland, M., Watson, P.R., & Grazier, K.L. (2012). An examination of costs, charges, and payments for inpatient psychiatric treatment in community hospitals. *Psychiatric Services, 63*(7), 66–71.

Stewart, S.M., Simmons, A., & Habibpour, E. (2012). Treatment of culturally diverse children and adolescents with depression. *Journal of Child and Adolescent Psychopharmacology, 22*(1), 72–79.

Streeton, C., & Whelan, G. (2001). Naltrexone, a relapse prevention maintenance treatment of alcohol dependence: A meta-analysis of randomized controlled trials. *Alcohol and Alcoholism, 36*(6), 544–552.

Sue, D.W. (2001). Multidimensional facets of cultural competence. *Counseling Psychologist, 29*(6), 790–821.

Sue, D.W. (2004). Multicultural counseling and therapy (MCT). In J. A. Banks and C. Banks (Eds.), *Handbook of research on multicultural education* (2nd ed., pp. 813–827). Jossey-Bass.

Sue, D.W., & Sue, D. (2007). *Counseling the culturally different: Theory and practice* (5th ed.). Wiley.

Sussman, L.K., Robins, L.N., & Earls, F. (1987). Treatment–seeking for depression by Black and White Americans. *Social Science & Medicine*, 24, 187–196.

Szasz, T.S. (1960). The Myth of Mental Illness. *American Psychologist*, 15, 113–118.

Thomas, K.C., & Snowden, L.R. (2002). Minority response to health insurance coverage for mental health services. *Journal of Mental Health Policy and Economics*, 4, 35–41.

Tiffany, F. (2012/1891). *Life of Dorothea Lynde Dix* (7th ed.). Houghton, Mifflin.

Torrey, E.F. (1997). *Out of the shadows: Confronting America's mental illness crisis*. Wiley.

Torrey, E.F., Zdanowicz, M.T., Kennard, A.D., Lamb, H.R., Eslinger, D.F., Biasotti, M.C., & Fuller, D.A. (2014, April 8). *The treatment of persons with mental illness in prisons and jails: A state survey*. Arlington, VA: Treatment Advocacy Center. http://tacreports.org/storage/documents/treatment-behind-bars/treatment-behind-bars.pdf

Townes D. L., Cunningham N. J., & Chavez-Korell, S. (2009). Reexaming the relationships between racial identity, cultural mistrust, help-seeking attitudes, and preference for a Black counselor. *Journal of Counseling Psychology*, *56*(2), 330–336.

U.S. Department of Agriculture. (2013, December 10). USDA announces support for mental health facilities in rural areas [Press release No. 0234.13]. http://www.usda.gov/wps/portal/usda/usdahome?contentid=2013/12/0234.xml

U.S. Department of Health and Human Services. (1999). *Mental health: A report of the Surgeon General*. Rockville, MD: U.S. Department of Health and Human Services, Substance Abuse and Mental Health Services Administration, Center for Mental Health Services, National Institutes of Health, National Institute of Mental Health.

U.S. Department of Health and Human Services, Health Resources and Services Administration, Office of Rural Health Policy. (2005). *Mental health and rural America: 1984-2005*. ftp://ftp.hrsa.gov/ruralhealth/RuralMentalHealth.pdf

U.S. Department of Health and Human Services, Substance Abuse and Mental Health Services Administration, Center for Behavioral Health Statistics and Quality. (2011, September). *Results from the 2010 National Survey on Drug Use and Health: Summary of National Findings* (NSDUH Series H-41, HHS Publication No. [SMA] 11-4658). http://www.samhsa.gov/data/NSDUH/2k10ResultsRev/NSDUHresultsRev2010.htm

U.S. Department of Health and Human Services, Substance Abuse and Mental Health Services Administration, Center for Behavioral Health Statistics and Quality. (2013, September). *Results from the 2012 National Survey on Drug Use and Health: Summary of National Findings* (NSDUH Series H-46, HHS Publication No. [SMA] 13-4795). http://www.samhsa.gov/data/NSDUH/2012SummNatFindDetTables/NationalFindings/NSDUHresults2012.htm#ch2.2

U.S. Department of Health and Human Services, Substance Abuse and Mental Health Services Administration, Center for Behavioral Health Statistics and Quality. (2013, December). *Results from the 2012 National Survey on Drug Use and Health: Mental Health Findings* (NSDUH Series H-47, HHS Publication No. [SMA] 13-4805). http://www.samhsa.gov/data/NSDUH/2k12MH_FindingsandDetTables/2K12MHF/NSDUHmhfr2012.htm

U.S. Department of Housing and Urban Development, Office of Community Planning and Development. (2011). *The 2010 Annual Homeless Assessment Report to Congress*. Washington, DC. http://www.hudhre.info/documents/2010HomelessAssessmentReport.pdf

U.S. Department of Labor. (n.d.). *Mental health parity*. Retrieved from: http://www.dol.gov/ebsa/mentalhealthparity/

U.S. Public Health Service. (2000). *Report of the Surgeon General's conference on children's mental health: A national action agenda*. Washington, DC: Department of Health and Human Services.

Wagenfeld, M.O., Murray, J.D., Mohatt, D.F., & DeBruiynb, J.C. (Eds.). (1994). *Mental health and rural America: 1980–1993* (NIH Publication No. 94-3500). U.S. Government Printing Office.

Wampold, B.E. (2007). Psychotherapy: The humanistic (and effective) treatment. *American Psychologist*, 62, 857–873. https://doi.org/10.1037/0003-066X.62.8.857

Weil, E. (2012, March 2). Does couples therapy work? *The New York Times*. http://www.nytimes.com/2012/03/04/fashion/couples-therapists-confront-the-stresses-of-their-field.html?pagewanted=all&_r=0

Weiss, R.D., Jaffee, W.B., de Menil, V.P., & Cogley, C.B. (2004). Group therapy for substance abuse disorders: What do we know? *Harvard Review of Psychiatry*, *12*(6), 339–350.

Willard Psychiatric Center. (2009). *Echoes of Willard*. http://www.echoesofwillard.com/willard-psychiatric-centre/

Wolf, M., & Risley, T. (1967). Application of operant conditioning procedures to the behavior problems of an autistic child: A follow-up and extension. *Behavior Research and Therapy*, *5*(2), 103–111.

Wolpe, J. (1958). *Psychotherapy by reciprocal inhibition*. Stanford University Press.

Photo Credits

Chapter 1

Chapter 2

Chapter 5

Chapter 6

Chapter 7

Chapter 9

Chapter 10

Chapter 11

Chapter 12

Chapter 13

Chapter 14

Notes